England

Newcastle &
Northeast England
p616

The Lake District
& Cumbria
p578

Yorkshire
p487

Manchester, Liverpool
& Northwest England
p543

Birmingham,
the Midlands &
the Marches
p397

Cambridge &
East Anglia
p357

Oxford, Cotswolds
& Around
p174

London
p52

Bath &
Southwest
England
p219

Canterbury &
Southeast England
p138

THIS EDITION WRITTEN AND RESEARCHED BY

Neil Wilson,

Oliver Berry, Fionn Davenport, Marc Di Duca, Belinda Dixon,

Peter Dragicevich, Damian Harper, Catherine Le Nevez

Contents

BEACHY HEAD P162

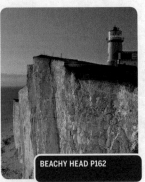

TOWER OF LONDON P70

PAUL THOMPSON /GETTY IMAGES ©

BRUCE YUANYUE BI /GETTY IMAGES ©

Contents

ON THE ROAD

JOHN FINNEY PHOTOGRAPHY /GETTY IMAGES ©

SCAFELL PIKE P600

Contents

Welcome to England

This green and pleasant land, this sceptred isle, this crucible of empire and pioneer of parliamentary democracy, is the most eccentric, extraordinary and downright intriguing place on Earth.

Variety Packed

From the Roman remains of Hadrian's Wall to London's incomparable theatre scene, England is full of astounding variety. In the cities, the streets buzz day and night, filled with tempting shops and restaurants, and some of the finest museums in the world. After dark, cutting-edge clubs, top-class performing arts and formidable live music provide a string of nights to remember. Next day, you're deep in the English countryside or enjoying a classic seaside resort. There really is something for everyone, whether you're eight or 80, going solo or travelling with your friends, your kids or your grandma.

Time Travel

A journey through England is a journey through history. But not history that's dull and dusty, history you can feel and relive. Lay your hands on the ancient megaliths of a 5000-year-old stone circle, or walk the battlements of a medieval fortress – just as they were patrolled by the chain-mail-clad many centuries ago. Visit the sites of the legend of King Arthur, the locations described in Shakespeare's sonnets and the palaces of royals – past and present. Then fast forward to the future and you're admiring 21st-century architecture in Manchester, or exploring the space-age domes of Cornwall's Eden Project.

English Spoken Here

And while England has developed a culture and tradition that may appear complex, on the surface at least it's familiar to many visitors thanks to a vast catalogue of British film and TV exports. The same applies when it comes to communication; this is home turf for the English language. For many visitors this means no need to carry a phrasebook – although you might get a little confused by local accents in places such as Devon or Liverpool.

Easy Does It

Travel here is a breeze. Granted, it may not be totally effortless, but it's easy compared with many parts of the world. And although the locals may grumble (in fact, it's a national pastime), public transport is very good, and a train ride through the English landscape can be a highlight in itself. But whichever way you get around, in this compact country you're never far from the next town, the next pub, the next restaurant, the next national park or the next impressive castle on your hit list of highlights. The choice is endless, and we've hand-picked the best places for you – but don't let this stop you from making your own discoveries.

Why I Love England

By Neil Wilson, Author

England's most appealing feature is the aura of deep-rooted history that emanates from almost every corner of the land. There's a sense that its towns and villages, castles and cathedrals have grown organically over many centuries, to create calming and comfortable landscapes that the mind settles into like a favourite armchair. It's a place that encourages leisurely contemplation, whether gazing at dreaming spires from a thousand-year-old bridge, taking in the view at the top of a not-too-tiring hill or – best of all – ensconced in the corner of a thatch-roofed, stone-floored country pub with a well-earned pint in hand.

For more about our authors, see page 720

Above: Big Ben & Houses of Parliament (p57), London

England

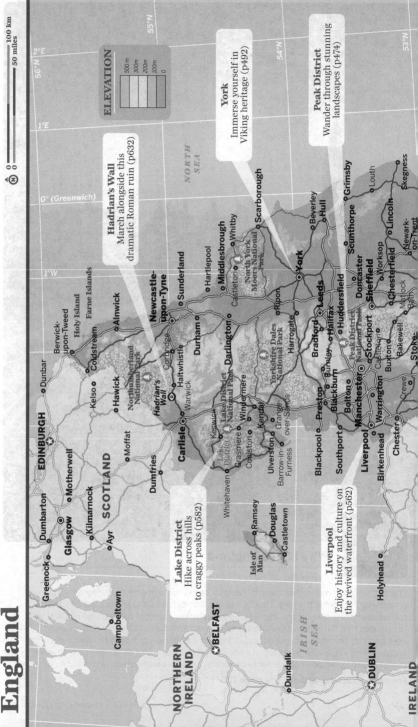

Hadrian's Wall
March alongside this dramatic Roman ruin (p632)

York
Immerse yourself in Viking heritage (p492)

Peak District
Wander through stunning landscapes (p474)

Lake District
Hike across hills to craggy peaks (p582)

Liverpool
Enjoy history and culture on the revived waterfront (p562)

ELEVATION

| 500 m |
| 300m |
| 200m |
| 100m |
| 0 |

100 km
50 miles

Shrewsbury
See a Shakespeare play at the Bard's birthplace (p417)

Oxford
Wonder at archaic colleges and traditions (p176)

The Cotswolds
Enjoy classic chocolate-box English countryside (p190)

Bath
Admire beautiful Georgian architecture (p310)

Eden Project
Marvel at Cornwall's three gigantic greenhouses (p349)

Stonehenge
Go mystic at England's famous prehistoric site (p261)

London
Don't miss its world-class theatre scene (p52)

Seven Sisters
Stroll across England's iconic white cliffs (p163)

Canterbury
Be awed by its historic place of worship (p139)

Cambridge
Attempt to punt on the picturesque 'Backs' (p361)

England's
Top 20

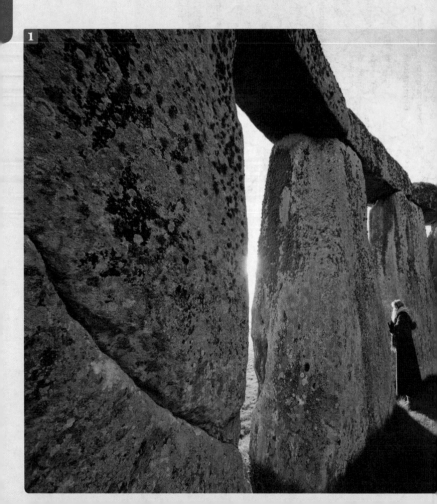

Stonehenge

1 Mysterious and compelling, Stonehenge (p261) is England's most iconic ancient site. People have been drawn to this myth-rich ring of boulders for more than 5000 years, and we still don't know quite why it was built. Most visitors gaze at the 50-tonne stones from behind the perimeter fence, but with enough planning you can arrange an early-morning or evening tour and gain access to the inner ring itself. In the slanting sunlight, away from the crowds, it's an ethereal place. This is an experience that stays with you.

Oxford

2 A visit to Oxford (p176) is as close as most of us will get to the brilliant minds and august institutions that have made this city famous across the globe. But you'll catch a glimpse of this rarefied world in the cobbled lanes and ancient quads where student cyclists and dusty academics roam. The beautiful college buildings, archaic traditions and stunning architecture have changed little over the centuries, leaving the city centre much as Einstein or Tolkien would have found it. Below: Radcliffe Camera (p181), University of Oxford

EURASIA PRESS / GETTY IMAGES ©

ALLAN BAXTER / GETTY IMAGES ©

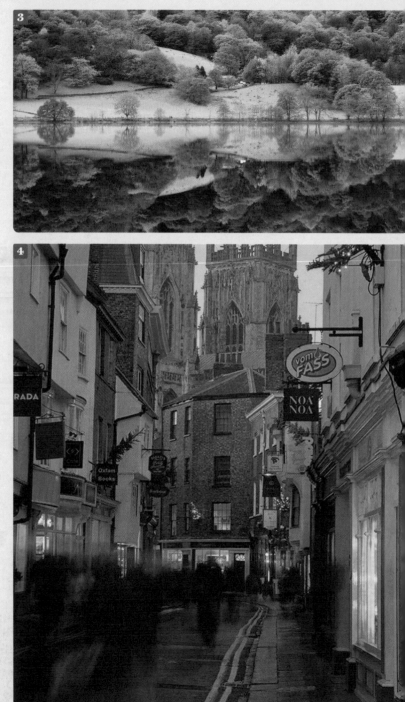

The Lake District

3 William Wordsworth and his Romantic friends were the first to champion the charms of the Lake District (p582) and it's not hard to see what stirred them. The dramatic landscape of whale-backed hills, deep valleys, misty mountain lakes and high peaks (including England's highest summit) makes this craggy corner of the country the spiritual home of English hiking. Strap on the boots, stock up on mint cake and drink in the views: inspiration is sure to follow. Top left: Grasmere (p594)

York

4 With its Roman and Viking heritage, ancient city walls and maze of cobbled streets, York (p492) is a living showcase for the highlights of English history. Join one of the city's many walking tours and plunge into the network of snickelways (narrow alleys), each one the focus of a ghost story or historical character. Explore the intricacies of York Minster, the biggest medieval cathedral in all of northern Europe, or admire the exhibits from more recent times at the National Railway Museum, the world's largest collection of historic locomotives.

Bath

5 In a nation packed with pretty cities, Bath (p310) still stands out as the belle of the ball. Founded by the Romans, who established the spa resort of Aquae Sulis to take advantage of the area's hot springs, Bath hit its stride in the 18th century when the rich industrialist Ralph Allen and architects John Wood the Elder and John Wood the Younger oversaw the city's reinvention as a model of Georgian architecture. Awash with amber town houses, sweeping crescents and Palladian mansions, Bath demands your undivided attention. Above: Pulteney Bridge (p314)

CHRIS MELLOR / GETTY IMAGES ©

Liverpool Museums

6 After a decade of development, the reborn waterfront is once again the heart of Liverpool (p562). The focal point is Albert Dock, a World Heritage Site of iconic and protected buildings, including a batch of top museums: the Merseyside Maritime Museum and International Slavery Museum ensure the good and bad sides of Liverpool's history are not forgotten, while the Tate Liverpool and the Beatles Story museum celebrate popular culture and the city's most famous musical sons (still). Above: Albert Dock & Beatles Story (p565)

Hadrian's Wall

7 Hadrian's Wall (p632) is one of the country's most revealing and dramatic Roman ruins, its 2000-year-old procession of abandoned forts, garrisons, towers and milecastles (small forts every Roman mile) marching across the wild and lonely landscape of northern England. This wall was about defence and control, but this edge-of-empire barrier also symbolised the boundary of civilised order – to the north lay the unruly land of the marauding Celts, while to the south was the Roman world of orderly taxpaying, underfloor heating and bathrooms.

The Cotswolds

8 The most wonderful thing about the Cotswolds (p190) is that no matter where you go or how lost you get, you'll still end up in an impossibly quaint village of rose-clad cottages and honey-coloured stone. There'll be a charming village green, a pub with sloping floors and fine ales, and a view of the lush green hills. It's easy to leave the crowds behind and find your very own slice of medieval England here – and some of the best boutique hotels in the country. Above: Snowshill (p202)

England's Pubs

9 Despite the growth of stylish clubs and bars, the traditional neighbourhood or village pub – Ye Olde Trip to Jerusalem (p451) is the country's oldest – is still the centre of social life in England, A lunchtime or evening visit can be one of the best ways to get under the skin of the nation. A drink or two may be necessary as well, and ideally that means traditional beer. To outsiders it may be 'warm and flat', but give it a chance and you'll soon learn to savour the complex flavours and the many regional varieties. Below: Ye Olde Trip to Jerusalem, Nottingham

Cambridge

10 One of England's two great historic university cities, Cambridge (p361) highlights include a tour of at least one of the ancient colleges, and time spent marvelling at the intricate vaulting of King's College Chapel. But no trip to Cambridge is complete without an attempt to take a punt (flat-bottomed boat) along the picturesque 'Backs' – the leafy lawns behind the city's finest colleges. Polish off the day with a pint in one of the many historic pubs. You'll soon wonder how you could have studied anywhere else. Bottom: Cambridge University (p361)

Peak District

11 Curiously, you won't find many peaks in the Peak District (p474). But you will find blissful miles of tumbling moorland, plunging valleys, eroded gritstone crags, lush farmland and ancient pocket-sized villages. This beautiful landscape attracts an army of outdoor enthusiasts on summer weekends, while those seeking more relaxing enjoyment can admire the rural market and famous puddings of Bakewell, the Victorian pavilions of spa-town Buxton, and the architectural drama of Chatsworth House.

Below: Chatsworth House (p485), Bakewell

Tower of London

12 The Tower of London (p70) is Europe's best-preserved medieval fortress and one of England's best-known attractions. At almost 1000 years old (more if you count the Roman foundations) it's an enduring landmark of the capital, and over the centuries this sturdy fortress has served the nation as a palace, prison, arsenal and mint. Today it's home to the legendary 'Beefeaters' and ravens that are attributed mythical powers.

ADINA TOVY / GETTY IMAGES ©

MICHAEL ENGLAND / GETTY IMAGES ©

Afternoon Tea

13 Among England's many and varied traditions, afternoon tea is one of the most enticing, and certainly one of the tastiest. Centre of the ritual is the iconic beverage itself – brewed in a pot (ideally silver-plated) and poured carefully into fine bone-china cups with saucers. Depending where you are in the country, this hot drink is served with scones and cream, fruit cake or wafer-thin cucumber sandwiches. Fancy city hotels and traditional tearooms, such as Betty's (p501) in Harrogate, are among the best places to sample this epicurean delight.

Stratford-upon-Avon

14 The pretty town of Stratford-upon-Avon (p417) is where William Shakespeare, the world's most famous playwright, was born and later shuffled off this mortal coil. Today, its tight knot of Tudor streets form a living map of Shakespeare's life and times. Huge crowds of thespians and theatre lovers come to take in a play at the famous theatre. Visit the five historic houses owned by Shakespeare and his relatives, then take a respectful detour to the old stone church where the Bard was laid to rest.

Top right: Nash's House & New Place (p417)

Canterbury Cathedral

15 Few other English cathedrals come close to Canterbury Cathedral (p142), the very fulcrum of the Anglican Church and a place of worship for over 15 centuries. Its intricate tower dominates the Canterbury city skyline, while at its heart lies a 12th-century crime scene where Archbishop Thomas Becket was put to the sword on the orders of the king – an event that launched a million pilgrimages and still pulls in the crowds today. A lone candle mourns the gruesome deed, the pink sandstone before it smoothed by 800 years' worth of devout kneeling.

CHRIS HEPBURN / GETTY IMAGES ©

Walking in England

16 Call it hiking, rambling or (most often) simply walking, England is the perfect place to explore on two feet, thanks to its compact nature and protected network of 'rights of way'. You can stroll the narrow streets and hidden alleyways of the nation's famous historic towns, then head for the national parks and open countryside where a gentle walk alongside meandering southern rivers or a serious trek over the Peak District hills can be an excellent way to get to know England and the English people a little better. Above left: Peak District National Park (p474)

Football

17 Much of the world may call it 'soccer' but to the English the name of the national sport is definitely 'football'. And despite what the fans may say in Italy or Brazil, the English Premier League has some of the finest football teams in the world, with many of the world's best (and richest) players. The most famous club on the planet is still Manchester United (p551), while other big names include rival Manchester City, Arsenal, Liverpool and Chelsea. Tickets for the biggest matches are like gold dust, but most stadiums are open to visitors outside match days. Top right: Old Trafford (p551), Manchester

Seven Sisters Chalk Cliffs

18 Dover's iconic white cliffs grab the most attention, but the colossal chalky walls of the Seven Sisters (p163) are a much more spectacular affair. This 4-mile roller coaster of sheer white rock rollicks along the Sussex shore overlooking the waters of the English Channel, an impressive southern border to the South Downs National Park and at its most dramatic at the towering headland of Beachy Head. Hikes through the grassy clifftop fields provide wide sea views, breathtaking in every sense.

The Eden Project

19 Looking like a cross between a lunar landing station and a James Bond villain's lair, the three gigantic semi-spherical greenhouses of the Eden Project (p349) have become a symbol of Cornwall's renaissance. Dreamt up by ex-record producer Tim Smit, and built in an abandoned clay pit near St Austell, Eden's three 'biomes' re-create the world's habitats in microcosm, from the lush jungles of the Amazon rainforest to the temperate plains of the African savannah.

London's Theatre Scene

20 However you budget your time and money in London, make sure you take in a show (p128). For big names, head for the West End (London's equivalent to Broadway), where famous spots include the National Theatre, Old Vic, Shaftesbury and Theatre Royal at Drury Lane. For new and experimental works, try the Donmar Warehouse and Royal Court. Either way, you'll see that London's theatre scene easily lives up to its reputation as one of the finest in the world – whatever New Yorkers say.

Need to Know

For more information, see Survival Guide (p689)

Currency
Pound sterling (£)

Language
English

Visas
Generally not needed for stays of up to six months. Not a member of the Schengen Zone.

Money
ATMs widely available; credit cards widely accepted.

Mobile Phones
The UK uses the GSM 900/1800 network, which covers the rest of Europe, Australia and New Zealand, but isn't compatible with the North American GSM 1900. Most modern mobiles can function on both networks, but check before you leave home just in case.

Time
GMT plus one hour during summer daylight saving time, UTC plus zero the rest of the year.

When to Go

Carlisle
GO May–Sep

York
GO May–Sep

Liverpool
GO May–Sep

Norwich
GO May–Sep

London
GO Any time

Exeter
GO Apr–Sep

High Season
(Jun–Aug)

➡ Weather at its best. Accommodation rates high, particularly in August (school holidays).

➡ Roads busy, especially in seaside areas, national parks and popular cities such as Oxford, Bath and York.

Shoulder
(Easter–May, mid-Sep–Oct)

➡ Crowds reduce. Prices drop.

➡ Weather often good: March to May sun mixes with sudden rain; September to October can feature balmy 'Indian summers'.

Low Season
(Dec–Feb)

➡ Wet and cold is the norm. Snow can fall, especially up north.

➡ Opening hours reduced October to Easter; some places shut for the winter. Big-city sights (especially London's) operate all year.

Useful Websites

BBC (www.bbc.co.uk) News and entertainment.

Enjoy England (www.enjoy-england.com) Official tourism website.

Lonely Planet (www.lonely-planet.com/england) Destination information, hotel bookings, traveller forums and more.

National Traveline (www.traveline.org.uk) Great portal site for all public transport around England.

British Arts Festivals (www.artsfestivals.co.uk) Lists festivals – art, literature, dance, folk and more.

Important Numbers

England (and UK) country code	📞44
International access code	📞00
Emergency (police, fire, ambulance, mountain rescue or coastguard)	📞112 or 📞999

Exchange Rates

Australia	A$1	£0.54
Canada	C$1	£0.56
Eurozone	€1	£0.79
Japan	Y100	£0.54
New Zealand	NZ$1	£0.50
USA	US$1	£0.63

For current exchange rates see www.xe.com.

Daily Costs

**Budget:
Less than £55**

➡ Dorm beds: £15–25

➡ Cheap meals in cafes and pubs: £7–11

➡ Long-distance coach: £15–40 (200 miles)

**Midrange:
£55–120**

➡ Double room in midrange hotel or B&B: £60–130 (London £100–200)

➡ Main course in midrange restaurant: £10–20

➡ Long-distance train: £20–80 (200 miles)

**Top End:
More than £120**

➡ Four-star hotel room: from £130 (London from £200)

➡ Three-course meal in a good restaurant: around £40

➡ Car rental per day: from £35

Opening Hours

Opening hours may vary throughout the year, especially in rural areas where many places have shorter hours, or close completely, from October or November to March or April.

Banks 9.30am to 4pm or 5pm Monday to Friday; some are open 9.30am to 1pm Saturday.

Pubs and Bars 11am to 11pm Monday to Thursday, 11am to 1am Friday and Saturday, 12.30pm to 11pm Sunday.

Restaurants Lunch is noon to 3pm, dinner 6pm to 9pm/10pm (or later in cities).

Shops 9am to 5.30pm (or 6pm in cities) Monday to Saturday, and often 11am to 5pm Sunday. London and other cities have convenience stores open 24/7.

Arriving in England

Heathrow airport (p698) Train to central London (London Paddington station) every 15 minutes (from £18). Taxi £40 to £50.

Gatwick airport (p698) Train to central London (London Victoria station) every 15 minutes (from £16). Taxi £70 to £90 (more at peak hours).

Eurostar trains (p698) From Paris or Brussels, arrive at London St Pancras International station in central London.

Getting Around

Transport in England can be expensive compared to the rest of Europe; bus and rail services are sparse in the more remote parts of the country. For timetables, check out www.traveline.org.uk.

Car Useful for travelling at your own pace, or for visiting regions with minimal public transport. Cars can be hired in every town or city.

Train Relatively expensive, with extensive coverage and frequent departures throughout most of the country.

Bus Cheaper and slower than trains, but useful for more remote regions that aren't serviced by rail.

For much more on **getting around**, see p699

PLAN YOUR TRIP NEED TO KNOW

First Time England

For more information, see Survival Guide (p689)

Checklist

➡ Check the validity of your passport

➡ Check any visa or entry requirements

➡ Make any necessary bookings (sights, accommodation, travel)

➡ Check the airline baggage restrictions

➡ Put all restricted items (eg hair gel, pocketknife) in your check-in baggage

➡ Inform your credit-/debit-card company

➡ Organise travel insurance

➡ Check mobile (cell) phone compatibility

➡ Check rental-car requirements

What to Pack

➡ Passport

➡ Credit card

➡ Drivers licence

➡ Electrical plug adaptor (UK-specific)

➡ Waterproof jacket

➡ Umbrella

➡ Comfortable shoes

➡ Taste for warm beer

Top Tips for Your Trip

➡ At major London airports, tickets for express trains into central London are usually available in the baggage arrivals hall; this saves queuing or dealing with machines on the station platform.

➡ The best way to get local currency is usually from an ATM, but this term is rarely used in England; the colloquial term 'cash machine' is more common.

➡ If staying more than a few days in London, get an Oyster card, the travel card the locals use.

➡ Pickpockets and hustlers lurk in the more crowded tourist areas, especially in London. No need to be paranoid, but do be on your guard.

➡ Britain's electrical plugs are unlike those in the rest of Europe, so bring (or buy) a UK-specific plug adaptor.

What to Wear

A rain jacket is essential, as is a backpack to carry it in when the sun comes out. In summer you'll need sunscreen and an umbrella; you're bound to use both – possibly on the same day.

For sightseeing, comfortable shoes can make or break a trip. If you plan to enjoy England's great outdoors, suitable hiking gear is required in higher/wilder areas, but not for casual strolls in the countryside.

Some bars and restaurants have dress codes banning jeans, T-shirts and trainers (sneakers or runners).

Sleeping

Booking your accommodation in advance is recommended, especially in summer, at weekends and on islands (where options are often limited). Book at least two months ahead for July and August.

➡ **B&Bs** These small, family-run houses generally provide good value. More luxurious versions are more like a boutique hotel.

➡ **Hotels** English hotels range from half-a-dozen rooms above a pub to restored country houses and castles, with a commensurate rates.

➡ **Hostels** There's a good choice of both institutional and independent hostels, many housed in rustic and/or historic buildings.

Money

ATMs (usually called 'cash machines') are common in cities and towns, but watch out for tampering; one ruse by scammers is to attach a card-reader to the slot. Visa and MasterCard are widely accepted in England, except at some smaller B&Bs, which take cash or cheque only. Other credit cards, including Amex, are not so widely accepted. Cities and larger towns have banks and exchange bureaux for changing money into pounds, but some bureaux offer poor rates. You can change money at some post offices, which is very handy in country areas; exchange rates are fair.

Bargaining

A bit of mild haggling is acceptable at flea markets and antique shops, but everywhere else you're expected to pay the advertised price.

Tipping

➡ **Restaurants** Around 10% in restaurants and tearooms with table service. Nearer 15% at smarter restaurants. Tips may be added to your bill as a 'service charge'. However, paying tips or the service charge is not compulsory – it's up to you.

➡ **Pubs and Bars** If you order drinks (or food) and pay at the bar, tips are not expected. If you order at the table and your meal is brought to you, then 10% is usual.

➡ **Taxis** Usually around 10%, or rounded up to the nearest pound, especially in London.

Etiquette

➡ **Manners** The English have a reputation for being polite, and good manners are considered important in most situations. When asking directions, 'Excuse me, can you tell me the way to...' is better than 'Hey, where's...'

➡ **Queues** In England, queuing ('standing in line') is sacrosanct, whether to board a bus, buy tickets at a kiosk or enter the gates of an attraction. Any attempt to 'jump the queue' will result in an outburst of tut-tutting and hard stares – which is about as angry as most locals get in public.

➡ **Escalators** If you take an escalator (especially at London tube stations) or a moving walkway (eg at an airport) be sure to stand on the right, so folks can pass on the left.

Eating

It's wise to book ahead for midrange restaurants, especially at weekends. Top-end restaurants should be booked at least a couple of weeks in advance. See Food & Drink (p662) for more information.

➡ **Restaurants** England's restaurants range from cheap-and-cheerful to Michelin-starred, and cover every cuisine you can imagine.

➡ **Cafes** Open during daytime (rarely after 6pm), cafes are good for a casual breakfast or lunch, or simply a cup of coffee.

➡ **Pubs** Most of England's pubs serve reasonably priced meals, and many can compete with restaurants on quality.

Underground station, London

What's New

Cycling

There has been a huge upsurge in interest in road cycling after Yorkshire hosted the first two days of the Tour de France bike race in 2014. Apart from an increase in the numbers of cyclists testing themselves against the hills of the Yorkshire Dales and the Lake District, England is now enjoying an abundance of new bike trails, rental outlets and specialist bike cafes such as Your Bike Shed in York. (p500)

Stonehenge

A £27-million revamp of England's most famous prehistoric site has seen the area around the stones returned to grassland, and the opening of an impressive new visitor centre. (p261)

Shangri-La at the Shard

The first opening in the UK for the luxury Asian hotel chain, this is Europe's first elevated hotel, occupying levels 34 to 52 of London's Shard skyscraper. (p109)

The Making of Harry Potter

Prospective Hogwarts pupils can waggle their wands and practise their spells during this spectacular new tour at Warner Bros Studios, just outside London. (p213)

Eden Project

Cornwall's iconic eco-centre has an added attraction in the form of a new treetop walkway through the rainforest biome. (p349)

King Richard III: Dynasty, Death & Discovery

The amazing story of the discovery of the skeletal remains of King Richard III beneath a Leicester car park in 2012 is celebrated in this new, high-tech visitor centre. (p465)

Bleak House

Snooze in the very bedroom occupied for 12 productive summers by one Charles Dickens at this new hotel overlooking Broadstairs' tight curve of beach. (p150)

Liverpool International Music Festival

Liverpool's old Mathew St Festival has been expanded into a showcase of local and international talent spread over two weeks in late August. (p568)

Black Sail Youth Hostel

One of England's most remote youth hostels, perched high in the Lake District fells above Ennerdale, now sports double glazing and solar-panel-powered lighting following a major upgrade. (p601)

Northumberland National Park

England's least populous national park was awarded dark-sky status by the International Dark Skies Association in late 2013 (the largest such designation in Europe), adding to the stargazing appeal of Kielder Observatory. (p639)

For more recommendations and reviews, see lonelyplanet.com/England

If You Like...

Royal England

Queen Elizabeth II celebrated her Diamond Jubilee in 2012 after 60 years on the throne. With a monarch at the top for a virtually unbroken 1500-year stretch, it's no surprise that many reminders of England's royal heritage dot the country today.

Buckingham Palace The Queen's official London residence, best known for its balcony from which the royals wave and the Changing of the Guard. (p59)

Westminster Abbey Where English monarchs are crowned and married – most recently William and Kate. (p56)

Tower of London A castle and royal palace for centuries, now holding the Crown Jewels; 900 years of history in one iconic building. (p70)

Sandringham House The monarch's country residence, with a royal memorabilia museum. (p395)

Royal Pavilion Opulent and fantastical palace built for King George IV. (p163)

Althorp House Ancestral home and burial place of Diana, Princess of Wales. (p462)

Osborne House Royal retreat on the Isle of Wight, built for Queen Victoria. (p236)

Castles

Windsor Castle Largest and oldest occupied fortress in the world, and the Queen's weekend retreat. (p214)

Warwick Castle One of the finest castles in England; this well-preserved castle is both impressive and romantic. (p414)

Tintagel Castle Atmospheric clifftop ruin, and the legendary birthplace of King Arthur. (p330)

Bamburgh Castle Spectacularly positioned and largely rebuilt fortress on the Northumberland coast; a sharp contrast to the nearby ruins of Dunstanburgh Castle. (p644)

Richmond Castle Among England's oldest castles, with fantastic views from the medieval keep. (p526)

Skipton Castle Little-known, but probably the best-preserved medieval castle in the country. (p521)

Cathedrals

St Paul's Cathedral Symbol of London for centuries, and still an essential part of the city's skyline. (p72)

York Minster One of the largest medieval cathedrals in all of Europe, especially renowned for its windows. (p492)

Canterbury Cathedral Mothership of the Anglican Church, still attracting pilgrims and visitors in their thousands. (p142)

Salisbury Cathedral Truly majestic cathedral and an English icon, topped by the tallest spire in England. (p257)

Ely Cathedral Visible for miles across the flatlands of eastern England, and locally dubbed the 'Ship of the Fens'. (p374)

Liverpool Cathedral Liverpool's is the largest Anglican cathedral in the world, and then there's the striking Catholic cathedral; both are comparatively modern – two for the price of one. (p563)

Museums

British Museum England's largest and most visited museum is also one of the oldest and finest in the world. (p93)

National Railway Museum The epicentre of the nation's obsession with steam engines and railway history. (p493)

Natural History Museum A sure-fire hit with kids of all ages, with dinosaur skeletons, earthquake simulators and interactive exhibits. (p85)

Museum of Liverpool The city's multilayered past is celebrated at this interactive exploration of cultural and historical milestones including, of course, the Beatles. (p567)

Ashmolean Museum England's oldest museum, established in 1683, crammed with Egyptian mummies, rare porcelain and priceless musical instruments. (p183)

Mary Rose Museum Superb modern facility built around the remains of King Henry VIII's 16th-century flagship. (p228)

Historic Houses

Blenheim Palace Monumental baroque fantasy, Winston Churchill's birthplace and one of England's greatest stately homes. (p189)

Castle Howard Another impressive baroque edifice, best known as the setting for *Brideshead Revisited*. (p503)

Audley End One of England's grandest country houses set amid glorious Lancelot 'Capability' Brown–landscaped gardens. (p378)

Chatsworth House Quintessential stately home and gardens; a treasure trove of heirlooms and works of art. (p485)

Longleat The first of England's stately homes to be opened to the public, complemented by a safari park on the grounds. (p264)

Wilton House Home for generations of earls of Pembroke, this house packed with exquisite art and period furniture gives a glimpse into the rarefied existence of English aristocracy. (p259)

Quaint Villages

Clovelly A picture-postcard fishing village with cute cottages tumbling down a steep cobbled hill to the harbour. (p299)

Top: Clovelly (p299)

Bottom: Glastonbury music festival (p323)

Lavenham One of England's most beautiful spots: a collection of exquisitely preserved medieval buildings in East Anglia virtually untouched since the 15th century. (p381)

Painswick The Cotswold Hills has many pretty villages, with hilltop Painswick an absolute gem, unassuming and gloriously noncommercial. (p204)

Goathland One of Yorkshire's most attractive villages, complete with village green and traditional steam railway station. (p519)

Hawkshead Surrounded by dramatic natural scenery, this maze of cobbled lanes and whitewashed cottages is the Lake District's most handsome village. (p595)

Moors & Mountains

North York Moors National Park Wild and windswept, with whaleback hills stretching all the way to the sea, topped by England's largest expanse of heather. (p512)

Lake District A feast of mountains, valleys, views and – of course – lakes; the place to hike the hilltops that inspired William Wordsworth. (p582)

Yorkshire Dales National Park With scenic valleys, high hills and deep caves, the Dales are designed for hiking, biking and caving. (p520)

Dartmoor Exhilarating wilderness, hidden valleys and southern England's highest hills. (p290)

Peak District OK, so it's the most visited national park in Europe, but all those outdoor enthusiasts can't be wrong. (p474)

Shopping

Portobello Road London has shopping galore, with Portobello Rd one of the best-known street markets, surrounded by quirky boutiques and gift stores. (p132)

Victoria Quarter In Leeds; lovely arcades of wrought iron-work and stained glass, home to several top fashion boutiques. (p532)

North Laine The perfect place in Brighton to pick up vegetarian shoes, Elvis outfits and circus monocycles. (p169)

Tetbury An upper-class shopping experience, with stylish shops, and an outlet for goodies from the Prince of Wales' estate at nearby Highgrove. (p205)

Ludlow Foodie heaven, where almost everything is organic, artisan, sustainable or locally sourced. (p444)

Art Galleries

Tate Britain The best-known gallery in London, full to the brim with the finest works. (p85)

Tate Modern London's other Tate focuses on modern art in all its wonderful permutations. (p78)

BALTIC – Centre for Contemporary Art The 'Tate of the North' features work by some of contemporary art's biggest show-stoppers. (p623)

Hepworth Wakefield An award-winning gallery of contemporary sculpture, anchored by a world-class collection of works by local lass Barbara Hepworth. (p534)

Barber Institute of Fine Arts With works by Rubens, Turner and Picasso, this provincial gallery is no lightweight. (p407)

Turner Contemporary In seaside Margate, the south coast's newest art space occupies a purpose-built structure next to the sea, named for one of England's finest artists. (p148)

Yorkshire Sculpture Park England's biggest outdoor sculpture collection, dominated by the works of Henry Moore and Barbara Hepworth. (p534)

Festivals

Notting Hill Carnival London's Caribbean community shows the city how to party. (p107)

Glastonbury More than 40 years on and still going strong, England's biggest and best-loved music festival. (p323)

Brighton Festival You know a festival's matured when it grows a fringe, and this gathering of all things arts is now firmly placed on the calendar. (p165)

Latitude An eclectic mix of music, literature, dance, drama and comedy, with a stunning location in Southwold and manageable size. (p386)

Grassington Festival A village in the scenic Yorkshire Dales hosts this amazing two-week cultural extravaganza. (p522)

Reading Festival Venerable rock gathering that traces its roots back to the 1960s. (p217)

Leeds Festival Northern companion to the long-established Reading Festival. (p529)

Coastal Beauty

Holkham Bay Pristine 3-mile beach; the vast expanse of sand gives a real sense of isolation with giant skies stretching overhead. (p394)

Royal Pavilion (p163), Brighto

Jurassic Coast Exhilarating 3D geology lesson, with towering rock stacks, sea-carved arches and fossils aplenty, plus some of the best beaches in the country. (p245)

Beachy Head & Seven Sisters Where the South Downs plunge into the sea, these mammoth chalk cliffs provide a dramatic finale. (p162)

Robin Hood's Bay Picturesque fishing village nestled in a nook amid impressive sea-cliff scenery. (p519)

Land's End The cliffs and coves at England's far western tip are some of the most dramatic in the country (if you can ignore the theme park). (p341)

Seaside Towns

Scarborough The original English seaside resort, where it all began back in the 17th century. (p506)

Southwold A genteel seaside town with lovely sandy beach, charming pier and rows of colourful beach huts. (p386)

Bournemouth Seven miles of sandy beach, 3000 deckchairs, 1800 beach huts and a pair of Edwardian cliff lifts. (p240)

Brighton Away from the ubercool scene there are still plenty of naughty postcards and kiss-me-quick hats in 'London-by-the-Sea'. (p163)

Eastbourne South-coast favourite, once known as the nation's retirement home, where new attractions and lively ambience now attract a considerably younger crowd. (p161)

Month by Month

January

After the festivities of Christmas and New Year's Eve, the first few weeks of the year can feel a bit of an anticlimax – never helped by the often-bad weather.

✨ The London Parade

A ray of light in the gloom, the New Year's Day Parade in London (www.london-parade.co.uk.) is one of the biggest events of its kind in the world, featuring marching bands, street performers, classic cars, floats and displays, winding their way through the streets.

February

February is midwinter in England. The country may be scenic under snow and sunshine, but more likely grey and gloomy. Festivals and events to brighten the mood are still thin on the ground.

✨ Jorvik Viking Festival

In chilly mid-February, the ancient Viking capital of York becomes home once again to invaders and horned helmets galore, with the intriguing addition of longship races. (p498)

March

Spring starts to show itself, with daffodil blooms brightening up the month. Some people cling to the winter mood, but hotels and inns offer special weekend rates to tempt them out from under their duvets.

☆ University Boat Race

Annual race down the River Thames in London between the rowing teams from Cambridge and Oxford Universities – an institution (since 1856) that still enthrals the country. Late March. (p107)

April

The weather is looking up, warmer and drier days bringing out the spring blossoms. Sights and attractions that closed for the low season open up around the middle of the month or at Easter.

☆ Grand National

Half the country has a flutter on the highlight of the three-day horse race meeting at Aintree, a steeplechase with a testing course and high jumps. First Saturday in April. (p568)

🏃 London Marathon

In early April, superfit athletes cover 26 miles, 385 yards in just over two hours. Others dress up in daft costumes and take considerably longer. (p107)

May

With sunny spring days, the calendar fills with more events. Two public holidays (the first and last Mondays of May) mean road traffic is very busy over the adjoining long weekends.

☆ FA Cup Final

The highlight of the football season for more than a century. All winter, teams from all of England's football divisions have been battling it out in a knockout tournament, culminating in this heady spectacle at Wembley Stadium – the home of English football. Held in early May. (p686)

🎏 Brighton Festival

The lively three-week arts fest takes over the streets of buzzy south-coast resort Brighton during May. Alongside the mainstream performances there's a festival 'fringe' as well. (p165)

🎏 Chelsea Flower Show

The Royal Horticultural Society flower show in late May is the highlight of the gardener's year. Top garden designers take gold, silver and bronze medals (and TV accolades), while the punters take the plants in the last-day giveaway. (p107)

☆ Glyndebourne

From late May till the end of August, this open-air festival of world-class opera enlivens the pastoral surroundings of Glyndebourne House in East Sussex.

🎏 Cotswold Food & Farming Festival

A celebration (www.thecotswoldfoodandfarmingfestival.com) of local food and farming at the Cotswold Farm Park near Cheltenham, with stalls, displays, activities and demonstrating chefs. Main festival in May; others later in the year.

June

Now it's almost summer. You can tell because June sees the music-festival season kick off properly, while sporting events – from rowing to racing – fill the calendar.

☆ Derby Week

Horse racing, people-watching and clothes-spotting are on the agenda at this weeklong race meeting (www.epsomderby.co.uk) in Epsom, Surrey, in early June.

☆ Cotswold Olimpicks

Welly-wanging, pole-climbing and shin-kicking are the key disciplines at this traditional Gloucestershire sports day in early June, held each year since 1612. (p201)

☆ Isle of Wight Festival

Originally held from 1968 to 1970 during the high point of hippie counterculture, this musical extravaganza (www.isleofwightfestival.com) was resurrected in 2002. Today it attracts top bands, especially from the indie and rock fraternities. Held in mid-June. (p237)

☉ Trooping the Colour

Military bands and bear-skinned grenadiers march down London's Whitehall in this mid-June martial pageant to mark the monarch's birthday. (p107)

☆ Royal Ascot

It's hard to tell which matters more – the fashion or the fillies – at this highlight of the horse-racing year, held in mid-June at Berkshire's Royal Ascot racetrack. Expect top hats, designer frocks and plenty of frantic betting. (p216)

☆ Wimbledon Lawn Tennis Championships

Correctly titled the All England Club Championship, and the best-known grass-court tennis tournament in the world, Wimbledon attracts all the big names. Held in late June. (p107)

☆ Glastonbury Festival

England's favourite pop and rock fest held (nearly) every year on a dairy farm in Somerset in late June. Invariably muddy and still a rite of passage for every self-respecting British music fan. (p323)

☆ Meltdown Festival

In late June, London's Southbank Centre (www.southbankcentre.co.uk) hands over the curatorial reigns to a legend of contemporary music (David Bowie, Morrissey, Patti Smith) to pull together a full program of concerts, talks and films. (p107)

☆ Royal Regatta

In late June or early July, boats of every description take to the water for an upper-crust river regatta at Henley-on-Thames. (p218)

🎏 Rochester Dickens Festival

Charles Dickens is one of England's best-known writers, celebrated at this literary festival in the town where he lived and based many of his novels.

Pride

The big event on the gay-and-lesbian calendar, a technicolour street parade through London's West End, culminating in a concert in Trafalgar Sq. Late June or early July. (p107)

July

This is it: summer, with weekly festivals and country shows. Schools break up at the end of the month, so there's a holiday tingle in the air, dulled only by busy Friday-evening roads.

Great Yorkshire Show

In July the charming town of Harrogate plays host to one of England's largest county shows (www greatyorkshireshow.co.uk). Expect Yorkshire grit, Yorkshire tykes, Yorkshire puddings, Yorkshire beef... (p505)

International Birdman Competition

In the first weekend in July, competitors dressed as batmen, fairies and flying machines compete in an outlandish celebration of self-powered flight at West Sussex' Bognor Regis. The furthest flight takes home a £30,000 prize. So far no one's got near the hallowed 100m goal. See www.bird-man.org.uk.

Latitude Festival

Popular and eclectic festival held near the lovely Suffolk seaside town of Southwold, with top names from the alternative-music scene complemented by theatre,

cabaret and literary events. Held in mid-July. (p386)

Cowes Week

The country's biggest yachting spectacular hits the choppy seas around the Isle of Wight in late July.

Womad

In late July roots and world music take centre stage at this former Reading-based festival (www.womad.org), now in a country park near Malmesbury in the south Cotswolds.

Truck

Held in late July, this indie-music festival (www.thisi-struck.com) in Steventon, Oxfordshire, has a loyal following and is known for its eclectic acts.

August

Schools and colleges are closed, parliament is in recess, the sun is shining (hopefully), most people go on holiday for a week or two (some of them abroad), and England is in a holiday mood.

Notting Hill Carnival

A multicultural, Caribbean-style street carnival in late August in London's district of Notting Hill. Steel drums, dancers and outrageous costumes. (p107)

Reading Festival

England's second-oldest music festival. Originally a rock fest, it veers a bit more towards pop these days, but it's still a good bet for big-name bands. Happens in late August. (p217)

Leeds Festival

Leeds' major music festival, and the northern sister of the festival in Reading. The two festivals are the same late-August weekend, with the same line-up. If they play Reading on the Friday they'll play Leeds on Saturday, and vice versa. (p529)

Manchester Pride

One of England's biggest celebrations of gay, bisexual and transgender life. Happens in late August; see www.manchesterpride.com. (p552)

International Beatleweek

In the last week of August, the world's biggest tribute to the Beatles features six days of music, exhibitions, tours and memorabilia sales in Liverpool. (p568)

September

The first week of September feels more like August, but then the schools open up again, motorway traffic returns to normal and the summer party's over for another year. Good weather is still a chance.

Bestival

Quirky music festival in early September, with a different fancy-dress theme every year. Held at Robin Hill Country Park on the Isle of Wight. (p237)

World Gurning Championships

Gurning is face-pulling, and this has to be one of the weirdest events of the year. Elastic-faced contestants come to Egremont in Cumbria in mid-September every year, contorting their features in a bid to pull the most grotesque expressions.

🏃 Great North Run

England's biggest marathon is in London, but the Great North Run in Tyneside in September is the biggest half-marathon in the world, with the greatest number of runners of any race over this distance.

October

October means autumn. Leaves turn golden-brown and, unless there's an 'Indian summer', the weather starts to get cold. Sights and attractions start to shut down for the low season, and accommodation rates drop.

🍴 Falmouth Oyster Festival

The Westcountry port of Falmouth hosts this event to mark the start of the traditional oyster-catching ('dredging') season, and to celebrate local food from the sea and farmland of Cornwall.

☆ Horse of the Year Show

The country's major indoor horse show, with dressage, showjumping and other equine activi-

ties. Held in early October at the NEC arena near Birmingham.

November

Winter's here, and November is dull. The weather's often cold and damp, summer is a distant memory and Christmas seems far away: suitably sombre for Remembrance Day, while Guy Fawkes Night sparks up some fun.

☆ Guy Fawkes Night

Also called Bonfire Night (www.bonfirenight.net) and Fireworks Night, 5 November sees fireworks filling the country's skies in commemoration of a failed attempt to blow up parliament in 1605. Effigies of Guy Fawkes, the leader of the Gunpowder Plot, often burn on bonfires.

◉ Remembrance Day

On 11 November, red poppies are worn and wreaths are laid in towns and cities around the country. The day (www.poppy.org.uk.) commemorates military personnel killed and injured in the line of duty, from the World Wars to modern conflicts.

☆ World's Biggest Liar Contest

Another whacky event, and it's Cumbria again. Fibbers from all walks of life go

head-to-head in a battle of mid-November mendacity at the Bridge Inn in Wasdale.

December

Schools break up around mid-December, but most shops and businesses keep going until Christmas Eve. Many towns and cities hold Christmas markets, ideal places for picking up Christmas presents. Holidaymakers hit the roads on the weekend before Christmas Day, driving to see family or heading for the airports.

🎎 Victorian Festival of Christmas

Portsmouth's historic dockyard, home to HMS *Victory* and the Mary Rose Museum, gets a Dickensian makeover for this celebration (www.christmasfestival.co.uk) of Victorian Christmas traditions including street entertainment, carol singing and a Christmas market. First weekend in December or last weekend in November.

☆ New Year Celebrations

On 31 December, fireworks and street parties happen in town squares across the country, lighting up the nation to welcome in the New Year.

Itineraries

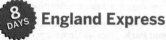 **8 DAYS England Express**

Just over a week is long enough to tick off many of England's highlights. This tour takes in a dozen of the nation's top sights, from London to the Lakes.

Start with a full day in the nation's capital, **London**, simply walking the streets to admire the world-famous sights: Buckingham Palace, Tower Bridge, Trafalgar Sq and more. Then head west for one or both of the grand cathedral cities of **Winchester** and **Salisbury**. Next stop: ancient history – the iconic megaliths of **Stonehenge**.

A short hop northwest leads to the beautiful city of **Bath,** for Roman history and fabulous Georgian architecture. Then cruise across the classic English countryside of the **Cotswolds** to reach **Oxford**, the ancient seat of learning. Not far away is **Stratford-upon-Avon**, for everything Shakespeare.

Next, strike out north for the **Lake District**, one of the country's most scenic areas, then across to **York** for Viking remains and the stunning Minster. End your trip with a visit to **Cambridge**, England's other great university city. Then a final day back in **London**, immersed in galleries, museums, luxury shops, street markets, West End shows or East End cafes – or whatever takes your fancy.

The Full Monty

4 WEEKS

With a month to spare you can enjoy a trip taking in all the very best that England offers, without the pressure of a crowded schedule. This circuit of the country covers all the bases.

Kick off in **London**, and spend a couple of days seeing the big-ticket attractions, but make the time for exploratory saunters as well – along the south bank of the River Thames, or through the markets of the East End. Next, go down to the sea at the buzzy coastal resort of **Brighton**; then west, via **Portsmouth** for the historic dockyard, to reach the picturesque **New Forest**. Head inland to the grand cathedral cities of **Winchester** and **Salisbury**, and on to **Stonehenge**, England's best-known ancient site, and nearby **Avebury Stone Circle** – bigger than Stonehenge but a more intimate experience.

Onwards into deepest Wessex, via Thomas Hardy's hometown, **Dorchester**, to reach the wide and wild expanse of **Dartmoor National Park**. Then it's time for yet another historic city, **Wells**, with its beautiful cathedral, en route to the Georgian masterpiece of **Bath** and the southwest's big little city, **Bristol**. Next comes the classic English countryside of the **Cotswolds**, with a pause at delightful Stow-on-the-Wold, and maybe Broadway or Chipping Campden, before reaching **Oxford**, England's oldest seat of learning. Not far away is Shakespeare central at **Stratford-upon-Avon** – plan on seeing a play by the Bard himself. Continue journeying north via the heather-clad moors and tranquil limestone dales of the **Peak District** to reach England's second city **Manchester** and neighbouring cultural crossroads **Liverpool**.

Then it's back to the wilds again with a short hop to the scenic wonders of the **Lake District**. From the sturdy bordertown of **Carlisle**, follow the ancient Roman landmark of **Hadrian's Wall** all the way to revitalised city **Newcastle-upon-Tyne**. Then it's into the home stretch, south via **Durham** and its world-class cathedral, and then **York** for its Viking remains and stunning Minster, to reach **Cambridge**, England's other great university city. From here it's a hop back to **London**, to use up the last few days of your grand tour, taking in highlights such as the Trafalgar Sq, the National Gallery, Tate Modern, the Tower of London, all polished off with a stroll across Westminster Bridge as Big Ben chimes the hour.

The Wild Side

This is a tour through the best of England's natural landscape, the inspiration for generations of poets, writers and composers. So put on your hiking boots, or have a camera at the ready, as we take a northeast–southwest meander through some of the country's finest national parks and stretches of open countryside.

Start at the spectacular Roman remains of **Hadrian's Wall**, one of England's finest reminders of the classical era, where you can explore the ancient forts and stride beside the ramparts centurion-style. Then continue into Cumbria for the high peaks of the **Lake District National Park**, once the spiritual home of Wordsworth and the Romantic poets, now a mecca for outdoor enthusiasts, with hikes and strolls for all abilities, plus cosy inns and traditional country hotels.

Travelling east from the Lakes carries you across the Pennines – the chain of hills known as the backbone of England – to reach the green hills and valleys of the **Yorkshire Dales National Park**. Nearby are the moors around **Haworth** – inspiration for Emily Brontë's *Wuthering Heights*.

Travel south through the hills and dales of the **Peak District National Park** – stopping off to explore the great park around Chatsworth if time allows – then through central England, via Elgar's beloved **Malvern Hills**, to reach the classic English countryside of the **Cotswolds**. Then continue southwards again to enjoy the epic emptiness of **Salisbury Plain**, home to **Stonehenge** and other archaeological intrigues. Nearby is **Avebury**, England's other great stone circle. A few miles more and you're on Dorset's spectacular fossil-ridden **Jurassic Coast**.

Then head into England's toe, the Westcountry Peninsula, jutting deep into the Atlantic. Take in the lush farmland of Devon and the heathery hills and sandy coves of **Exmoor National Park**, then it's on to the eerie granite tors of **Dartmoor National Park**, which offers some of the country's most bleakly beautiful views. Next stop: **Cornwall**, for pretty ports, gorse-clad cliffs and sparkling bays. Then finish this bucolic excursion at **Land's End**, where the English mainland finally runs out of steam and plunges headlong into the restless ocean.

Legend:
- Heart of England
- Urban Adventure

Map locations: SCOTLAND, NORTHERN IRELAND, Isle of Man, Newcastle-upon-Tyne, Angel of the North, IRISH SEA, IRELAND, Leeds, Pennines, National Coal Mining Museum, Liverpool, Manchester, NORTH SEA, ENGLAND, WALES, Birmingham, Warwick, Stratford-upon-Avon, The Cotswolds, Oxford, LONDON, Cirencester, Windsor, Bristol, Leeds Castle, Canterbury, Bath, BELGIUM, Salisbury, Winchester, English Channel, FRANCE

8 DAYS Urban Adventure

Start in **Bristol**, a thriving regional capital famed for its engineering heritage and lively cultural scene. Then to **Birmingham**, in the heart of the English Midlands, once forlorn and now a byword for successful urban renewal.

Continue north to reach **Manchester**, famous for its music and football team. Architectural highlights include the stunning Imperial War Museum North. Nearby **Liverpool** is reinventing itself as a cultural capital, with the redevelopment most apparent at the historic waterfront, Albert Dock.

Cross the **Pennines** to reach **Leeds**, the 'Knightsbridge of the North' where rundown factories and abandoned warehouses are now loft apartments and ritzy boutiques. But don't forget the past: go underground at the **National Coal Mining Museum**.

Further north is **Newcastle-upon-Tyne** and neighbouring Gateshead, former kings of coal, ships and steel, where heavy industries have given way to art and architecture, most notably the BALTIC contemporary gallery and the Sage concert hall. Conclude your urban tour with a visit to England's best-known public art, the iconic **Angel of the North**.

2 WEEKS Heart of England

Start in **London**, with its biggest landmarks: Westminster Abbey, the Tower of London, St Paul's Cathedral and Buckingham Palace. Out of the centre, the gorgeous gardens at Kew, Eton College and **Windsor Castle** are also must-see sights.

Beyond the capital lies old England proper, especially around the market towns of Kent, where **Canterbury Cathedral** and **Leeds Castle** are top historic sights.

Then loop through Sussex and into Hampshire, where **Winchester**, the ancient capital, boasts another fine cathedral. Jostling for prominence is nearby **Salisbury**, with its famous cathedral spire dominating the landscape for miles around.

Out west, **Bath** is crammed with Georgian architecture, while the picture-perfect **Cotswolds** conceal a host of pretty towns and villages, such as Northleach, Wantage and **Cirencester**, as well as the grand stately home of Blenheim Palace. On to picturesque **Oxford**, crammed with college buildings carved from honey-coloured stone, and **Stratford-upon-Avon**, home of Shakespeare and classic half-timbered houses, leaving just enough time to top up on English history at stunning **Warwick Castle**.

Southwestern Wander
2 WEEKS

Start in **Bristol**, the capital of the West-country, then saunter down through Somerset to **Glastonbury** – famous for its annual music festival and the best place to stock up on candles or crystals at any time of year. South leads to Dorset, where highlights include picturesque **Shaftesbury**.

West leads to heathery **Exmoor National Park**, then its onwards into Devon, where there's a choice of coasts, as well as **Dartmoor National Park**, the highest and wildest hills in southern England.

Cross into Cornwall to explore the space-age biodomes of the **Eden Project**. Nearby, but in another era entirely, is Tintagel Castle, the legendary birthplace of King Arthur. Depending on your tastes, you can hang 10 in surf-flavoured party-town **Newquay**, or browse the galleries at **St Ives**.

Land's End is the natural finish to this wild west meander where the English mainland comes to a final full stop. Sink a drink in the First & Last Inn at nearby Sennen, and promise yourself a return trip some day...

Edge of England
2 WEEKS

Start in **Colchester**, then visit sleepy **Suffolk**, where quaint villages and market towns such as Sudbury and Lavenham dot the landscape. Along the coast you'll discover wildlife reserves, shingle beaches, fishing ports such as **Aldeburgh**, and the delightfully retro seaside resort of **Southwold**.

Things get even quieter in Norfolk, especially around the misty lakes and windmill-lined rivers of the **Norfolk Broads**. For beach strolls or historic country pubs head for the coastal villages near **Wells-next-the-Sea**.

North of Norfolk lies the eerie, flat landscape of the **Fens**, now a haven for otters and birdlife. Then it's north again into Yorkshire to the heather-clad **North York Moors**, where humpbacked hills roll all the way to the coast to drop dramatically into the choppy waters of the North Sea.

Round things off with a stroll between the castles of Bamburgh and Dunstanburgh on the wild **Northumberland Coast**, finishing your tour at the island of **Lindisfarne**.

Plan Your Trip

The Great Outdoors

What's the best way to slow down, meet the locals and get off the beaten track as you travel around England? Simple: go for a walk or get on a bike. Getting involved in the great outdoors is much more rewarding than staring at it through a car window or a camera lens.

Best Outdoors

Best Long-Distance Walks
Coast to Coast, Hadrian's Wall, Cotswold Way, South West Coast Path

Best Areas for Short Walks
Lake District, Yorkshire Dales, Cotswolds, Dartmoor

Best for Coast Walks
Northumberland, Devon and Cornwall, Norfolk and Suffolk, Dorset

Best Time to Go
Summer (June to August) The best time for walking: weather usually warm and hopefully dry; plenty of daylight too.

Late spring (May) and early autumn (September) The seasons either side of summer can be great for walking: fewer crowds; days often mild and sunny.

Best Maps for Walking
Ordnance Survey (UK's national mapping agency) Explorer series 1:25,000 scale.

Harvey Maps (specially designed for walkers) Superwalker series 1:25,000 scale.

Walking

Walking is the most popular outdoor activity in England, for locals and visitors alike: first, because it opens up some beautiful corners of the country, and secondly because it can be done virtually on a whim. In fact, compared to hiking and trekking in some other parts of the world, it doesn't take much planning at all.

Getting Started

An established infrastructure for walkers already exists in England, so everything is easy for visitors or first-timers. Most villages and country towns in areas where walking is popular will have shops selling maps and local guidebooks, while the local tourist office can nearly always provide leaflets and other information. In national parks, suggested routes or guided walks are often available. This all means you can arrive in a place for the first time, pick up some info, and within an hour you'll be walking through some of England's finest landscape. No fees. No permits. No worries. It really is almost effortless.

England's Footpath Network

England is covered in a vast network of footpaths, many of which are centuries old, dating from the time when walking was the only way to get from farm to village, from village to town, from town to coast, or valley to valley. Any walk you do today will follow these historic paths. Even England's longest walks simply link up these networks of many shorter paths. You'll also sometimes walk along 'bridleways' originally for horse transport, and old unsurfaced roads called 'byways'.

Rights of Way

Nearly all footpaths in England are 'rights of way' – public paths and tracks across private property. Even though most land in England is privately owned, from tiny cultivated areas to vast mountain ranges, a right of way across the land cannot be overruled by the owner.

If you come from Australia, America or a country where a lot of land is jealously guarded with padlocked gates and barbed-wire fences, this can be a major revelation.

So if there is a right of way, you can follow it through fields, woods, pastures, paddocks, even farmhouse yards, as long as you keep to the correct route and do no damage.

In some mountain and moorland areas, it gets even better: walkers can move beyond the rights of way, and explore at will. Known as 'freedom to roam', where permitted it's clearly advertised with markers on gates and signposts.

Experience Required?

When deciding which area of England to visit for walking, a lot may depend on your own experience. Generally speaking, the lower and more cultivated the landscape, the easier the walking, with clear paths and signposts – ideal for beginners.

As the landscape gets higher, conditions tend to get more serious. In mountain and moorland areas, if the route is popular there will be a path (although sometimes this is faint), but not many signposts. This option is suitable if you already have a bit of walking/hiking experience.

In the more remote areas, if the route is rarely trodden, there may be no visible path at all, and absolutely no signposts, so you'll need to know what you're doing – and take a detailed map and compass for navigation.

England's Best Walking Areas

Although you can walk pretty much anywhere in England, some areas are better than others. Here's a rundown of favourite places, suitable for short walks of a couple of hours, or longer all-day outings.

Cotswolds

One of the most popular areas for walkers in southern England, the Cotswold Hills (p190) offer classic English countryside, where paths meander through neat fields, past pretty villages with cottages of honey-coloured stone. The eastern side of the Cotswolds tends to be a gentler landscape, while the paths undulate more on the western side, especially along the Cotswold Escarpment – although the views are better here.

Dartmoor

In England's southwest, Dartmoor National Park (p290) boasts the highest hills for miles around, and a great sense of space on the uplands, where much of the landscape is devoid of trees and surprisingly wild. Meanwhile, below the hills, delightful valleys cut into the edges of the moor, perfect for picnics and riverside strolls in summer.

Exmoor

Just to the north of Dartmoor, and sometimes overshadowed by its larger neighbour, southwest England's other national park is Exmoor (p268). Heather-covered hills cut by deep valleys make it a perfect walking area, edged with the added bonus of a spectacular coastline of cliffs and beaches.

> ### WALKING WEBSITES
> Before you set off, take a look at the comprehensive website of the **Ramblers** (www.ramblers.org.uk), the country's leading organisation for walkers. Also available is the annually updated *Walk Britain* handbook listing walker-friendly accommodation across the country.
>
> Also great for specifics on some longer routes is www.nationaltrail.co.uk.

Lake District

If anywhere is the heart and soul of walking in England, it's the Lake District (p582), a wonderful area of soaring peaks, endless views, deep valleys and, of course, beautiful lakes. Protected by the Lake District National Park (and often abbreviated to simply 'the Lakes', but never the 'Lakes District'), it is loved by walkers, partly because of the landscape, and partly because of the history; thanks to poet Wordsworth and his Romantic chums this is where walking for enjoyment really began.

Isle of Wight

Off the south coast of England, this island (p235) is a great spot if you're new to recreational walking, or simply not looking for high peaks and wilderness. Many routes are signposted, and there's a range of short and long options.

New Forest

In England's deep south lies the New Forest (p231). Visitors love this name, as the area is more than 1000 years old and there aren't *that* many trees – but the beautiful open areas of gorse and grassland are ideal for easy strolls.

Northumberland

On northern England's frontier, the starkly beautiful moors of Northumberland National Park (p633) are loved by

keen walkers. For a change of scene, the high cliffs and vast empty beaches on the nearby Northumberland coast are less daunting but just as dramatic – perfect for wild seaside strolls.

Norfolk & Suffolk

In the eastern counties of Norfolk (p387) and Suffolk (p379) the landscape is generally flat, with quiet paths through farmland and beside rivers and lakes, linking picturesque villages, lakes and welcoming country pubs, while the coastline offers a mix of salt marsh, bird reserves, shingle beaches and holiday resorts.

North Downs & South Downs

Between London and the south coast (and within easy reach of both), the North and South Downs (p139) are two parallel ranges of broad chalky hills. On the map, the North Downs appear hemmed in by motorways and conurbations, and while this area can never be described as wilderness, the walking here is often unexpectedly tranquil. The South Downs are higher and not so cramped by urban expansion, with more options for walks, and a landscape protected by England's newest national park.

Peak District

Despite the name, the Peak District (p474) has very few soaring summits. But there are plenty of hills, valleys and moors, making it a favoured walking area in northern England. Protected as a national park, the landscape falls into two zones: the south is mainly farmland, cut by limestone valleys; in the north are high peaty moors with rocky outcrops, and a more austere character.

Southwest Coast

Westcountry gems Cornwall (p327) and Devon (p273) enjoy the best of the English climate and some of the finest scenery in the country, especially on the coast. But the rugged landscape means tough days on the trail. Thanks to those beautiful rivers flowing down steep valleys to the sea, you're forever going up or down. The coastline in neighbouring Dorset – known as the Jurassic Coast thanks to the proliferation of fossils – is less arduous and another great area for seaside walks.

WEATHER WATCH

While enjoying your walking in England, it's always worth remembering the fickle nature of English weather. The countryside can appear gentle and welcoming, and often is, but sometimes conditions can turn nasty – especially on the higher ground. At any time of year, if you're walking on the hills or open moors, it's vital to be well equipped. You should carry warm and waterproof clothing (even in summer), a map and compass (that you know how to use), some water, food and high-energy fuel such as chocolate. If you're really going off the beaten track, leave details of your route with someone.

Yorkshire Dales

With rolling hills, wild moors, limestone outcrops and green valleys cut by scenic streams, the Yorkshire Dales National Park (p520) is one of the most popular walking areas in England. Paths are a little gentler and conditions a little less serious than in the Lake District, with the happy addition of some delightful villages nestling in the dales – many with pubs and tearooms providing refreshments for walkers.

Best Long-Distance Walks

Some long-distance routes traverse the country from west to east, while many more follow the coastline or traverse national parks and other scenic areas. Below is a list of some of the absolute classics.

Coast to Coast Walk

➡ 190 miles; 12-14 days; www.wainwright.org.uk/coasttocoast.html

Also known as Wainwright's Coast to Coast (after the man who devised it), this is not a national trail, but it is England's number-one favourite long-distance route, for locals and visitors alike – through three national parks via a spectacular mix of valleys, plains, mountains, dales and moors.

Hadrian's Wall

➡ 84 miles; 7-8 days; www.nationaltrail.co.uk/hadrianswall

A new national trial following the world-famous Roman structure across northern England, via forts, castles, ramparts and battlements, and giving the Coast to Coast a run for its money in the popularity stakes.

Cotswold Way

➡ 102 miles; 7-10 days; www.nationaltrail.co.uk/cotswold

A picturesque and dramatic route, delivering England at its most enchanting, from villages in intimate valleys to escarpment ridges with bird's-eye views. It's also a trail through time, passing prehistoric hill forts, Romans reminders and fine stately homes.

South West Coast Path

➡ 630 miles; 8-10 weeks; www.southwestcoastpath.com

A roller-coaster romp around England's southwest peninsula, past beaches, bays, shipwrecks, seaside resorts, fishing villages and clifftop castles. Given its length, most walkers do it in sections: the two-week stretch between Padstow and Falmouth around Land's End is most popular.

Pennine Way

➡ 256 miles; 14-21 days; www.nationaltrail.co.uk/pennineway

The granddaddy of them all, an epic trek on a national trail along the mountainous spine of northern England, via some of the highest, wildest countryside in the country. Even in the summer, the elements can be dire, and many walkers find it an endurance test – but not one without rewards.

South Downs Way

➡ 100 miles; 7-9 days; www.nationaltrail.co.uk/southdowns

A sweeping hike through southeast England, along an ancient chalky highway from Winchester to the sea, mostly following a line of rolling hills, meaning big skies and wonderful views, plus picture-perfect villages and prehistoric sites.

Dales Way

➡ 85 miles; 6 days; www.dalesway.org.uk

A nonstrenuous walk through the delightful Yorkshire Dales, via some of the most scenic valleys in northern England, to end at Windermere in the Lake District.

LONG-DISTANCE TRAILS

Some long-distance walking routes – such as the Pennine Way and South West Coast Path – are well known and well maintained, with signposts and route markers along the way, as well as being highlighted on Ordnance Survey maps. The most high-profile of these are the national trails, usually very clearly marked on the ground and on the map – so ideal for beginners or visitors from overseas (although just because they're easy to follow, it doesn't mean they're necessarily easy underfoot). A downside of these famous routes is that they can be crowded at holiday times, making accommodation harder to find. An upside is the great feeling of camaraderie with other walkers on the trail.

Cycling & Mountain Biking

A bike is the perfect mode of transport for exploring back-road England. Once you escape the busy main highways, a vast network of quiet country lanes winds through fields and peaceful villages, ideal for cycle touring. You can cruise through gently rolling landscapes, taking it easy and stopping for cream teas, or you can thrash all day through hilly areas, revelling in steep ascents and swooping downhill sections. You can cycle from place to place, camping or staying in B&Bs (many of which are cyclist-friendly), or you can base yourself in one area for a few days and go out on rides in different directions. All you need is a map and a sense of adventure.

Mountain bikers can go further into the wilds on the tracks and bridleways that criss-cross England's hills and high moors, or head for the many dedicated mountain-bike trail centres where specially built single-track winds through the forests. Options at these centres vary from delightful dirt roads ideal for families to gnarly rock gardens and precipitous drop-offs for hard-core riders, all classified from green to black in ski-resort style.

Sustrans (www.sustrans.org.uk) Details of Britain's national network of cycling trails.

Forestry Commision (www.forestry.gov.uk/england-cycling) Guide to forest cycling trails in England.

Horse Riding & Pony Trekking

If you want to explore the hills and moors but walking or cycling is too much of a sweat, seeing the wilder parts of England from horseback is highly recommended. In rural areas and national parks such as Dartmoor and Northumberland, riding centres cater to all levels of proficiency, with ponies for kids and beginners and horses for the more experienced.

British Horse Society (www.bhs.org.uk) Lists approved riding centres offering day rides or longer holidays on horseback.

Fishing

After walking, fishing is England's most popular outdoor activity. As well as sea angling, there is excellent fishing for brown trout, grayling, pike, perch, carp and other coarse fish all over the country, while the famous chalk streams of Hampshire and Wiltshire offer some of the world's finest fly-fishing for trout.

Fishing rights to most inland waters are privately owned and you must obtain a permit to fish in them – these are usually readily available from the local fishing-tackle shop or hotel, which are also great sources of advice and local knowledge. Permits cost from around £5 to £20 per day but salmon fishing on some rivers – notably the Tyne in northeast England – can be much more expensive (up to £150 a day).

As well as a permit you will need a rod licence, which can be purchased online (www.postoffice.co.uk/rod-fishing-licence) or from post offices all over the country. This costs £3.75/8/27 for one day/eight days/one year for all freshwater fish except salmon and sea trout, which cost £8/23/72.

Fishing in the sea is generally free (except for salmon and sea trout), and neither permit nor rod licence is needed.

FishPal (www.fishpal.com) Information and booking portal for fishing (mostly salmon and trout) all over Britain.

Surfing & Windsurfing

England may not seem an obvious destination for surfing, but conditions are surprisingly good and the large tidal range often means a completely different set of breaks at low and high tides. If you've come from the other side of the world, you'll be delighted to learn that summer water temperatures in southern England are roughly equivalent to winter temperatures in southern Australia (ie you'll still need a wetsuit). At the main spots, it's easy enough to hire boards and wetsuits.

Top of the list are the Atlantic-facing coasts of Cornwall and Devon (Newquay is surf-central, with all the trappings from Kombi vans to bleached hair), and there are smaller surf scenes elsewhere, notably Norfolk and Yorkshire in eastern England.

Windsurfing is hugely popular all around the coast. Top areas include Norfolk, Suffolk, Devon and Cornwall, and the Isle of Wight.

UK Windsurfing Association (www.ukwindsurfing.com) Good source of info on windsurfing.

Surfing Great Britain (www.surfinggb.com) Listings of approved surf schools, courses, competitions and so on.

Sailing & Boating

The south coast of England, with its superb scenery and challenging winds and tides, is one of Europe's most popular yachting areas, while the English canals offer a classic narrow-boating experience. Beginners can take a Royal Yachting Association training course in yachting or dinghy sailing at many sailing schools around the coast. Narrow-boaters only need a quick introductory lesson at the start of their trip.

Royal Yachting Association (www.rya.org.uk) The Royal Yachting Association's website.

CanalHolidays.com (www.canalholidays.com) For more info on narrow boats and lessons.

Rock Climbing

England has a long history of rock climbing and mountaineering, with many of the classic routes having been pioneered in the 19th century. The main rock-climbing areas include the Lake District, the Peak District and Yorkshire, plus the sea cliffs of Devon and Cornwall, but there are also hundreds of smaller crags situated all over the country.

Comprehensive climbing guidebooks are published by the **Fell & Rock Climb-**ing Club (www.frcc.co.uk) and the **Climbers Club** (www.climbers-club.co.uk).

UKClimbing.com (www.ukclimbing.com) The UK Climbing website is full of useful information.

Canoeing & Kayaking

Southwest England's coast, with its sheltered inlets and indented shoreline, is ideal for sea kayaking, while inland lakes and canals across the country are great for Canadian canoeing. Although tame by comparison with alpine torrents, the turbulent spate rivers of the Lake District, Northumberland and Devon offer challenging whitewater kayaking.

Equipment rental and instruction are readily available in major centres such as Cornwall, Devon and the Lake District.

GoCanoeing (www.gocanoeing.org.uk) Lists approved canoeing centres in England

Coasteering

If sometimes a simple clifftop walk doesn't cut the mustard, then coasteering might appeal. It's like mountaineering, but instead of going up a mountain, you go sideways along a coast – a steep and rocky coast – with waves breaking around your feet. And if the rock gets too steep, no problem – you jump in and start swimming. Coasteering centres provide wetsuits, helmets and buoyancy aids; you provide an old pair of training shoes and a sense of adventure. The sport can be done all around England, but the mix of sheer cliffs, sandy beaches and warm water make Cornwall and Devon prime spots.

Coasteering.org (www.coasteering.org) Info on coasteering in Devon and Cornwall.

Plan Your Trip
Travel with Children

England is ideal for travelling with children because of its compact size, packing a lot of attractions into a small area. So when the kids in the back of the car say 'are we there yet?' your answer can often be 'yes, we are'.

Best Regions for Kids

London
Children's attractions galore – some put a strain on parental purse strings, but many others are free.

Southwest England
Some of the best beaches in England, and fairly reliable holiday weather – though crowded in summer.

Peak District
Former railways that are now traffic-free cycle routes make the Peak District perfect for family outings by bike.

Oxford & the Cotswolds
Oxford has kid-friendly museums plus Harry Potter connections; the Cotswold countryside is ideal for little-leg strolls.

Shropshire
The historic England–Wales borderland has many castles to explore, plus excellent museums for inquisitive minds.

Lake District & Cumbria
This is Outdoor Activity Central: zip wires and mountain bikes for teenagers; boat rides and Beatrix Potter for the youngsters.

England for Kids

Many places of interest cater for kids as much as adults. At the country's historic castles, for example, mum and dad can admire the medieval architecture, while the kids will have great fun striding around the battlements or watching falconry demonstrations. In the same way, many national parks and holiday resorts organise specific activities for children. Everything ramps up in the school holidays.

Bargain Hunting

Most visitor attractions offer family tickets – usually two adults plus two children – for less than the sum of the individual entrance charges. Most offer cheaper rates for solo parents and kids too. Be sure to ask, as these are not always clearly displayed.

On the Road

If you're going by public transport, trains are great for families: intercity services have plenty of room for luggage and extra stuff like 'buggies' (prams), and the kids can move about a bit if they get bored. In contrast, they need to stay in their seats on long-distance coaches.

If you're hiring a car, most (but not all) rental firms can provide child seats; you'll need to check this in advance. Most will not actually fit the child seats; you must do that yourself, for insurance reasons.

Dining, not Whining

When it comes to refuelling, most cafes and teashops are child friendly. Restaurants are mixed: some offer high chairs and kiddy portions; others firmly say 'No children after 6pm'.

In some pubs, those under 18 are not allowed, but most pubs in tourist areas serve food, making them 'family friendly'. If in doubt, simply ask the bar staff.

And finally, a word on another kind of refuelling: England is still slightly buttoned up about breastfeeding. Older folks may tut-tut a bit if you give junior a top-up in public, but if done modestly it's usually considered OK.

Children's Highlights

Best Hands-on Action

'Please Do Not Touch'? No chance! Here are some places where grubby fingers and enquiring minds are positively welcomed:

Science Museum, London (p85) Seven floors of educational exhibits at the mother of all science museums.

Discovery Museum, Newcastle (p620) Tyneside's rich history on display; highlights include a buzzers-and-bells science maze.

National Railway Museum, York (p493) Clambering into the driver's cab on a steam locomotive, exploring a Royal Mail train, taking part in engineering demonstrations...it's all here.

Action Stations!, Portsmouth (p229) Toys with a military spin; your chance to fly a helicopter, control an aircraft carrier, or up-periscope in a submarine.

Enginuity, Ironbridge (p439) Endless interactive displays at the birthplace of the Industrial Revolution.

Best Fresh-Air Fun

If the kids tire of England's castles and museums, you're never far from a place for outdoor activities to blow away the cobwebs:

Conkers, Leicestershire (p469) Play indoors, outdoors or among the trees in the heart of the National Forest.

Puzzlewood, Forest of Dean (p210) A wonderful woodland playground with mazelike paths, weird rock formations and eerie passageways to offer a real sense of discovery.

Whinlatter Forest Park, Cumbria (p602) Highlights include a 'Go Ape' adventure park, excellent mountain-bike trails, plus live video feeds from squirrel-cams.

Bewilderwood, Norfolk (p390) Zip wires, jungle bridges, tree houses, marsh walks, boat trips, mazes and all sorts of old-fashioned outdoor adventure.

North York Moors, Yorkshire (p490) Easy, scenic bike trails at Sutton Bank, hard-core mountain biking at Dalby Forest.

Lyme Regis & the Jurassic Coast, Dorset (p253, p245) Guided tours show you how to find your very own prehistoric fossil.

Tissington Trail, Derbyshire (p377) Cycling this former railway is fun and almost effortless. You can hire kids' bikes, tandems and trailers. Don't forget to hoot in the tunnels!

Best Rainy-Day Distractions

On those inevitable gloomy days, head for the indoor attractions, including the nation's great collection of museums. Alternatively, try outdoor stuff like coasteering in Cornwall or canyoning (check conditions) in the Lake District – always fun, wet or dry.

ALL CHANGE

On the sticky topic of dealing with nappies (diapers), most museums and other attractions in England have good baby-changing facilities. Elsewhere, some city-centre public toilets have baby-changing areas, although these can be a bit grimy; your best bet for clean facilities is an upmarket department store. On the road, baby-changing facilities are usually OK at motorway service stations or out-of-town supermarkets.

Cadbury World, Birmingham (p407) Your dentist may cry, but kids love the story of chocolate. And yes, there are free samples.

Eden Project, Cornwall (p349) It may be raining outside, but inside these gigantic semispherical greenhouses it's forever tropical forest or Mediterranean climate.

Cheddar Gorge Caves, Wessex (p321) Finally nail the difference between stalactites and stalagmites in the Westcountry's deep caverns.

Underground Passages, Exeter (p274) Explore medieval catacombs – the only system of its kind open to the public in England.

National Media Museum, Bradford (p533) Atractions include a TV studio where you can film yourself, a gallery of 1980s video games (yes, you can play them) and an IMAX cinema.

Best Stealth Learning

Secretly exercise their minds while the little darlings think they are 'just' having fun.

At-Bristol Science Centre (p303) One of the best interactive science museums in England, covering space, technology and the human brain.

Jorvik Viking Centre, York (p495) An excellent smells-and-all Viking-settlement reconstruction.

Natural History Museum, London (p85) Animals everywhere! Highlights include the life-size blue whale and the animatronics dinosaurs.

Thinktank, Birmingham (p405) Every display comes with a button or a lever at this edu-taining science museum.

National Space Centre, Leicester (p465) Spacesuits, zero-gravity toilets and mini-astronaut training – all guaranteed to fire up little minds.

Planning

When to Go

The best time for families to visit England is pretty much the best time for everyone else – any time from April/May till the end of September. It's worth avoiding August – the heart of school summer holidays – when prices go up and the roads are busy, especially near the coast.

Accommodation

Some hotels welcome kids (with their parents!) and provide cots, toys and babysitting services, while others maintain an adult atmosphere. Many B&Bs offer 'family suites' – two adjoining bedrooms with one bathroom – and an increasing number of hostels (YHA and independent) have family rooms with four or six beds, some even with private bathroom attached. If you want to stay in one place for a while, renting a holiday cottage is ideal. Camping is very popular with English families, and there are lots of fantastic campsites, but you'll usually need all your own equipment.

Useful Websites

Baby Goes 2 (www.babygoes2.com) Advice, tips and encouragement – and a stack of adverts – for families on holiday.

Enjoy England (www.visitengland.com) Official tourism website for England, with lots of useful info for families.

Mumsnet (www.mumsnet.com) No-nonsense advice on travel and more from a gang of UK mothers.

Lonely Planet (www.lonelyplanet.com/family-travel) Inspirational articles about travelling as a family.

Regions at a Glance

From the multicultural melting pot of London to the lonely spiritual outpost of Lindisfarne, England's regions offer a kaleidoscope of classic experiences. Southern England is where you'll find the archetypal English countryside of lush meadows, thatched cottages and games of cricket on the village green. The southwestern counties of Devon and Cornwall are wilder in nature, known for their surf beaches and seafood restaurants. Lovers of moor and mountain will be spoilt for choice in the Lake District and Peak District, while those who prefer gritty industrial heritage and lively nightlife will enjoy the northern cities of Manchester, Liverpool and Newcastle. And bang in the middle is Yorkshire, with everything from the gorgeous city of York to the rolling hills of the Yorkshire Dales.

London

History
Entertainment
Museums

Historic Streets

London's ancient streets contain many of England's most famous and history-steeped landmarks. The echoes of the footfalls of monarchs, poets, whores and saints can still be detected in places like the Tower of London, Westminster Abbey and St Paul's Cathedral, as well as the pubs and coaching inns that once served Dickens, Shelley, Keats and Byron.

Venues & Arenas

From West End theatres to East End clubs, from Camden's rock venues to Covent Garden's opera house, from tennis at Wimbledon to cricket at Lord's or football at Wembley, London's world-famous venues and arenas offer a perpetual clamour of entertainment.

Museums & Galleries

While the British Museum is the big crowd-puller, the capital has museums and galleries of every shape and size – and many of the very best are free.

p52

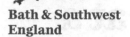

Canterbury & Southeast England

Cathedral
History
Food & Drink

Canterbury Cathedral

A major reason to visit southeast England, Canterbury Cathedral is one of the finest in Europe, and one of the most holy places in Christendom. Write your own Canterbury tale as you explore its atmospheric chapels, cloisters and crypts.

Invasion Heritage

The southeast has always been a gateway for arrivals from the Continent, some more welcome than others. Castles and fortresses, the 1066 battlefield and Dover's secret wartime tunnels all tell the region's story of invasion and defence.

Hops & Grapes

Kent is deservedly known as the Garden of England, long celebrated for its hops, which are still used to flavour traditional English beers. Sussex isn't far behind, with England's finest sparkling wine giving the French stuff a run for its euro.

p138

Oxford, Cotswolds & Around

Architecture
Stately Homes
Villages

Oxford Colleges

Oxford's architecture will never leave you indifferent, whether you gaze across the 'dreaming spires' from the top of Carfax Tower, or explore the medieval streets on foot, or simply admire the fantastic gargoyles on college facades.

Blenheim Palace

Favoured by the rich and powerful for centuries, this region is scattered with some of the finest country houses in England. Top of the pile is the baroque masterpiece of Blenheim Palace, birthplace of Sir Winston Churchill.

Cotswold Villages

Littered with picturesque 'chocolate box' scenes of honey-coloured stone cottages, thatched roofs, neat greens and cobbled lanes, the villages of the Cotswolds provide a charming snapshot of rural England.

p174

Bath & Southwest England

Coastline
History
Activities

Cornish Beaches

England's southwest peninsula juts determinedly into the Atlantic, fringed by an almost endless chain of sandy beaches, from the picturesque scenery of Kynance Cove to the rolling surf of Newquay.

Roman Remains

The handsome Georgian city of Bath – the whole town is a Unesco World Heritage Site – is home to one of the best preserved Roman bath complexes in the world.

Hiking & Surfing

If you like to take it nice and easy, come to walk the moors or tootle along cycle trails. If you prefer life fast and furious, come to surf the best waves in England or learn to dive or kitesurf.

p219

Cambridge & East Anglia

Architecture
Coastline
Waterways

Historic Churches

From the magnificent cathedrals of Ely, Norwich and Peterborough to Cambridge's King's College Chapel, Trinity's Great Court and the New Court at St John's, East Anglia's architectural splendour is second to none.

Seaside Resorts

With wide sandy beaches, great seafood, delightful old pubs, globally important bird reserves, historic villages still proud of their nautical heritage, and classic seaside resorts like Southwold and Cromer, the coastline of East Anglia is rich and varied.

The Broads

The Norfolk and Suffolk Broads are a tranquil haven of lakes and meandering rivers, and an ideal spot for boating, birding, canoeing, cycling or walking, or just getting back to nature at a leisurely pace.

357

Birmingham, the Midlands & the Marches

Activities
Stately Homes
Food & Drink

Hiking & Biking

The Peak District National Park, Cannock Chase, the Shropshire Hills, the Roaches, the Malvern Hills, Offa's Dyke Path, the Tissington Trail and the Pennine Cycleway all make this region great for hiking and biking.

Chatsworth

Grand houses like Haddon Hall, Burghley House and especially Chatsworth promise sprawling deer-filled grounds and grand interiors full of priceless heirlooms and walls dripping with oil paintings.

Curry Capital

Foodies take note: Birmingham is the curry capital of the country (and, increasingly, a magnet for Michelin-starred chefs), while the tiny town of Ludlow is an epicentre of gastronomic exploration.

p397

Yorkshire

Activities
Food & Drink
History

Hiking & Biking

With rolling hills, scenic valleys, high moors and a cliff-lined coast, all protected by national parks, Yorkshire is a natural adventure playground for hiking, biking, surfing and rock climbing.

Roast Beef & Real Ale

Lush pasture means Yorkshire beef and lamb is sought after, while the famous breweries of Masham turn out excellent real ales, best sampled in one of Yorkshire's equally excellent traditional pubs.

Ancient Abbeys

From York's Viking heritage and the ancient abbeys of Rievaulx, Fountains and Whitby to the industrial archaeology of Leeds, Bradford and Sheffield, you can follow several of England's most important historical narratives.

p387

Manchester, Liverpool & Northwest England

History
Sport
Seaside Resorts

Historical Museums

The northwest's collection of heritage sites, from the wonderful People's History Museum in Manchester to the International Slavery Museum in Liverpool, is testament to the region's rich history and its ability to keep it alive.

Football

Two cities, Liverpool and Manchester, give the world four famous clubs, including the two most successful in English history. The National Football Museum in Manchester is just another reason for football fans to visit this region.

Blackpool

The epitome of the classic English seaside resort just keeps on going, thanks to the rides of the Pleasure Beach amusement park, where adrenalin junkies can always find a fix.

p543

The Lake District & Cumbria

Scenery
Activities
Literature

Lakes & Mountains

The Lake District National Park is the most mountainous part of England, home to Scafell (England's highest summit) and countless scenic lakes. Some are big and famous – Windermere, Coniston, Ullswater – while others are small, hidden and little known.

Walking

If anywhere is the heart and soul of walking in England, it's the Lake District. Casual strollers find gentle routes through foothills and valleys, while serious hikers hit the high fells and mountains – many heading to the top of Scafell Pike, England's highest point.

William Wordsworth

The beauty of the Lake District famously moved William Wordsworth to write his ode to 'a host of golden daffodils', and visiting Wordsworth landmarks such as Dove Cottage and Hawkshead Grammar School is one of the region big draws.

p578

Newcastle & Northeast England

History
Landscapes
Castles

Hadrian's Wall

One of the world's premier Roman sites, this potent symbol of imperial power stretches for over 70 miles across the neck of England, from Tyneside to the Solway Firth. You can travel its length, stopping off at forts along the way.

Northumberland National Park

If it's widescreen vistas you're after, the broad moors, stone villages and expansive views of England's most northerly national park never fail to please.

Alnwick Castle

Northumberland is dotted with some of England's finest castles, including the coastal fortresses of Bamburgh and Dunstanburgh, but Alnwick – setting for the *Harry Potter* movies – is the most famous.

p616

On the Road

London

⌨ 020 / POP 8.3 MILLION / AREA 609 SQ MILES

Best Places to Eat

➡ Dinner by Heston Blumenthal (p118)

➡ Five Fields (p118)

➡ Koya (p113)

➡ Brasserie Zédel (p116)

➡ Ledbury (p119)

Best Places to Stay

➡ Haymarket Hotel (p108)

➡ Zetter Hotel (p113)

➡ Hoxton Hotel (p113)

➡ Citizen M (p109)

Why Go?

Everyone comes to London with preconceptions shaped by a multitude of books, movies, TV shows and songs. Whatever yours are, prepare to have them exploded by this endlessly fascinating, amorphous city. You could spend a lifetime exploring it and still find that the slippery thing's gone and changed on you. One thing though is constant: that great serpent of a river enfolding the city in its sinuous loops, linking London both to the green heart of England and the world.

From Roman times people from around the globe have come to London, put down roots and complained about the weather. This is one of the world's most multicultural cities – any given street yields a rich harvest of languages, and those narrow streets are also steeped in fascinating history, magnificent art, imposing architecture and popular culture. When you add an endless reserve of cool to this mix, it's hard not to conclude that London is one of the world's great cities, if not the greatest.

When to Go

➡ London is a place that you can visit any time of the year. That said, different months and seasons boast different charms.

➡ Spring in the city sees daffodils in bloom and blossom in the trees.

➡ In June the parks are filled with people, there's Trooping the Colour, summer arts festivals, Field Day in Victoria Park, other music events, gay pride and Wimbledon.

➡ Although the days are getting shorter, autumn in London is alive with festivals celebrating literature, the arts and culture.

➡ London in December is all about Christmas lights on Oxford and Regent Sts, and perhaps a whisper of snow.

History

London first came into being as a Celtic village near a ford across the River Thames, but the city only really took off after the Roman conquest in AD 43. The invaders enclosed their 'Londinium' in walls that still find refrain in the shape of the City (with a capital 'C') of London today.

By the end of the 3rd century AD, Londinium was home to some 30,000 people. Internal strife and relentless barbarian attacks wore the Romans down, however, and they abandoned Britain in the 5th century, reducing the settlement to a sparsely populated backwater.

The Saxons moved in next, their 'Lundenwic' prospering and becoming a large, well-organised town. As the city grew in importance, it caught the eye of Danish Vikings, who launched numerous invasions. In 1016 the Saxons, finally beaten down, were forced to accept the Danish leader Knut (Canute) as King of England, after which London replaced Winchester as capital. In 1042, the throne reverted to the Saxon Edward the Confessor, who built Westminster Abbey.

The Norman Conquest of 1066 saw William the Conqueror march into London, where he was crowned king. He built the White Tower (the core of the Tower of London), negotiated taxes with the merchants, and affirmed the city's right to self-government. From then until the late 15th century, London politics were largely taken up by a three-way power struggle between the monarchy, the church and city guilds. An uneasy political compromise was reached between the factions, and the city expanded rapidly in the 16th century under the House of Tudor.

In a rerun of the disease that wiped out half of London's population between 1348 and 1350, the Great Plague struck in 1665, and by the time the winter cold arrested the epidemic, 100,000 Londoners had perished. The cataclysm was followed by further devastation when the Great Fire of 1666 sent the city skywards. One upshot of the conflagration was a blank canvas for master architect Sir Christopher Wren to build his magnificent churches.

Despite these setbacks, London continued to grow, and by 1700 it was Europe's largest city, with 600,000 people. An influx of foreign workers brought expansion to the east and south, while those who could afford it headed to the more salubrious environs of the north and west. Georgian London saw a surge in artistic creativity, with the likes of Dr Johnson, Handel, Gainsborough and Reynolds enriching the city's culture, while architects fashioned an elegant new metropolis.

In 1837, 18-year-old Victoria began her epic reign, as London became the fulcrum of the British Empire. The Industrial Revolution saw the building of new docks and railways (including the first underground line in 1863), while the Great Exhibition of 1851 showcased London to the world. During the Victorian era, the city's population mushroomed from just over two million to 6.6 million.

Although London suffered a relatively minor bruising during WWI, it was devastated by the Luftwaffe in WWII, when huge swaths of the centre and East End were flattened and 32,000 people were killed. Ugly housing and low-cost developments followed, and pollutants – both residential and industrial – rose steadily into the air. On 6 December 1952, the Great Smog (a lethal combination of fog, smoke and pollution) descended, killing some 4000 people.

Prosperity gradually returned to the city, and creative energy bottled up in the postwar years was suddenly unleashed. In the 'Swinging Sixties', London became the capital of cool in fashion and music – a party followed morosely by the austere 1970s. Since then the city has surfed up and down the waves of global fortunes, hanging on to its position as the world's leading financial centre.

In 2000, the modern metropolis won its first mayor of London, an elected role covering the City and all 32 urban boroughs. Bicycle-riding Boris Johnson, a Tory (Conservative) with a shock of blond hair and an affable persona, was elected in 2008, and retained his post in the 2012 mayoral election.

Triggered by the shooting of a man by police in Tottenham in August 2011, numerous London boroughs were rocked by riots characterised by looting and arson. Analysts still debate the causes of the disorder, ascribing any number of factors from single-parent families to gang culture, unemployment and criminal opportunism.

Both the Olympics and the Queen's Diamond Jubilee concocted a splendid display of pageantry for London in 2012. New overground train lines opened, a cable car was flung across the Thames and a once rundown and polluted area of East London was regenerated for the Olympic Park. The games themselves were a universally applauded success, kicked off by a stupendous Opening Ceremony orchestrated by Danny Boyle.

London Highlights

1 Watching the world pass by on a sunny day in **Regent's Park** (p92) or any of London's other green oases

2 Sifting through the booty of an empire at the **British Museum** (p93)

3 Losing your head in history at the **Tower of London** (p70)

4 Sizing up the awe-inspiring architecture of **Westminster Abbey** (p56)

5 Raising a glass while overlooking the Thames from the **Dove** (p119) or another riverside London pub

◉ Sights

The city's main geographical feature is the murky Thames, which snakes around, but roughly divides the city into north and south. The old City of London is the capital's financial district, covering roughly a square mile bordered by the river and the many gates of the ancient (long-gone) city walls: Newgate, Moorgate etc. The areas east of the City are collectively known as the East End. The West End, on the City's other flank, is effectively the centre of London gravity. It actually falls within the City of Westminster, one of London's 32 boroughs and long the centre of government and royalty.

Surrounding these central areas are dozens of former villages (Camden Town, Islington, Clapham etc), each with its own High St, long ago swallowed by London's sprawl.

When the sun shines make like a Londoner and head to the parks.

◉ Westminster & St James's

Purposefully positioned outside the old City (London's fiercely independent burghers preferred to keep the monarch and parliament at arm's length), Westminster has been the centre of the nation's political power for nearly a millennium. The area's many landmarks combine to form an awesome display of authority, pomp and gravitas.

St James's is an aristocratic enclave of palaces, famous hotels, historic shops and elegant edifices, with some 150 historically noteworthy buildings in its 36 hectares.

★Westminster Abbey   CHURCH
(Map p58; ☑020-7222 5152; www.westminster -abbey.org; 20 Dean's Yard, SW1; adult/child £18/8, verger tours £3; ⊙9.30am-4.30pm Mon, Tue, Thu & Fri, to 7pm Wed, to 2.30pm Sat; ⊜Westminster) One of London's most imposing treasures, Westminster Abbey serves up the country's venerable history on cold slabs of stone. For centuries, the nation's greatest have been interred here, including most of the monarchs from Henry III (died 1272) to George II (1760). Every sovereign since William the Conqueror has been crowned here, with the exception of a couple of unlucky Eds who were murdered (Edward V) or abdicated (Edward VIII) before the magic moment.

The abbey is not only a sublime place of worship, it's etched with enough history and architectural detail to fill several days' exploration. It has never been a cathedral

(the seat of a bishop). It's what is called a 'royal peculiar' and is administered directly by the Crown. Look out for the curiously underwhelming Coronation Chair.

The building itself is an arresting spectacle. Though a mixture of architectural styles, it is considered the finest example of Early English Gothic in existence. The original church was built in the 11th century by King (later Saint) Edward the Confessor, who is buried in the chapel behind the main altar. Henry III began work on the new building in 1245 but didn't complete it; the French Gothic nave was finished in 1388. Henry VII's astonishing Late Perpendicular–style Lady Chapel was consecrated in 1519 after 16 years of construction.

Apart from the royal graves, keep an eye out for the many famous commoners interred here, especially in Poets' Corner, where you'll find the resting places of Chaucer, Dickens, Hardy, Tennyson, Dr Johnson and Kipling, as well as memorials to other literary titans (Shakespeare, Austen, Brontë etc). Elsewhere you'll find the graves of Handel and Sir Isaac Newton.

The octagonal Chapter House dates from the 1250s and was where the monks would meet for daily prayer before Henry VIII's suppression of the monasteries in 1536. The door on your right as you enter is the oldest in Britain, dating to around 1050 AD. Used as a treasury and 'Royal Wardrobe', the cryptlike Pyx Chamber dates from about 1070. The neighbouring Abbey Museum has as its centrepiece the death masks of generations of royalty.

Parts of the Abbey complex are free to visitors. This includes the 900-year-old College Garden (10am-6pm Tuesday to Thursday April to September, to 4pm Tuesday to Thursday October to March) and the Cloister, where drinks and snacks are available at the Coffee Club. For a proper sit-down meal head for the new Cellarium (Map p58; ☑020-7222 0516; www.cellariumcafe.com; mains £9.50-14.50; ⊙9am-6pm Mon-Fri, to 4.30pm Sat), part of the original 14th-century Benedictine monastery with stunning views of the Abbey's architectural detailing.

Adjacent to the abbey is St Margaret's Church (Map p58; ⊙9.30am-3.30pm Mon-Fri, to 1.30pm Sat, 2-4.30pm Sun), the House of Commons' place of worship since 1614. There are windows commemorating churchgoers Caxton and Milton, and Sir Walter Raleigh is buried by the altar.

Verger-led tours are held several times a day (except Sunday); call ahead to secure a place. Of course, admission to the Abbey is free if you wish to attend a service. On weekdays, Matins is at 7.30am, Holy Communion at 8am and 12.30pm, and Choral Evensong at 5pm. There are services throughout the day on Sunday. You can sit and savour the atmosphere, even if you're not religious.

★**Houses of Parliament**   HISTORIC BUILDING
(Map p58; www.parliament.uk; Parliament Sq, SW1; Ⓔ Westminster) **FREE** Coming face to face with one of the world's most recognisable landmarks can be a surreal moment, but in the case of the Houses of Parliament, it's a revelation. Photos just don't do justice to the ornate stonework and golden filigree of Charles Barry and Augustus Pugin's neo-Gothic masterpiece (1840). Its most famous feature is its clock tower, aka Big Ben (Map p58) (actually the 13-ton bell, named after Benjamin Hall, commissioner of works when the tower was completed in 1858).

Officially called the Palace of Westminster, the oldest part is Westminster Hall (1097), one of only a few sections that survived a catastrophic fire in 1834. Its roof, added between 1394 and 1401, is the earliest known example of a hammerbeam roof and has been described as the greatest surviving achievement of medieval English carpentry.

At the business end, parliament is split into two houses. The green-hued House of Commons is the lower house, where the 650 elected Members of Parliament sit. Traditionally the home of hereditary bluebloods, the scarlet-decorated House of Lords now has peers appointed through various means. Both houses debate and vote on legislation, which is then presented to the Queen for her Royal Assent (in practice, this is a formality; the last time Royal Assent was denied was 1708). At the annual State Opening of Parliament (usually in November), the Queen takes her throne in the House of Lords, having arrived in the gold-trimmed Irish State Coach from Buckingham Palace. It's well worth lining the route for a gawk at the crown jewels sparkling in the sun.

When parliament is in session, visitors are admitted to the House of Commons Visitors' Gallery. The best time to watch a debate is during Prime Minister's Question Time at noon on Wednesday, but it's also the busiest. Enter via St Stephen's Entrance (Map p58). The House of Lords Visitors' Gallery can also be accessed.

On Saturdays year-round and when Parliament is in summer recess (from mid-July to early September), visitors can join a 75-minute guided tour (Ⓙ 0844 847 1672; www.ticketmaster.co.uk/housesofparliament; 75min tour adult/child £16.50/7) of both chambers, Westminster Hall and other historic buildings conducted by qualified Blue Badge Tourist Guides in six languages. Tour schedules change with every recess, so check (and book) ahead.

LONDON IN...

Two Days

Only two days? Start in **Trafalgar Sq** and see at least the outside of all the big-ticket sights – **London Eye**, **Houses of Parliament**, **Westminster Abbey**, **St James's Park and Palace**, **Buckingham Palace**, **Green Park**, **Hyde Park** and **Kensington Gardens and Palace**– and then motor around the **Tate Modern** until you get booted out. In the evening, explore **Soho**. On day two, race around the **British Museum**, then head to the **City**. Start with our **walking tour** and finish in the **Tower of London**. In the evening, head to **Clerkenwell** for international eats, then **Hoxton** and **Shoreditch** for hip bars.

Four Days

Take the two-day itinerary but stretch it to a comfortable pace, spending extra time in the Tate Modern, British Museum and Tower of London. Stop at the **National Gallery** while you're in Trafalgar Sq and explore inside Westminster Abbey and **St Paul's Cathedral**. On your extra evenings, check out **Camden** and **Islington** or enjoy a no-expenses-spared dinner in **Kensington** or **Knightsbridge**.

One Week

As above, but slap on a day each for **Greenwich**, **Kew Gardens** and **Hampton Court Palace**.

Westminster & St James's

River Thames

Victoria Embankment

Whitehall Pl

Whitehall 6

Horse Guards Parade

Treasury

HorseGuards Rd

The Mall

Richmond Tce

Foreign & Commonwealth Office

King Charles St

Great George St

11

8

21
22
Westminster
Bridge St
10 Big Ben
3 Houses of Parliament
St Margaret St 17
Abingdon St
Millbank
16
4
Westminster Abbey
18
Parliament Sq

Great College St
Tufton St
Great Smith St Marsham St
Monck St
Great Peter St
Medway St
Old Pye St
Tothill St
Old Queen St

St James's Park

St James's Park Lake

Birdcage Walk

St James's Park
Broadway
Petty France
Caxton St
Victoria St

10

Carlton Gdns

ST JAMES'S

Pall Mall
Marlborough Rd
15
St James's St
St James's St

14

Queen's Walk

Queen Victoria Monument
Spur Rd
Buckingham Gate
Castle La

Buckingham Palace
2
7
12

Victoria St
Howick Pl
Ashley Pl
20

Green Park
9
Green Park

Piccadilly

Palace St
Cardinal Walk
Bressenden Pl
Lower Grosvenor Pl
Buckingham Palace Rd
13
23
Eaton La
Victoria

Victoria St
Victoria

Buckingham Palace Gardens
Constitution Hill

Duke of Wellington Pl
Memorial Gates
1

Hyde Park

Serpentine Rd

Rotten Row

Curzon St
Market Mews
Shepherd St
Hertford St
Brick St
25

Old Park La
Hamilton Pl
5

Park La

Hyde Park Corner
19
Grosvenor Pl
Grosvenor Cres
Halkin St
24
Chapel St
Chester St
Upper Belgrave St
Wilton St
BELGRAVIA
Hobart Pl
Eaton Sq

Belgrave Sq
Belgrave Square
Belgrave Pl
Eaton Pl
Lyall Mews

Whitehall Pl

500 m
0.25 miles

Tate Britain (500m)
Victoria Tower Gardens

Green Park

★ **Buckingham Palace**   PALACE
(Map p58; ☎020-7766 7300; www.royalcollection.
org.uk; Buckingham Palace Rd, SW1; adult/child
£19.75/11.25; ⊙9.30am-7.30pm late Jul-Aug, to
6.30pm Sep; ⊜St James's Park, Victoria, Green
Park) Built in 1703 for the Duke of Buckingham, Buckingham Palace replaced St
James's Palace as the monarch's official
London residence in 1837. When she's not
giving her famous wave to far-flung parts
of the Commonwealth, Queen Elizabeth
II divides her time between here, Windsor
and Balmoral. To check if she's at home, see
whether the yellow, red and blue standard
is flying. Nineteen lavishly furnished State
Rooms are open to visitors when HRH (Her
Royal Highness) takes her holidays.

The two-hour tour includes the Throne
Room, with his-and-hers pink chairs ini-
tialed 'ER' and 'P'. Access is by timed tickets
with admission every 15 minutes (audioguide included). Needless to say, the gardens
are an absolute picture.

Your ticket to Buckingham Palace is good
for a return trip if bought direct from the
palace ticket office (ask to have it stamped).
A 'Royal Day Out' is a combined ticket including the State Rooms, Queen's Gallery
and Royal Mews (adult/child £34.50/19.50).

➡ **Changing of the Guard**
At 11.30am daily from April to July, and
on alternate days (weather permitting)
from August to March, the old guard (Foot
Guards of the Household Regiment) comes
off duty to be replaced by the new guard on
the forecourt of Buckingham Palace. Highly
popular, the show lasts about forty minutes

(brace for crowds). If you're here in November, the procession leaving the palace for the
State Opening of Parliament is much more
impressive.

➡ **Queen's Gallery**
(www.royalcollection.org.uk; Southern wing, Buckingham Palace; adult/child £9.50/4.80, with Royal
Mews £16.25/9.10; ⊙10am-5.30pm) Originally
designed by John Nash as a conservatory,
the Queen's Gallery showcases some of the
palace's treasures on a rotating basis, through
temporary exhibitions. Entrance to the gallery
is through Buckingham Gate.

➡ **Royal Mews**
(www.royalcollection.org.uk; adult/child £8/5, with
Queen's Gallery £16.25/9.10; ⊙10am-5pm Apr-
Oct, to 4pm Mon-Sat Nov & Dec;) Indulge your
Cinderella fantasies while inspecting the
exquisite state coaches in the Royal Mews,
a working stable looking after the immaculately groomed horses and opulent vehicles
the royals use for getting from A to B. Highlights include the magnificent gold coach of
1762 and the 1910 Glass Coach (Prince William and Catherine Middleton actually used
the 1902 State Landau for their wedding in
2011).

Supreme Court   LANDMARK
(Map p58; www.supremecourt.gov.uk; Parliament
Sq, SW1; ⊙9.30am-4.30pm Mon-Fri; ⊜Westmin-
ster) **FREE** The Supreme Court, the highest court in the UK, is now housed in the
neo-Gothic Middlesex Guildhall (1913) on
Parliament Square. Members of the public
can observe cases when the court is sitting
four days a week (Monday to Thursday). On

LONDON SIGHTS

Westminster & St James's

the lower ground floor is a permanent exhibition on the UK's highest court as well as the history of the building.

St James's Park & Palace   PARK

(⊖ St James's Park, Green Park) With its manicured flower beds and ornamental lake, St James's Park is delightful for strolling and taking in the surrounding palaces. The striking Tudor gatehouse of St James's Palace (Map p58; www.royal.gov.uk; Cleveland Row, SW1; ⊖ Green Park), initiated by the palace-mad Henry VIII in 1530, is best approached from St James's St, to the north of the park. This was the residence of Prince Charles and his sons before they shifted next door to Clarence House (1828), following the death of its previous occupant, the Queen Mother.

Green Park   PARK

(Map p58; www.royalparks.gov.uk; ⊙24hr; ⊖ Green Park) Green Park's 47-acre expanse of meadows and mature trees links St James's Park to Hyde Park and Kensington Gardens, forming a green corridor from Westminster all the way to Kensington. Once a duelling ground, the park became a vegetable garden during WWII. Although it doesn't have lakes, fountains or formal gardens, it's blanketed with daffodils in spring and semi-naked bodies whenever the sun shines.

Westminster Cathedral   CHURCH

(Map p58; www.westminstercathedral.org.uk; Victoria St, SW1; tower adult/child £5/2.50; ⊙9.30am-5pm Mon-Fri, to 6pm Sat & Sun; ⊖ Victoria) Begun in 1895, this neo-Byzantine cathedral remains a work in progress, with new areas completed as funds allow. Look out for Eric Gill's highly regarded stone Stations of the Cross (1918). The Treasures of the Cathedral exhibition is rewarding, there's a cafe near the Baptistry and topping it all, the distinctive 83m red-brick and white-stone tower offers tantalising views of London and, unlike St Paul's dome, you can take the lift.

The Chapel of the Blessed Sacrament and other parts of the interior are ablaze with Eastern Roman mosaics and ornamented with 100 types of marble; other areas are just bare brick.

Banqueting House   PALACE

(Map p58; www.hrp.org.uk/banquetinghouse; Whitehall, SW1; adult/child £6.60/free; ⊙10am-5pm; ⊖ Westminster) Beautiful Banqueting House was conceived by Inigo Jones for James I in 1622. It's the only surviving part of Whitehall Palace after the Tudor bit went

🏃 City Walk
Royal London Tour

START: HOUSES OF PARLIAMENT
END: HOUSES OF PARLIAMENT
LENGTH: 4 MILES; THREE TO FOUR HOURS

From Westminster underground station, cross Bridge St to the Palace of Westminster, aka the ❶ **Houses of Parliament** (p57). Originally built in 1097, Westminster Hall is the oldest surviving part of the original palace, much of which burned down in October 1834. Following the length of the Houses of Parliament along Abingdon St (which becomes Old Palace Yard) brings you to the ❷ **Jewel Tower**, the only other still-extant chunk of the old palace, built in the 14th century for storing Edward III's royal treasures.

Exit the Jewel Tower to breathtaking ❸ **Westminster Abbey** (p56), London's West Minster (as distinct from the minster in the east – St Paul's Cathedral) and traditional venue of coronation for the English monarchy. Walking around Parliament Sq, note the ❹ **Supreme Court** (p59), within the ornate Middlesex Guildhall, dating from 1913.

Round the corner and walk west along Great George St. Turn left down Storey's Gate and then right into Old Queen St, before trotting down ❺ **Cockpit Steps**, said to be haunted by a headless woman dressed in red! The steps lead down to lovely Birdcage Walk, named after the royal Aviary, which was once situated here. Cross over the road and walk into ❻ **St James's Park** (p60) to walk alongside the lake. Near the southwestern end of the park is the ❼ **Guards Museum** on the far side of Birdcage Walk.

Walk up Buckingham Gate to the ❽ **Queen's Gallery** (p59) and the ❾ **Royal Mews** (p59) before walking back to ❿ **Buckingham Palace** (p59) and the ⓫ **Queen Victoria Memorial**, dating from 1911, with its grumpy-looking monarch staring down the Mall. Follow the ceremonial route of the Mall (rhymes with 'shall') and cross into ⓬ **Green Park** (p60) to head up Queen's Walk to grand ⓭ **Spencer House** (p64) before retracing your steps back to the Mall and on to

14 Clarence House, residence of Prince Charles and former home of Queen Elizabeth the Queen Mother.

Continue east along the Mall then walk north up Marlborough Road to **15 St James's Palace** (p60) and the **16 Queen's Chapel** opposite. Open during services only, the church interior has exquisite 17th-century fittings. Return to the Mall briefly, then take the steps up alongside a **17 bronze statue** of Queen Elizabeth the Queen Mother with King George VI behind her.

Head up Carlton Gardens and take the first left (also Carlton Gardens) and cross over the pedestrian crossing in Pall Mall to reach **18 St James's Sq**, surrounded by handsome Georgian architecture. With a statue of King William III at its centre, the private gardens at the heart of the square are open from 10am to 4.30pm on weekdays.

Head up Duke of York St towards the side-on form of St James's Piccadilly, designed by Christopher Wren, turn left along Jermyn St to cross Duke St St James's and walk up colon-naded Piccadilly Arcade to exit into Piccadilly. On the far side of the road is the impressive entrance of the **19 Royal Academy of Arts** (p65), founded by George III in 1768, and located within Burlington House. Head back across the road to mint-green **20 Fortnum & Mason** (p131), London's oldest grocery store and holder of many royal warrants.

Walk east along Piccadilly and turn right down Church Pl, then left onto Jermyn St. Take a right at Regent St, then left onto King Charles II St and walk down **21 Royal Opera Arcade**, London's oldest shopping arcade (designed by John Nash). From Pall Mall, walk along Cockspur St to pass Trafalgar Sq and head down Whitehall. Walking past the old Admiralty Building, you will reach **22 Horse Guards Parade**, where the mounted troopers of the Household Cavalry change guard daily at 11am (10am Sunday) and a lite-pomp version takes place at 4pm when the dismounted guards are changed. Open daily, the Household Cavalry Museum is here as well. On the far side of Whitehall stands **23 Banqueting House** (p60), with its bust of Charles I on the corner above the door, while continuing south along Whitehall takes you past **24 No 10 Downing Street** (p64) and returns you to the **25 Houses of Parliament**.

Royal London

Along with Stonehenge and Big Ben, the current monarch, Queen Elizabeth II, is one of the most potent symbols of England. Pretty much anything connected to the country's royal heritage is a guaranteed attraction – especially the capital's fine collection of palaces and castles.

The Tower of London

The Tower of London (p70) has a 1000-year-old history and foundations that date back to Roman times. Over the centuries it's been a royal residence, treasury, mint, prison and arsenal. Today it's home to the spectacular Crown Jewels, as well as red-coated Beefeaters and ravens attributed with mythical power.

. Windsor Castle **2.** Tower of London
3. Hampton Court Palace **4.** Buckingham Palace

Windsor Castle

Although not actually in London, Windsor Castle (p214) is near enough to visit on a day trip. This is the largest and oldest occupied fortress in the world, an astounding edifice of defensive walls, towers and battlements, used for state occasions and as the Queen's weekend retreat.

Buckingham Palace

Buckingham Palace (p59) has been the monarch's London residence since 1837, and the current Queen divides her time between here, Windsor Castle and Balmoral in Scotland. If she's at home, the 'royal standard' flag flies on the roof. If she's out, you can take a tour to see inside. Either way, don't miss the famous Changing of the Guard.

Hampton Court Palace

Hampton Court Palace (p102) is England's largest and grandest Tudor structure, used by King Henry VIII as a riverside hideaway. After admiring the grand interior, you can relax in the extensive gardens, but don't get lost in the 300-year-old maze.

heavenwards in a 1698 conflagration. The chief attraction is the ceiling, painted by Rubens in 1635 at the behest of Charles I. The king didn't get to savour it for long, in 1649 he was frogmarched out of the 1st-floor balcony to lose his head for treason.

No 10 Downing Street
HISTORIC BUILDING

(Map p58; www.number10.gov.uk; 10 Downing St, SW1; ⊖Westminster) It's fittingly British that the official seat of the prime minister is a nondescript Georgian town house in Whitehall. The street was cordoned off with a rather large iron gate during Margaret Thatcher's tenure, so you can't get up close.

Churchill War Rooms
MUSEUM

(Map p58; www.iwm.org.uk; Clive Steps, King Charles St, SW1; adult/child £17.50/free; ⊗9.30am-6pm, last entry 5pm; ⊖Westminster) Winston Churchill coordinated the Allied resistance against Nazi Germany on a Bakelite telephone from this underground military HQ during WWII. The Cabinet War Rooms remain much as they were when the lights were flicked off in 1945, capturing the drama and dogged spirit of the time, while the museum affords intriguing insights into the resolute, cigar-smoking wartime leader.

Institute of Contemporary Arts
ARTS CENTRE

(ICA; Map p58; ✆020-7930 9493; www.ica.org. uk; Nash House, The Mall, SW1; ⊗11am-11pm Tue-Sun, exhibition times vary; ⊖Charing Cross) FREE A one-stop contemporary-art bonanza, the excitingly cerebral program at the ICA embraces film, photography, theatre, installations, talks, performance art, DJs, digital art and book readings. Stroll around the galleries, watch a film, browse the left-field bookshop, then hit the bar for a beer.

Spencer House
HISTORIC BUILDING

(Map p58; ✆020-7514 1958; www.spencerhouse. co.uk; 27 St James's Pl, SW1; adult/child £12/10; ⊗10.30am-5.45pm Sun Feb-Jul & Sep-Dec; ⊖Green Park) The ancestral home of Princess Diana's family, Spencer House was built in the Palladian style between 1756 and 1766. It was converted into offices after the Spencers moved out in 1927, but 60 years later an £18 million restoration returned it to its former glory. Visits are by guided tour.

Apsley House
HISTORIC BUILDING

(Map p58; www.english-heritage.org.uk; 149 Piccadilly, Hyde Park Cnr, W1; adult/child £6.90/4.10, with Wellington Arch £8.90/5.30; ⊗11am-5pm Wed-Sun Apr-Oct, to 4pm Wed-Sun Nov-Mar; ⊖Hyde Park Corner) This stunning house, containing exhibits devoted to the Duke of Wellington, was designed by Robert Adam for Baron Apsley in the late 18th century. It was later sold to the first Duke of Wellington, who cut Napoleon down to size in the Battle of Waterloo and lived here for 35 years until his death in 1852. With 10 of its rooms open to visitors, the house has a stairwell dominated by Antonio Canova's staggering 3.4m-high statue of a fig-leafed Napoleon with titanic shoulders.

Don't miss the elaborate Portuguese silver service or the impressive Egyptian service, a divorce present from Napoleon to Josephine (she declined it).

Wellington Arch
MUSEUM

(Map p58; www.english-heritage.org.uk; Hyde Park Corner, W1; adult/child £4.20/2.50, with Apsley House £8.90/5.30; ⊗10am-5pm Wed-Sun Apr-Oct, to 4pm Wed-Sun Nov-Mar; ⊖Hyde Park Corner) Throttled by the Hyde Park Corner roundabout, this is London's answer to the Arc de Triomphe (except this one commemorates France's *defeat* at the hands of the Duke of Wellington). Erected in 1826, the monument is topped with Europe's largest bronze sculpture: *Peace Descending on the Quadriga of War* (1912). Until the 1960s, it housed the capital's smallest police station (complete with pet moggy). The open-air balconies afford unforgettable views of Hyde Park, Buckingham Palace and the Houses of Parliament.

On the inside is an exhibition on the history of the arch and the newly opened Quadriga Gallery.

◉ West End

A strident mix of culture and consumerism, but more a concept than a fixed geographical area, the West End is synonymous with roof-raising musicals, bright lights, outstanding restaurants and bag-laden shoppers. It casts its net around Piccadilly Circus and Trafalgar Sq to the south, Regent St to the west, Oxford St to the north, Covent Garden to the east and the Strand to the southeast.

Named after the elaborate collars (picadils) that were the sartorial staple of a local 17th-century tailor, Piccadilly became the fashionable haunt of the well-heeled (and collared), and still boasts establishment icons such as the Ritz hotel and the Fortnum & Mason department store. It meets Regent St, Shaftesbury Ave and Haymarket at the neon-lit swirl of Piccadilly Circus, home to the ever-popular and ever-misnamed Eros statue.

Mayfair, west of Piccadilly Circus, hogs all of the most expensive streets from the Monopoly board, including Park Lane and Bond St, which should give you an idea of what to expect: lots of pricey shops, Michelin-starred restaurants, society hotels and gentlemen's clubs. The elegant bow of Regent St and frantic Oxford St are the city's main shopping strips. At the heart of the West End lies Soho, a boho grid of narrow streets and squares hiding gay bars, strip clubs, cafes and advertising agencies. Carnaby St was the epicentre of the swinging London of the 1960s, but is now largely given over to chain fashion stores. Lisle St and, in particular, Gerrard St (north of Leicester Sq) form the heart of Chinatown, a convergence of reasonably priced Asian restaurants, decorative Chinese arches and aromatic Cantonese supermarkets. Heaving with tourists and dominated by huge cinemas (with occasional star-studded premieres), neighbouring Leicester Sq (*les*-ter) has undergone a facelift. Described by Benjamin Disraeli in the 19th century as Europe's finest street, the Strand still boasts a few classy hotels, including the Savoy, but its lustre has dimmed.

Piccadilly Circus SQUARE
(Map p66; ⊜ Piccadilly Circus) Designed in the 1820s and named after the street Piccadilly (heading west to Hyde Park Corner from the square) as it greets the grand sweep of Regent St and Shaftesbury Avenue, Piccadilly Circus is today a tumult of stop-start traffic, blinking neon advertisement panels and camera-toting out-of-towners. At the heart of the action stands the famous aluminium statue of Anteros (Map p66), twin brother of Eros, dedicated to the philanthropist and child-labour abolitionist Lord Shaftesbury.

The statue has long been mistaken for Eros, the God of Love, and the misnomer has stuck (it's even marked on the London A-Z, and signs for 'Eros' lead from the underground).

★Trafalgar Square SQUARE
(Map p66; ⊜ Charing Cross) Trafalgar Sq is the public heart of London, hosting rallies, marches and feverish New Year's festivities. Londoners congregate here to celebrate anything from football victories to the ousting of political leaders. The square is one of the world's grandest public places, with a sandstone Admiral Nelson surveying his fleet from the 43.5m-high Nelson's Column at its heart, erected in 1843 to commemorate his 1805 victory over Napoleon off Spain's Cape Trafalgar.

The square is flanked by splendid buildings: Canada House to the west, the National Gallery and National Portrait Gallery to the north, South Africa House and the church of St Martin-in-the-Fields to the east. Further south stands Admiralty Arch, built in honour of Queen Victoria in 1910 (and with a mysterious stone nose around seven foot up from the ground on one of the northernmost arches), and beyond that, the Mall (rhymes with 'shall', not 'shawl') is the ceremonial route leading to Buckingham Palace (p59).

★National Gallery GALLERY
(Map p66; www.nationalgallery.org.uk; Trafalgar Sq, WC2; ⊙10am-6pm Sat-Thu, to 9pm Fri; ⊜ Charing Cross) FREE Gazing grandly over Trafalgar Sq through its Corinthian columns, the National Gallery is the nation's most important repository of largely pre-modern art. Four million visitors flock annually to admire its 2300-plus Western European paintings, ranging from the 13th to the early 20th centuries. Highlights include Turner's *The Fighting Temeraire,* Botticelli's *Venus and Mars* and van Gogh's *Sunflowers.* The medieval religious paintings in the Sainsbury Wing are delightful. The comprehensive audioguides (£3.50) are recommended, as are the free introductory tours.

For sustenance, nothing beats the National Dining Rooms (p116) in the Sainsbury Wing.

★National Portrait Gallery GALLERY
(Map p66; www.npg.org.uk; St Martin's Pl, WC2; ⊙10am-6pm Sat-Wed, to 9pm Thu & Fri; ⊜ Charing Cross, Leicester Sq) FREE The National Portrait Gallery is like stepping into a picture book of English history. Founded in 1856, the permanent collection (around 11,000 works) kicks off with the Tudors on the 2nd floor and descends to contemporary figures (from pop stars to scientists), including Marc Quinn's *Self,* a frozen self-portrait of the artist's head cast in blood and recreated every five years. An audiovisual guide (£3) is available.

The Portrait (☑020-7312 2490; www.npg.org.uk/visit/shop-eat-drink.php; 3rd fl; mains £18.50; ⊙11.45am-2.45pm daily & 5.30-8.15pm Thu-Sat; ⊜ Charing Cross) restaurant pairs superb views towards Westminster with tantalising food.

Royal Academy of Arts GALLERY
(Map p66; www.royalacademy.org.uk; Burlington House, Piccadilly, W1; adult/child £10/6; prices vary for exhibitions; ⊙10am-6pm Sat-Thu, to 10pm Fri;

West End

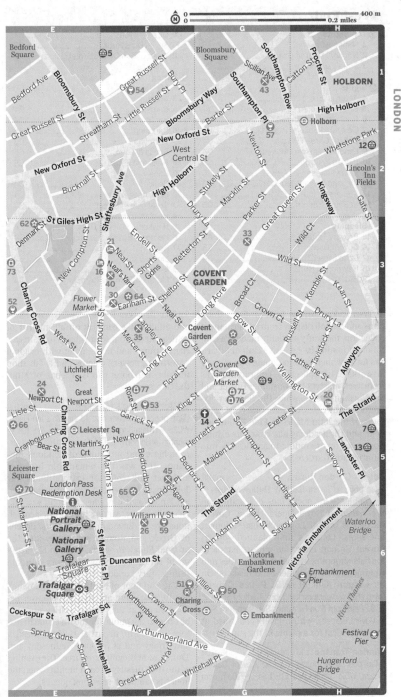

West End

◉Green Park) Hosting high-profile exhibitions and a small display from its permanent collection, the crafty academy made it a condition of joining its exclusive club of 80 artists for new members to donate one of their artworks. The collection embraces works from such masters as Constable, Turner and Sir Norman Foster, while the Summer Exhibition showcases contemporary art. Free tours of the John Madesjki Fine Rooms are held, and the academy has grown its exhibition space by expanding magnificently into 6 Burlington Gardens.

Covent Garden Piazza SQUARE
(Map p66; ◉Covent Garden) Hallowed turf – or cobbles – for opera fans descending on the esteemed Royal Opera House, Covent Garden is one of London's biggest tourist hot spots. London's first planned square, Covent Garden Piazza now hosts bands of tourists shopping in quaint old arcades and ringing street entertainers and buskers. On its western flank rises St Paul's Church (Map p66; www.actorschurch.org; Bedford St, WC2; ◎8.30am-5pm Mon-Fri, varies Sat, 9am-1pm Sun; ◉Covent Garden), with a lovely courtyard at the back, ideal for a picnic in the sun.

London Transport Museum MUSEUM
(Map p66; www.ltmuseum.co.uk; Covent Garden Piazza, WC2; adult/child £15/free; ◎10am-6pm Sat-Thu, 11am-6pm Fri; ◉Covent Garden) Kids and adults alike can tick off all manner of vehicles here, from sedan chairs to train carriages, trams and taxis, along with original advertising posters, photos and a fab shop for tube-map boxer shorts or a pair of 'Mind the Gap' socks.

Sir John Soane's Museum MUSEUM
(Map p66; www.soane.org; 13 Lincoln's Inn Fields, WC2; ◎10am-5pm Tue-Sat & 6-9pm 1st Tue of month; ◉Holborn) FREE One of the most atmospheric and intriguing of London's museums, this was the remarkable home of architect and collector extraordinaire Sir John Soane (1753–1837). The house has been left largely as it was when Sir John was taken out in a box. Among his eclectic acquisitions are an Egyptian sarcophagus, dozens of Greek and Roman antiquities and the original *Rake's Progress*, William Hogarth's set of caricatures telling the story of a late 18th-century London cad.

The 2nd floor of No 13, including Soane's private apartment and model room, was being restored at the time of writing and will be open to the public for the first time in history. Tours (£10) depart at 11.30am Tuesday and Friday and at 3.30pm Wednesday and Thursday. Audioguides are free. The evening of the first Tuesday of each month, when the house is candle-lit, sees long queues.

Somerset House HISTORIC BUILDING
(Map p66; www.somersethouse.org.uk; The Strand, WC2; ⏱galleries 10am-6pm, Safra Courtyard 7.30am-11pm; 🚇Charing Cross, Embankment, Temple) The first Somerset House was built for the Duke of Somerset, brother of Jane Seymour, in 1551. For two centuries it played host to royals (Elizabeth I once lived here), foreign diplomats, wild masked balls, peace treaties, the Parliamentary army (during the Civil War) and Oliver Cromwell's wake. Having fallen into disrepair, it was pulled down in 1775 and rebuilt in 1801 to designs by William Chambers.

Among other weighty organisations, it went on to house the Royal Academy of the Arts, the Society of Antiquaries, the Navy Board and, that most popular of institutions, the Inland Revenue.

The tax collectors are still here, but that doesn't dissuade Londoners from attending open-air events in the grand Safra courtyard, such as films (Film4 Summer Screen) over 12 days in summer and ice skating in winter. Behind the house, there's a sunny terrace and cafe overlooking the embankment.

Near the Strand entrance, the **Courtauld Gallery** (Map p66; www.courtauld.ac.uk; Somerset House, The Strand, WC2; adult/child Tue-Sun £6/free, Mon £3/free; ⏱10am-6pm; 🚇Charing Cross, Embankment or Temple) displays a wealth of 14th- to 20th-century art, including a room of Rubens and works by van Gogh, Renoir and Cézanne. Downstairs, the **Embankment Galleries** are devoted to temporary exhibitions; prices and hours vary.

Burlington Arcade SHOPPING ARCADE
(Map p66; www.burlington-arcade.co.uk; 51 Piccadilly, W1; ⏱10am-9pm Mon-Fri, 9am-6.30pm Sat, 11am-5pm Sun; 🚇Green Park) The illustrious Burlington Arcade, built in 1819, is famously patrolled by the Burlington Beadles, uniformed guards who constitute one of the world's smallest private police forces.

Broadcasting House TV LOCATION
(📞0370 901 1227; www.bbc.co.uk/showsandtours; Portland Pl, W1; adult/child £13.75/9.25; ⏱tour days & times vary; 🚇Oxford Circus) The BBC began radio broadcasting in 1932 from this splendid building north of Oxford Street, and the BBC World Service, other radio broadcasting and TV broadcasting in London recently moved in. Join frequent 1½-hour behind-the-scenes tours, peeking at studios and the state-of-the-art newsroom; check the website for details. No children under nine; pre-booking (at least the day before) essential.

The City

With beguiling churches, hidden gardens and atmospheric lanes stuffed between iconic corporate towers and office blocks, you could spend weeks exploring the City of London, which, for most of its history, *was* London. Its boundaries have changed little since the Romans first founded their gated community here two millennia ago.

It's only in the last 250 years that the City has gone from being the very essence of London and its main population centre to just its central business district. But what a business district it is – the 'square mile' remains at the very heart of world capitalism.

Currently fewer than 10,000 people actually live here, although some 300,000 descend on it each weekday, to generate almost three-quarters of Britain's GDP before squeezing back onto the tube. On Sundays the City (capital 'C') becomes a virtual ghost town; it's nice and quiet, but come with a full stomach – most shops, eateries and pubs are closed.

★ **Tower of London** CASTLE
(Map p70; ☎ 0844 482 7777; www.hrp.org.uk/toweroflondon; Tower Hill, EC3; adult/child £22/11, audioguide £4/3; ☉ 9am-5.30pm Tue-Sat, 10am-

The City

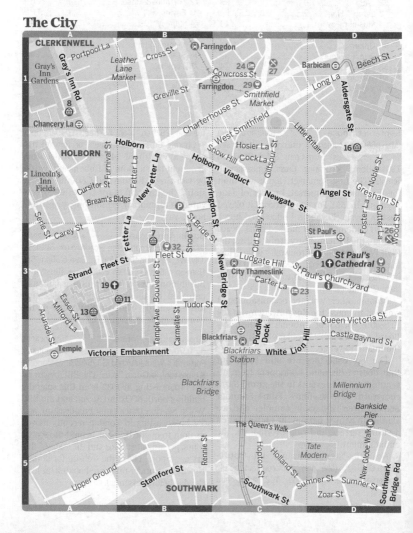

5.30pm Sun & Mon, to 4.30pm Nov-Feb; ⊖ Tower Hill) A World Heritage Site, the Tower possesses a gruesome and compelling history. In the 1070s, William the Conqueror started work on the White Tower to replace the earlier castle. By 1285, two walls with towers and a moat encompassed it and the defences have barely been altered since. A former royal residence, treasury, mint and arsenal, it became most famous as a prison when Henry VIII moved to Whitehall Palace in 1529 and started meting out his preferred brand of punishment.

The most striking building is indeed the central White Tower, with its solid Romanesque architecture and four turrets. Today it

houses a collection from the Royal Armouries, including Henry VIII's commodious suit of armour. On the 2nd floor is St John's Chapel, dating from 1080 and therefore the oldest church in London. To the north stands Waterloo Barracks, which now contains the spectacular Crown Jewels, including the platinum crown of the late Queen Mother, set with the 105-carat Koh-i-Noor (Mountain of Light) diamond, and the Imperial State Crown. On the far side of the White Tower rises the Bloody Tower, where the 12-year-old Edward V and his little brother were held 'for their own safety' and later murdered, probably by their uncle, the future Richard

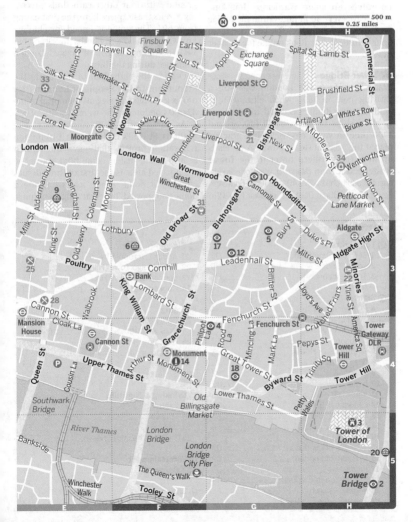

III. Sir Walter Raleigh did a 13-year stretch here, when he wrote his *History of the World*.

On the small green in front of the Chapel Royal of St Peter ad Vincula stood Henry VIII's scaffold, where seven people, including Anne Boleyn and her cousin Catherine Howard (Henry's second and fifth wives) were beheaded.

Look out for the latest in the Tower's long line of famous ravens, which legend says could cause the White Tower to collapse should they leave (their wings are clipped in case they get any ideas).

To get your bearings, take the hugely entertaining free guided tour with any of the Beefeaters (Yeoman Warders). Hour-long tours leave every 30 minutes from the bridge near the main entrance; the last tour is an hour before closing. Book online for cheaper rates.

★ Tower Bridge   BRIDGE
(Map p70; ⊖ Tower Hill) London was still a thriving port in 1894 when elegant Tower Bridge was built. Designed to be raised to allow ships to pass (it still lifts around 1000 times a year), electricity has now replaced the original steam power. A lift leads up from the northern tower to the Tower Bridge Exhibition (Map p70; www.towerbridge. org.uk; adult/child £8/3.40; ⊙10am-6pm Apr-Sep, 9.30am-5.30pm Oct-Mar; ⊖ Tower Hill) 42m

above the water, from where you can walk along the east and west-facing walkways.

The exhibition ticket also gets you into the engine rooms below the southern tower, for the mechanical lowdown.

★ St Paul's Cathedral   CHURCH
(Map p70; www.stpauls.co.uk; St Paul's Churchyard, EC4; adult/child £16.50/7.50; ⊙8.30am-4.30pm Mon-Sat; ⊖ St Paul's) Dominating the City with one of the world's largest church domes (around 65,000 tons worth), St Paul's Cathedral was designed by Christopher Wren after the Great Fire and built between 1675 and 1710. The site is ancient hallowed ground with four other cathedrals preceding Wren's masterpiece here, the first dating from 604. The dome is famed for eludling Luftwaffe incendiary bombs in December 1940, becoming an icon of dogged London resilience during the Blitz.

Outside the cathedral, to the north, the Monument to the People of London (Map p70) is a simple and elegant memorial to the 32,000 Londoners who weren't so lucky.

As part of the 300th anniversary celebrations, St Paul's underwent a £40 million renovation project that gave the church a deep clean. Inside, some 30m above the main paved area, is the first of three domes (actually a dome inside a cone inside a dome) supported by eight huge columns.

The City

LOCAL KNOWLEDGE

ALAN KINGSHOTT: CHIEF YEOMAN WARDER AT THE TOWER

Make the Most of Your Visit To understand the Tower's full history, I suggest visitors take a guided tour (in English) by a Yeoman Warder. With such a vast amount of history within the walls, you should allow at least three hours to fully enjoy your experience.

The Crown Jewels The new presentation of the Crown Jewels is a must-see with a new layout, which will help visitors easily explore our sometimes complex history and ceremonies. Just ask a member of the Jewel House staff about any item: you will be amazed at their wealth of knowledge and it will enhance your visit.

The Ravens of the Tower We must have six ravens at the Tower at any one time by a Royal Decree put in place by Charles II. According to an old legend, should the birds leave, the Monarchy and the White Tower will crumble and fall. We tend not to provoke legends so generally we have eight birds.

Recommended Ceremonies There are many ceremonies at the Tower of London, most of which can be viewed by visitors. However, many happen around royal events such as the Queen's Birthday and the State Opening of Parliament. Alternatively there is the Ceremony of the Keys (the locking up of the Tower of London), which takes place, as it has done for 700 years, at 9.30pm every night. (Note: attendance is free but requires that you apply by post at least two months in advance and supply a return-address envelope.)

The walkway around its base, 257 steps up a staircase on the western side of the southern transept, is called the Whispering Gallery because if you talk close to the wall, your words will carry to the opposite side 32m away. A further 119 steps brings you to the Stone Gallery, 152 iron steps above which is the Golden Gallery at the very top, which rewards you with unforgettable views of London.

The Crypt has memorials to up to 300 military demigods, including Wellington, Kitchener and Nelson, whose body lies below the dome. But the most poignant memorial is to Wren himself. On a simple slab bearing his name, a Latin inscription translates as: 'If you seek his memorial, look about you'. Also in the crypt is a cafe and the excellent Restaurant at St Paul's (☎020-7248 2469; www.restaurantatstpauls.co.uk; 2-/3-course lunch £21.50/25.95; ⏰lunch noon-3pm, tea 2.30-4.30pm Mon-Sat; ☏; ⬤St Paul's).

The Oculus in the former treasury projects four short films onto its walls (you'll need the iPad audiotour to hear the sound). If you're not up to climbing the dome, experience it here (audiovisually). Free audio tours lasting 1½ hours are available. Free 1½-hour guided tours leave the tour desk half-a-dozen times a day (10.30am, 10.45am, 11.15am, 1pm, 1.30pm and 2pm); head to the desk just past the entrance to check times and book a place. Choral evensong is held most days at 5pm.

Museum of London MUSEUM
(Map p70; www.museumoflondon.org.uk; 150 London Wall, EC2; ⏰10am-6pm; ⬤Barbican) FREE
This riveting museum peels back the layers of historical London for valuable perspectives on this great city. The first gallery, London before London, illustrates the settlements predating the Roman era. The Roman section explores the ancient roots of the modern city as we know it, while Saxon, medieval, Tudor and Stuart London are intriguingly brought to life. The museum's new £20 million Galleries of Modern London encompasses everything from 1666 (the devastating Great Fire of London) to the present day. While the Lord Mayor's ceremonial coach is the centrepiece, an effort has been made to create an immersive experience: you can enter reconstructions of an 18th-century debtors' prison, a Georgian pleasure garden and a Victorian street.

Guildhall HISTORIC BUILDING
(Map p70; ☎020-7606 3030; www.guildhall.city oflondon.gov.uk; Gresham St, EC2; ⬤Bank) FREE
The Guildhall has been the seat of the City's local government for eight centuries and the present building dates from the early 15th century. Visitors can see the Great Hall, where the city's mayor is sworn in – it's an impressive space decorated with the shields and banners of London's 12 principal livery companies, carved galleries and a beautiful oak-panelled roof. Beneath it is London's largest medieval crypt (visit by free guided tour only, bookings essential).

Tower of London

TACKLING THE TOWER

Although it's usually less busy in the late afternoon, don't leave your assault on the Tower until too late in the day. You could easily spend hours here and not see it all. Start by getting your bearings on one of the Yeoman Warder (Beefeater) tours; they are included in the cost of admission, entertaining and the easiest way to access the **Chapel Royal of St Peter ad Vincula** ❶, which is where they finish up.

When you leave the chapel, the **Tower Green Scaffold Site** ❷ is directly in front. The building immediately to your left is Waterloo Barracks, where the **Crown Jewels** ❸ are housed. These are the absolute highlight of a Tower visit, so keep an eye on the entrance and pick a time to visit when it looks relatively quiet. Once inside, take things at your own pace. Slow-moving travelators shunt you past the dozen or so crowns that are the treasury's centrepiece, but feel free to double-back for a second or even third pass – particularly if you ended up on the rear travelator the first time around. Allow plenty of time for the **White Tower** ❹, the core of the whole complex, starting with the exhibition of royal armour. As you continue onto the 1st floor, keep an eye out for **St John's Chapel** ❺. The famous **ravens** ❻ can be seen in the courtyard south of the White Tower. Head next through the towers that formed the **Medieval Palace** ❼, then take the **East Wall Walk** ❽ to get a feel for the castle's mighty battlements. Spend the rest of your time poking around the many other fascinating nooks and crannies of the Tower complex.

Chapel Royal of St Peter ad Vincula
This chapel serves as the resting place for the royals and other members of the aristocracy who were executed on the small green out front. Several other historical figures are buried here too, including Thomas More.

Dry Moat

Tower Green Scaffold Site
Seven people, including three queens (Anne Boleyn, Catherine Howard and Jane Grey), lost their heads here during Tudor times, saving the monarch the embarrassment of public executions on Tower Hill. The site now features a sculpture by Brian Catling.

Beauchamp Tower

Main Entrance

Middle Tower

Byward Tower

Bell Tower

White Tower
Much of the White Tower is taken up with an exhibition on 500 years of royal armour. Look for the virtually cuboid suit made to match Henry VIII's bloated body, complete with an oversized armoured codpiece to protect, ahem, the crown jewels.

t John's Chapel

pt as plain and
adorned as it
uld have been in
rman times, the
ite Tower's 1st-floor
apel is the oldest
rviving church in
ndon, dating from
80.

TOM HANLEY/ALAMY ©

Crown Jewels

When they're not being
worn for ceremonies of
state, Her Majesty's bling
is kept here. Among the
23,578 gems, look out for
the 530-carat Cullinan I
diamond at the top of the
Sovereign's Sceptre with
cross, the largest part of
what was then the largest
diamond ever found.

Bowyer Tower

Martin Tower

Queen's House

Constable Tower

Bloody Tower

Broad Arrow Tower

New Armouries

itors'
e & St
mas's
wer

Wakefield & St Thomas's Towers

Salt Tower

River Thames

Medieval Palace

his part of the Tower
omplex was begun
round 1220 and was
ome to England's
nedieval monarchs.
ook for the recreations
f the bedchamber of
dward I (1272–1307)
n St Thomas's Tower
nd the throne room
f his father, Henry
I (1216–72) in the
Vakefield Tower.

DAVID GARRY/GETTY IMAGES ©

Ravens

This stretch of green
is where the Tower's
half-dozen ravens are
kept, fed on raw meat
and blood-soaked bird
biscuits. According to
legend, if the birds were
to leave the Tower, the
kingdom would fall.

East Wall Walk

Follow the inner
ramparts, starting
from the 13th-century
Salt Tower, passing
through the Broad
Arrow and Constable
Towers, and ending
at the Martin Tower,
where the Crown
Jewels were stored till
the mid-19th century.

The **Clockmakers' Museum** charts 500 years of horology with an intriguing collection of more than 700 clocks; the **Guildhall Art Gallery** displays around 250 artworks. Included in the art gallery admission is entry to the remains of an ancient **Roman** amphitheatre.

Bank of England Museum   MUSEUM

(Map p70; www.bankofengland.co.uk/museum; Bartholomew Lane, EC2; ◷10am-5pm Mon-Fri; ◉Bank) **FREE** Guardian of the country's current shaky financial system, the Bank of England was established in 1694 when the government needed to raise cash to support a war with France. The centrepiece of this museum is a reconstruction of architect John Soane's original Bank Stock Office, complete with original mahogany counters. A series of rooms leading off the office are packed with exhibits ranging from silverware and coins to a 13kg gold bar you can lift up (and leave behind).

Monument   TOWER

(Map p70; www.themonument.info; Fish Street Hill, EC3; adult/child £4/2, incl Tower Bridge Exhibition £10.50/4.70; ◷9.30am-6pm Apr-Sep, to 5.30pm Oct-Mar; ◉Monument) Designed by Wren to commemorate the Great Fire, the towering Monument is 60.6m high, the exact distance from its base to the bakery on Pudding Lane where the blaze began. Corkscrew your way up the 311 tight spiral steps (claustrophobes beware) for some of London's best wraparound views and twist down again to collect a certificate commemorating your climb.

Dr Johnson's House   MUSEUM

(Map p70; www.drjohnsonshouse.org; 17 Gough Sq, EC4; adult/child £4.50/1.50, audioguide £2; ◷11am-5.30pm Mon-Sat May-Sep, to 5pm Oct-Apr; ◉Chancery Lane) The Georgian house where Samuel Johnson and his assistants compiled the first English dictionary (between 1748 and 1759) is full of prints and portraits of friends and intimates, including the good doctor's Jamaican servant to whom he bequeathed this grand residence.

Inns of Court   HISTORIC BUILDINGS

All London barristers work from within one of the four atmospheric Inns of Court, positioned between the walls of the old City and Westminster. It would take a lifetime working here to grasp all the intricacies of their arcane protocols, originating in the 13th-century. It's best just to soak up the dreamy ambience of the alleys and open spaces and consider the roll call of former members that

---

🏃 City Walk
City of London

START: ST BARTHOLOMEW-THE-GREAT
END: HERON TOWER
LENGTH: 2 MILES; TWO TO FOUR HOURS

It's fitting to start at ❶ **St Bartholomew-the-Great** (a five-minute walk southwest from Barbican tube station), as this history-steeped 12th-century church was once a pilgrimage stop for travellers to London.

Head out through the Tudor gatehouse and to your right you'll see the Victorian arches of Smithfield's meat market, on this site just north of the old city walls for 800 years. Executions were held here, most famously the torching of Protestants under Mary I and the grisly killing of Scottish hero William Wallace (Braveheart) in 1305; a plaque on the front of ❷ **St Bartholomew's Hospital** commemorates him.

Head back towards the gate and turn right into Little Britain. Follow it as it curves to the right and look out for the large tree marking the entrance to ❸ **Postman's Park**. This lovely space includes a touching legacy of Victorian socialism: a tiled wall celebrating everyday heroes.

Coming out of the park, turn right onto Aldersgate, then left and left again into Noble St. You're now inside what was once the old City's ❹ **walls**, remnants of which you'll pass on your left. This section was only uncovered after WWII bombs destroyed the buildings covering it. Take the stairs up to the footbridge crossing the street called London Wall towards the ❺ **Museum of London** (p73).

Turn left when leaving the museum and follow the Highwalk past ❻ **ruins** of the barbicans (defensive towers) that once guarded the northwestern corner of the walls, on your left, with the ❼ **Barbican Centre** (p129) behind (filling a space bombed out during WWII). At its heart is an arts centre consisting of concert halls, cinemas, galleries, eateries, a library and a school.

Follow the painted lines on the Highwalk for a closer look, or turn right at Pizza Express, take the escalator down to Wood St and head towards the remaining tower of ❽ **St Alban's**, a Wren-designed church destroyed in WWII. Turn left and you'll find a sweet garden on the site of **9 St Mary Aldermanbury**, with a bust of Shakespeare.

Turn right on to Aldermanbury and head to the **10 Guildhall** (p73). Take King St down to Cheapside, cross the road and head right to elegant **11 St Mary-le-Bow**. The church was rebuilt by Wren after the Great Fire, and then rebuilt again after WWII. The term 'Cockney' traditionally refers to someone born within the sound of this church's bell.

Walk down the west flank of the church and turn left into Bow Churchyard to reach Bow Lane; follow this narrow path south to **12 St Mary Aldermary**, rebuilt in the Perpendicular Gothic style in 1682 following the Great Fire. Turn left on to Queen Victoria St and then right into Bucklersbury, to spot **13 St Stephen's Walbrook** directly in front of you. Rebuilt after the Great Fire, the current St Stephen's is one of Wren's greatest masterpieces, with elegant Corinthian columns supporting a beautifully proportioned dome.

Leaving the church, you'll pass **14 Mansion House**, built in 1752 as the official residence of the Lord Mayor. As you approach the busy Bank intersection, lined with neoclassical temples to commerce, you might think you've stumbled into the ancient Roman forum (the

actual forum was a couple of blocks east). Head for the **15 equestrian statue of the Iron Duke**, behind which a metal pyramid details the many significant buildings here. Directly beyond the statue is the **16 Royal Exchange**; walk through it and exit through the door on the right, then turn left onto Cornhill.

If you're still not churched out, cross the road to **17 St Michael's**, a 1672 Wren design that still has its box pews. Hidden in the warren of tiny passages behind the church is its **18 churchyard**. Head through to Gracechurch St, turn left and cross the road to wonderful **19 Leadenhall Market**. As you wander out the far end, the famous **20 Lloyd's of London** displays its metallic innards for all to see. To the south rises the bulbous, top-heavy form of **21 20 Fenchurch St** (aka the 'Walkie-Talkie') – most impressive from a distance.

Turn left onto Lime St and you'll soon reach the uncompromising wedge of the **22 Leadenhall Building** (aka the 'Cheese Grater'). Ahead of you rises Norman Foster's 180m **23 30 St Mary Axe** (the 'Gherkin'). A short walk beyond, the **24 Heron Tower** is currently the tallest building in the City, from where it's a short walk north to Liverpool Street tube station.

LONDON'S NEW SKYSCRAPERS

A recent scramble for high-altitude, futuristic towers – given further lift by the Olympics – has shaken up the otherwise rather staid, low-lying London skyline. Most famous is the Shard (p83), rising over London Bridge like a vast glass splinter and home to the high-altitude five-star Shangri-La hotel. The City of London's tallest building, the straight-edged **Heron Tower** (Map p70; 110 Bishopsgate, EC2; Aldgate or Bank) was completed just up the road from **30 St Mary Axe** (Gherkin; Map p70; www.30stmaryaxe.co.uk; 30 St Mary Axe, EC3; Aldgate) in 2011. The top-heavy and bulging **20 Fenchurch St** (Walkie Talkie; Map p70) will be topped with a vast sky garden boasting magnificent views over town, while the wedge-shaped 48-storey, 225m-high **Leadenhall Building** (Cheese Grater; Map p70; 122 Leadenhall St, EC3) cuts into the sky just north of the Lloyd's building. Construction on the concrete stub of the radically-designed **Pinnacle** (Helter Skelter; Map p70; 22-24 Bishopsgate, EC2; Aldgate or Bank) – which has earned its nickname due to its cork-screwing top – was on hold at the the time of writing.

includes Oliver Cromwell, Charles Dickens, Mahatma Gandhi and Margaret Thatcher.

Lincoln's Inn (www.lincolnsinn.org.uk; Lincoln's Inn Fields, Newmans Row, WC2; grounds 7am-7pm Mon-Fri, chapel noon-2.30pm Mon-Fri; Holborn) still has some original 15th-century buildings. It's the oldest and most attractive of the bunch, with a 17th-century chapel and pretty landscaped gardens.

Gray's Inn (Map p70; www.graysinn.org.uk; Gray's Inn Rd, WC1; grounds 10am-4pm Mon-Fri, chapel 10am-6pm Mon-Fri; Chancery Lane) was largely rebuilt after the Luftwaffe levelled it.

Middle Temple (Map p70; www.middletemple.org.uk; Middle Temple Lane, EC4; grounds 10-11.30am & 3-4pm Mon-Fri; Temple) and **Inner Temple** (Map p70; www.innertemple.org.uk; King's Bench Walk, EC4; grounds 10am-4pm Mon-Fri, gardens 12.30-3pm Mon-Fri; Temple) sit between Fleet St and Victoria Embankment. The former is the best preserved, while the latter is home to the 12th-century **Temple Church** (Map p70; 020-7353 8559; www.templechurch.com; adult/concession £4/2; 11am-1pm & 2-4pm Mon-Fri, hours vary), built by the Knights Templar and featuring nine stone effigies of knights in its round chapel. Check the church's website or call ahead for opening hours.

St Katharine Docks   HARBOUR

(Tower Hill) A centre of commerce for 1000 years, St Katharine Docks is today a buzzing waterside area of pleasure boats, shops and eateries. It was badly damaged during WWII, but survivors include the popular **Dickens Inn**, with its original 18th-century timber framework, and **Ivory House** (built 1854), which used to store ivory, perfume and other precious goods. It's the perfect starting point for exploring Wapping and Limehouse.

☉ South Bank

Londoners once crossed the river to the area controlled by the licentious Bishops of Southwark for all manner of bawdy frolicking frowned upon in the City. It's a much more seemly and temperate area these days, but the frisson of theatre and entertainment survives. While South Bank only technically refers to the area of river bank between Westminster and Blackfriars Bridges (parts of which are actually on the east bank due to the way the river bends), we've used it as a convenient catch-all for those parts of Southwark and Lambeth that sit closest to the river.

★**Tate Modern**   MUSEUM

(Map p82; www.tate.org.uk; Queen's Walk, SE1; 10am-6pm Sun-Thu, to 10pm Fri & Sat; Southwark, St Paul's) **FREE** One of London's biggest attractions, this outstanding modern and contemporary art gallery is housed in the creatively revamped **Bankside Power Station** south of the Millennium Bridge. A riveting synthesis of funky modern art and capacious industrial brick design, the result is an art-going tour de force. Tate Modern has also been extraordinarily successful in bringing challenging work to the masses, while a stunning extension is under construction, aiming for a 2016 completion date.

The multimedia guides (£3.50) are worthwhile and there are free 45-minute guided tours of the collection's highlights (Level 3 at 11am and midday; Level 5 at 2pm and 3pm).

★**Shakespeare's Globe**   HISTORIC BUILDING

(Map p82; www.shakespearesglobe.com; 21 New Globe Walk, SE1; adult/child £13.50/8; 9am-5.30pm; London Bridge) Today's Londoners may flock to Amsterdam to misbehave, but back in the bard's day they'd swarm across London Bridge to Southwark. Free from the city's constraints, men could settle down to a diet of whoring, bear-baiting and heckling of actors. The most famous theatre was the Globe, where a genius playwright was penning box-office hits such as *Macbeth* and *Hamlet*. Admission includes the exhibition hall and a guided tour of the theatre (departing every 15 to 30 minutes).

The original Globe – known as the 'Wooden O' after its circular shape and roofless centre – was erected in 1599. Rival to the Rose Theatre, all was well but did not end well when the Globe burned down within two hours during a performance in 1613 (a stage cannon ignited the thatched roof). A tiled replacement fell foul of the party-pooping Puritans in 1642, who saw the theatre as the devil's workshop, and it was dismantled two years later. Its present-day incarnation – faithfully reconstructed from oak beams, handmade bricks, lime plaster and thatch – is the vision of American actor

and director Sam Wanamaker, who sadly died before the opening night in 1997.

From April to October plays are performed, and while Shakespeare and his contemporaries dominate, modern plays are also staged (see the website for upcoming performances). As in Elizabethan times, seatless 'groundlings' (up to 700 of them) can watch in all-weather conditions (£5; seats are £15 to £39) for the best views. There's no protection from the elements (or over-flying jetliners) and you'll have to stand, but it's an unforgettable experience.

The Globe has recently added a new Sam Wanamaker Playhouse, an indoor Jacobean theatre, to its repertoire.

Tours of the theatre shift to the nearby Rose Theatre instead when matinees are being staged in season.

★ London Eye   VIEWPOINT
(Map p82; ☑ 0871 781 3000; www.londoneye.com; adult/child £21/15; ⊘ 10am-8pm; ⊜ Waterloo) This 135m-tall, slow-moving and refurbed Ferris-wheel-like attraction is the world's tallest 'cantilevered observation wheel'. You

---

TATE MODERN HIGHLIGHTS

Over 50 million eager art-goers poured through Tate Modern in its first decade since opening, making it one of the most-visited of London's sights. The ambitiously run exhibition space is growing with the conversion of two underground oil tanks, while a funky 11-storey extension is slated for a 2016 opening date.

Note that special exhibitions are held on levels 2 and 3. Free guided highlights tours depart at 11am, noon, 2pm and 3pm daily – no booking is required. Handy multimedia guides are also available. Don't forget that Tate Modern is open till 10pm on Friday and Saturday.

The collection is in perpetual rotation so while the essential themes of the various galleries remain constant, the paintings and art works that represent each concept may vary.

A major highlight of Tate Modern is the architecture. The 4.2 million bricks of the Sir Gilbert Scott–designed Bankside Power Station – generating its last watt in 1981 when rising oil prices finally switched off its turbines – were ambitiously transformed into this modern and contemporary art gallery in 2000.

You can't exactly miss the cavernous 3300-sq-metre Turbine Hall, but try to join everyone else streaming down the ramp from Holland St to maximise its impact. Originally housing the power station's colossal turbines, the hall is the imposing venue for large-scale, temporary exhibitions from October to April.

The permanent collection is grouped thematically on levels 2, 3 and 4. For the surrealist dreamscapes of Paul Delvaux, Yves Tanguy, Max Ernst and other artists, immerse yourself in Poetry & Dream on Level 2. On Level 3, Transformed Visions explores works of expressive abstraction forged in the aftermath of WWII.

Focusing on the evolution of abstraction and radical art on Level 4, Structure & Clarity celebrates the abstract work of the interwar years, pieces that tilt towards utopian and universal themes. Also on Level 4, Energy & Process takes Art Povera, the revolutionary art of the 1960s, as its focus.

After you have had your fill of modern art, cap your visit with a trip to the restaurant and bar on Level 7 for sublime views of St Paul's and the River Thames. A popular cafe can also be found on Level 2.

The River Thames

A FLOATING TOUR

London's history has always been determined by the Thames. The city was founded as a Roman port nearly 2000 years ago and over the centuries since then many of the capital's landmarks have lined the river's banks. A boat trip is a great way to experience the attractions.

There are piers dotted along both banks at regular intervals where you can hop on and hop off the regular services to visit places of interest. The best place to board is Westminster Pier, from where boats head downstream, taking yo from the City of Westminster, the seat of government, to the original City of London, now th financial district and dominated by a growing band of skyscrapers. Across the river, the once shabby and neglected South Bank now bristles with as many top attractions as its northern counterpart, including the slender Shard.

In our illustration we've concentrated on the to highlights you'll enjoy from a waterborne vesse

MARK DAFFEY / GETTY IMAGES ©

St Paul's Cathedral
Though there's been a church here since AD 604, the current building rose from the ashes of the 1666 Great Fire and is architect Christopher Wren's masterpiece. Famous for surviving th Blitz intact and for the wedding of Charles and Diana, it's looking a good as new after a major clean-up for its 300th anniversary.

Blackfriars

Somerset House
This grand neoclassical palace was once one of many aristocratic houses lining the Thames. The huge arches at river level gave direct access to the Thames until the Embankment was built in the 1860s.

3 ⊖ Temple

Blackfriars Pier

Blackfriars Bridge

Charing Cross

Savoy Pier

Waterloo Bridge

Victoria Embankment Gardens

National Theatre

OXO Tower

Embankment

Queen Elizabeth Hall

Southbank Centre

London Eye
Built in 2000 and originally temporary, the Eye instantly became a much-loved landmark. The 30-minute spin takes you 135m above the city fro where the views are unsurprisingly amazing.

Waterloo Millennium Pier

Westminster Pier

Houses of Parliament
Rebuilt in neo-Gothic style after the old palace burned down in 1834, the most famous part of the British parliament is the clocktower. Generally known as Big Ben, it's named after Benjamin Hall who oversaw its construction.

Westminster

Westminster Bridge

RICHARD I'ANSON / GETTY IMAGES ©

These are, from west to east, the **Houses of Parliament** ❶, the **London Eye** ❷, **Somerset House** ❸, **St Paul's Cathedral** ❹, **Tate Modern** ❺, **Shakespeare's Globe** ❻, the **Tower of London** ❼ and **Tower Bridge** ❽.

Apart from covering this central section of the river, boats can also be taken upstream as far as Kew Gardens and Hampton Court Palace, and downstream to Greenwich and the Thames Barrier.

BOAT HOPPING

Thames Clippers hop-on/hop-off services are aimed at commuters but are equally useful for visitors, operating every 15 minutes on a loop from piers at Embankment, Waterloo, Blackfriars, Bankside, London Bridge and the Tower. Other services also go from Westminster. Oyster cardholders get a discount off the boat ticket price.

Tower of London
It's not the tallest building in London anymore, but with the Crown Jewels and execution site, the 900-year-old Tower still overshadows the city's other attractions. From the river you can clearly see Traitors' Gate through which enemies of the crown entered the prison.

30 St Mary Axe (Gherkin)

Leadenhall Building (Cheese Grater)

20 Fenchurch St (Walkie Talkie)

Cannon St

Monument

Millennium Bridge

Southwark Bridge

Bankside Pier

London Bridge

London Bridge Pier

HMS Belfast

Tower Pier

Southwark Cathedral

London Bridge

Shard

ate Modern
irectly across the river from St Paul's, this useum of modern art is the world's most visited. uilt as a power station in the late 1940s, its dustrial architecture is as popular with visitors s the paintings on the walls.

DOUG MCKINLAY / GETTY IMAGES ©

Shakespeare's Globe
The reconstructed Globe stands on the river a few hundred metres from where the original stood (and burnt down in 1613 during a performance). The life's work of American actor Sam Wanamaker, the theatre runs a hugely popular season from April to October each year.

City Hall
Tower Bridge
It might look as old as its namesake neighbour but one of the world's most iconic bridges was only completed in 1894. Not to be confused with London Bridge upstream, this one's famous raising bascules allowed tall ships to dock at the old wharves to the west and are still lifted up to 1000 times a year.

LONDON

South Bank

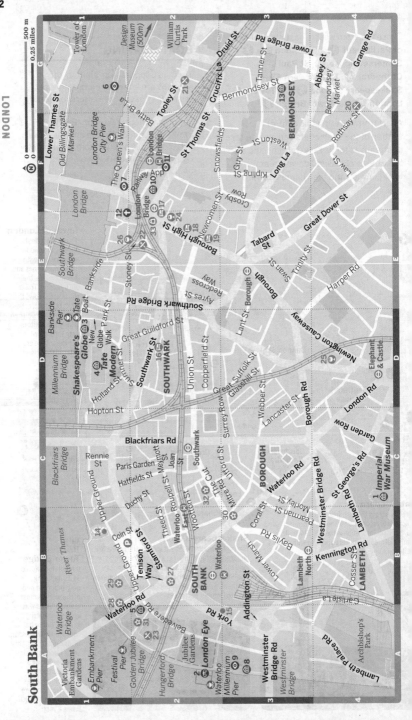

N

0   500 m
0   0.25 miles

ride in enclosed egg-shaped pods; the wheel takes 30 minutes to rotate completely, offering 25-mile views on clear days. Drawing 3.5 million visitors annually, at peak times (July, August and school holidays), it can seem like they are all in the queue with you. Save money and shorten queues by buying tickets online, or cough up an extra £10 to showcase your fast-track swagger.

Alternatively, visit before 11am or after 3pm to avoid peak density.

★ **Imperial War Museum**   MUSEUM

(Map p82; www.iwm.org.uk; Lambeth Rd, SE1; ⊙10am-6pm; ⊜Lambeth North) **FREE** Reopened in July 2014 after a massive refurbishment and fronted by a pair of intimidating 15in naval guns that could lob a 1938lb shell over 16 miles, this riveting museum is housed in what was once Bethlehem Royal Hospital, known notoriously as Bedlam.

As well as terrific new World War I galleries and a stunning new Foster+Partners atrium, exhibits include Lawrence of Arabia's 1000cc motorbike, a German V-2 rocket, a doodlebug, a lifelike replica of Little Boy (the atomic bomb dropped on Hiroshima), a Spitfire, Harrier Jet and other classic fighter planes dangling from the ceiling, plus a WWII bomb shelter and a Holocaust exhibition.

Shard   NOTABLE BUILDING

(Map p82; www.the-shard.com; 32 London Bridge St, SE1; adult/child £29.95/23.95; ⊙9am-10pm; ⊜London Bridge) Puncturing the skies above London, the crystalline splinter-like form of the Shard – the tallest building in Western Europe – has rapidly become a dramatic icon of town. The tower boasts the brand new, five-star Shangri-La Hotel at the Shard (p109), restaurants and viewing platforms on floors 68, 69 and 72 – book online to save £5.

Old Operating Theatre Museum & Herb Garret   MUSEUM

(Map p82; www.thegarret.org.uk; 9a St Thomas St, SE1; adult/child £6.50/3.50; ⊙10.30am-5pm; ⊜London Bridge) The highlight of this unique museum, 32 steps up the spiral stairway of the tower of St Thomas Church (1703), focuses on the nastiness of 19th-century hospital treatment. A fiendish array of amputation knives presages the operating theatre, where doctors operated in rough-and-ready (pre-ether, pre-chloroform, pre-antiseptic) conditions. A demonstration on Victorian speed surgery kicks off at 2pm on Saturdays and one on how drugs were made at 2pm on Sundays. Also browse the natural remedies in the herb garret, including snail water for venereal disease and bladderwrack for goitre and tuberculosis.

LONDON SIGHTS

South Bank

Southwark Cathedral CHURCH

(Map p82; ☑020-7367 6700; http://cathedral.
southwark.anglican.org; Montague Close, SE1; donations welcome; ☺8am-6pm Mon-Fri, 9am-6pm
Sat & Sun; ☻London Bridge) The earliest surviving chunks of this relatively small cathedral
are the retrochoir at the eastern end, some
ancient arcading by the southwest door,
12th-century wall cores in the north transept and an arch that dates to the original
Norman church, although most of the cathedral is Victorian. In the south aisle of the
nave, hunt down the green alabaster monument to William Shakespeare, next to which
is a plaque to Sam Wanamaker (1919–93).

Not far away hangs a splendid icon of
Jesus Christ illuminated by devotional can-
dles, and don't overlook the exceedingly fine
Elizabethan sideboard in the north transept.

Design Museum MUSEUM

(www.designmuseum.org; 28 Shad Thames, SE1;
adult/child £12.40/6.20; ☺10am-5.45pm; ⊕; ☻Tower
Hill) Housed in a 1930s-era warehouse, the
rectangular galleries here stage a revolving
program of special exhibitions devoted to
contemporary design, host the annual *Brit
Insurance Design Awards* competition for
design innovations, and display a permanent
collection of modern British design. The museum is moving to a new site in the former
Commonwealth Institute south of Kensington's Holland Park in November 2015.

HMS Belfast SHIP

(Map p82; www.iwm.org.uk/visits/hms-belfast;
Queen's Walk, SE1; adult/child £15.50/free; ☺10am-
5pm; ⊕; ☻London Bridge) White ensign flapping on the Thames breeze, HMS *Belfast* is
a magnet for naval-gazing kids. This large,
light cruiser served in WWII, helping sink
the German battleship *Scharnhorst* and
shelling the Normandy coast on D-Day.
Explore the nine decks and see the engine
room, gun decks, galley, chapel, punishment
cells, canteen and dental surgery. The excellent audioguide takes you on a 1½-hour tour
of the ship, only available until 3.30pm.

London Dungeon HISTORIC BUILDING

(Map p82; www.thedungeons.com/london/; County Hall, Westminster Bridge Rd, SE1; adult/child
£25.20/19.80; ☺10am-5pm, extended hours holidays; ⊕; ☻Westminster, Waterloo) Older kids
will enjoy the London Dungeon: it's all macabre free-fall hangman's drops, spooky boat
rides, fake blood and actors hamming it up
as gory criminals (including Jack the Ripper
and Sweeney Todd), torturers and judges,
plus ghastly interactive mayhem, with doses
of salacious humour to boot. It recently
moved from its old haunt to County Hall, by
the London Eye.

London Bridge Experience
& London Tombs HISTORIC ATTRACTION

(Map p82; www.thelondonbridgeexperience.com;
2-4 Tooley St, SE1; adult/child £23/17; ☺10am-5pm
Mon-Fri, to 6pm Sat & Sun; ⊕; ☻London Bridge)
Kicking off with the relatively tame London
Bridge Experience, where actors bring to
life the bridge's history with the assistance
of severed heads, the London Tombs turns
up the terror once the education bit is out
of the way. Adding to the creepiness is the
knowledge that these were once plague pits
and therefore actual tombs. The experience
takes about 45 minutes, with the tombs an
optional additional 25 minutes.

Save up to 50% by buying online.

London Sea Life Aquarium AQUARIUM

(Map p82; www.visitsealife.com; Westminster
Bridge Rd, SE1; adult/child £22.20/16.50; ☺10am-
7pm; ☻Westminster, Waterloo) This is one of the
largest aquariums in Europe, with a beautiful and educational array of aquatic (many
endangered) creatures from the briny deep
grouped into different zones (coral cave,
rainforest, River Thames), kicking off with
a shark walkway. Check the website for
shark-feeding times and book online for a
10% discount.

White Cube Bermondsey GALLERY

(Map p82; www.whitecube.com; 144-152 Bermondsey St, SE1; ☺10am-6pm Tue-Sat, noon-6pm Sun;
☻London Bridge) FREE The new White Cube
Bermondsey has ample exhibition space,
designed to showcase large and ambitious
installation pieces.

Hayward Gallery GALLERY

(Map p82; www.southbankcentre.co.uk; Belvedere
Rd, SE1; ☺10am-6pm Sat-Wed, to 8pm Thu & Fri;
⊕; ☻Waterloo) The 1968 Brutalist architecture is as opinion-dividing as you can get,
but the popular international contemporary
art shows held here constitute a further rich
seam of culture in the Southbank Centre.

⊙ Pimlico

The origins of its name highly obscure, Pimlico is a grand part of London, bordered by
the Thames but lacking a strong sense of
neighbourhood, becoming prettier the further you stray from Victoria station.

★**Tate Britain**   GALLERY
(www.tate.org.uk; Millbank, SW1; ⊙10am-6pm, to 10pm 1st Fri of month; ⊕Pimlico) **FREE** Splendidly refurbished with a stunning new staircase and a rehung collection, the more elderly and venerable of the two Tate siblings – in a riverside Portland stone edifice – celebrates paintings from 1500 to the present, with works from Blake, Hogarth, Gainsborough, Barbara Hepworth, Whistler, Constable and Turner – in particular – whose light-infused visions dominate the **Clore Gallery**. It doesn't stop there and vibrant modern and contemporary art finds expression in pieces from Lucian Freud, Francis Bacon and Tracey Emin.

The controversial **Turner Prize** (inviting annual protests outside the gallery) is held here every year between October and January, while a fantastic cafe with an excellent terrace facing the river provides sustenance and views. Free one-hour thematic **tours** are held daily at 11am, noon, 2pm and 3pm, and don't overlook the Late at Tate night (first Friday of the month), when doors are open to 10pm.

⊙ Chelsea & Kensington

Known as the royal borough, Chelsea and Kensington lays claim to the highest income earners in the UK. Kensington High St has a lively mix of chains and boutiques, while even the charity shops along King's Rd resemble fashion outlets. Some of London's most beautiful and fascinating museums, clustered together in South Kensington, are must-sees come rain or shine.

★**Victoria & Albert Museum**   MUSEUM
(V&A; Map p88; www.vam.ac.uk; Cromwell Rd, SW7; ⊙10am-5.45pm Sat-Thu, to 10pm Fri; ⊕South Kensington) **FREE** This outstanding museum boasts an unparalleled collection of decorative art and design with some 4.5 million objects from Britain and around the globe. The museum setting and gorgeous architecture is as inspiring as the sheer diversity and rarity of its exhibits. Part of Prince Albert's legacy to Londoners in the wake of the Great Exhibition of 1851, the museum is a bit like the nation's attic, spread generously through nearly 150 galleries.

The museum is epic, but it's open late on Friday evenings, for smaller crowds. For food and drink, make for the **V&A Café** in the magnificent Refreshment Rooms, dating from the 1860s, or the **Garden Café** in the John Madesjki Garden in summer.

TATE-A-TATE

Whisking art lovers between London's Tate galleries, the colourful **Tate Boat** (Map p82; www.tate.org.uk/visit/tate-boat; one-way adult/child £6.50/3.25) stops en route at the London Eye. Services from Bankside Pier run from 9.57am to 4.44pm daily at 40-minute intervals (10.20am to 4.27pm from Millbank Pier). Discounts are available for Travelcard holders.

Free one-hour guided tours leave the main reception area four times daily.

★**Natural History Museum**   MUSEUM
(Map p88; www.nhm.ac.uk; Cromwell Rd, SW7; ⊙10am-5.50pm; ⊕South Kensington) **FREE** This ornate building is one of London's finest and a masterpiece: pale blue and honey-coloured stone, broken by Venetian arches decorated with all manner of carved critters. A sure-fire hit with kids of all ages, this awesome museum is crammed with fascinating discoveries, starting with the giant Diplodocus skeleton that greets you in the main hall. In the **dinosaur gallery**, the roaring 4m-high animatronic Tyrannosaurus Rex is a heart-thumping highlight .

Other galleries are equally impressive. An escalator slithers up into a hollowed-out globe where **Volcanoes and Earthquakes** explores the forces that shape our planet; highlights include a plate tectonics room and the mock-up of the Kobe earthquake, a bone-rattling lesson in fault lines.

The **Darwin Centre** houses a team of biologists and a staggering 20-million-plus repertoire of animal and plant specimens. Take a lift to the top of the **Cocoon**, a seven-storey egg-shaped structure encased within a glass pavilion, and make your way down through the floors of interactive displays. Glass windows allow you to watch the scientists at work.

Finally, don't overlook **Sensational Butterflies** by the East Lawn and the charming **Wildlife Garden**, a slice of English countryside in SW7.

★**Science Museum**   MUSEUM
(Map p88; www.sciencemuseum.org.uk; Exhibition Rd, SW7; ⊙10am-6pm; ⊕South Kensington) **FREE** With seven floors of interactive and educational exhibits, this scientifically

Victoria & Albert Museum

HALF-DAY HIGHLIGHTS TOUR

The art- and design-packed V&A is vast: we have devised an easy-to-follow tour of the museum highlights to help cover some signature pieces while also allowing you to appreciate some of the grandeur of the museum architecture.

Enter the V&A by the Grand Entrance off Cromwell Rd and immediately turn left to explore the Islamic Middle East Gallery and to discover the sumptuous silk-and-wool **Ardabil Carpet ❶**. Among the pieces from South Asia in the adjacent gallery is the terrifying automated **Tipu's Tiger ❷**. Continue to the outstanding **Fashion Room ❸** with its displays of clothing styles through the ages. The magnificent gallery opposite, which houses the Raphael Cartoons, offers a shortcut via stairs on its far side to Level 2 and the Britain 1500–1760 Gallery; turn left in the gallery to

DAMIAN HARPER ©

Fashion Gallery
With clothing from the 18th century to the present day, this circular and chronologically arranged gallery showcases evening wear, undergarments and iconic fashion milestones, such as 1960s dresses designed by Mary Quant.

The Great Bed of Ware
Created during the reign of Queen Elizabeth I, its headboard and bedposts etched with ancient graffiti, the 16th-century oak Great Bed of Ware is famously name-dropped in Shakespeare's *Twelfth Night*.

Britain 1500-1760 Gallery

Raphael Cartoons

Stairs to Level 2

❸

❷

❶

Main Entrance

Gift Shop

John Madejski Garden

T.T.Tsui China collection

Japan Gallery

Cast Courts

Stairs from Level 1

❹

❺ Stairs to Level 3

LEVEL 1

LEVEL 2

The Ardabil Carpet
One of the world's most beautiful carpets, the Ardabil was completed in 1540, one of a pair commissioned by Shah Tahmasp, ruler of Iran. The piece is most astonishing for the artistry of the detailing and the subtlety of design.

Tipu's Tiger
This disquieting 18th-century wood-and-metal mechanical automaton depicts a European being savaged by a tiger. When a handle is turned, an organ hidden within the feline mimics the cries of the dying man, whose arm also rises.

INDIAN SCHOOL / GETTY IMAGES ©

find the **Great Bed of Ware** ④, beyond which rests the exquisitely crafted artistry of **Henry VIII's writing box** ⑤. Head up the stairs into the Metalware Gallery on Level 3 for the **Hereford Screen** ⑥. Continue through the Ironwork and Sculpture Galleries and through the Leighton Corridor to the glittering **Jewellery Gallery** ⑦, from where a succession of galleries bordering the John Madejski Garden lead you to the **Design Since 1946** ⑧ gallery, opposite the 20th Century Gallery (at the end of which are stairs and a lift to the rest of the museum).

TOP TIPS

» **More Info** Museum attendants are always at hand along the route.

» **Photography** Allowed in most galleries, except the Jewellery Gallery, the Raphael Cartoons and the China Gallery.

» **Evening Exploration** Avoid daytime crowds: visit the V&A till 10pm on Friday.

Henry VIII's Writing Box
This exquisitely ornate walnut and oak 16th-century writing box has been added to over the centuries, but the original decorative motifs are superb, including Henry's coat of arms, flanked by Venus holding Cupid) and Mars.

Design Since 1946
Weigh up some innovative classics that defined much of the late 20th century, when mobile phones were seriously chunky and portable audio cassette players were the latest must-have gadget.

Stairs to other Levels

20th Century Gallery

airs from level 2

⑧

National Art Library

⑥

Ironwork Gallery

⑦

Leighton Corridor

Sculpture Gallery

Photographers Gallery

LEVEL 3

LEVEL 4

Jewellery Gallery
The beautifully illuminated Jewellery Gallery has a stunning collection of items from ancient Greece to the modern day, including a dazzling gold Celtic breastplate, art-nouveau jewellery and animals fashioned by Fabergé.

The Hereford Screen
Designed by Sir George Gilbert Scott, this awe-inspiring choir screen is a labour of love, originally fashioned for Hereford Cathedral. An almighty conception of wood, iron, copper, brass and hardstone, there were few parts of the V&A that could support its great mass.

Knightsbridge, South Kensington & Chelsea

Marble Arch (150m)

Paddington (300m)

MAYFAIR

KNIGHTSBRIDGE

Hyde Park

Kensington Gardens

The Serpentine

The Long Water

Round Pond

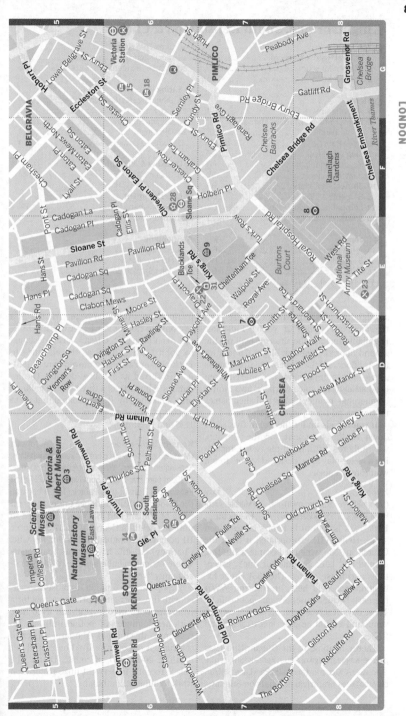

Knightsbridge, South Kensington & Chelsea

spellbinding museum will mesmerise even the most precocious of young Einsteins. Highlights include the **Energy Hall** on the ground floor, the riveting **Flight Gallery** on the 3rd floor and the flight simulator. There's also a 450-seat **Imax cinema**. Some children head straight for voice warpers, lava lamps, boomerangs, bouncy globes and alien babies in the ground-floor shop, and stay put.

If you've kids under the age of five, scoot down to the basement for the **Garden**, where there's a fun-filled play zone, including a water-play area, besieged by tots in red waterproof smocks.

Hyde Park
PARK

(Map p88; ⊙5.30am-midnight; ⊖Marble Arch, Hyde Park Corner, Queensway) At 145 hectares, Hyde Park is central London's largest open space. Henry VIII expropriated it from the Church in 1536, when it became a hunting ground and later a venue for duels, executions and horse racing. The 1851 Great Exhibition was held here, and during WWII the park became an enormous potato field. These days, it serves as an occasional concert venue and a full-time green space for fun and frolics.

There's boating on the **Serpentine** (Map p88; ⊖Knightsbridge or South Kensington), while **Speakers' Corner** (Map p88; Park Lane; ⊖Marble Arch) sees oratorical acrobats on Sundays,

maintaining a tradition begun in 1872 as a response to rioting. A wee bit north is **Marble Arch** (Map p92; ⊖Marble Arch), designed by John Nash in 1828 as the entrance to Buckingham Palace and moved here in 1851; it once served as a police lookout. The infamous Tyburn Tree, a three-legged gallows, once stood nearby. It is estimated that up to 50,000 people were executed here between 1196 and 1783.

Kensington Palace
PALACE

(Map p110; www.hrp.org.uk/kensingtonpalace; Kensington Gardens, W8; adult/child £16.50/free; ⊙10am-6pm Mar-Oct, to 5pm Nov-Feb; ⊖High St Kensington) Kensington Palace (1605) became the favourite royal residence under the joint reign of William and Mary and remained so until the death of George II (in 1762, George III bought Buckingham Palace for his wife, Charlotte). It still has private apartments where various members of the royal extended family live.

In popular imagination it's most associated with three intriguing princesses: Victoria (who was born here in 1819 and lived here with her domineering mother until her accession to the throne), Margaret (sister of the current queen, who lived here until her death in 2002) and, of course, Diana. The palace recently underwent huge restoration work totalling £12 million.

Kensington Gardens
GARDENS

(Map p110; ⊙dawn-dusk; ⊖High St Kensington) Blending in with Hyde Park, these royal gardens are part of Kensington Palace and hence popularly associated with Princess Diana. Diana devotees can visit the Diana, Princess of Wales Memorial Fountain (Map p88; ⊖Knightsbridge), a soothing structure fashioned from 545 pieces of Cornish granite, channeling a circular stream drawn from chalk aquifers more than 100m underground that cascades gently and flows together in a pool at the bottom; paddling is encouraged.

The astonishing Albert Memorial (Map p88; tours adult/concession £6/5; ⊙tours 2pm & 3pm 1st Sun of month Mar-Dec; ⊖Knightsbridge, Gloucester Rd) FREE is a unique chunk of Victorian bombast, a lavish marble, mosaic and gold affair opposite the Royal Albert Hall, built to honour Queen Victoria's husband, Albert (1819–61).

The gardens also house the Serpentine Gallery (Map p88; www.serpentinegallery.org; ⊙10am-6pm Tue-Sun; ⊖Lancaster Gate or Knightsbridge) FREE, one of London's edgiest contemporary art spaces; the recently opened Serpentine Sackler Gallery (Map p88; www.serpentinegallery.org; West Carriage Drive; ⊙10am-6pm Tue-Sun; ⊖Lancaster Gate) is on the far side of the Serpentine Bridge, in the former Magazine. The Sunken Garden, near the palace, is at its prettiest in summer, while tea in the Orangery (Map p110; ☑020-3166 6112; www.hrp.org.uk; Kensington Palace, Kensington Gardens, W8; afternoon tea £24, with champagne £34; ⊙10am-6pm Mar-Oct, to 5pm Nov-Feb; ⊖Queensway, Notting Hill Gate, High St Kensington) ⏺ is a treat any time of the year.

King's Road
STREET

(Map p88; ⊖Sloane Sq) Named after King Charles II who would return to Hampton Court Palace along a farmer's track here after amorous interludes with Nell Gwyn, this street was almost synonymous with London fashion during the '60s and '70s. Its days at the counter-cultural forefront of London fashion long gone, King's Road today is more a stamping ground for the leisure-class shopping set.

Saatchi Gallery
GALLERY

(Map p88; www.saatchi-gallery.co.uk; Duke of York's HQ, King's Rd, SW1; ⊙10am-6pm; ⊖Sloane Sq) FREE This enticing gallery hosts temporary exhibitions of experimental and thought-provoking work across a variety of media. The white, sanded bare-floorboard galleries are sharply presented, but save some wonder for Gallery 15, where Richard Wilson's *20:50* is on permanent display. Mesmerising, impassive and ineffable, it's a riveting tour de force. A cool bookshop chips in down in the basement.

Royal Hospital Chelsea
HISTORIC BUILDINGS

(Map p88; www.chelsea-pensioners.co.uk; Royal Hospital Rd, SW3; ⊙grounds 10am-noon & 2-4pm Mon-Sat, museum 10am-noon & 2-4pm Mon-Fri; ⊖Sloane Sq) FREE Designed by Wren, the Royal Hospital Chelsea was built in 1692 to provide shelter for ex-servicemen. Today it houses hundreds of war veterans known as Chelsea Pensioners, charming old chaps generally regarded as national treasures. The Chelsea Flower Show takes place in the hospital grounds in May.

Chelsea Physic Garden
GARDENS

(www.chelseaphysicgarden.co.uk; 66 Royal Hospital Rd, SW3; adult/child £9.90/6.60; ⊙11am-6pm Tue-Fri & Sun Apr-Oct, to 10pm Wed Jul & Aug; ⊖Sloane Sq) This gorgeous botanical enclave was established by the Apothecaries' Society in 1676 for students working on medicinal plants and healing. One of Europe's oldest of its kind, the small grounds are a compendium of botany from carnivorous pitcher plants to rich yellow flag irises, a cork oak from Portugal, delightful ferns and a treasure trove of rare trees and shrubs. Free tours are held three times daily.

Fulham Palace
HISTORIC BUILDING

(www.fulhampalace.org; Bishop's Ave; ⊙palace & museum 12.30-4.30pm Mon-Thu, noon-5pm Sun, gardens dawn-dusk daily; ⊖Putney Bridge) FREE Summer home of the bishops of London from 704 to 1975, this genteel palace near the Thames has an adorable courtyard that draws watercolourists on sunny days, a splendid cafe in the drawing room at the rear (looking out onto a magnificent lawn), a pretty walled garden and a Tudor Revival chapel.

Guided tours usually take in the Great Hall, the Victorian chapel, Bishop Sherlock's Room and the museum and last about 1¼ hours. There are also garden tours (£5); check the website for details on evening walks (for a nightfall perspective). Hiking around the extensive and partially excavated palace moat (once the longest in England) is enjoyable. Films are screened on the lawn in summer, when art fairs and musical festivals are also held.

◉ Marylebone

Not as exclusive as its southern neighbour Mayfair, hip Marylebone has one of London's most pleasant high streets and the famous, if rather disappointing, Baker St, immortalised in the hit song by Gerry Rafferty and strongly associated with Victoria-era sleuth Sherlock Holmes (there's a museum and gift shop at his fictional address, 221b).

Regent's Park PARK
(www.royalparks.org.uk; ⊘5am-dusk; ⊜Regent's Park, Baker St) A former royal hunting ground, Regent's Park was designed by John Nash early in the 19th century, although what was actually laid out is only a fraction of the celebrated architect's grand plan. Nevertheless, it's one of London's most lovely open spaces – at once serene and lively, cosmopolitan and local – with football pitches, tennis courts, a boating lake, ZSL London Zoo, and Regent's canal along its northern side.

Queen Mary's Gardens, towards the south of the park, are particularly pretty, with spectacular roses in summer. **Open Air Theatre** (☎0844 826 4242; www.openairtheatre.org) hosts performances of Shakespeare and other classics here on summer evenings, along with comedy and concerts.

Marylebone

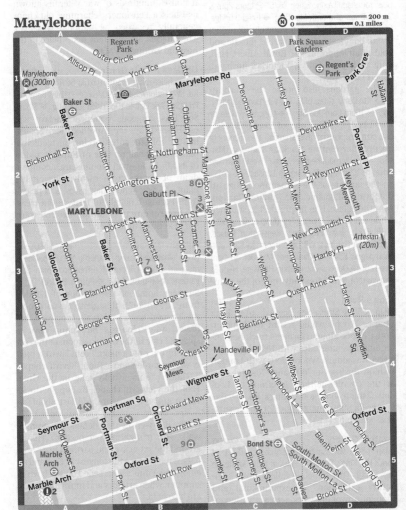

ZSL London Zoo ZOO

(www.londonzoo.co.uk; Outer Circle, Regent's Park, NW1; adult/child £26/18.50; ⊙ 10am-5.30pm Mar-Oct, to 4pm Nov-Feb; ⊜ Camden Town) These famous zoological gardens have come a long way since being established in 1828, with massive investment making conservation, education and breeding the name of the game. Highlights include Tiger Territory, Penguin Beach, Gorilla Kingdom, Rainforest Life, Nightlife and Butterfly Paradise. Feeding sessions or talks take place during the day. Save 20% off the admission price by booking online.

Regent's Canal CANAL

To flee the crowded streets and enjoy a picturesque, waterside angle on North London, take to the canals that once played such a vital role in the transport of goods across the capital. The towpath of Regent's Canal also makes an excellent shortcut across North London, either on foot or by bike.

In full, the ribbon of water runs 9 miles from Limehouse to Little Venice (where it meets the Grand Union Canal), but you can make do with walking from Little Venice to Camden in under an hour, passing Regent's Park and London Zoo, as well as beautiful villas designed by architect John Nash and redevelopments of old industrial buildings. Allow 15 to 20 minutes between Camden and Regent's Park, and 25 to 30 minutes between Regent's Park and Little Venice. The London Waterbus Company (p146) and Jason's Trip (p146) run canal boats between Camden Lock and Little Venice.

Madame Tussauds MUSEUM

(Map p92; ☑ 0870 400 3000; www.madametussauds.com/london; Marylebone Rd, NW1; adult/

Marylebone

⊙ Sights

1	Madame Tussauds	B1
2	Marble Arch	A5

⊗ Eating

3	La Fromagerie	B2
4	Locanda Locatelli	A4
5	Providores & Tapa Room	C3
6	Roti Chai	B5

⊙ Drinking & Nightlife

7	Purl	B3

⊜ Shopping

8	Daunt Books	B2
9	Selfridges	B5

child £30/26; ⊙ 9.30am-5.30pm; ⊜ Baker St) Tickets may cost a (wax) arm and a (wax) leg and the crowds can be as awesome as the exhibits, but the opportunity to pose beside Posh and Becks has clear-cut kudos. Most of the life-size wax figures – such as Leonardo Di Caprio – are fantastically lifelike and as close to the real thing as most of us will get, but queues for the Queen (and Barack Obama) can get leg-numbing.

Honing her craft making effigies of victims of the French revolution, Tussaud brought her wares to England in 1802. Her Chamber of Horrors still survives (complete with the actual blade that took Marie Antoinette's head), but it's joined by Scream!, where actors lunge at terrified visitors in the dark. The Spirit of London ride in a black cab is tremendous fun and the 4-D Marvel film is top-drawer entertainment, the audience sprayed with air jets and mist and jabbed in the back during a spectacular action film centred on London. Try to arrive early in the morning to avoid long queues.

Tickets are cheaper when ordered online; combined tickets with the London Eye, London Dungeon and London Sealife Aquarium are also available.

⊙ Bloomsbury & St Pancras

With the University of London and British Museum within its genteel environs, it's little wonder that Bloomsbury has attracted a lot of very clever, bookish people over the years. Between the world wars, these pleasant streets were colonised by a group of artists and intellectuals known collectively as the Bloomsbury Group, which included novelists Virginia Woolf and EM Forster and the economist John Maynard Keynes. Russell Sq, its very heart, was laid out in 1800 and is one of London's largest and loveliest.

The conversion of spectacular St Pancras station into the Eurostar terminal and a ritzy apartment complex is reviving the area's fortunes.

★ British Museum MUSEUM

(Map p66; ☑ 020-7323 8000; www.britishmuseum. org; Great Russell St, WC1; ⊙ 10am-5.30pm Sat-Thu, to 8.30pm Fri; ⊜ Russell Sq, Tottenham Court Rd) **FREE** The country's largest museum and one of the oldest and finest in the world, this monumental accumulation of treasures boasts vast Egyptian, Etruscan, Greek, Roman, European and Middle Eastern galleries, among many others. Begun in 1753 with a 'cabinet of

The British Museum

A HALF-DAY TOUR

The British Museum, with almost eight million items in its permanent collection, is so vast and comprehensive that it can be daunting for the first-time visitor. To avoid a frustrating trip – and getting lost on the way to the Egyptian mummies – set out on this half-day exploration, which takes in some of the museum's most important sights. If you want to see and learn more, join a tour or hire a multimedia iPad.

A good starting point is the **Rosetta Stone** ❶, the key that cracked the code to ancient Egypt's writing system. Nearby treasures from Assyria – an ancient civilisation centred in Mesopotamia between the Tigris and Euphrates Rivers – including the colossal **Khorsabad Winged Bulls** ❷, give way to the **Parthenon Sculptures** ❸, highpoints of classical Greek art that continue to influence

Winged Bulls from Khorsabad
This awesome pair of alabaster winged bulls with human heads once guarded the entrance to the palace of Assyrian King Sargon II at Khorsabad in Mesopotamia, a cradle of civilisation in present-day Iraq.

Parthenon Sculptures
The Parthenon, a white marble temple dedicated to Athena, was part of a fortified citadel on the Acropolis in Athens. There are dozens of sculptures and friezes with models and interactive displays explaining how they all once fitted together.

Ancient Greece & Rome ❸

Lion Hunt Reliefs from Nineveh ❷

West Stairs

❶ ❹

South Stairs

Main Entrance

Great Court

Reading Room

Great Court Shop

China, India & Southeast Asia

North America

Paul Hamlyn Library

Ticket Desk
(Temporary Exhibitions)

GROUND FLOOR

Rosetta Stone
Written in hieroglyphic, demotic (cursive ancient Egyptian script used for everyday use) and Greek, the 762kg stone contains a decree exempting priests from tax on the first anniversary of young Ptolemy V's coronation.

Bust of Ramesses the Great
The most impressive sculpture in the Egyptian galleries, this 7.5-tonne bust portrays Ramesses II, scourge of the Israelites in the Book of Exodus, as great benefactor.

us today. Be sure to see both the sculptures and the monumental frieze celebrating the birth of Athena. En route to the West Stairs is a huge bust of **Pharaoh Ramesses II ④**, just a hint of the large collection of **Egyptian mummies ⑤** upstairs. (The earliest, affectionately called Ginger because of its wispy reddish hair, was preserved simply by hot sand.) The Romans introduce visitors to the early Britain galleries via the rich **Mildenhall Treasure ⑥**. The Anglo-Saxon **Sutton Hoo Ship Burial ⑦** and the medieval **Lewis Chessmen ⑧** follow.

EATING OPTIONS

» **Court Cafes** At the northern end of the Great Court; takeaway counters with salads and sandwiches; communal tables

» **Gallery Cafe** Slightly out of the way near Room 12; quieter; offers hot dishes

» **Court Restaurant** Upstairs overlooking the former Reading Room; sit-down meals

Lewis Chessmen
The much-loved 78 chess pieces portray faceless pawns, worried-looking queens, bishops with their mitres turned sideways and rooks as 'warders', gnawing away at their shields.

FEARGUS COONEY / GETTY IMAGES ©

Egyptian Mummies
Among the rich collection of mummies and funerary objects is 'Ginger', who was buried at the site of Gebelein, in Upper Egypt, more than 5000 years ago, and Katebet, a one-time chantress (ritual performer) at the Amun temple in Karnak.

Greece & Rome

Stairs

Medieval Europe

Ancient Egypt

Court Restaurant ⑤

⑧

⑦ ⑥

Ancient Middle East

UPPER FLOOR

Sutton Hoo Ship Burial
This unique grave of an important (but unidentified) Anglo-Saxon royal has yielded drinking horns, gold buckles and a stunning helmet with face mask.

Mildenhall Treasure
Roman gods such as Neptune and Bacchus share space with early Christian symbols like the *chi-rho* (short for 'Christ') on the find's three dozen silver bowls, plates and spoons.

North Central London

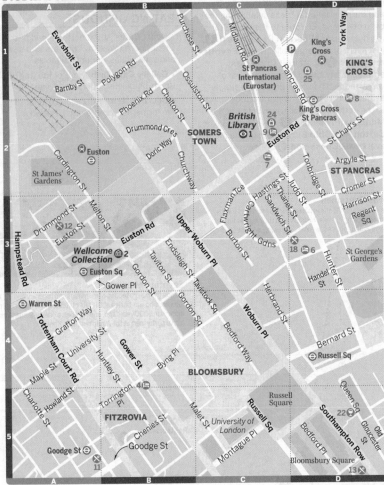

curiosities' bequeathed by Sir Hans Sloane to the nation on his death, the collection mushroomed over the ensuing years partly through plundering the empire. The grand Enlightenment Gallery was the first section of the redesigned museum to be built (in 1820).

Among the must-sees are the Rosetta Stone, the key to deciphering Egyptian hieroglyphics, discovered in 1799; the controversial Parthenon Sculptures, stripped from the walls of the Parthenon in Athens by Lord Elgin (the British ambassador to the Ottoman Empire), and which Greece wants returned; the stunning Oxus Treasure of 7th- to 4th-century-BC Persian gold; and the Anglo-Saxon Sutton Hoo burial relics. The Great Court was restored and augmented by Norman Foster in 2000 and now has a spectacular glass-and-steel roof, making it one of the most impressive architectural spaces in London. In the centre is the Reading Room, with its stunning blue-and-gold domed ceiling, where Karl Marx wrote the Manifesto of the Communist Party.

The museum is huge, so make a few focused visits if you have time, and consider the 15 free 30- to 40-minute eyeOpener tours of individual galleries per day. The museum also has excellent multimedia iPad tours (adult/child £5/3.50), offering six themed one-hour tours, and eight 35-minute children's trails. Highlights tours (adult/child £12/free) depart at 11.30am and 2pm Saturday and Sunday.

The British Museum's long-awaited new extension, the **World Conservation and Exhibitions Centre** in its northwestern corner, opened in 2014, with an exhibition on the Vikings.

When museum fever strikes you down, pop across the way to the lovely **Museum Tavern** (Map p66; 49 Great Russell St, WC1; ⊙11am-11.30pm Mon-Sat, 10am-10pm Sun; ⊖Holborn, Tottenham Court Rd) where Karl Marx used to polish off a drink or two after a hard day's graft in the Reading Room of the British Library.

★ **British Library**   LIBRARY
(Map p96; www.bl.uk; 96 Euston Rd, NW1; Ritblat Gallery free, special exhibition cost varies; ⊙9.30am-6pm Mon & Wed-Fri, to 8pm Tue, to 5pm Sat, 11am-5pm Sun; ⊖King's Cross St Pancras) For visitors, the real highlight of the British Library is a visit to the **Sir John Ritblat Gallery**, where the most precious manuscripts, spanning almost three millennia, are held. Here you'll find the *Codex Sinaiticus* (the

North Central London

first complete text of the New Testament), a Gutenberg Bible (1455), the stunningly illustrated Jain sacred texts, Leonardo da Vinci's notebooks, a copy of the *Magna Carta* (1215), explorer Captain Scott's final diary and Shakespeare's First Folio (1623).

Further choice selections include the lyrics to 'A Hard Day's Night' (scribbled on the back of Julian Lennon's birthday card) plus original scores by Handel, Mozart and Beethoven.

★ **Wellcome Collection**   MUSEUM
(Map p96; www.wellcomecollection.org; 183 Euston Rd, NW1; ◷10am-6pm Tue, Wed, Fri & Sat, to 10pm Thu, 11am-6pm Sun; ◉Euston Sq) **FREE** Focusing on the interface of art, science and medicine, this museum – 'a free destination for the incurably curious' – is fascinating. The core of the permanent collection includes objects from around the world collected by Sir Henry Wellcome (1853–1936), a pharmacist, entrepreneur and collector who amassed more than a million objects from different civilisations.

Charles Dickens Museum   MUSEUM
(Map p96; www.dickensmuseum.com; 48 Doughty St, WC1; adult/child £8/4; ◷10am-5pm, last admission 4pm; ◉Chancery Lane, Russell Sq) Recently refurbished, Dickens' sole surviving London residence is where his work really flourished – *The Pickwick Papers*, *Nicholas Nickleby* and *Oliver Twist* were all written here. The handsome four-storey house narrowly dodged demolition and opened as a museum in 1925.

◉ Camden Town

Once well outside the city limits, the former hamlets of North London were long ago gobbled up by the metropolis, yet they still harbour a village feel and distinct local identity. Neither as resolutely wealthy as the west (although there are highly desirable pockets) or as gritty as the east (but there's attitude), the 'Norf' is a mix of genteel terrace houses and featureless council estates, containing some of London's hippest neighbourhoods.

Technicolor hairstyles, facial furniture, elaborate tattoos and alternative threads are the look of bohemian Camden Town, a vibrant neighbourhood of pubs, live-music venues, appealing boutiques and, most famously, Camden Market (p132).

◉ Hoxton, Shoreditch & Spitalfields

These revitalised and hip areas northeast of the City have enough sightseeing allure to keep daytime travellers occupied, but things really get going in the evening, when the late-night pubs, clubs and restaurants come into their own. Vibrant Hoxton and Shoreditch form the centre of gravity for nightlife, while Sunday is optimum for strolling leisurely through Spitalfields after a Saturday night out. Over the centuries, waves of immigrants have left their mark here, and it's a great place to come for diverse cuisine and vibrant nightlife.

Dennis Severs' House MUSEUM
(Map p114; ☑ 020-7247 4013; www.dennissevers house.co.uk; 18 Folgate St, E1; ⊖ Liverpool St) This Georgian House is set up as if its occupants (a family of Huguenot silk weavers) had just walked out the door, with half-drunk cups of tea, lit candles and, with perhaps more detail than necessary, a full chamber pot by the bed. More than a museum, it's an opportunity to meditate on the minutiae of everyday Georgian life through silent exploration.

Bookings are required for the Monday- and Wednesday-evening candlelit sessions (£14; 6pm to 9pm), but you can just show up on Sundays (£10; noon to 4pm) or selected Mondays (£7; noon to 2pm).

Geffrye Museum MUSEUM
(Map p114; www.geffrye-museum.org.uk; 136 Kingsland Rd, E2; ⊙ 10am-5pm Tue-Sun; ⊖ Hoxton, Old St) FREE If you like nosing around other people's homes, you'll love this museum. Devoted to middle-class domestic interiors, these former almshouses (1714) have been converted into a series of living rooms dating from 1630 to the current Ikea generation. On top of the interiors, the back garden has been transformed into period garden 'rooms' and a lovely walled herb garden (April to October only).

◉ The East End & Docklands

A huge area, the East End and Docklands are not rich in sights, but a dramatic new focus has emerged in the Olympic Park, while recently opened Overground lines make transport a breeze.

The Docklands' Canary Wharf and Isle of Dogs are an island of tower blocks, rivalling those of the City itself. London's port was once the world's greatest, the hub of the enormous global trade of the British Empire. Since being pummelled by the unpleasant Luftwaffe in WWII, its fortunes have been topsy-turvy, but massive development of Canary Wharf replaced its crusty seadogs with battalions of dark-suited office workers.

Museum of London Docklands MUSEUM
(www.museumoflondon.org.uk/docklands; Hertsmere Rd, West India Quay, E17; ⊙ 10am-6pm; 🚈 DLR West India Quay) FREE Housed in a heritage-listed warehouse, this museum combines artefacts and multimedia to chart the history of the city through its river and docks. There's a lot to see here, including an informative section on the slave trade. The museum faces West India Quay; head west (towards the City) from the DLR station.

Queen Elizabeth Olympic Park PARK
(www.queenelizabetholympicpark.co.uk; ⊖ Stratford) From 2008, a vast swath of industrial East London was ambitiously regenerated, becoming London's Olympic Park for the 2012 Games. The 560-acre parkland was renamed the Queen Elizabeth Olympic Park and fully opened to public use in 2014. Complementing its iconic sporting architecture (much of which has been opened to public use) the park was thoughtfully designed with a diverse mix of wetland, woodland, meadow and other wildlife habitats as an environmentally fertile legacy for the future.

LONDON FOR CHILDREN

London is terrific for kids. Many of the city's museums – among the best in the world – are free and will fascinate all ages, with bundles of activities on offer, from storytelling at the National Gallery (p65) to arts and crafts workshops at the Victoria & Albert Museum (p85) and fun sleepovers at the British Museum (p93), Natural History Museum (p85), Science Museum (p85) and others. Theatre, dance and music performances are perfect for older kids and teens. Playgrounds and parks are ideal for relaxation or wearing the young tykes out. On top of that, city farms (see www.london-footprints.co.uk/visitfarms.htm) and the big galleries have activities for children. Ice rinks glisten across London in winter months, at Somerset House (p69), the Natural History Museum (p85), the Tower of London (p70), and Hampton Court Palace (p102). For the Hogwarts fan club, the Making of Harry Potter (Warner Bros studio tour; p223) is a short train trip away from Euston station.

All top-range hotels offer in-house babysitting services. Prices vary enormously from hotel to hotel, so ask the concierge about hourly rates. Get a babysitter or nanny at Greatcare (www.greatcare.co.uk), a site that provides all manner of childcare options.

Under-16s travel free on buses, under-11s travel free on the tube and under-5s go free on the trains.

ⓘ EMIRATES AIR LINE CABLE CAR

Capable of ferrying 2400 people per hour across the Thames in either direction, the Emirates Air Line (www.emiratesairline.co.uk; adult/child single £4.40/2.30, return £8.80/4.60, with Oyster or Travelcard single £3.20/1.60, return £6.40/3.20; ⊙ 7am-9pm Mon-Fri, 8am-9pm Sat, 9am-9pm Sun Apr-Sep, closes 1hr earlier Oct-Mar; ⑥ DLR Royal Victoria, ⊖ North Greenwich) cable car staples together the Greenwich Peninsula and the Royal Docks in a five- to 10-minute journey.

Designed to help regenerate both sides of the river around each embarkation point, the UK's first urban cable car system has cabins every half minute; Oyster card and Travelcard holders nab discounts for journeys, which are bike-friendly, too.

Arriving at Royal Docks, you can hop on the DLR at Royal Victoria DLR station, while in Greenwich, the underground interchange is with North Greenwich station. Open return tickets (£10) can be used any time on the same day and include entry to the Emirates Aviation Experience.

The signature buildings are the sustainably-built Olympic Stadium, the uplifting Aquatics Centre (now open to swimmers of all abilities), the cutting-edge Lee Valley VeloPark (⌨ 0845 6770 603; ⊙ 9am-10pm), with cycling sessions now bookable, and the Copper Box Arena, an indoor venue for sports and concerts. The twisted, abstract tangle of metal overlooking everything is the ArcelorMittal Orbit (www.arcelormittalorbit.com; Queen Elizabeth Olympic Park, E20; adult/child £15/7; ⊙ 10am-6pm Apr-Sep, to 4pm Oct-Mar; ⊜ Stratford), a 115m-high observation tower that opened during the games. Panoramic views of the park can also be had from the View Tube (www.theviewtube.co.uk; The Greenway; ⊙ 9am-5pm; ⑥ DLR Pudding Mill Lane) on the Greenway. Right alongside the park, Westfield Stratford City (p134) is Europe's largest urban shopping mall.

House Mill   HISTORIC BUILDING
(www.housemill.org.uk; Three Mill Lane, E3; adult/child £3/free; ⊙ 11am-4pm Sun May-Oct, 1st Sun only Mar, Apr & Dec; ⊜ Bromley-by-Bow) One of two remaining mills from a trio that once stood on this small island in the River Lea, House Mill (1776) operated as a sluice tidal mill, grinding grain for a nearby distillery until 1941. Tours, which run according to demand and last about 45 minutes, take visitors to all four floors of the mill.

Crystal   MUSEUM
(One Siemens Brothers Way, Royal Victoria Docks, E16; adult/child £8/free; ⊙ 10am-5pm Tue-Fri, to 7pm Sat & Sun; ⑥ DLR Royal Victoria, cable car Emirates Royal Docks) Housed in a dramatically modern structure, this creative, highly interactive and thoroughly engaging Siemens-sponsored exhibition focuses on urban

sustainability and the pressures facing the modern city, from water to energy consumption, transport needs and beyond. Engaging for both adults and youngsters, you can tie it in with the Emirates Air Line cable car journey across the river from North Greenwich. The ticket includes a complimentary return within two weeks.

⊙ Greenwich

Greenwich (*gren*-itch) straddles the hemispheres and the ages, retaining its own sense of identity based on historic associations with the sea and science and an extraordinary cluster of buildings that have earned 'Maritime Greenwich' a Unesco World Heritage listing.

Greenwich is easily reached on the DLR or via train from London Bridge. Thames River Services (www.thamesriverservices.co.uk; adult/child single £12.25/6.10, return £16/8) has boats departing from Westminster Pier (one hour, every 40 minutes), or alternatively take the cheaper Thames Clippers (www.thamesclippers.com; adult/child £6.50/3.25) ferry.

★ **Old Royal Naval College** HISTORIC BUILDING
(www.oldroyalnavalcollege.org; 2 Cutty Sark Gardens, SE10; ⊙ 10am-5pm, grounds 8am-6pm; ⑥ DLR Cutty Sark) **FREE** Designed by Wren, the Old Royal Naval College is a magnificent example of monumental classical architecture. Parts are now used by the University of Greenwich and Trinity College of Music, but you can visit the chapel and the extraordinary Painted Hall, which took artist Sir James Thornhill 19 years to complete. The complex was built on the site of the 15th-century Palace of Placentia, the birthplace of Henry VIII and Elizabeth I.

The Tudor connection, along with Greenwich's industrial and maritime history, is explored in the **Discover Greenwich** (www.ornc.org; Pepys Building, King William Walk; ⊘10am-5pm) **FREE** centre. The tourist office is based here, along with a cafe/restaurant and microbrewery. Yeomen-led tours of the complex leave at 2pm daily, taking in areas not otherwise open to the public (£6, 90 minutes).

★**National Maritime Museum**   MUSEUM
(www.rmg.co.uk/national-maritime-museum; Romney Rd, SE10; ⊘10am-5pm, Sammy Ofer Wing & ground fl galleries to 8pm Thu; 🚇DLR Cutty Sark) **FREE** With its recently opened **Sammy Ofer Wing**, the National Maritime Museum houses a splendid collection of nautical paraphernalia recounting Britain's brine-soaked seafaring history. Exhibits range from **Miss Britain III** (the first boat to top 100mph on open water) from 1933, the 19m-long **golden state barge** built in 1732 for Frederick, Prince of Wales, humdingers such as **Cook's journals** and **Nelson's uniform**, complete with bullet hole, and interactive educational displays. Tours depart from the ship's propeller at noon, 1pm and 3pm.

★**Royal Observatory**   HISTORIC BUILDING
(www.rmg.co.uk; Greenwich Park, SE10; adult/child £7.70/3.60; ⊘10am-5pm; 🚇DLR Cutty Sark, 🚇DLR Greenwich, 🚇Greenwich) Affording sublime views of London from a hilltop position within idyllic Greenwich Park, the Royal Observatory was commisioned in 1675 by Charles II to help solve the riddle of longitude. Success was confirmed in 1884 when Greenwich was designated as the prime meridian of the world, and Greenwich Mean Time (GMT) became the universal measurement of standard time.

In the north of the observatory is lovely **Flamsteed House** and the **Meridian Courtyard** (where you can stand with your feet straddling the western and eastern hemispheres); admission is by ticket. The southern half contains the highly informative (and free) **Astronomy Centre** and the **Peter Harrison Planetarium** (adult/child £6.50/4.50).

Queen's House   HISTORIC BUILDING
(📞020-8858 4422; www.rmg.co.uk/queens-house; Romney Rd, SE10; ⊘10am-5pm; 🚇Greenwich or DLR Cutty Sark) **FREE** The elegant Queen's House is a Palladian peach, designed by Inigo Jones in 1616 for the wife of Charles I. Don't miss the ceremonial **Great Hall** or the delightful helix-shaped **Tulip Staircase**.

Cutty Sark   SHIP
(www.rmg.co.uk/cuttysark; King William Walk, SE10; adult/child £13.50/7; ⊘10am-5pm; 🚇DLR Cutty Sark) The last of the great clipper ships to sail between China and England in the 19th century has reopened after a serious fire almost scuttled her forever. The vessel has been raised to allow visitors to view the ship from below.

O2   NOTABLE BUILDING
(www.theo2.co.uk; Peninsula Sq, SE10; ⊖North Greenwich) The 380m-wide circular O2 cost £750 million to build. Once *the* definitive white elephant, it finally found a winning direction as a multipurpose venue hosting big-ticket concerts, sporting events (it was the gymnastics and basketball venue for the London Olympics) and blockbuster exhibitions. There are dozens of bars and restaurants inside. The O2 is located on the Greenwich Peninsula, just 10 minutes by bus from Greenwich itself.

⊙ Hampstead & Highgate

These quaint and well-heeled villages, perched on hills north of London, are home to a litany of A- and B-list celebrities.

Hampstead Heath   PARK
(🚇 Gospel Oak, Hampstead Heath, ⊖Hampstead) With its 320 hectares of rolling meadows and wild woodlands, Hampstead Heath is a million miles away – approximately four, actually – from central London. A walk up **Parliament Hill** affords one of the most spectacular views of the city, and on summer days it's picnic heaven. Also bewilderingly popular are the murky brown waters of the single-sex and mixed bathing ponds.

WORTH A TRIP

ESTORICK COLLECTION OF MODERN ITALIAN ART

The outstanding concentration of art in the **Estorick Collection of Modern Italian Art** (www.estorickcollection.com; 39a Canonbury Sq, N1; adult/child £5/free; ⊘11am-6pm Wed-Sat, noon-5pm Sun; ⊖Highbury & Islington) in Islington boasts one of the world's leading collections of futurist painting, from such dazzling talents as Umberto Boccioni, Giacomo Balla and Gino Severini.

WORTH A TRIP

ABBEY ROAD

Beatles aficionados can't possibly visit London without making a pilgrimage to Abbey Road Studios (www.abbeyroad.com; 3 Abbey Rd, NW8) in St John's Wood. The fence outside is covered with decades of fans' graffiti. Stop-start local traffic is long accustomed to groups of tourists lining up on the zebra crossing to reenact the cover of the fab four's 1969 masterpiece and penultimate swan song *Abbey Road*. In 2010, the crossing was rewarded with Grade II listed status.

For an entertaining live view of the crossing and highlights of the day's action, check out the fun webcam at www.abbeyroad.com/crossing. To get here, take the tube to St John's Wood, cross the road, follow Grove End Rd to its end and turn right.

Kenwood House HISTORIC BUILDING

(www.english-heritage.org.uk; Hampstead Lane, NW3; ⊙10am-5pm; ⏷Gospel Oak, Hampstead Heath) FREE Kenwood House is a magnificent neoclassical mansion (1764) on the northern side of Hampstead Heath that houses a collection of paintings by English and European masters including Rembrandt, Vermeer, Turner and Gainsborough.

Highgate Cemetery CEMETERY

(www.highgatecemetery.org; Swain's Lane, N6; East Cemetery adult/child £4/free; ⊙10am-4pm Mon-Fri, 11am-4pm Sat & Sun; ⏷Archway) A Gothic wonderland of shrouded urns, obelisks, broken columns, sleeping angels, classical tomb porticoes and overgrown graves, this boneyard is a sublime Victorian Valhalla. On the eastern side you can pay your respects to the graves of Karl Marx and George Eliot (Mary Ann Evans), but the highlight is the overgrown West Cemetery, where a maze of winding paths leads to the Circle of Lebanon, rings of tombs flanking a circular path and topped with a majestic cedar of Lebanon tree.

Admission to the West Cemetery is by tour only (adult/child £12/6); bookings are essential for weekday tours. Tours of the East Cemetery take place on Saturdays at 2pm (adult/child £8/4). From Archway station, walk up Highgate Hill until you reach Waterlow Park on the left. Go through the park; the cemetery gates are opposite the exit.

⊙ Outside Central London

★ **Kew Gardens** GARDENS

(www.kew.org; Kew Rd; adult/child £15/free; ⊙9.30am-6.30pm Apr-Aug, earlier closing Sep-Mar; ⏷Kew Pier, ⏷Kew Bridge, ⏷Kew Gardens) In 1759 botanists began rummaging around the world for specimens they could plant in the 3-hectare plot known as the Royal Botanic Gardens. They never stopped collecting, and the gardens, which have bloomed to 120 hectares, provide the most comprehensive botanical collection on earth. The beautiful gardens are now recognised as a Unesco World Heritage Site.

No worries if you don't know your golden slipper orchid from your fengoky or your quiver tree from your alang-alang, a visit to Kew is a journey of discovery for everyone. You can easily spend a whole day wandering around, but if you're pressed for time, the Kew Explorer (adult/child £2/1) is a hop-on/hop-off road train that rolls from Victoria Gate, visiting the gardens' main sights.

Highlights include the enormous early Victorian Palm House, a hothouse of metal and curved sheets of glass; the impressive Princess of Wales Conservatory; the red-brick, 1631 Kew Palace (www.hrp.org.uk/kewpalace; ⊙9.30am-5.30pm Apr-Sep), formerly King George III's country retreat; the celebrated Great Pagoda designed by William Chambers in 1762; the Temperate House, the world's largest ornamental glasshouse; and the fun Rhizotron and Xstrata Treetop Walkway, 18m up in the air.

Several fabulous vistas (Cedar Vista, Syon Vista and Pagoda Vista) are channelled by trees from vantage points within Kew Gardens. The idyllic, thatched Queen Charlotte's Cottage (⊙11am-4pm Sat & Sun Apr-Sep) in the southwest of the gardens was popular with 'mad' George III and his wife; the nearby carpets of bluebells are a drawcard in spring. The Orangery near Kew Palace contains a restaurant, cafe and shop.

The gardens are easily reached by tube, but you might prefer to cruise by riverboat from the Westminster Passenger Services Association (Map p58; ☎020-7930 2062; www.wpsa.co.uk; return adult/child to Kew Gardens £18/9), which runs several daily boats from April to October from Westminster Pier (90 minutes).

★ **Hampton Court Palace** PALACE

(www.hrp.org.uk/HamptonCourtPalace; adult/child £18.20/9.10; ⊙10am-6pm Apr-Oct, to 4.30pm Nov-Mar; ⏷Hampton Court Palace, ⏷Hampton Court) Built by Cardinal Thomas Wolsey in 1514 but coaxed from him by Henry VIII just before Wolsey (as chancellor) fell from favour, Hampton Court Palace is England's largest and grandest Tudor structure. It was already one of the most sophisticated palaces in Europe when, in the 17th century, Wren was commissioned to build an extension. The result is a beautiful blend of Tudor and 're-strained baroque' architecture.

Take a themed tour led by costumed historians or, if you're in a rush, visit the highlights: **Henry VIII's State Apartments**, including the **Great Hall** with its spectacular hammer-beamed roof; the **Tudor Kitchens**, staffed by 'servants'; and the **Wolsey Rooms**. You could easily spend a day exploring the palace and its 24 hectares of riverside gardens, especially if you get lost in the 300-year-old **maze**.

Hampton Court is 13 miles southwest of central London and is easily reached by train from Waterloo. Alternatively, the riverboats that head from Westminster to Kew continue here (return adult/child £22.50/11.25, three hours).

Richmond Park PARK

(☺ 7am-dusk; ⊕Richmond) London's wildest park – and the largest urban parkland in Europe – spans more than 1000 hectares and is home to all sorts of wildlife, most notably herds of red and fallow deer.

To get there from Richmond tube station, turn left along George St then left at the fork that leads up Richmond Hill.

Strawberry Hill HISTORIC BUILDING

(www.strawberryhillhouse.org.uk; 268 Waldegrave Rd, TW1; adult/child £10.80/free; ☺house 2-6pm Mon-Wed, noon-6pm Sat & Sun Mar-Oct, garden 10am-6pm daily; ⊕Richmond, then bus R68) With its snow-white walls and Gothic turrets, this fantastical and totally restored 18th-century creation in Twickenham is the whimsical work of art historian, author and politician Horace Walpole. Studded with elaborate stained glass, the building reaches its astonishing apogee in the gallery, with its magnificent papier-mâché ceiling. For the full magic, join a twilight tour (£20).

LOCAL KNOWLEDGE

IAN FRANKLIN: HAMPTON COURT PALACE STATE APARTMENT WARDER

An enthusiastic communicator, Ian Franklin has been a State Apartment Warder at Hampton Court Palace for 17 years.

Costumed Guides & State Apartment Warders Trained historians, our interpreters wear extremely accurate representations of period clothes, bringing historic scenarios to life. Warders, such as myself, are found in most of the rooms and can answer questions face to face in a very personal way.

Fascinating Palace Facts The Palace is home to the largest indigenous spider in England. *Tegenaria parietina,* nick-named the Cardinal Spider after Cardinal Wolsey, can measure up to 20cm from leg-tip to leg-tip. You probably won't encounter one, but their webs are often seen in places like the Tudor Kitchens and King's Stairs. If you don't like spiders – watch out!

And another snippet – Jane Seymour, Henry VIII's third wife, died at Hampton Court Palace. It is said that as there was no burial place ready, her body was laid out in the Chapel Royal. To prevent Jane's body decomposing too quickly, her internal organs were removed, and her heart placed in a casket and buried beneath the Chapel altar. There's no evidence the casket was ever dug up, so the heart could still be buried at the palace.

Favourite Part of the Palace I love the Chapel Royal. As it's still used as a place of worship, and visitors are welcome to attend Sunday services, it gives a sense of life and community to the palace.

Recommended Palace Events Check out the special cooking days in the Tudor Kitchens on the first full weekend in any month, and at Easter and Christmas. Where else in the UK can you regularly see cooks creating Tudor dishes, or meals from period recipes, in the greatest surviving Tudor Kitchens in the country?

Spooky Treats Our famous ghost tours, which run from Halloween to March, allow visitors to enter the palace after dark, and take in the most 'haunted' areas. You can visit the infamous 'Haunted Galley' in almost total darkness!

Hampton Court Palace

A DAY AT THE PALACE

With so much to explore and seemingly infinite gardens, it can be tricky knowing where to begin. It helps to understand how the palace has grown over the centuries and how successive royal occupants embellished Hampton Court to suit their purposes and to reflect the style of the time.

As soon as he had his royal hands upon the palace from Cardinal Thomas Wolsey, Henry VIII began expanding the **Tudor architecture ①**, adding the **Great Hall ②**, the exquisite **Chapel Royal ③**, the opulent Great Watching Chamber and the gigantic **kitchens ④**. By 1540 it had become one of the grandest and most sophisticated palaces in Europe. James kept things ticking over, while Charles I added a new tennis court and did some serious art-collecting – including acquiring the **Triumphs of Caesar ⑤**.

Tudor Kitchens
These vast kitchens were the engine room of the palace. With a staff of 200 people, there were six spit-rack-equipped fireplaces, with roast meat always on the menu (to the tune of 8200 sheep and 1240 oxen per year).

VISITBRITAIN / GETTY IMAGES ©

⑦ The Maze
Around 150m north of the main bulding
Created from hornbeam and yew and planted in around 1700, the maze covers a third of an acre within the famous palace gardens. A must-see conclusion to Hampton Court, the maze takes the average visitor about 20 minutes to reach the centre.

Tudor Architecture
Dating to 1515, the heart of the palace serves as one of the finest examples of Tudor architecture in the nation. Cardinal Thomas Wolsey was responsible for transforming what was originally a grand medieval manor house into a stunning Tudor palace.

Main Entrance
Base Court
Anne Boleyn Gateway

↑ North Direction

CHRIS MELLOR / GETTY IMAGES ©

The Triumphs of Caesar
Acquired by Charles I in 1629, Italian artist Andrea Mantegna's nine-painting series *The Triumphs of Caesar* portray Julius Caesar returning to Rome in a triumphant procession, accompanied by the spoils of war.

After the Civil War, puritanical Oliver Cromwell warmed to his own regal proclivities, spending weekends in the comfort of the former Queen's bedroom and selling off Charles I's art collection. In the late 17th century, William and Mary employed Sir Christopher Wren for baroque extensions, chiefly the William III Apartments, reached by the **King's Staircase 6**. William III also commissioned the world-famous **maze 7**.

TOP TIPS

» Ask one of the red-tunic-garbed warders for anecdotes and information.

» Tag along with a themed tour led by costumed historians or join a Salacious Gossip Tour for scandalous royal stories.

» Grab one of the audio tours from the Information Centre.

The Great Hall
This grand dining hall is the defining room of the palace, displaying what is considered England's finest hammer-beam roof, 16th-century Flemish tapestries telling the story of Abraham, and some exquisite stained-glass windows.

Chapel Court Garden

Fountain Court

ck urt

3

6

Chapel Royal
The blue-and-gold vaulted ceiling was originally intended for Christ Church, Oxford, but was installed here instead; the 18th-century oak reredos was carved by Grinling Gibbons. Books on display include a 1611 1st edition of the King James Bible, printed by Robert Barker.

The King's Staircase
One of five rooms at the palace painted by Antonio Verrio and a suitably bombastic prelude to the King's Apartments, the overblown King's Staircase adulates William III by elevating him above a cohort of Roman emperors.

DAMIAN HARPER ©

OPEN FOR INSPECTION

The palace was opened to the public by Queen Victoria in 1838.

POUND SAVERS

As many of London's very best sights are free, you can easily spend a busy week without paying much on admission charges. However, if you're hanging around for longer and have particular attractions that you're keen to see, there are options for saving a few pounds.

London Pass (www.londonpass.com; 1/2/3/6 days £49/68/81/108) The London Pass is a smart card that gains you fast-track entry to over 60 different attractions, including pricier ones such as the Tower of London and St Paul's Cathedral. You'd have to be racing around frantically to get real value from a one-day pass, but you could conceivably save quite a bit with the two- or three-day version.

Passes can be booked online and either shipped or collected from the **London Pass Redemption Desk** (Map p66; 11a Charing Cross Rd, WC2; ⏰10am-4.30pm; ⊖Leicester Square) opposite the Garrick Theatre. It also sells a version with a preloaded Transport For London (TFL) travel pass, but it's cheaper to buy this separately.

Historic Royal Palaces (www.hrp.org.uk; individual/joint membership £43/65) If you're a royalty buff, taking out an annual membership to the Historic Royal Palaces allows you to jump the queues and visit the Tower of London, Kensington Palace, Banqueting House, Kew Palace and Hampton Court Palace as often as you like.

If you were intending to visit all five anyway, membership will save you £32 (£87 for a couple). There can be a lengthy wait for membership cards, but temporary cards are issued immediately.

Wimbledon Lawn Tennis Museum MUSEUM
(☏020-89466131; www.wimbledon.com/museum; Gate 4, Church Rd, SW19; adult/child £12/7, museum & tour £22/13; ⏰10am-5pm; ☒Wimbledon, then bus 93, ⊖Wimbledon) This museum in leafy Wimbledon details the history of tennis – from its French precursor *Jeu de paume* to the supersonic serves of today's champions. It's a state-of-the-art presentation, with plenty of video clips and a projection of John McEnroe in the dressing room at Wimbledon, but the highlight is the chance to see Centre Court from the 360-degree viewing box. During the championships, the museum is only open to ticket holders.

Regular tours of Wimbledon take in Centre Court, the No 1 Court and other areas of the All England Club, and include access to the museum.

☞ Tours

One of the best ways to orient yourself when you first arrive in London is with a 24-hour hop-on/hop-off pass for the double-decker bus tours. The buses loop around interconnecting routes throughout the day, providing commentaries as they go, and the price includes a river cruise and three walking tours. Save a few pounds by booking online.

Original Tour BUS TOUR
(www.theoriginaltour.com; adult/child/family £29/14/86; ⏰every 20min 8.30am-5.30pm) A hop-on/hop-off option with a river cruise thrown in as well as three themed walks – Changing of the Guard, Rock 'n' Roll and Jack the Ripper.

Big Bus Tours BUS TOUR
(www.bigbustours.com; adult/child/family £32/12/76; ⏰every 20min 8.30am-6pm Apr-Sep, to 5pm Oct & Mar, to 4.30pm Nov-Feb) Informative commentaries in eight languages. The ticket includes a free river cruise with City Cruises and three thematic walking tours (Royal London, Harry Potter film locations and Ghosts by Gaslight). Online booking discounts available.

London Beatles Walks WALKING TOUR
(☏020-8200 3438; www.beatlesinlondon.com; adult/child £9/free) Following the footsteps of the Fab Four.

London Walks WALKING TOUR
(☏020-7624 3978; www.walks.com; adult/child £9/free) Harry Potter tours, ghost walks and the ever-popular Jack the Ripper tours.

London Mystery Walks WALKING TOUR
(☏07957 388280; www.tourguides.org.uk; adult/child/family £10/9/25) Tour Jack the Ripper's old haunts at 7pm on Monday, Wednesday and Friday. You must book in advance.

Greenwich Guided Walks
WALKING TOUR

(☑ 07575 772298; www.greenwichtours.co.uk; adult/child £8/free; ⊙ 12.15pm & 2.15pm) Guided tours of Greenwich's sights, leaving twice daily from the tourist office (no need to book).

City Cruises
BOAT TOUR

(Map p58; ☑ 020-7740 0400; www.citycruises. com; single/return from £9.75/13, day pass £18) Ferry service between Westminster, Waterloo, Tower and Greenwich piers.

Capital Taxi Tours
TAXI TOUR

(☑ 020-8590 3621; www.capitaltaxitours.co.uk; 2hr daytime tour per taxi £165, 2½hr evening tour per taxi £235) Takes up to six people on a variety of tours with Blue Badge, City of London and City of Westminster registered guides/ drivers, cheeky Cockney Cabbie option and foreign language availability.

London Bicycle Tour
CYCLING TOUR

(Map p82; ☑ 020-7928 6838; www.londonbicycle. com; 1a Gabriel's Wharf, 56 Upper Ground, SE1; tour incl bike from £23.95; ⊜ Waterloo) Themed 2½- to 3½-hour tours of the 'West End', 'East', 'Central' or 'Night Tour'.

London Duck Tours
ADVENTURE TOUR

(Map p82; ☑ 020-7928 3132; www.londonduck-tours.co.uk; County Hall, SE1; adult/child £24/16; ⊜ Waterloo) Cruise the streets in the same sort of amphibious landing craft used on D-Day before making a dramatic plunge into the Thames.

✯✯ Festivals & Events

Chinese New Year
CULTURE

Late January or early February sees Chinatown snap, crackle and pop with fireworks, a colourful street parade, lion dances and dim sum aplenty.

University Boat Race
ROWING

(www.theboatrace.org) A grudge match on the Thames held annually since 1829 between the rowing crews of Oxford and Cambridge Universities. Late March.

Virgin Money London Marathon
MARATHON

(www.virginmoneylondonmarathon.com) Up to half a million spectators applaud whippet-thin champions and outlandishly clad greenhorns charging down London's streets in late April.

Chelsea Flower Show
HORTICULTURE

(www.rhs.org.uk/chelsea; Royal Hospital Chelsea; admission from £23) Held in May, arguably the world's most renowned horticultural show attracts green fingers from all corners.

Trooping the Colour
PAGEANT

Celebrating the Queen's official birthday (in June), this ceremonial procession of troops, marching along the Mall for their monarch's inspection, is a pageantry overload.

Field Day
MUSIC

(www.fielddayfestivals.com; Victoria Park; tickets £29.50-59.50; ⊜ Mile End) Fabulously popular indie and alternative music festival, held over a June weekend in Victoria Park.

Royal Academy Summer Exhibition
ART

(www.royalacademy.org.uk; adult/child £9.50/5) Running from mid-June to mid-August, this is an annual showcase of works submitted by artists from all over Britain.

Meltdown Festival
MUSIC

(www.southbankcentre.co.uk) The Southbank Centre hands over the curatorial reigns to a legend of contemporary music (such as Nick Cave, Morrissey or Patti Smith) to pull together a program of concerts, talks and films in late June.

Wimbledon Lawn Tennis Championships
TENNIS

(www.wimbledon.com) Held at the end of June, the world's most prestigious tennis event is as much about strawberries, cream and tradition as supersonic aces.

Wireless
MUSIC

(www.wirelessfestival.co.uk; Queen Elizabeth Olympic Park, E20) One of London's flagship music festivals, with an emphasis on R&B, Wireless moved from Hyde Park to its new home at the Queen Elizabeth Olympic Park in 2013. Usually held in July. Book in advance.

Pride
GAY & LESBIAN

(www.prideinlondon.org) The big event on the LGBT calendar; usually held in June or July.

Lovebox
MUSIC

(www.loveboxfestival.com; Victoria Park, E9) A popular contribution to the summer music festival circuit, held in Victoria Park in mid-July.

Notting Hill Carnival
CARNIVAL

(www.thenottinghillcarnival.com) Held over two days in August, Europe's largest (and London's most vibrant outdoor carnival) sees the Caribbean community showing the city how to party.

🛏 Sleeping

When it comes to finding a place for a good night's kip, London is one of the most expensive places in the world. 'Budget' is pretty much anything below £100 per night for a double; at the top end, how does an £18,000-per-night suite on Hyde Park Corner sound? Double rooms ranging between £90 and £180 per night are considered midrange; more expensive options fall into the top-end category.

London, however, has a delightful selection of characterful hotels, whether brimming with history, zany modern decor or all-stops-out charm. Most of the ritzier places offer substantial discounts on the weekends, for advance bookings and at quieter times.

Public transport is good, so you don't need to be sleeping at Buckingham Palace to be at the heart of things.

Budget accommodation is scattered about, with good options in Bloomsbury and St Pancras, Earl's Court and the South Bank. For something a little nicer, check out Bayswater, Notting Hill Gate or Belgravia. To splash some cash, consider the West End, Kensington and Knightsbridge. Most budget and midrange places offer free wi-fi (top-end properties may charge).

Prices listed here include 20% VAT, when it applies.

🛏 West End

Like in Monopoly, land on a Mayfair hotel and you may have to sell your house, or at least remortgage. This is the heart of the action, and a couple of hostels cater for would-be Soho hipsters of more modest means.

YHA London Oxford Street HOSTEL £
(Map p66; ☎ 020-7734 1618; www.yha.org.uk; 14 Noel St, W1; dm/tw from £18/46; @🛜; ⊖ Oxford Circus) The most central of the YHA London fold, this hostel is a tip-top choice for its location, bright and colourful shared facilities, cleanliness and manageable 104-bed size. There are doubles, twins and three/four-bed dorms, with a charge for wi-fi.

Dean Street Townhouse BOUTIQUE HOTEL ££
(Map p66; ☎ 020-7434 1775; www.deanstreettownhouse.com; 69-71 Dean St, W1; r £140-310; ❋🛜; ⊖ Tottenham Court Rd) This Soho gem of a 39-bedroom boutique hotel enjoys a delightful boudoir atmosphere with choice rooms – everything faultlessly in its place – from 'tiny' options upwards.

Seven Dials Hotel HOTEL ££
(Map p66; ☎ 020-7240 0823; www.sevendialshotellondon.com; 7 Monmouth St, WC2; s/d/tr/q £95/105/130/150; 🛜; ⊖ Covent Garden, Tottenham Court Rd) The clean, comfortable and affordable Seven Dials offers a highly central location and rooms at the front looking out over delightful Monmouth St and quieter rooms at the back, with less of a view.

★ Haymarket Hotel HOTEL £££
(Map p66; ☎ 020-7470 4000; www.haymarkethotel.com; 1 Suffolk Pl, off Haymarket, SW1; r £325-425, ste from £505; ❋🛜☒; ⊖ Piccadilly Circus) An exquisite place to hang your well-trimmed hat, the Tim and Kit Kemp–designed Haymarket is a super-stylish and eye-catching treat, with a knockout swimming pool bathed in serene mood lighting.

Hazlitt's HISTORIC HOTEL £££
(Map p66; ☎ 020-7434 1771; www.hazlittshotel.com; 6 Frith St, W1; s £216, d/ste from £288/660; ❋🛜; ⊖ Tottenham Court Rd) Envelop yourself in Georgian finery at this lovely 1718 house and journey back to the days of four-poster beds, claw-foot baths and panelled walls. Each of the 30 individually decorated rooms overflows with Georgian antiques and days-gone-by charm (plus up-to-the-minute mod cons).

One Aldwych HOTEL £££
(Map p66; ☎ 020-7300 1000; www.onealdwych.co.uk; 1 Aldwych, WC2; d £255-470, ste £465-1005; ❋🛜☒; ⊖ Covent Garden) Check in for a tremendous presentation of granite bathrooms, modern art, a majestic bar and restaurant, and a long, chlorine-free swimming pool (with underwater music). The circular suites serve up fabulous views of the Strand and Waterloo Bridge.

Brown's Hotel HOTEL £££
(Map p66; ☎ 020-7493 6020; www.brownshotel.com; 30 Albemarle St, W1; r/ste from £460/2000; ❋🛜; ⊖ Green Park) A stunning five-star choice, this 117-room hotel dates to 1837 when 11 houses were joined together; lovely old-world traditional features (Edwardian oak panelling, working fireplaces) complement individually decorated rooms.

Covent Garden Hotel BOUTIQUE HOTEL £££
(Map p66; ☎ 020-7806 1000; www.coventgardenhotel.co.uk; 10 Monmouth St, WC2; d/ste from £310/490; ❋🛜; ⊖ Covent Garden) Housed in an old French hospital, this well-positioned 58-room Firmdale hotel concocts a classy display of antiques, bright and vibrant

fabrics, quirky bric-a-brac and a winning bar-restaurant.

The City

It bristles with bankers during the week, but you can often net considerable bargains in the City come weekends.

London St Paul's YHA
HOSTEL £

(Map p70; 020-7236 4965; www.yha.org.uk; 36 Carter Lane, EC4; dm £17-25, d £40-50; @ 🛜; 🚇 St Paul 's) Perfectly placed for hoovering up the sights of the City and the South Bank, this 213-bed hostel in a heritage-listed building is just down the road from St Paul's (the bells, the bells!). There's a licensed cafeteria, but no self-catering, no lift and a seven-night maximum stay.

Hotel Indigo Tower Hill
BOUTIQUE HOTEL ££

(Map p70; 0843 208 7007; www.hotelindigo.com/lontowerhill; 142 Minories, EC3; r weekend/weekday from £100/200; ❄ @ 🛜) The 46 differently styled rooms at this crisp and affordable hotel north of the Tower of London feature four-poster beds and iPod docking stations.

Andaz Liverpool Street
HOTEL ££

(Map p70; 020-7961 1234; www.london.liverpool-street.andaz.com; 40 Liverpool St, EC2; r weekend/weekday from £145/290; ❄ 🛜; 🚇 Liverpool St) The former Great Eastern Hotel is now the London flagship for Hyatt's youth-focused Andaz chain. There's no reception here, just black-clad staff who check you in on mini laptops. Rooms are a little generic, but have free juice, snacks and wi-fi.

South Bank

Immediately on the south side of the Thames is a fab perch for reaching the central sights, while gauging the personality of South London.

St Christopher's Village
HOSTEL £

(Map p82; 020-7939 9710; www.st-christophers.co.uk; 163 Borough High St, SE1; dm/r from £14/62; @ 🛜; 🚇 London Bridge) The Village – a huge, up-for-it party hostel, with a hopping bar, roof terrace (plus bar), cinema and tons of beds – is the main hub of three locations on the same street. Dorms have four to 14 beds. The other locations are much smaller, quieter and, frankly, more pleasant. St Christopher's Inn (Map p82; 121 Borough High St, SE1) is above a very nice pub, while Oasis (Map p82; 59 Borough High St) is women-only.

★ Citizen M
BOUTIQUE HOTEL ££

(Map p82; 020-3519 1680; www.citizenm.com/london-bankside; 20 Lavington St, SE1; r £109-189; ❄ @ 🛜; 🚇 Southwark) Aimed squarely at young, trendy and Tate-going artsy travellers, this Dutch boutique hotel pulls out all the design stops (and rummages around to pull out a few more). Rooms are titchy, but have swish Samsung tablet–controlled mod-cons and free movies on tap. Space comes from the funky lounge area, conceived to hang around in.

New openings in Tower Hill and St Pauls are on the cards for 2014.

Shangri-La Hotel at the Shard
HOTEL £££

(Map p82; 020-7234 8000; www.shangri-la.com/london/shangrila; 31 St Thomas St, SE1; d/ste £575/3000; ❄ @ 🛜 🌊; 🚇 London Bridge, 🚇 London Bridge) The Shangri-La's first UK opening gives London its first five-star hotel south of the Thames and breathtaking views from the highest hotel in Western Europe, occupying levels 34 to 52 of the Shard. From the 35th floor sky lobby to the rooms, the Shangri-La concocts a stylish blend of Chinese aesthetics, Asian hospitality and sharp modernity.

The Shard's tapering shape puts the suites on lower floors, while each guestroom is slightly different in design. For drop-dead views, zip up to Gŏng on the 52nd floor, but book way ahead.

Pimlico & Belgravia

Lime Tree Hotel
B&B ££

(Map p88; 020-7730 8191; www.limetreehotel.co.uk; 135-137 Ebury St, SW1; s/tr/f £110/205/225, d £165-205; @ 🛜; 🚇 Victoria) Family-run for over 40 years, this smartly renovated Georgian town-house hotel has a pleasant back garden to catch the late afternoon rays, while contemporary renovations and polite staff make it an appealing choice. No lift.

B+B Belgravia
B&B ££

(Map p88; 020-7259 8570; www.bb-belgravia.com; 64-66 Ebury St, SW1; s £89-120, d £100-140, apt £225; @ 🛜; 🚇 Victoria) This lovely place marries contemporary chic with Georgian elegance (and a pleasant courtyard garden out back). Rooms are neat and, although not very spacious, fine studio rooms with compact kitchens are along the road at No 82. No lift.

★ Goring
HOTEL £££

(Map p58; 020-7396 9000; www.thegoring.com; Beeston Place; r £575-4350; ❄ @ 🛜; 🚇 Victoria) Kate Middleton spent her last night as a commoner in the Royal Suite here before joining the ranks of the Royal Family, propelling the Goring into an international media glare. Glistening with chandeliers and overseen by magnificent staff, this family-owned hotel is a supremely grand, albeit highly relaxed slice of England and Englishness.

Knightsbridge

Named after a bridge over the River Westbourne, Knightsbridge is where you'll find some of London's best-known department stores and some top hotels.

Levin Hotel   HOTEL £££

(Map p88; ☎ 020-7589 6286; www.thelevinhotel.co.uk; 28 Basil St, SW3; r from £379; ❀ ☎; ⊖Knightsbridge) As close as you can get to sleeping in Harrods, the 12-room Levin knows its market. Elegance and sophistication permeate this tiny hotel from top to toe, fashioning a highly personable choice in the heart of Knightsbridge.

Chelsea & Kensington

Well-turned out Chelsea and Kensington offer easy access to the museums, natty

Notting Hill & Bayswater

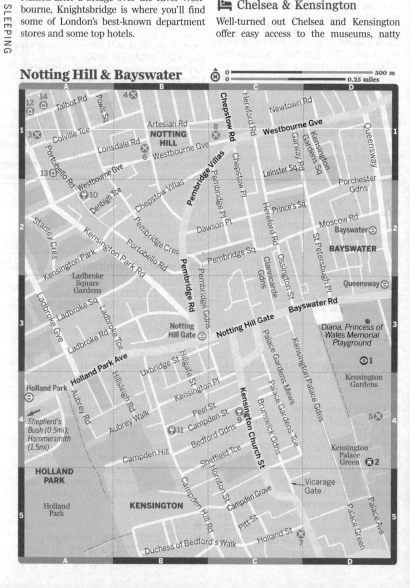

shopping choices and some of London's best-looking streets.

Meininger
HOSTEL £
(Map p88; ☑020-3318 1407; www.meininger-hostels.com; Baden Powell House, 65-67 Queen's Gate, SW7; dm £16-22, s/tw from £75/90; ❇@☎; ⊖Gloucester Rd, South Kensington) In late-1950s Baden Powell House, opposite the Natural History Museum, this 48-room German-run 'city hostel and hotel' has spic-and-span rooms, most of which are dorms of between four and 12 beds, with pod-like showers, plus 11 private rooms all with bathroom. There's a bar in-house plus a great roof terrace.

Ampersand Hotel
BOUTIQUE HOTEL £££
(Map p88; ☑020-7589 5895; www.ampersandhotel.com; 10 Harrington Road; s & d £372; ❇@☎; ⊖South Kensington) Housed in the old Norfolk Hotel building, the Ampersand boasts a light, fresh and bubbly feel: its (narrow) corridors and (stylish but smallish) rooms decorated with wallpaper designs celebrating the nearby arts and sciences of South Kensington's museums, a short stroll away. Apero, the cellar Mediterranean restaurant, is excellent.

Halkin by Como
HOTEL £££
(Map p58; ☑020-7333 1000; www.comohotels.com/thehalkin; Halkin St, SW1; r/ste from £390/540; ❇@☎; ⊖Hyde Park Corner) With muted Asian influences, the chichi Halkin is for business travellers of a minimalist bent. Bedroom

Notting Hill & Bayswater

doors are hidden within curved wooden hallways, and the 41 swish rooms are filled with natural light, boasting cream walls, burlwood panelling and large all-marble bathrooms.

Number Sixteen
HOTEL £££
(Map p88; ☑020-7589 5232; www.firmdalehotels.com/hotels/london/number-sixteen; 16 Sumner Pl, SW7; s from £174, d £228-360; ❇@☎; ⊖South Kensington) This is four properties in one delightful whole and a stunning place to stay, with 42 individually designed rooms, a cosy drawing room, a fully stocked library and a simply idyllic back garden.

Gore
HOTEL £££
(Map p88; ☑020-7584 6601; www.gorehotel.com; 190 Queen's Gate, SW7; r from £204; ❇@☎; ⊖Gloucester Rd) With obliging staff in tails, twinkling chandeliers, walls crowded with portraits and prints, this superb 50-room hotel wallows in old England charm. Rolling Stones fans can celebrate the 1968 *Beggars Banquet* album launch in the bar; Judy Garland aficionados can sleep on her bed.

⌂ Earl's Court & Fulham

West London's Earl's Court is lively, cosmopolitan and so popular with travelling Antipodeans it's nicknamed Kangaroo Valley. There are no real sights, but it has inexpensive digs, an infectious holiday atmosphere and it's a short hop to the action. Further west and abutting the Thames, Fulham is the home of its famous riverside palace.

★Barclay House
B&B ££
(☑020-7384 3390; www.barclayhouselondon.com; 21 Barclay Rd, SW6; r £110-125; @☎; ⊖Fulham Broadway) The two dapper, thoroughly modern and comfy bedrooms in this charmingly shipshape Victorian house are a dream, from the Philippe Starck shower rooms, walnut furniture, new double-glazed sash windows and underfloor heating to the small, thoughtful details (fumble-free coat hangers, drawers packed with sewing kits and maps). A four-night minimum stay usually applies.

Rockwell
BOUTIQUE HOTEL ££
(☑020-7244 2000; www.therockwell.com; 181-183 Cromwell Rd, SW5; s/ste from £90/160, d £100-150; ❇@☎; ⊖Earl's Court) With an understated-cool design ethos, things are muted, dapper and a tad minimalist at 'budget boutique' 40-room Rockwell. All rooms have a shower, the mezzanine suite is an absolute peach, and the three rooms (LG1, 2 and 3) onto the

garden are fine. Rooms on Cromwell Rd are triple-glazed to stifle the roar.

🛏 Notting Hill, Bayswater & Paddington

Don't be fooled by Julia Roberts' and Hugh Grant's shenanigans, Notting Hill and the areas immediately north of Hyde Park are as shabby as they are chic, but they're still cool. There are some gorgeous gated squares surrounded by Georgian town houses, but the area is better exemplified by the Portobello Road Market and the Notting Hill Carnival.

Scruffy Paddington has lots of cheap hotels, with a major strip of unremarkable ones along Sussex Gardens that may be worth checking if you're short on options.

Tune Hotel   HOTEL £
(📞 020-7258 3140; www.tunehotels.com; 41 Praed St, W2; r £35-80; ✳@🛜; ⊖Paddington) This 137-room Malaysian-owned budget hotel offers super-duper rates for early birds who book way in advance. You get the bare bones – a twin or double room, the cheapest without window – and pay for add-ons (towel, wi-fi, TV) as you see fit, giving you the chance to simply put a roof over your head. You don't even get a wardrobe, just hangers.

★ La Suite West   BOUTIQUE HOTEL £££
(📞 020-7313 8484; www.lasuitewest.com; 41-51 Inverness Tce, W2; r £179-489; ✳@🛜; ⊖Bayswater) The black-and-white foyer of the Anouska Hempel–designed La Suite West – bare walls, a minimalist slit of a fireplace, an iPad for guests' use on a bare white marble reception desk – presages the OCD neatness of rooms hidden away down dark corridors. Think impeccable bathrooms, comfortable beds and warm service. Downstairs suites have gardens and individual gated entrances.

🛏 Bloomsbury & St Pancras

One step from the West End and crammed with Georgian town-house conversions, these are more affordable neighbourhoods. A stretch of lower-priced hotels runs along Gower St and on the pretty Cartwright Gardens crescent. While St Pancras is handy with some excellent budget options.

Clink78   HOSTEL £
(Map p96; 📞 020-7183 9400; www.clinkhostels. com; 78 King's Cross Rd, WC1; dm/r from £10/25; @🛜; ⊖King's Cross St Pancras) If anyone can

think of a more right-on London place to stay than the courthouse where The Clash went on trial, please let us know. You can watch TV from the witness box or sleep in the converted cells, but the majority of the rooms are custom-built, quite comfortable and all were undergoing a repaint in 2014.

Generator   HOSTEL £
(Map p96; 📞 020-7388 7666; www.generatorhostels.com/london; 37 Tavistock Pl, WC1; dm/r from £12/50; @🛜; ⊖Russell Sq) Lashings of primary colours and shiny industrial metal are the hallmarks of this huge hostel. This former police barracks has over 850 beds, a bar that stays open until 2am and hosts themed parties, and a large eating area (but no kitchen). Dorm rooms have between four and 12 beds.

London St Pancras YHA   HOSTEL £
(Map p96; 📞 020-7388 9998; www.yha.org.uk; 79 Euston Rd, NW1; dm/r from £20/61; @🛜; ⊖King's Cross St Pancras) Renovations have converted this 185-bed hostel into a dependable central London choice – despite the busy road. Rooms range from private doubles to six-bed dorms; most have bathrooms. There's a good bar and cafe, but no kitchen.

Arosfa Hotel   B&B ££
(Map p96; 📞 020-7636 2115; www.arosfalondon. com; 83 Gower St, WC1; s/tr/f £78/145/175, d £130-145; 🛜; ⊖Goodge St) While the immaculately presented rooms are understated, Arosfa's guest lounge is blinged up with chandeliers and clear plastic chairs. Recent refurbishments have added en suites to all bedrooms, but they're tiny. There are a couple of family rooms; room 4 looks onto a small garden.

St Pancras Renaissance London Hotel   LUXURY HOTEL £££
(Map p96; 📞 020-7841 3540; www.marriott.co.uk; Euston Rd, NW1; d from £230; ✳🛜🛏; ⊖King's Cross St Pancras) This iconic George Gilbert Scott–designed Gothic masterpiece is a red-brick Victorian fantasy, its lobby a magnificent conversion of the former train station taxi rank boasting a splendid double-staircase. Disappointingly, only 38 of the 245 rooms are in the original building; the rest are in an extension at the back and rather bland. You can toast the former booking office architecture from the 29m-long bar.

Rough Luxe   BOUTIQUE HOTEL £££
(Map p96; 📞 020-7837 5338; www.roughluxe.co. uk; 1 Birkenhead St, WC1; r £229-289; ✳🛜; ⊖King's Cross St Pancras) Half rough, half luxury goes

the blurb, and the shabby/chic blend at this Grade-II listed property is compelling. Rooms treat you to the finest quality bed linen, eclectic art works cling to walls, you may get a free-standing copper bath and service is top-notch, but the wallpaper is fetchingly distressed and the 1970s TV doesn't quite work. A lovely patio chips in at the rear.

🛏 Clerkenwell & Farringdon

These now-fashionable districts just north of centre contain few echoes of the notorious 'rookeries' of the 19th century, where families were crammed into damp, foetid basements, living in possibly the worst conditions in the city's history (the London documented so vividly by Dickens).

The availability of accommodation hasn't kept pace with Clerkenwell's revival, but it's still a great area to hang your hat. The best pickings aren't exactly cheap.

★ Zetter Hotel & Townhouse
BOUTIQUE HOTEL **£££**

(Map p96; ✆ 020-7324 4444; www.thezetter.com; 86-88 Clerkenwell Rd, EC1; d from £235, studio £300-450; ❄ 🛜; ◉ Farringdon) 🌱 Guided by a sustainable ethos (water is supplied by its own bore hole), the 59-room Zetter is lovely, from the fine furnishings to the cutting-edge facilities. The rooftop studios with private patios and long views are the icing on this cake. Bistrot Bruno Loubet (Map p96; ✆ 020-7324 4455; www.bistrotbrunoloubet. com; mains £12-17; ⏱ 7.30-10.30am, noon-2.30pm & 6-10pm; 🛜) takes care of the fine food end.

Rookery
LUXURY HOTEL **£££**

(Map p70; ✆ 020-7336 0931; www.rookeryhotel. com; 12 Peter's Lane, Cowcross St, EC1; s £222, d £288-660, ste £474; ❄ 🛜; ◉ Farringdon) Named after London's notorious slums (Fagin's house in *Oliver Twist* was nearby), this antique-strewn charmer fashions an 18th-century ambience with none of the attendant grime or crime. For a bird's-eye view of St Paul's, book the two-storey Rook's Nest, but be warned: Fagin never had a lift.

🛏 Hoxton, Shoreditch & Spitalfields

Its rough-edged reputation well-smoothed by gentrification and the attentions of cash-loaded twenty-somethings, this is a knockout area to roost for some of London's best bars and nightlife.

★ Hoxton Hotel
HOTEL **£**

(Map p114; ✆ 020-7550 1000; www.hoxtonhotels. com; 81 Great Eastern St, EC2; r from £59; ❄ @ 🛜; ◉ Old St) A revolutionary pricing structure means that while all the rooms are identical, the hip Hoxton aims at constantly full occupancy. Book three months ahead (sign up on the website) and you can, if fortunate, nab a room for £1; you'll also need to book early for £49 to £69 deals.

The reasonably sized rooms have comfy beds, quality linen, a desk and fridge with complimentary bottled water and milk.

🛏 East End & Docklands

40 Winks
BOUTIQUE HOTEL **££**

(✆ 020-7790 0259; www.40winks.org; 109 Mile End Rd, E1; s/d £110/185; 🛜; ◉ Stepney Green) This fun Queen Anne town house spills over with charm, eclectic style and whimsy, so much so that the two bedrooms (one single) are devoid of TVs. Fashionistas make this their first port of call, so book way ahead. Breakfast included.

🍴 Eating

Dining out in London has become so fashionable that you can hardly open a menu without banging into some celebrity chef or other. The range and quality of eating options has increased exponentially over the last few decades. Waves of immigrant flavours have deeply infused London cuisine and the expectations of modern-day Londoners are demanding.

In this section we have sieved out choice restaurants and cafes noted for their location, value for money, unique character, ambience and, of course, good food. Vegetarians needn't fret: London has a host of dedicated meat-free joints, while most others have veggie offerings.

🍴 West End

Mayfair, Soho and Covent Garden are the gastronomic heart of London, with a blinding choice of restaurants and cuisines at budgets to suit booze hounds, theatregoers or determined grazers.

★ Koya
NOODLES **£**

(Map p66; www.koya.co.uk; 49 Frith St, W1; mains £7-15; ⏱ noon-3pm & 5.30-10.30pm; ◉ Tottenham Court Rd, Leicester Sq) Koya's speciality is udon noodles (a type of thick wheat flour noodle) – devoured either with a cold sauce or

Hoxton, Shoreditch & Spitalfields

plunged into a variety of hot broths (from plain to duck or smoked mackerel). The noodles are divine and the simple wooden-table decor wholesome; arrive early or late to avoid queues.

Ceviche SOUTH AMERICAN £

(Map p66; www.cevicheuk.com; 17 Frith St, W1; mains £5-11; ⊙noon-11.30pm Mon-Sat, to 10.30pm Sun; ⊙; ⊙Leicester Sq) A big hit with Soho gastronomes, this colourful, vibrant and fabuloso bodega is a must for lovers of Pe-

LONDON EATING

ruvian food, or those keen to kick-start an instant passion for *anticuchos* (grilled skewers), ceviche (citrus-marinated raw fish) and heart-warming shots of pisco.

Orchard
VEGETARIAN £

(Map p66; www.orchard-kitchen.co.uk; 11 Sicilian Ave, WC1; mains £6.50-7; ⊗8am-4pm Mon-Fri; ✐; ⊜Holborn) Delightfully ensconced amid the charming buildings of Sicilian Ave, this homely eatery is a must for roving vegetarians. The traditional menu is a wholesome delight, from dandelion leaves, baby spinach and poached garlic milk to crushed turnips with pink peppercorns.

Roti Chai
INDIAN £

(Map p92; www.rotichai.com; 3 Portman Mews South, W1; mains from £5-12; ⊗noon-11pm Mon-Sat, 1-9pm Sun; ☎; ⊜Marble Arch) With a refreshing street kitchen menu from India, colourful Roti Chai cooks up a roaring trade in *bel puris*, spiced lamb *chapli kebabs*, *papri chaat* and railway lamb curries for upstairs snackers, with a more expansive dining room menu down below.

Wahaca
MEXICAN £

(Map p66; www.wahaca.com; 66 Chandos Pl, WC2; mains £7-10; ⊗noon-11pm; ☎; ⊜Covent Garden) ✿ A branch of a chain peppering central London, this delightful cantina is a superb pitstop for Mexican street snacks (tacos, *tostadas, quesadillas*), more traditional mains such as marinated, grilled chicken or fish tacos, and a strong list of tequila and mezqal. Award-winning sustainable credentials to boot.

Nordic Bakery
SCANDINAVIAN £

(Map p66; www.nordicbakery.com; 14a Golden Sq, W1; snacks £4-5; ⊗8am-8pm Mon-Fri, 9am-7pm Sat, 10am-7pm Sun; ⊜Piccadilly Circus) As unfussy and stylish as you'd expect from the Scandinavians, this small cafe has bare wooden walls and uncomplicated Nordic snacks, such as sticky Finnish cinnamon buns, Scandinavian smoked-fish sandwiches, goat's cheese and beetroot salad, and oatmeal cookies.

Monmouth Coffee Company
CAFE £

(Map p66; www.monmouthcoffee.co.uk; 27 Monmouth St, WC2; pastry & cakes from £2.50; ⊗8am-6.30pm Mon-Sat; ⊜Tottenham Court Rd, Leicester Sq) There's an array of treats on the counter, but it's the coffee that's the star, nay god, here. Chat to a caffeinated stranger on one of the tight tables at the back, or grab a takeaway and slink off to a nearby lane for your fix. There's a second outlet in **Borough** (Map p82; 2 Park St, SE1; ⊗7.30am-6pm; underground rail London Bridge).

Hummus Bros
CAFE £

(Map p66; www.hbros.co.uk; 88 Wardour St, W1; mains £3.50-6.50; ⊗noon-10pm Mon-Sat, to 9pm Sun; ☎✐; ⊜Piccadilly Circus) ✿ Don't come here if you're chickpea-challenged, because this informal place is hummus heaven. It comes in small or regular bowls with a choice of meat or veggie toppings and a side of pita bread. Other branches can be found in **Holborn** (Map p96; 37-63 Southampton Row, W1; ⊗11am-9pm Mon-Fri, noon-5pm Sat; ☎✐; ⊜Holborn) ✿, **Cheapside** (Map p70; 128 Cheapside, EC2; ⊗7.30am-9pm Mon-Thu, to 4pm

Fri; ☎🔔; ⊖St Paul's) 🍴or **Exmouth Market**
(Map p96; 62 Exmouth Market; ⊘8am-9pm Mon-
Sat; ☎🔔) 🍴.

Fernandez & Wells
CAFE £

(Map p66; www.fernandezandwells.com; 73 Beak
St, W1; dishes £4.50-6; ⊘7.30am-6pm Mon-Fri,
9am-6pm Sat & Sun; ⊖Piccadilly Circus) One of
four central London branches of Fernandez
& Wells, each occupying small, friendly and
elegant spaces. Both the cafe and the espresso bar do sandwiches and first-rate coffee.

Mildreds
VEGETARIAN £

(Map p66; www.mildreds.co.uk; 45 Lexington St,
W1; mains £8-10.50; ⊘noon-11pm Mon-Sat; ☎🔔;
⊖Oxford Circus, Piccadilly Circus) Ceaselessly
busy, long-standing Mildred's seduces all
manner of vegetarians, omnivores and de-
toxers, so don't be shy about sharing a table
in the sky-lit dining room. Vegan and gluten-
free options available.

Baozi Inn
CHINESE £

(Map p66; 25 Newport Ct, WC2; mains £5-7.50;
⊘noon-10.30pm; ⊖Leicester Sq) Decorated vin-
tage-style with kitsch communist pop, Baozi
Inn serves authentic Beijing- and Cheng-
du-style street food, such as piquant *dan dan*
noodles (a Sichuan staple) and *baozi* (steamed
buns with stuffing), handmade daily.

★ Brasserie Zédel
FRENCH ££

(Map p66; 📞020-7734 4888; www.brasseriezedel.
com; 20 Sherwood St, W1; mains £8.75-30;
⊘11.30am-midnight Mon-Sat, to 11pm Sun; ☎;
⊖Piccadilly Circus) This triumphant basement
brasserie in the grandly renovated art-deco
ballroom of a former Piccadilly hotel offers excellent value set menus (£8.95/11.75
for two/three courses) and *plats du jour*
(£12.95), all in a terrific setting.

Great Queen Street
BRITISH ££

(Map p66; 📞020-7242 0622; 32 Great Queen St,
WC2; mains £12-16; ⊘noon-2.30pm & 6-10.30pm
Mon-Sat, noon-3pm Sun; ⊖Holborn) The menu
at what is one of Covent Garden's best places
to eat is seasonal (and changes daily), with
an emphasis on quality, hearty dishes and
good ingredients – with perennial delicious
stews, roasts and simple fish dishes. The atmosphere is lively, with a small bar tucked
below. Booking is essential.

National Dining Rooms
BRITISH ££

(Map p66; 📞020-7747 2525; www.peytonand-
byrne.co.uk; 1st fl, Sainsbury Wing, National Gallery,
Trafalgar Sq, WC2; mains £15.50-20.50; ⊘10am-
5.30pm Sat-Thu, to 8.30pm Fri; ⊖Charing Cross)

It's fitting that this acclaimed restaurant
should celebrate British food, being in the
National Gallery and overlooking Trafalgar
Sq. For a much cheaper option with the
same views, ambience, quality produce and
excellent service, try a salad, pie or tart at
the adjoining bakery.

Bocca di Lupo
ITALIAN ££

(Map p66; 📞020-7734 2223; www.boccadilupo.
com; 12 Archer St, W1; mains £8-27.50; ⊘12.30-
3.45pm & 5.30-11pm Mon-Sat, to 9pm Sun;
⊖Piccadilly Circus) Hidden on a dark Soho
backstreet, Bocca radiates elegant sophistication, setting taste buds a quiver with a
mouth-watering menu spanning Italy's culinary regions.

Barrafina
SPANISH ££

(Map p66; 📞020-7813 8016; www.barrafina.
co.uk; 54 Frith St, W1; tapas £5-18.50; ⊘noon-
3pm & 5-11pm Mon-Sat, 1-3.30pm & 5.30-10pm
Sun; ⊖Tottenham Court Road) The tapas here
(bar seating) may not be as good value as
in Spain, but they're standout. No reservations, so prepare to queue. There is a second
branch newly opened in **Covent Garden**
(Map p66; 10 Adelaide St, WC2).

Canela
PORTUGUESE ££

(Map p66; www.canelacafe.com; 33 Earlham St,
WC2; mains £9-13; ⊘11am-11pm Mon-Sat, to 9pm
Sun; ☎; ⊖Covent Garden) This sweet Covent
Garden cafe flings together a tempting range
of Portuguese and Brazilian dishes, including
feijoada (bean stew with smoked meat) and
pão de queijo (bread and cheese roll). Great
for satiating pre-theatre munchies.

Bar Shu
CHINESE ££

(Map p66; 📞020-7287 6688; www.barshurestau-
rant.co.uk; 28 Frith St, W1; mains £10-31; ⊘noon-
11pm; ⊖Piccadilly Circus, Leicester Sq) Authentic
Sichuan food long eluded the sweet-toothed
Cantonese chefs of Chinatown, but Bar Shu
hits all the right *mala* (numb-spicy) notes
with dishes steeped in smoked chillies and
the crucial aromatic peppercorn (*hua jiao*).

Pitt Cue Co
BARBECUE ££

(Map p66; www.pittcue.co.uk; 1 Newburgh St, W1;
mains £11.50-16.50; ⊘noon-3pm & 5.30-11pm Mon-
Sat, noon-4pm Sun; ⊖Oxford Circus) With only
30 seats jammed into this titchy upstairs-bar,
downstairs-dining room affair, prepare to
line up (no reservations) for a table and tin
trays loaded with slow-cooked meats (pulled
pork, beef ribs), classic American BBQ–style.
Tuck your elbows in and enjoy.

Hawksmoor Seven Dials STEAKHOUSE £££
(Map p66; ☑020-7420 9390; www.thehawksmoor.
co.uk; 11 Langley St, WC2; steak £20-34,
2-/3-course express menu £23/26; ⊙noon-
3pm & 5-10.30pm Mon-Sat, noon-9.30pm Sun;
📶; ⊜Covent Garden) 🥢 Legendary among
London carnivores for its mouth-watering
and flavour-rich steaks from British cattle,
Hawksmoor's sumptuous Sunday roasts,
burgers and well-executed cocktails are also
show-stoppers. Book ahead.

Arbutus MODERN EUROPEAN £££
(Map p66; ☑020-7734 4545; www.arbutusrestau-
rant.co.uk; 63-64 Frith St, W1; mains £18-20; ⊙noon-
2.30pm & 5-11pm Mon-Sat, noon-3pm & 5.30-
10.30pm Sun; 📶; ⊜Tottenham Court Rd) With
seasonal produce and inventive dishes, Anthony Demetre's Michelin-starred brainchild
is a winner. The well-priced 'working lunch'
menu at £17.95 for two courses and £19.95 for
three is a bargain. Bookings crucial.

✘ The City

You'll be sorely dismayed if you've got an
empty belly on a Sunday morning in the
City. Even during the busy weekdays, the
chain eateries are often your best option.

Café Below CAFE £
(Map p70; ☑020-7329 0789; www.cafebelow.
co.uk; St Mary-le-Bow Church, Cheapside, EC2;
mains £8.75-10.50; ⊙7.30am-2.30pm Mon-Fri;
🖋; ⊜Mansion House) This atmospheric cafe-
restaurant, in the crypt of one of London's
most famous churches, is breakfast and
lunch only these days, but offers excellent
value, with many vegetarian choices. In summer there are tables in the shady courtyard.

Duck & Waffle BRASSERIE ££
(Map p70; ☑020-3640 7310; www.duckandwaffle.
com; 40th fl, Heron Tower, 110 Bishopsgate, EC2;
mains £7-32; ⊙24hr; ⊜Liverpool St) The highest
restaurant in the UK matches a thoroughly
smart (no sportswear, beachwear or flip-
flops) and modern perch on the 40th floor
of the Heron Tower and a confident British
menu (small plates to encourage sharing) –
plus waffles – with wrap-around views and
round-the-clock hours.

Sweeting's SEAFOOD £££
(Map p70; ☑020-7248 3062; www.sweetingsres-
taurant.com; 39 Queen Victoria St, EC4; mains £15-
45; ⊙11.30am-3pm Mon-Fri; ⊜Mansion House)
🥢 Hauling in diners since 1889, Sweetings
is a massively popular fixture, serving deli-

cious and sustainably sourced fish (grilled,
fried or poached), fried whitebait, dover sole
and the outstanding chef's fish pie (£15).

✘ South Bank

Popular restaurants feast on iconic riverside
views, but cast your net wider and gems
crop up everywhere. For a feed with a local
feel, head to Borough Market (p132) or Bermondsey St.

M Manze BRITISH £
(Map p82; www.manze.co.uk; 87 Tower Bridge Rd,
SE1; mains £2.40-6.25; ⊙11am-2pm Mon-Thu,
10am-2.30pm Fri & Sat; ⊜Borough) Dating to
1902, classic M Manze (Italian roots) began
as an ice-cream seller before moving into pie
territory. There's lovely tile work and a traditional London working-man's menu: pie
and mash, pie and liquor (parsley sauce);
take your eels jellied or stewed.

★Skylon MODERN EUROPEAN ££
(Map p82; ☑020-7654 7800; www.skylon-
restaurant.co.uk; 3rd fl, Royal Festival Hall, Southbank
Centre, Belvedere Rd, SE1; grill mains £12.50-30,
restaurant 2-/3-course £42/48; ⊙grill noon-11pm,
restaurant noon-2.30pm & 5.30-10.30pm Mon-Sat,
noon-4pm Sun; 📶; ⊜Waterloo) This looker atop
the Royal Festival Hall divides into grill and
fine-dining sections. Design is cutting-edge
1950s, with floor-to-ceiling windows rewarding diners with Thames and the City views.
Weekday two-/three-course lunches are a
tempting £18/21 in the grill. Booking is advised, especially for the restaurant. Dress
smart casual (no sportswear).

Magdalen MODERN BRITISH ££
(Map p82; ☑020-7403 1342; www.magdalenres-
taurant.co.uk; 152 Tooley St, SE1; mains £14.50-21,
2-/3-course lunch £15.50/18.50; ⊙noon-2.30pm
Mon-Fri & 6.30-10pm Mon-Sat; 📶; ⊜London Bridge)
A diamond in the Tooley St rough, Magdalen
hits the spot for anyone eager to corner some
of London's best Modern British fare. With a
focus on charcuterie, lovingly cooked and presented, it's not the place to bring a vegetarian
or a weight-conscious waif on a date.

✘ Belgravia

★Pimlico Fresh CAFE £
(86 Wilton Road, SW1; mains from £6; ⊙7.30am-
7.30pm Mon-Fri, 9am-6pm Sat & Sun; ⊜Victoria)
A wholesome choice for a healthy breakfast
or lunch, this friendly two-room cafe cooks
up fine homemade dishes from pies, soups,

baked beans on toast and lasagne to warming bowls of porridge laced with honey, maple syrup, banana, yoghurt or sultanas, while making regular forays into creative cuisine.

✗ Knightsbridge

★ Dinner by Heston Blumenthal
MODERN BRITISH **£££**

(Map p88; 020-7201 3833; www.dinnerbyheston.com; Mandarin Oriental Hyde Park, 66 Knightsbridge, SW1; 3-course set lunch £38, mains £28-42; ⊙noon-2.30pm & 6.30-10.30pm; ⬦; ⬧Knightsbridge) Double Michelin-star Dinner is a gastronomic tour de force, taking diners on a journey through British culinary history (with inventive modern inflections). Dishes carry dates to convey historical context – the cod in cider (c 1940) is a joy – but unless you order the set lunch (Monday to Friday), your bill may rapidly spiral out of control. Book ahead.

Zuma
JAPANESE **£££**

(Map p88; 020-7584 1010; www.zumarestaurant.com; 5 Raphael St, SW7; mains £15-75; ⊙noon-2.30pm Mon-Fri, 12.30-3.30pm Sat & Sun, 6-11pm daily; ⬦; ⬧Knightsbridge) A modern-day take on the traditional Japanese *izakaya*, where drinking and eating harmonise, Zuma oozes style, but it's the excellent sushi, sashimi and *robata* (char-grilled) dishes that steal the show. Sake fiends will find more than 40 different types of their favourite tipple at the bar.

✗ Chelsea & Kensington

These highbrow neighbourhoods harbour some of London's very best (and priciest) restaurants.

Wasabi
JAPANESE **£**

(www.wasabi.uk.com; Kensington Arcade, Kensington High St, W8; mains £5-8; ⊙10am-10pm Mon-Sat, 11am-9pm Sun; ⬧High St Kensington) Large, bright sit-down and take-out branch of this superb Japanese sushi and bento chain, with delicious rice sets, noodles, rolls and salads, all good value and perfect for a fast lunch. Branches dot central London.

★ Five Fields
MODERN BRITISH **£££**

(Map p88; 020-7838 1082; www.fivefieldsrestaurant.com; 8-9 Blacklands Terrace, SW3; 3-course set meal £50; ⊙6.30-10pm Tue-Sat; ⬦; ⬧Sloane Square) The inventive British cuisine, consummate service and enticingly light and inviting decor at this triumphant Chelsea restaurant has won an immediate fan base, but plan early to get a seat.

★ Medlar
MODERN EUROPEAN **£££**

(020-7349 1900; www.medlarrestaurant.co.uk; 438 King's Rd, SW10; 3-course lunch £27-30, dinner £35-45; ⊙noon-3pm & 6.30-10.30pm; ⬦; ⬧South Kensington, Fulham Broadway, Sloane Sq) With its uncontrived yet crisply modern green-on-grey design, immaculate, Michelin star–rated Medlar has quickly become a King's Rd sensation. With no à la carte menu and scant pretentiousness, the prix fixe modern European cuisine is delightfully assured, with kitchen magic cooked up by chef Joe Mercer Nairne (from Chez Bruce).

Gordon Ramsay
FRENCH **£££**

(Map p88; 020-7352 4441; www.gordonramsay.com; 68 Royal Hospital Rd, SW3; 3-course lunch/dinner £55/95; ⊙noon-2.30pm & 6.30-11pm Mon-Fri; ⬧Sloane Sq) One of Britain's finest restaurants and London's longest-running with three coveted Michelin stars, you'll need to book ahead and hop into your best togs: jeans and T-shirts don't get past the door. And if you've seen the chef in action, you'll know not to argue.

✗ Notting Hill, Shepherd's Bush & Hammersmith

Notting Hill teems with good places to eat, from cheap takeaways to atmospheric pubs and restaurants worthy of the fine-dining tag. Shepherd's Bush and Hammersmith to the west pitch in with some fine contenders.

Taqueria
MEXICAN **£**

(Map p110; www.taqueria.co.uk; 139-143 Westbourne Grove; tacos £5-7.50; ⊙noon-11pm Mon-Fri, 10am-11.30pm Sat, noon-10.30pm Sun; ⬦; ⬧Notting Hill Gate) 🖉 Its sustainable credentials as exacting and appealing as its authentic soft-corn, freshly made tortillas, this place instantly elbows other Mexican restaurants into the Tex-Mex shade. Fish is all sustainably sourced and the pork, chicken and eggs come free range. Great mezcal and tequila menu, too.

Electric Diner
AMERICAN **££**

(Map p110; www.electricdiner.com; 191 Portobello Rd, W11; mains from £8-19; ⊙8am-midnight Mon-Thu, to 1am Fri-Sun; ⬦; ⬧Ladbroke Grove) A kitchen fire saw last orders for the Electric Brasserie, prompting redesign as a slender American-style diner with long counter, red-leather booths and a satisying French-American menu of breakfasts, burgers, steak frites and hot dogs.

★ **Ledbury** FRENCH £££
(Map p110; ☑020-7792 9090; www.theledbury.
com; 127 Ledbury Rd, W11; 4-course set lunch £45,
4-course dinner £90; ⊘noon-2pm Wed-Sun & 6.30-
9.45pm daily; ☎; ⊜Westbourne Park, Notting Hill
Gate) Two Michelin stars and swooningly
elegant, Brett Graham's artful French restaurant attracts well-heeled diners in jeans
with designer jackets. Dishes – such as roast
sea bass with broccoli stem, crab and black
quinoa, or saddle of roe deer with beetroot,
pinot lees and bone crisp potato – are triumphant. London gastronomes have Ledbury
on speed-dial, so reservations are crucial.

✖ **Marylebone**

You won't go too far wrong planting yourself on a table anywhere along Marylebone's
charming High St.

La Fromagerie CAFE ££
(Map p92; www.lafromagerie.co.uk; 2-6 Moxon St,
W1; mains £7-16.50; ⊘8am-7.30pm Mon-Fri, 9am-
7pm Sat, 10am-6pm Sun; ⊜Baker St) This deli-
cafe has bowls of delectable salads, antipasto,
peppers and beans scattered about the long
communal table. Huge slabs of bread invite
you to tuck in, and all the while the heavenly
waft from the cheese room beckons.

Locanda Locatelli ITALIAN ££
(Map p92; ☑020-7935 9088; www.locandalocatelli.
com; 8 Seymour St, W1; mains from £13.50; ⊘noon-
3pm daily, 6.45-11pm Mon-Sat, to 10.15pm Sun; ☎;
⊜Marble Arch) Known for its sublime but pricey
pasta dishes, this dark but quietly glamorous
restaurant in an otherwise unremarkable hotel is one of London's hottest tables.

Providores & Tapa Room FUSION £££
(Map p92; ☑020-7935 6175; www.theprovidores.
co.uk; 109 Marylebone High St, W1; 2-/3-/4-/5-course
dinner £33/47/57/63; ⊘9am-10.30pm Mon-Fri,
10am-10pm Sat & Sun; ☎; ⊜Baker St) New Zealand's most distinctive culinary export since
kiwi fruit, chef Peter Gordon works his fusion
magic here, matching his creations with NZ
wines. Downstairs, in a cute play on words,
the Tapa Room (as in the Polynesian bark-
cloth) serves sophisticated tapas, along with
excellent breakfasts.

✖ **Bloomsbury & St Pancras**

Diwana Bhel Poori House INDIAN £
(Map p96; 121-123 Drummond St, NW1; mains £7-
9; ⊘noon-11.30pm Mon-Sat, to 10.30pm Sun; ☑;
⊜Euston, Euston Sq) This ace Indian vegetarian eatery specialises in *bhel poori* (sweet-
and-sour, soft and crunchy 'party mix'
snacks), dosas (filled rice-flour pancakes),

WORTH A TRIP

HAMMERSMITH & SHEPHERD'S BUSH

Well within reach of Notting Hill, Hammersmith and Shepherd's Bush are well worth a
detour for their eclectic restaurants and pubs.

Potli (www.potli.co.uk; 319-321 King St, W6; weekday 1-/2-course set lunch £6.95/9.95, mains
£6.50-13.50; ⊘noon-2.45pm & 6-10.30pm Mon-Sat, noon-10.30pm Sun; ⊜Stamford Brook,
Ravenscourt Park) With its Bollywood posters, scattered pieces from Mumbai's Thieves
Market, Indian market kitchen/bazaar cuisine, homemade pickles and spice mixes, and
accent on genuine flavour, Potli deftly captures the aromas of its culinary home. Downstairs there's an open kitchen and service is very friendly, but it's the alluring menu that's
the real crowd-pleaser.

Kerbisher & Malt (www.kerbisher.co.uk; 164 Shepherd's Bush Rd, W6; mains £5.80-6.90;
⊘noon-2.30pm & 4.30-10pm Tue-Thu, noon-10pm Fri & Sat, to 9pm Sun; ⊜Hammersmith) The
sustainably sourced, delectable, battered-or-grilled coley, haddock, pollock, cod and
plaice at popular, blue-fronted Kerbisher & Malt has won over shoals of approving fish
fans. The chip butties, crispy servings of whitebait and tasty double-fried chips merit
equal applause.

Dove (☑020-8748 9474; www.dovehammersmith.co.uk; 19 Upper Mall, W6; ⊘11am-11pm Mon-
Sat, noon-10.30pm Sun; ⊜Hammersmith, Ravenscourt Park) Severely inundated by the epic
floodwaters of 1928, this gem of a 17th-century Fuller's pub revels in historic charm and
superb Thames views. Scottish poet James Thompson was reputedly inspired to write
the lyrics to 'Rule Britannia' here in the 18th century, it was Graham Greene's local, and
Hemingway and Dylan Thomas drank here, too, while William Morris lived nearby.

thali and the all-you-can-eat, lunchtime buffet (£6.95) is a legendary blowout.

Caravan
MEDITERRANEAN ££

(☎ 020-7101 7661; www.caravankingscross.co.uk; Granary Bldg, 1 Granary Sq, N1C; mains £7-15; ⊗ 8am-10.30pm Mon-Thu, to midnight Fri, 10am-midnight Sat, 10am-4pm Sun; ⊛ ⊅; ⊜ King's Cross St Pancras) In the freshly renovated Granary Building by the eye-catching piazza of Granary Sq alongside Regent's Canal, Caravan is a vast, tasty and trendy (industrial chic) stop for fusion Mediterranean cuisine. Book ahead.

North Sea Fish Restaurant
FISH & CHIPS ££

(Map p96; www.northseafishrestaurant.co.uk; 7-8 Leigh St, WC1; mains £10-20; ⊗ noon-2.30pm & 5.30-11pm Mon-Sat, 1-6pm Sun; ⊜ Russell Sq) Every day is fryday at the North Sea, a classic chippie for eat-in or takeaway with jumbo-sized plaice or halibut steaks, deep-fried or grilled, and lashings of chips.

✖ Fitzrovia

Tucked away behind busy Tottenham Court Rd, Fitzrovia's Charlotte and Goodge Sts form one of central London's most vibrant eating precincts.

Dabbous
MODERN EUROPEAN ££

(Map p96; ☎ 020-7323 1544; www.dabbous.co.uk; 39 Whitfield St, W1; mains £12-16; ⊗ noon-3pm & 5.30-11.30pm Tue-Sat; ⊜ Goodge St) You'll need to book ahead for dinner or come for lunch (four courses £28) at this creation from Ollie Dabbous. The rather stark and pared down ambience may not suit all tastes, but it's offset by an inventive menu stuffed with surprises and ideas; the basement cocktail bar is just the place for a pre-meal libation.

★ Lima
SOUTH AMERICAN £££

(Map p66; ☎ 020-3002 2640; www.limalondon. com; 31 Rathbone Place, W1; mains £10-29; ⊗ noon-2.30pm & 5.30-10.30pm Mon-Sat; ⊛; ⊜ Tottenham Court Rd) Sublimely zestful Peruvian flavours percolate at the heart of this neat and unassuming Fitzrovia restaurant. The stunningly presented cuisine has pulled a Michelin star and helpful staff take pride in their work.

Hakkasan Hanway Place
CHINESE £££

(Map p66; ☎ 020-7927 7000; www.hakkasan.com; 8 Hanway Place, W1; mains £11-100; ⊗ noon-3pm Mon-Fri, to 4pm Sat & Sun, 5.30-11pm Sun-Wed, to 12.15am Thu-Sat; ⊛; ⊜ Tottenham Court Rd) Michelin-starred Hakkasan elegantly pairs fine Chinese dining with stunning design

and some persuasive cocktail chemistry. The low-lighting hits all the right romantic notes and the expansive menu runs from *Szechuan mabo tofu* to grilled Shanghai dumplings, Peking duck and beyond.

✖ Camden Town

Camden is great for cheap eats, while neighbouring Chalk Farm and Primrose Hill are salted with gastropubs and upmarket restaurants.

Dirty Burger
BURGERS £

(www.eatdirtyburger.com; 79 Highgate Rd, NW5; burgers £5.50; ⊗ 5pm-midnight Mon-Fri, noon-midnight Sat, to 10pm Sun; ⊛ Gospel Oak, ⊜ Kentish Town) More chic shack than restaurant, Dirty Burger is all about burgers (beyond sausages and bacon till 11am) and crinkle-cut fries. And what burgers: thick, juicy and messy, with mustard, gherkin and cheese. The shakes are good, too.

Mango Room
CARIBBEAN ££

(Map p122; ☎ 020-7482 5065; www.mangoroom. co.uk; 10-12 Kentish Town Rd, NW1; mains £8-15; ⊗ noon-11pm; ⊜ Camden Town) Mango Room is an upmarket Caribbean experience serving a mix of modern and traditional dishes – Creole snapper, goat curry, jerk chicken – set to ska and reggae beats.

✖ Islington

Allow at least an evening to explore Islington's Upper St, along with the lanes leading off it.

Trullo
ITALIAN ££

(☎ 020-7226 2733; www.trullorestaurant.com; 300-302 St Paul's Rd, N1; mains £8.50-16, 2-/3-course lunch £15/19; ⊗ 12.30-3pm daily, 6-10.30pm Mon-Sat; ⊜ Highbury & Islington) Alongside fine service, the big plus here is an enjoyable variety beyond pasta or pizza. There are some exquisite pasta dishes, for sure, but the star attraction is the charcoal grill, which churns out succulent T-bone steaks or tasty pork chops with baked borlotti beans or polenta. Bookings essential.

Le Mercury
FRENCH ££

(☎ 020-7354 4088; www.lemercury.co.uk; 140a Upper St, N1; mains £9.95; ⊗ noon-1am Mon-Sat, to 11pm Sun; ⊜ Highbury & Islington, Angel) A cosy Gallic haunt ideal for cash-strapped Casanovas, given that it appears much more expensive than it is. Sunday lunch by the open fire upstairs is a treat, though you'll have to book. There's another branch up the road at **Le Mercury Deuxieme** (www.lemercury.co.uk; 154-155 Upper St, N1; mains £9.95; 5pm-midnight Mon-Thu, noon-midnight Fri & Sat, to 11pm Sun; Highbury & Islington).

Ottolenghi   BAKERY, MEDITERRANEAN ££
(020-7288 1454; www.ottolenghi.co.uk; 287 Upper St, N1; mains £9-12; 8am-11pm Mon-Sat, 9am-7pm Sun; ; Highbury & Islington, Angel) Mountains of meringues tempt you through the door, where a sumptuous array of bakery treats and salads greets you. Meals are as light and tasty as the lovely white interior design. Vegetarians are well catered for. There are further branches in **Belgravia** (Map p88; 13 Motcomb St, SW1; 8am-8pm Mon-Fri, to 7pm Sat, 9am-6pm Sun; Knightsbridge), **Kensington** (Map p110; 1 Holland St, W8; 8am-8pm Mon-Fri, to 7pm Sat, 9am-6pm Sun; High St Kensington) and **Notting Hill** (Map p110; 63 Ledbury Rd, W11; 8am-8pm Mon-Fri, to 7pm Sat, 8.30am-6pm Sun; Notting Hill Gate).

✕ Clerkenwell & Farringdon

Clerkenwell's hidden gems are well worth digging for. Pedestrianised Exmouth Market is a good place to start.

Little Bay   EUROPEAN £
(Map p96; 020-7278 1234; www.little-bay.co.uk; 171 Farringdon Rd, EC1; mains before/after 7pm £6.45/8.45; Farringdon) The crushed-velvet ceiling, handmade twisted lamps that im-

prove around the room (as the artist got better) and elaborately painted bar and tables showing frolicking nymphs are weird but fun. The hearty food is very good value.

Prufrock Coffee   CAFE £
(Map p96; www.prufrockcoffee.com; 23-25 Leather Lane, EC1; mains £5.50-9.50; 8am-6pm Mon-Fri, 10am-5pm Sat & Sun; ; Chancery Lane, Farringdon) Coffee-holics and caffeine geeks must trek to Clerkenwell for some of the finest brews in town, served by a talented line-up of staff in an inviting and light-filled space, with practice sessions and classes for baristas-to-be.

Morito   TAPAS ££
(Map p96; 020-7278 7007; www.morito.co.uk; 32 Exmouth Market, EC1; tapas £4.50-9.50; noon-4pm daily, 5-11pm Mon-Sat; ; Farringdon, Angel) This titchy venue is an authentic take on a Spanish tapas bar. Seats are at the bar, along the window, or on one of the small tables inside or out. It's relaxed, convivial and often completely crammed. The food is excellent; you can book at lunch, but not in the evening.

St John   BRITISH £££
(Map p70; 020-7251 0848; www.stjohnrestaurant.com; 26 St John St, EC1; mains £17-23; noon-3pm & 6-11pm Mon-Sat, 1-3pm Sun; Farringdon) Bright whitewashed brick walls, high ceilings and simple wooden furniture keep diners free to concentrate on the world-famous nose-to-tail offerings. Expect chitterlings and ox tongue.

CHAIN-CHAIN-CHAIN, CHAIN OF FOODS

Among the endless Caffe Neros and Pret a Mangers are some fab fallback options. Here are some of the best:

Konditor & Cook (www.konditorandcook.com) London's best bakery chain, serving excellent cakes, pastries, bread and coffee.

Jamie's Italian (www.jamieoliver.com) Good Italian food in a modern setting.

Masala Zone (www.masalazone.com) Fantastic Indian chain specialising in thalis (a meal made of several small dishes).

Nando's (www.nandos.co.uk) Loved by Londoners for fantastic value, mouth-watering spicy chicken *a la portuguesa* – with some blindingly hot peri-peri sauces.

Pizza Express (www.pizzaexpress.com) Excellent pizza, neat ambience and standout locations across London.

Wagamama (www.wagamama.com) Japanese noodles taking over the world from their London base.

Wahaca (www.wahaca.com) Working the Mexican street-food angle in fresh, colourful settings.

Wasabi (www.wasabi.uk.com) Cooking up a Japanese storm down the high street.

Zizzi (www.zizzi.co.uk) Wood-fired pizza.

Modern Pantry
FUSION £££

(Map p96; 020-7553 9210; www.themodern-pantry.co.uk; 47-48 St John's Sq, EC1; mains £14-21.50; noon-3pm Tue-Fri, 11am-4pm Sat & Sun, 6-10.30pm Tue-Sat; ; Farringdon) One of London's most talked-about eateries, this three-floor Georgian town house in the heart of Clerkenwell has a cracking innovative, all-day menu.

Hoxton, Shoreditch & Spitalfields

From the hit-and-miss Bangladeshi restaurants of Brick Lane to the Vietnamese strip on Kingsland Rd, and the Jewish, Spanish, French, Italian and Greek eateries in between, the East End's cuisine is as multicultural as its residents.

Sông Quê Café
VIETNAMESE £

(Map p114; www.songque.co.uk; 134 Kingsland Rd, E2; mains £6-9; noon-3pm & 5.30-11pm Mon-Fri,

noon-11pm Sat & Sun; Hoxton) Arrive after 7.30pm and you can expect to queue: this humble eatery is one of the best Vietnamese restaurants in London and you'll be shunted out shortly after your last bite.

Brick Lane Beigel Bake
BAGELS £

(Map p114; 159 Brick Lane, E2; bagels £1-4; 24hr; Shoreditch High St, Liverpool St) Always busy, this relic of London's Jewish East End is more takeaway than cafe and sells dirt-cheap bagels, a top late-night snack on a bellyful of booze.

Poppies
FISH & CHIPS ££

(Map p114; www.poppiesfishandchips.co.uk; 6-8 Hanbury St, E1; mains £7-16; 11am-11pm Mon-Thu, to 11.30pm Fri & Sat, to 10.30pm Sun; ; Shoreditch High St, Liverpool St) Frying since 1945, this fantastic Spitalfields chippie is a retro delight, a throwback to the 1950s with iconic jukebox, wall-to-wall memorabilia, waitresses in pinnies and hairnets and classic fish and chips (plus jellied eels).

Camden Town

Albion

BRITISH ££

(Map p114; ☑020-7729 1051; www.albioncaff.
co.uk; 2-4 Boundary St, E2; mains £9-13; ⊙8am-
11pm; 🐾; ⊜Old St) For those wanting to be
taken back to Dear Old Blighty's cuisine,
but with rather less grease and stodge,
this self-consciously retro 'caff' serves up
top-quality bangers and mash, along with
steak-and-kidney pies, devilled kidneys and,
of course, fish and chips.

✖ The East End

Formans

BRITISH ££

(☑020-8525 2365; www.formans.co.uk; Stour Rd,
Fish Island, E3; mains £11.50-19.50; ⊙7-11pm Thu
& Fri, 10am-2pm & 7-11pm Sat, noon-5pm Sun; 🐾;
⊜Hackney) Curing fish since 1905, riverside
Formans boasts prime views over the Olympic stadium alongside a delectable choice
of smoked salmon (including the signature
London cure) and seafood, plus a choice of
other mouth-watering British dishes. A viewing gallery into the smokery and a lounge
bar rounds out an attractive picture.

🍸 Drinking & Nightlife

As long as there's been a city, Londoners
have loved to drink – and, as history shows,
often immoderately. The pub is the hub of
social life and, despite depleting numbers,
there's always one near at hand. When
the sun shines, drinkers spill out into the
streets, parks and squares.

Soho is undoubtedly the heart of bar culture, with enough variety to cater to all tastes.
Still great for grungy boozers and rock kids,
Camden has lost ground on the bohemian-
cool front to Hoxton and Shoreditch.

Camden Town

◎ **Sights**
1 Camden Market C3

✖ **Eating**
2 Mango Room D3

🍸 **Drinking & Nightlife**
3 Lock Tavern B2

🎭 **Entertainment**
4 Barfly B2
5 Dublin Castle C4
6 Roundhouse A2

🛍 **Shopping**
7 Camden Lock Market...........................C2
8 Stables Market B2

Neighbourhoods such as Clerkenwell, Islington, Southwark, Notting Hill and Earl's
Court are bursting at their beer-addled
seams with pub-crawl potential.

Mirroring its worker-base, the City is a
Monday to Friday spot and several of its historic pubs shut up shop at weekends or on
Sundays. South London has some fine historic haunts near the river. The price of beer in
pubs is enough to drive you to drink – expect
to pay upwards of £3.25 per pint of lager.

The volume and variety of nightclubs in
London is staggering. Megaclubs are scattered throughout town wherever there's a
venue big enough, cheap enough or quirky
enough. The big nights are Friday and Saturday, although some of the most cutting-edge
sessions are midweek. Admission prices
vary widely; it's often cheaper to arrive early
or prebook tickets.

🍸 West End

★ Gordon's Wine Bar

BAR

(Map p66; www.gordonswinebar.com; 47 Villiers
St, WC2; ⊙11am-11pm Mon-Sat, noon-10pm Sun;
⊜Embankment) What's not to love about this
cavernous, candlelit wine cellar that's been
practically unchanged for the last 120 years?
Get here before the office crowd (generally
around 6pm) or forget about getting a table.

Opium

COCKTAIL BAR

(Map p66; ☑020-7734 7276; www.opiumchina-
town.com; 15-16 Gerrard St, W1; ⊙5pm-midnight
Mon-Wed, to 2am Thu-Sat, noon-midnight Sun)
Towering above Chinatown's main drag, this
self-proclaimed 'cocktail and dim sum parlour' could easily pass as an opium den-cum-
brothel, with a jade-coloured door leading
to a scarlet-drenched interior and byzantine
cocktails.

Spuntino

BAR

(Map p66; www.spuntino.co.uk; 61 Rupert St, W1;
mains £6-10; ⊙noon-midnight Mon-Wed, to 1am
Thu-Sat, to 11pm Sun; ⊜Piccadilly Circus) Speakeasy decor meets creative fusion American–Italian food at Rupert St cool customer
Spuntino. Grab a seat at the bar or one of the
counters at the back, but put aside time to
queue (no reservations and no phone).

French House

BAR

(Map p66; www.frenchhousesoho.com; 49 Dean
St, W1; ⊙noon-11pm; ⊜Leicester Sq) French
House is Soho's legendary boho boozer
with a history to match: the meeting place
of the Free French Forces during WWII, De

Gaulle is said to have knocked back shots here, while Dylan Thomas, Peter O'Toole, Brendan Behan and Francis Bacon all conspired to drink the place dry. The no-phones, no-music and no-TV ruling only amplifies the mystique.

Princess Louise PUB

(Map p66; 208 High Holborn, WC1; ⏰11.30am-11pm; ⊖Holborn) This late 19th-century Victorian boozer is arguably London's most beautiful pub. Spectacularly decorated with fine tiles, etched mirrors, plasterwork and a gorgeous central horseshoe bar, it gets packed with the after-work crowd.

Terroirs WINE BAR

(Map p66; www.terroirswinebar.com; 5 William IV St, WC2; ⏰noon-11pm Mon-Sat; ⊖Charing Cross

Road) Fab two-floor spot for a pre- or post-theatre glass or some expertly created charcuterie, with informative staff, affordable £10 lunch specials, a convivial atmosphere and a breathtaking list of organic wines.

Lamb & Flag PUB

(Map p66; www.lambandflagcoventgarden.co.uk; 33 Rose St, WC2; ⏰11am-11pm Mon-Sat, noon-10.30pm Sun; ⊖Covent Garden) Everyone's Covent Garden 'find', this historic pub is often as jammed with punters as it is packed with history. Built in 1623 and formerly called the 'Bucket of Blood', inside it's all brass fittings and creaky wooden floors.

Galvin at Windows BAR

(Map p58; www.galvinatwindows.com; London Hilton on Park Lane, 28th fl, 22 Park Lane, W1; ⏰11am-1am

---

GAY & LESBIAN LONDON

The West End, particularly Soho, is the visible centre of gay and lesbian London, with venues clustered around Old Compton St and its surrounds. However, Soho doesn't hold a monopoly on gay life. Vauxhall is a hub for the hirsute, hefty and generally harder-edged sections of the community. The railway arches are filled with dance clubs, leather bars and a sauna. Clapham (South London), Earl's Court (West London), Islington (North London) and Limehouse (East End) have their own miniscenes.

Generally, London is a safe place for lesbians and gays. It's rare to encounter any problem with sharing rooms or holding hands in the inner city, although it would pay to keep your wits about you at night and be conscious of your surroundings.

Some venues to get you started include the following:

George & Dragon (Map p114; 2 Hackney Rd, E2; ⏰6-11pm; ⊖Old St) Appealing corner pub where the crowd is often as eclectically furnished as the venue.

She Soho (☏0207 437 4303; www.she-soho.com; 23a Old Compton St, W1D; ⏰4-11.30pm Mon-Thu, to 12.30am Fri & Sat, to 10.30pm Sun; ⊖Leicester Square) Soho Lesbian bar with DJs at weekends, comedy and live music.

Duke of Wellington (Map p66; 77 Wardour St, W1; ⏰noon-11pm Sun-Wed, to midnight Thu-Sat; ⊖Leicester Sq) Friendly hang-out for the 30-somethings (and above) gay set.

Edge (Map p66; www.edgesoho.co.uk; 11 Soho Sq, W1; ⏰3pm-1am Mon-Thu, to 3am Fri & Sat, to 11.30pm Sun; ⊖Tottenham Court Rd) London's largest gay bar, hopping nightly across four floors.

Heaven (Map p66; www.heavennightclub-london.com; Villiers St, WC2; ⏰11pm-5am Mon, Thu & Fri, 10pm-5am Sat; ⊖Embankment, Charing Cross) Perennially popular gay club under the arches beneath Charing Cross station with fab club nights.

RVT (www.rvt.org.uk; 372 Kennington Lane, SE11; ⏰7pm-midnight Mon, Wed & Thu, 6pm-midnight Tue, 9pm-2am Fri & Sat, 2pm-midnight Sun; ⊖Vauxhall) Much-loved pub with crazy cabaret and drag acts. Head under the arches from Vauxhall tube station onto Kennington Lane, where you'll see the tavern immediately to your left.

Two Brewers (www.the2brewers.com; 114 Clapham High St, SW4; admission after 10pm £3-6; ⏰4pm-2am Sun-Thu, to 4am Fri & Sat; ⊖Clapham Common) Popular bar with regular acts and a nightclub out the back. From the tube station, head north along Clapham High St (away from the common).

Village (Map p66; www.village-soho.co.uk; 81 Wardour St, W1; ⏰4pm-1am Mon-Sat, to 11.30pm Sun; ⊖Piccadilly Circus) Glitzy gay bar with excellent, lengthy happy hours.

Mon-Wed, to 3am Thu-Sat, to 11pm Sun; 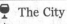 Hyde Park Corner) Be stunned by both the views and the cocktail prices at this 28th-floor eyrie at the Hilton, overlooking Hyde Park.

LAB
COCKTAIL BAR

(Map p66; ☎ 020-7437 7820; www.labbaruk.com; 12 Old Compton St, W1; ⊙ 4pm-midnight Mon-Sat, to 10.30pm Sun; ⊖ Leicester Sq, Tottenham Court Rd) The decor of the London Academy of Bartending has been left behind, but a frisson of creativity runs through the cocktail menu and LAB's mixologists can have your tastebuds singing.

⊖ The City

★Vertigo 42
BAR

(Map p70; ☎ 020-7877 7842; www.vertigo42.co.uk; Tower 42, 25 Old Broad St, EC2; ⊙ noon-3.45pm Mon-Fri & 5-11pm Mon-Sat; ⊖ Liverpool St) Book a two-hour slot in this 42nd-floor champagne bar (no shorts, caps or flip-flops) with vertiginous views across London from the former National Westminster Tower. Reservations only.

Madison
COCKTAIL BAR

(Map p70; www.madisonlondon.net; Roof Terrace, One New Change, EC4; ⊙ 10am-midnight Mon-Sat, to 8pm Sun; ⊖ St Paul's) Perched atop One New Change with a full-frontal view of St Paul's and beyond, Madison offers one of the largest public open-air roof terraces you'll ever encounter. There's a full restaurant on one side and a cocktail bar with outdoor seating on the other.

Ye Olde Cheshire Cheese
PUB

(Map p70; Wine Office Court, 145 Fleet St, EC4; ⊙ 11am-11pm Mon-Fri, noon-11pm Sat; ⊖ Chancery Lane) Rebuilt six years after the Great Fire, this hoary pub was popular with Dr Johnson, Thackeray, Dickens and the visiting Mark Twain. Touristy but always atmospheric and enjoyable for a pub meal.

⊖ South Bank

★Rake
PUB

(Map p82; www.uttobeer.co.uk; 14 Winchester Walk, SE1; ⊙ noon-11pm Mon-Sat, to 8pm Sun; ⊖ London Bridge) The resourceful Rake crams a range of over 100 beers, bitters and real ales into pea-sized premises. There's valuable elbow space on the bamboo-decorated decking outside.

George Inn
PUB

(Map p82; www.nationaltrust.org.uk/george-inn; 77 Borough High St, SE1; ⊙ 11am-11pm; ⊖ London Bridge) This glorious old boozer is London's last surviving galleried coaching inn, dating from 1676 and now a National Trust property. Getting a mention in Dickens' *Little Dorrit*, it also stands on the site of the Tabard Inn, where the pilgrims in Chaucer's *Canterbury Tales* gathered before hitting the road.

Ministry of Sound
CLUB

(Map p82; www.ministryofsound.com; 103 Gaunt St, SE1; admission £16-25; ⊙ 11pm-6.30am Fri & Sat; ⊖ Elephant & Castle) Where the global brand started, it's London's most famous club and still packs in a diverse crew with big local and international names.

⊖ Chelsea & Kensington

★Queen's Arms
PUB

(Map p88; www.thequeensarmskensington. co.uk; 30 Queen's Gate Mews, SW7; ⊙ noon-11pm; ⊖ Gloucester Rd) Just around the corner from the Royal Albert Hall, this godsend of a blue-grey painted pub in an adorable cobbled mews setting off bustling Queen's Gate beckons with a cosy interior and a right royal selection of ales and ciders on tap.

⊖ Bloomsbury & St Pancras

★Queen's Larder
PUB

(Map p96; www.queenslarder.co.uk; 1 Queen Sq, WC1; ⊙ 11.30am-11pm Mon-Sat, noon-10.30pm Sun; ⊖ Russell Sq) This small and supremely cosy pub in a gorgeous square gets its name from Queen Charlotte, wife of 'Mad' King George III, who rented part of the pub's cellar to store special foods for him while he was undergoing treatment nearby. Poets Sylvia Plath and Ted Hughes married in the church opposite.

Newman Arms
PUB

(Map p66; www.newmanarms.co.uk; 23 Rathbone St, W1; ⊙ noon-11.30pm Mon-Fri; ⊖ Goodge St) One of the few family-run pubs in central London, this tiny one-room affair with upstairs pie room packs a big history; George Orwell and Dylan Thomas drank here and a scene from Michael Powell's *Peeping Tom* was filmed in the passageway alongside the pub in 1960.

69 Colebrooke Row
COCKTAIL BAR

(69 Colebrooke Row, N1; ⊙ 5pm-midnight Sun-Wed, to 1am Thu, to 2am Fri & Sat; ⊖ Angel) London cocktail lovers gravitate to this popular bar run by mixer-maestro Tony Conigliaro, but reserve ahead as seats go faster than a down-in-one. The seasonal drinks menu is steeped in ambitious flavours and blends,

with classic drinks for less adventurous palates. Classes are also offered in cocktail mixing (£40).

Big Chill House
DJ BAR

(Map p96; www.wearebigchill.com; 257-259 Pentonville Rd, N1; ⊙ 9am-midnight Mon-Thu, to 3am Fri & Sat, 11am-midnight Sun; 🛜; ⊜ King's Cross St Pancras) Come the weekend, the only remotely chilled-out space in this busy bar, split over two levels, is its first-rate and generously proportioned rooftop terrace.

Draft House
BAR

(Map p66; www.drafthouse.co.uk; 43 Goodge St, W1; ⊙ noon-11pm Mon-Sat; ⊜ Goodge Street) You can line your tummy with ace food, but Draft House is all about the beer choice it crams into its pint-sized premises. This is a public house for ale aficionados, where you can corner a Flying Dog Gonzo Imperial Porter or a head-spinning Samichlaus 14%.

🍷 Notting Hill, Bayswater & Paddington

★ Churchill Arms
PUB

(Map p110; www.churchillarmskensington.co.uk; 119 Kensington Church St, W8; ⊙ 11am-11pm Mon-Wed, to midnight Thu-Sat, noon-10.30pm Sun; 🛜; ⊜ Notting Hill Gate) Adorned with a gob-smacking array of flower baskets and Union Jacks, this magnificent old boozer is a London classic, famed for its atmosphere, Winston memorabilia, knick-knacks and attached conservatory serving fine Thai food (mains from £7.50).

Windsor Castle
PUB

(Map p110; www.thewindsorcastlekensington. co.uk; 114 Campden Hill Rd, W11; ⊙ noon-11pm; 🛜; ⊜ Notting Hill Gate) A fine pub with oak partitions separating the original bars at the crest of Campden Hill Rd. One of the loveliest walled gardens of any pub in London is tucked away through the side entrance. The bones of Thomas Paine (*Rights of Man* author) are rumoured to be in the cellar.

Earl of Lonsdale
PUB

(Map p110; 277-281 Portobello Rd, W11; ⊙ noon-11pm; ⊜ Notting Hill Gate, Ladbroke Grove) Named after the bon vivant founder of the AA (Automobile Association), the Earl is peaceful during the day, with a mixture of old biddies and young hipsters inhabiting the reintroduced snugs. There's a fab backroom with sofas, banquettes and open fires, and a fine beer garden.

🍷 Marylebone

Purl
COCKTAIL BAR

(Map p92; ☑ 020-7935 0835; www.purl-london .com; 50-54 Blandford St, W1; ⊙ 5-11.30pm; ⊜ Baker St, Bond St) Coined after an old English early morning drink of warm beer, gin, wormwood and spices, Purl is all low lighting, subterranean mellowness and some magnificently presented and unusual cocktails. If you're with a group, book an alcove table. On the musical menu is swing and jazz. Reserve ahead.

Artesian
BAR

(☑ 020-7636 1000; www.artesian-bar.co.uk; Langham Hotel, 1c Portland Pl, W1; ⊙ 11am-2am Mon-Sat, to midnight Sun; ⊜ Oxford Circus) For doses of colonial glamour with a touch of China, the sumptuous bar at the Langham hits the mark. Rum is the speciality here – award-winning cocktails (from £14) are concocted from the 60 varieties on offer.

🍷 Camden Town

Lock Tavern
PUB

(Map p122; www.lock-tavern.com; 35 Chalk Farm Rd, NW1; ⊙ noon-midnight Mon-Thu, to 1am Fri & Sat, to 11pm Sun; ⊜ Chalk Farm) The archetypal Camden pub, the Lock has both a rooftop terrace and a beer garden and attracts an interesting crowd with its mix of ready conviviality and regular live music.

🍷 Clerkenwell & Farringdon

★ Jerusalem Tavern
PUB

(Map p96; www.stpetersbrewery.co.uk; 55 Britton St, EC1; ⊙ 11am-11pm Mon-Fri; 🛜; ⊜ Farringdon) Pick a wood-panelled cubbyhole to park yourself in at this tiny 1720 coffee shop–turned-inn (named after the Priory of St John of Jerusalem) and select from St Peter's fantastic beers and ales, brewed in North Suffolk.

Fabric
CLUB

(Map p70; www.fabriclondon.com; 77a Charterhouse St, EC1; admission £8-18; ⊙ 10pm-6am Fri, 11pm-8am Sat, 11pm-6am Sun; ⊜ Farringdon) Consistently rated by DJs as one of the world's greatest, Fabric's three dance floors occupy a converted meat cold-store opposite the Smithfield meat market. Friday's FabricLive offers drum and bass, breakbeat and hip hop, Saturdays see house, techno and electronica, while hedonistic Sundays are delivered by the Wetyourself crew.

🍸 Hoxton, Shoreditch & Spitalfields

★ BrewDog
BAR

(Map p114; ✆020-7729 8476; www.brewdog.com; 51-55 Bethnal Green Rd, EC1; ⏰noon-midnight Sun-Thu, to 1am Fri & Sat; 🛜; 🚇Shoreditch High St) Ale aficionados can migrate to this bar, which overflows with a seasoned and expertly selected choice of cask and bottled beers. There's a strong showing of microbrewery beers, including the Camden Town Brewery and the Redchurch Brewery.

Book Club
BAR

(Map p114; ✆020-7684 8618; www.wearetbc.com; 100 Leonard St, EC2A; ⏰8am-midnight Mon-Wed, to 2am Thu & Fri, 10am-2am Sat & Sun; 🛜; 🚇Old St) A cerebral/creative vibe animates this fantastic one-time Victorian warehouse in Shoreditch that hosts cultural events (life drawing, workshops, dance lessons) and DJ nights to complement the drinking, enthusiastic ping-pong-playing and pool-playing shenanigans. Early birds can catch breakfast from 8am weekdays and food continues through the day.

Ten Bells
PUB

(Map p114; cnr Commercial & Fournier Sts, E1; ⏰11am-11pm Mon-Sat, noon-10.30pm Sun; 🚇Liverpool St) The most famous Jack the Ripper pub, Ten Bells was patronised by his last victim before her grisly end, and possibly by the slayer himself.

Plastic People
CLUB

(Map p114; www.plasticpeople.co.uk; 147-149 Curtain Rd, EC2; admission £5-10; ⏰10pm-2am Thu, to 4am Fri & Sat; 🚇Old St) Taking the directive 'underground club' literally, Plastic People provides a low-ceilinged subterranean den of dubsteppy, wonky, funky, no-frills fun times.

XOYO
CLUB

(Map p114; www.xoyo.co.uk; 32-37 Cowper St, EC2; ⏰hours vary; 🚇Old St) This excellent Shoreditch warehouse club throws together a pulsingly popular mix of gigs, club nights and art events.

Cargo
CLUB

(Map p114; www.cargo-london.com; 83 Rivington St, EC2; admission free-£16; ⏰noon-1am Mon-Thu, to 3am Fri & Sat, to midnight Sun; 🚇Old St) A popular club with a courtyard where you can simultaneously enjoy big sounds and the great outdoors. Also hosts live bands.

Happiness Forgets
COCKTAIL BAR

(Map p114; ✆020-7613 0325; www.happinessforgets.com; 8-9 Hoxton Sq, N1; ⏰5.30-11pm; 🚇Hoxton, 🚇Old St) Take the stairs down to this trendy basement nook where bar staff know their cocktails, and the seductive, subdued ambience hits all the right moody notes (short hours though).

Worship St Whistling Shop
COCKTAIL BAR

(Map p114; ✆020-7247 0015; www.whistlingshop.com; 63 Worship St, EC2; ⏰5pm-midnight Tue, to 1am Wed & Thu, to 2am Fri & Sat; 🚇Old St) This drinking den's busy master mixologists are content to visit the more unexplored outer regions of cocktail chemistry and aromatic science, concocted within the on-site lab and its rotary evaporators. Many ingredients are made in-house.

Sager & Wilde
WINE BAR

(Map p114; www.sagerandwilde.com; 193 Hackney Rd, E2; ⏰5-11pm Mon-Fri, 2-11pm Sat & Sun; 🛜; 🚇Hoxton) Slightly beyond the Hoxton action along Hackney Rd, this fresh wine bar is a neat, unpretentious and good-looking addition to London drinking culture, with a modish bar bites menu, eye-catching iron- and glass-bricks bar counter and excellent wines by the glass and bottle.

🍸 Greenwich

Greenwich Union
PUB

(www.greenwichunion.com; 56 Royal Hill, SE10; ⏰noon-11pm Mon-Fri, 11am-11pm Sat & Sun; 🚈DLR Cutty Sark) The award-winning and handsome Greenwich Union peddles six or seven local microbrewery beers, including raspberry and wheat varieties, and a strong list of ales and bottled international brews. Sink into a distressed leather armchair or find space in the conservatory and beer garden at the rear.

Cutty Sark Tavern
PUB

(www.cuttysarktavern.co.uk; 4-6 Ballast Quay, SE10; ⏰11am-11pm Mon-Sat, noon-10.30pm Sun; 🚈DLR Cutty Sark) Housed in a delightful bow-windowed, wood-beamed Georgian building facing the Thames, this historic gem has half a dozen cask-conditioned ales on tap, and riverside seating outside.

🍸 Hampstead & Highgate

Holly Bush
PUB

(www.hollybushhampstead.co.uk; 22 Holly Mount, NW3; ⏰noon-11pm; 🚇Hampstead) Dating from the early 19th century, this beautiful pub has a secluded hilltop location, open fires in winter and a knack for making you stay a bit longer than you had intended. It's above Heath St, reached via the Holly Bush Steps.

🍺 Outside Central London

White Cross PUB

(www.thewhitecrossrichmond.com; Water Lane, TW9; ☉ 10am-11pm; ⊕ Richmond) The riverside location and fine food and ales make this bay-windowed pub on the site of a former friary a winner. There are entrances for low and high tides, but when the river is at its highest, Cholmondeley Walk running along the Thames floods and the pub is out of bounds to those not willing to wade. Wellies are provided.

Quirky detail: there's a tiny working fireplace *under* the window on your right as you enter.

☆ Entertainment

From West End luvvies to East End geezers, Londoners have always loved a spectacle. With bear-baiting and public executions long on the no-no list, they've fallen back on what London does well: some of the world's best theatre and live-music choices.

For a comprehensive list of what to do on any given night, check out free weekly listings mag *Time Out* and listings in the *Evening Standard* and *Metro*.

Theatre

London is a world capital for theatre across the spectrum from mammoth musicals to thoughtful drama for the highbrow crowd. Blockbuster musicals run and run, with mindboggling longevity. *Les Misérables* and *Phantom of the Opera* lead the pack, but the theatrical biscuit goes to Agatha Christie's *The Mousetrap*, keeping audiences guessing since 1952.

On performance days, you can buy half-price tickets for West End productions (cash only) from the official agency **TKTS** (Map p66; www.tkts.co.uk; Leicester Sq, WC2; ☉ 10am-7pm Mon-Sat, noon-4pm Sun; ⊕ Leicester Sq) on the southern side of Leicester Sq. The booth is the one with the clocktower; beware of touts selling dodgy tickets.

The term 'West End' – as with Broadway – generally refers to the big-money productions such as musicals, but also includes other heavyweights. Off West End – including venues such as Almeida and Young Vic – is where you'll generally find the most original works.

National Theatre THEATRE

(Map p82; ☑ 020-7452 3000; www.nationaltheatre. org.uk; South Bank, SE1; ⊕ Waterloo) Flagship South Bank venue with three theatres and excellent-value tickets for classic and contemporary productions.

Royal Court Theatre THEATRE

(Map p88; ☑ 020-7565 5000; www.royalcourtthe-atre.com; Sloane Sq, SW1; ⊕ Sloane Sq) Progressive theatre and champion of new talent.

Old Vic THEATRE

(Map p82; ☑ 0844 871 7628; www.oldvictheatre. com; The Cut, SE1; ⊕ Waterloo) Kevin Spacey continues his run as artistic director (and occasional performer) at this venue, which features classic, highbrow drama.

Donmar Warehouse THEATRE

(Map p66; ☑ 0844 871 7624; www.donmarware-house.com; 41 Earlham St, WC2; ⊕ Covent Garden) A 251-seat theatre that has forged itself a West End reputation.

Almeida THEATRE

(☑ 020-7359 4404; www.almeida.co.uk; Almeida St, N1; ⊕ Highbury & Islington) A plush Islington venue that can be relied on for an essential program of imaginative theatre.

Young Vic THEATRE

(Map p82; ☑ 020-7922 2922; www.youngvic.org; 66 The Cut, SE1; ⊕ Waterloo) One of the capital's most respected theatre troupes, the Young Vic stages winning performances.

Live Music

It goes without saying that London is a crucible of musical talent, with young bands gigging around venues citywide.

★**Vortex Jazz Club** JAZZ

(www.vortexjazz.co.uk; 11 Gillet St, N16; ☐ 73, ☐ Dalston Kingsland, Dalston Junction) Vortex has an outstanding program of musicians from the UK, US, Europe, Africa and beyond, and hosts jazz musicians, singers and songwriters. It's a small venue, so make sure you book if there is an act you particularly fancy.

★**O2 Academy Brixton** LIVE MUSIC

(www.o2academybrixton.co.uk; 211 Stockwell Rd, SW9; ⊕ Brixton) This Grade II–listed art-deco venue is always winning awards for 'best live venue' (something to do with the artfully sloped floor, perhaps) and hosts big-name acts in a relatively intimate setting (5000 capacity).

KOKO
LIVE MUSIC

(www.koko.uk.com; 1a Camden High St, NW1; ⊗ 7-11pm Sun-Thu, to 4am Fri & Sat; ⊜ Mornington Cres) Occupying the grand Camden Palace theatre, Koko hosts live bands most nights and the regular Club NME (New Musical Express; £5) on Friday.

12 Bar Club
LIVE MUSIC

(Map p66; www.12barclub.com; Denmark St, WC2; admission £6-10; ⊗ 7pm-3am Mon-Sat, to 12.30am Sun; ⊜ Tottenham Court Rd) Small and intimate with a rough-and-ready feel, the 12 Bar is a favourite live-music venue, with anything from solo acts to bands performing nightly. The emphasis is on songwriting and the music is very much indie rock, with anything from folk and jazzy influences to full-on punk and metal sounds.

Dublin Castle
LIVE MUSIC

(Map p122; ☑ 020-7485 1773; www.thedublincastle. com; 94 Parkway, NW1; ⊜ Camden Town) There's live punk or alternative music most nights in this pub's back room (cover usually £6).

Barfly
LIVE MUSIC

(Map p122; www.mamacolive.com/thebarfly; 49 Chalk Farm Rd, NW1; gigs from £8, club nights £3-5; ⊗ 7pm-3am Mon-Sat, to midnight Sun; ⊜ Chalk Farm) This grungy, indie-rock Camden venue hosts small-time artists looking for their big break. The Killers, Kasabian and Franz Ferdinand have all been on the billing. The lean is clearly towards rock from the US and UK, with alternative-music radio station Xfm hosting regular nights.

Ronnie Scott's
JAZZ

(Map p66; ☑ 020-7439 0747; www.ronniescotts. co.uk; 47 Frith St, W1; ⊗ 6.30pm-3am Mon-Sat, to midnight Sun; ⊜ Leicester Sq, Tottenham Court Rd) London's legendary jazz club has been pulling in jazz titans since 1959.

100 Club
LIVE MUSIC

(Map p66; ☑ 020-7636 0933; www.the100club. co.uk; 100 Oxford St, W1; admission £8-20; ⊗ check website for gig times; ⊜ Oxford Circus, Tottenham Court Rd) Hosting live music for 70 years, this legendary London venue once showcased the Stones and was at the centre of the punk revolution. It now divides its time between jazz, rock and even a little classical and swing.

606 Club
BLUES, JAZZ

(☑ 020-7352 5953; www.606club.co.uk; 90 Lots Rd, SW10; music fee Sun-Thu £10, Fri & Sat £12; ⊗ 7-11.15pm Sun-Thu, 8pm-12.30am Fri & Sat; ⊜ Im-perial Wharf) Named after its old address on the King's Road, this fantastic tucked-away basement jazz club and restaurant gives centre stage to contemporary British-based jazz musicians nightly. To consume alcohol you'll need to dine to meet some rather antique licensing requirements. There's no entry charge, but a music fee will go on your food/drink bill. Booking advised.

The club is also open most Sundays from 12.30pm to 4.30pm.

Roundhouse
LIVE MUSIC

(Map p122; www.roundhouse.org.uk; Chalk Farm Rd, NW1; ⊜ Chalk Farm) Built in 1847 as a railway shed, Camden's Roundhouse has been an iconic concert venue since the 1960s (capacity 3300), hosting the likes of the Rolling Stones, Led Zeppelin and The Clash. Theatre and comedy are also staged.

Classical Music

With four world-class symphony orchestras, two opera companies, various smaller ensembles, brilliant venues, reasonable prices and high standards of performance, London is a classical capital. Keep an eye out for the free (or nearly so) lunchtime concerts held in many of the city's churches.

Royal Albert Hall
CONCERT VENUE

(Map p88; ☑ 020-7589 8212, 0845 401 5045; www.royalalberthall.com; Kensington Gore, SW7; ⊜ South Kensington) This landmark elliptical Victorian arena – classically based on a Roman ampitheatre – hosts classical concerts and contemporary artists, but is best known as the venue for the annual classical music festival, the Proms.

Barbican
PERFORMING ARTS

(Map p70; ☑ 020-7638 8891, 0845 121 6823; www. barbican.org.uk; Silk St, EC2; ⊜ Barbican) Home to the excellent **London Symphony Orchestra** (www.lso.co.uk), this famously hulking complex has a rich program of film, music, theatre, art and dance, including concerts.

Southbank Centre
CONCERT VENUE

(Map p82; ☑ 020-7960 4200; www.southbankcentre.co.uk; Belvedere Rd, SE1; ⊜ Waterloo) Home to the **London Philharmonic Orchestra** (www. lpo.co.uk), **Sinfonietta** (www.londonsinfonietta. org.uk) and the **Philharmonia Orchestra** (www.philharmonia.co.uk), among others, this centre hosts classical, opera, jazz and choral music in three premier venues: the **Royal Festival Hall**, the smaller **Queen Elizabeth Hall** and the **Purcell Room**.

Opera & Dance

Royal Opera House OPERA

(Map p66; 020-7304 4000; www.roh.org.uk; Bow St, WC2; tickets £4-250; Covent Garden) Covent Garden is synonymous with opera thanks to this world-famous venue, home of the Royal Ballet, Britain's premier classical ballet company. Backstage tours take place three times a day on weekdays and five times on Saturdays (£8.50 to £12, book ahead).

Sadler's Wells DANCE

(Map p96; 0844 412 4300; www.sadlerswells. com; Rosebery Ave, EC1; tickets £10-49; Angel) A glittering modern venue that was, in fact, first established in the 17th century, Sadler's Wells has been given much credit for bringing modern dance to the mainstream.

London Coliseum OPERA

(Map p66; 020-7845 9300; www.eno.org; St Martin's Lane, WC2; Leicester Sq) Home of the progressive English National Opera; the English National Ballet also performs here.

Comedy

When London's comics aren't being outrageously funny on TV, you might find them doing stand-up somewhere in your neighbourhood.

Comedy Store COMEDY

(Map p66; 0844 871 7699; www.thecomedy store.co.uk; 1a Oxendon St, SW1; admission £16.50-26; Piccadilly Circus) One of London's first comedy clubs, featuring the capital's most famous improvisers, the Comedy Store Players, on Wednesdays (8pm) and Sundays (7.30pm).

Comedy Cafe COMEDY

(Map p114; 020-7739 5706; www.comedycafe. co.uk; 68 Rivington St, EC2; admission free-£12; Wed-Sat; Old St) Have dinner and watch comedy; the free New Act Night on Wednesday is good for toe-curling entertainment.

Soho Theatre COMEDY

(Map p66; 020-7478 0100; www.sohotheatre. com; 21 Dean St, W1; £15-20; Tottenham Court Rd) This is where grown-up comedians graduate to once crowds start paying attention.

Cinemas

Glitzy premieres usually take place in one of the mega multiplexes in Leicester Sq.

Electric Cinema CINEMA

(Map p110; 020-7908 9696; www.electriccinema.co.uk; 191 Portobello Rd, W11; tickets £8-22.50; Ladbroke Grove) Getting Londoners buzzing since 1911, the Electric can help you grab a glass of wine from the bar, head to your leather sofa and snuggle down for a flick.

BFI Southbank CINEMA

(Map p82; 020-7928 3232; www.bfi.org.uk; Belvedere Rd, SE1; tickets £8-12; 11am-11pm; Waterloo) A film-lover's fantasy, screening some 2000 flicks a year, from classics to foreign art-house. There's also the Mediatheque viewing stations, for exploring the British Film Institute's extensive archive of movies and watching whatever you like for free.

BFI IMAX Cinema CINEMA

(Map p82; www.bfi.org.uk/bfi-imax; 1 Charlie Chaplin Walk, SE1; adult/child from £9/5.75; Waterloo) Watch 3D movies and cinema releases on the UK's biggest screen: 20m high (nearly five double-decker buses) and 26m wide.

Prince Charles CINEMA

(Map p66; www.princecharlescinema.com; 7 Leicester Pl, WC2; tickets £7.50-16; Leicester Sq) Given the eye-watering prices of West End cinema ticket prices, wait till the first-runs have finished and come here, central London's cheapest picturehouse. Completing the score are mini-festivals, old classics and sing-along screenings.

Football (Soccer)

As the capital of a football-mad nation, expect half of London to be watching the beautiful game during the cooler months.

The home ground for England's national football team, and the venue for the FA Cup final, is Wembley Stadium (0844 980 8001; www.wembleystadium.com; tours adult/child £16/9).

Tickets for Premier League football matches are like gold dust, but you could try your luck.

London's leading football clubs include the following:

Arsenal STADIUM

(www.arsenal.com/tours; 75 Drayton Park, N5; self-guided tour adult/child £17.50/9; 10am-6pm Mon-Sat, to 4pm Sun; Arsenal, Finsbury Park, Highbury & Islington) Arsenal Emirates Stadium is the third largest in England. Daily tours available.

Chelsea STADIUM

(0871 984 1955; www.chelseafc.com; Stamford Bridge, Fulham Rd, SW6; stadium tours & museum adult/child £20/13; museum 9.30am-5pm; Fulham Broadway)

Fulham STADIUM
(www.fulhamfc.com; Craven Cottage, Stevenage Rd, SW6; tours adult/child £12/9; ⊙9am-5pm Mon-Fri; ⊖Putney Bridge)

Tottenham Hotspur STADIUM
(www.tottenhamhotspur.com; White Hart Lane, 748 High Rd, N17; tour adult/child £20/9; ⊠White Hart Lane)

West Ham STADIUM
(www.whufc.com; Boleyn Ground, Green Street, Upton Park, E13; ⊖Upton Park) In 2016, the Olympic Stadium will become the new home of West Ham United FC.

Rugby

Twickenham (www.rfu.com; Rugby Rd, TW1; ⊠Twickenham) is the home of English rugby union, but as with football, tickets for international matches are difficult to get unless you have contacts. The ground also has the **World Rugby Museum** (☑020-8892 8877; www.rfu.com; adult/child £8/6; ⊙10am-5pm Tue-Sat, 11am-5pm Sun), which can be combined with a tour of the stadium (adult/child £16/10, bookings recommended).

Cricket & Tennis

Cricket is as popular as ever in the home land. Test matches take place at two venerable grounds: Lord's Cricket Ground (which also hosts tours) and the **Brit Oval** (☑0871 246 1100; www.kiaoval.com; Surrey County Cricket Club, Kennington Oval, SE11; ⊖Oval). Tickets cost from £20 to £80, but if you're a fan it's worth it.

The Wimbledon Lawn Tennis Championships (p107) is one of the biggest events on the city's summer calendar.

Lord's Cricket Ground CRICKET GROUND
(www.lords.org; St John's Wood Rd, NW8; tours adult/child £18/12; ⊖St John's Wood) The next best thing to watching a test at Lord's is the absorbingly anecdotal 100-minute tour of the ground and facilities, held when there's no play. It takes in the famous (members only) Long Room and the **MCC Museum**, featuring evocative memorabilia, including the tiny Ashes trophy.

🅐 Shopping

From world-famous department stores to quirky backstreet retail revelations, London is a mecca for shoppers with an eye for style and a card to exercise.

London's famous department stores are a tourist attraction in themselves, and if there's a label worth having, you'll find it in central London. The capital's most famous designers (Paul Smith, Vivienne Westwood, Stella McCartney, the late Alexander McQueen) have their own stores scattered about and are stocked in major department stores. Look out for dress agencies that sell second-hand designer clothes, bags and shoes – there are particularly rich pickings in the wealthier parts of town.

Nick Hornby's book *High Fidelity* may have done for London music-store workers what *Sweeney Todd* did for barbers, but those obsessive types still lurk in wonderful independent stores all over the city.

🅐 West End

Oxford St is the place for high-street fashion, while Regent St cranks it up a notch. Bond St has designers galore, Savile Row is all about bespoke tailoring and Jermyn St is the place for smart clobber (particularly shirts).

Selfridges DEPARTMENT STORE
(Map p92; www.selfridges.com; 400 Oxford St, W1; ⊙9.30am-9pm Mon-Sat, 11.30am-6.15pm Sun; ⊖Bond St) Famed for its innovative window displays – especially at yuletide – the funkiest of London's one-stop shops bursts with fashion labels and tempts with an unparalleled food hall and the world's largest shoe department.

Fortnum & Mason DEPARTMENT STORE
(Map p66; www.fortnumandmason.com; 181 Piccadilly, W1; ⊙10am-9pm Mon-Sat, noon-6pm Sun; ⊖Piccadilly Circus) It's the byword for quality and service from a bygone era, steeped in 300 years of tradition. The old-world basement food hall is where Britain's elite come for their pantry provisions and epicurean morsels. A new branch opened in 2013 at **St Pancras International** (Map p96; www.fortnumandmason.com; Unit 1a, St Pancras International Station, Pancras Rd, N1; ⊙7am-9pm Mon-Sat, 8am-9pm Sun; ⊖King's Cross St Pancras).

Liberty DEPARTMENT STORE
(Map p66; www.liberty.co.uk; Great Marlborough St, W1; ⊙10am-8pm Mon-Sat, noon-6pm Sun; ⊖Oxford Circus) An irresistible blend of contemporary styles and indulgent pampering in a mock-Tudor fantasyland of carved wood.

Topshop CLOTHING
(Map p66; www.topshop.co.uk; 36-38 Great Castle St, W1; ⊙9am-9pm Mon-Sat, 11.30am-6pm Sun; ⊖Oxford Circus) Billed as the 'world's largest fashion

ROLL OUT THE BARROW

London has over 350 markets selling everything from antiques and curios to flowers and fish. Some, such as Camden and Portobello Rd, are tourist-packed, while others are just for locals.

Columbia Road Flower Market (Map p114; Columbia Rd, E2; ⊘8am-3pm Sun; ⊖Old St) The best place for East End barrow boy banter ('We got flowers cheap enough for ya muvver-in-law's grave'). Unmissable.

Borough Market (Map p82; www.boroughmarket.org.uk; 8 Southwark St, SE1; ⊘11am-5pm Thu, noon-6pm Fri, 8am-5pm Sat; ⊖London Bridge) A farmers market sometimes called London's Larder, it has been here in some form since the 13th century. It's wonderfully atmospheric and you'll find everything from organic falafel to boars' heads.

Maltby Street Market (www.maltby.st; Maltby St, SE1; ⊘10am-4pm Sat; ⊖London Bridge) Hailed as the new Borough Market, Maltby Street is small, delicious and a joy to spend a Saturday afternoon in.

Camden Market (Map p122; Camden High St, NW1; ⊘10am-6pm; ⊖Camden Town, Chalk Farm) London's most famous market is actually a series of markets spread along Camden High St and Chalk Farm Rd. Despite a major fire in 2008, the Camden Lock Market (Map p122; www.camdenlockmarket.com; 54-56 Camden Lock Pl, NW1; ⊘10am-6pm; ⊖Camden Town, Chalk Farm) and Camden Stables Market (Map p122; Chalk Farm Rd, NW1; ⊘10am-6pm; ⊖Chalk Farm) are still the places for punk fashion, cheap food, hippy chic and a whole lotta craziness.

Portobello Road Market (Map p110; www.portobellomarket.org; Portobello Rd, W10; ⊘8am-6.30pm Mon-Wed, Fri & Sat, to 1pm Thu; ⊖Notting Hill Gate, Ladbroke Grove) One of London's most famous street markets, in Notting Hill. New and vintage clothes are its main attraction, with antiques at its south end and food at the north.

Old Spitalfields Market (Map p114; www.oldspitalfieldsmarket.com; Commercial St, btwn Brushfield & Lamb Sts, E1; ⊘10am-4pm Sun-Fri; ⊖Liverpool St) It's housed in a Victorian warehouse, but the market's been here since 1638. Thursdays are devoted to antiques and vintage clothes and Fridays to fashion and art. Sunday's the big day, with a bit of everything.

Broadway Market (www.broadwaymarket.co.uk; London Fields, E8; ⊘9am-5pm Sat; ⊖Bethnal Green) Graze from the organic food stalls, choose a cooked meal and then sample one of the 200 beers on offer at the neighbouring Dove Freehouse. It's a bit of a schlep from the tube.

Brixton Village (www.brixtonmarket.net; Atlantic Rd; ⊘10.30am-6pm Mon-Wed, to 10pm Thu-Sat, 10.30am-5pm Sun; ⊖Brixton) Revitalised and hip transformation of Granville Arcade near Brixton Market, with a host of inventively inclined shops and fantastic restaurants and cafes.

Sunday UpMarket (Map p114; www.sundayupmarket.co.uk; Old Truman Brewery, Brick Lane, E1; ⊘10am-5pm Sun; ⊖Liverpool St) Handmade handbags, jewellery, new and vintage clothes and shoes, plus food if you need refuelling.

Brick Lane Market (Map p114; www.visitbricklane.org; Brick Lane, E1; ⊘8am-2pm Sun; ⊖Liverpool St) An East End pearler, this is a sprawling bazaar featuring everything from fruit and veggies to paintings and bric-a-brac.

Camden Passage Market (www.camdenpassageislington.co.uk; Camden Passage, N1; ⊘8am-2pm Wed, to 5pm Sat; ⊖Angel) Get your fill of antiques and trinkets galore. Not in Camden (despite the name).

Greenwich Market (www.greenwichmarketlondon.com; College Approach, SE10; ⊘10am-5.30pm; ⊖DLR Cutty Sark) Rummage through antiques, vintage clothing and collectables (Thursday and Friday), arts and crafts (Wednesday and weekends), or just chow down in the food section.

Petticoat Lane Market (Map p70; Wentworth St & Middlesex St, E1; ⊘9am-2pm Sun-Fri; ⊖Aldgate) A cherished East End institution overflowing with cheap consumer durables and jumble-sale ware.

store', the Topshop branch on Oxford Circus is a frenzy of shoppers searching for the latest look at reasonable prices. It's home to a range by London's favourite local supermodel rock chick, Kate Moss. Topman is upstairs.

Foyles
BOOKS

(Map p66; www.foyles.co.uk; 107 Charing Cross Rd, WC2; ⊘9.30am-9pm Mon-Sat, 11.30am-6pm Sun; ⊜Tottenham Court Rd) Flogging books since 1906, Foyles is a bookselling institution and retail landmark.

Stanford's
BOOKS, MAPS

(Map p66; www.stanfords.co.uk; 12-14 Long Acre, WC2; ⊘9am-8pm Mon-Fri, 10am-8pm Sat, noon-6pm Sun; ⊜Leicester Sq, Covent Garden) A wonderland of travel titles and maps, with 160 years of experience.

Hamleys
TOYS

(Map p66; www.hamleys.com; 188-196 Regent St, W1; ⊘10am-8pm Mon-Sat, noon-6pm Sun; ⊜Oxford Circus) Reputedly the oldest and largest toy store in the world, Hamleys is five floors of games and toys topped off with Lego world and a cafe.

Waterstones
BOOKS

(Map p66; www.waterstones.com; 203-206 Piccadilly, W1; ⊘9am-10pm Mon-Sat, noon-6pm Sun; ⊜Piccadilly Circus) The chain's mega Piccadilly store is the largest bookstore in Europe, boasting knowledgeable staff and regular author readings and signings. Check out the roof-top 5th View (Map p66; ☑020-7851 2433; www.5thview.co.uk; mains £9-15; ⊘9am-10pm Mon-Sat, noon-5pm Sun) bar-restaurant.

Benjamin Pollock's Toy Shop
TOYS

(Map p66; www.pollocks-coventgarden.co.uk; 1st fl, 44 Market Bldg, Covent Garden, WC2; ⊘10.30am-6pm Mon-Sat, 11am-4pm Sun; ⊜Covent Garden) All manner of treasures await at this gem of a traditional toy shop selling Victorian paper toy theatres, children's masks, spinning tops, finger puppets, antique teddy bears, dolls and more.

Moomin Shop
CHILDREN

(Map p66; www.themoominshop.com; 43 Market Bldg, Covent Garden, WC2; ⊘10am-8pm Mon-Sat, 11am-7pm Sun; ⊜Covent Garden) A tiny shrine to Tove Jansson's adorable Moomintrolls: mugs, hot-water bottle sleeves, tea towels, T-shirts, fridge magnets. The whole moomin shebang.

🔒 Knightsbridge, Kensington & Chelsea

Knightsbridge draws the hordes with quintessentially English department stores.

Harrods
DEPARTMENT STORE

(Map p88; www.harrods.com; 87 Brompton Rd, SW1; ⊘10am-8pm Mon-Sat, 11.30am-6pm Sun; ⊜Knightsbridge) Simultaneously stylish and garish, Harrods is an obligatory stop for visitors, both cash-strapped and big spenders alike. The spectacular food hall is a sight in itself.

John Sandoe Books
BOOKS

(Map p88; www.johnsandoe.com; 10 Blacklands Tce, SW3; ⊘9.30am-6.30pm Mon-Sat, 11am-5pm Sun; ⊜Sloane Sq) This atmospheric little bookshop is a treasure trove of literary gems and hidden surprises. In business for decades, loyal customers swear by it and the knowledgeable booksellers spill forth with well-read pointers.

Harvey Nichols
DEPARTMENT STORE

(Map p88; www.harveynichols.com; 109-125 Knightsbridge, SW1; ⊘10am-8pm Mon-Sat, 11.30am-6pm Sun; ⊜Knightsbridge) London's temple of high fashion, jewellery and perfume.

🔒 Bloomsbury & St Pancras

Harry Potter Shop
CHILDREN

(Map p96; www.harrypotterplatform934.com; departure concourse, King's Cross station, N1; ⊘10am-6pm; ⊜King's Cross St Pancras) For all things Potter and Hogwartish.

🔒 Notting Hill, Bayswater & Paddington

Portobello Rd and the lanes surrounding it are the main focus, both for the famous market and the quirky boutiques and gift stores.

Ceramica Blue
HOMEWARES

(Map p110; www.ceramicablue.co.uk; 10 Blenheim Cres, W11; ⊘10am-6.30pm Mon-Sat, noon-5pm Sun; ⊜Ladbroke Grove) For original and eye-catching crockery and coloured glass imported from more than a dozen countries, with Japanese eggshell-glaze teacups, serving plates with traditional South African designs, and more.

🏠 Marylebone

Daunt Books BOOKS

(Map p92; www.dauntbooks.co.uk; 83 Marylebone High St, W1; ⊙9am-7.30pm Mon-Sat, 11am-6pm Sun; ⊖Baker St) An exquisitely beautiful store, Daunt is one of London's loveliest travel bookshops (and stocks general fiction and nonfiction titles as well).

🏠 Hoxton, Shoreditch & Spitalfields

Rough Trade East MUSIC

(Map p114; www.roughtrade.com; Dray Walk, Old Truman Brewery, 91 Brick Lane, E1; ⊙8am-8pm Mon-Fri, 11am-7pm Sat & Sun; ⊖Liverpool St) At the forefront of the punk explosion of the 1970s, Rough Trade East – or West (Map p110; ☑020-7229 8541; www.roughtrade.com; 130 Talbot Rd, W11; ⊙10am-6.30pm Mon-Sat, 11am-5pm Sun; ⊖Ladbroke Grove) – is the best place to come for anything of an indie or alternative music bent.

Start CLOTHING

(Map p114; www.start-london.com; 42-44 Rivington St, EC2; ⊙10.30am-6.30pm Mon-Wed & Fri, 11am-6pm Sat, noon-5pm Sun; ⊖Old St) Spilling over three stores on the same lane (womenswear, menswear and men's formal), your quest for designer jeans starts here.

🏠 The East End & Docklands

Westfield Stratford City MALL

(http://uk.westfield.com; 2 Stratford Place, Montifichet Road, Queen Elizabeth Olympic Park, E20; ⊙10am-9pm Mon-Fri, 9am-9pm Sat, noon-6pm Sun; ⊖Stratford) Right by the Queen Elizabeth Olympic Park, this is Europe's largest mall, a shopping behemoth with over 250 shops, dozens of restaurants, a 17-screen cinema, and a casino.

ℹ Information

DANGERS & ANNOYANCES

Considering its size and wealth disparities, London is generally safe. That said, keep your wits about you and don't flash your cash unnecessarily. Instances of youth-on-youth knife crime is cause for concern, so walk away if you sense trouble brewing and take care at night. When travelling by tube, choose a carriage with other people in it and avoid deserted suburban stations. Following reports of robberies and sexual attacks, shun unlicensed or unbooked minicabs.

Nearly every Londoner has a story about a wallet/phone/bag being nicked from under their noses – or arses, in the case of bags on floors in bars. Watch out for pickpockets on crowded tube trains, night buses and streets.

When using ATMs, guard your PIN details carefully. Don't use an ATM that looks like it's been tampered with as there have been incidents of card cloning.

EMERGENCY

Police/Fire/Ambulance (☑999)

Rape & Sexual Abuse Support Centre (☑0808 802 9999; www.rasasc.org.uk; ⊙noon-2.30pm & 7-9.30pm)

Samaritans (☑08457 90 90 90; www.samaritans.org)

INTERNET ACCESS

You'll find free wireless (wi-fi) access at many bars, cafes and hotels (although a few, particularly top-end hotels, continue to charge for the service).

INTERNET RESOURCES

BBC London (www.bbc.co.uk/london)

Evening Standard (www.standard.co.uk)

Londonist (www.londonist.com) London-centric blog.

Lonely Planet (www.lonelyplanet.com/london)

Time Out (www.timeout.com/london)

View London (www.viewlondon.co.uk)

Walk It (www.walkit.com) Enter your destination and get a walking map, time estimate and information on calories burnt and carbon dioxide saved.

MEDIA

Two free newspapers bookend the working day – *Metro* in the morning and the *London Evening Standard* in the evening – both available from tube stations. Also free, *Time Out* is the local listing guide par excellence.

MEDICAL SERVICES

To find a local doctor, pharmacy or hospital, consult the local telephone directory or call ☑0845 46 47.

Hospitals with 24-hour accident and emergency units include the following:

St Thomas' Hospital (☑020-7188 7188; Lambeth Palace Rd, SE1; ⊖Waterloo)

University College London Hospital (☑0845 155 5000, 020-3456 7890; www.uclh.org; 235 Euston Rd, NW1; ⊖Euston Sq, Warren St)

TOILETS

If you're caught short around London, public toilets can be elusive. Only a handful of tube stations have them, but the bigger National Rail stations usually do (often coin operated). If you can face five floors on an escalator, department stores are a good bet.

TOURIST INFORMATION

There are tourist information desks at Heathrow Airport, King's Cross St Pancras station, Liverpool Street station, Piccadilly Circus underground station and Victoria Station. **Visit London** (☑ 0870 156 6366; www.visitlondon.com) can fill you in on everything from attractions and events to tours and accommodation.

City of London Information Centre (Map p70; www.visitthecity.co.uk; St Paul's Churchyard, EC4; ⊙ 9.30am-5.30pm Mon-Sat, 10am-4pm Sun; ⊜ St Paul's) Tourist information, fast-track tickets to City attractions and guided walks (adult/child under 12 £7/free).

Greenwich Tourist Office (www.visitgreenwich. org.uk/tourist-information-centre; Pepys House, 2 Cutty Sark Gardens, SE10; ⊙ 10am-5pm; ® DLR Cutty Sark) Information plus guided tours.

ⓘ Getting There & Away

London is the major gateway to England.

AIR

There are a number of London airports. For more information, see p698.

BUS

Most long-distance coaches leave London from **Victoria Coach Station** (Map p88; 164 Buckingham Palace Rd, SW1; ⊜ Victoria).

CAR

Check reservation numbers of the main car-hire firms, all of which have airport and various city locations.

TRAIN

London's main-line terminals are linked by the tube and each serves different destinations. Most stations have left-luggage facilities (around £4) and lockers (20p), toilets (around £3), newsstands and bookshops, and a range of eating and drinking outlets. St Pancras, Victoria and Liverpool St stations have shopping centres.

If you can't find your destination in the list of main-line terminals, consult the journey planner at www.nationalrail.co.uk.

Charing Cross Canterbury.

Euston Manchester, Liverpool, Carlisle, Glasgow.

King's Cross Cambridge, Hull, York, Newcastle, Scotland.

Liverpool Street Stansted Airport, Cambridge.

London Bridge Gatwick Airport, Brighton.

Marylebone Birmingham.

Paddington Heathrow Airport, Oxford, Bath, Bristol, Exeter, Plymouth, Cardiff.

St Pancras Gatwick and Luton airports, Brighton, Nottingham, Sheffield, Leicester, Leeds, Paris.

Victoria Gatwick Airport, Brighton, Canterbury.

Waterloo Windsor, Winchester, Exeter, Plymouth.

ⓘ Getting Around

TO/FROM THE AIRPORTS

Gatwick

There are **National Rail** (☑ 0845 748 4950; www.nationalrail.co.uk) services between Gatwick's South Terminal and Victoria station (from £15, 37 minutes), running every 15 minutes during the day and hourly through the night. Other trains head to London St Pancras International (from £10, 56 minutes) and London Bridge (£10, 30 minutes, every 15 minutes). Fares are cheaper the earlier you book. If you're racing to make a flight, the **Gatwick Express** (www.gatwickexpress.com; one way/return £19.90/34.90) departs Victoria every 15 minutes from 5am to 11.45pm (30 minutes, first/last train 3.30am/12.32am).

Prices start from £2, depending on when you book, for the **EasyBus** (www.easybus.co.uk) minibus service between Gatwick and Earls Court (allow 1¼ hours, every 30 minutes from 4.20am to 1am). You'll be charged extra if you have more than one carry-on and one check-in bag. Book online for the cheapest deals.

Heathrow

Transport connections to Heathrow are excellent, and the journey to and from the city is usually painless. The cheapest option is the Underground. The Piccadilly line is accessible from every terminal (£5.70, one hour to central London, every five minutes from around 5am to 11.30pm). If there are vast queues at the ticket office, use the automatic machines instead; some accept credit cards as well as cash.

You might save some time on the considerably more expensive **Heathrow Express** (www. heathrowexpress.com; one way/return £21/34), an ultramodern train to Paddington station (15 minutes, every 15 minutes 5.12am to 11.48pm). You can purchase tickets on board (£5 extra), from self-service machines (cash and credit cards accepted) at both stations, or online.

There are taxi ranks for black cabs outside every terminal; a fare to the centre of London will cost between £45 and £85.

London City

The Docklands Light Railway (DLR) connects London City Airport to the tube network, taking 22 minutes to reach Bank station (£4.70). A black taxi costs around £30 to/from central London.

Luton

There are regular **National Rail** (www.nationalrail. co.uk) services from St Pancras (£13.90, 29 to 39 minutes) to Luton Airport Parkway station, where a shuttle bus (£1.60) will get you to the airport within 10 minutes. EasyBus minibuses head from Victoria, Earl's Court and Baker St to Luton (one-way £10, allow 1½ hours, every 30 minutes). A taxi to central London costs around £100 to £110.

Stansted

The **Stansted Express** (☑ 0845 8500150; www. stanstedexpress.com) connects with Liverpool St station (one way/return £23.40/33.20, 46 minutes, every 15 to 30 minutes 6am to 12.30am).

EasyBus (www.easybus.co.uk; one way £10, return from £12) services run between Stansted and Baker St (1¼ hours, every 20 minutes). The **Airbus A6** (☑ 0870 580 8080; www.nationalexpress.com) links with Victoria Coach station (£11, allow 1¾ hours, at least every 30 minutes). **National Express** (www.nationalexpress.com) also runs buses to Stansted from Liverpool St station (£9 one way, 80 mins, every 30 mins).

Terravision (www.terravision.eu) coaches link Stansted to both Liverpool St train station (bus A51, one way/return from £9/15, 55 minutes) and Victoria coach station (bus A50, one way/return from £8/14, 75 minutes) every 20 to 40 minutes between 6am and 1am.

A taxi cab to/from central London costs about £125.

The central city is flat and relatively compact and traffic moves slowly – all good news for cyclists. Operating 24 hours a day, the excellent **Barclays Cycle Hire Scheme** (☑ 0845 026 3630; www.tfl. gov.uk.) allows you to hire a bike from one of 400 docking stations around London. The access fee is £2 for 24 hours or £10 per week; after that, the first 30 minutes are free (making the bikes perfect for short hops), or £1/4/6/15 for one hour/90 minutes/two hours/three hours. Cycle as often as you like, but leave five minutes between each trip. Visitors to London can pay either online or using a credit or debit card at a docking station. The minimum age for buying access is 18, the minimum age for riding a Barclays Bike is 14.

The M25 ring road encompasses the 609 sq miles that is broadly regarded as Greater London. For motorists it's the first circle of hell; London's streets can be congested beyond belief. Traffic is heavy, roadwork continuous, parking is either impossible or expensive, and wheel-clampers are diligent. If you drive into central London from 7am to 6pm on a weekday, you'll need to pay a £10 per day congestion charge (visit www.tfl.gov.uk for payment options) or face a hefty fine. If you're hiring a car to continue your trip from London, take the tube to Heathrow and pick it up from there.

Although complaining about it is a local sport, London's public transport is excellent, with tubes, trains, buses and boats getting you wherever you need to go. **TFL** (www.tfl.gov.uk), the city's public transport provider, is the glue that binds the network together. Its website has a handy journey planner and information on all services, including cabs. Get yourself an Oyster card and make the most of it.

Boat

Boats plying the Thames are a great way to travel, avoiding traffic jams while affording great views. Passengers with daily, weekly or monthly travelcards (including on Oyster) get a third off all fares.

Thames Clippers (www.thamesclippers. com) runs regular commuter services between Embankment, Waterloo, Blackfriars, Bankside, London Bridge, Tower, Canary Wharf, Greenwich, North Greenwich and Woolwich piers (adult/child £6.80/3.40) from 6am and between 10pm and midnight depending on the day of the week (from 9.30am weekends). Leisure services include the Tate-to-Tate boat (p85) and Westminster–Greenwich services. There are also boats to Kew Gardens and Hampton Court Palace.

London Waterbus Company (☑ 020-7482 2660; www.londonwaterbus.com; single/return £8.20/11.50) and **Jason's Trip** (www.jasons. co.uk; opposite 42 Blomfield Rd, W9; single/return £9/14) both run canal boat journeys between Camden Lock and Little Venice; see websites for times. London has some 40 miles of inner-city canals, mostly built in the 19th century.

Bus

Travelling around London by double-decker bus is great for seeing the city, but it's usually slower than the tube. Heritage 'Routemaster' buses with conductors operate on route 9 (from Aldwych to Royal Albert Hall) and 15 (between Trafalgar Sq and Tower Hill); these are the only buses without wheelchair access. A new fleet of freshly designed hybrid diesel/electric hop-on/hop-off (and wheelchair-accessible) Routemasters is now running on some routes, and will number 600 buses by 2016.

Buses run regularly during the day, while less frequent night buses (prefixed with the letter 'N') wheel into action when the tube stops. Single-journey bus tickets (valid for two hours) cost £2.40 (£1.45 on Oyster, capped at £4.40 per day); a weekly pass is £20.20. Children ride for free. At stops with yellow signs, you must buy your ticket from the automatic machine (or use an Oyster) before boarding. Buses stop on request, so clearly signal the driver with an outstretched arm.

LONDON'S OYSTER DIET

To get the most out of London, you need to be able to jump on and off public transport like a local, not scramble to buy a ticket at hefty rates each time. The best and cheapest way to do this is with an Oyster card, a reusable smartcard on which you can load prepaid credit or Travelcards, valid for periods from a day to a year. The card itself is £5, which is fully refundable when you leave.

London is divided into concentric transport zones, although most visitor destinations are in Zones 1 and 2. Travelcard tickets will give you unlimited transport on the tube, buses and rail services within these zones. All you need to do is touch your card to the yellow sensors on the station turnstiles or at the front of the bus.

For pay-as-you-go, the fare will be deducted from the credit on your card at a much lower rate than if you were buying a one-off paper ticket. An oyster bus trip costs £1.45 as opposed to £2.40 for an individual fare, while a Zone 1 tube journey is £2.20 as opposed to £4.70. Even better, in any single day your fares will be capped at the equivalent of the Oyster day-pass rate for the zones you've travelled in (Zones 1 and 2 peak/off-peak £8.40/7).

Assuming you avoid peak hours (6.30am to 9.30am and 4pm to 7pm), this ready reckoner gives the cheapest options for your length of stay:

One to four days Prepay

Five to 24 days Weeklies topped up with prepay for any remaining days

Twenty-five to 31 days Monthly

London Underground, DLR & Overground

'The tube', as it's universally known, burrows throughout London and into the surrounding counties, with services running every few minutes from roughly 5.30am to 12.30am (from 7am to 11.30pm Sunday).

It's easy to use. Tickets (or Oyster card top-ups) can be purchased from counters or machines at the entrance to each station using either cash or credit card. They're then inserted into the slot on the turnstiles (or you touch your Oyster card on the yellow reader), and the barrier opens.

Also included within the network are the driverless Docklands Light Railway (DLR), and the train lines shown on tube maps as 'Overground'. The DLR links the City to Docklands, Greenwich and London City Airport.

The tube map itself is an acclaimed graphic design work, using coloured lines to show how the 14 different routes intersect. However, it's not remotely to scale. The distances between stations become greater the further from central London you travel, while Leicester Sq and Covent Garden stations are only 250m apart.

Train

Particularly south of the river, where tube lines are in shorter supply, the various rail companies are an important part of the public transport picture. Most stations are now fitted with Oyster readers and accept Travelcards. If you travel outside your zone you'll need to have enough prepay credit on your Oyster card to cover the additional charge. As not all stations have turnstiles, it's important to remember to tap-in and tap-out at the Oyster reader at the station or your card will register an unfinished journey and you're likely to be charged extra. You can still buy a paper ticket from machines or counters at train stations.

TAXI

London's famous black cabs are available for hire when the yellow light above the windscreen is lit. To get an all-London licence, cabbies must do 'The Knowledge', which tests them on up to 25,000 streets within a 6-mile radius of Charing Cross and all points of interest from hotels to churches. Fares are metered, with flag fall of £2.40 and the additional rate dependent on time of day, distance travelled and taxi speed. A one-mile trip will cost between £5.60 and £8.80. To order a black cab by phone, try **Computer Cabs** (📞 cash 020-7908 0207, credit card 020-7432 1432; www.comcablondon.com); it charges a £2 booking fee. Find the nearest black cab by downloading the **Hailo** (www.hailocab.com) app to your mobile.

Licensed minicabs operate via agencies (most busy areas have a walk-in office with drivers waiting). They're a cheaper alternative to black cabs and quote trip fares in advance. To find a local minicab firm, visit www.tfl.gov.uk.

There have been many reports of sexual assault and theft by unlicensed minicab drivers. Only use drivers from proper agencies; licensed minicabs aren't allowed to tout for business or pick you up off the street without a booking, so avoid the shady characters who hang around outside nightclubs or bars.

Canterbury & Southeast England

Best Places to Eat

➜ Deeson's (p146)

➜ Allotment (p155)

➜ Iydea (p167)

➜ Terre à Terre (p167)

➜ Town House (p170)

Best Places to Stay

➜ Bleak House (p150)

➜ Jeake's House (p158)

➜ Wallett's Court (p155)

➜ Reading Rooms (p149)

➜ Hotel Una (p166)

Why Go?

Rolling chalk hills, venerable Victorian resorts, fields of hops and grapes sweetening in the sun: welcome to England's southeast, four soothing counties' worth of country houses, fairy-tale castles and the country's finest food and drink. That fruit-ripening sun shines brightest and longest on the coast, warming a string of seaside towns wedged between formidable chalk cliffs. There's something for everyone here, from the medieval quaintness of Sandwich to the bohemian spirit of hedonistic Brighton and the more genteel air of Eastbourne.

The southeast is also pock-marked with reminders of darker days. The region's position as the front line against Continental invaders has left a wealth of turbulent history, including the 1066 battlefield, Dover Castle's secret war tunnels and scattered Roman ruins.

England's spiritual heart is Canterbury; its cathedral and ancient Unesco-listed attractions are essential viewing for any 21st-century pilgrim.

When to Go

➜ May is a good time to get creative in Brighton at Great Britain's second-largest arts festival.

➜ During June, don your top hat and breeches to revel in frilly Victoriana at the Dickens Festival in Broadstairs.

➜ Any time between May and October is ideal for a hike along the South Downs Way, which runs the length of England's newest national park.

➜ In summer head to Thanet's glorious beaches for some proper seaside fun.

🏃 Activities

The southeast of England may be Britain's most densely populated corner, but there are still plenty of off-the-beaten-track walking and cycling routes to enjoy.

Cycling

Finding quiet roads for cycle touring takes a little extra perseverance in the southeast of England, but the effort is richly rewarded. Long-distance routes that form part of the National Cycle Network (NCN; www.sustrans. org.uk) include the following:

Downs & Weald Cycle Route (110 miles; NCN Routes 2, 20 & 21) London to Brighton and on to Hastings.

Garden of England Cycle Route (165 miles; NCN Routes 1 & 2) London to Dover and then Hastings.

You'll also find less demanding routes on the NCN website. Meanwhile, there are plenty of uppers and downers to challenge mountain bikers on walking trails, such as the South Downs Way National Trail, which takes between two and four days to complete.

Walking

Two long-distance trails meander steadily westward through the region, and there are plenty of shorter ambles to match your schedule, stamina and scenery wishlist.

South Downs Way National Trail (www. nationaltrail.co.uk/southdowns) This 100-mile National Trail through England's newest national park is a beautiful roller-coaster walk along prehistoric drove roads between Winchester and Eastbourne.

North Downs Way National Trail (www. nationaltrail.co.uk/northdowns) This 153-mile walk begins near Farnham in Surrey, but one of its most beautiful sections runs from near Ashford to Dover; a loop takes in Canterbury near its end.

1066 Country Walk Heads from Pevensey Castle to Rye (32 miles) and serves as a continuation of the South Downs Way.

🛈 Information

Kent Attractions (www.kentattractions.co.uk)
Tourism South East (www.visitsoutheastengland.com) The official website for south and southeast England.
Visit Kent (www.visitkent.co.uk)
Visit Surrey (www.visitsurrey.com)
Visit Sussex (www.visitsussex.org)

🛈 Getting There & Around

The southeast is easily explored by train or bus, and many attractions can be visited in a day trip from London. Contact the National Traveline (www.travelinesoutheast.org.uk) for comprehensive information about public transport.

BUS

Explorer Tickets (adult/child £6.20/3.10) provide unlimited day-long travel on most buses throughout the region. Buy them on the first bus you board.

TRAIN

Secure 33% discounts on most rail fares in the southeast by purchasing a Network Railcard (www.network-railcard.co.uk; per year £30). Three adults can travel with you for the same discounted fare, and you save 60% on fares for children under 15.

KENT

Kent isn't described as the garden of England for nothing. Within its sea-lined borders you'll find a fragrant landscape of gentle hills, fertile farmland, cultivated country estates and fruit-laden orchards. It could also be described as the beer garden of England as it produces the world-renowned Kent hops and some of the country's finest ales and wines from its numerous vineyards. At its heart is spellbinding Canterbury, crowned by its enthralling cathedral.

You'll also find beautiful coastal stretches dotted with beach towns and villages, from old-school Broadstairs to gentrified Whitstable and the aesthetically challenged port town of Dover.

Canterbury

POP 151,200

Canterbury tops the charts for English cathedral cities and is one of southern England's top attractions. Many consider the World Heritage–listed cathedral that dominates its centre to be one of Europe's finest, and the town's narrow medieval alleyways, riverside gardens and ancient city walls are a joy to explore. But Canterbury isn't just a showpiece for the past – it's a spirited place with an energetic student population and a wide choice of contemporary bars, restaurants and arts venues. Book ahead for the best hotels and eateries: pilgrims may no longer flock here in their thousands, but tourists certainly do.

Canterbury & Southeast England Highlights

1 Shopping, tanning and partying in **Brighton & Hove** (p163), hedonist capital of the southeast

2 Making a pilgrimage to **Canterbury** (p139), one of England's most important religious sites

3 Exploring the atmospheric WWII tunnels beneath sprawling **Dover Castle** (p153)

4 Wandering the cobbled lanes of **Rye** (p158), one of England's prettiest towns

5 Kicking back at the moated marvel that is **Leeds Castle** (p148)

6 Scrambling up **Beachy Head** (p162), a spectacular headland in snow-white chalk

7 Shaking out your beach towel for some seaside fun on the **Isle of Thanet** (p149)

8 Getting hopelessly lost in the crooked medieval streets of **Sandwich** (p151)

History

Canterbury's past is as rich as it comes. From AD 200 there was a Roman town here, which later became the capital of the Saxon kingdom of Kent. When St Augustine arrived in England from Africa in 597 to bring the Christian message to the pagan hordes, he chose Canterbury as his *cathedra* (primary seat) and set about building an abbey on the outskirts of town. Following the martyrdom of Thomas Becket, Archbishop of Canterbury, the town became northern Europe's most important pilgrimage destination, which in turn prompted Geoffrey Chaucer's *The Canterbury Tales,* one of the most outstanding works in English literature.

Despite its blasphemous murders and rampant tourism, the city of Canterbury still remains the primary seat for the Church of England.

◉ Sights

★ **Canterbury Cathedral**   CATHEDRAL
(www.canterbury-cathedral.org; adult/concession £10.50/9.50, tour adult/concession £5/4, audio tour adult/concession £4/3; ⊙ 9am-5pm Mon-Sat, 12.30pm-2.30pm Sun) A rich repository of more than 1400 years of Christian history, the Church of England's mother ship is a truly extraordinary place with an absorbing history. This Gothic cathedral, the highlight of the city's World Heritage Sites, is southeast England's top tourist attraction as well as a place of worship. It's also the site of English history's most famous murder: Archbishop Thomas Beckett was done in here in 1170. Allow at least two hours.

The cathedral is an overwhelming edifice crammed with enthralling stories, arresting architecture and a real and enduring sense of spirituality – although visitors can't help but pick up on the ominous undertones of violence and bloodshed.

Canterbury

This ancient structure is packed with monuments commemorating the nation's battles. Also here are the grave and heraldic tunic of one of the nation's most famous warmongers, Edward the Black Prince (1330–76). The spot in the northwest transept where Becket met his grisly end has drawn pilgrims for more than 800 years and is marked by a flickering candle and a striking modern altar.

Beside the altar is the doorway to the crypt. This cavernous space is the cathedral's highlight, the only survivor from the last fire in 1174, which destroyed the rest of the building. Look for the amazingly well-preserved carvings among the forest of pillars.

The wealth of detail in the cathedral is immense and unrelenting, so it's well worth joining a one-hour tour (three daily, from Monday to Saturday) or taking a 40-minute self-guided audio tour.

Canterbury Heritage Museum　MUSEUM
(www.canterbury-museums.co.uk; Stour St; adult/child £8/free; ⊙11am-5pm daily) This fine 14th-century building, once the Poor Priests' Hospital, now houses the city's captivating museum. It contains a jumble of exhibits ranging from pre-Roman times to the assassination of Thomas Becket, and from the likes of Joseph Conrad to locally born celebs. The kids' room is excellent, with a memorable glimpse of real medieval poo among other fun activities. Train fans can admire the *Invicta* locomotive, which ran on the world's third passenger railway, the 'Crab & Winkle' Canterbury–Whitstable line.

The building also houses the Rupert Bear Museum (Rupert's creator, Mary Tourtel, was born in Canterbury) and a gallery celebrating another old-time children's favourite TV show, *Bagpuss*.

St Augustine's Abbey　RUIN
(EH; Longport; adult/child £5/3; ⊙10am-6pm Jul & Aug, to 5pm Wed-Sun Apr-Jun & Sep-Oct, to 4pm Sat & Sun Nov-Mar) An integral but often overlooked part of the Canterbury World Heritage Site, St Augustine's Abbey was founded in AD 597, marking the rebirth of Christianity in southern England. Later requisitioned as a royal palace, it fell into disrepair and now only stumpy foundations remain. A small museum and a worthwhile free audio tour do their best to underline the site's importance and put flesh back onto its now-humble bones.

St Martin's Church　CHURCH
(www.martinpaul.org; North Holmes Rd; ⊙11am-4pm Tue, Thu & Sat Apr-Sep, to 3pm Oct-Mar) This stumpy little building just off the road from Canterbury to Sandwich is thought to be England's oldest parish church in continuous use. It's also where Queen Bertha (wife of the Saxon King Ethelbert) welcomed St Augustine when he arrived in England in the 6th century. The original Saxon church was swallowed up by a medieval refurbishment, but is still worth the walk out of town to see.

CANTERBURY & SOUTHEAST ENGLAND CANTERBURY

Canterbury

Eastbridge Hospital
HISTORIC BUILDING

(www.eastbridgehospital.org.uk; 25 High St; adult/child £2/1; ⊙10am-5pm Mon-Sat) A 'place of hospitality' for pilgrims, soldiers and the elderly since 1180, Eastbridge Hospital of St Thomas the Martyr is the last of many such buildings in Canterbury still open to the public. It's worth a visit for the Romanesque undercroft and historic chapel. The 16th-century almshouses, still in use, sit astride Britain's oldest road bridge, dating back more than 800 years.

Roman Museum
MUSEUM

(Butchery Lane; adult/child £6/free; ⊙10am-5pm) Given a facelift in 2013 after a reprieve from council cuts, this fascinating subterranean archaeological site gives an insight into Canterbury's everyday life almost two millennia ago. Visitors can stroll a reconstructed Roman marketplace and rooms, including a kitchen, as well as view Roman mosaic floors. Everything you see here was only discovered after WWII bombs did a bit of impromptu excavation.

West Gate Towers
MUSEUM

(St Peter's St) The city's only remaining medieval gateway has become Canterbury's most-discussed sight in recent years. Under threat from council cuts in 2011, it was taken over by a local businessman who spent lavishly turning it into a family attraction. His sudden death in early 2012 left the towers closed (again) and it's still uncertain what will become of them. Until they reopen, entertain yourself watching buses, their wing mirrors folded back, as they squeeze through the medieval archway.

Greyfriars Chapel
CHURCH

(⊙2-4pm Mon-Sat Easter-Sep) You'll find Greyfriars Chapel in serene riverside gardens behind Eastbridge Hospital. The first mon-astery built in England by Franciscan monks in 1267, its grounds are a tranquil spot to unfurl the picnic blanket.

Canterbury Tales
EXHIBITION

(www.canterburytales.org.uk; St Margaret's St; adult/child £8.50/6.25; ⊙10am-5pm Mar-Oct) This ambitious three-dimensional interpretation of Chaucer's classic tales using jerky animatronics and audioguides is certainly entertaining, but could never do full justice to the original work. It does, however, provide a lighthearted introduction for the young or uninitiated.

Beaney House of Art & Knowledge
MUSEUM

(18 High St; ⊙9am-5pm Mon-Wed, Fri & Sat, to 7pm Thu, 10am-5pm Sun) FREE This mock-Tudor edifice is the grandest on the main shopping thoroughfare, if not the most authentic. Formerly called the Royal Museum & Art Gallery, it has housed Canterbury's main library, a museum and an art gallery since 1899 – it's current name is in honour of the 19th-century benefactor who funded the original building. In addition to the city's main library and the tourist office, the mixed bag of museum exhibitions is worth half an hour between the main sights.

There's also a good cafe and interesting temporary exhibitions (admission sometimes charged).

☞ Tours

Canterbury Historic River Tours
BOAT TOUR

(☏07790-534744; www.canterburyrivertours.co.uk; Kings Bridge; adult/child £8.50/5; ⊙10am-5pm Mar-Oct) Knowledgeable guides double up as energetic oars on these fascinating River Stour mini cruises, which depart from behind the Old Weaver's House.

THE MARTYRDOM OF THOMAS BECKET

Not one to shy away from cronyism, in 1162 King Henry II appointed his mate Thomas Becket to the highest clerical office in the land, figuring it would be easier to force the increasingly vocal religious lobby to fall into line if he was pals with the archbishop. Unfortunately for Henry, he underestimated how seriously Thomas would take the job, and the archbishop soon began to disagree with almost everything the king said or did. By 1170 Henry had become exasperated with his former favourite and suggested to four of his knights that Thomas was too much to bear. Becket was murdered on 29 December. Becket's martyrdom – and canonisation in double-quick time (1173) – catapulted Canterbury Cathedral to the top of the league of northern European pilgrimage sites. Mindful of the growing criticism of his role in Becket's murder, Henry arrived in Canterbury in 1174 for a dramatic *mea culpa* and, after allowing himself to be whipped and scolded, was granted absolution.

Canterbury River Navigation Company
BOAT TOUR

(☑ 07816-760869; www.crnc.co.uk; Westgate Gardens; adult/child from £9/4; ☺ Apr-Oct) Weather permitting, this company offers relaxing punt trips on the River Stour.

Canterbury Guided Tours
WALKING TOUR

(☑ 01227-459779;www.canterburyguidedtours.com; adult/child/concession£7/5/6.50; ☺ 11am Feb-Oct, 11am & 2pm Jul-Sep) Guided walking tours leave from opposite the Canturbury Cathedral entrance. Tickets can be purchased from the tourist office.

✸ Festivals & Events

Canterbury Festival
PERFORMING ARTS

(☑ 01227-787787; www.canterburyfestival.co.uk; ☺ Oct) Myriad musicians, comedians, theatre groups and other artists from around the world come to party during this festival, which runs for the last two weeks in October.

🛏 Sleeping

Kipp's Independent Hostel
HOSTEL £

(☑ 01227-786121; www.kipps-hostel.com; 40 Nunnery Fields; dm/s/d £19.50/28.50/57; @ 🗢) Occupying a red-brick town house in a quietish residential area less than a mile from the city centre, these superb backpacker digs enjoy a homely atmosphere, clean (though cramped) dorms and rave reviews.

Yew Tree Park
CAMPSITE £

(☑ 01227-700306; www.yewtreepark.com; Stone St; sites per tent & 2 adults £14.20-24.50; ☺ Apr-Sep; 🅿@🗢🏊) Family-run campsite set in gentle rolling countryside 5 miles southeast of the city. Phone ahead for directions and transport information.

House of Agnes
HOTEL ££

(☑ 01227-472185; www.houseofagnes.co.uk; 71 St Dunstan's St; r from £85-130; @🗢) This rather wonky 13th-century beamed inn, mentioned in Dickens' *David Copperfield,* has eight themed rooms bearing names such as 'Marrakesh' (Moorish), 'Venice' (carnival masks), 'Boston' (light and airy) and 'Canterbury' (antiques and heavy fabrics). If you prefer your room to have straight lines and right angles, there are eight less exciting, but no less comfortable, rooms in an annexe in the walled garden.

Arthouse B&B
B&B ££

(☑ 07976-725457; www.arthousebandb.com; 24 London Rd; r £75; 🅿🗢) A night at Canterbury's most laid-back digs, which are

ⓘ CANTERBURY ATTRACTIONS PASSPORT
Canterbury Attractions Passport (adult/child £28/13) The Canterbury Attractions Passport gives entry to the Canterbury Cathedral, the Canterbury Tales and any one of the city's museums as well as other discounts. It's available from the tourist office.

housed in a 19th-century fire station, is a bit like sleeping over at a really cool art student's pad. The theme is funky and eclectic, with furniture by local designers and artwork by the instantly likeable artist owners, who have a house-studio out back.

The organic continental breakfast is laid out in the guest kitchen, with a hostel-like vibe. Only one of the three rooms is en suite.

Cathedral Gate Hotel
HOTEL ££

(☑ 01227-464381; www.cathgate.co.uk; 36 Burgate; s/d £50/112, without bathroom £50/81.50; 🗢) Predating the spectacular cathedral gate it adjoins, this quaint 15th-century hotel is a medieval warren of steep staircases and narrow passageways leading to 27 pleasingly old-fashioned rooms with angled floors, low doors and cockeyed walls. Some have cathedral views, while others overlook pretty Buttermarket. There's no lift.

Magnolia House
B&B ££

(☑ 01227-765121;www.magnoliahousecanterbury.co .uk; 36 St Dunstan's Tce; s/d from £50/95; 🅿@🗢) An alluringly cosy Georgian guesthouse, Magnolia House comes complete with beautifully appointed if slightly over-filled rooms, lovely gardens and big cooked breakfasts. Head up St Dunstan's St from the West Gate for about 400m until you reach a roundabout; turn left and St Dunstan's Terrace is the second on the left.

★ Abode Canterbury
HOTEL £££

(☑ 01227-766266; www.abodehotels.co.uk; 30-33 High St; r from £143; 🗢) The 72 rooms at this supercentral hotel, the only boutique hotel in town, are graded from 'comfortable' to 'fabulous', and for the most part live up to their names. They come with features such as handmade beds, cashmere throws, velour bathrobes, beautiful modern bathrooms and little tuckboxes of locally produced snacks. There's a splendid champagne bar, restaurant and tavern, too.

THE CANTERBURY TALES

If English literature has a father figure, then it is Geoffrey Chaucer (1342–1400). Chaucer was the first English writer to introduce characters – rather than 'types' – into fiction, and he did so to greatest effect in his best-known work, *The Canterbury Tales*.

Written between 1387 and his death, in the hard-to-decipher Middle English of the day, Chaucer's *Tales* is an unfinished series of 24 vivid stories told by a party of pilgrims journeying between London and Canterbury. Chaucer successfully created the illusion that the pilgrims, not Chaucer (though he appears in the tales as himself), are telling the stories, which gave him unprecedented freedom as an author. *The Canterbury Tales* remains one of the pillars of the literary canon. But more than that, it's a collection of rollicking good yarns of adultery, debauchery, crime and edgy romance, and is filled with Chaucer's witty observations about human nature.

✗ Eating

Boho
INTERNATIONAL £

(43 St Peter's St; snacks £4-14; ⊙9am-6pm Mon-Sat, 10am-5pm Sun) This hip eatery in a prime spot on the main drag is extraordinarily popular and you'll be lucky to get a table on busy shopping days. Cool tunes lilt through the chic retro dining space while chilled diners chow down on humungous burgers, full-monty breakfasts and imaginative, owner-cooked international mains. Boho doesn't do bookings, so be prepared to queue.

Veg Box Cafe
VEGETARIAN £

(www.thevegboxcafe.co.uk; 1 Jewry Lane; mains £7; ⊙10am-6pm Mon-Sat; 🖉) Perched above Canterbury's top veggie food store, this laid-back and welcoming spot uses only the freshest, locally sourced organic ingredients in its dishes.

Tiny Tim's Tearoom
CAFE £

(34 St Margaret's St; mains £7-9; ⊙9.30am-5pm Tue-Sat, 10.30am-4pm Sun) Swish 1930s English tearoom offering hungry shoppers big breakfasts bursting with Kentish ingredients, and tiers of cakes, crumpets, cucumber sandwiches and scones plastered in clotted cream.

★ Deeson's
BRITISH ££

(📞01227-767854; 25-27 Sun St; mains £6-16; ⊙noon-3pm & 5-10pm Mon-Sat, noon-10pm Sun) Put the words 'local', 'seasonal' and 'tasty' together and you have this superb British eatery. Local fruit and veg; award-winning wines, beers and ciders; fish from Kent's coastal waters; and the odd ingredient from the proprietor's own allotment are all served in a straightforward, contemporary setting just a Kentish apple's throw from the Canterbury Cathedral gates.

Goods Shed
MARKET, RESTAURANT ££

(www.thegoodsshed.co.uk; Station Rd West; mains £12-20; ⊙market 9am-7pm Tue-Sat, 10am-4pm Sun, restaurant 8am-9.30pm Tue-Sat, 9am-3pm Sun) Farmers market, food hall and fabulous restaurant rolled into one, this converted warehouse by the Canterbury West train station is a hit with everyone from self-caterers to sit-down gourmets. The chunky wooden tables sit slightly above the market hubbub but in full view of its appetite-whetting stalls, and daily specials exploit fresh farm goodies.

🍷 Drinking & Nightlife

Parrot
PUB

(1-9 Church Lane; ⊙noon-11pm) Built in 1370 on Roman foundations, Canterbury's oldest boozer has a snug, beam-rich pub downstairs and a much-lauded dining room upstairs under yet more ageing oak. Needless to say, many a local microbrewed ale is pulled in both venues.

Thomas Becket
PUB

(21 Best Lane; ⊙noon-3pm & 5-9pm Mon-Thu, to 9.30pm Fri, to 9.30pm Sat, to 9pm Sun) A classic English pub with a garden's worth of hops hanging from its timber frame, Thomas Becket has several quality ales to sample. Traditional decor includes copper pots, comfy seating and a fireplace to cosy up to on winter nights. It also serves decent pub grub.

Micro Roastery
CAFE

(www.microroastery.co.uk; 4 St Margaret's St; ⊙8am-6pm Mon-Fri, from 9am Sat, 10am-5pm Sun; 🛜) Owned by an Anglo-Peruvian couple, this new cafe imports, roasts, grinds and sells its unsurpassed beans and blends. There's local art on the walls; the furniture is upholstered in coffee-bean sacks; and a La Marzocco espresso machine pumps out strong brews.

Alberry's Wine Bar
CLUB

(www.alberrys.co.uk; 38 St Margaret's St; ⊙11am-3am) An after-hours music bar that puts on everything from smooth live jazz to DJ-led drum and bass to commercial pop. Relax over a French Kiss cocktail upstairs before heading down to the basement bar.

Chill Nightclub
CLUB

(www.chill-nightclub.com; 41 St George's Pl) Small, cheesy nightclub with Alphabeats theme nights on Wednesdays and a big Sound of Saturday that runs well into Sunday morning.

☆ Entertainment

New Marlowe Theatre
THEATRE

(✆01227-787787; www.newmarlowetheatre.org.uk; The Friars) Canterbury's main theatre attracts top acts and fast-selling productions. Check out the bizarre auditorium, with its dark faux veneers contrasting sharply with the lifejacket-orange seating.

🔒 Shopping

Canterbury has Kent's best shopping. For mainstream stores head for the east end of the main street (High St, St George's St) but for quirkier independents try the west end of High St, St Peter's St and the so-called 'King's Mile' (Palace St, Borough and Northgate).

Revivals
CLOTHING

(42 St Peter's St; ⊙10am-5pm Mon-Sat, to 4pm Sun) One of the southeast's best vintage-clothing emporia.

Chaucer Bookshop
BOOKS

(6-7 Beer Cart Lane; ⊙10am-5pm Mon-Sat, 11am-4pm Sun) Antiquarian and used books.

ℹ Information

Post Office (19 St George's St; ⊙9am-5.30pm Mon-Sat) On the 1st floor of WH Smiths.

Tourist Office (✆01227-378100; www.canterbury.co.uk; 18 High St; ⊙9am-5pm Mon-Wed, Fri & Sat, to 7pm Thu, 10am-5pm Sun) In the Beaney House of Art & Knowledge. Staff can help book accommodation, excursions and theatre tickets.

ℹ Getting There & Away

The city's **bus station** (St George's Lane) is just within the city walls on St George's Lane. There are two train stations, Canterbury East for London Victoria and Canterbury West for London's Charing Cross/St Pancras stations.

BUS

Canterbury connections:

Dover National Express; £4.90, 40 minutes, hourly

London Victoria National Express; £14.40, two hours, hourly

Margate £5.10, 50 minutes, three per hour

Ramsgate £5.10 45 minutes, hourly

Sandwich £3.50, 40 minutes, three hourly

Whitstable £4.50, 30 minutes, every 10 minutes

TRAIN

Canterbury connections:

Dover Priory £8, 25 minutes, every 30 minutes

A SWIG OF KENT & SUSSEX

With booze cruises over to Calais almost a thing of the past, many Kent and Sussex drinkers are rediscovering their counties' superb home-grown beverages. Both counties produce some of the most delicious ales in the country and the southeast's wines are even outgunning some traditional Continental vintners.

Kent's **Shepherd Neame Brewery** (✆01795-542016; www.shepherdneame.co.uk; 10 Court St, Faversham; tours £12.50; ⊙call ahead or see website for tour times) is Britain's oldest and produces aromatic ales brewed from Kent-grown premium hops. Sussex's reply is **Harveys Brewery** (✆01273-480217; www.harveys.org.uk; Bridge Wharf, Lewes; per person £2.50; ⊙evenings three times a week Jun-Jul & Sep-Nov), which perfumes Lewes town centre with a hop-laden scent. Book in advance for tours of either brewery.

Mention 'English wine' not too long ago and you'd likely hear a snort of derision. Not any more. Thanks to warmer temperatures and determined winemakers, English wine, particularly of the sparkling variety, is developing a fan base all of its own.

Award-winning vineyards can be found in both Sussex and Kent, whose chalky soils are likened to France's Champagne region. Many vineyards now offer tours and wine tastings. Some of the most popular are **Biddenden Vineyards** (✆01580-291726; www.biddenden vineyards.com; admission free ; ⊙tours 10am Wed & Sat), 1.2 miles from Wealden, and **Chapel Down Vinery** (✆01580-766111; www.englishwinesgroup.com; Tenterden; admission £10; ⊙tours daily Jun-Sep, weekends May & Oct), located 2.5 miles south of Tenterden on the B2082.

WHITSTABLE

Perhaps it's the oysters, harvested since Roman times... Maybe it's the weatherboard houses and shingle beach... Perhaps it's the pleasingly old-fashioned main street with petite galleries, been-there-forever outfitters and emporia of vintage clothing... Most likely it's for all of these reasons that Whitstable has become a bit of a weekend mecca for metropolitan types looking for refuge from the city hassle.

If it's the oysters you fancy, **Wheeler's Oyster Bar** (☏01227-273311; 8 High St; mains £18.50-22.50; ⊙10.30am-9pm Mon & Tue, from 10.15am Thu, 10.15am-9.30pm Fri, 10am-10pm Sat, 11.30am-9pm Sun) is the place to head, but you'll have to book ahead and bring your own wine. Sittings are at 1pm, 3pm, 5pm & 7.30pm. While you're here, take a stroll along the beach or a spin around the **Whitstable Museum & Gallery** (www.whitstable -museum.co.uk; 5 Oxford St; adult/concession £3/2; ⊙11am-4.30pm), which has a corner dedicated to actor Peter Cushing, star of several Hammer Horror films and the town's most famous resident, who died in 1994

Whitstable has no tourist office, but you can pick up maps and other information at the **library** (31-33 Oxford St; ⊙9am-6pm Mon-Fri, to 5pm Sat, 10am-4pm Sun). Bus 4 departs for Canterbury (30 minutes) every 10 minutes.

London St Pancras High-speed service; £33.70, one hour, hourly

London Victoria/Charing Cross £28.40, 1¾ hours, two hourly

ⓘ Getting Around

Canterbury's centre is mostly set up for pedestrians. Car parks are dotted along and just inside the walls, but to avoid heavy traffic day-trippers may prefer to use one of three Park & Ride sites, which cost £3 per day and connect to the centre by bus every eight minutes (7am to 7.30pm Monday to Saturday).

Leeds Castle

This immense moated pile just east of Maidstone is for many the world's most romantic **castle** (www.leeds-castle.com; adult/child £21/13.50; ⊙10am-6pm Apr-Sep, to 5pm Oct-Mar), and it's certainly one of the most visited in Britain. The formidable, hefty structure balancing on two islands is known as something of a 'ladies castle'. This stems from the fact that in its more than 1000 years of history, it has been home to a who's who of medieval queens, most famously Henry VIII's first wife, Catherine of Aragon.

The castle was transformed from fortress to lavish palace over the centuries, and its last owner, the high-society hostess Lady Baillie, used it as a princely family home and party pad to entertain the likes of Errol Flynn, Douglas Fairbanks and John F Kennedy.

The castle's vast estate offers enough attractions of its own to justify a day trip: peaceful walks, a duckery, aviary and falcon-

ry demonstrations. You'll also find possibly the world's sole dog-collar museum, plenty of kids' attractions and a hedge maze, overseen by a grassy bank from where fellow travellers can shout encouragement or misdirections.

Since Lady Baillie's death in 1974, a private trust has managed the property. This means that some parts of the castle are periodically closed for private events.

Trains run from London Victoria to Bearsted, where you catch a special shuttle coach to the castle.

Margate

POP 40,400

A popular resort for more than two centuries, Margate's late 20th-century slump was long and bleak as British holidaymakers ditched Victorian frump for the carefree *costas* of Spain. But this grand old seaside, with fine-sand beaches and artistic associations, has bounced off the bottom. Major cultural regeneration projects – including the spectacular Turner Contemporary art gallery – are slowly reversing the town's fortunes, and on busy days even the odd non-English speaker can be overheard in the newly minted cafes and rejuvenated old town.

◉ Sights

★**Turner Contemporary**   GALLERY
(www.turnercontemporary.org; Rendezvous (Seafront); ⊙10am-6pm Tue-Sun) FREE This blockbuster contemporary art gallery, bolted together on the site of the seafront guest-

house where master painter JMW Turner used to stay, is one of East Kent's top attractions. Within the strikingly featureless shell, the only thing distracting the eye, apart from the artwork on display, is the sea view from the floor-to-ceiling windows. These allow you to appreciate the very thing Turner loved so much about Margate – the sea, sky and refracted light of the north Kent coast.

The gallery is attracting top-notch contemporary installations by high-calibre artists such as Tracey Emin (who grew up in Margate) and Alex Katz, so catch a free gallery tour (Fridays and weekends at 11.30am).

Shell Grotto   GROTTO, CAVE
(www.shellgrotto.co.uk; Grotto Hill; adult/child £3.50/1.50; ⊙10am-5pm Apr-Oct, 11am-4pm Sat & Sun Nov-Mar) Margate's unique attraction is a mysterious subterranean grotto, discovered in 1835. It's a claustrophobic collection of rooms and passageways embedded with 4.6 million shells arranged in symbol-rich mosaics. It has inspired feverish speculation over the years; some think it a 2000-year-old pagan temple, others an elaborate 19th-century hoax. Either way, it's an exquisite place worth seeing.

🛏 Sleeping & Eating

★ **Reading Rooms**   B&B £££
(☎01843-225166; www.thereadingroomsmargate.
co.uk; 31 Hawley Sq; r £180; 🐾) Occupying an unmarked 18th-century Georgian town house on a tranquil square just five minutes' walk from the sea, this luxury boutique B&B is as stylish as they come. Generously cut rooms with waxed wooden floors and beautiful French antique reproduction furniture contrast with the 21st-century bathrooms fragrant with Ren cosmetics. Breakfast is served in your room. Booking essential.

Sands Hotel   BOUTIQUE HOTEL £££
(☎01843-228228; www.sandshotelmargate.co.uk; 16 Marine Dr; r £120-190; 🏵🐾) This beautifully styled boutique hotel sits right on the Margate seafront. It features an understated sand-hued theme throughout; the southeast's best bathrooms; and a restaurant with spectacular bay views, which around half of the rooms also share. The entrance is hidden under the arches on the seafront next to the hotel's very own summertime ice cream parlour.

Mad Hatter   CAFE £
(9 Lombard St; snacks & light meals £3.50-11; ⊙11am-5.30pm Sat) This unmissable cuckoo eatery run by a top-hatted proprietor packs two rooms of a 1690s house with regalia and knick-knackery from down the ages. Christmas decorations stay up all year and the toilets are original Victorian porcelain. The yummy cakes and snacks are all homemade.

Great British Pizza Company   PIZZA £
(14a Marine Dr; pizzas £6-9; ⊙noon-9pm Tue-Sat, to 3pm Sun) A world away from your normal 'British pizza', the delicious cheese-topped wheels at this new hang-out are made using the best local and Italian ingredients. Right on the seafront, this popular feeding spot has a funkily eclectic but simple dining space, heart-pumping coffees and gelato containing nothing that it shouldn't.

ℹ Information

Tourist Office (☎01843-577577; www.visit thanet.co.uk; Droit House, Stone Pier; ⊙10am-5pm daily Easter-Oct, to 5pm Tue-Sat Nov-Easter) Next to the Turner Contemporary art gallery, the tourist office serves all of the Isle of Thanet. It hands out *The Isle*, a glossy magazine crammed with Thanet listings.

ℹ Getting There & Away

Departure and arrival points for local buses are Queen St and adjacent Cecil St. The train station is just a few steps from the beach.

BUS

Broadstairs Thanet Loop Bus; £1.80, up to every ten minutes

Canterbury £5.10, 50 minutes, three hourly

London Victoria National Express; £16, 2½ hours, four daily

Ramsgate Thanet Loop Bus; £2.20, up to every ten minutes

ISLE OF THANET

You won't need a wetsuit or a ferry to reach the Isle of Thanet and its towns of Margate, Ramsgate and Broadstairs: the 2-mile-wide Wantsum Channel, which divides the island from the mainland, silted up in the 16th century, transforming the East Kent landscape forever. In its island days, Thanet was the springboard for several epoch-making episodes in English history. It was here that the Romans kicked off their invasion in the 1st century AD and where St Augustine landed in AD 597 to launch his conversion of the pagans.

TRAIN

London St Pancras High-speed service, £38.10, 1½ hours, hourly

London Victoria £22.30, one hour and 50 minutes, two hourly

Broadstairs

POP 24,370

While its bigger, brasher neighbours seek to revive and regenerate themselves, quaint little Broadstairs quietly gets on with what it's done best for the past 150 years – wowing visitors with its tight sickle of reddish sand (Viking Bay) and sun-warmed lapping sea. Charles Dickens certainly thought it a pretty spot, spending most summers here between 1837 and 1859. The resort now plays the Victorian nostalgia card at every opportunity and names every second business after the works of its most famous holidaymaker.

👁 Sights

Dickens House Museum   MUSEUM

(www.dickensfellowship.org; 2 Victoria Pde; adult/child £3.60/2; ⊙2-5pm Easter-May, 10am-5pm Jun-Sep) Given a fresh lick of paint for Charles Dickens' 200th birthday in 2012, this quaint museum is Broadstairs' top attraction and the former home of Mary Pearson Strong – Dickens' inspiration for the character of Betsey Trotwood in *David Copperfield*. Diverse Dickensiana on display includes letters from the author.

🎊 Festivals & Events

Dickens Festival   ARTS

(www.broadstairsdickensfestival.co.uk) Broadstairs' biggest bash, this annual, nine-day festival held in mid-June culminates in a banquet and ball in Victorian fancy dress.

🛏 Sleeping & Eating

Copperfields Guest House   B&B ££

(☑01843-601247; www.copperfieldsbb.co.uk; 11 Queen's Rd; s/d £50/75; 🛜) 🍽 This vegetarian B&B offers three homely rooms with en suite, and a warm welcome from the owners and pet Yorkie. It also caters for vegans, and all products in the bathrooms are cruelty-free.

★ Bleak House   HISTORIC HOTEL £££

(☑01843-865338; www.bleakhousebroadstairs.co.uk; Fort Rd; r £155-250, apt £300; 🛜) Recently reopened, this former Napoleonic-era fortress overlooking the beach was converted into an opulent Victorian residence just in time for one Charles Dickens to rent it for 12 summers (1837–1859). From the lounge bar to the Copperfield suite with its Viking Bay views and five-star bathroom, the whole caboodle oozes unique period character. Building tours run from 10am to 6pm.

It was here that Dickens penned *David Copperfield* and the outline of *Bleak House*, declaring the building his favourite place to stay – when you see the views it's not hard to see why. But the highlight must be Dickens' very own bedroom and semicircular seaview study where he would write looking out across the Channel. It's worth every penny of the £250 a night rate and what a place to update your travel journal! There's a labyrinthine smuggling museum in the basement, a fancy restaurant, and a tearoom.

Oscar's Festival Cafe   CAFE £

(15 Oscar Rd; snacks £4-6.50; ⊙10.30am-5.30pm Thu-Sun) Just back from the bandstand at the southern end of Viking Bay, this hidden gem successfully recreates the buttered-toast-and-railways brand of sunny 1950s austerity that the British find so comforting.

Wyatt & Jones   BRITISH ££

(www.wyattandjones.co.uk; 23-27 Harbour St; mains £6-17; ⊙9-11am, noon-3pm & 6-11pm Mon-Sat, 12.30-5pm Sun) Broadstairs was clamouring for a contemporary British restaurant and now, just a few steps off the beach, it has one. Savour unashamedly local dishes such as partridge in crab-apple glaze, or try local bream, mussels and chips or breakfast in the uncluttered interior of gun-metal blue and scratched timber floors. Then admire your expanding waistline in the retro mirror wall.

ℹ Getting There & Away

BUS

Canterbury £5.10, 1½ hours, up to three times an hour

London Victoria National Express, £13.90, three hours, seven daily

Margate Thanet Loop Bus; £1.80, up to every ten minutes

Ramsgate Thanet Loop Bus; £1.80, up to every ten minutes

TRAIN

London St Pancras High-speed service, £38.10, one hour 20 minutes, hourly

London Victoria £22.30, two hours, twice hourly

Ramsgate

POP 40,000

The most varied of Thanet's towns, Ramsgate has a friendlier feel than rival Margate and is more vibrant than its quaint little neighbour Broadstairs. A forest of masts whistles serenely in the breeze below the handsomely curved walls of Britain's only royal harbour, and the seafront is surrounded by bars and cosmopolitan street cafes. Just one celebrity chef away from being described as 'up and coming', Ramsgate retains a shabbily undiscovered charm, its sweeping, environmentally sanctioned Blue Flag beaches and some spectacular Victorian architecture making it well worth the visit.

◉ Sights & Activities

Spitfire Memorial Museum   MUSEUM
(www.spitfiremuseum.org.uk; Manston Rd; ⊙10am-5pm Apr-Oct, to 4pm Nov-Mar) FREE Around 4 miles northwest of Ramsgate's town centre at Manston Airport, this purpose-built museum stores two WWII planes: one a Spitfire, the other a Hurricane. Both look factory-fresh but are surprisingly delicate and so, sadly, there's no clambering on board. Take bus 38 (hourly) from King St and alight at the airport, then walk about 10 minutes along Manston Rd.

Gathered around the planes are myriad flight-associated exhibits, many relating to Manston's role as an airfield during the Battle of Britain.

Ramsgate Maritime Museum   MUSEUM
(www.ramsgatemaritimemuseum.org; The Clock House, Royal Harbour; adult/child £2/1; ⊙10am-5pm Tue-Sun Easter-Sep) Interesting but erratically opening museum displaying loot from the more than 600 ships that have been wrecked on the notorious Goodwin Sands off this stretch of coast.

⌂ Sleeping & Eating

Ramsgate has two restaurant rows: Harbour St and Westcliff Arcade.

Glendevon Guesthouse   B&B ££
(☑01843-570909; www.glendevonguesthouse.co.uk; 8 Truro Rd; s/d from £52.50/70; ⊠⊙) ⊘ Run by energetic young hosts, this comfy guesthouse takes the whole ecofriendly thing very seriously, with guest recycling facilities, eco-showers and even energy-saving hairdryers. The hallways of this grand Victorian house, a block back from the Ramsgate seafront, are decorated with work by local artists. All rooms have kitchenettes, and breakfast is a convivial affair taken around a communal table.

Bon Appetit   FRENCH ££
(4 Westcliff Arcade; mains £7-21; ⊙noon-2.30pm & 7pm-late) The best eatery on Westcliff, this first-rate bistro serves up French-inspired dishes in a simple dining room or with alfresco harbour views. Ingredients on the menu are of the seasonal and locally sourced ilk, with finely crafted mains including delights such as pan-fried Kentish pheasant, line-caught sea bass, and lamb rump with rosemary and red-currant preserve.

ⓘ Information

Tourist Office (☑01843-598750; Customs House, Harbour Pde; ⊙10am-4pm Mon-Sun) A small, staffed visitor centre with out-of-hours brochure stands.

ⓘ Getting There & Away

BOAT

Euroferries (☑0844 414 5355; www.euroferries.co.uk) High-speed ferries to Boulogne (from £49 per car, 1¼ hours, four times daily)

BUS

Broadstairs Thanet Loop Bus; £1.80, up to every ten minutes

London Victoria National Express, £13.90, three hours, seven daily

Margate Thanet Loop Bus; £2.20, up to every ten minutes

Sandwich £2.90, 25 minutes, hourly

TRAIN

London Charing Cross £22.30, two hours, two hourly

London St Pancras High-speed service, £38.50, 1¼ hours, hourly

Sandwich

POP 5000

As close as you'll get to a living museum, Sandwich was once England's fourth city (after London, Norwich and Ipswich). It's a fact hard to grasp as you ponder its drowsy medieval lanes, ancient churches, Dutch gables, crooked peg-tiled roofs and overhanging timber-framed houses. Once a port to rival London, Sandwich began its decline when the entrance to the harbour silted up in the 16th century, and this once-vital gateway to and from the Continent spent the next 400 years retreating into quaint rural obscurity. Preservation is big here, with huge local interest in period authenticity. The tiny 100-seat cinema is preserved as an art deco museum piece and the 1920s garage deals more in classic cars than modern vehicles. Within the town's historical core, unlisted buildings are the exception.

Of course, Sandwich indirectly gave the world its favourite snack when the Fourth Earl of Sandwich called for his meat to be served between two slices of bread, thus freeing him to gamble all night without leaving the table or smudging his cards. From then on, it became *de rigueur* to ask for meat 'like Sandwich' and the rest is fast-food history, although the town makes precious little of it.

◉ Sights & Activities

Sandwich's web of medieval and Elizabethan streets is perfect for ambling through and getting pleasantly lost (as many do). Strand Street in particular has one of the country's highest concentrations of half-timbered buildings. Ornate brickwork on some houses betrays the strong influence of 350 Protestant Flemish refugees (referred to as 'the Strangers'), who settled in the town in the 16th century at the invitation of Elizabeth I.

Richborough Roman Fort RUIN
(EH; Richborough Rd; adult/child £5.20/3.10; ⊙10am-6pm Apr-Sep, to 5pm Wed-Sun Oct, to 4pm Sat & Sun Nov-Mar) Roman Britain began here amid the windswept ruins of Richborough's Roman Fort, just 2 miles north of Sandwich. This is where the successful AD 43 invasion of Britain was launched. To celebrate their victory, the Romans planted a colossal triumphal arch here, the base of which remains.

The fort's clearest features today – high walls and scores of deep defensive ditches – came later when the Romans were forced to stave off increasingly vicious seaborne attacks.

To arrive as the Romans did, by boat, you can take the Sandwich River Bus from the Quay.

Sandwich Quay WATERFRONT
Several attractions line the River Stour. First up is a cute little flint-chequered Barbican tollgate built by Henry VIII, which controls traffic flow over the river's only road bridge. Nearby rises Fishergate, built in 1384 and once the main entrance to the town, through which goods from the Continent and beyond once passed. On fair-weather days, hop aboard the Sandwich River Bus (☑07958 376183; www.sandwichriverbus.co.uk; adult/child 30min trip £7/5, 1hr £12/8; ⊙every 30-60min 11am-6pm Thu-Sun Apr-Sep) beside the toll bridge for seal-spotting trips along the River Stour and in Pegwell Bay, or for an interesting way to reach Richborough.

Guildhall Museum MUSEUM
(adult/child £1/50p; ⊙10.30am-12.30pm & 2-4pm Tue, Wed, Fri & Sat, 2-4pm Thu & Sun Apr-Nov) Sandwich's small but thorough museum is a good place to start exploring the town. Exhibitions examine the town's rich past as a Cinque Port, its role in various wars, and the gruesome punishments meted out to felons, fornicators and phoney fishers.

Salutation Gardens GARDENS
(www.the-secretgardens.co.uk; The Salutation, Knightrider St; adult/child £6.50/3; ⊙10am-5pm) Just along from Fishergate, this set of exquisite gardens was laid out behind a 1912

CINQUE PORTS

Due to their proximity to Europe, southeast England's coastal towns were the frontline against raids and invasion during Anglo-Saxon times. In the absence of a professional army and navy, these ports were frequently called upon to defend themselves, and the kingdom, on land and at sea.

In 1278 King Edward I formalised this ancient arrangement by legally defining the Confederation of Cinque Ports (pronounced 'sink ports'). The five original ports – Sandwich, Dover, Hythe, Romney and Hastings – were awarded numerous perks and privileges in exchange for providing the king with ships and men. At their peak, the ports were considered England's most powerful institution after Crown and Church.

The ports' importance eventually evaporated when the shifting coastlines silted up several Cinque Port harbours and a professional navy was based at Portsmouth. But still the pomp and ceremony remain. The Lord Warden of the Cinque Ports is a prestigious post now bestowed on faithful servants of the Crown. The Queen Mother was warden until she passed away, succeeded by Admiral Lord Boyce. Previous incumbents include the Duke of Wellington and Sir Winston Churchill.

mansion by leading early 20th-century garden designers Jekyll and Lutyens. There's a superb tearoom in the grounds.

St Peter's
CHURCH

(King St; ⊘10am-5pm) The oldest church in Sandwich is now no longer used for worship. It's a real mixture of styles and years: its tower collapsed in dramatic fashion in 1661 and it was rebuilt with a bulbous cupola by the Flemish 'Strangers'.

St Mary's
CHURCH

(www.stmarysartscentre.org.uk; cnr Church St & Strand St; ⊘10am-5pm) This former church is now a multipurpose venue hosting some surprisingly big acts, and is open during the day for perusal.

🛏 Sleeping & Eating

★ Bell Hotel
HOTEL ££

(🖉01304-613388; www.bellhotelsandwich.co.uk; The Quay; s/tw/d from £95/120/165; 🕿) Today the haunt of celebrity golfers, the Bell Hotel has been sitting on the town's quay since Tudor times, though much of the remaining building is from the 19th century. A splendid sweeping staircase leads to luxurious rooms, some with pretty quay views. The Old Dining Room restaurant is one of East Kent's poshest nosh spots.

King's Arms
INN ££

(🖉01304-617330; www.kingsarms-sandwich.co.uk; cnr Church St St Mary's & Strand St; light meals £3-9, mains £10-17; 🕿) This cosy 15th-century inn opposite St Mary's church serves quality English food and very popular Sunday lunches in a beamed dining room heated by large fireplaces. There are six B&B rooms upstairs.

No Name Shop
DELI, BISTRO ££

(www.nonameshop.co.uk; No Name St; snacks £1.60-6.75, meals £6.50-14.50; ⊘8am-5pm Mon-Sat, 9am-4pm Sun) This far-from-anonymous French-owned deli (downstairs) and bistro (upstairs) near the bus stop is a pleasantly aromatic spot for a quick sandwich in Sandwich or an 'oozylicious' *croque-monsieur,* as well as more sophisticated dishes, followed by a relaxing glass of something Gallic. Very popular among locals, some of whom seem to regularly prefer it over their own kitchens.

ℹ Information

Tourist Office (🖉01304-613565; www.open-sandwich.co.uk; Guildhall, Cattle Market; ⊘10am-4pm Mon-Sat Apr-Oct) Located in the historic Guildhall.

ℹ Getting There & Away

Trains run from Dover Priory train station (22 minutes, hourly), Ramsgate (12 minutes, hourly) and London Charing Cross (£33.20, 2½ hours, hourly).

Buses also go to Ramsgate (£2.90, 22 minutes, hourly), Dover (£5.50, 45 minutes, hourly) and Canterbury (£3.50, 40 minutes, three hourly).

Dover
POP 37,090

Down-in-the-dumps Dover has certainly seen better days. Its derelict postwar architecture and shabby town centre of vacant shops is a sad introduction to England for travellers arriving on cross-Channel ferries and cruise ships, most of whom pass through quickly. Lucky, then, that the town has a couple of stellar attractions to redeem it. The port's vital strategic position so close to mainland Europe gave rise to a sprawling hilltop castle, which has some 2000 years of history to its credit. The spectacular white cliffs, as much a symbol of English wartime resilience as Winston Churchill or the Battle of Britain, rear in chalky magnificence to the east and west.

◉ Sights & Activities

★ Dover Castle
CASTLE

(EH; www.english-heritage.org.uk; adult/child £17/10.20; ⊘10am-6pm Apr-Jul & Sep, 9.30am-6pm Aug, to 5pm Oct, 10am-4pm Sat & Sun Nov-Mar; 🅿) Occupying top spot, literally and figuratively, in Dover's townscape, this most impressive of castles was built to bolster the country's weakest point at the shortest sea crossing to mainland Europe. The highlights here are the unmissable secret wartime tunnels and the Great Tower, but the huge area it sprawls across has a lot of other bits, so allow at least three hours for your visit, more if you stand to admire the views across the Channel to France.

The site has been in use for as many as 2000 years. On the vast grounds are the remains of a Roman lighthouse, which dates from AD 50 and may be the oldest standing building in Britain. Beside it lies the restored Saxon Church of St Mary in Castro.

The robust 12th-century Great Tower, with walls up to 7m thick, is a medieval warren filled with interactive exhibits and light-and-sound shows that take visitors back to the times of Henry II.

The biggest draw of all is the network of secret wartime tunnels. The claustrophobic

Dover

Dover

◎ Top Sights
1 Dover Castle C1

◎ Sights
2 Dover Museum B2
3 Roman Painted House B2

⬤ Sleeping
4 Dover Marina Hotel B3
5 East Lee Guest House B1

⊗ Eating
6 Allotment A1
7 La Salle Verte B2

chalk-hewn passageways were first excavated during the Napoleonic Wars and then expanded to house a command post and hospital in WWII. The highly enjoyable 50-minute guided tour (every 20 minutes) tells the story of one of Britain's most famous wartime operations, code-named Dynamo, which was directed from here in 1940 and saw hundreds of thousands of men evacuated from the beaches at Dunkirk. The story is told in a very effective way, with video projected sharply onto the tunnel walls and sounds rumbling through the rock. At one point the entire passageway is consumed in flames and at others visitors are plunged into complete darkness.

Dover Museum   MUSEUM
(www.dovermuseum.co.uk; Market Sq; adult/child £3.50/2.25; ⊘9.30am-5pm Mon-Sat year-round, 10am-3pm Sun Apr-Sep) By far the most enthralling exhibit in the town's three-storey museum is an astonishing 3600-year-old Bronze Age boat, discovered here in 1992. Vaunted as the world's oldest-known seagoing vessel, it measures a thumping 9.5m by 2.4m and is kept in a huge, low-lit, climate-controlled glass case.

Roman Painted House   RUIN
(New St; adult/child £3/2; ⊘10am-5pm Tue-Sun Jun-Sep) A crumbling 1960s bunker is the unlikely setting for some of the most extensive, if stunted, Roman wall paintings north of the Alps. Several scenes depict Bacchus (Roman god of wine and revelry), which makes perfect sense as this large villa was built around AD 200 as a *mansio* (hotel) for travellers needing a little lubrication to unwind.

🛏 Sleeping

B&Bs are clustered along Castle St, Maison Dieu Rd and Folkestone Rd.

Blériot's GUESTHOUSE £

(☑ 01304-211394; www.bleriotsguesthouse.co.uk; 47 Park Ave; s/d £35/52; P 🎧) Spacious eight-room guesthouse in a quiet residential location but within walking distance of all the sights. Some of the light-filled rooms have original Victorian fireplaces; there's a cosy lounge; and the hosts are the friendliest you'll meet in the southeast. Breakfast is £6 extra.

Dover Marina Hotel HOTEL ££

(☑ 01304-203633; www.dovermarinahotel.co.uk; Waterloo Cres; r £89-130; 🎧) Just a few steps from Dover's beach, this seafront hotel crams 81 rooms of varying dimensions into a gently curving 1870s edifice. The undulating corridors show the building's age, but there's nothing wonky about the rooms with their trendy ethnic fabrics, big-print wallpaper and contemporary artwork. Half the rooms have unrivalled sea views and 10 boast much-sought-after balconies.

East Lee Guest House B&B ££

(☑ 01304-210176; www.eastlee.co.uk; 108 Maison Dieu Rd; d £65-75; P 🎧) This lovely terracotta-shingled town house impresses with its grand, elegantly decorated communal areas, scrupulously maintained rooms, energetic hosts and excellent, varied breakfasts.

★**Wallett's Court** HOTEL £££

(☑ 01304-852424; www.wallettscourt.com; Westcliffe, St Margaret's-at-Cliffe; d £120-330; P 🎧🏊) With its soothing spa, first-rate restaurant and perky service, this is one relaxing country retreat. Digs at this country house set in rolling farmland range from spacious Jacobean guestrooms to beamed converted barns to a canvas wigwam (for a night of 'glamping'). Heading towards Deal, turn right off the A258 after almost 2 miles for Westcliffe.

🍴 Eating

La Salle Verte CAFE £

(14-15 Cannon St; snacks £2-6; ⊙9am-4.30pm Mon-Sat) A much-loved coffee or lunch halt with fascinating black-and-white images of old Dover lining the walls, an intimate cellar and friendly staff. Fills up at lunch, even on winter Wednesdays.

★**Allotment** BRITISH ££

(www.theallotmentdover.com; 9 High St; mains £7.50-16; ⊙8.30am-10pm Tue-Sat) Dover's best dining spot plates up local fish and regional meat, seasoned with herbs from the tranquil garden out back, for breakfast, lunch and dinner. Cleanse your palette with a Kentish wine in a relaxed setting as you admire the view of the Maison Dieu (13th-century pilgrims' hospital) directly opposite through the exquisite stained-glass frontage.

ℹ️ Information

Post Office (68-72 Pencester Rd; ⊙7am-10pm Mon-Sat, 8am-8pm Sun)

Tourist Office (☑ 01304-201066; www.whitecliffscountry.org.uk; Market Sq; ⊙9.30am-5pm Mon-Sat year-round, 10am-3pm Sun Apr-Sep) Located in the Dover Museum.

ℹ️ Getting There & Away

BOAT

Ferries depart for France from the Eastern Docks below the castle. Fares vary according to season and advance purchase. These days services seem to be in a constant state of flux.

DFDS (☑ 0871 5747235; www.dfdsseaways.co.uk) Services to Dunkirk (two hours, every two hours).

MyFerryLink (☑ 0844 2482 100; www.myferrylink.com) Services to Calais (1½ hours, five times daily).

P&O Ferries (☑ 0871 6642020; www.poferries.com) Runs to Calais (1½ hours, every 40 to 60 minutes).

BUS

Dover connections:

Canterbury £4.90, 40 minutes, four hourly

London Victoria Coach 007; £14.80, 2½ to 3½ hours, 12 daily

Sandwich £5.50, 40 minutes, hourly

TRAIN

Dover connections:

London Charing Cross £22.30, two hours, twice hourly

London St Pancras High-speed service, £38.50, one hour, hourly

Ramsgate (via Sandwich) £9.30, 35 minutes, hourly

ℹ️ Getting Around

Between 7am and 9pm, a **port shuttle bus** (£2, five minutes, every 20 minutes) runs between the Eastern Docks and the train station, a long walk apart.

Around Dover

The White Cliffs

Immortalised in song, film and literature, these iconic cliffs are embedded in the national consciousness, and are a big 'Welcome Home' sign to generations of travellers and soldiers. The cliffs rise to 100m high and extend on either side of Dover, but the best bit is the 6-mile stretch that starts about 2 miles east of town, properly known as the Langdon Cliffs.

The Langdon Cliffs are managed by the National Trust, which has a tourist office (☑01304-202756; ☉10am-5pm Mar-Oct, 11am-4pm Nov-Feb) and car park (nonmembers £3 per park per day) 2 miles east of Dover along Castle Hill Rd and the A258 road to Deal, or off the A2 past the Eastern Docks. From the tourist office, follow the stony path east along the clifftops for a bracing 2-mile walk to the stout Victorian South Foreland Lighthouse (NT; adult/child £5/2.50; ☉guided tours 11am-5.30pm Fri-Mon mid-Mar–Oct). This was the first lighthouse to be powered by electricity and is the site of the first international radio transmissions, in 1898.

A mile further on the same trail brings you to delightful St Margaret's Bay, a gap in the chalk with a sun-trapping shingle beach and the welcoming Coastguard Pub (www.thecoastguard.co.uk; mains £10-16; ☉10.30am-11pm). This is the closest point to France and many a cross-Channel swimmer has stepped into the briny here. From the top of the hill, bus 15 shuttles back to Dover or onward to Deal every hour.

To see the cliffs in all their full-frontal glory, Dover White Cliffs Tours (☑01303-271388; www.doverwhiteclifftours.com; adult/child £10/5; ☉daily Jul & Aug, Sat & Sun Apr-Jun & Sep-Oct) runs 40-minute sightseeing trips at least three times daily from the Western Docks. Dover Sea Safari (☑01304-212880; www.doverseasafari.co.uk; Dover Sea Sports Centre, Esplanade; adult/child £25/13; ☉year round) offers exciting, fast-moving rigid inflatable tours of the Cliffs and beyond.

EAST SUSSEX

Home to rolling countryside, medieval villages and gorgeous coastline, this inspiring corner of England is besieged by weekending Londoners whenever the sun pops out. And it's not hard to see why as you explore the cobbled medieval streets of Rye; wander around historic Battle, where William the Conqueror first engaged the Saxons in 1066;

🏃 Driving Tour
Dover to Rye

START DOVER EASTERN DOCKS
END RYE
LENGTH 35.5 MILES; AT LEAST FOUR HOURS (WITHOUT DUNGENESS PENINSULA DETOUR)

If you've just rolled off a cross-Channel ferry or have a day away from a cruise ship docked in Dover, instead of heading north to London, why not take this fascinating route along the white cliffs and across the flat marshes of the Kent–Sussex border to discover some of the southeast's hidden corners. Buses 100, 101 and 102 follow this route between Dover, Lydd and Hastings.

Starting at the exit to Dover's frantic ❶ Eastern Docks, where all cross-Channel ferries tie up, take the A20 along the seafront. After a few minutes this dual-carriageway begins to climb onto the famous white cliffs west of Dover. Your first stop is just outside town – take the turning for ❷ Samphire Hoe nature park, a ledge of parkland created between the white cliffs and the sea using 5 million cu metres of chalk excavated during the construction of the Channel tunnel. It's a fine spot for a picnic as you watch the 30 local species of butterfly flutter by.

Back on the A20, it's a mere 1.75 miles to the exit for the village of Capel-Le-Ferne (on the B2011). Well signposted at the end of the village is the ❸ Battle of Britain Memorial, a striking monument to the airmen who took part in the decisive struggle with the Luftwaffe in the skies above Kent and Sussex. An airman seated at the centre of a huge Spitfire propeller looks out serenely across the Channel. At the time of writing a new visitor centre was under construction nearby. Returning to the B2011, a few gear changes will have you on the outskirts of ❹ Folkestone. Take a left at the first roundabout then the sixth right onto Dover Rd. This will take you into the centre of this formerly grand old resort, once a favourite stomping ground of royal bon viveur King Edward VII and a forgotten piece of England's seaside past. Take a stroll through the seafront Leas Coastal Park with its subtropical flora, then halt for fish and chips at the old fish market before ambling up through the Creative Quarter, Folkestone's old town now occupied by artists studios and craft shops.

Heading out of Folkestone to the west on the A259 Sandgate Rd, you pass through Sandgate with its antique shops and shingle beach. From there it's another 2.5 miles to fascinating little **⑤ Hythe**. You could spend a full day in this original Cinque Port. Not only is it the eastern terminus of the fascinating narrow-gauge Romney, Hythe and Dymchurch Railway (RH&D Railway), but the Royal Military Canal also flows through the town and there's a quaint high street and beach to explore.

Heading ever west, a series of not-so-attractive shingle resorts such as Dymchurch and St Mary's are strung along the A259, cowering below their huge dykes, which keep the high tides from turning this stretch of the coast into sea bottom.

You've now left the white cliffs behind and are entering the **⑥ Romney Marsh**, a flat, sparsely populated landscape of reed beds and sheep-dotted fields. There's a visitor centre (www.kentwildlifetrust.org.uk) between St Mary's Bay and New Romney (on the A259) for those with time.

Having negotiated New Romney, another of the original five Cinque Ports, just outside the town take the turning to the left onto the B2075, which leads to **⑦ Lydd**, a quaint former corporate member of the Cinque Ports. From here detour along the lonely Dungeness Rd, which heads across the flats of the eerie **⑧ Dungeness Peninsula**, a low shingle spit dominated by a brooding nuclear power station. As well as boasting the southeast's largest seabird colony, it's also the western terminus of the RH&D Railway.

Back in Lydd stick with the B2075 heading west for 6 miles until you reach Camber. Thought the entire south coast had just shingle beaches? Well, the main attraction here is **⑨ Camber Sands**, a wide expanse of golden grains and dunes, ideal for picnicking and strolling.

The B2075 winds through shingly, scrubby wetlands until it rejoins the A259 at the hamlet of East Guldeford, where you should turn left towards Rye. Along the roads around here you will see the main source of revenue from the Romney Marsh – thousands of sheep grazing on the verdant flats. The A259 barrels across the marshes, eventually depositing you in **⑩ Rye**, one of the southeast's quaintest towns.

and peer over the edge of the breathtaking Seven Sisters chalk cliffs and Beachy Head near the genteel seaside town of Eastbourne. Brighton, a highlight of any visit, offers some kicking nightlife, offbeat shopping and British seaside fun. Off the beaten track, you can stretch your legs on the South Downs Way, which traverses England's newest national park, the South Downs National Park.

Rye

POP 4500

Often described as England's quaintest town, Rye is a little nugget of the past, a medieval settlement that looks like it's been dunked in formaldehyde and left for all to admire. Even the most hard-boiled cynic can't fail to be softened by Rye's cobbled lanes, mysterious passageways and crooked half-timbered Tudor buildings. Tales of resident smugglers, ghosts, writers and artists abound.

Rye was once one of the Cinque Ports, occupying a high promontory above the sea. Today the town rises 2 miles from the briny; sheep graze where the Channel's strong tides once swelled.

◉ Sights

Most start their exploration of Rye in famous Mermaid St, a short walk from the Rye Heritage Centre. It bristles with 15th-century timber-framed houses with quirky house names such as 'The House with Two Front Doors' and 'The House Opposite'.

Ypres Tower　　　　　　　　MUSEUM
(www.ryemuseum.co.uk; adult/child £3/free; ⊙ 10.30am-5pm Apr-Oct, to 3.30pm Nov-Mar) Just off Church Sq stands the sandcastle-esque Ypres Tower (pronounced 'wipers'). You can scramble through the 13th-century building to learn about its long history as a fort, prison, mortuary and museum (the last two at overlapping times), but it's the views of Rye Bay, Dungeness nuclear power station and even France on very clear days, that will hold your attention longest.

Lamb House　　　　　　　HOUSE, MUSEUM
(NT; West St; adult/child £5/2.60; ⊙ 2-6pm Tue & Sat late Mar-Oct) This Georgian town house is a favourite stomping ground for local apparitions, but its most famous resident was American writer Henry James, who lived here from 1898 to 1916, during which time he wrote *The Wings of the Dove*.

Church of St Mary the Virgin　　CHURCH
(Church Sq; tower adult/child £3/1; ⊙ 9.15am-5.30pm Apr-Sep, to 4.30 Nov-Mar) Rye's church is a hotchpotch of medieval and later styles, and its turret clock is the oldest in England (1561) still working with its original pendulum, which swings above your head as you enter. Climb the tower for pretty views of the town and surroundings.

⌂ Sleeping

★ **Jeake's House**　　　　　　HOTEL ££
(☎ 01797-222828; www.jeakeshouse.com; Mermaid St; s/d from £70/90; P 🅿 🛜) Situated on Mermaid St, this 17th-century town house once belonged to US poet Conrad Aitken. The 11 rooms are named after writers who stayed here. The decor was probably slightly less bold then, minus the beeswaxed antiques and lavish drapery. Take a pew in the snug book-lined bar and, continuing the theme, enjoy breakfast in an 18th-century former Quaker chapel.

Mermaid Inn　　　　　　　HOTEL £££
(☎ 01797-223065; www.mermaidinn.com; Mermaid St; s/d from £90/150; P) Few inns can claim to be as atmospheric as this ancient hostelry, dating from 1420. Each of the 31 rooms is different, but all are thick with dark beams and lit by leaded windows, and some are graced by secret passageways that now act as fire escapes. It also has one of Rye's best restaurants.

George in Rye　　　　　　　HOTEL £££
(☎ 01797-222114; www.thegeorgeinrye.com; 98 High St; d from £135; @ 🛜) This old coaching inn has managed to reinvent itself as a contemporary boutique hotel while staying true to its roots. Downstairs, an old-fashioned wood-panelled lounge is warmed by roaring log fires, while the guestrooms in the main building, created by the set designer from the film *Pride & Prejudice*, are chic and understated.

✕ Eating

Haydens　　　　　　　　　　CAFE £
(www.haydensinrye.co.uk; 108 High St; snacks/meals from £4-9; ⊙ 10am-5pm) Staunch believer in organic and fair-trade produce, Haydens dishes up delicious omelettes, ploughman's lunches, salads and bagels in a light, breezy cafe. There's a wonderful elevated terrace at the back with great views over town and country. Also runs an excellent seven-room ecofriendly guesthouse upstairs.

Landgate Bistro
BRITISH **££**

(www.landgatebistro.co.uk; 5-6 Landgate; mains £13-20; ⊙noon-3pm Sat & Sun, 7-9pm Wed-Sat) Escape the medieval excesses of Rye's central eateries to this fresh-feeling bistro slightly off the tourist trail near the impressive 14th-century Landgate. The focus here is on competently crafted dishes using local lamb and fish; locals who eat here love it.

❶ Information

Post Office (Unit 2, Station Approach; ⊙8.30am-5.30pm Mon-Fri, to 1pm Sat)

Rye Heritage Centre (☑ 01797-226696; www.ryeheritage.co.uk; Strand Quay; ⊙10am-5pm Apr-Oct, reduced hours Nov-Mar) See a town-model audiovisual history for £3.50 and, upstairs, a freaky collection of penny-in-the-slot novelty machines.

Tourist Office (☑ 01797-229049; www.visit1066country.com; 4-5 Lion St; ⊙10am-5pm Apr-Sep, to 4pm Oct-Mar) Accommodation bookings, and train and bus tickets.

❶ Getting There & Away

BUS

Dover Bus 100, two hours, hourly

Hastings Bus 344 or 100, 40 minutes, two per hour

TRAIN

London Charing Cross £22.30, two hours, hourly (change in Ashford)

Battle

POP 6170

'If there'd been no battle, there'd be no Battle,' goes the saying in this unassuming village, which grew up around the hillside where invading French duke William of Normandy, aka William the Conqueror, scored a decisive victory over local king Harold in 1066. The epicentre of 1066 country, visitors flock here to see the spot where Harold got it in the eye, with the biggest crowd turning up mid-October to witness the annual re-enactment on the original battlefield.

◉ Sights

Battle Abbey
HISTORIC SITE

(EH; adult/child £7.80/4.70; ⊙10am-6pm Apr-Sep, to 4pm Sat & Sun Oct-Mar) On this spot raged the pivotal battle in the last successful invasion of England in 1066: an event that had an unparalleled impact on the country's subsequent social structure, language and, well,

pretty much everything. Four years after, the Normans began constructing an abbey on the battlefield, a penance ordered by the pope for the loss of life incurred here. Only the foundations of the original church remain, the altar's position supposedly the spot King Harold famously took an arrow in his eye.

Other impressive monastic buildings survive and make for atmospheric explorations. The battlefield's innocently rolling lush hillsides do little to evoke the ferocity of the event, but high-tech interactive presentations and a film at the visitors centre, as well as blow-by-blow audio tours, do their utmost to bring the battle to life.

Yesterday's World
MUSEUM

(www.yesterdaysworld.co.uk; 89-90 High St; adult/child £7.95/5.75; ⊙10am-5.30pm Apr-Sep, 11am-4pm Oct-Mar) Overshadowed literally and figuratively by the Battle Abbey, this excellent museum constitutes an incredible repository of England's retail past. The first building houses entire streets of quaint old shops where costumed dummies proffer long-discontinued brands, every space in between stuffed with yesteryear products, enamel advertising signs, battered toys, wartime memorabilia and general nostalgia-inducing knick-knackery. The second building houses the Royalty Room where a cardboard cut-out illustrates just how tiny Queen Victoria was (1.40m).

❶ Information

The town's tourist information point is housed in Yesterday's World (p159) museum.

❶ Getting There & Away

Bus 304/305 goes to Hastings (26 minutes, hourly).

Trains travel to Hastings (£4.10, 15 minutes, twice hourly) and to London Charing Cross (£22.10, one hour and 20 minutes, twice hourly).

Hastings

POP 90,300

Forever associated with the Norman invasion of 1066 (even though the crucial events took place 6 miles away), Hastings thrived as one of the Cinque Ports and, in its Victorian heyday, was one of the country's most fashionable resorts. After a period of steady decline, the town is enjoying a mini-renaissance, and these days is an intriguing mix of tacky resort, fishing port and arty New Age hang-out.

◉ Sights

Stade NEIGHBOURHOOD

(Rock-A-Nore Rd) The seafront area known as the Stade (below East Hill) is home to distinctive black clapboard structures known as Net Shops. These were built to store fishing gear back in the 17th century, but some now house fishmongers who sell off the catch of Europe's largest beach-launched fishing fleet, usually hauled up on the shingle behind. All these fishy goings-on keep the Stade very much a working place, with the combined pong of diesel and guts scenting the air.

Hastings Museum & Art Gallery MUSEUM

(www.hmag.org.uk; Johns Place, Bohemia Rd; ⊙10am-5pm Tue-Sat, noon-5pm Sun Apr-Sep, shorter hours Oct-Mar) FREE A short walk west of the train station, this marvellous little museum is housed in a red-brick mansion. Highlights inside include the intricately Moorish Durbar Hall and a section on John Logie Baird, who invented television while recuperating from an illness in Hastings between February 1923 and November 1924.

Jerwood Gallery GALLERY

(www.jerwoodgallery.org; Rock-A-Nore Rd; adult/child £8/3.50; ⊙11am-4pm Tue-Fri, to 6pm Sat & Sun) Large, purpose-built exhibition venue at the end of the Stade used for temporary shows of contemporary British art as well as themed installations from the Jerwood collection. The building has a great cafe with Channel views.

Fishermen's Museum MUSEUM

(Rock-A-Nore Rd; ⊙10am-5pm Apr-Oct, 11am-4pm Nov-Mar) FREE Shoals of barnacled exhibits swim around the huge *Enterprise* fishing boat at this Stade museum, housed in a former fishers' church.

Hastings Castle RUIN

(www.discoverhastings.co.uk; Castle Hill Rd; adult/child £4.35/3.60; ⊙10am-4pm Easter-Sep) This fortress was built by William the Conquerer, and an exhibition in the grounds tells the story of the castle and the Battle of Hastings.

Smugglers Adventure CAVE

(www.smugglersadventure.co.uk; St Clement Caves; adult/child £7.50/5.50; ⊙10am-5pm Easter-Sep) On West Hill, a short walk east of the Hastings Castle, is the Smugglers Adventure, where you can explore underground caverns and hear smuggling yarns from the Sussex coast.

Shipwreck Museum MUSEUM

(www.shipwreckmuseum.co.uk; Rock-a-Nore Rd; ⊙10am-5pm Apr-Oct, 11am-4pm Sat & Sun Nov-Mar) FREE An old-school repository of junk salvaged from various vessels that have sunk in the Channel, plus sections on fossils and diving.

🛏 Sleeping & Eating

Swan House B&B ££

(☎01424-430014; www.swanhousehastings.co.uk; 1 Hill St; s/d from £80/120; @ 🐶) Inside its 15th-century timbered shell, this place blends contemporary and vintage chic to perfection. The four rooms feature organic toiletries, fresh flowers, hand-painted walls and huge beds. The guest lounge, where pale sofas, painted floorboards and striking modern sculpture rub shoulders with beams and a huge stone fireplace, is a stunner.

Dragon Bar RESTAURANT ££

(71 George St; mains £10-18, weekday lunch menu £7; ⊙noon-11pm Mon-Sat, to 10.30pm Sun; 🐶) The younger end of the alternative old-town crowd is attracted to this atmospheric bar-restaurant hang-out. It's full of dark walls, mismatched furniture and beaten leather sofas, and the eclectic menu features everything from Thai curry to Winchelsea lamb and pizzas.

🍷 Drinking & Nightlife

Hanushka Coffee House CAFE

(28 George St; ⊙9.30am-6pm) Hastings' best caffeine stop resembles a well-stocked secondhand bookshop with every inch of wall space packed with titles. The low-lit and tightly packed space in between provokes inter-table interaction, or you can seek sanctuary on the sofas and perches in the window. No wi-fi.

❶ Information

Tourist Office (☎01424-451111; www.visit 1066country.com; Aquila House, Breeds Pl; ⊙9am-5.30pm Mon-Fri, to 5pm Sat, 10.30am-4pm Sun Apr-Sep, shorter hours Oct-Mar)

A PIER INTO THE FUTURE

Hastings last hit the national news in October 2010 when its Victorian pier burnt down. The ballroom at the end of the structure, where the likes of the Clash, Sex Pistols, Rolling Stones, The Who, Jimi Hendrix and Pink Floyd once performed, was completely destroyed. Work is now under way to rebuild the pier as an open performance space, however, with some of the funding coming from local people.

CANTERBURY & SOUTHEAST ENGLAND EASTBOURNE

THE LAST INVASION OF ENGLAND

If there's one date that seared itself into every English schoolchild's brain, it's 1066, the year of the most famous battle in the country's history. The punch-up in question was the Battle of Hastings, which began when King Harold's army arrived in a field near what is now the village of Battle on 14 October and created a three-ringed defence consisting of archers, cavalry and massed infantry at the rear. Invading French duke William of Normandy, aka William the Conqueror, marched north from Hastings and took up a position about 400m south of the English. He tried repeatedly to break the cordon, but Harold's men held fast. William's knights then feigned retreat, drawing some of Harold's troops after them. It was a fatal mistake. Seeing the gap in the English wall, William ordered his remaining troops to charge through, and the battle was as good as won. Among the English casualties was King Harold who, as tradition has it, was hit in the eye by an arrow and struck down by Norman knights as he tried to pull it out. At news of his death, the last English resistance collapsed.

In their irreverent parody of a British history textbook, *1066 and All That* (1930), Sellar and Yeatman suggest that 'the Norman conquest was a Good Thing, as from this time onward England stopped being conquered and thus was able to become top nation...'

ⓘ Getting There & Away

BUS

Eastbourne Bus 99, 80 minutes, four per hour

London Victoria National Express, £14.40, three hours, daily

Rye Buses 100 & 344, 40 minutes, twice hourly

TRAIN

Brighton Via Eastbourne, £12.90, one hour to 80 minutes, twice hourly

London Victoria £17.30, two hours, hourly

ⓘ Getting Around

Hastings has two delightful Victorian funiculars.

East Hill Cliff Railway (Rock-A-Nore Rd; adult/child £2.50/1.50; ◷10am-5.30pm Apr-Sep, 11am-4pm Sat & Sun Oct-Mar) The East Hill Cliff Railway funicular ascends from the Stade to Hastings Country Park.

West Hill Cliff Railway (George St; adult/child £2.50/1.50; ◷10am-5.30pm Mar-Sep, 11am-4pm Oct-Feb) The West Hill Cliff Railway funicular saves visitors' legs when climbing up to Hastings Castle.

Eastbourne

POP 99,000

Despite its official title as 'Britain's sunniest town', Eastbourne has been slow to throw off its unattractive image as death's waiting-room by the chilly Channel, all snoozing octogenarians in deckchairs and fusty guesthouses populated by vitamin D–deprived bank-holidaying Scots. But while much of this is still to be found here, in the last decade an influx of students and the arrival of the southeast's largest Polish community have given the town a sprightlier feel.

Eastbourne's 3.5-mile sweeping, palm-tree-lined seafront is one of the UK's grandest. Add to this a fresh modern art gallery and the recently created South Downs National Park that nudges its western suburbs and Eastbourne certainly makes an enjoyable day trip from London or Brighton. It's also the start and end point for a hike along the 100-mile South Downs Way.

◉ Sights & Activities

Towner Art Gallery   ART GALLERY

(☑01323-434670; www.townereastbourne.org.uk; Devonshire Park, College Rd; ◷10am-5pm Tue-Sun, tours 11.30am & 2pm) **FREE** One of the southeast's most exciting exhibition spaces, this purpose-built structure has temporary shows of contemporary work on the ground and 2nd floors, while the first floor is given over to rotating themed shows created from the gallery's 5000-piece collection. Building tours include a peek inside the climate-controlled art store.

Pier   LANDMARK

(☑01323-410466; www.eastbournepier.com; ◷24hr) Until the summer of 2014, Eastbourne's ramshackle pier was a lovable piece of rusty Victoriana jutting into the Channel. But on 30 July 2014 a fire broke out in the amusement arcade at the land end of the structure, destroying a third of the pier as thousands of tanning holidaymakers looked on. Some clever firefighting saved the other two-thirds, however, and Eastbourne's finest landmark is set to reopen in 2015.

Museum of Shops
MUSEUM

(20 Cornfield Tce; adult/child £5/4; ⊙10am-5pm, closed Jan) This small museum is swamped by an obsessive collection of how-we-used-to-live memorabilia.

👉 Tours

Sussex Voyages
BOAT TOUR

(🖉01293-888780; www.sussexvoyages.co.uk; Lower Quayside, The Waterfront, Sovereign Harbour Marina; adult/child £25/14) Hour-long Beachy Head and Seven Sisters boat tours leaving from Sovereign Harbour (take hourly bus 51) on rigid-hulled inflatables. Reservations essential.

🎊 Festivals & Events

Airbourne
AIR SHOW

(www.airshows.org.uk; ⊙mid-Aug) Arguably the UK's best airshow – as it's free! Takes place over the Channel.

🛏 Sleeping

Big Sleep
HOTEL ££

(🖉01323-722676; www.thebigsleephotel.com; King Edward's Pde; s/d from £45/60; 🛜) Hip, fresh and friendly, this seafront hotel has 50 gob-smacking rooms with big-print wallpaper, retro furnishings, and curtains that resemble sheep that might have been grazing on Beachy Head just a few hours prior. A trendy bar, big basement games room and Channel views make this Eastbourne's coolest kip.

Albert & Victoria
B&B ££

(🖉01323-730948; www.albertandvictoria.com; 19 St Aubyns Rd; s/d from £35/70; 🛜) Book ahead to stay at this delightful Victorian terraced house, whose fragrant rooms, canopied beds, crystal chandeliers and secluded walled garden for summer breakfasts are mere paces from the seafront promenade. The four rooms are named after four of Queen Victoria's offspring.

🍴 Eating

Lamb Inn
PUB ££

(www.thelamb.eu; 36 High St; mains £8.50-11; ⊙11am-11.30pm) This Eastbourne institution located less than a mile northwest of the train station in the undervisited Old Town has been plonking Sussex ales on the bar for eight centuries, and now also serves gourmet British pub grub. A holidaying Charles Dickens also left a few beer rings and smudged napkins here when he stayed across the road. Buses 1, 1A and 12 stop nearby.

Belgian Cafe
BELGIAN ££

(www.thebelgiancafe.co.uk; 11-23 Grand Pde; mains £11-22.50) If you didn't know that Belgian beer can taste of fruit; the national dish is mussels and chips; and Tintin hails from its capital, Brussels, you will once you've experienced this popular cafe near the pier. Fifty types of mussel dishes and the same number of Belgian ales are available.

☆ Entertainment

Eastbourne International Tennis Tournament
TENNIS

(www.devonshireparkltc.co.uk; Devonshire Park; ⊙mid-Jun) One of the UK's top tennis tournaments played in the week before Wimbledon. Attracts some of the biggest names.

🛍 Shopping

Camilla's Bookshop
BOOKS

(www.camillasbookshop.com; 57 Grove Rd; ⊙10am-5pm Mon-Sat) Literally packed to the rafters with half a million musty volumes, this incredible secondhand-book repository, an interesting amble from the train station, fills three floors of a crumbling Victorian town house.

ℹ Information

Tourist Office (🖉0871 6630031; www.visiteastbourne.com; Cornfield Rd; ⊙9.15am-5.30pm Mon-Fri, to 5pm Sat, 10am-1pm Sun Apr-Oct, closed Sun & shorter hours Nov-Mar)

ℹ Getting There & Away

BUS

Brighton Bus 12, 75 minutes, up to four hourly

Hastings Bus 98/99, 70 minutes, three per hour

TRAIN

Brighton £10.30, 30 to 40 minutes, twice hourly

London Victoria £17.30, 1½ hours, twice hourly

Around Eastbourne

The South Downs National Park, more than 600 sq miles of rolling chalk downs, stretches west from Eastbourne for about 100 miles. The South Downs Way extends its entire length.

Beachy Head

The famous cliffs of Beachy Head are the highest point of the chalky rock faces that slice across the rugged coastline at the southern end of the South Downs. It's off the B2103, from the A259 between Eastbourne and Newhaven. From here the stunning Seven Sisters Cliffs undulate their way west. A clifftop path (a branch of the South Downs Way) rides the waves of chalk as far as picturesque Cuckmere Haven.

Eastbourne's City Sightseeing (www. city-sightseeing.co.uk; Eastbourne Pier; adult/child £9/5; ☉ every 30min 10am-5pm mid-Mar–Oct) tour bus stops at the clifftop.

Beachy Head is a spot of thrilling beauty. Unfortunately it is also known as one of Europe's suicide spots.

Along the clifftop path, you'll stumble upon the tiny seaside hamlet of Birling Gap, where you can stop for a drink, snack or ice cream at the Birling Gap Hotel (Seven Sisters Cliffs). The secluded beach is a sun-trap popular with locals and walkers taking a breather.

Pevensey Castle

The ruins (EH; Castle Rd, Pevensey; adult/child £5/3; ☉ 10am-6pm Apr-Sep) of William the Conqueror's first stronghold sit 5 miles east of Eastbourne, just off the A259. Regular train services between London Victoria and Hastings via Eastbourne stop at Westham, half a mile from Pevensey. Picturesquely dissolving into its own moat, the castle marks the point where William the Conqueror landed in 1066, just two weeks before the Battle of Hastings.

He wasted no time after his landing by building upon sturdy Roman walls to create this castle, which was used time and again through the centuries, right up to WWII.

Brighton & Hove

POP 273,400

Raves on the beach, Graham Greene novels, mods and rockers in bank-holiday fisticuffs, naughty weekends for Mr and Mrs Smith, classic car runs from London, the UK's biggest gay scene and the Channel's best clubbing – this city by the sea evokes many images for the British. One thing is certain: with its bohemian, cosmopolitan and hedonistic vibe, Brighton is where England's seaside experience goes from cold to cool.

Brighton is without doubt Britain's most colourful and outrageous city, and one with many faces. Here, burlesque meets contemporary design; Spanish students leave Starbucks to rub shoulders with stars in Spanish bars; the southeast's grottiest hostels share thin walls with kinky boutique hotels; microbrew ales costing £4 a pint occupy bar space with £1 buckets of 'sex on the beach'; and stags watch drag. This is the city that returned the UK's first Green Party MP, where Valentine's Day is celebrated with more gusto than Christmas, and is the place, according to the 2001 census, with the highest UK population of Jedi.

Brighton rocks all year round, but really comes to life during the summer months when tourists, language students and revellers from London pour into the city, keen to explore the city's legendary nightlife, summer festivals and quirky shops. The highlight for the sightseeing visitor is, without doubt, the weird and wonderful Royal Pavilion, a 19th-century party palace built by the Prince Regent, who kicked off Brighton's enduring love of the outlandish.

◉ Sights

★ Royal Pavilion   PALACE
(www.royalpavilion.org.uk; Royal Pavilion Gardens; adult/child £11/6; ☉ 9.30am-5.45pm Apr-Sep, 10am-5.15pm Oct-Mar) The city's must-see attraction is the Royal Pavilion, the glittering party pad and palace of Prince George, later Prince Regent and then King George IV. It's one of the most opulent buildings in England, certainly the finest example of early 19th-century chinoiserie anywhere in Europe and an apt symbol of Brighton's reputation for decadence. An unimpressed Queen Victoria called the Royal Pavilion 'a strange, odd Chinese place', but for visitors to Brighton it's an unmissable chunk of Sussex history.

The entire palace is an eye-popping spectacle, but some interiors stand out even amid the riot of decoration. The dragon-themed banqueting hall must be the most incredible in all England; more dragons and snakes writhe in the music room, with its ceiling of 26,000 gold scales; and the then state-of-the-art kitchen must have wowed Georgians with its automatic spits and hot tables. Prince Albert carted away all of the furniture, some of which has been loaned back by the present queen.

Brighton Museum
& Art Gallery   MUSEUM, GALLERY
(www.brighton-hove-museums.org.uk; Royal Pavilion Gardens; ☉ 10am-5pm Tue-Sun) FREE Set in the Royal Pavilion's renovated stable block, this museum and art gallery has a glittering

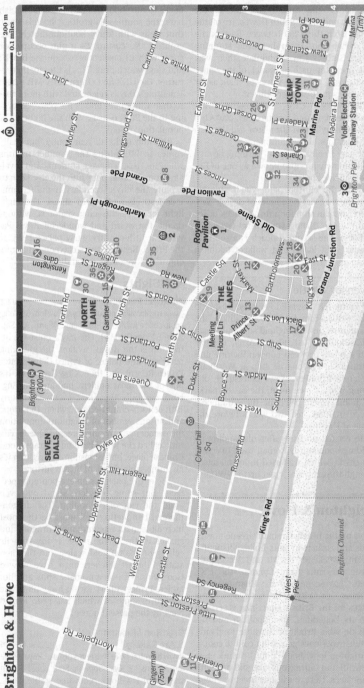

Brighton & Hove

collection of 20th-century art and design, including a crimson Salvador Dalí sofa modelled on Mae West's lips. There's also an enthralling gallery of world art, an impressive collection of Egyptian artefacts, and an 'images of Brighton' multimedia exhibit containing a series of oral histories and a model of the defunct West Pier.

Brighton Pier   LANDMARK
(www.brightonpier.co.uk; Madeira Dr) This grand century-old pier is the place to experience Brighton's tackier side. There are plenty of stomach-churning fairground rides and dingy amusement arcades to keep you amused, and candy floss and Brighton rock to chomp on while you're doing so.

Look west and you'll see the sad remains of the West Pier, a skeletal iron hulk that attracts flocks of starlings at sunset. It's a sad end for this Victorian marvel, where the likes of Charlie Chaplin and Stan Laurel once performed.

So far there's no sign of the i360 observation tower ('Hurray!' some may cry), a spectacularly space-age piece of architecture from the creators of the London Eye that may one day loom 175m above the seafront (the completion date of 2015 is unlikely). The venue would include a West Pier Heritage Centre – a pavilion with audiovisual exhibits relating the pier's history.

🎉 Festivals & Events

Brighton Festival   FESTIVAL
(☎01273-709709; www.brightonfestival.org; ⊙May) After Edinburgh, this is the UK's biggest arts festival. It draws star performers from around the globe for three weeks by the sea.

Brighton Pride   GAY, LESBIAN
(www.brighton-pride.org; ⊙early Aug) One of the UK's biggest gay bashes with a rainbow-hued parade and concerts in Preston Park.

🛏 Sleeping

Brighton has lots of places to sleep to suit every budget and taste, but beds can be scarce on summer weekends and during events such as the Brighton Festival, when booking ahead is recommended.

Baggies Backpackers   HOSTEL £
(☎01273-733740; www.baggiesbackpackers.com; 33 Oriental Pl; dm/d £15/40; @) This place may have recently changed hands, but the new proprietors are determined to maintain the warm, familial atmosphere, worn-in charm, attentive service and clean, snug dorms that have made this long-established hostel an institution. The cosy basement music and chill-out room, and a TV lounge piled high with video cassettes have also survived the changeover, as well as the digital revolution.

Kipps Brighton
HOSTEL £

(☑ 01273-604182; www.kipps-brighton.com; 76 Grand Pde; dm/s/d from £15/25/25; @ ☎) The owners of Canterbury's award-winning hostel have created equally commendable budget digs here in Brighton. There's a real cafe vibe around reception, and facilities include a communal kitchen. Free movie, pizza and pub nights successfully separate guests from their wi-fi-enabled devices.

Hotel Pelirocco
HOTEL ££

(☑ 01273-327055; www.hotelpelirocco.co.uk; 10 Regency Sq; s £59-75, d £109-155; ☎) One of Brighton's sexiest and nuttiest places to stay, the Pelirocco has become the ultimate venue for a flirty rock-and-roll weekend. Flamboyant rooms, some designed by artists, include the Soviet-chic room with vodka bottles frozen into the walls, the Pin-up Parlour dedicated to Diana Dors, and the Pretty Vacant double, a shrine to the Sex Pistols.

There's also a Play Room suite with 3m circular bed, mirrored ceiling and a pole-dancing area.

Neo Hotel
BOUTIQUE HOTEL ££

(☑ 01273-711104; www.neohotel.com; 19 Oriental Pl; s incl breakfast £55-65, d incl breakfast £100-150; ☎) You won't be surprised to learn the owner of this gorgeous hotel is an interior stylist. The nine rooms could have dropped straight from the pages of a design magazine, each finished in rich colours and tactile fabrics, with bold floral and Asian motifs, and black-tiled bathrooms. Wonderful breakfasts include homemade smoothies and pancakes.

Snooze
HOTEL ££

(☑ 01273-605797; www.snoozebrighton.com; 25 St George's Tce; s/d from £55/65; ☎) The retro styling at this eccentric Kemptown pad features everything from vintage posters and bright '60s and '70s wallpaper to Bollywood film posters, floral sinks and mad clashes of colour. It's more than just a gimmick – the rooms are comfortable and spotless, and there are great meat-free breakfasts. You'll find it just off St James' St, about 500m east of New Steine.

Motel Schmotel
B&B ££

(☑ 07557-947449; www.motelschmotel.co.uk; 37 Russell Sq; d £63-120; ☎) If you can overlook the petite rooms and miniscule bathrooms, this 11-room B&B in a Regency town house, a short stroll from virtually anywhere, is a sound and central place to hit the sack. Rooms are accented with colourful oversized prints and an uncluttered design, and guests

heap praise on the breakfast cooked by the always-there-to-help couple who run things.

Paskins Town House
B&B ££

(☑ 01273-601203; www.paskins.co.uk; 18-19 Charlotte St; s £50-75, d £100-150; @ ☎) ✔ Around a kilometre east of Brighton Pier along the seafront, this environmentally friendly B&B is spread between two elegant town houses. Paskins prides itself on using ecofriendly products such as recycled toilet paper, low-energy lightbulbs and biodegradable cleaning materials. The individually designed rooms are beautifully maintained, and excellent organic and vegetarian breakfasts are served in the art deco–inspired breakfast room.

myhotel
HOTEL ££

(☑ 01273-900300; www.myhotels.com; 17 Jubilee St; r £70-320; ☎) There's nothing square about this place: trendsetting rooms look like space-age pods with curved white walls, floor-to-ceiling observation windows and suspended flatscreen TVs, enlivened by the odd splash of neon orange or pink. Hook up your iPod and play music through speakers in the ceiling. There's also a cocoon-like cocktail bar downstairs and, if you've currency to ignite, a suite with a steamroom and harpooned vintage carousel horse.

★ Hotel Una
BOUTIQUE HOTEL £££

(☑ 01723-820464; www.hotel-una.co.uk; 55-56 Regency Sq; s incl breakfast £55-75, d incl breakfast £115-200; ✸ ☀ ☎) All of the 19 generous rooms here wow guests with their bold-patterned fabrics, supersized leather sofas, in-room free-standing baths and vegan/veggie/carnivorous breakfast in bed. Some, such as the two-level suite with its own mini-cinema, and the underpavement chambers with their own spa and jacuzzi, are truly show-stopping and not as expensive as you might expect.

All this plus a cool cocktail bar and lots of timewarp period features make the Una our numero uno.

Drakes
BOUTIQUE HOTEL £££

(☑ 01273-696934; www.drakesofbrighton.com; 43-44 Marine Pde; r £115-345; P ✸ @ ☎) This minimalist boutique hotel oozes understated class. So understated is the entrance, in fact, you could easily miss it. All rooms have similar decor in bold fabrics and funky European elm panelling, but it's the feature rooms everyone wants – their giant freestanding tubs are set in front of full-length bay windows with widescreen Channel views. The basement restaurant is superb.

✖ Eating

Brighton easily has the best choice of eateries on the south coast, with cafes, diners and restaurants to fulfil every dining whim. It's also one of Britain's best destinations for vegetarians, and its innovative meat-free menus are terrific value for anyone on a budget. For food from the former British Empire and beyond, head for Preston St, which has an incredible concentration of ethnic eateries.

★ Iydea VEGETARIAN £

(www.iydea.co.uk; 17 Kensington Gardens; mains £6-7.50; ⊙9.30am-5.30pm Mon-Sat, from 10am Sun; 🛜📷) Even by Brighton's lofty standards, the food at this award-winning vegetarian cafe is a treat. The daily changing choices of curries, lasagnes, falafel, enchiladas and quiches are full of flavour and can be washed down with a selection of vegan wines, organic ales and homemade lemonades. If you're on the hop, you can get any dish to takeaway in environmentally friendly packaging.

Infinity Foods Cafe VEGETARIAN £

(www.infinityfoodscafe.co.uk; 50 Gardner St; mains £3.50-8; ⊙10.30am-5pm Mon-Fri, from 10am Sat, noon-4pm Sun; 🛜📷) The sister establishment of Infinity Foods wholefoods shop (healthfood cooperative and Brighton institution) serves a wide variety of vegetarian and organic food, with many vegan and wheat- or gluten-free options including tofu burgers, mezze platters and veggie sausage sandwiches.

Foodilic BUFFET £

(www.foodilic.com; 60 North St; buffet £6.45, takeaway per 100g £1.20; ⊙9am-9.30pm Mon-Sat, to 6pm Sun) It's as good for breakfast (£2) as for a late dinner, but it's the eat-till-you-burst buffet of scrumptious healthy fare that packs out this funky place all day long.

Tea Cosy CAFE £

(www.theteacosy.co.uk; 3 George St; teas £3.50-12; ⊙noon-5pm Wed-Fri & Sun, to 5.30pm Sat) Tearoom offering cakes and sandwiches, though you can hardly get in the door due to the royal family memorabilia, including ample Kate and Wills paraphernalia.

Mock Turtle CAFE £

(4 Pool Valley; mains £4-7; ⊙9am-6pm Mon-Sat, to 6.30pm Sun) Little has changed at this wonderfully quaintly English tearoom since the mid-20th century. Those who've sipped and munched here that long claim the myriad homemade cakes, Sussex cream teas and light meals are as tasty now as they were back then.

Scoop & Crumb ICE CREAM £

(5-6 East St; snacks £3-6, sundaes £2.50-6; ⊙10am-6pm Sun-Fri, to 7pm Sat) This ice-cream parlour belongs to the city's artisan ice-cream producer, and the sundaes (more than 50 types) are second to none. Freshly cut sandwiches and monster toasties are also available.

★ Terre à Terre VEGETARIAN ££

(📞01273-729051; www.terreaterre.co.uk; 71 East St; mains £15; ⊙noon-10.30pm Mon-Fri, 11am-11pm Sat, to 10pm Sun; 📷) Even staunch meat-eaters will rave about this legendary vegetarian restaurant. A sublime dining experience, from the vibrant modern space to the entertaining menus and inventive dishes stuffed with excitingly zingy ingredients. There's also plenty for vegans. Desserts are on the steep side.

Riddle & Finns SEAFOOD ££

(www.riddleandfinns.co.uk; 12 Meeting House Lane; mains £13-18; ⊙noon-last customer) Regarded as the town's most refined seafood spot, R&F is light on gimmicky interiors (think white butcher's shop tiles, marble tables and candles) but heavy on taste. With the kitchen open to the street outside, chefs put on a public cooking class with every dish as they prepare your smoked haddock in champagne sauce or wild sea bass.

There's an elite wine list to choose from as you wait.

JB's American Diner FAST FOOD ££

(http://jbsdiner.co.uk; 31 King's Rd; burgers £8-10, mains £6.50-12; ⊙10am-10pm Mon-Sat, from 9am Sun) The waft of hotdogs as you push open the door, the shiny red-leather booths, the stars and stripes draped across the wall, the 1950s soundtrack twanging in the background and the colossal portions of burgers, fries and milkshakes – in short, this is a hefty slab of authentic Americana teleported to the Brighton seafront.

Food for Friends VEGETARIAN ££

(www.foodforfriends.com; 17-18 Prince Albert St; mains £11-13; 📷) An ever-inventive choice of vegetarian and vegan food keeps bringing locals back for seconds and thirds at this place to see and be seen – literally, by every passerby through the huge streetside windows. Be prepared to wait for a table on busy shopping days.

English's Oyster Bar
SEAFOOD ££

(www.englishs.co.uk; 29-31 East St; mains £9-30; ⊙noon-10.15pm Mon-Sat, 12.30-4pm Sun) An almost 70-year-old institution and celebrity haunt, this Brightonian seafood paradise dishes up everything from Essex oysters to locally caught lobster and Dover sole. It's converted from fishers' cottages, with shades of the elegant Edwardian era inside and alfresco dining on the pedestrian square outside.

Gingerman
MODERN EUROPEAN £££

(☑01273-326688; 21a Norfolk Sq; 2-/3-course menu £15/18; ⊙12.30-2pm & 7-10pm Tue-Sun) Hastings seafood, Sussex beef, Romney Marsh lamb, local sparkling wines and countless other seasonal, local and British treats go into the adroitly flash-fried and slow-cooked dishes served at this snug 32-cover eatery. Reservations are advised. Norfolk Sq is a short walk west along Western Rd from the Churchill Square shopping centre.

🍸 Drinking & Nightlife

With the exception of London, Brighton's nightlife is the best in the south, with its unique mix of seafront clubs and bars, and visits by top DJs. On West St, drunken stag and hens' parties and charmless, tacky nightclubs rule. For more ideas, visit www.drinkinbrighton.co.uk or search out publications such as *The List, Source* and *What's On*.

Brighton Rocks
BAR

(www.brightonrocksbar.co.uk; 6 Rock Pl; ⊙4-11pm Mon-Thu, to 1am Sat, from noon Sun; 🛜) Incongruously located in an alley of garages and used-car lots, this cocktail bar is firmly established on the Kemptown gay scene, but welcomes all-comers with 'Shocktails', a 'grazing' menu and theme parties.

Dorset
PUB

(www.thedorset.co.uk; 28 North Rd; ⊙9am-late; 🛜) In fine weather this laid-back Brighton institution throws open its doors and windows, and tables spill out onto the pavement. You'll be just as welcome for a morning coffee as for an evening pint here, and should you not leave between the two, there's a decent gastropub menu.

Black Dove
PUB

(www.blackdovebrighton.com; 74 St James's St; ⊙4pm-late) Eclectic hang-out with shabby-chic furnishings, huge antique ceiling fans, a bar stocked with unusual tipples and a quirky basement snug. Live acoustic music and local DJs provide the soundtrack for evening quaffing that spills out onto the pavements when the mercury is high.

Coalition
BAR

(171-181 Kings Rd Arches; ⊙10am-late) On a summer's day, there's nowhere finer to sit and watch the world go by than at this popular

---

GAY & LESBIAN BRIGHTON

Brighton has the most vibrant gay community in the country outside London and Kemptown (aka Camptown). On and off St James's St is where it's all at. The old Brunswick Town area of Hove is a quieter alternative to the traditionally cruisy (and sometimes seedy) scene in Kemptown. For up-to-date information on the gay scene in Brighton, check out www.gay.brighton.co.uk and www.realbrighton.com, or pick up the free monthly magazine *Gscene* (www.gscene.com) from gay venues.

For Drinking

Poison Ivy (129 St James's St) In-your-face pub featuring drag acts and camp karaoke.

A Bar (www.amsterdam.uk.com; 11-12 Marine Pde; ⊙noon-2am) Extremely hip bar and sauna in the Amsterdam hotel; its sun terrace is a particular hit.

Bulldog (www.bulldogbrighton.com; 31 St James's St) Longest-running gay bar in Brighton, mostly frequented only by men.

Queen's Arms (www.queensarmsbrighton.com; 7 George St; ⊙3pm-late) And they ain't talking Victoria or Elizabeth! Plenty of camp cabaret and karaoke at this pub.

For Dancing

Revenge (www.revenge.co.uk; 32-34 Old Steine) Nightly disco with occasional cabaret.

Legends Club (31-34 Marine Pde) Located beneath the Legends Hotel, arguably the best gay hotel in town and 2009 winner of the Golden Handbag award.

beach bar, diner and club. All sorts of events happen here, from comedy to live music and club nights.

Concorde 2 — CLUB
(www.concorde2.co.uk; Madeira Dr) Brighton's best-known and best-loved club is a disarmingly unpretentious den, where DJ Fatboy Slim pioneered the Big Beat Boutique and still occasionally graces the decks. Each month there's a huge variety of club nights, live bands and concerts by international names.

Audio — CLUB
(www.audiobrighton.com; 10 Marine Pde) Some of the city's top club nights are held at this ear-numbing venue. The music's top priority here, attracting a young, up-for-it crowd.

Digital — CLUB
(www.yourfutureisdigital.com/brighton; 187-193 Kings Rd Arches) Seafront club hosting indie, house and student nights.

☆ Entertainment

Brighton Dome — THEATRE
(01273-709709; www.brightondome.org; Church St) Once the stables for King George IV's horses, this art deco complex houses three theatre venues within the Royal Pavilion estate. ABBA famously won the 1974 Eurovision Song Contest here.

Theatre Royal — THEATRE
(08448 717 650; New Rd) Built by decree of the Prince of Wales in 1806, this grand venue hosts musicals, plays and operas.

Komedia Theatre — COMEDY
(0845 293 8480; www.komedia.co.uk; 44-47 Gardner St) A stylish comedy, theatre and cabaret venue attracting top stand-up acts.

🛍 Shopping

In the market for a pair of vegetarian shoes, a gauche portrait of a Lego man or a letter opener in the shape of something naughty? Whatever item you yearn for, old or new, you'll probably find it in Brighton. The tightly packed Lanes is the most popular shopping district, its every twist and turn jam-packed with jewellers and gift shops, coffee shops and boutiques selling everything from antique firearms to hard-to-find vinyls. There's another, less-claustrophobic shopping district in North Laine, a series of partially pedestrian thoroughfares north of the Lanes, including Bond, Gardner, Kensington and Sydney Sts, lined with retro-cool boutiques

and bohemian cafes. Mainstream chains gather within the Churchill Square shopping centre and along Western Rd.

ℹ Information

Incredibly, Brighton closed its busy tourist office in 2013.

Brighton City Guide (www.brighton.co.uk)
City Council (www.brighton-hove.gov.uk) A rich seam of city information.
Jubilee Library (Jubilee St; ⊙10am-7pm Mon, Tue & Thu, to 5pm Wed, Fri & Sat, 11am-5pm Sun) Bring ID to sign up for free internet sessions.
Post Office (2-3 Churchill Sq; ⊙9am-5.30pm Mon-Sat) Located within WH Smiths.
Visit Brighton (01273-290337; www.visit-brighton.com) There's no tourist office but you can still call or log on for information.

ℹ Getting There & Away

Transport between London and Brighton is fast and frequent. If arriving by car, parking is plentiful but pricey, and the city-centre traffic, bus-clogged lanes and road layouts can be confusing.

BUS
Standard connections:
Arundel Bus 700, two hours, twice hourly
Chichester Bus 700, 2¾ hours, twice hourly
Eastbourne Bus 12, 70 minutes, up to every 10 minutes
London Victoria National Express, from £8, 2¼ hours, hourly

TRAIN
London-bound services pass through Gatwick Airport (£9.80, 25 to 40 minutes, up to five hourly).
Chichester £12.60, 50 minutes, half-hourly
Eastbourne £10.30, 30 to 40 minutes, half-hourly
Hastings £13, 80 minutes, half-hourly
London St Pancras £22.40, 1¼ hours, half-hourly
London Victoria £24, one hour, three-hourly
Portsmouth £15, 1½ hours, hourly

ℹ Getting Around

Day bus tickets (£4.60) are available from the drivers of all Brighton and Hove buses. Alternatively a £2 PlusBus ticket on top of your rail fare gives unlimited bus travel for the day.

The city operates a pricey pay-and-display parking scheme. In the town centre, it's usually £3.50 per hour for a maximum stay of two hours. Alternatively, there's a Park & Ride 2.5 miles northwest of the centre at Withdean, from where bus 27 zips into town.

Cab companies include **Brighton Stream-line Taxis** (☑ 01273-202020) and **City Cabs** (☑ 01273-205205), and there's a taxi rank at the junction of East St and Market St.

WEST SUSSEX

West Sussex offers a welcome respite from fast-paced adventures. The serene hills and valleys of the South Downs ripple across the county, fringed by sheltered coastline. Beautiful Arundel and cultured Chichester make good bases from which to explore the county's winding country lanes and remarkable Roman ruins.

Arundel

POP 3410

Arguably the prettiest town in the county, Arundel is clustered around a vast fairy-tale castle, and its hillside streets overflow with antique emporiums, teashops and a host of eateries. While much of the town appears medieval – the whimsical castle has been home to the Dukes of Norfolk for centuries – most of it dates back to Victorian times.

⊙ Sights

Arundel Castle   CASTLE
(www.arundelcastle.org; adult/child £18/9; ⊙ 10am-5pm Tue-Sun Apr-Oct) Arundel Castle was first built in the 11th century but all that's left of the early structure are the modest remains of the keep. It was ransacked during the English Civil War, and most of what you see today is the result of reconstruction by the eigth, 11th and 15th dukes of Norfolk between 1718 and 1900. The current duke still lives in part of the castle, whose highlights include the atmospheric keep, the massive Great Hall and the library.

The castle does a good impression of Windsor Castle and St James's Palace in the popular 2009 film *The Young Victoria,* and occasionally is closed for other film shoots.

Arundel Cathedral   CATHEDRAL
(www.arundelcathedral.org; London Rd; ⊙ 9am-6pm Apr-Oct, to dusk Nov-Mar) Arundel's ostentatious 19th-century Catholic cathedral is the other dominating feature of the town's impressive skyline. Commissioned by the 15th duke of Norfolk in 1868, this impressive structure was designed by Joseph Aloysius Hansom (inventor of the Hansom cab) in the French Gothic style, but shows much Victorian economy and restraint. Although small for a cathedral – it holds just 500 worshippers – Hansom's clever layout makes the building seem a lot bigger.

A 1970s shrine in the north transept holds the remains of St Philip Howard, a canonised Catholic martyr who was banged up in the Tower of London by Elizabeth I until his death in 1595 for reverting to Catholicism. The building attracts only a trickle of tourists, rare indeed for a cathedral in southern England.

Arundel Museum   MUSEUM
(www.arundelmuseum.org; Mill Rd; adult/child £3/2.50; ⊙ 10am-4pm) Located opposite the Arundel Castle gates, this small, brand-new museum has sections on the castle, the South Downs National Park and the River Arun's role in 19th-century trade, as well as various other bits of Arundelia.

🍴 Sleeping & Eating

Arundel House   B&B ££
(☑ 01903-882136; www.arundelhouseonline.com; 11 High St; d/ste from £85/120; ⊛) The contemporary chambers at this lovely 'restaurant with rooms' may be slightly low-ceilinged, but they're clean-cut and very comfortable, with showers big enough for two. The restaurant downstairs serves some of the best food in Arundel, which, happily, extends to breakfast.

Arden Guest House   B&B ££
(☑ 01903-882544; www.ardenguesthouse.net; 4 Queens Lane; s/d £58/78, without bathroom £48/68; ℗⊛) For the classic British B&B experience, head to this eight-room guesthouse just over the river from the historical centre. Rooms are kept fresh and tick all the boxes; the hosts are amiable; and the breakfasts are cooked. No pets or children under 14.

★ Town House   BRITISH £££
(☑ 01903-883847; 65 High St; set lunch/dinner from £17.50/25.50; ⊙ noon-2.30pm & 7-9.30pm Tue-Sat) The only thing that rivals the 16th-century Florentine gilded-walnut ceiling in this compact and very elegant eatery is the sparkling atmosphere and acclaimed British cuisine with a European twist. Book ahead. Town House also has well-appointed rooms to let.

🛍 Shopping

Arundel is antiques central as far as West Sussex is concerned. If you've come to splurge on old stuff, **Tarrant Street** must have the highest concentration of collectibles shops anywhere in the southeast.

ℹ Getting There & Away

Trains run to London Victoria (£17.30, 1½ hours, twice hourly) and to Chichester (£4.50, 20 minutes, twice hourly); change at Ford or Barnham. There are also links to Brighton (£10.10, 1¼ hours, twice hourly); again, change at Ford or Barnham.

Bus 700 runs to Brighton (two hours, twice hourly).

Chichester

POP 23,700

A lively Georgian market town still almost encircled by its medieval town walls, the administrative capital of West Sussex keeps watch over the plains between the South Downs and the sea. Visitors flock to Chichester's splendid cathedral, streets of handsome 18th-century town houses and its famous theatre, and of course to its pedestrianised shopping streets. A Roman port garrison in its early days, the town is also a launch pad to other fascinating Roman remains, as well as to Arundel and the coast.

◉ Sights

Chichester Cathedral   CATHEDRAL
(www.chichestercathedral.org.uk; West St; ⊙ 7.15am-7pm, tours 11.15am & 2.30pm Mon-Sat) This understated cathedral was begun in 1075 and largely rebuilt in the 13th century. The free-standing church tower went up in the 15th century; the spire dates from the 19th century, when its predecessor famously toppled over. Inside, three storeys of beautiful arches sweep upwards and Romanesque carvings are dotted around. Interesting features to track down include a smudgy stained-glass window added by artist Marc Chagall in 1978 and a glassed-over section of Roman mosaic flooring. Free guided tours last 45 minutes.

The excellent cathedral choir is guaranteed to give you goosebumps during the daily evensong (5.30pm).

Pallant House Gallery   GALLERY
(www.pallant.org.uk; 9 North Pallant; adult/child £9/3.50; ⊙ 10am-5pm Tue, Wed, Fri & Sat, to 8pm Thu, from 11am Sun) A Queen Anne mansion built by a local wine merchant, handsome Pallant House and a 21st-century wing host this superb gallery. The focus is on, mostly British, 20th-century art. Show-stoppers Patrick Caulfield, Lucian Freud, Graham Sutherland, Frank Auerbach and Henry Moore are interspersed with internation-

al names such as Emil Filla, Le Corbusier and RB Kitaj. Most of these older works are in the mansion, while the newer wing is packed with pop art and temporary shows of modern and contemporary work.

Novium Museum   MUSEUM
(www.thenovium.org; Tower St; adult/child £7/2.50; ⊙ 10am-5pm Mon-Sat, to 4pm Sun Apr-Oct, to 5pm Tue-Sat Nov-Mar) Chichester's purpose-built museum provides a home for the eclectic collections of the now-defunct District Museum, as well as many artefacts from Fishbourne Palace and a huge mosaic from Chilgrove Roman villa. The highlight is the set of Roman baths discovered in the 1970s, around which the six-million-pound museum was designed.

🛌 Sleeping

Accommodation is very thin on the ground in the city centre. Beds fill when there are goings-on at Goodwood racecourse, just to the north of Chichester.

Ship Hotel   BOUTIQUE HOTEL **££**
(☏ 01243-778000; www.theshiphotel.net; North St; r from £124; 🖥) The grand central staircase in this former Georgian town house climbs to 36 fairly spacious rooms of commanding period chic. It's the most enticing option in the city centre and it also boasts a brand-new and very snazzily styled restaurant. Book well ahead.

Jubilee House   B&B **££**
(☏ 01243-536558; www.jubileehousechichester.co.uk; 13 New Park Rd; s £60-80 d £70-90; 🖥) Two-room B&B on the edge of the historical centre with crisp, well-maintained quarters, a communal breakfast table and all of Chichester's sights a short amble away. Book ahead.

🍴 Eating

St Martin's Tearooms   CAFE **£**
(3 St Martins St; mains £4-10; ⊙ 10am-6pm Mon-Sat) A little cocoon of nooks and crannies tucked away in a part-18th-century, part-medieval town house, this organic cafe serves freshly ground coffee with wholesome, mostly vegetarian, food and a sinful selection of desserts. There's also a guest piano with which to shatter the tranquil scene, if you so wish. St Martin's St is off East St.

Wests Bar   BRITISH **£**
(14 West St; mains £5-9; ⊙ 11am-11pm Mon-Sat, to 10.30pm Sun; 🖥) In a large deconsecrated church opposite Chichester Cathedral, this

temple of food and ale allows you to refuel and kick back in an incongruously ecclesiastical setting. The sinful menu of British pub favourites, including some typically spicy fare, is sure to bust your belt and invoke a holy thirst.

☆ Entertainment

Chichester Festival Theatre THEATRE
(☑ 01243-781312; www.cft.org.uk; Oakland's Park) Built in 1962, this somewhat Soviet-looking playhouse has a long and distinguished history. Sir Laurence Olivier was the theatre's first director, and Ingrid Bergman, Sir John Gielgud and Sir Anthony Hopkins have all played here.

ℹ Information

Post Office (10 West St; ⊘ 9am-5.30pm Mon & Wed-Fri, from 9.30am Tue, 9am-3pm Sat)
Tourist Office (☑ 01243-775888; www. visitchichester.org; Tower St; ⊘ 10am-5pm Mon-Sat, to 4pm Sun) Located in the Novium Museum.

ℹ Getting There & Away

BUS
Brighton Bus 700, 2½ hours, twice hourly
London Victoria National Express, change at Gatwick Airport; £15.60, three hours 40 minutes, every two hours
Portsmouth Bus 700, 70 minutes, twice hourly

TRAIN
Chichester has train connections to the following destinations:
Arundel Change at Ford or Barnham; £4.50, 20 minutes, twice hourly
Brighton £12.60, 50 minutes, twice hourly
London Victoria £17.30, 1½ hours, half-hourly
Portsmouth £7.50, 30 to 40 minutes, twice hourly

Around Chichester

Fishbourne Palace & Museum

Fishbourne Palace (www.sussexpast.co.uk; Roman Way; adult/child £8.70/4.30; ⊘ 10am-5pm Mar-Oct, reduced hours & days rest of the year) is the largest-known Roman residence in Britain. The palace lies 1.5 miles west of Chichester, just off the A259 (take bus 700 from outside Chichester Cathedral). Happened upon by labourers in the 1960s, it's thought that this once-luxurious mansion was built

around AD 75 for a romanised local king. Housed in a modern pavilion are its foundations, hypocaust and painstakingly re-laid mosaics.

The centrepiece is a spectacular floor depicting Cupid riding a dolphin, flanked by sea horses and panthers. There's also a fascinating little museum and replanted Roman gardens.

SURREY

Surrey is popular with affluent London commuters who've had kids, moved out of the city and bought a country pad. For the most part, though, it's made up of uninspiring towns and dull, sprawling suburbs. Further away from the roaring motorways and packed rush-hour trains, the county reveals some inspiring landscapes made famous by authors Sir Arthur Conan Doyle, Sir Walter Scott and Jane Austen.

Farnham
POP 39,500

Nudging the border with Hampshire and joined at the hip with the garrison settlement of Aldershot, affluent Farnham is Surrey's prettiest town and its best destination. Blessed with lively shopping streets of Georgian symmetry, a 12th-century castle and some soothing river walks, this easygoing market town makes for an undemanding day trip from London, just an hour away.

◉ Sights

Farnham Castle CASTLE
(EH; ☑ 01252-721194; www.farnhamcastle.com; Castle St; palace adult/child £3.50/2.50, keep admission free; ⊘ palace 2-4pm Wed, keep 9am-5pm Mon-Fri, 10am-4pm Sat & Sun, closed Jan) Farnham Castle was constructed in 1138 by Henry de Blois, the grandson of William the Conqueror. There's not much left of the castle keep today except the beautiful old ramparts. Even if the keep is closed, it's worth walking around the outside for the picturesque views.

Open only one afternoon a week, the residential palace was built in the 13th century as a stopover for the bishops of Winchester on London journeys. From 1926 to the 1950s, it was used by the bishops of Guildford.

The palace is now a private function venue, hence the limited opening hours.

Museum of Farnham
MUSEUM

(38 West St; ⊙ 10am-5pm Tue-Sat) FREE This engaging little museum is located in the splendid Willmer House, a Georgian mansion built in 1718 for the wealthy hop merchant and maltster John Thorne.

Themed rooms trace Farnham's history from flint-tool days to Bakelite nostalgia. A corner is dedicated to William Cobbett, the town's most famous son, a 19th-century reformer, radical member of parliament, writer and journalist who established Hansard (the official record of what is said in Parliament).

Cobbett's bust takes pride of place in the peaceful garden out back, where you'll also find a timber gallery housing temporary exhibitions.

🛏 Sleeping & Eating

Bush Hotel
HOTEL **££**

(☑ 01252-234800; www.mercure-uk.com; The Borough; r from £109; P ❄ 🛜) This 17th-century inn is right in the heart of the action. Rolling renovations keep things fresh, and there's a snug beamed bar and recommended restaurant that spills into the pretty courtyard.

Vintage Cake House
CAFE **£**

(www.thevintagecakehouse.co.uk; 5 Downing St; light lunch & tea £5-10; ⊙ 9.30am-5pm) Classic English tearoom with wedges of homemade cake, tinkling tea china, staff in vintage attire and lashings of clotted cream.

Brasserie Blanc
FRENCH **££**

(www.brasserieblanc.com; 5 Castle St; mains £10-18; ⊙ 9-11am, noon-3pm, 6-10pm Mon-Thu, to 10.30pm Fri, noon-10.30pm Sat, to 9pm Sun) For a bit of Gallic class, head to this understated eatery near Farnham Castle. The simply laid tables, low-Watt art deco lighting and art-packed walls create a modestly stylish atmosphere, and there's a walled garden out the back. The menu is a mostly seasonal list of finely crafted dishes cooked using choice ingredients shipped in from France.

ℹ Information

Farnham has no tourist office, but maps and leaflets are available from the town hall on South St.

ℹ Getting There & Away

BUS

London Victoria National Express; £9.70, two hours, daily

TRAIN

London Waterloo £15.30, one hour, twice hourly

Winchester Change at Woking; £19.40, 60 to 80 minutes, twice hourly

Hindhead

The tiny hamlet of Hindhead, 8 miles south of Farnham off the A287, lies in the middle of the largest area of open heath in Surrey. During the 19th century a number of prominent Victorians bought up property in the area, including Sherlock Holmes' mastermind Sir Arthur Conan Doyle (1859–1930). One of three founders of the National Trust, Sir Robert Hunter lived in nearby Haslemere, and today much of the area is administered by the foundation.

The most beautiful part of the area is to the northeast, where you'll find a natural depression known as the Devil's Punchbowl. There are a number of excellent trails and bridleways here. To get the best view, head for Gibbet Hill (280m), which was once an execution ground. The Hindhead YHA Hostel (☑ 0845 371 9022; www.yha.org. uk; Devil's Punchbowl, Thursley, Godalming; dm from £16) is a completely secluded cottage run by the National Trust on the northern edge of the Punchbowl – perfect digs for walkers.

Buses 18 and 19 run every 30 minutes between Hindhead and Farnham.

Oxford, Cotswolds & Around

Why Go?

Dotted with gorgeous little villages, this part of the country is as close to the old-world English idyll as you'll get. It's a haven of lush rolling hills, rose-clad cottages, graceful stone churches and thatched roofs. Add to this mix the legendary university city of Oxford, with its gracious architecture and lively student vibe, and it's easy to see why the region is a magnet for visitors.

Although the roads and the most popular villages are busy in summer, it's easy to get off the tourist trail. The Cotswolds are at their best when you find a romantic refuge of your own, and discover the fire-lit inns and grandiose manors that persuade A-list celebrities and the moneyed to buy property here.

Most of the area is an easy day trip from London, but Oxford and the Cotswolds deserve at least a couple of leisurely days.

When to Go

➜ On 1 May you can welcome the dawn with Oxford's Magdalen College Choir, which sings hymns from the college tower.

➜ In July you can sip champagne and watch the rowing at Henley's Royal Regatta and Festival.

➜ September is the best time to sample England's finest ales at the four-day St Albans Beer Festival.

➜ Rambling in the Cotswolds is ideal in spring, early summer and September, when the weather is in your favour, without the July and August crowds.

Best Places to Eat

➜ Paris House (p212)

➜ Waterside Inn (p218)

➜ Rickety Press (p186)

➜ Horse & Groom (p200)

➜ Edamame (p185)

Best Places to Stay

➜ Bradley (p207)

➜ Glove House (p189)

➜ Star Cottage (p196)

➜ Hope House (p189)

Oxford, Cotswolds & Around Highlights

1 Following in the footsteps of JRR Tolkien, CS Lewis, Evelyn Waugh and Oscar Wilde as you tour the **Oxford colleges** (p177)

2 Having a wizard of a time at the **Making of Harry Potter studio tour** (p213) in Leavesden

3 Getting a glimpse of the regal life at the Queen's weekend hideaway, **Windsor Castle** (p214)

4 Touring the elegant cloisters at the magnificent **Gloucester Cathedral** (p207)

5 Lording it up in **Blenheim Palace** (p189), one of the country's greatest stately homes

6 Meandering around **Painswick** (p204), one of the most beautiful and unspoilt towns in the Cotswolds

7 Exploring the anthropological treasure trove that is the **Pitt Rivers Museum** (p177) in Oxford

🏃 Activities

Cycling

Gentle gradients and scenic vistas make the Cotswolds ideal for cycling, with only the steep western escarpment offering a challenge to the legs. Plenty of quiet country lanes and byways criss-cross the region, or you can follow the signposted Thames Valley Cycle Way (NCN Routes 4 and 5) from Windsor to Oxford.

Mountain bikers can use a variety of bridleways in the Cotswolds and Chilterns. In the west of the region, the Forest of Dean has many dirt-track options and some dedicated mountain-bike trails.

Walking

The Cotswolds offers opportunities for day hikes. If you're looking for something more ambitious, the 102-mile Cotswold Way (www.nationaltrail.co.uk/cotswold) from Bath to Chipping Campden takes about a week to walk.

Alternatively, the Thames Path (www.nationaltrail.co.uk/thamespath) follows the river downstream from its source near Cirencester to London. In Oxfordshire (www.oxfordshire.gov.uk/countryside) there's also the Oxfordshire Way, a 65-mile signposted trail running from Bourton-on-the-Water to Henley-on-Thames, and the Wychwood Way, a 37-mile loop route from Woodstock, which runs through an ancient royal forest.

The picturesque 87-mile Ridgeway National Trail (www.nationaltrail.co.uk/ridgeway) meanders along the chalky grassland of the Wiltshire downs near Avebury, down into the Thames Valley and then along the spine of the Chilterns to Ivinghoe Beacon near Aylesbury in Buckinghamshire.

ℹ️ Getting There & Around

A car will give you the most freedom, especially for exploring the small villages of the Cotswolds.

Oxford, Moreton-in-Marsh, Stroud, Cheltenham, Gloucester, Bletchley, St Albans and Windsor are plugged into the train network and all have direct services to London. Other direct trains go as far afield as Birmingham, Manchester and Newcastle (from Oxford), and Cardiff and Edinburgh (from Cheltenham).

National Express coaches head from London and further-flung destinations to Oxford, Cirencester, Stroud, Cheltenham, Gloucester, Newent and Windsor.

Local buses connect larger towns to each other and to their surrounding villages. Services are run by various operators. To view timetables, use the journey planner tool on www.traveline.info.

OXFORD

POP 171,000

One of the world's most famous university cities, Oxford is a privileged place. It is steeped in history and studded with august buildings, yet it maintains the feel of a young town, thanks to its large student population. The elegant honey-coloured buildings of the colleges that make up the university wrap around tranquil courtyards along narrow cobbled lanes, and inside their grounds, a studious calm reigns. Just as in Cambridge, the existence of 'town' beside 'gown' makes it more than simply a bookish place of learning.

Oxford is a wonderful place to ramble: the oldest colleges date back 750 years, and little has changed inside the hallowed walls since then. But along with the rich history, tradition and lively academic life, there is a world beyond the college walls. Oxford has a long industrial past and the working majority still outnumber the academic elite.

The university buildings are scattered throughout the city, with the most important and architecturally significant in the centre. Jericho, in the northwest, is the trendy, artsy end of town, with slick bars, restaurants and an art-house cinema, as well as the wonderfully tranquil Port Meadow. East Oxford is a gritty, ethnically diverse area packed with cheap places to eat and drink. Further out, in the salubrious northern suburb of Summertown, you'll find upmarket restaurants and bars.

History

Strategically placed at the confluence of the Rivers Cherwell and Thames (called the Isis here, from the Latin *Tamesis*), Oxford was a key Saxon town, heavily fortified by Alfred the Great during the war against the Danes.

By the 11th century, the Augustinian abbey in Oxford had begun training clerics, and when Anglo-Norman clerical scholars were expelled from the Sorbonne in 1167, the abbey began to attract students in droves. Alongside Oxford's growing prosperity grew the enmity between the new students and the local townspeople, culminating in the St Scholastica's Day Massacre in 1355, which started as an argument over beer. Thereafter, the king ordered that the university be broken up into colleges, each of which then developed its own traditions.

The university, largely a religious entity at the time, was rocked in the 16th century by the Reformation; the public trials and burning at the stake of Protestant heretics under Mary I; and by the subsequent hanging, drawing and quartering of Catholics under her successor Elizabeth I. As the Royalist headquarters, Oxford backed the losing side during the Civil War, but flourished after the restoration of the monarchy, with some of its most notable buildings constructed at that time.

The arrival of the canal system in 1790 had a profound effect on the rest of Oxford. By creating a link with the Midlands' industrial centres, work and trade suddenly expanded beyond the academic core. This development was further strengthened by the construction of the railways.

The city's real industrial boom came, however, when William Morris began producing cars here in 1913. With the success of his Bullnose Morris and Morris Minor, his Cowley factory went on to become one of the largest motor plants in the world. Although the works have been scaled down since their heyday, Minis still run off BMW's Cowley production line today.

◉ Sights

University of Oxford

Much of the centre of Oxford is taken up by graceful university buildings and elegant colleges, each one individual in its appearance and academic specialities. The first colleges (Balliol, Merton and University) were built in the 13th century, with at least three more being added in each of the following three centuries. Newer colleges, such as Keble, were added in the 19th and 20th centuries to cater for an ever-expanding student population. Tradition dies hard at Oxford, however, and it wasn't until 1877 that lecturers were allowed to marry, and another year before female students were admitted. It took another 42 years before women were granted degrees.

Today, there are 38 colleges catering to more than 21,000 students. Not all are open to the public. For those that are, visiting hours change with the term and exam schedule; check www.ox.ac.uk for full details of visiting hours.

Oxford University Museum of Natural History MUSEUM
(www.oum.ox.ac.uk; Parks Rd; ⊙10am-5pm; 👶) FREE Housed in a glorious Victorian Gothic building with slender, cast-iron columns, ornate capitals and a soaring glass roof, this museum is worth visiting for its architecture alone. The real draw, however, is the collection of more than five million exhibits. These range from exotic insects and fossils to a towering T Rex skeleton and the remains of the first dinosaur ever to be mentioned in a written text (in 1677).

★ Pitt Rivers Museum MUSEUM
(www.prm.ox.ac.uk; Parks Rd; ⊙noon-4.30pm Mon, 10am-4.30pm Tue-Sun; 👶) FREE Hidden away through a door at the back of the main exhibition hall of the Oxford University Museum of Natural History, this wonderfully creepy anthropological museum houses a treasure trove of objects from around the world – more than enough to satisfy any armchair adventurer. One of the reasons this museum is so brilliant is because there are no computers here or shiny modern gimmicks. The dim light lends an air of mystery to the glass cases stuffed with the prized booty of Victorian explorers.

Objects are divided into themes, rather than culture, with subjects such as 'Smoking' or 'Treatment of Dead Enemies' (a particularly disturbing ensemble). Among the feathered cloaks, necklaces of teeth, blowpipes, magic charms, Noh masks, totem poles, fur parkas, musical instruments and shrunken heads, you may spot ceremonial headgear from Uganda worn during circumcision ceremonies, ancient dental implements and a porcupine fish helmet from Kiribati.

Trinity College COLLEGE
(www.trinity.ox.ac.uk; Broad St; adult/child £2/1; ⊙10am-noon Mon-Fri, 2-4pm daily) Founded in 1555, this small college is worth a visit to see the lovely garden quad, designed by Christopher Wren. Its exquisitely carved chapel is one of the most beautiful in the city and a masterpiece of English baroque. Famous students have included William Pitt the Elder and Cardinal Newman.

LOCAL KNOWLEDGE

ACADEMIC ATTIRE

Don't be surprised to see students wandering around Oxford in black gowns, black 'mortarboard' caps, white bowties and (for graduates) colourful hoods. Oxford students are required to wear their academic dress to take their exams, and some colleges require it every night when dining in the hall.

Oxford

OXFORD, COTSWOLDS & AROUND OXFORD

Exeter College COLLEGE
(www.exeter.ox.ac.uk; Turl St; ⊘2-5pm) FREE Exeter is known for its elaborate 17th-century dining hall and its ornate Victorian Gothic chapel housing *The Adoration of the Magi*, a William Morris tapestry, and a psychedelic bombast of gold mosaic and stained glass.

Museum of the History of Science MUSEUM
(www.mhs.ox.ac.uk; Broad St; ⊘noon-5pm Tue-Fri, 10am-5pm Sat, 2-5pm Sun) FREE Science, art, celebrity and nostalgia come together at this fascinating museum, where the exhibits include everything from a blackboard used by Einstein to the world's finest collection

of historical scientific instruments. It's all housed in a beautiful 17th-century building.

Sheldonian Theatre THEATRE
(www.sheldon.ox.ac.uk; Broad St; adult/child £3.50/2.50; ⊘10am-4.30pm daily Jul & Aug, closed Sun Sep-Jun, closed Sat Dec & Jan) Built in 1663, this monumental building was the first major work of Christopher Wren, at that time a professor of astronomy. Inspired by the classical Theatre of Marcellus in Rome, it has a rectangular front end and a semicircular back, while the ceiling of the main hall is blanketed by a fine 17th-century painting of the triumph

of truth over ignorance. What's remarkable about the ceiling is its length, made possible by ingenious braces made of shorter timbers, for want of trees large enough.

The Sheldonian is now used for college ceremonies and public concerts, but you can climb to the cupola for good views of the surrounding buildings.

New College COLLEGE
(www.new.ox.ac.uk; Holywell St; adult/child £3/2 Mar-Sep, free Oct-Feb; ☉11am-5pm Mar-Sep, 2-4pm Oct-Feb) This 14th-century college was the first in Oxford for undergraduates and is a fine example of the glorious Perpendicular Gothic style. The chapel here is full of treasures, including superb stained glass, much of it original, and Sir Jacob Epstein's disturbing statue of Lazarus. During term time, visitors can attend the beautiful Evensong, a choral church service held nightly at 6pm.

William Spooner was once a college warden here, and his habit of transposing the first consonants of words gave rise to the term 'spoonerism'. Local lore suggests that he once reprimanded a student by saying, 'You have deliberately tasted two worms and can leave Oxford by the town drain'. Spooner

Oxford

aside, other famous alumni include Hugh Grant and Kate Beckinsale.

New College is also famous for a bizarre medieval ritual. Every three years, the Lord Major of Oxford has to walk along the ruins of the city wall, which is part of New College, to fulfill a medieval obligation that the wall would be repaired if need be (the walk is merely symbolic).

Access for visitors is through the New College Lane gate from Easter to early October, and through the Holywell St entrance the rest of the year. As you walk along New College Lane, look up at the steeped **Bridge of Sighs** linking the two halves of Hertford College to New College. It's sometimes erroneously referred to as a copy of the famous bridge in Venice, but it bears a much closer resemblance to that city's Rialto Bridge.

Bodleian Library　　　　　　LIBRARY
(☎ 01865-287400; www.bodley.ox.ac.uk; Catte St; tours £5-13; ⊙ 9am-5pm Mon-Sat, 11am-5pm Sun)

Oxford's Bodleian Library is one of the oldest public libraries in the world and quite possibly the most impressive one you'll ever see. Casual visitors are welcome to wander around the central quad and visit the exhibition space in the foyer. For £1 you can also access the Divinity School, but the rest of the complex can only be visited on guided tours (check online or at the information desk for times; it pays to book ahead).

The Bodleian Library has its roots in a 15th-century collection of books and its present state is largely due to the efforts of Sir Thomas Bodley, a 16th-century fellow of Merton College. He came to the agreement with the Stationers' Company of London that the library would receive a copy of every single book published in the UK – an agreement that still stands today. It currently holds more than 11 million items, contains 117 miles of shelving and has seating space for up to 2500 readers. A staggering 4000 books and articles arrive every week, all of which need to be catalogued and stored.

The oldest part of the library surrounds the Jacobean Gothic Old Schools Quadrangle, which dates from the early 17th century and sports some of Oxford's odder architectural gems. On the eastern side of the quad is the Tower of Five Orders, an ornate building depicting the five classical orders of architecture. On the west side is the Divinity School, the university's first teaching room. It is renowned as a masterpiece of 15th-century English Gothic architecture and has a superb fan-vaulted ceiling; it featured as the Hogwarts hospital wing in the *Harry Potter* films.

Half-hour mini tours (£5) include the Divinity School and the medieval Duke Humfrey's library, where no fewer than five kings, 40 Nobel Prize winners, 25 British prime ministers, and writers such as Oscar Wilde, CS Lewis and JRR Tolkien studied amid rows filled with grand ancient tomes chained to the shelves. Those wishing to read here (the books may not be borrowed) still have to swear Bodley's Oath, which involves vowing 'not to bring into the Library or kindle therein any fire or flame'.

Hour-long standard tours (£7) also visit the 17th-century Convocation House, where parliament was held during the Civil War, and the Chancellor's Court. Extended tours (£13) run for 90 minutes and include the Radcliffe Camera and either the Upper Reading Room or underground Gladstone Link.

Radcliffe Camera   LIBRARY

(Radcliffe Sq) The Radcliffe Camera is the quintessential Oxford landmark and one of the city's most photographed buildings. The spectacular circular library/reading room, filled with natural light, was built between 1737 and 1749 in grand Palladian style, and has Britain's third-largest dome. The only way to see the interior is to join one of the extended tours (£13; 90 minutes) of the Bodleian Library (p180).

Brasenose College   COLLEGE

(www.bnc.ox.ac.uk; Radcliffe Sq; admission £2; ⊘10-11.30am & 2-4.30pm) Founded in 1509, this small, select and elegant place is named after a 'brass nose', or a brazen door-knocker, to be precise. It's believed that wayward students took the knocker all the way to Stamford, Lincolnshire, in 1533. In 1890 the college purchased a house in Stamford, convinced that the knocker on its front door was the original. The door-knocker in question now takes pride of place above the high table in the dining hall.

Also of interest is the chapel, with its fine painted, vaulted ceiling. Famous alumni include *Lord of the Flies* author William Golding, Monty Python's Michael Palin and British prime minister David Cameron. If the sign outside says that it's shut during supposed open hours, check with the porters as they sometimes hang it to deter tour groups.

University Church of St Mary the Virgin   CHURCH

(www.university-church.ox.ac.uk; High St; ⊘9am-5pm Mon-Sat, 11.30am-5pm Sun) With a tower dating from 1280 and a perpendicular Gothic nave, this relatively unadorned church is most famous as the site of the 1556 trial of three Anglican bishops (including Thomas Cranmer, the first Protestant archbishop of Canterbury) during the reign of Mary I. All three were later burnt at the stake for heresy on Broad St. Inside, there's a memorial to the victims of the Reformation – both Protestant and Catholic.

Mahatma Gandhi spoke here in the 1930s, and his image is inscribed on a ceiling boss above the loft at the rear of the church. A trek to the top of the tower (adult/child £4/3) offers excellent views of the Radcliffe Camera.

All Souls College   COLLEGE

(www.all-souls.ox.ac.uk; High St; ⊘2-4pm Mon-Fri) FREE One of the wealthiest Oxford colleges, All Souls was founded in 1438 as a centre of prayer and learning. It's one of several graduate colleges, though it doesn't accept just any old Oxford graduate. Each year, the university's top finalists sit a fellowship exam, with an average of only two making the grade. Today fellowship of the college is one of the highest academic honours in the country.

Much of the college facade dates from the 1440s and, unlike other older colleges, the front quad is largely unchanged in five centuries. It also contains a beautiful 17th-century sundial designed by Christopher Wren. Most obvious, though, are the twin mock-Gothic towers on the north quad. Designed by Nicholas Hawksmoor in 1710, they were lambasted for ruining the Oxford skyline when first erected.

St Edmund Hall
COLLEGE

(www.seh.ox.ac.uk; Queen's Lane; ⊙10am-4pm) FREE St Edmund Hall ('Teddy Hall' to its residents) is the sole survivor of the original medieval halls, the teaching institutions that preceded colleges in Oxford. The Mohawk chief Oronhyatekha studied here in 1862 (and eloped with the principal's daughter). The college is best known for its small chapel decorated by William Morris and Edward Burne-Jones.

Magdalen College
COLLEGE

(www.magd.ox.ac.uk; High St; adult/child £5/4; ⊙1-6pm) Set amid 40 hectares of lawns, woodlands, river walks and deer park, Magdalen (*mawd*-lin), founded in 1458, is one of the wealthiest and most beautiful of Oxford's colleges. It has a reputation as an artistic college, and some of its famous students have included writers Julian Barnes, Alan Hollinghurst, CS Lewis, John Betjeman, Seamus Heaney and Oscar Wilde, not to mention Edward VIII, TE Lawrence 'of Arabia' and Dudley Moore.

An elegant Victorian gateway leads into a medieval chapel (with its glorious 15th-century tower) and on to the remarkable cloisters (with strange animals perching on the buttresses), some of the finest in Oxford. The fantastic gargoyles and grotesques along the frontage here are said to have inspired CS Lewis' stone statues in *The Chronicles of Narnia*. Behind the cloisters, the lovely Addison's Walk leads through the grounds and along the banks of the River Cherwell for just under a mile. Were you here in the mid-1870s, you would have encountered Oscar Wilde taking his pet lobster for a walk.

The college also has a fine choir that sings Hymnus Eucharisticus at 6am on May Day (1 May) from the top of the 42m bell tower. The event now marks the culmination of a solid night of drinking for most students as they gather in their glad rags on Magdalen Bridge to listen to the dawn chorus.

Botanic Garden
GARDENS

(www.botanic-garden.ox.ac.uk; High St; adult/child £4.50/free; ⊙9am-5pm) Sweeping along the banks of the River Cherwell, this peaceful garden was founded in 1621 for the study of medicinal plants, and it's still a department of the university. The bench that Lyra and her extra-universal lover Will intend to haunt in Phillip Pullman's *His Dark Materials* is usually well-attended by mooning students.

Merton College
COLLEGE

(www.merton.ox.ac.uk; Merton St; admission £3; ⊙2-5pm Mon-Fri, 10am-5pm Sat & Sun) Founded in 1264, Merton is the oldest of the three original colleges and the first to adopt collegiate planning, bringing scholars and tutors together into a formal community and providing a planned residence for them. Its distinguishing architectural features include large gargoyles whose expressions suggest that they're about to throw up, and the charming 14th-century Mob Quad – the first of the college quads.

Just off the quad is a 13th-century chapel and the Old Library (admission on guided tour only), the oldest medieval library in use (look for the chained books). It is said that Tolkien spent many hours here writing *The Lord of the Rings* and that the trees in the Fellows' Garden inspired the ents of Middle Earth. Other literary giants associated with the college include TS Eliot and Louis MacNeice.

During the summer holidays it may be possible to join a guided tour of the college grounds (£4). Also in summer, look out for posters advertising candlelit concerts in the chapel.

Behind Merton College is the ominously named Dead Man's Walk, so called because the medieval Jewish community, who were not allowed to bury their dead within the city, would take bodies along this route to the Jewish cemetery (now the Botanic Garden).

★ Christ Church
COLLEGE

(www.chch.ox.ac.uk; St Aldate's; adult/child £8/6.50; ⊙10am-4.30pm Mon-Sat, 2-4.30pm Sun) The largest of all of Oxford's colleges and the one with the grandest quad, Christ Church is also its most popular. Its magnificent buildings, illustrious history and latter-day fame as a location for the *Harry Potter* films have tourists coming in droves. The college was founded in 1524 by Cardinal Thomas Wolsey, who suppressed the monastery existing on the site to acquire the funds for his lavish building project.

Over the years numerous luminaries have been educated here, including philosopher John Locke, poet WH Auden, Charles Dodgson (Lewis Carroll), and no less than 13 British prime ministers. The main entrance is below the imposing Tom Tower, the upper part of which was designed by former student Sir Christopher Wren. Great Tom, the 7-tonne tower bell, still chimes 101 times each evening at 9.05pm (Oxford is five minutes west of Greenwich) to sound the curfew imposed on the original 100 students – plus the one added in 1663.

Visitors must go further down St Aldate's to the side entrance. Immediately on entering is the 15th-century cloister, a relic of the ancient Priory of St Frideswide, whose shrine was once a focus of pilgrimage. From here, you go up to the Great Hall, the college's magnificent dining room, with its hammerbeam roof and imposing portraits of past scholars; it was replicated in the film studios as the dining hall at Hogwarts for the *Harry Potter* films.

Coming down the grand staircase (where Professor McGonagall welcomed Harry in the first film), you'll enter Tom Quad, Oxford's largest and arguably most impressive quadrangle, and from here, 12th-century Christ Church Cathedral. It was originally the abbey church and then the college chapel, but it was declared a cathedral by Henry VIII when he broke from the Catholic Church, suppressed more monasteries and convents, and gave the college its current name. It was formerly known as Cardinal's College.

Inside, brawny Norman columns are topped by elegant vaulting, and beautiful stained-glass windows illuminate the walls. Look out for the depiction of the murder of Thomas Becket, dating from 1320, above the side altar on the right. As this is a working Anglican cathedral, there's no charge to visit it for private prayer or to attend a service – talk to the porters at the main gate. Evensong is held at 6pm most days.

To the south of the college is Christ Church Meadow, a leafy expanse bordered by the Rivers Cherwell and Isis, ideal for leisurely walking.

The hall often closes between noon and 2pm and the cathedral in late afternoon.

Christ Church Picture Gallery   GALLERY
(www.chch.ox.ac.uk/gallery; Oriel Sq; adult/child £3/free; ☺10.30am-4.30pm Mon-Sat, 2-4.30pm Sun, closed Tue Oct-Jun) Christ Church's stash of precious masterpieces dates from 1300 to 1750, and has a particular focus on the Italian Renaissance. Paintings by the likes of Tintoretto, Veronese and Anthony van Dyck take pride of place, and there's an exalted collection of drawings by the likes of Michelangelo, Leonardo da Vinci and Raphael. Admission is half price with a valid Christ Church ticket.

Other Sights

★Ashmolean Museum   MUSEUM
(www.ashmolean.org; Beaumont St; ☺10am-5pm Tue-Sun; ⓘ) FREE Britain's oldest public museum, second in repute only to London's British Museum, was established in 1683 when Elias Ashmole presented the university with the collection of curiosities amassed by the well-travelled John Tradescant, gardener to Charles I. A 2009 makeover has left the museum with new interactive features, a giant atrium, glass walls revealing galleries on different levels and a beautiful rooftop restaurant.

Its collections, displayed in bright, spacious galleries within one of Britain's best examples of neoclassical architecture, span the world and include Egyptian mummies, Islamic art, ancient documents, rare porcelain, tapestries, silverware, priceless musical instruments and extensive displays of European art.

Oxford Union   LIBRARY
(www.oxford-union.org; Frewin Ct; admission £1.50; ☺9.30am-5pm Mon-Fri, longer during university term) Oxford's legendary members' society is famous for its feisty debates, heavyweight international speakers and Pre-Raphaelite murals. Although most of the building is off-limits to nonmembers, you can visit the library to see the murals, which were painted between 1857 and 1859 by Dante Gabriel Rossetti, William Morris and Edward Burne-Jones. They depict scenes from the Arthurian legends but are difficult to see on bright days, as they surround the windows.

Carfax Tower   TOWER
(Queen St; adult/child £2.50/1.30; ☺10am-5.30pm) This central landmark, towering over what has been a crossroads for 1000 years, is the sole reminder of medieval St Martin's Church and offers good views over the city centre.

LOCAL KNOWLEDGE

TOLKIEN'S RESTING PLACE

Lord of the Rings author JRR Tolkien is buried with his wife Edith at Wolvercote Cemetery, 2 miles north of the city along Banbury Rd. The names Beren and Luthien are carved on their gravestone, a reference to the love between a mortal man and an elf maiden who gave up her immortality to be with him.

Oxford Castle Unlocked CASTLE

(www.oxfordcastleunlocked.co.uk; 44-46 Oxford Castle; adult/child £10/7; ☺ tours 10am-4.20pm) It's not England's most imposing fortress, but Oxford Castle dates back more than 1000 years. Access is by tours, departing every 20 minutes, led by costumed guides.

Tours include St George's Tower, offering excellent views of the city; the 11th-century crypt of St George's Chapel (possibly the first formal teaching venue in Oxford); the Victorian prison cells; and the 18th-century Debtors' Tower, where you learn about the inmates' grisly lives, daring escapes and cruel punishments. You can also clamber up the original medieval motte.

🏃 Activities

A quintessential Oxford experience, **punting** is all about sitting back and quaffing Pimms (the typical English summer drink) as you watch the city's glorious architecture float by. Which, of course, requires someone else to do the hard work – punting is far more difficult than it appears. If you decide to go it alone, a deposit for the punt is usually charged. Most punts hold five people including the punter.

Magdalen Bridge Boathouse BOATING

(☑ 01865-202643; www.oxfordpunting.co.uk; High St; chauffered per 30min £25, self-punt per hour £20; ☺ 9.30am-dusk Feb-Nov) The most central location to hire a punt, chauffered or otherwise. From here, you can head downstream around the Botanic Garden and Christ Church Meadow or upstream around Magdalen Deer Park. You can also hire row boats and pedaloes.

Cherwell Boat House BOATING

(☑ 01865-515978; www.cherwellboathouse.co.uk; 50 Bardwell Rd; per hour £15-18; ☺ 10am-dusk mid-Mar–mid-Oct) Head a mile north of the centre for a countryside punt on the River Cherwell, where the most popular destination is the busy pub, the Victoria Arms. Row boats and Canadian canoes are also available. To get here, head north on Banbury Rd and then turn right into Bardwell Rd.

Salter Bros BOATING, CRUISE

(☑ 01865-243421; www.salterssteamers.co.uk; Folly Bridge; punt/row boat/motor boat per hr £20/20/35; ☺ May-late Sep) Rents punts, row boats and motor boats, and offers a range of cruises along the River Isis from Oxford. The most popular is the scenic journey to the historic market town of Abingdon (adult/child £13/6.80). The trip takes two hours and passes the college boathouses and several popular riverside pubs en route.

👉 Tours

Bill Spectre's Ghost Trails WALKING TOUR

(☑ 07941 041811; www.ghosttrail.org; adult/child £8/6; ☺ 6.30pm Fri & Sat) For a highly entertaining and informative look at Oxford's dark underbelly, join Victorian undertaker Bill Spectre on a 1¾-hour tour of the city's most haunted sites. It departs from Oxford Castle Unlocked (p184); audience participation likely.

Footprints Tours WALKING TOUR

(☑ 020-7558 8706; www.footprints-tours.com) There's no need to book for the 'free' two-hour walking tours (payment is by way of tips), just turn up at the departure point on Broad St at 11am or 2pm. Bookings are required though for the themed pub, bike, *Harry Potter* and Blenheim Palace tours – check times and prices online.

Oxford City Walk WALKING TOUR

(☑ 07530 951320; www.oxfordcitywalk.co.uk; 2hr tour for up to 5 people £50) Bespoke tours tweaked to your party's interests, whether that be architecture, literature, history, science, music, university life or detective series *Inspector Morse*.

Oxford Official Guided Walking Tours WALKING TOUR

(☑ 01865-252200; www.visitoxfordandoxfordshire. com; 15-16 Broad St; adult/child from £9/8) Book at the tourist office for tours of Oxford city and colleges (10.45am and 1pm year-round, plus 11am and 2pm at busy times) or a bewildering array of themed tours, including *Inspector Morse, Alice in Wonderland* and *Harry Potter*, and family walking tours in the school holidays. Check the website for details.

Oxon Carts TOUR

(☑ 07747 024600; www.oxoncarts.com; tours £25) Flexible hour-long tours conducted by a fleet of pedicabs. Passengers receive a copy of a 1904 map of the city and a personal guide to its buildings and history.

🛏 Sleeping

Book ahead between May and September and on weekends. If you're stuck, you'll find a string of B&Bs along Iffley, Abingdon, Banbury and Headington Rds.

Central Backpackers
HOSTEL £

(☑ 01865-242288; www.centralbackpackers.co.uk; 13 Park End St; dm £22-28; @🗺) A friendly budget option located above a bar and right in the centre of town, this small hostel has basic, bright and simple rooms that sleep four to 12 people, a rooftop terrace and a small lounge with satellite TV.

Oxford YHA
HOSTEL £

(☑ 0845 371 9131; www.yha.org.uk; 2a Botley Rd; dm/r from £17/56; @🗺) Particularly convenient for budget travellers arriving by train, this hostel has simple but comfortable four- and six-bed en suite dorms, private rooms and loads of facilities, including a restaurant, library, garden, laundry and a choice of lounges.

★ Oxford Coach & Horses
B&B ££

(☑ 01865-200017; www.oxfordcoachandhorses.co.uk; 62 St Clements St; s/d from £115/130; P🗺) Once a coaching inn, this 18th-century building has been painted powder blue and given a fresh, modern makeover. Rooms are spacious and light-filled, and the ground floor has been converted into a large, attractive breakfast room.

Burlington House
B&B ££

(☑ 01865-513513; www.burlington-house.co.uk; 374 Banbury Rd, Summertown; s/d from £70/97; P🗺) Twelve big, bright and elegant rooms with patterned wallpaper and splashes of colour are available at this Victorian merchant's house. The fittings are luxurious and the bathrooms immaculate; the service is attentive; and breakfast comes complete with organic eggs and granola. It has good public transport links to town.

Remont Guesthouse
B&B ££

(☑ 01865-311020; www.remont-oxford.co.uk; 367 Banbury Rd, Summertown; r £112-142; P@🗺) All modern style, subtle lighting and plush furnishings, this 25-room guesthouse has rooms decked out in cool neutrals with silky bedspreads, abstract art and huge plasma-screen TVs. There's also a sunny garden.

Buttery Hotel
HOTEL ££

(☑ 01865-811950; www.thebutteryhotel.co.uk; 11-12 Broad St; s/d from £75/125; 🗺) Right in the heart of the city, the Buttery is wonderfully central and offers views over college grounds from the front rooms. The rooms are spacious but rather modest, so it's the location that you're paying for. Rooms at the rear are smaller but quieter.

University Rooms
Oxford
UNIVERSITY ACCOMMODATION ££

(www.universityrooms.com; s/d from £45/60; 🗺) You can sleep inside hallowed colleges and breakfast in a grand hall by staying in student rooms. Most rooms are functional singles with basic furnishings and shared bathrooms, though there are some en suite, twin and small flats available. Some have views over college quads. They're only available during university holidays (Christmas, Easter and summer).

Old Bank Hotel
HOTEL £££

(☑ 01865-799599; www.oldbank-hotel.co.uk; 92 High St; r from £250; P🗺) Slap bang in the centre of Oxford, this grand hotel's front rooms look over St Mary's Church and into the very heart of Oxford University. The elegant, pale-hued bedrooms are sleek and spacious, and the whole place is strewn with interesting contemporary art. Downstairs there's a buzzing restaurant.

Malmaison
HOTEL £££

(☑ 01865-268400; www.malmaison-oxford.com; 3 New Rd; d/ste from £180/315; P🗺) This former Victorian prison is one place you'd wish to be locked up in. Attached to Oxford Castle, it has been converted into a sleek hotel with plush interiors, sultry lighting and giant beds. Each room is made from three cells.

Old Parsonage Hotel
HOTEL £££

(☑ 01865-310210; www.oldparsonage-hotel.co.uk; 1 Banbury Rd; r from £250; P🗺) Wonderfully quirky, this small boutique hotel inhabits a 17th-century stone building covered with wisteria, and has just the right blend of period charm and modern luxury. Inside, there's a contemporary art collection, artfully mismatched furniture, and chic bedrooms with handmade beds and marble bathrooms. Oscar Wilde once made it his home.

✗ Eating

✗ City Centre

★ Edamame
JAPANESE £

(www.edamame.co.uk; 15 Holywell St; mains £6-8; ⏱11.30am-2.30pm Wed-Sun, 5-8.30pm Thu-Sat) The queue out the door speaks volumes about the quality of food here. This tiny joint, all light wood and friendly bustle, is the best place in town for authentic Japanese cuisine. Arrive early and be prepared to wait.

WORTH A TRIP

LE MANOIR AUX QUAT'SAISONS

As Oxford has no Michelin-starred restaurants of its own, local foodies make the pilgrimage 10km east to the famous **Le Manoir aux Quat'Saisons** (☎01844-278881; www.manoir.com; Church Rd, Great Milton; five-course lunch/dinner £79/134; �7.30-10am, 11.45am-2.15pm & 6.45-9.30pm; ✐) for special occasions. Chef Raymond Blanc has been working his magic at this impressive stone manor house for more than 30 years, presenting imaginative, complex and exquisitely presented dishes to his adoring fans. If you're one of them, consider staying overnight in one of the luxurious rooms. Book well ahead and dress up.

Missing Bean   CAFE £
(www.themissingbean.co.uk; 14 Turl St; mains £3-4; �8am-6.30pm Mon-Sat, 10am-5.30pm Sun) Oxford's best coffee can be found here, as well as loose-leaf teas and smoothies for those less caffeine inclined. The fresh muffins, cakes and ciabatta sandwiches make this a great lunchtime stop.

Chiang Mai Kitchen   THAI ££
(☎01865-202233; www.chiangmaikitchen.co.uk; 130a High St; mains £7-16; �noon-10.30pm; ✐) Authentic Thai cuisine in the heart of Oxford, complete with tear-jerkingly spicy *som tum* (spicy papaya salad), a range of curries (including, unusually, venison), noodle dishes and standout classics such as chicken with cashew nuts. There's an extensive separate menu for vegetarians.

✗ Jericho

Al-Shami   LEBANESE £
(☎01865-310066; www.al-shami.co.uk; 25 Walton Cres; mains £7-12; �noon-midnight; ✐) The service can be patchy but the food's tasty and authentic at this long-standing Lebanese eatery. Start with a selection of hot and cold mezze before tucking into charcoal-grilled lamb and chicken. There's a great vegetarian selection, too.

Manos   GREEK £
(☎01865-311782; www.manosfoodbar.com; 105 Walton St; mains £7-9; �10.30am-9pm; ✐) For delicious home-cooked tastes of the Mediterranean, head for this Greek deli and restaurant, where you'll find the likes of spinach and feta tart, chicken souvlaki and a great selection of mezze. The ground floor cafe and deli serves inexpensive wraps and salads, while downstairs offers more style and comfort.

★Rickety Press   MODERN BRITISH ££
(☎01865-424581; www.thericketypress.com; 67 Cranham St; mains £13-17; �noon-2.30pm & 6-9.30pm) Hidden in the back streets of Jericho, this old corner pub serves up beautifully presented, tasty food in casual surrounds. Call in for lunch or before 7pm for a great-value express menu (two/three courses £13/15).

Branca   ITALIAN ££
(☎01865-556111; www.branca.co.uk; 110-111 Walton St; mains £10-18; �10am-11pm; ✐) Big, bustling and bright, this glitzy Italian eatery serves delicious cocktails and all the requisite pizza, pasta, and meat and seafood grills that you'd expect. It also runs the deli next door.

✗ East Oxford

Oli's Thai   THAI £
(☎01865-790223; www.olisthai.com; 38 Magdalen Rd; mains £7-10; �4-10pm Tue, 11am-10pm Wed-Sat) With a sunny front terrace and a small, brightly coloured interior, this little hot spot is off the tourist track but well worth seeking out. A Thai chef lends authenticity to the short but zingy menu. From Magdalen Bridge, head along Iffley St and turn left at the Magdalen Arms pub; book ahead.

Atomic Burger   AMERICAN £
(www.atomicburger.co.uk; 96 Cowley Rd; mains £7-11; �11.30am-10.30pm) Atomic comes with the Fallout Challenge, which involves consuming a triple burger stack complete with fear-inducing ghost-chilli hot sauce. Not keen on killing your taste buds? Try the Chuck Norris, Dead Elvis, barbeque ribs, nachos or curly fries, all washed down with mega shakes.

Magdalen Arms   BRITISH ££
(☎01865-243159; www.magdalenarms.com; 243 Iffley Rd; mains £12-19; �5-11pm Mon, 11am-11pm Tue-Sun) Claret-coloured walls and mismatched furniture set the scene for a cosy pub, popular with students and foodies alike. It's well worth the 20-minute walk from Magdalen Bridge for hearty fare such as steak-and-ale pie, venison and duck.

Café Coco
MEDITERRANEAN ££

(☑ 01865-200232; www.cafecoco.co.uk; 23 Cowley Rd; breakfast £4-10, lunch £7-12; ⊗ 10am-midnight Thu-Sat, to 5pm Sun) This Cowley Rd institution is a popular brunching destination for the hip and hungry, and is decorated with classic posters on the walls and a bald plaster-cast clown in an ice bath. The menu ranges from cooked breakfasts and waffles to pizza, salads, Mediterranean mains and pecan pie.

Door 74
MODERN BRITISH ££

(☑ 01865-203374; www.door74.co.uk; 74 Cowley Rd; mains £10-14; ⊗ noon-3pm & 5-11pm Tue-Fri, 10am-11pm Sat, 11am-4pm Sun) This cosy little place woos its fans with a rich mix of British and Mediterranean flavours and friendly service. The menu is limited and the tables tightly packed, but the food is consistently good and weekend brunches (full English breakfast, pancakes etc) supremely filling. Book ahead.

🍸 Drinking & Nightlife

Oxford is blessed with some wonderful traditional pubs (see www.oxfordpubguide.co.uk), as well as a good selection of funky bars. Despite a large student population, Oxford's club scene is fairly limited, with several large, run-of-the-mill clubs on the train-station side of the town centre. Paradise St has a couple of gay bars.

Bear Inn
PUB

(www.bearoxford.co.uk; 6 Alfred St; ⊗ 11am-11pm; 🛜) Arguably Oxford's oldest pub (there's been a pub on this site since 1242), this atmospherically creaky place requires all but the most vertically challenged to duck their heads when passing through doorways. There's a curious tie collection on the walls and ceiling (though you can no longer exchange yours for a pint), and there are usually a couple of worthy guest ales.

Eagle & Child
PUB

(www.nicholsonspubs.co.uk/theeagleandchildoxford; 49 St Giles; ⊗ 11am-11pm; 🛜) Affectionately known as the 'Bird & Baby', this atmospheric place, dating from 1650, was once the favourite haunt of author JRR Tolkien and CS Lewis. Its wood-panelled rooms and selection of real ales still attract a mellow crowd.

Turf Tavern
PUB

(www.theturftavern.co.uk; 4 Bath Pl; ⊗ 11am-11pm) Hidden down a narrow alleyway, this tiny medieval pub (dating from at least 1381) is one of the town's best loved; it's where US president Bill Clinton famously 'did not inhale'. Home to 11 real ales, it's always packed with a mix of students, professionals and lucky tourists who manage to find it. Plenty of outdoor seating.

White Horse
PUB

(www.whitehorseoxford.co.uk; 52 Broad St; ⊗ 11am-11pm) This tiny 16th-century pub was a favourite retreat for TV detective Inspector Morse, and it can get pretty crowded in the evenings. It's a great place for a quiet afternoon pint of whatever the guest ale happens to be.

Raoul's
COCKTAIL BAR

(www.raoulsbar.com; 32 Walton St; ⊗ 4pm-midnight) Perfectly mixed cocktails and funky music at Jericho's finest retro-look bar.

Kazbar
BAR

(www.kazbar.co.uk; 25-27 Cowley Rd; ⊗ 5pm-midnight Mon-Fri, noon-12.30am Sat, noon-11pm Sun) This funky Moroccan-themed bar has giant windows, low lighting, warm colours and a cool vibe. It's buzzing most nights with hip young things sipping cocktails and filling up on Spanish and North African tapas.

Trout
PUB

(www.thetroutoxford.co.uk; 195 Godstow Rd, Wolvercote; ⊗ 11am-11pm) A 2.5-mile walk northwest along the Thames from the centre of Oxford will bring you to this charming old-world pub, a favourite hang-out since the 17th century. Immortalised by British TV detective series *Inspector Morse*, it's generally crammed with people enjoying the riverside garden.

☆ Entertainment

If you're a fan of classical music you'll be spoilt for choice in Oxford, which has a host of excellent venues and regular concerts throughout the year. See www.dailyinfo.co.uk or www.musicatoxford.com for listings.

★ Creation Theatre
THEATRE

(☑ 01865-766266; www.creationtheatre.co.uk) Performing in a variety of nontraditional venues, including city parks, the BMW plant and Oxford Castle, this theatre company produces highly original, mostly Shakespearean, shows featuring plenty of magic and special effects.

Oxford Playhouse
THEATRE

(☑ 01865-305305; www.oxfordplayhouse.com; Beaumont St) The city's main stage for quality drama also hosts an impressive selection of touring music, dance and theatre performances. The Burton Taylor Studio often features quirky student productions.

Catweazle Club   LIVE MUSIC

(www.catweazleclub.com; East Oxford Social Club, 44 Princes St; admission £6; ☺8pm Thu) Legendary open-mic night, featuring musos, poets and all sorts of bohemian performers.

O2 Academy   LIVE MUSIC

(www.o2academyoxford.co.uk; 190 Cowley Rd) Oxford's best club and live-music venue hosts everything from big-name DJs and international touring artists to indie bands, hard rock and funk nights across three performance spaces.

Cellar   LIVE MUSIC

(www.cellaroxford.co.uk; Frewin Crt; ☎) There's live music or DJs most nights at this independent venue, covering a wide spread of genres including indie rock, reggae, folk, hip hop, and drum and bass.

🛍 Shopping

★ Blackwell's   BOOKS

(www.blackwell.co.uk; 48-51 Broad St; ☺9am-6.30pm Mon-Sat, 11am-5pm Sun) The most famous bookshop in the most studenty of cities, Blackwell's doesn't disappoint with its vast range of literature, academic treatises and guilty pleasures. Separate branches on the same street focus on sheet music and art posters. In summer Blackwell's runs literary-themed walking tours.

Make sure you visit the Norrington Room in the basement – an immense inverted step pyramid lined with shelves.

Oxford Covered Market   MARKET

(www.oxford-coveredmarket.co.uk; Market St; ☺9am-5.30pm Mon-Sat, 10am-4pm Sun) A haven of traditional butchers, fishmongers, cobblers, barbers, eateries and independent shops, this is the place to go for Sicilian sausage, funky T-shirts and wacky hats for weddings and/or the Ascot horse races. At Christmas the market is a must for its displays of freshly hung deer, wild boar, ostrich and turkey. Be sure to join the queue at Ben's Cookies

ℹ Information

John Radcliffe Hospital (☎01865-741166; www.ouh.nhs.uk; Headley Way, Headington) Located 3 miles east of Oxford city centre.

Post Office (102 St Aldate's; ☺9am-5.30pm Mon-Sat)

Tourist Office (☎01865-252200; www.visitoxfordandoxfordshire.com; 15-16 Broad St; ☺9.30am-5pm Mon-Sat, 10am-3.30pm Sun)

ℹ Getting There & Away

BUS

Oxford's main bus/coach station is at Gloucester Green, near the corner of Worcester and George Sts.

Destinations include the following:

Cambridge (X5) £12.50, 3¾ hours

Chipping Norton (S3) £4.30, 56 minutes

Cheltenham (853) £7.50, 1½ hours

London Victoria (Oxford Tube/X90) £14, 1¾ hours

Woodstock (S3) £3.50, 25 minutes

Oxford Bus Company (☎01865-785400; www.oxfordbus.co.uk) Runs 'The Airline' service to/from Heathrow (£23, 1½ minutes) and Gatwick (£28, two hours).

National Express (☎08717 818178; www.nationalexpress.com) Coach destinations include London Victoria (£15, two hours), Bath (£6.50, two hours), Bristol (£7.50, 2¾ hours) and Birmingham (£8.50, two hours).

CAR

Driving and parking in central Oxford is a nightmare. There are five Park & Ride car parks on major routes leading into town. Parking costs from £2 to £4 per day; buses leave roughly every 15 minutes into town and cost about £2.70 (journey time from 12 to 25 minutes) .

TRAIN

Oxford's train station is conveniently placed to the west of the city centre. Destinations include the following:

Birmingham £27, 1¼ hours

London Paddington £25, 1¼ hours

Manchester £60, three hours

Newcastle £106, 4¾ hours

Winchester £17, 1¼ hours

ℹ Getting Around

BICYCLE

Cyclo Analysts (☎01865-424444; www.cycloanalysts.com; 150 Cowley Rd; per day/week from £10/36; ☺9am-6pm Mon-Sat) Sells, repairs and rents out bikes, including hybrids.

BUS

Oxford Bus Company and Stagecoach service an extensive local network with regular buses on the major routes. A short journey costs £1.70 (return £2.80); consider a day pass (£4). Tickets can be purchased on the bus.

TAXI

There are taxi ranks at the train station and bus station, as well as on St Giles and at Carfax.

AROUND OXFORD

Rustic charm is in abundant supply in the villages and towns surrounding Oxford. They make excellent day-trip options or stop-off destinations if you're heading on to the Cotswolds.

Woodstock

POP 2520

Don't come expecting tie-dyed clothing, rock music or illicit scents in the English Woodstock; the attractions here are considerably more genteel. Old pubs and antique stores dominate the stone buildings of the well-heeled town centre, but what really draws the crowds is Blenheim Palace, the extravagant baroque pile that was the birthplace of Sir Winston Churchill.

◉ Sights

★**Blenheim Palace**   PALACE
(www.blenheimpalace.com; adult/child £22/12, park & gardens only £13/6.50; ⊙10.30am-5.30pm daily, closed Mon & Tue Nov–mid-Feb) One of the country's greatest stately homes, Blenheim Palace is a monumental baroque fantasy designed by Sir John Vanbrugh and Nicholas Hawksmoor, and was built between 1705 and 1722. The land and funds to build the house were granted to John Churchill, Duke of Marlborough, by a grateful Queen Anne after his decisive victory at the 1704 Battle of Blenheim. Now a Unesco World Heritage Site, Blenheim (pronounced *blen*-num) is home to the 11th duke and duchess.

Inside, the house is stuffed with statues, tapestries, ostentatious furniture, priceless china and giant oil paintings in elaborate gilt frames. Visits start in the Great Hall, a vast space topped by 20m-high ceilings adorned with images of the first duke. Next up is the Churchill Exhibition, which is dedicated to the life, work and writings of Sir Winston Churchill, who was born at Blenheim in 1874. The British prime minister was a descendant of the Dukes of Marlborough, as was Princess Diana.

From here you can choose to wander through the various grand state rooms at your own pace or wait to join one of the free guided tours, which depart regularly throughout the day (except Sundays). Highlights include the famous Blenheim Tapestries, a set of 10 large wall hangings commemorating the first duke's achievements; the State Dining Room, with its painted walls and ceilings; and the magnificent Long Library.

Afterwards, head upstairs to the 'Untold Story', where a ghostly chamber maid leads you through a series of tableaux recreating important scenes from the palace's history.

If the crowds in the house become too oppressive, retire to the lavish gardens and vast parklands, parts of which were landscaped by Lancelot 'Capability' Brown. A minitrain takes visitors to the Pleasure Gardens, which feature a yew maze, adventure playground and butterfly house. For quieter and longer strolls, there are glorious walks leading to an arboretum, cascade and temple.

🛏 Sleeping & Eating

★**Glove House**   B&B £££
(☑01993-813475; www.theglovehouse.co.uk; 24 Oxford St; r/ste from £155/165; 🖭) Luxuriously renovated but proudly displaying evidence of its venerable age, this elegant 400-year-old town house offers the added bonus of a glorious rear garden. The largest suite has a wonderful free-standing copper bathtub, while another has a rolltop bath.

★**Hope House**   BOUTIQUE HOTEL £££
(☑01993-815990; www.hopehousewoodstock. co.uk; 14 Oxford St; s/d from £250/350; 🅿❄🖭) Wallow in pure indulgence in this sumptuous 1708 town house, which has been meticulously restored and furnished with effortless style. Original features blend seamlessly with high-tech gadgetry in the three enormous suites.

WORTH A TRIP

KELMSCOTT MANOR

Tucked away in the countryside 20 miles west of Oxford (near Faringdon), Kelmscott Manor (☑01367-252486; www.kelmscottmanor.org.uk; Kelmscott; adult/child £9/4.50; ⊙11am-5pm Wed & Sat Apr-Oct) is a gorgeous Tudor pile that was once the summer home of William Morris, a poet, artist and founder of the Arts and Crafts Movement. The interior is true to his philosophy that one should not own anything that is neither beautiful nor useful, and the house contains many of Morris' personal effects, as well as fabrics and furniture designed by him and his associates.

La Galleria
ITALIAN **££**

(📞 01993-813381; www.lagalleriawoodstock.com; 2 Market Pl; mains £11-24; ⏲ noon-2pm & 7-10pm Tue-Sun) Big windows bathe the simple interior of this much-loved restaurant in light. It's an old-fashioned kind of place, with heavy swag curtains, pink tablecloths and flowers on every table, but the food is excellent. Primarily Sardinian, the menu ranges from silky pastas to perfectly cooked veal and fish.

ℹ Getting There & Away

Stagecoach (📞 01865-772250; www.stage-coachbus.com) Buses head to/from Oxford (route S3; £3.50, 25 minutes), Chipping Norton (S3; £3.80, 25 minutes) and Witney (242; £3.40, 28 minutes).

Witney

POP 29,100

The sleepy town of Witney is firmly on Oxford's commuter belt. Make your way through the traffic and new housing developments to the centre of town, however, and you'll find a charming village green flanked by pretty stone houses. At one end is a glorious 13th-century church and 18th-century almshouses, and at the other a 17th-century covered market.

Witney built its wealth through blanket production, which incredibly was its main trade from the Iron Age until 2002. Its mills, wealthy merchants' homes and blanket factories can still be seen today. The baroque 18th-century Blanket Hall dominates genteel High St, while at Wood Green you'll find a second village green and a cluster of old stone cottages.

🛏 Sleeping & Eating

Fleece
PUB **££**

(📞 01993-892270; www.fleecewitney.co.uk; 11 Church Green; mains £12-26, s/d from £69/89; 🅿🛜) Facing the main village green, this roomy pub has an ambitious seasonal menu, with some wonderful smoked fish, steaks, deli platters and Sunday roasts. Upstairs, the rooms are sleek and spacious.

ℹ Information

Tourist Office (📞 01993-861000; www.west-oxon.gov.uk; 3 Welch Way; ⏲ 9am-5pm Mon-Sat) Stocks brochures outlining local walks.

ℹ Getting There & Away

Witney Shuttle (📞 01993-705993; www.witney-shuttle.com) minibuses head to/from Heathrow (£48, 1½ hours) and Gatwick (£68, 2½ hours) airports every two hours. Other destinations:

Burford (route 233) £3, 19 minutes
Chipping Norton (233/X9) £3.40, 45 minutes
Minster Lovell (233/853) £2.50, six minutes
Oxford (11/S1/S2/853) £4.50, 30 minutes
Woodstock (242) £3.40, 28 minutes

Vale of the White Horse

Lying southwest of Oxford, this verdant valley is notable for the historic market town of Wantage, the birthplace of Alfred the Great (in AD 849). But it's most interesting attractions are far older.

Sitting just below the crest of the highest point in Oxfordshire, the Uffington White Horse is the oldest chalk figure in Britain, dating from the Bronze Age. Around 3000 years ago this highly stylised image of a horse was created by cutting trenches out of the hill and filling them with blocks of chalk; local people have maintained the figure for centuries. Perhaps it was designed with the gods in mind, as it's designed to be seen at its best if you're floating in the air above it.

Just below the figure is Dragon Hill, so called because it was believed by locals to be the site where St George slew the dragon, although it's possibly an Iron Age ritual site. Above the figure is Uffington Castle, a hill fort dating from around 700 BC. One mile east from the White Horse along the Ridgeway (an ancient road which may have existed for more than 5000 years) is Waylands Smithy, a neolithic long barrow and chamber tomb named after the Saxon god of smiths.

THE COTSWOLDS

Glorious villages riddled with beautiful old mansions of honey-coloured stone; thatched cottages; atmospheric churches; and rickety almshouses draw crowds of visitors to the Cotswolds. If you've ever coveted exposed beams or lusted after a cream tea in the mid-afternoon, there's no finer place to fulfill your fantasies

The booming medieval wool trade brought the area its wealth and left it with a proliferation of beautiful buildings. In 1966 it was declared an Area of Outstanding Natural Beauty (AONB), and at 790 sq miles, it's the second-largest protected area in England after the Lake District. Spreading from north of Chipping Campden to south of Bath, the Cotswolds cuts across six different counties, although the bulk of it is in Gloucestershire. More than 86% is farmland but, even so, around 158,000 people live within the AONB itself, not counting those in the large towns and small cities on its fringes, such as Cirencester, Cheltenham and Gloucester.

While there are bus routes between the major towns and villages, for flexibility and the option of getting off the beaten track, you can't beat having your own car. The gentle hills are also perfect for walking, cycling and horse riding, as a network of long-distance tracks pass through, most notably the 102-mile **Cotswold Way** (www.nationaltrail.co.uk/cotswold).

Cirencester

POP 17,200

Refreshingly unpretentious, charming Cirencester (siren-sester) is nonetheless an affluent, elegant town. The lovely market square – the heart of the town – is surrounded by Victorian architecture, and the nearby streets showcase a harmonious medley of buildings from various eras.

It's difficult to believe that under the Romans (who called the town Corinium), Cirencester was second only to London in terms of size and importance and, although little of this period remains, you can still see the grassed-over ruins of one of the largest amphitheatres in the country. The medieval wool trade was also good to the town, with wealthy merchants funding the building of a superb church.

Today, Cirencester is the most significant town in the southern Cotswolds, and the lively Monday and Friday markets are as important as the expensive boutiques and trendy delis that line its narrow streets.

◉ Sights & Activities

Corinium Museum MUSEUM
(www.coriniummuseum.org; Park St; adult/child £5/2.50; ◷ 10am-4pm Mon-Sat, 2-4pm Sun; 🖽) The largest part of this well-presented modern museum is, understandably, dedicated to Cirencester's Roman past. Highlights include an incredible set of floor mosaics and the 'Jupiter column', a carved capital depict-

ing Bacchus and his drunken mates. Reconstructed rooms and interactive displays bring the era to life, and the kids can dress up as Roman citizens and medieval monks.

St John the Baptist's Church CHURCH
(www.cirenparish.co.uk; Market Sq; suggested donation £3; ◷ 9.30am-4pm) Commenced in 1100, the cathedral-like St John's is one of England's largest parish churches. It boasts an outstanding Perpendicular Gothic tower with flying buttresses (circa 1400) and a majestic three-storey south porch, which was built as an office by late-15th-century abbots but subsequently became the medieval town hall.

Soaring arches, magnificent fan vaulting and a Tudor nave adorn the light-filled interior, where you'll also find a 15th-century painted stone pulpit and some columns recycled from ancient Roman buildings. The east window contains fine 15th- and 16th-century stained glass, and a wall safe displays the Boleyn Cup, made for Anne Boleyn in 1535.

New Brewery Arts ARTS CENTRE
(www.newbreweryarts.org.uk; Brewery Ct; ◷ 9am-5pm Mon-Sat, 10am-4pm Sun) **FREE** Home to a theatre and more than a dozen resident artisans, this converted Victorian brewery hosts regular exhibitions, workshops and classes.

Cirencester Park PARK
(www.cirencesterpark.co.uk; Cecily Hill; ◷ 8am-5pm) Unusually for a stately home, the Earl of Bathurst's mansion sits right on the edge of town, hidden behind a giant yew hedge. The extensive landscaped grounds are open to the public daily, free of charge.

🛏 Sleeping

Old Brewhouse B&B ££
(☎ 01285-656099; www.theoldbrewhouse.com; 7 London Rd; s/d from £68/79; 🅿 🛜) Set in a charming 17th-century town house, this

The Cotswolds

lovely B&B has pretty rooms with cast-iron beds and country-style floral or patchwork quilts. The courtyard rooms are newer and larger.

Greensleeves
B&B ££

(☎ 01285-642516; www.greensleeves4u.co.uk; Baunton Lane, Stratton; s/d £50/65; P ☎) Farmland fringes this modern house on the outskirts of town (off Gloucester Rd). The three comfortable guest rooms share their own wing with a communal kitchenette. Breakfasts include homemade bread.

No 12
B&B ££

(☎ 01285-640232; www.no12cirencester.co.uk; 12 Park St; d/ste £120/140) This Georgian town house right in the centre of Cirencester has four gloriously unfussy rooms kitted out with a tasteful mix of antiques and modern furnishings. Think piles of feather pillows, extra-long beds and slick modern bathrooms.

✖ Eating

Lick the Spoon
CAFE £

(www.lickthespoon.co.uk; 3 Black Jack St; cakes £1-2.50; ⊙ 9.30am-5pm Mon-Sat) One word: chocolate. It comes both in award-winning solid form, all boxed up for you to take away, and in glorious liquid form. Coffee is roasted on the premises for those desiring a caffeine kick alongside the sugar rush.

Made by Bob
MODERN BRITISH ££

(www.foodmadebybob.com; Corn Hall, 26 Market Pl; breakfast £5-10, lunch £10-19; ⊙ 7.30am-6.30pm Mon-Sat; ✎) Part deli, part hip brasserie, Bob's has a casual atmosphere and features inventive, sophisticated fare on the daily changing menu. The breakfast selection's the best in town, and light lunch options include soup, salads and charcuterie plates.

Jesse's Bistro
MODERN BRITISH £££

(☎ 01285-641497; www.jessesbistro.co.uk; 14 Black Jack St; mains £18-19; ⊙ noon-2.15pm Mon-Sat,

Stroud (54) £3.50, 36 minutes
Tetbury (881) £3.50, 37 minutes

National Express coach destinations:
Birmingham £15, 2½ hours
Leeds £52, 6¾ hours
London £17, 2½ hours
Newcastle-upon-Tyne £68, 10 hours
Nottingham £27, 5¼ hours

Bibury
POP 625

Once described by William Morris as 'the most beautiful village in England', Bibury is the Cotswolds at its most picturesque, with a cluster of riverside cottages and a tangle of narrow streets flanked by wayward stone buildings. Arlington Row, a perfectly rustic sweep of cottages, has served as a backdrop for many films (most notably *Stardust*) and is thought to be a contender for the title of the most photographed street in Britain. Also worth a look is the 17th-century Arlington Mill, just a short stroll away across Rack Isle, a wildlife refuge once used as a cloth-drying area.

⊙ Sights

Church of St Mary the Virgin   CHURCH
(Church Rd) The village's Saxon-built church has been much altered since its original construction, but there are many 8th-century features still visible among the 12th- and 13th-century additions.

Bibury Trout Farm   FARM
(www.biburytroutfarm.co.uk; adult/child £4/3, catch per lb £4; ⊙9am-5pm) You can fish for your supper at this trout farm, located at the edge of the village, where the B4425 crosses the River Coln. Otherwise, take the easy option and buy some smoked fish at the little shop.

⊨ Sleeping

The best options are in the nearby villages of Coln St Aldwyns (2 miles east) and Barnsley (3 miles southwest).

New Inn   PUB ££
(☑01285-750651; www.new-inn.co.uk; Coln St Aldwyns; r £100-150; ℙ☎) The jasmine-clad New Inn offers quirky luxury in 16th-century surroundings, both in the main building and a neighbouring cottage. The 15 bedrooms are spacious and atmospheric, with bold colours and smart furnishings.

6.45-9.15pm Tue-Sat) Hidden away in a cobbled stable yard, Jesse's is a great little place, with flagstone floors, wrought-iron chairs and mosaic tables. The dishes feature local, seasonal produce, such as Cornish crab and Cotswold beef.

❶ Information

Tourist Office (☑01285-654180; www.cotswolds.com; Corinium Museum, Park St; ⊙10am-4pm Mon-Sat, 2-4pm Sun) Stocks a leaflet detailing a self-guided walk around the town (£1.20).

❶ Getting There & Away

Most buses stop outside the Corn Hall on Market Pl. They run to the following from Monday to Saturday:
Cheltenham (route 51) £3.60, 40 minutes
Gloucester (852) £2.60, one hour
Northleach (855) £2.20, 30 minutes

Barnsley House HOTEL £££
(☏ 01285-740000; www.barnsleyhouse.com; B4425, Barnsley; r from £290; ᴘ 🕏 ☒) For pure indulgence and romance, this 1697 house and its famous garden takes some beating. All of the 18 rooms are different and while some have disco balls and jacuzzis, most are demure in their decor. Facilities include a spa centre, private cinema and restaurant.

❶ Getting There & Away

Pulhams Coaches (www.pulhamscoaches.com) bus 855 heads to/from Cirencester (£2.20, 15 minutes) and Northleach (£1.70, 19 minutes); no Sunday service.

Burford

POP 1190

Slithering down a steep hill to a medieval crossing point on the River Windrush, the remarkable village of Burford is little changed since its glory days at the height of the wool trade. It's a particularly picturesque place with higgledy-piggledy stone cottages, fine Cotswold town houses and the odd Elizabethan or Georgian treasure. Antique shops, tearooms and specialist boutiques peddle nostalgia to the hordes of visitors who make it here in summer, but despite the crowds it's easy to get off the main drag and wander along quiet side streets seemingly lost in time.

◉ Sights

St John the Baptist's Church CHURCH
(www.burfordchurch.org; Church Lane) Commenced in 1175 and added to over the years, Burford's sturdy stone church has managed to survive reformers and Roundheads (supporters of parliament against the king in the English Civil War) with its fine fan-vaulted ceiling and several grand tombs intact. The best of these is the macabre 1626 Tanfield tomb, which has effigies of a noble couple in all their finery on top and as skeletons below.

During the Civil War, 340 Levellers were imprisoned here – Roundhead soldiers who mutinied due to their leaders' failure to uphold the notion of equality of all men before the law. One of them carved his name in the lead lining of the font. A plaque outside the church entrance commemorates the three ringleaders who were executed in the churchyard.

Just outside the churchyard, you'll find the town's 15th-century almshouses

🏃 Driving Tour
Classic Cotswolds

START BURFORD
END WINCHCOMBE
LENGTH 50 MILES; ONE DAY

Given its large network of winding country lanes linking ancient market towns, timeless villages and magnificent stately homes, it's impossible to cover all of the Cotswolds' highlights in one day. This tour spans three counties and ticks off some of the most picturesque parts of the northern half of the range. It can easily be driven in a day, but could be stretched into two or three.

Begin in Oxfordshire at the pretty market town of ❶ **Burford** (p194) and then head west on the A40 into Gloucestershire and follow the signs to ❷ **Northleach** (p197). The Escape to the Cotswolds visitor centre on the edge of this classic Cotswolds town has excellent displays covering all you need to know about the history, geography, flora and fauna of the Cotswolds Area of Outstanding Natural Beauty (AONB). From here, head northeast on the A429 and follow the signs to ❸ **Lower Slaughter** (p198), a picture-perfect village lined with houses made of the golden stone so typical of the area. If you've got time, take the 1 mile walk to ❹ **Upper Slaughter** (p198), less often visited than its sibling but no less attractive due to its idyllic setting between a small ford and the hills. If you've had the wherewithal to book ahead, stop for lunch at Michelin-starred Lords of the Manor, housed in a Jacobean mansion.

Continue on to ❺ **Stow-on-the-Wold** (p198), the highest of the Cotswold villages at 244m and a market town since the 12th century. After perusing the market square, take the A429 north following the route of the ancient Roman road, the Fosse Way. After 4 miles you'll reach ❻ **Moreton-in-Marsh** (p199), a town known for its weekly market and excellent local food shops.

From Moreton, take the A44 west through tiny ❼ **Bourton-on-the-Hill**, lined with attractive 17th- and 18th-century cottages and famous for two things: the gibbeting cage in which the bodies of dead highwaymen were hung in the 19th century, and horse training – there are several stud farms in the vicinity of the village. This is a good alternative spot to pause for lunch.

Continuing on, turn right onto the B4081 and head to **8** **Chipping Campden** (p200), one of the Cotswold's prettiest towns. After admiring the buildings on the main street (and if you're not tempted to stay the night), backtrack to the A44, cross into the Worcestershire corner of the Cotswolds and head down the hill to **9** **Broadway** (p202). After cruising along the broad main street, take the B4632 south in the direction of Cheltenham.

After three miles, take the left turn-off to **10** **Stanton**. A little stunner of a village, its houses are crafted out of that golden Cotswolds stone, with not a shop or quaint tearoom in sight. The buildings most likely to catch your eye are the Jacobean Stanton Court and the fine Perpendicular tower of St Michael & All Angels' Church, which has an absolutely beguiling medieval interior. Stanton Court once belonged to civil architect Sir Philip Stott (1858–1937), who was responsible for the restoration of many other houses in the village.

You'll undoubtedly see walkers passing through the village, heading south along the Cotswold Way to the village of **11** **Stanway**, just a mile south; follow the narrow road that runs parallel to the trail. There is little more to Stanway than a few thatched-roofed cottages, a church and Stanway House, a magnificent Jacobean mansion hidden behind a triple-gabled gatehouse. Its baroque water gardens feature Britain's tallest fountain, which erupts, geyser-like, to a height of 300ft. The manor has been the private home of the Earls of Wemyss for 500 years and has a delightful, lived-in charm with much of its original furniture and character intact. It's only open to the public on Tuesday and Thursday afternoons from June to August (adult/child £7/2).

After passing through Stanway, turn right onto the B4077 and then left back onto the B4632. The next stop is **12** **Winchcombe** (p202), an ancient Saxon town with some great eating and sleeping options. You'll probably want to stop here for the night so that you can explore wonderful Sudeley Castle in the morning. Otherwise, continue on to the relatively bright lights of Cheltenham.

Tolsey House
NOTABLE BUILDING

(cnr High & Sheep Sts) Perched on sturdy pillars, this unusual 16th-century building was originally the place to pay market tolls.

Cotswold Wildlife Park
ZOO

(☏01993-823006; www.cotswoldwildlifepark.co.uk; adult/child £15/10; ⏰10am-5pm; 🅿) Younger visitors will enjoy a visit to this hugely popular place, 3 miles south of Burford. It's home to a vast menagerie of penguins, zebras, white rhinos, lions and much more. A miniature train (£1) and petting zoo take the excitement up a notch. Last admission is 1½ hours before closing time.

🏃 Activities

There are several picturesque walks from Burford, including the one along the river path to the untouched and rarely visited village of Swinbrook (3 miles), where 12th-century St Mary's Church has the remarkably jaunty tombs of the Fettiplace family who dominated the area for 500 years. *Downton Abbey* fans will recognise the pub as the place where Lady Sybil and Branson stayed while planning their elopement.

🛏 Sleeping & Eating

⭐ Star Cottage
B&B ££

(☏01993-822032; www.burfordbedandbreakfast.co.uk; Meadow Lane, Fulbrook; s/d from £70/80; 🛜) In the village of Fulbrook, a 15-minute walk from Burford, this wonderful old Cotswold cottage has two comfortable and character-filled en suite rooms, the smaller of which has a grand canopied bed. The cooked breakfasts are excellent.

Bull
HOTEL ££

(☏01993-822220; www.bullatburford.co.uk; 105 High St; s/d from £65/80; 🅿🛜) You'll be following in the footsteps of guests as illustrious as Charles II and Horatio Nelson if you stay at this 15th-century hotel. The plusher rooms feature four-poster beds and antique furniture, and the restaurant is pure gourmet, with beautifully executed dishes making the most of local ingredients.

Lamb Inn
PUB £££

(☏01993-823155; www.cotswold-inns-hotels.co.uk/lamb; Sheep St; s/d from £150/160; 🛜) At this atmospheric 15th-century inn, expect flagstone floors, exposed beams, creaking stairs, a laid-back vibe and luxurious period-style rooms with antique furniture. The restaurant serves

top-notch modern British food (two-/three-course dinner £33/39); there's less-formal dining in the bar (mains from £8 to £15).

Angel
PUB ££

(☏01993-822714; www.theangelatburford.co.uk; 14 Witney St; mains £14-17; ⏰noon-11.30pm; 🛜) Set in a lovely 16th-century coaching inn, this atmospheric pub serves up a tasty menu of modern British food. Dine by roaring fires in winter, or eat alfresco in the lovely walled garden in warmer weather. There are three traditionally decorated rooms upstairs (£90 to £120) if you wish to linger.

Spice Lounge
INDIAN, BANGLADESHI ££

(☏07833 292255; www.spiceloungeburford.co.uk; 81 High St; mains £7-13; ⏰noon-2pm Sat-Thu, 6-11pm daily; 🛜🍴) White linen and brown-leather chairs set the scene for this upmarket restaurant serving excellent Bangladeshi and Indian fare. All your favourite curries and tandoori dishes feature here, along with some lesser-known regional specialities.

Huffkins
BAKERY, CAFE ££

(www.huffkins.com; 98 High St; mains £7-12; ⏰8am-5pm Mon-Sat, 10am-5pm Sun) Huffkins has been baking and serving delicious scones, cakes and pies since 1890. More substantial fare includes cooked breakfasts, macaroni cheese, Welsh rarebit and burgers.

ℹ Information

Tourist Office (☏01993-823558; www.oxfordshirecotswolds.org; 33a High St; ⏰9.30am-5pm)

ℹ Getting There & Away

Most buses stop on the High St or Sheep St. Bus destinations to/from Burford:

Cheltenham (route 853) £3.80, 45 minutes

Gloucester (853) £5, 1¼ hours

Oxford (853) £4.20, 45 minutes

Minster Lovell (233/853) £1.60, nine minutes

Witney (233/853) £3.10, 19 minutes

Minster Lovell
POP 1340

Set on a gentle slope leading down to the meandering River Windrush, Minster Lovell is a gorgeous village with a cluster of stone cottages nestled beside an ancient pub and riverside mill. One of William Morris' favourite spots, the village has changed little since medieval times. It's divided into two halves: Old Minster, recorded in the Domesday Book (1086) and the rather newer Minster Lovell, across the river and up the hill.

◎ Sights

Minster Lovell Hall   HISTORIC BUILDING
The main sight in Old Minster is Minster Lovell Hall, the 15th-century manor house that was home to Viscount Francis Lovell. The manor is now in ruins; you can peek past the blackened walls into the roofless great hall and the interior courtyard, while the wind whistles eerily through the gaping windows.

Lovell fought with Richard III at the Battle of Bosworth in 1485 and joined Lambert Simnel's failed rebellion after the king's defeat and death. Lovell's mysterious disappearance was never explained, and when a skeleton was discovered inside a secret vault in the house in 1708, it was assumed he had died while in hiding.

🛏 Sleeping & Eating

Old Swan & Minster Mill   HOTEL, PUB £££
(☑ 01993-774441; www.oldswanandminstermill.com; Old Minster; d/ste from £165/285, mains £14-22; ☺ Old Swan noon-3pm & 6-9pm; P 🛜 ♿ 🐾) This luxurious complex has charming period-style rooms in a 600-year-old pub and sleek, contemporary design in the converted 19th-century mill. Spa treatments are available at the mill, while the Old Swan serves excellent gastropub food, with doorstep sandwiches for lunch, and handmade sausages, daily fish and game for dinner.

❶ Getting There & Away

Buses service the following destinations:
Burford (route 233/853) £1.60, nine minutes
Cheltenham (853) £4.60, 52 minutes
Gloucester (853) £5.60, 1½ hours
Oxford (S2/853) £3.90, 46 minutes
Witney (233/S2/853) £2.60, six minutes

Northleach

POP 1860

Little visited and underappreciated, Northleach has been a little market town since 1227 and comprises late-medieval cottages, imposing merchants' stores and half-timbered Tudor houses. A wonderful mix of architectural styles clusters around the market square and the narrow laneways leading off it.

◎ Sights

Escape to the Cotswolds   INTERPRETATION CENTRE
(www.cotswoldsaonb.co.uk; A429; ☺ 9.30am-4.30pm; ☎) FREE Housed in the Old Prison (an attraction in itself), this is the official visitor centre for the Cotswolds Area of Outstanding Natural Beauty (AONB), and has displays outlining the area's history, ecology and attractions. There's also a cafe and a collection of agricultural wagons in the rear courtyard.

Church of St Peter & St Paul   CHURCH
(www.northleach.org; Church Walk; ☺ 10am-dusk) The grandeur and complexity of this masterpiece of the Cotswold Perpendicular style is testimony to its wool-era wealth. Although the chancel dates to around 1350, the building was extensively reworked during the 15th century wool boom. A modern highlight is the large 1964 stained-glass window behind the altar depicting Christ in Glory.

Keith Harding's World of Mechanical Music   MUSEUM
(www.mechanicalmusic.co.uk; High St; adult/child £8/3.50; ☺ 10am-5pm) Near Northleach's market square is Oak House, a 17th-century wool house containing this fascinating museum of lovingly restored self-playing musical instruments. Entry is by way of hour-long guided tours.

Chedworth Roman Villa   ARCHAEOLOGICAL SITE
(NT; www.nationaltrust.org.uk; Yanworth; adult/child £9/4.50; ☺ 10am-4pm Feb-Nov) Rediscovered in 1864 by a gamekeeper out ferreting, these extensive ruins represent one of the largest and most luxurious Roman villas in England. The earliest section dates to around AD 175, but it's thought to have been at its most magnificent in around AD 362, with two sets of bathhouses, a formal dining room with underfloor heating and a water shrine. It's 4.5 miles southwest of town, signposted from the A429.

🛏 Sleeping & Eating

★ Wheatsheaf   PUB £££
(☑ 01451-860244; www.cotswoldswheatsheaf.com; West End; d £140-180, mains £11-20; ☺ 8-10am, noon-3pm & 6-9.30pm; P 🛜 ♿ 🐾) The 14 rooms at this former coaching inn blend nice period touches, such as free-standing baths, with modern comforts, such as power showers. The restaurant is excellent, serving a menu of hearty British dishes including diabolically good devilled kidneys.

❶ Getting There & Away

Buses head to/from the following:

Cheltenham (route 801/853) £1.80, 30 minutes

Cirencester (855) £2.20, 30 minutes

Gloucester (853) £3, one hour

Moreton-in-Marsh (801) £2.20, 40 minutes

Oxford (853) £6, one hour

The Slaughters

POP 400

The picture-postcard villages of Upper and Lower Slaughter manage to maintain their unhurried medieval charm in spite of receiving a multitude of visitors. The village names have nothing to do with abattoirs; they are derived from the Old English 'sloughtre', meaning slough or muddy place. Today the River Eye is contained within limestone banks and meanders peacefully through the village past the 17th-century Lower Slaughter Manor to the Old Mill (www.oldmill-lower-slaughter.com; adult/child £2.50/1; ☉10am-6pm), which houses a small museum, cafe and ice cream parlour.

🛏 Sleeping & Eating

Lords of the Manor HOTEL £££
(☎01451-820243; www.lordsofthemanor.com; Upper Slaughter; d £199-495, 3-course meal £69; ☉restaurant noon-3pm Sun, 6-9pm daily; P🕾) 'Countryside splendour' is what comes to mind when you clap your eyes on this 17th-century mansion. Its rooms are spacious and supremely tasteful, and the Michelin-starred restaurant is one of the best in the Cotswolds, concocting imaginative, beautifully presented dishes.

❶ Getting There & Away

Pulhams (www.pulhamscoaches.com) bus 801 heads between Lower Slaughter and Northleach (£1.80, 20 minutes), Stow-on-the-Wold (£1.70, seven minutes), Moreton-in-Marsh (£1.70, 17 minutes) and Cheltenham (£3, 33 minutes); no Sunday service.

Stow-on-the-Wold

POP 2050

The highest town in the Cotswolds (244m), Stow is anchored by a large market square surrounded by handsome buildings and steep-walled alleyways, originally used to funnel the sheep into the fair. It's still an important market town and has long held a strategic place in Cotswold history, standing as it does on the Roman Fosse Way and at the junction of six roads. Today, it's famous for its twice-yearly Stow Horse Fair (May and October), where Romany people and other travellers have gathered for more than 500 years.

🛏 Sleeping

Stow-on-the-Wold YHA HOSTEL £
(☎0845 3719540; www.yha.org.uk; Market Sq; dm £19; @🕾🚼) You can't get more central than this location on the market square. The Cotswolds' only YHA is located in a wonderful 16th-century town house, with compact dorms, a children's play area and its own onsite cafe, which serves inexpensive hot meals.

Number 9 B&B ££
(☎01451-870333; www.number-nine.info; 9 Park St; s/d from £45/65; 🕾) Centrally located and wonderfully atmospheric, this friendly B&B is all sloping floors, low ceilings and exposed beams. The three rooms are cosy but spacious and each has its own bathroom.

Number Four at Stow HOTEL £££
(☎01451-830297; www.hotelnumberfour.co.uk; Fosse Way; s/d from £115/130; P🕾) While not exactly 'at Stow' (it's a steep mile's walk from town on the main road to Burford), Number Four has a popular restaurant and 18 modern rooms with bathrooms. Standard rooms are a little cramped (especially for the prices charged), but nicely furnished.

🍴 Eating

Bell at Stow PUB ££
(☎01451-870916; www.thebellatstow.com; Park St; mains £13-16; ☉11am-11pm) Stow has plenty of cool old pubs but the Bell is the best. Lurking on the eastern edge of town, it serves a lively and varied menu stretching from Wiener schnitzel to jerk chicken to jambalaya. A selection of fresh fish dishes is chalked up on the blackboard daily.

Vine Leaf CAFE ££
(☎01451-832010; www.thevineleaf.co.uk; 10 Talbot Ct; mains £9-16, 2-/3-course menu £12/15; ☉11.30am-9pm Tue-Sat Apr-Sep, Wed-Sat Oct-Mar) A wonderful little catch-all cafe, serving chunky lunchtime sandwiches with locally baked bread, burgers, Mediterranean-style mezze and more substantial bistro-style mains crafted from locally sourced produce.

ⓘ Getting There & Away

➻ Pulhams bus 801 heads to/from Moreton-in-Marsh (£1.70, 15 minutes), Lower Slaughter (£1.70, seven minutes), Northleach (£2.10, 26 minutes) and Cheltenham (£3, one hour), Monday to Saturday.

➻ The Witney Shuttle (www.witneyshuttle.com) has scheduled runs to/from Heathrow (£88, two hours) and Gatwick (£108, three hours) airports.

Chipping Norton

POP 5720

The hilly town of Chipping Norton ('Chippy', to locals) has plenty of quiet side streets to wander and none of the Cotswold crowds. Handsome Georgian buildings and old coaching inns cluster around the market square, while on Church St you'll find a row of beautiful honey-coloured almshouses built in the 17th century.

⊙ Sights

St Mary's Church   CHURCH
(www.stmaryscnorton.com) This secluded church is a classic example of the Cotswold wool churches, with a magnificent Perpendicular nave and clerestory. While most of the church was built in 1448, two of the arches in the chancel date to around 1200. In the hexagonal porch, take time to gaze up at the carved ceiling bosses that include the possibly pagan but common visitor to British churches, the Green Man.

Bliss Mill   LANDMARK
Chipping Norton's most enduring landmark is the arresting Bliss Mill on the western outskirts of town. This monument to the industrial architecture of the 19th century is more like a stately home than a factory, topped by a domed tower and chimney stack of the Tuscan order. It's been converted into luxury flats, so content yourself with admiring it as you drive along the A44.

✕ Eating

Wild Thyme   MODERN BRITISH £££
(☑ 01608-645060; www.wildthymerestaurant.co.uk; 10 New St; mains £18-19, 2-/3-course lunch £18/23; ⊙ noon-2pm Wed-Sun, 7-9pm Tue-Sat) This little 'restaurant with rooms' thrills the palate with top-notch dishes such as goat's-cheese soufflé with red-onion marmalade. The desserts are nothing short of sublime, and the three upstairs rooms (single/double from

WORTH A TRIP

COTSWOLD FARM PARK

Owned by TV presenter Adam Henson, **Cotswold Farm Park** (www.cotswold-farmpark.co.uk; Guiting Power; adult/child £9/8; ⊙ 10.30am-4.30pm Mar-Nov; ﹩) is designed to introduce little ones to the world of farm animals while also preserving rare breeds. There are milking and shearing demonstrations, an adventure playground and pedal tractors to ride on. It's located in Guiting Power, halfway between Stow-on-the-Wold and Winchcombe, signposted from the B4077.

£65/75) have feather duvets and Egyptian cotton bedding.

🛍 Shopping

★ **Jaffé & Neale Bookshop Cafe**   BOOKS
(www.jaffeandneale.co.uk; 1 Middle Row; ⊙ 9.30am-5.30pm Mon-Sat, 11am-5pm Sun) This great little independent bookshop serves delicious cakes to tables squeezed between the bookshelves. Upstairs there's a good second-hand selection.

ⓘ Getting There & Away

Buses head to/from the following:
Oxford (route S3) £4.30, 56 minutes
Stratford-upon-Avon (50) £5.40, 45 minutes
Witney (233/X9) £3.40, 45 minutes
Woodstock (S3) £3.80, 25 minutes
On Sundays buses head to Burford (233; £3.80, 30 minutes).

Moreton-in-Marsh

POP 3500

Home to some beautiful buildings but plagued by heavy traffic that clogs up its broad High St (built on top of the Roman Fosse Way), Moreton-in-Marsh is a major transport hub known for its excellent food shops stocking Cotswold produce. On Tuesdays, the town bursts into life for its weekly market, and if you're here in September, don't miss the one-day **Moreton Show** (www.moretonshow.co.uk), the ultimate agricultural extravaganza, attracting up to 20,000 people with the best of local food and gussied-up livestock competitions.

◉ Sights & Activities

Chastleton House HOUSE

(NT; www.nationaltrust.org.uk; adult/child £8.50/4; ⊘12.30-3pm Wed-Sun Mar-Oct) Five miles east of Moreton (off the A44), Chastleton is one of England's finest and most complete Jacobean houses. Full of rare tapestries, family portraits and antique furniture, its Long Gallery is particularly resplendent. Outside, there's a wonderful topiary garden.

Batsford Arboretum PARK

(www.batsarb.co.uk; Batsford Park; adult/child £7/3; ⊘10am-5pm; 🅿) Created by Bertie Mitford (Lord Redesdale) in 1880, these exotic woodlands feature more than 3300 labelled trees, bamboos and shrubs from Nepal, China, Japan and North America. Highlights include vast American redwoods, flowering Japanese cherries (at their best in spring) and the strangely churchlike 'cathedral' lime.

★ Cotswold Falconry Centre AVIARY

(www.cotswold-falconry.co.uk; Batsford Park; adult/child £10/5; ⊘10.30am-5pm mid-Feb–mid-Oct) Home to numerous species of owl, vulture, eagle and, of course, falcon, this interesting place offers displays of the ancient practice of falconry at 11.30am, 1.30pm and 3pm daily (plus 4.30pm in summer). The birds fly at their best on windy days. Various hands-on experiences are also offered (from £40).

🛏 Sleeping & Eating

White Hart Royal Hotel HOTEL ££

(🖉01608-650731; www.whitehartroyal.co.uk; High St; s/d from £72/86) The 'Royal' in the name relates to the fact that Charles I once stayed here during the Civil War, and while he probably didn't make use of the iPod docks, flatscreen TVs and en suite bathrooms, he certainly would have walked down the atmospheric half-timbered corridors. The downstairs restaurant has plenty of charm, as well.

★ Horse & Groom PUB ££

(🖉01386-700413; www.horseandgroom.info; mains £14-20; ⊘noon-2pm daily, 7-9pm Mon-Sat; 🅿🛜) In the village of Bourton-on-the-Hill, 2 miles from Moreton-in-Marsh, this relaxed pub excels at upmarket country cooking showcasing local lamb and beef, alongside flavour-filled fish dishes. It's a firm favourite with the well-heeled horsey types who live hereabouts. It also has rooms upstairs (single/double £80/120).

❶ Getting There & Away

BUS

From Monday to Saturday buses head to/from the following:

Broadway (route 21/973) £3, 25 minutes

Cheltenham (801/813) £3.30, 1¼ hours

Chipping Campden (21/22/816) £3, 40 minutes

Stow-on-the-Wold (801/817) £1.70, 15 minutes

Stratford-upon-Avon (21/22/23) £5, one hour

TRAIN

Trains head to/from the following:

Hereford £18, two hours

Ledbury £17, 1½ hours

London Paddington £33, 1¾ hours

Oxford £9.60, 35 minutes

Worcester £12, 45 minutes

Chipping Campden

POP 2290

An absolute gem in an area full of pretty towns, Chipping Campden is a glorious reminder of life in the Cotswolds in medieval times. The graceful curving main street is flanked by a picturesque array of stone cottages, fine terraced houses, ancient inns and historic homes, many made of that honey-coloured stone that the Cotswolds is so famous for. Despite its obvious allure, the town remains relatively unspoiled by visiting crowds, though it is very popular with walkers rambling along the Cotswold Way.

While the village's name derives from the Old English 'ceapen', meaning 'market', 'Chippy's' visible prosperity derives from its past as a successful wool town.

◉ Sights & Activities

St James' Church CHURCH

(www.stjameschurchcampden.co.uk; Church St; ⊘10am-5pm Mon-Sat, 2-5.45pm Sun Apr-Oct, 11am-3pm Mon-Sat, 2-4pm Sun Nov-Mar) Built in the 15th century in Perpendicular Gothic style, imposing St James' has a magnificent tower and some graceful 17th-century monuments. Nearby on Church St is a remarkable row of almshouses dating from 1612.

Court Barn Museum MUSEUM

(🖉01386-841951; www.courtbarn.org.uk; Church St; adult/child £4/free; ⊘10am-4pm Tue-Sun) Chipping Campden has been linked with the Arts and Crafts Movement since architect and designer Charles Robert Ashbee moved his Guild of Handicrafts from East London to here in 1902. This small but interesting design museum features work from luminaries of the movement, which celebrated the work of the traditional artisan in an age of industrialisation.

The barn once belonged to Campden House, a grand 17th-century merchant's pad that was burned down by Royalist soldiers during the Civil War. Some of its lodges have since been restored and are available for holiday lets through the Landmark Trust (www.landmarktrust.org.uk); it's closed to non-residents but you can peer through the gates.

Grevel House
HISTORIC BUILDING

(High St) One of the grandest residences on the High St, 14th-century Grevel House was home to the highly successful wool merchant William Grevel. It's not open to the public, but you can admire the splendid Perpendicular Gothic–style gabled window from the street.

Market Hall
HISTORIC BUILDING

(High St) In the middle of the High St stands the highly photogenic 17th-century Market Hall, an open-sided building where dairy farmers used to sell their produce. It looks like a cross between a barn and a chapel, with its simple arches, uneven stone floors, multiple gables and elaborate timber roof.

Guild Craft Workshops
ARTS CENTRE

(www.thegalleryattheguild.co.uk; Sheep St; ⊘ 10am-4.30pm) FREE This former silk mill (circa 1790) was the home of Charles Ashbee's Guild of Handicrafts from 1902 until it went bust in 1908. Many of the artisans stayed on, however, including Hart Gold & Silver-smiths, who are still here to this day. Downstairs there's a cafe and a gallery showcasing the work of a cooperative of local artists and craftspeople.

Hidcote
GARDENS

(NT; www.nationaltrust.org.uk; Hidcote Bartrim; adult/child £10/5; ⊘ 10am-6pm) About 4 miles northeast of Chipping Campden, this is one of the finest examples of Arts and Crafts landscaping in Britain, with outdoor 'rooms' filled with flowers and rare plants for the arboreally inclined.

Cotswold Country Cycles
CYCLING

(☑ 01386-438706; www.cotswoldcountrycycles.com; Longlands Farm Cottage; tours from £265) Arranges maps, luggage transfers and B&B accommodation for a range of self-guided cycling itineraries through the Cotswolds countryside.

🛏 Sleeping & Eating

Volunteer Inn
B&B £

(☑ 01386-840688; www.thevolunteerinn.net; Lower High St; s/d £35/50, with bathroom £45/60, mains £8-20; 🛜) Attached to a busy locals' pub, this clutch of simple rooms is a favourite haunt of walkers and cyclists travelling along the Cotswold Way. Maharaja, the pub's popular Indian restaurant, covers all the classics as well as more unusual dishes such as venison *tikka masala*. The Inn also rent bikes.

Eight Bells Inn
PUB ££

(☑ 01386-840371; www.eightbellsinn.co.uk; Church St; s/d from £80/115, mains £13-19) This 14th-century inn is an atmospheric place to stay, featuring bright, modern rooms with iron bedsteads, soothing neutral decor and warm accents. The pub downstairs wins points for its flagstone floors and good modern British country cooking.

Cotswold House & Spa
HOTEL £££

(☑ 01386-840330; www.cotswoldhouse.com; The Square; r from £162; ⊘ restaurant 6.30-9.30pm Tue-Sat, noon-2.30pm Sun; 🅿🛜🐾) This chic Regency town-house-turned-boutique hotel has ultracomfortable king-sized beds, lush furnishings and, in the top rooms, private gardens and hot tubs. Indulge in a spa treatment and then dine in style in the Dining Room (three-course set dinner £45).

ℹ Information

Tourist Office (☑ 01386-841206; www.campdenonline.org; High St; ⊘ 9.30am-5pm daily Apr-Oct, to 4pm Fri-Sun Nov-Mar) Pick up a town guide (£1.50) for a self-guided walk around the most significant buildings. Enquire about the guided tours run

---

LOCAL KNOWLEDGE

THE COTSWOLDS OLIMPICKS

The medieval sport of shin-kicking lives on in Chipping Campden, where each year the townspeople gather annually to compete in the Cotswold Olimpicks (www.olimpickgames.co.uk; ⊘ late May or early Jun), a traditional country sports day first celebrated in 1612. It is one of the most entertaining and bizarre sporting competitions in England, and many of the original events, such as tug o' war, the sack race and climbing a slippery pole, are still held.

by the Cotswold Voluntary Wardens (from May to September; suggested donation £3).

ℹ Getting There & Around

Johnsons Excelbus (www.johnsonscoaches.co.uk) services head to/from Moreton-in-Marsh (route 21/22/816; £3, 40 minutes), Broadway (21/608; £3, 17 minutes) and Stratford-upon-Avon (21/22; £4, 35 minutes), from Monday to Saturday.

Broadway

POP 2540

A quintessentially English place with a smattering of antique shops, tearooms and art galleries, Broadway has inspired writers, artists and composers in times past with its graceful, golden-hued cottages set at the foot of a steep escarpment. Take the time to wander down to the lovely 12th-century St Eadburgha's Church, a signposted 1-mile walk from town.

If the neighbouring village of Snowshill looks familiar, that's because it featured in the film *Bridget Jones's Diary;* a local house was used as Bridget's parents' home.

◉ Sights

Broadway Tower   TOWER
(www.broadwaytower.co.uk; Middle Hill; adult/child £4.80/3; ⊙10am-5pm) Near St Eadburgha's Church, a mile from Broadway, a path leads uphill for 2 miles to Broadway Tower, a crenulated 18th-century Gothic folly on the crest of the escarpment, where you'll find all-encompassing views from the top.

Snowshill Manor   HOUSE
(NT; www.nationaltrust.org.uk; adult/child £9.80/4.90; ⊙noon-5pm Wed-Sun Apr-Jun, Sep & Oct, 11.30am-4.30pm Wed-Mon Jul & Aug) About 3 miles south of Broadway lies Snowshill Manor, a wonderful Cotswold mansion that was once home to the marvellously eccentric poet and architect Charles Paget Wade (1883–1956). The house contains Wade's extraordinary collection of crafts and design, with everything from musical instruments to Victorian perambulators and Japanese samurai armour. The impressive gardens were designed as an extension of the house, with pools, terraces and wonderful views.

🛏 Sleeping & Eating

Crown & Trumpet   PUB **££**
(☑ 01386-853202; www.cotswoldholidays.co.uk; 14 Church St; r £60; P🐾) For modern comfort within a 300-year-old exterior, this friendly pub offers five en suite rooms complete with sloped floors, exposed beams and low ceilings. Downstairs is a good bet for real ales and a proper roast dinner.

Russell's   HOTEL **££**
(☑ 01386-853555; www.russellsofbroadway.co.uk; 20 High St; r from £115, 2-/3-course menu £14/17; ⊙restaurant noon-2.30pm daily, 6-9.30pm Mon-Sat; P🐾) Sleek and stylish Russell's has seven spacious, individually designed rooms, some with exposed beams and four-poster beds, and all with modern luxuries such as contemporary bathrooms and iPod docks. It's known for its beautifully executed modern British fare.

Lygon Arms   HOTEL **£££**
(☑ 01386-852255; www.pumahotels.co.uk; High St, Broadway; r from £126; P🐾🏊) Choose medieval splendour or modern chic at this 16th-century inn in the heart of Broadway. It's a grand old place, with a golden stone exterior and half-timbered walls inside. There's also a good restaurant.

ℹ Information

Tourist Office (☑ 01386-852937; www.beautifulbroadway.com; Russell Sq; ⊙10am-5pm Mon-Sat, 11am-3pm Sun Apr-Oct, 10am-4pm Mon-Sat Nov-Mar)

ℹ Getting There & Away

Buses head to/from the following:
Cheltenham (route 606/608) 47 minutes
Chipping Campden (21/22/608) £3, 17 minutes
Moreton-in-Marsh (21/22/973) £3, 25 minutes
Stratford-upon-Avon (21) £4, 52 minutes
Winchcombe (606) 30 minutes

Winchcombe

POP 4540

Winchcombe is very much a working, living town, with butchers, bakers and small independent shops lining the main streets. It was capital of the Saxon kingdom of Mercia and one of the most important towns in the Cotswolds until the Middle Ages. Today, the remnants of its illustrious past can still be seen in its stone and half-timbered buildings. Keep an eye out for the picturesque cottages on Vineyard St and Dents Tce, and the grotesque gargoyles that adorn St Peter's Church.

Winchcombe is ideally situated for walkers, with a spider's web of long-distance trails branching out in every direction including the Cotswold Way, the Gloucestershire Way and the Worcestershire-bound St Kenelm's Way.

◉ Sights & Activities

Sudeley Castle
CASTLE
(www.sudeleycastle.co.uk; adult/child £14/5; ⊙10am-5pm mid-Mar–Oct) Winchcombe's main attraction, this magnificent castle has welcomed many a monarch over its thousand year history, including Richard III, Henry VIII and Charles I. It is most famous as the home of Catherine Parr (Henry VIII's widow) and her second husband, Thomas Seymour. Princess Elizabeth (before she became Elizabeth I) was part of the household for a time until Seymour's inappropriate displays of affection towards her prompted Catherine to banish her from the premises.

Lady Jane Grey – the ill-fated 'Nine Days Queen' – was also sent here to live with the Seymours, and she was the chief mourner at Catherine's funeral. You'll find Catherine's tomb in the chapel, making this the only private house in England where a queen is buried.

The house is still used as a family home and some of the interior is off-limits to visitors, but you can get a good sense of its grand proportions while visiting the exhibitions of costumes, memorabilia and paintings, and the surrounding grounds. The gardens include spectacular avenues of sculpted yews, an intricate knot garden and aviaries containing magnificently coloured pheasants.

Enquire at the visitor centre about the 5-mile loop walk from here that leads to a well-preserved Roman mosaic floor hidden within the surrounding woods. Allow 2½ hours for the walk.

Belas Knap Long Barrow
ARCHAEOLOGICAL SITE
Dating from more than 5500 years ago, Belas Knap is one of the best-preserved neolithic burial chambers in the country, and the views down to Sudeley Castle and across the surrounding countryside are breathtaking. The remains of 38 people were found when its four chambers were excavated. The barrow can be accessed from Winchcombe by a 2½-mile hike along the Cotswold Way. Otherwise you can park on Corndean Lane and take a steep but shortish walk up across the fields.

Hailes Abbey
RUIN
(EH; www.english-heritage.org.uk; Hailes; adult/child £4.50/2.70; ⊙10am-5pm Apr-Nov) Two miles northeast of Winchcombe are the meagre ruins of this Cistercian abbey, once one of the country's main pilgrimage centres, due to a long-running medieval scam. The abbey was said to possess a vial of Christ's blood, which turned out to be merely coloured water. Before the deception came to light, thousands of pilgrims contributed to the abbey's wealth.

⌨ Sleeping & Eating

Wesley House
B&B ££
(☎01242-602366; www.wesleyhouse.co.uk; High St; s/d from £65/90, mains £17-20; ⊙restaurant noon-2pm Tue-Sun, 7-9pm Tue-Sat; ☎) Methodist founder John Wesley once stayed in this wonderful 15th-century half-timbered house. The rooms are pleasantly indulgent, especially 'Almsbury', which has its own balcony overlooking the countryside. Downstairs is split between a relaxed bar and grill, and a more formal restaurant serving fabulous Modern British cuisine.

White Hart Inn
HOTEL ££
(☎01242-602359; www.whitehartwinchcombe. co.uk; High St; s/d from £60/70, without bathroom £40/50; ☎) Appealingly old-fashioned, this central inn caters well to walkers. Choose one of the three cheaper 'rambler' rooms, with shared bathrooms and iron bedsteads, or go for greater luxury in a superior room.

★5 North St
MODERN EUROPEAN £££
(☎01242-604566; www.5northstreetrestaurant. co.uk; 5 North St; 2-/3-course lunch £24/28, 3–7-course dinner £44-70; ⊙7-9.30pm Tue-Sat) This Michelin-starred restaurant is a treat from start to finish, from its splendid 400-year-old timbered exterior to what you eventually find on your plate. Marcus Ashenford's cooking is rooted in traditional ingredients, but the odd playful experiment (such as Guinness ice cream) adds that extra magic.

❶ Information

Tourist Office (☎01242-602925; www. winchcombe.co.uk; High St; ⊙10am-4pm daily Apr-Oct, Sat & Sun Nov-Mar)

❶ Getting There & Away

Castleways (www.castleways.co.uk) bus 606 travels to/from Broadway (30 minutes) and Cheltenham (20 minutes); no Sunday services.

Painswick

POP 1770

One of the most beautiful and unspoilt towns in the Cotswolds, hilltop Painswick sees only a trickle of visitors, so you can wander the narrow winding streets and admire the picture-perfect cottages, handsome stone town houses and medieval inns in your own good time. Look out for Bisley St, the original main drag, which was superseded by the now ancient-looking New St in medieval times.

◉ Sights & Activities

St Mary's Church CHURCH
(www.stmaryspainswick.org.uk; New St; ◷ 9.30am-6pm Apr-Sep, to 4pm Oct-Mar) The village centres on this fine 14th-century, Perpendicular Gothic wool church, surrounded by tabletop tombs and clipped yew trees that resemble giant lollipops. Legend had it that only 99 trees could ever grow here, as the devil would appear and shrivel the 100th tree were it ever planted. They planted it anyway, to celebrate the millennium and – lo and behold! – one of the trees toppled several years later. We're assured it's now making a good recovery.

Just behind the churchyard, a rare set of iron stocks stand in the street.

Painswick Rococo Garden GARDENS
(www.rococogarden.org.uk; adult/child £6.50/3; ◷ 11am-5pm mid-Jan–Oct) A mile north of town, this is the only garden of its type in England, designed by Benjamin Hyett in the 1740s and now restored to its former glory. Winding paths soften the otherwise strict geometrical precision, bringing visitors around the central vegetable garden to the many Gothic follies dotted in the grounds. There's also a children's nature trail and maze.

CHEESE-ROLLING AT COOPER'S HILL

Cooper's Hill in Cranham, near Painswick, is the location of the Cotswolds' most dangerous sport: the annual Cheese-Rolling (www.cheese-rolling. co.uk; ◷ last bank holiday in May). This 200-year-old tradition sees locals running, tumbling and sliding down a steep hill in pursuit of a 7lb round of Double Gloucester cheese; it's only a 90m run, but people get hurt every year. The prize? The cheese itself, and the glory of catching it.

⌖ Sleeping & Eating

Troy House B&B ££
(☎ 01452-812339; www.troy-house.co.uk; Gloucester St; s/d £50/75; ☏) At this great little B&B the two spacious guest rooms occupy their own separate rear cottage accessed from a pretty courtyard. They're nicely decked out with quality toiletries, magazines and *Tintin* books.

Cardynham House HOTEL ££
(☎ 01452-814006; www.cardynham.co.uk; Tibbiwell St; s/d from £70/90, lunch £12-14, dinner £14-17; ◷ bistro noon-3pm Tue-Sun, 6.30-9.30pm Tue-Sat; ☏▣) Each of the differently themed rooms at 15th-century Cardynham House has four-poster beds and heavy patterned fabrics. For a private pool and garden, book the Pool Room. Downstairs, the bistro (mains from £10 to £20) serves hearty British fare.

Cotswolds88 HOTEL £££
(☎ 01452-813688; www.cotswolds88.com; Kemps Lane; r/ste from £110/250, 2-/3-course lunch £15/20, dinner £43/50; ◷ restaurant noon-2.30pm & 7-9.30pm Wed-Sun; ℗☏) This is a happy marriage of 18th-century architecture and over-the-top decor – from the wallpaper to the psychedelic lighting. Spacious, individually decorated rooms come with every creature comfort, and the suites have four-poster beds and spa baths. The restaurant is also excellent, featuring sophisticated yet playful fare.

ⓘ Getting There & Away

Stagecoach (www.stagecoachbus.com) bus 46 heads to/from Cheltenham (£3.40, 42 minutes) and Stroud (£2, 10 minutes).

Stroud

POP 32,700

Stroud once hummed with the sound of more than 150 cloth mills operating around the town, but when the bottom fell out of the market, the town went into decline. Although a handful of the handsome old mills are still operating, the hilly town has become a bohemian enclave known for its fairtrade shops, delis and independent stores.

This is still one of the most important market towns in the Cotswolds, with dozens of stallholders converging every Saturday for the farmers market. Another great place for organic food, books, craft and more is the Shambles Market (www.shamblesmarket-stroud.co.uk), which takes place in the historic Shambles on Fridays and Saturdays.

◉ Sights

Museum in the Park   MUSEUM
(www.museuminthepark.org.uk;   Stratford   Pk;
⊙11am-4pm Tue-Sun; ⊕) `FREE` Set in an
18th-century mansion surrounded by parkland, this museum tells the history of the
town and its cloth-making, and there are
interactive displays of everything from dinosaurs to Victorian toys. A separate gallery
hosts eclectic contemporary art exhibitions.

✕ Eating

Star Anise   CAFE £
(www.staranisearticscafe.com; Gloucester St; mains
£6-8; ⊙8am-5pm Mon-Sat; ⊘) Local produce
features heavily in the inventive dishes at
this mostly vegetarian cafe (there are some
fish dishes). It often hosts live music and
other community events.

No 23   TAPAS ££
(⊘01453-298525; www.facebook.com/no23barand
bistrostroud; 23 Nelson St; tapas £5-10; ⊙10am-
10pm; ⊛⊘) Tuck into proper Spanish tapas,
wine, sherry and brandy at this chilled-out
little place. Head upstairs to the balcony for
great views of the countryside.

ⓘ Information

Tourist Office (⊘01453-760960; www.
visitthecotswolds.org.uk; George St; ⊙10am-
5pm Mon-Sat)

ⓘ Getting There & Away

➜ Buses head to/from Cirencester (route 54;
£3.50, 36 minutes), Uley (21/35; £4, 30 minutes), Painswick (46; £2, nine minutes), Cheltenham (46; £3.60, 46 minutes) and Gloucester
(14/93; £3.70, 1¼ hours).

➜ National Express coaches head to/from
London Victoria (£25, 2¾ hours), Bristol (£8,
45 minutes), Birmingham (£15, 2½ hours),
Hereford (£8, 1½ hours) and Scarborough (£56,
10 hours).

➜ Trains head to/from London Paddington
(£22, 1½ hours), Gloucester (£4.50, 20 minutes) and Cheltenham (£5.90, 40 minutes).

Tetbury

POP 5480

Once a prosperous wool-trading centre, Tetbury's busy streets are lined with medieval
cottages, sturdy old town houses and Georgian gems. The Georgian Gothic Church of
Sts Mary the Virgin & Mary Magadelene
has a towering spire and wonderful interior,

COTSWOLDS FOOD & FARMERS MARKETS

When the locally sourced, seasonal food
movement took off, the Cotswolds were
already there. Organic, ethically produced produce has long been a staple in
its villages. In the delis and independent
food shops all over the region, visiting
foodies will make tempting discoveries.
Edible goodies to look out for include
cheese from **Simon Weaver Organic**
(www.simonweaver.net), from a farm
near Upper Slaughter; organic beef
from **LoveMyCow** (www.lovemycow.
com) in Bourton-on-the-Water; smoked
fish and meats from **Upton Smokery**
(www.uptonsmokery.co.uk) in Burford;
and fantastic ice cream from Chedworth's **Cotswold Ice Cream Company** (www.cotswold-icecream.co.uk).

Farmers markets take place monthly
or fortnightly in many of the villages and
towns, with a multitude of local producers selling their seasonal delights to the
general public. The best is held every
Saturday morning in Stroud.

including its original box pews. From here,
it's a short stroll to Market Sq, where the
17th-century Market House stands as if on
stilts.

Tetbury is also a great place for antiques
fans, with a shop of old curios on almost
every corner. A good time to visit is the last
Monday in May for the **Woolsack Races**
(www.tetburywoolsack.co.uk) – a nod to the
town's past – or in August for the **Festival
of British Eventing** (www.gatcombe-horse.
co.uk) at Princess Anne's Gatcombe Park estate. Her big brother, Charles, also lives near
here, at Highgrove.

Buses head to/from Stroud (route 29/129;
£3.50, 36 minutes) and Cirencester (881;
£3.50, 37 minutes); no Sunday services.

Uley

POP 1000

This lovely little hamlet, with its quaint village
green and jumble of pretty houses, sits below
the overgrown remains of **Uley Bury**, the largest Iron Age hill fort in England. Dating from
about 300 BC, the fort and its perimeter walk
provide spectacular views over the Severn
Vale; follow the steep path that runs from the

village church. If you're driving, access to the car park is off the B4066, north of the village.

Virtually untouched since the mid-1870s, **Woodchester Mansion** (www.woodchester-mansion.org.uk; adult/child £6.50/free; ⏰11am-5pm Sat & Sun Apr-Oct) was abandoned before it was finished, yet it's still amazingly grand and graceful. Doors open to nowhere, fireplaces are stuck halfway up walls, and corridors end at ledges with views of the ground below. The house also features an impressive set of gruesome gargoyles and is home to one of England's most important colonies of horseshoe bats and several resident ghosts. It's a mile north of Uley on the B4066.

Buses 21 and 35 head to/from Stroud (£4, 30 minutes) on weekdays.

WESTERN GLOUCESTERSHIRE

West of the Cotswolds, Gloucestershire's greatest asset is the elegant Regency town of Cheltenham. It's home to tree-lined terraces, upmarket boutiques and a tempting collection of dining options. The county capital, Gloucester, is well worth a visit for its magnificent Gothic cathedral, while to the west, the picturesque Forest of Dean is a leafy backwater perfect for cycling and walking.

Berkeley

POP 2040

Tucked away in the thin strip of land between the Cotswolds and the River Severn, Berkeley is a bucolic little place that's none-the-less featured prominently in history.

◉ Sights

Berkeley Castle CASTLE
(www.berkeley-castle.com; adult/child £10/5.50; ⏰11am-5pm Sun-Wed Apr-Oct) Little changed since it was built as a sturdy fortress in Norman times, this fine fortress has been the home of the Berkeleys for nearly 900 years. Edward II was imprisoned and then murdered here in 1327 (allegedly with a hot poker up his rectum) on the order of his wife and her lover. Visits include the King's Gallery (with its cell and dungeon), the medieval Great Hall and the kitchen.

Dr Jenner's House MUSEUM
(www.jennermuseum.com; Church Lane; adult/child £6.95/5.95; ⏰noon-5pm Sun-Wed Apr-Sep)

This beautiful Queen Anne house honours the life and work of Edward Jenner (1749–1823), the country doctor who discovered the principle of vaccination, fundamentally changing the lives of us all. It was here that the doctor performed the first smallpox vaccination in 1796.

① Getting There & Away

Berkeley is best visited with your own wheels, as public transport is extremely limited. It's 16 miles south of Gloucester; take the A38 and follow the signs.

Cheltenham

POP 117,000

Cheltenham retains an air of gracious refinement left over from its heyday as a spa resort in the 18th century. At the time, it rivalled Bath as the place for sick rich people to go, and today it still has many Regency buildings and manicured squares. These days, however, it's best known for its racecourse (www.cheltenham.co.uk), which in mid-March attracts up to 40,000 people for one of England's premier steeplechase events.

Cheltenham's excellent accommodation and restaurants make it a more appealing base to the region than the county town of Gloucester, but this mid-tier city is unlikely to be the highlight of your trip.

◉ Sights

Wilson MUSEUM, GALLERY
(www.thewilson.org.uk; Clarence St; ⏰9.30am-5.15pm) FREE Cheltenham's excellent museum depicts local life through the ages and has wonderful displays on William Morris and the Arts and Crafts Movement, as well as British ceramics and fine art. A section on Scott's ill-fated expedition to Antarctica highlights the role of local lad Edward Wilson.

Holst Birthplace Museum MUSEUM
(www.holstmuseum.org.uk; 4 Clarence Rd; adult/child £5/4.50; ⏰10am-5pm Tue-Sat, 1.30-5pm Sun Jun-Sep, 10am-4pm Tue-Sat Feb-May & Oct–mid-Dec) Gustav Holst was born in Cheltenham in 1874, and the rooms of his childhood home are laid out in typical period fashion. They feature many of his personal possessions, including the piano on which most of his orchestral suite *The Planets* was composed, as well as photos of the notoriously camera-shy composer.

GLOUCESTER

Gloucester (*glos*-ter) is the county town of Gloucestershire and a major transport hub, with plenty of train, bus and coach connections. It was originally a settlement for retired Roman soldiers but it came into its own in medieval times, when the pious public flocked to see the grave of Edward II and financed the building of what remains one of England's most beautiful cathedrals.

Gloucester Cathedral (www.gloucestercathedral.org.uk; 12 College Green; tower tours adult/child £4/1; ⊙7.40am-5.30pm Mon-Sat, to 3pm Sun) Gloucester Cathedral is among the first and finest examples of the Perpendicular Gothic style. Originally the site of a Saxon abbey, a Norman church was built here by a group of Benedictine monks in the 12th century. When Edward II was murdered in 1327, the church was chosen as his burial place.

Inside, the best of Norman Romanesque and Gothic design are skillfully combined with sturdy columns, creating a sense of gracious solidity. From the elaborate 14th-century wooden choir stalls, you'll get a good view of the imposing Great East Window, one of the largest in England. Beneath the window in the northern ambulatory is Edward II's magnificent tomb, and nearby is the late 15th-century Lady Chapel, a glorious patchwork of carved stone and stained glass.

One of the cathedral's treasures is the exquisite Great Cloister (used in the first two *Harry Potter* films). Completed in 1367, it is the first example of fan vaulting in England and only matched in beauty by Henry VII's chapel at Westminster Abbey.

Gloucester Quays (www.gloucesterquays.co.uk; St Ann Way; ⊙10am-8pm Mon-Sat, to 5pm Sun) This set of old brick warehouses is filled with bargain outlet stores for many of the big fashion brands. It's also home to the excellent three-story Gloucester Antiques Centre.

Pittville Pump Room NOTABLE BUILDING
(www.pittvillepumproom.org.uk; Pittville Park; ⊙10am-4pm Wed-Sun) **FREE** Built in 1830 as a centrepiece to a large housing subdivision, the Pittville Pump Room is Cheltenham's finest Regency building, based on an ancient Athenian temple. Wander into the main auditorium and sample the pungent spa waters from the fountain, or just explore the surrounding park with its lake, lawns, playground and aviary.

🛏 Sleeping

Accommodation books up well in advance for Cheltenham's horse-racing festival in March, not just in Cheltenham but throughout the surrounding villages as well.

★**Bradley** B&B **££**
(☎01242-519077; www.thebradleyhotel.co.uk; 19 Royal Parade, Bayshill Rd; s/d from £80/88; P🖕) It was the present owner's eccentric great-aunt Madge who brought this lovely Regency house into the family more than 100 years ago. It's lost none of its character in its transition into a fabulous B&B. Each of the six rooms has its own individual style.

Battledown B&B **££**
(☎01242-233881; www.thebattledown.co.uk; 125 Hales Rd; s/d £60/80; P🖕) If you don't mind a 20-minute walk to the city centre, this family-run French colonial–style villa is an especially warm and friendly option. Hales Rd branches off London Rd, just southeast of central Cheltenham.

Wyastone Townhouse B&B **££**
(☎01242-245549; www.wyastonehotel.co.uk; Parabola Rd; s/d from £80/112; P🖕) A young couple has taken over this big white Victorian house in the centre of Cheltenham and freshened up the decor. Rooms in the main house are grander than those in the annexe facing the pretty rear courtyard, but all are very comfortable.

Ellenborough Park HOTEL **£££**
(☎01242-545454; www.ellenboroughpark.com; Southam Rd; r from £207; P🖕🏊) Oozing tradition, this majestic 500-year-old country house has 62 individually designed rooms, mixing original fittings with modern features such as comfy beds and iPod docks. It's 3 miles northeast of the city centre; take Prestbury Rd and follow the signs.

Cowley Manor HOTEL **£££**
(☎01242-870900; www.cowleymanor.com; Cowley; r from £195; P🖕🏊) In the village of Cowley, 5 miles south of Cheltenham (off the A435), this superb Italianate sandstone mansion

Cheltenham

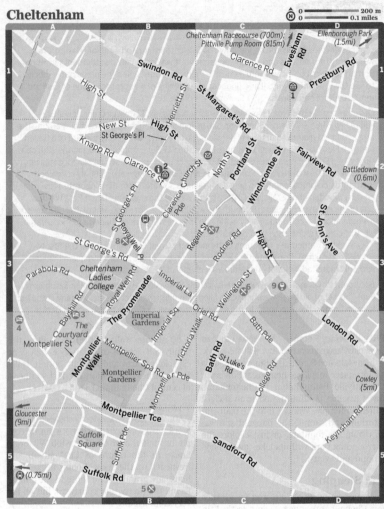

OXFORD, COTSWOLDS & AROUND CHELTENHAM

sets both the comfort and the kookiness levels to extreme. Handmade furniture and fabrics by young British designers adorn the bright but elegant rooms; downstairs, oddball art juts out from the walls.

✕ Eating

The Tavern PUB **££**
(☎01242-221212; www.thetaverncheltenham.com; 5 Royal Well Pl; mains £10-20; ☺9am-10pm; ✸) Delivering 'dude food' at its best, this hiply dishevelled bar (exposed bricks, bare wooden tables) serves fancy burgers, hot dogs, steaks, macaroni cheese, devilled Scotch eggs, calves livers and, for that extra dude pep, Thai-style oysters. There's free popcorn and sparkling water, and the sliders alone justify repeat visits.

Prithvi INDIAN **££**
(☎01242-226229; www.prithvirestaurant.com; 37 Bath Rd; mains £11-16; ☺noon-1.30pm Wed-Sun, 6-9.45pm Tue-Sun) Prithvi's top-notch service and white-linen ambience matches its immaculate dishes. Each mouth-watering offering is presented with great attention to detail. Various set menus are available, including a good-value lunch option (two/ three courses £15/19).

Cheltenham

Red Pepper   CAFE **££**
(✆ 01242-253900; www.redpeppercheltenham.
co.uk; 13 Regent St; brunch £5-9, dinner £11-17;
☺ 9.30am-4pm Sun & Mon, to 9.30pm Tue-Sat)
Despite the main dining area being in the
basement, this central cafe still manages
to be surprisingly bright and peppy. In the
evening the lighter meals give way to bistro
fare, with 'steak night' on Wednesdays and
'sausages and wine night' on Thursdays.

★ **Le Champignon Sauvage**   FRENCH **£££**
(✆ 01242-573449; www.lechampignonsauvage.
co.uk; 24-28 Suffolk Rd; 3-course menu £32-59;
☺ 12.30-3pm & 7.30-10pm Tue-Sat) For nearly 30
years this Cheltenham institution has been
delighting visitors and locals alike with chef
David Everitt-Matthias' finely executed dishes and imaginative flavour combinations.
We're not alone in thinking it Gloucestershire's best restaurant.

Sandford Park Ale House   PUB
(www.spalehouse.co.uk; 20 High St; ☺ noon-midnight) With 10 hand-pulled ales and ciders,
more than 80 bottled beers and 16 taps of Belgian and German brews, this is Cheltenham's
premier beer den. The large back garden is
more appealing than the starkly lit interior.

❶ Information

Tourist Office (✆ 01242-237431; www.visit
cheltenham.com; The Wilson, Clarence St;
☺ 9.30am-5.15pm)

❶ Getting There & Away

BUS
Bus destinations:
Oxford (route 853) £7.50, 1½ hours

Cirencester (51) £3.60, 40 minutes
Gloucester (4/10/94/97-99/377) £3.20, 45
minutes
Stroud (23/46) £3.60, 1¾ hours
Winchcombe (606) 20 minutes

National Express coach destinations:
Birmingham £12, 1½ hours
Leeds £42, 5½ hours
London Victoria £17, three hours
Newcastle-upon-Tyne £55, 8¾ hours
Nottingham £24, four hours

TRAIN
Trains run to/from the following:
Bristol £8.70, 40 minutes
Cardiff £18, 1½ hours
Edinburgh £84, six hours
Exeter £22, 1¾ hours
London Paddington £29, 2¼ hours

Forest of Dean

The Forest of Dean is the oldest oak forest
in England and a wonderfully scenic place to
walk, cycle or paddle. The 42-sq-mile woodland, designated England's first National
Forest Park in 1938, was formerly a royal
hunting ground and a centre of iron and coal
mining. Its mysterious depths supposedly
inspired the forests of JRR Tolkien's Middle
Earth books, and key scenes in *Harry Potter
& the Deathly Hallows* were set here.

The Forest of Dean also gives its name
to one of Gloucestershire's districts, which
includes the small towns of Newent and
Coleford, north and south (respectively) of
the forest itself. A good place to begin your
explorations of the forest proper is the Dean
Forest Centre, near the village of Soudley,
within its eastern fringe. To the west, the forest spills over the Herefordshire border near
the village of Goodrich. The River Wye skirts
its edge, offering glorious views to canoeists
who paddle out from the pretty village of
Symonds Yat.

◎ Sights

Three Choirs Vineyard   WINERY
(✆ 01531-890223; www.threechoirs.com; B4215,
Newent; mains £16-19; ☺ shop 9am-5pm, restaurant noon-2pm & 7-9pm Tue-Sun) While the
phrase 'quality English wine' might sound
like an oxymoron, a handful of English producers are making just that. Three Choirs is
England's third biggest winery, producing
250,000 bottles annually from varietals such

as pinot noir, bacchus and siegerrebe. Call in for a tasting (five wines, beers or ciders for £6) or take a guided tour of the winery (£12.50, 2.30pm daily). The attached restaurant serves classic brasserie dishes, using locally sourced produce wherever possible.

★ International Centre for Birds of Prey
AVIARY

(✆ 01531-820286; www.icbp.org; adult/child £11/7; ◷ 10.30am-4.30pm Feb-Nov) Watch raptors swoop and dive at this large complex in the countryside 2 miles from Newent (follow the signs). There are at least three flyings per day, along with aviaries housing an extensive collection of owls, falcons, kestrels, eagles, buzzards and hawks from all over the world.

Dean Heritage Centre
MUSEUM

(www.deanheritagecentre.com; Camp Mill, Soudley; adult/child £7.20/5.40; ◷ 10am-4pm; ⊛) This entertaining museum looks at everything from the Forest of Dean's geology to the Roman occupation, medieval hunting laws, cottage crafts and coal mining. There are plenty of sights for kids, too, from a mini-zoo with pigs, rabbits and weasels to the current pride and joy – the Gruffalo Trail, featuring life-sized wooden carvings from Julia Donaldson's classic picture book.

Puzzlewood
FOREST, FARM

(www.puzzlewood.net; Perrygrove Rd, Coleford; adult/child £6.50/5; ◷ 10am-5pm Apr-Oct, to 3.30pm Sat & Sun Mar, Nov & Dec; ⊛) A pre-Roman open-cast ore mine, overgrown with eerie moss-covered trees, Puzzlewood has a web of paths, weird rock formations, tangled vines and dark passageways seemingly designed to leave you disorientated and uneasy. If it seems familiar, that's because episodes of *Dr Who* and *Merlin* were shot here. Kids will love interacting with the farm animals, and there's also an indoor and outdoor maze. Puzzle Wood is 1 mile south of Coleford on the B4228.

Clearwell Caves
CAVE

(www.clearwellcaves.com; adult/child £6.50/4.50, Christmas display £8.50; ◷ 10am-5pm mid-Feb–Dec; ⊛) Descend into the damp subterranean world of a 4500-year-old iron mine, comprising a warren of dimly lit passageways, caverns and pools, and home to several species of bats. From November the caves are transformed into a hugely popular Christmas grotto. Clearwell is signposted off the B4228, a mile south of Coleford.

Symonds Yat
VILLAGE

Right on the edge of the Forest of Dean, squeezed between the River Wye and the towering limestone outcrop known as Symonds Yat Rock (504m), Symonds Yat is an endearing tangle of pubs, guesthouses and campsites, with great walks and a canoeing centre. It's split into two halves by the river, connected by an ancient hand-hauled ferry (adult/child/bicycle £1.20/60p/60p). Strong currents make the river dangerous for swimming.

The scenic Peregrine Path follows the River Wye River from Symonds Yat East to Monmouth. Another popular walk from the eastern side picks its way up the side of Symonds Yat Rock, with fabulous views of river and valley. In July and August, you may be lucky enough to spot peregrine falcons soaring by the drop-off. A kiosk atop the rock sells drinks and snacks, and peaceful walking trails continue through the forest.

Experienced rock climbers follow a series of mainly trad routes directly up the face of the cliff, but routes in the easier grades tend to be very polished, and rock falls are common – bring a varied rack and wear your helmet.

Goodrich Castle
CASTLE

(EH; ✆ 01600-890538; www.english-heritage.org.uk; Castle Lane, Goodrich; adult/child £6/3.60; ◷ 10am-5pm daily Apr-Oct, to 4pm Sat & Sun Nov-Mar) Seemingly part of its craggy red bedrock, Goodrich is a partly ruined castle topped by a 12th-century keep that affords spectacular views. An audioguide tells the story of the castle from its origins to its demise in the Civil War.

🏃 Activities

Wyedean Canoe & Adventure Centre
ADVENTURE SPORTS

(✆ 01600-890238; www.wyedean.co.uk; Symonds Yat East; half-day hire from £24) Hires out canoes and kayaks, and organises white-water trips, archery, high ropes, abseiling, caving and rock climbing.

Way2Go Adventures
ADVENTURES SPORTS

(✆ 01594-800908; www.way2goadventures.co.uk; per person £55) Offers canoeing, kayaking, raft-building and Nordic walking expeditions.

Kingfisher Cruises
CRUISE

(✆ 01432 267862; Symonds Yat East; adult/child £8/3.50) Fair-weather water-babies can enjoy the Wye without the hard work on a sedate 40-minute gorge cruise leaving Symonds Yat East from beside the ferry crossing.

Pedalabikeaway   CYCLING

(☑ 01594-860065; www.pedalabikeaway.co.uk; Cannop Valley; hire per day from £18; ⊙ 9am-6pm Apr-Oct) Hires both leisure bikes and full suspension mountain bikes, and offers advice on routes. In Cannop Valley, near Coleford.

🛏 Sleeping & Eating

Wye Valley YHA   HOSTEL £

(☑ 0845 371 9666; www.yha.org.uk; dm/r from £16/46; ⊙ Apr-Oct; P) This austere former Victorian rectory surveys the countryside from its lovely riverside grounds. It's on the Wye Valley Walk, 1.5 miles from Goodrich. Drivers should be prepared for a steep and difficult access road; follow the signed road near Goodrich Castle and take the right fork where the road splits.

Garth Cottage   B&B ££

(☑ 01600-890364; www.garthcottage-symondsyat. com; Symonds Yat East; s/d £43/85; ⊙ mid-Mar-Oct; P ⍻) This exceedingly friendly, family-run B&B sits by the river near the ferry crossing, and has spotlessly maintained, chintzy rooms with river views. There are discounted rates for longer stays.

Old Court Hotel   HOTEL ££

(☑ 01600-890367; www.oldcourthotel.co.uk; s/d/ ste from £63/85/155; P ⍻ 🐾) Set in gardens on the outskirts of Symonds Yat West, on the main road into the village from the A40, this 16th-century manor house still has its original dining room. The spic-and-span rooms in the newer block are fine but the 'feature rooms' and barn suites (timbered charmers with four-posters) have all the atmosphere.

Ye Olde Ferrie Inn   PUB ££

(☑ 01600-890232; www.yeoldferrieinn.com; Ferrie Lane; mains £9-11; ⊙ noon-11pm; P ⍻) Since 1473 this diamond-in-the-rough has been filling bellies on the western shores of Symonds Yat. Options include ploughman's boards, juicy burgers and all the usual pub-grub suspects (steaks, sausages etc). The upstairs rooms all have bathrooms and river views.

ℹ Getting There & Away

➡ Buses head from Gloucester to Coleford (route 23/30/31; £3.40, 1¼ hours) and to Newent (32/132; £2.40, 30 minutes); and from Monmouth to Coleford (35; £2.40, 22 minutes) and Goodrich (34; £2.20, 19 minutes).

➡ National Express coaches head to Newent from London Victoria (£25, 3¾ hours), Cirencester (£6, 1¼ hours), Gloucester (£3, 25 minutes) and Hereford (£5, 45 minutes).

BUCKINGHAMSHIRE, BEDFORDSHIRE & HERTFORDSHIRE

Now on the edge of London's commuter belt, these counties once served as rural bolt-holes for the city's rich and titled, especially when the stench and grime of the industrial age was at its peak. The sweeping valleys and forested hills are still scattered with majestic stately homes and grand gardens, many of which are open to the public.

Stowe

Located 3 miles northwest of the market town of Buckingham, Stowe has had a manor since before the Norman conquest. While the current incarnation of the house is suitably grand, the real attraction here is the extraordinary Georgian garden. The most spectacular approach is by way of the 1.5-mile-long tree-lined Stowe Ave.

◉ Sights

Stowe Gardens   GARDENS

(NT; www.nationaltrust.org.uk; adult/child £9/5; ⊙ 10am-6pm Mar-Oct, to 4pm Nov-Feb) Covering 400 hectares, these glorious gardens were shaped in the 18th century by Britain's greatest landscape gardeners, including Lancelot 'Capability' Brown. They are best known for their 32 temples and other follies, commissioned by the superwealthy Richard Temple (1st Viscount Cobham), whose family motto was *Templa Quam Delecta* (How Delightful are Your Temples).

Stowe House   HOUSE

(☑ 01280-818166; www.stowe.co.uk/house; adult/ child £5.70/free, incl Stowe Gardens £14) Neoclassical Stowe House now houses a private school so exclusive that its driveway is half a mile long. Mere mortals are permitted to visit the eight state rooms by way of guided tours; call or check the website for times. Although the rooms are left bare (the house's contents were sold off to rescue the original owners from financial disaster), the sheer scale and ornamentation of the building is highly impressive.

Bletchley

Once England's best-kept secret, Bletchley Park (www.bletchleypark.org.uk; adult/child £15/9; ⊙ 9.30am-4pm) was the scene of a huge code-breaking operation during WWII, dramatised in the 2001 film *Enigma*. Almost 8500 people worked here in total secrecy – intercepting, decrypting, translating and interpreting enemy correspondence.

Bletchley is just south of Milton Keynes off the B4034. Regular trains head here from London Euston (£19, 40 minutes).

Entry includes an optional hour-long guided tour of the grounds and a multi-media guide. It gives you a real insight into the complex code-breaking process and the hard work, frustration and successes that shaped this secret war effort. Inside Station X you can also see the Enigma machine itself – crucial to the breaking of the code.

Woburn

POP 935

Blissfully set within the Bedfordshire countryside, this peaceful village has existed since the 10th century. Despite having a couple of big attractions and a Michelin-starred restaurant, it's still charmingly sleepy.

◉ Sights

Woburn Abbey   HOUSE
(www.woburn.co.uk; Park St; adult/child £15/7.25; ⏰house 11am-5pm Easter-Oct) Originally a Cistercian abbey but dissolved by Henry VIII and awarded to the Earl of Bedford (the current Duke of Bedford still calls it home), Woburn Abbey is a wonderful country pile set within a 1200-hectare deer park. The opulent house displays paintings by Gainsborough, van Dyck and Canaletto. Highlights include Queen Victoria's bedroom, the beautiful wall hangings and cabinets of the Chinese Room, plus the mysterious story of the Flying Duchess.

Woburn Safari Park   ZOO
(www.woburnsafari.co.uk; adult/child £21/16; ⏰10am-5pm) This is the country's largest drive-through animal reserve. Rhinos, tigers, lions, zebras, bison, monkeys, elephants and giraffes roam the grounds, while in the 'foot safari' area, you can see sea lions, penguins and lemurs.

✖ Eating

★ Paris House   MODERN BRITISH £££
(📞01525-290692; www.parishouse.co.uk; London Rd; lunch £39, dinner £71-98; ⏰noon-2pm & 7-10pm Wed-Sat, noon-8pm Sun) On the Woburn Estate, Paris House is a pretty black-and-white structure that a previous duke of Bed-

ford took a shine to on a visit to the French capital and had shipped back here. During WWII the Queen often stayed here. Now it's Bedfordshire's best restaurant, serving exquisite set tasting menus of beautifully presented contemporary cuisine.

❶ Information

The Woburn Passport ticket (adult/child £27/20) can be used on two separate days within any 12-month period and gives access to both Woburn Abbey and Safari Park.

Waddesdon

POP 1800

A remarkable French Rensaissance chateau-style fairy-tale palace, **Waddesdon Manor** (NT; www.waddesdon.org.uk; adult/child £18/9, garden only £8/4; ⏰10am-5pm Wed-Sun Apr-Dec) was completed in 1889 for the Baron Ferdinand de Rothschild so that he could showcase his collection of French decorative arts and throw glamorous parties. Taking in the ostentatious magnificence of the house, it's not difficult to imagine the great and good of Victorian society living it up in the palatial rooms.

Very little space is left unadorned – only the Bachelor's Wing stands out as being noticeably more restrained. On display is the outstanding collection of Dutch Old Masters and English portraits, Sèvres porcelain, ornate furniture and the extensive wine cellar. The beautiful gardens boast formal parterres, contemporary sculptures and a rococo-revival aviary filled with exotic birds.

On the edge of the grounds, in Waddeson village, **Five Arrows Hotel** (📞01296-651727; www.thefivearrows.co.uk; s/d from £75/105; 🅿🐾) is an elaborate half-timbered inn that was originally built to house the artisans working on the manor. Inside, the 16 rooms are nicely renovated, and the downstairs restaurant serves a great cooked breakfast. Guests are entitled to free access to the manor gardens.

Waddesdon is on the A41, 5 miles northwest of Aylesbury.

St Albans

POP 57,800

Under the name Verulamium, this was the third biggest city in Roman Britain. Its current name derives from Alban, a Christian Roman soldier who was martyred here in about AD 250, becoming the first English martyr. These days it's a bustling and prosperous market town with a host of crooked Tudor buildings and elegant Georgian town houses.

Things look a little more crooked and less elegant in late September during the very popular beer and cider festival (http://st albansbeerfestival.org.uk).

◉ Sights

★ St Alban's Cathedral   CATHEDRAL
(www.stalbanscathedral.org; off High St & Holywell Hill; ⊘8.30am-5.45pm, free tours 11.30am & 2.30pm Mon-Sat, 2.30pm Sun) Built by King Offa of Mercia in 793 around the tomb of St Alban, this massive cathedral is a magnificent melange of Norman Romanesque and Gothic architecture. The longest medieval nave in the country gives way to ornate ceilings, semi-lost wall paintings, an elaborate nave screen and, of course, the shrine of St Alban, hiding behind a stone reredos.

Verulamium Museum   MUSEUM
(www.stalbansmuseums.org.uk; St Michael's St; adult/child £5/2.50; ⊘10am-5.30pm Mon-Sat, 2-5.30pm Sun) This fantastic exposé of everyday life under the Romans includes household objects, legionnaires' armour, statuary, jewellery, glassware and grave goods. The

highlight, however, is the Mosaic Room, where five superb mosaic floors, uncovered between 1930 and 1955, are laid out.

Adjacent Verulamium Park has the remains of a basilica, bathhouse and parts of the city wall, and across the busy A4147 are the grassy foundations of a Roman theatre, which once seated 2000 spectators.

✕ Eating

Lussmanns Fish & Grill   MODERN BRITISH ££
(☑01727-851941; www.lussmans.com; Waxhouse Gate, off High St; mains £12-20; ⊘noon-9.30pm) This bright, modern restaurant just off the main street serves a changing menu of creative British dishes with Mediterranean touches. Ingredients are ethically and mostly locally sourced.

❶ Information

Tourist Office (☑01727-864511; www.enjoyst albans.com; Market Pl; ⊘10am-4.30pm Mon-Sat)

❶ Getting There & Away

Regular trains run between London St Pancras and St Albans (£12, 30 minutes), with less frequent services from London Blackfriars.

DON'T MISS

WARNER BROS STUDIO TOUR: THE MAKING OF HARRY POTTER

Whether you're a fairweather fan or a full-on Pothead, the Warner Bros Studio Tour: the Making of Harry Potter (☑0845 084 0900; www.wbstudiotour.co.uk; Studio Tour Drive, Leavesden; adult/child £31/24; ⊘9am-9.30pm) is well worth the admittedly hefty admission price. You'll need to prebook your visit for an allocated timeslot and then allow two- to three-hours to do the complex justice. It starts with a short film before you're ushered through giant doors into the actual set of Hogwarts' Great Hall – the first of many 'wow' moments.

From here, you're left to explore the rest of the complex on your own, including a large hangar featuring all of the most familiar interior sets (Dumbledore's office, the Gryffindor common room, Hagrid's hut) and an outdoor section with the exterior of Privet Drive, the purple triple-decker Knight Bus and a shop selling butterbeer (super sweet, but worth trying). Along the way, video screens burst into life to discuss elements of the production. The attention to detail is fascinating: there's even a section devoted to the graphic design of elements such as the cereal boxes in the Weasley kitchen!

Other highlights include the animatronic workshop (say 'hi' to the Hippogriff) and a stroll along Diagon Alley. But the most magical treat is kept to last – a giant, gasp-inducing scale-model of Hogwarts, which was used for the exterior shots. Then comes the biggest challenge for true fans and parents, a quite extraordinary gift shop stocked with all your wizardry accessories, including uniforms for each of the Hogwarts houses and replicas of the individually designed wands used by pretty much any character you can think of.

If you're driving, there's a large free car park and extensive directions on the website. Otherwise, train to Watford Junction from London Euston (£9.50, 20 minutes), Bletchley (£15, 34 minutes), Northampton (£22, 40 minutes), Coventry (£20, 45 minutes) or Birmingham (£20, 1½ hours) and then catch the shuttle bus (return £2).

THE THAMES VALLEY

This rather posh and prosperous part of the world acts as a country getaway for some of England's most influential figures. Within easy reach of London and yet entirely different in character, the pastoral landscape features handsome villages and historic houses, as well as some of the top attractions in the country.

Windsor & Eton

POP 33,400

Dominated by the massive bulk of Windsor Castle, these twin towns have a rather surreal atmosphere, with the morning pomp and ceremony of the changing of the guards in Windsor, and the sight of school boys dressed in formal tailcoats wandering the streets of tiny Eton.

Windsor town centre is full of expensive boutiques, grand cafes and trendy restaurants. Eton, by comparison, is far quieter, its one-street centre lined with antique shops and art galleries. Both are easily doable as a day trip from London.

◉ Sights

★Windsor Castle   CASTLE, PALACE
(www.royalcollection.org.uk; Castle Hill; adult/child £19/11; ⊘ 9.45am-5.15pm) The largest and oldest occupied fortress in the world, Windsor Castle is a majestic vision of battlements and towers. It's used for state occasions and is one of the Queen's principal residences; if she's at home, you'll see the Royal Standard flying from the Round Tower. Join a free guided tour (every half-hour) or take a multilingual audio tour of the lavish state rooms and beautiful chapels. Note, some sections may be off-limits on any given day if they're in use.

William the Conqueror first established a royal residence in Windsor in 1070; since then successive monarchs have rebuilt,

Windsor & Eton

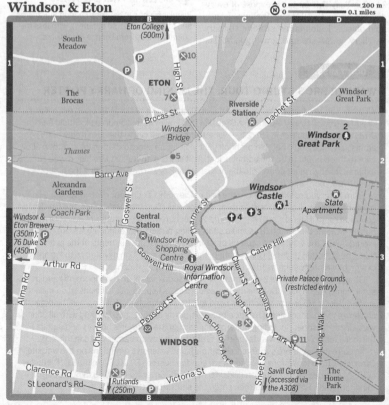

remodelled and refurbished the castle complex to create the massive and sumptuous palace that stands here today. Henry II replaced the wooden stockade in 1165 with a stone round tower and built the outer walls to the north, east and south; Charles II gave the state apartments a baroque makeover; George IV swept in with his preference for Gothic style; and Queen Victoria refurbished a beautiful chapel in memory of her beloved Albert.

➡ Queen Mary's Dolls' House

Your first stop is likely to be the incredible dolls' house designed by Sir Edwin Lutyens for Queen Mary in 1924. The attention to detail is spellbinding – there's running water, electricity and lighting, tiny Crown Jewels and vintage wine in the cellar!

➡ State Apartments

The **Grand Staircase** sets the tone for a set of absolutely spectacular rooms, dripping in gilt and screaming 'royal' from every painted surface and sparkling chandelier. Highlights include **St George's Hall**, used for state banquets of up to 160 people. For more intimate gatherings (just 60 people), the Queen entertains in the **Waterloo Chamber**, its paintings commemorating the victory over Napoleon.

➡ St George's Chapel

This elegant chapel, commissioned for the Order of the Garter by Edward IV in 1475, is one of Britain's finest examples of Perpendicular Gothic architecture. The nave and fan-vaulted roof were completed under Henry VII, but the final nail was struck under Henry VIII in 1528.

Along with Westminster Abbey, it serves as a royal mausoleum, housing the remains of numerous royals, including Henry VIII, Charles I and the present queen's father (King George VI), mother (Queen Elizabeth) and sister (Princess Margaret).

St George's Chapel closes on Sunday, but time your visit well and you can attend a morning service or Evensong at 5.15pm daily.

➡ Albert Memorial Chapel

Built in 1240 and dedicated to St Edward the Confessor, this small chapel was the place of worship for the Order of the Garter until St George's Chapel snatched that honour. After the death of Prince Albert at Windsor Castle in 1861, Queen Victoria ordered its elaborate redecoration as a tribute to her husband. A major feature of the restoration is the magnificent vaulted roof, whose gold mosaic pieces were crafted in Venice. There's a monument to the prince, although he's actually buried with Queen Victoria in the Frogmore Royal Mausoleum in the castle grounds.

➡ Changing of the Guard

A fabulous spectacle, with triumphant tunes from a military band and plenty of foot stamping, the changing of the guard draws crowds to the castle gates each day to watch the smartly attired lads in red uniforms and bear-fur hats do their thing. The spectacle takes place at 11am Monday to Saturday from April to July, and on alternate days from August to March. Stay to the right of the crowd for better views.

Eton College   NOTABLE BUILDING
(www.etoncollege.com) Eton is the largest and most famous public (meaning very private) school in England, and arguably the most enduring and illustrious symbol of England's class system. At the time of writing, it wasn't possible to visit the school due to building work, but check the visitors tab on their website to see whether tours have resumed.

Eton was founded by Henry VI in 1440 with a view towards educating 70 highly qualified boys awarded a scholarship from a fund endowed by the king. Every year since then, 70 King's Scholars (aged 12 to 14) have been chosen based on the results of a highly competitive exam; these pupils are housed in separate quarters from the rest of the 1300 or so other students. All the boys are boarders and must wear

ROYAL ASCOT

Get out your Sunday best and join the glitterati for the biggest racing meet (www.ascot.co.uk; Silver Ring per day £25, Grandstand per day £65; ⊘ mid-June) of the year. The royal family, A-list celebrities and the rich and famous gather here to show off their Jimmy Choos and place the odd bet. It's essential to book tickets for this five-day festival well in advance.

You can soak up the atmosphere from the Silver Ring for a mere £25 or head for the Grandstand, where you can rub shoulders with the posh ladies in fancy hats for £65 a day.

formal tailcoats, waistcoats and white collars to lessons (though the top hats went out in 1948).

Those who have studied here include 19 prime ministers, countless princes, kings and maharajahs, famous explorers, authors and economists – among them Princes William and Harry, George Orwell, Ian Fleming, Aldous Huxley, John Maynard Keynes and Bear Grylls.

★ **Windsor Great Park**   PARK

Stretching behind Windsor Castle almost all the way to Ascot, Windsor Great Park covers about 8 sq miles and features a lake, walking tracks, a bridleway and gardens. The Long Walk is a 3-mile jaunt along a tree-lined path from King George IV Gate to the Copper Horse statue (of George III) on Snow Hill, the highest point of the park.

Savill Garden   GARDENS

(www.theroyallandscape.co.uk; Wick Lane, Englefield Green; adult/child £9.50/4.25; ⊘10am-6pm Mar-Oct, to 4.30pm Nov-Feb) Created in the 1930s in the southern reaches of the Windsor Great Park, this pretty 14-hectare garden includes ornamental beds and woodlands. Head southeast on the A308 and follow the brown signs. It's 4.5 miles from Windsor Castle.

Runnymede   HISTORIC SITE

(NT; www.nationaltrust.org.uk; Windsor Rd, Old Windsor; parking per hr £1.50; ⊘car park 8.30am-7pm Apr-Sep, to 5pm Oct-Mar) FREE In June 1215, King John met his barons in a field 3 miles southeast of Windsor, and over the next few

days they hammered out an agreement on a basic charter of rights guaranteeing the liberties of the king's subjects and restricting the monarch's absolute power. The document they signed was the Magna Carta, the world's first constitution. Today, the field remains pretty much as it was, except that it now features two lodges (1930) designed by Edward Lutyens.

The Magna Carta formed the basis for statutes and charters throughout the world's democracies. Both the national and state constitutions of the USA, drawn up more than 500 years later, paraphrase it. To recognise its importance, the American Bar Association erected a memorial here in 1957 in the form of a Greek temple. Nearby, an acre of land was gifted to the US in 1963 as a memorial to President John F Kennedy.

After stomping through the muddy field to the two memorials (wear sensible shoes), it's possible to continue up the hill on a two-hour loop track to the moving Commonwealth Airforces Memorial, where the names of 20,000 WWII airmen without graves from the UK, Canada, New Zealand, Australia, India and South Africa are inscribed.

Runnymede is on the A308, 3 miles southeast of Windsor.

☞ Tours

French Brothers   BOAT TOUR

(☏ 01753-851900; www.frenchbrothers.co.uk; Windsor Promenade, Barry Ave; ⊘11am-5pm Easter-Oct) Offers a variety of boat trips to Runnymede (adult/child £13/8.65) and around Windsor (adult/child from £6.70/4.50).

Royal Windsor Town Walks   WALKING TOUR

(☏ 01753-743900; www.windsor.gov.uk; adult/child £7/6; ⊘11.30am Sat & 2.30pm Sun Apr-Sep) Book at the tourist office or online.

🛏 Sleeping

Windsor is an easy day trip from London but overnighting allows you to see the town return to its normally sleepy state after the hordes of visitors have gone home.

76 Duke Street   B&B ££

(☏ 01753-620636; www.76dukestreet.co.uk; 76 Duke St; s/d £85/100; ☏) Presided over by a welcoming hostess, this centrally located B&B offers two immaculate double rooms. The second bedroom is only available if booked along with the first, so it's ideal for a family or two couples.

Rutlands
B&B ££

(✆ 01753-859533; www.therutlandsbedandbreak-fast.co.uk; 102 St Leonards Rd; s/d from £55/85, s without bathroom £40; [P] 🛜) Close to the town centre and with two extremely handy car spaces, this six-room B&B is a comfortable choice. The rooms are smartly renovated; some have chandeliers and moulded fireplaces.

Macdonald Windsor Hotel
HOTEL £££

(✆ 0844 879 9101; www.macdonaldhotels.co.uk/Windsor; 23 High St; r from £149; [P] 🛜) Looking small and quaint from the road but magically hiding 120 spacious rooms within, the Windsor is the slickest choice in town. Dark browns and creams add a rich earthy feel to the resolutely modern decor.

✖ Eating

✖ Windsor

Meimo
MOROCCAN, MEDITERRANEAN ££

(✆ 01753-862222; www.meimo.co.uk; 69-70 Peascod St; mains £9-17; ⊙ 11am-10pm) Bright colours, glass lanterns and draped fabrics bring North African sunshine into this bastion of Englishness. The tagines are excellent, delivered bubbling to the table. Pasta, steaks and fish dishes round out the menu.

Green Olive
GREEK ££

(✆ 01753-866655; www.green-olive.co.uk; 10 High St; mains £13-20; ⊙ noon-3pm & 6-10pm; 🍴) A great spot for a light lunch, Green Olive dishes up generous portions of traditional Greek mezze and some interesting dessert choices in bright, simple surroundings.

✖ Eton

Zero 3
SANDWICHES, CAFE £

(www.facebook.com/zero3eton; 45 High St; mains £4-9; ⊙ 8.30am-4pm) A posh take on a diner, with lots of shiny chrome and Hollywood headshots, Zero 3 delivers a lengthy menu of cooked breakfasts, grills, pasta, salads, burgers and jacket potatoes. Alternatively, grab a sandwich to eat by the river.

Gilbey's
MODERN BRITISH £££

(✆ 01753-854921; www.gilbeygroup.com; 82-83 High St; 2-/3-course menu £20/26; ⊙ noon-3pm Tue-Sun, 6-10pm daily) Small but perfectly formed, this restaurant is one of the area's best. Terracotta tiling, and a sunny courtyard garden and conservatory give Gilbey's a Continental cafe feel, complemented by a superb modern British menu.

🍷 Drinking & Nightlife

Two Brewers
PUB

(www.twobrewerswindsor.co.uk; 34 Park St; ⊙ 11.30am-11pm) Posh folk with dogs congregate in this atmospheric 17th-century inn perched on the edge of Windsor Great Park. Think low beamed ceilings, dim lighting, hearty pub meals and a roaring fire in winter.

Windsor & Eton Brewery
BREWERY

(www.webrew.co.uk; Duke St; ⊙ 9am-6pm Mon-Fri, to 3pm Sat) Call into this boutique brewery to sample and stock up on hoppy delights such as the award-winning Knight of the Garter pale ale, Guardsman Best Bitter or the royal-wedding special, the Windsor Knot.

ℹ Information

Royal Windsor Information Centre (www.windsor.gov.uk; Old Booking Hall, Windsor Royal Shopping Arcade; ⊙ 9.30am-5pm) Pick up a heritage walk brochure (50p).

ℹ Getting There & Away

➡ Buses head to/from Bray (route 6/16; £4, 36 minutes) and Heathrow terminal 5 (60/61/71/77; £4.70, 52 minutes).

➡ Green Line (www.greenline.co.uk) coaches head to London (£5, 1½ hours).

➡ Trains from Windsor Riverside station go directly to London Waterloo (£9.80, one hour), although trains from Windsor Central, changing at Slough for London Paddington, are considerably quicker (between 26 and 44 minutes).

Bray

It's strange to think that this tiny village of flint, brick and half-timbered cottages strung along the Thames could be the gastronomic capital of Britain. Yet Bray is home to two of only four restaurants in the UK to be rated

---

READING FESTIVAL

Each August Bank Holiday weekend, up to 87,000 revellers descend on the industrial town of Reading for one of the country's biggest rock-music events. The **Reading Festival** (www.reading-festival.com; tickets £100-213; ⊙ Aug) is a three-day extravaganza featuring a top line-up of rock, indie, punk and alternative artists. Tickets will set you back about £100 per day or £213 for a three-day pass.

three-star (the highest possible honour) by foodie bible, the Michelin guide. On top of that, two of the local pubs also sport a star.

Arguably the most famous restaurant in the country, The Fat Duck – whizz-bang chef Heston Blumenthal's signature eatery – is exceedingly difficult to get into at the best of times (even at £195 per head), but with the news that he's going to be shifting the entire operation to Melbourne, Australia, for six months in 2015, you might want to leave it on your bucket list a little longer.

Eating

★ Waterside Inn   FRENCH £££

(☑ 01628-620691; www.waterside-inn.co.uk; Ferry Rd; mains £50-59, 2-/3-course lunch £46/60; ☺ noon-2pm & 7-10pm Wed-Sun, closed end Dec–end Jan) From the moment the uniformed valet opens your car door, until the last tray of *petits fours* is served, you know you're somewhere special. For more than 40 years chef Alain Roux has been working his magic here, constructing exceptional dishes for the small army of staff to serve, in a room looking straight out to the Thames. It also has rooms.

★ Hind's Head   GASTROPUB £££

(☑ 01628-626151; www.hindsheadbray.com; High St; mains £16-33; ☺ 11.30am-11pm Mon-Sat, noon-4pm Sun) Oozing atmosphere, this 15th-century pub offers a chance to experience some of Heston Blumenthal's creative cuisine in a relatively affordable and informal setting. The food's less zany than at his signature restaurant, The Fat Duck, but there are still plenty of whimsical touches – try the fish pie topped with 'surf' (crispy kale) and 'sand' (anchovy crumb).

ℹ Getting There & Away

Courtney (www.courtneybuses.com) has buses to/from Windsor (route 6/16; £4; 36 minutes).

Henley-on-Thames

POP 11,500

The attractive commuter town of Henley is synonymous with the Henley Royal Regatta (www.hrr.co.uk; tickets £18-24 ; ☺ Jul), a world-famous rowing tournament that sees the town bursting into action in July. The five-day regatta has grown into a major fixture in the social calendar of the upwardly mobile, and although rowers of the highest calibre take part, the main event is rather overshadowed by the champagne-fuelled antics of the wealthy who come here to see and be seen. Still, picnicking in the public enclosure and watching the rowers' straining muscles as the boats whizz by makes for a good day out in sunny weather.

Taking place each July in the week following the famous Henley Royal Regatta, the Henley Festival (www.henley-festival.co.uk; ☺ Jul) is a vibrant dressed-up affair that features everything from opera to rock, jazz, comedy and swing. The main events take place on a floating stage on the Thames.

Bath & Southwest England

Why Go?

England's southwest is simply spectacular. Here the past is ever present – prepare for close encounters with iconic stone circles, Iron Age hill forts and Roman baths. Blockbuster stately homes border romantic castles; serene cathedrals frame sumptuous Georgian cityscapes. The landscape immerses you in the myths of Kings Arthur and Alfred the Great, and the writings of Thomas Hardy, Jane Austen and Daphne du Maurier.

But the southwest also has an eye to the future. Here you can tour alternative eco-towns, pioneering restaurants and cool surfer hang-outs, and sleep in campsites peppered with chic yurts and retro campervans. Then there are three wildlife-rich national parks, fossil-studded shores, England's best surf spots and a coastline flecked with exquisite bays, towering rock formations and tranquil sweeps of sandy beach. It all gives you a bit of a dilemma – with the Westcountry you won't know what to do first.

Best Places to Eat

➡ Restaurant Nathan Outlaw (p333)

➡ Riverford Field Kitchen (p285)

➡ Circus (p318)

➡ The Pig (p233)

Best Places to Stay

➡ Vintage Vacations (p237)

➡ Scarlet (p334)

➡ Lulworth Cove (p246)

➡ Tide House (p339)

When to Go

➡ Cliffs, hillsides and formal gardens burst into fragrance and blooms in April and May, when seasonal attractions also reopen and boat trips start.

➡ Music festival fever takes hold in June at ultra-cool Glastonbury (p323), on the funky Isle of Wight (p237).

➡ The peak holiday season and the best weather (in theory) is in July and August.

➡ The end of school summer holidays in September brings cheaper sleep spots, quieter beaches and warmer seas. The Isle of Wight goes all groovy at bohemian Bestival (p237).

➡ Bigger waves draw surfers to Cornwall and north Devon in October; meanwhile Exmoor's deer rut sees huge stags battle for supremacy and the winter storm watching season begins.

Bath & Southwest England Highlights

1 Securing a space on a magical dawn walk inside the massive sarsen ring at **Stonehenge** (p261)

2 Soaking up beach life on the white sands of Porthcurno

or at a quaint surf spot, such as **Croyde** (p298)

3 Strolling England's most glorious Georgian street, Bath's **Royal Crescent** (p313)

4 Striding the high hills of **Exmoor** (p268), Dartmoor and Bodmin Moor

5 Staring at Henry VIII's warship the Mary Rose, in **Portsmouth** (p228)

GLOUCESTERSHIRE

Oxford

Newport

Southern Cotswolds

Swindon

Severn Estuary

Bristol ⑨

Chippenham

Avebury

Reading

diff

Severn

M4

M4

ston-Mare

Cheddar

Mendip Hills

Bath

Lacock

Pewsey Vale

Devizes

Newbury

Farnborough

Burnham-on-Sea

Wells

Frome

Trowbridge

③

A36

Salisbury Plain

Stonehenge

A34

Basingstoke

Bridgwater

Warminster

①

Chawton

M3

Jane Austen's House Museum

Glastonbury

WILTSHIRE

A303

ey

SOMERSET

Taunton

Yeovil

A303

Sherborne

Salisbury ⑧

Winchester

HAMPSHIRE

A36

Shaftesbury

Southampton

M5

locks

gton

A354

Moors

New Forest National Park

Chichester

Cerne Abbas

Lyndhurst

Beaulieu

⑤**Portsmouth**

ton

Axminster

DORSET

A31

Brockenhurst

Bucklers Hard

Osborne House

A435

Bridport

Maiden Castle

Dorchester

Bournemouth

Lymington

Cowes

Ryde

e Regis

⑦

Abbotsbury

Wareham

Poole

Yarmouth

Newport

rassic

Chesil Beach

Purbeck Peninsula

The Needles

ISLE OF WIGHT

Coast

Weymouth

Lulworth Cove

Corfe Castle

Swanage

Shanklin

Lyme Bay

Fortuneswell

Ventnor

Portland Bill

Le Havre (France, 100mi);
Caen (France, 120mi)

English Channel

N 0 _____ 40 km
   0 _____ 20 miles

St-Peter Port
(England, 80mi)

St Helier
(England, 100mi)

Cherbourg (France, 75mi);
St-Malo (France, 140mi)

⑥ Marvelling at the space-age biomes of the **Eden Project** (p349)

⑦ Foraging for 200-million-year-old fossils on Dorset's **Jurassic Coast** (p253)

⑧ Savouring the serene cathedrals at **Salisbury** (p257), Exeter, Winchester and Wells

⑨ Stepping on the deck of Brunel's groundbreaking

steamship, the **SS Great Britain** (p300) in Bristol

⑩ Discovering the locations behind the murder plots at Agatha Christie's enchanting home, **Greenway** (p282)

🏃 Activities

Cycling

Cycling the southwest is a superb, if strenuous, way to experience England's great outdoors. The region's National Cycle Network (NCN) routes include the West Country Way (NCN Route 3), a 240-mile jaunt from Bristol to Padstow via Glastonbury, Taunton and Barnstaple, and the 103-mile Devon Coast to Coast Cycle Route (NCN Route 27) between Ilfracombe and Plymouth.

The 160-mile, circular Wiltshire Cycleway skirts the county's borders. In Hampshire, the New Forest's hundreds of miles of cycle paths snake through a wildlife-rich environment, while the Isle of Wight boasts 62 miles of bike-friendly routes and its very own cycling festival.

Off-road mountain-biking highlights include the North Wessex Downs, Exmoor National Park and Dartmoor National Park. Many cycle trails trace the routes of old railway lines, including Devon's 11-mile Granite Way between Okehampton and Lydford, and Cornwall's popular 18-mile Camel Trail linking Padstow with Bodmin Moor.

For more information contact Sustrans (www.sustrans.org.uk) and local tourist offices.

Walking

Often called the 630-mile adventure, the South West Coast Path (www.southwestcoastpath.com) is Britain's longest national walking trail, stretching from Minehead on Exmoor, via Land's End to Poole in Dorset. You can pick it up along the coast for short and spectacular day hikes or tackle longer stretches. The South West Coast Path Association (www.swcp.org.uk) publishes an annual guide.

For wilderness hikes, the national parks of Dartmoor and Exmoor are hard to beat. Dartmoor is bigger and more remote; Exmoor's ace in the pack is a cracking 34 miles of precipitous coast. The region's third national park, the New Forest, is a gentler affair, offering hundreds of miles of heritage trails.

Other hiking highlights are Exmoor's 51-mile Coleridge Way (www.coleridgeway.co.uk), the Isle of Wight and Bodmin Moor, while Wiltshire's 87-mile Ridgeway National Trail (www.nationaltrail.co.uk/ridgeway) starts near Avebury and winds through chalk downland and the wooded Chiltern hills.

Surfing & Boating

North Cornwall, and to a lesser extent north Devon, serve up the best surf in England. Party-town Newquay is the epicentre; other top spots are Bude in Cornwall and Croyde in Devon. Region-wide surf conditions can be found at www.magicseaweed.com.

Sailing highlights includes Britain's 2012 Olympic sailing venues at Weymouth and Portland and the yachting havens of the Isle of Wight, Falmouth, Dartmouth and Poole.

Other Activities

The southwest is also prime territory for kitesurfing, windsurfing, diving, sea kayaking, white-water kayaking and wakeboarding. The sport of stand-up paddleboarding (SUP) continues to grow in popularity, especially in calm water spots.

Plenty of firms also offer caving, coasteering, mountain boarding, climbing and kite-buggying. Check out www.visitsouthwest.co.uk for operators.

ℹ️ Getting Around

It is possible to travel the southwest using public transport, but services to remote areas are limited; using your own wheels gives you more flexibility. **Traveline South West** (☑ 0871 200 2233; www.travelinesw.com) provides region-wide bus and train timetable info.

BUS

The region's bus network is fairly comprehensive, but becomes patchy away from main towns. **National Express** (www.nationalexpress.com) often provides the quickest bus link between cities and larger towns. **PlusBus** (www.plusbus.info) adds local bus travel to your train ticket (from £2 per day). Participating cities include Bath, Bournemouth, Bristol, Exeter, Plymouth, Salisbury, Truro and Weymouth. Buy tickets at train stations.

First (www.firstgroup.com) The region's largest bus company. The FirstDay Southwest ticket (adult/child £7/6) is valid for one day on many First buses. Weekly passes (adult/child from £37/23) are also available.

More (Wilts & Dorset; www.wdbus.co.uk) Useful service across Wiltshire and Dorset. Does day tickets (adult/child £8.50/5.50) and seven-day network tickets (£25/20) for south coast routes.

Stagecoach (www.stagecoachbus.com) A key provider in Hampshire and Devon. Offers a range of one-day tickets (adult/child from £4/3) and weekly Megarider fares from £8 (no child fare).

Western Greyhound (www.westerngreyhound.com) Key operator in Cornwall. Its day explorer tickets cost adult/child £8.50/5.50.

CAR

The main car-hire firms have offices at the region's airports and main-line train stations; rates reflect those elsewhere in the UK.

TRAIN

Bristol is a main train hub with links including those to London Paddington, Scotland and Birmingham, plus services to Bath, Swindon, Chippenham, Weymouth, Southampton and Portsmouth. Trains from London Waterloo travel to Bournemouth, Salisbury, Southampton, Portsmouth and Weymouth.

Stops on the London Paddington–Penzance service include Exeter, Plymouth, Liskeard, St Austell and Truro. Spur lines run to Barnstaple, Paignton, Gunnislake, Looe, Falmouth, St Ives and Newquay.

The Freedom of the South West Rover pass (adult/child £110/55) allows eight days' unlimited travel over 15 days in an area west of, and including, Salisbury, Bath, Bristol and Weymouth.

HAMPSHIRE

Hampshire's history is regal and rich. Kings Alfred the Great, Knut and William the Conqueror all based their reigns in its ancient cathedral city of Winchester, whose jumble of historic buildings sits in the centre of undulating chalk downs. The county's coast is awash with heritage too – in rejuvenated Portsmouth you can clamber aboard the pride of Nelson's navy, HMS *Victory,* and wonder at the *Mary Rose* (Henry VIII's flagship), before wandering wharfs buzzing with restaurants, shops and bars. Hampshire's southwestern corner claims the open heath and woods of the New Forest and, just offshore, the hip holiday hot spot that is the Isle of Wight.

Winchester

POP 116,600

Calm, collegiate Winchester is a mellow must-see. The past still echoes strongly around the flint-flecked walls of this ancient cathedral city. It was the capital of Saxon kings and a power base of bishops, and its statues and sights evoke two of England's mightiest myth-makers: Alfred the Great and King Arthur (he of the round table). Winchester's architecture is exquisite, from the handsome Elizabethan and Regency buildings in the narrow streets to the wondrous cathedral at its core, while its river valley location means there are charming waterside trails to explore.

History

The Romans built a defended settlement at Winchester in AD 70, but the city really took off when the powerful West Saxon bishops moved their episcopal see here in AD 670. Thereafter, Winchester was the most important town in the powerful kingdom of Wessex. King Alfred the Great (r 871–99) made it his capital, and it remained so under Knut (r 1016–35) and the Danish kings. After the Norman invasion of 1066, William the Conqueror commissioned local monks to write the ground-breaking Domesday Book (1086), an administrative survey of the entire country and the most significant clerical accomplishment of the Middle Ages. Winchester thrived until the 12th century, when a fire gutted most of the city – after this, London took its crown. In the 18th century the city was revived as a trading centre.

◉ Sights

★**Winchester Cathedral**   CATHEDRAL
(☑ 01962-857225; www.winchester-cathedral.org.uk; The Close; adult/child incl cathedral body & crypt tours £7.50/free; ⊙ 9.30am-5pm Sat, 12.30-3pm Sun) One of southern England's most awe-inspiring buildings, 11th-century Winchester Cathedral boasts a fine Gothic facade, one of the longest medieval naves in Europe (164m), and a fascinating jumble of features from all eras. Other highlights include the intricately carved medieval choir stalls, which sport everything from mythical beasts to a mischievous green man, and one of the UK's finest illuminated manuscripts. The cathedral's three separate, excellent tours (p226) of the ground floor, crypt and tower can get busy – book ahead.

Today's cathedral sits beside foundations that mark Winchester's original 7th-century minster church. The cathedral was begun in 1070 and completed in 1093, and was subsequently entrusted with the bones of its patron saint, St Swithin (Bishop of Winchester from 852 to 862). He is best known for the proverb stating if it rains on St Swithin's Day (15 July), it will rain for a further 40 days and 40 nights.

Soggy ground and poor workmanship spelled disaster for the early church. The original tower collapsed in 1107 and major restructuring continued until the mid-15th century. Look out for the monument at the far end of the building to diver William Walker; he saved the cathedral from collapse by delving repeatedly into its waterlogged underbelly from 1906 to 1912 to bolster rotting wooden foundations with vast quantities of concrete and brick.

Choral evensong (5.30pm Monday to Saturday and 3.30pm Sunday) is intensely

Winchester

Winchester

atmospheric; Sunday services take place at 7.40am, 8am and 10am.

➡ **Winchester Bible & Triforium Gallery**
(◎10.30am-4pm Tue-Sat, 2-4pm Mon) As the biggest, brightest and best-surviving 12th-century English bible, the dazzling Winchester Bible has vivid illuminated pages. It was commissioned in 1160, possibly by the grandson of William the Conqueror. The treasures in the Triforium Gallery include rare late-Saxon glass and a 15th-century Madonna and child, part of the medieval Great Screen. Admission is included with Winchester Cathedral.

→ Jane Austen's Grave

Jane Austen, one of England's best-loved authors, is buried near the entrance in the cathedral's northern aisle. Austen died a stone's throw away in 1817 at Jane Austen's House, where she spent her last six weeks. It's now a private residence and is marked by a slate **plaque** (8 College St). Another of her former homes, now a museum (p226), is 18 miles away.

→ Cathedral Grounds

The cathedral's tree-fringed lawns make for tranquil spots to take time out, especially on the quieter south side beyond the cloisters; the permanent secondhand book stall in the **Deanery Porch** provides great bargain hunting.

★ **Wolvesey Castle**　　　　CASTLE

(EH; ☑02392-378291; www.english-heritage.org.uk; College St; ☺10am-5pm Apr-Oct) **FREE** The fantastical, crumbling remains of early-12th-century Wolvesey Castle huddle in the protective embrace of the city's walls. Completed by Henry de Blois, it served as the Bishop of Winchester's residence throughout the medieval era, with Queen Mary I and Philip II of Spain celebrating their wedding feast here in 1554. According to legend, its name comes from a Saxon king's demand for an annual payment of 300 wolves' heads. Today the bishop lives in the (private) **Wolvesey Palace** next door.

★ **Winchester College**　　HISTORIC BUILDING

(☑01962-621100; www.winchestercollege.org; College St; adult/child £6/5; ☺10.45am & noon Mon-Sat, plus 2.15pm & 3.30pm Mon, Wed, Fri-Sun) Winchester College delivers a rare chance to nose around a prestigious English private school. It was set up by William Wykeham, Bishop of Winchester in 1393, 14 years after he founded Oxford's New College. Hour-long guided tours take in the 14th-century Gothic chapel, complete with wooden vaulted roof, the dining room (called College Hall), and a vast 17th-century open classroom (called School), where exams are still held. A revealing insight into how the other half learns.

City Museum　　　　　　MUSEUM

(www.winchester.gov.uk/heritage-conservation/museums/city-museum; The Square; ☺10am-4pm Mon-Sat, noon-4pm Sun) **FREE** A canter through Winchester's past with jewellery, mosaics, sculpture, coins and tobacco tins charting a narrative from the Iron Age, via the Romans and Anglo Saxons to the present.

Round Table & Great Hall　HISTORIC BUILDING

(☑01962-846476; www.hants.gov.uk/greathall; Castle Ave; suggested donation £2; ☺10am-5pm) **FREE** Winchester's cavernous Great Hall is the only part of 11th-century Winchester Castle that Oliver Cromwell spared from destruction. Crowning the wall like a giant-sized dartboard of green and cream spokes is what centuries of mythology has dubbed King Arthur's Round Table. It's actually a 700-year-old copy, but is fascinating nonetheless. It's thought to have been constructed in the late 13th century and then painted in the reign of Henry VIII (King Arthur's image is unsurprisingly reminiscent of Henry's youthful face).

This hall was also the stage for several gripping English courtroom dramas, including the trial of adventurer Sir Walter Raleigh in 1603, who was sentenced to death but received a reprieve at the last minute.

Royal Green Jackets Museum　　MUSEUM

(The Rifles; ☑01962-828549; www.winchestermilitarymuseums.co.uk; Peninsula Barracks, Romsey Rd; adult/child £4/1.50; ☺10am-5pm Tue-Sat, plus Sun Jul-Sep) The pick of Winchester's cluster of army museums, with a mini rifle-shooting range, a room of 6000 medals and an impressive blow-by-blow diorama of Napoleon's downfall, the Battle of Waterloo.

Hospital of St Cross　　HISTORIC BUILDING

(☑01962-853525; www.stcrosshospital.co.uk; St Cross Rd; adult/child £4/2; ☺9.30am-5pm Mon-Sat, 1-5pm Sun Apr-Oct, 10.30am-3.30pm Mon-Sat Nov-Mar) Welcome to the oldest charitable institution in the country, founded in 1132 by the grandson of William the Conqueror, Henry de Blois. As well as healing the sick and housing the needy, the hospital was built to care for pilgrims and crusaders en route to the Holy Land. Today, it's roamed by elderly black- and red-gowned brothers, who hand out the Wayfarer's Dole; a crust of bread and horn of ale (now a small swig of beer) from the Porter's Gate.

Make sure you visit the stumpy church, the brethren hall, the kitchen and the peaceful gardens. The best way to arrive is via the 1-mile Keats' Walk through the water meadows; pick up the trail near Wolvesey Castle.

🏃 **Activities**

Winchester's tempting walks include the 1-mile **Keats' Walk** through the water meadows to the Hospital of St Cross. Its beauty is said to have prompted the poet to pen the ode *To Autumn;* pick up the trail near

JANE AUSTEN'S HOUSE MUSEUM

There's more than a touch of the period dramas she inspired about the former home of Jane Austen (1775–1817). The appealing red-brick house, where the celebrated English novelist lived with her mother and sister from 1809 to 1817, is now a **museum** (☑ 01420-83262; www.jane-austens-house-museum.org.uk; Chawton; adult/child £7.50/2.50; ☉ 10.30am-4.30pm mid-Feb–Dec). While here, she wrote *Mansfield Park*, *Emma* and *Persuasion*, and revised *Sense and Sensibility, Pride and Prejudice* and *Northanger Abbey*.

The interior showcases a typical well-to-do Georgian family home, complete with elegant furniture and copper pans in the kitchen, plus the occasional table Austen used as a desk, first editions of her novels and the delicate handkerchief she embroidered for her sister.

The museum is 18 miles east of Winchester in Chawton village; take bus 64 from Winchester to Alton Butts (£8, 45 minutes, hourly) then walk 800m to Chawton village.

Wolvesey Castle. Alternatively, head down Wharf Hill, through the water meadows to St Catherine's Hill (1 mile), or take the tranquil **Riverside Walk** from Wolvesey Castle along the River Itchen's banks to High St.

⏱ Tours

Cathedral Tours WALKING TOUR

The highly informative, one-hour **Cathedral Body Tours** (Monday to Saturday, 10am to 3pm) and atmospheric **Crypt Tours** (10.30am, 12.30pm and 2.30pm, Monday to Saturday) are included in the admission price for Winchester Cathedral (p223). **Tower and Roof Tours** (2.15pm Monday to Saturday, plus 11.30am Saturday, May to September) cost £6 and take you onto the roof for views as far as the Isle of Wight. These tours are popular – book well in advance.

On the Crypt Tour look out for *Sound II*, an enigmatic life-sized depiction of a contemplative man by Anthony Gormley. The Tower and Roof Tour will see you clambering 213 steps up narrow stairwells, navigating an interior gallery high above the nave and visiting the bell chamber.

Guided Walks WALKING TOUR

(adult/child £6/free; ☉ Mon-Sat Apr-Oct, weekly Nov-Mar) These 90-minute walks include City Highlights and Roman and Saxon Winchester. Up to four leave daily from the tourist office in peak season.

🛏 Sleeping

★ St John's Croft B&B ££

(☑ 01962-859976; www.st-johns-croft.co.uk; St John's St; s/d £45/85; P �) You may well fall in love with this oh-so-casually stylish, rambling Queen Anne town house, where rattan carpets are teamed with bulging bookcases, and Indian art with shabby-chic antiques.

The rooms are vast, the garden is tranquil and breakfast is served beside the Aga in the country-house kitchen.

5 Clifton Terrace B&B ££

(☑ 01962-890053; cliftonterrace@hotmail.co.uk; 5 Clifton Tce; s £65-70, d £75-90, f £110-125; �) There's a captivating air of easygoing elegance about this tall Georgian town house. Family heirlooms sit beside candy-striped rugs and peppermint-green, claw-footed baths – it's great value too.

No 5 B&B ££

(☑ 01962-863838; www.no5bridgestreet.co.uk; 5 Bridge St; d £99-130; ⏛) Subtle tweedy-meets-tartan motifs are used to good effect here, with soft, checked throws book-ending beds draped in gentle grey. Spacious bathrooms, feature fireplaces, while a downstairs bistro adds to the appeal.

Magdalen House B&B ££

(☑ 01962-869634; www.magdalen-house.co.uk; 5 Magdalen Hill; s/d/f £50/65/75; P ⏛) Smart bedrooms are arranged over three floors in this peaceful, modern hillside house. The family room opens out directly onto a sunny terrace – the doubles trump that though, with views over rooftops to Winchester Cathedral.

★ Wykeham Arms INN £££

(☑ 01962-853834; www.wykehamarmswinchester.co.uk; 75 Kingsgate St; s/d/ste £65/150/180; P ⏛) At 250-odd years old, the Wykeham bursts with history – it used to be a brothel and also put Nelson up for a night (some say the events coincided). Creaking stairs lead to plush bedrooms that manage to be both deeply established but also on-trend; brass bedsteads meet jazzy throws, oak dressers sport stylish lights. Simply smashing.

✗ Eating

Chesil Rectory BRITISH ££
(☑ 01962-851555; www.chesilrectory.co.uk; 1 Chesil St; mains £14-20; ⊘ noon-2.20pm & 6-9.30pm) It's almost as if they created a checklist for a great date: hushed tones, flickering candles, dark beams. They get the food right too, from lighter offerings such as white onion risotto, to flavourful braised ox cheek, or roasted guinea fowl with red wine.

Wykeham Arms PUB ££
(☑ 01962-853834; www.wykehamarmswinchester. co.uk; 75 Kingsgate St; mains £14-23; ⊘ noon-3pm & 6-9pm; 🕾 ☑) The menu range here is remarkable, from juicy burgers and fish and chips, to satisfying creations adorned with cheffy flourishes: ham-hock terrine, roasted venison and seared scallops come complete with purees, creams, gels, 'snow' and 'sand'.

Old Vine PUB ££
(☑ 01962-854616; www.oldvinewinchester.com; 8 Great Minster St; mains £10-20; ⊘ noon-2.30pm & 6.30-9pm) Ask for a table with a view of Winchester's captivating Cathedral Green, soak up the mellow, old-inn atmosphere, then choose between comfort food (pork pies and baked eggs) or fancier fare: flaky grilled salmon and hefty rib-eye steaks.

★ Black Rat FINE DINING £££
(☑ 01962-844465; www.theblackrat.co.uk; 88 Chesil St; mains £23, 2-/3-course lunch £23/26; ⊘ 7-9pm daily, noon-2.15pm Sat & Sun) The aromas are irresistible, the food frankly fabulous, the cooking highly technical and the ingredients dare to surprise – expect cuttlefish, rabbit saddle, black garlic, seaweed salt, loveage and blowtorched back fat. That'll be why the Black Rat deserves its Michelin star.

🍷 Drinking & Entertainment

★ Wykeham Arms PUB
(www.wykehamarmswinchester.co.uk; 75 Kingsgate St; ⊘ 11am-11pm; 🕾) Winchester's mustn't-miss inn envelops you in an eccentric embrace. Tankards and school canes hang from the ceiling, and worn school desks lend pint-supping an illicit air. The sizzling sausages (75p each) served nightly at 6pm help make it hard to imagine drinking anywhere else. Ever.

Black Boy PUB
(www.theblackboypub.com; 1 Wharf Hill; ⊘ noon-11pm Mon-Thu, to midnight Fri & Sat, to 10.30pm Sun) This adorable old boozer is worth visiting just for the bizarre collections of pocket watches, wax facial features, bear traps and sawn-in-half paperbacks. Then there's the beer: the pumps here produce five well-kept, locally produced real ales.

Railway Inn LIVE MUSIC
(www.railwaylive.co.uk; 3 St Paul's Hill; ⊘ 5pm-midnight Sun-Thu, to 2am Fri, to 1am Sat) One of the region's best live-music and DJ spaces, the two-venue Railway puts on everything from indie to country, plus poetry, comedy and even retro gaming (yep).

❶ Information

Discovery Centre (www3.hants.gov.uk/wdc; Jewry St; ⊘ 9am-7pm Mon-Fri, to 5pm Sat, 11am-3pm Sun; 🕾) Free internet access.
Tourist Office (☑ 01962-840500; www. visitwinchester.co.uk; High St; ⊘ 10am-5pm Mon-Sat, plus 11am-4pm Sun May-Sep)

❶ Getting There & Away

Winchester is 65 miles west of London. Direct National Express buses shuttle to London Victoria every two hours (£14, 1¾ hours). Trains leave half-hourly to hourly for London Waterloo (£33, 1¼ hours) and hourly for Portsmouth (£11, 1¼ hours). There are also fast links to the Midlands.

❶ Getting Around

Bikes can be hired from the Tourist Office, per half/full day £7/10. Park & Ride car parks (per day £3) are signed off junctions 10 and 11 of the M3.

There are taxi ranks on the High St, and outside the train station and tourist office.
Wintax (☑ 01962-878727; www.wintaxcars. com) Operates 24 hours.

Portsmouth
POP 209,100

The world-class collection of maritime heritage at Portsmouth demands a day trip. Here you can roam around three stunning historic ships, a submarine and an impressive cluster of museums. Nauticalia done, the city's Point district tempts with cobbled streets and ancient pubs, the Spinnaker Tower delivers jaw-dropping views, and the port makes a prime jumping-off point for the Isle of Wight.

◉ Sights

★ Portsmouth
Historic Dockyard HISTORIC SHIPS
(☑ 02392-728060; www.historicdockyard.co.uk; Victory Gate; All Attractions ticket adult/child/family £28/21/78; ⊘ 10am-6pm Apr-Oct, to 5.30pm

Portsmouth

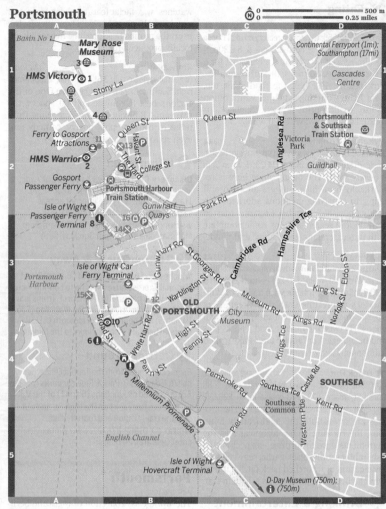

Nov-Mar) Portsmouth's blockbuster draw sees you gazing at the evocative hulk of Henry VIII's flagship, the *Mary Rose,* and jumping aboard HMS *Victory* – the warship Nelson captained at the Battle of Trafalgar. Then there's the Victorian HMS *Warrior,* the WWII-era submarine HMS *Alliance* and a wealth of imaginative, maritime-themed museums, along with water-borne harbour tours. Visiting more than one exhibit makes the All Attraction ticket (rather than single attraction versions) the best value. Last admission is 1½ hours before closing. Harbour Tours (p230) are also included in the All Attractions ticket.

➡ ★ Mary Rose Museum

(www.maryrose.org; adult/child £18/13) The raising of the 16th-century warship the *Mary Rose* in 1982 was an extraordinary feat of marine archaeology. Now the new £35 million, boat-shaped Mary Rose Museum has been built around her. It showcases the massive hull which can be seen from tiered galleries reconstructing life on each deck, using some of the 19,000 artefacts that were raised with her.

This 700-tonne floating fortress was Henry VIII's favourite vessel, but she sank suddenly off Portsmouth while fighting the French in

Portsmouth

1545. Of a crew of 400, it's thought 360 died. Items on display range from the military, including scores of cannons and hundreds of longbows, to the touchingly prosaic: water jugs, hair combs, leather shoes and even the skeleton of Hatch, the ship's dog.

➡ ★**HMS Victory**

(www.hms-victory.com; adult/child £18/13) As resplendent as she is venerable, HMS *Victory* was Lord Nelson's flagship at the Battle of Trafalgar (1805) and the site of his famous dying words 'Kiss me, Hardy', after victory over the French had been secured. This remarkable ship is topped by a forest of ropes and masts, and weighted by a swollen belly filled with cannon and paraphernalia for an 850-strong crew. Clambering through the low-beamed decks and crew's quarters is an evocative experience.

➡ ★**HMS Warrior**

(www.hmswarrior.org; adult/child £18/13) Anywhere else, the magnificent warship HMS *Warrior* would grab centre stage. This stately dame was at the cutting edge of technology when she was built in 1860, riding the transition from wood to iron and sail to steam. The gleaming upper deck, vast gun deck and dimly lit cable lockers conjure up vivid pictures of life in the Victorian navy.

➡ **National Museum of the Royal Navy**

(www.royalnavalmuseum.org; adult/child £13/8) Cannon fire, recoiling guns and injured sailors appear in this museum's multimedia re-creation of the Battle of Trafalgar; Nelson and Napoleon even pop up to give a tactical briefing. The site also features William Wyllie's 42ft painting *The Panorama of the Battle of Trafalgar,* Nelson's 1800 Life Mask and an Enigma machine, used by British WWII code-breakers to crack German signals.

➡ **Action Stations!**

(adult/child £12/9) Stroll into Action Stations!, a warehouse full of child-friendly interactive gadgets, to command a warship, gaze at an astronaut's view of earth, and up a periscope. The whole set-up is a thinly disguised recruitment drive for the modern navy, but it's fun nonetheless.

➡ **Explosion!**

(www.explosion.org.uk; Priddy's Hard, Gosport; adult/child £10/6) This 1771 powder magazine is packed full of ordnance tracing the story of naval munitions from gunpowder to Exocet missiles. Explosion! is in Gosport, on the west side of Portsmouth Harbour – a free waterbus (15 minutes) links it with the main historic dockyard site.

➡ **HMS Alliance at the Submarine Museum**

(www.submarine-museum.co.uk; Haslar Jetty Rd, Gosport; adult/child £14/10) Taking a trip deep into the bowels of the the WWII-era sub HMS *Alliance* is compelling, thanks to the lights, sounds and even smells used to create a sense of dropping by just as the crew has gone ashore. HMS *Alliance* is in Gosport, across the harbour from Portsmouth; free water buses (30 minutes) shuttle to the site from Portsmouth Historic Dockyard.

Your tour leads through the submarine's service years, from the 1940s to the 1970s, and sees you navigating cramped quarters and peering up through periscopes onto the harbour outside.

The Point   HISTORIC SITE
The Point's characterful cobbled streets are dotted with higgledy-piggledy houses and

ⓘ HMS VICTORY

In the summer, tours of Nelson's flagship are self-guided. But between autumn and spring, hugely popular 40-minute guided tours are held. Arrive early to bag a place – you can't book in advance.

salty sea-dog pubs – their terraces prime places to watch streams of ferries and navy ships. Here you can also climb Henry V's Round Tower and stroll along the fort's walls to the 15th-century Square Tower. Underneath, cavernous vaults frame Sally Ports; openings in the defences that used to give captains access to the sea, and now lead sun worshippers onto a tiny shingle beach.

Spinnaker Tower
TOWER

(☑ 02392-857520; www.spinnakertower.co.uk; Gunwharf Quays; adult/child £9/7; ☉ 10am-6pm) The Spinnaker Tower soars 170m above Gunwharf Quays, its two sweeping white arcs resembling a billowing sail from some angles, and a skeletal ribcage from others. The 23-mile views take in Portsmouth, the Isle of Wight and the South Downs. Observation Deck 1 has a hair-raising view through the glass floor, while the roofless Crow's Nest on Deck 3 allows you to feel the wind on your face. Tickets are 15% cheaper when booked online.

D-Day Museum
MUSEUM

(☑ 02392-826722; www.ddaymuseum.co.uk; Clarence Esplanade, Southsea; adult/child £7/5; ☉ 10am-5pm) The exhibits here recount the assault mounted by Allied D-Day forces in 1944 and Portsmouth's key role in the operation.

Tours

Harbour Tours
BOAT TOUR

(☑ 01983-864602; Portsmouth Historic Dockyard; adult/child £7/5; ☉ 10.30am-4pm Apr-Oct, 11am-3pm Nov-Mar) These 45-minute voyages (weather permitting) provide salt-sprayed views of HMS *Warrior* and HMS *Victory*, and you'll go past modern warships too. The tours are included in the All Attractions ticket (p227). The free waterbus to HMS *Alliance*, the Submarine Museum and Explosion! leaves from the same pontoon.

Walking Tours
HERITAGE TOUR

(adult/child £3/free; ☉ 2.30pm Sun) Themes include Nelson, the Point and Old Fortifications; there are Sunday evening Ghost Walks too. The tourist office has full details.

Eating & Drinking

Still & West
PUB £

(www.stillandwest.co.uk; 2 Bath Sq; mains £8; ☉ 9am-9pm Mon-Thu, to 10pm Fri & Sat, to 8pm Sun) Genius: two great British institutions in one – a fish and chip shop inside a pub (open 11am to 11pm). Your fried delights come wrapped in traditional chippy paper, so buy a pint, bag a window table and tuck in while watching the close-up panorama of passing boats.

Lady Hamilton
PUB £

(☑ 02392-870505; 21 The Hard; mains £7.50; ☉ kitchen 11am-3pm & 6-9pm Mon-Sat, noon-9pm Sun) Cutlasses and paintings of valiant sea battles plaster the walls of a proper old boozer (open 11am to 11pm) that's named after naval hero Horatio Nelson's mistress. The daily roasts are legendary, the vibe is un-gimmicky and the decor is definitely not smart – and it's all the better for it.

A Bar
BISTRO ££

(☑ 02392-811585; www.abarbistro.co.uk; 58 White Hart Rd; mains £10-19; ☉ 11am-11pm; 🐾) A laid-back spot to sample local produce and soak up local life – the menu is strong on fish that's been landed just yards away, while cider-drinking fishermen prop up the bar. The wine list is seriously good; the same people run a specialist retailer from upstairs.

Old Customs House
PUB ££

(www.theoldcustomshouse.com; Gunwharf Quays; mains £10-16; ☉ 9am-9pm Sun-Thu, to 10pm Fri & Sat; 🐾) The best of Gunwharf Quays' numerous eateries, this smart pub occupies an 18th-century former Royal Marine hospital. Now better-than-average bar food (think mussels steamed in cider, steak and ale pie and Welsh rarebit) is served up alongside its raspberry-red walls and gilt-framed mirrors.

❶ Information

Net Cafe (www.netcafeportsmouth.com; 4 Market Way; per hr £3; ☉ 10am-5.30pm Mon-Fri, to 5pm Sat) Some 1.5 miles east of the Historic Dockyard.

Tourist Office (☑ 02392-826722; www. visitportsmouth.co.uk; Clarence Esplanade; ☉ 10am-5pm Apr-Sep, to 4.30pm Nov-Mar) In the D-Day Museum in Southsea.

❶ Getting There & Away

Portsmouth is 100 miles southwest of London.

BOAT

Ferries link Portsmouth to the Isle of Wight (p235).

Several routes run from Portsmouth to France. Prices vary wildly depending on times and dates of travel – an example fare is £120 one way for a car and two adults on the Portsmouth–Cherbourg route. Book in advance, be prepared to travel off-peak and look out for special deals.

Brittany Ferries (www.brittanyferries.co.uk) Services run regularly from Portsmouth to St Malo (10¾ hours), Caen (four hours), Cherbourg (three hours) and Le Havre (3¾ hours) in France, and twice-weekly to Santander (13 hours) and Bilbao in Spain.

Condor Ferries (www.condorferries.co.uk) Runs a weekly car-and-passenger service from Portsmouth to Cherbourg (6½ hours) between June and September.

LD Lines (www.ldlines.co.uk) Shuttles daily to Le Havre (five to eight hours) in France.

BUS

There are hourly, direct National Express buses from London Victoria (£14, 1¾ hours). Bus 700 runs to Chichester (£4.40, one hour) and Brighton (£4.70, four hours) at least hourly.

TRAIN

Direct trains run hourly from London Victoria (£35, two hours) and half-hourly from London Waterloo (£35, two hours). For the Historic Dockyard get off at the final stop, Portsmouth Harbour.

Other departures include:

Brighton (£16, 1½ hours, hourly)
Chichester (£8, 40 minutes, two per hour)
Southampton (£10, one hour, three per hour)
Winchester (£15, 1¼ hours, half-hourly)

❶ Getting Around

Bus 1 runs every 20 minutes between Portsmouth Harbour bus station and South Parade Pier in Southsea, via Old Portsmouth. An all-day ticket is £4.

Ranks for taxis are near the Portsmouth Harbour bus and train stations. Or call **Aquacars** (☏ 02392-811111; www.aquacars.co.uk).

NEW FOREST

With typical, accidental, English irony the New Forest is anything but new – it was first proclaimed a royal hunting preserve in 1079. It's also not much of a forest, being mostly heathland ('forest' is from the Old French for 'hunting ground'). Designated a national park in 2005, the forest's combined charms make it a joy to explore. Wild ponies mooch around pretty scrubland, deer flicker in the distance and rare birds flit among the foliage. Genteel villages dot the landscape, connected by a web of walking and cycling trails.

🏃 Activities

The forest is prime hiking territory. Ordnance Survey (OS) produces a detailed, 1:25,000 Explorer map (*New Forest; No 22, £8*); Pathfinder's *New Forest Short Walks* (£8) features 20 day hikes.

New Forest Activities　　ADVENTURE SPORTS
(☏ 01590-612377; www.newforestactivities.co.uk; High St, Beaulieu) Runs sessions in canoeing (adult/child per two hours £32/25), kayaking (per two hours £32) and archery (adult/child per 1½ hours £22/17).

Cycling

The New Forest makes for superb cycling country, with 100 miles of routes linking the main villages and the key railway station at Brockenhurst.

Cycling in the New Forest (£3.25) shows approved off-road and quieter 'on-road' routes. The *New Forest Cycle Experience Route Pack* (£4) features seven trips, ranging from 4 to 24 miles. The *Forest Leisure Cycling Route Pack* (£4) has nine circular trails for all abilities – all start from the village of Burley.

Maps and guides can be bought from Lyndhurst tourist office (p232) or via its website.

To rent bikes you'll need to pay a deposit (usually £20) and provide identification.

AA Bike Hire　　BICYCLE RENTAL
(☏ 02380-283349; www.aabikehirenewforest.co.uk; Fern Glen, Gosport Lane, Lyndhurst; adult/child per day £10/5)

Country Lanes　　BICYCLE RENTAL
(☏ 01590-622627; www.countrylanes.co.uk; train station, Brockenhurst; adult/child/family per day £16/9/43)

New Forest Cycle Hire　　BICYCLE RENTAL
(Cyclexperience; ☏ 01590-624204; www.newforestcyclehire.co.uk; 2-4 Brookley Rd, Brockenhurst; adult/child per day £16/6)

Forest Leisure Cycling　　BICYCLE RENTAL
(☏ 01425-403584; www.forestleisurecycling.co.uk; The Cross, Burley; adult/child per day £16/6)

Horse Riding

A number of stables welcome beginners.

---

❶ CAMPING IN THE NEW FOREST

The New Forest is a haven for campers. The **Forestry Commission** (www.campingintheforest.co.uk) runs 10 relatively rural sites. Lyndhurst's tourist office (p232) has a free brochure detailing other designated areas; see also www.thenewforest.co.uk.

Arniss Equestrian Centre HORSE RIDING
(☑ 01425-654114; www.arnissequestrian.co.uk; God-shill, Fordingbridge; per hr £27)

Burley Manor HORSE RIDING
(☑ 01425-403489; www.burleymanorridingstables.com; Ringwood Rd, Burley; per 1/2hr £33/60)

Burley Villa HORSE RIDING
(☑ 01425-610278; www.burleyvilla.co.uk; near New Milton; per hr £42)

☞ Tours

Ranger Walks WALKING TOUR
(☑ 03000 680400; www.forestry.gov.uk; from £5) Day walks including those themed around ecology, flowers and ponies, plus memorable early evening deer-watching strolls.

ℹ Information

Tourist Office (☑ 02380-282269; www.thenewforest.co.uk; main car park, Lyndhurst; ◷10am-5pm) The national park's main tourist office, set in the New Forest Centre, has a wealth of information, including walking and cycling maps, and camping guides

ℹ Getting There & Around

BUS

Regular services run to Bournemouth (£8.50) and Southampton (£7.20).
New Forest Tour (www.thenewforesttour.info; adult per 1/2/5 days £14/19/28, child £7/9/14; ◷ hourly 10am-6pm mid-Jun–mid-Sep) Three connecting routes of hop-on/hop-off buses, passing through Lyndhurst's main car park, Brockenhurst station, Lymington, Beaulieu and Exbury.

TRAIN

Two trains an hour run to Brockenhurst from London Waterloo (£15, two hours) via Winchester (£12, 30 minutes) and on to Bournemouth (£8, 25 minutes). Local trains also shuttle twice an hour between Brockenhurst and Lymington (£4, 10 minutes).

Lyndhurst, Brockenhurst & Around

POP 6579

The quaint country villages of Lyndhurst and Brockenhurst are separated by just 4 miles. Their picturesque sleeping spots and superb eateries ensure they're atmospheric bases from which to explore the New Forest.

Lyndhurst also has the New Forest Centre, which contains the tourist office, and a library (main car park; ◷ 9.30am-1pm Mon, Wed & Sat, 2-5.30pm Tue & Fri) with free internet access.

◉ Sights

New Forest Museum MUSEUM
(www.newforestcentre.org.uk; main car park, Lyndhurst; adult/child £4/free; ◷10am-5pm) Features a local labourer's cottage (complete with socks drying beside the fire), potato dibbers and a cider press. The mini-film makes for an accessible introduction to the park – listen too for recordings of the autumn pony sales, which take place after the annual drifts (roundups).

Beaulieu HISTORIC BUILDING
(www.beaulieu.co.uk; adult/child £10/10; ◷10am-6pm Jun-Sep, to 5pm Oct-May) Petrolheads, historians and ghost-hunters gravitate to Beaulieu (pronounced *bew*-lee), a vintage car museum, stately home and tourist complex based on the site of a key 13th-century Cistercian monastery. Motor-maniacs will be in raptures at Lord Montague's National Motor Museum. Beaulieu is on the Lymington/Brockenhurst route of the New Forest Tour (p232).

Following Henry VIII's monastic land grab of 1536, the abbey fell to the ancestors of current proprietors, the Montague family. Today the motor museum presents a splendid collection that spans early classics, F1 cars and jet-powered land-speed record-breakers including *Bluebird,* which broke the 403mph (649km/h) limit in 1964. Celebrity wheels include those driven by James Bond and Mr Bean.

Beaulieu's grand but homely palace began life as a 14th-century Gothic abbey gatehouse, but received a 19th-century Scottish baronial makeover from Baron Montague in the 1860s. Listen out for eerie Gregorian chanting – the abbey is supposedly one of England's most haunted buildings.

🛏 Sleeping

Lyndhurst House B&B ££
(☑ 02380-282230; www.lyndhursthousebb.co.uk; 35 Romsey Rd, Lyndhurst; s £55, d £70-76; 🅿 🛜) Pine furniture fills floral-themed rooms; steeply slanting eaves add character to those on the top floor. But a real surprise sits in an outhouse: a mini hot tub and sauna combo, for soothing limbs tested by New Forest cycling, hiking or riding.

Daisybank Cottage
BOUTIQUE B&B ££

(☑ 01590-622086; www.bedandbreakfast-newforest. co.uk; Sway Rd, Brockenhurst; s £75, d £90-135; P🗲) The five gorgeous themed suites here are mini pamper palaces. Expect aromatic smellies in gleaming bathrooms, stylish, luxurious furnishings and lots of little extras: breakfasts laden with New Forest goodies, handmade chocolates and range-baked cakes on arrival.

★ The Pig
BOUTIQUE HOTEL £££

(☑ 01590-622354; www.thepighotel.co.uk; Beaulieu Rd, Brockenhurst; r £139-169; P🗲) One of the New Forest's classiest hotels remains an utter delight: log baskets, croquet mallets and ranks of guest gumboots give things a country-house air; espresso machines and mini-larders lend bedrooms a luxury touch. In fact, all this effortless elegance makes it feel like you've just dropped by a friend's (very stylish) rural retreat.

✖ Eating

Oak Inn
PUB ££

(☑ 02380-282350; www.oakinnlyndhurst.co.uk; Pinkney Lane, Bank; mains £8-16; ⊘ noon-2.30pm & 6-9.30pm Mon-Fri, noon-9pm Sat & Sun) Beams, panelling, horse brasses, and dried hops hanging over the bar – this flower-framed New Forest inn is as English as they come. The grub though is pure gastropub: monkfish and squid salad; goat-cheese mousse. It's a mile southwest of Lyndhurst in the hamlet of Bank.

★ The Pig
MODERN BRITISH ££

(☑ 01590-622354; www.thepighotel.co.uk; Beaulieu Rd, Brockenhurst; mains £10-17; ⊘ noon-2.30pm & 6.30-9.30pm; 🗲) Add this to your must-eat-in list. The '25 mile menu' at this über-cool hotel is all sourced locally – most is home-grown, own-reared or foraged. That means imaginative combos featuring earthy chard from the kitchen garden, punchy own-smoked ham and a creamy risotto of just-picked mushrooms. You can even join them for a foraging trip.

❶ Getting There & Away

Bus 6 shuttles between Lyndhurst, Brockenhurst and Lymington (£3.60, hourly Monday to Saturday, five on Sunday); so does the New Forest Tour (p232).

Trains run twice an hour between Brockenhurst and Lymington (£4, 10 minutes).

SOUTHAMPTON

Southampton is a useful transport hub. **Southampton International Airport** (www.southamptonairport.com) sits between Winchester, Portsmouth and Bournemouth and connects with more than 30 UK and European destinations, including Amsterdam, Glasgow, Paris and Dublin.

Trains run direct from the airport to Bournemouth (£13, 30 minutes, three per hour) via Brockenhurst in the New Forest (£9, 25 minutes). Five trains an hour link the airport to Southampton's main train station (seven minutes). From there, three trains an hour run to Portsmouth (£10, one hour) and Winchester (£7, 25 minutes).

Ferries (www.redfunnel.co.uk) shuttle from Southampton to the Isle of Wight.

Buckler's Hard

For such a tiny place, this picturesque huddle of 18th-century cottages, near the mouth of the River Beaulieu, has a big history. It started in 1722, when a duke of Montague built a port to finance a Caribbean expedition. His dream faltered, but when war with France came, this embryonic village and sheltered gravel waterfront became a secret boatyard where several of Nelson's triumphant Battle of Trafalgar warships were built. In the 20th century it played its part in the preparations for the D-Day landings.

Buckler's Hard is 2 miles downstream from Beaulieu; a riverside walking trail links the two.

◉ Sights

Buckler's Hard Story
MUSEUM

(☑ 01590-616203; www.bucklershard.co.uk; adult/ child £6.20/4.40; ⊘ 10am-5.30pm Apr-Sep, to 4.30pm Oct-Mar) The hamlet's fascinating Maritime Museum and heritage centre chart the inlet's shipbuilding history and WWII role and feature immaculately preserved 18th-century labourers' cottages.

⊨ Sleeping

Master Builder's House Hotel
HOTEL ££

(☑ 01590-616253; www.themasterbuilders.co.uk; Buckler's Hard; d £93-158; P) The luxurious

Master Builder's House Hotel is part of the Buckler's Hard Story complex. This beautifully restored 18th-century hotel has 25 stately but stylish rooms, featuring soft lighting, burnished trunks and plush fabrics. The atmospheric **restaurant** (lunch two/three courses £16/19, dinner mains £16) overlooks the river, while the wood-panelled **Yachtsman's Bar** serves quality pub grub from £7.

Lymington

POP 15,425

A yachting haven, New Forest base and jumping-off point to the Isle of Wight, the appealing Georgian harbour town of Lymington has several strings to its tourism bow. This former smuggler's port offers nautical shops, prime eating and sleep spots and, in Quay St, an utterly quaint cobbled lane.

◉ Sights

St Barbe Museum MUSEUM
(☑01590-676969; www.stbarbe-museum.org.uk; New St; adult/child £4/2; ⊙10am-4pm Mon-Sat) This place explores tales of boat-builders, sailors, smugglers, salt-makers and farmers through a mix of models, hands-on displays and artefacts.

☞ Tours

Puffin Cruises BOAT TOUR
(☑07850-947618; www.puffincruiseslymington. com; Town Quay) The best trip is an exhilarating, three-hour surge across the Solent to the Isle of Wight (adult/child £19/8, 6pm Wednesday and Friday, May to October), where the Needles lighthouse and towering chalk stacks loom from the water. There is also a 1½-hour evening cruise and a one-hour picnic voyage.

⊨ Sleeping

Auplands B&B ££
(☑01590-675944; www.auplands.com; 22 Southampton Rd; s £45, d £60-70; ⓟ☎) Your genial hosts have been running this B&B for more than 30 years, and it shows in their supremely efficient systems and easy charm. Snug rooms feature pine and big plants, while the eateries of Lymington are only a short stroll away.

★ Mill at Gordleton BOUTIQUE HOTEL £££
(☑01590-682219; www.themillatgordleton.co.uk; Silver St, Hordle; d/ste £150/195; ⓟ☎) Step inside here and you know, instantly, you're going to be looked after, beautifully. Wicker, velvet and gingham dot exquisite rooms (each one comes with a sweet soft toy duck), while the garden is a magical mix of rushing water, fairy lights and modern sculpture. The acclaimed restaurant (two-course lunch/dinner £16/23, open noon to 2pm daily and 7pm to 9pm Monday to Saturday) focuses firmly on the homemade and the home-grown. The Mill is 4 miles west of Lymington.

Stanwell House BOUTIQUE HOTEL £££
(☑0844 7046820; www.stanwellhouse.com; 14 High St; d £140-180, ste £220; @☎) There are boutique tweaks everywhere at Stanwell. Swish Georgian rooms manage to be both period and modern, the Four Poster ones feature dark woods and zingy colours, while the high-tech suites are simply irresistible – two even have their own roof terrace for sunny days and moonlit nights.

✗ Eating

Fish & Chips FISH & CHIPS £
(130 High St; mains £7.50; ⊙11.30am-2.30pm & 4.30-8.30pm Mon-Thu, 11.30am-9pm Fri & Sat, to 7pm Sun) They're often queuing out the door at this classic British chippy, which boasts great fish, formica tables and pickled eggs. Eat in or take away.

Ship Inn PUB ££
(www.theshiplymington.co.uk; The Quay; mains £9-17; ⊙kitchen noon-9pm; ☞) A pub for all seasons: knock back summertime drinks on the waterside terrace; in winter a toasty log burner gets you warm. Hearty food ranges from prosciutto and poached egg to a sticky marinated chicken; drinks totter from tangy real ales to vintage champagne.

Elderflower MODERN BRITISH £££
(☑01590-676908; www.elderflowerrestaurant.co. uk; 5 Quay St; mains £15-23; ⊙noon-2.30pm & 6.30-9.30pm Wed-Sat, noon-3.30pm Sun) The man running things here used to be head chef at one of the New Forest's finest hotels, and this venture is as ambitious and innovative as you'd expect: prepare for assured rarities like hay-smoked goats' cheese, Dorset snails and cigar-smoked chocolate. The three-course lunch (£25) is a snip.

ⓘ Information

Library (North Close; ⊙9am-5pm Mon, Wed, Thu & Sat, to 7pm Tue & Fri; ☎) Free internet access.

ℹ Getting There & Away

Lymington has two train stations: Lymington Town and Lymington Pier. Isle of Wight ferries connect with Lymington Pier. Trains run to Southampton (£11, 40 minutes), via Brockenhurst, every hour.

Wightlink Ferries (☎ 0871 376 1000; www.wightlink.co.uk) Car and passenger ferries run hourly to Yarmouth on the Isle of Wight (30 minutes). An adult/child foot passenger day return costs £14/7. Car fares start at around £60 for a short-break return.

ISLE OF WIGHT

On the Isle of Wight these days there's something groovy in the air. For decades this slab of rock anchored off Portsmouth has been a magnet for family holidays, and it still has seaside kitsch by the bucket and spade. But now the proms and amusement arcades are framed by pockets of pure funkiness. A brace of music festivals draws party-goers, just-caught seafood is served in kooky fishermen's cafes, and cool camping rules – here sites are dotted with ecoyurts and vintage campervans. Yet still the isle's principal appeal remains: a mild climate, myriad outdoorsy activities and a 25-mile shore lined with beaches, dramatic white cliffs and tranquil sand dunes.

🏃 Activities

Water sports are serious business on the Isle of Wight. Cowes is the sailing centre, surfers and wind- and kite-surfers flock to the southwest, especially around Compton Bay, while power boats run trips out to the Needles rocks. See the island's visitor website (www.visitisleofwight.co.uk) for more.

Isle of Wight Adventure   ADVENTURE SPORTS
(☎ 01983-755838; www.isleofwightadventureactivities.co.uk; Freshwater) Runs activities ranging from surfing, stand-up paddleboarding and kayaking (per two hours adult/child £40/25), to archery (£12) and fossil hunting (adult/child £4/3).

Isle of Wight Steam Railway   HERITAGE RAILWAY
(☎ 01983-882204; www.iwsteamrailway.co.uk; ☉ mid-Apr–Sep) Chugs regularly from Smallbrook Junction to Wootton Common (return adult/child £12/6, 1st class £17/12, one hour).

Cycling

With 200 miles of cycle routes, the Isle of Wight makes pedal-pushers smile. The island's official visitor website lists suggested trips (complete with maps), ranging from family-friendly tootles along former railway routes to the 50-mile, cliff-climbing **Chalk Ridge Extreme**. A **Cycling Festival** (☎ 01983-821000; www.sunseaandcycling.com) is held every September.

Bike rentals start at around £13/45 per day/week. Many firms deliver and collect on orders over £30.

Tavcycles   BICYCLE RENTAL
(☎ 01983- 812989; www.tavcycles.co.uk; 140 High St, Ryde)

Top Gear   BICYCLE RENTAL
(☎ 01983-299056; www.top-gearhire.com; 1 Terminus Rd, Cowes)

Wight Cycle Hire   BICYCLE RENTAL
(☎ 01983-761800; www.wightcyclehire.co.uk; Station Rd, Yarmouth)

Walking

This is one of the best spots in southern England for rambling, with 500 miles of well-marked walking paths, including 67 miles of coastal routes. The island's two-week **Walking Festival** (www.isleofwightwalkingfestival.co.uk) each May is billed as the UK's largest.

ℹ Information

At time of writing, the Isle of Wight doesn't have a tourist office. Small-scale info points include one at the Yarmouth Harbour Office.

Visit Isle of Wight (www.visitisleofwight.co.uk) The isle's official tourism website.

ℹ Getting There & Away

Hovertravel (☎ 08434 87 88 87; www.hovertravel.co.uk; day return adult/child £18/9) Shuttles foot passengers between Southsea (a Portsmouth suburb) and Ryde half hourly to hourly.

Red Funnel (☎ 0844 844 9988; www.redfunnel.co.uk) Operates car-and-passenger ferries between Southampton and East Cowes (day return adult/child £16/8, from £40 with car,

---

ℹ CAR FERRY COSTS

The cost of car ferries to the Isle of Wight can vary enormously. Make savings by booking ahead, asking about special offers and travelling off-peak (midweek and later in the day). Long stays are cheaper and some deals include admission to island attractions. Booking online can mean paying £20 less.

Isle of Wight

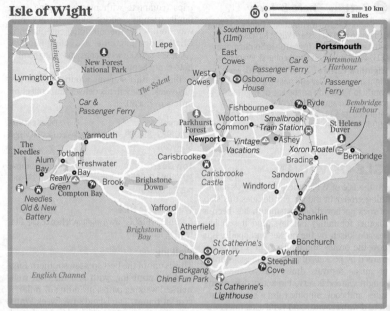

60 minutes, hourly) and high-speed passenger ferries between Southampton and West Cowes (day return adult/child £23/11, 25 minutes, one to two per hour).

Wightlink Ferries (☑ 0871 376 1000; www. wightlink.co.uk) Operates passenger ferries every half hour from Portsmouth to Ryde (day-return adult/child £17/9, 22 minutes). It also runs hourly car-and-passenger ferries from Portsmouth to Fishbourne (40 minutes) and from Lymington to Yarmouth (30 minutes). For both, an adult/child foot passenger day return costs £14/7. Car fares start at around £60 for a short-break return.

ℹ Getting Around

BUS

Southern Vectis (www.islandbuses.info) Runs buses between the eastern towns roughly every 30 minutes. Regular services to the remoter southwest, especially between Blackgang Chine and Brook, are less frequent, but between April and September the Island Coaster makes four return circuits a day along the southern shore from Ryde around to Yarmouth, in the west. Rover Tickets are available for one day (adult/child £10/5), two days (adult/child £15/7.30) and a week (adult/child £24/12).

CAR

1st Call (☑ 01983-400055; www.1stcallcar-sales.com; 15 College Close, Sandown; per day/week from £22/160) Collects and delivers island wide.

TRAIN

Island Line (www.southwesttrains.co.uk/island-line) Trains run twice-hourly from Ryde to Shanklin (day return £5.40, 25 minutes), via Smallbrook Junction, Brading and Sandown.

Cowes & Around

POP 10,437

Pack your yachting cap – the hilly Georgian harbour town of Cowes is famous for Cowes Week (www.aamcowesweek.co.uk) in late July; first held in 1826, it's one of the biggest and longest-running sailing regattas in the world. Fibreglass playthings and vintage sailboats line Cowes' waterfronts, which are lopped into East and West Cowes by the River Medina; a chain ferry shuttles regularly between the two (foot passengers free, cars £2).

The island's capital, Newport, is 5 miles south.

◉ Sights

★**Osborne House**   HISTORIC BUILDING
(EH; ☑ 01983-200022; www.english-heritage.org.uk; York Ave, East Cowes; adult/child £14/8; ⊙10am-5pm Apr-Oct; ℗) Lemon-frosted and

Italianate, Osborne House is pure Victorian pomp. Built in the 1840s at the behest of Queen Victoria, the monarch grieved here for many years after her husband's death. Extravagant rooms include the opulent Royal Apartments and Durbar Room; other highlights are horse and carriage rides, the Swiss Cottage – where the royal ankle-biters would play – and the stroll down Rhododendron Walk to Her Majesty's private beach.

Carisbrooke Castle   CASTLE
(EH; ☑01983-522107; www.english-heritage.org.uk; Castle Hill, Newport; adult/child £8/5; ☺10am-5pm Apr-Oct; ℗) Charles I was imprisoned here before his execution in 1649. Today you can clamber the sturdy ramparts and play bowls on the very green the doomed monarch used.

🛏 Sleeping

onefiftycowes   B&B ££
(☑07795-296399; www.onefiftycowes.co.uk; 150 Park Rd, West Cowes; s £60-70, d £85-95; ℗🛜) Modern art dots the walls, sea-smoothed pebbles are scattered around – this is a crisp, contemporary B&B with beautifully turned-out rooms. Two overlook the water; the pick is top-floor Solent, which comes with mini-binoculars to help you drink in the sea views.

Fountain   HOTEL ££
(☑01983-292397; www.fountaininn-cowes.co.uk; High St, West Cowes; s £40-100, d £50-110; 🛜) Georgian-repro style rules at this appealing harbourside inn, where mock-flock wallpaper and old, wooden furniture define comfy rooms; number 15 has prime views of the bustling quay. The snug bar and sunny terrace are top places to sample pints and pub-grub classics (mains £9; open noon to 10pm).

Ryde to Shanklin

The nippiest foot-passenger ferries between Wight and Portsmouth alight in **Ryde**, a workaday Victorian town rich in the trappings of the British seaside. Next come the cutesy village of **Brading**, with its fine Roman villa; photogenic **Bembridge Harbour**, fringed by sandy beaches; and the twin resort towns of **Sandown** and **Shanklin**, boasting promenades and hordes of families wielding buckets and spades. The area also features unique places to sleep – including a decommissioned warship and vintage Airstream trailers.

👁 Sights

Brading Roman Villa   RUIN
(☑01983-406223; www.bradingromanvilla.org.uk; Morton Old Rd, Brading; adult/child £6.50/3.75; ☺9.30am-5pm) The exquisitely preserved mosaics here (including a famous cockerel-headed man) make this one of the finest Romano-British sites in the UK. Wooden walkways lead over rubble walls and brightly painted tiles, allowing you to gaze right down onto the ruins below.

St Helens Duver   NATURE RESERVE
(NT; www.nationaltrust.org.uk; ☺24hr; ℗) At this idyllic sand-and-shingle spit bordering the mouth of the River Yar, trails snake past swaths of sea pink, marram grass and rare clovers. It's signed from the village of St Helens, near Bembridge Harbour.

🛏 Sleeping

★Vintage Vacations   CAMPSITE £
(☑07802-758113; www.vintagevacations.co.uk; Ashey, near Ryde; 4-person caravans per week £460-680; ☺Apr-Oct; ℗) The bevy of 1960s Airstream trailers on this farm are vintage chic personified. The gleaming aluminium shells shelter lovingly selected furnishings ranging from cheerful patchwork blankets to vivid tea cosies. Alternatively, opt for a beach-shack retreat, a 1930s Scout Hut or the Mission: a late-Victorian tin chapel.

Xoron Floatel   B&B ££
(☑01983-874596; www.xoronfloatel.co.uk; Bembridge Harbour; d £70; ℗) A truly unique spot to drop off – this former WWII gunboat is

---

ISLE OF WIGHT MUSIC FESTIVALS

The isle's festival tradition kicked off in the early 1970s, when 600,000 hippies came to see the Doors, the Who, Joni Mitchell and rock icon Jimi Hendrix's last performance. A generation on, its gatherings are still some of England's top musical events. Mid-June's Isle of Wight Festival (www.isleofwightfestival.org) has been headlined by Muse, the Red Hot Chili Peppers, the Kings of Leon and the Rolling Stones, while Bestival (www.bestival.net), in early September, delights in an eclectic, alternative feel, drawing the Super Furry Animals, Scissor Sisters, Candi Staton and more.

now a cheery, bunting-draped houseboat. Comfy cabins come complete with tiny bathrooms, while the harbour views from the flower-framed sun deck are simply superb.

Townhouse
B&B ££

(07703-171365; www.thetownhouseryde.co.uk; 1 Monkton St, Ryde; d £70-90; 🐾) Swish and quirky sums up the Townhouse; expect smoothly stylish furnishings, brass bedsteads, and a fireside roll-top bath in the poshest room. Breakfast is available until 1.30pm (gasp!), and is either in a nearby, seafront cafe, or is a bacon sandwich delivered to your room.

✗ Eating

Pilot Boat
PUB ££

(01983-872077; www.thepilotboatinn.com; Station Rd, Bembridge; mains £9; ⊘noon-2pm & 6-8pm; 🅿🐾) It's a good sign when customers can just sit down and play the pub's piano and guitars – a convivial atmosphere added to by a log-burner, ships' flags and quality homemade grub (think local crab salad and big bowls of chilli). Meanwhile, the spicand-span bedrooms (doubles £90) are attractively nautically themed.

Black Sheep
BISTRO ££

(www.theblacksheepbar.co.uk; 53 Union St, Ryde; tapas £5-7; ⊘10am-11pm Sun-Thu, to 2am Fri & Sat) Fancy sitting on a sunny terrace, sipping an Isle of Wight-brewed beer and eating tapas-style treats – perhaps chargrilled chorizo or buffalo mozzarella with honey and thyme? Then join the cool crowd at this elegant lounge club, with its art-deco vibe.

Ventnor & Around
POP 6300

The Victorian town of Ventnor slaloms so steeply down the island's southern coast that it feels like the south of France. The winding streets are home to a scattering of boutiques, while local hotels, eateries and the atmospheric Steephill Cove are well worth a detour.

To the west, the island's southernmost point is marked by the stocky 19th-century St Catherine's Lighthouse and its 14th-century counterpart St Catherine's Oratory. Nearby, kid-friendly Blackgang Chine Fun Park (01983-730330; www.blackgangchine. com; admission £17; ⊘10am-5pm Apr-Jul, to 6pm Aug, to 4pm Sep-Mar) features water gardens, animated shows and a hedge maze.

🛏 Sleeping

★ Lighthouse
APARTMENT £

(07801-899747; www.theboathouse-steephillcove. co.uk; Steephill Cove; 6 people per week £1400-1850) This is the sea-view sleep spot of your dreams. A white, two-storey, clapperboard lighthouse where the style is pure New England beach chic and the setting is right on the shore. Lie in bed watching the waves, take a few steps to the beach to swim in the sea, stroll out to dine on your private deck. Heavenly. The same people run a house (sleeping six, £700 to £1400 per week) and the romantic, two-person Crow's Nest (£350 to £550) nearby.

St Augustine Villa
B&B ££

(Harbour View; 01983-852285; www.harbourviewhotel.co.uk; Esplanade, Ventnor; s £94, d £88-103; 🅿🐾) Country house collectibles dot this Italianate Victorian villa, wing-backed chairs sit in stately bedrooms and rich red fabrics frame sea views. And what views: watch the sun set from your sofa or the waves roll from your four-poster bed. The window-seated Tower Room sees light pour in from three sides.

Hambrough
BOUTIQUE HOTEL £££

(01983-856333; www.thehambrough.com; Hambrough Rd, Ventnor; d £190-280; 🅿🐾) It's hard to say which is better: the 180-degree vistas out to sea, or the super-sleek rooms where espresso machines and heated floors keep luxury levels set sky-high.

✗ Eating

Crab Shed
CAFE £

(Steephill Cove; snacks £5; ⊘noon-3pm Apr-Sep) Lobster pots and fishing boats line the slipway outside a shack that's a riot of seasmoothed spas, cork floats and faded buoys. Irresistible treats include meaty crab salads, mackerel ciabatta and crumbly crab pasties.

★ Boathouse
SEAFOOD ££

(01983-852747; www.theboathouse-steephillcove. co.uk; Steephill Cove; mains £18-35; ⊘noon-3pm Thu-Tue late May-early Sep) Arrive early enough, and you'll see Steephill Cove's fishermen (Jimmy and Mark) landing your lunch – the sanded wooden tables here are just steps from the sea. It makes a spellbinding spot to sip chilled wine, sample succulent lobster and revel in Wight's new-found driftwood chic. Book.

Pond Cafe
MODERN BRITISH ££

(01983-855666; www.thehambrough.com; Bonchurch; mains £15; ⊘10.30am-3pm & 6-9.30pm Thu-Mon) Chef Joanne Bennetts loves giving Italian

STEEPHILL COVE

Steephill Cove's tiny, sandy beach is fringed by buildings that range from stone cottages to rickety-looking shacks. Beach finds festoon porches dotted with driftwood furniture and draped with fishing nets; a tiny clapper-board lighthouse presides over the scene. That lighthouse is let out as a fabulous self-catering apartment (p238) sleeping six. Two atmospheric places to eat, the Boathouse (p238) and the Crab Shed (p238), add to the appeal.

Steephill Cove is 1 mile west of Ventnor and is off limits to cars. Walk from the nearby Botanical Gardens, or hike from the hillside car park 200m west of Ventnor Esplanade, then follow the (sometimes steep) coast path until you arrive.

twists to prime island ingredients; perhaps roast local pigeon with pancetta, parmesan-flecked island beef carpaccio, or the day's catch with cannellini bean mash. Canny locals book a terrace table for a set lunch or early evening meal (two/three courses £18/22).

Ale & Oyster BISTRO ££
(www.thealeandoyster.co.uk; The Esplanade, Ventnor; £8-22; ⊘noon-2.30pm & 6-9pm Tue-Sun) Modern takes on pub and bistro standards include monkfish scampi and chips, ham-hock terrine with poached egg, and Isle of Wight cheeses.

West Wight

Rural and remote, Wight's westerly corner is where the island really comes into its own. Sheer white cliffs rear from a surging sea as the stunning coastline peels west to Alum Bay and the most famous chunks of chalk in the region: the Needles. These jagged rocks rise, shard-like out of the sea, looking like the backbone of a prehistoric sea monster. West Wight is also home to arguably the isle's best beach: sandy, windswept Compton Bay.

⊙ Sights

★ **Needles Old & New Battery** FORT
(NT; ☑ 01983-754772; www.nationaltrust.org.uk; The Needles; adult/child £5.30/2.65; ⊘11am-4pm mid-Mar–Oct) The Victorian fort complex at the Isle of Wight's western tip houses two gun emplacements where engrossing displays convey how the site was established in 1862, served in two world wars and then became a secret Cold War rocket-testing base. Walk to the battery along the cliffs from Alum Bay (1 mile) or hop on the tourist bus (www.islandbuses.info; per 24hr adult/child £10/5; ⊘10am-5pm mid-Mar–Sep) that runs twice-hourly between battery and bay.

The whiff of gunpowder seems to linger still at Old Battery: shells and powder kegs

lie around, uniforms hang on pegs. You get to pinpoint ships' positions with the rangefinders, then scramble down an ornate spiral staircase, along an echoey 60m tunnel to a searchlight post with close-up views of the eroded cliffs.

In the 1950s the batteries staged top-secret trials of Black Knight rockets, built at East Cowes, that were later used to launch Cold War surveillance satellites into space from Australia. In the tiny underground bunker at New Battery, exhibits evoke how this remote location and the existing fortifications proved ideal for keeping clandestine activities away from prying eyes.

⚑ Tours

Needles Pleasure Cruises BOAT TOUR
(☑ 01983-761587; www.needlespleasurecruises.co.uk; Alum Bay; adult/child £5.50/3.50; ⊘10.30am-4.30pm Apr-Oct) Twenty-minute voyages run half hourly from Alum Bay beach to the towering Needles chalk stacks, providing close-up views of those soaring white cliffs.

⮿ Sleeping

★ **Really Green** CAMPSITE £
(☑ 07802-678591; www.thereallygreenholidaycompany.com; Blackbridge Rd, Freshwater Bay; yurt per week £375-700; ⊘Apr-Oct; 🅿) ⌖ Roughing it has never been so smooth. The two- to five-person, fully furnished yurts on this tree-shaded site feature four-poster beds, futons, wood-burning stoves and time-worn antiques. It's set amid secluded fields with river views, and a local farm shop-cum-deli is just a few minutes' walk away.

Totland Bay YHA HOSTEL £
(☑ 01983-752165; www.yha.org.uk; Hirst Hill, Totland Bay; dm/d £17/22; 🅿) Creaking, cheerfully run Victorian house with a maximum of eight beds per room and staff happy to share local info.

DORSET

Holiday hot spot Dorset offers a checklist of charms. Its shoreline is one of Britain's best, boasting the Jurassic Coast – a World Heritage Site flecked with sea-carved bays, crumbly cliffs and beaches loaded with fossilised souvenirs. No wonder the swimming, kayaking and hiking here are truly memorable. Inland Thomas Hardy's lyrical landscape serves up vast Iron Age hill forts, rude chalk figures, fairy-tale castles and must-see stately homes. Then there are resorts packed with party animals, golden beaches much loved by multi-millionaires, and Olympic-class sailing waters. Dorset is worth adding to your list.

ⓘ Information

Visit Dorset (www.visit-dorset.com) The county's official tourism website.

ⓘ Getting Around

One main train line runs from Bristol and Bath through Dorchester West to Weymouth. The other connects London with Weymouth, via Southampton, Bournemouth, Poole and Dorchester South.

First (www.firstgroup.com) Runs key bus routes linking the main towns.

More (Wilts & Dorset; www.morebus.co.uk) Key bus operator in Bournemouth, Poole and surrounding rural areas.

Bournemouth

POP 186,700

If one thing has shaped Bournemouth it's the beach. This glorious, 7-mile strip of soft sand first drew holiday-makers in the Victorian days. Today the resort attracts both grey-haired coach parties and boozed-up stag parties – on Saturday nights fancy-dress is everywhere; angels in L-plates meet men in mankinis. But Bournemouth is more than just a full-on party town. It also boasts some hip hideaways, great restaurants, tempting water sports, and in Boscombe, 2 miles east of the centre, a suburb with a cool urban-surfer vibe.

◉ Sights & Activities

Bournemouth Beach   BEACH

Bournemouth's sandy shoreline regularly clocks up seaside awards. It stretches from Southborne in the far east to Alum Chine in the west – an immense promenade backed by 3000 deckchairs, ornamental gardens, kids' playgrounds and cafes. The resort also has

two piers. Around **Bournemouth Pier** you can hire brightly painted **beach huts** (✆0845 055 0968; www.bournemouthbeachhuts.co.uk; per day/week £36/145), deckchairs (per day £2.50), windbreaks (£3) and parasols (£4.50). Boscombe Pier is a focus for water sports.

East Cliff Lift Railway   HERITAGE RAILWAY

(✆01202-451781; Undercliff Dr; adult/child £1.25/85p; ⊙Easter-Oct) These box-like passenger cars on rails whiz up bracken-covered slopes. First built in 1908, the system cuts out the short, steep hike up the zigzag paths from the seafront promenade to the road above.

Alum Chine   GARDENS

(Mountbatten Rd; ⊙24hr) Bournemouth's 1920s heyday is beautifully evoked at a subtropical enclave containing plants from the Canary Islands, New Zealand, Mexico and the Himalayas; their bright-red bracts, silver thistles and purple flowers are set against a glittering sea. Its 1.5 miles west of Bournemouth Pier.

Russell-Cotes   MUSEUM

(✆01202-451858; www.russell-cotes.bournemouth .gov.uk; Russell-Cotes Rd; adult/child £5/4; ⊙10am-5pm Tue-Sun) Ostentation oozes from almost every inch of this arresting structure: a mash up of Italianate villa and Scottish Baronial pile. It was built at the end of the 1800s for Merton and Annie Russell-Cotes as somewhere to showcase the remarkable range of souvenirs gathered on their world travels. Look out for a plaster version of the Parthenon frieze, Maori woodcarvings and Persian tiles. Paintings include those by Rossetti, Edwin Landseer and William Frith.

Sorted Watersports   WATER SPORTS

(✆01202-300668; www.sortedsurfschool.co.uk; Overstrand Bldg, Undercliff Dr) From its base beside Boscombe Pier, Sorted runs lessons in surfing (per two hours adult/child £30/25) and stand-up paddleboarding (per two hours £30). It also hires out wetsuits (two/ eight hours £10/30), surfboards (two/eight hours £10/30), stand-up paddleboards (one/ two hours £15/20) and kayaks (one/four hours £15/45).

Coastal Activity Park   OUTDOORS

(www.coastalactivitypark.co.uk; Boscombe Promenade) Still in development at time of writing, this 1-mile-long cluster of activities is set to bring bouldering, slacklining, snorkelling, beach volleyball, beach football, table tennis and gym machines to the Boscombe shore.

🛏️ Sleeping

Bournemouth Backpackers
HOSTEL £

(☎01202-299491; www.bournemouthbackpackers.co.uk; 3 Frances Rd; dm/d £18/33; P🐕🛜) Three-to six-bed dorms in a suburban house dotted with travellers' totems – one wall is lined with chocolate bar wrappers from around the world. It's for non-UK citizens only; reservations by email, or by phone: 5pm to 7pm Sunday.

★ B&B By The Beach
B&B ££

(☎01202-433632; www.bedandbreakfastbythebeach.co.uk; 7 Burtley Rd; d £88-92; P🛜) Gorgeous rooms, fruit-packed breakfasts and charming, quick-to-laugh owners make this light-filled B&B one of the best in town. Bright, fresh bedrooms sport white shutters and subtle seaside themes, while the sunny patio is perfect for breakfast waffles or a slice of homemade cake.

Mory House
B&B ££

(☎01202-433553; www.moryhouse.co.uk; 31 Grand Ave; s £50-65, d £72-93, f from £108; P🛜) There's a delightful air of calm at Mory, where stained glass and an elegant stairwell hint at the house's Edwardian age. The pick of the contemporary bedrooms is no 3, where a pint-sized balcony is an ideal spot to nibble one of the cookies and sweets you'll find scattered around.

Amarillo
B&B ££

(☎01202-553884; www.amarillohotel.co.uk; 52 Frances Rd; s £30-35, d £60-70; P🛜) Amarillo's smart, stylish rooms remain ridiculously good value; expect jazzy wallpaper, snazzy throws and subtle lighting.

★ Urban Beach
BOUTIQUE HOTEL ££

(☎01202-301509; www.urbanbeach.co.uk; 23 Argyll Rd; s £72, d £100-145; P@🛜) Still the slumber-spot of choice for Bournemouth's hip visitors, Urban Beach revels in a 'no worries' air that sees free loans of wellingtons, umbrellas and DVDs. Bold black, dark grey and deep brown colour schemes define bedrooms, while the decked terrace is full of dudes tucking into fare from the upscale bistro (open 8am to 10pm).

🍴 Eating

★ Urban Reef
BISTRO ££

(☎01202-443960; www.urbanreef.com; Undercliff Dr, Boscombe; mains £7-35; ⊗8am-11pm Mon-Sat, to 6pm Sun; 🛜) On sunny weekends a cool crowd is queuing out the door at funky Urban Reef. No wonder: a waterfront deck and balcony, punchy coffee, top-notch snacks and quality, sustainable restaurant fare. On stormy days snuggle down beside the log burner and listen to the sound of the sea.

West Beach
SEAFOOD ££

(☎01202-587785; www.west-beach.co.uk; Pier Approach; mains £13-40; ⊗noon-2.30pm & 6-9pm) The seafood and setting are hard to beat – bag a chair on the decked terrace jutting out over the sand, watch the waves lap Bournemouth Pier and tuck into perfectly cooked, perfectly fresh fish; perhaps plaice braised in cider or a shellfish platter piled high with oysters, langoustines, cockles and clams.

Reef Encounter
BISTRO ££

(www.reef-encounter.com; 42 Sea Rd, Boscombe; mains £7-15; ⊗11am-10pm, from 9am Sat & Sun; 🛜) Big squishy sofas, rough wood walls, a mellow soundtrack and a sea-view terrace give this chilled-out eatery a surf-bar vibe. Graze your way through a meat, fish or veggie platter, or just sit alfresco, sipping a tall, cool beer, watching the waves.

🍸 Drinking & Nightlife

Most of the main entertainment venues are clustered around Firvale Rd, St Peter's Rd and Old Christchurch Rd. The gay scene kicks off around the Triangle.

Sixty Million Postcards
PUB

(www.sixtymillionpostcards.com; 19 Exeter Rd; ⊗noon-midnight Sun-Thu, to 2am Fri & Sat) An oasis of pure funkiness amid drinks-promotion Bournemouth, Sixty Million draws a decidedly beatnik crowd. Worn wooden floors and fringed lampshades frame events encompassing DJ sets, live music (think indie-pop and punk grunge) and musical bingo.

Old Firestation
CLUB

(www.oldfirestation.co.uk; 36 Holdernhurst Rd; ⊗10pm-3am Thu-Sat) Mixes gigs, club nights and student parties; music takes in D&B, dubstep, electro and old skool.

ℹ️ Information

Rio Internet Cafe (☎01202-312021; 130 Commercial Rd; per hr £1.80; ⊗9am-7pm)

Tourist Office (☎08450-511700; www.bournemouth.co.uk; Westover Rd; ⊗10am-5pm Mon-Sat, to 4pm Sun, closed Sun Nov-Feb)

ⓘ Getting There & Away

BUS

Morebus Zone A Dayrider (adult/child £4.10/3.60) Gives a day's unlimited travel in much of Poole, Bournemouth and neighbouring Christchurch.

Direct National Express routes include:

Bristol (£20, four hours, one service Monday to Saturday)

London (£23, 2½ hours, half-hourly)

Oxford (£22, three hours, three daily)

Southampton (£7, 50 minutes, hourly)

Local buses:

Poole (£2, 25 minutes, every 15 minutes) Bus M1/M2.

Salisbury (£6.30, 1¼ hours, at least hourly) Bus X3.

TRAIN

Destinations include Dorchester South (£12, 45 minutes, hourly), London Waterloo (£20, 2¾ hours, half-hourly), Poole (£4, 12 minutes, half-hourly) and Weymouth (£15, one hour, hourly).

Poole

POP 148,600

In the quaint old port of Poole there's a whiff of money in the air: the town borders Sandbanks, a gorgeous beach backed by some of the world's most expensive chunks of real estate. Big bucks aside, Poole also boasts excellent eateries and is the springboard for water sports and some irresistible boat trips.

⊙ Sights

Brownsea Island   ISLAND
(NT; ☎ 01202-707744; www.nationaltrust.org.uk; adult/child £6/3; ⊙ 10am-5pm late Mar-Oct)

On this small, wooded island in the middle of Poole Harbour trails weave through heath and woods, past peacocks, red squirrels, red deer and a wealth of bird life: the water-framed views onto the Isle of Purbeck are stunning. Free guided walks (at 11.30am and 2pm) focus on the wartime island, smugglers and pirates. Boats, run by **Brownsea Island Ferries** (☎ 01929-62383; www.brownseaislandferries.com; ⊙ 10am-5pm late Mar-Oct), leave from Poole Quay (adult/child return £10/6) and Sandbanks (adult/child return £6/4.50) half-hourly.

Brownsea also played a key role in a global movement famous for three-fingered salutes, shorts and toggles - Lord Baden-Powell staged the first ever scout camp here in 1907.

Poole Old Town   HISTORIC AREA
Poole Quay's attractive historic buildings include the Tudor **King Charles pub** on Thames St; the cream **Old Harbour Office** (1820s) next door; and the impressive red-brick **Custom House** (1813) opposite, complete with Union Jack and gilded coat of arms. The tourist office sells the *Poole Cockle Trail* guide to the old town (30p).

Waterfront Museum   MUSEUM
(☎ 01202-262600; www.boroughofpoole.com/museums; 4 High St; ⊙ 10am-5pm Mon-Sat, noon-5pm Sun) FREE The building alone is worth seeing: a beautifully restored 15th-century warehouse. The star exhibit though is a 2300-year-old **Iron Age logboat** dredged up from Poole Harbour. At 10m long and 14 tonnes, it's the largest to be found in southern Britain and probably carried 18 people. It was hand-chiselled from a single tree; millennia later you can still see the blade marks in the wood.

WATER SPORTS – POOLE HARBOUR

Poole Harbour's sheltered coasts may inspire you to get on the water. Operators cluster near the start of the Sandbanks peninsula.

Pool Harbour Watersports (☎ 01202-700503; www.pooleharbour.co.uk; 284 Sandbanks Rd) This operator does lessons in stand-up paddleboarding (SUP; per two hours £40), windsurfing (per three hours £45) and kitesurfing (per day £99), plus memorable kayak and SUP tours (per three hours £40).

FC Watersports (☎ 01202-707757; www.fcwatersports.co.uk; 19 Banks Rd, Sandbanks) Provides kitesurfing lessons (per day £99).

Watersports Academy (☎ 01202-708283; www.thewatersportsacademy.com; Banks Rd) Offers kitesurfing lessons, and also runs windsurfer taster sessions (per hour £25), plus sailing courses (per two hours/days £55/165) and wakeboarding and water-skiing (per 15 minutes £20).

Sandbanks
BEACH

A 2-mile, wafer-thin peninsula of land that curls around the expanse of Poole Harbour, Sandbanks is studded with some of the most expensive houses in the world. But the white-sand beaches that border them are free, and have some of the best water quality standards in the country. They're also home to a host of water-sports operators. Brownsea Island Ferries (p242) shuttle between Poole Quay and Sandbanks (adult/child return £10/6).

🛏 Sleeping

Corkers
B&B ££

(☑ 01202-681393; www.corkers.co.uk; 1 High St; s £61-77, d £83-94; 🛜) The decor may be unremarkable, but this neat 'n' tidy B&B punches way above its weight, thanks to a setting right on bustling Poole Quay and the tiny harbour-view roof terrace attached to the Brownsea and Purbeck rooms.

Quayside
B&B ££

(☑ 01202-683733; www.poolequayside.co.uk; 9 High St; s £35-50, d £60-80, f £80; 🛜) Snug rooms in pine and bright, blocky prints in the heart of the old harbour.

Merchant House
BOUTIQUE B&B £££

(☑ 01202-661474; www.themerchanthouse.org.uk; 10 Strand St; s £100, d £140-180) Tucked just one street back from the water's edge, tall, red-brick Merchant House is boutiquey at its best. Hefty wood sculptures, wicker rocking chairs and crisp linen ensure it's stylish; the odd teddy bear keeps it cheery too.

🍴 Eating

Storm
SEAFOOD ££

(☑ 01202-674970; www.stormfish.co.uk; 16 High St; mains £16-20; ⊘ 6-10pm Mon-Sat) Ah, Storm. They've been cooking up one here since 1991 and it's still just as good. Dishes depend on what fisherman-owner, Pete, has caught; it might be intense Goan fish curry, buttery local plaice or fragrant local clams steamed in white wine. They also open some summer lunchtimes; call to check.

Poole Arms
PUB ££

(www.localbiztoday.com/poole-arms; The Quay; mains £9-16; ⊘ noon-2.30pm & 6-8.30pm) The grub at this ancient pub is strong on locally landed seafood – try the homemade fish pie, local crab or pan-fried herring roe. Order some New Forest beer, then settle down in the snug wood-lined bar with the locals, or on the terrace overlooking the quay.

⭐ Guildhall Tavern
FRENCH £££

(☑ 01202-671717; www.guildhalltavern.co.uk; 15 Market St; mains £20, 2-course lunch/dinner £15/22; ⊘ noon-3pm & 5.30-10pm Tue-Sat; 🅿) Poole's top table delights as it works local ingredients with French flair. Try chargrilled sea bass flambéed with Pernod or the superb-value set menus, where double-baked cheese soufflé and beef bourguignon are followed by *crepe au chocolat* and ripe cheese.

ℹ️ Information

Tourist Office (☑ 0845 234 5560; www. pooletourism.com; Poole Quay; ⊘ 10am-5pm, to 6pm Jul & Aug, closed Sun Nov-Apr)

ℹ️ Getting There & Around

BOAT

Brittany Ferries (☑ 0871 244 0744; www. brittany-ferries.com) Sails between Poole and Cherbourg in France (4½ hours, one daily). Summer return prices range from around £80 for foot passengers to £320 for a car and two adults.
Sandbanks Ferry (☑ 01929-450203; www. sandbanksferry.co.uk; per pedestrian/car £1/3.50; ⊘ 7am-11pm) Makes the four-minute trip from Sandbanks to Studland every 20 minutes. It's a short cut from Poole to Swanage, Wareham and the Isle of Purbeck, but the summer queues can be a pain.

BUS

Bournemouth (£2, 25 minutes, every 15 minutes) Bus M1/M2.
London Victoria (£20, 2¾ hours, every two hours) National Express.
Sandbanks (£3.40, 30 minutes, hourly Monday to Saturday) Bus 52.

TAXI

Dial-a-Cab (☑ 01202-666822; www.pooletaxis. co.uk)

TRAIN

Bournemouth (£4, 12 minutes, half-hourly)
Dorchester South (£10, 30 minutes, hourly)
London Waterloo (£25, 2¾ hours, half-hourly)
Weymouth (£14, 45 minutes, hourly)

Southeast Dorset

With its string of glittering bays and towering rock formations, the southeast of Dorset can claim the county's most beautiful shores. Also known as the 'Isle' of Purbeck (although it's a peninsula), it's also the start of the Jurassic Coast and the scenery and geology, especially around Lulworth Cove, make swimming here irresistible and hiking memorable. The hinterland harbours the huge, fairy-tale ruins of Corfe Castle, while Wareham sheds light on the mysterious figure of Lawrence of Arabia.

Wareham & Around

POP 5492

Saxons established the sturdy settlement of Wareham beside the River Frome in the 10th century, and their legacy lingers in the remaining defensive walls and one of Dorset's last remaining Saxon churches. Wareham is also famous for its links to the enigmatic TE Lawrence, the British soldier immortalised in the 1962 David Lean epic *Lawrence of Arabia*.

◉ Sights

★ **Clouds Hill**   HOUSE
(NT; ☑ 01929-405616; www.nationaltrust.org.uk; near Bovington; adult/child £5.50/2.50; ⊙ 11am-5pm Wed-Sun mid-Mar–Oct; P) The tiny cottage that was home to TE Lawrence (1888–1935) provides a compelling insight into a complex man. The British soldier became legendary after working with Arab tribes against Turkish forces in WWI. Look out for Lawrence's evocative desert campaign photos, his French crusader castle sketches and the desk where he abridged *Seven Pillars of Wisdom*. The four idiosyncratic rooms include a surprisingly comfortable cork-lined bathroom, an aluminium foil–lined bunk room and a heavily beamed music room.

The house is much as Lawrence left it – he died at the age of 46 after a motorbike accident on a nearby road.

St Martin's on the Walls   CHURCH
(North St, Wareham; ⊙ 9am-5pm) This 11th-century church features a 12th-century fresco on the northern wall, and a marble effigy of TE Lawrence. If it's locked during normal shop hours, get the key from Joy's Outfitters in North St.

Monkey World   ZOO
(☑ 01929-462537; www.monkeyworld.co.uk; Longthorns; adult/child £12/8.50; ⊙ 10am-5pm, to 6pm Jul & Aug; P) An appealing sanctuary for rescued chimpanzees, orang-utans, gibbons, marmosets and some utterly adorable ring-tailed lemurs.

⫸ Sleeping & Eating

Red Lion   INN ££
(☑ 01929-550099; www.redlionwareham.co.uk; 1 North St, Wareham; d £90-115; P) Gorgeous, elegant and full of fancy touches, the supremely stylish makeover of this old inn sees vast rooms sport brass bedsteads, sweet armchairs and wind-up alarm clocks. The menu (mains £6 to £16, kitchen open noon to 8pm) spans Dorset pâté to Sunday roast.

Anglebury   INN ££
(☑ 01929-408094; www.angleburyhouse.co.uk; 15 North St; s/d/f £50/75/95) In an inn that's more than 450 years old you expect a bit of atmosphere, and that's just what you get. A creaking, twisting staircase leading to sedate, traditionally styled bedrooms, and dark wood and beams galore in the bar.

ⓘ Information

Purbeck Tourist Office (☑ 01929-552740; www.visitswanageandpurbeck.com; South St, Wareham; ⊙ 9.30am-4pm Mon-Sat)

ⓘ Getting There & Away

Rail links include London Waterloo (£25, 2½ hours, half-hourly) and Weymouth (£10, 30 minutes, half-hourly).

Bus 40 runs hourly north to Poole (£4.90, 35 minutes) and south to Swanage (£4.90, 30 minutes) via Corfe Castle (£4, 15 minutes). Bus 104 goes to Lulworth (£4.90, 35 minutes, two daily, Monday to Saturday).

Corfe Castle

The massive, shattered ruins of Corfe Castle loom so dramatically from the landscape it's like blundering into a film set. The defensive fragments tower over an equally photogenic village, which bears the castle's name and makes for a romantic spot for a meal or an overnight stay.

◉ Sights

★ **Corfe Castle**   CASTLE
(NT; ☑ 01929-481294; www.nationaltrust.org.uk; The Square; adult/child £8/4; ⊙ 10am-6pm Apr-Sep, to 4pm Oct-Mar) The startling, fractured battlements of one of Dorset's most iconic landmarks were once home to Sir John Bankes, Charles I's right-hand man. The Civil War saw the castle besieged by Cromwellian forces; in 1646 the plucky Lady Bankes directed a six-week defence and the castle fell only after being betrayed from within. The Roundheads then gunpowdered Corfe Castle apart; today turrets and soaring walls still sheer off at precarious angles, while the splayed-out gatehouse looks like it's just been blown up.

JURASSIC COAST

The kind of massive, hands-on geology lesson you wish you had at school, the Jurassic Coast is England's first natural World Heritage Site, putting it on a par with the Great Barrier Reef and the Grand Canyon. This striking shoreline stretches from Exmouth in East Devon to Swanage in Dorset, encompassing 185 million years of the earth's history in just 95 miles. It means you can walk, in just a few hours, many millions of years in geological time.

It began when layers of rocks formed, their varying compositions determined by different climates: desert-like conditions gave way to higher then lower sea levels. Massive earth movements then tilted all the rock layers, forcing most of the oldest formations to the west, and the youngest to the east. Next, erosion exposed the different strata.

The differences are very tangible. Devon's rusty-red Triassic rocks are 200–250 million years old. Lyme Regis' fossil-rich, dark-clay Jurassic cliffs are 190 million years old. Pockets of much younger, creamy-coloured Cretaceous rocks (a mere 140–65 million years old) pop up, notably around Lulworth Cove, where erosion has sculpted a stunning display of bays, stacks and rock arches.

The coast's website (www.jurassiccoast.com) is a great information source; also look out locally for the highly readable *Official Guide to the Jurassic Coast* (£4.95), or buy it at www.jurassiccoasttrust.org.

Swanage Steam Railway HERITAGE RAILWAY
(☑ 01929-425800; www.swanagerailway.co.uk; adult/child return £11.50/7; ☺ daily Apr-Oct, Sat & Sun Nov-Mar) Vintage steam trains run (roughly hourly) between Swanage and Norden (25 minutes), stopping at Corfe Castle.

🛏 Sleeping & Eating

Ammonite B&B £
(☑ 01929-480188; www.ammonite-corfecastle.co.uk; 88 West St; s £55, d £65-75; P 🐾) The pleasing bedrooms at this tranquil edge-of-village B&B feature pastels and pine, while the Aga-cooked breakfast includes local eggs, homemade jams and crusty bread from Corfe Castle's bakery.

Olivers B&B ££
(☑ 01929-477111; www.oliverscorfecastle.com; 5 West St; s £75-85, d £85-95) Tucked away in the heart of the old village in a charismatic street, Olivers combines honey-coloured beams with 21st-century chic: brown leather armchairs, tree silhouette wallpaper and chunky wood furniture – stylish, restful, great-value rooms.

Castle Inn PUB ££
(www.castleinncorfe.com; 63 East St; mains £10-17; ☺ noon-3pm & 6-9pm Mon-Sat, noon-9pm Sun; 🍴) The locals' choice. Prepare to dine beside flagstone floors and ancient beams festooned with fairy lights on tasty pub classics, plus some surprises: try the sea bass given a kick by smoked paprika, or the chickpea stew.

ℹ Getting There & Away

Bus 40 shuttles hourly between Poole, Wareham, Corfe Castle and Swanage. The 15-minute trip to Wareham costs £4.

Lulworth Cove & Around

POP 740

South of Corfe Castle the coast steals the show. For millions of years the elements have been creating an intricate shoreline of curved bays, caves, stacks and weirdly wonderful rock formations – most notably the massive natural arch at Durdle Door.

At charismatic Lulworth Cove, a pleasing jumble of thatched cottages and fishing gear leads down to a perfect crescent of white cliffs.

◎ Sights & Activities

★**Durdle Door** LANDMARK
The poster-boy of Dorset's Jurassic Coast, this immense, sea-fringed, 150-million-year-old Portland stone arch was created by a combination of massive earth movements and erosion. Today it's framed by shimmering bays; bring your swimsuit and head down the hundreds of steps for an unforgettable dip.

You can park at the top of the cliffs, but it's best to hike the coast path from Lulworth Cove (1 mile), passing the delightfully named Lulworth Crumple, where layers of rock form dramatically zigzagging folds.

Lulworth Castle
CASTLE

(EH; ☑01929-400352; www.lulworth.com; East Lulworth; adult/child £5/3; ⊙10.30am-5pm Sun-Fri, to 4pm Nov-Mar) A confection in creamy, dreamy white, this baronial pile looks more like a French chateau than a traditional English castle. Built in 1608 as a hunting lodge, it's survived extravagant owners, extensive remodelling and a disastrous fire in 1929. It has been extensively restored – check out the reconstructed kitchen and cellars, then climb the tower for sweeping coastal views. It costs £3 to park.

Lulworth Cove
Heritage Centre
INTERPRETATION CENTRE

(☑01929-400587; www.lulworth.com; main car park, Lulworth Cove; ⊙10am-5pm) Excellent displays outline how geology and erosion have combined to shape the area's remarkable shoreline. Staff can advise about walks as well.

★ Jurassic Coast Activities
KAYAKING

(☑01305-835301; www.jurassiccoastactivities.co.uk; Lulworth Cove; per person £50; ⊙up to 3 tours daily) This unmissable, three-hour paddle offers jaw-dropping views of Dorset's heavily eroded coast. Starting at Lulworth Cove, you glide through Stair Hole's caves and stacks, across Man O'War Bay then under the stone arch at Durdle Door, stopping for swims and picnics along the way.

🛏 Sleeping & Eating

Lulworth YHA
HOSTEL £

(☑0845 371 9331; www.yha.org.uk; School Lane, West Lulworth; dm £18-23; ℗) Hills stretch up behind and sheep bleat outside at this cosy, chalet-style, edge-of-village hostel.

Durdle Door Holiday Park
CAMPSITE £

(☑01929-400200; www.lulworth.com; sites £25-35; ⊙Mar-Oct; ℗) Spacious site, just minutes from the creamy cliffs and 1.5 miles west of Lulworth Cove.

★ Lulworth Cove
INN ££

(☑01929-400333; www.lulworth-coveinn.co.uk; Main Rd, Lulworth Cove; d £110-120; ℗🤶) Prepare for a vision of driftwood chic – whitewashed floorboards, aquamarine panels, painted wicker chairs and roll-topped baths. It's on the lane leading down to the cove, so add cracking sea views, a mini roof terrace and top-quality gastropub grub (mains £8 to £14, kitchen open noon to 9pm) and you have an irresistible inn.

Cove House
B&B ££

(☑01929-400137; www.covehouse.net; Main Rd, West Lulworth; s £80-95, d £80-100; ℗) Fragrant, calm, pristine rooms set amid West Lulworth's soaring hills.

Cove Fish
SEAFOOD £

(☑01929-400807; Lulworth Cove; ⊙10am-4pm Tue-Sun Easter-Oct, Sat & Sun Nov-Easter) The seafood piled high in this shed by the path to the beach has been caught by 9th-generation fisherman Joe. Bag a fish kebab for the BBQ, or settle at the wobbly table and tuck into Lulworth Cove crab – a meal that's travelled food yards not miles.

🍷 Drinking & Nightlife

★ Castle
PUB

(www.thecastleinn-lulworthcove.co.uk; West Lulworth; ⊙noon-10pm; 🤶) A head-spinning array of 40-plus ciders make this thatched pub a magnet for fans of the golden elixir. From quaffable Bumble Berry (4%) to epic Old Rosie (7.3%), this 'permanent cider festival' thoughtfully offers sampler trays (three different thirds of a pint) to help you get through a few.

ℹ Getting There & Away

Bus 104 links Lulworth with Wareham (£4.90, 35 minutes, two daily, Monday to Saturday).

Dorchester & Around

POP 19,143

With Dorchester, you get two towns in one: a real-life, bustling county town and Thomas Hardy's fictional Casterbridge. The Victorian writer was born nearby and his literary locations can still be found among Dorchester's white- and red-brick Georgian terraces. Here you can also visit Hardy's former homes and see his original manuscripts. Add cracking archaeological sites and attractive places to eat and sleep and you have an appealing base for a night or two.

◉ Sights

Thomas Hardy fans will want to hunt down the *Mayor of Casterbridge* locations hidden among modern Dorchester. They include Lucetta's House, a grand Georgian affair with ornate door posts in Trinity St, while in parallel South St, a red-brick, mid-18th-century building (now a bank) is named as the inspiration for the house of the mayor himself. The tourist office sells book location guides.

★ Dorset County Museum   MUSEUM

(☎01305-262735; www.dorsetcountymuseum.org;
High West St; adult/child £6.35/3.60; ☺10am-5pm
Mon-Sat, to 4pm Nov-Mar) The Thomas Hardy
collection here is the world's largest, offering
extraordinary insights into his creative process. Reading Hardy's cramped handwriting,
you can see where he's crossed out one word
and substituted another. There's also an atmospheric reconstruction of his study at
Max Gate and a letter in which Siegfried Sas-
soon requests permission to dedicate his first
book of poems to Hardy. In other collections,
Jurassic Coast fossil exhibits feature a huge
ichthyosaur and 6ft plesiosaur fore paddle.

Bronze and Iron Age finds from Maiden
Castle include a treasure trove of coins and
neck rings, while Roman artefacts include
70 gold coins, nail cleaners and (toe-curling)
ear picks.

Max Gate   HISTORIC BUILDING

(NT; ☎01305-262538; www.nationaltrust.org.uk;
Alington Ave; adult/child £5.50/2.50; ☺11am-5pm
Wed-Sun mid-Mar–Oct; 🅿) Novelist Thomas
Hardy was a trained architect and designed
this attractive house, where he lived from
1885 until his death in 1928. *Tess of the
D'Urbervilles* and *Jude the Obscure* were
both written here, and the house contains
several pieces of original furniture. It's a
mile east of Dorchester, on the A352.

Hardy's Cottage   HISTORIC BUILDING

(NT; ☎01305-262366; www.nationaltrust.org.uk;
adult/child £5.50/2.50; ☺11am-5pm Wed-Sun
mid-Mar–Oct; 🅿) This picturesque cob-and-
thatch house is the birthplace of Thomas Hardy and features evocative, sparsely
furnished rooms and a lush garden. It's in
Higher Bockhampton, 3 miles northeast of
Dorchester.

Roman Town House   HISTORIC BUILDING

(www.romantownhouse.co.uk;   Northern   Hay;
☺24hr) FREE The knee-high flint walls and
beautifully preserved mosaics here powerfully conjure up the Roman occupation of
Dorchester (then Durnovaria). Peek into the
summer dining room to see the underfloor
heating system (hypocaust), where charcoal-
warmed air circulated around pillars to produce a toasty 18°C (64°F).

🛏 Sleeping

★ Beggars Knap   BOUTIQUE B&B ££

(☎01305-268191; www.beggarsknap.co.uk; 2 Weymouth Ave; s £60-70, d £80-90, f £85-130; 🅿)
Despite the name, this altogether fabulous,
vaguely decadent guesthouse is far from
impoverished. Opulent rooms drip with
chandeliers and gold brocades; beds draped
in fine cottons range from French sleigh
to four-poster. You could pay much, much
more and get something half as nice.

Yalbury Cottage   HOTEL ££

(☎01305-262382; www.yalburycottage.com; Lower Bockhampton; s £85, d £120) With its flower-
framed patios and quaint village setting,
serene Yalbury draws you deftly into rural
Westcountry life. Fresh, simple cottage-style
rooms overlook fields, the intimate restaurant is acclaimed (two/three courses cost
£33/38, booking required) and the superb
English tapas (£8, available noon to 4pm
Tuesday to Saturday May to September) are
packed with prime Dorset goodies.

Westwood   B&B ££

(☎01305-268018; www.westwoodhouse.co.uk; 29
High West St; s/d/f £75/95/130; 🖥) For a delightful dollop of 18th-century elegance, head
to Westwood. Plush bedrooms are decked
out in olive, dove grey or duck-egg blue; and

BATH & SOUTHWEST ENGLAND DORCHESTER & AROUND

WORTH A TRIP

MAIDEN CASTLE

Occupying a massive slab of horizon on the southern fringes of Dorchester, Maiden
Castle (EH; www.english-heritage.org.uk; ☺dawn-dusk; 🅿) FREE is the largest and most
complex Iron Age hill fort in Britain. The huge, steep-sided chalk ramparts flow along a
hill's contour lines and surround 48 hectares – the equivalent of 50 football pitches. The
first hill fort was built on the site around 500 BC and in its heyday was densely populated
with clusters of roundhouses and a network of roads. The Romans besieged and captured it in AD 43 – an ancient Briton skeleton with a Roman crossbow bolt in the spine
was found at the site. Up close, the sheer scale of the ramparts is awe-inspiring and the
winding complexity of the west entrance reveals just how hard it would be to storm. Finds
from the site are displayed at Dorset County Museum (p247). Maiden Castle is 1.5 miles
southwest of Dorchester.

mini-armchairs and shaded reading lights are dotted around. Breakfast is a veritable feast.

Eating

No 6 FRENCH ££
(☑ 01305-267679; www.no6-restaurant.co.uk; 6 North Sq; mains £17; ⊙ noon-2pm & 6.30-9pm Tue-Fri, 6-10pm Sat) The locally sourced produce appearing here is dished up with more than a soupçon of French finesse. Expect rich red wine–laced game crock, plump Lyme Bay king scallops and simply cooked but stunning fish. Canny foodies book Tuesday through to Thursday evenings, when a main and a pud is a mere £16.

Trinity SEAFOOD ££
(☑ 01305-757428; www.trinitybistro.co.uk; Trinity St; mains from £9; ⊙ 11.30am-3pm Tue-Sat, 6-9.30pm Thu-Sat) Mouth-watering aromas waft around you, and the open-plan kitchen is only yards away. The chalked-up menu might include lemon-fragranced sea bass, Scillian mussel or clams – it's no frills but fun and the fish is super fresh.

Sienna MODERN BRITISH £££
(☑ 01305-250022; www.siennarestaurant.co.uk; 36 High West St; 2-course lunch/dinner £26/39; ⊙ 12.30-2pm Wed-Sat, 7-9pm Tue-Sat) At tiny, Michelin-starred Sienna innovation, exquisite presentation and seasonal produce cast a fine culinary spell. Look out for duck egg and asparagus, brill with caviar, and cheeseboards bearing the very best of the west. Reservations required.

Information

Tourist Office (☑ 01305-267992; www.visit-dorset.com; Antelope Walk; ⊙ 9am-5pm Mon-Sat Apr-Oct, to 4pm Nov-Mar)

Getting There & Around

BICYCLE

Dorchester Cycles (☑ 01305-268787; www.dorchestercycles.co.uk; 31 Great Western Rd; per day £12; ⊙ 9am-5.30pm Mon-Sat)

BUS

London (£20, four hours, one daily) National Express.
Lyme Regis (£4.50, 1¾ hours, hourly) Bus 31.
Poole (£4.30, 1¼ hours, one daily Tuesday and Friday) Bus 186.
Sherborne (£4.10, one hour, four to six daily Monday to Saturday) Bus 216; via Cerne Abbas.
Weymouth (£3, 20 minutes, half-hourly) Bus 10.

TRAIN

There are services, every two hours, from Dorchester West to Bath (£30, two hours) and Bristol (£20, 2½ hours).

Hourly trains from Dorchester South:
Bournemouth (£12, 45 minutes)
London Waterloo (£25, 2¾ hours)
Southampton (£25, 1½ hours)
Weymouth (£5, 10 minutes)

Cerne Abbas & the Cerne Giant

If you had to describe an archetypal sleepy Dorset village, you'd come up with something a lot like Cerne Abbas: houses run the gamut of English architectural styles, roses climb countless doorways and half-timbered houses frame a honey-coloured, 12th-century church. But this village also packs one heck of a surprise: the Cerne Giant, a vast chalk figure of a naked man.

Sights

Cerne Giant LANDMARK
(⊙ 24hr; P) FREE Rarely do you find such a nudge-nudge, wink-wink tourist attraction. Nude, full frontal and notoriously well endowed, this hill-side chalk figure is revealed in all his glory. And he's in a stage of excitement that wouldn't be allowed in most magazines. The giant is around 60m high and 51m wide and his age remains a mystery; some claim he's Roman but the first historical reference comes in 1694, when three shillings were set aside for his repair.

The Victorians found it all deeply embarrassing and allowed grass to grow over his most outstanding feature. Today the hill is grazed by sheep and cattle, though only the sheep are allowed to do their nibbling over the giant – the cows would do too much damage to his lines.

Sleeping

Abbots B&B ££
(☑ 01300-341349; www.abbotsbedandbreakfast.co.uk; 7 Long St; s/d/f £60/85/130; ☎) The top-floor rooms here are big on atmosphere and small on head space, with duck-or-regret-it lintels for those over 6ft. It's charming throughout though, with rooms decked out in light grey, lemon and blue. The cakes in the cafe (open 10am to 5pm) are real diet busters.

★ New Inn

INN ££

(☑ 01300-341274; www.thenewinncerneabbas.co.uk; 14 Long St; d £95-140, ste £170; P 🛜) What do you get when a retired Michelin inspector runs a 16th-century English inn? Sleekly styled boltholes in outhouses, and luxurious main-building rooms rich in dark beams. The bar has the easy atmosphere of a country estate (think mounted antlers and honey-brown tartan) and rustles up prime gastropub (mains £9 to £18) delights from noon to 2pm and 7pm to 9pm.

❶ Getting There & Away

Dorchester is 8 miles south. Bus 216 (four to six daily Monday to Saturday) goes to Dorchester (£2.40, 30 minutes) and Sherborne (£2.80, 30 minutes).

Weymouth

POP 65,000

An immense harbour ensured this strip of Dorset coast was the 2012 Olympic sailing venue – a state-of-the-art water-sports centre and a soaring viewing tower are among the legacies. Otherwise, the area's core character remains: fishing boats pack Weymouth's bustling harbour and candy-striped beach kiosks line its 3-mile beach.

Weymouth has been a popular seaside spot since King George III took an impromptu dip here in 1789. More than 225 years later, the town is still popular with holidaymakers, drawn by a curling, golden beach, a revitalised historic harbour and oodles of seaside kitsch.

⊙ Sights & Activities

Weymouth Beach

BEACH

The nostalgia-inducing offerings along Weymouth's fine sandy shore could see you marvelling at highly skilled sand sculptors, renting a deckchair or pedalo (per hour £7), watching Punch and Judy shows, and taking a donkey ride. Alternatively, go all Californian and join a volleyball game.

Nothe Fort

FORT

(☑ 01305-766626; www.nothefort.org.uk; Barrack Rd; adult/child £7/1; ⊙10.30am-5.30pm Apr-Oct) Weymouth's 19th-century defences are studded with cannons, searchlights and 12in coastal guns. Exhibits detail Dorset's Roman invasion, a Victorian soldier's drill and Weymouth in WWII. Commanding an armoured car and clambering around the magazine prove popular with regiments of children.

Sea Life

AQUARIUM

(☑ 0871 423 2110; www.sealifeweymouth.com; Lodmoor Country Park; admission £23; ⊙10am-5pm; P) Aquarium highlights include sharks, penguins and seahorses. Admission includes a trip up the 53m Sea Life Tower on Weymouth seafront, which rotates to reveal expansive views. Tickets are 25% cheaper online.

Coastline Cruises

BOAT CRUISE

(☑ 01305-785000; www.coastlinecruises.com; Brewers Quay; adult/child return £9/6; ⊙2 boats daily Apr-Oct) This wind-blown 40-minute jaunt crosses Portland Harbour's vast 2012 Olympic sailing waters, before dropping you off at Portland Castle. Boats leave from Weymouth Harbour.

🛏 Sleeping

★ B+B

B&B ££

(☑ 01305-761190; www.bb-weymouth.com; 68 The Esplanade; s £60-70, d £80-95; P 🛜) This hip hotel remains remarkable value with its sleek, minimalist rooms (some have sea views) and host of freebies; the mineral water, biscuits

---

WORTH A TRIP

ABBOTSBURY SWANNERY

Every May some 600 free-flying swans choose to nest at the Abbotsbury Swannery (☑ 01305-871858; www.abbotsbury-tourism.co.uk; New Barn Rd, Abbotsbury; adult/child £11/8; ⊙10am-5pm late Mar-Oct), which shelters in the Fleet lagoon, protected by the ridge of Chesil Beach. The swannery was founded by local monks about 600 years ago, and feathers from the Abbotsbury swans are still used in the helmets of the Gentlemen at Arms (the Queen's official bodyguard). Wandering the network of trails that wind between the swans' nests is an awe-inspiring experience that is punctuated by occasional territorial displays (think snuffling, coughing and stand-up flapping), ensuring that even the liveliest children are stilled.

The swannery is at the picturesque village of Abbotsbury, 10 miles from Weymouth off the B3157.

THE CHANNEL ISLANDS

Clustering just off the coast of France, the islands of Jersey, Guernsey, Sark, Herm and Alderney overflow with exquisite coastlines, beautiful harbours, shaded lanes and old-world charm. The warm Gulf of St Malo ensures subtropical plants, superb local seafood and an incredible array of bird life.

The larger islands of Guernsey and Jersey are the main entry points, with a plethora of flights and ferries from both England and France. Air links between Guernsey, Jersey and Alderney are good, while fleets of ferries also connect them and the other islands. Accommodation and eating options abound; for details and transport information, see the islands' websites.

During WWII, the Channel Islands were the only British soil to be occupied by the Nazis, and poignant museums – some housed in old war tunnels and bunkers – provide an insight into the islanders' fortitude.

The islands are proudly independent, self-governing British Crown dependencies and sport a wealth of quirky anachronisms. English is the main language and although place names may look French, local pronunciation is very different. The islands print their own version of the British pound – it isn't legal tender on the mainland, but you can use British money on the islands. The Channel Islands aren't covered by NHS or EHIC cards, so make sure your travel insurance includes medical treatment. Tourist entry requirements are the same as for the UK.

Jersey

At 9 miles by 5 miles, Jersey (www.jersey.com) is the biggest of the Channel Islands. An offshore finance centre with a rugged north coast, key sights are the Durrell Wildlife Park (www.durrell.org) and the thought-provoking Jersey War Tunnels (www.jerseywartunnels.com), a former WWII underground military hospital.

Guernsey

The second-largest island, Guernsey (www.visitguernsey.com) features a captivating capital, St Peter Port and stunning sea cliffs and sandy bays. Victor Hugo's former home, Hauteville House (www.victorhugo.gg), and Castle Cornet (www.museums.gov.gg) are the big draws.

Alderney

Remote Alderney (www.visitalderney.com) is the third-largest island. Its village capital St Anne is picture-perfect; its wealth of bird and wildlife includes blonde hedgehogs and 7000 squawking seabirds.

Sark

On steep-sided, car-free Sark (www.sark.co.uk) transport is by bike, tractor or horse and cart – the island (measuring 3 miles by 1.5 miles) has a magical, castaway feel.

Herm

Tiny, traffic-free Herm (www.herm.com) is just 1.5 miles long and half a mile wide. Flower-strewn hills are framed by white sandy shores – Shell Beach is a superb spot for a swim.

and espresso machine coffee are best enjoyed in the funky 1st-floor lounge overlooking the bay. They'll loan you a bike as well.

Roundhouse　　　　B&B ££

(☑ 01305-761010; www.roundhouse-hotel-weymouth.com; 1 The Esplanade; d £105-145; ☎) Soak up Weymouth's seaside charms from your bedroom – almost all here have superb views of the beach out front and the harbour behind. Inside, vivid decor combines sky blue, pur-

ple and shocking pink, while fluffy cushions sit beside snazzy modern art.

Old Harbour View　　　　B&B ££

(☑ 01305- 774633; www.oldharbourviewweymouth.co.uk; 12 Trinity Rd; s/d £78/98; P ☎) In this pristine Georgian terrace you get boating themes in the fresh, white bedrooms and boats right outside the front door. One room overlooks the busy quay, the other faces the back.

✕ Eating

Marlboro FISH & CHIPS £
(www.marlbororestaurant.co.uk; 46 St Thomas St; mains £7.50; ⊗noon-9.45pm) There's a sustainable slant to this traditional chippy, just metres from Weymouth's quay, with mackerel featuring among the long list of super-fresh fish. Take it away or get munching in the bay-windowed, licensed cafe (open till 8pm).

Dining Room MODERN BRITISH ££
(✆01305-783008; www.thediningroomweymouth. co.uk; 67 St Mary St; mains £11-24; ⊗noon-2pm daily, 7-9.30pm Mon-Sat) Stand by to see fresh flavours transform local foods – the open-plan design means you watch the chefs beavering away. They might make you lime-cured, Weymouth-landed fish, or red wine–laced Westcountry chorizo – the chocolate cheesecake with Dorset wasabi is a feisty meal's end.

Dorset Burger Co BURGERS ££
(DBC; www.thedorsetburgercompany.co.uk; 97 St Mary St; burgers £9; ⊗noon-3pm Wed-Sun, 6-9pm Wed-Sat) These hand-patted, juicy, chargrilled burgers are made mostly from Dorset produce.

ℹ Information

Tourist Office (✆01305-783225; www. visit-dorset.com; The Esplanade; ⊗10am-6pm) Inside the Weymouth Pavilion theatre.

ℹ Getting There & Away

BUS

Axminster (£6, 2¼ hours, hourly) Bus 31.

Dorchester (£3, 20 minutes, half-hourly) Bus 10.

Fortuneswell (£2.50, Isle of Portland; 30 minutes, four per hour) Bus 1.

Jurassic Coast Bus X53 (£7.20, four daily to hourly, no service winter Sundays) Travels from Weymouth to Wareham (50 minutes), Poole (1½ hours), Abbotsbury (35 minutes), Lyme Regis (1¾ hours) and Exeter (three hours).

London (£17, 4¼ hours, one direct daily) National Express.

Lyme Regis (£6, two hours, hourly) Bus 31.

Portland Bill (£2.50, Isle of Portland; 45 minutes, from four daily May to September only) Bus 501.

BOAT

Condor Ferries (✆0845 609 1024; www.condorferries.co.uk) Sails to the Channel Islands of Guernsey and Jersey. Prices range from around £50 return for a foot passenger, to £300 return for a car and two passengers.

TRAIN

Hourly services:

Bournemouth (£15, one hour)

Dorchester South (£5, 10 minutes)

London Waterloo (£30, three hours)

Services every two hours:

Bath (£17, two hours)

Bristol (£18, 2¾ hours)

Isle of Portland

The 'Isle' of Portland is really a hard, high comma of rock fused to the rest of Dorset by the ridge of Chesil Beach. Its strip of once-waste waterfront now features a sailing centre, business units and new homes. But inland, on the 500ft central plateau, a quarrying past still holds sway, evidenced by huge craters and large slabs of limestone. Portland also offers jaw-dropping views down onto 18-mile Chesil Beach, which is backed by the Fleet, Britain's biggest tidal lagoon – home to 600 nesting swans. Proud, bleak and rough around the edges, Portland is decidedly different from the rest of Dorset, and is all the more compelling because of it. Its industrial heritage, water-sports, rich bird life and starkly beautiful cliffs make it worth at least a day trip. The population clusters of Fortuneswell and Chiswell are towards the north of the isle; Portland Bill is 4 miles south at the tip.

◉ Sights

★**Tout Quarry** OUTDOORS
(near Fortuneswell; ⊗24hr; ℗) **FREE** Portland's white limestone has been quarried for centuries, and has been used in some of the world's finest buildings, such as the British Museum and St Paul's Cathedral. Tout Quarry's disused workings now house 53 sculptures that have been carved into the rock in situ, resulting in a fascinating combination of the raw material, the detritus of the quarrying process and the beauty of chiselled works. Labyrinthine paths snake through hacked-out gullies and around jumbled piles of rock, revealing the half-formed bears, bison and lizards that emerge out of stone cliffs. Highlights include *Still Falling* by Antony Gormley, *Woman on Rock* by Dhruva Mistry and the well-hidden *Green Man*. Tout Quarry is signed off the main road, just south of Fortuneswell.

Portland Lighthouse LIGHTHOUSE
(✆01255-245156; www.trinityhouse.co.uk; Portland Bill; adult/child £4/3; ⊗11am-5pm Sun-Thu

WATER SPORTS – PORTLAND HARBOUR

At 890-hectare Portland Harbour, just south of Weymouth, you can glide in 2012 Olympic sailing waters. The Weymouth & Portland National Sailing Academy (☑ 01305-866000; www.wpnsa.org.uk; Portland Harbour) is home to the Andrew Simpson Sailing Centre (☑ 0753 201 6281; www.andrewsimpsonsailing.org), which runs lessons (adult/child per two days £180/210) and hires lasers (per two hours/day £32/75). Also on-site, OTC (☑ 07817-717904; www.uk.otc-windsurf.com) does lessons in stand-up paddleboarding (SUP; one/two hours £25/40) and windsurfing (per two hours/one day/two days £45/90/165). It also rents out SUP boards (per hour £10) and windsurf boards and sails (per hour £15).

Local waters offer superb diving, with a huge variety of depths, seascapes and wrecks. Operators include Underwater Explorers (☑ 01305-824555; www.underwaterexplorers.co.uk; Mereside, Portland) and Old Harbour Dive Centre (☑ 01305-760888; www.oldharbourdivecentre.co.uk; 11 Nothe Pde, Weymouth). Lessons range from around £50 a day to £475 for a five-day PADI openwater dive course.

late Apr-Aug; P) For a real sense of Portland's remote nature, head to its southern tip, Portland Bill. Then climb the 41m-high, candy-striped lighthouse for breathtaking views of rugged cliffs and the Race, a surging vortex of conflicting tides.

Portland Castle
CASTLE

(EH; ☑ 01305-820539; www.english-heritage.org.uk; Liberty Rd, Chiswell; adult/child £5/3; ⊙ 10am-6pm Apr-Sep, to 5pm Oct) A particularly fine product of Henry VIII's castle-building spree, with expansive views over Portland harbour.

🛏 Sleeping & Eating

Portland YHA
HOSTEL £

(☑ 0845 371 9339; www.yha.org.uk; Castle Rd; dm/d £18/32) Comfy, rambling Edwardian house with sea views from most dorms.

Queen Anne House
B&B ££

(☑ 01305-820028; www.queenannehouse.co.uk; 2 Fortuneswell; s £45-55, d £75-90; 🛜) It's impossible to know which room to pick: White, with skylight, beams and a hobbit-esque door; Lotus, with its grand furniture; Oyster with its half tester bed, or the suite with French bath and mini-conservatory. It doesn't matter though – they're all great value and gorgeous.

★ Crab House Cafe
SEAFOOD ££

(☑ 01305-788867; www.crabhousecafe.co.uk; Portland Rd, Wyke Regis; mains £16-21; ⊙ noon-2.30pm & 6-9pm Wed-Sat, noon-3.30pm Sun) This is the place for fresh-as-it-gets seafood and beach-shack-chic. The funky cabin has views onto the cafe's own Fleet Lagoon oyster beds, while the waterside terrace is a prime place to sample clam and cockle spaghetti or cracked whole crab, best washed down with lip-smacking Somerset cider.

Cove House
PUB ££

(www.thecovehouseinn.co.uk; Chiswell Seafront; mains £10-18; ⊙ noon-2.30pm & 6-9pm Mon-Fri, noon-9pm Sat & Sun) Extraordinary Chesil Beach views, memorable sunsets and great grub (try the crunchy whitebait) in a history-rich fishermen's inn.

ℹ Getting There & Away

Bus 1 runs from Weymouth to Fortuneswell (£2.50, 30 minutes, four per hour). Between May and September bus 501 goes from Weymouth to Portland Bill (£2.50, from four daily).

Coastline Cruises (p249) runs ferries to Portland Castle from Weymouth.

Chesil Beach

One of the most breathtaking beaches in Britain, Chesil is 18 miles long, 15m high and moving inland at the rate of 5m a century. This mind-boggling, 100-million-tonne pebble ridge is the baby of the Jurassic Coast. A mere 6000 years old, its stones range from pea-sized in the west to hand-sized in the east.

◉ Sights & Activities

Chesil Beach Visitors Centre
INTERPRETATION CENTRE

(☑ 01305-206191; www.chesilbeach.org; Ferrybridge; ⊙ 10am-4pm) FREE Just over the bridge to Portland, this centre is a great gateway to the beach. The pebble ridge is at its highest here – 15m compared to 7m at Abbotsbury. From the car park an energy-sapping hike up sliding pebbles leads to the constant surge and rattle of waves on stones and dazzling views of the sea, with the thin pebble line and the expanse of the Fleet Lagoon behind.

The centre details an ecosystem that includes ringed plover, redshank and oyster-catchers, as well as drifts of thrift and sea campion. There's also the Taste cafe here, open 10am to 4pm.

Fleet Observer BOATING
(☏ 01305-759692; www.thefleetobserver.co.uk; adult/child £7/4; ☺ daily Easter-Sep) Offers glass-bottom boat trips on the Fleet Lagoon.

Lyme Regis

POP 3662

Fantastically fossiliferous Lyme Regis packs a heavyweight historical punch. Rock-hard relics of the past pop out repeatedly from the surrounding cliffs – exposed by the landslides of a retreating shoreline. Now a pivot point of the Unesco-listed Jurassic Coast, fossil fever is definitely in the air and everyone, from proper palaeontologists to those out for a bit of fun, can engage in a spot of coastal rummaging. Add sandy beaches and some delightful places to sleep and eat, and you have a charming base for explorations.

◉ Sights

Lyme Regis Museum MUSEUM
(☏ 01297-443370; www.lymeregismuseum.co.uk; Bridge St; adult/child £10/5; ☺ 10am-5pm Easter-Oct, 11am-4pm Wed-Sun Nov-Easter) In 1814 local teenager Mary Anning found the first full ichthyosaurus skeleton near Lyme Regis, propelling the town onto the world stage. An incredibly famous fossilist in her day, Miss Anning did much to pioneer the science of modern-day palaeontology. The museum, on the site of her former home, tells her story and exhibits spectacular fossils and other prehistoric finds.

Dinosaurland MUSEUM
(☏ 01297-443541; www.dinosaurland.co.uk; Coombe St; adult/child £5/4; ☺ 10am-5pm mid-Feb–Nov) This joyful, mini, indoor Jurassic Park overflows with fossilised remains; look out for belemnites, plesiosaurus and an impressive locally found ichthyosaur. Lifelike dinosaur models will thrill youngsters – the rock-hard tyrannosaurus eggs and 73kg dinosaur dung will have them in raptures.

Cobb LANDMARK
(☺ 24hr) First built in the 13th century, Lyme's iconic, curling sea defences have been strengthened and extended over the years, so don't present the elegant line they once did, but it's still hard to resist wandering their length to the tip.

Town Mill HISTORIC BUILDING
(www.townmill.org.uk; Mill Lane; ☺ 11am-2pm Mon-Fri, to 4pm Sat & Sun Apr-Oct) FREE An atmospheric, creaking, grinding, 14th-century working watermill. Cafes, art galleries, a cheese deli and microbrewery sit alongside.

🛏 Sleeping

Sanctuary B&B £
(☏ 01297-445815; www.lyme-regis.demon.co.uk; 65 Broad St; s/d £45/56) A B&B for bibliophiles: the charming, chintzy, volume-filled bedrooms here are part of a four-floor, 18-room bookshop. Ancient tomes that just beg to be perused are everywhere – they can delay you en route to (the excellent) breakfast, but handily there's a wonderfully relaxed vibe.

Coombe House B&B ££
(☏ 01297-443849; www.coombe-house.co.uk; 41 Coombe St; s £35, d £62-70, 5-person flat per week £370-650; ᴘ) The airy, easygoing, stylish

---

FOSSIL HUNTING

Fossil fever is catching. Lyme Regis sits in one of the most unstable sections of Britain's coast, and regular landslips mean nuggets of prehistory keep tumbling from the cliffs.

Joining a guided walk aids explorations. Three miles east of Lyme, the Charmouth Heritage Coast Centre (☏ 01297-560772; www.charmouth.org) runs one to seven trips a week (adult/child £7.50/3). Or, in Lyme itself, Lyme Regis Museum holds three to seven walks a week (adult/child £11/6); local expert Brandon Lennon (☏ 07944-664757; www.lymeregisfossilwalks.com; adult/child £8/6; ☺ Sat-Mon) also leads expeditions. All are popular; book early.

For the best chances of a find, visit within two hours of low water. If you do hunt by yourself, official advice is to check tide times and collect on a falling tide, observe warning signs, keep away from cliffs, only pick up from the beach and always leave some behind for others. Oh, and tell the experts if you find a stunner.

FORDE ABBEY

This abbey (☑ 01460-220231; www.
fordeabbey.co.uk; Chard; house adult/child
£11/free, gardens £9/free; ☺ house noon-
4pm Tue-Fri & Sun Apr-Oct, gardens 10am-
4.30pm) was built in the 12th century as
a Cistercian monastery, but has been a
private home since 1649. The building
boasts magnificent plasterwork ceilings
and fine tapestries but it's the gardens
that are the main attraction: 12 hectares
of lawns, ponds, shrubberies and flower
beds with hundreds of rare and beautiful species.

It's 10 miles north of Lyme Regis;
public transport is a nonstarter.

bedrooms in this fabulous-value guesthouse
are full of bay windows, wicker and white
wood. Breakfast is delivered to your room on
a trolley, complete with homemade bread and
a toaster – perfect for a lazy lie-in in Lyme.

★ **Hix Townhouse**　　BOUTIQUE B&B **£££**
(☑ 01297-442499; www.hixtownhouse.co.uk; 1
Pound St; d £130-150, ste £165; 🛜) With its witty designer decor, luxury flourishes and in-
town location, this 18th-century terrace is
hard to resist. Each room echoes a leisure
theme (think gardening, fishing etc); the
pick is Sailing with its mock portholes, artfully arranged ropes, mini roof terrace and
gorgeous sea views.

✖ Eating

★ **Alexandra**　　CAFE **£**
(☑ 01297-442010; www.hotelalexandra.co.uk; Pound
St; afternoon tea £6.50-28; ☺ 3-5.30pm; 🅿) It's
like the setting for an Agatha Christie, minus
the murder. Wicker chairs dot manicured
lawns, a glittering Lyme Bay sweeps out
behind. The perfect spot for a proper English afternoon tea, complete with scones,
jam and dainty sandwiches. The hotel's
best bedrooms (singles £90, doubles £177 or
£235) boast bay windows and sea views; the
back-facing ones are charming too.

Mill Cafe　　BISTRO **££**
(☑ 01297-445757; www.townmillcafe.co.uk; The
Town Mill, Mill Lane; lunch mains £8, 2-course dinner £20; ☺ 10am-4pm Thu-Sun, 7-9pm Fri & Sat)
The Italian home cooking here is so authentic it feels more like Lombardy than Lyme.
Expect flavour-packed sweet pepper stews,

Sicilian-style cod and irresistible home-
baked bread, best devoured on the tucked-
away terrace out back.

Harbour Inn　　PUB **££**
(www.harbourinnlymeregis.co.uk; Marine Pde;
mains £10-19; ☺ noon-2.30pm & 6-9pm) A flower-
framed, beach-side verandah, smart but
snug interior and some of the best bistro-
pub grub in town – the bouillabaisse is suitably intense.

★ **Hix Oyster & Fish House**　　SEAFOOD **£££**
(☑ 01297-446910; www.hixoysterandfishhouse.co.
uk; Cobb Rd; mains £14-25; ☺ 10am-10pm) Expect
sweeping views of the Cobb and dazzling
food at this super-stylish, open-plan cabin.
Local asparagus comes with cuttlefish ink
dressing; succulent Portland Race sea bass
comes with kelp broth. Perhaps start by
slurping oysters: Brownsea Island or Portland molluscs come at £2.25 a pop.

ℹ Information

Tourist Office (☑ 01297-442138; www.vis-
it-dorset.com; Church St; ☺ 10am-5pm Mon-
Sat, to 4pm Sun, to 3pm Mon-Sat Nov-Mar)

ℹ Getting There & Away

Bus 31 runs to Dorchester (1¾ hours) and Weymouth (two hours) hourly. Bus X53 goes west
to Exeter (£7, six daily, 1¾ hours) and east to
Weymouth (£7.20, hourly, 1¾ hours); it doesn't
run on winter Sundays.

Sherborne

POP 9495

Sherborne gleams with mellow, orangey-
yellow stone; it's been used to build a
cluster of 15th-century buildings and the
impressive abbey church at their core. This
serene town exudes wealth; the five local fee-
paying schools include the famous Sherborne School, and its pupils are a frequent
sight. Evidence of splashing the cash 16th-
and 18th-century style lies on the edge of
town with two castles: one a crumbling ruin,
the other a marvellous manor house, complete with a Lancelot 'Capability' Brown lake.

◉ Sights

Sherborne Abbey　　CHURCH
(☑ 01935-812452; www.sherborneabbey.com; suggested donation £3.50; ☺ 8am-6pm) **FREE** At the
height of its influence, the magnificent Abbey Church of St Mary the Virgin was the

central cathedral of 26 succeeding Saxon bishops. Established early in the 8th century, it became a Benedictine abbey in 998 and functioned as a cathedral until 1075. The church has mesmerising fan vaulting that's the oldest in the country, a central tower supported by Saxon-Norman piers and an 1180 Norman porch.

The abbey's tombs include the elaborate marble effigy belonging to John Lord Digby, Earl of Bristol, and those of the elder brothers of Alfred the Great, Ethelred and Ethelbert.

Sherborne Old Castle
CASTLE
(EH; ☑ 01935-812730; www.english-heritage.org.uk; adult/child £3.70/2.20; ⊙ 10am-5pm Apr-Oct; Ⓟ) These days the epitome of a picturesque ruin, Sherborne's Old Castle was built by Roger, Bishop of Salisbury, in 1120 – Elizabeth I gave it to her one-time favourite Sir Walter Raleigh in the late 16th century. It became a Royalist stronghold during the English Civil War, but Cromwell reduced it to rubble after a 16-day siege in 1645, leaving just the fractured southwest gatehouse, great tower and north range.

Sherborne New Castle
CASTLE
(☑ 01935-812072; www.sherbornecastle.com; New Rd; house & gardens adult/child £11/free, gardens only £6/free; ⊙ 11am-4.30pm Tue-Thu, Sat & Sun Apr-Oct; Ⓟ) Sir Walter Raleigh began building the impressive Sherborne New Castle in 1594, but only got as far as the central block before being imprisoned by James I. James promptly sold the castle to Sir John Digby who added the splendid wings you see today. In 1753 the grounds received a mega-makeover at the hands of landscape-gardener extraordinaire Capability Brown who added a massive lake and 12-hectare waterside gardens.

☞ Tours

Walking Tours
HERITAGE TOUR
(tours £5; ⊙ 11am Fri Jul-Sep) Ninety-minute trips exploring the photogenic old town, leaving from the tourist office.

🛏 Sleeping

Cumberland House
B&B ££
(☑ 01935-817554; www.bandbdorset.co.uk; Green Hill; s £55-60, d £70-85; Ⓟ🖕) Artistry oozes from these history-rich rooms – bright scatter rugs sit on flagstone floors; lemon and oatmeal walls undulate between wonderfully wonky beams. Gourmet breakfasts include freshly squeezed orange juice; arrive around 4pm and expect an offer of tea, taken in the garden or beside the fire.

Stoneleigh Barn
B&B ££
(☑ 01935-389288; www.stoneleighbarn.co.uk; North Wootton; s/d £60/80; Ⓟ🖕) Outside, this glorious 18th-century barn delights the senses – it's smothered in bright, fragrant flowers. Inside, exposed trusses frame spacious rooms delicately decorated in lilac and turquoise. Stoneleigh is 3 miles southeast of Sherborne.

✕ Eating

Green
MODERN BRITISH ££
(☑ 01935-813821; www.greenrestaurant.co.uk; 3 The Green; mains £13-25; ⊙ noon-2.30pm & 6.30-9.30pm Tue-Sat) In this affable, elegant eatery gently distressed furniture is more chic than shabby, while the food is pure Westcountry élan – local goodies might include a trio of Lyme Bay crab, sole escabeche or wild venison carpaccio. Or plump for the cracking-value *menu du jour* (three courses £20).

George
PUB ££
(www.thegeorgesherborne.co.uk; 4 Higher Cheap St; mains £7-10; ⊙ noon-2.30pm & 6-9pm; 🖕) It's five centuries since Sherborne's oldest, cosiest inn pulled its first pint; today it signals its age with wooden settles polished smooth by countless behinds. The food is enduring pub grub fare: robust steaks, ham and eggs, homemade pud and both Sunday and Saturday roasts.

ℹ Information

Tourist Office (☑ 01935-815341; www.visit-dorset.com; Digby Rd; ⊙ 9.30am-4pm Mon-Sat, to 3pm Dec-Mar) Stocks a self-guided walking tour leaflet (50p).

ℹ Getting There & Away

BUS
Dorchester (£4.10, one hour, four to six daily Monday to Saturday) Bus 216; via Cerne Abbas (30 minutes).

Shaftesbury (£6, 30 minutes, daily) National Express.

Yeovil (£4.10, 15 minutes, every two hours Monday to Saturday) Bus 58.

TRAIN
Hourly services to Exeter (£20, 1¼ hours), London Waterloo (£30, 2½ hours) and Salisbury (£13, 40 minutes).

Shaftesbury & Around

POP 7707

Crowning a ridge of hogbacked hills and overlooking pastoral meadows, the agreeable market town of Shaftesbury circles around its medieval abbey ruins. A charismatic castle and a postcard-pretty, ancient street add to the town's appeal.

⊙ Sights

Shaftesbury Abbey   RUIN

(☎ 01747-852910; www.shaftesburyabbey.org.uk; Park Walk; adult/child £3/free; ⊙10am-5pm Apr-Oct) These hilltop ruins mark the site of what was England's largest and richest nunnery. Founded in 888 by King Alfred the Great, Alfred's daughter, Aethelgifu, was its first abbess. St Edward is thought to have been buried here while King Knut died at the abbey in 1035. Most of the buildings were dismantled by Henry VIII, but you can wander its foundations and search out statuary and illuminated manuscripts in the museum.

Old Wardour Castle   CASTLE

(EH; ☎ 01747-870487; www.english-heritage.org.uk; adult/child £4.20/2.50; ⊙10am-5pm Apr-Oct, to 4pm Sat & Sun Nov-Mar; P) Six-sided Old Wardour Castle was built around 1393 and suffered severe damage during the English Civil War, leaving these imposing remains. The views from the upper levels are fabulous while its grassy lawns make a fine spot for a picnic. It's open until 6pm in July and August and is 4 miles west of Shaftesbury.

Gold Hill   STREET

This often-photographed, painfully steep, quaint cobbled slope, lined by chocolate-box cottages, starred in a famous TV advert for Hovis bread.

⎙ Sleeping & Eating

Old Chapel   B&B ££

(☎ 01747-852404; www.theoldchapelbb.co.uk; 9 Breach Lane; s/d £60/90; P⊜) Sleep spots don't come much more characterful than this: a converted Victorian chapel with slender, two-storey windows, light-filled atriums and massive support beams. Smoothly comfy bedrooms feature fresh flowers and cookie jars; from the guest lounge you can see all the way to Salisbury Plain.

Updown   COTTAGE ££

(☎ 07710-307202; www.updowncottage.co.uk; 12 Gold Hill; per week £700-1300; P⊜) A supreme-

ly picturesque whitewashed, six-person cottage clinging to charming Gold Hill with snug, beam-lined rooms, open fires and a hillside garden.

Fleur de Lys   HOTEL £££

(☎ 01747-853717; www.lafleurdelys.co.uk; Bleke St; s £95-110, d £130-170; P@⊜) A place to be pampered, whether in the deeply luxurious bedrooms or the acclaimed restaurant (open 7am to 10pm Monday to Saturday; two/three courses cost £27/34).

Mitre   PUB ££

(www.youngs.co.uk/pubs/mitre; 23 High St; mains £9; ⊙noon-3pm Mon-Fri, to 9pm Sat & Sun) It's the decked terrace that'll draw you into this old inn – its cracking views out over Blackmore Vale make for a memorable spot to tuck into homemade pizzas, fish and chips and beefy burgers.

ⓘ Information

Tourist Office (☎ 01747-853514; www.shaftesburydorset.com; 8 Bell St; ⊙10am-4pm Mon-Sat)

ⓘ Getting There & Away

Buses include:

London Victoria (£22, four hours, one daily) National Express; goes via Heathrow.

Salisbury (£4.20, 1¼ hours, five daily Monday to Saturday) Bus 29.

Sherborne (£6, 30 minutes, one daily) National Express.

WILTSHIRE

Wiltshire is rich in the reminders of ritual and packed with not-to-be-missed sights. Its verdant landscape is littered with more mysterious stone circles, processional avenues and ancient barrows than anywhere else in Britain. It's a place that teases and tantalises the imagination – here you'll experience the prehistoric majesty of Stonehenge and the atmospheric stone ring at Avebury. Add the serene 800-year-old cathedral at Salisbury, the supremely stately homes at Stourhead and Longleat and the impossibly pretty village of Lacock, and you have a county crammed full of English charm waiting to be explored.

ⓘ Information

There's a tourist office in Salisbury (p261).

Visit Wiltshire (www.visitwiltshire.co.uk)

ⓘ Getting Around

Wiltshire's bus coverage can be patchy, especially in the northwest.

First (www.firstgroup.com) Serves west Wiltshire.

Salisbury Reds (www.salisburyreds.co.uk) Covers Salisbury and many rural areas. Offers one-day Explorer Tickets (£8.50) and seven-day passes (Salisbury area £15, network-wide £27).

TRAIN

Rail lines run from London Waterloo to Salisbury and beyond to Exeter and Plymouth, branching off north to Bradford-on-Avon, Bath and Bristol.

Salisbury & Around

POP 40,300

Centred on a majestic cathedral that's topped by the tallest spire in England, Salisbury makes an appealing Wiltshire base. It's been an important provincial city for more than a thousand years, and its streets form an architectural timeline ranging from medieval walls and half-timbered Tudor town houses to Georgian mansions and Victorian villas. Salisbury is also a lively, modern town, boasting plenty of bars and restaurants, plus a concentrated cluster of excellent museums.

◉ Sights

★Salisbury Cathedral   CATHEDRAL
(☑01722-555120; www.salisburycathedral.org.uk; Cathedral Close; requested donation adult/child £6.50/3; ⊘9am-5pm Mon-Sat, noon-4pm Sun) England is endowed with countless stunning churches, but few can hold a candle to the grandeur and sheer spectacle of 13th-century Salisbury Cathedral. This early English Gothic–style structure has an elaborate exterior decorated with pointed arches and flying buttresses, and a sombre, austere interior designed to keep its congregation suitably pious. Its statuary and tombs are outstanding; don't miss the daily tower tours and the cathedral's original, 13th-century copy of the Magna Carta. It's best experienced on a Tower Tour (p259).

The cathedral was built between 1220 and 1258. Beyond its highly decorative West Front, a small passageway leads into the 70m-long nave, lined with handsome pillars of Purbeck stone. In the north aisle look out for a fascinating medieval clock dating from 1386, probably the oldest working timepiece in the world. At the eastern end of the ambulatory the glorious Prisoners of Conscience stained-glass window (1980) hovers above the ornate tomb of Edward Seymour (1539–1621) and Lady Catherine Grey. Other monuments and tombs line the sides of the nave, including that of William Longespée, son of Henry II and half-brother of King John. When the tomb was excavated a well-preserved rat was found inside Longespée's skull.

Salisbury's 123m crowning glory, its spire, was added in the mid-14th century, and is the tallest in Britain. It represented an enormous technical challenge for its medieval builders; it weighs around 6500 tons and required an elaborate system of cross-bracing, scissor arches and supporting buttresses to keep it upright. Look closely and you'll see the additional weight has buckled the four central piers of the nave.

Sir Christopher Wren surveyed the cathedral in 1668 and calculated that the spire was leaning by 75cm. A brass plate in the floor of the nave is used to measure any shift, but no further lean was recorded in 1951 or 1970. Despite this, reinforcement of the notoriously 'wonky spire' continues to this day.

The cathedral really comes into its own during evensong, which takes place at 5.30pm Monday to Saturday and 3pm on Sunday, during term time only.

➡ Magna Carta
(⊘10am-4.30pm Mon-Sat, 12.45-4.30pm Sun) Tucked into Salisbury Cathedral's Chapter House is one of only four surviving original copies of the Magna Carta, the historic agreement made between King John and his barons in 1215 that acknowledged the fundamental principle that the monarch was not above the law. It's a still-powerful document; beautifully written and remarkably well preserved.

BATH & SOUTHWEST ENGLAND SALISBURY & AROUND

WORTH A TRIP

CANAL TRIPS

The 87-mile-long Kennet & Avon (www.katrust.org) runs all the way from Bristol to Reading. Sally Boats (☑01225-864923; www.sallyboats.ltd.uk) hires out narrowboats. Weekly rates for a four-berth boat range from around £750 in winter to £995 in high summer.

Salisbury

★ **Cathedral Close**   HISTORIC AREA

Salisbury's medieval cathedral close, a hushed enclave surrounded by beautiful houses, has an other-worldly feel. Many of the buildings date from the 13th century, although the area was heavily restored during an 18th-century clean-up by James Wyatt. The close is encircled by a sturdy outer wall, constructed in 1333; the stout gates leading into the complex are still locked every night.

Just inside the narrow High St Gate is the **College of Matrons**, founded in 1682 for widows and unmarried daughters of clergymen. South of the cathedral is the **Bishop's Palace**, now the private Cathedral School, parts of which date from 1220.

★ **Salisbury Museum**   MUSEUM

(☎01722-332151; www.salisburymuseum.org.uk; 65 Cathedral Close; adult/child £5/2; ☺10am-5pm Mon-Sat, plus noon-5pm Sun Jun-Sep) The hugely important archaeological finds here include

the Stonehenge Archer; the bones of a man found in the ditch surrounding the stone circle – one of the arrows found alongside probably killed him. With gold coins dating from 100 BC and a Bronze Age gold necklace, it's a powerful introduction to Wiltshire's prehistory.

Mompesson House   HISTORIC BUILDING

(NT; ☎01722-335659; www.nationaltrust.org.uk; Cathedral Close; adult/child £6/3; ☺11am-5pm Sat-Wed mid-Mar–Oct) Magnificent plasterwork ceilings, exceptional period furnishings and a sweeping carved staircase grace this fine Queen Anne (1701) building. All that made it the perfect location for the 1995 film *Sense and Sensibility*.

Rifles   MUSEUM

(The Wardrobe; ☎01722-419419; www.thewardrobe.org.uk; 58 Cathedral Close; adult/child £5/2; ☺10am-5pm Mon-Sat, closed Dec & Jan) Collections include a cannonball from the

Salisbury

American War of Independence, Victorian redcoat uniforms and displays on 19th- and 21st-century conflicts in Afghanistan.

Old Sarum ARCHAEOLOGICAL SITE
(EH; ☏ 01722-335398; www.english-heritage.org.uk; Castle Rd; adult/child £4/2.40; ⊙10am-5pm Sep-Jun, 9am-6pm Jul & Aug; ℗) The huge ramparts of Old Sarum sit on a grass-covered hill 2 miles north of Salisbury. You can wander the grassy ramparts, see the original cathedral's stone foundations, and look across the Wiltshire countryside to the spire of Salisbury's new cathedral. Medieval tournaments, open-air plays and mock battles are held on selected days. Bus X5/8 runs twice an hour from Salisbury to Old Sarum (£2.20, hourly on Sundays). It's also a stop on the Stonehenge Tour bus (p263).

It began life as a hill fort during the Iron Age, and was later occupied by both the Romans and the Saxons. By the mid-11th century it was a town – one of the most important in the west of England. William the Conqueror convened one of his earliest councils here and the first cathedral was built in 1092, snatching the bishopric from nearby Sherborne Abbey. But Old Sarum had problems: it was short on water and exposed to the elements, and in 1219 the bishop was given permission to move the cathedral, so founding the modern-day city of Salisbury. By 1331 Old Sarum's cathedral had been demolished for building materials and the settlement was practically abandoned.

Wilton House HISTORIC BUILDING
(☏ 01722-746700; www.wiltonhouse.com; Wilton; house & grounds adult/child £15/8; ⊙11.30am-5pm Sun-Thu mid-Apr–Aug; ℗) Stately Wilton House provides an insight into the rarefied world of the British aristocracy. One of England's finest stately homes, the earls of Pembroke have lived here since 1542, and it's been expanded, improved and embellished by successive generations. Highlights are the Single and Double Cube Rooms, designed by the pioneering 17th-century architect Inigo Jones.

Wilton House is 2.5 miles west of Salisbury; bus R3 runs from Salisbury (£2.60, 10 minutes, one to three hourly).

The result of centuries of embellishments is quite staggering: magnificent period furniture, frescoed ceilings and elaborate plasterwork frame paintings by Van Dyck, Rembrandt and Joshua Reynolds. All the architectural eye candy makes the house a favoured film location: *The Madness of King George*, *Sense and Sensibility* and *Pride and Prejudice* were all shot here. But Wilton was serving as an artistic haven long before the movies – famous guests include Ben Jonson, Edmund Spenser, Christopher Marlowe and John Donne. Shakespeare's *As You Like It* was performed here in 1603, shortly after the bard had written it. The fine landscaped grounds (adult/child £6/4.50; ⊙11am-5.30pm early Apr–Sep) were largely laid out by Capability Brown.

☞ Tours

Tower Tour WALKING TOUR
(adult/child £10/8; ⊙1-5 daily) The best way to experience Salisbury Cathedral is on a 90-minute tower tour which sees you climbing 332 vertigo-inducing steps to the base of the spire for jaw-dropping views across the city and the surrounding countryside. Booking required.

Salisbury Guides HERITAGE TOUR

(📞07873-212941; www.salisburycityguides.co.uk; adult/child £5/free; ⏰11am daily Apr-Oct, 11am Sat & Sun Nov-Mar) These 90-minute trips leave from the tourist office.

✨ Festivals & Events

Salisbury Festival ARTS FESTIVAL

(📞01722-33224; www.salisburyfestival.co.uk) A prestigious, eclectic event running from late May to early June, encompassing classical, world and pop music, plus theatre, literature and art.

🛏 Sleeping

Salisbury YHA HOSTEL £

(📞0845 371 9537; www.yha.org.uk; Milford Hill; dm/d £18/28; P @ 🕸) A real gem: neat rooms in a rambling Victorian house, with a cafe-bar, laundry and dappled gardens too.

★ St Ann's House BOUTIQUE B&B £

(📞01722-335657; www.stannshouse.co.uk; 32 St Ann St; s £59-64, d £89-110; 🕸) The aromas wafting from breakfast may well spur you from your room: great coffee; baked peaches with raspberry, honey and almonds; poached eggs and Parma ham. Utter elegance reigns upstairs, where well-chosen antiques, warm colours and Turkish linen ensure a supremely comfortable stay.

Spire House B&B ££

(📞01722-339213; www.salisbury-bedandbreakfast.com; 84 Exeter St; s/d/f £60/75/90; P 🕸) In this B&B of beautifully kept, sweet rooms the easygoing vibe extends to breakfast (add £5): chalk up your choice on a blackboard the night before. Options include slow-cooked, blueberry-studded porridge, croissants and pastries, or local bacon and eggs.

Lazy Cow INN ££

(📞01722-412 028; www.thelazycowsalisbury.co.uk; 9 St Johns St; d £75-95, tr £120; 🕸) Bordering on bonkers but beautifully done, a bovine theme is everywhere here. Highland cattle peer from walls topped by snaking beams, cowhide-framed mirrors sit on oak-panelled walls. Your room key is attached to a tethering ring, and the mainstay of the restaurant? Steaks galore.

Cathedral View B&B ££

(📞01722-502254; www.cathedral-viewbandb.co.uk; 83 Exeter St; s £70-80, d £75-99; P 🕸) Admirable attention to detail defines this Georgian town house. Miniature flower displays and home-baked cookies sit in quietly elegant rooms. Breakfasts include prime Wiltshire sausages and homemade bread and jam. And the owner's daily what's-on list features self-guided town trails.

🍴 Eating

Fish Row DELI, CAFE £

(www.fishrowdelicafe.co.uk; 3 Fish Row; snacks from £5; ⏰8.30am-5.30pm Mon-Sat, 9.30am-4.30pm Sun) Local produce is piled high at this heavily beamed deli-cafe – the New Forest Blue, Old Sarum and Nanny Williams cheeses come from just a few miles away. Grab some potato salad and a wedge of quiche to go, or duck upstairs to eat alongside weathered wood, stained glass and old church pews.

Anokaa INDIAN ££

(📞01722-414142; www.anokaa.com; 60 Fisherton St; mains £11-32; ⏰noon-2pm & 5.30-11pm; 🍴) The pink neon and multicoloured bubble displays signal what's in store here: a supremely modern version of Indian cuisine. The spice and flavour combos make the ingredients sing; the meat-free menu range makes vegetarians beam.

Cloisters PUB ££

(www.cloisterspubsalisbury.co.uk; 83 Catherine St; mains £9-13; ⏰11am-9pm Sat & Sun, 11am-3pm & 6-9pm Mon-Fri) The building dates from 1350, it's been a pub since the 1600s and today improbably warped beams reinforce an age-old vibe. It's a convivial spot for tasty beef-and-ale pie, sausage and mash or fancier foods such as an impressive lamb shank slow-braised in red wine.

Charter 1227 BRITISH £££

(📞01722-333118; www.charter1227.co.uk; 6 Ox Row, Market Pl; mains £15-26; ⏰noon-2.30pm & 6-9.30pm Tue-Sat, noon-2.30pm Sun) Ingredients that speak of ancient England have a firm foothold here – feast on suckling pig, Wiltshire ham hock or roast John Dory. Canny locals eat between 6pm and 8pm Tuesday to Thursday (two/three courses for £20/25) or at lunchtime, when dishes are £5.50 each.

🍷 Drinking & Nightlife

Haunch of Venison PUB

(1 Minster St; ⏰11am-11pm Mon-Sat, to 6pm Sun) Featuring wood-panelled snugs, spiral staircases and wonky ceilings, this 14th-century drinking den is packed with atmosphere – and ghosts. One is a cheating whist player

whose hand was severed in a game – look out for his mummified bones on display inside.

Chapel   BAR, CLUB
(www.chapelnightclub.com; 34 Milford St; ☺5pm-3am Wed-Sat) Buzzing bar with adjoining club where the DJ sets range from funk to '90s hip-hop and chart 'n' cheese.

MusicBox   CLUB
(www.themusicboxsalisbury.co.uk; 46 Catherine St; ☺9pm-3am Thu-Sun) Three-floor venue filled by gigs, open-mic events and DJ sets featuring '80s pop, reggae and dub.

☆ Entertainment

Salisbury Arts Centre   ARTS CENTRE
(☑01722-321744; www.salisburyartscentre.co.uk; Bedwin St) An innovative arts centre showcasing cutting-edge theatre, indie films, dance and live gigs.

Salisbury Playhouse   THEATRE
(☑01722-320333; www.salisburyplayhouse.com; Malthouse Lane) A producing theatre that also hosts top touring shows and musicals.

❶ Information

Library (Market Pl; internet per hr £1; ☺10am-7pm Mon-Tue & Fri, 9am-5pm Wed-Thu & Sat; ☎)
Tourist Office (☑01722-342860; www.visit-wiltshire.co.uk; Fish Row; ☺9am-5pm Mon-Fri, 10am-4pm Sat, 10am-2pm Sun)

❶ Getting There & Away

BUS

Direct National Express services include those to Bath (£11, 1¼ hours, one daily), Bristol (£11, 2¼ hours, one daily) and London (£17, three hours, three daily) via Heathrow.

Local services include bus 29 to Shaftesbury (£4.20, 1¼ hours, five daily Monday to Saturday) and bus 2 to Devizes (£5, one hour, hourly Monday to Saturday).

Tour buses leave Salisbury for Stonehenge regularly (p263).

TRAIN

Half-hourly connections include:
Bath (£10, one hour)
Bradford-on-Avon (£13, 40 minutes)
Bristol (£11, 1¼ hours)
London Waterloo (£38, 1¾ hours)
Southampton (£10, 30 minutes)

Hourly connections include:
Exeter (£25, two hours)
Portsmouth (£20, 1¾ hours)

Stonehenge

Welcome to Britain's most iconic archaeological site. This compelling ring of monolithic stones has been attracting a steady stream of pilgrims, poets and philosophers for the last 5000 years and is still a mystical, ethereal place – a haunting echo from Britain's forgotten past, and a reminder of those who once walked the ceremonial avenues across Salisbury Plain.

◉ Sights

★**Stonehenge**   ARCHAEOLOGICAL SITE
(EH; ☑0870 333 1181; www.english-heritage.org.uk; adult/child incl visitor centre £14/8.30; ☺9am-8pm Jun-Aug, 9.30am-7pm Apr, May & Sep, 9.30am-5pm Oct-Mar; ℗) Ancient Stonehenge has had an ultramodern, £27 million makeover. It's brought an impressive new visitor centre and the closure of an intrusive nearby road – now restored to grassland. The result: a far stronger sense of historical context; dignity and mystery returned to an archaeological gem.

A pathway frames the ring of massive stones, and although you can't walk in the circle, unless on a recommended Stone Circle Access Visit (p263), you can get close-up views. Admission is only through prebooked tickets, so secure a place well in advance.

Stonehenge is one of Britain's great archaeological mysteries: despite countless theories about the site's purpose, ranging from a sacrificial centre to a celestial timepiece, in truth no one knows for sure what drove prehistoric Britons to expend so much time and effort on its construction.

The first phase of building started around 3000 BC, when the outer circular bank and ditch were erected. A thousand years later, an inner circle of granite stones, known as bluestones, was added. It's thought that these mammoth 4-tonne blocks were hauled from the Preseli Mountains in South Wales, some 250 miles away – an almost inexplicable feat for Stone Age builders equipped with only the simplest of tools. Although no one is entirely sure how the builders transported the stones so far, it's thought they probably used a system of ropes, sledges and rollers fashioned from tree trunks – Salisbury Plain was still covered by forest during Stonehenge's construction.

Around 1500 BC, Stonehenge's main stones were dragged to the site, erected in a circle and crowned by massive lintels to make

Stonehenge

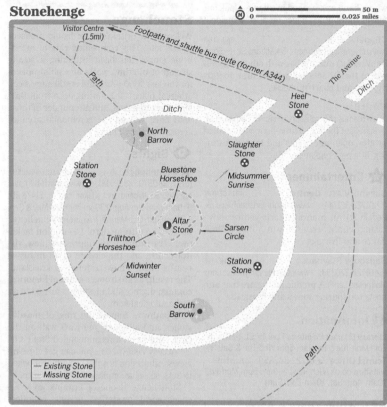

the trilithons (two vertical stones topped by a horizontal one). The sarsen (sandstone) stones were cut from an extremely hard rock found on the Marlborough Downs, 20 miles from the site. It's estimated dragging one of these 50-tonne stones across the countryside would require about 600 people.

Also around this time, the bluestones from 500 years earlier were rearranged as an inner bluestone horseshoe with an altar stone at the centre. Outside this the trilithon horseshoe of five massive sets of stones was erected. Three of these are intact; the other two have just a single upright. Then came the major sarsen circle of 30 massive vertical stones, of which 17 uprights and six lintels remain.

Much further out, another circle was delineated by the 58 Aubrey Holes, named after John Aubrey, who discovered them in the 1600s. Just inside this circle are the South and North Barrows, each originally topped by a stone. Like many stone circles in Britain (including Avebury, 22 miles away) the inner horseshoes are aligned to coincide with sunrise at the midsummer solstice, which some claim supports the theory that the site was some kind of astronomical calendar.

Prehistoric pilgrims would have entered the site via the Avenue, whose entrance to the circle is marked by the Slaughter Stone and the Heel Stone, located slightly further out on one side.

Admission includes an audioguide and is free for EH and NT members.

Visitor Centre INTERPRETATION CENTRE
(EH; ☑ 0870 333 1181; www.english-heritage.org. uk; 9am-8pm Jun-Aug, 9.30am-7pm Apr, May & Sep, 9.30am-5pm Oct-Mar) Stonehenge's swish new visitor centre sees you standing in the middle of an atmospheric 360-degree projection of the stone circle through the ages and seasons – complete with midsummer sunrise and swirling starscape.

The visitor centre is 1.5 miles from the stones. A fleet of trolley buses makes the 10-minute trip – it's more atmospheric to walk.

Engaging audiovisual displays detail the transportation of the stones and the building stages, while 300 finds from the wider site include flint chippings, bone pins and arrowheads, there's also a striking re-creation of the face of a neolithic man whose body was found nearby.

Tours

Stone Circle Access Visits WALKING TOUR
(0870 333 0605; www.english-heritage.org.uk; adult/child £21/12.60) Circle-access visits are an unforgettable experience. Visitors normally have to stay outside the stone circle itself, but on these self-guided walks, you can wander around the core of the site, getting up-close views of the iconic bluestones and trilithons. They take place in the evening or early morning so the quieter atmosphere and the slanting sunlight add to the effect. Each visit takes only 26 people; to secure a place book at least two months in advance.

Salisbury Guided Tours GUIDED TOUR
(07775-674816; www.salisburyguidedtours.com; per person from £80) Runs a wide range of expert-led trips to Stonehenge, the wider ritual landscape and Salisbury.

Getting There & Around

BUS
No regular buses go to the site.
Stonehenge Tour (0845 0727 093; www.thestonehengetour.info; adult/child £26/16) Leaves Salisbury's railway station half-hourly from June to August, and hourly between September and May. The ticket includes admission to Stonehenge and the Iron Age hill fort at Old Sarum (p259); it stops there on the return leg.

Around Stonehenge

Stonehenge actually forms part of a huge complex of ancient monuments.

Sights & Activities

North of Stonehenge and running roughly east–west is the Cursus, an elongated embanked oval; the smaller Lesser Cursus is nearby. Theories abound as to what these sites were used for, ranging from ancient sporting arenas to processional avenues for the dead. Two clusters of burial mounds,

the Old and New Kings Barrows, sit beside the ceremonial pathway the Avenue, which originally linked Stonehenge with the River Avon, 2 miles away.

The National Trust (www.nationaltrust.org.uk) website has a downloadable 3.5-mile circular walk (A King's View) that traces tracks across the chalk downland from Stonehenge, past the Cursus and Kings Barrows and along a section of the Avenue itself. The Stonehenge visitor centre also has leaflets detailing walking routes.

Woodhenge ARCHAEOLOGICAL SITE
(EH; 0870 3331181; www.english-heritage.org.uk; dawn-dusk) FREE Some 1.5 miles east of Stonehenge, near Amesbury, is Woodhenge, a series of concentric rings that would once have been marked by wooden posts. It's thought there might be some correlation between the use of wood and stone in both henges. Excavations in the 1970s at Woodhenge revealed the skeleton of a child with a cloven skull, buried near the centre.

Stourhead

Overflowing with vistas, temples and follies, Stourhead (NT; 01747-841152; www.nationaltrust.org.uk; Mere; house or garden adult/child £8/4, house & garden £13/7; house 11am-4.30pm mid-Mar–Oct, 11am-3pm Sat & Sun Nov–mid-Mar; P) is landscape gardening at its finest. The Palladian house has some fine Chippendale furniture and paintings by Claude and Gaspard Poussin, but it's a sideshow to the magnificent 18th-century gardens (open 9am to 5pm, to 7pm April to September), which spread out across the valley. Stourhead is off the B3092, 8 miles south of Frome (in Somerset).

A picturesque 2-mile circuit takes you past the most ornate follies, around the lake and to the Temple of Apollo; a 3.5-mile side trip can be made from near the Pantheon to King Alfred's Tower (adult/child £3/2; ⊙noon-4pm Sat & Sun Mar-Oct), a 50m-high folly with wonderful views.

Longleat

Half ancestral mansion, half safari park, Longleat (⏱01985-844400; www.longleat.co.uk; all-inclusive ticket adult/child £34/22, house & grounds £15.50/10.50; ⊙10am-7pm Jul & Aug, to 5pm Apr-Jun, to 4pm Mar, Sep & Oct; P) was transformed into Britain's first safari park in 1966, turning Capability Brown's landscaped grounds into an amazing drive-through zoo, populated by a menagerie of animals more at home in the African wilderness than the fields of Wiltshire. Longleat also has a throng of attractions, including a narrow-gauge railway, Dr Who exhibit, Postman Pat village, pets' corner and butterfly garden.

Longleat House is just off the A362, 3 miles from both Frome and Warminster.

It was the first English stately home to open its doors to the public, prompted by finance: heavy taxes and mounting post-WWII bills meant the house had to earn its keep.

The house itself contains fine tapestries, furniture and decorated ceilings, as well as seven libraries containing around 40,000 tomes. The highlight, though, is an extraordinary series of paintings and psychedelic murals by the present-day marquess, who was an art student in the '60s and upholds the long-standing tradition of eccentricity among the English aristocracy – check out his website (www.lordbath.co.uk).

Malmesbury

The mellow hilltop town of Malmesbury is peppered with ancient buildings constructed out of honey-coloured Cotswold stone. It's the oldest borough in England, having been awarded that status in AD 880, and boasts one of the county's finest market crosses – a 15th-century crown-like structure built to shelter the poor from the rain.

Bus 31 runs to Swindon (£3, one hour, hourly Monday to Saturday); bus 92 heads to Chippenham (£2.70, 45 minutes, hourly Monday to Saturday).

◎ Sights

Malmesbury Abbey   ABBEY
(⏱01666-826666; www.malmesburyabbey.info; suggested donation £3; ⊙9am-4pm) Malmesbury's big draw is Malmesbury Abbey, a blend of ruin and living church, with a somewhat turbulent history. Notable features include the Norman doorway decorated with biblical figures, the Romanesque Apostle carvings and a four-volume illuminated bible dating from 1407. A window at the western end of the church depicts Elmer the Flying Monk, who in 1010 strapped on wings and jumped from the tower. Although he broke both legs during this leap of faith, he survived and became a local hero.

The abbey began life as a 7th-century monastery, which was later replaced by a Norman church. By the mid-15th century the building had been embellished with a spire and twin towers, but in 1479 a storm toppled one tower and spire, destroying the eastern end of the church. The west tower followed suit in 1662, destroying much of the nave. The present-day church is about a third of its original size, and is flanked by ruins at either end.

Just below the abbey are the Abbey House Gardens (⏱01666-827650; www.abbeyhousegardens.co.uk; adult/child £8/3; ⊙11am-5.30pm mid-Mar–Oct), which include a herb garden, river, waterfall and 2 hectares of colourful blooms.

Lacock

POP 1000

With its geranium-covered cottages and higgledy-piggledy rooftops, pockets of the medieval village of Lacock seem to have been preserved in mid-19th-century aspic. The village has been in the hands of the National Trust since 1944, and in many places is remarkably free of modern development: there are no telephone poles or electric street lights and the main car park on the outskirts keeps it largely traffic-free. Unsurprisingly, it's a popular location for costume dramas and feature films – the village and its abbey pop up in the Harry Potter films, *The Other Boleyn Girl* and BBC adaptations of *Moll Flanders* and *Pride and Prejudice*.

◎ Sights

Lacock Abbey   ABBEY
(NT; ⏱01249-730459; www.nationaltrust.org.uk; adult/child £11.20/5.60; ⊙10.30am-5.30pm Mar-Oct, 11am-4pm Nov-Feb) Lacock Abbey is a window into a medieval world. Founded as an Augustinian nunnery in the 13th century, its deeply atmospheric rooms and stunning Gothic entrance hall are lined with bizarre terracotta figures; spot the scapegoat with a

lump of sugar on its nose. Some of the original structure is evident in the cloisters and there are traces of medieval wall paintings too. On Tuesdays year-round and winter weekdays, access is limited to the cloisters.

Ela, Countess of Salisbury established the abbey in 1232. After the Dissolution it was sold to Sir William Sharington in 1539, who converted the nunnery into a home, demolished the church, built a tower and added a brewery.

The ticket into the abbey also includes admission to the Fox Talbot Museum, which profiles the man who pioneered the photographic negative: William Henry Fox Talbot (1800–77). A prolific inventor, he began developing the system in 1834 while working at the abbey. The museum details his ground-breaking work and displays a superb collection of his images.

A cheaper ticket (adult/child £8.50/4.50) gets you into the grounds, museum and abbey cloisters, but not the abbey building itself.

🍴 Sleeping & Eating

★ Red Lion
INN ££
(☎ 01249-730456; www.redlionlacock.co.uk; 1 High St; d £120; P �&) In atmospheric Lacock where better to sleep than a Georgian coaching inn that oozes ambience. Step on flagstone floors past open fires, up a grand staircase to sweet rooms where padded cushions line mullioned windows with picture-postcard views of ancient streets. The food's notable too (mains £11, served 9am to 8.30pm).

King John's Hunting Lodge
B&B ££
(☎ 01249-730313; www.kingjohnslodge.2day.ws; 21 Church St; d/f £95/110; P) An air of peace pervades Lacock's oldest building. The decor matches the beam-lined, irregular-shaped rooms; expect tapestries, dainty chairs and china figurines in meticulous rooms. Afternoon tea in the cafe is a must (served 10.30am to 4pm Wednesday to Sunday).

Lacock Pottery
B&B ££
(☎ 01249-730266; www.lacockbedandbreakfast.com; Church St; s £56-66, d £89-110; P �&) A serene, airy former workhouse featuring peat fires, organic breakfasts and, appropriately, fine ceramics.

George Inn
PUB £
(www.georgeinnlacock.co.uk; 4 West St; mains £11-19; �},noon-2.30pm & 6-9pm) Sample good grub and local ales at this 14th-century, horse brass-hung pub.

❶ Getting There & Away

Bus 234 runs hourly, Monday to Saturday, from Chippenham (£2.40, 15 minutes).

Avebury

POP 235

While the tour buses head straight for Stonehenge, prehistoric purists make for the massive stone circle at Avebury. Though it lacks the dramatic trilithons of its sister site across Salisbury Plain, Avebury is just as rewarding to visit. It's bigger and older, and a large section of the village is actually inside the stones – footpaths wind around them, allowing you to really soak up the extraordinary atmosphere. Avebury also boasts an encircling landscape that's rich in prehistoric sites and a manor house where restored rooms span five completely different eras.

◎ Sights

★ Avebury Stone Circle
ARCHAEOLOGICAL SITE
(NT; ☎ 01672-539250; www.nationaltrust.org.uk; �},24hr; P) FREE With a diameter of 348m, Avebury is the largest stone circle in the world. It's also one of the oldest, dating from 2500 to 2200 BC. Today, more than 30 stones are in place; pillars show where missing stones would have been. Wandering between them reveals the sheer scale of the site, evidenced also by the massive bank and ditch that lines the circle; the quieter northwest

RITUAL LANDSCAPE

Avebury is surrounded by a network of ancient monuments, including Silbury Hill (p267) and West Kennet Long Barrow (p267). To the south of the village, the West Kennet Avenue stretched out for 1.5 miles, lined by 100 pairs of stones. It linked the Avebury circle with a site called the Sanctuary. Post holes indicate that a wooden building surrounded by a stone circle once stood at the Sanctuary, although no one knows quite what the site was for.

The Ridgeway national trail (www.nationaltrail.co.uk/ridgeway) starts near Avebury and runs eastwards across Fyfield Down, where many of the sarsen stones at Avebury (and Stonehenge) were collected.

Avebury

⊙ **Top Sights**

⊙ **Sights**

🛏 **Sleeping**

🍴 **Eating**

🍷 **Drinking & Nightlife**

🛍 **Shopping**

quadrant is particularly atmospheric. The National Trust holds guided tours daily.

Avebury Henge originally consisted of an outer circle of 98 standing stones of up to 6m in length, many weighing 20 tonnes. The stones were surrounded by another circle delineated by a 5m-high earth bank and ditch up to 9m deep. Inside were smaller stone circles to the north (27 stones) and south (29 stones).

In the Middle Ages, when Britain's pagan past was an embarrassment to the church, many of the stones were buried, removed or broken up. In 1934, wealthy businessman and archaeologist Alexander Keiller supervised the re-erection of the stones. He later bought the site for posterity using funds from his family's marmalade fortune.

Modern roads into Avebury neatly dissect the circle into four sectors. Starting at High St, near the Henge Shop, and walking round the circle in an anticlockwise direction, you'll encounter 11 standing stones in the southwest sector. They include the Barber Surgeon Stone, named after the skeleton of a man found under it – the equipment buried with him suggests he was a barber-cum-surgeon.

The southeast sector starts with the huge portal stones marking the entry to the circle from West Kennet Avenue. The southern inner circle stood in this sector and within this ring was the obelisk and a group of stones known as the Z Feature. Just outside this smaller circle, only the base of the Ring Stone survives.

In the northern inner circle in the northeast sector, three sarsens remain of what would have been a rectangular cove. The northwest sector has the most complete collection of standing stones, including the massive 65-tonne Swindon Stone, one of the few never to have been toppled.

★Avebury Manor   HISTORIC BUILDING
(NT; ☑01672-539250; www.nationaltrust.org.uk; adult/child £9/4.50; ☉11am-5pm Thu-Tue Apr-Oct) The mother of all makeovers took place at this 16th-century manor house as part of the BBC TV series *The Manor Reborn*. It used original techniques and materials to recreate interiors spanning five periods, so now you can sit on beds, play billiards and listen to the gramophone in rooms that range from Tudor, through Georgian to the 1930s.

In the garden, the topiary and box hedges create a series of rooms that inspired Vita Sackville-West, creator of Sissinghurst gardens (☑01580-710700; www.nationaltrust.org.uk/sissinghurst; adult/concession/family £8.80/4.40/22; ☉11am-6.30pm, last entry 5.30pm Mon, Tue & Fri, 10am-6.30pm, last entry 5.30pm Sat & Sun mid-Mar–Nov) in Kent. Visits are by timed tickets only; arrive early to bag a slot.

Silbury Hill   ARCHAEOLOGICAL SITE
(www.english-heritage.org.uk; P) FREE Rising abruptly from the fields just south of Avebury, 40m high Silbury Hill is the largest artificial earthwork in Europe. It was built in stages from around 2500 BC, but the reason for its construction remains unclear. Direct access to the hill isn't allowed, but you can view it from a lay-by on the A4. For more atmospheric views, from Avebury head through the main car park, cross the road, then pick up the footpath south across the fields (3 miles return) to the hill's north side.

West Kennet
Long Barrow   ARCHAEOLOGICAL SITE
(EH; ☑01672-539250; www.english-heritage.org.uk; ☉dawn-dusk) FREE England's finest burial mound dates from around 3500 BC. Its entrance is guarded by huge sarsens and its roof is made out of gigantic overlapping capstones. About 50 skeletons were found when it was excavated; finds are on display at the Wiltshire Heritage Museum in Devizes. A footpath leads from Avebury to West Kennet (2 miles), passing Silbury Hill en route.

🛏 Sleeping

★Manor Farm   B&B ££
(☑01672-539294; www.manorfarmavebury.com; High St; s £70-80, d £90-100; P🐾) Offering a rare chance to sleep in style inside a stone circle, this red-brick farmhouse snuggles just inside Avebury henge. The elegant, comfy rooms blend old woods with bright furnishings, while the windows provide spine-tingling views of those 4000-year-old standing stones.

Avebury Lodge   B&B £££
(☑01672-539023; www.aveburylodge.co.uk; High St; d £175; P🐾) It's as if gentlemanly archaeologists are still in situ: antiquarian prints of stone circles smother the walls, pelmets and chandeliers are dotted around. And whenever you glance from a window, a bit of Avebury henge appears.

🍴 Eating & Drinking

Circle   CAFE £
(www.nationaltrust.org.uk; mains from £7; ☉10am-6pm Apr-Oct, to 4pm Nov-Mar; 🐾) A veggie and wholefood cafe beside the Great Barn serving homemade quiches and cakes, chunky sandwiches and afternoon teas.

Red Lion   PUB
(www.oldenglishinns.co.uk; High St; ☉11am-11pm) Having a pint here means downing a drink at the only pub in the world inside a stone circle. The food (served noon to 9pm, mains £7 to £13) is firmly traditional – think pork belly and sausage and mash.

❶ Getting There & Away

Bus 49 runs hourly to Swindon (£4.40, 30 minutes) and Devizes (£4, 20 minutes).

EXMOOR NATIONAL PARK

Exmoor is more than a little addictive. Even when you get home, your mind could well return to its broad, russet views. In the middle sits the higher moor, an empty, expansive, other-worldly landscape of tawny grasses and huge skies. Here picturesque Exford makes an ideal village base. In the north, sheer, rock-strewn river valleys cut into the plateau and coal-black cliffs lurch towards the sea. Amid these towering headlands, charismatic Porlock, and the twin villages of Lynton and Lynmouth, are atmospheric places to stay. Relaxed Dulverton delivers a country-town vibe, while appealing Dunster boasts cobbled streets and a russet-red castle. And everywhere on Exmoor life is attuned to the rhythm of the seasons; it's a glimpse into another world. Visit – but you're likely to be planning to return before you leave.

🏃 Activities

Exmoor Adventures   OUTDOORS
(☑ 01643-863536; www.exmooradventures.co.uk) Runs kayaking, canoeing, mountain biking, coasteering and rock-climbing sessions.

Cycling
Despite the formidable hills, cycling is hugely popular on Exmoor. Several sections of the National Cycle Network (NCN; www.sustrans. org.uk) cross the park, including the Westcountry Way (NCN route 3) from Bristol to Land's End, and the Devon Coast to Coast (NCN route 27), between Illfracombe and Plymouth, via Dartmoor and Exmoor.

Exmoor is also one of the county's most exhilarating off-road cycling destinations, with a wealth of bridleways and permitted tracks. The Exmoor National Park Authority (p269) has produced a colour-coded, off-road cycle map (£10); buy it at tourist offices or from the ENPA website.

Exmoor Adventures (p268) runs a five-hour mountain-biking skills course (£50) and also hires bikes (adult per day £25).

Exmoor Cycle Hire   BICYCLE RENTAL
(☑ 01598-753967; www.exmoorcyclehire.co.uk; adult per day/week £14/50, child £8/28)

Pompys   BICYCLE RENTAL
(☑ 01643-704077; www.pompyscycles.co.uk; Mart Rd, Minehead; per day £15; ⊙ 9am-5pm Mon-Sat)

Pony Trekking & Horse Riding
Exmoor is prime riding country, with stables offering pony and horse treks from around £40 to £45 for a two-hour ride.

Brendan Manor Stables   HORSE RIDING
(☑ 01598-741246; www.ridingonexmoor.co.uk; Brendon Manor, near Lynton)

Burrowhayes Farm   HORSE RIDING
(☑ 01643-862463; www.burrowhayes.co.uk; West Luccombe, near Porlock)

Outovercott Stables   HORSE RIDING
(☑ 01598-753341; www.outovercott.co.uk; near Lynton)

Walking
The open moors and profusion of marked bridleways make Exmoor an excellent area for hiking. The best-known routes are the Somerset & North Devon Coast Path,

Exmoor National Park

WILDLIFE WATCHING

Exmoor supports one of England's largest wild red deer populations, best experienced in autumn when the annual 'rutting' season sees stags bellowing, charging and clashing horns in an attempt to impress prospective mates. Despite their numbers, these skittish creatures are notoriously difficult to spot without some local knowledge.

The Exmoor National Park Authority (see below) runs regular wildlife-themed guided walks (£3 to £5), or head out on an organised jeep safari to combine scenic sightseeing with a couple of hours of off-road wildlife-spotting.

Barle Valley Safaris (☑ 01643-841326; www.exmoorwildlifesafaris.co.uk; adult/child £30/25) Runs from Dulverton and Dunster, with pick-ups from Wheddon Cross.

Discovery Safaris (☑ 01643-863444; www.discoverysafaris.com; per person £25) Twice-daily trips from Porlock.

Exmoor Safari (☑ 01643-831229; www.exmoorsafari.co.uk; adult/child £35/16) This long-running operator also does special photography-themed trips.

Red Stag Safari (☑ 01643-841831; www.redstagsafari.co.uk; safari £25-38) Departs from a wide range of Exmoor towns.

which is part of the **South West Coast Path** (www.southwestcoastpath.com), and the Exmoor section of the **Two Moors Way**, which starts in Lynmouth and travels south to Dartmoor and beyond.

Other superb routes include the **Coleridge Way** (www.coleridgeway.co.uk) which winds for 51 miles through Exmoor, the Brendon Hills and the Quantocks. Part of the 180-mile **Tarka Trail** cuts through the park; join it at Combe Martin, hike along the cliffs to Lynton/Lynmouth, then head across the moor towards Barnstaple.

Organised walks run by the ENPA (p269) are held throughout the year and include deer safaris, nightjar walks and dark sky strolls.

ℹ Information

INTERNET RESOURCES

Active Exmoor (www.activeexmoor.com) Info on outdoor activities.

Visit Exmoor (www.visit-exmoor.co.uk) Official visitor website with useful advice on activities, events and accommodation.

TOURIST INFORMATION

There are three **Exmoor National Park Authority** (ENPA; www.exmoor-nationalpark.gov.uk) tourist offices.

Dulverton Tourist Office (☑ 01398-323841; www.exmoor-nationalpark.gov.uk; 7-9 Fore St, Dulverton; ⊙10am-5pm)

Dunster Tourist Office (☑ 01643-821835; www.exmoor-nationalpark.gov.uk; Dunster Steep, Dunster; ⊙10am-5pm)

Lynmouth Tourist Office (☑ 01598-752509; www.exmoor-nationalpark.gov.uk; The Esplanade, Lynmouth; ⊙10am-5pm)

ℹ Getting Around

The **MoorRover** (☑ 01643-709701) is an on-demand minibus that can take you anywhere on Exmoor. Prices range from £10 to £30, depending on distances involved. It'll also carry bikes and provide a luggage transfer service. Book at least a day ahead.

Exmoor's bus routes are listed at the **ExploreMoor** (www.exploremoor.co.uk) website. Be aware: some services are seasonal, and the more remote ones are particularly prone to change.

300 (one to three daily Monday to Saturday, no Sunday service October to May) Heads along the coast from the resort of Minehead to Lynmouth, via Porlock. One to two services go onto Ilfracombe on Saturday and Sunday.

309/310 (nine daily, Monday to Saturday) Year round; runs from Barnstaple, via Parracombe to Lynmouth.

398 (six daily Monday to Saturday) Year round; cuts through the moor from Minehead to Tiverton via Dunster, Wheddon Cross and Dulverton. One bus a day stops at Exford.

Dulverton

POP 1500

The southern gateway to Exmoor National Park, Dulverton sits at the base of the Barle Valley near the confluence of two key rivers: the Exe and Barle. A traditional country town, it's home to a collection of gun-sellers,

> ### STARGAZING ON EXMOOR
>
> All over Exmoor people are chuffed to bits that it's been named Europe's first International Dark Sky Reserve. The ENPA runs free night-time stargazing strolls; eerie hilltop hikes where the inky blackness is punctuated by mesmerising constellations. The authority's (free) Dark Sky Discovery leaflets feature star-charts and maps. For optimum views, central, higher Exmoor is best; try the hills around Dunkery Beacon.

fishing-tackle stores and gift shops, and makes an attractive edge-of moor base.

◉ Sights

Tarr Steps　　　　　　　　　LANDMARK
(⊙24hr) FREE Exmoor's most famous landmark is an ancient stone clapper bridge shaded by gnarled old trees. Its huge slabs are propped up on stone columns embedded in the River Barle. Local folklore aside (which declares it was used by the devil for sunbathing), it first pops into the historical record in the 1600s and has had to be rebuilt after 21st-century floods. The steps are signed off the B3223 Dulverton to Simonsbath road 5 miles northwest of Dulverton.

Or hike there from Dulverton along the banks of the River Barle (12 miles return).

🛏 Sleeping

★ Streamcombe Farm　　　　　B&B ££
(✆01398-323775; www.streamcombefarm.co.uk; Streamcombe Lane, near Dulverton; s £60-65, d £75-100; ℗) In this enchanting, 18th-century farmhouse stylish, rustic-chic bedrooms feature chimney breasts and reclaimed joists, and the only sounds are the sheep, deer and pheasants outside. There's woodland camping (per person £10) and a two-person shepherd's hut (£75) too.

Town Mills　　　　　　　　　B&B ££
(✆01398-323124; www.townmillsdulverton.co.uk; High St; s/d £85/95; ℗🖈) The top choice if you want to stay in town is a thoroughly contemporary riverside mill with creamy carpets, magnolia walls and bursts of floral art.

Tarr Farm　　　　　　　　　HOTEL £££
(✆01643-851507; www.tarrfarm.co.uk; Tarr Steps; s/d £85/150; ℗) This is the place to really lose yourself: a farmhouse nested among the woods near Tarr Steps, 7 miles from Dulverton. The nine rooms are spacious and luxurious, with spoil-yourself extras like organic bath goodies and homemade biscuits.

🍴 Eating

Exclusive Cake Co　　　　　　BAKERY £
(www.exclusivecakecompany.co.uk; 19 High St; items from £3; ⊙9am-5pm Mon-Fri, to 2pm Sat) Real rarities stack the shelves here: Exmoor ale, cheese and wholegrain mustard bread; Somerset cider cake; venison and port pie (note the typically Exmoor warning: 'Game pies may contain lead shot').

Mortimers　　　　　　　　　CAFE £
(✆01398-323850; 13 High St; mains from £6; ⊙9.30am-5.15pm Thu-Tue) Top-class teas (including many rare estate varieties) are the order of the day at this charmingly frilly and floral tearoom, but it's worth leaving room for the Welsh rarebits and crumbly cakes.

★ Woods　　　　　　　　　BISTRO £££
(✆01398-324007; www.woodsdulverton.co.uk; 4 Bank Sq; mains £19; ⊙noon-2pm & 6-9.30pm) Woods has country-but-classy down to a fine art, both in decor and dishes. Deer antlers hang on rough stone walls, and trestle tables sit beside wood-panelled booths. Exmoor beef, lamb, pigeon and cheeses fill the menu; truffle purée, pickled mushrooms and caramelised walnuts add élan.

Lynton & Lynmouth

Tucked in amid precipitous cliffs and steep, tree-lined slopes, these twin coastal towns are a landscape painter's dream. Bustling Lynmouth sits beside the shore, a busy harbour lined with pubs and souvenir shops. On the cliff top, Lynton feels much more genteel and well-to-do. A cliffside railway links the two; it's powered by the rushing West Lyn river, which feeds numerous cascades and waterfalls nearby.

◉ Sights

Cliff Railway　　　　　　HERITAGE RAILWAY
(✆01598-753486; www.cliffrailwaylynton.co.uk; adult single/return £2.50/3.50, child £1.50/2; ⊙10am-5pm Feb-Oct, to 7pm Jun-Aug) This extraordinary piece of Victorian engineering sees two cars linked by a steel cable descend or ascend the sloping cliff face according to the weight of water in the cars' tanks. All burnished wood and polished brass, it's

been running since 1890 and makes for an unmissable ride.

Flood Memorial Hall   INTERPRETATION CENTRE
(The Esplanade, Lynmouth; ⊙9am-5pm Easter-Oct) FREE On 16 August 1952 a huge wave of water swept through Lynmouth after torrential rain. The devastation was immense – 34 people lost their lives; four bridges and countless houses were washed away. This exhibition features a scale model of the pre-flood village, photos of the destroyed buildings and personal testimonies of those involved.

🏃 Activities

Popular hiking trails among Lynton and Lynmouth's spectacular scenery include ones to the lighthouse at Foreland Point, to Watersmeet, 2 miles east of Lynmouth (reached via the gorgeous East Lyn River glade), and along the scenic Glen Lyn Gorge.

Valley of the Rocks   WALKING
The dramatic geology in this valley was described by poet Robert Southey as 'rock reeling upon rock, stone piled upon stone, a huge terrifying reeling mass'. Look out for the formations dubbed the Devil's Cheesewring and Ragged Jack – and also the feral goats that wander the tracks. It's a mile's walk west of Lynton along a cracking coast path.

🛏 Sleeping

⭐**Rock House**   B&B ££
(☑01598-753508; www.rock-house.co.uk; Manor Green, Lynmouth; s £45, d £100-120) The setting is simply superb: set right on Lynmouth's pocket-sized harbour, steep hills slope up on three sides. Contemporary rooms sport leather headboards, lilac scatter-cushions and mini-armchairs. All have extraordinary views; the best is number four, where the window is next to the beach.

North Walk House   B&B ££
(☑01598-753372; www.northwalkhouse.co.uk; North Walk, Lynton; d £60-80; P🐾) Stripped wooden floors, stripy bedspreads and colourful rugs give North Walk House a gently funky feel. The views over the sea and rugged cliffs are fantastic, while the all-organic breakfasts feature Exmoor bacon and sausages, and Aga-baked eggs.

Castle Hill   B&B ££
(☑01598-752291; www.castlehill.biz; Castle Hill, Lynton; d £70-95, f £140; 🐾) Despite a stately

Victorian exterior, the rooms in this central Lynton guesthouse are decidedly modern; oatmeal colours combine with chunky wood furniture and the odd cherry-red settee. The mini-suites have tiny balconies with fine hill and town views.

⭐**Millers at the Tors**   BOUTIQUE HOTEL £££
(☑01598-753236; www.millerslynmouth.co.uk; Countisbury Hill, Lynmouth; d £180-300; P) With lashings of sculpture, paintings and exotic artefacts, eccentric doesn't even begin to describe this objet d'art–packed enclave. It was set up by the late Martin Miller, of the *Miller's Antiques* books, which explains the delightfully over-the-top furnishings. It's set partway up precipitous Countisbury Hill, which explains the wraparound views.

🍴 Eating

Charlie Friday's   CAFE £
(www.charliefridays.co.uk; Church Hill, Lynton; items from £3; ⊙10am-5pm Feb-Nov) A funky, friendly hang-out serving melting pastries, thick sarnies and fair-trade, two-shot espresso that really packs a punch.

Rising Sun   FUSION ££
(☑01598-753223; www.risingsunlynmouth.co.uk; mains £12-19; ⊙noon-2.30pm & 6-9pm) Head chef Ben Meill delights in pairing Westcountry produce with European flavours, so tuck into soft, seared scallops with crisp pancetta, or crab with coriander and lime. The building itself has plenty of smugglers' character too, with higgledy-piggledy floors and hefty beams.

ℹ Information

Lynmouth has an ENPA tourist office (p269).

ℹ HOSTELS & CAMPING BARNS

The only YHA hostel inside Exmoor National Park is at Exford (☑0845 3719 634; www.yha.org.uk; Exe Mead; dm £18; P). For more basic accommodation, there are camping barns at Mullacott Farm (YHA; ☑0800 0191 700; www.yha.org.uk; Mullacott Cross, near Ilfracombe; per person £10) near Ilfracombe and Northcombe Farm (YHA; ☑0800 0191 700; www.yha.org.uk; Hollam, near Dulverton; per person £9) near Dulverton; you'll need all the usual camping supplies.

Porlock & Around

POP 2300

The coastal village of Porlock is one of the prettiest on the north Exmoor coast; the huddle of thatched cottages lining its main street is framed on one side by the sea, and on the other by houses clinging to the steeply sloping hills behind. Winding lanes lead to the charismatic breakwater of Porlock Weir, 2 miles to the west, with its arching pebble beach and striking coastal views.

◉ Sights

Holnicote Estate   HISTORIC BUILDINGS
(NT; ☑ 01823-451587; www.nationaltrust.org.uk; near Porlock; ⊙24hr; P) **FREE** The 5060-hectare Holnicote Estate sweeps southeast out of Porlock, taking in a string of impossibly pretty villages. Picturesque Bossington leads to charming Allerford, with its 15th-century packhorse bridge. The biggest, Selworthy, offers eye-catching Exmoor views, a cafe, shop, and cob-and-thatch cottages clustering around the village green.

⬛ Sleeping & Eating

★ Millers at the Anchor   BOUTIQUE HOTEL **££**
(☑ 01643-862753; www.millersuk.com/anchor; Porlock Weir; s £65-95, d £90-155; P🖥) Stuffed with antiques, overflowing with piled-up books, and scattered with exotic rugs, Millers delivers an enjoyably overwhelming dose of English eccentricity. Gilt-framed mirrors jostle with marble busts, vast beds and captivating views of Porlock Weir. But the chess set in the lounge and the quirky home cinema may tempt you from your room.

ⓘ DRIVING TO PORLOCK

If you're driving, you can choose from two picturesque routes into Porlock village. The New Road Toll Road sweeps through pine forests and round U-bends, while Porlock Hill (A39) is a brake-burning 1:4 descent. Another toll road, the Porlock Scenic (Worthy) Toll Road, provides an alternative, bouncing, route up out of Porlock Weir.

Culbone   BRITISH **££**
(☑ 01643-862259; www.theculbone.com; near Porlock; mains £13-25; ⊙noon-10pm Tue-Sat, to 4pm Sun; P) The menu at this smart restaurant (with rooms) is stuffed with local produce – plump for the 28-day aged Devon-red steaks and choose from three different cuts or a huge chateaubriand for two. The contemporary-chic setting, with slate floors and black leather chairs, runs into the upstairs rooms (£85 to £100).

Ship Inn   PUB **£**
(www.shipinnporlock.co.uk; High St, Porlock; mains £8-16; ⊙noon-2.30pm & 6-9pm; P) Coleridge and pal Robert Southey both downed pints in this thatched Porlock inn – you can even sit in 'Southey's Corner'. Substantial pub food – mainly steaks, roasts and stews – is served in the bar, and there are 10 light bedrooms (doubles £70) in pine and cream.

ⓘ Information

Porlock Tourist Office (☑ 01643-863150; www.porlock.co.uk; High St, Porlock; ⊙10am-5pm Mon-Sat, to 1pm Sun)

Dunster

POP 850

Centred on a scarlet-walled castle and a medieval yarn market, Dunster is one of Exmoor's oldest villages, a tempting tangle of cobbled streets, bubbling brooks and packhorse bridges.

◉ Sights

Dunster Castle   CASTLE
(NT; ☑ 01643-821314; www.nationaltrust.org.uk; adult/child £9.30/4.60; ⊙11am-5pm Mar-Oct; P) Rosy-hued Dunster Castle crowns a densely wooded hill. Built by the Luttrell family, who once owned much of northern Exmoor, the oldest sections are 13th century, although the turrets and exterior walls are 19th-century additions. Look out for Tudor furnishings, 17th-century plasterwork and a ridiculously grand staircase. Leave time to explore the colourful terraced gardens, with their riverside walks and views across Exmoor's shores.

St George's Church   CHURCH
Dunster's beautiful church dates mostly from the 15th century and boasts an intricately carved fan-vaulted rood screen. Just behind the church is a 16th-century dovecote, used for breeding edible squabs (young pigeons) for the dinner table at Dunster Castle.

Watermill
MILL

(📞 01643-821759; Mill Lane; adult/child £3.75/2.75; ⏰ 11am-4.45pm Apr-Oct) Most of the original cogs, wheels and grinding stones still rotate away in this working 18th-century mill. There's a picturesque riverside tearoom alongside.

🛏 Sleeping & Eating

Mill Stream Cottage
B&B ££

(📞 01643-821966; www.millstreamcottagedunster. co.uk; 2 Mill Lane; s £55, d £74-84) In the 1600s this was Dunster's workhouse, but now it's a sweet-as-pie guesthouse with country-cottage-style rooms. There are homemade cakes on arrival and home-baked biscuits on the tea tray, plus an oh-so-comfy guest lounge, where you can snooze in front of the wood-burner.

Dunster Castle Hotel
HOTEL ££

(📞 01643-823030; www.thedunstercastlehotel.co. uk; 5 High St; d £70-160; ⏰ noon-2.30pm & 6-9pm; 🛜) Everything feels rich in this former coaching inn, from the dark purple furnishings and gleaming wooden furniture, to the plush, heraldic-style throws. The bar is comfy, while the buzzy restaurant (mains £14 to £22) specialises in intense flavours; expect beef with chorizo, and scallops with air-dried ham.

Spears Cross
B&B ££

(📞 01643-821439; www.spearscross.co.uk; 1 West St; d £97-107; 🅿 🛜) One for the connoisseur – of cuisine and beams. Age-old elm supports are everywhere, along with panels, floral furnishings and raspberry-red walls. Breakfast features bucks fizz with freshly squeezed orange juice, home-cured bacon, locally smoked trout and spelt and honey artesanal bread.

Reeve's
BRITISH ££

(📞 01643-821414; www.reevesrestaurantdunster. co.uk; 20 High St; mains £12-25; ⏰ noon-1.30pm Sat & Sun, 7-9pm Tue-Sat) Seriously stylish Reeve's dishes up Dunster's best food. Complex, satisfying creations include piled-up confit of duck and chicken, saffron-fragranced turbot, and a still-warm, zesty lemon meringue.

Cobblestones
CAFE ££

(📞 01643-821595; www.cobblestonesofdunster.co. uk; 24 High St; mains £5-10; ⏰ 10am-3.30pm daily, 6.30-8.30pm Wed-Sat) Plump for a ham or cheese platter or potted prawns on toast at this village cafe, or drop in for a superior cream tea.

ℹ Getting There & Awa
Bus 28 stops at Dunster on its way b…
Taunton and Minehead (£4, half-hour
to Saturday, hourly on Sunday).

The **West Somerset Railway** (📞 01…
704996; www.west-somerset-railway.…uk;
24hr rover ticket adult/child £17/8.50) stops at Dunster during the summer, with four to seven trains daily from May to October.

DEVON

Devon offers freedom. Its rippling, beach-fringed landscape is studded with historic homes, vibrant cities and wild, wild moors. So here you can ditch schedules and to-do lists and hike a rugged coast path, take a scenic boat trip, or get lost in hedge-lined lanes that aren't even on your map. Discover collegiate Exeter, touristy Torquay, yachting haven Dartmouth and alternative Totnes. Or escape to wilderness Dartmoor and the remote, surf-dashed north coast. Sample wine made from the vines beside you and food that's fresh from field, furrow or sea. Go surfing, cycling, kayaking, horse riding, sea xswimming and barefoot beachcombing. Heading to Devon? Then prepare for freedom and sandy feet.

ℹ Information
Visit Devon (www.visitdevon.co.uk)

ℹ Getting Around
Traveline South West (www.travelinesw.com) Searchable database of bus and train times.

BUS
The Devon interactive **bus map** (www.journeydevon.info) helps in route-planning. Central Dartmoor is covered by a fleet of smaller operators.

First (www.firstgroup.com) A key operator in Plymouth and south Devon.

Stagecoach Devon (www.stagecoachbus.com) Runs services around Exeter, north Devon, south Dartmoor and Torquay.

Bus Passes
First Seven Day (adult/child/family £37/23/58) Weeklong pass for most First buses in Devon.

Firstday Southwest (adult/child £7.40/5.30) A day's unlimited bus travel on First buses in Devon and Cornwall.

MegaRiderGold (1/4 weeks £26/94) Unlimited travel on all southwest Stagecoach buses.

ecoach Explorer (adult/child/family .50/5/15) One day's travel on Stagecoach's southwest network.

TRAIN

Devon's main line skirts southern Dartmoor, running from Exeter to Plymouth and on to Cornwall. Branch lines include the 39-mile Exeter–Barnstaple Tarka Line, the 15-mile Plymouth–Gunnislake Tamar Valley Line and the scenic Exeter–Torquay Paignton line.

Freedom of Devon & Cornwall Rover Allows unlimited train travel in Devon and Cornwall for three days out of seven (adult/child £45/23), or eight days out of 15 (£65/39).

Exeter & Around

POP 117,800

Well heeled and comfortable, Exeter exudes evidence of its centuries-old role as the spiritual and administrative heart of Devon. The city's Gothic cathedral presides over pockets of cobbled streets; medieval and Georgian buildings, and fragments of the Roman city stretch out all around. A snazzy new shopping centre brings bursts of the modern, thousands of university students ensure a buzzing nightlife, and the vibrant quayside acts as a launch pad for cycling or kayaking trips. Throw in some stylish places to stay and eat and you have a relaxed but lively base for explorations.

History

Exeter's past can be read in its buildings. The Romans marched in around AD 55 – their 17-hectare fortress included a 2-mile defensive wall, crumbling sections of which remain, especially in Rougemont and Northernhay Gardens. Saxon and Norman times saw growth: a castle went up in 1068, the cathedral 40 years later. The Tudor wool boom brought Exeter an export trade, riches and half-timbered houses; prosperity continued into the Georgian era when hundreds of merchants built genteel homes. The Blitz of WWII brought devastation. In 1942, in just one night 156 people died and 12 hectares of the city were flattened. In the 21st century the £220 million Princesshay Shopping Centre has added shimmering glass and steel lines to the architectural mix.

◉ Sights

★ **Exeter Cathedral**   CATHEDRAL
(Cathedral Church of St Peter; ☑01392-285983; www.exeter-cathedral.org.uk; The Close; adult/child

£6/free; ⊙9.30am-4.45pm Mon-Sat, 11.30am-3.30pm Sun) Magnificent in warm, honey-coloured stone, Exeter's cathedral is one of Devon's most prestigious sights. Dating largely from the 12th and 13th centuries, one end of the exterior is framed by extraordinary medieval statuary, while inside the ceiling is mesmerising – the longest unbroken Gothic vaulting in the world, it sweeps up to meet ornate ceiling bosses in gilt and vibrant colours. Other highlights include elegant wood carvings and striking sculptures.

The site has been a religious one since at least the 5th century but the Normans started the current building in 1114; the towers of today's cathedral date from that period. In 1270 a 90-year remodelling process began, introducing a mix of Early English and Decorated Gothic styles.

Above the Great West Front scores of weather-worn figures line a once brightly painted screen that now forms England's largest collection of 14th-century sculpture. Inside, the exquisitely symmetrical ceiling soars up and along, towards the north transept and the 15th-century Exeter Clock: in keeping with medieval astronomy it shows the earth as a golden ball at the centre of the universe with the sun, a fleur-de-lys, travelling round. Still ticking and whirring, it chimes on the hour.

The huge oak canopy over the Bishop's Throne was carved in 1312, while the 1350 minstrels' gallery is decorated with 12 angels playing musical instruments. Cathedral staff will point out the famous sculpture of the lady with two left feet and the tiny St James Chapel, built to repair the one destroyed in the Blitz. Look out for its unusual carvings: a cat, a mouse and, oddly, a rugby player.

The Roof Tours (p275) are superb; as are the 45-minute ground-floor guided tours (incl in admission; ⊙11am, 12.30pm & 2.30pm Mon-Sat). Evocative choral evensong services are held at 5.30pm Monday to Friday, and 4pm Saturday and Sunday.

In the adjoining Refectory (Serlo's; mains £6; ⊙10am-4.45pm Mon-Sat) you can tuck into cakes, quiches and soups at trestle tables surrounded by vaulted ceilings, stained glass and busts of the great, the good and the dead.

★ **Underground Passages**   UNDERGROUND
(☑01392-665887; www.exeter.gov.uk/passages; Paris St; adult/child £6/4; ⊙9.30am-5.30pm Mon-Sat, 10am-4pm Sun Jun-Sep, 11.30am-4pm Tue-Sun Oct-May) Prepare to crouch down, don a hard

hat and possibly get spooked in what is the only publicly accessible system of its kind in England. These medieval vaulted passages were built to house pipes bringing fresh water to the city. Guides lead you on a scramble through the network telling tales of ghosts, escape routes and cholera. The last tour is an hour before closing; they're popular – book ahead.

★ RAMM   MUSEUM
(Royal Albert Memorial Museum & Art Gallery; ☑01392-265858; www.rammuseum.org.uk; Queen St; ⊙10am-5pm Tue-Sun) FREE The imposing, red-brick exterior looks every inch the Victorian museum, but a £24 million revamp has brought the exhibits bang up to date. Interactive displays focus on Exeter's heritage from prehistory to the present, as well as global exploration and the concept of collecting. Look out for Exeter's Roman-era artefacts, local Tudor carvings and the striking ethnographic displays which include African masks, samurai armour and the mummy of Shep en-Mut.

Bill Douglas Centre   MUSEUM
(☑01392-724321; www.billdouglas.org; Old Library, Prince of Wales Rd; ⊙10am-5pm; ℗) FREE A delightful homage to film and fun, the Bill Douglas Centre is a compact collection of all things celluloid, from magic lanterns to Mickey Mouse. Inside discover just what the butler did see and why the flicks are called the flicks. Among the mass of movie memorabilia are Charlie Chaplin bottle stoppers, Ginger Rogers playing cards, James Bond board games and Star Wars toys. It's set on the Exeter University campus, a mile northwest of the city centre.

St Nicholas Priory   HISTORIC BUILDING
(☑01392-265858; www.exeter.gov.uk/priory; The Mint; adult/child £4.20/1.60; ⊙10am-5pm Sat, plus Mon-Fri school holidays) For a vivid glimpse of life inside a late-Elizabethan town house, head to this 900-year-old former Benedictine monastery. Its beautiful russet stone walls shelter interiors alive with brightly coloured furnishings, elaborate plaster ceilings and intricate oak panelling.

Powderham Castle   HISTORIC BUILDING
(☑01626-890243; www.powderham.co.uk; adult/child £11/10; ⊙11am-4.30pm Sun-Fri Apr-Oct; ℗) The historic, and current, home of the Earl of Devon, Powderham is a stately but still friendly place that was built in 1391 and remodelled in the Victorian era. A visit takes

CATHEDRAL ROOF TOURS

DON'T MISS

CATHEDRAL ROOF TOURS

For a sensational view of Exeter Cathedral (p274) book one of these high-rise guided walks (☑01392-285983; www.exeter-cathedral.org.uk; adult/child £10/5; ⊙2pm Tue-Thu, 11am Sat Apr-Sep). Climb 251 steps up spiral staircases, head out onto the sweeping roof, then gaze down on the city from the edge of the North Tower. They're popular so book two weeks ahead.

in a fine wood-panelled Great Hall, parkland with 650 deer and glimpses of life 'below stairs' in the kitchen. Powderham is on the River Exe near Kenton, 8 miles south of Exeter. Bus 2 runs from Exeter (£3.80, 30 minutes, every 20 minutes Monday to Saturday).

A La Ronde   HISTORIC BUILDING
(NT; ☑01395-265514; www.nationaltrust.org.uk; Summer Lane; adult/child £8/4; ⊙11am-5pm early Feb-Oct, noon-4pm Sat & Sun Nov-Jan; ℗) This quirky 16-sided cottage was built in 1796 so two spinster cousins could display a mass of curiosities acquired on their 10-year European grand tour. Its glass alcoves, low lintels and tiny doorways mean it's like clambering through a doll's house – highlights are a delicate feather frieze in the drawing room and a gallery smothered with a thousand seashells. The house is 10 miles south of Exeter, near Exmouth; bus 57 (£4.30, 30 minutes, every 15 minutes) runs close by.

Activities

The River Exe and the Exeter Canal are framed by foot and cycle paths which wind south from the Quay, past pubs, beside an ever-broadening estuary towards the sea, 10 miles away.

Saddles & Paddles   OUTDOORS
(☑01392-424241; www.sadpad.com; Exeter Quay; ⊙9azzm-6pm) Rents out bikes (adult per hour/day £6/15), kayaks (£10/35) and Canadian canoes (£15/50); the tourist office stocks maps.

Tours

★ Redcoat Tours   WALKING TOUR
(☑01392-265203; www.exeter.gov.uk/visiting; ⊙3-6pm daily Apr-Oct, 2 daily Nov-Mar) FREE For an informed and entertaining introduction to Exeter's history, tag along on one of these

Exeter

Exeter

◎ Top Sights
1	Exeter Cathedral	C3
2	RAMM	C2
3	Underground Passages	D2

◎ Sights
4	St Nicholas Priory	B3

◉ Activities, Courses & Tours
	Exeter Cathedral Guided Tours	(see 1)
	Exeter Cathedral Roof Tours	(see 1)
5	Redcoat Tours	C3
6	Saddles & Paddles	C4

◎ Sleeping
7	ABode Exeter	C3
8	Globe Backpackers	C4
9	Magdalen Chapter	D4
10	Raffles	D1

11	Townhouse	A1
12	White Hart	C4

◎ Eating
13	@Angela's	B4
14	Herbies	B3
15	Michael Caines	C3
	Refectory	(see 1)
16	Ruby	C2
17	Rusty Bike	C1

◎ Drinking & Nightlife
18	Mamma Stone's	B3
19	Old Firehouse	D2
20	Timepiece	C2

◎ Entertainment
21	Bike Shed	B3
22	Exeter Picturehouse	B4
23	Phoenix	C2

1½-hour tours. Themes range from murder and trade to the Tudors and religion – there are even torchlit prowls through the catacombs and evening ghost walks. Tours leave from Cathedral Yard or the Quay; there's no need to book.

Sleeping

★ Wood Life   CAMPSITE £
(☑ 01392-832509; www.thewoodlife.org; The Linhay; 5/7 nights from £550/800; ☺ Apr–Oct; P) The trappings that come with this luxurious, six-person safari-style tent don't just include brass bedsteads draped with Egyptian cotton and thick rugs on decked floors. There's also a firepit (plus campfire kettle), tub of fresh herbs and vintage games chest. Add firewood-warmed showers and your very own 3.5-hectare wood, and you have comfy camping heaven. It's on the outskirts of Kenn village, 7 miles south of Exeter.

Globe Backpackers   HOSTEL £
(☑ 01392-215521; www.exeterbackpackers.co.uk; 71 Holloway St; dm/d £17.50/45; P ☎) Rightly a firm favourite among budget travellers, this spotlessly clean, relaxed, rambling house boasts three doubles, roomy dorms and wet room showers that are positively luxurious.

ABode Exeter   HOTEL ££
(☑ 01392-319955; www.abodehotels.co.uk/exeter; Cathedral Yard; r £90-300; ☎) At ABode, Georgian grandeur meets minimalist chic. Wonky floors and stained glass combine with recessed lighting, pared-down furniture and neutral tones. The rooms range from 'comfortable' and 'enviable' to 'fabulous', where slanted ceilings frame grandstand cathedral views. Prices depend on availability; book ahead to bag bargains.

Raffles   B&B ££
(☑ 01392-270200; www.raffles-exeter.co.uk; 11 Blackall Rd; s/d/f £55/78/88; P ☎) The antique dealer owner has peppered each room of this late-Victorian town house with heritage features – look out for Bakelite radios, wooden plant stands and polished trunks. Largely organic breakfasts and a walled garden add to the appeal.

White Hart   INN ££
(☑ 01392-279897; www.whitehartpubexeter.co.uk; 66 South St; s/d £74/84; P ☎) They've been putting people up here since the Plantagenets were on the throne in the 1300s. The courtyard is a wisteria-fringed bobble of cobbles and the bar is book-lined and

beamed. Rooms are tasteful modern affairs with suede chairs, honey and gold hues and glinting bathrooms.

Townhouse   B&B ££
(☑ 01392-494994; www.townhouseexeter.co.uk; 54 St David's Hill; s/d/f £40/80/90; P ☎) Expect simple but delightful rooms with stripped wooden floors and clean, pared-down lines, spiced up by dashes of intense colour. The Victorian exterior drips with ivy and all the rooms are named after literary characters – will you opt for Moneypenny, Lorna Doone or Darcy?

★ Magdalen Chapter   BOUTIQUE HOTEL £££
(☑ 01392-281000; www.themagdalenchapter.com; Magdalen St; d £160-250; @ ☎ ☀) Undoubtedly Exeter's coolest hotel (staff wear Converse trainers and low-slung slacks) the Magdalen is replete with funky flourishes. Lush purple corridors lead to dove-grey bedrooms, each with iPad, coffee machine, complimentary mini bar and mood lighting. There's even a tiny, heated outdoor pool that leads into an indoor enclave made toasty by a log burner.

Eating

★ Rusty Bike   MODERN BRITISH ££
(☑ 01392-214440; www.rustybike-exeter.co.uk; 67 Howell Rd; mains £15-19; ☺ 6-10pm daily, noon-3pm Sat & Sun) A vintage football table and bashed-about chairs set the scene for some seriously stylish rustic cuisine. Menus change daily depending on deliveries from local suppliers. So expect rarities like confit goose and pistachio; beef chuck and carrots; or truffle-laced pheasant breast – delivered, of course, by the local gamekeeper.

Ruby   BURGERS ££
(www.rubyburgers.com; 74 Queen St; mains £5.50-10; ☺ 10am-10pm) The vibe might be retro-hip,

WORTH A TRIP

RIVER COTTAGE CANTEEN

TV chef Hugh Fearnley-Whittingstall campaigns on sustainable food, so it's fitting his east Devon canteen (☎ 01297-631715; www.rivercottage.net; Trinity Sq, Axminster; mains £8-16; ⊙ 9am-5pm daily, 6.30-9pm Tue-Sat; ☑), 30 miles east of Exeter, champions local, seasonal and organic ingredients. Hearty flavours feature cured wild boar, venison scotch eggs, and sharing platters of local meats, fish and cheese. Drinks include Stinger Beer; brewed from (carefully) hand-picked Dorset nettles. Alternatively, book a four-course gastronomic delight at the nearby River Cottage HQ (☎ 01297-630300; www.rivercottage.net; 2-course lunch £55, 4-course dinner £70-90; ⊙ noon-3pm Sun, 7.30-11pm Fri & Sat); booking required. There's another River Cottage Canteen in Plymouth (p289).

but the focus on prime local ingredients is pure zeitgeist: succulent beef patties from Devon herds, outdoor-reared pork, free-range chicken. Add Devon Blue cheese and edge-of-Exeter veg and you have modern-diner dining that's a cut above the rest.

Herbies VEGETARIAN ££
(15 North St; mains £7-11; ⊙ 11am-2.30pm Mon-Sat, 6.30-9.30pm Tue-Sat; ☑) Cosy and gently groovy, Herbies has been cheerfully feeding Exeter's veggies for more than 20 years. Tuck into delicious Tuscan mushrooms, Moroccan tagine or butter bean, thyme and squash risotto. They take good culinary care of vegans too.

★ **Michael Caines** FINE DINING £££
(☎ 01392-319955; www.michaelcaines.com; Cathedral Yard; mains £24; ⊙ noon-2.30pm & 6-9pm Mon-Sat) Run by the eponymous, double Michelin-starred chef, the food here is a complex blend of prime Westcountry ingredients and full-bodied French flavours. Gastronomes linger over the seven-course tasting menu (£65), but the set lunches (two/three courses £13/18) are some of the best deals in town.

@Angela's MODERN BRITISH £££
(☎ 01392-499038; www.angelasrestaurant.co.uk; 38 New Bridge St; mains £20; ⊙ 6-9.30pm Mon-Sat) Dedication to sourcing local ingredients sometimes sees the chef here rising before dawn to bag the best fish at Brixham Market. The garlic-infused roasted monkfish is worth the trip alone, while the Devon duck is made memorable by a rich caramelised orange sauce. Also open for reservations only at lunch Friday and Saturday.

🍷 Drinking & Nightlife

★ **Old Firehouse** PUB
(www.oldfirehouseexeter.co.uk; 50 New North Rd; ⊙ noon-2am Mon-Wed, to 3am Thu-Sat, to 1am Sun)

Step into the snug, candlelit interior of this Exeter institution and feel instantly at home. Here, dried hops hang from rafters above flagstone floors and walls of exposed stone. The range of draught ciders and cask ales is truly impressive while the pizzas, served after 9pm, have kept countless students fed.

Timepiece CLUB
(www.timepiecenightclub.co.uk; Little Castle St; ⊙ 9.30pm-1.30am Mon-Wed, 10pm-2am Fri & Sat) DJ sets range from salsa (Tuesday) and indie electro (Friday), to multi-genre club classics on Saturday nights.

☆ Entertainment

Mamma Stone's LIVE MUSIC
(www.mamastones.com; 1 Mary Arches St; ⊙ 6pm-midnight) A cool venue showcasing everything from acoustic sets to pop, folk and jam nights; many of the acts have been schooled at the artist-development program which operates alongside. Mama Stone's daughter, Joss (yes, *the* Joss Stone) plays sometimes too. It's open 9pm to 3am when bands play.

Phoenix PERFORMING ARTS
(www.exeterphoenix.org.uk; Gandy St; ⊙ 10am-11pm Mon-Sat; ☎) Exeter's art and soul; the Phoenix is a buzzing blend of indy cinema, performance space, galleries and a cool cafe-bar (snacks to 9pm).

Exeter Picturehouse CINEMA
(☎ 0871 902 5730; www.picturehouses.co.uk; 51 Bartholomew St West) An intimate, independent cinema, screening mainstream and art-house movies.

Bike Shed THEATRE
(☎ 01392-434169; www.bikeshedtheatre.co.uk; 162 Fore St; ⊙ noon-midnight Mon-Thu, to 2am Fri & Sat, 5-11pm Sun) Emerging writers are profiled in the Bike Shed's rough 'n' ready subterranean,

brick-lined performance space. Its vintage cocktail bar makes a hip setting for live music and DJ sets on Friday and Saturday nights.

❶ Information

Exeter Library (Castle St; per 30min £3; ⊙9am-6pm Mon, Tue, Thu & Fri, 10am-5pm Wed, 9am-4pm Sat; 🛜) Internet access and free wi-fi.

Main Tourist Office (📋01392-665700; www. heartofdevon.com; Dix's Field; ⊙9.30am-4.30pm)

Police Station (📋08452-777444; Heavitree Rd; ⊙24hr)

Royal Devon & Exeter Hospital (Barrack Rd) Accident and emergency.

Tourist Office at the Quay (📋01392-271611; www.heartofdevon.com; The Quay; ⊙10am-5pm Apr-Oct, 11am-4pm Sat & Sun Nov-Mar)

❶ Getting There & Away

AIR

Exeter International (www.exeter-airport. co.uk) Flights connect with Europe and the UK, including Amsterdam, Glasgow, the Isles of Scilly, Manchester, Newcastle and Paris, plus the Channel Islands.

BUS

Services include:

Bude (£6.50, two hours, five daily Monday to Saturday) Bus X9; runs via Okehampton.

Jurassic Coast Bus/Bus X53 Four to six daily to Lyme Regis (£7), Weymouth (£7.20) and Poole (£7.20); no service on winter Sundays.

Moretonhampstead (£3.50, one hour, six daily Monday to Saturday) Bus 359.

Plymouth (£6.50, 1¼ hours, two-hourly Monday to Saturday, three on Sunday) Bus X38.

Totnes (£5.80, 50 minutes, seven daily Monday to Saturday, two on Sunday) Bus X64.

Transmoor Link/Bus 82 Runs on summer Saturdays and Sundays only (mid-May to mid-September), making one trip each way from Exeter to Tavistock (£5.80) via Moretonhampstead, Postbridge, Princetown and Yelverton.

TRAIN

Main-line trains stopping at Exeter St David's include.

Barnstaple (£10, 1¼ hours, one to two hourly)

Bristol (£15, 1¼ hours, half-hourly)

Exmouth (£4, hourly, 40 minutes)

London Paddington (£46, 2½ hours, half-hourly)

Paignton (£7, 50 minutes, half-hourly)

Penzance (£15, three hours, half-hourly to hourly)

Plymouth (£9, one hour, half-hourly)

Torquay (£6, 45 minutes, half-hourly to hourly)

Totnes (£7, 35 minutes, half-hourly)

Some branch-line services also go through Exeter Central.

❶ Getting Around

TO/FROM THE AIRPORT

Bus 56 runs from the bus station and Exeter St David's train station to Exeter Airport (£2.80, 30 minutes, hourly 7am to 6pm).

BICYCLE

Saddles & Paddles (p275) rents out bikes, kayaks and canoes.

BUS

Bus H (two to four per hour) links St David's train station with Central Station and the High St, passing near the bus station.

CAR

Hire options include **Europcar** (www.europcar. co.uk).

Park & Ride buses (adult/child £2.40/1.60) operate every 20 minutes, running from Sowton (near M5, junction 30) and Matford (near M5, junction 31) Monday to Saturday, and from Honiton Rd (near M5, junction 29) daily.

TAXI

There are ranks at St David's train station and on High St and Sidwell St.

Capital Taxis (📋01392-434343; ⊙24hr)

Club Cars (📋01392-213030; ⊙24hr)

Gemini (📋01392-666666; ⊙24hr)

Torquay & Around

POP 114, 266

It may face the English Channel, rather than the Med, but the coast around Torquay has long been dubbed the English Riviera; famous for palm trees, piers and russet-red cliffs. At first glance, Torquay itself is the quintessential English seaside resort in flux, beloved by both the coach-tour crowd and stag- and hen-party animals. But a mild microclimate and an azure circle of bay have also drawn a smarter set and Torquay now competes with foodie-hub Dartmouth for fine eateries. The area also boasts unique attractions that range from an immense aviary to a surreal model village. Add an Agatha Christie connection, fishing boats and steam trains, and it all adds up to some grand days out beside the sea.

Torquay's neighbouring resort, Paignton, sits 3 miles south; the fishing port of Brixham is 5 miles further south again.

◉ Sights & Activities

Torquay boasts no fewer than 20 beaches and an impressive 22 miles of coast. Holidaymakers flock to the central (but tidal) **Torre Abbey Sands**; locals head for the sand-and-shingle beaches beside the 240ft red-clay cliffs around **Babbacombe**.

Living Coasts ZOO
(📞 0844 474 3366; www.livingcoasts.org.uk; Beacon Quay; adult/child £12/9; ⊙ 10am-5pm) An enormous open-plan aviary bringing you up close to free-roaming penguins, punk-rocker style tufted puffins and disarmingly cute bank cormorants.

Babbacombe Model Village EXHIBITION
(📞 01803-315315; www.model-village.co.uk; Hampton Ave; adult/child £11/7; ⊙ 10am-4pm) Prepare for a fabulously eccentric, 1.6-hectare world in miniature, complete with small-scale Stonehenge, football stadium, beach, castle (under attack from a fire-breathing dragon) and thatched village where firefighters are tackling a blaze. Visit in the evening for illuminations; think pocket-sized Piccadilly Circus, complete with flashing banner ads. It's open until 9pm on some summer evenings.

Paignton Zoo ZOO
(📞 0844 474 2222; www.paigntonzoo.org.uk; Totnes Rd, Paignton; adult/child £16/12; ⊙ 10am-5pm; 🅿) A conservation charity runs this innovative, 80-acre zoo, where spacious enclosures re-create habitats as varied as savannah, wetland, tropical forest and desert. High spots include the orang-utan island, vast glass-walled lion enclosure and a lemur

wood, where you walk over a plank suspension bridge as the primates leap around in the surrounding trees. Then there's the steamy crocodile swamp with pathways winding over and beside Nile, Cuban and saltwater crocs, some up to 6m long.

Babbacombe Cliff Railway HERITAGE RAILWAY
(📞 01803-328750; www.babbacombecliffrailway. co.uk; adult/child return £2/1.40; ⊙ 9.30am-4.55pm Feb-Oct) At Babbacombe a glorious 1920s funicular railway sees you climbing into a tiny wooden carriage and rattling up and down rails set into the cliff.

Ferry to Brixham FERRY TRIP
(📞 01803-882811; www.greenwayferry.co.uk; Princess Pier; adult/child return £6/4; ⊙ 12 sailings daily Apr-Oct) This blast across Tor Bay offers spray-dashed views of beaches, crumbling cliffs and grand Victorian hotels. Competition can cause prices to dip wildly; check out the stands lining Torquay's harbour.

🛏 Sleeping

Torquay Backpackers HOSTEL £
(📞 01803-299924; www.torquaybackpackers.co.uk; 119 Abbey Rd; dm/d £17/34; @🖥) Photos of grinning past guests plaster noticeboards; flags of all nations drape the walls at this budget stalwart. There are luxuries too: a DVD den and a decked, alfresco pool table terrace.

Orestone HOTEL ££
(📞 01803-328098; www.orestonemanor.com; Rock House Lane; s £90-275, d £105-190, ste £185-285; 🅿🖥) At this Georgian country house winter brings blazing log fires; summer brings breakfast on a sea-backed terrace. In the bay-view bedrooms, period elegance meets modern comforts: muted blues and greens surround snazzy bathrooms. It's all tucked

---

AGATHA CHRISTIE

Torquay is the birthplace of the 'Queen of Crime', Agatha Christie (1890–1976), author of 75 novels and 33 plays, and creator of Hercule Poirot, the moustachioed, immodest Belgian detective, and Miss Marple, the surprisingly perceptive busybody spinster. Born Agatha Miller, she grew up, courted and honeymooned in Torquay and also worked as a hospital dispenser here during WWI, thus acquiring her famous knowledge of poisons.

The tourist office stocks the free Agatha Christie Mile leaflet, which guides you round significant local sites, while **Torquay Museum** (📞 01803-293975; www.torquaymuseum. org; 529 Babbacombe Rd; adult/child £6/3; ⊙ 10am-4pm Mon-Thu & Sat) has a collection of photos, handwritten notes and displays devoted to her famous detectives. The highlight, though, is Greenway (p282), her summer home near Dartmouth. The Greenway Ferry (p283) sails there from Torquay's Princess Pier – it's best to book. Boats also go from Dartmouth and Totnes; a steam train runs from Paignton.

away in a wooded valley 3 miles north of Torquay. There's also a restaurant open noon to 2pm and 7pm to 9pm.

Seabreeze
B&B ££

(☑ 01803-322429; www.seabreezebabbacombe.co. uk; 39 Babbacombe Downs Rd; s £60-80, d £70-90; P ⌂) The smart rooms here are done out in cheery colours – choose from sea-themed aquamarine or bright 'n' breezy red, white and blue. Swish bathrooms and mini bay-view balconies seal the deal.

Headland View
B&B ££

(☑ 01803-312612; www.headlandview.com; 37 Babbacombe Downs Rd; d £72-75; P ⌂) Set high on the cliffs at Babbacombe, this delightful terrace is peppered with subtle nautical flourishes, from jaunty model lighthouses to boat motifs on the curtains. The wicker chairs on the tiny balconies have grandstand views of a cracking stretch of sea.

★ Cary Arms
BOUTIQUE HOTEL £££

(☑ 01803-327110; www.caryarms.co.uk; Babbacombe Beach; d £195-275, ste £375) The great British seaside has just gone seriously stylish. At this boutique bolthole New England tones are jazzed up by candy-striped cushions; balconies directly overlook the beach and children are given a fishing net and bait on arrival. Prices fall by up to £80 in low season.

✗ Eating & Drinking

At time of writing, sustainable seafood restaurateur Mitch Tonks was about to open one of his aclaimed Rockfish (www.therockfish.co.uk) eateries on Torquay Harbour.

Number 7
SEAFOOD ££

(☑ 01803-295055; www.no7-fish.com; 7 Beacon Tce; mains £14-20; ⏲ noon-1.45pm Wed-Sat year-round, 7-9pm daily Jul-Sep, Tue-Sat Oct-Jun) Fabulous smells fill the air at this bustling harbourside bistro, where the chalked-up menus are crowded with crab, lobster and fish fresh from the boats. Accompaniments range from garlic and brandy to Moroccan spices.

Orange Tree
MODERN BRITISH ££

(☑ 01803-213936; www.orangetreerestaurant.co. uk; 14 Park Hill Rd; mains £15-25; ⏲ 7-9pm Tue-Sat) English-meets-European cuisine here in dishes majoring in local fish, meat and game; prepare to enjoy rich Brixham crab bisque with scallops, cod with nutty Serrano ham or south Devon steaks with a Madeira and mushroom sauce.

★ The Room at the Elephant
FINE DINING £££

(☑ 01803-200044; www.elephantrestaurant.co.uk; 3 Beacon Tce; 7 courses £72; ⏲ 6.30-8.30pm Tue-Sat) A restaurant to remember. Torbay's Michelin-starred eatery is defined by a tasting menu showcasing intricate presentation and imaginative flavour fusions: Brixham crab with lovage; roe deer with onion ash; beetroot with smoked blueberries. The window frames bright marina views; a ground-floor brasserie (open noon to 2pm and 6.30pm to 9pm, Tuesday to Saturday) serves simpler fare (mains £16 to £23).

Hole in the Wall
PUB

(www.holeinthewalltorquay.co.uk; 6 Park Lane; ⏲ 11am-11pm) A heavily beamed, Tardis-like boozer with a tiny terrace; an atmospheric spot for a pint.

ℹ Information

Tourist Office (☑ 0844 474 2233; www. theenglishriviera.co.uk; Vaughan Pde, the Harbour; ⏲ 9.30am-5pm Mon-Sat)

ℹ Getting There & Away

BUS

Brixham (£4.10, 50 minutes, half-hourly) Bus 12, via Paignton.

Dartmouth (£4.50, 1¼ hours, hourly Monday to Saturday) Stagecoach Gold.

Totnes (£3.50, 45 minutes, half-hourly Monday to Saturday, seven on Sunday) Stagecoach Gold.

FERRY

Regular ferries (p280) shuttle between Torquay and Brixham.

TRAIN

Trains run from Exeter via Torquay (£6, 45 minutes, half-hourly to hourly) to Paignton (£6, 52 minutes).

Dartmouth Steam Railway (www.dartmouthrailriver.co.uk; Paignton Station; adult/child return £14/8; ⏲ 3-9 trains daily Apr-Oct) These steam trains puff from Paignton via Greenway Halt to Kingswear, which is linked by ferry (p284) to Dartmouth.

Brixham
POP 17,457

An appealing, pastel-painted tumbling of fishermen's cottages leads down to Brixham's horseshoe harbour where arcades and gift shops coexist with winding streets, brightly coloured boats and one of England's busiest fishing ports. Although picturesque, Brixham is far from a neatly packaged resort, and its brand of gritty charm offers an insight into work-a-day life along Devon's coast.

◎ Sights

Golden Hind
SAILING SHIP

(☑01803-856223; www.goldenhind.co.uk; The Quay; adult/child £4/3; ⊙10am-4pm Mar-Oct) Devon explorer Sir Francis Drake carried out a treasure-seeking circumnavigation of the globe aboard the *Golden Hind,* in the late 1500s. This full-sized replica sees you crossing the gangplank, clambering below decks, peering into the captain's cabin and prowling around the poop deck.

Brixham Heritage Museum
MUSEUM

(☑01803-856267; www.torbaymuseums.com; Bolton Cross; adult/child £2/free; ⊙10am-4pm Tue-Sat Apr-Oct, to 1pm Nov-Mar) An eclectic collection of exhibits explores the town's salty history, foscusing on sailboats, smuggling, ship-building and sea rescues.

⚐ Tours

★ Fish Market
MARKET TOUR

(☑0741 0617931; www.brixhamtourismpartnership. co.uk; The Quay; tours incl breakfast £10; ⊙twice monthly late Jun-Sep) Book early for one of these memorable, early-morning tours around a normally off-limits world. You'll see ice-lined fish trays, white-coated buyers and a bustling auction, then have breakfast at the Fishermen's Mission. If you miss a space on the tours, head to the fish market's viewing platform around 6am to watch the fleet's manoeuvrings.

✗ Eating & Drinking

David Walker
SEAFOOD £

(www.davidwalkerandson.com; unit B, Fish Market; ⊙9am-3pm Mon-Fri, 8am-3pm Sat) *The* place to connect with Brixham's fishing industry and stock up for your BBQ – the counters are piled high with the day's catch. Picnic goodies include huge, cooked shell-on prawns and dressed crab.

Beamers
SEAFOOD ££

(☑01803-854777; www.beamersrestaurant.co.uk; 19 The Quay; mains £16-20; ⊙6-9pm Wed-Mon; ✍) Each morning Head Chef Simone strolls to Brixham Fish Market to select the best of the day's catch. The result? Fresh, superbly cooked fish. Samphire, saffron and Pernod spring some menu surprises; bagging a window table secures an absorbing harbour view.

Maritime
PUB

(www.themaritime.co.uk; 79 King St; ⊙7-11pm) Eccentric old boozer smothered in thousands of key rings, stone jugs and chamber pots, presided over by a chatty parrot called Mr Tibbs.

❶ Getting There & Away

Regular ferries (p280) shuttle between Brixham and Torquay.

Bus 22 to Kingswear (£3.20, 15 minutes, half-hourly to hourly) Ferry (p284) connections continue to Dartmouth.

Bus 12 to Torquay (£4.10, 50 minutes, half-hourly) Via Paignton.

Dartmouth & Around
POP 10,716

A bewitching blend of primary-coloured boats and delicately shaded houses, Dartmouth is irresistible. Buildings cascade down steep, wooded slopes towards the River Dart; 17th-century shops with splendidly carved and gilded fronts line narrow lanes. Its charms have drawn a yachting crowd and a string of top-notch eateries, but fleets of fishing vessels, ferries and pleasure boats ensure it's still a busy working port with an authentic tang of the sea. Hiking trails lead up the river or onto the cliffs, while a unique art-deco house and Agatha Christie's Greenway estate wait in the wings.

Dartmouth is on the west side of the Dart estuary. It's linked to the village of Kingswear on the east bank by fleets of car and foot ferries, providing a key transport link to Torquay.

◎ Sights & Activities

★ Greenway
HISTORIC BUILDING

(NT; ☑01803-842382; www.nationaltrust.org.uk; Greenway Rd, Galmpton; adult/child £9.40/5.20; ⊙10.30am-5pm Wed-Sun Mar-Oct, plus Tue late Jul-late Aug) High on Devon's must-see list, the captivating summer home of crime writer Agatha Christie sits beside the placid River Dart. Part-guided tours allow you to wander between rooms where the furnishings and knick-knacks are much as she left them. The bewitching waterside gardens include features that pop up in her mysteries, so you get to spot locations made notorious by fictional murders. Car parking places have to be prebooked; the best way to arrive is by ferry or on foot.

Christie owned Greenway between 1938 and 1959, and the house feels frozen in time: check out the piles of hats in the lobby, the books in her library, the clothes in her wardrobe, and listen to her speak (via a replica radio) in the drawing room. In the gardens, woods speckled with splashes of magnolias, daffodils and hydrangeas frame the water, while the planting creates intimate, secret spaces – the boathouse and views over the river are sublime. In Christie's book *Dead Man's Folly*, Greenway doubles as Nasse House, with the boathouse making an appearance as a murder scene.

The **Greenway Ferry** (☎01803-882811; www.greenwayferry.co.uk) runs to the house from Dartmouth (adult/child return £8/6, eight daily), Totnes (return fare £8, two to seven per week) and Torquay (one daily adult/child return £15/10). It only operates when the house is open – booking is advised. Alternatively, take the Dartmouth Steam Railway (p284) from Paignton to Greenway Halt (adult/child £8.50/5) then walk half a mile through the woods, or hike along the picturesque **Dart Valley Trail** from Kingswear (4 miles).

Coleton Fishacre
HISTORIC BUILDING
(NT; ☎01803-842382; www.nationaltrust.org.uk; Brownstone Rd, near Kingswear; adult/child £9.40/5.20; ◷10.30am-5pm Sat-Thu mid-Feb–Oct; P) For an evocative glimpse of Jazz Age glamour, drop by the former home of the D'Oyly Carte family of theatre impresarios.

Built in the 1920s, its faultless art-deco embellishments include original Lalique tulip uplighters, comic bathroom tiles and a stunning saloon – complete with tinkling piano. The croquet terrace leads to deeply shelved subtropical gardens and suddenly revealed vistas of the sea. Hike the 4 miles along the cliffs from Kingswear, or drive.

Dartmouth Castle
CASTLE
(EH; ☎01803-833588; www.english-heritage.org.uk; adult/child £5.50/3.30; ◷10am-6pm Apr-Sep, to 5pm Oct, to 4pm Sat & Sun Nov-Mar) Encounter mazy passages, atmospheric guardrooms and great views from the battlements. Get there via the tiny, open-top **Castle Ferry** (www.dartmouthcastleferry.co.uk; adult/child return £4/2; ◷10am-4.45pm Apr-Oct).

Blackpool Sands
BEACH
Sun-loving locals head 3 miles south of Dartmouth to this curl of coarse sand, lured by beautiful views, kayaking (per hour/day £15/40) and a licensed cafe stacked with organic, local produce. Take bus 93 from Dartmouth (20 minutes, hourly Monday to Saturday).

Dartmouth Steam Railway & River Boat Co
BOAT CRUISE
(☎01803-555872; www.dartmouthrailriver.co.uk) Cruises along the River Dart to Totnes (adult/child return £14/8.50, 1¼ hours, two to four daily April to September).

LOCAL KNOWLEDGE

EATING & DRINKING LIKE A LOCAL

The southwest is a veritable foodie hot spot. Here are some locals' favourites:

Cornish Pasties Now awarded EU protected status, sample the savoury at bakeries county-wide.

Seafood Net-fresh fish abounds. Prime specialist restaurants include the Seahorse (p284) in Dartmouth, the Wheelhouse (p347) in Falmouth, and the Crab House Cafe (p252) on the Isle of Portland.

Cream Teas Homemade jam, just-baked scones and utterly gooey clotted cream; get stuck in at Alexandra (p254), Brimpts Farm (p293) and the Dwelling House (p350) in Fowey.

Organic & Slow Food Around a quarter of UK-registered organic producers are southwest-based. Try sustainable fare at Riverford (p285) and **River Cottage** (☎01297-630300; www.rivercottage.net; near Axminster; 4-course lunch/dinner £50/80; ◷noon-4pm Fri-Sun, 7.30-11pm Fri & Sat; ✐).

Drinks Top spots to try regional tipples include the Castle inn (p246) for cider, Camel Valley (p329) and Sharpham (p284) for wine, Grain Barge (p308) in Bristol and the Salamander (p319) in Bath for beer, and Plymouth (p287) for gin.

🛏 Sleeping

⭐ Bayard's Cove
B&B ££

(📞 01803-839278; www.bayardscoveinn.co.uk; 27 Lower St; d £115-125, ste £135-180, f from £155; 🛜) Crammed with character and bursting with beams, Bayard's Cove sees you sleeping amid whitewashed stone walls and huge church candles. The lavish family suites feature grand double beds and kids' cabins, complete with bunk beds and tiny TVs; there are even estuary glimpses from the rooms.

Just B
GUESTHOUSE ££

(📞 01803-834311; www.justbdartmouth.com; reception 17 Fosse St; r £70-94) The nine chichi options here range from bedrooms with bathrooms to mini-apartments, all featuring snazzy furnishings, crisp cottons and comfy beds. They're scattered over three central properties, and the 'just B' policy (no '&B' means no breakfast) keeps prices down.

Hill View House
B&B ££

(📞 01803-839372; www.hillviewdartmouth.co.uk; 76 Victoria Rd; s/d £47/70; P🛜) ⌖ At this price, you'll be asking, 'what's the catch?' There isn't one. Lloyd loom-style furniture and angle-poise lamps sit in relaxed, beautifully styled rooms above a retro guest lounge. It's a 10-minute walk into Dartmouth.

🍴 Eating

⭐ Alf Resco
CAFE £

(📞 01803-835880; www.cafealfresco.co.uk; Lower St; mains from £6; ⏰7am-2pm; 🛜) An eclectic crowd hangs out at Alf's – you'll be eating among hipsters, families, tourists and riverboat crews. The same menu spans breakfast through to lunch; expect piled-high fry-ups, irresistible pastries and eye-opening espressos. The gorgeous B&B rooms (£75) are pure shabby-chic.

Rockfish
FISH & CHIPS ££

(📞 01803-832800; www.rockfishdevon.co.uk; 8 South Embankment; mains £10-14; ⏰noon-9.30pm) With its weathered boarding and chilled soundtrack, this place feels more like a beatnik boathouse than your average chippy. The menu is a cut above too; along with sustainable cod there's also monkfish, scallops, oysters and good wine. Eat in (enjoy the atmosphere) or take away (fight the seagulls).

⭐ Seahorse
SEAFOOD £££

(📞 01803-835147; www.seahorserestaurant.co.uk; 5 South Embankment; mains £23-32; ⏰noon-3pm Tue-Sun, 6-10pm Tue-Sat) The seafood served at Mitch Tonks' eatery is so fresh, the menu changes daily. So depending on what's been landed at Brixham (7 miles away) or Dartmouth (a few yards) you might get cuttlefish in Chianti, garlicky roast scallops, or *fritto misto di mare*. Their speciality is sublime, charcoal-roasted fish; their two-course lunch menu (£20, Wednesday to Sunday) is a snip.

ℹ Information

Tourist Office (📞 01803-834224; www.discoverdartmouth.com; Mayor's Ave; ⏰10am-4pm Mon-Sat, to 2pm Sun Apr-Oct, closed Wed & Sun Nov-Mar)

ℹ Getting There & Away

BUS

Plymouth (£6.25, 2½ hours, hourly Monday to Saturday) Bus 93; runs via Kingsbridge (one hour).

Torquay (£4.50, 1¼ hours, hourly Monday to Saturday) Stagecoach Gold.

Totnes (£3.50, 50 minutes, hourly Monday to Saturday) Stagecoach Gold.

FERRY

Dartmouth–Kingswear Ferries (www.dartmouthhigherferry.com; car/pedestrian one way £4.70/1.50; ⏰7am-10.20pm) Dartmouth's Higher and Lower Ferries both take cars and foot passengers, shuttling across the river to Kingswear every six minutes.

TRAIN

Regular **steam trains** (📞 01803-555872; www.dartmouthrailriver.co.uk) link Kingswear with Paignton (adult/child return £14/8).

Totnes & Around
POP 8041

Totnes has such a reputation for being alternative that local jokers wrote 'twinned with Narnia' under the town sign. For decades famous as Devon's hippie haven, eco-conscious Totnes also became Britain's first 'transition town' in 2005, when it began trying to wean itself off a dependence on oil. Sustainability aside, Totnes boasts a tempting vineyard, a gracious Norman castle and a mass of fine Tudor buildings, and is the springboard for a range of adrenaline sports.

👁 Sights & Activities

⭐ Sharpham Wine & Cheese
WINERY

(📞 01803-732203; www.sharpham.com; ⏰10am-5pm Mar-Sep; booking required for some tours; P) The vine-lined hills here are more reminiscent of Chablis than south Devon. Opt for self-guided rambles (£2.50), wine and cheese tastings (£9) or an expert-led walk, tutored tasting, lunch and bottle of Dart Valley Reserve (£65). The gourmet meals dished up in the award-winning cafe (p285) are a true treat. The vineyard is 3 miles south of Totnes, off the A381. A more atmospheric option is to hike from town along the Dart Valley Trail. Booking is required for some tours.

Totnes Castle   CASTLE
(EH; ☎01803-864406; www.english-heritage.org.uk; Castle St; adult/child £3.70/2.20; ⊙10am-6pm Apr-Sep, to 5pm Oct, to 4pm Sat & Sun Nov-Mar) The outer keep of Totnes' Norman motte-and-bailey fortress crowns a hill at the top of town, providing engrossing views over higgledy-piggledy rooftops and the river valley. Hunt out the medieval loo, too.

★Dynamic Adventures   ADVENTURE SPORTS
(☎01803-862725; www.dynamicadventurescic.co.uk; The Shops at Dartington, Dartington) The superb activities on offer here include canoeing and kayaking (per half/full day £30/60) and sea kayaking (from £75), as well as rock climbing and archery (both per hour £12). Plus, in the winter, exhilarating white-water kayaking on the River Dart (from £30). They're based 2 miles northwest of Totnes.

Totnes Kayaks   KAYAKING
(☎07799-403788; www.totneskayaks.co.uk; The Quay, Stoke Gabriel; per 1/6hr £15/40) On these self-guided paddles beside unspoilt hills, it's best to go with the tide (owner Tom will advise); so either upriver past Sharpham Vineyard, or downriver to the charming village of Dittisham. You set off from sleepy Stoke Gabriel, 5 miles southeast of Totnes.

🛏 Sleeping

★Dartington Hall   B&B ££
(☎01803-847147; www.dartington.org; Dartington, near Totnes; d £59-115; 🅿🛜) The wings of this idyllic, ancient manor house have been carefully converted into rooms that range from heritage-themed to deluxe-modern. Ask for one overlooking the grassy, cobble-fringed courtyard and settle back for a truly tranquil night's sleep.

Sea Trout   INN ££
(☎01803-762274; www.theseatroutinn.co.uk; Staverton, near Totnes; d £95-150; 🅿🛜) Most of the rooms here are the epitome of carefully judged, contemporary good taste. The feature room though is a deliberately over-the-

top rococo delight, all ornate black-wood, mock chandeliers and a slipper bath. The great-value restaurant (mains £13, open noon to 2pm and 6pm to 9pm) regularly notches up awards.

Steam Packet   INN ££
(☎01803-863880; www.steampacketinn.co.uk; St Peters Quay; s/d £85/105; 🅿) It's almost as if the minimalist bedrooms of this wharf-side former warehouse have been plucked from the pages of a design magazine; expect painted wood panels, willow arrangements and neutral tones. Opt for a river-view room, then watch the world float by.

🍴 Eating

★Riverford Field
Kitchen   MODERN BRITISH ££
(☎01803-762074; www.riverford.co.uk; Wash Barn; 2/3 courses £23/27; ⊙noon-2.30pm daily, 6-10pm most evenings; 🖊) 🌱 Eco-friendly Riverford's bistro is set in a farm, meaning minimal food miles: vegetables are picked to order from the fields outside; meats are organic and locally sourced. Big trestle tables fill a futuristic hangar-like canteen, with diners passing around platters laden with richly flavoured food. Imaginative treatments might include marinated, grilled Moroccan lamb and British veg transformed by cumin or saffron. Bookings required.

Sharpham Vineyard Café   BISTRO ££
(☎01803-732178; www.vineyardcafe.co.uk; Sharpham Estate; mains £10-15, snacks £4-7; ⊙noon-2pm May-Sep; 🖊) Rustic, organic fare fills the tables of this decked cafe, anchored just yards from Sharpham's vines. Treats include smoked-fish or charcuterie boards, local crab salads and hearty fare such as belly pork and bean cassoulet. And, of course, the

---

DARTINGTON HALL

Henry VIII gave this beguiling 320-hectare estate (☎01803-847000; www.dartington.org) to two of his wives (Catherines Howard and Parr); now it's home to B&B accommodation (p285), the Barn art-house cinema, a mellow pub (p286), landscaped grounds and a medieval great hall that hosts events ranging from classical music to the Ways With Words Literature Festival (☎01803-867373; www.wayswithwords.co.uk). The estate is 2 miles northwest of Totnes.

vineyard's own, simply superb cheese and wine. It's 3 miles south of Totnes.

White Hart
PUB ££

(☑ 01803-847111; www.dartingtonhall.com; Dartington Estate, near Totnes; tapas £6, mains £12-17; ☺ noon-9pm; ☑) To its already-acclaimed gastropub dishes, the White Hart has added a British tapas menu, so now grazing options include ham hock, lamb cutlets, scallops or wild-mushroom risotto. Winter brings a blazing fire; on fine evenings the lawnside tables are the place to be.

Rumour
PUB ££

(☑ 01803-864682; www.rumourtotnes.com; 30 High St, Totnes; mains £9-18; ☺ noon-3pm Mon-Sat, 6-9pm daily) ☑ Rumour is a local institution – a narrow, cosy pub-restaurant with low lighting, funky local art and free newspapers. Famous for its crispy pizzas (£9), it also rustles up stylish cuisine, such as pollock roasted with avocado butter, and irresistible 28-day matured 8oz steaks.

ℹ️ Information

Tourist Office (☑ 01803-863168; www.totnesinformation.co.uk; Coronation Rd; ☺ 9am-5pm Mon-Fri, 10am-4pm Sat Apr-Oct, 10am-4pm Mon-Fri, to 1pm Sat Nov-Mar)

ℹ️ Getting There & Away

BOAT

Boats (p283) shuttle downriver to Dartmouth.

BUS

Dartmouth (£3.50, 50 minutes, hourly Monday to Saturday) Stagecoach Gold.

Torquay (£3.50, 45 minutes, every half hour Monday to Saturday, seven on Sunday) Stagecoach Gold.

TRAIN

Trains go at least hourly to Exeter (£8, 35 minutes) and Plymouth (£8, 30 minutes). The privately run **South Devon Steam Railway** (www.southdevonrailway.org; adult/child return £12/7; ☺ 4-9 trains daily Apr-Oct) chuffs to Buckfastleigh, on the edge of Dartmoor.

Plymouth & Around

POP 258,000

For decades, some have dismissed Plymouth as sprawling and ugly, pointing to architectural eyesores and sometimes palpable poverty. But the arrival of high-profile chefs Hugh Fearnley-Whittingstall and Mitch Tonks, and ongoing waterfront regeneration begs a rethink. Yes the city, an important Royal Naval port, suffered WWII bomb damage, and today it is still sometimes more gritty than pretty, but Plymouth is also packed with possibilities: swim in an art-deco lido; tour a gin distillery; learn to kayak; roam an aquarium; take a boat trip across the bay; then see a top-class theatre show and party till dawn. And the ace in the pack? Plymouth Hoe – a cafe-dotted, wide grassy headland offering captivating views of a boat-studded bay.

History

Plymouth's history is dominated by the sea. The first recorded cargo left in 1211 and by the late 16th century it was the port of choice for explorers and adventurers. It's waved off Sir Francis Drake, Sir Walter Raleigh, the fleet that defeated the Spanish Armada, the pilgrims who founded America, Charles Darwin, Captain Cook and countless boats carrying emigrants to Australia and New Zealand.

During WWII Plymouth suffered horrendously at the hands of the Luftwaffe – more than 1000 civilians died in the Blitz, which reduced the city centre to rubble. The 21st century has brought regeneration to waterfront areas, a £200 million Drake Circus shopping centre and a growing university, bringing a burst of new buildings and 30,000 students to the heart of town.

⊙ Sights

★ Plymouth Hoe
HEADLAND

Francis Drake supposedly spied the Spanish fleet from this grassy headland overlooking Plymouth Sound (the city's wide bay); the bowling green on which he finished his game was probably where his statue now stands. The wide villa-backed promenade features scores of war memorials, including the immense Plymouth Naval Memorial, which commemorates Commonwealth WWI and WWII sailors who have no grave but the sea.

Smeaton's Tower
LIGHTHOUSE

(☑ 01752-304774; www.plymouth.gov.uk/museumsmeatonstower; The Hoe; adult/child £2.60/1.30; ☺ 10am-4.30pm Apr-Sep, to 3pm Tue-Sat Oct, Nov, Feb & Mar) The red-and-white stripes of Smeaton's Tower rise from the middle of the Plymouth Hoe headland. The whole 70ft structure used to stand on the Eddystone Reef, 14 miles offshore, and was transferred here, brick by brick, in the 1880s. For an insight into past lighthouse keepers' lives, head up 93 stone steps and through the circular rooms to emerge onto an open-air platform with stunning views of the city, Dartmoor and the sea.

⭐ **Barbican**   NEIGHBOURHOOD
(www.plymouthbarbican.com) In the historic Barbican district, part-cobbled streets are lined with Tudor and Jacobean buildings, galleries, restaurants and funky bars. The Pilgrim Fathers' *Mayflower* set sail to found America from here in 1620. The Mayflower Steps (⏱24hr) **FREE** mark the approximate embarcation point; track down the passenger list on the side of Island House nearby. Other famous departures are also commemorated at the steps, including Captain James Cook's 1768 voyage of discovery, and the first emigrant ships to Australia and New Zealand.

⭐ **Plymouth Gin Distillery**   DISTILLERY
(📞01752-665292; www.plymouthdistillery.com; 60 Southside St; tours £7; ⏱6 tours daily) They've been concocting gin at this heavily beamed distillery since 1793, making it the oldest producer of the spirit in the world. The Royal Navy ferried it round the world in countless officers' messes and the brand was specified in the first recorded recipe for a dry martini in the 1930s. Tours thread past the stills and take in a tutored tasting before retiring to the medieval bar for a complimentary G&T. Book.

National Marine Aquarium   AQUARIUM
(📞0844 893 7938; www.national-aquarium.co.uk; Rope Walk; adult/child £14/10; ⏱10am-5pm, to 6pm Apr-Sep) The sharks here swim in coral seas that teem with moray eels and vividly coloured fish – there's even a loggerhead turtle called Snorkel who was rescued from a Cornish beach. Walk-through glass arches ensure huge rays glide over your head, while the gigantic Atlantic reef tank reveals just what's lurking a few miles offshore.

Buckland Abbey   HISTORIC BUILDING
(NT; 📞01822-853607; www.nationaltrust.org.uk; near Yelverton; adult/child £9/4.50; ⏱10.30am-5.30pm Mar-Oct, 11.30am-4.30pm Dec & Feb; P) Founded as a Cistercian monastery and abbey church in the 13th century, Buckland Abbey was one of Henry VIII's 'acquisitions' during the Dissolution. Sir Richard Grenville bought it from the land-hungry king, before selling it to his cousin and nautical rival Sir Francis Drake. Highlights include Drake's Drum, said to beat by itself when Britain is in danger of being invaded, exquisite modelled ceilings, a Great Barn, fine Elizabethan gardens and woodland walks. Buckland Abbey is 11 miles north of Plymouth.

🏃 **Activities**

⭐ **Tinside Lido**   SWIMMING
(📞01752-261915; www.everyoneactive.com; Hoe Rd; adult/child £3.90/2.80; ⏱10am-6pm Jun-Sep) Taking a dip at this Jazz Age, open-air swimspot is an unforgettable experience. Its 1935, art-deco design sees cream curves and light- and dark-blue tiles sweep gracefully out from the foot of the Hoe. Plunge into the chilly saltwater to join the regulars doing laps and the youngsters larking around beside the fountains.

Mount Batten Centre   WATER SPORTS
(📞01752-404567; www.mount-batten-centre.com; 70 Lawrence Rd) Two-hour taster sessions include those for sail dinghies, stand-up paddleboarding and canoeing (each £20). Two-day courses include kayaking (£90), sailing (£170) and windsurfing (£145). It's on the Mount Batten peninsula. Ferries run from the Barbican Pontoon.

Mount Batten Ferry   FERRY TRIPS
(www.mountbattenferry.com; adult/child return £3/2) A little yellow ferry shuttling from the Barbican Pontoon across to the Mount Batten Peninsula (10 minutes, half-hourly).

👉 **Tours**

Plymouth Boat Trips   BOAT TOUR
(📞01752-253153; www.plymouthboattrips.co.uk; Barbican Pontoon; ⏱4 daily Apr–mid-Oct) The pick of this firm's trips is the 30-minute blast-across-the-bay to quaint, pub-packed

---

ROYAL WILLIAM YARD

This cluster of 1830s waterfront warehouses once supplied stores for countless Royal Navy vessels. Today it's home to sleek apartments, a couple of art galleries, a relaxed pub, chic wine bar and a string of eateries; the best being River Cottage Canteen (p289) and the Royal William Bakery (p289).

The yard is 2 miles west of the city centre; bus 34 (£1.20, eight minutes, half-hourly) runs there; better still catch the ferry (📞07979-152008; www.royal-williamyardharbour.co.uk; adult/child single £3/1.50; ⏱10am-5pm May-Sep, to 6pm Jul & Aug) from the Barbican Pontoon.

Plymouth

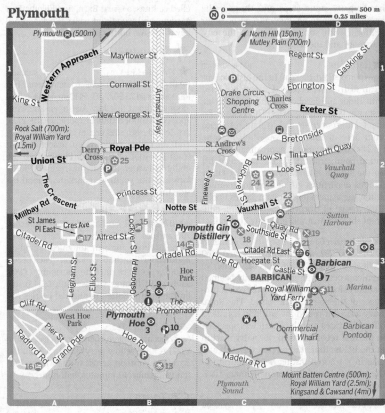

Cornish fishing villages of Kingsand and Cawsand (adult/child return £8/4). They also run one-hour harbour cruises (adult/child £7.50/4) to the warships at Plymouth's naval base.

🛏 Sleeping

⭐ **St Elizabeth's House** BOUTIQUE HOTEL **££**
(☎01752-344840; www.stelizabeths.co.uk; Longbrook St, Plympton St Maurice; d £99-119, ste £150; 🅿🛜) Prepare to be pampered. In this 17th-century manor house turned boutique bolthole, free-standing slipper baths, oak furniture and Egyptian cotton grace the rooms; the suites feature palatial bathrooms and private terraces. It's set in the suburb-cum-village of Plympton St Maurice, 5 miles east of Plymouth.

Imperial HOTEL **££**
(☎01752-227311; www.imperialplymouth.co.uk; Lockyer St; s £60, d £62-86, f £92-100; 🅿🛜) In the

1840s an admiral used to slumber in this elegant town house. Now you get to sleep amid heritage features, swish modern furnishings and all the mod-cons, before breakfasting on top-notch local produce (the homemade kedgeree is quite a treat). It's all very high quality for the price.

Sea Breezes B&B **££**
(☎01752-667205; www.plymouth-bedandbreakfast.co.uk; 28 Grand Pde; s/d/f £45/72/97; 🅿) The fresh decor at this deeply comfortable guesthouse ranges from subtle gingham to groovy swirls. The bathrooms gleam, the towels are fluffy and the breakfasts feature melon, strawberries and hand-cut toast. Bag a front-facing bedroom (go for the one with the window seat) for smashing sea views.

Acorns & Lawns B&B **££**
(☎01752-229474; www.acornsandlawnsguesthouse.com; 171 Citadel Rd; d £60-75; 🛜) Simplicity and serenity seem to seep from the walls here.

Plymouth

The guest lounge and breakfast room are all light colours and varnished floors; a bright-white stairwell leads to light-filled rooms. Ask for a front-facing bedroom to look out over the lower slopes of grassy Plymouth Hoe.

Squires   B&B ££
(📞 01752-261459; www.squiresguesthouse.com; 7 St James Pl East; s/d £32/65; 🛜) Unfussy, squeaky-clean rooms, a quiet but central location and a friendly welcome.

✗ Eating

Royal William Bakery   CAFE, BAKERY £
(www.royalwilliambakery.com; Royal William Yard; mains £5; ⊙8.30am-4pm; 🅿) Piles of huge, just-cooked loaves, tureens full of soup, crumbly pastries and irresistible cakes – this is a bakery like few others. The serve-yourself style is so laid-back you don't get a bill – just tell them what you've eaten and they'll tot it up at the end. The Royal William Yard is 2 miles west of the city centre, on bus route 34.

Cap'n Jaspers   CAFE £
(www.capn-jaspers.co.uk; Whitehouse Pier, Quay Rd; snacks £3-5; ⊙7.30am-midnight) Beloved by bikers, fishermen, families and tourists, this cabin-kiosk is a local institution thanks to its late hours, motorised gadgets and resolutely burger-van fare – trying to finish the 'half a yard of hot dog' is a Plymouth rite of passage; the Barbican crab rolls are an easier eat.

★ Rock Salt   MODERN BRITISH ££
(📞01752-225522; www.rocksaltcafe.co.uk; 31 Stonehouse St; mains £7-20; ⊙10am-9.30pm, from 8am Wed-Sat; 🛜) First-class ingredients and creative flavours – no wonder Rock Salt keeps bagging awards. Their range is remarkable: from stylish all-day breakfasts and afternoon cupcakes to confit Dartmoor lamb. And all in a friendly setting that feels like a funky neighbourhood brasserie.

River Cottage Canteen   MODERN BRITISH ££
(📞01752-252702; www.rivercottage.net; Royal William Yard; mains £10-17; ⊙11am-10.30pm Mon-Sat, to 4pm Sun; 🅿) Hugh Fearnley-Whittingstall's gaff focuses firmly on local, sustainable, seasonal, organic goodies. Expect meats to be roasted beside an open fire, fish to be simply grilled and familiar veg to be given a revelatory makeover. It's in the Royal William Yard, 2 miles west of the city centre; catch bus 34.

Barbican Kitchen   MODERN BRITISH ££
(📞01752-604448; www.barbicankitchen.com; 60 Southside St; mains £10-20; ⊙noon-2.30pm & 5-9.30pm) The assured menus at this stylish eatery take in everything from chilli dogs and wild-garlic risotto to chateaubriand for two. The express menu (two/three courses £13/16), served at lunch and Monday to Thursday evenings, is a superb deal.

Rockfish   SEAFOOD ££
(📞01752-255974; www.therockfish.co.uk; 3 Rope Walk; mains £12; ⊙noon-9.30pm) In Mitch Tonks' cheery bistro (handily set right beside the fish market) perfectly cooked cod comes with as many chips as you can eat; roasted scallops, steamed prawns and sweet Devon crab feature on the imaginative menu too.

🍷 Drinking & Nightlife

Like any Royal Navy city, Plymouth has a more-than-lively nightlife. Union St is clubland; Mutley Plain and North Hill have a studeny vibe, while the Barbican has more restaurants amid the bars. All three areas can get rowdy, especially at weekends.

★ Dolpin   PUB
(14 The Barbican; ⊘10am-11pm) This gloriously unreconstructed Barbican boozer is all scuffed tables, padded bench seats and an authentic, no-nonsense atmosphere. Feeling peckish? Get a fish-and-chip takeaway from next-door-but-one, then settle down with your pint.

Minerva   PUB
(www.minervainn.co.uk; 31 Looe St; ⊘11.30am-11pm Sun-Wed, to midnight Thu-Sat; 🎤) Stone walls, wooden benches, chunks of sailing ships, real ales, live music and Thursday night jam sessions make this 16th-century drinking den a locals' favourite.

Vignoble   WINE BAR
(www.levignoble.co.uk; Royal William Yard; ⊘noon-11.30pm) A bijou hang-out where you can sample taster-sized glasses of your chosen vintages. It's at the Royal William Yard, 2 miles west of the centre.

☆ Entertainment

★ Annabel's   CABARET, CLUB
(www.annabelscabaret.co.uk; 88 Vauxhall St; ⊘9pm-2am Thu, 8.30pm-3am Fri & Sat) The stage spots in this fabulously quirky venue are filled by an eclectic collection of acts (expect anything from comedy or bellydancing to burlesque). Crowd-pleasing tunes fill the dance floor while classy cocktails fill your glass.

Plymouth Arts Centre   CINEMA
(📞01752-206114; www.plymouthartscentre.org; 38 Looe St; ⊘10am-8.30pm Tue-Sat, from 4pm Sun) Combines a cracking independent cinema, modern-art exhibitions, and a licensed, vegetarian-friendly bistro (closed Sunday).

Theatre Royal   THEATRE
(TRP; 📞01752-267222; www.theatreroyal.com; Royal Pde) Plymouth's main theatre stages large-scale touring and home-grown productions; its studio space, the Drum, is renowned for featuring new writing.

ℹ Information

Plymouth Library (Drake Circus; per 30min £2; ⊘9am-6pm Mon-Fri, to 5pm Sat; 🎤) Internet access and free wi-fi.

Police Station (Charles Cross; ⊘24hr)

Tourist Office (📞01752-306330; www.visit-plymouth.co.uk; 3 The Barbican; ⊘9am-5pm Mon-Sat, 10am-4pm Sun Apr-Oct, 10am-4pm Mon-Sat Nov-Mar)

ℹ Getting There & Away

BUS
National Express services include:
Birmingham (£30, five hours, five daily)
Bristol (£20, three hours, four daily)
London (£25, five to six hours, six daily)
Penzance (£10, 3¼ hours, four daily)

Other services:
Exeter (£6.50, 1¼ hours, two-hourly Monday to Saturday, three on Sunday) Bus X38.
Tavistock (£6.20, one hour, one to three hourly) Bus 83/84/86; runs via Yelverton.

TRAIN
Services include:
Bristol (£20, two hours, two or three per hour)
Exeter (£9, one hour, half-hourly)
London Paddington (£40, 3¼ hours, half-hourly)
Penzance (£10, two hours, half-hourly)
Totnes (£8, 30 minutes, half-hourly to hourly)

Dartmoor National Park

Dartmoor is an ancient, compelling landscape, so different from the rest of Devon that a visit feels like falling straight into Tolkien's *Return of the King*. Exposed granite hills (called tors) crest on the horizon, linked by swaths of honey-tinged moors. Streams tumble over moss-smothered boulders in woods of twisted trees. The centre of this 368-sq-mile national park is the higher moor; a vast, treeless expanse.

On sunny, summer days Dartmoor is idyllic; ponies wander at will and sheep graze beside the road; a cinematic location that features in Steven Spielberg's WWI epic *War Horse*. But Dartmoor is also the setting for Sir Arthur Conan Doyle's *The Hound of the Baskervilles*, and in sleeting rain and swirling mists you suddenly see why; the moor morphs into a bleak wilderness where tales of a phantom hound can seem very real indeed.

Dartmoor's settlements range from brooding Princetown and picturesque Widecombe-in-the-Moor to tiny Postbridge and genteel Chagford. In between, lies a natural breakout zone offering superb hiking, cycling, riding, climbing and white-water kayaking; rustic pubs and fancy restaurants; wild camping nooks and country-house hotels – perfect boltholes when the fog rolls in.

Dartmoor is administered by the Dartmoor National Park Authority (DNPA; www.dartmoor.gov.uk).

🏃 Activities

Walking

Some 730 miles of public footpaths snake across Dartmoor's open heaths and rocky tors. The Pathfinder *Dartmoor Walks* (£12) guide has 28 hikes of up to 9 miles, while its *Dartmoor Short Walks* (£8) focuses on family-friendly treks.

For multiday hikes, see p292.

★ Moorland Guides   WALKING
(www.moorlandguides.co.uk; adult/child £5-10/free) Wide range of walks, from one-hour rambles to strenuous all-day hikes, on themes spanning heritage, geology, wildlife, myths and navigation.

DNPA Guided Walks   WALKING
(www.dartmoor.gov.uk/visiting; adult/child £5/free) One- to six-hour, ranger-led outings.

Cycling

Routes include the 11-mile Granite Way, which runs, now entirely off-road, along a former railway line between Okehampton and Lydford. The 13-mile Princetown & Burrator Mountain Bike Route is a challenging moorland circuit along tracks and bridleways taking in Princetown, Sheepstor village and Burrator Reservoir. Tourist offices also sell the *Dartmoor Cycling Map* (£13).

Devon Cycle Hire   BICYCLE RENTAL
(☑ 01837-861141; www.devoncyclehire.co.uk; Sourton Down, near Okehampton; per day adult/child £14/10; ⏱ 9am-5pm Thu-Tue Apr-Sep) On the Granite Way.

Princetown Cycle Hire   BICYCLE RENTAL
(Fox Tor Cafe; ☑ 01822-890238; www.princetowncyclehire.co.uk; Two Bridges Rd, Princetown; per day

Dartmoor National Park

Ⓝ 0 — 10 km
0 — 5 miles

Bideford (28mi);
Barnstaple (32mi)
Okehampton
Okehampton Castle
Granite Way
Finch Foundry
Sticklepath
Cheriton Bishop
Tedburn St Mary
A30
Okehampton
Bracken Tor YHA
Yes Tor
Belstone Tor
Sandy Park
Castle Drogo
Teign
Dunsford
Bodmin (28mi)
A30
Granite Way
High Willhays
Gidleigh Park
Easton Cross
Brat Tor
Scorhill
Chagford
Moreton-hampstead
Christow
Exeter (6mi)
White Lady
A386
Range Danger Area
Grey Wethers
B3212
Tottiford Reservoir
A38
Lydford
Lydford Gorge
Warren House Inn
Grimspound
Chudleigh
Dartmoor Way
Postbridge
Haytor
Dartmoor Way
Bovey Tracey
Tavistock
Merrivale Stone Rows
Two Bridges
Widecombe-in-the-Moor
Vixen Tor
Princetown
Dartmeet
Brimpts Farm
Newton Abbot
A390
B3212
Princetown & Burrator Mountain Bike Route
Poundsgate
Ashburton
Templer Way
Yelverton
Buckland Abbey
Shaugh Prior
South Brent
A38
Buckfastleigh
Totnes
Paignton (1mi); Torquay (3mi)
Plymouth
A38
Ivybridge
A385
Plymouth Sound

adult/child £18.50/10; ⊙9am-5pm) Handy for the Princetown & Burrator Mountain Bike Route.

Horse Riding

A number of local stables cater to all abilities.

Eastlake HORSE RIDING
(☎01837-52513; www.eastlakeridingstables.co.uk; Eastlake, near Okehampton; per 2hr £35)

Shilstone Rocks HORSE RIDING
(☎01364-621281; www.dartmoorstables.com; Widecombe-in-the-Moor; per 1/2hr £40/55)

Tor Royal HORSE RIDING
(☎01822-890189; www.dartmoorhorseriding.co.uk; Princetown; per 1/2hr £25/40)

White-Water Sports

The raging River Dart makes Dartmoor a top spot for thrill seekers. Experienced kayakers can get permits from the DNPA (p291). For white-water kayaking, go for Dynamic Adventures (p285), near Totnes. Rivers are only open from October to mid-March.

CRS Adventures WATER SPORTS
(☎01364-653444; www.crsadventures.co.uk) For white-water rafting (per two people £100), try this operator near Widecombe-in-the-Moor.

Climbing

Adventure Okehampton OUTDOORS
(☎01837-53916; www.adventureokehampton.com; Klondyke Rd, Okehampton; per day from £60;

school holidays only) Runs wall- and rock-climbing sessions, plus activities including archery, abseiling and wild camping.

ℹ Information

DNPA Haytor (☎01364-661520; ⊙10am-5pm Apr-Sep, to 4pm Mar & Oct, 10.30am-3.30pm Thu-Sun Nov-Feb)

DNPA Postbridge (☎01822-880272; ⊙10am-5pm Apr-Sep, to 4pm Mar & Oct, 10.30am-3.30pm Thu-Sun Nov-Feb)

Higher Moorland Tourist Office (DNPA; ☎01822-890414; www.dartmoor.gov.uk; Princetown; ⊙10am-5pm Apr-Sep, to 4pm Mar & Oct, 10.30am-3.30pm Thu-Sun Nov-Feb) Dartmoor's main tourist office also stocks walking guides, maps and clothes.

ℹ Getting There & Around

Public transport is an option, but planning is needed and some services are seasonal. Tourist offices stock bus timetables. See www.journeydevon.info.

BUS

The **Dartmoor Sunday Rover** (adult/child/family £8/6/17) offers unlimited Sunday travel on most moorland bus routes; buy from drivers or at Plymouth train station.

Bus 83/84/86 (one to three hourly) From Plymouth to Tavistock, via Yelverton.

Bus 118 (two to six daily) From Barnstaple to Tavistock (2¼ hours), via Lydford and Okehampton.

Bus 359 (six daily Monday to Saturday) From Exeter to Moretonhampstead.

Bus 98 (three daily Monday to Saturday) A year-round service, which runs from Tavistock to Princetown, via Merrivale; one bus a day goes onto Two Bridges and Postbridge.

Haytor Hoppa Runs on Saturdays between April and October only, providing four buses between Newton Abbot, Bovey Tracey, Haytor and Widecombe-in-the-Moor (daily fare £5).

Transmoor Link/Bus 82 Runs on Saturdays and Sundays between mid-May and mid-September only, making one trip each way from Exeter to Tavistock (£5.80) via Moretonhampstead, Postbridge, Princetown and Yelverton. It leaves Exeter in the morning and Tavistock in the afternoon.

Princetown

POP 1767

Set in the heart of the remote, higher moor, Princetown is dominated by the grey, foreboding bulk of Dartmoor Prison and on bad weather days the town can have a bleak feel. But it's also a useful insight into the harsh realities of moorland life and makes an atmospheric base for some excellent walks.

DARTMOOR HIKES

The 18-mile Templer Way is a two- to three-day leg stretch from Haytor to Teignmouth, while the West Devon Way forms a 36-mile trek linking Okehampton and Plymouth. The 95-mile Dartmoor Way circles from Buckfastleigh in the south, through Moretonhampstead, northwest to Okehampton and south through Lydford to Tavistock. The 117-mile Two Moors Way runs from Wembury on the south Devon coast, across Dartmoor and Exmoor to Lynmouth, on the north coast.

Be prepared for Dartmoor's notoriously fickle weather and carry a map and compass – many trails are not waymarked. The Ordnance Survey (OS) Explorer 1:25,000 map No 28, Dartmoor (£8), is the most comprehensive and shows park boundaries and Ministry of Defence firing-range areas.

For shorter hikes, see p291.

⊙ Sights

Dartmoor Prison Museum   MUSEUM
(☑01822-322130; www.dartmoor-prison.co.uk; Princetown; adult/child £3.50/2.50; ⊙9.30am-12.30pm & 1.30-4pm; ℗) In the early 1800s Princetown's jail was home to French and American Prisoners of war, becoming a convict jail in 1850. Just up from the looming gates, this museum provides a chilling glimpse of life inside. Look out for straitjackets, manacles, escape stories and the makeshift knives made by modern prisoners. You can also book a guided walk (adult/child £6.50/5.50) which skirts the prison perimeter and heads into otherwise out-of-bounds French and American cemeteries.

**Higher Moorland
Tourist Office**   INTERPRETATION CENTRE
(DNPA; ☑01822-890414; ⊙10am-5pm Apr-Sep, to 4pm Mar & Oct, 10.30am-3.30pm Thu-Sun Nov-Feb) Heritage displays include those on tin workings, gunpowder factories, legends and a stunning time-lapse video. The office used to be the Duchy Hotel; one former guest was Sir Arthur Conan Doyle, who went on to write *The Hound of the Baskervilles*. Dartmoor lore recounts local man Henry Baskerville took the novelist on a carriage tour, and the brooding landscape he encountered, coupled with legends of huge phantom dogs, inspired the thriller.

🛏 Sleeping & Eating

★ Prince of Wales   HOSTEL £
(☑01822-890219; www.theprinceofwalesprincetown.co.uk; Tavistock Rd; dm/s/d £14/40/60; ℗) The pick of Dartmoor's bunkhouses, with central heating, double glazing (on the moor, this matters) and – joy of joys – a drying room. The rustic pub (mains £5 to £16, served 11am to 2.30pm and 5.30pm to 8pm) next door is famous for its three open fires, mixed-grill platters the size of tea trays and pints of own-brewed, full-bodied, Jail Ale.

★ Tor Royal Farm   B&B ££
(☑01822-890189; www.torroyal.co.uk; Tor Royal Lane, near Princetown; s £55, d £85-100; ℗🤖) This is just what a middle-of-the-moor retreat should be – an easygoing, country cottage–styled farmhouse packed with lived-in charm. Their own-reared pork appears on the breakfast menu, and you can book horse-riding lessons at their stables right next door.

ℹ WARNING

The military uses three adjoining areas of Dartmoor as training ranges where live ammunition is used. Tourist offices can outline their locations; they're also marked on Ordnance Survey (OS) maps. You're advised to check if the route you're planning falls within a range; if it does, find out if firing is taking place when you want to walk via the **Firing Information Service** (☑0800 458 4868; www.mod.uk/access). During the day, red flags fly at the edges of in-use ranges, while red flares burn at night. Even when there's no firing, beware of unidentified metal objects lying in the grass. Don't touch anything you find: note its position and report it to the **Commandant** (☑01837-650010).

Two Bridges   HOTEL £££
(☑01822-892300; www.twobridges.co.uk; Two Bridges; s £95-120, d £140-190; ℗🤖) Perhaps the definitive historic moorland hotel: polished wood panels, huge inglenook fireplaces and a guest list that includes Wallis Simpson, Winston Churchill and Vivien Leigh. It's 1.5 miles northeast of Princetown.

ℹ Getting There & Away

Bus 98 runs from Tavistock to Princetown (£2.30, three daily, Monday to Saturday). One service a day goes on to Two Bridges and Postbridge.

Postbridge

POP 170

The quaint hamlet of Postbridge owes its popularity, and its name, to its medieval stone slab or clapper bridge; a 13th-century structure with four, 10ft-long slabs propped up on sturdy columns of stacked stones. Walking over takes you across the rushing East Dart river; a picturesque spot to whip off your boots and plunge your feet into water that's quite possibly never felt so cold.

🛏 Sleeping & Eating

★ Brimpts Farm   B&B £
(☑0845 0345968; www.brimptsfarm.co.uk; site per person £3, s/d/f £33/55/83; ℗) The brightly painted, rustic bedrooms above this farmhouse have views over *War Horse* location Combestone Tor; the back-to-nature camping fields are idyllic and the cream teas are some

🏃 Driving Tour
A Dartmoor Road Trip

START TAVISTOCK
END CHAGFORD
LENGTH 20 MILES; ONE DAY

Driving on Dartmoor is like being inside a feature film: compelling 360-degree views are screened all around. This scenic, west-to-east transmoor traverse sweeps up and through this wilderness, taking in a bleak prison, prehistoric remains, a rustic pub and a unique castle.

Start by strolling among the fine 19th-century architecture of ❶ **Tavistock**, perhaps dropping by its Pannier Market to rummage for antiques. Next take the B3357 towards Princetown. It climbs steeply (expect ears to pop), crosses a cattle grid (a sign you're on the moor 'proper') and crests a hill to reveal swaths of honey-coloured tors. Soon you're at ❷ **Merrivale** (p296). Park up on the right, just after the Dartmoor Inn, and stroll over the rise (due south) to discover a snaking stone row; a tiny stone circle and a standing stone are just 100m further on.

Back in the car, after a short climb, turn right towards Princetown, glimpsing the brooding bulk of Dartmoor Prison (you can't stop here; there's a better vantage point later). Call in at the ❸ **Dartmoor Prison Museum** (p293) to explore the jail's grim story. Cut through rugged ❹ **Princetown** (p292), before picking up the B3212 towards Two Bridges; the ❺ **lay-by** immediately after you leave Princetown provides prime Dartmoor Prison views. As you follow signs for Moretonhampstead, an expansive landscape unfurls. At ❻ **Postbridge** (p293), park and stroll over the 700-year-old bridge, then dangle hot feet in the cold River Dart. A few miles further on, the ❼ **Warren House Inn** (p295) makes an atmospheric spot for lunch. Around ❽ **Lettaford** take one of the signed, plunging lanes to ❾ **Chagford** (p295) to visit its quaint, thatch-dotted square. Scour some of its wonderfully old-fashioned shops, then head to ❿ **Castle Drogo** (p295) to explore a unique 1920s stately home. Finish the day back at Chagford at ⓫ **22 Mill Street** (p296); a truly classy spot to eat and sleep.

of the moor's best: freshly baked scones, home-made jams and utterly gooey clotted cream (£5) served 11.30am to 5.30pm on weekends and school holidays. Brimpts is signed off the B3357, Two Bridges–Dartmeet road.

Runnage YHA HUT £
(☎ 0800 0191 700; www.yha.org.uk; dm £10; P) A converted hayloft on a working farm where you bed down to a soundtrack of bleating sheep. It's 1.5 miles east of Postbridge: take the 'Widecombe' turning off the B3212 Moretonhampstead road.

Dartmoor YHA HOSTEL £
(Bellever; ☎ 0845 371 9622; www.yha.org.uk; dm/d £15/48; P) A characterful former farm on the edge of a conifer plantation, with a huge kitchen, lots of rustic stone walls and cosy dorms. It's a mile south of Postbridge.

★**Warren House Inn** PUB £
(www.warrenhouseinn.co.uk; mains £6-14; ⊗ kitchen noon-8.30pm, shorter hours winter) Marooned amid miles of moorland, this Dartmoor institution exudes a hospitality only found in pubs in the middle of nowhere. A fire that's been burning (apparently) since 1845 warms stone floors, trestle tables and hikers munching robust food; the Warreners' Pie (local rabbit) is legendary. It's on the B3212, some 2 miles northeast of Postbridge. The bar's open 11am to 11pm.

❶ Getting There & Away
Bus 98 runs to Princetown (£1.25, one per day Monday to Saturday). Postbridge is also served by the Transmoor Link (p292).

Widecombe-in-the-Moor
POP 566
This is archetypal Dartmoor, down to the ponies grazing on a village green encircled by 15th-century buildings of honey-grey stone. The village features in the traditional English folksong, 'Widecombe Fair, an event that takes place on the second Tuesday of September.

◉ Sights

St Pancras Church CHURCH
St Pancras' immense 40m tower has seen it dubbed the Cathedral of the Moor. Inside search out the boards telling the fire-and-brimstone tale of the violent storm of 1638 – it knocked a pinnacle from the roof, killing several parishioners. As ever on Dartmoor, the devil was blamed, said to be in search of souls.

❶ DRIVING ON DARTMOOR
Dartmoor's roads are exciting to drive, but large stretches have unfenced grazing so you'll come across Dartmoor ponies, sheep and even cows in the middle of the road. Many sections have a 40mph speed limit. Car parks on the moor can be little more than lay-bys; their surface can be rough to very rough.

🛏 Sleeping & Eating

Manor Cottage B&B £
(☎ 01364-621218; www.manorcottagedartmoor.co.uk; d £50-60; P🐾) Roses climb around the doorway of this quaint, ancient, village-centre cottage. The best billet is a bedroom-bathroom suite at the top of its own spiral staircase. Breakfasts feature berry compote, local sausages and eggs freshly laid by the hens clucking around outside.

Rugglestone Inn PUB ££
(www.rugglestoneinn.co.uk; mains £11; ⊗ kitchen noon-2pm & 6.30-9pm) You'll find plenty of locals in front of this intimate old pub's wood-burning stove. Its stone floor and low beams set the scene for hearty dishes; pies are a speciality, including fishermen's, beef in ale, and a rich steak and Stilton.

❶ Getting There & Away
Bus 672 stops once a week (Wednesday) en route to Buckfastleigh (£1.60, 40 minutes) and Newton Abbot (£2.60, one hour). On summer Saturdays Widecombe is served by the Haytor Hoppa (p292).

Chagford & Around
POP 1446
With its wonky thatches and cream-and white-fronted buildings, Chagford clusters on the edge of Dartmoor around a picturesque square. But this apparently timeless moorland scene is also now home to some supremely stylish places to eat and sleep.

The bustling market town of Moretonhampstead sits 5 miles east.

◉ Sights

★**Castle Drogo** HISTORIC BUILDING
(NT; ☎ 01647-433306; www.nationaltrust.org.uk; near Drewsteignton; adult/child £8.70/4.30; ⊗ 11am-5pm mid-Mar–Oct; P) Magical, unique Castle Drogo really shouldn't be missed.

Designed by Sir Edwin Lutyens for self-made food-millionaire Julius Drewe, it was built between 1911 and 1931. The brief was to combine the medieval grandeur of a castle and the comforts of a 20th-century country house, so today you see Tudor, Georgian and Edwardian styling along with both crenellated battlements and cosy carpeted interiors. The woodland trails have extraordinary alpine-esque views over the plunging Teign Gorge. It's 3 miles northeast of Chagford.

Sleeping & Eating

Sparrowhawk HOSTEL £

(☑01647-440318; www.sparrowhawkbackpackers.co.uk; 45 Ford St, Moretonhampstead; dm/d/f £17/38/46) ✿ At this long-standing backpackers' favourite, primary colours meet beams and exposed stone in light dorms overlooking a central courtyard that's ringed by rickety outbuildings.

★Gidleigh Park HOTEL £££

(☑01647-432367; www.gidleigh.com; Gidleigh; d £315-515, ste £1100-1220; P✿) At Devon's most luxurious hotel crests, crenellations and roaring fires meet shimmering blue-marble bathrooms, complete with waterproof TVs. Culinary alchemy occurs in the double Michelin-starred restaurant where the eight-course tasting menu costs £140 – thrifty cognoscenti opt for the £44 two-course lunch. It's 2 miles west of Chagford.

22 Mill Street B&B £££

(☑01647-432244; www.22millst.com; 22 Mill St, Chagford; d £130-170; ✿) The elegant rooms of this sleek retreat feature wooden floorboards, satin cushions and bursts of modern art. Its intimate restaurant (two-course lunch/dinner £19/36, served noon

to 2.30pm and 7pm to 9pm Wednesday to Saturday) delivers creative twists on local, seasonal fare: expect scallops with black pudding, and garlic-laced Dartmoor lamb.

★Horse GASTROPUB ££

(☑01647-440242; www.thehorsedartmoor.co.uk; 7 George St; mains £5-19; ⊘12.30-2.30pm Tue-Sat, 6.30-9pm daily) With a style somewhere between boho-chic and casual country house, this funky gastropub makes for a chilled-out hang-out. Mediterranean-themed goodies crowd a menu which ranges from pizzas and Dartmoor beef bresaola, to worth-forking-out-for à la carte.

Sandy Park BISTRO ££

(☑01647-433267; www.sandyparkinn.co.uk; Sandy Park; mains £8-12; ⊘noon-2.30pm & 6-9pm Mon-Fri, noon-9pm Sat & Sun; P) A 17th-century thatch with exposed-beam bar, quality restaurant and brightly furnished rooms (£60 to £80).

Getting There & Away

Bus 173 Goes from Chagford to Exeter (£3.60, one hour, five daily Monday to Saturday), with two services also stopping at Moretonhampstead.

Bus 178 (one daily Monday to Saturday) Runs from Moretonhampstead to Okehampton (£2.40, one hour), via Chagford (45 minutes).

Bus 359 (£3.50, six daily Monday to Saturday) Links Moretonhampstead with Exeter. Moretonhampstead is also served by the Transmoor Link (p292).

Okehampton & Lydford

POP 7831

Okehampton huddles on the edge of an uninhabited tract of bracken-covered slopes and granite tors – the mind-expanding land-

---

PREHISTORIC DARTMOOR

With an estimated 11,000 monuments Dartmoor is ripe for archaeological explorations. It has the largest concentration of Bronze Age (c 2300–700 BC) remains in the country, 75 stone rows (half the national total), 18 stone circles and 5000 huts.

The Merrivale Stone Rows, near Princetown, are a handy one-stop shop for most monument types. The site has a parallel stone row, a stone circle, a menhir, burial chambers and dozens of hut circles. To the northeast, near Chagford, the Grey Wethers stone circles stand side by side on a stretch of open moor; another stone circle is 400m away near Fernworthy. Also nearby, at Gidleigh, Scorhill stone circle is sometimes called the Stonehenge of Dartmoor, although only half of the original stones remain. The biggest site is the Bronze Age village of Grimspound, just off the B3212, where you can wander inside the circular stone wall that once surrounded an entire village, and the ruins of several granite roundhouses.

You can buy guides to some sites (£4) from tourist offices.

scape known as the higher moor. The town has a staging-post feel, and its traditional shops and pubs are good places to prepare for a foray into the wilderness.

Some 9 miles southwest, the village of Lydford has an archetypal inn, a string of weathered granite cottages and a stunning gorge.

⊙ Sights & Activities

★ Lydford Gorge WATERFALL
(NT; ☎ 01822-820320; www.nationaltrust.org.uk; Lydford; adult/child £7/3.50; ⊙ 10am-5pm mid-Mar–Oct) The 1.5-mile rugged riverside hikes here snake past a series of bubbling whirlpools (including the fearsome Devil's Cauldron) to the thundering, 30m-high White Lady waterfall.

Okehampton Castle CASTLE
(EH; ☎ 01837-52844; www.english-heritage.org.uk; Castle Lodge, Okehampton; adult/child £4/2.40; ⊙ 10am-5pm Apr-Oct, to 6pm Jul & Aug) The towering ruined Norman motte and keep of what was once Devon's largest castle cling to a wooded spur, setting the scene for some picturesque rampart clambering.

Finch Foundry HISTORIC SITE
(NT; ☎ 01837-840046; www.nationaltrust.org.uk; Sticklepath; adult/child £5/3; ⊙ 11am-5pm mid-Mar–Oct; P) The last working waterpowered forge in England sits at the end of a 4-mile (3½-hour) walk east along the Tarka Trail from Okehampton.

🛌 Sleeping & Eating

Okehampton Bracken Tor YHA HOSTEL £
(☎ 0844 293 0555; www.yha.org.uk; Saxongate; dm £20; P @ �🛜) Budget-conscious outdoors types love this one: a 100-year-old country house, set in 1.6-hectare grounds on the fringe of the higher moor – it also offers climbing, canoeing and bike hire. It's a mile south of Okehampton; be aware, there's another YHA hostel in Okehampton itself.

★ Dartmoor Inn INN ££
(☎ 01822-820221; www.dartmoorinn.com; Moorside, Lydford; d £100; P) They've pulled off the ancient-meets-modern trick superbly here. Distressed furniture, lavish fabrics and Roberts radios fill chic bedrooms; flagstone floors, roaring open fires and horse brass–hung beams frame diners tucking into elegant gastropub meals (mains £13 to £22, served noon to 2.30pm and 6.45pm to 9pm Tuesday to Saturday, plus noon to 2.30pm Sunday). Irresistible.

Castle INN ££
(☎ 01822-820241; www.castleinndartmoor.co.uk; Lydford; d £60-95; P 🛜) The bedrooms in this Elizabethan inn range from smallish 'n' simple to spacious and luxurious – bag room 1 for a private deck and views of tiny, ruined Lydford Castle. The bar is the ultimate snug: lamplight bathes bow ceilings and high-backed benches, while the food, served noon to 3pm and 5pm to 9pm, is tried and tested Dartmoor pub fare (mains £9 to £22).

❶ Information

Tourist Office (☎ 01837-53020; www.oke-hamptondevon.co.uk; Museum Courtyard, 3 West St, Okehampton; ⊙ 10am-5pm Mon-Sat Apr-Oct, to 4pm Mon, Fri & Sat Nov-Mar)

❶ Getting There & Away

Bus 118 (two to six daily) Stops at Okehampton and Lydford, en route from Barnstaple to Tavistock (£6.15, 2¼ hours).

Bus 178 (one daily Monday to Saturday) Runs to Okehampton from Moretonhampstead (£2.40, one hour), via Chagford (45 minutes).

Bus X9 (five daily Monday to Saturday) Links Okehampton with Exeter (£3.40, 50 minutes) and Bude (£4.40, one hour).

Croyde & Braunton
POP 8131

The cheerful, chilled village of Croyde is Devon's surf central. Here olde worlde meets new wave: thatched roofs peep out over racks of wetsuits; crowds of cool types in board shorts sip beer outside 17th-century inns.

The businesslike town of Braunton is 4 miles inland.

⊙ Sights & Activities

The water's hard to resist in Croyde. **Ralph's** (☎ 01271-890147; Hobbs Hill, Croyde; surfboard & wetsuit per 4/24hr £12/18, bodyboard & wetsuit £10/15; ⊙ 9am-dusk mid-Mar–Dec) is among those hiring equipment. Lessons are provided by **Surf South West** (☎ 01271-890400;

www.surfsouthwest.com; Croyde Burrows, Croyde; per half/full day £32/62; ☺Mar-Nov) and **Surfing Croyde Bay** (☑01271-891200; www.surfing-croydebay.co.uk; 8 Hobbs Hill, Croyde; per half day adult/child £40/35).

★ **Museum of British Surfing** MUSEUM
(☑01271-815155; www.museumofbritishsurfing.org.uk; Caen St, Braunton; adult/child £3.60/free; ☺10am-4pm Wed-Mon Easter-Dec) Few museums are this cool. Vibrant surfboards and vintage wetsuits line the walls, sepia images catch your eye. The stories are compelling: 18th-century British sailors riding Hawaiian waves; England's 1920s home-grown surf pioneers – here heritage meets hanging ten.

🛏 Sleeping & Eating

Croyde gets very busy in the summer – book ahead, even for campsites.

★ **Baggy** HOSTEL, B&B £
(www.baggys.co.uk; Baggy Point; dm/d £30/110; 🛜) It doesn't get much sleeker than this surf lodge-cum-cafe set right on the coast path beside Croyde Bay. The dorms here are super-smart, the sea-view doubles positively boutiquey, and breakfast (served till 11am) can be eaten on decking watching the waves.

Bay View Farm CAMPSITE £
(☑01271-890501; www.bayviewfarm.co.uk; Croyde; site per 2 adults £24; ☺Apr-Oct; 🅿🛜) One of the area's best campsites, with laundry, showers and surf-view pitches. Often requires a week's minimum booking in summer.

Ocean Pitch CAMPSITE £
(☑07581-024348; www.oceanpitch.co.uk; Moor Lane, Croyde; site per 2 adults £29-33; ☺mid-Jun–Aug; 🅿🛜) Set at the northern end of Croyde Bay, a well-equipped site that's two minutes' walk to the beach and has cracking sea views.

Thatch INN ££
(☑01271-890349; www.thethatchcroyde.com; 14 Hobbs Hill, Croyde; d £50-110, f £130) A legendary venue among surfers, this cavernous, thatched pub's trendy bedrooms feature subtle creams, stripes and checks; the owners offer similar billets above another pub and in the cottage opposite. The pick though are at their nearby (quieter) Priory, where elegant beams frame exposed stone.

ℹ Information

Tourist Office (☑01271-816688; www.visit-braunton.co.uk; Caen St, Braunton; ☺10am-3pm Mon-Fri, to 1pm Sat) Inside Braunton's museum.

ℹ Getting There & Away

Bus 21/21A (half-hourly Monday to Saturday, hourly Sunday) Runs between Ilfracombe and Barnstaple (£2.30, 40 minutes), via Braunton.
Bus 308 (hourly Monday to Saturday, five on Sunday) Goes from Barnstaple to Braunton, Saunton Sands and Croyde (£2.40, 50 minutes).

Ilfracombe & Around

POP 11,509

Ilfracombe's geology is startling. Precipitous headlands plummet down to pint-sized beaches; waterfront walkways cling to the sides of sheer cliffs. The town seems at first a classic, well-worn Victorian watering hole. Streets slope to a historic harbour lined by touristy shops; crazy golf greens and ropes of twinkling lights line the promenade. But the resort also has a snazzier side, as evidenced by an immense Damien Hirst statue, a string of smart eateries and places to sleep, and some enchanting Victorian bathing pools.

◉ Sights & Activities

★ **Verity** LANDMARK
(The Pier) FREE Pregnant, naked and holding aloft a huge spear, Damien Hirst's 20m statue, *Verity*, towers above Ilfracombe's harbour mouth. On the seaward side her skin is peeled back, revealing sinew, fat and foetus. Critics say she detracts from the scenery, the artist says she's an allegory for truth and justice. Either way, she's drawing the crowds.

Ilfracombe Aquarium AQUARIUM
(☑01271-864533; www.ilfracombeaquarium.co.uk; The Pier; adult/child £4.25/3.25; ☺10am-4.30pm, to 5.45pm late Jul & Aug) Recreates aquatic environments from Exmoor to the Atlantic, via estuary, rock pool and harbour.

★ **Tunnelsbeaches** SWIMMING
(☑01271-879882; www.tunnelsbeaches.co.uk; Granville Rd; adult/child £2.50/2; ☺10am-5pm Apr-Oct, to 7pm Jul & Aug) It was a remarkable feat – in 1823 hundreds of Welsh miners hacked, by hand, the four tunnels here out of solid rock. They lead to a strip of beach where you can still plunge into the sea from Victorian tidal bathing pools. Extensive exhibits include sepia photos depicting the site in the 19th century, conveying a world of woollen bathing suits, segregated swimming and boating etiquette ('Gentlemen who cannot swim should never take ladies upon the water').

🛏 Sleeping & Eating

Ocean Backpackers
HOSTEL £

(☑ 01271-867835; www.oceanbackpackers.co.uk; 29 St James Pl; dm £15-19, d £45; P @ ☎) Brightly painted en suite dorms, a convivial kitchen and free coffee lend this long-established indie hostel a laid-back vibe; the giant world map in the lounge has kick-started countless travellers' tales.

★ Norbury House
B&B ££

(☑ 01271-863888; www.norburyhouse.co.uk; Torrs Park; d £85-110, f £120-145; P ☎) Each of the rooms in this gorgeous guesthouse is done up in a different style: choose from pop art, art deco or contemporary chic. Fabulous soft furnishings, a light-filled sitting room (complete with baby grand piano), charming hosts and cracking sea-and-town views seal the deal.

Olive Branch & Room
B&B ££

(☑ 01271-879005; www.olivebranchguesthouse.co. uk; 56 Fore St; s £42-95, d £75-105; ☎) Georgian trimmings (bay windows and ceiling roses) meet modern furnishings (oval armchairs and beautifully carved wood) in swish rooms that, mostly, have grandstand views over the bay and steeply sloping Capstone Hill. The buzzing bistro downstairs (mains £12, open 6.30pm to 9pm Wednesday to Monday) rustles up tasty treats.

11 The Quay
EUROPEAN ££

(☑ 01271-868090; www.11thequay.co.uk; 11 The Quay; mains £8-25; ⊙10am-10pm) Ilfracombe's hippest harbourside hang-out by far is owned by Damien Hirst. His creations line the walls, so you get to tuck into lobster macaroni or Exmoor Angus steaks while studying models of his statue *Verity* and, with delicious irony, fish in formaldehyde.

❶ Information

Tourist Office (☑ 01271-863001; www.visit-ilfracombe.co.uk; The Seafront; ⊙9.30am-4.30pm Mon-Fri, from 10.30am Sat & Sun) Inside the Landmark Theatre.

❶ Getting There & Away

Bus 21/21A (half-hourly Monday to Saturday, hourly Sunday) Runs to Barnstaple (£2.30, 40 minutes), via Braunton.

Bus 300 Heads to Lynton and Lynmouth (£3.70, 45 minutes) twice on Saturday and once on Sunday; on Sunday the service goes onto Minehead (£5.40, 1¾ hours).

Clovelly & Around

POP 440

Clovelly is the quintessential, picture-postcard Devon village. Its cottages cascade down cliffs to meet a curving crab claw of a harbour which is lined with lobster pots and set against a deep-blue sea. A clutch of impossibly picturesque inns and B&Bs make it even harder to leave.

⊙ Sights

Clovelly Historic Village
HISTORIC SITE

(☑ 01237-431644; www.clovelly.co.uk; adult/child £7/4; ⊙9am-6.30pm Jun-Sep, 9.30am-5pm Apr-May & Oct, 10am-4pm Nov-Mar; P) Clovelly is privately owned, and admission is charged at the hilltop visitor centre. The village's cobbled streets are so steep that cars can't cope, so supplies are still brought in by sledge; you'll see these big bread baskets on runners leaning outside homes. Charles Kingsley, author of the children's classic *The Water Babies,* spent much of his early life in Clovelly – don't miss his former house, or the highly atmospheric fisherman's cottage and the village's twin chapels.

Hartland Abbey
HISTORIC BUILDING

(☑ 01237-441496; www.hartlandabbey.com; adult/child £11/5; ⊙house 2-5pm, grounds 11.30am-5pm Sun-Thu Apr-Sep; P) History seems to flow from the walls of this enchanting, warm-grey manor house. Built in the 12th century, it was a monastery until Henry VIII grabbed it in the Dissolution; he then gave it to the sergeant of his wine cellar. Today its sumptuous interiors house vivid murals, an ornate Alhambra Passage and a Regency library designed in the Strawberry Hill Gothic style.

It's 5 miles west of Clovelly, off the A39 between Hartland and Hartland Quay.

🛏 Sleeping & Eating

Donkey Shoe Cottage
B&B £

(☑ 01237-431601; www.donkeyshoecottage.co.uk; 21 High St; s/d £30/60) A country-style B&B plumb on Clovelly's crazily steep hill, with wooden floors, raspberry-red walls and sea views – the best is from number 3, under the eaves.

★ Berridon Farm
CAMPSITE ££

(☑ 01409-241552; www.berridonfarm.co.uk; near Bradworthy; 3 nights £400-515, 7 nights £575-975; ⊙Easter–mid-Oct; P) At Berridon camping goes seriously comfy. Here five- or six-person, insulated safari-style tents sport a leather sofa and wood burner/oven, plus proper beds and a flushing loo. If it's wet, head for the shabby-chic sitting-eating-play space in a converted barn. It's all tucked away 11 miles south of Clovelly.

Red Lion   INN £££
(☎ 01237-431237; www.clovelly.co.uk; d £150-180) Set right beside the water, the Red Lion has plush bedrooms with either harbour or sea views, a quality restaurant (two/three courses £25/30, booking required), and a welcoming bar (mains £8, served noon to 2.30pm and 6pm to 8.30pm).

❶ Getting There & Away

Bus 319 (five daily Monday to Saturday) runs between Clovelly, Hartland Village, Bideford (£2.10, 40 minutes) and Barnstaple (£2.70, one hour).

BRISTOL

POP 393,300

If ever there was a British city on the rise, it's Bristol. Once a centre for heavy industry, over the last few decades the southwest's largest city has reinvented itself as a hub of culture and creativity. From Clifton's iconic suspension bridge to Brunel's groundbreaking steamship, the SS *Great Britain*, it's a city that's awash with historical interest. But Bristol is also known for its offbeat, alternative character, and you'll find a wealth of art collectives, community-run cafes and music venues dotted around the city's streets – not to mention murals left behind by the city's most notorious son, the mischievous street artist Banksy.

Throw in the revamped harbourside, the landmark new M-Shed history museum and a fast-growing foodie reputation, and it's little wonder that Bristol was recently named Britain's most liveable city. Gert lush, as they might say round these parts.

History

The city began as a Saxon village and developed into the medieval river-port of Brigstow, an important trading centre for cloth and wine.

In 1497, 'local hero' John Cabot (actually a Genoese sailor called Giovanni Caboto) sailed from Bristol to discover Newfoundland in 1497. The city subsequently become one of Britain's major ports, growing rich on the 'Triangular Trade' (in which African slaves were shipped across the Atlantic to New World colonies, where they were bartered for luxury goods such as sugar, rum, tobacco and cotton that fetched a healthy profit back home). Much of Bristol's 18th-century splendour – including Clifton's terraces and the Old Vic theatre – were part-financed on profits from the trade.

After being usurped by rival ports in London and Liverpool, Bristol repositioned itself as an industrial and shipbuilding centre, and in 1840 became the western terminus for the newly built Great Western Railway line from London.

In the early 20th century, local engineers pioneered the development of a groundbreaking aeroplane design, known as the Bristol Boxkite, and the city became a hub for aeronautics; many parts for Concorde were made in nearby Filton. Unfortunately, Bristol's industrial importance made it a target for German bombing during WWII, and much of the city centre and harbourside was reduced to rubble.

In 2006, the city celebrated the bicentenary of the birth of Isambard Kingdom Brunel, the pioneering Victorian engineer responsible (among many other things) for the Great Western Railway, the Clifton Suspension Bridge and SS *Great Britain*.

◉ Sights

★**SS Great Britain**   HISTORIC SHIP
(☎ 0117-926 0680; www.ssgreatbritain.org; Great Western Dock, Gas Ferry Rd; adult/child/family £13.75/7/36.50; ⊙ 10am-5.30pm Apr-Oct, to 4.30pm Nov-Mar) Bristol's pride and joy is the mighty steamship SS *Great Britain*, designed by the genius engineer Isambard Kingdom Brunel in 1843. Driven by a revolutionary screw propeller, this massive vessel was one of the largest and most technologically advanced steamships ever built, measuring 322ft (98m) from stern to tip. Originally built as a luxury transatlantic liner, she later fell into disrepair but has since been painstakingly restored to her full glory.

The ship has had a chequered history. Between 1843 and 1886, the SS *Great Britain* served her intended duty as a passenger liner, completing the transatlantic crossing between Bristol and New York in just 14 days. Unfortunately, enormous running costs and mounting debts led her towards an ignominious end: she was eventually sold off and subsequently served as a troop vessel, quarantine ship, emigration transport and coal-hulk, before finally being scuttled near Port Stanley in the Falklands in 1937.

Happily, that wasn't the end. The ship was towed back to Bristol in 1970, and has since undergone a 30-year restoration program. The ship's interior has been impeccably refurbished, including the galley, surgeon's quarters, dining saloon and a working model of the original steam engine (weighing 340 tons and measuring three storeys high). The highlight is the 'glass sea' on which the ship sits, enclosing an airtight dry dock that preserves the hull and allows visitors to view the screw propeller.

Tickets remain valid for a year, and also include admission to the nearby **Brunel Institute** (⏏ 0117-926 0680; Great Western Dockyard; ⏰ 10.30am-4.30pm Tue-Fri & first 2 Sats per month) **FREE**, which houses a wealth of research materials relating to Bristol's maritime past.

Matthew HISTORIC SHIP
(⏏ 0117-927 6868; www.matthew.co.uk; Princes Wharf; ⏰ 10am-4pm Tue-Sun) **FREE** For much of the year, a replica of John Cabot's ship, the *Matthew,* is moored in Bristol's Floating Harbour. It's a reconstruction of the vessel in which the explorer made his landmark voyage from Bristol to Newfoundland in 1497. The *Matthew* allows visits Tuesday to Sunday, and also runs trips around the city's harbour (adult/child £10/8) and along the Avon Gorge; see the website for dates.

M Shed MUSEUM
(⏏ 0117-352 6600; www.mshed.org; Princes Wharf; ⏰ 10am-5pm Tue-Fri, to 6pm Sat & Sun; ⏏) **FREE** Opened in 2011 alongside the iconic cranes of Bristol's dockside, this impressive museum is a treasure trove of memorabilia rummaging through the city's past. The exhibits are divided into three sections (People, Place and Life), and provide a panoramic overview of Bristol's history – from slaves' possessions and vintage buses to Wallace and Gromit figurines and a set of decks once used by Massive Attack. It's all highly interactive, child-friendly – and, best of all, free.

In summer, look out for special weekend activities including the chance to ride on the dock cranes, watch the old Pyronaut fireboat in action or catch a lift aboard the little steam locomotives of the Bristol Harbour

BANSKY

If there's one Bristolian nearly everyone has heard of, it's **Banksy** (www.banksy.co.uk) – the guerrilla street artist whose distinctive stencilled style and provocative artworks have earned him worldwide notoriety.

Though his true identity is a secret, it's believed Banksy was born in 1974 in Yate, 12 miles from Bristol, and honed his artistic skills in a local graffiti outfit. His works take a wry view of 21st-century culture – especially capitalism, consumerism and the cult of celebrity. Among his best-known pieces are the production of spoof banknotes (featuring Princess Diana's head instead of the Queen's), a series of murals on Israel's West Bank barrier (depicting people digging holes and climbing ladders over the wall) and a painting of a caveman pushing a shopping trolley at the British Museum (which the museum promptly claimed for its permanent collection). His documentary *Exit Through The Gift Shop,* about an LA street artist, was nominated for an Oscar in 2011.

Long despised by the authorities, Banksy has become an unlikely tourist magnet. Though many of his works are short-lived, a few still survive around the city. Look out for the **Well Hung Lover** (Frogmore St) on Frogmore St, featuring an angry husband, a two-timing wife, and a naked man dangling from a window; a stencil of the **Grim Reaper** on the side of the Thekla (p309); the **Paint-Pot Angel** outside the Bristol Museum & Art Gallery (p304), a reminder of the artist's hugely popular 2009 exhibition there; and **Mild Mild West** (featuring a Molotov cocktail–wielding teddy bear) on Cheltenham Rd.

Banksy hit the headlines again in 2014 when one of his murals unexpectedly appeared on a wooden panel outside the Broad Plain Boys' Club in April 2014. Known as *Mobile Lovers*, the mural depicted a young couple who appear to be embracing but are actually staring into their phones. Predictably enough, a furore over ownership ensued, but the artist made it clear that he had painted the mural as a gift to the boys' club, which he is thought to have attended as a young man. After a few months on display at the Bristol City Museum, the work was sold for £400,000 to a private collector in August 2014, with all the proceeds going to fund the boys' club's ongoing projects. Good on ya, Banksy.

Bristol

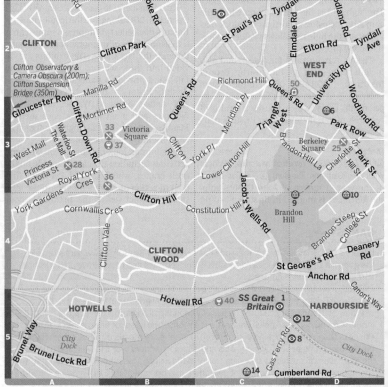

Railway (consult the website for timetables). The museum also runs guided tours exploring the harbour's history.

Spike Island
GALLERY

(☎ 0117-929 2266; www.spikeisland.org.uk; 133 Cumberland Rd; ☺ gallery noon-5pm Tue-Sun, cafe 8.30am-5pm Mon-Fri, noon-5pm Sat & Sun) Culture vultures should make time to visit Spike Island, a lively centre for visual arts that's home to a collective of artists' studios, a contemporary art gallery and a cracking little cafe. It's a short walk south from the SS *Great Britain*.

Arnolfini
GALLERY

(☎ 0117-917 2300; www.arnolfini.org.uk; 16 Narrow Quay; ☺ 10am-6pm Tue-Sun) The city's avant-garde art gallery occupies a hulking red-brick warehouse by the river, and remains the top venue in town for modern art, as well as occasional exhibitions of dance, film and photography.

Bristol Aquarium
AQUARIUM

(☎ 0117-929 8929; www.bristolaquarium.co.uk; Harbourside; adult/child/family £13.50/9.25/43.50; ☺ 10am-5pm Mon-Fri, to 6pm Sat & Sun) Bristol's harbourside aquarium has underwater habitats including a Bay of Rays, a Coral Sea, a

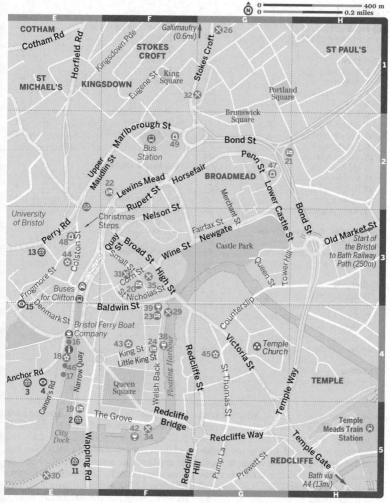

Shark Tank, and an Amazon River Zone, as well as a resident giant Pacific octopus and an underwater viewing tunnel. There's a £2 discount per ticket for buying online.

At-Bristol MUSEUM
(☑ 0845 345 1235; www.at-bristol.org.uk; Anchor Rd; adult/child/family £12.05/7.70/34.15; ☉ 10am-5pm Mon-Fri, to 6pm Sat & Sun; ☝) Bristol's interactive science museum has several zones spanning space, technology and the human brain. In the Curiosity Zone you get to walk through a tornado, spin on a human gyroscope and strum the strings of a virtual harp. There's also a great planetarium. It's fun and interactive, and should keep kids entertained for hours.

Georgian House HISTORIC BUILDING
(7 Great George St; ☉ 10am-4pm Tue-Sun Apr-Aug) **FREE** Once the home of the wealthy West Indian merchant John Pinney, this 18th-century house provides an evocative insight into aristocratic life in Bristol during the Georgian era. It's decorated in period style, typified by the huge kitchen (complete with cast-iron roasting spit), the book-lined library and the grand drawing rooms, as well as Pinney's cold-water plunge-pool in the basement.

Bristol

Cabot Tower
HISTORIC BUILDING

(⊙8am-dusk) **FREE** Located in the small park of Brandon Hill, this red-brick tower was built between 1896 and 1898 to commemorate John Cabot's pioneering voyage in search of Canada. It was closed in 2007 when suspicious cracks appeared, but was reopened in 2011 and offers an unparalleled bird's-eye panorama over the whole of Bristol.

Bristol Museum & Art Gallery
MUSEUM

(☏0117-922 3571; Queen's Rd; ⊙10am-5pm Mon-Fri, to 6pm Sat & Sun) **FREE** A classic old Edwardian museum that's full of mix-and-match exhibits, taking in everything from dinosaurs and Asian antiques to Assyrian reliefs. The French and Eastern Art sections are particularly strong: look out for paintings by Pissarro and Renoir, and a new 'Red Gate' sculpture by the Chinese artist Guan Donghai. As you enter, look up to see the famous Bristol Boxkite, an early design of propeller-powered biplane, dangling from the ceiling.

Red Lodge
HISTORIC BUILDING

(Park Row; ⊙10am-4pm Tue-Sun Apr-Aug) **FREE** Built in 1590 but remodelled in 1730, this red-brick house is a mix of Elizabethan, Stuart and Georgian architecture. The highlight is the Great Oak Room, which still features its original Elizabethan oak panelling, plasterwork ceiling and carved chimney piece.

Clifton
NEIGHBOURHOOD

During the 18th and 19th centuries, wealthy Bristol merchants transformed the former spa resort of Clifton into an elegant hilltop suburb packed with impressive Georgian mansions. Some of the finest examples can be seen along **Cornwallis Crescent** and **Royal York Crescent**. These days, Clifton is still the poshest postcode in Bristol, with fancy shops and a villagey atmosphere that's far removed from the rest of the city.

Clifton Suspension Bridge
BRIDGE

(www.cliftonbridge.org.uk) Clifton's most famous (and photographed) landmark is a

Brunel masterpiece, the 76m-high Clifton Suspension Bridge, which spans the Avon Gorge. Construction began in 1836, but Brunel died before its completion in 1864. Designed to carry light horse-drawn traffic and foot passengers, these days the bridge carries around 12,000 cars every day – testament to the vision of Brunel's design. It's free to walk or cycle across; car drivers pay a £1 toll.

There's an information point near the tower on the Leigh Woods side. Free tours take place at 3pm on Saturdays and Sundays from Easter to October.

The Downs PARK

(🚻🛝) Near the Clifton Suspension Bridge, the grassy parks of Clifton Down and Durdham Down (often referred to as just the Downs) make a fine spot for a picnic. Nearby, the small **Clifton Observatory** (📞0117-974 1242; Clifton Down; adult/child £2/1; ⏱11.30am-5.30pm Mon-Fri, from 10.30am Sat & Sun) houses a **camera obscura** (📞0117-974 1242; adult/child £2/1; ⏱10.30am-5.30pm) and a tunnel leading down to the **Giant's Cave** (adult/child £1.50/50p), a natural cavern that emerges halfway down the cliff with dizzying views across the Avon Gorge. At the time of writing, the observatory was up for sale for a cool £2 million – so things may have changed by the time you visit. Ring ahead to check.

Bristol Zoo ZOO

(📞0117-974 7399; www.bristolzoo.org.uk; adult/child £14.50/8.86; ⏱9am-5.30pm; 🅿♿) The city's zoo is on the north side of Clifton. Highlights include a brand-new £1 million house for the zoo's family of seven gorillas, as well as reptile and bug zones, a butterfly forest, a lion enclosure, a monkey jungle and the **Zooropia** (adult/child £8/7) treetop adventure park. There's a 10% discount for online tickets. To get there from the city centre, catch bus 15A or 8/9.

Blaise Castle House Museum MUSEUM

(Henbury Rd; ⏱10am-5pm Wed-Sat) FREE In the northern suburb of Henbury is this late-18th-century house and social-history museum. Displays include vintage toys, costumes and other Victorian ephemera. Bus 42/42A (45 minutes, every 15 minutes) passes the castle from Colston Ave; bus 1 (20 minutes, every 10 minutes) runs from the station and St Augustine's Pde.

🔎 Tours

Bristol Highlights Walk WALKING TOUR

(www.bristolwalks.co.uk; adult/under 12yr £5/free; ⏱11am Sat Apr-Sep) Tours of the old town, city centre and Harbourside. It's run every Saturday at 11am; just turn up outside the tourist office (p309). Themed tours exploring Clifton, medieval Bristol and the history of Bristol's slave and wine trades run on request.

BRISTOL'S HOT SPRINGS

Bath isn't the only southwest city with its own outdoor hot tub. It's a little-known fact that Bristol sits on its own system of hot springs, which bubble up through the rocks beneath the Avon Gorge. During the 19th century, these geothermally heated waters turned the area around Hotwells into a popular spa resort, where Georgian bathers flocked to try the curative waters (which were believed to alleviate a variety of conditions including consumption, asthma, dropsy and venereal diseases). The area even had its own funicular railway between Hotwells and Clifton, which served as a bomb shelter during WWII.

Though Bristol's days as a spa town may be over, you can still experience a flavour of its hot-water heyday, thanks to the wonderful **Bristol Lido** (📞0117-933 9530; www.lido-bristol.com; Oakfield Pl; nonmembers £20; ⏱nonmembers 1-4pm Mon-Fri). Originally opened as the Clifton Lido in 1849, the baths fell into disrepair and were closed in 1990, but have been carefully restored over the last few years. They're now a real local's secret, with a beautiful 24m outdoor swimming pool that's kept at a constant temperature of around 24°C. Spa treatments and massage sessions are also available, and there's even an excellent bistro.

The only drawback for nonlocals is that priority is given to members. On weekends and busy days the lido is closed for day visitors, so phone ahead to make sure there's space.

MP3 Tours
WALKING TOUR

(www.visitbristol.co.uk/about-bristol/video-and-audio/audio-tours) FREE Free downloadable MP3 guides covering Bristol's quayside, the slave trade, heritage architecture, historic churches and the city's literary connections.

Bristol Packet Boat Trips
BOAT TOUR

(☑ 0117-926 8157; www.bristolpacket.co.uk; Wapping Wharf, Gas Ferry Rd; ⊙ 11am-4.15pm Sat & Sun) This boat company cruises around the harbour area (adult/child £5.75/3.75, departures every 45 minutes on weekends, daily during school holidays). There are also weekly cruises along the Avon from May to October (adult/child £16/12) and a Sunday afternoon trip to Beese's Tea Gardens (£11/7). Cruises to Bath (£26.50/20) run once a month from May to September.

Cycle The City
CYCLING

(☑ 07873-387167; www.cyclethecity.org; 1 Canon's Rd; bike hire per day £16; ⊙ 10am-5.30pm Mon-Sat) Bike rental and cycling tours from Bristol's waterfront. It's based at No 1 Harbourside.

⭐ Festivals & Events

Bristol Shakespeare Festival THEATRE FESTIVAL

(www.bristolshakespeare.org.uk) Britain's biggest outdoor festival devoted to the Bard, held between May and September.

Bristol Harbour Festival COMMUNITY FESTIVAL

(www.bristolharbourfestival.co.uk) Bands, events and historic ships take over the city's docks in early August.

International Balloon Fiesta HOT-AIR BALLOONS

(www.bristolballoonfiesta.co.uk) Hot-air balloons fill the skies at Ashton Court in August.

Encounters FILM FESTIVAL

(www.encounters-festival.org.uk) Bristol's largest film fest is in November.

🛏 Sleeping

Bristol's hotels are geared towards the business crowd, but there are some great-value chains and B&Bs dotted around the city centre.

Bristol YHA
HOSTEL £

(☑ 0845 371 9726; bristol@yha.org.uk; 14 Narrow Quay; dm £13-22, d from £70; @) Few hostels can boast a position as good as this one, beside the river in a red-brick warehouse. Facilities include kitchens, cycle store, games room and the Grainshed coffee lounge – but the dorms are functional, and the doubles are expensive.

Brooks Guest House
B&B ££

(☑ 0117-930 0066; www.brooksguesthousebristol.com; Exchange Ave; d £85-120; 🖥) If you want to be in the heart of things, this brilliantly central B&B is a fine bet. It's in a modern building opposite St Nick's Market. Rooms are boxy, but pleasantly finished with flock wallpaper, John Lewis bed linen and Hansgröhe power showers. Discounted parking is available for £14 a day at the nearby Queen Charlotte St car park.

Future Inn Cabot Circus
HOTEL ££

(☑ 0845 094 5588; www.futureinns.co.uk/bristol-hotels; Bond St South; d £59-99; P 🖥) This hotel mini-chain has outlets in Plymouth, Cardiff and Bristol. It's modern and businessy, but the rooms are the best value in town, simply decorated in beige, white and MDF. Prices include parking at the Cabot Circus car park.

Mercure Brigstow Hotel
HOTEL ££

(☑ 0117-929 1030; H6548@accor.com; Welsh Back; d £63-125; 🖥) A harbourside location and attractive modern design make the Mercure a good, central option. All rooms boast 'floating' beds, curved panel walls and tiny TVs set into bathroom tiles (gimmicky, yes, but fun). Upper rooms have great city views.

Premier Inn, King Street
HOTEL ££

(☑ 0871 527 8158; www.premiertravelinn.com; King St; r £59-89; ✳ 🖥) Yes, we realise this is a Premier Inn, but stop being snobby and just appreciate the cheap rates and riverside location. Rooms have big beds, desk and wi-fi, and some even have glimpses of the harbour. Worth considering – although the Llandoger Trow pub next door gets rowdy at weekends. Discounted parking is available at the NCP on Queen Charlotte St.

Greenhouse
B&B ££

(☑ 0117-902 9166; www.thegreenhousebristol.co.uk; 61 Greenbank Rd, Southville; s/d £70/105; P 🖥) 🖉 No bells and whistles here – just a lovely, friendly, quiet B&B in Southville, a few minutes' stride to the river and the centre. Cream rooms, white sheets and an excellent organic breakfast make it worth considering. Free parking's an extra bonus.

⭐ Number 38
B&B £££

(☑ 0117-946 6905; www.number38clifton.com; 38 Upper Belgrave Rd, Clifton; d £135-210; P 🖥) Perched on the edge of the Downs, this upmarket B&B is one for the style-conscious. The rooms are huge and contemporary –

sombre greys and smooth blues dictate the palette, luxury is provided by waffle bathrobes and REN bath goodies, and city views unfold from the roof terrace. The two suites have old-fashioned tin baths.

Hotel du Vin HOTEL **£££**
(📞0117-925 5577; www.hotelduvin.com; Narrow Lewins Mead; r £139-254; 🅿🛜) This luxury British hotel brand is a fave with well-heeled city-breakers. Their Bristol outpost occupies an old sugar warehouse, and mixes industrial chic and sleek minimalism: exposed brick and iron pillars meet futon beds and clawfoot baths. The rooms are named after vintage champagnes; the best are the split-level mezzanine suites. The **bistro** is great, too.

🍴 Eating

Bristol's lively food scene takes in everything from ethnic restaurants to wholefood cafes. For a quick lunch, local tips include **Boston Tea Party** (www.bostonteaparty.co.uk; Park St; sandwiches & salads £4-6) and **Bagel Boy** (📞0117-922 0417; 39-41 St Nicholas St; bagels £3-5; ⏲9.30am-5.30pm).

Canteen CAFE **£**
(📞0117-923 2017; www.canteenbristol.co.uk; 80 Stokes Croft; mains £4-10; ⏲10am-10pm) 🍴 Occupying the ground floor of an old office block in gritty Stokes Croft, this community-run cafe sums up Bristol's alternative character: it's all about slow food, local suppliers and fair prices, whether you pop in for a bacon butty, veggie chilli or sit-down supper. There's regular live music, and artists' studios to explore.

St Nicholas Market MARKET **£**
(Corn St; ⏲9.30am-5pm Mon-Sat) The city's lively street market has a bevy of food stalls selling everything from mezze platters to pulled-pork rolls from BBQ specialists **Grillstock**. Lines can be long at lunchtime, but it's worth the wait. Look out for **farmers markets** on Wednesdays and a **slow-food market** on the first Sunday of each month.

Thali Café INDIAN **£**
(📞0117-974 3793; www.thethalicafe.co.uk; 1 Regent St; meals £5.95-10.95; ⏲noon-10pm) This long-standing Indian canteen now has four outlets, including this one in Clifton. It specialises in thalis (multicourse Indian meals), showcasing different curry styles from across India. You can even get takeaway in a reusable tiffin tin.

Gallimaufry BRITISH **£**
(📞0117-942 7319; www.thegallimaufry.co.uk; 26-28 The Promenade; lunch mains £5.50-7, dinner £11.50-13.50; ⏲11am-midnight) The definition of a locals' cafe, favoured by Gloucester Rd's cool crowd. All the elements are there – upcycled furniture, quirky artworks, scruffy decor – along with a dedication to Bristolian suppliers. The food covers all bases, from quick 'Gallimouthfuls' to plates of pork belly and champ mash.

Pieminister BRITISH **£**
(24 Stokes Croft; pies around £4.50; ⏲10am-7pm Sat, 11am-4pm Sun) A Bristol institution: gourmet pies with quirky names (Chicken of Aragon, Deerstalker, Moo and Blue), all drowned in lashings of gravy (meat-free if you wish). The main shop is on Stokes Croft, but there's an outlet in St Nick's market.

Olive Shed BISTRO **£**
(📞0117-929 1960; www.theoliveshed.com; Princes Wharf; mains £4-8; ⏲6.30-10pm Wed, noon-10pm Thu-Sat, noon-4pm Sun) A good spot for a harbourside lunch, especially after a visit to the SS *Great Britain* or the M Shed. It serves tapas and Med food, with tables on the quayside.

★ Riverstation BRITISH **££**
(📞0117-914 4434; www.riverstation.co.uk; The Grove; 2-/3-course lunch £12.75/15.50, dinner mains £15.50-19.50; ⏲noon-2.30pm & 6-10pm) One of Bristol's original dining-out destinations, and still leading the pack. The riverside location is hard to beat, with a view over the Floating Harbour, but it's the food that keeps the punters coming back: classic in style with a strong European flavour, from French fish soup to steak *à la béarnaise*. The **bar+kitchen** downstairs is open all day for coffee and cakes.

Ox BRITISH **££**
(📞0117-922 1001; www.theoxbristol.com; 43 Corn St; dinner mains £12.50-16; ⏲12.30-2.30pm Thu & Fri, 5-10.30pm Tue-Sat, noon-4pm Sun) This new addition to Corn St offers a refined dining experience. Located in a basement bank vault, it now resembles a posh Pullman dining car, with wood panelling, a mahogany bar and Pre-Raphaelite murals. As its name suggests, it's for the carnivores – charcuterie platters, gourmet burgers and five choices of steak cut.

Fishers SEAFOOD **££**
(📞0117-974 7044; www.fishers-restaurant.com; 35 Princess Victoria St; mains £11.95-15.50; ⏲noon-2.30pm & 6.30-10pm) Top choice for a fish

TYNTESFIELD

Formerly the aristocratic home of the Gibbs family, **Tyntesfield** (NT; ☑ 01275-461900; www.nationaltrust.org.uk/tyntesfield; adult/child £13.90/7, gardens only £8.55/4.30; ⊙ house 11am-5pm Fri-Wed, grounds 10am-6pm) is one of the National Trust's most important acquisitions of recent years. A fairy-tale mansion bristling with pinnacles and turrets, brimful of sweeping staircases and cavernous, antique-filled rooms, the house gives an insight into the lavish lives once enjoyed by England's aristocratic families. Entry is via timed ticket and includes a guided tour. The house is 7 miles southwest of Bristol, off the B3128.

Built in grand Gothic Revival style by the architect John Norton, it was in danger of collapse when the Trust acquired it in 2001, but has since undergone extensive (and very expensive) renovations. Outside, work continues on the orangery and walled gardens.

supper, from baked bream to megrim sole; the hot shellfish platter (£43 for two people) is made for sharing. The simple setting, with its whitewashed walls, ships' lanterns and nautical knick-knacks, contributes to the maritime vibe.

Cowshed BRITISH ££
(☑ 0117-973 3550; www.thecowshedbristol.com; 46 Whiteladies Rd; 3-course lunch £10, dinner mains £12.95-21.50; ⊙ noon-3pm & 6-10pm) Country food with a modern twist is served at the Cowshed. The focus is on quality, locally sourced meat – aged beef, wild rabbit, pork belly, plus the *pièce de la résistance* 'steak on stone', served sizzling on a hot lava rock. The three-course lunch and sharing boards (£15.30 to £18.50 for four people) are great value.

Primrose Café BISTRO ££
(☑ 0117-946 6577; www.primrosecafe.co.uk; 1-2 Boyce's Ave; lunch mains £6-12, dinner £13.50-18.50; ⊙ 9am-5pm & 6-10pm Tue-Sat, 9.30am-3pm Sun, 9am-5pm Mon) A Clifton classic, as perfect for morning coffee as for a proper sit-down dinner. With its pavement tables and wooden interior, it feels like a Bristolian version of a Parisian street cafe. It's particularly choice for breakfast: the *croque-monsieurs* and Belgian waffles are legendary.

Glassboat FRENCH ££
(☑ 0117-929 0704; www.glassboat.co.uk; Welsh Back; 2-/3-course lunch menu £10/12, dinner mains £15-22; ⊙ 8-11am, noon-5pm & 5.30-10pm Mon-Sat, to 4pm Sun) This converted river barge is great for a romantic dinner, with candlelit tables and harbour views through a glass extension. The food revolves around French and Italian flavours.

Soukitchen MIDDLE EASTERN ££
(☑ 0117-966 6880; www.soukkitchen.co.uk; 277 North St; mains £9.50-12.50; ⊙ noon-3pm & 6-10pm) Middle Eastern market food is

the stock in trade at this friendly diner in Southville, with characteristic dishes such as *bourek* (filo pies stuffed with meat or vegetables), mix-and-match mezze platters and flame-grilled kebabs. Honest food with heart.

Maitreya Social VEGETARIAN ££
(☑ 0117-951 0100; www.cafemaitreya.co.uk; 89 St Marks Rd; mains £8.95-10.95; ⊙ 10am-11.30pm Tue-Sat, to 4pm Sun; ☑) This Easton eatery has won awards for its innovative veggie food, and it's recently branched out with a funky new arts-space-cum-music-venue.

🍷 Drinking & Nightlife

Grain Barge PUB
(www.grainbarge.com; Mardyke Wharf, Hotwell Rd; ⊙ noon-11pm Sun-Thu, to 11.30pm Fri & Sat) Built in 1936, this barge opposite the SS *Great Britain* is owned by the Bristol Beer Factory. Descend the decks to down a pint of No. 7 Bitter or dark Exhibition ale.

Highbury Vaults PUB
(164 St Michaels Hill; ⊙ noon-midnight Mon-Sat, to 11pm Sun) This endearingly scruffy boozer has a warren of wood-panelled rooms and hallways, and at least eight real ales on tap.

Albion PUB
(www.thealbionclifton.co.uk; Boyce's Ave; ⊙ 9am-midnight Mon-Sat, to 11pm Sun) A lovely old-fashioned pub that's popular with evening drinkers from Clifton's well-heeled streets.

BrewDog Bristol PUB
(www.brewdog.com/bars/bristol; 58 Baldwin St; ⊙ noon-midnight) Britain's punk brewery has a new Bristol outlet, serving craft beers such as Libertine Black Ale, Dead Pony Club and Hardcore IPA.

Apple BAR
(www.applecider.co.uk; Welsh Back; ⊙ noon-midnight Mon-Sat, to 10.30pm Sun summer,

5pm-midnight Mon-Sat winter) Forty varieties of cider are served on this converted barge, including raspberry, strawberry and six perries (pear ciders).

Thekla CLUB
(www.thekla.co.uk; The Grove) Bristol's club-boat has nights for all moods: electro-punk, indie, disco and new wave, plus regular live gigs.

☆ Entertainment

Watershed CINEMA
(www.watershed.co.uk; 1 Canon's Rd) Bristol's digital media centre hosts regular art-house programs and film-related events, including the Encounters Festival in November.

Bristol Old Vic THEATRE
(www.bristololdvic.org.uk; 103 The Cut) Bristol's stately theatre (one of England's oldest) hosts big touring productions in its ornate auditorium, plus more experimental work in its smaller studio.

Colston Hall LIVE MUSIC
(www.colstonhall.org; Colston St) Bristol's historic concert hall tends to attract the best bands and big-name comedy acts.

Fleece LIVE MUSIC
(www.fleecegigs.co.uk; St Thomas St) A gig-pub favoured by indie artists.

🛍 Shopping

Bristol is good for shopping, but you'll need to get out of the centre if you want to avoid the high street chains, which cluster around Cabot Circus (www.cabotcircus.com) and Broadmead.

Stokes Croft and Gloucester Rd are the best areas for independent shops, especially vintage clothing, crafts and secondhand music. Clifton is more upmarket, with high-end designers, homewares and antiques shops.

Rise Music MUSIC
(☎0117-929 7511; bristol@rise-music.co.uk; 70 Queens Rd; ☉10am-7pm Mon-Sat, noon-6pm Sun) Bristol's top independent record shop, with racks of CDs and vinyl, and a coffee bar downstairs.

Dig Haüshizzle VINTAGE
(☎07789-145 175; www.dig-haushizzle.co.uk; 51 Colston St; ☉11am-6pm Mon-Fri, 10am-6pm Sat, noon-4pm Sun) Vintage furniture and retro design pieces, from pine chests to apothecary jars.

Loot CLOTHING
(☎0117-922 0633; facebook.com/LOOTvintagewarehouse; 6-9 Haymarket Walk; ☉10am-5.30pm Mon-Sat, noon-5pm Sun) The city's largest vintage clothing shop.

ℹ Information

Bristol Tourist Information Centre (☎0906 711 2191; www.visitbristol.co.uk; E-Shed, 1 Canon's Rd; ☉10am-4pm Mon-Sat, 11am-4pm Sun) Calling the phone number costs the premium rate of 50p per minute.

ℹ Getting There & Away

The **Travel Bristol** (www.travelbristol.org) website lists comprehensive information on public transport in and around Bristol city.

AIR

Bristol International Airport (☎0871 3344344; www.bristolairport.co.uk) Bristol's airport is 8 miles southwest of the city. Destinations include UK airports such as Newcastle, Edinburgh, Glasgow and Aberdeen (mainly handled by Ryanair and EasyJet) as well as direct flights to cities in Ireland and mainland Europe.

LOCAL KNOWLEDGE

BRISTOL & BATH RAILWAY PATH

This bike trail (www.bristolbathrailwaypath.org.uk) between Bristol and Bath is a delightful way to explore the countryside between the two cities. It runs for 13 miles along an old railway track that was decommissioned during Beeching's cuts in the 1950s, and passes several interesting sights, including disused mills and a delightful old station at Bitton (now part of the restored Avon Valley Railway). It also links up with other bike trails including the Dramway Path (www.southglos.gov.uk/Documents/The%20Dramway.pdf) and the River Avon Trail (www.riveravontrail.org.uk).

The official starts of the path are at St Phillips Lane in Bristol and Brassmill Lane in Bath, but you can access it at various points along the route.

For bike hire, see p310 and p320.

On-the-day parking at the airport is expensive; booking online in advance gets much cheaper rates.

BUS

National Express coaches go to Birmingham (£21.30, two hours, six to eight daily), London (£18.90, 2½ hours, hourly), Cardiff (£6, 1¼ hours, every two hours) and Exeter (£15, two hours, five daily).

Useful local buses:

Bath (£5.50, 50 minutes, several per hour) Express bus X39/339.

Wells (£5.50, one hour, half-hourly Monday to Saturday, hourly on Sunday) Bus 376, with onward connections to Glastonbury (£5.50, 1¼ hours).

TRAIN

Bristol is an important rail hub, with regular services to London Paddington provided by **First Great Western** (www.firstgreatwestern.co.uk) and services to northern England and Scotland mainly covered by **CrossCountry** (www.cross countrytrains.co.uk). Book in advance for cheaper tickets than those listed here.

Birmingham (£51.50, 1½ hours, hourly)
Edinburgh (£163.10, 6½ hours, hourly)
Exeter (£26.90, one hour, hourly)
Glasgow (£148, 6½ hours, hourly)
London (£42, 1¾ hours, hourly)
Penzance (£45, 5½ hours, hourly)
Truro (£45, five hours, hourly)

ⓘ Getting Around

TO/FROM THE AIRPORT

Bristol International Flyer (http://flyer.bristol airport.co.uk) Runs shuttle buses (one way/return £11/7, 30 minutes, every 10 minutes at peak times) from the bus station and Temple Meads.

Checker Cars (☑ 01275-475000; www. checkercars.com) Bristol Airport's official taxi service. Fares start from around £25 to £30 from the city centre.

ⓘ DRIVING IN BRISTOL

Heavy traffic and pricey parking make driving in Bristol a headache. If you do drive, make sure your hotel has parking, or use the **Park & Ride buses** (☑ 01179-222910; return before 10am Mon-Fri £3.50, after 10am Mon-Fri £2.50, Sat £2.50; ⊙ every 10min Mon-Sat) from Portway, Bath Rd and Long Ashton. Note that overnight parking is not permitted at the Park & Ride car parks.

BICYCLE

Bristol Bike Project (☑ 07983-417231; www. thebristolbikeproject.org; City Rd; bike hire per day Mon-Fri £12, Sat & Sun £25; ⊙ 9am-5.30pm Mon-Fri) A community-run bike shop and rental outlet in Stokes Croft.

Roll for the Soul (☑ 07596-917963; www. rollforthesoul.org; 2 Quay St; ⊙ 9am-5.30pm Mon-Fri, 10am-5.30pm Sat) Not-for-profit bike cafe and bike workshop – great for meeting like-minded cycling buddies.

BOAT

Bristol Ferry Boat Company (☑ 0117-927 3416; www.bristolferry.com; adult/child return £4.80/3.80, day pass £6/5) Regular ferry service around the harbour. There are two hourly routes: the red route runs west towards Hotwells, with stops including Millennium Sq and the SS *Great Britain;* the blue route runs east to Temple Meads, with stops including Castle Park (for Cabot Circus), Welsh Back, Millennium Sq and the SS *Great Britain*. Boats leave from the dock near the tourist office.

BUS

Bus journeys in Bristol's city centre cost £1 for up to three stops, otherwise they cost £1.50.

Bus 8/9 to Clifton (10 minutes), Whiteladies Rd and Bristol Zoo Gardens every 15 minutes from St Augustine's Pde. Add 10 minutes from Temple Meads.

Bus 73 Runs from Parkway Station to the centre (30 minutes).

TAXI

You can usually find a cab at the taxi rank on St Augustine's Pde, but there are plenty of dial-a-fares: try **Streamline Taxis** (☑ 0117-926 4001) or **1st Call Taxi** (☑ 0117-955 8880; www.1stcall-taxis.net). If you're taking a non-metered cab, agree on the fare in advance.

BATH

POP 90,144

Britain's littered with beautiful cities, but precious few compare to Bath. Home to some of the nation's grandest Georgian architecture – not to mention one of the world's best-preserved Roman bathhouses – this slinky, sophisticated, snooty city has been a tourist draw for nigh-on 2000 years.

Founded on top of natural hot springs, Bath's heyday really began during the 18th century, when local entrepreneur Ralph Allen and his team of father-and-son architects, John Wood the Elder and Younger, turned this sleepy backwater into the toast of Georgian society, and constructed fabulous landmarks such as the Circus and Royal Crescent.

History

Legend has it King Bladud, a Trojan refugee and father of King Lear, founded Bath some 2800 years ago when his pigs were cured of leprosy by a dip in the muddy swamps. The Romans established the town of Aquae Sulis in AD 44 and built the extensive baths complex and a temple to the goddess Sulis-Minerva.

Long after the Romans left, the Anglo-Saxons arrived, and in 944 a monastery was founded on the site of the present abbey. Throughout the Middle Ages, Bath was an ecclesiastical centre and a wool-trading town, but it wasn't until the early 18th century that Ralph Allen and the celebrated dandy Richard 'Beau' Nash made Bath the centre of fashionable society. Allen developed the quarries at Coombe Down, constructed Prior Park and employed the two John Woods (father and son) to create Bath's signature buildings.

During WWII, Bath was hit by the Luftwaffe during the so-called Baedeker raids, which targeted historic cities in an effort to sap British morale. Several houses on the Royal Crescent and the Circus were badly damaged, and the city's Assembly Rooms were gutted by fire, although all have since been restored.

In 1987, Bath became the only city in Britain to be declared a Unesco World Heritage Site in its entirety, leading to many subsequent wrangles over construction and development, most recently concerning the design of the redeveloped Thermae Bath Spa and SouthGate shopping centre.

◉ Sights

★ Roman Baths   MUSEUM
(☑ 01225-477785; www.romanbaths.co.uk; Abbey Churchyard; adult/child/family £13.50/8.80/38; ☺ 9am-6pm, to 9pm Jul & Aug) In typically ostentatious style, the Romans constructed a complex of bathhouses above Bath's three natural hot springs, which emerge at a steady 46°C (115°F). Situated alongside a temple dedicated to the healing goddess Sulis Minerva, the baths now form one of the best-preserved ancient Roman spas in the world, encircled by 18th- and 19th-century buildings. As Bath's premier attraction, the Roman Baths can get very, very busy. Avoid the worst crowds by buying tickets online,

visiting early on a midweek morning, and avoiding July and August.

The heart of the complex is the Great Bath, a lead-lined pool filled with steaming, geothermally heated water from the so-called 'Sacred Spring' to a depth of 1.6m. Though now open-air, the bath would originally have been covered by a 45m-high, barrel-vaulted roof.

More bathing pools and changing rooms are situated to the east and west, with excavated sections revealing the hypocaust system that heated the bathing rooms. After luxuriating in the baths, Romans would have reinvigorated themselves with a dip in the circular cold-water pool, which now has life-size films of bathers projected onto the walls.

The King's Bath was added sometime during the 12th century around the site of the original sacred spring. Every day, 1.5 million litres of hot water still pour into the pool. Beneath the Pump Room are the remains of the Temple of Sulis-Minerva.

There is also a fascinating museum displaying artefacts discovered on the site. Look out for the famous gilded bronze head of Minerva and a striking carved Gorgon's Head, as well as some of the 12,000-odd Roman coins thrown into the spring as votive offerings to the Goddess.

The complex of buildings around the baths were built in stages during the 18th and 19th centuries. The two John Woods designed the buildings around the Sacred Spring, while the famous Pump Room (Stall St) was built by their contemporaries, Thomas Baldwin and John Palmer, in neoclassical style, complete with soaring Ionic and Corinthian columns. The building now houses a restaurant which serves a magnificent afternoon tea (£21, or £27.50 with champagne). Should you wish, you can also sample the spring waters, which were believed in Victorian times to have curative properties. If you're lucky, you might even have music provided by the Pump Room's string trio.

Admission includes an audioguide, featuring a commentary in eight languages. The one in English is read by bestselling author Bill Bryson. Free hourly guided tours start at the Great Bath.

★ Bath Abbey   CHURCH
(☑ 01225-422462; www.bathabbey.org; requested donation £2.50; ☺ 9am-6pm Mon-Sat, 1-2.30pm & 4.30-5.30pm Sun) Looming above the city centre, Bath's huge abbey church was built

Bath

between 1499 and 1616, making it the last great medieval church raised in England. Its most striking feature is the west facade, where angels climb up and down stone ladders, commemorating a dream of the founder, Bishop Oliver King.

Tower tours (towertours@bathabbey.org; adult/child £6/3; ⏰11am-5pm Apr-Aug, to 4pm Sep-Oct, to 3pm Dec-Mar) leave on the hour from Monday to Friday, or every half-hour on Saturdays, but don't run on Sundays. Unfortunately, there's no way out of the 212

Bath

steps to the top, but the view's worth the slog. If you're feeling really romantic, you can also book a private tour for two.

On the abbey's southern side, the small **Vaults Heritage Museum** explores the abbey's history. Among those buried here are Sir Isaac Pitman (who devised Pitman shorthand) and the celebrated bon viveur Beau Nash.

Jane Austen Centre　　　　MUSEUM
(☎01225-443000; www.janeausten.co.uk; 40 Gay St; adult/child £8/4.50; ☺9.45am-5.30pm) Bath is known to many as a location in Jane Austen's novels, including *Persuasion* and *Northanger Abbey*. Though Austen only lived in Bath for five years from 1801 to 1806, she remained a regular visitor, and a keen student of the city's social scene. This museum houses memorabilia relating to the writer's life in Bath, and there's a Regency tearoom which serves crumpets and cream teas in suitably frilly surroundings.

Herschel Museum of Astronomy　　MUSEUM
(☎01225-446865; www.herschelmuseum.org.uk; 19 New King St; adult/child £6/3; ☺1-5pm Mon-Fri, 11am-5pm Sat & Sun) In 1781 astronomer William Herschel discovered Uranus from the garden of his home, now converted into a museum. The house is little changed since the 18th century; an astrolabe in the garden marks the position of Herschel's telescope.

★**Royal Crescent**　　　　HISTORIC AREA
Bath is justifiably celebrated for its glorious Georgian architecture, and it doesn't get any grander than on Royal Crescent, a semicircular terrace of majestic town houses overlooking the green sweep of Royal Victoria Park. Designed by John Wood the Younger (1728–82) and built between 1767 and 1775, the houses appear perfectly symmetrical from the outside, but the owners were allowed to tweak the interiors to their own specifications; consequently no two houses on the Crescent are quite the same.

A walk east along Brock St from the Royal Crescent leads to the **Circus**, a ring of 33 houses divided into three semi-circular terraces. Plaques on the houses commemorate famous residents such as Thomas Gainsborough, Clive of India and David Livingstone.

City Walk
Bath's Architecture

START BATH ABBEY
END ROYAL CRESCENT
LENGTH 1.5 MILES, TWO HOURS

Start this architectural amble at ❶ **Bath Abbey** (p311), the city's iconic ecclesiastical edifice, built on the site of an 8th-century chapel. From the abbey square, head south along Stall St for a view of the 19th-century ❷ **Pump Room** (p311). Turn left onto York St, and follow it west to ❸ **Parade Gardens**, a landscaped Victorian park framed by the River Avon.

From here, the Grand Parade leads north; look out for the building on the corner, ❹ **The Empire**, built as a luxurious hotel in 1901. At the northern end of the Grand Parade is ❺ **Pulteney Bridge**, designed by Robert Adams in 1773, and one of only a handful in the world to be lined with shops (the most famous example is Florence's Ponte Vecchio). West of the bridge, ❻ **Upper Borough Walls** marks the northern extent of medieval Bath; if you look closely, you might spot some sections of the medieval wall that remain.

At Saw Close, you'll see the elaborate facade of Bath's ❼ **Theatre Royal** (p319), which has been staging productions since 1805. From here, follow Barton St onto ❽ **Queen Square**, the oldest of Bath's Georgian squares, built as a showpiece development between 1728 and 1736 to demonstrate the talents of its architect, John Wood the Elder.

Turn north onto Gay St, and right onto George St. Next to the Porter pub, an alley leads north, emerging next to the ❾ **Assembly Rooms** (p315), the heart of Georgian Bath's social life. Continue to Bennett St and turn left until you reach the ❿ **Circus**, designed to echo the Colosseum in Rome. The three-tiered pillars exhibit the key styles of classical architecture (Doric, Ionic and Corinthian).

From here, Brock St leads west to Bath's Georgian glory, the ⓫ **Royal Crescent** (p313). Constructed by John Wood the Younger in 1774, the terrace is now Grade-I listed, making it as architecturally significant as Buckingham Palace. The elegant Royal Crescent Hotel is at number 16.

The terrace was designed by John Wood the Elder, but he died in 1754, and the terrace was completed by his son in 1768.

To the south along Gravel Walk is the Georgian Garden, restored to resemble a typical 18th-century town-house garden.

No 1 Royal Crescent
HISTORIC HOUSE

(☑01225-428126; www.bath-preservation-trust.org.uk; 1 Royal Cres; adult/child/family £8.50/3.50/17; ⊙10.30am-5pm Tue-Sun late Feb–mid-Dec) For a glimpse into the splendour and razzle-dazzle of Georgian life, head for the beautifully restored house at No 1 Royal Crescent, given to the city by the shipping magnate Major Bernard Cayzer, and since restored using only 18th-century materials. Among the rooms on display are the drawing room, several bedrooms and the huge kitchen, complete with massive hearth, roasting spit and mousetraps. Costumed guides provide historical background.

Bath Assembly Rooms
HISTORIC BUILDING

(www.nationaltrust.org.uk/main/w-bathassemblyrooms; 19 Bennett St; adult/child £2.50/free; ⊙10.30am-6pm) Opened in 1771, the city's glorious Assembly Rooms were where fashionable Bath socialites once gathered to waltz, play cards and listen to the latest chamber music. Rooms open to the public include the card room, tearoom and ballroom, all lit by their original 18th-century chandeliers.

It's free to enter if you already have a ticket to the Fashion Museum.

Fashion Museum
MUSEUM

(☑01225-477282; www.fashionmuseum.co.uk; Assembly Rooms, Bennett St; adult/child £8/6; ⊙10.30am-5pm) In the basement of the Assembly Rooms, this museum contains costumes worn from the 16th to late-20th centuries. Exhibitions are changed annually, so check the website for the latest.

Building of Bath Museum
MUSEUM

(☑01225-333895; www.bath-preservation-trust.org.uk; The Vineyards, The Paragon; adult/child £5/2.50; ⊙2-5pm Tue-Fri, 10.30am-5pm Sat & Sun mid-Feb–Nov) This museum explores the story of Bath's architecture, with antique tools, displays on Georgian construction methods and a 1:500 scale model of Bath.

Holburne Museum
GALLERY

(☑01225-388569; www.holburne.org; Great Pulteney St; ⊙10am-5pm) FREE Sir William Holburne, the 18th-century aristocrat and art fanatic, amassed a huge collection that now forms the core of the Holburne Museum, in a lavish mansion at the end of Great Pulteney St. Fresh from a three-year refit, the museum houses a roll-call of works by artists including Turner, Stubbs, William Hoare and Thomas Gainsborough, as well as 18th-century majollica and porcelain. Temporary exhibitions incur a fee.

Beckford's Tower
HISTORIC BUILDING

(www.beckfordstower.org.uk; adult/child £4/1.50; ⊙10.30am-5pm Sat & Sun Mar-Oct) Built as a study and library for the aristocrat William Beckford in 1827, this 39m neoclassical tower is worth visiting for its eye-popping panoramic view over Bath. A spiral staircase leads to the top-floor Belvedere, while a small collection of paintings and artefacts explores Beckford's eccentric life.

The tower is about 2 miles north of the Royal Crescent along Lansdown Rd.

American Museum in Britain
MUSEUM

(☑01225-460503; www.americanmuseum.org; Claverton Manor; adult/child £9/5; ⊙noon-5pm) Britain's largest collection of American folk art, including First Nations textiles, patchwork quilts and historic maps, is housed in a fine mansion a couple of miles from the city centre. Several rooms have been decorated to resemble a 17th-century Puritan house, an 18th-century tavern and a New Orleans boudoir c 1860. Catch bus 18/418/U18 from the bus station.

Activities

Various cruise operators offer boat trips up and down the River Avon from Pulteney

---

🛈 MUSEUM DISCOUNTS

If you're spending time exploring Bath and Somerset, pick up a Bath Visitor Card (http://visitbath.co.uk/special-offers/bath-visitor-card; £3) from the tourist office, which gives discounts at museums and attractions as well as several restaurants and shops.

Alternatively, joint tickets covering the Roman Baths and the Fashion Museum cost adult/child/family £17/10.25/48. There's also a joint ticket covering the Fashion Museum and No 1 Royal Crescent for £13/7.50/32; as long as you hold on to your first ticket, you can 'top-up' if you decide to visit the second museum later.

WORTH A TRIP

PRIOR PARK

Partly designed by the landscape architect Capability Brown, the grounds of this **18th-century estate** (NT; ☑ 01225-833422; www.nationaltrust.org. uk/priorpark; Ralph Allen Dr; adult/child £6/3.30; ☉ 10am-5.30pm Feb-Nov) on Bath's southern fringe feature cascading lakes and a graceful **Palladian bridge**, one of only four such structures in the world (look out for the period graffiti, some of which dates back to the 1800s).

It was built by the entrepreneur Ralph Allen, who founded Britain's first postal service, and owned many of the local quarries from which the city's amber-coloured Bath stone was mined. The house itself is now occupied by a private school, but there are several lovely pathways around the estate, including the **Bath Skyline**, a 6-mile circular trail offering truly inspirational views.

The park is a mile south of Bath's centre. Bus 2 (every 10 minutes) stops nearby, as does the Bath City Sightseeing's 'City Skyline' tour (p316).

Bridge, including **Pulteney Cruisers** (☑ 01225-312900; www.bathboating.com; adult/child £8/4), the **Pulteney Princess** (☑ 07791-910650; www.pulteneyprincess.co.uk; adult/child £8/4) and **Bath City Boat Trips** (☑ 07974-560197; www.bathcityboattrips.com; adult/child £8/4). There's not much difference between the tours; most last around an hour. Depending on the season, there's at least one boat an hour, or more during peak holiday times.

★ **Thermae Bath Spa**   SPA
(☑ 0844 888 0844; www.thermaebathspa.com; Bath St; ☉ 9am-10pm, last entry 7.30pm) Taking a dip in the Roman Baths might be off limits, but you can still sample the city's curative waters at this fantastic modern spa complex, housed in a shell of local stone and plate glass. Tickets include steam rooms, waterfall showers and a choice of two swimming pools. The showpiece attraction is the open-air rooftop pool, where you can bathe with a backdrop of Bath's cityscape – a mustn't-miss experience, best appreciated at dusk.

Bathwick Boating Station   BOATING
(☑ 01225-312900; www.bathboating.co.uk; Forrester Rd; 1st hr adult/child £7/3.50, additional hr £4/2;

☉ 10am-6pm Easter-Oct) You can pilot your own vessel down the Avon from this Victorian-era boathouse, which rents out traditional skiffs, rowboats and Canadian canoes. It's in the suburb of Bathwick, a 20-minute walk northeast from the city centre.

☞ Tours

Mayor's Guide Tours   WALKING TOUR
(☑ 01225-477411; www.bathguides.org.uk; ☉ 10.30am & 2pm Sun-Fri, 10.30am Sat) **FREE** Excellent historical tours provided free by the Mayor's Corp of Honorary guides, leaving from outside the Pump Room. There are extra tours at 7pm on Tuesdays and Thursdays May to September. They cover about 2 miles and are wheelchair accessible.

Jane Austen's Bath   WALKING TOUR
(☑ 01225-443000; www.janeausten.co.uk/jane-austen-centre-walking-tours; adult/child £12/10; ☉ 11am Sat & Sun) A guided tour of the Georgian city, organised by the Jane Austen Centre. The 1½-hour tours leave from the Abbey churchyard.

Bizarre Bath Comedy Walk   WALKING TOUR
(☑ 01225-335124; www.bizarrebath.co.uk; adult/student £8/5; ☉ 8pm Mar-Oct) Daft city tour mixing street theatre and live performance. Leaves from outside the Huntsman Inn on North Parade Passage. Most of the walk is wheelchair accessible.

Bath City Sightseeing   BUS TOUR
(☑ 01225-330444; www.city-sightseeing.com; adult/child £14/8; ☉ 9.30am-6.30pm Mar-Nov) Hop-on/hop-off city tour on an open-topped bus, with commentary in seven languages.

✯ Festivals & Events

Bath has lots of festivals. All bookings are handled by **Bath Festivals** (☑ 01225-463362; www.bathfestivals.org.uk; 2 Church St; ☉ 9.30am-5.30pm Mon-Sat).

Bath Literature Festival   BOOK FESTIVAL
(www.bathlitfest.org.uk) Major book festival in late February or early March.

Bath International
Music Festival   MUSIC FESTIVAL
(www.bathmusicfest.org.uk) Mainly classical and opera, plus smaller gigs of jazz, folk and world. Mid-May to early June.

Bath Fringe Festival   THEATRE FESTIVAL
(www.bathfringe.co.uk) Major theatre festival around mid-May to early June.

🛏 Sleeping

Bath gets very busy in the height of summer, when prices are at a premium. Few hotels have on-site parking, although some offer discounted rates at municipal car parks.

Bath YHA
HOSTEL £

(☑ 0845 371 9303; www.yha.org.uk; Bathwick Hill; dm £13-20, d from £29; ⊙ reception 7am-11pm; P @ 🛜) Split across an Italianate mansion and a modern annexe, this impressive hostel is a steep climb (or a short hop on bus 18) from the city centre. The listed building means the rooms are huge, and some have period features such as cornicing and bay windows.

Grays Boutique B&B
B&B ££

(☑ 01225-403020; www.graysbath.co.uk; Upper Oldfield Park; d £120-195; 🛜) An elegant B&B straight out of an interiors magazine. All the rooms are individual: some with feminine flowers or polka-dot prints, others with maritime stripes, but all simple and stylish (we particularly liked Room Two, with its French bed and bay window). Breakfast is served in the conservatory, with eggs, milk and bacon from local farms.

The owners run a smaller but equally smart B&B on the east side of town, **Brindleys** (☑ 01225-310444; www.brindleysbath.co.uk; 14 Pulteney Gardens; d £110-185).

139 Bath
B&B ££

(☑ 01225-314769; www.139bath.co.uk; 139 Wells Rd; r £125-195; P 🛜) It's a bit out of the centre, but this swish B&B has been thoughtfully designed, with swirly fabrics and supremely comfy beds, plus spoils such as cafetière coffee and spa baths in some rooms. Posh, but perhaps pricey for what you get.

Hill House Bath
B&B ££

(☑ 01225-920520; www.hillhousebath.co.uk; 25 Belvedere; s £85, d £110-140) This six-room B&B feels like staying with friends. Renovated in 2011, its decor showcases the quirky tastes of its owners – dog-print cushions, retro pictures and objets d'art abound. Breakfast is served buffet style by owner Douglas – ask him to show you the house's wine cellars. On-street parking permits available.

Henry
B&B ££

(☑ 01225-424052; www.thehenry.com; 6 Henry St; d £95-125, f £155-165; 🛜) This tall town house has one of the best positions in Bath, literally steps from the centre. Seven rooms and a self-catering apartment are finished in crisp whites and smooth beiges, and offer decent value considering the location, but there's no parking, and the house's architecture means some rooms feel cramped. Two-night minimum stay at weekends.

Three Abbey Green
B&B ££

(☑ 01225-428558; www.threeabbeygreen.com; 3 Abbey Green; d £100-160; 🛜) You literally can't get more central – step out of the front door and you're on the abbey's doorstep. It's on a leafy square, and the house has an old-fashioned, country house feel, with original fireplaces and armchairs; three rooms are named after Jane Austen characters. The suites have adjoining singles, ideal for families.

★ Queensberry Hotel
HOTEL £££

(☑ 01225-447928; www.thequeensberry.co.uk; 4 Russell St; d £115-225; P 🛜) The quirky Queensberry is Bath's best boutique spoil. Four Georgian town houses have been combined into one seamlessly stylish whole. Some rooms are cosy in gingham checks and country creams, others feature bright upholstery, original fireplaces and free-standing tubs. The Olive Tree Restaurant is excellent, too. Rates exclude breakfast.

★ Halcyon
HOTEL £££

(☑ 01225-444100; www.thehalcyon.com; 2/3 South Pde; d £125-145; 🛜) Just what Bath needed: a smart city-centre hotel that doesn't break the bank. Situated on a terrace of town houses off Manvers St, the Halcyon offers style on a budget: uncluttered rooms, contemporary bed linen and Philippe Starck bath fittings.

Rooms vary in size and are spread out over three floors – inconvenient as there's no lift. Self-catering apartments (£150 to £300 per night) are also available in a separate building at 15a George St.

Haringtons Hotel
HOTEL £££

(☑ 01225-461278; www.haringtonshotel.co.uk; Queen St; d £148-200) Bath's classical trappings aren't to everyone's taste, so things are kept strictly modern at this city-centre crash pad, with searingly bright colour schemes and clashing wallpapers giving it a fun, young vibe. The location is fantastic, but there's no lift and some rooms are shoebox-sized. Off-site parking costs £11.

✗ Eating

Many bakeries and cafes serve the city's famous 'Bath Bun', somewhere between a brioche and a bread, and not to be confused with the London Bath Bun, which is small and sweet.

There's a Saturday morning food market at **Green Park Station** (Green Park; ⊙ 8am-1pm), where you can pick up local cheeses, meats and ciders, plus bread from the **Thoughtful Bread Company** (www.thethoughtfulbreadcompany.com; Green Park Railway Station; ⊙ 9am-6pm Tue-Sat).

Sam's Kitchen Deli
CAFE £

(☑ 01225-481159; www.samskitchendeli.co.uk; 61 Walcot St; lunch £8-10; ⊙ 8am-5pm Mon-Sat, to 10pm every 2nd Fri) Situated on Bath's hippest street, Sam's is a perfect lunch spot, with set dishes (including a daily roast) served from pans on the counter. With its dilapidated piano and reclaimed furniture, it's the epitome of a shabby-chic cafe, and very popular. There are live gigs every other Friday.

Bertinet Bakery
BAKERY, CAFE £

(www.bertinet.com/bertinetbakery; 6 New Bond St Pl; ⊙ 8am-6pm Mon-Sat, 10.30am-4pm Sun) Renowned baker Richard Bertinet now has his own cafe in Bath, where you can try his feather-light cakes and French-inspired pastries. He also runs a bakery school off George St.

Café Retro
CAFE £

(☑ 01225-339347; 18 York St; mains £5-11; ⊙ 9am-5pm Mon-Sat, 10am-5pm Sun) A poke in the eye for the corporate coffee chains. The paint job's scruffy, the crockery's ancient and none of the furniture matches, but that's all part of the charm: this is a cafe from the old school, and there's nowhere better for burgers, butties or cake. Takeaways (in biodegradable containers) are available from Retro-to-Go next door.

Sally Lunn's
TEAROOM £

(4 North Pde Passage; mains £5-15; ⊙ 10am-9pm) Eating a bun at Sally Lunn's is just one of those things you have to do in Bath. It's all about proper English tea here, brewed in bone-china teapots, with finger sandwiches and dainty cakes served by waitresses in frilly aprons.

The trademark Sally Lunn's Bun is the house speciality – but there are heartier plates too, such as Welsh rarebit and 'Trencher' dishes (with the 'bun' acting as plate).

★ Circus
MODERN BRITISH ££

(☑ 01225-466020; www.thecircuscafeandrestaurant.co.uk; 34 Brock St; mains lunch £8.30-13.50, dinner £16.50-18.50; ⊙ 10am-10pm Mon-Sat) Chef Ali Golden has turned this bistro into one of Bath's destination addresses. Her taste is for British dishes with a continental twist, à la Elizabeth David: rabbit, guinea-fowl, roast chicken, spring lamb, infused with herby flavours and rich sauces. It occupies the ground floor and basement of a town house near the Circus. Reservations recommended.

Tasting Room
TAPAS ££

(☑ 01225-483070; www.tastingroom.co.uk; 6 Green St; 3-course tapas £10; ⊙ 10am-4.30pm Sun & Mon, 9.30am-11pm Tue-Sat) Plates of tapas and high-class vintages are the *modus operandi* of this slinky cafe-bar, located above Bath's premier wine merchant.

Marlborough Tavern
GASTROPUB ££

(☑ 01225-423731; www.marlborough-tavern.com; 35 Marlborough Bldgs; lunch £9-13, dinner mains £13.50-21.50; ⊙ noon-11pm) The queen of Bath's gastropubs, with food that's closer to a fine-dining restaurant – think duo of venison and pork tenderloin rather than bog-standard meat-and-two-veg. Chunky wooden tables and racks of wine behind the bar give it an exclusive, classy feel.

Sotto Sotto
ITALIAN ££

(☑ 01225-330236; www.sottosotto.co.uk; 10a North Pde; pasta £9, mains £13-17; ⊙ noon-2.30pm & 5-10.30pm) Bath's best Italian, hidden away in a vaulted cellar. Ingredients are shipped in from Italy and everything's just like mamma made, from the classic house lasagne to more unusual options such as veal, grilled swordfish and sea bass in Parma ham.

Chequers
GASTROPUB ££

(☑ 01225-360017; www.thechequersbar.com; 50 Rivers St; lunch mains £6.95-13.50, dinner £14.50-21.95; ⊙ noon-11pm) A local's favourite, this pub has been in business since 1776, but the menu is bang up-to-date thanks to young chef Leigh Evans. Forget bangers and mash – here it's Bath chorizo and spring onion champ. You'll need to book for Sunday lunch.

Yen Sushi
JAPANESE ££

(11-12 Bartlett St; sushi £4-6; ⊙ noon-3pm & 5.30-10.30pm) Bath's own *kaiten* (conveyor-belt) restaurant, with colour-coded dishes of nigiri, sushi and sashimi.

Hudson Steakhouse
STEAKHOUSE £££

(☑ 01225-332323; www.hudsonbars.com; 14 London St; steaks £22-34; ⊙ 5-10.30pm) Steak, steak and more steak is this place's raison d'être. Tuck into top-quality cuts from porterhouse to prime fillet, all sourced from a Staffordshire farmers' co-op.

Allium MODERN BRITISH £££

(☑ 01225-805870; www.alliumbrasserie.co.uk; North Pde; 2-/3-course lunch £17.50/23, dinner mains £16.50-21; ☺noon-3pm & 5.30-9pm) It's not often you find Michelin-level dining inside a Best Western – but that's what you get at the Abbey Hotel, where renowned chef Chris Staines is in charge. This is serious fine dining, awash with emulsions and purées and foams, blending Asian and European flavours.

Menu Gordon Jones MODERN BRITISH £££

(☑ 01225-480871; www.menugordonjones.co.uk; 2 Wellsway; 5-course lunch £40, 6-course dinner £50; ☺12.30-2pm & 7-9pm Tue-Sat) If you enjoy dining with an element of surprise, then Gordon Jones' restaurant will be right up your culinary boulevard. Menus are dreamt up daily by the chef, and showcase his taste for experimental ingredients (candied citrus, cod tongues, biodynamic wines) and madcap presentation (test tubes, edible cups, slate plates). It's superb value given the skill on show. Reservations essential.

🍷 Drinking & Nightlife

⭐ **Colonna & Smalls** CAFE

(www.colonnaandsmalls.co.uk; 6 Chapel Row; ☺8am-5.30pm Mon-Sat, 10am-4pm Sun) This is a connoisseur's coffee house. The espressos and cappuccinos are, quite simply, second to none – so if you care about your caffeine, you won't want to miss it. Proper coffee nuts can even take a barista training course.

⭐ **Star Inn** PUB

(www.star-inn-bath.co.uk; 23 The Vineyards, off The Paragon; ☺noon-11pm) Not many pubs are registered relics, but the Star is – it still has many of its 19th-century bar fittings. It's the brewery tap for Bath-based Abbey Ales; some ales are served in traditional jugs, and you can even ask for a pinch of snuff in the 'smaller bar'.

Same Same But Different CAFE, BAR

(7a Prince's Bldgs, Bartlett St; ☺8am-6pm Mon-Wed, to 11pm Thu-Sat, 10am-5pm Sun) Boho hang-out for the town's trendies, tucked down an alley off George St. Savour wine by the glass, snack on tapas or sip a cappuccino with the Sunday papers.

Door 34 COCKTAIL BAR

(www.door34.co.uk; 34 Monmouth St; cocktails from £8; ☺from 7pm) This cocktail bar touts itself as a 'liquid alchemist's lounge', and it certainly mixes a mean martini.

Salamander PUB

(☑ 01225-428889; www.bathales.com/pubs/salamander.html; 3 John St; mains £10-14; ☺10am-midnight Mon-Thu, to 1am Fri & Sat, to 11pm Sun) Owned by Bath Ales, the Sally serves in-house beers such as amber Gem and Golden Hare and the stronger, darker Rare Hare. There's an upstairs supper club.

☆ Entertainment

Moles LIVE MUSIC

(www.moles.co.uk; 14 George St) Bath's main music venue suffered a serious fire in March 2014; it was closed at the time of writing, and won't reopen until 2015 at the earliest.

Theatre Royal THEATRE

(www.theatreroyal.org.uk; Sawclose) Bath's historic theatre dates back 200 years. Major touring productions go in the main auditorium, while smaller shows appear in the Ustinov Studio.

Komedia CABARET, COMEDY

(www.komedia.co.uk; 22-23 Westgate St) Live comedy and cabaret at this Bath offshoot of the Brighton-based original.

Little Theatre Cinema CINEMA

(St Michael's Pl) Bath's excellent art-house cinema screens fringe films as well as foreign-language flicks.

🛍 Shopping

Bath's main shopping centre is Southgate (www.southgatebath.com), where you'll find all the major chain stores.

Smaller shops tend to be situated north from the centre. Milsom St is good for up-market fashion, while Walcot St is lined by quirky independent food shops, design stores and vintage clothing retailers.

ℹ Information

Bath Visitor Centre (☑ 0906 711 2000, accommodation bookings 0844 847 5256; www.visitbath.co.uk; Abbey Churchyard; ☺9.30am-5pm Mon-Sat, 10am-4pm Sun) Sells the Bath Visitor Card (p315). The general enquiries line is charged at the premium rate of 50p per minute.

Main Post Office (27 Northgate St)

Police Station (Manvers St; ☺7am-midnight)

ℹ Getting There & Away

BUS

Bath's **bus and coach station** (Dorchester St; ☺9am-5pm Mon-Sat) is near the train station.

National Express coaches run direct to London (£17, 3½ hours, eight to 10 daily) via Heathrow. Services to most other destinations change at Bristol or Heathrow.

Local buses:

Bristol (£5.50, 50 minutes, four per hour Monday to Saturday, half-hourly on Sunday) Bus X39/339.

Wells (£5.50, one hour 10 minutes, hourly Monday to Saturday, five on Sunday) Bus 173.

TRAIN

Bath Spa station is at the end of Manvers St. Many services connect through Bristol, especially to the north of England.

Direct services include:

Bristol (£7.10, 15 minutes, several per hour)

Cardiff Central (£19.40, one hour, hourly)

Exeter (£32, 1¼ hours, hourly)

London Paddington (£42, 1½ hours, half-hourly)

Salisbury (£16.90, one hour, hourly)

🛈 Getting Around

BICYCLE

Bath's hills make getting around by bike challenging, but the canal paths along the Kennet and Avon Canal and the 13-mile Bristol & Bath Railway Path (p309) are great to explore by bike.

Bath Bike Hire (☎01225-447276; www.bath-narrowboats.co.uk/bathbikehirecom; Sydney Wharf; half/full day £13/19; ⏰9am-11pm) Ten minutes' walk from the centre. Handy for the canal and railway paths.

Bath by Cycle (☎01225-807881; www.bathbycycle.com; 3 George's Pl; bike rental from £5; ⏰9am-6pm) Rents standard and electric bikes.

BUS

Bus 18 runs from the bus station, High St and Great Pulteney St up Bathwick Hill past the YHA to the university every 10 minutes. Bus 4 runs every 20 minutes to Bathampton.

CAR & MOTORCYCLE

Bath has serious traffic problems, especially at rush hour. **Park & Ride services** (☎01225-464446; return Mon-Fri £3, Sat £2.50; ⏰6.15am-7.30pm Mon-Sat) operate from Lansdown to the north, Newbridge to the west and Odd Down to the south. It takes about 10 minutes to the centre; buses leave every 10 to 15 minutes.

The best-value car park is underneath the SouthGate shopping centre (two/eight hours £3.30/10, after 6pm £2).

SOMERSET

With its pastoral landscape of hedgerows, fields and hummocked hills, sleepy Somerset is the very picture of the rural English countryside, and makes the perfect escape from the bustle of Bath and the hustle of Bristol. Things certainly move at a drowsier pace around these parts – it's a place to wander, ponder and drink in the sights at your leisure. The cathedral city of Wells is a handy base for exploring the limestone caves and gorges around Cheddar, while the hippie haven of Glastonbury is handy for venturing onto the wetlands of the Somerset Levels and the high hills of the Quantocks.

🛈 Information

Somerset Visitor Centre (☎01934-750833; www.visitsomerset.co.uk; Sedgemoor Services M5 South; ⏰9.15am-5pm daily Easter-Oct, Mon-Fri Nov-Easter)

Visit South Somerset (www.visitsouthsomerset.co.uk)

🛈 Getting Around

Most buses in Somerset are operated by **First** (☎08456 064446; www.firstgroup.com). For timetables and general information contact **Traveline South West** (www.travelinesw.com).

Key train services link Bath, Bristol, Bridgwater, Taunton and Weston-super-Mare. The M5 heads south past Bristol, to Bridgwater and Taunton, with the A39 leading west across the Quantocks to Exmoor.

Wells & Around

POP 10,406

In Wells, small is beautiful. This is England's smallest city, and only qualifies for the title thanks to a magnificent medieval cathedral, which sits beside the grand Bishop's Palace – the official residence of the Bishop of Bath and Wells since the 12th century. Medieval buildings and cobbled streets radiate out from the cathedral green to a marketplace that has been the bustling heart of Wells for some nine centuries (Wednesday and Saturday are market days). Film buffs might also recognise it from the hit British comedy, *Hot Fuzz* – the film's final shootout was filmed here.

�‍ Sights

Wells Cathedral   CATHEDRAL
(Cathedral Church of St Andrew; www.wellscathedral.org.uk; Cathedral Green; requested donation

adult/child £6/3; ⏰7am-7pm) Wells' gargantu-an Gothic cathedral sits plum in the centre of the city, surrounded by one of the largest cathedral closes anywhere in England. It was built in stages between 1180 and 1508, and consequently showcases several Gothic styles. Among its notable features are the West Front, decorated with more than 300 carved figures, and the famous scissor arch-es – an ingenious architectural solution to counter the subsidence of the central tower.

In the north transept is a mechanical clock dating from 1392 – the second oldest in England after the one at Salisbury Cathe-dral – which shows the position of the plan-ets and the phases of the moon.

Other highlights include the elegant Lady Chapel (1326), the fan-vaulted Chapter House (1306) and the celebrated chained library, which contains books and man-uscripts dating back to 1472. Outside, the covered cloister known as the Chain Bridge enabled clerics to reach the cathedral with-out getting their robes wet.

Free guided tours run every hour from Monday to Saturday, but you'll need a pho-tography permit (£3) to take pictures.

Cathedral Close   HISTORIC SITE
Wells Cathedral forms the centrepiece of a cluster of ecclesiastical buildings dating back to the Middle Ages. Facing the west front, on the left are the 15th-century Old Deanery and the Wells & Mendip Muse-um (www.wellsmuseum.org.uk; 8 Cathedral Green; adult/child £3/1; ⏰10am-5.30pm Easter-Oct, 11am-4pm Wed-Mon Nov-Easter), with exhibits on local life, cathedral architecture and the infamous Witch of Wookey Hole.

Further along, Vicars' Close is a stun-ning 14th-century cobbled street, with a chapel at the end; members of the cathedral choir still live here. It is thought to be the oldest complete medieval street in Europe.

Penniless Porch, a corner gate leading onto Market Sq, is so-called because beggars asked for alms here.

Bishop's Palace   HISTORIC BUILDING
(www.bishopspalacewells.co.uk; adult/child £7/3; ⏰10am-6pm Apr-Oct, to 4pm Nov-Mar) Built for the bishop in the 13th century, this moat-ringed palace is purportedly the oldest inhab-ited building in England. Inside, the palace's state rooms and ruined great hall are worth a look, but it's the gardens that are the real draw. The natural springs after which Wells is named bubble up in the palace's grounds.

Famously, the palace's population of mute swans have been trained to ring a bell when they want to be fed.

Guided tours are included in the admis-sion price and run at 11.30am and 2.30pm during summer.

Wookey Hole   CAVE
(www.wookey.co.uk; adult/child £18/12; ⏰10am-5pm Apr-Oct, 10.30am-4pm Nov-Mar) On the edge of the Mendip Hills, the River Axe has gouged out deep limestone caverns collective-ly known as Wookey Hole. They're famous for their stalagmites and stalactites, one of which is the legendary Witch of Wookey Hole, who was turned to stone by a local priest. Admis-sion to the caves is by guided tour, while up on top you'll find tacky tourist attractions ranging from a penny arcade to a mirror maze. Wookey Hole is 3 miles northwest of Wells; look out for brown signs on the A371.

At weekends, you might even be greeted by the witch herself. Tickets remain valid for the whole day, and there's a 15% discount for booking online.

Cheddar Gorge   CAVE
(www.cheddargorge.co.uk; Explorer Ticket adult/child £18.50/12; ⏰10am-5.30pm) Carved out by glacial meltwater during the last Ice Age, the limestone cliffs of Cheddar Gorge form England's deepest natural canyon, in places towering 138m above the twisting B3135. Beneath the cliffs, the gorge is riddled with miles of subterranean caves. Cox's Cave and Gough's Cave are the easiest to reach, dec-orated with impressive displays of stalactites and stalagmites, but you'll need to sign up for a caving trip (p322) if you want to venture deeper underground. The gorge begins about 20 miles northwest of Wells on the A371.

The Cheddar caves have been inhabited since the last Ice Age; a 9000-year-old skel-eton (imaginatively named Cheddar Man) was discovered here in 1903, although car-bon dating has suggested Gough's Cave was inhabited several thousand years earlier. Ru-mours of prehistoric cannibalism also seem to have been confirmed by recent discov-eries of polished human skulls that are be-lieved to have been used as drinking vessels.

Cheddar is very popular, so expect traffic during summer and school holidays. You can escape the crowds by climbing the 274-step staircase known as Jacob's Ladder, which leads to a spectacular viewpoint over the gorge and a 3-mile clifftop trail. There's a 15% discount for online booking.

Cheddar Gorge Cheese Company
CHEESEMAKER

(☑ 01934-742810; www.cheddargorgecheeseco.co.uk; adult/child £2.25/free; ⊙ 10am-5pm Easter-Oct) Along with its caves, Cheddar is also famous as the home of the nation's favourite cheese, produced here since the 12th century (Henry II considered it 'the best cheese in Britain', and the king's accounts from 1170 record that he purchased 10,240lb of the stuff). Take a guided tour at this cheesemaker and purchase top-quality cheddars at the shop.

Activities

X-Treme
ADVENTURE SPORTS

(☑ 01934-742343; www.cheddargorge.co.uk/x-treme; 1½-hr trip adult/child £21/19) The Cheddar Gorge's main outdoors company offers guided caving trips lasting around 1½ hours. Inevitably you'll get wet and dirty, and it might not be a great idea if you're averse to small spaces. Rock-climbing trips are also available.

Sleeping

Beryl
B&B ££

(☑ 01749-678738; www.beryl-wells.co.uk; Hawkers Lane; d £100-150; P ⊛) This grand gabled mansion offers a taste of English eccentricity. Every inch of the house is crammed with antique atmosphere, and the rooms boast grandfather clocks, chaises longues and four-posters galore. It's about a mile from Wells.

Swan Hotel
HOTEL ££

(☑ 01749-836300; www.swanhotelwells.co.uk; Sadler St; d £100-149) A former coaching inn that's a distinct cut above your average Best Western. The building's part-15th-century architecture is packed with period detail, and many rooms have views across the cathedral green – although square footage can be variable, so it might be worth viewing a few before you settle.

Ancient Gate House Hotel
HOTEL ££

(☑ 01749-672029; www.ancientgatehouse.co.uk; Browne's Gate; s £90-100, d £110-130; ☎) This old hostelry is partly built right into the cathedral's west gate. Rooms are decorated in regal reds and duck-egg blues; the best have four-poster beds and knockout cathedral views through latticed windows. They're £15 extra, but worth it.

Stoberry House
B&B ££

(☑ 01749-672906; www.stoberryhouse.co.uk; Stoberry Park; d £85-145; P ☎) Just outside the city outskirts, this modern house offers a swanky B&B experience: plush cushions and swags above the beds in the rooms, plus a guest lounge with books to browse and Nespresso coffee on tap.

Eating

Good Earth
VEGETARIAN £

(☑ 01749-678600; www.thegoodearthwells.co.uk; 4-6 Priory Rd; lunch £8-12; ⊙ 9am-4.30pm) A wholefood store that's branched out into homewares and a fantastic veggie cafe, which offers two daily dishes in a sunny dining room or a secret patio garden.

Strangers with Coffee
CAFE £

(31 St Cuthbert St; cakes £2-5; ⊙ 10am-5.30pm Mon-Sat) This little cafe does the best flat white in town, and has a tempting selection of cakes to match.

Old Spot
BRITISH ££

(☑ 01749-689099; www.theoldspot.co.uk; 12 Sadler St; lunch £18.50, dinner mains £14-21.50; ⊙ 12.30-2.30pm Wed-Sun, 7-9.30pm Tue-Sat) Run by husband-and-wife team Ian and Clare Bates, this restaurant focuses on British classics with a streak of Italian spice – rump of lamb with polenta and peperonata, or guinea-fowl with risotto.

Goodfellows
BISTRO, CAFE £££

(☑ 01749-673866; www.goodfellows.co.uk; 5 Sadler St) There's a choice of settings at Goodfellows: a continental-style cafe (lunch £10-17, dinner £20-25; ⊙ 8.30am-4pm Mon & Tue, 8.30am-5pm & 6-10pm Wed-Sat) for quick lunches, cakes and pastries, or a full-blown seafood bistro (3-/6-course menu £42/55; ⊙ noon-2pm Tue-Sat, 6.30-9.30pm Wed-Sat) for sit-down dining. The quality at both is excellent.

Information

Tourist office (☑ 01749-672552; www.wellstourism.com; Market Pl; ⊙ 9.30am-5.30pm Apr-Oct, 10am-4pm Nov-Mar) Stocks the *Wells City Trail* leaflet (30p) and sells discount tickets to Wookey Hole and Cheddar Gorge.

Getting There & Away

The bus station is south of Cuthbert St, on Princes Rd. Useful services:

Bath (£5.50, 1¼ hours, hourly Monday to Saturday, five on Sunday) Bus 173.

Bristol (£5.50, one hour, half-hourly Monday to Saturday, hourly on Sunday) Bus 376.

Cheddar (£4.50, 25 minutes, hourly Monday to Saturday, four on Sunday) Bus 126; continues to Weston-super-Mare (£5.50, 1½ hours).

Glastonbury (£3.50, 15 minutes, several per hour) Bus 377.

Taunton (day rover £10, 1¼ hours, hourly Monday to Saturday) Bus 29 stops in Glastonbury.

Glastonbury

POP 8429

Ley lines converge, white witches convene and every shop is filled with the aroma of smouldering joss-sticks in good old Glastonbury, the southwest's undisputed capital of alternative culture. Now famous for its annual musical mudfest held on Michael Eavis' farm in nearby Pilton, Glastonbury has a much more ancient past: the town's iconic tor was an important pagan site, and is rumoured by some to be the mythical Isle of Avalon, King Arthur's last resting place. It's also allegedly one of the world's great spiritual nodes, marking the meeting point of many mystical lines of power – so if you feel the need to get your chakras realigned, this is definitely the place. Whatever the truth of the various legends swirling round Glastonbury, one thing's for certain – watching the sunrise from the top of the tor is an experience you won't forget in a hurry.

◉ Sights

★ **Glastonbury Tor**   LANDMARK
(NT; www.nationaltrust.org.uk/glastonbury-tor) Topped by the ruined medieval **Chapel of St Michael**, the iconic hump of Glastonbury Tor is visible for miles around, and provides Somerset with one of its most unmistakable landmarks. It takes half an hour to walk up from the start of the trail on Well House Lane; the steepest sections are stepped. You can walk to the trailhead from the town centre in about 20 minutes, or catch the regular Tor Bus, which shuttles from Dunstan's car park near the Abbey to the trailhead on Well House Lane.

The tor is the focal point for a wealth of local legends. According to Celtic legend, the tor is the home of Arawn or Gwyn ap Nudd, king of the Underworld and lord of the faeries. A more famous legend identifies the tor as the mythic Isle of Avalon, where King Arthur was taken after being mortally wounded in battle, and where Britain's 'once and future king' sleeps until his country calls again. Others believe that the Tor marks an ancient mystical node where invisible lines of energy known as ley lines converge.

It's easy to see why the tor has inspired so many myths. It's a strange presence in an

---

GLASTONBURY FESTIVAL

To many people, Glastonbury is synonymous with the **Glastonbury Festival of Contemporary Performing Arts** (www.glastonburyfestivals.co.uk), a majestic (and frequently mud-soaked) extravaganza of music, theatre, dance, cabaret, carnival, spirituality and general all-round weirdness that's been held on and off on farmland in Pilton, just outside Glastonbury, for the last 40-something years (bar the occasional off-year to let the farm recover).

The first event was held in 1970, when young dairy farmer Michael Eavis decided to stage his own British version of Woodstock on his land at Worthy Farm. Eavis borrowed £15,000 and invited some bands to play on a couple of makeshift stages in a field. Entry was £1, which included a pint of milk from Eavis' dairy herd; among the acts who performed was Marc Bolan of T-Rex, who arrived in typically flamboyant style in his own velvet-covered Buick.

Forty years later, the festival has become the world's longest-running pop-music festival, attracting crowds of more than 120,000. It's even had a feature-length film made about it, directed by Julien Temple. Eavis' daughter Emily has since taken over the day-to-day-running of the festival, and her decision to give headline slots to artists such as Jay-Z and U2 has led many people to grumble that Glastonbury's gone mainstream – but with acts such as the Rolling Stones and the Arctic Monkeys still lining up to play, Glastonbury's status as the UK's premier outdoor party looks safe for years to come.

More importantly, even the local councillors seem to have come around; after years of wrangling, in 2014 the festival was granted an unprecedented 10-year licence, a sign that the powers-that-be have recognised the festival's status as a national treasure. Tickets (which cost £210 in 2014) usually go on sale in the autumn, but always sell out within a matter of minutes, so you need to get in lightning-quick if you want to go.

Glastonbury

Glastonbury

otherwise pan-flat landscape, and in ancient times (when the area around Glastonbury was covered by water for much of the year), the Tor would indeed have appeared as an island, wreathed in mists and cut off by rivers, marshes and bogs.

Chalice Well & Gardens   GARDENS
(☑ 01458-831154; www.chalicewell.org.uk; adult/child £4/2; ◉10am-6pm Apr-Oct, to 4.30pm Nov-Mar) Shaded by yew trees and criss-crossed by quiet paths, the Chalice Well and Gardens have been sites of pilgrimage since the days of the Celts. The iron-red waters from the 800-year-old well are rumoured to have healing properties, good for everything from eczema to smelly feet; some legends also identify the well as the hiding place of the Holy Grail. In fact, the reddish waters are caused by iron deposits in the soil. You can drink the water from a lion's-head spout, or rest your feet in basins surrounded by flowers.

The Chalice Well is also known as the 'Red Spring' or 'Blood Spring'; its sister, White Spring, surfaces across Well House Lane.

★ **Glastonbury Abbey**   RUIN
(☑ 01458-832267; www.glastonburyabbey.com; Magdalene St; adult/child £6/4; ◉9am-8pm) The scattered ruins of Glastonbury Abbey give little hint that this was once one of England's great seats of ecclesiastical power. It was torn down following Henry VIII's dissolution of the monasteries in 1539, and the last abbot, Richard Whiting, was hung, drawn and quartered on the tor. Precious little now remains save for a few nave walls, the ruined

St Mary's chapel, and the crossing arches, which may have been scissor-shaped like those in Wells Cathedral.

The grounds also contain a museum, cider orchard and herb garden. According to legend, the abbey's famous holy thorn tree sprang from the staff of Joseph of Arimathea, Jesus' great-uncle, who supposedly visited the abbey following Christ's death. It blooms at Christmas and Easter.

The abbey even has an Arthurian connection. In the 12th century, monks purportedly uncovered a tomb in the abbey grounds inscribed *Hic iacet sepultus inclitus rex arturius in insula avalonia*, or 'Here lies buried the renowned King Arthur in the Isle of Avalon'. Inside the tomb were two entwined skeletons, supposedly those of Arthur and his wife Guinevere. The bones were reburied beneath the altar in 1278, but were lost following the abbey's destruction.

Lake Village Museum
MUSEUM
(The Tribunal, 9 High St; adult/child £3/1.50; ⊙10am-3pm) Upstairs from Glastonbury's tourist office, the Lake Village Museum displays finds from a prehistoric bog village discovered in nearby Godney. The houses were clustered in about six groups and built from reeds, hazel and willow. It's thought they were occupied by summer traders who lived the rest of the year around Glastonbury Tor.

🛏 Sleeping

Crown Glastonbury Backpackers
HOSTEL £
(☑01458-833353; www.glastonburybackpackers.com; 4 Market Pl; dm £16.50, d £35-60; P @) Basic but friendly hostel above the old Crown pub, with small, clean rooms as well as a kitchen and laundry.

Covenstead
B&B ££
(☑07970-615251; www.covenstead.co.uk; Magdalene St; s £60, d £70-90) Well, what else would you expect in mystical Glastonbury but a witchcraft-themed B&B? There are four rooms, all with their own pagan theme, and the house is a mix of suburban semi and spooky knick-knacks – oil paintings, horned bedside lamps, candelabra and velvet chairs. Thankfully no eye of newt or toe of frog for breakfast, though.

Glastonbury White House
B&B ££
(☑01458-830886; www.theglastonburywhitehouse.com; 21 Manor House Rd; s £60-65, d £75-95; P) There are only two rooms here, but owner Carey has made them super-cosy, with extra

touches such as fridges, fresh milk and bottles of White Spring water. Breakfast is extra (£5 continental, £7.50 cooked). It's about five minutes' walk from High St.

Glastonbury Townhouse
B&B ££
(☑01458-831040; www.glastonburytownhouse.co.uk; Street Rd; d £90-120) Nothing too outlandish about this place – just a solid, red-brick, Edwardian town house, with three quiet rooms, lots of antique furniture and a friendly owner, Greg, who has all the local tips.

Parsnips
B&B ££
(☑01458-835599; www.parsnips-glastonburyco.uk; 99 Bere Lane; s £55, d £70-75; P @) This modern B&B is a solid bet, with bright rooms in gingham and cream, complimentary coffee on arrival, and a range of holistic treatments by arrangement. Breakfast is in an attractive conservatory.

🍴 Eating & Drinking

Rainbow's End
VEGETARIAN £
(☑01458-833896; www.rainbowsendcafe.com; 17a High St; mains £4-8; ⊙10am-5.30pm Mon-Sat, to 4pm Sun; 🍴) 🖉 This psychedelic cafe sums up the Glastonbury spirit, with its all-veggie food, potted plants and mix-and-match furniture. Tuck into homity pie or a hot quiche, followed by scrumptious homemade cake. There's a small patio out back.

Bocabar
BRITISH ££
(☑01458-440558; http://glastonbury.bocabar.co.uk; Morland Rd; lunch £5-10, dinner £13.50-19.95; ⊙9.30am-midnight Tue-Sat, to 5pm Sun & Mon) In an old factory once occupied by Morlands the sheepskin makers, this has turned into Glastonbury's hippest hang-out. There are live bands and events several times a week, and a pan-global menu that takes in Thai chillies, classic steaks, gourmet burgers and adventurous crêpes. The industrial-chic vibe adds appeal. It's about 1.5 miles southwest of the town centre along Morland Rd.

Hundred Monkeys Cafe
BISTRO ££
(www.hundredmonkeyscafe.com; 52 High St; mains £8-15; ⊙8am-8.30pm Mon-Fri, to 9pm Fri & Sat, 9am-4pm Sun; 🍴) A cosy bistro with a laid-back, fair-trade, seasonal ethos, decorated in homely fashion with pine furniture and handwritten blackboards. Mezze platters, pasta dishes, curries and risottos are the order of the day – with plenty of gluten-free and vegan options (this is Glastonbury, after all). The tea selection is enormous and the wines are all biodynamic.

Who'd a Thought It Inn GASTROPUB ££
(17 Northload St; mains £10.95-13.95; ⊘ noon-2pm & 6-9pm) A pleasantly peculiar local's pub, covered in paraphernalia including antique bottles and old signs, an old red telephone box and an upside-down bike on the ceiling. The food is solid pub fare – think sausages, pies and steaks – but there are usually specials chalked above the bar.

George & Pilgrim PUB
(1 High St; mains £7-15; ⊘ 11am-11pm) Partly 15th-century inn with one of the town's most authentically historic interiors – timbers, flagstones and all.

ⓘ Information

Glastonbury Tourist Office (⌕ 01458-832954; www.glastonburytic.co.uk; The Tribunal, 9 High St; ⊘ 10am-5pm)

ⓘ Getting There & Away

There is no train station in Glastonbury. Bus 377 (several times per hour) travels north to Wells (£3.50, 15 minutes). Bus 29 travels to Taunton (£5.50, 50 minutes, hourly Monday to Saturday).

Taunton & Around

Taunton is in the heart of Somerset in more ways than one; it's bang in the middle of the county geographically, and is also the area's county town and commercial centre.

It's worth a look for its part-12th-century castle, which now houses the Museum of Somerset and the Somerset Military Museum (⌕ 01823-255088; Castle Green, Taunton; ⊘ 10am-5pm Tue-Sat) FREE.

It's also a useful gateway to the Quantocks and handy for exploring several local sights.

ⓞ Sights

Fleet Air Arm Museum MUSEUM
(⌕ 01963-840565; www.fleetairarm.com; adult/child £14/10; ⊘ 10am-5.30pm daily Apr-Oct, 10am-4.30pm Wed-Sun Nov-Mar) This excellent aviation museum houses hundreds of naval aircraft from Sopwiths to Phantom fighters. You can walk onto the flight deck of the first British-built Concorde and take a simulated flight onto the aircraft carrier HMS *Ark Royal*. The museum is 4 miles north of Somerset, near Yeovilton.

West Somerset Railway HERITAGE RAILWAY
(⌕ 01643-704996; www.west-somerset-railway.co.uk; 24hr rover ticket adult/child £17/8.50) The chuffing steam trains of this vintage railway are a fine way to see the Somerset countryside. The 20-mile route runs from Bishops Lydeard to Minehead, stopping at Dunster, Watchet, Williton, Crowcombe Heathfield and several other stations en route. There are four to eight trains daily from March to October, with a more limited service for the rest of the year. Bikes can be carried on board for £2.

There are discounts if you book online.

Montacute House HISTORIC BUILDING
(NT; ⌕ 01935-823289; montacute@nationaltrust.org.uk; adult/child £11.20/5.60; ⊘ 11am-4pm Wed-Mon summer, gardens 10am-5pm year-round) This manor was built in the 1590s for Sir Edward

---

OFF THE BEATEN TRACK

THE SOMERSET LEVELS

Flat as a pancake, sub-sea-level and criss-crossed with canals (known locally as rhynes), the Somerset Levels are one of England's largest native wetlands. Covering over 64,000 hectares between the Quantock and Mendip Hills, they're brilliant for bird-spotters, particularly in October and November, when huge flocks of starlings (properly known as 'murmurations') descend on the area. Nature reserves have been established at Ham Wall, Shapwick Heath, Sedgemoor and Westhay.

More recently, the Levels made the headlines thanks to the serious floods that struck in 2014, submerging the area under several metres of water for much of the winter. In truth, the land here has always been flood-prone, but it's been claimed that the recent floods have been exacerbated by climate change and the cessation of river-dredging.

Along with agriculture, many traditional industries survive on the Levels, including peat digging, reed harvesting and willowcraft, which you can see in action at the Willows & Wetlands Visitor Centre (⌕ 01823-490249; www.englishwillowbaskets.co.uk; ⊘ 9.30am-5pm Mon-Sat) near Stoke St Gregory.

The flat landscape of the Levels also makes it ideal for cycling. Several trails pass through the village of Langport, including the long-distance River Parrett Trail.

THE QUANTOCKS

The range of red sandstone hills known as the Quantocks traces a 12-mile curve across Somerset's northern edge. A mix of moors, valleys and ancient woods of coppiced oak, these little-visited hills offer stirring views across the Bristol Channel: when the weather's fine, you can see across to the Gower coastline in south Wales.

Designated as an Area of Outstanding Natural Beauty (AONB), the Quantocks receive far fewer visitors than Exmoor and Dartmoor, making them perfect for hikers and bikers in search of quiet trails. The Quantocks AONB (www.quantockhills.com; Fyne Ct; ⊙9am-5pm Mon-Fri) runs walks.

Literary buffs might also like to make a stop at the village of Nether Stowey, best known for its association with the poet Samuel Taylor Coleridge, who moved to the village with his wife Sara and son Hartley in 1796. Coleridge Cottage (NT; ☑01278-732662; 35 Lime St, Nether Stowey; adult £5.80/2.90; ⊙11am-5pm Thu-Mon) is now owned by the National Trust; the poet is thought to have composed some of his greatest works during his three-year stay here, including *The Rime of the Ancient Mariner*, *Kubla Khan* and *This Lime Tree Bower My Prison*.

Phelips, a Speaker of the House of Commons, and contains some of the finest 16th- and 17th-century interiors in the country. The house is particularly renowned for its plasterwork, chimney pieces and tapestries, but the highlight is the Long Gallery, the longest such hall in England. It's decorated with Elizabethan portraits on loan from the National Portrait Gallery in London. It's 24 miles southeast of Taunton on the A358 and A303, or 5 miles west of Yeovil on the A3088.

The house is only open on selected days in winter, so phone ahead.

Ham Hill
VIEWPOINT

(www.southsomerset.gov.uk/hamhill; near Stoke-sub-Hamdon) FREE Looming above the village of Stoke-sub-Hamdon, this is the highest point in Somerset. It's served a variety of purposes – Iron Age hill fort, medieval village, stone quarry – but it's now a delightful park covering 156 hectares. Recent archaeological excavations have revealed a huge Iron Age bone-pit that – at least for now – remains a mystery.

Stoke-sub-Hamdon is 7 miles west of Yeovil off the A303; follow the brown signs.

🛏 Sleeping & Eating

Queen's Arms
INN ££

(☑01963-220317; www.thequeensarms.com; Corton Denham; d £85-130, mains £15-25; ⊙restaurant noon-3pm & 6-9pm; P 🌐) Somerset's not short on lovely pubs, but this one in Corton Denham is worth the trip. Rugs, reclaimed pews and flagstones nod to its 18th-century heritage, but the gastropub menu and rustic-chic rooms are altogether modern.

It's scooped numerous awards, including CAMRA's Somerset Cider Pub of the Year. It's 8 miles northeast of Yeovil.

Frog St Farmhouse
B&B ££

(☑01823-481883; www.frogstreet.co.uk; Hatch Beauchamp; d £90-120; P 🌐) The name of this amber-stoned longhouse in nearby Hatch Beauchamp derives from the Anglo-Saxon for 'meeting place'. It's a beauty, with four rooms mixing rusticity (beams, stone, wonky doors) with luxurious furnishings (rolltop baths, cotton linen, wood floors).

★ Lord Poulett Arms
GASTROPUB ££

(☑01460-73149; www.lordpoulettarms.com; Hinton St George; mains £14-16, r £85-95; ⊙noon-2.30pm & 6-9pm; P) Hinton St George's deliciously olde-worlde village pub has been named Somerset Dining Pub of the Year three times, most recently in 2014. The hearty food is fantastic, and the building oozes country atmosphere, with beams, roaring fires and stacks of ale barrels behind the bar. It even has quirky rooms upstairs. Hard to fault.

It's roughly 15 miles from Yeovil and Taunton.

CORNWALL

You can't get further west than the ancient Celtic kingdom of Cornwall (or Kernow, as it's known to Cornish-speakers). Blessed with the southwest's wildest coastline and most breathtakingly beautiful beaches, this proudly independent peninsula has always marched to its own tune.

BATH & SOUTHWEST ENGLAND TAUNTON & AROUND

While the staple industries of old – mining, fishing and farming – have all but disappeared, Cornwall has since reinvented itself as one of the nation's creative corners. Whether it's exploring the space-age domes of the Eden Project, sampling the culinary creations of a celebrity chef or basking on a deserted beach, you're guaranteed to feel the itch of inspiration. Time to let a little Kernow into your soul.

Since 2006, Cornwall's historic mining areas have formed part of the UK's newest Unesco World Heritage Site, the Cornwall & West Devon Mining Landscape (www.cornish-mining.org.uk).

ⓘ Getting Around

Bus, train and ferry timetables can be found on the **Traveline South West** (☑ 0871 200 2233; www.travelinesw.com) website.

The useful **Great Scenic Railways** (www.greatscenicrailways.com) website features online booking and timetables for Cornwall's regional railways.

BUS

Cornwall has two main bus operators. First Cornwall operates the routes between main towns, and the majority of services in the west of the county, while Western Greyhound operates services between coastal villages and most services in the east of the county.

First Cornwall (☑ customer service 0845 600 1420, timetables 0871 200 2233; www.firstgroup.com/ukbus/devon_cornwall)

Western Greyhound (☑ 01637-871871; www.westerngreyhound.com)

TRAIN

Cornwall's main railway line follows the coast as far as Penzance, with branch lines to Gunnislake, Looe, Falmouth, St Ives and Newquay.

CrossCountry (☑ 0844 811 0124; www.crosscountrytrains.co.uk) Operates services to the north of England, the Midlands and Scotland.

First Great Western (☑ 08457 000125; www.firstgreatwestern.co.uk) Operates the main line from London Paddington via Exeter, Plymouth, St Austell, Truro and Penzance, as well as the regional branch lines.

TRANSPORT PASSES

Several passes cover public transport in Cornwall. Ride Cornwall is the best all-round value covering bus and train. There are also Day Ranger tickets for all of Cornwall's branch railway lines, as well as 'Two Together' and 'Groupsave' tickets for two and four adults travelling together.

FirstDay Southwest (adult/child/family £7.60/6.20/18.70) One-day pass offering unlimited bus travel on First buses in Devon and Cornwall.

Freedom of Devon & Cornwall Rover (3-day adult/child £45, 8-day adult/child £69) Three days' train travel in seven, or eight days' travel in 14. Valid after 9am and anytime weekends.

Ride Cornwall (adult/child/family £10/7.50/20) The best-value all-round travel pass, covering one day's rail and bus travel between Cornwall and Plymouth. Valid after 9am Monday to Friday and weekends.

Western Greyhound Day Explorer (adult/child/family £8.50/5.50/17) Covers one day's travel on any of Western Greyhound's bus routes in Cornwall.

Day Ranger Rail Tickets

Atlantic Coast Line (1-day ranger adult/child £4.60/2.30) Branch line from Newquay to Par.

Looe Valley Line (1-day ranger adult/child £5/3.15) Scenic line from Liskeard to Looe.

Maritime Line (1-day ranger adult/child £4.10/2.05) Truro to Falmouth Docks, with stops at Penryn and Falmouth Town.

Tamar Valley Line (1-day ranger adult/child £5.40/2.70) Plymouth to Gunnislake, with stops including Devonport Dockyard, St Budeaux, Bere Alston and Calstock.

St Ives Bay Line (1-day ranger adult/child/family £4/2/10) Lovely line that runs between St Erth, Carbis Bay and St Ives.

Bude

POP 9242

Just a scant few miles across the Devon border, Bude is a breezy seaside town with a bevy of impressive beaches, as well as a lovely seawater lido built in the 1930s. The town itself isn't much to look at, but the stunning coastline on its doorstep makes it worthy of a stop.

◉ Sights

Bude's beaches are definitely its main asset. Closest is Summerleaze, a bucket-and-spade affair with lots of space at low tide, and the beautiful Bude Sea Pool (www.budeseapool.net). North across Summerleaze Down is Crooklets, offering golden sand and rock pools at low tide.

To reach Bude's other beaches requires either a car or a hike along the coast path. Three miles south of town is Widemouth Bay (pronounced 'widmouth'), a broad, sandy beach good for both families and surfers. Two miles further is the shingly beach of Millook, followed by the dramatic cliffs around Crackington Haven.

Three miles north of town are the National Trust–owned Northcott Mouth and Sandymouth.

A mile further on is pebbly Duckpool, often quiet even in summer.

Bude Castle   MUSEUM

(www.thecastlebude.org.uk; The Castle; ⏱10am-5pm Easter-Oct, 10am-4pm Nov-Easter) FREE Housed in a peculiar folly behind Summerleaze Beach, Bude Castle was built by local inventor Sir Goldsworthy Gurney, whose creations included theatrical limelight and steam carriages. The building now houses a small heritage centre which roves through Bude's maritime, geological and social history. There's also a cafe on the top floor.

🛏 Sleeping

Dylan's Guesthouse   B&B £

(☎01288-354705; www.dylansguesthouseinbude.co.uk; Downs View; s £40-50, d £60-75; P🛜) This snazzy B&B has rooms decked out in white linen, chocolate throws, pine furniture and quirky curios. Most look across the town's golf course and downlands.

Elements Hotel   HOTEL ££

(☎01288-275066; www.elements-life.co.uk; Marine Dr; d £99-120; P🛜) Smart clifftop hotel with 11 rooms in whites and creams, big views from the outdoor deck, a gym and Finholme sauna, and surf packages courtesy of nearby Raven Surf School.

Beach at Bude   HOTEL £££

(☎01288-389800; www.thebeachatbude.co.uk; Summerleaze Cres; r £95-185; P🛜) The main sell at this swish hotel are the fine views over Summerleaze beach, but the rooms are attractive too: spacious and smart, with slate-lined bathrooms featuring his-and-hers sinks and Lloyd Loom chairs. They're styled to resemble a New England beach cabin.

🍴 Eating

Scrummies   CAFE £

(Lansdown Rd; mains £6-8; ⏱8am-10pm) The best place for fish and chips in town (the skate and monkfish are caught by the owner). For something fancier, try their scallops and lobster (half/whole £12/24).

Life's a Beach   CAFE ££

(☎01288-355222; www.lifesabeach.info; Summerleaze; lunch mains £6-10, dinner £16.50-19; ⏱10.30am-3.30pm & 7-10pm Mon-Sat, 10.30am-3.30pm Sun) This bistro overlooking Summerleaze has a split personality: by day a beach caff serving coffees, panini and ice cream; by night a smart seafood restaurant.

ℹ Information

Bude Tourist Office (☎01288-354240; www.visitbude.info; The Crescent; ⏱10am-5pm Mon-Sat, plus 10am-4pm Sun summer) Beside the main car park near the Castle.

ℹ Getting There & Away

Bus 594/595 (six daily Monday to Saturday, four on Sunday in summer) travels to Boscastle (£4.50 single) via Widemouth and Crackington Haven (£3 or £4).

Boscastle

POP 641

Nestled in the crook of a steep coombe (valley) at the confluence of three rivers, Boscastle's sea-going heritage stretches back to Elizabethan times. With its quaint cottages, flower-clad cliffs, tinkling streams and sturdy quay, it's almost impossibly photogenic.

But the peaceful setting belies some turbulent history: in 2004 Boscastle was devastated by one of Britain's largest-ever flash floods, which carried away cars, bridges and buildings. The village has since been rebuilt, but look closely and you'll still spot reminders of the floods dotted around.

WORTH A TRIP

VINTAGE CORNWALL

Cornwall might not seem like an obvious place for winemaking, but local entrepreneur Bob Lindo has been producing award-winning vintages at his Camel Valley Vineyard (☎01208-77959; www.camelvalley.com; ⏱10am-5pm Mon-Sat) since 1989. The range includes award-winning whites and rosés, and a bubbly that's champagne in all but name. Aficionados say the wines have a fresh, light quality that comes from the mild climate and pure sea air. Vineyard tours run regularly, and you can taste and buy the goods in the on-site shop.

◎ Sights

Museum of Witchcraft   MUSEUM
(☑ 01840-250111; www.museumofwitchcraft.com; The Harbour; adult/child £5/4; ◷ 10.30am-6pm Mon-Sat, 11.30am-6pm Sun Mar-Nov) This odd-ball museum claims to house the world's largest collection of witchy memorabilia, from haunted skulls to hags' bridles and voodoo dolls. It's half-tacky, half-spooky, and some of the more 'controversial' exhibits might perturb kids of a sensitive disposition (or adults, for that matter).

🛏 Sleeping

Boscastle YHA   HOSTEL £
(☑ 01840-250928, 0845 371 9006; boscastle@yha.org.uk; Palace Stables, The Harbour; dm £20-22.50; ◷ Apr-Nov) Boscastle's shoebox-sized hostel was all but washed away by the floods, but it's been completely renovated. It's in one of the village's oldest buildings beside the harbour, but be prepared for small dorms, especially considering the price.

Boscastle House   B&B ££
(☑ 01840-250654; www.boscastlehouse.co.uk; Tintagel Rd; s/d from £50/102; ℗ 🤶) The fanciest of Boscastle's B&Bs, in a Victorian house overlooking the valley, with five classy rooms with a bright, contemporary feel, mixing neutral colours with bold print wallpapers. Charlotte has bay window views, Nine Windows has his-and-hers sinks and a free-standing bath, and Trelawney has ample space and a sofa.

Orchard Lodge   B&B ££
(☑ 01840-250418; www.orchardlodgeboscastle.co.uk; Gunpool Lane; d £89-99, 2-night minimum in summer; ℗ 🤶) Uphill from the harbour, Geoff and Shirley Barratt have turned their white-washed house into a charming B&B bolthole, with each room boasting its own mix-and-match furnishings and fabrics, and hallways plastered with Thomas Hardy quotes. There's a two-night minimum in summer, and rates get cheaper the longer you stay.

✖ Eating

For good pub grub, try the cosy **Cobweb** (☑ 01840-250278; www.cobwebinn.co.uk; The Bridge; mains £8-14) and the old-time **Napoleon** (☑ 01840-250204; High St; mains £6-12).

Boscastle Farm Shop   CAFE £
(☑ 01840-250827; www.boscastlefarmshop.co.uk; cakes & teas £3-5; ◷ 10am-5pm; ℗) Half-a-mile from the harbour on the B3263, this excellent farm shop sells its own produce, including ruby-red beef and possibly the best sausages on the north coast. In the cafe, tall windows look onto fields and coast – the perfect setting for a cream tea.

Waterloo Restaurant   BRITISH £££
(☑ 01840-250202; www.wellingtonhotelboscastle.com; The Harbour; 2-/3-course menu £30/37.50) This turreted coaching inn dates back to the 16th century (previous guests include King Edward VII and Guy Gibson of Dambusters fame). It's an old-fashioned place – flock carpets, burnished furniture, upholstered chairs – and the restaurant continues the trad theme. It's now run by Kit Davis, who previously ran his own restaurant in Bude.

ⓘ Information

Boscastle Tourist Office (☑ 01840-250010; www.visitboscastleandtintagel.com; The Harbour; ◷ 10am-5pm Mar-Oct, 10.30am-4pm Nov-Feb)

Tintagel
POP 1822

The spectre of King Arthur looms large over Tintagel and its spectacular clifftop castle. Though the present-day ruins mostly date from the 13th century, archaeological digs have revealed the foundations of a much earlier fortress, fuelling speculation that Arthur may indeed have been born at the castle as locals like to claim.

The village itself isn't terribly exciting, but if you're looking for a cheesy king Arthur souvenir, you'll find them in ample supply.

◎ Sights

★ Tintagel Castle   CASTLE
(EH; ☑ 01840-770328; adult/child £6.10/3.70; ◷ 10am-6pm Apr-Sep, to 5pm Oct, to 4pm Nov-Mar) Famous as the supposed birthplace of King Arthur, Tintagel's stunning clifftop castle has been occupied since Roman times and once served as a residence for Cornwall's Celtic kings. The present castle is largely the work of Richard, Earl of Cornwall, who established the fortress to cash in on its Arthurian connections and curry favour with the local populace.

Though the Arthurian links may be tenuous, there's no doubt that Tintagel's builders chose a fine spot for a fortress. Clinging to the black granite cliffs, surrounded by booming surf and wheeling gulls, it's most people's idea of a fairy-tale castle.

Though much of the structure has crumbled away, it's still possible to make out several walls and much of the original layout. Part of the castle stands on a rocky outcrop cut off from the mainland, and is accessed via a wooden bridge and a very steep staircase (vertigo sufferers beware). Trails lead along the headland to the atmospheric medieval chapel of St Glebe's.

It's a steep walk down to the castle from the village car parks; however, in summer Land Rover taxis shuttle up and down throughout the day.

Old Post Office HISTORIC BUILDING

(NT; ☑ 01840-770024; Fore St; adult/child £3.70/1.80; ☺ 10.30am-5.30pm mid-Mar–Sep, 11am-4pm Oct) One of the National Trust's oldest properties, this is also one of the best-preserved examples of a traditional 16th-century Cornish longhouse, and is topped by pepper-pot chimneys and riddled with tiny rooms. As its name suggests, it was used as a post office during the 19th century.

ⓘ Getting There & Away

Tintagel is on the route for the 594/595 bus (£4 to £5.50, six daily Monday to Saturday), with connections to Bude, Boscastle and Newquay.

Port Isaac

A few miles southwest of Tintagel is the classic Cornish fishing harbour of Port Isaac, a cluster of cobbled alleyways, slender opes (lanes) and cobwalled cottages collected around a medieval harbour and slipway.

Though still a working harbour, Port Isaac is best known as a filming location: the Brit film *Saving Grace* and the TV series *Doc Martin* have both used the village as a ready-made backdrop (a sign near the quayside directs tourists straight to Doc Martin's cottage). A short walk west leads to the neighbouring harbour of Port Gaverne, while a couple of miles west is Port Quin, now owned by the National Trust.

Cornwall's *chef du jour,* Nathan Outlaw, has opened his latest restaurant right beside the quay. Outlaw's Fish Kitchen (☑ 01208-881183; www.outlaws.co.uk/fishkitchen; 1 Middle St; mains £6-10; ☺ noon-3pm & 6-9pm daily Jun-Dec, Tue-Sat Feb-Jun) serves up seafood tasting plates, with the menu dictated by whatever's brought in on the day by Port Isaac's fishermen. The restaurant is tiny, but bookings are only taken for dinner.

Padstow & Rock

POP 3162

If anywhere symbolises Cornwall's changing character, it's Padstow. This once-sleepy fishing port has been transformed into one of the county's most cosmopolitan corners thanks to celebrity chef Rick Stein, whose property portfolio encompasses several restaurants, shops and hotels, as well as a seafood school and fish-and-chip bar.

The 'Stein Effect' has certainly changed the place: Padstow feels more Kensington-chic than Cornish-quaint these days, with a rash of fancy restaurants and chichi boutiques sitting alongside the old pubs and pasty shops. Whether the town's managed to hold on to its soul in the process is debatable, but it's still hard not to be charmed by the setting.

Across the Camel Estuary from Padstow is Rock, a once-quiet village that's been reinvented as an über-exclusive holiday destination. It's worth a trip for the chance to dine at the Michelin-starred restaurants of Nathan Outlaw, the county's top seafood chef.

Between the two resorts is the silvery sweep of the Doom Bar, a treacherous sandbank that's claimed many ships down the centuries.

◉ Sights & Activities

Padstow is surrounded by fine beaches, including the so-called Seven Bays: Trevone, Harlyn, Mother Ivey's, Booby's, Constantine, Treyarnon and Porthcothan. Bus 556 runs close to most of them.

Between Easter and October, cruise boats including the Jubilee Queen (☑ 07836-798457; www.padstowboattrips.co.uk; adult/child £11/6) and Padstow Sealife Safaris (☑ 01841-521613; www.padstowsealifesafaris.co.uk; 2hr cruise adult/child £39/25) run trips to local seal and seabird colonies.

National Lobster Hatchery NATURE DISPLAY

(☑ 01841-533877; www.nationallobsterhatchery.co.uk; adult/child £3.75/1.50; ☺ 10am-7.30pm Jul & Aug, to 4pm or 5pm Sep-Jun) 🕊 In an effort to combat falling lobster stocks, this harbourside hatchery rears baby lobsters in tanks before returning them to the wild. Displays detail the crustaceans' life cycle, and there are viewing tanks where you can watch the residents in action.

Prideaux Place HISTORIC BUILDING

(☑ 01841-532411; www.prideauxplace.co.uk; house & grounds adult £8.50, grounds only £3; ☺ house

DON'T MISS

BEDRUTHAN STEPS

Roughly halfway between Newquay and Padstow loom the stately rock stacks of Bedruthan (Carnewas; NT; www.nationaltrust.org.uk/carnewas-and-bedruthan-steps). These mighty granite pillars have been carved out by the relentless action of thousands of years of wind and waves, and now provide a stirring spot for a sunset stroll. The area is owned by the National Trust, who also run the car park and cafe. The beach itself is accessed via a steep staircase and is submerged at high tide. Towards the north end is a rocky shelf known as Diggory's Island, which separates the main beach from another little-known cove.

1.30-4pm Sun-Thu, grounds & tearoom 12.30-5.30pm Apr-Oct) Much favoured by directors of costume dramas, the stately manor was built by the Prideaux-Brune family, purportedly descendants of William the Conqueror. Guided tours last around an hour and take in state rooms, staircases and Prideaux-Brune heirlooms.

Camel Trail   CYCLING
The old Padstow–Bodmin railway was closed in the 1950s, and has now been turned into Cornwall's most popular bike trail. The main section starts in Padstow and runs east through Wadebridge (5.75 miles), but the trail runs all the way to Poley Bridge on Bodmin Moor (18.3 miles).

Bikes can be hired from Padstow Cycle Hire (☑01841-533533; www.padstowcyclehire.com; South Quay; adult/child per day £14/6; ☺9am-5pm, to 9pm summer) or Trail Bike Hire (☑01841-532594; www.trailbikehire.co.uk; Unit 6, South Quay; adult £12, child £5-8; ☺9am-6pm) at the Padstow end, or from Bridge Bike Hire (☑01208-813050; www.bridgebikehire.co.uk; adult £12-15, child £6-9; ☺10am-5pm) at the Wadebridge end. Pumps and helmets are usually included, but tandems and kids' trailers cost extra.

🛏 Sleeping

Treyarnon Bay YHA   HOSTEL £
(☑0845 371 9664; treyarnon@yha.org.uk; Treyarnon Bay; dm £17-23; P @) A super 1930s-built beach hostel on the bluffs above Treyarnon Bay. Rooms are big and there's a good cafe, plus barbecues in summer. It's 4.5 miles east of Padstow. Bus 556 stops nearby at Constantine.

Althea Library   B&B ££
(☑01841-532579; www.altheahouse-padstow.co.uk; 64 Church St, Padstow; d £98-124; P 🕾) If you want to be in the heart of Padstow, this charming ivy-clad house is hard to better. The rooms are both suites, and quite rightly, with sofas, Nespresso coffee machines, in-room fridges and roll-top baths. Rafters is

accessed via a private staircase, while Driftwood has a pine four-poster bed, and there's a cottage for longer stays.

Treann House   B&B ££
(☑01841-553855; www.treannhousepadstow.co.uk; 24 Dennis Rd, Padstow; d £100-130; 🕾) This stylish number makes a fancy place to stay. The three rooms are finished with stripped floors, crisp sheets and antique beds, and the Estuary Room has its own dinky balcony with a panorama over Padstow's rooftops.

Treverbyn House   B&B ££
(☑01841-532855; www.treverbynhouse.com; Station Rd, Padstow; d £120-125; P 🕾) This town house offers four colour-themed rooms (pink, green, lilac or yellow) plus an extra-romantic turret hideaway. The style is classic (oriental rugs, brass bedsteads, traditional tea trays), the rooms are huge, and breakfast includes homemade jams and smoked kippers.

🍴 Eating

Chough Bakery   BAKERY £
(☑01841-533361; www.thechoughbakery.co.uk; 1-3 The Strand, Padstow; pasties £2-4) This family-run bakery makes Padstow's best pasties, bar none.

Stein's Fish & Chips   CAFE £
(South Quay, Padstow; takeaway £6.65-10.95; ☺9-11.30am, noon-3pm & 5-8pm) Stein's fish-and-chips bar uses beef dripping batter for a crisp finish, and often has unusual fish options such as monkfish, John Dory and lemon sole.

Margot's Bistro   BRITISH ££
(☑01840-533441; www.margotsbistro.co.uk; 11 Duke St, Padstow; mains £14.50-17.50; ☺noon-2pm Wed-Sat, 7-10pm Tue-Sat) While the food snobs head for Stein's, Margot's is where you'll be sent by the locals. Run by madcap chef Adrian Oliver, known for his chaotic style and seasonal food, it's a fantastically convivial place, but the tables are packed in sardine-tight.

Rojano's in the Square
ITALIAN ££

(☑ 01841-532796; www.rojanos.co.uk; 9 Mill Sq, Padstow; pizzas & pastas £12-15) Now run by Paul Ainsworth, this excellent little Italian bistro turns out fantastic wood-fired pizzas, spicy pastas and antipasti.

Rick Stein's Cafe
EUROPEAN ££

(☑ 01841-532700; Middle St, Padstow; mains £10-18; ⊙ 8am-9.30pm) Stein's backstreet bistro takes its inspiration from the chef's globetrotting travels, with dishes ranging all the way from the Far East to the Mediterranean: classic mussels with saffron, or Thai-spiced seafood broth. It's a lot more relaxed than its sister restaurant, but you'd still be wise to book.

Basement
CAFE ££

(☑ 01841-532846; 11 Broad St, Padstow; lunch mains £5-10, dinner £10-14; ⊙ 8am-10pm) Harbourside cafe that's good for a quick morning coffee, or a bowl of mussels for lunch.

★ Paul Ainsworth at No 6
BRITISH £££

(☑ 01840-532093; www.number6inpadstow.co.uk; 6 Middle St, Padstow; 2-/3-course lunch £19/25, dinner mains £26-30; ⊙ noon-2.30pm & 6.30-9pm) Paul Ainsworth is Padstow's hottest chef, and thanks to a shiny Michelin star, his restaurant has become the town's most desirable table. Known for his modern take on surf-and-turf, Ainsworth's cooking combines local seafood, meat and game into fresh, surprising concoctions. His signature dessert, 'A Trip to the Fairground', was created for BBC2's *Great British Menu* in 2011.

★ Restaurant Nathan Outlaw
SEAFOOD £££

(☑ 01208-862737; www.nathan-outlaw.com; Rock Rd, Rock; tasting menu £99; ⊙ 7-9pm Tue-Sat) A former Rick Stein trainee, Nathan Outlaw has now established his own stellar seafood reputation with two Michelin stars – the only chef in Cornwall to do so. There's a choice of Outlaw venues, both in Rock. Foodies plump for the flagship restaurant, which serves a superb £99 tasting menu. Expensive, but very much a never-to-be-forgotten experience.

Nathan's style is surprisingly classic, and relies on the quality of the seafood rather than cheffy tricks to provide the fireworks. The more relaxed Outlaw's (mains £16-25; ⊙ noon-2.30pm & 6-9.30pm) serves similar quality seafood at more affordable prices, while Nathan has also recently opened a new place, Outlaw's Fish Kitchen (p331), in Port Isaac.

Seafood Restaurant
SEAFOOD £££

(☑ 01841-532700; www.rickstein.com; Riverside, Padstow; mains £25-65; ⊙ noon-2pm & 6.30-10pm) Rick Stein's flagship seafooderie needs no introduction: it's one of Britain's foremost fish addresses, with an expensive menu offering treats such as fresh Padstow lobster and sumptuous *fruits de mer*. You'll generally need to book months in advance – although last-minute lunch tables sometimes crop up.

ⓘ Information

Padstow Tourist Office (☑ 01841-533449; www.padstowlive.com; North Quay, Padstow; ⊙ 10am-5pm Mon-Sat)

ⓘ Getting There & Away

There are a couple of car parks beside the harbour in Padstow, but they fill up quickly, so it's usually a better idea to park at one of the large car parks at the top of town and walk down.

Useful bus routes include:

Bude Bus 594/595 (£8, six daily Monday to Saturday) via Wadebridge (£7.50), Boscastle and Tintagel.

Newquay Bus 556 (£6.50, hourly Monday to Saturday, five on Sunday) runs via Padstow's main beaches along the coast to Newquay.

Newquay
POP 19,423

If Padstow is Cornwall's Cannes, then Newquay is its Costa del Sol. Perched on the cliffs above a cluster of white-sand beaches, and packed with enough pubs, bars and dodgy clubs to give Ibiza a run for its money, it's become the summer venue of choice for beer boys, beach bums and surf addicts alike, all of whom descend on the town in their droves in summer. It's also the capital of Cornish surfing, and if you're looking to learn how to brave the waves, this is the place to do it.

⊙ Sights

Newquay has a truly stunning location among some of North Cornwall's finest beaches. The best known is Fistral, England's most famous surfing beach. It's nestled on the west side of Towan Head, a 10-minute walk from the town centre.

To the east of Towan Head are Newquay's other main beaches. Just below town are Towan, Great Western and Tolcarne, followed by nearby Lusty Glaze. All offer good swimming and lifeguard supervision throughout the summer.

You'll need transport to reach Newquay's other beaches. North of Lusty Glaze is Porth, a long, narrow beach that's popular with families, followed a couple of miles later by the massive curve of Watergate Bay, home to Jamie Oliver's much-vaunted restaurant, Fifteen Cornwall. Two miles north brings you to Mawgan Porth, a horseshoe-shaped bay which often stays quieter than its neighbours.

You'll find even more beaches to the southwest of Newquay, including the large, sandy, family-friendly beaches of Crantock (about 3 miles from town) and Holywell Bay (6 miles from town).

Blue Reef Aquarium   AQUARIUM

(✆ 01637-878134; www.bluereefaquarium.co.uk/newquay; Towan Promenade; adult/child/family £10/7.75/33.50; ◷ 10am-5pm; ⛟) Small aquarium on Towan Beach, with touch-pools and various deep-sea denizens including reef sharks, loggerhead turtles and a giant Pacific octopus. There's a £1 discount for online bookings.

Newquay Zoo   ZOO

(✆ 01637-873342; www.newquayzoo.org.uk; Trenance Gardens; adult/child/family £11.75/9.05/35; ◷ 9.30am-5pm Apr-Sep, 10am-5pm Oct-Mar; ⛟) Newquay's miniature zoo isn't a world-beater, but its population of penguins, lemurs, parrots and snakes will keep the kids happy. The Tropical House and Toad Hall are particularly good fun.

Trerice   HISTORIC BUILDING

(NT; ✆ 01637-875404; www.nationaltrust.org.uk/trerice; adult/child £7.65/3.80; ◷ house 11am-5pm, gardens 10.30am-5pm) This Elizabethan manor (1751) is most famous for the elaborate barrel-roofed ceiling of its Great Chamber. It's 3.3 miles southeast of Newquay.

🏃 Activities

Newquay's brimming with surf schools, but the quality is variable. Choose one that offers small-group sessions, and ideally has a no-stag-party policy. Ask about teachers' accreditation and experience, and whether they travel to beaches other than Fistral – good schools follow the best waves.

English Surf School   SURFING

(✆ 01637-879571; www.englishsurfschool.com) This is one of the most experienced and efficient large schools, linked with Rip Curl and staffed by fully English Surfing Federation–

approved instructors (including the British team coach).

Extreme Academy   ADVENTURE SPORTS

(✆ 01637-860840; www.extremeacademy.co.uk; Watergate Bay) A well-organised surf school and water-sports centre with a large base at Watergate Bay.

Errant Surf School   SURFING

(✆ 07581-397038; www.errantsurfschool.co.uk; Trebarwith Cres) A small, independent surf school that offers small class sizes, friendly tutors and optional one-to-one lessons. Based at the Trebarwith Hotel.

Kingsurf Surf School   SURFING

(✆ 01637-860091; www.kingsurf.co.uk) A good option if you prefer to avoid the Fistral hustle, this school at Mawgan Porth has five young instructors and gets a tick for personal attention and small class sizes.

EboAdventure   OUTDOORS

(✆ 0800 781 6861; www.eboadventure.co.uk) Surfing's not the only sport in Newquay – you could also try kitebuggying, kayaking, paddle surfing and coasteering (a mix of rock climbing, scrambling and wild swimming). This multi-activity centre is based at the Penhale Training Camp, at the northern end of Holywell Bay.

🛏 Sleeping

Newquay Townhouse   B&B £

(✆ 01637-620009; www.newquaytownhouse.co.uk; 6 Tower Rd; d £50-70; ⓟ 🛜) A great B&B near Newquay's town centre, with bright rooms livened up with stripy cushions and wicker furniture.

★ Scarlet   HOTEL £££

(✆ 01637-861600; www.scarlethotel.co.uk; r winter/summer from £155/285; ⓟ 🛜 🏊) For out-and-out luxury, Cornwall's fabulously chic, adults-only eco-hotel takes the crown. In a regal location above Mawgan Porth, 5 miles from Newquay, it screams designer style, from the huge sea-view rooms with their funky furniture and minimalist decor to the luxurious spa, complete with meditation lounge, outdoor hot tubs and wild swimming pool. The restaurant's a beauty, too.

★ Bedruthan Hotel   HOTEL £££

(✆ 01637-860555; www.bedruthan.com; Mawgan Porth; d from £130; ⓟ 🛜 🏊) Run by the same team as the Scarlet, the Bedruthan is a family-friendly version but with the same attention to style and detail. It offers contemporary rooms in bright primary colours, artworks and bold pattern prints, plus villas and apartments for longer stays. Activities aplenty will keep the small ones occupied.

✖ Eating

Café Irie CAFE **£**
(✆01637-859200; www.cafeirie.co.uk; 38 Fore St; lunch £3-8; ⊕9am-5.30pm Mon-Sat) A surfer's favourite in the centre of Newquay, perfect for hot chocolate, sticky cakes and jacket spuds after hitting the waves.

Beach Hut BISTRO **££**
(✆01637-860877; Watergate Bay; mains £10-18; ⊕9am-9pm) Lodged beneath Jamie Oliver's Fifteen Cornwall, this beachside bistro is a great bet for simple surf 'n' turf: sticky pork ribs, 'extreme' burgers and a different fish every day.

Lewinnick Lodge GASTROPUB **££**
(✆01637-878117; www.lewinnick-lodge.info; Pentire Head, Newquay; mains £10-16; ⊕9am-11pm) Perched on the dramatic outcrop of Pentire Head, the Lewinnick is a super lunch spot. The wraparound views over the clifftops are the main selling point here, but there's a decent choice of gourmet burgers, mussels and Thai-style salads on the menu.

Fifteen Cornwall ITALIAN **£££**
(✆01637-861000; www.fifteencornwall.com; Watergate Bay; lunch/dinner menu £28/60; ⊕8.30-10am, noon-2.30pm & 6.15-9.15pm) Owned by celeb chef and self-marketing mogul Jamie Oliver, this restaurant on Watergate Bay serves Jamie's trademark Italian food while simultaneously training young apprentices. The vibe is relaxed and the beach view is stunning, but the prices are on the high side.

▾ Drinking & Nightlife

Newquay's town centre gets rowdy on Friday and Saturday nights.

Chy BAR
(www.thekoola.com/the-chy-bar; 12 Beach Rd; ⊕9am-11pm) Chrome, wood and leather dominate this cafe-bar overlooking Towan Beach. The action continues till late at the Koola nightclub downstairs.

Central PUB
(11 Central Sq; ⊕11am-midnight Sun-Thu, to 1am Fri & Sat) As its name suggests, this pre-club pub is in the heart of town, and is usually packed at weekends.

❶ Information

Newquay Tourist Office (✆01637-854020; www.visitnewquay.com; Marcus Hill; ⊕9.30am-5.30pm Mon-Sat, to 12.30pm Sun)

❶ Getting There & Away

The 585/586 is the fastest bus service to Truro (50 minutes, twice hourly Monday to Saturday), while the hourly 587 (£3.40 to any stop on the route) follows the coast via Crantock (14 minutes), Holywell Bay (25 minutes) and Perranporth (50 minutes).

There are trains every couple of hours on the branch line between Newquay and Par (£4.50, 45 minutes) on the main London–Penzance line.

Newquay Airport (✆01637-860600; www.newquaycornwallairport.com) Five miles from town, Newquay's airport currently offers direct flights to Belfast, Edinburgh, Glasgow, Manchester, Newcastle and London Gatwick. Bus 556 (22 minutes, hourly Monday to Saturday, five on Sunday) runs from the bus station. A taxi will cost from £15 to £25.

Perranporth to Porthtowan

Southwest of Newquay, Cornwall's craggy northern coastline dips and curves through a stunning panorama of wild, sea-smacked cliffs and golden bays, including the family-friendly beach of Perranporth, the old mining town of St Agnes and the surfy hang-out of Porthtowan.

⊙ Sights

Perranporth Beach BEACH
(🅿) Perranporth's huge, flat, sandy beach is popular with bucket-and-spading families and surfers alike. It's over a mile long, backed by dunes and rocky cliffs, and usually has space even on the busiest days. It's also home to the Watering Hole (p336).

★ Chapel Porth COVE
Two miles from St Agnes is one of Cornwall's most beautiful coves, Chapel Porth, a wild, rocky beach framed by steep, gorse-covered cliffs, owned by the National Trust. Above the cove is the ruined engine stack of Wheal Coates, which still boasts its chimney and winding house, from where the coast path winds all the way to the blustery outcrop of St Agnes Head.

Trevaunance Cove COVE
St Agnes' main beach is great for paddling and rock-pooling, and has old-fashioned

beach huts to change in. Koru Kayaking (p345) runs trips from the cove.

Blue Hills Tin Streams   EXHIBITION

(☑ 01872-553341; www.bluehillstin.com; adult/child £6.50/3; ☺ 10am-4pm Tue-Sat mid-Apr–mid-Oct) A mile east of St Agnes (signed to Wheal Kitty) is the rocky valley of Trevellas, home to one of Cornwall's last tin manufacturers where you can watch the whole tinning process, from mining and smelting through to casting and finishing. Handmade jewellery is sold in the shop.

✗ Eating & Drinking

Chapel Porth Cafe   CAFE £

(Chapel Porth; sandwiches & cakes £2-4; ☺ 10am-5pm) The Chapel Porth Cafe is a local institution, serving hot chocolate, cheesy baguettes and the house speciality, hedgehog ice-cream (vanilla ice-cream topped with clotted cream and hazelnuts).

★ No 4 Peterville   BISTRO ££

(☑ 01872-554245; Peterville Sq, St Agnes; mains £12-16.95; ☺ 7-10.30pm Wed-Sat, 10am-1pm Sat & Sun) An impressive address at the bottom of St Agnes that's earned a loyal following with its continental-style bistro food: whole plaice with curried mussel butter, or rib-eye steak with rosemary-salted fries. Pine tables and kilner-jar candles continue the dining-with-friends atmosphere.

Driftwood Spars   PUB ££

(☑ 01872-552428; www.driftwoodspars.com; Trevaunance Cove, St Agnes; mains £8-16; ☺ 11am-11pm; P) This classic old inn by Trevaunance Cove has something to suit all-comers: home-brewed beers, good pub food, and nautically themed upstairs rooms.

Bolingey Inn   PUB ££

(☑ 01872-571626; Penwartha Rd, Bolingey; mains £10-16; ☺ noon-11pm) The ivy-covered Bolingey Inn is the best pub around Perranporth for food, and has a valley location about 2 miles' drive inland.

Blue Bar   BISTRO ££

(☑ 01209-890329; www.blue-bar.co.uk; Porthtowan; mains £8-16; ☺ 10am-11pm) For a seaside sundowner or a lunchtime snack by the sand, this Porthtowan cafe is tough to beat (unfortunately everyone knows about it, so arrive early).

Watering Hole   BAR

(www.the-wateringhole.co.uk; Perranporth Beach) One of Cornwall's oldest beach bars, the Watering Hole, which was nearly washed away during heavy storms in 2014.

❶ Getting There & Away

First bus 85 travels at least hourly between Truro and St Agnes (£2.50). Western Greyhound's bus 587 runs twice an hour from Truro to St Agnes (£1.70), and then continues from St Agnes to Perranporth (£2.20) and Newquay (£3.40).

St Ives

POP 9870

Even if you've seen St Ives many times before, it's still hard not to be dazzled as you gaze across its improbably pretty jumble of slate roofs, church towers and turquoise bays. Once a busy pilchard harbour, St Ives later became the centre of Cornwall's arts scene in the 1920s and '30s, and the town is still an artistic centre, with numerous galleries and craft shops lining its winding cobbled streets, as well as the southwestern outpost of the renowned Tate Museum.

DON'T MISS

GWITHIAN & GODREVY TOWANS

Four miles' drive east of St Ives across the Hayle Estuary, the dune-backed flats of Gwithian and Godrevy unfurl in a glimmering golden curve that joins together at low tide to form Hayle's '3 miles of golden sand'. This is one of Cornwall's most glorious beach panoramas, fringed by hectares of rockpools and grassy dunes (known in Cornish as towans) and, at the northern end, the lighthouse that inspired Virginia Woolf's stream-of-consciousness classic, To The Lighthouse. Don't miss it.

There are several good cafes nearby, including the timber-framed Godrevy Cafe (☑ 01736-757999; www.godrevycafe.com; lunch £6-10; ☺ 10am-5pm), as well as an excellent farm shop, Trevaskis Farm (☑ 01209-713931; www.trevaskisfarm.co.uk; 12 Gwinear Rd, Hayle; ☺ 9am-6pm Jun-Aug, to 5pm Sep-May).

West Cornwall

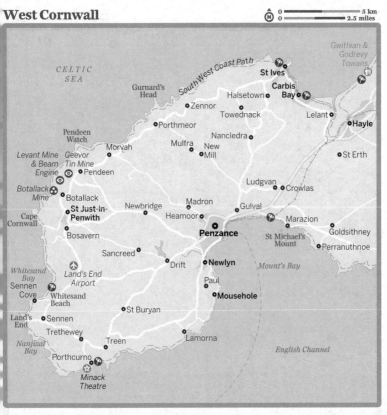

◎ Sights & Activities

The largest town beaches are **Porthmeor** and **Porthminster**, both of which have sand and space aplenty. Between them juts the grassy promontory known as the **Island**, topped by the tiny pre-14th-century **Chapel of St Nicholas**. On the peninsula's east side is the little cove of **Porthgwidden**, often a good place to escape the crowds.

★ **Tate St Ives**   GALLERY
(☑ 01736-796226; www.tate.org.uk/stives; Porthmeor Beach; adult/child £7/4.50, with Barbara Hepworth Museum £10/6; ☉ 10am-5pm Mar-Oct, to 4pm Nov-Feb) Hovering like a concrete curl above Porthmeor Beach, St Ives' celebrated art museum focuses on the key artists of the 'St Ives School', including luminary names such as Terry Frost, Patrick Heron, Naum Gabo, Ben Nicholson and Barbara Hepworth, displayed alongside more contemporary artists. Of particular local interest are the naive works of fisherman-turned-artist Alfred Wallis, who didn't start painting until the ripe old age of 67.

The top-floor cafe has super views over Porthmeor Beach.

Barbara Hepworth Museum   MUSEUM
(☑ 01736-796226; Barnoon Hill; adult/child £6/4, with Tate St Ives £10/6; ☉ 10am-5pm Mar-Oct, to 4pm Nov-Feb) Barbara Hepworth (1903–75) was one of the leading abstract sculptors of the 20th century and a key figure in the St Ives art scene. Her studio on Barnoon Hill has remained almost untouched since her death and the adjoining garden contains several of her most notable sculptures. Hepworth's work is scattered throughout St Ives; look for works outside the Guildhall and inside the 15th-century parish church of St Ia.

St Ives Boats   BOATING
(☑ 0777 300 8000; www.stivesboats.co.uk; adult/child £10/8) From the harbourfront, several

St Ives

operators including St Ives Boats offer fishing trips and scenic cruises, including to the grey seal colony on Seal Island. If you're really lucky, you might even spot a porpoise or a basking shark in summer.

🛏 Sleeping

No 1 St Ives
B&B **££**

(☏ 01736-799047; www.no1stives.co.uk; 1 Fern Glen; d £95-139; P �ⓢ) Despite its pretentious 'bouchique' tag, this 19th-century granite cottage is still one of the nicest B&Bs in St Ives. Rooms vary in size, but all sport the same palette of cool greys and off-whites,

and have extra spoils such as filtered water, goose-down duvets, iPod docks and White Company bath-stuffs. It's five minutes' walk from town, but there's only space for four cars.

Little Leaf Guest House
B&B **££**

(☏ 01736-795427; www.littleleafguesthouse.co.uk; Park Ave; r £65-120; 🗟) A friendly and cosy five-roomer, on a terrace overlooking the town's rooftops. Rooms are sweet and simple, finished in creamy colours and pine furniture. Ask for rooms 2 or 5 if you're after a sea view.

St Ives

Gekko Lodge B&B ££

(✆ 01736-796591; www.gekkolodge.co.uk; 7 Carthew Tce; d £70-90) A bit of a find, this one: a pebble-dash Victorian house with just two rooms, both of which are enormous and have sea views through bay windows. The style is contemporary, with futon-style beds and funky circular sinks.

Treliska B&B ££

(✆ 01736-797678; www.treliska.com; 3 Bedford Rd; d £60-80; ☎) This B&B is a bargain in pricey St Ives, especially given the location, just steps from the town centre. The trade-off is the room size: most are on the small side (ask for No 5 if it's space you're after).

★Tide House HOTEL £££

(✆ 01736-791803; www.thetidehouse.co.uk; Skidden Hill; d £140-240) Even in increasingly chi-chi St Ives, this beautiful hotel feels unusually special. It has everything going for it: 16th-century building, harbourside location, gorgeous design and seriously luxurious rooms (all named after Cornish light-houses), ranging from a romantic penthouse to a split-level mezzanine. Definitely the place to push the boat out.

Trevose Harbour House B&B £££

(✆ 01736-793267; www.trevosehouse.co.uk; 22 The Warren; d £140-195; ☎) A stylish six-room town house on the winding Warren, restored with a sea-themed combo of fresh whites and stripy blues. It's been beautifully finished – Neal's Yard bathstuffs, iPod docks and retro design pieces in the rooms, plus a book-lined lounge and minimalist courtyard patio – but the rooms are quite small given the price.

Boskerris HOTEL £££

(✆ 01736-795295; www.boskerrishotel.co.uk; Boskerris Rd, Carbis Bay; d £130-265; P ☎) In nearby Carbis Bay, this upmarket mini-hotel feels uncluttered, contrasting cool monotones with snazzy design features: pattern-print bedsteads, scatter cushions, minimalist ceramic sinks. The decked patio is an absolute beauty, with grandstand views over the bay.

✗ Eating

Blas Burgerworks CAFE £

(✆ 01736-797272; The Warren; burgers £5-10; ⊙ noon-9.30pm) ✔ A fantastic boutique burger joint, with an eco-friendly manifesto and an imaginative menu. Go for a 6oz Classic Blasburger, or branch out with a guacamole and corn salsa–topped Rancheros, or a Smokey with beetroot, aged cheddar and homemade piccalilli (plenty of veggie options, too). The owners also run the excellent **Halsetown Inn** (✆ 01736-795583; www.halsetowninn.co.uk), just outside St Ives.

Pengenna Pasties BAKERY £

(www.pengennapasties.co.uk; 9 High St; pasties £3-4; ⊙ 10am-5pm Mon-Sat) Generously-stuffed pasties, with a controversial top crimp and flakier texture.

★Porthminster Beach Café BISTRO ££

(✆ 01736-795352; www.porthminstercafe.co.uk; Porthminster Beach; mains £10.50-16.50, dinner £10-22; ⊙ 9am-10pm) This is no ordinary beach cafe: it's a full-blown bistro with a gorgeous suntrap terrace and a superb Mediterranean-influenced menu, specialising in seafood. Tuck into rich bouillabaisse, seafood curry or Provençal fish soup, and settle back to enjoy the breezy beach vistas.

Rum & Crab Shack SEAFOOD ££

(✆ 01736-796353; Wharf Rd; mains £9.95-12.95; ⊙ 9am-9pm; ♠) If the thought of cracking your own spider crab and eating it from the shell appeals, then this place will be happy to oblige (aprons and tools are provided). Alternatively, you could just tackle the claws, or tuck into a plate of seafood gumbo or scrowlers on toast (aka sardines). Great fun, and great food to match.

Alba
MODERN BRITISH ££

(📞01736-797222; www.thealbarestaurant.com; Old Lifeboat House; 2-/3-course dinner menu £16.95/19.95; ⊙noon-2pm & 6-10pm) In a converted boathouse near the lifeboat station, this long-standing restaurant has been consistently turning out some of the town's top food for many years. With its banquette seats and sharp decor, it feels classy, especially if you get one of the prime tables next to the panoramic window. The menu is a mix of British and European flavours.

Alfresco
BISTRO ££

(📞01736-793737; info@alfrescocafebar.co.uk; The Wharf; 2-/3-course dinner menu £16.95; ⊙7-9pm daily, noon-3pm Thu & Fri) Sliding doors onto the quayside allow this tiny restaurant to make the most of its harbourside position, and when the sun's shining it feels positively continental. The Alfresco fish stew is particularly recommended.

Seagrass
MODERN BRITISH ££

(📞01736-793763; www.seagrass-stives.com; Fish St; 2-/3-course menu £16.95/19.95; ⊙6-9pm) A popular, small bistro just off the wharf, focusing mainly on local seafood – there's a special Oyster and Shells menu, featuring langoustines, whole crab, lobster and oysters.

🍷 Drinking & Entertainment

Hub
CAFE, BAR

(www.hub-stives.co.uk; The Wharf; ⊙9am-11pm) The open-plan Hub is the heart of St Ives' (limited) nightlife: coffee and burgers by day, cocktails after-dark.

Sloop Inn
PUB

(📞01736-796584; www.sloop-inn.co.uk; The Wharf; ⊙11am-11pm) This beam-ceilinged boozer is as comfy as an old pair of slippers, with a few tables on the harbour and lots of local ales.

Guildhall
CONCERT VENUE

(1 Street-an-Pol) St Ives' concert hall hosts music and theatre, especially during the annual St Ives September Festival (www.stivesseptemberfestival.co.uk).

❶ Information

St Ives Tourist Office (📞01736-796297; www.stivestic.co.uk; Street-an-Pol; ⊙9am-5.30pm Mon-Fri, 9am-5pm Sat, 10am-4pm Sun) Inside the Guildhall.

❶ Getting There & Away

The branch train line from St Ives is worth taking just for the coastal views: trains terminate at St Erth (£3, 14 minutes, half-hourly), where you can catch connections along the Penzance–London Paddington main line.

Bus 17/17A (£4, 30 minutes, half-hourly Monday to Saturday, hourly on Sunday) The quickest route to Penzance.

Bus 16/16A (£5, hourly Monday to Saturday) Round the coast road to Penzance; only the 16A travels via Zennor.

Zennor & St Just

The twisting B3306 from St Ives is a rollercoaster of a road, winding through a stark landscape of ancient drystone walls, barren moorland, tiny villages and rocky bluffs. The landscape here feels wild and ancient, a world away from some of Cornwall's more gentrified corners.

◉ Sights

Church of St Senara
CHURCH

(Zennor) This little church in the hamlet of Zennor dates from at least 1150. Inside, a famous carved chair depicts the legendary Mermaid of Zennor, who is said to have fallen in love with the singing voice of local lad Matthew Trewhella. Locals say you can still sometimes hear them singing down at nearby Pendour Cove – and even if you don't, the views along the coast path are reward enough.

⭐ Geevor Tin Mine
MINE

(📞01736-788662; www.geevor.com; adult/child £11/6.50; ⊙9am-5pm Sun-Fri Mar-Oct, to 4pm Nov-Feb) Just north of St Just near Pendeen, this historic mine closed in 1990 and now provides a powerful insight into the dark, dingy and dangerous conditions in which Cornwall's miners worked. Above ground, you can view the dressing floors and the original machinery used to sort the minerals and ores, before taking a guided tour into some of the underground shafts. Claustrophobes need not apply.

Botallack Mine   RUIN, MINE

Clinging to the cliffs near Levant, this dramatic engine house has abandoned mine shafts extending right out beneath the raging Atlantic waves. It's a treacherous climb down, so it's best viewed from a distance from nearby **Botallack Head**.

Levant Mine & Beam Engine   HISTORIC SITE

(www.nationaltrust.org.uk/main/w-levantmine-andbeamengine; adult/child £6.60/3.30; ⊙ 11am-5pm Sun-Fri) At this clifftop site, one of the world's only working beam engines is still in thunderous action. Built in 1840, these great engines were the powerhouses behind the Cornish mining boom, powering mineral trains and pumping water from the shafts. Lovingly restored by a team of enthusiasts, it's a sight to behold when it's in full steam.

Cape Cornwall   LANDMARK

Jutting out from the cliffs near St Just is Cornwall's only 'official' cape, a craggy finger of land topped by an abandoned minestack. Below the cape is the rocky beach of **Priest's Cove**, while nearby are the ruins of **St Helen's Oratory**, supposedly one of the first Christian chapels built in West Cornwall.

🛏 Sleeping & Eating

Tinner's Arms   INN ££

(☑ 01736-792697; www.tinnersarms.com; Zennor; s/d £60/100, mains £10-16; P) An old Cornish inn, complete with slate roof, roaring fireplaces, gleaming bar taps and a refreshing lack of commercial clutter (no TV, no juke-box, no mobile signal). Next door, the 'White House' provides fresh, spotless rooms. DH Lawrence drank here while he was writing *Women in Love*.

★**Gurnard's Head**   BRITISH ££

(☑ 01736-796928; www.gurnardshead.co.uk; mains £10-18.50, r £105-170; P 🐾 🍴) On the road between Zennor and St Just, you can't miss the Gurnard's – it's name is written on the roof. Run by the Inkin brothers (who also own Mousehole's Old Coastguard Hotel) this is a perfect country pub, with old-fashioned rooms, book-lined shelves and sepia prints conjuring a cosy, lived-in feel. It's renowned for its delicious, classic British food.

ⓘ Getting There & Away

St Just is 6 miles north of Land's End.

Bus 16A (£4, three or four daily Monday to Saturday) Travels from St Ives via Zennor to Penzance.

Bus 10/10A (£5, hourly Monday to Saturday, six on Sunday) Circular route from Penzance via Madron, St Just and Botallack.

Sennen & Land's End

Beyond St Ives, the coastline gets ever wilder and emptier as you near Cornwall's tip at **Land's End**, the westernmost point of mainland England, where the coal-black cliffs plunge into the pounding surf, and the views stretch all the way to the Isles of Scilly on a clear day.

DON'T MISS

MINACK THEATRE & PORTHCURNO

In terms of theatrical settings, the **Minack** (☑ 01736-810181; www.minack.com) takes top billing. Carved into the crags overlooking Porthcurno Bay and the azure-blue Atlantic, this amazing clifftop amphitheatre was the lifelong passion of local lady Rowena Cade, who dreamt up the idea in the 1930s and oversaw the theatre until her death in 1983. It's now a hugely popular place for alfresco theatre, with a 17-week season running from mid-May to mid-September. Experienced theatre-goers bring wine, picnic supplies, wet-weather gear and – most importantly, considering the seats are carved out of granite – a comfy cushion. Above the theatre, the **visitor centre** (adult/child £3.50/1.40; ⊙ 9.30am-5.30pm Apr-Sep, 10am-4pm Oct-Mar) recounts the theatre's history. It's closed when there's a matinée.

Below the theatre, the sandy wedge of **Porthcurno** is great for swimming and sunbathing, and the lesser-known beach of **Pednvounder** nearby is good if you like to sunbathe au naturel – it's one of Cornwall's few naturist beaches. Inland, the newly redeveloped **Porthcurno Telegraph Museum** (☑ 01736-810966; www.porthcurno.org.uk; adult/child £8.50/5; ⊙ 10am-5pm) recounts the area's role as Britain's first hub for transatlantic telecommunications.

The Minack is 3 miles from Land's End and 9 miles from Penzance. Bus 1/1A from Penzance stops several times daily.

Unfortunately, the decision to build the Legendary Land's End (www.landsend-landmark.co.uk; adult/child £10/7; ⏱10am-5pm Mar-Oct; 🅿) theme park on the headland in the 1980s hasn't done much to enhance the view. Take our advice: just pay for the car park, skip the tacky multimedia shows and opt for an exhilarating clifftop stroll instead. Look out for the slender profile of the historic Longships Lighthouse, perched on a rocky reef 1.25 miles out to sea.

From Land's End, you can follow the coast path west to the secluded cove of Nanjizal Bay, or east to the old harbour of Sennen, which overlooks the glorious – and appropriately named – beach of Whitesand Bay (actually pronounced Whitsand), the area's most impressive stretch of sand.

Land's End is 9 miles from Penzance. Bus 1/1A travels from Penzance (£5, one hour, six daily Monday to Saturday) to Land's End; 1 goes via Sennen, while the 1A travels via Treen and Porthcurno.

Mousehole

POP 697

With a tight tangle of cottages and alleyways gathered behind the granite breakwater, Mousehole (pronounced 'mowzle') looks like something from a children's storybook (a fact not unnoticed by the author Antonia Barber, who set her much-loved fairy-tale *The Mousehole Cat* here). In centuries past this was Cornwall's busiest pilchard port, but the fish dried up at the turn of the century, and the village now survives mostly on tourist traffic.

Packed in summer and deserted in winter, it's ripe for a wander, with a maze of slips, net-lofts and courtyards. It's also well-known for its Christmas lights, and as the home of 'stargazey pie', a pilchard pie in which the fish heads are left poking through the pie's crust. It's traditionally eaten on Tom Bawcock's Eve (23 December), named after a local lad who reputedly rescued the town from a famine by braving stormy seas to land a bumper haul of pilchards.

The Old Coastguard Hotel (☎01736-731222; www.oldcoastguardhotel.co.uk; d £120-245, mains £11-15; 🅿🛜🐾) is the pick of the places to stay, a swanky seaside hotel with to-die-for sea views on the edge of Mousehole.

Bus 6 makes the 20-minute journey (£3) to Penzance half-hourly.

Penzance

POP 21,168

Overlooking the sweep of Mount's Bay, the old harbour of Penzance has a salty, sea-blown charm that feels altogether more authentic than many of Cornwall's polished-up ports. Its streets and shopping arcades still feel real and a touch ramshackle, and there's nowhere better for a windy-day walk than the town's seafront Victorian promenade. The nearby harbour of Newlyn is still home to Cornwall's largest fishing fleet.

⊙ Sights & Activities

Penlee House Gallery & Museum GALLERY
(www.penleehouse.org.uk; Morrab Rd; adult/child £4.50/3; ⏱10am-5pm Mon-Sat Easter-Sep, 10.30am-4.30pm Oct-Easter) Penzance's historic art gallery displays paintings by artists of the Newlyn School (including Stanhope Forbes) and hosts regular exhibitions. Admission is free on Saturday.

Exchange GALLERY
(www.theexchangegallery.co.uk; Princes St; ⏱10am-5pm Mon-Sat Easter-Sep, Wed-Sat Oct-Easter) FREE Housed in Penzance's former telecoms building, this gallery hosts regular exhibitions of contemporary art. It's the sister gallery to the Newlyn Art Gallery (www.newlynartgallery.co.uk; ⏱10am-5pm Mon-Sat Easter-Sep, Wed-Sat Oct-Easter), a mile west along Penzance's prom.

Trengwainton GARDENS
(NT; ☑01736-363148; trengwainton@nationaltrust.org.uk; Madron; adult/child £6.80/3.40; ⏱10am-5pm Sun-Thu mid-Feb–Nov) Two miles north of Penzance near Madron is the walled garden of Trengwainton, which has a subtropical collection of ferns, shrubs, magnolias and rhododendrons.

Jubilee Pool SWIMMING
(www.jubileepool.co.uk) At the eastern end of town is Penzance's 1930s seawater lido. It's usually open in summer, but at the time of writing it was closed due to storm damage – check the website for news.

🛏 Sleeping

Penzance has lots of low-price B&Bs, especially along Alexandra Rd and Morrab Rd.

Penzance YHA HOSTEL £
(☎0845 371 9653; penzance@yha.org.uk; Castle Horneck, Alverton; dm £15-20; 🅿@) Penzance's

Penzance

N 0 — 500 m
0 — 0.25 miles

YHA is inside an 18th-century house on the edge of town. It's a rambling place, with a cafe, laundry and four- to 10-bed dorms. It's a 15-minute walk from the front; buses 5 and 6 stop nearby.

★ Venton Vean B&B **££**
(☑ 01736-351294; www.ventonvean.co.uk; Trewithen Rd; r £80-95; ☎) The picture of a modern B&B, finished in greys, blues and pistachios, with stripped wood floors and a keen eye for design. Rooms 1 and 2 are the most spacious; the former overlooks Penlee Memorial Park. The sumptuous breakfast choice includes smoked pollack and Spanish tortillas.

Artist Residence Penzance B&B **££**
(☑ 01736-365664; www.arthotelcornwall.co.uk; Chapel St; d £105-145; ☎) This quirky B&B on Chapel St is like sleeping inside an art gallery. All the rooms have their own design courtesy of a local artist: street-art murals by Jo Peel, seascapes by Pinky Vision, butterfly wallpapers by Dolly Divine. They're furnished with retro furniture and most peep across Penzance's rooftops. Great fun.

Hotel Penzance HOTEL **£££**
(☑ 01736-363117; www.hotelpenzance.com; Briton's Hill; d £140-205; ☎) Perched on a hill

Penzance

◎ Sights
1 Exchange C2
2 Penlee House Gallery & Museum B2

◎ Activities, Courses & Tours
3 Jubilee Pool D3

◎ Sleeping
4 Artist Residence Penzance C2
5 Venton Vean A3

◎ Eating
6 Archie Brown's B2
7 Bakehouse C2

◎ Drinking & Nightlife
8 Turk's Head C2
9 Zero Lounge C2

◎ Entertainment
10 Acorn Arts Centre B2

with views across Mount's Bay, this townhouse hotel makes a pleasant Penzance base. Bedrooms are staid in style, with cream-and-magnolia colours, varnished desks and vintage lamps: the best have bay windows looking out to sea. The hotel's restaurant, the Bay, serves quality food.

DON'T MISS

ST MICHAEL'S MOUNT

Looming from the waters of Mount's Bay and connected to the mainland via a cobbled causeway, this abbey-crowned island (NT; ☑ 01736-710507; www.stmichaelsmount.co.uk; adult/child £8.75/4.25; ☺ house 10.30am-5.30pm Sun-Fri late Mar-Oct, gardens Mon-Fri Apr-Jun, Thu & Fri Jul-Sep) is an unforgettable sight. There's been a monastery here since at least the 5th century, but the present abbey was mostly built by Benedictine monks during the 12th century. Highlights include the rococo drawing room, the armoury, the 14th-century church and the amazing clifftop gardens. Though owned by the St Aubyn family, the abbey is run by the National Trust.

Recent excavations including a Bronze Age axe head, dagger and metal clasp have proved the island has been inhabited since ancient times.

You can catch the ferry (adult/child £2/1) from nearby Marazion at high tide, but it's worth timing your arrival for low tide so you can walk across the causeway, just as the monks and pilgrims did centuries ago.

The 13/13A bus shuttles between Marazion and Penzance (£2) three times a day.

✕ Eating

Archie Brown's CAFE £
(☑ 01736-362828; Bread St; mains £4-10; ☺ 9am-5pm Mon-Sat) A wholefood cafe and health shop, serving quiches, homity pies and salads to Penzance's arty crowd.

★ Tolcarne Inn PUB ££
(☑ 01736-363074; www.tolcarneinn.co.uk; Tolcarne Pl, Newlyn; mains £12-18; ☺ noon-2.15pm & 7-9pm Tue-Sat, noon-2.15pm Sun) This old Newlyn inn is run by talented local chef Ben Tunnicliffe, who's fast turned it into the area's primo gastropub. The ethos is refreshingly honest – top-quality fish, seafood and locally sourced meat, served with minimal fuss. Bookings advisable, especially for Sunday lunch.

Ben's Cornish Kitchen BRITISH ££
(☑ 01736-719200; www.benscornishkitchen.com; Marazion; mains £14-23; ☺ noon-2pm & 7-8.30pm Tue-Sat; ☑) You could easily miss Ben Prior's restaurant as you zip along Marazion's main street, but you'd be sorry. Diners travel from far and wide to taste his classical cooking, which focuses on meaty Cornish flavours with a French influence. It's so popular he's recently expanded upstairs.

Bakehouse MEDITERRANEAN ££
(☑ 01736-331331; www.bakehouserestaurant.co.uk; Chapel St; mains £8.95-19.50; ☺ 6.15-10pm Mon-Sat) Down an alley off Chapel St, this no-nonsense bistro serves unpretentious food such as fish served with Med-style marinades, and steaks with spicy rubs.

🍷 Drinking & Entertainment

Turk's Head PUB
(Chapel St; ☺ 11am-11pm) This salty old boozer could have tumbled from the pages of *Treasure Island*. The bar's covered in maritime memorabilia, and it's said a secret smugglers' tunnel links the pub to the harbour.

Zero Lounge BAR
(Chapel St; ☺ 11am-11pm) More urban chic than olde worlde, this open-plan bar also has the town's best beer garden.

Acorn Arts Centre THEATRE
(www.acornartscentre.co.uk; Parade St) A small theatre hosting film, theatre, comedy and live-music gigs.

❶ Getting There & Away

BUS
Local destinations include:
Helston and Falmouth Bus 2/2A (£5, hourly Monday to Saturday, six on Sunday) via Marazion.
St Ives Buses 17/17A/17B (£4, 30 minutes, half-hourly Monday to Saturday, hourly on Sunday).

TRAIN
Penzance is the last stop on the line from London Paddington.
Exeter (£19.80, three hours)
London Paddington (£60.50, 5½ hours)
Truro (£6.40, 30 minutes)

The Lizard

Once notorious as a smugglers' haven and an ill-famed graveyard for ships, the rugged Lizard Peninsula offers Cornwall's wildest coastal panoramas. Wind-lashed in winter, in summer its heaths and cliffs blaze with wildflowers, and its numerous beaches and coves are perfect for a bracing swim.

The main town is Helston, which is famous for its annual street party, Flora Day, held on 8 May. Pretty villages are dotted all round the peninsula's coastline: the old harbour of Coverack, the beaches of Mullion and the idyllic thatched-cottage cove of Cadgwith are all well worth a visit.

Along the peninsula's northern edge runs the Helford River, lined by creeks and inlets which famously inspired Daphne du Maurier's smuggling yarn, *Frenchman's Creek*. Several local companies offer kayaking tours.

◉ Sights & Activities

Lizard Lighthouse Heritage Centre MUSEUM
(☑ 01326-290202; www.lizardlighthouse.co.uk; adult/child £2.75/1.75; ☺ 11am-5pm Sun-Thu Mar-Oct) Housed in a 1751 lighthouse above Lizard Point, this museum contains exhibits on seafaring and shipwrecks, and you can take guided tours (adult/child £7/4) into the tower to see the lamp room and foghorn.

★ Kynance Cove BEACH
A mile north of Lizard Point, this National Trust–owned inlet is a showstopper, studded with offshore islands rising out of searingly blue seas. The cliffs around the cove are rich in serpentine, a red-green rock popular with Victorian trinket-makers. Drinks and snacks are available at the eco-friendly cafe (www.kynancecovecafe.co.uk; mains £8-14).

National Seal Sanctuary WILDLIFE RESERVE
(☑ 0871 423 2110; www.sealsanctuary.co.uk; adult/child £14.40/12; ☺ 10am-5pm May-Sep, 9am-4pm Oct-Apr) Towards the northwest of the Lizard Peninsula, this sanctuary cares for sick and orphaned seals washed up along the Cornish coastline before returning them to the wild.

Koru Kayaking KAYAKING
(☑ 07794-321827; www.korukayaking.co.uk; 2hr trip £35) Kayaking trips to Frenchman's Creek from the north bank of the Helford River, as well as from Trevaunance Cove near St Agnes.

Aberfal Outdoor Pursuits KAYAKING
(☑ 07968-770756; www.aberfaloutdoorpursuits.co.uk; half/full day £35/50) Half- and full-day guided kayaking trips along the Helford on sit-on-top kayaks.

🛏 Sleeping & Eating

Lizard YHA HOSTEL **£**
(☑ 0845 371 9550; www.yha.org.uk; dm £17-22; ☺ Apr-Oct) The old lighthouse-keeper's cottage at the heritage centre has now been turned into the UK's most southerly hostel, the Lizard Point YHA.

Ann's Pasties BRITISH **£**
(☑ 01326-290889; www.annspasties.co.uk; pasties £2.85; ☺ 9am-3pm Mon-Sat) Approved by Rick Stein, no less, Ann Muller serves huge, traditional pasties from her tiny shop near Lizard Point.

Roskilly's ICE CREAM **£**
(The Harbour; ice cream £2-3; ☺ 9am-5pm) Harbourside outlet for the Lizard's renowned ice-cream maker.

★ Kota INTERNATIONAL **££**
(☑ 01326-562407; www.kotarestaurant.co.uk; 2-course menu £17.50, mains £12-20; ☺ 12.30-2.30pm & 6-9pm) New Zealander Jude Kereama takes his culinary inspiration from his globetrotting travels, and his menu is spiced with exotic flavours, from Szechuan to Thai and Malaysian. His main restaurant is in a converted mill in Porthleven, 3 miles south of Helston. He also has a new cafe-bistro, **Kota Kai** (☑ 01326-574411; www.kotakai.co.uk; mains £11.50-14.95; ☺ noon-2pm & 5.30-9.30pm; 🖘), along the quay.

Halzephron Inn PUB **££**
(☑ 01326-240406; www.halzephron-inn.co.uk; mains £9.95-21.95; ☺ 11am-11pm) On the cliffs above the cove of Gunwalloe, 5 miles south of Helston, this is a proper Cornish local, whitewashed and slate-topped, with brassy trinkets above the bar, beams on the ceiling and a menu of beer-battered fish and surf-and-turf steak.

❶ Getting There & Away

Services include:

Bus 2 Penzance to Falmouth, with stops at Porthleven and Helston (£5, hourly Monday to Saturday, six on Sunday).

Bus 36 Helston to Gunwalloe, Gweek, Coverack and St Keverne (£3, three or four daily Monday to Saturday).

Bus 37 Helston to Mullion (£3) and the Lizard (£5, every two hours Monday to Saturday, four on Sunday).

Bus 82 (£5, one hour, hourly, five on Sunday) Helston to Truro.

Falmouth & Around

POP 20,775

The world's third-deepest natural harbour, Falmouth made its fortune during the 18th and 19th centuries, when clippers, trading vessels and mail packets stopped off here to unload their cargoes. The town is still an important centre for ship repairs, although these days it's also a lively student town thanks to the ever-expanding campus of University College Falmouth in nearby Penryn.

It's an ideal base for exploring Cornwall's south coast, with a wealth of bars and bistros, a trio of beaches and the nation's foremost maritime museum on its doorstep.

◉ Sights

Falmouth has three beaches. Nearest to town is busy Gyllyngvase, a short walk from the town centre, where there's lots of sand and the lively Gylly Beach Café. Around the headland is little Swanpool, while Maenporth is another mile further west. The 500 bus stops at all three in summer.

National Maritime Museum   MUSEUM
(☑ 01326-313338; www.nmmc.co.uk; Discovery Quay; adult/child £11.50/8; ◎ 10am-5pm) This is the sister outpost to the National Maritime Museum in Greenwich, London. It focuses on Falmouth's history as a seafaring port, supplemented by regular nautically themed exhibitions. At the heart of the complex is the impressive Flotilla Gallery, where an array of small boats is suspended from the ceiling on steel wires. From the top floor of the Lookout tower, there's a 360-degree panorama across Falmouth Bay.

Pendennis Castle   CASTLE
(EH; ☑ 01326-316594; adult/child £7/4.20; ◎ 10am-6pm Jul & Aug, to 5pm Apr-Jun & Sep, to 4pm Oct-Mar) Designed to work in tandem with its sister castle in St Mawes, out across the estuary, this Tudor castle sits proudly on Pendennis Point, and was designed as part of Henry VIII's massive castle-building program to reinforce England's coastline. You can wander around several of the castle floors and the Tudor gun deck, as well as the Governor's bedroom, a WWI guard ouse and the WWII-era Half-Moon Battery. Listen out for the Noonday Gun blasting out at midday.

⊨ Sleeping

Falmouth Lodge Backpackers   HOSTEL £
(☑ 01326-319996; www.falmouthbackpackers.co.uk; 9 Gyllyngvase Tce; dm/s £19/26, d £28-35) In a mock-Tudor house at the top of town, this friendly hostel makes a fun budget stay. Rooms are small but clean and cosy, there's an Aga in the kitchen and a DVD lounge, and owner Judi often holds impromptu BBQs for guests.

Highcliffe Contemporary B&B   B&B ££
(☑ 01326-314466; www.highcliffefalmouth.com; 22 Melvill Rd; s £45-55, d £75-130; 🛜) Vintage furniture and upcycled design pieces give each of the rooms here its own individual feel. The pick of the bunch is the light-filled Attic Penthouse, with skylight windows overlooking Falmouth Bay. Room service breakfasts are served in picnic baskets, or you can tuck into pancakes and Hog's pudding in the dining room.

WORTH A TRIP

TREBAH & GLENDURGAN GARDENS

Two of Cornwall's great subtropical gardens sit side by side along the northern bank of the River Helford. First planted in 1840, Trebah (☑ 01326-252200; www.trebahgarden.co.uk; adult/child £9/3; ◎ 10.30am-4.30pm) is dramatically situated in a steep ravine filled with giant rhododendrons, huge Brazilian rhubarb plants and jungle ferns.

Next-door Glendurgan (NT; ☑ 01326-250906; www.nationaltrust.org.uk/glendurgan-garden; adult/child £7.20/3.60; ◎ 10.30am-5.30pm Tue-Sun) was established around the same time by the wealthy Fox family, and is now owned by the National Trust. It has amazing views of the River Helford, as well as an original yew-tree maze and a secluded beach near Durgan village.

They're about 4 miles from Falmouth: head for Mawnan Smith and follow the signs.

Bosanneth
B&B **££**

(☎ 01326-314649; www.bosanneth.co.uk; Gyllyngvase Hill; d from £90; 🛜) There's a mix-and-match decorative vibe running through this eight-room B&B. Some of the rooms feel vintage, with old mirrors, reclaimed furniture and classic colours, while others go for a more up-to-date look. The 'oasis' garden is a particular delight.

Greenbank
HOTEL **£££**

(☎ 01326-312440; www.greenbank-hotel.co.uk; Harbourside; r £99-245; 🅿🛜) The queen of Falmouth's old hotels, with a knockout position overlooking the boat-filled estuary towards Flushing. It feels rather like the setting for an Agatha Christie novel – nautical knick-knacks and ships in cabinets dot the public areas, and tall windows look out onto the water. The rooms are more modern, decorated in inoffensive beiges and creams. Sea views command premium prices.

✗ Eating

★ Oliver's
BISTRO **££**

(☎ 01326-218138; www.oliversfalmouth.com; 33 High St; mains £12.50-20.50; ⊙noon-2pm & 7-9pm Tue-Sat) Run by chef Ken Oliver, this little bistro is the place everyone wants to dine in Falmouth, but the tiny dining room means you'll have to book well ahead. White walls and pine tables provide a stripped-back match for Ken's no-fuss, Mediterranean-inspired food. Local foragers provide many ingredients.

Wheelhouse
SEAFOOD **££**

(☎ 01326-318050; Upton Slip; mains £8-15; ⊙6-10pm Wed-Sat) Hidden down a narrow alley, this backstreet shellfish bar is another Falmouth favourite. The dining here is DIY: crab, scallops, mussels and lobsters are served shell-on, complete with cracking tools. There are two sittings, but both are always packed out – book well ahead.

Courtyard Deli
DELI, CAFE **££**

(☎ 01326-319526; http:courtyarddeli.wordpress. com; 2 Bells Ct; mains £8-12; ⊙8.30am-5.30pm Mon-Wed, to 9.30pm Thu-Sat, 10.30am-4pm Sun) Small yet beautiful, as this fabulous deli-diner ably demonstrates. Charcuterie, tarts, salads and quiches fill the counter cabinets, and there are evening tapas sessions several times a week. It's up an easy-to-miss alley, next to Beerwolf Books.

Gylly Beach Café
CAFE **££**

(☎ 01326-312884; www.gyllybeach.com; Gyllyngvase Beach; mains £10.95-15.95; ⊙9am-11pm)

When the sun shines, everyone heads to the Gylly Beach for morning coffee or lunch with a sea view. Sliding doors open onto the glass-fronted patio, perched right above Gyllyngvase's sands. Burgers, kebabs, mussels and salads dominate the menu, and the breakfasts are great.

Rick Stein's Fish
FISH & CHIPS **££**

(☎ 01841-532700; Discovery Quay; takeaway £4.95-6.50, mains £10.50-14.50; ⊙noon-2.30pm & 5-9pm) Rick Stein's posh fish-and-chips shop now has a Falmouth branch.

🍷 Drinking & Nightlife

Dolly's
TEAROOM

(☎ 01326-218400; www.dollysbar.co.uk; 21 Church St; ⊙10am-10pm or 11pm Tue-Sat) Frilly and friendly, Dolly's captures the delights of the English tearoom – complete with charity-shop lamps, bone china teapots and cake stands. It kicks into a different gear after dark, with cocktails and jazz.

Espressini
CAFE

(39 Killigrew St; ⊙8am-6pm Mon-Sat, 10am-4pm Sun; 🛜) Cornwall's best coffee house, bar none. The choice of blends, roasts and coffees are enough to fill a 3m-long blackboard. Literally.

Beerwolf Books
PUB

(☎ 01326-618474; www.beerwolfbooks.co.uk; 3 Bells Ct; ⊙noon-midnight) Quite possibly the greatest idea ever, anytime, anywhere: a pub and bookshop rolled into one, meaning you can browse for reading material before settling down for a pint of real ale.

Front
PUB

(☎ 01326-212168; Custom House Quay; ⊙11am-11.30pm) Spit-and-sawdust pub favoured by beer buffs, with scuffed wood floors and real ales served straight from wooden casks.

Chain Locker
PUB

(Quay St; ⊙11am-11pm) A proper old sea-dog's pub, with outside seating on the harbour.

❶ Getting There & Away

Falmouth is at the end of the branch train line from Truro (£4, 20 minutes), which also stops at Penryn.

Bus 2 (£5, hourly Monday to Saturday) To Penzance via Helston.

Bus 35 (£5, twice daily Monday to Saturday) Stops at Glendurgan and Gweek en route to Helston.

Bus 88 (£5, hourly) Fastest bus to Truro.

Truro

POP 17,431

Centred on its three-spired 19th-century cathedral, Truro is Cornwall's capital city. Once a busy river port and one of Cornwall's five Stannary towns (where tin was assayed and stamped for export), these days it's a busy commercial city, with a lively centre dominated by the usual coffee shops and chain stores.

Remnants of the city's elegant Georgian past can be seen on Lemon St and Walsingham Pl.

◉ Sights

Royal Cornwall Museum   MUSEUM
(☑ 01872-272205; www.royalcornwallmuseum.org.uk; River St; ◷ 10am-5pm Mon-Sat) FREE Collections at the county's main museum encompass everything from geological specimens to Celtic torques and a ceremonial carriage. Upstairs there's an Egyptian section and a little gallery with some surprising finds: a Turner here, a van Dyck there, and several works by Stanhope Forbes.

Truro Cathedral   CATHEDRAL
(www.trurocathedral.org.uk; High Cross; suggested donation £4; ◷ 7.30am-6pm Mon-Sat, 9am-7pm Sun) Built on the site of a 16th-century parish church in soaring Gothic Revival style, Truro Cathedral was completed in 1910, making it the first cathedral built in England since St Paul's. Inside, the vast nave contains some fine Victorian stained glass and the impressive Father Willis Organ.

Trelissick Gardens   GARDENS
(NT; www.nationaltrust.org.uk/trelissick-garden; adult/child £8.60/4.30; ◷ 10.30am-5.30pm) At the head of the Fal estuary, 4 miles south of Truro, Trelissick is one of Cornwall's most beautiful estates, with a formal garden filled with magnolias and hydrangeas, and a huge expanse of fields and parkland criss-crossed by walking trails.

Lemon St Market   MARKET
(www.lemonstreetmarket.co.uk; Lemon St; ◷ 10.30am-5.30pm Mon-Sat) A covered market housing craft shops, cafes, delis and an upstairs gallery. The willow-and-paper lanterns hanging from the ceiling were built for Truro's Christmas street parade, the City of Lights, held in early December.

🛏 Sleeping

Mannings Hotel   HOTEL ££
(☑ 01872-270345; www.manningshotels.co.uk; Lemon St; r £79-109; P 🖅) The best place to stay in the city centre. The part-Georgian building has been tastefully modernised, with zingy colours and minimalist furniture. There are 'aparthotels' for longer stays (£129).

Merchant House Hotel   HOTEL ££
(☑ 01872-272450; www.merchant-house.co.uk; 49 Falmouth Rd; s £55, d £70-90, f £95; P) This smart Victorian house is handy for town, and refurbishment has brightened up the rooms. Some rooms have skylights, others overlook the garden. It's popular with business travellers and organised tours, so it's worth reserving well ahead.

WORTH A TRIP

THE ROSELAND

On the opposite side of the Fal Estuary from Truro and Falmouth, the Roseland peninsula gets its name not from flowers, but from the Cornish word *ros*, meaning promontory. Greener and gentler than the harsh granite cliffs of the north coast, it's a pastoral place, criss-crossed by hedgerows and spotted with quiet villages and sandy bays – including the large beaches of Carne and Pendower, which join together at low tide. It's also well worth visiting the chichi town of St Mawes, which has a beautifully preserved Tudor castle (EH; ☑ 01326-270526; adult/child £4.60/2.80; ◷ 10am-6pm Apr-Sep, to 5pm Oct-Mar), shaped like a clover leaf.

The quickest route to the Roseland is via the King Harry Ferry (☑ 01872-862312; www.falriver.co.uk/getting-about/ferries/king-harry-ferry; per car one way/return £5/8, bicycles & pedestrians free), which carries cars and pedestrians over the Fal River from near Trelissick Gardens to the opposite side at Philleigh. Otherwise it's a drive of around 14 miles from Truro.

CORNWALL'S GLOBETROTTING GARDENS

Lodged at the bottom of a disused clay-pit, the giant biomes of the Eden Project (☑ 01726-811911; www.edenproject.com; adult/child/family £23.50/13.50/68; ☺ 10am-6pm Apr-Oct, to 4.30pm Nov-Mar) – the largest greenhouses in the world – have become Cornwall's most celebrated landmark and a definite must-see. Looking like a Bond villain's lair, Eden's bubble-shaped biomes maintain miniature ecosystems that enable all kinds of weird and wonderful plants to flourish – from stinking rafflesia flowers and banana trees in the rainforest biome to cacti and soaring palms in the Mediterranean biome.

Exhibits around the complex explore ecological and conservation themes, covering everything from global warming to rubber production and chocolate-making. Landscaped gardens wind their way between the biomes, but the highlight is the gravity-defying treetop walkway that winds its way through the canopy of the Rainforest Biome.

In summer, the biomes provide a backdrop for live concerts during the Eden Sessions, and in winter host a full-size ice rink.

The Eden site is at Bodelva, about 5 miles' drive from St Austell. There are discounts for buying tickets online and arriving by public transport. Bus 101 runs regularly from St Austell train station; bus 527 travels from Newquay.

Not far away is Cornwall's real-life secret garden, the Lost Gardens of Heligan (☑ 01726-845100; www.heligan.com; adult/child £12/6; ☺ 10am-6pm Mar-Oct, to 5pm Nov-Feb). Formerly the family estate of the Tremaynes, Heligan's magnificent 19th-century gardens fell into disrepair following WWI, and have since been restored to their former splendour by the brains behind the Eden Project, Tim Smit, and a huge army of gardeners, horticulturalists and volunteers.

It's a horticultural wonderland: wandering round the grounds you'll discover formal lawns, working kitchen gardens, fruit-filled greenhouses, a secret grotto and an 25m-high rhododendron (claimed to be the world's largest). For many people, though, it's the jungle valley which really steals the show – a Lost World landscape of gigantic ferns, towering palms and tropical blooms.

Heligan is 7 miles from St Austell. Bus 526 links Heligan with Mevagissey and St Austell train station (£5).

✖ Eating

Bustopher's   BISTRO ££
(☑ 01872-279029; www.bustophersbarbistro.com; 62 Lemon St; mains £10-14; ☺ noon-10pm Wed-Sat, to 4pm Sun) Modern urban dining comes to Truro at Bustopher's, a classy bistro decked out with shiny wood, candles on the tables and lots of nooks and crannies. The menu is divided into 'Smalls' and 'Bigs', and runs the gamut from clam and fish stew to confit duck. It's really rather good.

Sam's in the City   BISTRO ££
(www.samscornwall.co.uk; 1-2 New Bridge St; mains £11.95-21.95; ☺ 9am-10pm) This long-standing restaurant has a snazzy new city address, in a former jeweller's on one of Truro's oldest streets. The menu is split between seafood classics, steaks, city salads and sharing platters – plus bouillabaisse and seafood feasts for the very hungry.

☕ Drinking & Entertainment

Old Ale House   PUB
(Quay St; ☺ noon-11pm) A proper ale-drinker's pub, with sawdust on the floor, beer mats on the ceiling and a menu of guest ales.

Old Grammar School   PUB
(19 St Mary St; ☺ 10am-late) Open-plan drinking den with big tables and sofas to sink into. Lunch is served from noon to 3pm; later it's cocktails, candles and Belgian and Japanese beers.

Hall for Cornwall   THEATRE
(☑ 01872-262466; www.hallforcornwall.co.uk; Lemon Quay) The county's main venue for touring theatre and music.

❶ Information

Tourist Office (☑ 01872-274555; tic@truro.gov.uk; Boscawen St; ☺ 9am-5.30pm Mon-Fri, to 5pm Sat)

❶ Getting There & Away

BUS

Truro's bus station is beside Lemon Quay.

Bus 88 (£5, hourly) Express to Falmouth.

Bus X18 (£5, hourly Monday to Saturday, six on Sunday) To Penzance.

Bus 14/14A (£5, 1½ hours, hourly Monday to Saturday) To St Ives.

TRAIN

Truro is on the main London Paddington–Penzance line and the branch line to Falmouth.

Bristol (£45, 3½ hours)

Exeter (£17.90, 2¼ hours)

Falmouth (£4, 30 minutes)

London Paddington (£60.50, 4½ hours)

Penzance (£6.40, 30 minutes)

Fowey

POP 2273

In many ways, Fowey feels like Padstow's south-coast sister; a workaday port turned well-heeled holiday town, with a tumble of pastel-coloured houses, portside pubs and tiered terraces overlooking the wooded banks of the Fowey River. The town's wealth was founded on the export of china clay from the St Austell pits, but it's been an important port since Elizabethan times, and later became the adopted home of the thriller writer Daphne du Maurier, who used the nearby house at Menabilly Barton as the inspiration for *Rebecca*.

These days, it's an attractive and increasingly upmarket town, handy for exploring Cornwall's southeastern corner.

◉ Sights

Readymoney Cove BEACH

From the town centre, the Esplanade leads down to this little cove and the remains of the small Tudor fort of St Catherine's Castle.

Polkerris Beach BEACH

(www.polkerrisbeach.com) A couple of miles west of Fowey, this is the area's largest and busiest beach. Sailing lessons, windsurfing and paddle-boarding are all available.

🏃 Activities

Hall Walk WALKING TRAIL

(www.nationaltrust.org.uk/item379352) This 3.5-mile circular walk starts across the river from Fowey in Bodinnick, winding along the wooded shores of Pont Pill Creek before

following the coastline to the harbour of Polruan, from where you can catch a ferry back to Fowey. You can download a route guide from the National Trust website.

Encounter Cornwall KAYAKING

(☑ 07976-466123; www.encountercornwall.com; Golant; adult/child £25/12.50) Three-hour trips from Golant, just north of Fowey, with a choice of exploring creek or coastline.

🛏 Sleeping

★ **Coriander Cottages** B&B ££

(☑ 01726-834998; www.foweyaccommodation.co.uk; Penventinue Lane; r £100-130; P⊠⚹) A delightfully rural cottage complex on the outskirts of Fowey, with ecofriendly accommodation in a choice of open-plan, self-catering barns, all with quiet country views. The stone barns have been beautifully modernised, and use a combination of solar panels, ground-source heating and rainwater harvesting to reduce environmental impact. A lovely retreat.

Cormorant Hotel HOTEL ££

(☑ 01726-833426; www.cormoranthotel.co.uk; Golant; d £115-170) Up the creek in Golant, this small hotel has a superb riverside location, and many of its rooms have water-view balconies. They're split into three comfort levels: go for a Superior with view for the premium price/comfort ratio.

Old Quay House HOTEL £££

(☑ 01726-833302; www.theoldquayhouse.com; 28 Fore St; d £145-395; ⚹) The epitome of Fowey's upmarket trend, this exclusive quayside hotel is all natural fabrics, rattan chairs and tasteful tones, and the rooms are a mix of estuary-view suites and attic penthouses. Very Kensington, not very Cornish.

🍴 Eating & Drinking

Lifebuoy Cafe CAFE £

(☑ 07715-075869; www.thelifebuoycafe.co.uk; 8 Lostwithiel St; mains £5-10; ⊗8am-5pm) Everyone's favourite brekkie stop in Fowey, this friendly cafe is a riot of character, from the brightly coloured furniture and polka-dot bunting to the vintage Action Men on the shelves. Wolf down a Fat Buoy brekkie or a classic fish-finger butty, washed down with a mug of good old English tea.

Dwelling House CAFE £

(☑ 01726-833662; 6 Fore St; tea £3-6; ⊗10am-6.30pm May-Sep, to 5.30pm Wed-Sun Oct-Apr)

Top spot for tea (20-plus varieties) and dainty cakes (decorated with sprinkles and icing swirls, and served on a proper cake stand).

Bistro
FRENCH ££

(☑01726-832322; www.thebistrofowey.co.uk; 24 Fore St; 2-/3-course menu £15.95/18.95) Solid bistro dining on Fowey's main street, offering a Cornish spin on French classics, with an especially strong focus on seafood. It's stylish inside, with mosaic floors and monochrome photos.

Sam's
BISTRO ££

(www.samsfowey.co.uk; 20 Fore St; mains £6.50-13.95; ☺noon-9pm) Sam's has been a stalwart in Fowey for years. Booth seats, day-glo menus and classic movie posters keep the feel laid-back, and the menu of burgers, fishy specials, salads and 'old favourites' all come in a choice of starter or main sizes. There's a beachside outpost beside Polkerris Beach. No bookings.

King of Prussia
PUB

(www.kingofprussia.co.uk; Town Quay; ☺11am-11pm) Fowey has lots of pubs, but you might as well go for the one with the best harbour view, named after notorious 'free trader' John Carter.

⊙ Getting There & Away

Buses to Fowey all stop at Par Station, where you can catch trains to the Penzance–London Paddington main line. Bus 524/525 (half-hourly) stops in Fowey, St Austell (£4) and Mevagissey (£5); the 525 continues to Heligan (£5).

Bodinnick Ferry (car & 2 passengers/pedestrian/bicycle £4.60/1.70/free; ☺last ferry 8.45pm Apr-Oct, 7pm Nov-Mar) Car ferry crossing the river to Bodinnick.

Polruan Ferry (adult/child/bicycle £1.80/80p/£1; ☺last ferry 9pm Sun-Thu, 11pm Fri & Sat) Passenger ferry to Polruan. In winter and on summer evenings, it runs from Town Quay; during the day, it runs from Whitehouse Slipway on the Esplanade.

Polperro
POP 1206

Even in a county where picturesque fishing harbours are 10-a-penny, it's hard not to fall for Polperro – a warren of cottages, boat stores and alleyways, all set around a stout granite harbour. Unsurprisingly, this was once a smugglers' hideout, and it's still a place with a salty, sea-dog atmosphere, despite the inevitable summer crowds. The coast path between Polperro and Looe is particularly scenic, especially around Talland Bay.

The main car park is 750m uphill from the village, from where it's a 15-minute stroll down to the quayside. Apart from simply wandering and soaking up the scenery, it's worth popping into the ramshackle Polperro Heritage Museum (☑01503-272423; The Warren; adult/child £1.75/50p; ☺10am-6pm Mar-Oct), which explores the town's seafaring and smuggling heritage.

The 573 bus (£2.80, hourly) runs between Liskeard, Looe and Polperro, while the 572 (£6.50, hourly Monday to Saturday, three on Sunday) continues to Plymouth.

Looe
POP 5280

Tucked into the long curve of coast between the Fowey River and Plymouth Sound, Looe is half historic fishing port, half bucket-and-spade resort. Split into East and West Looe and linked by a historic arched bridge, it's a pleasant base for exploring Cornwall's southeastern reaches, and has some lovely beaches nearby.

⊙ Sights & Activities

Half a mile offshore is tiny Looe Island, a 9-hectare nature reserve run by the Cornwall Wildlife Trust. The boat Islander (☑07814-139223; adult/child return £7/5, plus landing fee £3/1) crosses to the island in summer. Guided nature walks leave from the quay.

Wild Futures Monkey Sanctuary
WILDLIFE RESERVE

(☑01503-262532; www.monkeysanctuary.org; St Martins; adult/child £8/5; ☺11am-4.30pm Sun-Thu Easter-Sep; ⊕) Half a mile west of town, this wildlife centre is guaranteed to raise some 'aaahhhhs' over its woolly and capuchin monkeys, many of which were rescued from captivity.

Porfell Wildlife Park
ZOO

(☑01503-220211; www.porfell.co.uk; Lanreath; adult/child £9.50/7.50; ☺10am-6pm; ⊕) A lively animal park a couple of miles outside Looe, with wild denizens including macaws, parakeets, owls, lemurs, meerkats and zebras, as well as a venerable capybara called Bert.

Sleeping

Penvith Barns B&B £

(☎ 01503-240772; www.penvithbarns.co.uk; St-Martin-by-Looe; s £63-72, d £65-80; P 🛜 🐕) Escape the Looe crowds at this rural barn conversion in nearby of St-Martin-by-Looe. Rooms range from small to spacious: the Piggery is tiny and tucked under the eaves, while the Dairy has enough space for a spare bed and sofa.

Barclay House B&B £££

(☎ 01503-262929; www.barclayhouse.co.uk; St Martins Rd; d £95-130; P 🛜 🐕) This detached Victorian villa sits on 2.4-hectare gardens and has the best bedrooms in East Looe, with wraparound river views and graceful shades of peach, pistachio and aquamarine. It has self-catering cottages available.

ℹ Information

Looe Tourist Office (☎ 01503-262072; www.visit-southeastcornwall.co.uk; Guildhall, Fore St; ⊙ 10am-5pm Easter-Oct)

ℹ Getting There & Away

Bus 572 travels to Plymouth (1¼ hours, seven daily Monday to Saturday). Trains on the Looe Valley Line (every two hours Monday to Saturday, eight on Sunday, day ranger adult/child £5/3.15) trundle along a gorgeous stretch of track to Liskeard.

Southeast Cornwall & the Rame Peninsula

Often called 'Cornwall's forgotten corner', the Rame Peninsula remains one of Cornwall's most unspoilt pockets, and it's a fine place to head when you want to give the crowds the slip. This area was once parcelled up between some of Cornwall's old aristocratic families, and several grand country estates are open to the public. If you have time, it's also worth stopping at the little harbour villages of Kingsand and Cawsand, and the impressive 3-mile expanse of Whitsand Bay (not to be confused with Whitesand Bay, near Sennen). Further inland, Cornwall's southeast is also home to some impressive historic homes.

◉ Sights

Lanhydrock HISTORIC BUILDING

(NT; ☎ 01208-265950; www.nationaltrust.org.uk/lanhydrock; adult/child £11.30/5.60, grounds only £7/3.50; ⊙ house 11am-5.30pm Tue-Sat, grounds 10am-6pm daily) This huge house provides a fascinating insight into the 'upstairs, downstairs' lives of the Cornish gentry, namely the Robartes family. Extensively rebuilt after a fire in 1881, it's the quintessential Victorian manor, complete with gentlemen's smoking room, toy-strewn nursery and antique-filled dining room – as well as an enormous kitchen which has its original roasting spit. The house is 2.5 miles southeast of Bodmin.

Antony House HISTORIC BUILDING

(NT; ☎ 01752-812191; www.nationaltrust.org.uk/antony; adult/child £8.10/5.10, grounds only £4.10/2.10; ⊙ house 1-5pm, gardens noon-5pm Tue-Thu & Sun) Owned by the National Trust and occupied by the Carew-Pole family, this house's main claim to fame are its decorative gardens, designed by the 18th-century landscape architect Humphry Repton and filled with outlandish topiary, some of which featured in Tim Burton's *Alice in Wonderland*. It's 9 miles east of Looe or 6 miles west from Plymouth.

Port Eliot HISTORIC BUILDING

(☎ 01503-230211; www.porteliot.co.uk; house & grounds adult/child £8/4, grounds only £5/2; ⊙ 2-6pm Sat-Thu Mar-Jun) This glorious 2400-hectare estate is the family seat of the Earl of St Germans. The house is open for three months of the year, and the estate has lots and lots of fabulous walks. The annual Port Eliot Festival (www.porteliotfestival.com) of music and literature is held in July.

ℹ Getting There & Away

On the Rame Peninsula's east side, the **Torpoint Ferry** (www.tamarcrossings.org.uk/index.aspx?articleid=36386; cars £2.50, pedestrians & cyclists free; ⊙ 24hr) chugs across the River Tamar to Plymouth.

Bodmin Moor

It can't quite boast the wild majesty of Dartmoor, but Bodmin Moor has a bleak beauty all of its own. Pock-marked with heaths and granite hills, including Rough Tor (pronounced 'row-tor'; 400m) and Cornwall's highest point, Brown Willy (419m), it's a desolate place that works on the imagination; for years there have been reported sightings of the Beast of Bodmin, a large, black cat-like creature, although no one's ever managed to snap a decent picture.

Apart from the hills, the moor's main landmark is Jamaica Inn (☎ 01566-86250;

www.jamaicainn.co.uk; s£65, d£80-110; P), made famous by Daphne du Maurier's novel of the same name – although it's disappointingly been modernised since the author's day.

Bus services are very limited on the moor, so you'll need a car to explore.

◉ Sights & Activities

Golitha Falls   WATERFALL
Around 1.25 miles west of St Cleer, these crashing waterfalls are one of the most renowned beauty spots on the moor. Around the falls are the remains of the ancient oak woodland which once covered much of the moor. There is a car park half a mile's walk from the reserve near Draynes Bridge.

Carnglaze Caverns   CAVE
(☑01579-320251; www.carnglaze.com; adult/child £6/4; ☺10am-5pm) Slate was once extensively mined on the moor, leaving behind a network of deep caverns such as these ones outside St Neot. Several of the caves are open to the public and can be visited on an underground tour.

Bodmin & Wenford Railway   HERITAGE RAILWAY
(☑01208-73555; www.bodminandwenfordrailway.co.uk; rover pass adult/child £12/6; ☺Mar-Oct) Run by enthusiasts, this steam railway chuffs and clatters for 6.5 miles between Bodmin and Boscarne Junction. Many trains are still decked out in their original 1950s livery. At the Boscarne end, the line links up with the Camel Trail (p332); bikes can be taken on the trains if there's space. Look out for special trips in summer, including Pullman-style dining trains that include a silver-service supper.

Cardinham Woods   HIKING, BIKING
(☑01208-72577; www.forestry.gov.uk/cardinham) Just outside Bodmin, this large public forest is a great spot for a woody wander, and also has a network of mountain-bike trails if you're feeling more energetic. The Bodmin and Wenford Railway stops at nearby Coleslogget Halt, from where a 1.5-mile trail leads to Cardinham.

ISLES OF SCILLY

They might only be 28 miles west of the mainland, but in many ways the Isles of Scilly feel like a different world. Life on this archipelago of around 140 tiny islands seems hardly to have changed in decades: there are no traffic jams, no supermarkets, no multinational hotels, and the only noise pollution comes from the sound of breaking waves and cawing gulls. That's not to say that Scilly is behind the times – you'll find a mobile signal and broadband on the main islands – but the people seem perfectly content for life to tick along at their own island pace. Renowned for their glorious beaches, there are few places better to escape the outside world.

Only five islands are inhabited: St Mary's is the largest, followed by Tresco, while only a few hardy souls remain on Bryher, St Martin's and St Agnes. Regular ferry boats run between all five islands.

Unsurprisingly, summer is by far the busiest time. Many businesses shut down completely in winter. Hotels are expensive and the B&B supply is limited, so many people hire a cottage instead – the two main companies are Island Properties (☑01720-422082; www.scillyhols.com) and Sibley's Island Homes (☑01720-422431; www.sibleysonscilly.co.uk).

All the inhabited islands (except Tresco) have a campsite, but you'll need to reserve well ahead for July and August.

❶ Information

Isles of Scilly Tourist Board (☑01720-422536; tic@scilly.gov.uk; St Mary's; ☺8.30am-6pm Mon-Fri, 9am-5pm Sat, 9am-2pm Sun May-Sep, shorter hours Oct-Apr) The islands' only tourist office.

Simply Scilly (www.simplyscilly.co.uk) The official tourist site.

❶ Getting There & Away

Bookings for flights and ferries are handled by the **Isles of Scilly Travel Centre** (☑0845 710 5555; www.islesofscilly-travel.co.uk; Quay St; ☺8am-6.30pm Mon-Sat) in Penzance.

Isles of Scilly Skybus Since the closure of the helicopter service in 2013, planes provide the only air link to the islands. There are several flights daily from Land's End Airport, near Zennor, and Newquay Airport. Adult fares start at £70 to £80 one way. Summer flights also run from Exeter, Bristol and Southampton.

Scillonian III (☺Apr-Oct) Scilly's ferry plies the notoriously choppy waters between Penzance and St Mary's (adult fare from £47 each way). There's at least one daily crossing in summer, but there are no ferries in winter.

❶ Getting Around

St Mary's Boatmen Association (☑01720-423999; www.scillyboating.co.uk) Provides regular ferry services from St Mary's to Scilly's other islands. Returns to/from one island cost adult/child £8.50/4.25, or you can take a 'circular' return via another island for £13/6.50.

St Mary's

POP 2200

St Mary's is the largest and busiest island in Scilly, and the main point of arrival for flights and ferries. About a mile west of the airport is the main settlement of Hugh Town, home to most of the island's hotels, shops and guesthouses, as well as the main harbour.

Most people never get much further than Porthcressa, Hugh Town's narrow sandy beach, but there are plenty of other coves that can be reached on foot or by bike, including Porth Hellick, Watermill Cove and the remote Pelistry Bay.

Sights

Isles of Scilly Museum   MUSEUM
(Church St, Hugh Town; adult/child £3.50/1; ◷ 10am-4.30pm Mon-Fri, to noon Sat Easter-Sep, 10am-noon Mon-Sat Oct-Easter) The small Isles of Scilly Museum explores the islands' history, with an eclectic mix of archaeological finds and shipwreck artefacts.

Tours

Scilly Walks   WALKING TOUR
(☏ 01720-423326; www.scillywalks.co.uk; adult/child £6/3) Three-hour archaeological and historical tours, plus guided walking trips to other islands.

Island Wildlife Tours   WALKING TOUR
(☏ 01720-422212; www.islandwildlifetours.co.uk; half/full day £6/12) Regular birdwatching and wildlife walks with resident twitcher Will Wagstaff.

Island Sea Safaris   BOAT TOUR
(☏ 01720-422732; www.islandseasafaris.co.uk) Trips to see local seabird and seal colonies (adult/child £33/25). Also rents wetsuits and snorkelling gear.

Sleeping

Garrison Campsite   CAMPSITE £
(☏ 01720-422670; tedmoulson@aol.com; Tower Cottage, Garrison; sites £8.80-11; ☏) Several hectares of sea-view camping above Hugh Town, with electrical hook-ups, wi-fi and a laundry-cum-shower block. They'll even pre-pitch a tent for you.

Isles of Scilly Country Guesthouse   B&B ££
(☏ 01720-422440; www.scillyguesthouse.co.uk; High Lanes; d £100-124; ☏) Run by Bavarian expat Sabine Schraudolph, this guesthouse is one of the comfiest on St Mary's. The large rooms are chintz-free and look out across St Mary's fields. Sabine serves Bavarian goodies such as *apfelstrudel* in her conservatory-cum-coffee house.

Wingletang   B&B ££
(☏ 01720-422381; www.wingletangguesthouse.co.uk; The Parade; d £72-90) Simple and cosy rooms in a 200-year-old granite cottage in the heart of Hugh Town.

Star Castle Hotel   HOTEL £££
(☏ 01720-422317; www.star-castle.co.uk; The Garrison; r incl dinner £98-398; ☏☏) Shaped like an eight-pointed star, this former fort on Garrison Point is one of Scilly's star hotels, with heritage-style castle rooms and more modern garden suites. It's stuffy and expensive, but prices include dinner.

Eating

Dibble & Grub   CAFE ££
(☏ 01720-423719; www.dibbleandgrub.com; lunch £6-12, dinner £10-16; ◷ 10am-10pm Apr-Sep) Sleek new beach cafe beside Porthcressa in the island's old fire station. The menu dabbles in tapas and Mediterranean-style classics.

Juliet's Garden Restaurant   BISTRO ££
(☏ 01720-422228; www.julietsgardenrestaurant.co.uk; mains £8-16; ◷ noon-2pm & 6-9pm) St Mary's long-standing bistro, in business for three decades, and still the best place to eat. It's in a converted barn 15 minutes' walk from town: expect gourmet salads and sandwiches by day, plus classier plates of curried monkfish and spring lamb after dark, served by candlelight.

Getting Around

For taxis on St Mary's, try **Island Taxis** (☏ 01720-422126), **Scilly Cabs** (☏ 01720-422901) or **Toots Taxis** (☏ 01720-422142).

All flights are met by **Paulgers Transport** (☏ 01720-423701), who for a flat-rate fare of £4 will run you to wherever you're staying, or straight to the quayside if you're travelling to other islands.

Island Rover (☏ 01720-422131; www.islandrover.co.uk; tickets £8) St Mary's only bus service. Runs circular tours from Holgate's Green in Hugh Town at 10.15am and 3.30pm, plus extra tours in high summer.

Tresco

POP 175

Owned by the Duchy of Cornwall, the main attraction of Scilly's second-largest island is the magical **Tresco Abbey Garden** (☑ 01720-424105; www.tresco.co.uk/stay/abbey-garden; adult/child £12/free; ⊙ 10am-4pm), which boasts more than 5000 subtropical plants and a peculiar microclimate, nurtured by the Gulf Stream. Keep an eye out for the Valhalla collection, made up of figureheads and nameplates salvaged from the many ships that have foundered off Tresco's shores.

Most people visit Tresco on a day trip, as accommodation is ludicrously expensive in season, but you should be able to stretch to lunch at the island's lively pub, the **New Inn** (☑ 01720-422849; contactus@tresco.co.uk; mains £10-18).

Bryher

POP 70

Only around 70 people live on Bryher, Scilly's smallest and wildest inhabited island. Covered by rough bracken and heather, this chunk of rock takes the full force of Atlantic storms; Hell Bay in a winter gale is a truly powerful sight. Cloaked in sea-grass and heather, it's a lovely island to explore on foot. **Watch Hill** provides cracking views over the islands, and **Rushy Bay** is one of the finest beaches on Scilly. Several smaller beaches can be reached via the coast path.

🛏 Sleeping & Eating

Bryher Campsite   CAMPSITE £
(☑ 01720-422886; www.bryhercampsite.co.uk; sites £10.25; 🐾) Bare-bones camping near the quay. Hot showers and tractor transport are included in the rates.

Samson Hill   B&B ££
(☑ 01720-423951; www.samsonhill.co.uk; d £60-75; 🐾) Run by born-and-bred islander Issy Tibbs, this lovely two-room cottage offers a fabulous view towards Tresco. Issy's a keen cook, and breakfast choices range from Canadian pancakes to homemade granola; she also makes her own fudge. Husband Gareth cooks wood-fired pizza in the garden several nights a week.

Hell Bay Hotel   HOTEL £££
(☑ 01720-422947; www.hellbay.co.uk; d £190-320) Pretty much the poshest place to stay in Scilly – a true island getaway blending New England-style furnishings with sunny golds, sea blues and pale wood beams.

Fraggle Rock   CAFE ££
(☑ 01720-422222; www.bryher.co; mains £8-14; ⊙ 9am-9pm; 🐾) This relaxed cafe also doubles as Bryher's pub. The menu's mainly quiches, salads and burgers, but owners Chris and Kim use island suppliers wherever possible. There are a few timber-clad cabins if you feel like staying.

St Martin's

POP 136

The northernmost of the main islands, little St Martin's is rightly renowned for its beaches. Worth hunting out are **Lawrence's Bay** on the south coast, which becomes a broad sweep of sand at low tide; **Great Bay** on the north, arguably Scilly's finest beach; and the secluded cove of **Perpitch** in the southeast.

◎ Sights & Activities

St Martin's Vineyard   WINERY
(☑ 01720-423418; www.stmartinsvineyard.co.uk; ⊙ tours 10.45am-4pm Tue-Thu) The UK's smallest and most southwesterly vineyard produces its own range of white wines. Tours are conducted by owners Val and Graham.

Scilly Diving   DIVING
(☑ 01720-422848; www.scillydiving.com) Situated in Higher Town, this dive outfit offers diving courses and single dives.

🛏 Sleeping

Accommodation is limited apart from one super-expensive hotel, **St Martin's on the Isle** (☑ 01720-422090; www.stmartinshotel.co.uk; d £300-560), and a handful of B&Bs.

St Martin's Campsite   CAMPSITE £
(☑ 01720-422888; www.stmartinscampsite.co.uk; sites £9-11; ⊙ Mar-Oct) The second-largest campsite in Scilly at the western end of Lawrence's Bay, with 50 pitches spread across three fields. Coin-operated laundry and showers are available, and eggs and veg are available for your morning fry-up.

Polreath   B&B ££
(☑ 01720-422046; www.polreath.com; Higher Town; d £100-110) This friendly granite cottage has small rooms and a sunny conservatory serving cream teas, homemade lemonade and evening meals. Weekly stays only May to September.

✗ Eating

Adam's Fish & Chips
SEAFOOD £

(☎01720-422457; ⊙6-8.30pm Tue-Thu, noon-2.30pm Sat Jul & Aug, 6-8.30pm Tue & Thu Sep-Jun) The fish here is as fresh as it gets – whatever's caught on the day is what ends up in your batter. It's run by Adam and Emma, who live and work on Little Arthur Farm nearby.

Little Arthur Farm
CAFE £

(☎01720-422457; www.littlearthur.co.uk; ⊙10.30am-4pm daily, 6.30-8.30pm Mon-Fri) Home-grown produce, handmade shoes, farm-fresh milk: this organic farm and wholefood cafe does it all.

St Martin's Bakery
BAKERY £

(☎01720-423444; www.stmartinsbakery.co.uk; ⊙9am-6pm Mon-Sat, to 2pm Sun) This home-spun bakery turns out fresh bread, pizzas and, of course, homemade pasties.

St Agnes

POP 170

Scilly's southernmost island feels really remote, with a string of empty coves and a scattering of prehistoric sites. Visitors disembark at Porth Conger, near the decommissioned Old Lighthouse – one of the oldest lighthouses in the country.

Other points of interest include the 200-year-old stone Troy Town Maze and the island of Gugh, where you'll find intriguing standing stones and Bronze Age remains.

🛏 Sleeping & Eating

Troytown Farm
CAMPSITE £

(☎01720-422360; www.troytown.co.uk; adult £8.75, tents £2-8) Once a flower farm, St Martin's miniscule campsite offers meadow camping with superb sea views, and also rents three self-catering cottages (from £550 to £950 per week).

Covean Cottage
COTTAGE ££

(☎01720-422620; http://st-agnes-scilly.org/covean.htm; d £60-80) This is a little stone-walled cottage, with three pretty sea-view rooms. There's also a small cafe which serves brekkies and light meals cooked up by the owner.

Turk's Head
PUB ££

(☎01720-422434; mains £8-14; ⊙11am-11pm Mon-Sat, noon-10.30pm Sun) Britain's most southerly alehouse is a beauty. Model ships and seafaring photos line the walls, and you can down your pint of homebrewed Turk's Head beside the slipway. You might even be treated to a sea shanty if the lads are in the mood.

Cambridge & East Anglia

Best Places to Eat

➡ Midsummer House (p371)

➡ Roger Hickman's (p392)

➡ Company Shed (p376)

➡ Great House (p382)

Best Places to Stay

➡ Varsity (p370)

➡ Sutherland House (p386)

➡ Angel (p381)

➡ Peacocks (p375)

Why Go?

Unfurling gently eastwards to the sea, the vast flatlands of East Anglia are a rich web of lush farmland, melancholy Fens and sparkling rivers. The area is justly famous for its sweeping sandy beaches, big skies and the bucolic landscape that once inspired Constable and Gainsborough.

It's not all rural idyll though: rising out of the Fens is the world-famous university town of Cambridge, with its stunning classical architecture and earnest attitude, and to the east is the cosmopolitan city of Norwich. Around them magnificent cathedral cities, pretty market towns and implausibly picturesque villages are testament to the enormous wealth amassed here during medieval times, when the wool and weaving industries flourished.

Meanwhile, the meandering coastline is peppered with pretty fishing villages and traditional bucket-and-spade resorts, while inland is the languid, hypnotic charm of the Norfolk Broads, an ideal location for serious relaxation.

When to Go

➡ If the Cambridge colleges are high on your list, avoid Spring (early April to mid-June), when they close to visitors as students prepare for exams.

➡ The (hopefully) better weather between June and August means you'll see the Norfolk and Suffolk beaches and the Norfolk Broads at their best. But school holidays (late-July to August) bring plenty more people, and also push accommodation prices up.

➡ World-class classical music comes to Suffolk in the Aldeburgh Festival (p385) in June. In July, cool-culture fans chill at Southwold's eclectic Latitude Festival (p386).

➡ Come November, the Ways With Words (p386) literature festival draws big-name authors to Southwold.

➡ Exquisite, seasonal music fills Cambridge's King's College Chapel (p361) in December, culminating in the Festival of Nine Lessons and Carols on Christmas Eve.

Cambridge & East Anglia Highlights

1 Punting past historic colleges in Cambridge and enjoying the heavenly sounds of evensong at **King's College Chapel** (p361)

2 Soaking up the medieval atmosphere in topsy-turvy **Lavenham** (p381)

3 Marvelling at the exquisite rib vaulting at **Norwich Cathedral** (p387)

4 Walking the prom, dining on sublime food and just chilling out in understated **Aldeburgh** (p385)

5 Noseying around the drawing room of the Queen's country estate at **Sandringham** (p395)

6 Canoeing your way through the tranquil waterways of the **Norfolk Broads** (p390)

7 Pondering the history of British and American air forces at the **Imperial War Museum** (p374) in Duxford

8 Wandering barefoot along the immense, golden sands of **Holkham beach** (p394)

9 Delighting in one of Britain's grandest stately homes at **Audley End** (p378) in Saffron Walden

History

East Anglia was a major Saxon kingdom; the dazzling treasures unearthed in the ship burial at Sutton Hoo in Suffolk have revealed how complex a society it was.

The region's heyday came during the wool boom of the Middle Ages when Flemish weavers settled in the area; many of the grand local churches also date from this time – Cambridge University was founded too.

By the 17th century much of the region's marshland and bog had been drained and converted into arable land.

It was in East Anglia's emergent, Puritan bourgeoisie that the seeds of the English Civil War were sown. Oliver Cromwell, the uncrowned king of the Parliamentarians, was a small-time merchant residing in Ely when he answered God's call to take up arms against what he saw as the fattened and corrupt monarchy of Charles I.

East Anglia's fortunes waned in the 18th century, when the Industrial Revolution flourished in northern England. During WWII the region became an ideal base for the RAF and the United States Air Force in the fight against Nazi Germany, thanks to its flat, open landscape and close proximity to mainland Europe.

🏃 Activities

East Anglia is an appealing destination for walkers, cyclists and kayakers. Here you can discover miles of coastline, take time touring vast expanses of level land and glide along snaking inland waterways.

The coast and Norfolk Broads are also beloved by sailors, those without their own craft can easily hire boats and arrange lessons. Alternatively putt-putt your way gently around the Broads in a motorboat or paddle a kayak or canoe along the slow-moving rivers. Then there are the wide and frequently empty beaches of the Norfolk coast, which make great spots for land yachting and kite-surfing.

Visit East of England (www.visiteastofengland.com) has more info.

Cycling

Famously one of England's flattest regions, there's gorgeous cycling to be had along the Suffolk and Norfolk coastlines and in the Fens. Meanwhile, the Tour de France snaked its way through East Anglia in 2014. Mountain bikers should head for Norfolk's Thetford Forest (www.forestry.gov.uk/thetford

forestpark), while much of the popular on- and off-road Peddars Way (p360) walking route is also open to cyclists.

Walking

The Peddars Way and Norfolk Coast Path (www.nationaltrail.co.uk/peddarsway) is a seven-day, 93-mile national trail from Knettishall Heath near Thetford to Cromer. The first half winds along an ancient Roman road, then finishes by meandering along the beaches, sea walls, salt marshes (great for birdwatching) and fishing villages of the coast.

Curving further south, the 50-mile Suffolk Coast Path links Felixstowe and Lowestoft, via Snape Maltings, Aldeburgh, Dunwich and Southwold.

ℹ Getting There & Around

Public transport links between London, the Midlands and East Anglia are excellent. Services within the region are generally good; as ever there are fewer connections to smaller towns and villages.

Traveline East Anglia (www.travelineeastanglia.org.uk) Details local bus and train timetables.

BUS

A host of smaller firms, plus two main companies, run the region's bus networks.

First (www.firstgroup.com) Major provider in Essex, Norfolk and Suffolk.

Stagecoach (www.stagecoachbus.com) Services in Cambridge and around.

TRAIN

Greater Anglia (Abellio; www.greateranglia.co.uk) Runs rail services across East Anglia.

Anglia Plus Pass Secures off-peak train (and some bus) travel in Norfolk, Suffolk and parts of Cambridgeshire. One/three days out of seven costs £18/35. Up to four accompanying children can travel for £2 each.

CAMBRIDGESHIRE

Many visitors to Cambridgeshire never make it past the captivating university city of Cambridge, where august old buildings, student cyclists in academic gowns and glorious chapels await. But beyond this breathtaking seat of learning, the flat reclaimed Fen, lush farmland and myriad waterways make perfect walking and cycling territory, while the extraordinary cathedral at Ely and the rip-roaring Imperial War Museum at Duxford would be headline attractions anywhere else.

Getting Around

Public transport radiates from Cambridge, a mere 55-minute train ride from London. This line continues north through Ely to King's Lynn in Norfolk. Branch lines run east to Norwich and into Suffolk.

Cambridge

POP 123,900

Abounding with exquisite architecture, oozing history and tradition and renowned for its quirky rituals, Cambridge is a university town extraordinaire. The tightly packed core of ancient colleges, the picturesque 'Backs' (college gardens) leading on to the river and the leafy green meadows that surround the city give it a far more tranquil appeal than its historic rival Oxford.

Like 'the Other Place', as Oxford is known locally, the buildings here seem unchanged for centuries, and it's possible to wander the college buildings and experience them as countless prime ministers, poets, writers and scientists have done. The sheer academic achievement seems to permeate the very walls, with cyclists loaded down with books negotiating narrow cobbled passageways, students relaxing on manicured lawns and great minds debating life-changing research in historic pubs. Meanwhile, first-time punters zigzag erratically across the river, shoppers stroll unhurriedly through the Grand Arcade, and those long past their student days wonder what it would have been like to study in such splendid surroundings.

History

Despite roots stretching back to the Iron Age, Cambridge was little more than a rural backwater until the 11th century, when an Augustinian order of monks set up shop here – the first of the religious institutions that eventually became the colleges. When the university town of Oxford exploded in a riot between town and gown in 1209, a group of scholars, fed up with the constant brawling between locals and students, upped and joined what was to become the University of Cambridge. Cambridge wasn't spared by the riots, and brawls between town and gown took place with disturbing regularity here as well.

The first Cambridge college, Peterhouse (never Peterhouse *College*), was founded in 1284, and in 1318 Pope John XXII's papal bull declared Cambridge to be an official university.

By the 14th century, royalty, nobility, churches, trade guilds and anyone rich enough could court prestige by founding their own colleges, though the system was shaken up during the Reformation with the dissolution of the monasteries. It was 500 years before female students were allowed into the hallowed grounds, though, and even then they were only allowed into the women-only colleges Girton and Newnham, founded in 1869 and 1871 respectively. By 1948 Cambridge minds had broadened sufficiently to allow women to actually graduate.

The honour roll of famous Cambridge students reads like an international who's who of high achievers: 87 Nobel Prize winners (more than any other institution in the world), 13 British prime ministers, nine archbishops of Canterbury, an immense number of scientists, and a healthy host of poets and authors. This is the town where Newton refined his theory of gravity, Whipple invented the jet engine, and Crick and Watson discovered DNA. William Wordsworth, Lord Byron, Vladimir Nabokov, Stephen Hawking and Stephen Fry all studied here too.

Today the university remains one of the best for research worldwide. Thanks to some of the earth-shaking discoveries made here, Cambridge is inextricably linked to the history of learning.

Sights

Cambridge University

Cambridge University comprises 31 colleges, though not all are open to the public.

★ King's College Chapel　CHAPEL
(☑ 01223-331212; www.kings.cam.ac.uk/chapel; King's Pde; adult/child £7.50/free; ⊙ non-term 9.45am-4.30pm, term 9.45am-3.15pm Mon-Sat, 1.15-2.30pm Sun) In a city crammed with show-stopping buildings, this is the scene-stealer. Grandiose, 16th-century King's College Chapel is one of England's most extraordinary examples of Gothic architecture. Its inspirational, intricate 80m-long, fan-vaulted ceiling is the world's largest and soars upwards before exploding into a series of stone fireworks. This hugely atmospheric space is a fitting stage for the chapel's world-famous choir; hear it in full voice during the magnificent, free, evensong (in term time only – 5.30pm Monday to Saturday, 10.30am and 3.30pm Sunday).

King's steeples have long been a magnet for student night climbers and today images

Cambridge

Benson House (175m)

Hakka (100m); Worth House (500m)

51

Hertford St

Castle St

Pound Hill

Chesterton La

Chesterton Rd

Cam

28

27

40

Victoria Ave

Midsummer Common

14

Northampton St

16

Quayside

Thompson's La

32

New Park St

Park Pde

Portugal Pl

Jesus Green

47

Bridge St

Park St

13

Malcolm St

Jesus La

Maid's Causeway

The Backs

3

5

22

34

20

48

Trinity College

4

St John's St

Manor St

King St

36

Christ's Pieces

25

Senate House Passage

24

Trinity La

11

Green St

39

44

Rose Cres

21

12

2

35

Market Sq

49

30

33

50

46

Sidney St

Hobson St

6

Drummer St Bus Station

Emmanuel St

10

Emmanuel Rd

Clarendon St

Parker St

Garrett Hostel La

King's College Chapel

9

8

43

Benet St

Petty Cury

P

St Andrew's St

Parkside

National Express Coach Stop

Queen's La

19

17

King's Pde

38

Downing St

Downing Pl

Park Tce

Parker's Piece

Cotto (400m)

Queen's Rd

26

37

Mill La

15

29

Little St Mary's La

18

Silver St

Fitzwilliam Museum

1

Trumpington St

Tennis Court Rd

Regent Tce

Regent St

Gonville Pl

Cambridge YHA (650m); (800m)

45

Newnham Rd

Granta Pl

31

Cambridge University Botanic Garden (375m); Grantchester (3mi)

41

Lensfield Rd

23

CAMBRIDGE & EAST ANGLIA CAMBRIDGE

of the chapel adorn thousands of postcards, tea towels and choral CDs. But it was begun in 1446 as an act of piety by Henry VI and was only finished by Henry VIII around 1516.

The lofty **stained-glass windows** that flank the chapel's sides ensure it is remark-ably light. The glass is original, rare survivors of the excesses of the Civil War in this region. It's said that these windows were ordered to be spared by Cromwell himself, who knew of their beauty from his own studies in Cambridge.

Cambridge

The antechapel and the choir are divided by a superbly carved **wooden screen**, were designed and executed by Peter Stockton for Henry VIII. The screen bears his master's initials entwined with those of Anne Boleyn. Look closely and you may find an angry human face (possibly Stockton's) amid the elaborate jungle of mythical beasts and symbolic flowers. Above is the magnificent bat-wing **organ**, originally constructed in 1686, though much altered since.

Beyond the thickly-carved, dark-wood choir stalls light suffuses the high **altar**, which is framed by Rubens' masterpiece *Adoration of the Magi* (1634) and the magnificent east window. To the left of the altar in the side chapels, an **exhibition** charts the construction stages and methods.

Note the chapel itself (but not the grounds) *are* open during the exam period (April to June). Each Christmas Eve, King's College Chapel stages the **Festival of Nine Lessons and Carols**. It's broadcast globally by the BBC, and to around 300 American radio stations. You can also queue – if you start early enough (before 9am), you could well get in.

Senate House HISTORIC BUILDING
(Senate House Passage) This beautiful classical structure (not open to the public), tucked in beside King's College, was designed in 1730 by James Gibbs. Graduations are held here in summer, when gowned and mortar-boarded students parade the streets. Look out for the degree class-lists that are posted outside at the end of the academic year.

Gonville & Caius College COLLEGE
(www.cai.cam.ac.uk; Trinity St; ☉9am-2pm, closed early Apr–mid-Jun) FREE Known locally as Caius (pronounced 'keys'), Gonville and Caius boasts three fascinating **gates**: Virtue, Humility and Honour. They symbolise the progress of the good student, since the third gate (the Porta Honoris, a fabulous domed and sundial-sided confection) leads to the Senate House and thus graduation. Ex-students

ℹ VISITING THE COLLEGES

Colleges close to visitors over the Christmas break, and while students are preparing for and sitting exams – shutting between early April and mid-June. Be aware too, opening hours can vary from day to day, so if you have your heart set on visiting a particular college, contact it in advance to avoid disappointment.

include Francis Crick (of DNA-discoverers Crick and Watson) and Edward Wilson, of Scott's tragic Antarctic expedition. The megastar of astrophysics, Stephen Hawking, is currently a fellow here.

The college was actually founded twice, first by a priest called Gonville, in 1348, and then again in 1557 by Dr Caius (his given name was Keys – it was common for academics to use the Latin form of their names), a brilliant physician who supposedly spoiled his legacy by insisting in the statutes that the college admit no 'deaf, dumb, deformed, lame, chronic invalids, or Welshmen'.

Trinity Hall College   COLLEGE
(www.trinhall.cam.ac.uk; Trinity Lane; admission by donation; ⊘ 9.15am-noon & 2-4pm, closed early Apr–mid-Jun) Wedged cosily among the great and the famous, but unconnected to better-known Trinity, diminutive Trinity Hall was founded in 1350 as a refuge for lawyers and clerics escaping the ravages of the Black Death. The college's 16th-century library has original Jacobean reading desks and chained books on the shelves (to visit, book two weeks in advance), while the chapel is one of the most beautiful of all the colleges – drop by for evensong at 6.30pm Thursday and 6pm Sunday during term time. Writer JB Priestley, astrophysicist Stephen Hawking and actor Rachel Weisz are among Trinity Hall's graduates.

★ Trinity College   COLLEGE
(www.trin.cam.ac.uk; Trinity St; adult/child £2/1; ⊘10am-4.30pm, closed early Apr–mid-Jun) The largest of Cambridge's colleges, Trinity offers an extraordinary Tudor gateway, an air of supreme elegance and a sweeping Great Court – the largest of its kind in the world. It also boasts the renowned and suitably musty Wren Library (⊘noon-2pm Mon-Fri), containing 55,000 books dated before 1820 and more than 2500 manuscripts. Works include those by Shakespeare, St Jerome, Newton and Swift – and AA Milne's original

Winnie the Pooh; both Milne and his son, Christopher Robin, were graduates.

As you enter Trinity through the part-gilded gate, look at the statue of the college's founder, Henry VIII, that adorns it. His left hand holds a golden orb, while his right grips not the original sceptre but a table leg, put there by student pranksters and never replaced. It's a wonderful introduction to one of Cambridge's most venerable colleges, and a reminder of who really rules the roost.

In the Great Court beyond, scholastic humour gives way to wonderment, thanks to its imposing architecture and sheer size. To the right of the entrance is a small tree, planted in the 1950s and reputed to be a descendant of the apple tree made famous by Trinity alumnus Sir Isaac Newton. Other alumni include Francis Bacon, Lord Byron, Tennyson, HRH Prince Charles (legend has it his bodyguard scored higher in exams than he did), at least nine prime ministers (British and international) and some 32 Nobel Prize winners.

The college's vast hall has a dramatic hammerbeam roof and lantern, beyond lie the dignified cloisters of Nevile's Court. Henry VIII would have been proud to note, too, that his college would eventually come to throw the best party in town, the lavish May Ball in June, though you will need a fat purse, and a friend on the inside, to get an invitation.

St John's College   COLLEGE
(www.joh.cam.ac.uk; St John's St; adult/child £5/3.50; ⊘10am-5pm mid-Jun–Oct, to 3.30pm Nov-early Apr) Alma mater of six prime ministers, three saints and Douglas Adams (*The Hitchhiker's Guide to the Galaxy* author), St John's is superbly photogenic. It's also the second-biggest college after Trinity. Founded in 1511 by Henry VII's mother, Margaret Beaufort, it sprawls along both river banks, joined by the Bridge of Sighs (p367), a masterpiece of stone tracery and focus for student pranks. Going into St John's, or a punting tour, are the only ways to get a clear view of the structure.

Over the bridge, is the 19th-century New Court, an extravagant neo-Gothic creation, and out to the left are impressive views of the Backs. Parts of the college are much older and the chapel, though smaller than King's, is one of Cambridge's hidden gems.

Magdalene College   COLLEGE
(www.magd.cam.ac.uk; Magdalene St; ⊘8am-6pm, closed early Apr–mid-Jun) **FREE** Riverside

Magdalene often catches people out – the college name is properly pronounced 'Maudlyn'. This former Benedictine hostel's greatest asset is the Pepys Library (⊘2-4pm Mon-Fri, 11.30am-12.30pm & 1.30-2.30pm Sat May-Aug, 2-3pm Mon-Sat Oct-Apr) housing 3000 books bequeathed by the mid-17th-century diarist to his old college. This idiosyncratic collection of beautifully bound tomes is ordered by height, treasures include vivid medieval manuscripts and the *Anthony Roll,* a 1540s depiction of the Royal Navy's ships.

Magdalene has the dubious honour of being the last college to let women study there; when they were finally admitted in 1988, some male students wore black armbands and flew the college flag at half mast.

Jesus College
COLLEGE

(www.jesus.cam.ac.uk; Jesus Lane; ⊘9am-5pm, closed early Apr–mid-Jun) FREE This tranquil 15th-century college was once a nunnery of St Radegund before the Bishop of Ely, John Alcock, expelled the nuns for 'improvidence, extravagance and incontinence'. Highlights include a Norman arched gallery, a 13th-century chancel and art-nouveau features by Pugin, Ford Madox Brown, William Morris (ceilings) and Burne-Jones (stained glass). Illustrious alumni include Thomas Cranmer, burnt for his faith in Oxford during the Reformation, and long-running BBC and PBS radio journalist and presenter Alistair Cooke.

Christ's College
COLLEGE

(www.christs.cam.ac.uk; St Andrew's St; ⊘9.30am-4pm, closed early Apr–mid-Jun) FREE A great institution at more than 500 years old, Christ's gleaming Great Gate is emblazoned with heraldic carving of Tudor roses, portcullis and spotted Beaufort yale (antelope-like creatures). Its founder, Lady Margaret Beaufort, hovers above like a guiding spirit. A stout oak door leads into First Court, one of Cambridge's more picturesque front courts and the only circular one. Hunt out the gardens dedicated to alumnus Charles Darwin, they feature species brought back from his famous Galapagos voyage.

The Second Court has a gate to the Fellows' Garden, which contains a mulberry tree under which 17th-century poet John Milton reputedly wrote 'Lycidas'. Other notable alumni include Sacha Baron Cohen (aka Ali G and Borat) and historian Simon Schama.

Emmanuel College
COLLEGE

(www.emma.cam.ac.uk; St Andrew's St; ⊘9am-6pm, closed early Apr–mid-Jun) FREE The 16th-century Emmanuel College ('Emma' to students) is famous for its exquisite chapel designed by Sir Christopher Wren. The college has a prodigious collection of ducks, they roam the area freely and in early spring produce armies of bright-yellow ducklings. Here, too, is a plaque commemorating John Harvard (BA 1632), a scholar here who later settled in New England and left his money to a certain Cambridge College in Massachusetts – now Harvard University.

Corpus Christi College
COLLEGE

(www.corpus.cam.ac.uk; King's Pde; admission £2.50; ⊘10.30am-4.30pm mid-Jun–Sep, 2-4pm Oct-early Apr) One of Cambridge's ancient colleges, Corpus Christi was founded in 1352, a heritage reflected in its exquisite buildings – a monastic atmosphere still radiates from the medieval Old Court. Look out for the fascinating sundial and plaque to playwright and past student Christopher Marlowe (1564–93), author of *Doctor Faustus* and *Tamburlaine.* New Court (a mere 200 years old) leads to the Parker Library, which holds the world's finest collection of Anglo-Saxon manuscripts (open Thursday afternoons to tourist office–run tours).

Back outside, on the junction of Benet St and King's Pde, look out for the college's new Corpus Clock. Made from 24-carat gold, it displays the time through a series of concentric LED lights. A hideous-looking insect 'time-eater' crawls across the top. The clock is only accurate once every five minutes. At other times it slows or stops and then speeds up, which according to its creator, JC Taylor, reflects life's irregularity.

Queens' College
COLLEGE

(www.queens.cam.ac.uk; Silver St; admission £2.50; ⊘10am-4pm, closed early Apr–mid-Jun) Gorgeous 15th-century Queens' College sits elegantly

CHARIOTS OF FIRE

Trinity College's immense Great Court is the scene of the run made famous by the film *Chariots of Fire* – a 350m-sprint around the courtyard in 43 seconds (the time it takes the clock to strike 12). Although many students attempt it, Harold Abrahams (the hero of the film) never did, and the run in the movie was filmed at Eton. If you fancy your chances, remember that you'll need Olympian speed to even come close.

🚶 City Walk
The Colleges & the Backs

START KING'S COLLEGE CHAPEL
END FITZBILLIES
LENGTH 3 MILES; FOUR HOURS

From divine ❶ **King's** (p361), stroll north, diverting into ❷ **Great St Mary's** (p368) and climbing the tower for fine Cambridge views. Next, dodge the bicyclists and touting tour guides before ducking into atmospheric ❸ **Gonville & Caius** (p363) to marvel at its ornate gates. ❹ **Trinity's** (p364) elaborate entranceway towers up on the left; head through it into the college's (genuinely) Great Court; marvel in the architecture, then make for the absorbing ❺ **Wren Library** (p364), with its extraordinary historic books. Next, pause to admire the front of gorgeous ❻ **St John's** (p364), before dropping into the captivating, 12th-century ❼ **Round Church** (p368). Cut right between the sweet terraces of narrow Portugal Place – at the end, the ❽ **Maypole** (p372) pub is a friendly place to eat or drink. Next it's diagonally across Jesus Green, past lounging picnickers and tennis players, to consider a dip in the bijou open-air

❾ **pool** (p369). Then stroll south west beside the river, passing locks and houseboats before a waterside boardwalk leads to a punt launching pad. Cross at the bridge beside ❿ **Magdalene College** (p364), where the unique Peyps Library is well worth a detour. Northampton St reminds you the 21st century does exist, then it's onto the path through the Backs, where the stately sweep of St John's College shelters amid the trees, Trinity sits next door. Next play zigzag with college paths and the river: nip up ⑪ **Garret Hostel Lane** for a closer view of punts, bridges and college facades. Then it's back to the path, before another detour left leads to the often-open gates of ⑫ **Clare College** (p367), where the Fellow's Garden is a real must-see. Back on the Backs, next comes the impressive west end of Kings College Chapel; the Palladian ⑬ **Fellows' Building** is just to the right. After curving beside ⑭ **Queens'** (p365), cut left. On Silver St's bridge spy the chunky ⑮ **Mathematical Bridge** (p367) on the left, and the fleets of punts on the right. Time to rest. Where better than ⑯ **Fitzbillies** (p371) for a Chelsea bun and a steaming cup of tea.

astride the river, connected by the unscientific-looking Mathematical Bridge (p367). Highlights include two enchanting medieval courtyards: Old Court and Cloister Court, the beautiful half-timbered President's Lodge and the tower in which Dutch scholar and reformer Desiderius Erasmus lodged from 1510 to 1514. His verdict on Cambridge? That the wine tasted like vinegar, the beer was slop and the place was too expensive – he also noted the local women were good kissers.

Peterhouse COLLEGE
(www.pet.cam.ac.uk; Trumpington St; ⊘9am-5pm, closed early Apr–mid-Jun) FREE The oldest and smallest college, charming Peterhouse was founded in 1284. Much of the college was rebuilt or added to over the years, including the exceptional little chapel built in 1632, but the beautifully restored main hall is bona fide 13th century. Just to the north is Little St Mary's Church, which has a memorial to Peterhouse student Godfrey Washington, great-uncle of George. His family coat of arms was the stars and stripes – the inspiration for the US flag.

Rumours abound among students (vigorously denied by college authorities) of hauntings and spectral happenings on the site. Three Nobel Prize winners count themselves among Peterhouse's alumni.

★**The Backs** PARK
Behind the Cambridge colleges' grandiose facades and stately courts, a series of gardens and parks line up beside the river. Collectively known as the Backs, the tranquil green spaces and shimmering waters offer unparalleled views of the colleges and are often the most enduring image of Cambridge for visitors. The picture-postcard snapshots of college life and graceful bridges can be seen from the riverside pathways and pedestrian bridges – or the comfort of a chauffeur-driven punt.

The fanciful Bridge of Sighs, built in 1831 at St John's (p364), is best observed from the stylish bridge designed by Wren just to the south, also on St John's grounds. The oldest river crossing is at Clare College, built in 1639 and ornamented with decorative balls. Its architect was paid a grand total of 15p for his design and, feeling aggrieved at such a measly fee, it's said he cut a chunk out of one of the balls adorning the balustrade so the bridge would never be complete.

Most curious of all is the flimsy-looking wooden construction joining the two halves of Queen's College known as the Mathematical Bridge, first built in 1749. Despite what unscrupulous guides may tell you, it wasn't the handiwork of Sir Isaac Newton (he died in 1727), originally built without nails, or taken apart by academics who then couldn't figure how to put it back together.

Other Sights

★**Fitzwilliam Museum** MUSEUM
(www.fitzmuseum.cam.ac.uk; Trumpington St; donation requested; ⊘10am-5pm Tue-Sat, noon-5pm Sun) Fondly dubbed 'the Fitz' by locals, this colossal neoclassical pile was one of the first public art museums in Britain, built to house the fabulous treasures that the seventh Viscount Fitzwilliam bequeathed to his old university. Expect Roman and Egyptian grave goods, artworks by many of the great masters and some more quirky collections: banknotes, literary autographs, watches and armour.

PRANKSTERS, NIGHT CLIMBERS AND CUBES

In a city with so much concentrated mental prowess, it is perhaps inevitable that the student community would excel at all kinds of mischief. The most impressive prank ever to take place in Cambridge – lifting an Austin Seven van onto the roof of the landmark Senate House (p363) in 1958 – involved a great deal of planning from four Mechanical Sciences students and spawned a number of copycat pranks, including suspending another Austin Seven from the ornate Bridge of Sighs (p367).

King's College has long been a target of night climbers – students who get their thrills by scaling the lofty heights of out-of-bounds buildings at night. The sport is taken very seriously – to the point where a Trinity College student, Geoffrey Winthrop Young, wrote the *Roof Climber's Guide to Trinity* in 1900. If you're in Cambridge after a particularly spectacular climber excursion, you may find some out-of-place objects atop the pinnacles of King's College Chapel – anything from a traffic cone to a Santa hat.

Finally, there's the Cubes (Cambridge University Breaking and Entering Society); its objective is to access places members shouldn't be and leave distinctive calling cards – the most famous being the wooden mallard in the rafters of Trinity's Great Hall.

The building's unabashedly over-the-top appearance sets out to mirror its contents; this ostentatious jumble of styles mixes mosaic with marble, and Greek with Egyptian. The lower galleries are filled with priceless treasures spanning the ancient world; look out for a Roman funerary couch, an inscribed copper votive plaque from Yemen (c AD 100–200), a figurine of Egyptian cat goddess Bastet, splendid Egyptian sarcophagi and mummified animals, plus dazzling illuminated manuscripts. The upper galleries showcase works by Leonardo da Vinci, Titian, Rubens, the Impressionists, Gainsborough and Constable, right through to Rembrandt and Picasso; standout works include the tender *Pietà* by Giovanni del Ponte and Salvator Rosa's dark and intensely personal *L'Umana Fragilita*.

The Fitz has a tragic footnote: although begun by George Basevi in 1837, he didn't live to see its completion: while working on Ely Cathedral he stepped back to admire his handiwork, slipped and fell to his death.

One-hour guided tours (£6) of the museum are held at 2.30pm Saturday.

The Polar Museum
MUSEUM

(www.spri.cam.ac.uk/museum; Lensfield Rd; ⊙10am-4pm Tue-Sat) FREE Tales of hostile environments, dogged determination and, sometimes, life-claiming mistakes are evoked powerfully at this compelling museum. Its focus on polar exploration charts the feats of the likes of Roald Amundsen, Fridtjof Nansen and Captain Robert Falcon Scott. The affecting collections include paintings, photographs, clothing, equipment, maps, journals and last messages left for loved ones by Scott's polar crew.

Other engaging exhibits include models of ships that ventured into the frigid Arctic and Antarctic waters, innovative equipment such as the 'Nansen cooker' and interactive displays on ice and climate change. The section devoted to the people of the Arctic includes Inuit carvings and scrimshaw (etched bones), a Sámi knife with a carved reindeer-horn sheath, a walrus tusk with walrus hunt scenes etched on it, and particularly fine examples of *tupilaat* (carved caribou horn figures with ancestor souls captured inside) from Greenland. The museum is run by the Scott Polar Institute, founded with part of the relief fund set up in the wake of the explorer's ill-fated South Pole expedition – these days it takes a lead role in climate-change research.

Great St Mary's Church
CHURCH

(www.gsm.cam.ac.uk; Senate House Hill; ⊙10am-4pm Mon-Sat, 1-4pm Sun) FREE The foundations of Cambridge's sublime university church date from 1010. It was burnt to the ground in the 1290s and rebuilt in 1351. The major expansion of 1478–1519 resulted in the late-Gothic Perpendicular style you see today. Striking features include the mid-Victorian stained-glass windows, seating galleries and two organs – unusual in a church. The tower (adult/child £3.50/2) was added in 1690; climb it for superb vistas of Cambridge's dreamy spires.

Round Church
CHURCH

(www.christianheritageuk.org.uk; Bridge St; adult/child £2/free; ⊙10am-5pm) Cambridge's intensely atmospheric Round Church is one of only four such structures in England. It was built by the mysterious Knights Templar in 1130 and shelters an unusual circular nave ringed by chunky Norman pillars – the carved stone faces that crown them bring the 12th century vividly to life. The church's position on Bridge St reminds you of its original role; that of a chapel for pilgrims crossing the river.

Kettle's Yard
HOUSE

(www.kettlesyard.co.uk; Castle St; ⊙2-5pm Tue-Sun) FREE If you like snooping around other people's houses (and who doesn't?), you'll love this very personal glimpse into the incredible home of HS 'Jim' Ede, a former curator at the Tate Gallery in London. In his deceptively roomy cottage all the furniture, ceramics and art – such as the collection of 20th-century works by Miró, Henry Moore and others – is arranged just so, allowing you a real sense of the man's intriguing personality.

Cambridge University Botanic Garden
GARDENS

(www.botanic.cam.ac.uk; Bateman St; adult/child £4.50/free; ⊙10am-6pm Apr-Sep, to 4pm Oct-Mar) Founded by Charles Darwin's mentor, Professor John Henslow, the beautiful Botanic Garden is home to 8000 plant species, a wonderful arboretum, glasshouses (containing both fierce carnivorous pitcher plants and the delicate slipper orchid), a winter garden and flamboyant herbaceous borders. Hour-long guided tours (£7) are held at 11am on the first Saturday of the month and some Wednesdays. The gardens are 1200m south of the city centre via Trumpington St.

Activities

Jesus Green Pool
SWIMMING

(www.better.org.uk; Jesus Green; £4.20; ☺8am-6pm May-Sep) A long, thin, 1920s open-air swim-spot, popular with pool-side sunbathers too.

Punting

Gliding a self-propelled punt along the Backs is a blissful experience – once you've got the hang of it; it can also be a manic challenge to begin. If you wimp out you can always opt for a relaxing chauffeured punt.

Punt hire costs around £19 per hour, one-hour chauffeured trips of the Backs cost about £15, and a return trip to Grantchester (2½ hours) will set you back around £27.

Cambridge Chauffer Punts
PUNTING

(www.punting-in-cambridge.co.uk; Silver St Bridge) One of the biggest punting companies in Cambridge, with regular chauffeured punting tours.

Granta Canoe & Punt Hire Company
PUNTING

(www.puntingincambridge.com; Newnham Rd) Handily sited punt-rental company if you're heading towards Grantchester. Runs reduced services in the winter.

Scudamore's Punting Cambridge
PUNTING

(www.scudamores.com; Granta Pl) Hires punts, rowboats, kayaks and canoes. Offers up to £5 discount if you buy online.

Tours

As well as running escorted tours, the tourist office (p372) also has information about self-guided walks.

Walking Tours
WALKING TOUR

(☎01223-457574; www.visitcambridge.org; Peas Hill) The tourist office runs guided two-hour tours (adult/child £17.50/15.50) of central Cambridge, which take in two of the most memorable colleges; depending on opening hours they might include King's College Chapel, Queens', Pembroke or St John's. The price includes admission to the colleges. Year-round, tours run at 11am Monday to Friday, at 11am, noon and 2pm Saturday, and at 1pm Sunday. In July and August there are extra daily tours at noon and 2pm. They're popular: book.

Colourful, one-hour Ghost Tours (£6) take place on Fridays at 6pm, and – from May to August – on Saturdays at 8pm.

Riverboat Georgina
BOAT TOUR

(☎01223-929124; www.georgina.co.uk; Jesus Lock; ☺Apr-Sep) One-/two-hour cruises are £7/13, optional extras include lunch, fish and chips, wine or a cream tea.

City Sightseeing
BUS TOUR

(www.city-sightseeing.com; adult/child £14/7; ☺every 20min 10am-4.40pm) Hop-on/hop-off bus tours; tickets secure 24 hours' unlimited travel.

Festivals & Events

Cambridge has a jam-packed cultural schedule. For one-off events, check out the notices tied to railings all over the city centre, especially around St Mary's Church.

Bumps
BOAT RACE

(www.cucbc.org/bumps; ☺Feb & Jun) Traditional rowing races along the Cam (or the Granta as the Cambridge stretch is called), in

HOW TO PUNT

Punting looks pretty straightforward but, believe us, really – it's not. So here are some tips to stop you zigzagging wildly across the river, losing your pole and falling in.

➼ Standing at the back end of the punt, lift the pole out of the water at the side of the punt.

➼ Let the pole slide through your hands to touch the bottom of the river.

➼ Tilt the pole forward (that is, in the direction of travel of the punt) and push down to propel the punt forward.

➼ Twist the pole to free the end from the mud at the bottom of the river, and let it float up and trail behind the punt. You can then use it as a rudder to steer.

➼ If you haven't fallen in yet, raise the pole out of the water and into the vertical position to begin the cycle again.

➼ Hold on to the pole, particularly when passing under Clare Bridge, as students sometimes snatch them for a giggle.

which college boat clubs compete to 'bump' the crew in front.

Beer Festival
BEER

(www.cambridgebeerfestival.com; ☉ May) Hugely popular five-day beer and cider extravaganza on Jesus Green, featuring brews from all over the country as well as a great range of British cheeses.

Folk Festival
MUSIC

(www.cambridgefolkfestival.co.uk; ☉ late Jul–early Aug) Acclaimed four-day music fest in neighbouring Cherry Hinton Hall, which has hosted the likes of Van Morrison, Ladysmith Black Mambazo, Sinéad O'Connor, Paul Simon and kd lang.

May Balls
FORMAL BALLS

(☉ early Jun) The biggest student events of the year, the name of these formal balls don't match the month they're held in (June) because college authorities decided that May's traditional booze-fuelled revelry – just before the exams – wasn't such a great idea. Now they take place after the exams, but in a typically Cambridge quirk they keep the old name.

Cambridge Shakespeare Festival
THEATRE

(www.cambridgeshakespeare.com; ☉ Jul & Aug) The bard's best-loved works performed in outdoor settings.

🛏 Sleeping

Cambridge YHA
HOSTEL £

(☎ 0845 371 9728; www.yha.org.uk; 97 Tenison Rd; dm/d £21/30; @ 🛜) Busy, recently renovated, popular hostel with compact dorms and good facilities near the railway station.

Cambridge Rooms
B&B ££

(www.universityrooms.com/en/city/cambridge/home; s/d from £45/75) For an authentic taste of university life check into a student room in one of a range of colleges. Accommodation varies from functional singles (with shared bathroom) overlooking college courts to more modern, en suite rooms in nearby annexes. Breakfast is often in hall (the students' dining room).

Worth House
B&B ££

(☎ 01223-316074; www.worth-house.co.uk; 152 Chesterton Rd; s £65-75, d £65-100; P 🛜) The welcome is wonderfully warm; the great-value rooms utterly delightful. Soft grey and cream meets candy-stripe reds, fancy bathrooms boast claw-footed baths, and tea trays

are full of treats. There's also a three-person, self-catering apartment (per week £550) two doors down.

Benson House
B&B ££

(☎ 01223-311594; www.bensonhouse.co.uk; 24 Huntingdon Rd; s £70, d £90-115; P 🛜) Lots of little things lift Benson a cut above, meaning you can sleep among feather pillows and cotton linen, before breakfasting off Royal Doulton bone china, tucking into kippers, croissants and fresh fruit.

Tudor Cottage
B&B ££

(☎ 01223-565212; www.tudorcottageguesthouse. co.uk; 292 Histon Rd; s/d £45/75; P 🛜) Sweet features help make this neat-as-a-pin guesthouse feel like a home from home, from bedrooms boasting gleaming bathrooms, to the ranks of speciality teas, cereals, cakes and muffins at the breakfast table. It's 2 miles north of the City centre; bus 8 stops just outside.

Rosa's
B&B ££

(☎ 01223-512596; www.rosasbedandbreakfast. co.uk; 53 Roseford Rd; s £45-60; P 🛜) One for solo travellers: a friendly, family-run B&B with four cosy singles that are studies in cream and pale wood. The hosts are engaging without being intrusive, it's 2 miles north of the city centre and bus 8 runs nearby.

⭐ Varsity
BOUTIQUE HOTEL £££

(☎ 01223-306030; www.thevarsityhotel.co.uk; Thompson's Lane; d £180-345; 🛜) In the 48 individually styled rooms of riverside Varsity, wondrous furnishings and witty features (union-jack footstools, giant postage stamps) sit beside floor-to-ceiling glass windows, monsoon showers and iPod docks. The views from the roof terrace are frankly gorgeous.

⭐ Hotel du Vin
HOTEL £££

(☎ 01223-227330; www.hotelduvin.com; Trumpington St; d £200-230, ste £250-340; @ 🛜) Arguably the country's swishest, coolest chain delivers again here. Achingly beautiful rooms sport roll-top baths and Egyptian cotton sheets, the cosy cellar bar is vaulted, the bistro (mains £18) is chic and the modern mural in reception depicts a suitably wine-soaked May Ball.

Felix
BOUTIQUE HOTEL £££

(☎ 01223-277977; www.hotelfelix.co.uk; Whitehouse Lane, Huntingdon Rd; s £175, d £210-260, ste £305-325; P @ 🛜) It's the bold modern art and imaginative design (fuchsia-pink chairs amid stately polished wood) that nudges Felix into the boutique sleep spots. That and the silk curtains, luxurious linens and stone-and-slate bathrooms. The Penthouse, up in the eaves, is an utterly romantic retreat. Felix is 1.5 miles northwest of the city.

✖ Eating

Aromi   ITALIAN **£**

(www.aromi.co.uk; 1 Benet St; mains £4.50; ⊗ 9am-8pm Fri-Sun, to 5pm Mon-Thu; 🖋) Sometimes you should yield to temptation. So be drawn in by a window full of stunning Sicilian pizza and feast on light, crisp bases piled high with fresh spinach and Parma ham. Then succumb to the indecently thick hot chocolate; may as well make it a large.

Fitzbillies   BAKERY, CAFE **£**

(www.fitzbillies.com; 52 Trumpington St; cafe mains £6-16; ⊗ 9am-9.30pm Thu-Sat, 8am-5pm Mon-Wed, 10am-5pm Sun) Cambridge's oldest bakery has a soft, doughy place in the hearts of generations of students, thanks to its ultra-sticky Chelsea buns and other sweet treats. Pick up a bag-full to take away or munch in comfort in the quaint cafe next door.

Byron   BURGERS **£**

(www.byronhamburgers.com; 12 Bridge St; mains £8; ⊗ 11am-11pm) A bustling, better-than-average burger bar where students, families and business types perch on reclaimed banquettes tucking into prime patties and more.

Dojo   ASIAN **£**

(www.dojonoodlebar.co.uk; Mill Lane; mains £8; 🖋) Favoured by students from nearby Queens' and noodle lovers in general, this smart, aroma-filled eatery rustles up the kind of spicy street food you'll find in Thailand, Malaysia, Singapore, Japan and Vietnam.

Gardenia   GREEK **£**

(www.gardis.org.uk; 2 Rose Cres; mains £5; ⊗ noon-4am; 🖋) 'Gardi's' is responsible for the late-night nutrition for large numbers of students, and its walls are plastered with photos of happy customers munching on the lamb souvlaki and doner kebabs.

Clowns   CAFE **£**

(54 King St; mains £6; ⊗ 8am-11pm; 🖋) A friendly Italian family has created this Cambridge institution; a top spot for cooked breakfast, homemade lasagne, or lingering over a first-class coffee.

Kingston Arms   PUB **££**

(www.kingston-arms.co.uk; 33 Kingston St; mains £5-16; ⊗ noon-2pm & 6-10pm Mon-Fri, to 10pm Sat & Sun; 🖋) Great gastropub grub – from roasts to white-onion soup and recession-busting mains (held at £4.99), keeps stomachs satisfied at the award-winning Kingston. Meanwhile 12 real ales, stacked board games and a students-meet-locals clientele deliver a contemporary Cambridge vibe. It's 1 mile southeast of the centre, along Parkside then down student-central Mill Rd.

Oak   BISTRO **££**

(🖋 01223-323361; www.theoakbistro.co.uk; 6 Lensfield Rd; mains £12-20; set lunch 2/3 courses £13/16; ⊗ noon-2.30pm & 6-9.30pm Mon-Sat) Truffles (white and black), olive pesto and rosemary jus are the kind of flavour intensifiers you'll find at this friendly but classy neighbourhood eatery where locally sourced duck, fish and beef come cooked just so. The set lunch is a bargain.

Chop House   BRITISH **££**

(www.cambscuisine.com/cambridge-chop-house; 1 Kings Pde; mains £14-20; ⊗ noon-10.30pm Mon-Sat, to 9.30pm Sun) The window seats here deliver some of the best views in town – onto King's College's hallowed walls. The food is pure English establishment too: hearty steaks and chops and chips, plus a scattering of fish dishes and suet puds. Sister restaurant St John's Chop House (21-24 Northampton St) sits near the rear entrance to St John's College.

Hakka   CHINESE **££**

(www.hak-ka.co.uk; 24 Milton Rd; mains £10; ⊗ 6.30-9.30pm; 🖋) Chef Daniel's mother taught him the secrets of Hakka cooking and once you've tasted his signature salt-and-chilli chicken, you'll be inclined to give her a hug. The menu is extensive but the sizzling dishes stand out.

★ Midsummer House   FINE DINING **£££**

(🖋 01223-369299; www.midsummerhouse.co.uk; Midsummer Common; 5/7/10 courses £45/75/95; ⊗ noon-1.30pm Wed-Sat, 7-9pm Tue-Sat) At the region's top tables Chef Daniel Clifford's double Michelin-starred creations are distinguished by depth of flavour and immense technical skill. Sample braised oxtail, coal-baked celeriac and scallops with truffle before dollops of dark chocolate, blood orange and marmalade ice cream. Wine flights start at £55.

Cotto   INTERNATIONAL **£££**

(🖋 01223-302010; www.cottocambridge.co.uk; 183 East Rd; 3 courses £50; ⊗ 6.30-9pm Wed-Sat; 🖋) 🖋 An irresistible blend of artistry and precision ensure chef Hans Schweitzer's creations look gorgeous and taste fabulous. Delights might include saffron-infused Cromer crab and crayfish tian or herb-encrusted, salt marsh lamb, followed perhaps by a Caribbean palm sugar and vanilla bean brûlée.

🍷 Drinking & Nightlife

Eagle   PUB
(www.gkpubs.co.uk; Benet St; ⊙9am-11pm Mon-Sat, to 10.30pm Sun) Cambridge's most famous pub has loosened the tongues and pickled the grey cells of many an illustrious academic; among them Nobel Prize-winning scientists Crick and Watson, who discussed their research into DNA here (note the blue plaque by the door). Dating from the 15th-century, wood-panelled and rambling, its cosy rooms include one with WWII airmens' signatures on the ceiling. The food, served all day, is good too.

Granta   PUB
(www.gkpubs.co.uk; Newnham Rd; ⊙11am-11pm, to 10.30pm Sun) If the exterior of this picturesque waterside pub, overhanging a pretty mill pond, looks strangely familiar, it could be because it is the darling of many a TV director. No wonder, with its snug deck, riverside terrace and punts (p369) moored up alongside, it's a highly atmospheric spot to sup and watch the world drift by.

Maypole   PUB
(www.maypolefreehouse.co.uk; 20a Portugal Pl; ⊙11.30am-midnight Sun-Thu, to 2am Fri & Sat) A dozen pumps dispensing real ale, a roomy beer garden and a friendly, unreconstructed vibe make this red-brick pub popular with the locals. That and hearty, homemade Italian food and an annual festival championing regional and microbrewery beers.

Fez   CLUB
(www.cambridgefez.com; 15 Market Passage; ⊙10pm-3am) Hip-hop, dance, R&B, techno, funk, indie, big-name DJs and club nights – you'll find it all at Cambridge's most popular club, the Moroccan-themed Fez, strewn with Turkish rugs and cushions.

Lola Lo   CLUB
(www.lolalocambridge.com; 1 Corn Exchange St; ⊙10pm-3am Wed-Mon) Bringing a South Pacific vibe to the centre of Cambridge, Lola Lo specialises in cocktails and themed nights, featuring commercial dance, drum 'n' bass and club anthems. Grass skirts are de rigueur for ladies (though we might be lying).

☆ Entertainment

Portland Arms   LIVE MUSIC
(www.theportlandarms.co.uk; 129 Chesterton Rd; ⊙11am-11.30pm, to 12.30am Fri & Sat) A popular student haunt, the Portland is the best spot in town to catch a gig and see the pick of up-and-coming bands. It has a wood-panelled interior, a spacious terrace and a monthly comedy night too.

ADC   THEATRE
(www.adctheatre.com; Park St) This famous student-run theatre is home to the university's Footlights comedy troupe whose past members include Emma Thompson, Hugh Laurie and Stephen Fry.

Junction   PERFORMING ARTS
(☎01223-578000; www.junction.co.uk; Clifton Way) Theatre, dance, comedy, live bands and club nights at a contemporary performance venue near the railway station. It's 1.5 miles southeast of the city centre, down Regent St (later Hills Rd).

Cambridge Arts Theatre   THEATRE
(☎01223-503333; www.cambridgeartstheatre.com; 6 St Edward's Passage) Cambridge's biggest bona fide theatre puts on everything from highbrow drama and dance, to panto and shows fresh from London's West End.

Corn Exchange   PERFORMING ARTS
(☎01223-357851; www.cornex.co.uk; Wheeler St) Venue attracting the top names, from pop and rock to comedy.

ℹ Information

Addenbrooke's (www.cuh.org.uk; Hills Rd) Hospital 4 miles southeast of the centre.

CB1 (www.cb1.com; 32 Mill Rd; per hr £1.80; ⊙9.30am-8pm; 🛜) Internet cafe half a mile southeast of the centre.

Police Station (www.cambs.police.uk; Parkside; ⊙8am-10pm) On the north east corner of Parker's Piece.

Post Office (St Andrew's St; ⊙9.30am-5.30pm Mon-Sat)

Tourist Office (☎0871 226 8006; www.visitcambridge.org; Peas Hill; ⊙10am-5pm Mon-Sat, plus 11am-3pm Sun Apr-Oct)

ℹ Getting There & Away

BUS

Buses run by **National Express** (www.nationalexpress.com) leave from Parkside. Destinations include the following:
Gatwick £20, 4½ hours, hourly

OLIVER CROMWELL – THE SCOURGE OF KINGS

While some believe the enigmatic Cromwell was a regicidal dictator, others hail him as a hero of liberty – although the truth is probably more complex than either.

East Anglia's most notorious son was born in Huntingdon in 1599. His first 40 years or so on a smallholding were spent in obscurity, but after he underwent a religious conversion and became a militant Puritan there was no stopping him, driven as he was by ambition and clarity of purpose before God. After a spell as a Member of Parliament for Huntingdon and then Cambridge, 'Old Ironsides' excelled as a military commander during the English Civil War, fighting on the side of the victorious 'Roundheads' (ie those siding with parliament against the king). Despite the fact that he was only one of several signatories of the death warrant of Charles I, he is the one largely held responsible.

Though modern interpretation suggests Cromwell allowed Jews (expelled in 1290) back into Britain to 'stimulate the economy', the fact that he used the full weight of his office as lord protector to force through this unpopular decision shows how firmly he believed that the conversion of the Jews to Christianity was an essential precondition to the establishment of Christ's rule on earth: 'Was it not our duty in particular to encourage them to settle here, where alone they could be taught the truth?'

His other major actions were the conquests of Ireland and Scotland, acts that – together with the death of Charles I – won him widespread posthumous animosity, to the point where his body was exhumed from Westminster Abbey after the Restoration (of the monarchy) and then treated as if he had been a live rebel: hanged at Tyburn and decapitated. The body was almost certainly thrown into the common pit at Tyburn (the present-day site of Marble Arch), while the head was stuck on Westminster Hall and remained there for several decades, blowing down in a storm in the early 18th century. Picked up, it passed into private ownership and was occasionally exhibited as a curiosity. A descendant of its last owner deeded it to Sidney Sussex College in 1960 – Cromwell's alma mater – and it was buried in the chapel. There is a plaque on the wall but the exact location is kept secret, lest self-proclaimed Royalists dig it up and defile it.

Heathrow £17, four hours, hourly

Oxford £15, 3½ hours, every 30 minutes

Stansted £10, 50 minutes, hourly

CAR

Cambridge's centre is largely pedestrianised. The city's multistorey car parks charge between £2.50 and £4.80 for two hours.

Five free Park & Ride car parks circle the city on the major routes, with buses (return tickets £2.90) shuttling into the city centre every 10 to 15 minutes between around 7am and 8pm.

TRAIN

The **train station** is 1.5 miles southeast of the centre. Destinations include the following:

Birmingham New Street £32, four hours, hourly

Bury St Edmunds £10, 50 minutes, hourly

Ely £4, 15 minutes, three per hour

King's Lynn £10, 45 minutes, hourly

London Kings Cross £18, one hour, two to four per hour

Stansted £15, 30 minutes to 1¼ hours, two per hour

🛈 Getting Around

BICYCLE

Cambridge is incredibly bike-friendly, with two wheels providing an ideal, and atmospheric, way to get around town.

Station Cycles (www.stationcycles.co.uk; Corn Exchange St; per half-day/day/week £7/10/25; ⊙ 8am-6pm Mon-Fri, 9am-5pm Sat, 10am-4pm Sun) In the heart of town, underneath the Grand Arcade shopping centre. There's another branch on Station Rd at the train station.

City Cycle Hire (www.citycyclehire.com; 61 Newnham Rd; per half-day/day/week £7/10/25; ⊙ 9am-5.30pm Mon-Fri, plus 9am-5pm Sat Apr-Oct) A mile southwest of the city centre

BUS

Bus routes run around town from the **main bus station** (Drummer St). Many operate until around 11.30pm. C1, C3 and C7 stop at the train station. A Dayrider ticket (£3.90) provides 24 hours, unlimited, citywide bus travel.

Grantchester

POP 560

Old thatched cottages with gardens covered in flowers, breezy meadows and classic cream teas aren't the only reason to make the pilgrimage along the Cam to the picture-postcard village of Grantchester. You'll also be following in the footsteps of some of the world's greatest minds on a 3-mile walk, cycle or punt that has changed little since Edwardian times. After the idyllic journey, flop into a deck chair under a leafy apple tree and wolf down calorific cakes or light lunches at the quintessentially English Orchard Tea Garden (www.orchard-grantchester.com; Mill Way; lunch mains £4-9, cakes £3; ⊘ 9.30am-5pm Mar-Oct, 10am-4pm Nov-Feb). This was the favourite haunt of the Bloomsbury Group who came to camp, picnic, swim and discuss their work.

Imperial War Museum

The romance of the winged war machine is alive and well at Europe's biggest ★ aviation museum (www.iwm.org.uk; Duxford; adult/child £17.50/free; ⊘10am-6pm Easter-Oct, to 4pm Nov-Easter; P ♿), where almost 200 lovingly preserved vintage aircraft are housed in several enormous hangars. The vast airfield showcases everything from dive bombers to biplanes, Spitfire and Concorde.

The last admission is an hour before closing. Duxford is 9 miles south of Cambridge at Junction 10 of the M11. Bus C7 runs from Emmanuel St in Cambridge to Duxford (£3.50, 50 minutes, two-to-three per hour).

Make this a day trip, especially if you're bringing kids – the interactive rocket launchers and flight simulators prove irresistible.

The awe-inspiring American Air Museum hangar, designed by Norman Foster, pays homage to the daring of US WWII servicemen and hosts the largest collection of American civil and military aircraft outside the USA, while the slick AirSpace hangar houses an exhibition on British and Commonwealth aviation. The planes aren't here to just look pretty – a number, such as the legendary *Flying Fortress*, take to the skies during the ultra-popular June/July Winged Legends airshow – an exhilarating spectacle not least because there's considerable risk involved for pilots. Modern battles are also covered, including the latest desert warfare in Afghanistan and Iraq, complete with an assortment of tanks and artillery from WWII onwards.

Ely

POP 20,200

A small but charming city dominated by a jaw-dropping cathedral, Ely makes an excellent day trip from Cambridge. It takes its name (pronounced *ee-lee*) from the eels that once inhabited the undrained Fens surrounding the town. From the Middle Ages onwards, Ely was one of the biggest opium-producing centres in Britain, with high-class ladies holding 'poppy parties' and mothers in the Fens sedating their children with 'poppy tea'. Today, beyond the dizzying heights of the cathedral towers, Ely is a cluster of medieval streets lined with traditional tearooms and pretty Georgian houses; a quaint quayside adds extra appeal.

◉ Sights

Ely Cathedral   CATHEDRAL
(www.elycathedral.org; The Gallery; adult/child £8/free, entry & tower tour £14.50/free; ⊘ 7am-6.30pm, evensong 5.30pm Mon-Sat, 4pm Sun, choral service 10.30am Sun) Ely Cathedral's stunning silhouette dominates the whole area – it's dubbed the 'Ship of the Fens' because it's so visible across the vast, flat sweeps of land. The early-12th-century nave dazzles with clean, uncluttered lines and a lofty sense of space. Look out too for the entrancing ceiling, the masterly 14th-century Octagon, and towers that soar upwards in shimmering colours. Standard admission includes a ground-floor guided tour. The tower tours (three to five daily) deliver behind-the-scenes glimpses, 165 steps and remarkable views.

Ely has been a place of worship and pilgrimage since at least 673, when Etheldreda, daughter of the king of East Anglia, founded a nunnery here (shrugging off the fact that she had been twice married in her determination to become a nun). She was canonised shortly after her death. The nunnery was sacked by the Danes, rebuilt as a monastery, demolished and then resurrected as a church after the Norman Conquest. In 1109 Ely became a cathedral. Gothic arches were added later to support the weight of the mighty walls.

The vast 14th-century Lady Chapel is filled with eerily empty niches that once held statues of saints and martyrs. They were hacked out unceremoniously by iconoclasts during the English Civil War. But the delicate tracery remains, overseen by a rather controversial statue of *Holy Mary* by David Wynne, unveiled in 2000 to mixed reviews. The cathedral's beauty has made it a popular film location: you may recognise some of its fine details from scenes in *Elizabeth: The Golden Age* and *The Other Boleyn Girl*. For optimum atmosphere, visit during evensong or a choral service.

Oliver Cromwell's House
MUSEUM

(www.olivercromwellshouse.co.uk; 29 St Mary's St; adult/child £4.60/3.10; ⊙10am-5pm Apr-Oct, 11am-4pm Nov-Mar) England's premier Puritan lived in this attractive, half-timbered house with his family from 1636 to 1647, when he was the local tithe collector. The interior has been restored to reflect the fixtures and fittings that would have been part of their daily lives – expect flickering candles, floppy hats and writing quills. It's engaging and entertaining, and also challenges you to answer one question: was this complex character a hero or a villain?

Ely Museum
MUSEUM

(www.elymuseum.org.uk; Market St; adult/child £3.50/1; ⊙10.30am-5pm Wed-Sat & Mon, 1-5pm Sun Apr-Oct, to 4pm Nov-Mar) Housed in the Old Gaol House, this quirky little museum appropriately features gruesome prison tableaux inside prisoners' cells, plus displays on Romans, Anglo-Saxons, the Long Barrow burial ground at nearby Haddlington, and the formation of the Fens. You are also initiated into the mysteries of old Ely trades such as leatherwork and eel-catching.

🛏 Sleeping & Eating

★ Peacocks
B&B ££

(☑01353-661100; www.peacockstearoom.co.uk; 65 Waterside; d £125-150) Walk into the roomy suites here and feel instantly at home. In Cottage, floral Laura Ashley wallpaper graces a sweet sitting area and bedroom; in Brewery, the vintage books, gilt mirrors and burnished antiques are reminiscent of a grand gentlemen's club. Downstairs, the award-winning cafe (open 10.30am to 5pm Wednesday to Sunday) serves a vast selection of teas and cream teas (from £7), luscious homemade soups, salads, cakes and scones.

Riverside Inn
B&B ££

(☑01353-661677; www.riversideinn-ely.co.uk; 8 Annesdale; s/d £65/90; ℗) In this Georgian guesthouse on Ely's quay, rooms team with brocade bedspreads and dark furniture with sparkling new bathrooms. Just the place to gaze at the houseboats and rowers bobbing about on the River Great Ouse.

Old Fire Engine House
BRITISH ££

(☑01353-662582; www.theoldfireenginehouse. co.uk; 25 St Mary's St; lunch 2/3 courses £15/20, mains £16; ⊙noon-2pm & 7-9pm Mon-Sat, to 2pm Sun) 🍴 Eating here is like sampling the dishes cooked up in a (decidedly classy) classic East Anglian farmhouse kitchen. Seasonal and local produce rules, so treats might include Suffolk venison or quince and Stilton tart with Fen celery or Norfolk samphire, rounded off with some custard-smothered, steamed treacle pud.

ℹ Information

Tourist Office (☑01353-662062; www.visitely. org.uk; 29 St Mary's St; ⊙10am-4pm) Stocks leaflets (50p) on the picturesque 'Eel Trail' and Fen Rivers Way circular walks (£2).

ℹ Getting There & Away

You can walk to Ely from Cambridge, along the 17-mile, riverside Fen Rivers Way. Rail connections include:

Cambridge £4, 15 minutes, three per hour
King's Lynn £7, 30 minutes, hourly
Norwich £16, one hour, every 30 minutes

ESSEX

The county's inhabitants have been the butt of snobbery and some of England's cruellest jokes for years, thanks to pop-culture stereotypes. But beyond the fake Burberry bags and slots 'n' bumper car resorts, the county's still-idyllic medieval villages and rolling countryside provided inspiration for Constable, one of England's best-loved painters. Here, too, is the historic town of Colchester, while even Southend-on-Sea, the area's most popular resort, has a softer side in the traditional cockle-sellers and cobbled lanes of the sleepy suburb Leigh.

Colchester

POP 173,074

Dominated by its sturdy castle and extensive Roman walls, Colchester is Britain's oldest recorded city, dating from the 5th century BC. In AD 43, the Romans came, saw, conquered and constructed their northern capital Camulodunum. It was razed by Boudica just 17 years later. In the 11th century the invading Normans built a mighty castle; today it's set amid a maze of narrow streets that are home to a striking new arts space and some half-timbered gems.

◎ Sights

★ Colchester Castle
CASTLE

(www.cimuseums.org.uk; adult/child £7.50/4.75; ◎10am-5pm Mon-Sat, 11am-5pm Sun) Built in 1076 on the foundations of the Roman Temple of Claudius, England's largest surviving Norman keep is bigger than that of the Tower of London. Over the centuries it's been a royal residence, a prison and home to a Witchfinder General. Now a £4-million restoration has brought 21st-century technology to its 11th-century walls. Look out for mobile phone apps and tablet hire, and a cracking *son et lumiere* re-creating lost internal structures and bringing the building's history to life.

firstsite
ARTS CENTRE

(www.firstsite.uk.net; Lewis Gdns; ◎10am-5pm Tue-Sun; [wheelchair]) **FREE** Colchester's shiny curved, glass-and-copper arts centre brings the town bang up to date. It's as striking inside as out: installations flow seamlessly into one another amid a wealth of space and light. Temporary visual art display are cunningly juxtaposed with historical works; the one permanent exhibition is the magnificent Berryfield Mosaic – a Roman artefact found on firstsite's location in 1923, and now under glass in the centre of the gallery space.

Hollytrees Museum
MUSEUM

(www.cimuseums.org.uk; Castle Park; ◎10am-5pm Tue-Sat, 11am-5pm Sun) **FREE** It's like walking into a period drama: a Georgian town house dating from 1718, filled with toys and costumes, watches and clocks. Reminders of the domestic life of the wealthy owners and their servants are everywhere, with quirky exhibits that include a shipwright's baby carriage in the shape of a boat, a make-your-own Victorian silhouette feature and an intricate, envy-inducing dolls' house.

Dutch Quarter
HISTORIC NEIGHBOURHOOD

The best of the city's half-timbered houses and rickety roof lines are clustered together in this Tudor enclave just a short stroll north of High St. The area remains as a testament to the 16th-century Protestant weavers who fled here from Holland.

📙 Sleeping & Eating

North Hill
HOTEL **££**

(Green Room; ✆01206-574001; www.north-hillhotel.com; 50 North Hill; s £65-80, d/f/ste

£90/120/110; 🛜) Ask for a room in the more characterful, back building of this sleek sleep spot and you'll be rewarded with wonky beams, exposed red brick and plush modern furnishings. The restaurant (open noon to 2.30pm daily and 6pm to 9.30pm Monday to Saturday) delights in giving local, seasonal comfort food classics a contemporary twist. Dinner mains are around £15 and their working lunch (mains £7) is a snip.

Four Sevens
B&B **££**

(✆01206-546093; www.foursevens.co.uk; 28 Inglis Rd; s £55-60, d £65-75; [P][🛜]) The far-from-frilly furnishings here feature stand-alone bowl sinks, industrial-esque clothes rails and platform beds. Impressive breakfasts include eight cereal options, and guests are often welcomed with sponge cake or even tiramisu. It's a mile southwest of the centre, off the B1022 to Maldon.

★ Company Shed
SEAFOOD **££**

(✆01206-382700; www.the-company-shed.co.uk; 129 Coast Rd, West Mersea; mains £4-12; ◎9am-5pm Tue-Sat, 10am-5pm Sun) Bring your own bread and wine to this seaside shack to tuck into mussels, Colchester oysters, prawns, lobster, jellied eels and smoked fish, courtesy of the Howard family – eighth-generation oyster-men. It's set on Mersea Island, 9 miles south of Colchester; check the tides – it's cut off for an hour either side of particularly high water.

❶ Information

Tourist Office (✆01206-282920; www.visitcolchester.com; Castle Park; ◎9.30am-5pm Mon-Sat) Now set inside the Hollytrees Museum.

❶ Getting There & Away

National Express buses run to London Victoria every two hours (£15, 2½ hours).

Trains run to London Liverpool Street (£18, one hour, every 15 minutes).

Dedham Vale

John Constable's romantic visions of country lanes, springtime fields and babbling creeks were inspired by and painted in this serene vale. The artist was born and bred in East Bergholt in 1776 and, although you may not see the rickety old cart pictured in his renowned painting *The Hay Wain,* the picturesque cottages, rolling countryside and languid charm remains.

Now known as Constable Country, **Dedham Vale** (www.dedhamvalestourvalley.org) centres on the villages of Dedham, East Bergholt and Flatford. With leafy lanes, arresting pastoral views and graceful old churches, it's a glorious area to explore on foot or by bike.

Sights

Bridge Cottage HISTORIC BUILDING
(NT; 01206-298260; www.nationaltrust.org.uk; Flatford, nr East Bergholt; parking £3; 10.30am-5pm Apr-Oct, to 3.30pm Sat & Sun Nov-Mar; P) **FREE** Set right beside Flatford Mill – a feature of several Constable paintings – thatched Bridge Cottage has an exhibition that provides a fine introduction to the artist's life and works. Call ahead about the daily guided tours (£6.50) which take in Flatford Mill, Willy Lott's Cottage (which features in *The Hay Wain*) and other sites that pop up in Constable's paintings. There are also self-guided routes.

Flatford Mill HISTORIC BUILDING
(Flatford, nr East Bergholt; P) Constable fans will recognise red-brick Flatford Mill immediately, as it appears in many of his canvases and remains as idyllic a setting today. It was once owned by the artist's family and is now used as an education centre, so although you can take in picture-perfect views from front and back, you can't go in.

Courses

Painting Courses ART
(01206-323027; www.dedhamhall.co.uk; Brook St, Dedham; nonresidents per 3/7 days £295/325) For those inspired by Dedham Vale's bucolic landscapes, atmospheric Dedham Hall runs acclaimed painting courses in a converted, 14th-century barn. You can just visit each day for lessons, but it's more fun to stay, when the fee (per three/seven nights from £495/650) includes dinner, bed and breakfast.

Sleeping & Eating

Sun INN ££
(01206-323351; www.thesuninndedham.com; High St, Dedham; d £110-150; P) Choices, choices, choices. The Rocco-themed, duck-egg-blue room, or the one with a four-poster, beamed bathroom and its own ghost? The lamb kofka and mojitos or the Stilton ploughmans and real ale? Either way the 15th-century Sun delivers wonky walls, creaking floors and bags of charm. The restaurant (mains £13 to £19) is open noon to 2.30pm and 6.30pm to 9.30pm.

Milsoms HOTEL ££
(01206-322795; www.milsomhotels.com; Stratford Rd, Dedham; d £120-200; P) Sure-footed design gives the rooms here a real sense of fun: red-leather armchairs, Anglepoise lamps and retro phones meet vast leaning mirrors and jazzy modern art. But the peppery pistachio-crusted salmon or lemon posset in the funky brasserie (open noon to 9.30pm, mains £8 to £27) might tempt you from your room.

Dedham Hall B&B ££
(01206-323027; www.dedhamhall.co.uk; Brook St, Dedham; s/d £65/110, 3 courses £35; P) From the beamed bar and cosy lounge to the plump furnishings and shelves of vintage books, it's all atmosphere at this rambling, 15th-century house. Chairs and tables dot landscaped lawns, while the Fountain House restaurant (three courses £35, booking required) dishes up elegant, imaginative fare.

Maison Talbooth BOUTIQUE HOTEL £££
(01206-322367; www.milsomhotels.com; Stratford Rd, Dedham; ste £210-345; P) In secluded grounds overlooking Constable's Dedham Vale, this fabulous retreat sees guests luxuriating in swish suites with goose-feather duvets and don't-want-to-get-up beds, and de-stressing in its heated pool, hot tub, tennis courts and spa.

Getting There & Around

Buses 247 and 102 run from Colchester to Dedham (£2.20, 30 minutes, two to eight daily). Bus 93 links Colchester with East Bergholt (£2.60, 45 minutes, every two hours Monday to Saturday). If coming by train, Flatford Mill is a lovely 2-mile walk from Manningtree station.

Saffron Walden

POP 14,572

The 12th-century market town of Saffron Walden is a delightful knot of half-timbered houses, narrow lanes, crooked roofs and ancient buildings. It gets its name from the purple saffron crocus (source of the world's most expensive spice), which was cultivated in the surrounding fields between the 15th and 18th centuries. It makes an atmospheric day trip from Cambridge.

◉ Sights

Old Sun Inn   HISTORIC BUILDING
(Church St) Saffron Walden's most famous landmark sits at a crossroads surrounded by timber-framed buildings. An ornate, 14th-century structure, it was once used as Cromwell's HQ and its exterior walls still bear intricate 17th-century pargeting (decorative plaster work).

St Mary the Virgin   CHURCH
(www.stmaryssaffronwalden.org; Church St; ☺8am-5pm) FREE St Mary's oldest parts date back to 1250. A symbol of the town's saffron-inspired golden age, it is one of the largest churches in the county and features some impressive Gothic arches, and local landowner Lord Audley's tomb.

Saffron Walden Museum   MUSEUM
(www.saffronwaldenmuseum.org; Museum St; adult/child £1.50/free; ☺10am-4.30pm Tue-Sat, to 2pm Sun) Eclectic collections here range from local history, 18th-century costumes and Victorian toys to geology, ancient Egyptian artefacts and Inuit bone harpoons. The bramble-covered ruins of Walden Castle Keep, built about 1125, lie in the grounds.

Bridge End Gardens   GARDENS
(☺gardens 24hr, maze & kitchen garden 9am-3pm Mon-Thu, to 1pm Fri, 10am-4pm Sat & Sun) FREE Careful restoration of these seven interlinked gardens has brought them back to their former Victorian glory. Make sure you visit when the maze and produce-packed kitchen garden are open too.

✗ Eating

Eight Bells   PUB ££
(www.8bells-pub.co.uk; 18 Bridge St; mains £12-20; ☺noon-3pm & 6-10pm Mon-Sat, noon-6pm Sun; ✈)

A warm mix of medieval character and contemporary style, this 16th-century gastropub serves up the likes of pork tenderloin with sage-infused apple and home-cured gravlax. Scrubbed wooden floors, half-timbered walls, abstract art, deep leather sofas and roaring fires make it an attractive place to sip on a pint too.

Cafe Coucou   CAFE ££
(www.cafecoucou.co.uk; 17 George St; mains £7-10; ☺9am-5pm Mon-Sat) Delicious homemade quiches, huge scones, chunky doorstop sandwiches and salads sell like hotcakes at this cheerful family-run cafe.

ⓘ Information

Tourist Office (☎01799-524002; www.visitsaffronwalden.gov.uk; 1 Market Pl; ☺9.30am-5pm Mon-Sat) Stocks a good town trail leaflet on the historic buildings.

ⓘ Getting There & Around

Bus 7 runs between Saffron Walden and Cambridge (£4, one hour, hourly).

The nearest train station is 2 miles west of Saffron Walden at Audley End. Bus 301 links Audley End train station with Saffron Walden (£1.70, 15 minutes, hourly Monday to Friday). Train services from there include:

Cambridge £7, 20 minutes, every 20 minutes

London Liverpool Street £11, one hour, twice hourly Monday to Saturday, hourly Sunday

Southend-on-Sea

POP 173,600

Full of flashing lights and fairground rides, Southend is London's weekend playground, replete with gaudy amusements and packed nightclubs. But as well as all that, there's a glorious stretch of sandy beach, an absurdly

---

DON'T MISS

AUDLEY END HOUSE PARK

Positively palatial in its scale, style and the all-too-apparent ambition of its creator, the first earl of Suffolk, the fabulous early-Jacobean **Audley End House Park** (☺10am-6pm Wed-Sun) eventually did become a royal palace when it was bought by Charles II in 1668.

Audley End House is 1 mile west of Saffron Walden off the B1383. Audley End train station is 1.25 miles from the house. Taxis from the town marketplace cost around £5.

Today, the enormous building is one-third of its original size, but it's still magnificent. Lavishly decorated rooms glitter with silverware, priceless furniture and paintings, making it one of England's grandest country homes. The interior was remodelled in Gothic style by the third Baron Braybrooke in the 19th century, and much of his creation remains today.

The house is surrounded by a landscaped park (open 10am to 6pm Wednesday to Sunday) designed by Lancelot 'Capability' Brown and is host to summer concerts.

long pier and, in the suburb of Old Leigh, a traditional fishing village.

◉ Sights

Southend Pier
LANDMARK

(www.southend.gov.uk/pier; ⊘8am-6pm Mon-Fri, to 8pm Sat & Sun Apr-Sep, 9am-5pm Wed-Sun Oct-Mar) FREE Welcome to the world's longest pier – a staggering 1.34 miles long, to be precise – built in 1830 and a magnet for boat crashes, storms and fires, the last of which ravaged its tip in 2005. Today, a peaceful if windy stroll to the restored pier head reveals a cafe, artists' studios and the 185-seater Royal Pavilion. Hopping on the Pier Railway (single adult/child £3.50/2) saves the long slog back.

Pier Museum
MUSEUM

(www.southendpiermuseum.co.uk; Marine Pde; adult/child £1.50/50p; ⊘11am-5pm Sat, Sun, Tue & Wed Mar-Oct) Southend's seaside heyday springs to life in this charming museum, where a Victorian toast-rack tram from the pier sits beside a functioning signal box, sepia photos and period costumes. The best bits though are the still-working antique penny-slot machines.

Old Leigh
NEIGHBOURHOOD

Cobbled streets, cockle sheds, art galleries and craft shops define atmospheric Old Leigh. It's a long stroll west along Southend's seafront, or a short hop on the local train.

🛏 Sleeping & Eating

Roslin Beach
HOTEL ££

(☑01702-586375; www.roslinhotel.com; Thorpe Esplanade; s/d/ste £87/120/185, mains £14-22; P🕸📶) Seafront Roslin is all New England beach-house chic: sculptural driftwood features, seashell-framed mirrors and sand drifting up the steps. De-knot in the sauna, soak in the spa then sample locally-caught whitebait on the water-view terrace, framed by swaying palms. Food is served noon to 3pm and 6pm to 9pm.

Beaches
B&B ££

(☑01702-586124; www.beachesguesthouse.co.uk; 192 Eastern Esplanade; s/d from £40/90; P📶) A welcome respite from violent florals and heavy swag curtains, rooms at Beaches are bright, simple and tasteful, with white Egyptian-cotton bed linen, feather duvets and subtle colour schemes.

Osborne Bros
SEAFOOD £

(www.osbornebros.co.uk; High St, Leigh-on-Sea; snacks £2.50, mains £6; ⊘8am-5pm) Part fish stall, part bare-bones cafe, Osbourne's is set right on Old Leigh's waterfront and serves up expansive Thames Estuary views. As it's run by a seafood merchant there are also cockles, mussels, prawns and jellied eels to go with your salad or jacket spud.

ⓘ Information

Tourist Office (☑01702-618747; www.visit southend.co.uk; Western Esplanade; ⊘8am-6pm Arp-Oct, 9am-5pm Wed-Sun Nov-Mar) At the entrance to the pier.

ⓘ Getting There & Around

Southend has two train stations: Central (10 minutes' walk from the sea) and Victoria (15 minutes from the shore).

London Liverpool Street £15, one hour, four per hour, from Southend Victoria.

London Fenchurch St £11, 55 minutes, four per hour, from Southend Central.

Leigh-on-Sea £3, seven minutes, every 15 minutes, from Southend Central.

SUFFOLK

Suffolk is dotted with picturesque villages seemingly lost in time. The county made its money on the back of the medieval wool trade and magnificent churches and lavish Tudor homes attest to the area's wealthy past. To the west are the picture-postcard villages of Lavenham and Long Melford. Further north Bury St Edmunds ushers in historic buildings and a market-town vibe. While the appealing seaside resorts of Aldeburgh and Southwold overflow with genteel charm.

ⓘ Getting Around

Ipswich is the county's main transport hub. Search online for bus routes via Suffolk County Tourism (www.suffolkonboard.com) and Traveline (p360).

Trains connections from Ipswich include the following:

Bury St Edmunds £9, 30 minutes, two per hour

London Liverpool Street £30, 1¼ hours, every 20 minutes

Norwich £15, 40 minutes, two per hour

Long Melford

POP 2898

Two Elizabethan manors and some fine eateries make Long Melford deserving of a detour. Its expansive village green, antiques shops and string of independent stores provide other excellent reasons to meander on through.

⊙ Sights

Kentwell Hall
HISTORIC BUILDING

(☑ 01787-310207; www.kentwell.co.uk; adult/child £11.50/8; P) Gorgeous, turreted, haunted Kentwell Hall may date from the 1500s and be full of Tudor grandeur, but the manor house is still used as a private home, resulting in a wonderfully lived-in feel. It's framed by a rectangular moat, glorious gardens and an irresistible rare-breeds farm. Keep an eye out for the Tudor re-enactment events, when the whole estate bristles with bodices, codpieces and hose, and Scaresville – a costumed Halloween extravaganza. Opening hours are erratic, call to check, though it's open noon to 4pm most days in summer, plus other weekends.

Melford Hall
HISTORIC BUILDING

(NT; www.nationaltrust.org.uk; Hall St; adult/child £7/3.40; ⊙ 1-5pm Wed-Sun Apr-Oct; P) From outside, the romantic Elizabethan mansion of Melford Hall seems little changed since it entertained Queen Elizabeth I in 1578. Inside, there's a panelled banqueting hall, masses of Regency and Victorian finery, and a display on Beatrix Potter, who was a cousin of the Parkers, who owned the house from 1786 to 1960.

Holy Trinity
CHURCH

(www.longmelfordchurch.com; Church Walk; ⊙ 10am-5pm) Magnificent Holy Trinity is more cathedral-sized than church-sized, a spectacular example of a 15th-century wool church. The stained-glass windows and flint and stone flushwork are outstanding.

🛏 Sleeping & Eating

Black Lion
HOTEL ££

(☑ 01787-312356; www.blacklionhotel.net; The Green; s/d/ste £100/125/175, mains £16; P 🖘) There's more than a hint of the Scottish Highlands at the smashing Black Lion, thanks to tartan carpets, open fires and ancient-looking oil paintings. Flamboyant bedrooms, all swag curtains and feature beds, are named after classy wines – Yquem is, fittingly, floor-to-ceiling rich red. The food, served noon to 2pm and 7pm to 9pm, is a combo of contemporary style and traditional elegance too.

Bull
INN ££

(☑ 01787-378494; www.oldenglishinns.co.uk; Hall St; s/d £60/80, mains £8-12; P 🖘) They've been serving travellers at this rambling village pub since 1580, and its bars are pleasantly businesslike despite ornate carved ceilings and heraldic crests. For maximum atmosphere check into a front-facing bedroom; it'll be rich in aged beams and dark wood. Food is served noon to 9.30pm.

DON'T MISS

SUTTON HOO

Somehow missed by plundering grave robbers and left undisturbed for 1300 years, the hull of an enormous Anglo-Saxon ship was discovered at **Sutton Hoo** (NT; ☑ 01394-389700; www.nationaltrust.org.uk; Sutton Hoo, nr Woodbridge; adult/child £7.50/3.70; ⊙ 10.30am-5pm Easter-Oct, 11am-4pm Sat & Sun Nov-Easter; P 🚼) in 1939, buried under a mound of earth. The vessel was the final resting place of Raedwald, King of East Anglia until AD 625, and was stuffed with Saxon riches, reflecting a sophisticated culture that's conveyed beautifully in on-site displays.

The massive effort that went into Raedwald's burial gives some idea of just how important a man he was, while the elaborate nature of the treasures transformed perceptions of the era.

Many of the original finds and a full-scale reconstruction of his ship and burial chamber can be seen in the visitor centre. The finest treasures, including the king's exquisitely crafted helmet, shields, gold ornaments and Byzantine silver, are displayed in London's British Museum, but replicas are on show here, along with an original prince's sword.

Paths encircle the 18 burial mounds (which look like bumps in the ground) that make up the 'royal cemetery'. You can only walk onto them as part of a one-hour **guided tour** (adult/child £2.50/1.25), which provides a fascinating insight into the site. Call to check for tour times.

Sutton Hoo is 2 miles east of Woodbridge and 6 miles northeast of Ipswich off the B1083.

Scutcher's Bistro
BRITISH **£££**

(☑ 01787-310200; www.scutchers.com; Westgate St; mains £20-30; ⊘ noon-2pm & 7-9.30pm Thu-Sat) Beautiful reinventions of traditional ingredients ensure this unpretentious place is renowned throughout the Stour Valley. Local Gressingham duck might be given an Asian twist; wild seabass could be paired with Milanese risotto. It's modern, classy and assured.

ⓘ Getting There & Away

Bus links include the following:

Bury St Edmunds £3.95, 50 minutes, hourly Monday to Saturday.

Sudbury £1, 10 minutes, hourly Monday to Saturday.

Sudbury

POP 13,000

Besides giving us the celebrated portrait and landscape painter Thomas Gainsborough (1727–88) and being the model for Charles Dickens' fictional town Eatanswill in *The Pickwick Papers* (1837), Sudbury is a bustling market town that prospered during the wool trade, with small-scale silk weaving surviving to this day.

Most visitors to Sudbury come to see **Gainsborough's House** (www.gainsborough.org; 46 Gainsborough St; adult/child £6.50/2; ⊘10am-5pm Mon-Sat), the artist's birthplace and home to the world's largest collection of his work. The 16th-century house and gardens feature a Georgian facade built by the artist's father. Inside, look for his earliest surviving portrait, *A Boy and a Girl in a Landscape,* the exquisite *Portrait of Harriett, Viscountess Tracy,* celebrated for its delicate portrayal of drapery, and the landscapes that were his passion.

Sudbury's train station has hourly connections to London Liverpool Sreet (£26, 1¼ hours). Regular buses run to Ipswich (one hour), Long Melford (13 minutes), Lavenham (30 minutes), Bury St Edmunds (one hour) and Colchester (one hour).

Lavenham

POP 1413

One of East Anglia's most beautiful and rewarding towns, the former wool-trade centre of Lavenham is home to a collection of exquisitely preserved medieval buildings that lean and lurch to dramatic effect. Lavenham's 300 half-timbered, pargeted and thatched houses have been left virtually untouched since the 15th century; many are now superb places to eat and stay.

⊙ Sights

Guildhall of Corpus Christi HISTORIC BUILDING

(NT; www.nationaltrust.org.uk; Market Pl; adult/child £5.35/2.65; ⊘11am-5pm Apr-Oct, to 4pm Sat & Sun Mar & Nov) Lavenham's most enchanting buildings are clustered along High St, Water St and around the unusually triangular Market Pl. They're dominated by this early-16th-century whitewashed guildhall – a superb example of a close-studded, timber-framed building. It is now a local-history museum with displays on the wool trade and medieval guilds; in its tranquil garden you can see dye plants that produced the typical medieval colours.

Little Hall HISTORIC BUILDING

(www.littlehall.org.uk; Market Pl; adult/child £3.50/free; ⊘2-4.30pm Tue-Thu, Sat & Sun, 10am-1pm Mon Apr-Oct) Caramel-coloured, 14th-century Little Hall was once home to a successful wool merchant. Inside, the rooms of this gem had been restored to period splendour through the efforts of the Gayer-Anderson twins who made it their home in the 1920s and 1930s.

St Peter & St Paul CHURCH

(www.lavenhamchurch.wordpress.com; Church St; ⊘8.30am-5.30pm) This late-Perpendicular structure seems to lift into the sky, with its beautifully proportioned windows, soaring flint tower and gargoyle waterspouts. Built between 1485 and 1530, it was one of Suffolk's last great wool churches, completed on the eve of the Reformation, and is now a lofty testament to Lavenham's past prosperity.

ⓒ Tours

Guided Walks WALKING TOUR

(adult/child £4/free; ⊘2.30pm Sat, 11am Sun Easter-Oct) Delve deep into the stories behind Lavenham's beautiful buildings on these guided strolls. They leave from the tourist office; there's no need to book.

⊨ Sleeping & Eating

★ **Angel** HOTEL **££**

(☑ 01787-247388; www.wheelersangel.com; Market Pl; s £85, d £75-125, mains £12-19; Ⓟ ⓐ) For what you get, this is ridiculously good value. In Lavenham's oldest building, dark-green corridors lead to gorgeously renovated large, bright, beam-scored rooms. It also happens to be run by renowned chef Marco Pierre

White; the food (served noon to 2.30pm and 6pm to 9pm) is a seriously good version of bistro-meets-pub-grub.

Lavenham Priory
B&B ££

(☑ 01787-247404; www.lavenhampriory.co.uk; Water St; s/d from £87/120; ℙ ⏃) A rare treat – a sumptuously restored, 13th-century B&B that steals your heart as soon as you walk in. The history-rich bedrooms (here called 'bedchambers', naturally) feature cavernous fireplaces, leaded windows, oak floors, original wall paintings and canopied four-poster beds. Book well in advance.

Guinea House
B&B ££

(☑ 01787-249046; www.guineahouse.co.uk; 16 Bolton St; d £75-85) Get ready to duck – some of the doors in this superbly snug, 15th-century cottage are only 5ft tall. Sloping roofs meet sloping walls, slanting floors support wildly wonky beams. And the Aga-cooked breakfast is served in front of a vast fireplace. Perfect.

★ Swan
HOTEL £££

(☑ 01787-247477; www.theswanatlavenham.co.uk; High St; s £105, d £195-290, ste £350; ℙ ⏃) Marvellously medieval and utterly indulgent, the Swan might just spoil you in terms of other places to stay. Tasteful furnishings team oatmeal with olive and gentle reds, lattice works of ancient wood climb all around. The service is smooth, while the suites are simply stunning; expect soaring arched ceilings criss-crossed with beams.

★ Great House
FRENCH ££

(☑ 01787-247431; www.greathouse.co.uk; Market Pl; 3-course lunch/dinner £24/33; ⏰ noon-2.30pm Wed-Sun, 7-9.30pm Tue-Sat; ⏃) Contrasting cultures combine so well here: traditional meets modern, East Anglian ingredients meet French cuisine. Which could see you eating confit of Lavenham lamb or caramelised Suffolk pork, then dispatching melting chocolate moelleux or tangy morsels of French and Suffolk cheese.

ⓘ Information

Tourist Office (☑ 01787-248207; www.discoverlavenham.co.uk; Lady St; ⏰ 10am-4.45pm mid-Mar–Oct, 11am-3pm Sat & Sun Nov–mid-Mar) Tucked in beside central Market Pl.

ⓘ Getting There & Away

Bus 753/754 runs to Bury St Edmunds (£3.65, 30 minutes) and Sudbury (£3.55, 30 minutes) hourly, Monday to Saturday.

Bury St Edmunds

POP 41,113

In Bury the past is ever present. A centre of pilgrimage for centuries, its history-rich features include an atmospheric ruined abbey, handsome Georgian architecture and tranquil gardens. The chance to visit two breweries proves pretty tempting too.

The event that put Bury on the map was the burial, in 903, of St Edmund, the last Saxon king of East Anglia, He'd become a martyr after been decapitated by the Danes in 869 – his grave became a site of pilgrimage and part of one of Europe's most powerful medieval monasteries. In 1214 the English barons came to the abbey to draw up the petition that formed the basis of the Magna Carta, setting the country on the road to a constitutional government.

◉ Sights

Abbey Gardens
RUIN

(Mustow St; ⏰ dawn-dusk) FREE Now a picturesque ruin in parkland behind the cathedral, Bury's once-mighty abbey still impresses despite the townspeople having made off with much of the stone after the Dissolution. The walls are striking (especially on the west side), having crumbled and eroded into a series of fantastical shapes. Other highlights are the decorative Great Gate, the diminutive dovecote and the flower-filled gardens.

You enter the Abbey Gardens via one of two well-preserved old gates: opposite the tourist office, the staunch mid-14th-century **Great Gate** is intricately decorated and ominously defensive, with battlements, portcullis and arrow slits. The other entrance sits further up Angel Hill, where a gargoyle-studded early-12th-century **Norman Tower** looms.

Just beyond the Great Gate is a peaceful garden where the **Great Court** was once a hive of activity; further on a **dovecote** marks the only remains of the Abbot's Palace. Most impressive, however, are the remains of the western front, where the original abbey walls were burrowed into in the 18th century to make way for homes. The houses are still in use and look as if they've been carved out of the stone-like caves. Nearby is **Samson Tower** and in front of it a beautiful statue of St Edmund by Dame Elisabeth Frink (1976). The rest of the abbey spreads eastward like a ragged skeleton, with various lumps and pillars hinting at its immense size.

St Edmundsbury Cathedral   CATHEDRAL

(www.stedscathedral.co.uk; Angel Hill; requested donation adult/child £3/50p; ⊙8.30am-6pm) The 45m-high tower of this cathedral was only completed in 2005 and is a vision in Lincolnshire limestone – its traditional Gothic-style construction conveys how many English cathedrals must have looked fresh from the stonemason's chisel. Most of the building is early 16th century, though the eastern end is post-1945. The overall effect is light and lofty, with a gorgeous hammerbeam roof and a striking sculpture of the crucified Christ by Dame Elisabeth Frink in the north transept.

The impressive entrance porch has a tangible Spanish influence, a tribute to Abbot Anselm (1121–48), who opted against pilgrimage to Santiago de Compostela in favour of building a church dedicated to St James (Santiago in Spanish) right here.

Stop by the **Treasury** (Angel Hill; ⊙10am-4pm Mon-Sat, 12.30-3pm Sun) in the crypt for a glimpse of church silver and ornate medieval Bibles. Free, 30-minute guided **tours** (Angel Hill; ⊙11.30am Mon-Sat late-Apr–Sep) provide an in-depth insight into the cathedral's heritage.

St Mary's Church   CHURCH

(www.stmarystpeter.net/stmaryschurch; Honey Hill; donation requested; ⊙10am-4pm) St Mary's is one of the largest parish church in England and also contains the tomb of Mary Tudor – Henry VIII's sister and a one-time queen of France. Built around 1430, it's famous for its hammer-beam roof, which features a host of vampire-like angels swooping from the ceiling. A bell is still rung to mark curfew, as it was in the Middle Ages.

Greene King Brewery   BREWERY

(☎01284-714297; www.greeneking.co.uk; Crown St; visitor centre free; tours £10; ⊙10am-4.30pm Mon-Sat) They've been crafting some of England's favourite booze in this working brewery since 1799. These days it's a place to explore the town's 900-year-old brewing heritage in the visitor centre, then take a tour (2pm weekdays, plus 11am Wednesday to Sunday, plus 12.30pm and 3.30pm Saturday) that winds past the vats and pipes of the historic brewhouse, takes in sweeping town views from the roof, and heads to the Brewery Tap for tipples from the casks. The tours are popular – book.

Moyse's Hall   MUSEUM

(www.stedmundsbury.gov.uk/moyseshall; Cornhill; adult/child £4/2; ⊙10.30am-4.30pm Mon-Sat) Set in an impressive 12th-century undercroft,

rarities here include a locket containing some of Mary Tudor's hair and finds from Bury's ruined abbey. Displays chart the key episodes in the town's past, including the chilling Bury witch trials. There are also displays about one of England's most notorious murders – that of Maria Marten in the Red Barn at nearby Polstead in 1827. A huge crowd gathered in Bury to see her murderer hang.

Theatre Royal   HISTORIC BUILDING

(NT; www.theatreroyal.org; Westgate St; ⊙11.30am-3.30pm Wed-Sun early Aug, 11am-5pm Sat & Sun late-May to Jun) A real treat, Britain's only working Regency playhouse features ornate gilding, sweeps of boxes and a *trompe l'oeuil* ceiling, all revealed on self-led and guided front- and back-stage tours.

🛏 Sleeping

★ Fox   INN ££

(☎01284-705562; www.oldenglishinns.co.uk; 1 Eastgate St; d £90-150; P🐾) Slumber in these converted animal barns and be surrounded by carefully kept original features: whitewashed beams, weathered brick walls and even the livestock tethering rings. Painted wicker chairs and the odd chandelier add another layer of class.

The Glen   B&B ££

(☎01284-755490; rallov@aol.com; 84 Eastgate St; s £40, d £60-75; P🐾) A wood-burning stove and hanging tapestries lend the lounge of this late-Georgian B&B a cosy air. Upstairs it's all bright elegance, with bedrooms in cream and gentle gold.

Angel   HOTEL £££

(☎01284-714000; www.theangel.co.uk; 3 Angel Hill; d £115-180, ste £350; P🐾) The more expensive rooms at this ivy-clad Georgian coaching inn are pretty special; expect luxury bathrooms, quirky mock-1700s furnishings (the odd bright-pink plastic chair) and suites with stand-alone copper baths. The cheaper rooms have much less pizzaz.

✖ Eating & Drinking

★ Pea Porridge   INTERNATIONAL ££
(☑ 01284-700200; www.peaporridge.co.uk; 28-29 Cannon St; mains £13-18; ⊙ noon-2pm & 6.30-9.30pm Wed-Sat, 6.30-9.30pm Tue) Warmth, happy chatter and great aromas greet you at this intimate neighbourhood eatery. Imaginative dishes borrow from the cuisines of Turkey, Italy and France – choose from tagines, gnocchi, Normandy black sausage or pigs cheeks and polenta – you're onto a winner any which way.

★ Maison Bleue   FRENCH £££
(☑ 01284-760 623; www.maisonbleue.co.uk; 31 Churchgate St; mains £18-27; ⊙ noon-2pm & 7-9.30pm Tue-Sat) Settle onto an elegant chair here for modern French cuisine that's supremely stylish and bursting with flavour. Creations might include roasted Gressingham duck with chicken liver velouté, or a gingery tartar of gilt head bream. The set menus (three-course lunch/dinner £24/33) are great-value deals.

★ Old Cannon   PUB
(☑ 01284-768769; www.oldcannonbrewery.co.uk; 86 Cannon St) 🍴 How's this for a three-in-one? A microbrewery with its own pub and accommodation (singles/doubles £90/120) alongside. Gleaming mash tuns sit in the funky bar; try the Rusty Gun (ABV 4%) or more feisty Gunner's Daughter (5.5%). Then tuck into modish bistro-meets-pub-grub (mains £12-17, served 8.30am to 9pm Monday to Saturday, to 3pm on Sunday) before droping off in the converted brewery flanked by gentle checks and terracotta walls.

Nutshell   PUB
(www.thenutshellpub.co.uk; The Traverse; ⊙ 11am-11pm Mon-Fri, to midnight Sat, to 10.30pm Fri) See how many of your friends you can squeeze into this thimble-sized, memorabilia-packed, timber-framed pub, recognised by the Guinness Book of Records as Britain's smallest.

❶ Information

Tourist Office (☑ 01284-764667; www.visit-burystedmunds.co.uk; 6 Angel Hill; ⊙ 9.30am-5pm Mon-Sat, 10am-3pm Sun Easter-Oct, to 4pm Mon-Fri Nov-Easter)

❶ Getting There & Around

BUS
The main bus station is on St Andrew's St North.
Cambridge (£4.80, one hour, hourly Monday to Saturday) Stagecoach bus 11
London (£15, 2½ hours, five daily) National Express

TRAIN
The train station is 900m northwest of the tourist office, with frequent buses to the centre.
Cambridge £10, 45 minutes, hourly
Ely £10, 30 minutes, every two hours

Orford
POP 720

Secluded and seductive, the gorgeous village of Orford, 6 miles south of Snape Maltings, is well worth a detour. It's a laid-back place littered with pretty houses and dominated by a real rarity: curiously polygonal Orford Castle.

◉ Sights

Orford Castle   CASTLE
(EH; www.english-heritage.org.uk; adult/child £6/3.60; ⊙ 10am-6pm daily Apr-Oct, Sat & Sun Nov-Mar; ℗) This 12th-century structure has an innovative, 18-sided drum design with three square turrets. From the roof there are glorious views of Orford Ness.

Orford Ness   NATURE RESERVE
(NT; www.nationaltrust.org.uk; adult/child incl ferry crossing £4/2; ⊙ 10am-5pm Tue-Sat Jul-Sep, plus Sat Oct & late-Apr–Jun) The largest vegetated shingle spit in Europe was once used as a secret military testing ground; now it's a nature reserve and is home to rare wading birds, animals and plants. Ferries run from Orford Quay: the last leaves Orford at 2pm and returns from the reserve at 5pm. Spaces can be limited – arrive early to reserve a seat.

✖ Eating

Butley Orford Oysterage   FISH ££
(☑ 01394-450277; www.pinneysoforford.co.uk; Market Hill; mains £8-17; ⊙ noon-2pm daily, plus 6.30-9pm Jun–mid-Sep) Make sure you've booked a table at this place, lauded locally for the fish and seafood they catch and smoke themselves (it's open some evenings in low season as well); alternatively get some goodies to go from **Pinney's** (www.pinneysoforford.co.uk; The Quay; ⊙ 10am-4pm), their shop by the harbour.

Aldeburgh

POP 3225

The time-warped coastal town of Aldeburgh (pronounced 'orld-bruh') is one of the region's most charming. Its picturesque streets and sweeping shingle beach are lined with pastel-coloured houses, independent shops, art galleries and ramshackle fresh-fish kiosks. Connections with composer Benjamin Britten and two festivals might also draw you to town.

Sights

Scallop
LANDMARK

(Thorpe Rd car park) Maggi Hambling's sculpture commemorates Aldeburgh's links with 20th-century composer Benjamin Britten, who spent much of his life in the town. With 4m of inscribed, scallop shell–shaped steel, its beachside setting has proved controversial locally. It's a short stroll north of town along the seafront.

Moot Hall
MUSEUM

(www.aldeburghmuseum.org.uk; Market Cross Pl; adult/child £2/free; ⊙noon-5pm Jun-Aug, from 2.30pm Apr, May, Sep & Oct) Displays on fishing, shipbuilding, coastal defences and Regency-era tourism set in an intricately carved, timber-framed, 16th-century house.

Festivals

Aldeburgh Festival
MUSIC

(www.aldeburgh.co.uk; ⊙Jun) Founded by local composer Benjamin Britten in 1948, this exploration of classical music is one of East Anglia's biggest, taking in new, re-interpreted and rediscovered pieces, and visual arts.

Aldeburgh Food & Drink Festival
FOOD

(www.aldeburghfoodanddrink.co.uk; ⊙late-Sep) A two-day celebration of Suffolk produce and top-class cooking.

Sleeping & Eating

★ Ocean House
B&B, APARTMENT ££

(☑01728-452094; www.oceanhousealdeburgh.co.uk; 25 Crag Path; d £100, apt per week £1300) Just a pebble's throw from Aldeburgh's beach, many of the rustic-chic bedrooms here directly overlook the surging sea. The five-person self-catering flat comes with homely kitchen and pint-sized balcony, while the top floor double is a true delight: water views on three sides and a sitting room with a baby grand.

Dunan House
B&B ££

(☑01728-452486; www.dunanhouse.co.uk; 41 Park Rd; d £80-95, f from £117; P ⊛) Evidence of the artist owners' efforts are everywhere: bright abstracts, self-portraits and pottery galore. Vivid walls alternate between red, orange and lemon; vintage books and battered travelling chests lie around, while the top-floor family suite even has binoculars for zoomed-in estuary views.

Fish & Chip Shop
FISH & CHIPS £

(www.aldeburghfishandchips.co.uk; 226 High St; mains £5-6; ⊙noon-2pm Tue-Sat, 5-8pm Thu-Sat) Aldeburgh has a reputation for the finest fish and chips in the area; this is the best place to find out why.

★ Lighthouse
MODERN BRITISH ££

(☑01728-453377; www.lighthouserestaurant.co.uk; 77 High St; mains £11-16; ⊙noon-2pm & 6.30-10pm; ⊕) The bright lighthouse has plenty to keep fish fans happy, and plenty of choices for carnivores too. Flavourful dishes range from

---

WORTH A TRIP

DUNWICH & RSPB MINSMERE

Strung along the coastline north of Aldeburgh is a poignant trail of serene and little-visited coastal heritage towns that are gradually succumbing to the sea. Most dramatically, the once-thriving port town of Dunwich is now an eerie village, its 12 medieval churches lost under the waves.

The coast near Dunwich draws ranks of birdwatchers, thanks to Royal Society for the Protection of Birds Minsmere (RSPB; www.rspb.org.uk; nr Westleton; adult/child £7.50/3; ⊙reserve dawn-dusk, visitor centre 9am-5pm; P). The reserve is home to one of England's rarest birds, the bittern, with hundreds of migrant birds dropping by in the autumn. Year-round, binoculars are available for rent from the visitor centre, while the hides along the reserve's trails are prime bird-spotting sites.

With public transport lacking you'll need to drive, cycle or walk.

calves liver and mash, via beer-battered cod and chips, to prime duck confit.

Regatta Restaurant
SEAFOOD ££

(☑ 01728-452011; www.regattaaldeburgh.com; 171 High St; mains £14-20; ☺ noon-2pm & 6-10pm) Other restaurants must be so envious – your own smokery in the back garden. Oak-smoked treats include meaty salmon and memorable prawns, while the perfectly cooked catch of the day could come with anything from risotto or garlic butter to basil sauce.

ℹ Information

Tourist Office (☑ 01728 453637; www.the-suffolkcoast.co.uk; 48 High St; ☺ 10am-3pm Mon-Sat)

ℹ Getting There & Away

Bus 165 runs hourly, Monday to Saturday to Ipswich (£4.10, 1½ hours), where you can make connections to the rest of the region.

Southwold

POP 974

Southwold's reputation as a well-heeled holiday getaway has earned it the nickname 'Kensington-on-Sea' after the upmarket London borough, and its lovely sandy beach, pebble-walled cottages, cannon-dotted clifftop and rows of beachfront bathing huts are undeniably picturesque. It's all attracted many artists, including JMW Turner, Charles Rennie Mackintosh, Lucian Freud and Damien Hirst.

◉ Sights

Seafront & Pier
NEIGHBOURHOOD

(www.southwoldpier.co.uk; ☺ pier 10am-5pm, to 7pm Fri & Sat) **FREE** Southwold's shorefront is its main attraction. Amble along the promenade, admire the squat 19th-century lighthouse then drop by the 623ft pier, first built in 1899 but recently reconstructed. Its Under the Pier Show (open same hours as the pier) sports a cooky collection of handmade amusement machines which combine daft fun with political satire.

Adnams
BREWERY

(☑ 01502-727225; www.adnams.co.uk; Adnams Pl; tours £12; ☺ 2-4 tours daily Mar-Sep) Spend an hour touring the high-tech kit inside this Victorian brewery, indulge in a 30-minute tutored tasting, then select a free bottle of beer to take home. Book.

St Edmund's
CHURCH

(Church St; ☺ 9am-6pm) Worth a peek for its fabulous medieval screen and 15th-century, bloodshot-eyed 'Southwold Jack' effigy (believed to be part of a clock), grumpily overlooking the church's rear.

☞ Tours

Coastal Voyager
BOAT TOUR

(☑ 07887 525082.; www.coastalvoyager.co.uk; Southwold Harbour) Trips on offer include a 30-minute high-speed blast around the bay (adult/child £24/12), a leisurely 3½-hour cruise up the Blyth Estuary (£28/14) and a three-hour voyage to Scroby Sands (£35/18) to see a seal colony and wind farm.

✷ Festivals

Latitude Festival
ARTS

(www.latitudefestival.co.uk; Henham Park; ☺ Jul) An eclectic mix of music, literature, dance, drama and comedy set in a country estate.

Ways With Words
LITERATURE

(www.wayswithwords.co.uk; ☺ Nov) Talks and readings by big-name authors in venues around town.

🛏 Sleeping & Eating

Home@21
B&B ££

(☑ 01502-722573; www.homeat21.co.uk; 21 North Pde; d £80-100; 🐾) The rooms in this neat Victorian terrace may be super-compact and relatively simple, but the location is all: plumb on the seafront, with a prime view of Southwold's iconic pier and the surging waves.

★ Sutherland House
HOTEL £££

(☑ 01502-724544; www.sutherlandhouse.co.uk; 56 High St; d £140-220, mains £19; P 🐾) Past guests at this former mayor's house include a future James II and the Earl of Sandwich. They'd probably approve of the present appearance: pargeted ceilings, exposed beams and free-standing baths. Supper time (noon to 2pm and 7pm to 9pm, closed Monday) sees prime local ingredients transformed by bouillabaiss sauce, plantain crisps and clam ragù.

Swan
INN £££

(☑ 01502-722186; www.adnams.co.uk/hotels/the-swan; Market Sq; s/d from £115/185; 🐾) There's a timeless elegance to the 17th-century Swan where large fireplaces, grandfather clocks and old-fashioned lamps induce a soporific calm. Bedroom styles range from stately Georgian to contemporary coastal, the atmospheric restaurant (noon to 2pm and

7pm to 9pm) majors on local fish, while bar-staff are itching to serve you a Southwold-brewed Adnams beer.

Coasters
MODERN BRITISH ££
(☑ 01502-724734; www.coastersofsouthwold.co.uk; 12 Queen St; mains £10-20; ⊗9am-3pm & 6-9pm) Punchy flavours and rich ingredients are the mainstay of this bistro, where a wide-ranging menu skips nimbly from whole baked crab and Stilton-glazed beef, to Dingley Dell Suffolk pork sausages with mustard mash.

❶ Information

Tourist Office (☑ 01502-724729; www. visit-sunrisecoast.co.uk; Child's Yard; ⊗10am-5pm Mon-Sat, 11am-4pm Sun) Just off the High St, has extensive accommodation listings.

❶ Getting There & Away

Services are limited: catch bus 61 to Lowestoft (£3.90, 50 minutes, hourly) or bus 88 to Halesworth train station (£2.70, 20 minutes, hourly Monday to Saturday) and continue from there.

NORFOLK

Big skies, sweeping beaches, windswept marshes, meandering inland waterways and pretty flint houses combine to great effect in Norfolk. They say the locals have 'one foot on the land, and one in the sea' and you're never far from water here, whether it's beside the windmill-framed rivers of the tranquil Norfolk Broads or the wide, bird-life-rich sands of the shore. Inland, the bustling city of Norwich offers a fine castle and cathedral, a lively market and some truly excellent places to sleep and eat.

Norwich
POP 132,500

The affluent and easygoing city of Norwich (pronounced 'norr-ich') is a rich tapestry of meandering alleys liberally sprinkled with architectural jewels – spoils of the city's medieval wool boom. A magnificent cathedral and impressive Norman castle bookend the city centre; in between, crooked half-timbered buildings line quiet lanes. Thriving markets and a large student population enhance the city's easygoing vibe. Add easy access to the Broads and Norfolk's beaches, and you have an excellent base from which to explore.

◉ Sights

★ **Norwich Cathedral** CATHEDRAL
(www.cathedral.org.uk; The Close; donations welcome; ⊗7.30am-6pm) Norwich's most stunning landmark is the magnificent Anglican cathedral, its barbed spire soaring higher than any in England except Salisbury, while the size of its cloisters is second to none. Highlights include the mesmerising ceiling and striking modern features of the Hostry, where high-tech displays explore the cathedral's past. The one-hour guided tours (donation requested, hourly Monday to Saturday) are an engaging way to find out more.

Work started on the cathedral in 1096 and it remains one of the finest Anglo-Norman abbey churches in the country. The sheer size of its nave is striking, but its most renowned feature is the superb Gothic rib vaulting added in 1463. Among the spidery stonework are 1200 sculpted roof bosses depicting Bible stories. Together they represent one of the finest achievements of English medieval masonry.

HAUNTED BLICKLING HALL

Largely remodelled in the 17th century for Sir Henry Hobart, James I's chief justice, Blickling Hall (NT; www.nationaltrust.org.uk; Blickling; adult/child £12/7; ⊗noon-5pm Wed-Sun Easter-Oct, 11am-5pm Sat & Sun Nov-Mar; ℗) began life in the 11th century as a manor house and bishop's palace. Today this grand Jacobean mansion is set in vast parklands and is famous for ghostly sightings and a spectacular Long Gallery.

Blickling Hall is 15 miles north of Norwich off the A140. Buses run twice hourly from Castle Meadow and Tombland in Norwich. Aylsham is the nearest train station, 1.5 miles away.

In 1437 the isolated house was claimed by the Boleyn family and passed through the generations to Thomas, father of Anne Boleyn. Anne was executed by her husband Henry VIII in 1533, who opted to have her beheaded. It's said on the anniversary of her death a coach drives up to the house, drawn by headless horses, driven by headless coachmen and containing the queen with her head on her lap. Ghostly apparitions aside, Blickling's grand state rooms are stuffed with fine Georgian furniture, pictures and tapestries, while the Jacobean plaster ceiling in the Long Gallery is a feast for the eyes.

Norwich

Norwich

Similar bosses can be seen in closer detail in the cathedral's two-storey cloisters. Built between 1297 and 1430, they are unique in England and were originally built to house a community of about 100 monks.

Above the bronze font (which came from a nearby chocolate factory), look out for

Censing Angel (2012) – a suspended celestial figure woven out of willow branches by sculptor Joy Whiddett, trailing the words 'peace', 'hope' and 'love'.

Outside the cathedral's eastern end is the grave of the WWI heroine Edith Cavell, a Norfolk-born nurse who was executed for helping hundreds of Allied soldiers escape from German-occupied Belgium. The handsome cathedral close also contains the old chapel of King Edward VI School (where naval hero Admiral Nelson was educated). Today's students make up the choir, which performs in services daily.

Tombland & Elm Hill   NEIGHBOURHOOD

Leafy Tombland, near Norwich Cathedral, is where the market was originally located ('tomb' is an old Norse word for empty, hence space for a market). From there, follow Princes St to reach Elm Hill, Norwich's prettiest street, with its medieval cobblestones, crooked timber beams and doors, intriguing shops and tucked-away cafes.

★**Bridewell Museum**   MUSEUM

(www.museums.norfolk.gov.uk; Bridewell Alley; adult/child £5/3; ⊙10am-4.30pm Tue-Sat) Best be on your best behaviour: 14th-century Bridewell is a former house of correction, a 'prison for women, beggars and tramps'. Displays here explore Norwich's prominence as England's second city in the Middle Ages and its 19th-century industrial heritage. You can also play games in a 1950s parlour, listen to shoe workers' memories, and watch films in a pocket-sized cinema. Look out too for the eccentric, snake-proof boot.

★**Norwich Castle**
Museum & Art Gallery   CASTLE

(www.museums.norfolk.gov.uk; Castle Hill; adult/child £7/5; ⊙10am-4.30pm Mon-Sat, from 1pm Sun) Crowning a hilltop overlooking central Norwich, this massive, 12th-century castle is one of England's best-preserved examples of Anglo-Norman military architecture. Its superb interactive museum crams in lively exhibits on Boudica, the Iceni, Anglo-Saxons and Vikings. Perhaps the best bit though is the atmospheric keep itself with its graphic displays on grisly punishments meted out in its days as a medieval prison. Twice-daily, guided tours (£2) run around the battlements and creepy dungeons. The castle's art gallery houses works of the acclaimed 19th-century Norwich School of landscape painting founded by John Crome, and (drumroll) the world's largest collection of novelty teapots.

Dragon Hall   HISTORIC BUILDING

(www.dragonhall.org; 123 King St; adult/child £5/3; ⊙10am-4pm Tue-Thu, noon-4pm Sun Apr-Oct) A carved incarnation of the eponymous creature sits amid this medieval trading hall's crown-post roof – a stunning affair of carved and arching beams. The building dates from 1430 and is the only one of its kind to have belonged to one man, Robert Toppes, rather than a guild, suggesting that he was a successful entrepreneur. Engaging displays introduce you to the merchant himself, medieval trade, and 15th-century Norwich life.

Sainsbury Centre for Visual Arts   GALLERY

(www.scva.org.uk; University of East Anglia; ⊙10am-5pm Tue-Sun) **FREE** The region's most important centre for the arts is housed in the first major public building by renowned architect Norman Foster. Its eclectic collections include works by Picasso, Moore, Degas and Bacon, and are displayed beside curios from Africa, the Pacific and the Americas. The gallery is in the University of East Anglia's grounds, 2 miles west of the city centre. To get there take bus 25, 25A or X25 from Castle Meadow (20 minutes).

☞ Tours

Guided Walks   WALKING TOUR

(☑01603-213999; www.visitnorwich.co.uk; adult/child £4/1.50; ⊙11.30am or 2pm, 2-4 per week Easter-Oct) Art-nouveau Norwich, Georgian dandies and 1000 years of history are among the themes for these 1½-hour guided strolls. Run by the tourist office (p392), many leave from the Forum centre, where the office is based.

Ghost Walks   WALKING TOUR

(☑07831-189985; www.ghostwalksnorwich.co.uk; adult/child £7/5; ⊙2-3 walks per week mid-Apr-Dec) A lively immersion in Norwich's haunted history; the tours depart from the Adam & Eve pub (p392) on Bishopsgate at 7.30pm.

🛏 Sleeping

★**38 St Giles**   B&B ££

(☑01603-662944; www.38stgiles.co.uk; 38 St Giles St; s/d/ste £90/130/160; 🛜) Deep-red rugs sit on varnished floors; silk curtains hang in light rooms dotted with quirky art – this handsome B&B is boutique yet still relaxed. The breakfast table groans with local and organic meats and eggs, as well as home-baked bread.

Gothic House   B&B ££

(☑01603-631879; www.gothic-house-norwich.com; King's Head Yard, Magdalen St; s/d £65/95; P🛜)

Step through the door here and be whisked back to the Regency era. Original panelling, columns and cornices border the swirling stairs; fresh fruit and mini-decanters of sherry sit in elegant bedrooms that are studies in olive green, lemon yellow and duck-egg blue.

No 15
B&B **££**

(☎01603-250283; www.number15bedandbreakfast.co.uk; 15 Grange Rd; s/d £55/75; ☎) 🍃 The breakfasts at this vegetarian B&B are packed with treats: organic eggs, veggie sausages, artisan-baked walnut bread and grilled haloumi cheese. The furnishings are low allergy, but high on style – expect sanded wooden furniture, soft lights and bright throws. It's a mile west of the centre, bus 25 runs nearby.

Arrandale Lodge
B&B **££**

(☎01603-250150; www.norwichbedandbreakfast.co.uk; 431 Earlham Rd; s/d £50/70; 🅿☎) Few British B&Bs feature zebra prints and Irish food, but the South African/Southern Irish owners here like to celebrate their twin heritages. Tasteful, contemporary rooms feature springbok and giraffe motifs, while breakfast time brings both white and black pudding. It's 1.5 miles west of the centre.

St Giles House
HOTEL **£££**

(☎01603-275180; www.stgileshousehotel.com; 41 St Giles St; d/ste £130/200; 🅿☎) There's more than a whiff of art nouveau about luxurious St Giles House; built in 1919. Period flourishes echo on into bedrooms that are full of bold patterns and fluid curves, while the spa, bistro and cocktail terrace are rather splendid too.

🍴 Eating

Grosvenor Fish Bar
FISH & CHIPS **£**

(www.fshshop.com; 28 Lower Goat Lane; mains £5; ⊙11am-7pm Mon-Sat) At this groovy chippy-with-a-difference, chips come with fresh cod goujons, sea-bass wraps come with spicy mango salsa and a 'Big Mack' is crispy mackerel fillet tucked into a bread roll. Take away or chow down on the benches inside.

EXPLORING THE NORFOLK BROADS

Why Should I Wish To Visit a Swamp?

These vast wetlands were formed when the Rivers Wensum, Bure, Waveney and Yare flooded the big gaping holes inland which had been dug by 12th-century crofters looking for peat. They comprise fragile ecosystems and, protected as a national park, are home to some of the UK's rarest birds and animals. Apart from that, if you've ever envisioned yourself captaining your own boat and living afloat, there are 125 miles of lock-free waterways to explore. Or if paddling a canoe and losing yourself in the hypnotic lapping of water away from the rest of humanity appeals, there's plenty of scope for that, too.

What Is there to See & Do that Doesn't Involve Water?

Museum of the Broads (www.museumofthebroads.org.uk; The Staithe, Stalham; adult/child £5/2.50; ⊙10.30am-5pm Easter-Oct; 🐾) Five miles north of Potter Heigham off the A149, this museum features fine boats and colourful displays on the local marshmen, their traditional lifestyles, peat extraction and modern conservation.

Toad Hole Cottage (How Hill; ⊙10.30am-5pm Apr-Oct) FREE This tiny cottage delves deeper into the life of Fen-dwellers, showing how the eel-catcher's family lived and the tools they used to work surrounding marshes.

Bewilderwood (www.bewilderwood.co.uk; Hornig Rd, Hoveton; adult/child £14/12; ⊙10am-5.30pm Mar-Oct) A forest playground for children and adults alike, with zip wires, jungle bridges, tree houses and old-fashioned outdoor adventure involving plenty of mud, mazes and marsh walks.

St Helen's Church (Ranworth; ⊙8am-7pm) The Broads' most impressive ecclesiastical attraction is this 14th-century church, known locally as the 'Cathedral of the Broads', which dominates the pretty village of Ranworth and features a magnificent painted medieval rood screen and a 15th-century antiphonar – a rare illustrated book of prayers.

Bure Valley Steam Railway (www.bvrw.co.uk; Aylsham; adult/child return £12/6; ⊙2-6 trains daily Apr-Oct; 🅿) Siderodromophiles will love this train which puffs along 9 miles of narrow-gauge tracks between Aylsham and Wroxham.

Mustard CAFE £

(www.mustardcoffeebar.com; 3 Bridewell Alley; snacks/mains £2/6; ⏰7.30am-5.30pm Mon-Sat 10am-4pm Sun) Set on the site of the original Colman's Mustard shop, you'll find a suitably bright yellow colour scheme at this funky cafe. Quality dishes include rarities (Mexican style huevos rancheros with salsa), and delight in being home-made; expect own-baked Scotch eggs and sausage rolls and their own hand-roasted coffee beans.

Tea House CAFE £

(Elm Hill; snacks from £2; ⏰8.30am-5.30pm Mon-Sat; 🕿) Tuck into doorstep sarnies, steaming jacket potatoes, and top tea and scones.

Bishops MODERN BRITISH ££

(☑01603-767321; www.bishopsrestaurant.co.uk; 8 St Andrew's Hill; 2-course lunch/dinner £15/27; ⏰noon-2pm & 6-9.30pm) The unusual, the unexpected and Norfolk ingredients are the mainstays of menus at Bishops. Sample smoked eel with pork confit, a ballotine of Norfolk chicken, or a cockle, mussel and bacon chowder. Then tingle your tongue with roasted pineapple spiked with chilli.

Library BRASSERIE ££

(☑01603-616606; www.thelibraryrestaurant.co.uk; 1 Guildhall Hill; mains £12; ⏰noon-2pm & 6-10pm Mon-Sat, to 3pm Sun) Victorian bookcases still line the walls at this cosy former library, lending dining a club-like feel. The imaginative menu is strong on locally sourced produce, including Lowestoft fish, Havensfield eggs, East Anglian game and prime Norfolk cheese.

No 12 BISTRO ££

(www.number12norwich.org; 12 Farmers Ave; mains £12; ⏰noon-2.30pm & 5-9pm Mon-Sat, to 3pm Sun) Lounge music plays, heather-hued tartan covers the walls, beams sit above white-leather bar stools; it sounds weird but it works. Food ranges from homemade burgers, chilli and fish pie to tasty, breaded schnitzel.

How Do I Get There?

Driving around the Broads is missing the point and pretty useless. The main centres in the Broads – Wroxham, on the A1151 from Norwich, and Potter Heigham, on the A1062 from Wroxham – are reachable by bus from Norwich and Great Yarmouth, respectively, and from there you can either take to the water or to the trails.

Exploring by Boat

Launches range from large cabin cruisers to little craft with outboards; they can be hired for anything from a couple of hours' gentle messing about on the water to week-long trips. Tuition is given. Depending on boat size, facilities and season, a four-person boat costs from around £15 per hour, from £75 for four hours and from £100 for one day. Week-long rental ranges from around £650 to £1300, including fuel and insurance. Boats for the Broads (www.dayboathire.com) and Barnes Brinkcraft (www.barnesbrinkcraft.co.uk) do short- and long-term rental, Broads Tours (www.broads.co.uk) lets out boats by the week – all are Wroxham-based. Blakes (www.blakes.co.uk) arranges all manner of boating holidays.

Exploring by Canoe

Paddlers can find canoes for hire for around £33 per day; Rowan Craft (www.rowancraft.com; Geldeston) and Waveney River Centre (www.waveneyrivercentre.co.uk; Burgh St Peter) are recommended. Mark the Canoe Man (www.thecanoeman.com; half-day trip £25-45) knows the secrets of the Broads and arranges day and overnight guided trips to areas the cruisers can't reach, as well as canoe and kayak hire, weekend camping canoe trails (two nights £65) and bushcraft courses (two days adult/child £95/70).

Exploring by Foot/Bike

Walking trails stretch across the region, including the 61-mile Weavers' Way from Cromer to Great Yarmouth, taking in some choice parts of the landscape along the way. The Broads' highest point, How Hill, is just 12m above sea level, so superhero levels of fitness are not required. Parts of the trail are open to bicycles. Broadland Cycle Hire (www.norfolkbroadscycling.co.uk; Bewilderwood, Hoveton) and Martha's Cottage (www.marthascottagecyclehire.co.uk; Barnby) are among rental firms. Prices start at £16 per day, with child seats and tandems also available.

★ **Roger Hickman's**　　FINE DINING **£££**
(☎ 01603-633522; www.rogerhickmansrestaurant.
com; 79 Upper St Giles St; dinner 2/3/7 courses
£34/42/55; ☺ noon-2.30pm & 7-10pm Tue-Sat) Understated elegance is everywhere: pale floorboards, white linen and unobtrusive service.
Dishes might include venison and cherries,
salt-baked turnip, or blow-torched mackerel –
flair, imagination and a simple dedication to
quality run right through. The lunches (two/
three courses £18/22) are a cracking deal.

🍷 Drinking & Nightlife

★ **Birdcage**　　PUB
(www.thebirdcagenorwich.co.uk; 23 Pottergate;
☺ 11am-midnight; 🔊) Formica tables, chilled
tunes, cupcakes and cocktails make this
beatnik drinking den a one-of-a-kind delight. Drop by for a Bums Life Drawing session (yes, really) and classy nibbles; or ferry
in fish 'n' chips from the shop over the lane.

Adam & Eve　　PUB
(Bishopsgate; ☺ 11am-11pm Mon-Sat, noon-
10.30pm Sun) Norwich's oldest-surviving pub
has been slaking thirst since 1249, when the
cathedral builders used to drop by. Tiny,
with a sunken floor and part-panelled walls,
it attracts a mixed band of regulars, choristers and ghost hunters, drawn by the fine
malt whiskies and real ales.

❶ Information

Tourist Office (☎ 01603-213999; www.
visitnorwich.co.uk; Millenium Plain; ☺ 9.30am-
5.30pm Mon-Sat, plus 10.30am-3.30pm Sun
mid-Jul–mid-Sep) Inside the Forum centre.

❶ Getting There & Around

Norwich has free parking at six Park & Ride locations. Buses (£2.40) run to the city centre up to
every 15 minutes from around 6.30am to 7pm,
some routes don't operate at weekends.

AIR

Norwich International Airport (www.norwichinternational.com), 4 miles north of town;
has connections to Amsterdam, Aberdeen,
Edinburgh and Manchester year round, plus
summer flights to the Channel Islands.

BUS

The **bus station** (Queen's Rd) is 400m south
of the castle. Follow Red Lion St into Stephen's
St and then turn left onto Surrey St. **National
Express** (www.nationalexpress.com) and **First**
(www.firstgroup.com) run the following services:
Cromer £3.30, one hour, hourly

King's Lynn £8.60, 1½ hours, hourly
London £15, three hours, hourly

TRAIN

The train station is off Thorpe Rd, 600m east of
the castle.
Cambridge £18, 1¼ hours, hourly
Ely £16, one hour, twice hourly
London Liverpool Street £45, two hours, two
per hour

North Coast Norfolk

Norfolk's north coast has something of a split
personality, with busy seaside towns brim-full
of brash attractions in the east, and a string of
villages dotted with gastropubs and boutique
hotels in the west. In between sit vast sandy
beaches and marshes that attract unusually
rich concentrations of birds, including oystercatchers, plovers, curlews and brent geese.

❶ Getting There & Away

Coasthopper Bus (www.coasthopper.co.uk;
one-way fares from £2.70, passes per one/
three/seven days £9/18/32.) Runs from
Cromer to Kings Lynn. Stops include Cley,
Blakeney, Wells, Holkham, Burnham Deepdale
and Brancaster. Services range from every 30
minutes to five daily.

Cromer

POP 7294

The once-fashionable Victorian resort of
Cromer is slowly becoming gentrified again,
after years of amusement arcade and souvenir stand rule. Its main attractions remain
sweet-tasting Cromer crab, the atmospheric
pier and an appealing stretch of sandy shore.

◉ Sights

Henry Blogg Museum　　MUSEUM
(Lifeboat Museum; www.rnlicromer.org.uk; The
Gangway; ☺ 10am-4pm Tue-Sun Feb-Nov) FREE
Cromer's WWII lifeboat and hands-on gizmos help convey tales of remarkably brave
sea rescues in a museum named after one
of the Royal National Lifeboat Institution's
most decorated coxswains.

Felbrigg Hall　　HISTORIC BUILDING
(NT; www.nationaltrust.org.uk; Felbrigg; adult/child
£10/5; ☺ 11am-5pm Sat-Wed Mar-Oct; 🅿) This elegant Jacobean mansion boasts a fine Georgian interior and splendid facade, as well as
gorgeous walled gardens and an orangery. It's
2 miles southwest of Cromer, off the B1436.

🛏 Sleeping & Eating

⭐ Red Lion   INN ££
(📞 01263-514964; www.redlioncromer.co.uk; Brook
St; s £65, d £110, ste £125-180; 🅿 📶) If only all
seafront inns were this chic. Cool contem
porary rooms feature wood- or brass-framed
beds; colours vary from soft grey to purple
and red. The enormous Billiard Room suite
is superb value (£125), with its chandelier,
free-standing bath and chaise longue.

Rocket House   CAFE £
(www.rockethousecafe.co.uk; The Gangway; mains
£4-10; ⏱ 10am-5pm) Set right on the seafront
inside the Henry Blogg Museum, Rocket
House delivers an airy interior, water-view
terrace, soups, sandwiches and heaped
Cromer crab platters.

Davies   SEAFOOD £
(7 Garden St; ⏱ 8am-4.30pm daily May-Sep, Tue-
Sat Oct-Apr) The super-fresh catches here include cooked (and cracked) crab and lobster,
cockles, mussel and homemade fish pâté.

ℹ Getting There & Away

Trains run to Norwich (£7, 45 minutes) hourly
Monday to Saturday, and every two hours on
Sunday. The Coasthopper bus (p392) shuttles
west along the coast to King's Lynn roughly
every half-hour in summer.

Cley-next-the-Sea & Around
POP 420

As the name suggest, the sleepy village of
Cley (pronounced 'cly') huddles beside the
shore. Here a cluster of pretty cottages surrounds a photogenic windmill and bird-rich
marshes fan out all around.

⦿ Sights

Cley Marshes   NATURE RESERVE
(www.norfolkwildlifetrust.org.uk; nr Cley-next-the-
Sea; adult/child £5/free; ⏱ 10am-5pm Nov-Mar,
to 4pm Apr-Oct; 🅿) 🌿 One of England's premier birdwatching sites, Cley Marshes has
more than 300 resident bird species, plentiful migrants and a network of walking
and bird hides amid its golden reeds. Even
if you're not into birding, don't miss the
(free) cafe-cum-visitor centre (www.norfolk
wildlifetrust.org.uk; ⏱ 10am-5pm Nov-Mar, to 4pm
Apr-Oct) FREE where seats and telescopes
line up beside vast picture windows with
panoramic reserve views – this is birding for
softies; sip a latte enjoying zoomed-in images of marsh harriers.

🛏 Sleeping & Eating

Cookes   B&B ££
(📞 01263-740776; www.cookes-of-cley.co.uk; High
St; d/tr £70/80; 🅿 📶) Satin curtains and re-
strained checks bring a touch of the 21st century to this 18th-century coaching inn. Fluffy
hot water bottles raise a smile, while breakfast
is served in the beamed tea shop next door.

⭐ Cley Windmill   B&B £££
(📞 01263-740209; www.cleymill.co.uk; High St; d
£160-200, apt per week £570.; 🅿) With the kind
of wonky walls you'd expect from a circular, 18th-century agricultural building, Cley
Windmill is packed with character. Rooms
are named after their former functions (the
crazy-shaped Barley Bin is gorgeous), and
many look out directly over reed-filled salt
mashes. A sweet, four-person self-catering
cottage sits just next door.

Cley Smokehouse   DELI £
(www.cleysmokehouse.com; High St; ⏱ 9.30am-
4.30pm) Flavour-packed, home-smoked fish,
shellfish and cured meats.

Picnic Fayre   DELI £
(www.picnic-fayre.co.uk; High St; ⏱ 9am-5pm
Mon-Sat, 10am-4pm Sun) Head here for great
breads, cheeses, homemade pork pies and
cakes, Norfolk ice cream, jams and chutneys.

Blakeney Point
POP 700

Blakeney was once a busy fishing and trading
port before its harbour silted up. These days
it offers an inviting seafront walk lined with
yachts and boat trips out to a colony of common and grey seals that live, bask and breed
on nearby Blakeney Point. Several companies,
including Bishop's Boats (www.norfolksealtrips.
co.uk; Blakeney Quay), and Beans Boat Trips
(www.beansboattrips.co.uk; Morston, nr Cley-next-
the-Sea) run hour-long trips (adult/child £10/5,
one to four boats daily, April to October). The
best time to come is between June and August
when the common seals pup.

🛏 Sleeping & Eating

Kings Arms   INN ££
(📞 01263-740341; www.blakeneykingsarms.co.uk;
Westgate St; d £80; mains £6-15; 🅿) Sweet simple rooms (expect bright colours and pine)
in a pub that is so welcoming you might not
want to leave. Order some substantial pub
grub (served noon to 9pm) then, for some
great theatre gossip, ask landlady Marjorie
about her career on the stage.

Moorings

MODERN BRITISH ££

(☑ 01263-40054; www.blakeney-moorings.co.uk; High St; mains £7-17; ⊙ 10.30am-9pm Fri & Sat, 10am-5.30pm Sun & Tue-Thu) Perfectly pitched fish dishes have won this bistro a loyal following – try the sea salt–crusted bass or seafood platter; the classic meat and veg dishes are tempting too. Mustn't-miss puddings include pear-and-ginger strudel, and treacle sponge.

Wells-next-the-Sea

POP 2165

Charming Wells excels at both land and sea. Rows of attractive Georgian houses and flint cottages snake down to a boat-lined quay; to the north sits a vast golden beach, backed by pine-covered dunes.

☉ Sights

Wells Beach

BEACH

Fringed by dense pine forests and undulating dunes, Wells' sandy shore stretches for miles to the west, with brightly coloured beach huts clustering beside the water and wooden steps leading up into the woods. It's all tucked away at the end of a mile-long road; you can walk, drive, or hop on a miniature train. Parking is available.

Wells & Walsingham Railway

HERITAGE RAILWAY

(www.wellswalsinghamrailway.co.uk; Stiffkey Rd; adult/child return £9/7; ⊙ 3-6 trains daily Apr-Oct; P) The longest 10.25in narrow-gauge railway in the world puffs for five picturesque miles from Wells to the village of Little Walsingham, the site of religious shrines and the ruined but still impressive Walsingham Abbey.

🛏 Sleeping & Eating

Wells YHA

HOSTEL £

(☑ 0845 371 9544; www.yha.org.uk; Church Plains; dm/d £15/32; P) In the heart of town in an ornately gabled early-20th-century church hall.

Crugmeer

B&B ££

(☑ 01328-710622; www.crugmeer-wells.co.uk; Croft Yard; d £85; P 🌐) Walk 20 paces from Well's atmospheric quay and arrive at the perfect holiday bolthole. A lattice of beams criss-crosses the walls (and the walk-in cupboard), the bed is a study in burgundy and crisp white, and the standalone bath sits on a whitewashed floor.

Wells Beach Cafe

CAFE £

(Wells Beach; mains £4; ⊙ 10am-5pm Easter-Oct, to 4pm Nov-Easter; 🌐) This locals' favourite rustles up bacon baps, homemade chilli and an irresistible 'hot chocolate of the week'. Outside, sits a corral of picnic tables; inside there's a sofa-surrounded wood-burning stove for when the wind whips in.

Crown

RESTAURANT ££

(www.thecrownhotelwells.co.uk; The Buttlands; mains £12-22; ⊙ noon-2.30pm & 6-9pm) Renowned for robust dishes made from locally sourced ingredients.

❶ Information

Tourist Office (☑ 01328-710885; www.visitnorthnorfolk.com; Staithe St; ⊙ 10am-5pm Mon-Sat, to 1pm Sun Apr-Oct)

Holkham

The pretty village of Holkham is dominated by **Holkham Hall and Estate** (www.holkham.co.uk; Holkham; adult/child £13/5, parking £2.50; ⊙ noon-4pm Sun, Mon & Thu Apr-Oct; P), a severe Palladian mansion, largely unadorned on the outside, set in a vast deer park designed by William Kent.

For many, Holkham's true delight is the other part of the estate – the **Holkham National Nature Reserve**, where the expansive, pristine **beach** bordering Holkham Bay is perfumed by the pine forest growing alongside. Ribboning pathways lead to bird and wildlife hides and onto nearby villages.

The estate is the ancestral seat of the original Earl of Leicester and still belongs to his descendants. The interior is sumptuous, with a red velvet–lined saloon, copies of Greek and Roman statues, and fluted columns in the Marble Hall and luxurious Green State Bedroom. Admission to the hall includes entry to the **Bygones Museum** (www.holkham.co.uk; Holkham; museum only adult/child £7/3.50; ⊙ 10am-5pm Apr-Oct) in the stable block. Its 4000 exhibits feature everything from mechanical toys to vintage cars and steam engines.

Burnham Deepdale & Around

POP 800

Walkers flock to this lovely coastal spot, with its tiny twin villages of Burnham Deepdale and Brancaster Staithe strung along a rural road. Edged by the beautiful Norfolk Coastal Path, surrounded by beaches and reedy marshes, alive with bird life and criss-crossed by cycling routes, Burnham Deepdale is also a base for a whole host of water sports.

🛏 Sleeping & Eating

Deepdale Farm HOSTEL **£**
(☎01485-210256; www.deepdalefarm.co.uk; Burnham Deepdale; dm £13-18, d £30-60, camping £9-20, tipis from £60.; P@🛜) For backpackers it really doesn't get much better than Deepdale Farm: spic-and-span en suite dorms and doubles in a converted stables, a homely well-equipped kitchen, BBQ area, and cosy lounge warmed by a wood burning stove. Campers get to go glam – in a tipi or yurt – or casual, in a good old tent.

The hostel also operates a **tourist office** (☎01485-210256; ⊙10am-4pm), the best place to go to organise kitesurfing or windsurfing on nearby beaches. **Bike hire** (☎014852-10258; per half/full day £10/16) is also available.

White Horse HOTEL **£££**
(☎01485-210262; www.whitehorsebrancaster.co.uk; Main Rd, Brancaster Staithe; mains £10-14; ⊙11am-9pm; P🛜) The award-winning White Horse is a gastropub with a menu strong on seafood; the tapas-style dishes, featuring brown potted shrimp, seared tuna and tempura mackerel, more than set it apart from its competitors. The bedrooms (doubles £140 to £230) embody the seaside with their subtle colour schemes.

Titchwell & Around

Tiny Titchwell, just west of Burnham Deepdale, has a big asset: the **Titchwell Marsh Nature Reserve** (RSPB; www.rspb.org.uk; Titchwell; parking £5; ⊙dawn-dusk; P), where marshland, sandbars and lagoons attract vast numbers of birds. Summer brings marsh harriers, avocets, terns and nesting bearded tits; in winter you'll see more than 20 species of wading birds and countless ducks and geese.

Nearby, dreamy **Titchwell Manor** (☎01485-210221; www.titchwellmanor.com; Titchwell; d £125-215, mains £12-19; P@) is a swish, oh-so-contemporary hotel set in a grand Victorian house – one of its restaurants focuses on informal eating, the other fine dining. They're open noon to 2pm and 6pm to 9pm.

King's Lynn & Around

POP 12,200

Once one of England's most important ports, King's Lynn was long known as 'the Warehouse on the Wash'. It was said you could cross from one side of the River Great Ouse to the other by simply stepping from boat to boat in its heyday. Something of the salty port-town tang can still be felt in old King's Lynn, with its cobbled lanes, vibrant weekly markets, and narrow streets flanked by old merchants' houses.

◉ Sights

St Margaret's Church CHURCH
(www.stmargaretskingslynn.org.uk; Margaret Plain; ⊙8am-6pm) The patchwork of styles here includes Flemish brasses and a remarkable 17th-century moon dial, which tells the tide. You'll find historic flood-level markings by the west door. Opposite, the 1421 **Trinity Guildhall** has an attractive stone facade.

CAMBRIDGE & EAST ANGLIA KING'S LYNN & AROUND

DON'T MISS

SANDRINGHAM HOUSE

Both monarchists and those bemused by the English system will have plenty to mull over at this, the **Queen's country estate** (www.sandringhamestate.co.uk; Sandringham; adult/child £13/6.50; ⊙11am-4.30pm Easter-Oct; P). It's set in 25 hectares of beautifully landscaped gardens, and is open to the public when the royal family is not in residence. Sandringham is 6 miles northeast of King's Lynn off the B1440. Take Hunstanton-bound bus 11 from King's Lynn bus station (30 minutes, hourly Monday to Saturday, four on Sunday).

Queen Victoria bought Sandringham in 1862 for her son, the Prince of Wales (later Edward VII), and the features and furnishings remain much as they were in Edwardian days. Wandering around sumptuous reception rooms regularly used by the royals reveals a wealth of objets d'art and glinting gifts from European and Russian royal families. The stables house a flag-waving **museum** filled with diverse royal memorabilia, while the superb **vintage-car collection** includes the very first royal motor from 1900 and the buggy in which the Queen Mother would bounce around race tracks.

There are **guided tours** (£3.50, 11am and 2pm Wednesday and Saturday) of the gardens. The shop stocks organic goodies produced on the sprawling estate.

Old Gaol House
MUSEUM
(www.kingslynntownhall.com; Sat Market Pl; adult/child £3.30/2.20, Regalia Room free; ☉10am-4pm Wed-Sat Apr-Oct) Explore the old cells and hear grisly tales of smugglers, witches and highwaymen in the former jail. The Regalia Room houses the civic treasures, including the 650-year-old King John Cup, exquisitely decorated with scenes of hunting and hawking.

Lynn Museum
MUSEUM
(www.museums.norfolk.gov.uk; Market St; adult/child £3.70/2.10; ☉10am-5pm Tue-Sat) High points here include a large hoard of Iceni gold coins and the Seahenge Gallery, which tells the story behind the construction and preservation of the early–Bronze Age timber circle which survived for 4000 years, despite being submerged on the Norfolk shoreline – it was only discovered in 1998.

True's Yard
MUSEUM
(www.truesyard.co.uk; North St; adult/child £3/1.50; ☉10am-4pm Tue-Sat) Housed in two restored fishermen's cottages – the only remainder of the district's bustling, fiercely independent fishing community – this museum explores the lives and traditions of the fisherfolk, who were packed into cottages such as these like sardines.

Castle Rising
CASTLE
(www.castlerising.co.uk; Castle Rising; adult/child £4/2.50; ☉10am-5pm Apr-Oct, to 4pm Wed-Sun Nov-Mar; P) There's something bordering on ecclesiastical about the beautifully embellished keep of this castle, built in 1138 and set in the middle of a massive earthwork upon which pheasants scurry about like guards. It's well worth the trip 4 miles northeast of King's Lynn off the A149. Bus 10/11 runs here (20 minutes, hourly Monday to Saturday, four on Sunday) from the King's Lynn bus station.

So extravagant is the stonework that it's no surprise to learn that it shares stonemasons with some of East Anglia's finest cathedrals. It was once the home of Queen Isabella, who (allegedly) arranged the gruesome murder of her husband, Edward II.

Houghton Hall
HISTORIC BUILDING
(www.houghtonhall.com; nr King's Lynn; adult/child £13/5; ☉11am-4pm Wed, Thu & Sun May-mid-Oct; P) Built for Britain's first de-facto prime minister, Sir Robert Walpole, in 1730, the grand Palladian-style Houghton Hall is worth seeing for the ornate staterooms alone, where stunning interiors overflow with gilt, tapestries, velvets and period furniture. Even when the house is closed, the surrounding grounds, home to 600 deer, make for pleasant rambling. Houghton Hall is just off the A148, 13 miles east of Kings Lynn.

Intriguingly, there could have been a whole other dimension to your visit, were it not for the fact that Sir Robert Walpole's grandson sold the estate's splendid art collection to Catherine the Great of Russia to stave off debts – those paintings formed the foundation of the world-renowned collection at the State Hermitage in St Petersburg.

⚜ Festivals & Events

King's Lynn Festival
CULTURAL
(www.kingslynnfestival.org.uk; ☉Jul) East Anglia's most important cultural gathering, with a diverse mix of music, from medieval ballads to opera, as well as literary talks.

🛏 Sleeping & Eating

Bank House
B&B ££
(☎01553-660492; www.thebankhouse.co.uk; King's Staithe Sq; s/d from £90/110; P 🐕) ⚓ A quayside setting, gently funky decor and luxury bathrooms make this stylish Georgian town house pretty hard to turn down. Especially as the hip brasserie (mains £8 to £17) serves seriously good Modern British food.

Market Bistro
MODERN BRITISH ££
(☎01553-771483 01553-771483; www.marketbistro.co.uk; 11 Sat Market Pl; mains £10-18; ☉noon-2pm & 6-8.30pm Tue-Sat) ⚓ A commitment to Norfolk ingredients has won this family-run eatery heaps of fans. Seasonal specials might include succulent Cromer crab, locally smoked fish and tangy samphire from the marshes, not to mention home-made ice cream.

ⓘ Information

Tourist Office (☎01553-763044; www.visitwestnorfolk.com; Purfleet Quay; ☉10am-4pm Mon-Sat, noon-4pm Sun) Arranges guided heritage walks (adult/child £4/1) at 2pm Tuesdays, Fridays and Saturdays between May and October.

ⓘ Getting There & Away

There are hourly trains from Cambridge (£9, 50 minutes) via Ely and London Kings Cross (£31, 1¾ hours). The **Coasthopper 1** (www.coasthopper.co.uk) bus runs to Hunstanton (35 minutes, hourly) and connects with the Coasthopper 2 service, which runs along the north Norfolk coast. Services are frequent from April to September, less so the rest of the year.

Birmingham, the Midlands & the Marches

Best Places to Eat

➜ Hammer & Pincers (p467)

➜ Old Rectifying House (p426)

➜ Samuel Fox (p482)

➜ Trooper (p424)

Best Places to Drink

➜ Ye Olde Trip to Jerusalem (p451)

➜ Jekyll & Hyde (p410)

➜ Ludlow Brewing Company (p446)

➜ Old Bell Hotel (p470)

Why Go?

Few other places come so close to the dream of England as here, the country's heart. If you're searching for green valleys and chocolate-box villages of wonky timbered houses, the legend surrounding Nottingham's Robin Hood, or stately homes that look like the last lord of the manor just clip-clopped out of the stables, you'll find them here.

You'll also find the relics of centuries of industrial history, best exemplified by the World Heritage–listed mills of Ironbridge and the Derwent Valley. Then there are dynamic cities, including Britain's second-largest, Birmingham: a canal-woven industrial crucible reinvented as a cultural melting pot, with striking architecture and red-hot restaurants, bars and nightlife. And then there are tumbling hills where the air is so clean you can taste it. Walkers and cyclists flock to these areas, particularly the Peak District National Park and the Shropshire Hills, to vanish into the vastness of the landscape.

When to Go

➜ February and March see the wonderful chaos of Shrovetide football in Ashbourne.

➜ Literary buffs take note: Shakespeare takes a back seat to contemporary wordsmiths at Stratford's Literary Festival in April/May.

➜ If you're up for a belt-loosening, belly-stretching good time, head to Ludlow's famous Food and Drink Festival in September.

➜ On weekends from April to September, Shropshire Hills Shuttles provides access to wonderful walking trails on the Long Mynd and the Shropshire Hills, while June to September is the peak season for walking and cycling in the Peak District.

Birmingham, the Midlands & the Marches Highlights

1 Surveying the buzzing city of Birmingham from the rooftop 'secret garden' of its stunning new **library** (p401)

2 Hiking, cycling or driving through the rugged **Peak District National Park** (p474)

3 Contemplating the apple tree that inspired Isaac Newton's theories on gravity at **Woolsthorpe Manor** (p460)

4 Museum-hopping in **Ironbridge Gorge** (p437), birthplace of the Industrial Revolution

5 Learning about King Richard III's life, death and the extraordinary discovery of his remains in **Leicester** (p465)

6 Taking in a Shakespearean performance in the Bard's Tudor hometown **Stratford-upon-Avon** (p421)

7 Touring Great Malvern's **Morgan Motor Company** (p428) and taking a car for a spin through the surrounding hills

8 Wandering the opulent halls and grand gardens of Stamford's **Burghley House** (p459)

🏃 Activities

The Peak District is the Midlands' number-one spot to get in touch with nature. Famous walking trails such as the Pennine Way and Limestone Way struggle across the hills, while cyclists pit determination and muscle against challenging routes such as the Pennine Cycleway (NCN Route 68) from Derby to Buxton. Other activities include caving and rock climbing.

Tracing the border between England and Wales, the lush green hills of the Marches are scattered with ruined castles. Top walking and cycling areas include the Long Mynd and Stiperstones in Shropshire and the Malvern Hills in Worcestershire.

Sailors, windsurfers and water babies of all ages and levels of experience flock to Rutland Water near Leicester, while canoeing and kayaking are popular diversions in Hereford.

ℹ️ Getting There & Around

Birmingham Airport (☑ 0871 222 0072; www.birminghamairport.co.uk) and **East Midlands Airport** (☑ 0871 919 9000; www.eastmidlands airport.com) near Derby are the main air hubs.

There are excellent rail connections to towns across the Midlands. **National Express** (☑ 08717 818178; www.nationalexpress.com), at Birmingham Coach Station, and local bus companies connect larger towns and villages, though services are reduced in the low season. For general route information, consult **Traveline** (☑ 0871 200 2233; www.travelinemidlands.co.uk) or visit www.networkwestmidlands.com. Ask locally about discounted all-day tickets.

BIRMINGHAM

POP 1,085,800

Britain's second-largest city is also one of its most happening. A state-of-the-art £189 million library, a gleaming shopping centre atop the revitalised New St Station, beautifully restored Victorian buildings and a new 1.4km Midland Metro tram line extension through the city's heart are just some of the initiatives of its Big City Plan. There are also new parks, public spaces, and glitzy residential and commercial buildings. These come hot on the heels of the striking Mailbox and Bullring shopping malls and the 'bubblewrapped' facade of the iconic Selfridges building.

Alongside outstanding museums and galleries you'll find an increasing number of gastronomic restaurants, cool and/or secret cocktail bars, and picturesque canals with waterside bars, restaurants, attractions and cruises. Thriving legacies of Birmingham's industrial heritage include its Jewellery Quarter, Cadbury manufacturing plant and a former custard factory that's been transformed into a cutting-edge creative hub.

With construction on the High Speed Rail (HS2) line – connecting London with Birmingham in just 40 minutes by 2026 – set to boost employment and the economy, 'Brum', as it's dubbed by locals, is buzzing.

History

Birmingham was first mentioned in the Domesday Book of 1086, where it was described

---

EAT & DRINK LIKE A LOCAL

Look out for the following specialities in Birmingham, the Midlands and the Marches:

Balti This fiery one-pot curry, believed to derive from the Urdu word *balty* ('bucket'), is prepared in a cast-iron wok and traditionally served with a giant *karack* naan bread. It was first cooked up in the curry-houses of Sparkbrook in southern Birmingham by Pakistani workers who moved here in the 1970s; the area is now known as the Balti Triangle (p409).

Chocolate Iconic confectionery company Cadbury originated in Birmingham in 1824 when John Cadbury opened a grocer's shop at 93 Bull Street, selling his own preparations of cocoa and drinking chocolate. Learn about chocolate's evolution, watch it being made and taste it too at Cadbury World (p407).

Bakewell Pudding The Peak District's most famous dessert is more rustic than the glazed versions from commercial bakeries. This pastry shell, spread with jam and topped with frangipane, a mixture of egg and ground almonds, was invented following an accidental misreading of a recipe around 1820. Both the Old Original Bakewell Pudding Shop (p485) and Bloomers Original Bakewell Puddings (p485) in Bakewell claim to be the pudding's progenitor.

Cider Crisp, dry ciders have been produced in Herefordshire since medieval times – discover them on the Herefordshire Cider Route (p429).

BIRMINGHAM IN...

Two Days

Start off in the centre, dropping into the eclectic **Birmingham Museum & Art Gallery** (p404). Walk west through Centenary Sq, stopping to check out the **Library of Birmingham** (p401) before reaching the Birmingham Canals. From here you can take a **canal cruise** (p408) or while away an afternoon at the **National Sea Life Centre** (p406) or **Ikon Gallery** (p406). Dine that night at one of Birmingham's cutting-edge restaurants such as **adam's** (p409). On day two, indulge your inner shopaholic at the gleaming shopping malls of the **Bullring** (p411) and **Mailbox** (p411), which both have good options for lunch. In the afternoon, catch up on some social history at the museum **Birmingham Back to Backs** (p404). After dark, kick off a pub crawl at the **Lost & Found** (p410).

Four Days

On day three, head north from the centre to **Aston Hall** (p407) and **Soho House** (p407), or south to the famous **Barber Institute** (p407). End the day with a show at the **Repertory Theatre** (p411) or a concert at **Symphony Hall** (p411). Use day four to explore the fascinating **Jewellery Quarter** (p406) and spend the afternoon reliving *Charlie and the Chocolate Factory* fantasies at **Cadbury World** (p407).

as a small village, home to a handful of villagers and two ploughs, with a total value of £1. From these humble beginnings, Brum exploded into an industrial and mercantile hub, building its fortunes first on the wool trade and then on metal-working from the 16th century.

The Lunar Society brought together the leading geologists, chemists, scientists, engineers and theorists of the mid-18th century and Birmingham became the world's first industrialised town, attracting a tide of workers from across the nation.

In the mid-1800s enlightened mayors such as Joseph Chamberlain (1836–1914) cleaned out the slums and filled the centre with grand civic buildings. Later, WWII bombers and overzealous town planners took their toll, and swaths of the centre were demolished in a bid to transform Birmingham into 'Britain's Motor City'.

Recent years have seen an explosion of regeneration projects, with 21st-century landmarks appearing all over the city.

Sights & Activities

City Centre

Birmingham's grandest civic buildings are clustered around pedestrianised Victoria Square, at the western end of New St, dominated by the stately facade of Council House, built between 1874 and 1879. The square was given a facelift in 1993, with modernist sphinxes and a fountain topped

by a naked female figure, nicknamed 'the floozy in the jacuzzi' by locals, overlooked by a disapproving statue of Queen Victoria.

To the west, Centenary Sq is book-ended by the art deco Hall of Memory War Memorial, the International Convention Centre (ICC) and Symphony Hall. There's a gleaming golden statue of Birmingham's Industrial Revolution leading lights Matthew Boulton, James Watt and William Murdoch. Centenary Sq's showpiece is the spiffing new Library of Birmingham.

★ **Library of Birmingham** LIBRARY
(www.libraryofbirmingham.com; Centenary Sq; ⊙8am-8pm Mon-Fri, 9am-5pm Sat, 11am-4pm Sun) Resembling a glittering stack of gift-wrapped presents, the Francine Houben–designed Library of Birmingham is an architectural triumph. Opened in 2013, the library features a subterranean amphitheatre, a spiralling interior, viewing decks and a glass elevator to the 7th-floor 'secret garden', which provides panoramic views over the city. In addition to its archives, photography and rare-book collections, including Britain's most important Shakespeare collection, are gallery spaces, 160-plus computers and a cafe. The British Film Institute Mediatheque provides free access to the National Film Archive.

The former Central Library is to be demolished to make way for the Paradise Circus redevelopment between Centenary and Chamberlain Sqs, incorporating a new four-star hotel, shops and public squares, due for completion in 2017.

...st beef & Yorkshire pudding **2.** Sandwiches
...rnish pasty **4.** Cumberland sausage

Flavours of England

England has shaken off its reputation for bland food. Today, wherever you go in the country it's possible to find good quality dishes, which focus on locally sourced or seasonally grown ingredients. There's still no English equivalent of *'bon appetit'* but at least the term can be used genuinely these days – instead of with a dash of irony.

Breakfast

For many visitors to England, the culinary day begins in a hotel or B&B with the phenomenon known as the 'Full English' – a large plateful of mainly fried food that may be a shock if you usually have just a bowl of cereal. But perseverance is recommended, as there's enough fuel here to see you through hours of sightseeing.

Lunch & Dinner

For lunch or an evening meal, England has a good range of local and international options to suit all budgets, but you should definitely sample two quintessentially English eateries: the cafe and the pub.

In cities, cafes are a good cheaper option, while in country areas they're often called teashops – perfect for a traditional afternoon tea with scones, jam and cream.

Pubs are the obvious place to sample traditional English beer, as well as being a reliable option for good-value meals. The most food-focused establishments are now called 'gastropubs'.

ENGLISH CLASSICS

➡ **Fish & chips** Long-standing favourite, best sampled in coastal towns.

➡ **Sandwich** Global snack today, but an English 'invention' from the 18th century.

➡ **Ploughman's lunch** Bread and cheese, a pub menu regular, perfect with a pint.

➡ **Roast beef & Yorkshire pudding** Traditional English Sunday lunch.

➡ **Cumberland sausage** Northern speciality, so big it's coiled to fit on your plate.

➡ **Cornish pasty** Once restricted to the southwest, now available country-wide.

Birmingham Museum & Art Gallery

MUSEUM

(☑0121-303 2834; www.bmag.org.uk; Chamberlain Sq; ⏰10am-5pm Sat-Thu, 10.30am-5pm Fri; 🚻) **FREE** Major Pre-Raphaelite works by Rossetti, Edward Burne-Jones and others are among the highlights of the delightful Birmingham Museum & Art Gallery's impressive collection of ancient treasures and Victorian art.

Birmingham Back to Backs

HISTORIC BUILDING

(NT; ☑0121-666 7671; www.nationaltrust.org.uk; 55-63 Hurst St; tours adult/child £7.25/3.90; ⏰1-5pm Tue-Thu, 10am-5pm Fri-Sun, longer hours during school holidays) Quirky tours of this cluster of restored back-to-back terraced houses take you through four working-class homes, telling the stories of those who lived here between the 1840s and the 1970s. Book by phone for the compulsory guided tour.

For an even more vivid impression of what life was like here, you can book to stay in basic three-storey period cottages at 52 and 54 Inge St (doubles from £100). Guests receive a free Back to Backs tour.

Town Hall

HISTORIC BUILDING

(☑0121-345 0600; www.thsh.co.uk; Victoria Sq) Constructed in 1834 and styled after the

Birmingham

Temple of Castor and Pollux in Rome, Birmingham's neoclassical Town Hall is now used as a venue for classical concerts and stage performances.

Birmingham Cathedral
CATHEDRAL

(☎0121-262 1840; www.birminghamcathedral.com; Colmore Row; entry by donation; ☺7.30am-6.30pm Mon-Fri, 8.30am-5pm Sat & Sun) Dedicated to St Philip, this small but perfectly formed cathedral was constructed in a neoclassical style between 1709 and 1715. Pre-Raphaelite artist Edward Burne-Jones was responsible for the magnificent stained-glass windows.

Thinktank
MUSEUM

(☎0121-202 2222; www.thinktank.ac; Millennium Point, Curzon St; adult/child £12.25/8.40; ☺10am-5pm) A 10-minute walk northeast of the centre, surrounded by the footprints of vanished factories, the Millennium Point development contains this entertaining and ambitious attempt to make science accessible to children. Highlights include galleries on the past (Birmingham's industrial breakthroughs), present (how stuff works) and future, as well as an outdoor science garden and digital planetarium (included in the admission price). There's also a giant screen cinema

(☎0121-202 3333; www.giantscreencinema.co.uk; adult/child from £8.50/6).

◉ Birmingham Canals

During the industrial age, Birmingham was a major hub on the English canal network and today the city has more miles of canals than Venice. Narrow boats still float through the heart of the city, passing a string of swanky wharfside developments.

Ikon Gallery   GALLERY
(☎0121-248 0708; www.ikon-gallery.co.uk; 1 Oozells Sq; ⊙11am-6pm Tue-Sun) FREE Within the glitzy Brindley Pl development of banking offices and designer restaurants, a converted Gothic schoolhouse contains the cutting-edge Ikon Gallery. Prepare to be thrilled, bemused or outraged, depending on your take on conceptual art.

National Sea Life Centre   AQUARIUM
(☎0121-643 6777; www.visitsealife.com; 3a Brindley Pl; admission £20.95; ⊙10am-5pm Mon-Fri, to 6pm Sat & Sun) The Norman Foster–designed National Sea Life Centre is England's largest inland aquarium. Its tanks teem with exotic marine life including razor-jawed hammerhead sharks, turtles and otters. Tickets for two or more people cost £15 per person. Pre-purchase tickets online for fast-track entry and get discounts of up to 40% off on-the-spot rates.

◉ Jewellery Quarter

Birmingham has been a major jewellery player since Charles II acquired a taste for it in 17th-century France. The gentrifying Jewellery Quarter, three-quarters of a mile northwest of the centre, still produces 40% of UK-manufactured jewellery. Dozens of workshops open to the public are listed in the free booklet *Jewellery Quarter: the Essential Guide,* available from tourist offices and local businesses, or visit www.jewelleryquarter.net.

Take the metro from Snow Hill (£2.20, 10 minutes, frequent) or the train from Moor St (£1.80, six minutes, every 10 minutes) to Jewellery Quarter station.

Birmingham

Museum of the Jewellery Quarter   MUSEUM

(☑ 0121-554 3598; www.bmag.org.uk; 75 Vyse St; adult/child £5/free; ⊙ 10.30am-5pm Tue-Sat) The Smith & Pepper jewellery factory is preserved as it was on its closing day in 1981 after 80 years of operation. Guided tours lasting around one hour explain the long history of the trade in Birmingham and let you watch master jewellers at work. Entry to the temporary exhibition space and shop is free.

St Paul's Church   CHURCH

(www.saintpaulbrum.org; St Paul's Sq; ⊙ 10am-4pm Tue-Sat) St Paul's Sq is dominated by this beautiful 18th-century Georgian church, where 'Birmingham Brains' Matthew Boulton and James Watt came to pray.

Royal Birmingham
Society of Artists   ARTS CENTRE

(☑ 0121-236 4353; www.rbsa.org.uk; 4 Brook St; ⊙ 10.30am-5.30pm Mon-Fri, to 5pm Sat, 1-5pm Sun) **FREE** Local artists and artisans have exhibited their work at the Royal Birmingham Society of Artists since 1814.

Jewellery-Silversmithing
Design Academy   COURSE

(☑ 07780-671 870; www.jsdauk.com; Studio 214b, 120 Vyse St; ⊙ 1-day courses from £69) Learn how to create your own jewellery during master classes, short courses and workshops in the heart of the Jewellery Quarter.

⊙ Outlying Areas

Soho House   MUSEUM

(☑ 0121-554 9122; www.bmag.org.uk; Soho Ave, Handsworth; adult/child £4/free; ⊙ 11.30am-4pm Tue-Sun mid-Apr–Oct) About 1.5 miles northwest of Birmingham's Jewellery Quarter, Soho House is where industrialist Matthew Boulton lived from 1766 to 1809. Among the restored 18th-century chambers is the dining room where Boulton and members of the esteemed Lunar Society met to discuss their world-changing ideas during the greatest technological leap forward since the invention of the wheel. From Priory Queensway, take bus 74 or 75 (£1.70, 25 minutes, every 10 minutes) to the Lozells stop, from where it's a five-minute walk.

Barber Institute of Fine Arts   GALLERY

(☑ 0121-414 7333; www.barber.org.uk; ⊙ 10am-5pm Mon-Fri, 11am-5pm Sat & Sun) **FREE** At the University of Birmingham, 3 miles south of the centre, the Barber Institute of Fine Arts has an astonishing collection of Renaissance mas-

---

LOCAL KNOWLEDGE

DIGBETH'S CREATIVE QUARTER

Just over a mile southeast of the centre, Digbeth's creative quarter centres on the Custard Factory (☑ 0121-224 7777; www.custardfactory.co.uk; Gibb St), a hip art and design enclave set in the converted buildings of the factory that once churned out British favourite Bird's Custard. The open-plan space is now full of small galleries, quirky design boutiques, vintage clothes outlets, skateboard shops and affordable, off-beat cafes. There's also a mini skate ramp and free ping-pong tables.

Check out the artist-run experimental gallery Eastside Projects (www.eastsideprojects.org; 86 Heath Mill Lane; ⊙ noon-5pm Wed-Sat) nearby.

---

terpieces; European masters such as Rubens and Van Dyck; British greats including Gainsborough, Reynolds and Turner; and classics from modern titans Picasso, Magritte and others. Trains run from New St to University station (£2.10, seven minutes, every five minutes), from where it's a 10-minute walk.

Cadbury World   MUSEUM

(☑ 0844 880 7667; www.cadburyworld.co.uk; Linden Rd, Bournville; adult/child £15.95/11.70; ⊙ 10am-4.30pm) The next best thing to Willy Wonka's chocolate factory is Cadbury World, 4 miles south of Birmingham. It aims to educate visitors about the history of cocoa and the Cadbury family, but sweetens the deal with free samples, displays of chocolate-making machines, and chocolate-themed rides. Opening hours vary; bookings are essential at peak times. Last entry is 90 minutes before closing. Frequent trains run from Birmingham New St Station to Bournville (£2.40, 12 minutes, every 10 minutes), from where it's a sign-posted 10-minute walk.

Surrounding the aromatic chocolate works, pretty Bournville Village was built by the philanthropic Cadbury family to accommodate early 20th-century factory workers.

Aston Hall   HISTORIC BUILDING

(☑ 0121-675 4722; www.bmag.org.uk; Trinity Rd, Aston; house adult/child £4/free, grounds free; ⊙ noon-4pm Tue-Sun mid-Apr–Oct) About 3 miles north of the centre, set in lush grounds, this well-preserved hall was built in extravagant Jacobean style between 1618 and 1635. The sumptuous interiors are full of friezes, moulded ceilings and tapestries. Trains run from New St to Aston station (£2, eight minutes, every 10 minutes), from where it's a 10-minute walk.

Tours

Big Brum Buz BUS TOUR
(www.birmingham-tours.co.uk; day ticket adult/child £12/5; ⊘Sat & Sun May-Sep) Hop-on/hop-off bus tour. On the first Sunday of the month from May to October, it operates as the Museum Heritage Bus (adult/child £5/free) with a different schedule and stops.

Sherborne Wharf Boat Trips BOAT CRUISE
(☏0121-455 6163; www.sherbornewharf.co.uk; Sherborne St; adult/child £8/6; ⊘11.30am, 1pm, 2.30pm & 4pm daily mid-Apr–Oct, Sat & Sun Nov–mid-Apr) Nostalgic narrow-boat cruises from the quayside by the International Convention Centre.

Festivals & Events

Crufts Dog Show ANIMAL SHOW
(www.crufts.org.uk; ⊘Mar) The world's greatest collection of pooches on parade, held annually at the National Exhibition Centre.

Birmingham Pride GAY
(www.birminghampride.com; ⊘May) One of the biggest and most colourful celebrations of gay and lesbian culture in the country.

Frankfurt Christmas Market & Craft Fair CHRISTMAS MARKET
(www.birmingham.gov.uk/frankfurtmarket; ⊘mid-Nov–mid-Dec) Some 200 food, drink and craft stalls from Birmingham's twin city in Germany and from local purveyors fill the centre during the UK's largest Christmas market.

Sleeping

Most Birmingham hotels are aimed at business travellers, ensuring high prices during the week. Look out for cheap deals at weekends or for longer stays. B&Bs are concentrated outside the centre in Acocks Green (to the southeast) or Edgbaston and Selly Oak (to the southwest).

Birmingham Central Backpackers HOSTEL £
(☏0121-643 0033; www.birminghambackpackers.com; 58 Coventry St; dm/d from £14/36; @ ☏) Despite the railway-bridge-right-next-door setting, Birmingham's purple and turquoise backpacker hostel is recommendable for its convenience to the bus station and choice of clean, multicoloured dorms or Japanese-style pods. Excellent facilities include a lounge with DVDs, Wii, an Xbox and PlayStation, a bar and a self-catering kitchen. You mightn't need the latter – breakfast and an evening snack buffet are free.

★Hotel La Tour HOTEL £££
(☏0121-718 8000; http://hotel-latour.co.uk; Albert St; d from £100; ❊ ☏) Sunlight streams through floor-to-ceiling windows into the public areas and spacious rooms of this state-of-the-art boutique hotel, purpose-built in 2012. Tech-savvy room features include digitally controlled 'do not disturb' signs and media hubs. There's a 24-hour gym and a swish Modern British restaurant, Aalto.

Hotel du Vin BOUTIQUE HOTEL £££
(☏0121-200 0600; www.hotelduvin.com; Church St; d from £115; @ ☏) Housed in the handsome Victorian precincts of the former Birmingham Eye Hospital, this red-brick beauty has real class, with wrought-iron balustrades, classical murals and seasoned charms. Art deco–inspired rooms have spectacular bathrooms; there's a pampering spa and a gym; a bistro with shabby-chic worn floorboards and a stellar wine list; plus a pub and lounge bar with comfy, duffed-up leather furniture.

Bloc HOTEL £££
(☏0121-212 1223; www.blochotels.com; St Paul's, Caroline St; d from £90; ❊ ☏) In the Jewellery Quarter, Bloc excels in sharp, contemporary pod design. Rooms are tiny but space is cleverly stretched – flatscreen TVs are built into walls; storage is under-bed; and bathrooms are compact but with luxe shower-heads. Rooms come with window or without. Good online specials.

Westbourne Lodge B&B £££
(☏0121-429 1003; www.westbournelodge.co.uk; Fountain Rd; s/d/f from £49.50/69.50/79.50; P @ ☏) This popular B&B is conveniently located about 2 miles west out in the peaceful suburb of Edgbaston (follow the A456). Rooms are a little chintzy but spacious, and there's a pleasant terrace to enjoy in summer.

Eating

Dining options span cool cafes and cosy pubs to gastronomic extravaganzas. For cheap curries, try the Balti Triangle. Spice is also on the menu at inexpensive restaurants throughout Chinatown, on the southwestern side of the Bullring shopping mall.

Canalside Cafe
CAFE **£**

(☑0121-643 3170; 35 Worcester Bar, Gas St; dishes £3.95-4.95; ⊘9am-11pm) Narrow boats glide past the terrace of this 18th-century lock-keeper's cottage, where the low-ceilinged interior is strung with nautical paraphernalia and warmed by an open fire. Home-cooked meals such as cottage pie, lasagne and stroganoff are chalked on the blackboard alongside vegetarian (and vegan) specials. Drop by for a cuppa and cake, or a real ale or cider.

Le Truc
FRENCH **££**

(☑0121-622 7050; http://letruc.co.uk; 21 Ladywell Way; mains £11.50-23; ⊘5-10pm Mon-Fri, 10am-10pm Sat & Sun) Bulldog murals, chandeliers, Scrabble tiles and a cassette-covered DJ console at this funky independent bistro form the backdrop for authentic French regional dishes, served with a contemporary and/or British twist. Regular events include Sunday brunch with 'lashings of Bloody Marys'.

Pushkar
INDIAN **££**

(☑0121-643 7978; www.pushkardining.com; 245 Broad St; 2-/3-course lunch menus £10/13, mains £7.25-17; ⊘noon-2.30pm & 5-11.30pm Mon-Fri, 5-11.30pm Sat & Sun) Classy North Indian and Punjabi cuisine is served up in this glass-fronted, white tableclothed, gold-trimmed dining room. The elegant presentation extends to boxed menus and serviette-wrapped naan bread as well as stunning cocktails. Lunch menus are an excellent deal.

adam's
MODERN BRITISH **£££**

(☑0121-643 3745; www.adamsrestaurant.co.uk; 21a Bennett's Hill; 3-course lunch menu £32, 5-/9-course menu £50/80; ⊘noon-2pm & 7-9.30pm Tue-Sat) In a small but snazzy dining room with suspended lighting and a space-defying, trompe-l'œil-effect photo of a Victorian columned hallway, Birmingham's newest Michelin-starred restaurant wows with intricately prepared and presented flavour combinations. Five- and nine-course tasting menus are available at lunch and dinner (nine-course only Friday and Saturday). Book well ahead.

★Simpsons
MODERN BRITISH **£££**

(☑0121-454 3434; www.simpsonsrestaurant. co.uk; 20 Highfield Rd; 3-course lunch menu £40, mains £21-27; ⊘noon-2pm & 7-9.30pm Mon-Sat, to 2.30pm Sun) It's worth making the journey 2.5 miles southwest of the centre to this gorgeous Georgian mansion in leafy Edgbaston for Michelin-starred chef Andreas Antona's sensational creations. You can also stay the night in one of four luxurious bedrooms upstairs (£160 to £225; Tuesday to Saturday only), or take an all-day cookery class (£135 including three-course lunch, Saturdays). Reservations recommended.

Drinking & Nightlife

Nightlife hubs in Birmingham include Broad St (aka the 'golden mile' – some say for the prevalence of fake tan here), which has mainstream pubs and clubs as well as theatres and cinemas.

South of New St station, defunct pubs and warehouses have found new life as bars and clubs; Chinatown's **Arcadian Centre** (www. thearcadian.co.uk; Hurst St) is the gateway to this hedonistic quarter, with numerous party bars and dancing spots.

Post-industrial Digbeth has alternative clubs and club events in and around the Custard Factory (p407).

BALTI TRIANGLE

Birmingham's famous Balti Triangle (www.balti-birmingham.co.uk), 2.5 miles southeast of the centre, is formed by Ladypool Rd, Stoney Lane and Stratford Rd. Dozens of restaurants here serve balti, a Pakistani-inspired one-pot curry, as well as soft drinks, fruit juices and lassis (yoghurt shakes), and diners can bring their own beer or wine.

The Balti Triangle is liveliest at night, especially on Fridays. Take bus 3, 5, 6, 31 or 37 from Selfridges stop PA3 (£1.90, 30 minutes, every five minutes).

Saleem's Restaurant & Sweet House (☑0121-449 1861; www.saleemsrestaurant.com; 256-258 Ladypool Rd; mains £6-8; ⊘noon-midnight Mon-Sat, 9am-midnight Sun) This long-established Balti Triangle restaurant is understandably popular for its generous portions of balti and tasty milk-based Indian sweets.

Al Faisal's (☑0121-449 5695; www.alfaisal.co.uk; 136-140 Stoney Lane; mains £7-8; ⊘noon-midnight) This Balti Triangle favourite serves delicious dishes from the mountains of Kashmir, as well as for classic Birmingham baltis.

★ **Jekyll & Hyde**   PUB

(☎ 0121-236 0345; www.thejekyllandhyde.co.uk; 28 Steelhouse Lane; ☺ noon-11pm Mon-Thu, to 2am Fri & Sat) Potent cocktails (or rather 'elixirs, concoctions and potions') at this trippy spot are served in sweets jars, watering cans, teapots and miniature bathtubs – even a wash bag (with a rum-mint toothpaste and Kaffir lime). Downstairs, Mr Hyde's emporium has a cosy drawing room and *Alice in Wonderland*–themed courtyard; upstairs is Dr Jekyll's Gin Parlour.

If Jekyll & Hyde is your kind of place, check out some of independent Birmingham company Bitters 'n' Twisted's other unique properties, especially the South American–themed **Bodega Bar & Cantina** (www.bodegabirmingham.co.uk; 12 Bennett's Hill; ☺ noon-11pm Mon-Thu, to 2am Fri & Sat, to 8pm Sun); the 19th-century splendour of **Victoria** (www.thevictoriabirmingham.co.uk; 48 John Bright St; ☺ noon-midnight Sun-Wed, to 1am Thu, to 2am Fri & Sat), with awesome DJs; and rum specialist **Island Bar** (☎ 0121-632 5296; www.bar-island.co.uk; 14-16 Suffolk St Queensway; ☺ 5pm-midnight Mon-Wed, to 2am Fri & Sat, 8pm-2am Sun), with giant blow-ups of Hawaiian beaches. All serve top-notch food too.

Lost & Found   BAR

(www.the-lostandfound.co.uk; 8 Bennett's Hill; ☺ 11am-11pm Mon-Thu, to midnight Fri, 10am-midnight Sat, 11am-9pm Sun) Fictitious Victorian-era explorer/professor Hettie G Watson is the inspiration for the botanical library theme of this bar in an 1869-built former bank. Inside the domed entrance, elevated seating is surrounded by plants, birdcages, books and maps, while a bookcase conceals the entrance to Hettie's 'secret emporium' bar (try your luck around 7.30pm on a Friday or Saturday).

Wellington   PUB

(www.thewellingtonrealale.co.uk; 37 Bennett's Hill; ☺ 10am-midnight) The pastel wallpaper,

---

timber bar and polished brass give the impression the Welly is frozen in time, but this specialist real ale pub has just been spruced up and has gained a new roof terrace. Its 16 hand-pulled beers (and three ciders) include favourites from Black Country and Wye Valley as well as rare brews.

Bacchus   BA

(☎ 0121-632 5445; www.nicholsonspubs.co.uk; Burlington Arcade, New St; ☺ 11am-11pm Sun-Thu, to 1am Fri & Sat) Beneath the Burlington arcade, down a faux marble-encased staircase crumbling pillars and giant Grecian murals give way to soaring medieval-style stone arches, swords, suits of armour and candelabras. All of this gives the darkened drinking den the ambience of a decadent underworld

Old Joint Stock   PUB

(☎ 0121-200 1892; www.oldjointstocktheatre.co.uk; 4 Temple Row West; ☺ 11am-11pm Mon-Sat, noon-5pm Sun; ☎) A vast high-ceilinged temple of a pub, housed in a former bank and beloved by a high-spirited after-work crowd. Upstairs, an 80-seat theatre puts on plays and comedy shows.

Q Club   CLU

(www.qclub.co.uk; 212 Corporation St; ☺ hours vary) The old brick Central Hall that housed this legendary club is on its last legs, but the 'Q' is still going strong. DJs pump out boisterous electro, house, jungle and old-school club classics.

☆ **Entertainment**

Tickets for most Birmingham events can be purchased through entertainment mega corp **TicketWeb** (☎ 0870 060 0100; www.ticketweb.co.uk).

Free publications listing gigs and events include the excellent *Brum Notes* (www.brumnotes.com).

Live Music

The **National Indoor Arena** (☎ 0121-780 4141; www.thenia.co.uk; King Edwards Rd), north of Brindley Pl, and the **National Exhibition Centre Arena** (☎ 0121-780 4141; www.thenec.co.uk; off the M42), near Birmingham Airport, host stadium fillers from the world of rock and pop.

Sunflower Lounge   LIVE MUSIC

(☎ 0121-632 6756; www.thesunflowerlounge.com; 76 Smallbrook Queensway; ☺ hours vary) This quirky little indie bar matches a magnificent alternative soundtrack with a regular program of live gigs and DJ nights.

GAY & LESBIAN BIRMINGHAM

Birmingham's loud and lively gay scene is centred on the **Gay Village** south of the Bullring around Hurst St. The area throngs with the bold, bright and beautiful on weekend nights and peaks during May's Birmingham Pride (p408) festivities. For up-to-the-minute information on the Brummie scene, check www.visitgaybrum.com.

Jam House

LIVE MUSIC

(www.thejamhouse.com; 3-5 St Paul's Sq; ☺ 6pm-midnight Tue & Wed, to 1am Thu, to 2am Fri & Sat) Pianist Jools Holland was the brains behind this moody, smart-casual music venue (dress accordingly). Acts range from jazz big bands to famous soul crooners. Over 21s only.

Symphony Hall

CLASSICAL MUSIC

(☎ 0121-345 0600; www.symphonyhall.co.uk; Broad St) The City of Birmingham Symphony Orchestra's official home is the ultramodern Symphony Hall. Shows also take place in the handsome auditorium at the Town Hall.

O2 Academy

LIVE MUSIC

(www.o2academybirmingham.co.uk; 16-18 Horse-fair, Bristol St; ☺ box office 12-4pm Mon-Sat) Birmingham's leading venue for big-name rockers and tribute bands as well as up-and-coming talent.

Theatre & Cinema

Birmingham Repertory Theatre

THEATRE

(☎ 0121-236 4455; www.birmingham-rep.co.uk; Centenary Sq) Founded over a century ago, 'the Rep' now has three performance spaces – the Main House; the more experimental Door; and a new 300-seat studio theatre presenting edgy drama and musicals, with an emphasis on contemporary work.

Electric Cinema

CINEMA

(www.theelectric.co.uk; 47-49 Station St; standard/ deluxe seats £7.80/13.50) Topped by its art deco sign, this is the UK's oldest working cinema, operating since 1909. It screens mainly art-house films. Be waited upon in plush two-seater sofas or have a drink in the small bar (complete with an absinthe fountain).

Hippodrome

THEATRE

(☎ 0844 338 5000; www.birminghamhippodrome. com; Hurst St) Hosts the Birmingham Royal Ballet.

Sport

Birmingham has three football (soccer) clubs within striking distance: Birmingham City Football Club, West Bromwich Albion ('West Brom') and, most famously, Aston Villa Football Club.

Villa Park

FOOTBALL

(☎ 0800 612 0970; www.avfc.co.uk; Trinity Rd, Witton; tours adult/child from £12.95/7.95) Aston Villa Football Club's 19th-century Villa Park is one of the country's largest stadiums. Behind-the-scenes tours (three times weekly by reservation) include the dressing rooms, tunnel

and pitch. The ground is 2 miles north of Birmingham. Trains run from New St to Witton (£2, nine minutes, half-hourly), a five-minute walk away; and every 10 minutes to Aston, a 15-minute walk. Tickets and merchandise are available from the Aston Villa City Centre Store (☎ 0121-326 1559; www.avfc.co.uk; New St; ☺ 9.30am-6pm Mon-Sat, 11am-3pm Sun).

🛍 Shopping

Bustling markets sell fresh food and cheap imported clothes in the pedestrian precincts surrounding the Bullring.

Atop the revitalised New St train station, the gleaming Grand Central Birmingham shopping mall (www.grandcentralbirmingham.com), opening 2015, is anchored by a massive John Lewis department store.

Great Western Arcade

SHOPPING ARCADE

(www.greatwesternarcade.co.uk; btwn Colmore Row & Temple Row; ☺ arcade 9am-11pm Mon-Sat, 11am-8pm Sun, shop hours vary) This glass-roofed, tiled-floored Victorian-era arcade is a jewel filled with mostly independent shops.

Bullring

MALL

(www.bullring.co.uk; St Martin's Circus; ☺ 10am-8pm Mon-Fri, 9am-8pm Sat, 11am-5pm Sun) Split into two vast retail spaces – the East Mall and West Mall – the Bullring has all the international brands and chain cafes you could ask for, plus the standout architectural wonder of Selfridges, which looks out over the city like the compound eye of a giant robot insect.

Mailbox

MALL

(www.mailboxlife.com; Wharfside St; ☺ 10am-6pm Mon-Wed, to 7pm Thu-Sat, 11am-5pm Sun) Birmingham's stylish waterside shopping experience, the redevelopment of the former Royal Mail sorting office, comes complete with designer hotels, a fleet of upmarket restaurants, the luxury department store Harvey Nichols and designer boutiques. Its snazzy metallic extension, The Cube, houses Marco Pierre White's Steakhouse Bar and Grill on the 25th floor.

🛈 Information

As in most large cities, it's wise to avoid walking alone late at night in unlit areas. In particular, the centre – especially south of the Bullring – can be rowdy with revellers on weekend nights.

Digbeth bus station and its surrounds can be quite rough after dark.

Birmingham Children's Hospital (☎ 0121-333 9999; www.bch.nhs.uk; Steelhouse Lane) Has an Accident & Emergency department.

Heart of England Tourist Board (☑ 01905-887690; www.visitheartofengland.com)

Heartlands Hospital (☑ 0121-424 2000; www.heartofengland.nhs.uk; Bordesley Green East) Located 4 miles east of the centre; has an Accident & Emergency department.

Police Station (☑ 101; Steelhouse Lane)

Tourist Office (☑ 0844 888 3883; www.visit-birmingham.com; cnr Corporation & New Sts; ⊙ 9am-5pm Mon-Sat, 10am-4pm Sun) Kiosk with racks of info on activities, transport and sights. There's a branch at the Library of Birmingham (p401).

❶ Getting There & Away

AIR

Birmingham Airport is about 8 miles east of the centre, with direct flights to destinations around the UK and Europe as well as direct long-haul routes to Dubai, India, the USA and Canada.

BUS

Most intercity buses run from **Birmingham Coach Station** (Digbeth High St), but the X20 to Stratford-upon-Avon (£5, 1¼ hours, hourly) leaves from a stop on Moor St, just north of the Pavilions mall.

National Express runs coaches between Birmingham and major cities across the country, including the following destinations:

London Victoria £12.60, 2¾ hours, every 30 minutes

Manchester £14.40, 3 hours, 14 daily

Oxford £15.20, 1½ to four hours, eight daily

TRAIN

Most long-distance trains leave from New St station, but Chiltern Railways runs to London Marylebone (£49, 2½ hours, half-hourly) from Birmingham Snow Hill, and London Midland runs to Stratford-upon-Avon (£7.30, one hour, half-hourly) from Snow Hill and Moor St stations.

Services from New St include the following:

Derby £15.90, 45 minutes, four per hour

Leicester £12.90, one hour, two per hour

London Euston £27.50, 1½ hours, every 15 minutes

Manchester £34.40, 1¾ hours, every half hour

Nottingham £17.40, 1¼ hours, three per hour

Shrewsbury £13.60, one hour, two per hour

❶ Getting Around

TO/FROM THE AIRPORT

Fast and convenient trains run regularly between New St and Birmingham International station (£3.50, 20 minutes, every 10 minutes), or take bus 97 or 900 (£5, 30 minutes, every 30 minutes) from Moor St Queensway, which runs 24 hours.

A taxi from the airport to the centre costs about £30.

CAR

All the big car-hire companies have town offices.

Avis (☑ 0844 544 6038; www.avis.co.uk; 17 Horse Fair)

Enterprise Rent-a-Car (☑ 0121-643 7743; www.enterprise.co.uk; 9-10 Suffolk St Queensway)

PUBLIC TRANSPORT

Local buses run from a convenient hub on Corporation St, just north of the New St junction. For routes, pick up a free copy of the *Network Birmingham Map & Guide* from the tourist office. Single-trip tickets start from £1.70.

Commuter trains to destinations in the north of Birmingham (including Aston) operate from Moor St train station, close to Selfridges.

The 2015-opening extension of Birmingham's single tram line, the **Metro** (www.travelmetro.co.uk), links New St Station with Wolverhampton via the Jewellery Quarter, West Bromwich and Dudley. Tickets start from £2.20. A further extension from New St to Birmingham Town Hall and Centenary Sq is due to open in 2017.

Various saver tickets covering buses and trains are available from **Network West Midlands** (☑ 0121-2147 7550; www.networkwest-midlands.com; ⊙ 8.30am-5.30pm Mon-Sat) at New St Station.

TOA Taxis (☑ 0121-427 8888; www.toataxis.co.uk) is a reliable black-cab taxi firm.

WARWICKSHIRE

Warwickshire could have been just another picturesque English county of rolling hills and market towns were it not for the birth of a rather well-known wordsmith. William Shakespeare was born and died in Stratford-upon-Avon, and the sights linked to his life are a magnet for tourists from around the globe. Famous Warwick Castle attracts similar crowds. Elsewhere visitor numbers dwindle, but Kenilworth has atmospheric castle ruins and Coventry claims two extraordinary cathedrals and an unmissable motoring museum.

❶ Information

Shakespeare Country (www.shakespeare-country.co.uk)

❶ Getting There & Around

Coventry is the main transport hub, with frequent rail connections to London Euston and Birmingham New St.

Coventry

POP 325,950

Dominated today by its twin spires and identikit tower blocks, Coventry was once a bustling hub for the production of cloth, clocks, bicycles, automobiles and munitions. It was this last industry that drew the German Luftwaffe in WWII: on the night of 14 November 1940, the city was so badly blitzed that the Nazis coined a new verb, *coventrieren*, meaning 'to flatten'. Postwar planners filled in the gaps with dull concrete developments, and the city faced a further setback with the collapse of the British motor industry in the 1980s. A handful of medieval streets that escaped the bombers offer a glimpse of old Coventry.

⊙ Sights

★ **Coventry Transport Museum** MUSEUM
(☎024-7623 4270; www.transport-museum.com; Hales St; ⊙10am-5pm) FREE This stupendous museum has hundreds of 'cars' spanning the ages, from horseless carriages to jet-powered, land-speed record breakers. There's a brushed stainless steel DeLorean DMC-12 (of *Back to the Future* fame) with gull-wing doors, alongside a gorgeous Jaguar E-type, a Daimler armoured car and, for 1970s British design oddity enthusiasts, a Triumph TR7 and an Austin Allegro 'Special'. View the Thrust SCC, the current holder of the World Land Speed Record and the Thrust 2, the previous record holder.

Kids will be engrossed by the atmospheric 'Coventry Blitz Experience' and the Thrust speed simulator (£1.50).

Coventry Cathedral CATHEDRAL
(☎024-7652 1200; www.coventrycathedral.org.uk; Priory Row; adult/child £8/5.75; ⊙10am-4pm) The evocative ruins of St Michael's Cathedral, built around 1300 but destroyed by Nazi incendiary bombs in the Blitz, stand as a permanent memorial to Coventry's darkest hour and as a symbol of peace and reconciliation. Climb the Gothic spire's 180 steps for panoramic views (adult/child £2.75/1.50).

Symbolically adjoining St Michael's Cathedral's sandstone walls is the Sir Basil Spence–designed modernist architectural masterpiece, Coventry Cathedral, with a futuristic organ, stained glass and Jacob Epstein statue of the devil and St Michael.

Herbert Art Gallery & Museum GALLERY
(☎024-7623 7521; www.theherbert.org; Jordan Well; ⊙10am-4pm Mon-Sat, noon-4pm Sun) FREE Behind Coventry's twin cathedrals, the Herbert has an eclectic collection of paintings and sculptures (including work by TS Lowry and Stanley Spencer), a delightful cafe and lots of activities aimed at kids. The history gallery and thought-provoking gallery on peace and reconciliation are worth a look-in.

St Mary's Guildhall HISTORIC BUILDING
(☎024-7683 3328; www.stmarysguildhall.co.uk; Bayley Lane; ⊙10am-4pm Sun-Thu mid-Mar–Sep) FREE This hall is where the town's trades came together in the Middle Ages to discuss town affairs. As one of England's finest guildhalls, it was chosen to be a jail for Mary Queen of Scots. Stained-glass windows glorify the kings of England; further down the hall stands WC Marshall's statue of Lady

---

WORTH A TRIP

RUGBY

Warwickshire's second-largest hub, Rugby (population 100,500) is an attractive market town whose history dates back to the Iron Age. But it's most famous for the sport that takes its name, and is a place of pilgrimage for fans.

The game was invented at Rugby School in 1823 when William Webb Ellis is said to have caught the ball during a football match and broke the rules by running with it. The school itself is closed to the public, but you can peek at the hallowed ground through the gates just across from the Webb Ellis Rugby Football Museum (☎01788-533217; www.rugbyfootballmuseum.org.uk; 5-6 Matthews St; ⊙9.30am-5pm Mon-Sat) FREE. Intriguing exhibits at the little museum include the evolution of the ball and historic team photos from the Webb Ellis Cup (aka the Rugby World Cup). The museum is attached to the first rugby football workshop, established in 1842, which still manufactures footballs today.

Rugby is 13 miles east of Coventry, served by regular trains (£5.50, 10 minutes, up to four hourly). Trains also serve Birmingham (£9.20, 40 minutes, two to four per hour) and Leicester (£13.60, one hour, hourly).

Godiva. Look out for the medieval tapestry depicting Henry VI.

🛏 Sleeping & Eating

Coventry makes an easy day trip from Birmingham but if you want to stay, the tourist office can help find accommodation.

Spon St, better known as 'Medieval Spon St', has a smattering of restaurants, pubs and cafes as well as boutiques in its half-timbered buildings.

Playwrights   CAFE **££**
(📋024-7623 1441; www.playwrightsrestaurant.co.uk; 4-6 Hay Lane; mains £8-19.50; ⊘9am to late) On the lovely cobbled lane leading from Earl St to the cathedral, this bright, inviting cafe, bar and bistro is as good for breakfast as it is for lunch or an intimate dinner. Tables are flung out on the cobbles in warmer weather.

ℹ Information

Tourist Office (📋024-7622 5616; www.visitcoventry.co.uk; ⊘9.30am-4.30pm Mon-Fri, 10am-4.30pm Sat, 10am-noon & 1-4.30pm Sun) Housed in the restored tower of St Michael's Cathedral.

ℹ Getting There & Away

From the main bus station, National Express buses serve most parts of the country. Buses X17 and X19 (every 15 minutes) go to Kenilworth (£1.90, 25 minutes), Leamington Spa (£3.35, 50 minutes) and Warwick (£5, 1¼ hours).

Trains go south to London Euston (£45.90, 1¼ hours, every 10 to 20 minutes) and you will rarely have to wait for a train to Birmingham (£3.40, 30 minutes, every 10 minutes).

Warwick

POP 31,350

Regularly name-checked by Shakespeare, Warwick was the ancestral seat of the Earls of Warwick, who played a pivotal role in the Wars of the Roses. Despite a devastating fire in 1694, Warwick remains a treasure-house of medieval architecture with rich veins of history and charming streets, dominated by the soaring turrets of Warwick Castle.

◉ Sights

★**Warwick Castle**   CASTLE
(📋0871 265 2000; www.warwick-castle.com; castle adult/child £22.80/16.80, castle & dungeon £28.80/24, Kingdom Ticket incl castle, dungeon & exhibition £30.60/27; ⊘10am-6pm Apr-Sep, to 5pm

Oct-Mar; 🅿) Founded in 1068 by William the Conqueror, stunningly preserved Warwick Castle is the biggest show in town. The ancestral home of the Earls of Warwick remains impressively intact, and the Tussauds Group has filled the interior with attractions that bring the castle's rich history to life in a flamboyant but undeniably family-friendly way. As well as waxworks populating the private apartments there are jousting tournaments, daily trebuchet-firings, themed evenings and a dungeon. Discounted online tickets provide fast-track entry. Parking costs £6.

Collegiate Church of St Mary   CHURCH
(📋01926-492909; www.stmaryswarwick.org.uk; Old Sq; church entry by £2 donation, tower adult/child £2.50/1; ⊘10am-6pm Apr-Sep, to 4.30pm Oct-Mar) This 1123-founded Norman church was badly damaged in the Great Fire of Warwick in 1694 but is packed with 16th- and 17th-century tombs. Highlights include the Norman crypt with a 14th-century extension; the impressive Beauchamp Chapel, built between 1442 and 1464 to enshrine the mortal remains of the Earls of Warwick; and, up 134 steps, the tower, which provides supreme views over town (kids must be aged over eight).

Lord Leycester Hospital   HISTORIC BUILDING
(📋01926-491422; www.lordleycester.com; High St; adult/child £4.90/3.90, garden only £2; ⊘10am-5pm Tue-Sun Apr-Sep, to 4.30pm Oct-Mar) A survivor of the 1694 fire, the wonderfully wonky Lord Leycester Hospital has been used as a retirement home for soldiers (but not as a hospital) since 1571. Visitors can wander around the chapel, guildhall, regimental museum and restored walled garden, which includes a knot garden and a Norman arch.

Warwickshire Museum   MUSEUM
(📋01926-412501; Market Pl; ⊘10am-5pm Tue-Sat year-round, 11.30am-5pm Sun Apr-Sep) **FREE** Housed in Warwick's striking 17th-century market hall, Warwickshire Museum has some entertaining displays on local history and the Warwick sea dragons (Jurassic-era sea creatures).

🛏 Sleeping & Eating

Reasonably priced B&Bs line Emscote Rd, which runs northeast towards Leamington Spa (2 miles east of Warwick), a genteel spa town that's almost a suburb of Warwick.

Tilted Wig   PUB **££**
(📋01926-400110; www.tiltedwigwarwick.co.uk; 11 Market Pl; d £65-90, mains £8.50-14; 🅿🛜) Bang

Warwick

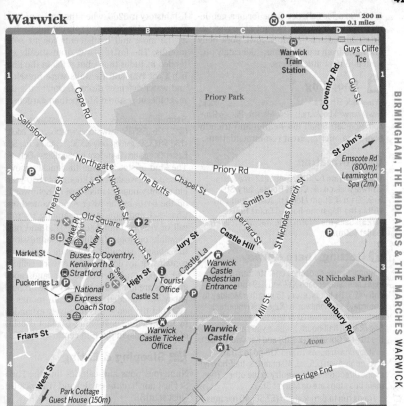

on the epicentral Market Pl, this brilliantly named 17th-century Georgian inn has four freshly refurbished, snug but comfortable rooms and some of the better pub grub in town, such as roast duck breast in port wine reduction. Guests get a three-course meal for just £10 per person.

Park Cottage Guest House B&B **££**

(☎01926-410319; www.parkcottagewarwick.co.uk; 113 West St; s £55-70, d £75-90; 🅿🐾) Southwest of the centre, this stand-alone 16th-century wattle-and-daub building once served as the dairy for Warwick Castle. There are seven pretty rooms, each with a teddy bear, original floors and a courtyard garden.

Merchants BRASSERIE **££**

(☎01926-403833; www.merchantswarwick.co.uk; Swan St; mains £10.50-19.90; ⊗noon-9pm Mon-Thu, to 9.30pm Fri & Sat) With stylish leather furniture and chalkboard menus, this restaurant and wine bar specialises in steaks.

Warwick

⊙ Top Sights
1 Warwick Castle C4

⊙ Sights
2 Collegiate Church of St Mary B3
3 Lord Leycester Hospital A4
4 Warwickshire Museum A3

⊜ Sleeping
5 Tilted Wig A3

⊗ Eating
6 Merchants B3
7 Tailors A3

⊜ Shopping
8 Warwick Books A3

Tailors MODERN BRITISH **£££**

(☎01926-410590; www.tailorsrestaurant.co.uk; 22 Market Pl; 2-/3-course lunch menu £15/19, 2-/3-course dinner menu £28/32.50; ⊗noon-1.45pm

& 6.30-9pm Tue-Sat) Set in a former gentlemen's tailor shop, this elegant eatery serves prime ingredients – guinea fowl, pork belly and lamb from named farms – delicately presented in neat little towers.

🔒 Shopping

Warwick Books BOOKS
(www.warwickbooks.net; 24 Market Pl; ⊙9am-5pm Mon-Sat) Small but helpful and friendly bookshop offering great recommendations.

ℹ️ Information

Tourist Office (✆01926-492212; www.visitwarwick.co.uk; Court House, Jury St; ⊙9.30am-4.30pm Mon-Fri, 10am-4pm Sat) Within the flagstone-floored Court House (1725). Sells the informative *Warwick Town Trail* leaflet (50p).

ℹ️ Getting There & Away

National Express coaches operate from Puckerings Lane. Stagecoach X17 and X19 run to Coventry (£3, 1¼ hours, every 15 minutes Monday to Saturday), via Kenilworth (£2.80, 30 minutes). On Sunday, take bus G1 or 18A for Leamington Sap (£3.35, half-hourly), where you can pick up the U17 for Coventry (£3.10) and Kenilworth (£2).

Stagecoach buses 16 and X18 go to Stratford-upon-Avon (£5.40, 40 minutes, half-hourly) in one direction, and Coventry in the other. The main bus stops are on Market St.

Trains run to Birmingham (£7.50, 40 minutes, half-hourly), Stratford-upon-Avon (£5.40, 30 minutes, hourly) and London (£28.80, 1½ hours, every 20 minutes), from the station, northeast of the centre.

Kenilworth

POP 22,410

A refreshing counterpoint to the commercialism of nearby Warwick's royal ruin, the atmospheric ruin of Kenilworth Castle was the inspiration for Walter Scott's *Kenilworth*, and it still feels pretty inspiring today. It's an easy deviation off the A46 between Warwick and Coventry.

👁️ Sights

Kenilworth Castle CASTLE
(EH; ✆01926-852078; www.english-heritage.org.uk; adult/child £9.30/5.60; ⊙10am-5pm Apr-Oct, reduced hours Nov-Mar; 🅿️) This spine-tingling ruin sprawls among fields and hedges on Kenilworth's outskirts. Built in the 1120s, the castle survived the longest siege in Eng-

lish history in 1266, when the forces of Lord Edward (later Edward I) threw themselves at the moat and battlements for six solid months. The fortress was dramatically extended in Tudor times, but it fell in the English Civil War and its walls were breached and water defences drained. Don't miss the magnificent restored Elizabethan gardens.

Stoneleigh Abbey HISTORIC BUILDING
(✆01926-858535; www.stoneleighabbey.org; adult/child £8/3.50, garden only £3.50; ⊙tours Tue-Sun Easter-Oct, garden 11am-5pm Tue-Sun Easter-Oct; 🅿️) The kind of stately home that makes movie directors go weak at the knees, this 850-year-old country house 2 miles east of Kenilworth, off the B4115 by the River Avon, name-drops Charles I and Jane Austen among its roll-call of visitors. Completed in 1726 and only viewable on tours (included in admission), the abbey's splendid Palladian west wing contains richly detailed plasterwork ceilings and wood-panelled rooms. The landscaped grounds are fine picnic territory. The original abbey was founded by Cistercian monks in 1154, but the house was massively expanded by the wealthy Leigh family (distant cousins of the Austens) in the 16th century.

🛏️ Sleeping & Eating

Numerous pubs and eateries line the High St (just north of the castle) and Warwick Rd (just south).

The Old Bakery B&B ££
(✆01926-864111; www.theoldbakery.eu; 12 High St; s/d from £75/95; 🅿️🛜) Located down High St east of the castle, this B&B has attractively attired modern rooms and a cosy, welcoming bar serving real ales on the ground floor.

Harringtons on the Hill MODERN BRITISH ££
(✆01926-852074; www.harringtonsonthehill.com; 42 Castle Hill; mains £10-19; ⊙noon-3pm & 6-11pm Mon-Sat, noon-4pm Sun) In an adorable bow-fronted cottage festooned with flower boxes opposite Kenilworth Castle, chef Ryan New recreates his success at some of London's top tables. Dishes include hot smoked salmon with bubble and squeak and soft poached egg, and char-grilled swordfish with chorizo – at impressively reasonable prices.

ℹ️ Information

Browse the tourist brochures at the town **library** (✆01908-276 2451; www.kenilworthlibrary.org; 11 Smalley Pl; ⊙9am-5.30pm Mon, Tue, Thu & Fri, 10.30am-5.30pm Wed, 9am-1pm Sat).

ℹ Getting There & Away

From Monday to Saturday, buses X17 and X19 run every 15 minutes from Coventry to Kenilworth (£3.10, 25 minutes) and on to Leamington Spa (£3.10, 15 minutes) and Warwick (£3.35, 20 minutes). On Sundays, take bus U17 for Coventry (£3.10) and Leamington Spa (£2). At Leamington Spa you can change to bus G1 or 18A for Warwick (£3.35, half-hourly).

Stratford-upon-Avon

POP 27,830

The author of some of the most quoted lines ever written in the English language, William Shakespeare was born in Stratford in 1564 and died here in 1616. The five houses linked to his life form the centrepiece of a tourist attraction that verges on a cult of personality.

Experiences in this unmistakably Tudor town range from the touristy (medieval re-creations and Bard-themed tearooms) to the humbling (Shakespeare's modest grave in Holy Trinity Church) and the sublime (taking in a play by the world-famous Royal Shakespeare Company).

◉ Sights & Activities

★ Shakespeare's Birthplace
HISTORIC BUILDING

(☑ 01789-204016; www.shakespeare.org.uk; Henley St; incl Nash's House & New Place and Halls Croft £15.90/9.50; ⊙9am-5.30pm Jul-Sep, to 5pm Oct-Jun) Start your Shakespeare quest at the house where the world's most popular playwright supposedly spent his childhood days. In fact, the jury is still out on whether this really was Shakespeare's birthplace, but devotees of the Bard have been dropping in since at least the 19th century, leaving their signatures scratched onto the windows. Set behind a modern facade, the house has restored Tudor rooms, live presentations from famous Shakespearean characters, and an engaging exhibition on Stratford's favourite son.

Nash's House & New Place
HISTORIC SITE

(☑ 01789-204016; www.shakespeare.org.uk; cnr Chapel St & Chapel Lane; incl Shakespeare's Birthplace & Halls Croft £15.90/9.50; ⊙10am-5pm mid-Mar–Oct) When Shakespeare retired, he swapped the bright lights of London for a comfortable town house at New Pl, where he died of unknown causes in April 1616. The house was demolished in 1759, but an attractive Elizabethan knot garden occupies part

of the grounds. Archaeologists recently dug beneath the plot in search of Shakespearean treasures; their finds are displayed in the adjacent Nash's House, where Shakespeare's granddaughter Elizabeth lived. Displays describe the town's history and there's a collection of 17th-century furniture and tapestries.

Hall's Croft
HISTORIC BUILDING

(☑ 01789-204016; Old Town; incl Shakespeare's Birthplace and Nash's House & New Place £15.90/9.50; ⊙10am-5pm mid-Mar–Oct) The handsome Jacobean town house belonging to Shakespeare's daughter Susanna and her husband, respected doctor John Hall, stands south of the centre. The exhibition offers fascinating insights into medicine in the 16th and 17th centuries, and the lovely walled garden sprouts with aromatic herbs employed in medicinal preparations.

Holy Trinity Church
CHURCH

(☑ 01789-266316; www.stratford-upon-avon.org; Old Town; Shakespeare's grave adult/child £2/1; ⊙8.30am-6pm Mon-Sat, 12.30-5pm Sun Apr-Sep, reduced hours Oct-Mar) The final resting place of the Bard is said to be the most visited parish church in all of England. Inside are handsome 16th- and 17th-century tombs (particularly in the Clopton Chapel), some fabulous carvings on the choir stalls and, of course, the grave of William Shakespeare, with its ominous epitaph: 'cvrst be he yt moves my bones'.

Anne Hathaway's Cottage
HISTORIC BUILDING

(☑ 01789-204016; www.shakespeare.org.uk; Cottage Lane, Shottery; adult/child £9.50/5.50; ⊙9am-5pm mid-Mar–Oct) Before tying the knot with Shakespeare, Anne Hathaway lived in Shottery, a mile west of the centre

ℹ SHAKESPEARE HISTORIC HOMES

Five of the most important buildings associated with Shakespeare contain museums that form the core of the visitor experience at Stratford. All are run by the Shakespeare Birthplace Trust (www.shakespeare.org.uk).

Tickets for the three houses in town – Shakespeare's Birthplace, Nash's House & New Place and Halls Croft – cost adult/child £15.90/9.50. If you also visit Anne Hathaway's Cottage and Mary Arden's Farm, buy a combination ticket covering all five properties (£23.90/14).

Stratford-upon-Avon

of Stratford, in this delightful thatched farmhouse. As well as period furniture, it has gorgeous gardens and an orchard and arboretum, with examples of all the trees mentioned in Shakespeare's plays. A footpath (no bikes allowed) leads to Shottery from Evesham Pl.

Mary Arden's Farm   HISTORIC SITE, FARM
(☑ 01789-204016; www.shakespeare.org.uk; Station Rd, Wilmcote; adult/child £12.50/8; ☺ 10am-5pm mid-Mar–Oct) Shakespeare genealogists can trace the family tree to the childhood home of the Bard's mother at Wilmcote, 3 miles west of Stratford. Aimed squarely at families, the working farm traces country life over the centuries, with nature trails, falconry displays and a collection of rare-breed farm animals. You can get here on the City Sightseeing bus, or cycle via Anne Hathaway's Cottage, following the Stratford-upon-Avon Canal towpath.

Falstaff's Experience   GHOST EXPERIENCE
(☑ 01789-298070; www.falstaffsexperience.co.uk; 40 Sheep St; adult/child £5.50/3; ☺ 10.30am-5.30pm) Set in an old timbered building, Falstaff's Experience offers a ghostly take on Shakespeare's tales, with oldey-worldey walk-throughs, mannequins of Tudor celebs and live actors hamming it up like Olivier. Night-time adults-only ghost tours are led by famous mediums.

☞ Tours

Guided Town Walks   WALKING TOUR
(☑ 07855-760377; www.stratfordtownwalk.co.uk; adult/child £5/2; ☺ 11am Mon-Thu, 2pm Fri, 11am & 2pm Sat & Sun) Popular and informative two-hour guided town walks departing from Waterside, opposite Sheep St.

Stratford Town Ghost Walk   WALKING TOUR
(☑ 07855-760377; www.stratfordtownwalk.co.uk; adult/child £6/4; ☺ 7.30pm Mon & Thu-Sat)

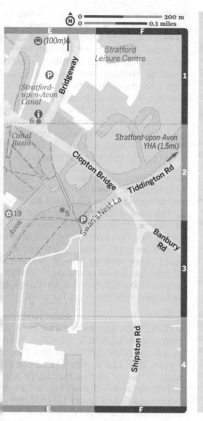

Stratford-upon-Avon

Chill-seekers can take the Stratford Town Ghost Walk departing from Waterside, opposite Sheep St.

City Sightseeing BUS TOUR
(☑ 01789-412680; www.city-sightseeing.com; adult/child £12.50/6.50; ☺ every 30min Apr-Sep, less frequently Oct-Mar) Open-top, hop-on/hop-off bus tours leave from the tourist office on Bridge Foot, rolling to each of the Shakespeare properties. Tickets are valid for 24 hours (there are also 48-hour tickets costing £19/9.50) and can be bought from the driver. On-board commentary comes in seven languages.

Avon Boating BOAT TOUR
(☑ 01789-267073; www.avon-boating.co.uk; The Boathouse, Swan's Nest Lane; river cruises adult/child £5.50/3/50; ☺ 9am-dusk Apr-Oct) Runs 40-minute river cruises that depart every 20 minutes from either side of the main bridge.

⛷ Festivals & Events

Stratford Literary Festival LITERATURE
(☑ 01789-207100; www.stratfordliteraryfestival.co.uk; ☺ Apr/May) The top event on Stratford's cultural calendar is the Stratford Literary Festival, which attracts literary big-hitters of the calibre of John Simpson and Jonathan Miller.

🛏 Sleeping

B&Bs are plentiful, particularly along Grove Rd and Evesham Pl, but vacancies can be hard to find during the high season – the tourist office can help with bookings for a £5 fee.

Stratford-upon-Avon YHA HOSTEL £
(☑ 0845 371 9661; www.yha.org.uk; Hemmingford House, Alveston; dm/d from £19/40; P@🖙) Set in a large 200-year-old mansion, 1.5 miles east of the town centre along Tiddington Rd, this superior hostel attracts travellers of all ages. Of its 32 rooms and dorms, 16 are en suite. There's a canteen, bar and kitchen.

Buses 18 and 18A run here from Bridge St. Wi-fi is available in common areas.

Legacy Falcon
HOTEL ££

(☑08444 119 005; www.legacy-hotels.co.uk; Chapel St; d/f from £83/113; P �🖥) Definitely request a room in the original 15th-century building, not the souless modern annexe or dingy 17th-century garden house of this epicentral hotel. This way you'll get the full Tudor experience – creaky floorboards, wonky timbered walls and all. Open fires blaze in the wi-fi'd public areas; rooms have wired broadband but the best asset is the unheard-of-for-Stratford free car park.

White Sails
GUESTHOUSE ££

(☑01789-550469; www.white-sails.co.uk; 85 Evesham Rd; d from £100; ❋) Plush fabrics, framed prints, brass bedsteads and shabby-chic tables and lamps set the scene at this gorgeous and intimate guesthouse on the edge of the countryside. The four individually furnished rooms come with flatscreen TVs, climate control and glamorous bathrooms.

Emsley Guesthouse
B&B ££

(☑01789-299557; www.theemsley.co.uk; 4 Arden St; d from £64; P🖥) This lovely five-bedroom Victorian property has a personable owner, very clean and attractive accommodation, and a large, pretty family room at the top with an exposed beam ceiling. Weekends require a two-night minimum stay.

Church Street Townhouse
BOUTIQUE HOTEL £££

(☑01789-262222; www.churchstreettownhouse.com; 16 Church St; d £110-200; 🖥) Some of the rooms at this exquisite hotel have free-standing baths, and all have iPod docks, flatscreen TVs and luxurious furnishings. Light sleepers should avoid room 1, nearest the bar. The building itself is a centrally located 400-year-old gem with a first-rate restaurant and bar. Minimum two-night stay on weekends.

Arden Hotel
HOTEL £££

(☑01789-298682; www.theardenhotelstratford.com; Waterside; d incl breakfast from £129; P🖥) Facing the Swan Theatre, this elegant property has a sleek brasserie and champagne bar. Rooms feature designer fabrics and bathrooms are full of polished stone.

✖ Eating

Sheep St is clustered with upmarket eating options, mostly aimed at theatre-goers (look out for good-value pre-theatre menus).

Fourteas
TEAROOM £

(☑01789-293908; www.thefourteas.co.uk; 24 Sheep St; dishes £3-7, afternoon tea with/without prosecco £17/12.50; ⏱9.30am-5pm Mon-Fri, 9am-5.30pm Sat, 11am-4pm Sun) Breaking with Stratford's Shakespearian theme, this tearoom takes the 1940s as its inspiration with beautiful old teapots, framed posters and staff in period costume. As well as premium loose-leaf teas and homemade cakes, there are hearty breakfasts, delicious sandwiches (fresh poached salmon, brie and grape), a hot dish of the day and indulgent afternoon teas.

Church Street Townhouse
BISTRO ££

(☑01789-262222; www.churchstreettownhouse.com; 16 Church St; mains £12.25-17; ⏱8am-11pm; 🖥) This lovely restaurant is a fantastic place for immersing yourself in Stratford's historic charms. The food is delightful and the ambience impeccably congenial and well presented. Music students from Shakespeare's old grammar school across the way tinkle the piano ivories daily at 5.30pm, though it can be hard to hear over the bar noise.

Lambs
MODERN EUROPEAN ££

(☑01789-292554; www.lambsrestaurant.co.uk; 12 Sheep St; mains £11.75-18.75; ⏱5-9.30pm Mon & Tue, noon-2pm & 5-9.30pm Wed-Sat, noon-2.30pm & 6-9pm Sun) Lambs swaps Shakespeare chintz in favour of Venetian blinds and modern elegance but throws in authentic 16th-century ceiling beams for good measure. The menu embraces Gressingham duck, deep-fried goats cheese and slow-roasted lamb shank, backed up by a strong wine list.

Edward Moon's
MODERN BRITISH ££

(☑01789-267069; www.edwardmoon.com; 9 Chapel St; mains £10-18; ⏱12.30-3pm & 5-10pm Mon-Fri, noon-10pm Sat & Sun) Named after a famous travelling chef who cooked up the flavours of home for the British colonial service, this snug eatery serves delicious, hearty English dishes, many livened up with herbs and spices from the East.

🍸 Drinking & Nightlife

★ Old Thatch Tavern
PUB

(http://oldthatchtavernstratford.co.uk; Greenhill St; ⏱11.30am-11pm Mon-Sat, noon-6pm Sun; 🖥) To truly appreciate Stratford's olde-worlde atmosphere, join the locals for a pint at the town's oldest pub. Built in 1470, this thatched-roofed, low-ceilinged treasure has great real ales and a gorgeous summertime courtyard.

Dirty Duck PUB

(Black Swan; Waterside; ⊙11am-11pm Mon-Sat, to 10.30pm Sun) Also called the 'Black Swan', this enchanting riverside alehouse is the only pub in England to be licensed under two names. It's a favourite thespian watering hole, with a roll-call of former regulars (Olivier, Attenborough et al) that reads like a who's who of actors.

Windmill Inn PUB

(Church St; ⊙11.30am-11pm Mon-Sat, 11am-11pm Sun) Ale was flowing here at the same time as rhyming couplets gushed from Shakespeare's quill – which means this pub with low ceilings has been around a while.

☆ Entertainment

★ **Royal Shakespeare Company** THEATRE

(RSC; ☑0844 800 1110; www.rsc.org.uk; Waterside; tickets £10-62.50) Coming to Stratford without seeing a Shakespeare production would be like visiting Beijing and bypassing the Great Wall. The three theatre spaces run by the world-renowned Royal Shakespeare Company have witnessed performances by such legends as Lawrence Olivier, Richard Burton, Judi Dench, Helen Mirren, Ian McKellan and Patrick Stewart.

Stratford has two grand stages – the Royal Shakespeare Theatre and the Swan Theatre on Waterside – as well as the smaller Courtyard Theatre (☑0844 800 1110; www.rsc.org.uk; Southern Lane). Contact the RSC for the latest news on performance times. There are often special deals for under 25-year-olds, students and seniors, and a few tickets are held back for sale on the day of the performance, but get snapped up fast. Book well ahead.

❶ Information

Tourist Office (☑01789-264293; www.shakespeare-country.co.uk; Bridge Foot; ⊙9am-5.30pm Mon-Sat, 10am-4pm Sun) Just west of Clopton Bridge on the corner with Bridgeway.

❶ Getting There & Away

CAR

If you're driving, be warned that town car parks charge high fees, 24 hours a day.

BUS

National Express coaches and other bus companies run from Stratford's Riverside bus station (behind the Stratford Leisure Centre on Bridgeway). Services include the following destinations:

Birmingham National Express; £8.40, one hour, twice daily

London Victoria National Express; £7, three hours, three daily

Oxford National Express; £10.70, one hour, twice daily

Warwick Bus 16; £3, 40 minutes, hourly.

TRAIN

From Stratford train station, London Midland runs to Birmingham (£7.30, 50 minutes, half-hourly); Chiltern Railways runs to London Marylebone (£9, 2 hours, up to two per hour).

The nostalgic **Shakespeare Express** (☑0121-708 4960; www.shakespeareexpress.com; adult/child £15/10) steam train chugs twice every Sunday in July and August between Stratford and Birmingham Snow Hill; journey time is one hour.

❶ Getting Around

From April to October, a 1937-built, hand-wound **chain ferry** yo-yos across the Avon (one way 50p).

A bicycle is handy for getting out to the outlying Shakespeare properties. **Stratford Bike Hire** (☑07711-776340; www.stratfordbikehire.com; 7 Seven Meadows Rd; per half-day/day from £10/15) will deliver to your accommodation.

Punts, canoes and rowing boats are available for hire from Avon Boating (p419) near Clopton Bridge. Prices for canoes/rowboats per 30 minutes start from £3/5; punts are £20.

Around Stratford-upon-Avon

Charlecote Park

A youthful Shakespeare allegedly poached deer in the grounds of this lavish Elizabethan pile (NT; ☑01789-470277; www.nationaltrust.org.uk; adult/child £9.35/7.40, garden only £5/2.50; ⊙noon-3.30pm Thu-Tue mid-Feb–mid-Mar, 11am-4.30pm Thu-Tue mid-Mar–Oct, noon-3.30pm Sat & Sun Nov & Dec, garden 10.30am-5.30pm Mar-Oct, to 4.30pm Nov-Feb) on the River Avon, 5 miles east of Stratford-upon-Avon. Fallow deer still roam the grounds today. The interiors were restored from Georgian chintz to Tudor splendour in 1823. Highlights include Victorian kitchens, filled with culinary-moulds, and an original 1551 Tudor gatehouse.

Bus 18 (18A on Sunday) runs to Charlecote hourly from Stratford (£2.30, 30 minutes), continuing to Leamington Spa (£2.30, 30 minutes).

STAFFORDSHIRE

Despite being wedged between the ever-expanding conurbations of Birmingham and Manchester, Staffordshire is surprisingly green, with the northern half of the county rising to meet the rugged hills of the Peak District.

ℹ️ Information

Staffordshire Tourism (www.enjoystaffordshire.com)

ℹ️ Getting There & Around

Regular trains and National Express buses serve Stafford and other major towns. The main local bus operator is **First Group** (☑ 08456 020 121; www.firstgroup.com). For details of services, browse the public transport pages at www.staffordshire.gov.uk.

Stafford

POP 68,470

The capital of Staffordshire is a quiet little place that seems somewhat overshadowed by other towns around the county, such as Lichfield. The main shopping street has some handsome Georgian and medieval buildings, but little evidence remains that this was once the capital of the Anglo-Saxon kingdom of Mercia.

◉ Sights

Ancient High House   MUSEUM
(☑ 01785-619131; www.staffordbc.gov.uk; Greengate St; ⊙ 10am-4pm Tue-Sat) **FREE** Surrounded by high-street shops, the Ancient High House is the largest timber-framed town house in the country, artistically assembled in 1595. Creaking stairways lead to carefully restored rooms, and to displays on the history of the town and medieval construction techniques.

Stafford Castle   RUIN
(☑ 01785-257698; www.staffordbc.gov.uk; Newport Rd; ⊙ visitor centre 11am-4pm Wed-Sun Apr-Oct, 11am-4pm Sat & Sun Nov-Mar) **FREE** The hilltop remains of Stafford Castle, a classic Norman moat and bailey, sit romantically in a forest glade about 1 mile southwest of town, just off the A518.

🛏️ Sleeping & Eating

Swan   PUB ££
(☑ 01785-258142; www.theswanstafford.co.uk; 46-46a Greengate St; s/d from £85/105 mains £9.50-

23; ⊙ kitchen noon-10pm Mon-Sat, noon-4.30pm & 6-8.30pm Sun; 🅿️🐶📶) Stafford's best place to sleep, eat and drink is a one-stop-shop. In the centre of town, this former coaching inn has 31 beautiful rooms (some with original stone fireplaces and wooden beams), an excellent brasserie-style restaurant, two bars (cocktail and traditional courtyard) and a cafe/tea-room. Parking's limited but free for overnight guests. The staff is a pleasure to deal with.

ℹ️ Information

Tourist Office (☑ 01785-619619; www.visit-stafford.org; Eastgate St; ⊙ 9.30am-5pm Mon-Sat) For local info, drop into the tourist office at the Stafford Gatehouse Theatre.

ℹ️ Getting There & Away

Bus 101 (£3.50, 1¼ hours, every 20 minutes, hourly on Sunday) runs between Stafford and Hanley (Stoke-on-Trent). Trains run to Birmingham (£10.20, 40 minutes, every 20 minutes).

Lichfield

POP 32,880

Even without its magnificent Gothic cathedral, one of the most spectacular in the country, this quaintly cobbled market town would be worth a visit to tread in the footsteps of lexicographer and wit Samuel Johnson, and natural philosopher Erasmus Darwin, grandfather of Charles. Johnson once described Lichfield folk as 'the most sober, decent people in England', which was rather generous considering that this was the last place in the country to stop burning people at the stake.

◉ Sights

Lichfield Cathedral   CATHEDRAL
(☑ 01543-306100; www.lichfield-cathedral.org; admission by donation; ⊙ 7.30am-6.15pm Sun-Fri, 8am-6.15pm Sat) Crowned by three dramatic towers, Lichfield Cathedral is a Gothic fantasy, constructed in stages from 1200 to 1350. The enormous vaulted nave is set slightly off line from the choir, creating a bizarre perspective when viewed from the west door, and carvings inside the cathedral still bear signs of damage caused by Civil War soldiers sharpening their swords.

In the octagonal Chapter House, you can view the illuminated *Chad Gospels*, created around AD 730; an ornate Anglo-Saxon bas-relief known as the *Lichfield Angel*; and a faded but glorious medieval wall painting above the door.

The grand west facade positively bows under the weight of 113 statues of bishops, saints and kings of England. Be sure to stroll the delightful, once-fortified Cathedral Close, ringed with imposing 17th- and 18th-century houses.

Erasmus Darwin House   HISTORIC BUILDING
(☑ 01543-306260; www.erasmusdarwin.org; Beacon St; adult/child £3/1; ☉11am-5pm Tue-Sun Apr-Oct, noon-4.30pm Thu-Sun Nov-Mar) After turning down the job of royal physician to King George III – perhaps a lucky escape, considering the monarch's descent into madness – Erasmus Darwin became a leading light in the Lunar Society, debating the origins of life with such luminaries as Wedgwood, Boulton and Watt decades before his grandson Charles came up with the theory of evolution. The former house of the 'Grandfather of Evolution' contains some intriguing personal effects.

At the back is a fragrant herb garden leading to Cathedral Close.

Samuel Johnson
Birthplace Museum   MUSEUM, HISTORIC BUILDING
(☑ 01543-264972; www.samueljohnsonbirthplace.org.uk; Breadmarket St; ☉10.30am-4.30pm Apr-Sep, 11am-3.30pm Oct-Mar) **FREE** This absorbing museum charts the life of the pioneering lexicographer, wit, poet and critic Samuel Johnson, who moved to London from his native Lichfield and devoted nine years to producing the first major dictionary of the English language. Ten years in the making, Johnson's first dictionary helped define the word 'dull' with this example: 'to make dictionaries is dull work'. On the 1st floor, a short dramatised film narrates Johnson's life story. It's a lovely property to explore.

Lichfield Heritage Centre   HERITAGE CENTRE
(☑ 01543-256611; www.stmaryslichfield.co.uk; Market Sq; adult/child £2.50/1, tower adult/child £2.75/1.25; ☉9.30am-4pm Mon-Fri, to 5pm Sat, 10am-4pm Sun) Exhibits cover 1300 years of Lichfield history inside the old St Mary's

THEME PARK SHENANIGANS

Staffordshire is famous for its theme parks, which resound with the screams of adrenalin junkies lured here by fast and furious thrills. Buckle up: it's going to be a bumpy ride...

Alton Towers
Phenomenally popular Alton Towers (☑ 0871 222 3330; www.altontowers.com; adult/child £48/40.80, water park £16.50/11.75; ☉10am-5pm, water park 10am-6pm, longer hours school holidays, weekends & high season, closed Nov-Mar), east of Cheadle off the B5032, offers maximum G-force for your buck. Roller-coaster fans are well catered for: as well as the vertical drop-ride Th13teen, you can ride lying down, sitting down or suspended from the rails on the Nemesis, Oblivion, Air and Rita; or brave 14 loops on the Smiler. Gentler thrills include log flumes, carousels, stage shows, a pirate-themed aquarium and a splashtastic water park. Book online for discounted entry fees and fast-track entry.

Most large towns in the area offer package coach tours (enquire at tourist offices), or you can ride bus 32A from Stoke-on-Trent (£7, 50 minutes, every two hours), or X52 Nottingham (£10, 40 minutes, hourly) and Derby (£8, 20 minutes, hourly).

Set in pleasant walking country, the miniature Dimmingsdale YHA (☑ 0845 371 9513; www.yha.org.uk; Oakamoor; dm from £16) is 2 miles northwest of Alton Towers.

Drayton Manor
Drayton Manor (☑ 0844 472 1960; www.draytonmanor.co.uk; adult/child £36/27; ☉10.30am-5pm Easter-Oct, longer hours May-Sep) has been serving up screams since 1949. Crowd-pleasers include the Apocalypse free-fall tower, voted Britain's scariest ride, and Shockwave, Europe's only stand-up roller coaster. Younger kids will be just as thrilled by Thomas Land, dedicated to the animated steam-train character.

The theme park is on the A4091, between junctions 9 and 10 of the M42. Package coach tours run from Birmingham, or you can take bus 110 from Birmingham Corporation St to Fazeley (£10, one hour, every 20 minutes hourly on Sunday) and walk the last 15 minutes.

The park currently has no on-site accommodation, but Tamworth is just 2 miles away and has plenty of B&Bs and hotels. Contact Tamworth Tourist Information (☑ 01827-709581; www.visittamworth.co.uk; Corporation St; ☉9am-7pm Mon-Fri, to 5pm Sat) for recommendations.

Church. Climb the tower's 120 steps for sweeping city views.

🛏 Sleeping

Bogey Hole
B&B £

(☎ 01543-264303; www.thebogeyhole.co.uk; 23 Dam St; s/d £40/60) A sweet little place near Lichfield Cathedral with bright and rather feminine en suite rooms, a lounge with TV, and a kitchen at the top and laundry room below. There's no signage; look for the quaint cream-coloured facade.

George Hotel
HOTEL ££

(☎ 01543-414822; www.thegeorgelichfield.co.uk; 12-14 Bird St; s £80, d £90-103; P @ 🖘) Part of the Best Western chain, this old Georgian pub has been upgraded into a comfortable midrange hotel, scoring points for location rather than atmosphere.

🍴 Eating & Drinking

Chapters Cathedral Coffee Shop
CAFE £

(☎ 01543-306125; 19 The Close; dishes £3.50-7.75; ⊙ 8.30am-4pm Mon-Sat, 10am-4pm Sun) A fine 18th-century house overlooking its 13th-century walled garden on one side and the cathedral on the other, serving morning and afternoon tea and Sunday lunches.

Damn Fine Cafe
CAFE £

(16 Bird St; dishes £4-8; ⊙ 9am-4pm Tue, Thu & Fri, to 3.30pm Wed, to 5pm Sat, 10am-4pm Sun; ⛄) Teeming with locals, this cafe is a handy spot for sandwiches, soup, filling bacon-and-sausage breakfasts or vegetarian toad-in-the-hole. Order and pay at the counter.

★ Trooper
GASTROPUB £

(☎ 01543-480413; www.thetrooperwall.co.uk; Watling St, Wall; mains £9.50-23; ⊙ kitchen noon-9.15pm Mon-Wed, to 9.45pm Thu-Sat, to 8pm Sun) Situated 3 miles southwest of Lichfield in the tiny village of Wall, this idyllic gastropub prides itself on ingredients such as aged steak (served with hand-cut, beef-dripping-fried chips and sweet tomato chutney) and pork belly (with apple and quince jus) as well as vegetarian options using herbs from the pub's gardens. Fabulous real ales too.

Wine House
MODERN BRITISH ££

(☎ 01543-419999; www.thewinehouselichfield. co.uk; 27 Bird St; mains £13-24; ⊙ noon-10pm Mon-Sat, to 6pm Sun) Astutely selected whites, reds, champagnes and rosés, including many by-the-glass options, complement the seriously good cooking at these smart, red-brick premises. Choices range from pancetta-wrapped, fig-stuffed pork fillet to steamed

---

WORTH A TRIP

THE POTTERIES

Situated at the heart of the Potteries – the famous pottery-producing region of Staffordshire – Stoke-on-Trent (population 248,720) is famed for its ceramics.

Don't expect cute little artisanal producers. This was where pottery shifted to mass production during the Industrial Revolution, and Stoke is a sprawl of industrial townships tied together by flyovers and bypasses. You really need your own wheels to get around.

There are dozens of active potteries; the **tourist office** (☎ 01782-236000; www.visit-stoke.co.uk; Victoria Hall, Bagnall St, Hanley; ⊙ 10am-4pm Tue-Sat), in Stoke-on-Trent's 'city centre' Hanley, has leaflets on all the potteries open to the public.

Potteries Museum & Art Gallery (☎ 01782-232323; www.stoke.gov.uk/museum; Bethesda St, Hanley; admission by donation; ⊙ 10am-5pm Mon-Sat & 2-5pm Sun) For a good overview of the history of the Potteries area, this Hanley museum houses an extensive ceramics display, from Toby jugs and jasperware to outrageous ornamental pieces such as the Minton Peacock. You can also see treasures from the outstanding Staffordshire Hoard; displays on the WWII Spitfire, created by the Stoke-born aviator Reginald Mitchell; and artworks by TS Lowry and Sir Henry Moore.

Wedgwood Visitor Centre (☎ 01782-282986; www.wedgwoodvisitorcentre.com; Wedgwood Dr, Barlaston; adult/child £10/8; ⊙ 10am-5pm Mon-Fri, to 4pm Sat & Sun) Set in attractive parkland 8 miles south of Hanley, the modern production centre for Josiah Wedgwood's porcelain empire displays an extensive collection of historic pieces, including plenty of Wedgwood's delicate, neoclassical blue-and-white jasperware. The fascinating industrial process is revealed, and there's an interesting film on Josiah's life and work, including his involvement in canal-building and opposition to slavery.

Scottish mussels with tail-on tiger prawns and squid-ink risotto.

Chandlers' Grande Brasserie MODERN EUROPEAN **££**
(☑01543-416688; www.chandlersrestaurant.co.uk; Conduit St; mains £9-24; ☺11am-2pm & 6-11pm Mon-Sat; 🐾) Set in the old Corn Exchange and decked out with natural wood and polished brass. This is where locals go for a big night out, as much for the ambience as for the Mediterranean-inspired cuisine.

ℹ Information

Tourist Office (☑01543-256611; www.stmarys lichfield.co.uk; Market Sq; ☺9.30am-3.30pm Mon-Sat) In the Lichfield Heritage Centre.

ℹ Getting There & Away

The bus station is opposite the main train station on Birmingham Rd. Bus 825 serves Stafford (£3.40, 1½ hours, half-hourly, hourly on Sunday).

Lichfield has two train stations. Trains to Birmingham (£5.80, 40 minutes, every 20 minutes) leave from Lichfield City station in the centre. Trains to London Euston (£34, 1¾ hours, two per hour) run from Lichfield Trent Valley station.

WORCESTERSHIRE

Famed for its eponymous condiment, invented by two Worcester chemists in 1837, Worcestershire marks the transition from the industrial heart of the Midlands to the peaceful countryside of the Welsh Marches. The southern and western fringes of the county burst with lush countryside and sleepy market towns, while the capital is a classic English county town, whose magnificent cathedral inspired the composer Elgar to write some of his greatest works.

🏃 Activities

The longest riverside walk in the UK, the 210-mile Severn Way winds its way through Worcestershire en route from Plynlimon in Wales to the sea at Bristol. A shorter challenge is the 100-mile Three Choirs Way, linking Worcester to Hereford and Gloucester. The Malvern Hills are also prime country for walking and cycling – information is available at www.malvernhillsaonb.org.uk.

ℹ Information

Visit Worcestershire (www.visitworcester-shire.org)

ℹ Getting Around

Worcester is a convenient rail hub. Kidderminster is the southern railhead of the quaint **Severn Valley Railway** (☑01299-403816; www.svr.co.uk; ☺daily May-Sep, Sat & Sun Oct-Apr).

Buses connect larger towns, but services to rural areas can be frustratingly infrequent – search the transport pages at www.worcestershire.gov.uk for bus companies and timetables.

Worcester

POP 100,150

Worcester (pronounced *woos*-ter) has enough historic treasures to forgive the architectural eyesores from the postwar love affair with all things concrete. The home of the famous Worcestershire sauce (an unlikely combination of fermented tamarinds and anchovies), this ancient cathedral city was the site of the last battle of the Civil War, the Battle of Worcester, which took place on 3 September 1651. The defeated Charles II only narrowly escaped the pursuing Roundheads by hiding in an oak tree, an event still celebrated in Worcester every 29 May, when government buildings are decked out with oak sprigs.

◉ Sights

Worcester Cathedral CATHEDRAL
(☑01905-732900; www.worcestercathedral.co.uk; admission by £5 donation, tower adult/child £4/2, tours £4/free; ☺7.30am-6pm, tower 11am-5pm Sat Apr-Oct, tours 11am & 2.30pm Mon-Sat Mar-Nov, 11am & 2.30pm Sat Dec-Feb; 🚼) Rising above the River Severn, Worcester's majestic cathedral is best known as the final resting place of Magna Carta signatory King John. The strong-legged can tackle the 249 steps to the top of the tower, from where Charles II surveyed his troops during the disastrous Battle of Worcester. Hour-long cathedral tours run from the gift shop. Several works by local composer Edward Elgar had their first public outings at the cathedral – to appreciate the acoustics, come for evensong (5.30pm Monday to Saturday, 4pm Sunday).

Commandery MUSEUM
(☑01905-361821; www.worcestercitymuseums.org .uk; College St; adult/child £5.50/2.50; ☺10am-5pm Mon-Sat, 1.30-5pm Sun) The town's history museum is housed in a splendid Tudor building that served as King Charles II's headquarters during the Battle of Worcester. Engaging audioguides and interactive exhibits tell the story of Worcester during

WORTH A TRIP

ELGAR BIRTHPLACE MUSEUM

England's most popular classical composer is celebrated with appropriate pomp and circumstance at Elgar Birthplace Museum (☑ 01905-333224; www.elgarmuseum.org; Crown East Lane, Lower Broadheath; adult/child £7.50/3.50; ☺ 11am-5pm Feb-late Dec) , housed in the humble cottage where Edward Elgar was born in 1857. Admission includes an audioguide with musical interludes so that you can appreciate what all the fuss is about.

Bus 308 goes from Worcester to Broadheath Common (£3.10, 15 minutes, three daily Monday to Saturday), from where it's a short walk to the museum.

key periods in its history. A highlight is the 'painted chamber', covered with intriguing 15th-century religious frescos.

Royal Worcester Porcelain Works MUSEUM
(☑ 01905-21247; www.museumofroyalworcester.org; Severn St; adult/child £6/free; ☺ 10am-5pm Mon-Sat Mar-Oct, to 4pm Mon-Sat Nov-Feb) Up there with Crown Derby and Wedgwood, the Royal Worcester porcelain factory gained an edge over its rivals by picking up the contract to provide fine crockery to the English monarchy. An entertaining audio tour reveals some quirkier sides to the Royal Worcester story, including its brief foray into porcelain dentures and 'portable fonts' designed for cholera outbreaks. The shop has some splendid pieces, from monk-shaped candle-snuffers to decorated thimbles and pill boxes.

☞ Tours

Worcester Walks WALKING TOUR
(☑ 01905-726311; www.worcesterwalks.co.uk; adult £5; ☺ 11am Mon-Fri Apr-Sep) Popular half-hour walking tours.

Worcester River Cruises BOAT TOUR
(☑ 01905-611060; www.worcesterrivercruises.co.uk; adult/child £6/4; ☺ hourly noon-4pm Apr-Sep) Offers a different perspective of Worcester on 45-minute cruises on the River Severn aboard the 1926-built *Earl*. Departure times and days can vary.

🛏 Sleeping

Lenchford Inn INN ££
(☑ 01905-620229; www.thelenchfordinn.co.uk; Shrawley; d from £75; P 🕾) An easy 8-mile drive

north of Worcester, this sprawling inn on the banks of the Severn is a tranquil haven. Its nine en suite rooms are old fashioned but spacious and clean, and all open onto a communal balcony or terrace with river views. There's a cavernous restaurant and sociable bar.

Barrington House B&B ££
(☑ 01905-422965; www.barringtonhouse.eu; 204 Henwick Rd; r £80-90; P @ 🕾) This lovely Georgian house by the river comes with wonderful views, a pretty walled garden and three plush bedrooms full of brocade, trim and super-king-sized beds. Hearty breakfasts include eggs from the owners' hens.

Ye Olde Talbot Hotel HOTEL ££
(☑ 01905-235730; www.oldenglishinns.co.uk; Friar St; s/d from £55/70; 🕾) Attached to a popular bar and bistro right in the centre, this tasteful inn dates back to the 13th century, but many of the rooms are housed in a modern extension. Ask for discounted parking in the nearby multistorey car park.

Diglis House Hotel HOTEL ££
(☑ 01905-353518; www.diglishousehotel.co.uk; Severn St; s/d from £70/105; P 🕾) Next to the boathouse in a waterside setting, this rambling yet cosy 28-room Georgian house is a short stroll from the cathedral. The best rooms have four-poster beds and luxe bathrooms. Guests can work out at the nearby gym for free.

🍴 Eating

Mac & Jac's DELI, CAFE £
(www.macandjacs.co.uk; 44 Friar St; mains £5-12; ☺ 9am-5pm Mon-Sat) This Friar St outfit has a lovely deli downstairs for quality titbits and a relaxing cafe upstairs for caffeine, sandwiches with fillings such as brie and grape, and a wholesome menu of hot dishes such as crispy pork belly with toasted almonds and coriander. There's a second location in Great Malvern (p428).

Little Ginger Pig CAFE, BISTRO £
(☑ 01905-338913; www.littlegingerpig.co.uk; 9-11 Copenhagen St; dishes £4.50-8; ☺ 10am-3.30pm Tue-Fri, 8.30am-4.30pm Sat, 10am-3pm Sun; 🖢) 🍃 The focus is on locally sourced, free-range produce and independent labels at this pleasant and frequently busy cafe, bistro and bar.

★ Old Rectifying House MODERN BRITISH ££
(☑ 01905-619622; www.theoldrec.co.uk; North Parade; light menu £6-14, mains £12-23.50; ☺ kitchen noon-3pm & 6-9pm Tue-Thu, to 9.30pm Fri & Sat, to 4pm Sun) Worcester's hippest dining

space has a candlelit, painted-brick interior and umbrella-shaded courtyard tables. A switched-on menu of light bites includes burgers (haloumi, wild boar or Wagyu) and mains range from fish pie with curly kale to rare-breed longhorn ribeye steak. DJs often hit the decks in the lounge bar, which mixes mighty cocktails including a sparkling wine-topped 'millionaire's martini'.

Drinking & Nightlife

Hand in Glove COCKTAIL BAR
(25 College St; ⊙4pm-midnight Mon-Thu, 3pm-1am Fri & Sat, 12.30pm-midnight Sun; 🛜) The muted charcoal-coloured facade doesn't give much away but inside this low-key, independent bar does whizz-bang cocktails.

Cardinal's Hat PUB
(www.the-cardinals-hat.co.uk; 31 Friar St; ⊙noon-11pm Mon-Sat, to 10.30pm Sun; 🛜) Despite looking as English as Tudor ruffs and claiming a resident ghost, this atmospheric Worcester institution with log-burning stoves sells Austrian beers in traditional steins and serves authentic Austrian delicacies at lunchtime.

Entertainment

Marr's Bar LIVE MUSIC
(📞01905-613336; www.marrsbar.co.uk; 12 Pierpoint St; ⊙8pm-late) The best live-music venue for miles around, Marr's still has its original sprung dance floors from its days as a dance studio. There's a lively schedule of gigs, acts, comedy shows, acoustic and jamming evenings most nights.

Shopping

Chocolate Deli FOOD
(📞01905-611324; www.chocolatedeli.biz; 53 New St; ⊙10am-5pm Mon-Sat) At this cherry-red deli you can buy handcrafted chocolates (such as strawberry and pepper, Jack Daniels truffles or milk-chocolate pencils that actually write); taste them over a cuppa; or sign up for a one-day chocolate-making course (£60 to £99).

Information

Tourist Office (📞01905-726311; www.visit-worcester.com; Guildhall, High St; ⊙9.30am-5pm Mon-Sat)

Getting There & Away

BUS
The bus station is inside the Crowngate Centre on Friary Walk.

Birmingham Bus 144; £3.50, 1¾ hours, every 20 minutes (hourly Sunday)

Great Malvern Bus 44; £3.50, 30 minutes, every 10 minutes Monday to Saturday (hourly on Sunday)

London Victoria National Express; £22.60, 3½ hours, three daily

TRAIN
Worcester Foregate is the main rail hub, but services also run from Worcester Shrub Hill. Regular trains include the following:

Birmingham £8.40, one hour, every 20 minutes

Hereford £8.90, 50 minutes, hourly

Ledbury £6.50, 25 minutes, half-hourly

London Paddington £30.50, 2½ hours, twice hourly

Great Malvern
POP 36,770

Tumbling down the side of a forested ridge about 7 miles southwest of Worcester, the picturesque spa town of Great Malvern is the gateway to the Malverns, a soaring 9-mile-long range of volcanic hills that rise from the surrounding meadows. In Victorian times, the medicinal waters were prescribed as a panacea for everything from gout to 'sore eyes' – you can test the theory by sampling Malvern water straight from the ground at public wells dotted around the town.

Sights

Great Malvern Priory MONASTERY
(📞01684-561020; www.greatmalvernpriory.org.uk; Church St; ⊙9am-5pm) FREE The 11th-century Great Malvern Priory is packed with remarkable features, from original Norman pillars to surreal modernist stained glass. The choir is enclosed by a screen of 15th-century tiles and the monks' stalls are decorated with delightfully irreverent 14th-century misericords, depicting everything from three rats hanging a cat to the mythological reptile, the basilisk. Charles Darwin's daughter Annie is buried here.

Malvern Museum of Local History MUSEUM
(📞01684-567811; www.malvernmuseum.co.uk; Priory Gatehouse, Abbey Rd; adult/child £2/50p; ⊙10.30am-5pm Mar-Oct) Straddling Abbey Rd in the grand Priory Gatehouse (c 1470), the town museum offers a thorough exploration of Great Malvern's claims to fame, including spring waters, medieval monasteries, the Malvern Hills and Morgan Motors.

★ **Morgan Motor Company** MUSEUM
(☎ 01684-584580; www.morgan-motor.co.uk; Pickersleigh Rd; tours adult/child £12.50/7.50; ⊗ 8.30am-5pm Mon-Thu, to 2.30pm Fri) **FREE** Morgan has been handcrafting elegant sports cars since 1909, and you can still see the mechanics at work on guided tours of the unassuming shed-like buildings comprising the factory (prebooking essential), and view a fleet of vintage classics. Bus 44 from Church St runs past the factory. If buying one of these beautiful machines is beyond your budget, you can rent one from £190 per day, including insurance, for a spin through the Malvern Hills.

☞ Tours

Great Malvern Walking Tours WALKING TOUR
(adult/child £3/50p; ⊗ tours 10.30am Sat & Sun Apr-Sep) Walking tours departing from the tourist office explore the town's medieval and Victorian history.

🛏 Sleeping

Bredon House HOTEL ££
(☎ 01684-566990; www.bredonhouse.co.uk; 34 Worcester Rd; s/d from £45/70; P @) A short saunter from the centre, this genteel family- and pet-friendly Victorian hotel backs onto a stunning vista. Rooms are decorated in a quirky but tasteful mix of new and old, and the books, magazines and family photographs dotted around the place mean it feels like staying with relatives.

Abbey Hotel HOTEL £££
(☎ 01684-892332; www.sarova-abbeyhotel.com; Abbey Rd; d £180-220; P @) Tangled in vines like a Brothers Grimm fairy-tale castle, this stately property has 103 elegant rooms in a prime location by the museum and priory.

✕ Eating

Mac & Jac's CAFE £
(www.macandjacs.co.uk; 23 Abbey Rd; dishes £4.50-11; ⊗ 9am-7pm Tue-Sat, 10am-4pm Sun) Creative salads, flatbreads, sharing plates, spelt risotto and a savoury tart of the day are served up at this fresh addition to the town's dining scene. It's the sister branch of the Worcester (p426) cafe, set in a chic white-painted shopfront near the Great Malvern Priory. Look out for supper evenings (two-/three-course menus £25/29; dates vary).

St Ann's Well Cafe CAFE £
(☎ 01684-560285; www.stannswell.co.uk; dishes £1.50-4; ⊗ 11.30am-3.30pm Tue-Fri, 10am-4pm Sat & Sun Easter-Sep) A s-t-e-e-p climb above St Ann's Rd (so best to check opening times beforehand with the tourist office), this quaint cafe is set in an early 19th-century villa, with mountain-fresh spring water bubbling into a carved basin by the door.

Fig Tree MODERN BRITISH ££
(☎ 01684-569909; www.thefigtreemalvern.co.uk; 99b Church St; mains £13-18; ⊗ 10am-10pm Tue-Sat) Tucked down an alleyway off Church St, this 19th-century former stable serves Mediterranean-inspired fare such as marinated pork chops with caramelised apple, red onion and rosemary potatoes, and char-grilled chicken with minted yoghurt and saffron rice.

☆ Entertainment

Malvern Theatres THEATRE
(☎ 01684-892277; www.malvern-theatres.co.uk; Grange Rd) One of the country's best provincial theatres, this long-established cultural hub packs in a lively program of classical music, dance, comedy, drama and cinema.

Theatre of Small Convenience THEATRE
(☎ 01684-568933; www.wctheatre.co.uk; Edith Walk; shows adult/child £2.50/1.50) Set in a converted Victorian public lavatory decked out with theatrical Italianate flourishes, this quirky place has just 12 seats and a program running from puppet shows to poetry and opera. Shows usually last five to 10 minutes.

WALKING IN THE MALVERN HILLS

The jack-in-the-box Malvern Hills, which dramatically pop up out of the Severn plains on the boundary between Worcestershire and Herefordshire, rise to the lofty peak of the Worcester Beacon (419m), reached by a steep 3-mile climb above Great Malvern. More than 100 miles of trails traipse over the various summits, which are mostly capped by exposed grassland, offering the kind of views that inspire orchestral movements.

The Great Malvern tourist office has racks of pamphlets covering popular hikes, including a map of the mineral-water springs, wells and fountains of the town and surrounding hills. The enthusiast-run website www.malvern-trail.co.uk is also a goldmine of useful walking information.

A single £3 parking ticket per day is valid at locations throughout the hills.

ℹ Information

Tourist Office (☑ 01684-892289; www.visit-themalverns.org; 21 Church St; ⊙10am-5pm Apr-Oct, to 4pm Nov-Mar) The tourist office is a mine of walking and cycling information.

ℹ Getting There & Around

National Express runs one bus daily to London Victoria (£21.70, five hours). For Worcester, take bus 44 (£3.50, 30 minutes, every 10 minutes Monday to Saturday, hourly on Sunday).

The train station is east of the centre, off Ave Rd. Services include the following:

Hereford £7.50, 35 minutes, hourly

Ledbury £4.80, 13 minutes, hourly

Worcester £5, 15 to 20 minutes, two or three hourly

HEREFORDSHIRE

Slumbering in the English countryside, Herefordshire is a patchwork of fields, hills and cute little black-and-white villages, many dating back to the Tudor era and beyond. Getting around is complicated by infrequent bus services and meandering country lanes, but taking the scenic route is part of the appeal of this laid-back rural idyll.

🏃 Activities

As well as the famous Offa's Dyke Path, walkers can follow the Herefordshire Trail (www.herefordshiretrail.com) on a 150-mile circular loop through Leominster, Ledbury, Ross-on-Wye and Kington. Only slightly less ambitious is the 136-mile Wye Valley Walk (www.wyevalleywalk.org), which runs from Chepstow in Wales through Herefordshire and back out again to Plynlimon. Then there's the Three Choirs Way, a 100-mile route connecting the cathedrals of Hereford, Worcester and Gloucester.

Cyclists can trace the Six Castles Cycleway (NCN Route 44) from Hereford to Leominster and Shrewsbury, or NCN Route 68 to Great Malvern and Worcester.

ℹ Information

Visit Herefordshire (www.visitherefordshire.co.uk)

ℹ Getting Around

For bus timetables, contact Traveline (p400). Alternatively, pick up the chunky *Bus and Train Timetable* from any tourist office (50p). Trains run frequently to Hereford, Leominster and Ledbury, with irregular bus connections on to the rest of the county.

Hereford

POP 60,410

Dozing in the midst of apple orchards and rolling pastures at the heart of the Marches, straddling the River Wye, Hereford is best known for prime steaks, cider and the Pretenders – three of the original band members (guitarist James Honeyman-Scott, bassist Pete Farndon and drummer Martin Chambers) were local boys.

SIPPING (AND SUPPING) YOUR WAY AROUND CIDER COUNTRY

Herefordshire Cider Route (www.ciderroute.co.uk) The Herefordshire Cider Route drops in on numerous local cider producers, where you can try before you buy, and then totter off to the next cidery. Mindful of road safety, tourist offices have maps and guide booklets to help you explore by bus or bicycle.

Westons Cider Mills (☑ 01531-660108; www.westons-cider.co.uk; The Bounds; tours adult/child £7.50/4; ⊙9am-5pm Mon-Fri, 10am-4.30pm Sat & Sun) If you only have time to visit one cider-maker, make it Westons Cider Mills, just under a mile west of the tiny village of Much Marcle, whose house brew is even served in the Houses of Parliament. Informative tours (1¼ hours) start at 11am, 12.30pm and 2.30pm, with free cider and perry tastings for the grown-ups. There's also a fascinating bottle museum.

Walwyn Arms (☑ 01531-660601; www.walwynarms.co.uk; Much Marcle; mains £9.50-17; ⊙kitchen noon-2.30pm & 6-9.30pm Mon-Sat, noon-4pm & 6-9pm Sun) Westons ciders are served at this welcoming country pub, just across from Westons Cider Mills. Cider is also used in many dishes, such as the scrumptious twice-baked, mature cheddar and Old Rosie scrumpy soufflé, and cider-battered haddock fillet, with chips and mushy peas. Great lunchtime sandwiches (eg prawn and Bloody Mary mayonnaise) on hand-cut bread, too.

◉ Sights

Hereford Cathedral CATHEDRAL
(☎01432-374200; www.herefordcathedral.org; 5 College Cloisters; cathedral entry by £5 donation, Mappa Mundi £6; ⊙9.15am to evensong, Mappa Mundi 10am-5pm Mon-Sat May-Sep, to 4pm Mon-Sat Oct-Apr, evensong 5.30pm Mon-Sat, 3.30pm Sun) After Welsh marauders torched the original Saxon cathedral, the Norman rulers of Hereford erected a larger, grander cathedral on the same site, which was subsequently remodelled in a succession of medieval architectural styles.

The signature highlight is the magnificent **Mappa Mundi**, a single piece of calfskin vellum intricately painted with some rather fantastical assumptions about the layout of the globe in around 1290. The same wing contains the world's largest surviving chained library of rare manuscripts manacled to the shelves.

Heated by four impressive Gurney stoves, the magnificent cathedral comes alive with **evensong**, and every three years in August it holds the famous Three Choirs Festival (www.3choirs.org), shared with Gloucester and Worcester Cathedrals.

In the cloisters you'll find an atmospheric cafe.

Old House MUSEUM
(☎01432-260694; ⊙10am-5pm Tue-Sat year-round, to 4pm Sun Apr-Sep) FREE This gloriously creaky black-and-white, three-storey wooden house was built in 1621. Climb upstairs for beautifully kept medieval rooms with period furniture (including 17th-century cradles), carved wood panelling and antique cast-iron firebacks.

Hereford Museum & Art Gallery MUSEUM
(☎01432-260692; www.herefordshire.gov.uk/museums; Broad St; ⊙10am-5pm Tue-Sat year-round, to 4pm Sun Apr-Sep) FREE The eclectic town museum has displays on just about everything from 19th-century witches' curses to Roman antiquities.

**Cider Museum &
King Offa Distillery** BREWERY
(☎01432-354207; www.cidermuseum.co.uk; 21 Ryeland St; adult/child £5.50/3; ⊙10am-5pm Mon-Sat Apr-Oct, 11am-3pm Mon-Sat Nov-Mar) Displays at this brewery and museum cover cider-making history and you can sample the delicious modern brews. Look for the fine *costrels* (minibarrels) used by agricultural workers to carry their wages, which were partially paid in cider. It's about half-a-mile west of the centre; follow Eign St and turn south along Ryelands St.

☞ Tours

Guided walks WALKING TOUR
(adult/child £3.50/free; ⊙11am Mon-Sat, 3pm Sun May-Sep) Guided walks start from the tourist office, exploring less well known historic sights in the centre.

Ultimate Left Bank CANOEING
(☎01432-264807; www.leftbankcanoehire.com; Bridge St; canoe hire half-day/day £20/25) Rents open canoes to paddle along the River Wye.

🛏 Sleeping

Kidwells Guest House B&B £
(☎01432-264625; www.kidwellshouse.com; 9 Newtown Rd; s/d with en suite £50/60, without bathroom £35/50; P🖥) This warm and welcoming B&B in the north of town has comfortable rooms in varying categories, some with big balconies. A sunlit conservatory opens onto a large garden. Guests can use a gym, located 3 miles from the guesthouse and run by the same owners, for free.

Charades B&B ££
(☎01432-269444; www.charadeshereford.co.uk; 32 Southbank Rd; s/d from £50/65; P@🖥) Handy for the bus station, this imposing Victorian house has five inviting rooms with high ceilings, big and bright windows, and

---

WORTH A TRIP

GOLDEN VALLEY

Nudging the foot of the Black Mountains, this lush valley was made famous by children's author CS Lewis, of *Narnia* acclaim.

Following the meandering River Dore, the valley is peppered with historic relics, including **Arthur's Stone**, a 5000-year-old Neolithic dolmen (chamber-tomb) near the village of Dorestone, and the handsome 12th-century **Dore Abbey** (www.doreabbey.org.uk; ⊙dawn-dusk) in the appropriately named village of Abbey Dore.

Bus 39 between Hereford and Hay-on-Wye (£3.50, one hour, five daily Monday to Saturday) follows the valley, stopping at Dorestone and Peterchurch. For accommodation and dining ideas, visit www.herefordholidays.co.uk.

some with soothing countryside views. The house itself has character in spades – look for old service bells in the hall and the plentiful Titanic memorabilia.

★ **Castle House** BOUTIQUE HOTEL **£££**
(📞 01432-356321; www.castlehse.co.uk; Castle St; s/d/ste from £130/150/195; 🅿 @ 🛜) Set in a regal Georgian town house that was once the luxurious digs of the Bishop of Hereford, this tranquil hotel has a sophisticated restaurant, sun-kissed garden spilling down to the river, and magnificent rooms and suites. Eight newer rooms are a short walk away at 25 Castle St. Wheelchair accessible.

🍴 Eating & Drinking

Hereford Deli DELI **£**
(http://thehereforddeli.com; 4 The Mews, St Owen St; sandwiches £2-3; ⏱ 8am-6pm Mon-Fri, 9am-5pm Sat) Great for lunch on the run or eaten at the clutch of tables, sandwiches at this gourmet emporium are a steal. Combinations include curried free-range chicken with mango chutney, Scottish smoked salmon with lemon-and-dill butter, or local roast beef with Cropwell Bishop Stilton and rosehip jelly. It's hidden down a narrow laneway near a large public car park.

Cafe@All Saints CAFE **£**
(📞 01432-370415; www.cafeatallsaints.co.uk; High St; mains £6-10; ⏱ 8am-5pm Mon-Sat; 🛜 ♿) Inside the renovated nave of All Saint's Church, this inviting licensed cafe serves wholesome daily specials, kicking off from 8am with bacon butties, eggy bread and breakfasts. There's outside seating for warmer days.

La Madeleine FRENCH **££**
(📞 01432-265 233; www.la-madeleine.co.uk; 17 Church St; mains £11-16; ⏱ 10am-4pm Mon, Tue & Thu, to 4pm & 6-9pm Wed, to 4pm & 6-10pm Fri, 9am-5pm Sat) 🍴 A pretty, bare-boards interior, outdoor tables in the vine-draped garden and a stylish French menu – breakfast croissants, lunchtime tarts and dinner dishes such as fillet steak with horseradish crème fraîche, fries and green-bean salad – are enough to make any Parisian homesick.

Lichfield Vaults PUB
(www.lichfieldvaultshereford.co.uk; 11 Church St; ⏱ 11am-midnight Sun-Thu, to 2am Fri & Sat) On a cobbled lane near the cathedral, sociable 18th-century pub 'The Lich' opens to a decked beer garden out back. Regular live-music events include a monthly jazz Sunday lunch. Jovial Greek Cypriot host

Andy serves up superior Greek food including meatballs, mezze plates and more.

Black Lion PUB
(www.theblacklionhereford.co.uk; 31 Bridge St; ⏱ 10am-11pm) The more real ales and local ciders you knock back in this traditional pub, the more you believe the tales of resident ghosts from the site's history as a monastery, an orphanage, a brothel and even a Chinese restaurant. There's regular live music.

Jailhouse CLUB
(http://thejailhouse.wordpress.com; Gaol St; ⏱ 10pm-3am Wed-Sat) Edgy, underground DJs and alternative sounds are constantly on the billing at Hereford's leading club. Look out for secret sets by big-name spinners.

ℹ Information

Tourist Office (📞 01432-268430; www.visit herefordshire.co.uk; 1 King St; ⏱ 9.30am-5pm Mon-Sat) Opposite the cathedral.

ℹ Getting There & Around

The bus station is on Commercial Rd, northeast of the town centre. National Express goes to London Victoria (£20.20, 4½ hours, five daily) and Gloucester (£5.50, one hour, four daily). Local services include the following:

Ross-on-Wye Bus 44; £3.50, 50 minutes, five daily Monday to Friday, four Saturday

Worcester Bus 420; £8.90, 1¼ hours, five daily Monday to Saturday, four Sunday

The train station is northeast of the centre, with hourly trains to Birmingham (£15.20, 1½ hours), Ledbury (£6.50, 20 minutes), London Paddington (£38.50, three hours) – either direct or with a change in Newport, South Wales. Half-hourly services head to Ludlow (£9.50, 30 minutes).

Ross-on-Wye

POP 10,580

Set on a red sandstone bluff over a kink in the River Wye, hilly Ross-on-Wye was propelled to fame in the 18th century by Alexander Pope and Samuel Taylor Coleridge, who penned tributes to philanthropist John Kyrle, Man of Ross, who dedicated his life and fortune to the poor of the parish.

◉ Sights

Market House HERITAGE CENTRE
(📞 01989-260675; ⏱ 10am-5pm Mon-Sat, 10.30am-4pm Sun Apr-Oct, to 4pm Mon-Sat Nov-Mar) **FREE** The 17th-century Market House sits atop weathered sandstone columns in Market Pl;

inside the salmon-pink building the heritage centre has local history displays.

St Mary's Church
CHURCH

(Church St; ⊙9am-5pm) Crowning the hilltop, pin-straight St Mary's Church is a 13th-century building with a fine east window and grand alabaster memorials, including the grave of John Kyrle and the outrageously ostentatious tombs of the noble Rudhall family. Behind the church, Royal Pde runs to the edge of the bluff, lined with realistic-looking but ersatz castle ruins, constructed in 1833.

🛏 Sleeping & Eating

White House Guest House
B&B ££

(☑01989-763572; www.whitehouseross.com; 13 Wye St; s/d/tr/f £50/70/90/100; P @ 🛜) This 18th-century stone house has a great location across the road from the River Wye. Vivid window boxes give it a splash of colour, and the quiet and comfortable rooms are decorated in shades of burgundy and crisp white.

Truffles Delicatessen
DELI £

(www.trufflesdeli.co.uk; 46 High St; dishes £2.50-3.50; ⊙8am-5pm Mon-Sat, 11am-5pm Sun) Packed to the rafters with local artisan products (cheeses, breads, chutneys et al), Truffles also has stellar sandwiches, soups and salad boxes to take away for a riverside picnic.

Pots & Pieces
CAFE £

(www.potsandpieces.com; 40 High St; mains £5-6; ⊙9am-5pm Mon-Fri, 10am-5pm Sat, 11am-4pm Sun) The best of the tearooms around the market place, with ceramics and crafts to browse.

BLACK-AND-WHITE VILLAGES

A triangle of Tudor England survives almost untouched in northwest Herefordshire, where higgledy-piggledy black-and-white houses cluster around idyllic village greens, seemingly oblivious to the modern world. A delightful 40-mile circular drive follows the Black and White Village Trail (www.blackandwhitetrail. org), meandering past the most handsome timber-framed buildings. It starts at Leominster and loops round through Eardisland and Kington, the southern terminus of the Mortimer Trail from Ludlow.

Pick up guides to exploring the villages by car, bus or bicycle at tourist offices.

King's Head
INN ££

(☑01989-763174; www.kingshead.co.uk; 8 High St; d £85-110, mains £11-21; ⊙kitchen noon-2.15pm & 6.30-9.00pm; 🛜) On the atmospheric High St, this unassuming 14th-century inn is a charmer. Dining highlights – in the low-lit front restaurant or glass conservatory – include seafood in champagne bisque, steaks and pies. Some of its chocolate-toned rooms have four-poster beds; there's limited guest parking. Two caveats: vegetarian options are limited and there's no access for travellers with disabilities.

ℹ Information

Tourist Office (☑01989-562768; www. herefordshire.gov.uk; Market House, Market Pl; ⊙10.30am-4.30pm Wed-Mon Apr-Sep, to 4pm Sun Oct-Mar) Has information on sights and walks – ask for the *Ross-on-Wye Heritage Trail* booklet (50p). Note that it closes every second Sunday throughout the year.

ℹ Getting There & Around

The bus stand is on Cantilupe Rd. Bus 44 runs hourly to Hereford (£3.50, 45 minutes, five daily Monday to Friday, four on Saturdays).

Ledbury
POP 8860

Creaking with history and dotted with antique shops, Ledbury's crooked black-and-white streets zero in on a delightfully leggy medieval Market House. The timber-framed structure is precariously balanced atop a series of wooden posts supposedly taken from the wrecked ships of the Spanish Armada.

Almost impossibly cute Church Lane runs its cobbled way from the High St to the town church, crowded with tilting timber-framed buildings.

At the top of the lane lies the 12th-century church of St Michael and All Angels (www. ledburyparishchurch.org.uk; ⊙9am-5.30pm), with a splendid 18th-century spire and tower divided from its medieval nave.

🛏 Sleeping & Eating

The town pubs offer reasonably priced meals, but budget travellers will struggle to find cheap accommodation.

Feathers Hotel
HOTEL £££

(☑01531-635266; www.feathers-ledbury.co.uk; High St; s/d from £97.50/145, mains £13.50-25; P 🛜 ⛲) This charming black-and-white Tudor hotel rooms over the main road in Ledbury. Rooms in the oldest part of the building come with sloping floorboards, painted beams and much more character than the modern rooms. There's an atmospheric wood-panelled restaurant and an indoor heated swimming pool.

Chez Pascal FRENCH ££
(☑ 01531-634443; Church Lane; mains £14-15; ☺ 9.30am-5.30pm Mon-Thu, to 11pm Fri & Sat) Set in a delightful courtyard with garden tables, this place is the go-to address of locals for fine dining. French owner/chef/patissier Pascal's mains include classics such as pan-fried pheasant in red wine, seafood ragout and fish gratin, but it's desserts such as ginger and lemon torte and raspberry tarts that are the stars of the show.

🔒 Shopping

Three Counties Cider Shop DRINK
(www.threecountiescider.co.uk; 5a The Homend; ☺ 10am-5.30pm Tue-Thu, to 6pm Fri & Sat) The aroma of apples pervades this charming little shop filled with artisan cider, perry and juices from producers in three counties (Herefordshire, Worcestershire and Gloucestershire). A dozen ciders and perries are on tap to try; you can also buy locally produced gourmet goods including cider chocolates, chutneys and jams.

ℹ️ Getting There & Away

Buses are limited but regular train services include the following:

Great Malvern £4.80, 10 minutes, hourly

Hereford £6.50, 15 minutes, hourly

Worcester £6.50, 30 minutes, hourly

SHROPSHIRE

Sleepy Shropshire is a glorious scattering of hills, castles and timber-framed villages tucked against the Welsh border. Highlights include food-obsessed Ludlow, industrial Ironbridge and the beautiful Shropshire Hills, which offer the best walking and cycling in the Marches.

🏃 Activities

Walking

The towering Shropshire Hills call out to walkers like a siren. Between Shrewsbury and Ludlow, the landscape rucks up into dramatic folds, with spectacular trails climbing the flanks of Wenlock Edge and the Long Mynd near Church Stretton. The county is also crossed by long-distance trails, including the famous Offa's Dyke Path and the popular Shropshire Way, which meanders around Ludlow and Church Stretton. For general information on walking in the county, visit www.shropshire walking.co.uk.

Cycling

Mountain bikers head for the muddy tracks that scramble over the Long Mynd near Church Stretton, while road riders aim for the Six Castles Cycleway (NCN 44), which runs for 58 miles from Shrewsbury to Leominster.

Tourist offices sell copies of *Cycling for Pleasure in the Marches*, a pack of five maps and guides covering the entire county. You can also download free cycling pamphlets from www.travelshropshire.co.uk.

ℹ️ Information

Secret Shropshire (www.secretsshropshire.org.uk)

Shropshire Tourism (www.shropshiretourism.co.uk)

ℹ️ Getting Around

Shrewsbury is the local transport hub, and handy rail services go to Church Stretton and Ludlow. The invaluable *Shropshire Bus & Train Map,* available free from tourist offices, shows useful routes. **Shropshire Hills Shuttles** (www.shropshirehillsshuttles.co.uk) runs useful bus services along popular hiking routes on weekends and bank holidays.

Shrewsbury

POP 71,710

A delightful jumble of winding medieval streets and timbered Tudor houses leaning at precarious angles, Shrewsbury (*shroos-bree*) was a crucial front in the conflict between English and Welsh in medieval days. Even today, the road bridge running east towards London is known as the English Bridge to mark it out from the Welsh Bridge leading northwest towards Holyhead. Shrewsbury is also the birthplace of Charles Darwin (1809–82).

👁️ Sights

The most handsome buildings can be found on the narrow lanes surrounding St Alkmond's Church (AD 912), particularly along Fish St and amorously named Grope Lane.

Shrewsbury

Shrewsbury

In a cute cobbled square, Shrewsbury's 16th-century **Old Market Hall** contains the town's pocket-sized cinema.

St Mary's Church CHURCH
(www.visitchurches.org.uk; St Mary's St; ⊙10am-5pm Mon-Sat May-early Dec, to 4pm Mon-Sat early Dec-Apr) The fabulous interior of this tall-spired medieval church contains an impressive collection of stained glass, including a 1340 window depicting the Tree of Jesse (a biblical representation of the lineage of Jesus) and a magnificent oak ceiling in the nave, which largely collapsed in a huge gale in 1894 when the top of the spire blew off. Much of the glass in the church is sourced from Europe, including some outstanding Dutch glass from 1500.

Shrewsbury Abbey CHURCH
(☏01743-232723; www.shrewsburyabbey.com; Abbey Foregate; admission by donation; ⊙10am-4pm Apr-Oct, 10.30am-3pm Nov-Mar) All that remains of a vast, cruciform Benedictine monastery founded in 1083 is the lovely red-sandstone Shrewsbury Abbey. Twice the setting for meetings of the English Parliament, the Abbey church lost its spire and

two wings when the monastery was dissolved in 1540. It sustained further damage in 1826 when engineer Thomas Telford ran the London–Holyhead road right through the grounds. Nevertheless, you can still see some impressive Norman, Early English and Victorian features, including an exceptional 14th-century west window.

It's famous as the setting for Ellis Peters' *Chronicles of Brother Cadfael*.

Shrewsbury Museum & Art Gallery   MUSEUM
(☑ 01743-258885; www.shrewsburymuseums.com; The Square; adult/child £4/2; ☺ 10am-5pm) Newly housed in the Music Hall along with the tourist office, the town museum has diverse exhibits covering everything from Roman treasures to Shropshire gold, including the Bronze Age Perry bracelet. Its Prehistory and Roman Gallery is free of charge.

Shrewsbury Castle   CASTLE
(☑ 01743-358516; www.shrewsburymuseum.org.uk; adult/child £2.50/1.50; ☺ 10.30am-5pm Mon-Wed, Fri & Sat, to 4pm Sun late May–mid-Sep, 10.30am-4pm Mon-Wed, Fri & Sat mid-Sep–late May) Hewn from flaking red Shropshire sandstone, the town castle contains the Shropshire Regimental Museum, plus fine views from Laura's Tower and the battlements. The lower level of the Great Hall dates from 1150.

Charles Darwin Statue   MONUMENT
The town's most famous son, naturalist Charles Darwin, was born in the Mount in Shrewsbury's Frankwell area in 1809. He's commemorated by a statue outside the town library, formerly the Shrewsbury School, where he was educated.

Tours

Shrewsbury Walking Tours   WALKING TOUR
(☑ 01743-258888; adult/child £4/2.50; ☺ 2.30pm Mon-Sat, 11am Sun May-Sep) Guided walking tours leave from the tourist office.

Sabrina   BOAT TOUR
(☑ 01743-369741; www.sabrinaboat.co.uk; adult/child £7.50/3.50; ☺ hourly 11am-4pm Mar-Oct) Enjoy Shrewsbury from the water on board the Sabrina, which cruises the River Severn. Trips leave from Victoria Quay near the Welsh Bridge. Ghost cruises run from 7.30pm to 10.30pm on Monday evenings (£7.50/3.50). There are music nights from 7.30pm to 10.30pm on Tuesdays (£5).

Sleeping

Pretty Abbey Foregate is lined with B&Bs.

Corbet Arms   PUB ££
(☑ 01743-709232; www.thecorbetarms.com; Church Rd, Uffington; d £65-95; P ☎) Situated 4 miles east of Shrewsbury in the pint-sized village of Uffington, this peaceful, family-friendly pub has nine beautifully appointed en suite rooms reached by a staircase. Try for top-floor room 10, which has exposed beams, a spacious sitting area and panoramic views of the surrounding countryside. Also serves high-quality food including outstanding Sunday roasts.

Old House Suites   HISTORIC HOTEL ££
(☑ 07813-610904; www.theoldhousesuites.com; The Old House, 20 Dogpole; ste £85-125; P @) Shrewsbury's most historic place to hang your tricorn, the Old House has three lavish suites, all with views of the garden from a gloriously crooked timbered Tudor town house that was once owned by one of Catherine of Aragon's courtiers. The owner conducts hour-long history tours of the property for guests. There's no sign, but it's up the steps from the Dogpole bus stop.

Lion Hotel   HOTEL ££
(☑ 01743-353107; www.thelionhotelshrewsbury.com; Wyle Cop; s/d/ste incl breakfast from £80/108/140; P) A gilded wooden lion crowns the doorway of this famous 16th-century coaching inn, decked out inside with portraits of lords and ladies in powdered wigs. Charles Dickens was a former guest, and the lounge is warmed by a grand stone fireplace. Rooms are lovely, right down to the period-pattern fabrics and ceramic water jugs.

Eating

Good Life
Wholefood Restaurant   VEGETARIAN £
(☑ 01743-350455; Barracks Passage; mains £3.50-7; ☺ 9am-4pm Mon-Sat; ☑) ⏻ Wholesome, freshly prepared vegetarian food is dished up at this healthy refuge off Wyle Cop. Favourites include quiches, nut loaf, salads, soups, veggie lasagne and a lovely spinach moussaka.

Appleyards Delicatessen   DELI £
(☑ 01743-240180; 85 Wyle Cop; ☺ 9am-5pm Tue-Sat) Fantastic traditional shop stuffed with a cornucopia of cheeses and beers.

Golden Cross
MODERN BRITISH ££

(☑ 01743-362507; www.goldencrosshotel.co.uk; 14 Princess St; lunch mains £10.50-14, dinner mains £11.50-19.50; ⊙kitchen noon-2.30pm & 6-10pm) Overwhelmingly romantic, this candlelit inn dating from 1428 has an inventive, impeccably executed menu, with dishes such as semolina-crusted ricotta-and-nutmeg dumplings, BBQ-glazed ribs with pineapple salsa and smoked garlic, and duck with plum sauce. Upstairs, five exquisite guest rooms (doubles £75 to £150) have luxurious touches including free-standing bathtubs and chaises longues.

Drapers Hall
FRENCH £££

(☑ 01743-344679; www.drapershallrestaurant.co.uk; 10 St Mary's Pl; mains £12-25; ⊙kitchen noon-2.30pm & 6.30-9pm; P 🐾) The sense of history is palpable in this beautifully preserved 16th-century hall, fronted by an elegant Elizabethan facade. Award-winning Anglo-French haute cuisine is served in rooms adorned with wood panelling and artwork, and upstairs there are spectacular heirloom-filled bedrooms (doubles £105 to £155).

🍷 Drinking & Nightlife

Henry Tudor House
PUB

(www.henrytudorhouse.com; Barracks Passage; ⊙11am-11pm Mon-Thu, to 1am Fri & Sat, noon-11pm Sun) Tucked off Wyle Cop, this seriously overhanging black-and-white beauty was built in the early 15th century and is where Henry VII stayed before the Battle of Bosworth. Today it melds old and new with a zinc bar, light-filled conservatory and birdcage-encased chandeliers. Live gigs regularly take to the stage. Good menu, too.

Three Fishes
PUB

(www.realaleshrewsbury.co.uk; 4 Fish St; ⊙11.30am-3pm & 5-11pm Mon-Thu, to 11pm Fri & Sat, noon-10.30pm Sun) The quintessential creaky Tudor alehouse, with a jolly publican, mellow regulars and hops hanging from the 15th-century beamed ceiling.

☆ Entertainment

Old Market Hall Film & Digital Media
CINEMA

(☑ 01743-281281; www.oldmarkethall.co.uk; The Square; ⊙10am-9pm Mon-Sat, noon-6pm Sun; 🐾) View mainstream and art-house movies in a charming Elizabethan setting.

Theatre Severn
THEATRE

(☑ 01743-281281; www.theatresevern.co.uk; Frankwell Quay) This much-acclaimed and expansive new riverside theatre and music venue hosts everything from pop gigs and comedy nights to plays and classical concerts.

ℹ Information

Tourist office (☑ 01743-258888; www.visit-shrewsbury.com; The Square; ⊙10am-5pm daily Apr-Oct, to 5pm Tue-Sun Nov-Mar) In the Music Hall along with the Shrewsbury Museum & Art Gallery (p435).

ℹ Getting There & Away

BUS

The **bus station** (Smithfield Rd) is beside the river. Bus 435 runs to Ludlow (£3.50, 1½ hours, hourly Monday to Friday, every two hours Saturday), via Church Stretton (£2.70, 45 minutes). Other useful services include the following:

Birmingham National Express; £7, 1½ hours, twice daily

Ironbridge Bus 96; £3, 50 minutes, every two hours Monday to Saturday

London Victoria National Express; £22.10, 4½ hours, twice daily

TRAIN

From the train station at the bottom of Castle Foregate, trains run to Birmingham (£13.60, one hour, half-hourly), Ludlow (£14.20, 30 minutes, half-hourly) and London Euston (£68, 2¾ hours, every 20 minutes).

If you're bound for Wales, **Arriva Trains Wales** (☑ 0845 606 1660; www.arrivatrainswales.co.uk) runs to Swansea (£44.20, 3¾ hours, hourly) and Holyhead (£57.20, three hours, hourly).

ℹ Getting Around

Dave Mellor Cycles (☑ 01743-366662; www.davemellorcycles.com; 9a New St, Frankwell; per half-day/day £7.50/15; ⊙9am-6pm Mon-Sat) Rents bikes for adults (no kids' bikes available).

Attingham Park

Straight from a bodice-ripping period drama, **Attingham Park** (NT; ☑ 01743-708123; www.nationaltrust.org.uk; house & grounds adult/child £9.45/5.25, grounds only £4.55/2.35; ⊙house 10.30am-5.30pm mid-Mar–early Nov, grounds 8am-7pm May-Sep, 9am-6pm Mar-Apr & Oct, to 5pm Nov-Mar) was built in imposing neoclassical style in 1785. It has a grand columned facade, manicured lawns, and a stagecoach turning-circle in the courtyard. Home to some 300 fallow deer, the landscaped grounds swirl around an ornamental lake. The restored walled garden is a picture.

Attingham Park is 4 miles southeast of Shrewsbury at Atcham – take bus 81 or 96 (£2.10, 20 minutes, six per day Monday to Saturday).

Ironbridge Gorge

Strolling or cycling through the woods, hills and villages of this peaceful river gorge, it's hard to believe such a sleepy enclave could really have been the birthplace of the Industrial Revolution. Nevertheless, it was here that Abraham Darby perfected the art of smelting iron ore with coke in 1709, making it possible to mass-produce cast iron for the first time.

Abraham Darby's son, Abraham Darby II, invented a new forging process for producing single beams of iron, allowing Abraham Darby III to astound the world with the first-ever iron bridge, constructed in 1779. The bridge remains the focal point of this World Heritage Site, and 10 very different museums tell the story of the Industrial Revolution in the buildings where it took place.

◎ Sights & Activities

★ Museum of the Gorge   MUSEUM
(☑ 01952-433424; www.ironbridge.org.uk; The Wharfage; adult/child £4.15/3.25; ☺10am-5pm Mar-early Nov, to 4pm early Nov-Feb) Kick off your visit at the Museum of the Gorge, which offers an overview of the World Heritage Site using film, photos and 3-D models. Housed in a Gothic warehouse by the river, it's filled with entertaining, hands-on exhibits.

★ Iron Bridge   BRIDGE
(www.ironbridge.org.uk; ☺toll house 10am-5pm Sat & Sun Mar-early Nov, to 4pm Sat & Sun early Nov-Feb, daily during school holidays) FREE The flamboyant, arching and gravel-strewn Iron Bridge, which gives the area its name, was built to flaunt the new technology invented by the pioneering Darby family. At the time of its construction in 1779, nobody could believe that anything so large – it weighs 384 tonnes – could be built from cast iron without collapsing under its own weight. There's a small exhibition on the bridge's history at the former toll house.

Blists Hill Victorian Town   MUSEUM
(☑ 01952-433424; www.ironbridge.org.uk; Legges Way; adult/child £16.50/11; ☺10am-5pm Mar-early Nov, to 4pm early Nov-Feb) Set at the top of the Hay Inclined Plane (a cable lift that once transported coal barges uphill from the Shropshire Canal), Blists Hill is a lovingly restored Victorian village repopulated with townsfolk in period costume, busy with day-to-day chores. There's even a bank, where you can exchange your modern pounds for shillings to use at the village shops. In summer, a Victorian fair is an added attraction for young ones.

Museum of Iron   MUSEUM
(www.ironbridge.org.uk; Wellington Rd; adult/child, £8.50/5.75, incl Darby Houses £9.25/6.75; ☺10am-5pm Mar-early Nov, to 4pm early Nov-Feb) Set in the brooding buildings of Abraham Darby's original iron foundry, the Museum of Iron contains some excellent interactive exhibits. As well as producing the girders for the Ironbridge, the factory became famous for heavy machinery and extravagant ornamental castings, including the gates for London's Hyde Park.

Darby Houses   MUSEUM
(☑ 01952-433522; www.ironbridge.org.uk; adult/child £5.25/3.75, incl Museum of Iron £9.25/6.75; ☺10am-5pm late Mar-early Nov) These beautifully restored 18th-century homes housed generations of the Darby family in gracious but modest Quaker comfort. They're just uphill from the Museum of Iron.

Coalport China Museum & Tar Tunnel   MUSEUM
(www.ironbridge.org.uk; museum adult/child £8.50/5.75, Tar Tunnel £3.25/2.50; ☺10.30am-4pm Mar-early Nov) As ironmaking fell into decline, Ironbridge diversified into manufacturing china pots, using the fine clay mined around Blists Hill. Dominated by a pair of towering bottle kilns, the atmospheric old china works now contains an absorbing museum tracing the history of the industry, with demonstrations of traditional pottery techniques.

> ### ⓘ IRONBRIDGE GORGE MUSEUM PASSPORT
>
> The 10 Ironbridge museums are administered by the **Ironbridge Gorge Museum Trust** (☑ 01952-433424; www.ironbridge.org.uk). You'll save considerably by buying a **passport ticket** (adult/child £27.50/16.50) at any of the museums or the tourist office. Valid for 12 months, it allows unlimited entry to all of Ironbridge Gorge's sites.

Ironbridge Gorge

Ironbridge Gorge

A short stroll along the canal brings you to the 200-year-old Tar Tunnel, an artificial watercourse that was abandoned when natural bitumen started trickling from its walls.

Jackfield Tile Museum MUSEUM
(☎ 01952-433424; www.ironbridge.org.uk; adult/child £8.50/5.75; ⊗10am-5pm late Mar-early Nov, to 4pm early Nov-late Mar) Once the largest tile factory in the world, Jackfield was famous for its encaustic tiles, with ornate designs produced using layers of different coloured clay. Tiles are still produced here today for period restorations. Gas-lit galleries re-create ornately tiled rooms from past centuries including Victorian public conveniences. The museum is on the south bank of the Severn – cross the footbridge at the bottom of the Hay Inclined Plane. Tile decorating workshops take place on Tuesdays (from 10am; £5).

Enginuity MUSEUM
(www.ironbridge.org.uk; Wellington Rd; adult/child £8.75/7.25; ⊗10am-5pm late Mar-early Nov, to 4pm early Nov-late Mar) If the kids are starting to look glazed, recharge their batteries at this levers-and-pulleys science centre beside the Museum of Iron, where you can control robots, move a steam locomotive with your bare hands (and a little engineering know-how) and power up a vacuum cleaner with self-generated electricity.

Broseley Pipeworks MUSEUM
(www.ironbridge.org.uk; adult/child £5.25/3.75; ⊗1-5pm mid-May–mid-Sep) This was once the biggest clay tobacco pipe-maker in the country, but the industry nose-dived after the introduction of prerolled cigarettes in the 1880s, and the factory was preserved much as it was when the lights were turned off in 1957. The pipeworks is a 1-mile walk south

of the river (cross the Ironbridge and follow the signs) on a winding lane that passes the old workers' cottages. Ask the tourist office for the *Jitties* leaflet, which has a walking tour of laneways around the pipeworks.

Bedlam Furnaces NOTABLE BUILDING
By the River Severn, you can see the remains of the 1750s-built coke-fired blast furnaces, which remained in use into the 19th century.

Ironbridge Leisure CANOEING, KAYAKING
(☎ 01952-433518; www.ironbridgeleisure.co.uk; 31 High St; kayak/canoe rental from £20/25; ⊗9am-5pm Tue-Sat) In summer, when the river is at a safe level, you can rent canoes and kayaks to explore the gorge and surrounding areas on 5-mile excursions (around three hours) or multiday camping trips.

⌂ Sleeping

Rooms are everywhere in Ironbridge and nearby Telford has modern hotels. Ironbridge has two YHA hostels but the Coalbrookdale hostel is reserved for groups.

Ye Olde Robin Hood PUB £
(☎ 01952-433071; www.yeolderobinhoodinn.co.uk; 33 Waterloo St; d from £55; P�) New managers are revitalising this quaint, white-washed, traditional inn on the banks of the River Severn. Its three spotless rooms come with king-size mattresses; the bar does well-priced, dependable food and you're treated like a regular from the moment you walk in the door.

Coalport YHA HOSTEL £
(☎ 0845 371 9325; www.yha.org.uk; High St; dm/d from £13/50; P☎) In a converted china factory in the quietest, prettiest corner of Ironbridge. Rooms are modern and functional

WORTH A TRIP

COSFORD ROYAL AIR FORCE MUSEUM

This famous aerospace museum (☑ 01902-376200; www.rafmuseum.org. uk; Shifnal; ⊘ 10am-6pm Mar-Oct, to 5pm Nov-Feb) 13 miles east of Ironbridge is run by the Royal Air Force, whose pilots steered many of these winged wonders across the skies. Among the 70 aircraft on display are the Vulcan bomber (which carried Britain's nuclear deterrent) and the tiny helicopter-like FA330 Bachstelze glider that was towed behind German U-boats to warn them of enemy ships. You can also try out a Black Hawk simulator. It's a half-mile walk from Cosford train station, on the Birmingham–Shrewsbury line.

The Red Arrows stunt team paint the sky with coloured smoke during the Cosford Air Show (www.cosfordair-show.co.uk) in June .

but the biggest drawcards are the facilities, which include a laundry, kitchen and licensed cafe, with wi-fi in common areas.

★ **Library House**　　B&B **££**
(☑ 01952-432299; www.libraryhouse.com; 11 Severn Bank; s/d from £75/90; P @ �rm) Up an alley off the main street, this lovingly restored Georgian library building is hugged by vines, backed by a beautiful garden and decked out with stacks of vintage books, curios, prints and lithographs. There are three charmingly well-preserved, individually decorated rooms, named Milton, Chaucer and Eliot. The affable dog whipping around is Millie.

Calcutts House　　B&B **££**
(☑ 01952-882631; www.calcuttshouse.co.uk; Calcutts Rd; s/tw/d from £55/70/90; P �
) This former ironmaster's pad dates from the 18th century. It's tucked away on the south bank around the corner from the Jackfield Tile Museum, about a mile east of the bridge. Its traditionally decorated rooms have heaps of character, and one is furnished with an out-sized two-hundred-year-old four-poster bed.

✖ Eating & Drinking

Most places to eat line the High St, but old-fashioned pubs dot both banks of the River Severn.

Deli-Dale　　DELI **£**
(Dale End, Coalbrookdale; dishes £3-5.50; ⊘ 8.30am-5.30pm Mon-Fri, 10am-4pm Sat, noon-4pm Sun; ☎ ♿) This wonderful deli is far and away the best place in the area for a light meal. Steaming-hot soups, salads, cakes and sandwiches are all freshly made; take them away or else dine in the cosy shop or at umbrella-shaded picnic tables in the courtyard. Very family-friendly.

D'arcys at the Station　　MEDITERRANEAN **££**
(☑ 01952-884499; www.darcysironbridge.co.uk; Ladywood; mains £12-14; ⊘ 6-9.30pm Tue-Sat) Just over the bridge by the river, the handsome old station building is the backdrop for flavoursome Mediterranean dishes, from Moroccan chicken to Cypriot kebabs and Tuscan bean casserole.

Restaurant Severn　　BRITISH, FRENCH **£££**
(☑ 01952-432233; www.restaurantsevern.co.uk; 33 High St; 2-/3-course lunch menu £18.95/20.95, 2-/3-course dinner menu from £25.95/27.95; ⊘ 6.30pm-8.30pm Wed-Sat, noon-1.30pm Sun; P) The highly praised fare at this small, unadorned riverside restaurant is a winning English–French hybrid. The locally sourced menu changes weekly but incorporates creations such as Shropshire venison medallions with cognac and sundried cranberry sauce. Menu prices rise slightly on Fridays and Saturdays.

ℹ Information

Tourist Office (☑ 01952-433424; www. ironbridge.co.uk; The Wharfage; ⊘ 10am-5pm) Located at the Museum of the Gorge.

ℹ Getting There & Away

The nearest train station is 6 miles away at Telford, from where you can travel to Ironbridge on bus 96 (£2.10, 15 minutes, six per day Monday to Saturday). The same bus continues from Ironbridge's tourist office to Shrewsbury (£5.10, 35 minutes). Bus 99 runs from Bridgnorth (£3.20, 45 minutes, nine per day Monday to Saturday) and bus 88 runs to Much Wenlock (£3.50, 30 minutes, every two hours Monday to Saturday).

ℹ Getting Around

At weekends and on bank holidays from Easter to October, the Gorge Connect bus (£1.65; Museum Passport holders £1) runs from Telford bus station to all of the museums on the north bank of the Severn. A Day Rover pass costs £2.20/1.55 per adult/child.

Much Wenlock

POP 2210

With one of those quirky names that abound in the English countryside, Much Wenlock is as charming as it sounds. Surrounding the time-worn ruins of Wenlock Priory, the streets are studded with Tudor, Jacobean and Georgian houses, and locals say hello to everyone. This storybook English village also claims to have jump-started the modern Olympics.

Sights

Guildhall   HISTORIC BUILDING

(01952-727509; admission £1; 10.30am-1pm & 2-4.30pm Mon-Sat & 2-4.30pm Sun Apr-Oct) Built in classic Tudor style in 1540, the wonky Guildhall features some splendidly ornate woodcarving. One of the pillars supporting it was used for public floggings in medieval times.

Holy Trinity Church   CHURCH

(www.muchwenlockchurch.co.uk; 9am-5pm) The ancient, eroded Holy Trinity Church was built in 1150 over Saxon foundations. Note the Norman arch as you enter with the (as yet) undeciphered initials 'AB' and 'RI' on either side. Also look out for the old police station nearby, dating from 1864.

Wenlock Priory   RUIN

(EH; 01952-727466; www.english-heritage.org.uk; adult/child incl audioguide £4.20/2.50; 10am-6pm Apr-Sep, to 5pm Oct, to 4pm Sat & Sun Nov-Mar; P) The maudlin Cluniac ruins of Wenlock Priory rise up from vivid green lawns, sprinkled with animal-shaped topiary. Raised by Norman monks over the ruins of a Saxon monastery from AD 680, the hallowed remains include a finely decorated chapterhouse and an unusual carved lavabo, where monks came to ceremonially wash before eating.

Sleeping & Eating

Raven Hotel   HOTEL ££

(01952-727251; www.ravenhotel.com; Barrow St; d £85-95, ste £105, lunch mains £11-13, dinner 2-/3-course menu £28/36; P) Much Wenlock's finest digs, this 17th-century coaching inn and converted stables has oodles of historical charm and rich country-chic styling. Overlooking a flower-filled courtyard, the excellent restaurant serves classic Mediterranean and British fare.

Fox   PUB ££

(01952-727292; www.the-fox-inn.co.uk; 46 High St; s/d from £65/85, mains £13.50-16.50; noon-2pm & 6-9.30pm Tue-Sat, to 2pm Sun; P@) Warm yourself by the massive fireplace, then settle down in the dining room to savour locally sourced venison, pheasant and beef, swished down with a pint of Shropshire ale. Candlelit dinners here are lovely. It also has five contemporary rooms.

Information

Tourist Office (01952-727679; www.much-wenlockguide.info; The Square; 10.30am-1pm & 1.30-5pm Apr-Oct, 10.30am-1pm & 1.30-4pm Fri-Sun Nov-Mar) Has a modest museum (admission free) of local history.

Getting There & Away

Bus 436 runs from Shrewsbury to Much Wenlock (£3.30, 35 minutes, hourly Monday to Saturday) and on to Bridgnorth (£3.30, 20 minutes). Bus 88 runs to Ironbridge (£2.60, 30 minutes, every two hours Monday to Saturday).

BIRMINGHAM, THE MIDLANDS & THE MARCHES MUCH WENLOCK

GRANDADDY OF THE MODERN OLYMPICS

All eyes were on London for the Olympic Games in 2012, but tiny Much Wenlock held its own Olympic Games in July the same year, as it has annually since 1850. The idea of holding a sporting tournament based on the games of ancient Greece was the brainchild of local doctor William Penny Brookes, who was looking for a healthy diversion for bored local youths. Accordingly, he created a tournament for 'every kind of man', with running races, high and long jumps, tilting, hammer throwing and wheelbarrow races – plus glee singing, knitting and sewing for every kind of woman.

The games soon piqued the interest of Baron Pierre Coubertin, who visited in 1890 and consulted Brookes extensively before launching the modern Olympic Games in Athens in 1896. Unfortunately, Brookes was effectively airbrushed out of the Olympic story until 1994, when then-International Olympic Committee President Juan Antonio Samaranch visited Much Wenlock to pay his respects to 'the founder of the Modern Olympic Games'.

The Much Wenlock Olympics are still held every July, with events that range from the triathlon to volleyball; for details visit www.wenlock-olympian-society.org.uk.

Around Much Wenlock

The spectacular limestone escarpment of Wenlock Edge swells up like an immense petrified wave, breaking over the Shropshire countryside. Formed from limestone that once lined the bottom of Silurian seas, the ridge sprawls for 15 miles from Much Wenlock to Craven Arms along the route of the B4371, providing a fantastic hiking backroute from Ludlow and Ironbridge Gorge.

Wilderhope Manor YHA (☑ 0845 371 9149; www.yha.org.uk; Longville-in-the-Dale; dm/d/f from £16/48/75; ☺ Fri, Sat & school holidays; P) is a gloriously atmospheric gabled grey-stone Elizabethan manor, with spiral stair-cases, wood-panelled walls, an impressive stone-floored dining hall and spacious, oak-beamed rooms – this is hostelling for royalty. Bus 155 from Ludlow (£3.70, 50 minutes) runs once daily Monday to Friday to Shipton, a half-mile walk from Wilderhope – call the hostel for timetables.

Bridgnorth & Around

POP 12,315

Cleaved into two by a dramatic sandstone bluff that tumbles down to the River Severn, Bridgnorth is one of Shropshire's finest-looking historic towns, with a wealth of architectural charm despite much of the High Town succumbing to fire in 1646 during the Civil War.

Around its namesake church, the High Town's adorable St Leonard's Close contains some of the most attractive buildings and almshouses in town, including a splendid six-gabled house, once part of the grammar school.

A 19th-century cliff railway and several narrow lanes drop down from the High Town to the Low Town, including the very steep pedestrian Cartway, at the bottom of which is Bishop Percy's House, dating from 1580.

◉ Sights & Activities

Northgate   MUSEUM
(www.bridgnorthmuseum.org.uk; Northgate; ☺ 1.30-4pm Sat, 11am-4pm Sun Easter-Oct, 11am-4pm Sun-Fri, 1.30-4pm Sat during school holidays) FREE Northgate is the last surviving gate of five that originally guarded the town, and contains a small museum on local history run by volunteers from the Historical Society.

Daniels Mill   MILL
(☑ 01746-762753; www.danielsmill.co.uk; adult/child £5/4; ☺ 11am-4pm Easter-Oct) One mile south of the centre, Daniels Mill is the largest working water-powered mill in the country, and still produces flour for local bakers. Visitors get a personal tour of the working machinery from the resident miller.

Bridgnorth Cliff Railway   HISTORIC RAILWAY
(☑ 01746-762052; www.bridgnorthcliffrailway.co.uk; return £1.20; ☺ 8am-8pm Mon-Sat & noon-8pm Sun May-Sep, to 6.30pm Oct-Apr) Britain's steepest inland railway has trundled up the cliff since 1892. At the top of the route, a pedestrian walkway (affording astonishing night-time panoramas) curves around the bluff to a pretty park dotted with scattered masonry, some leaning at an incredible angle (all that remains of Bridgnorth Castle), and passes the grand and imposing Thomas Telford-designed and cupola-topped St Mary's Church.

Severn Valley Railway   HISTORIC RAILWAY
(☑ 01299-403816; www.svr.co.uk; adult one-way/return £12.50/18, child £8/11.50; ☺ daily May-Sep, Sat & Sun Oct-Apr) Bridgnorth is the northern terminus of the Severn Valley Railway, whose historic steam or diesel locomotives chug down the valley to Kidderminster (one hour) starting from the station on Hollybush Rd. Check the calendar for additional event dates.

Cyclists can follow a beautiful 20-mile section of the Mercian Way (NCN Route 45) beside the railway line towards the Wyre Forest.

🛏 Sleeping & Eating

Severn Arms Hotel   HOTEL ££
(☑ 01746-764616; www.thesevernarms.co.uk; 3 Underhill St; s with/without en suite £32/46, d £64, f £75; ☎) At the bottom of the bluff right next to the cliff railway, this comfortable riverside Georgian property has gorgeous views over the bridge. The helpful owners can direct you to parking a few minute's walk away over the bridge.

Cinnamon Cafe   CAFE £
(☑ 01746-762944; Waterloo House, Cartway; mains £5-8; ☺ 9am-6pm Mon-Wed & Fri, 10am-4pm Sat & Sun; ☑) Sweeping views extend from the dining room and terrace of this licensed cafe near the top of the Cartway. It serves up savoury bakes (many vegetarian and vegan) plus quiches, homemade muesli and cakes.

Bridgnorth Delicatessen DELI £
(www.delicatessen.tv; 45 High St; ⊙ 9am-5pm Mon-Sat, 11am-4pm Sun) Pick up picnic ingredients from the well-stocked Bridgnorth Delicatessen, a lovely old shop full of gleaming jars.

❶ Information

Tourist Office (☑ 01746-763257; www.visit-bridgnorth.co.uk; ⊙ 9.30am-5pm Mon-Wed, Fri & Sat year-round, 10am-1pm & 2-5pm Thu Apr-Oct) Based at the town library.

❶ Getting There & Away

Bus 436 runs from Shrewsbury to Bridgnorth (£3.30, one hour, hourly Monday to Saturday), via Much Wenlock (£3.30, 25 minutes). Bus 99 runs to Ironbridge (£3.30, 30 minutes, every two hours Monday to Saturday).

Church Stretton & Around

POP 3700

Set in a deep valley formed by the Long Mynd and the Caradoc Hills, Church Stretton is an ideal base for walks or cycle tours through the Shropshire Hills. Although black-and-white timbers are heavily in evidence, most of the buildings in town are 19th-century fakes, built by the Victorians who flocked here to take the country air. The Norman-era St Laurence's Church features an exhibitionist sheila-na-gig over its north door.

⭐ Activities

Walking

Church Stretton clings to the steeply sloping sides of the Long Mynd, Shropshire's most famous hill, which rises to 517m. Dubbed 'Little Switzerland' by the Victorians, this desolate but dramatic bluff is girdled by walking trails that offer soaring views over the surrounding countryside. Most people start walking from the National Trust car park (per day £2.50) at the end of the Carding Mill Valley (www.cardingmillvalley.org.uk), half a mile west of Shrewsbury Rd. A small tearoom (dishes £3.50-5; ⊙ 10am-5pm Apr-Oct, to 4pm Nov-Mar) here provides refreshments.

A maze of single-track roads climbs over the Long Mynd to the adjacent ridge of Stiperstones, crowned by a line of spooky-looking crags. You can continue right over the ridge, passing the Bog (☑ 01743-792484; www.bogcentre.co.uk; ⊙ 10am-5pm Wed-Sun Easter-Oct) tourist office and cafe in a Victorian-era school by the ruins of an abandoned mining village, heading to the village

of Snailbeach (☑ 01743-790613; www.shropshiremines.org.uk; tours £7.50/3; ⊙ tours 11am-4pm Sun Jun-Sep), with its intriguing mining relics.

Other Activities

The tourist office has maps of local mountain-biking circuits and details of horse-riding stables (visit www.shropshireriding.co.uk for info).

Plush Hill Cycles CYCLING
(☑ 01694-720133; www.plushhillcycles.co.uk; 8 The Square; per half-day/day from £17/22; ⊙ 8.30am-6pm Mon, Tue, Thu & Fri, to 5pm Sat, 10am-4pm Sun) Handy range of mountain bikes and electric bikes. Rates include helmets, maps and child seats.

🛏 Sleeping

Bridges Long Mynd YHA HOSTEL £
(☑ 01588-650656; www.yha.org.uk; Bridges; dm from £16; ℗) On the far side of the Long Mynd, this wonderfully isolated hiker favourite is housed in a former school in the tiny hamlet of Bridges, 1.1 miles from Ratlinghope. Meals and liquid refreshment are available at the nearby Horseshoe Inn pub. No wi-fi, no phone reception, no credit cards. Cross the Mynd to Ratlinghope, or take the Long Mynd & Stiperstones Shuttle (p444) bus.

Mynd Guest House B&B ££
(☑ 01694-722212; www.myndhouse.co.uk; Ludlow Rd; s/d from £50/80; ℗@�) Just under 2 miles south of Church Stretton in Little Stretton, this inviting, family-friendly guesthouse has splendid views across the valley and backs directly onto the Mynd. The lovely rooms are named after local hills; there's a small bar and lounge stocked with local books; and a room for drying your boots.

🍴 Eating & Drinking

Several cosy pubs line Church Stretton's High St.

Berry's Coffee House CAFE £
(☑ 01694-724452; www.berryscoffeehouse.co.uk; 17 High St; mains £6-9.50; ⊙ 9am-5pm Sun-Thu, later Fri & Sat; ✋) 🌿 A cosy cafe with loads of rooms in an 18th-century house, Berry's offers an organic, free-range, fair-trade, home-cooked menu, including Shropshire breakfasts and wicked desserts. No credit cards.

Bridges PUB ££
(☑ 01588-650260; www.thebridgespub.co.uk; Ratlinghope; lunch mains £9-14, dinner mains £10.50-17.50; ⊙ kitchen noon-3pm & 6.30-9pm) Some 5

miles northeast of Church Stretton, at the base of Long Mynd (tucked away just 160m from Bridges Long Mynd YHA by the river), this is one of those secret country pubs revered for its live music, riverside terrace, relaxed accommodation (dorm/double from £15/50) and impressive food (pork belly in cider; mushroom and goats cheese strudel...). Hard to find but absolutely worth it.

ℹ Information

Tourist Office (☏ 01694-723133; www.church-stretton.co.uk; Church St; ⊙ 9.30am-3pm Mon, Tue & Thu-Sat) Adjoining the library. Has abundant walking information and free internet terminals.

ℹ Getting There & Around

Trains between Ludlow (£6.80) and Shrewsbury (£5.90) stop in Church Stretton hourly, taking 15 minutes from either end. Alternatively, take bus 435 from Shrewsbury or Ludlow (£2.70, 40 minutes, hourly Monday to Saturday).

Bus 553 runs from Shrewsbury to Bishop's Castle via Stiperstones and Snailbeach (£3.30, 40 minutes, four daily Monday to Saturday).

From Easter to September, the hail-and-ride **Long Mynd & Stiperstones Shuttle** (www.shropshirehillsaonb.co.uk; Day Rover ticket £7; ⊙ 7 daily Sat & Sun Apr-Sep) runs from the Carding Mill Valley near Church Stretton to the villages atop the Long Mynd, passing the YHA at Bridges, and Stiperstones near the Snailbeach mine.

Bishop's Castle

POP 1895

Set amid peaceful Shropshire countryside, Bishop's Castle is a tangle of timbered town houses and Old Mother Hubbard cottages. The High St climbs from the town church to the refurbished Georgian town hall (1765) abutting the crooked 16th-century House on Crutches (☏ 01588-630556; www.hocmuseum.org.uk; ⊙ 2-5pm Sat & Sun Apr-Sep) FREE, which also houses the town museum.

🏃 Activities

Walkers can hike from Bishop's Castle along the Shropshire Way, which joins up with the long-distance Offa's Dyke Path and Kerry Ridgeway to the west. The northern sections of the Shropshire Way climb to the high country of the Stiperstones and the Long Mynd near Church Stretton. Bishop's Castle also lies on the popular Six Castles Cycleway (NCN Route 44) between Shrewsbury and Leominster.

🛏 Sleeping & Eating

Castle Hotel   HOTEL **££**
(☏ 01588-638403; www.thecastlehotelbishopscastle.co.uk; The Square; s/d/f incl breakfast from £100/105/150, mains £11-20; P 🛜) This solid-looking 18th-century coaching inn was built with stones from the now-vanished Bishop's Castle, which also contributed the gorgeous wood panelling in the dining room. All eight en suite rooms are lovely, with modern fabrics meeting old antique furniture. The pub bar in the hotel is decidedly cosy and the garden delightful. Rates increase at the weekends.

Yarborough House   CAFE **£**
(www.yarboroughhouse.com; The Square; dishes £3.50-5; ⊙ 10am-5pm Tue & Thu-Sun) Coffee and cakes in a cosy secondhand bookshop with a simply vast collection of secondhand classical-music recordings.

🍷 Drinking & Nightlife

Three Tuns   PUB
(www.thethreetunsinn.co.uk; Salop St; ⊙ noon-11pm Mon-Sat, to 8.30pm Sun) Bishop's Castle's finest watering hole is attached to the tiny Three Tuns Brewery (www.threetunsbrewery.co.uk), which has been rolling barrels of nutbrown ale across the courtyard since 1642. It's a lively local, and the ales are delicious.

ℹ Information

Tourist Office (☏ 01588-630023; http://bishopscastletownhall.co.uk; ⊙ 10am-4pm Mon-Sat) In the restored Town Hall.

ℹ Getting There & Away

Bus 553 runs to and from Shrewsbury (£3.10, one hour, half-hourly Monday to Saturday). On Saturdays, Sundays and bank holidays from mid-April to September, you can jump on the Castle Connect Shuttle from Ludlow (Day Rover ticket/single £7/1.30, 1¼ hours, three per day).

Ludlow

POP 10,515

Exactly why this genteel market town fanning out from the rambling ruins of a fine Norman castle became a national gastronomic phenomenon is not entirely clear, but today Ludlow's delightful muddle of narrow streets are crammed with independent butchers, bakers, grocers, cheesemongers and exceptional restaurants.

◉ Sights & Activities

Ludlow is ringed by wonderful landscapes. Starting just outside Ludlow Castle entrance, the waymarked **Mortimer Trail** runs for 30 miles through idyllic English countryside to Kington in Herefordshire. The tourist office has various leaflets describing the route, or visit www.exploremortimercountry.com.

Ludlow Castle   CASTLE
(☑ 01584-873355; www.ludlowcastle.com; Castle Sq; adult/child £5/2.50; ☺ 10am-6pm daily Aug, to 5pm Apr-Jul & Sep, to 4pm Oct, Nov, Feb & Mar, to 4pm Sat & Sun Dec & Jan) Perched in an ideal defensive location atop a cliff that's above a crook in the river, the town castle was built to ward off the marauding Welsh – or to enforce the English expansion into Wales, perspective depending. Founded after the Norman conquest, the castle was dramatically expanded in the 14th century.

The Norman chapel in the inner bailey is one of the few surviving round chapels in England, and the sturdy keep (built around 1090) offers wonderful views over the hills.

Church of St Laurence   CHURCH
(www.stlaurences.org.uk; King St; admission by £3 donation; ☺ 10am-5.30pm Apr-Sep, 11am-4pm Oct-Mar) One of Britain's largest parish churches, the church of St Laurence contains grand Elizabethan alabaster tombs and delightfully cheeky medieval misericords carved into its medieval choir stalls, including a beer-swilling chap raiding his barrel. The Lady Chapel contains a marvellous **Jesse Window** originally dating from 1330 (although the glass is mostly Victorian). Four windows in St John's Chapel date from the mid-15th century, including the honey-coloured **Golden Window**. Climb 200 steps up the **tower** (included in donation) for stunning views.

☞ Tours

Town Tours   WALKING TOUR
(☑ 01584-874205; www.ludlowhistory.co.uk; adult/child £3/free; ☺ 2.30pm Sat & Sun Apr-Oct) Popular town tours leave from the Cannon in Castle Sq.

Ghost Walk   WALKING TOUR
(www.shropshireghostwalks.co.uk; adult/child £4/3; ☺ 8pm Fri) Search for spooks on the ghost walk from outside the Church Inn on the Buttercross.

☆ Festivals & Events

Ludlow Festival   ARTS
(www.ludlowartsfestival.co.uk; ☺ Jun) The town's cultural calendar peaks with this fortnight of theatre and music that uses the castle as its dramatic backdrop.

Ludlow Food & Drink Festival   FOOD
(www.foodfestival.co.uk; ☺ Sep) One of Britain's best foodie celebrations, spanning a long weekend in September.

⌨ Sleeping

Feathers Hotel   HISTORIC HOTEL ££
(☑ 01584-875261; www.feathersatludlow.co.uk; 21 Bull Ring; s/d from £95/130; ⓟ) Stepping through the impossibly ornate timbered Jacobean facade, you'll find this hotel is all tapestries, creaky wood furniture, timber beams and stained glass: you can almost hear the cavaliers toasting the health of King Charles. The best rooms are in the old building; rooms in the newer wing lack the character and romance. The restaurant is highly recommended (2-/3-course menus £32.50/39.95).

Charlton Arms   INN ££
(☑ 01584-872813; www.charltonarms.co.uk; Ludford Bridge; d £90-120; ⓟ ☜) The pick of the rooms at this landmark inn overlook the River Teme, and the pick of those rooms have terraces (one with an outdoor hot tub as well as a four-poster bed). Its restaurant, also opening to a terrace, serves Ludlow-quality Modern British cuisine, and there's a large free car park and superb service.

Dinham Hall Hotel   HOTEL £££
(☑ 01584-876464; www.dinhamhall.com; d £145-195, ste £245; ⓟ ☜) This resplendent 18th-century country manor has views of the castle and the river from gorgeous rooms full of heirloom furniture. There's a superb fine-dining restaurant, Elliots, and afternoon teas.

✕ Eating

Almost every pub and restaurant in town has caught the local-produce-and-deli-ingredients bug. Foodies shouldn't miss the Ludlow Food Centre (p446).

Fish House   SEAFOOD £
(☑ 01584-879790; www.thefishhouseludlow.co.uk; 50 Bull Ring; taster plates £4-9, shellfish platter £65; ☺ 9am-5pm Wed-Fri, to 4pm Sat) Except on Saturdays, when it's first-come, first-served,

bookings are recommended for the barrel tables at this stylish fish and oyster bar. It sources Britain's best seafood: Whitby dressed crab, Arbroath smokies and Bigbury Bay oysters included. The house shellfish platter, available Fridays and Saturdays only, is best washed down with champagne.

Green Cafe
CAFE £

(☑ 01584-879872; www.thegreencafe.co.uk; Mill on the Green, Linney; dishes £5-11; ⊗ 10.30am-4.30pm Tue-Sun) Overlooking the weir, the Green Cafe takes full advantage of its riverside position beneath Ludlow Castle with its 25 outdoor seats (plus another 30 inside). Outstanding food spans warm salt beef baps (soft bread rolls) to tagliatelle with pheasant sauce and parmesan shavings. Wines, beers and ciders are from small-scale producers. Its popularity means you should book ahead.

La Bécasse
MODERN FRENCH £££

(☑ 01584-872325; www.labecasse.co.uk; 17 Corve St; 2-/3-course lunch menu £28/32.50, 2-/3-course dinner menu £45/55; ⊗ noon-2pm & 7-9pm Tue-Fri, noon-2pm & 7-9.30pm Sat) Artistically presented and bursting with inventive flavours, meals are served in an oak-panelled, exposed-brick dining room in the 17th-century coach house. Head chef Chris O'Halloran creates remarkable dishes and also runs masterclasses on the second Monday of each month (£99 including lunch).

Mr Underhill's
MODERN BRITISH £££

(☑ 01584-874431; www.mr-underhills.co.uk; Dinham Weir; 8-course menu £67.50-75; ⊗ 7-9.30pm Wed-Sun) ⊘ This dignified Michelin-starred restaurant is set in a converted corn mill that dips its toes in the river. The Modern British food is exquisitely prepared, using market-fresh ingredients in a menu that changes daily. If you're too content to move, one of the four particularly elegant suites (£220 to £365) can oblige.

🍷 Drinking & Entertainment

Real ales are the order of the day in flavour-obsessed Ludlow.

★ Ludlow Brewing Company
BREWERY, PUB

(☑ 01584-873291; www.theludlowbrewingcompany. co.uk; The Railway Shed, Station Dr; ⊗ 10am-5pm Mon-Thu, to 6pm Fri, to 4pm Sat) Up an inconspicuous laneway, the Ludlow Brewing Company produces award-winning brews and sells directly from the brewery and its airy, post-industrial-style bar. Hour-long tours run at 3pm Monday to Friday and 2pm Saturday (£6 including three half-pints).

Church Inn
PUB

(http://www.thechurchinnludlow.com; Buttercross; ⊗ 10am-midnight Mon-Thu, to 1am Fri & Sat, to 11pm Sun) The hop-strewn Church Inn is a cosy little escape with a pulpit at the bar. It's tucked away on the narrow lane beside the old butter market.

Wheatsheaf Inn
PUB

(www.the-wheatsheaf-inn.co.uk; Lower Broad St; ⊗ noon-11pm) Under the medieval Broadgate, the quiet little Wheatsheaf Inn has a good choice of local ales.

Ludlow Assembly Rooms
CINEMA

(☑ 01584-878141; www.ludlowassemblyrooms. co.uk; adult standard/balcony £6.50/7, child £4/5) Overlooking the market square, Ludlow Assembly Rooms double as the town cinema.

🛍 Shopping

Delis, independent butchers and artisan bakers cluster around the market square and the surrounding lanes.

Ludlow Market
MARKET

(www.ludlowmarket.co.uk; ⊗ Mon, Wed, Fri & Sat) Ludlow Market takes place on the market square on the site of the old Victorian town hall, demolished overnight in 1986.

Ludlow Food Centre
FOOD & DRINK

(☑ 01584-856000; www.ludlowfoodcentre.co.uk; off Bromfield Rd, Bromfield; ⊗ 9am-5.30pm Mon-Wed & Sat, to 6.30pm Thu & Fri, to 4.30pm Sun) ⊘ More than 80% of the cheeses, meats, breads, fruit and vegetables are sourced from the surrounding region and tantalisingly displayed at this enormous farm shop stocking some 4000 products in all. Watch through viewing windows to see traditional preserves, pies, ice cream and more being made. It's signposted 4 miles northwest of Ludlow off Bromfield Rd (the A49).

Produce is utilised by the adjoining cafe/restaurant, the Ludlow Kitchen (www.ludlow kitchen.co.uk; breakfast £3.50-10, lunch mains £7-10, dinner mains £7-15; ⊗ 9am-5pm Mon & Tue, to 5pm & 6.30-10pm Wed-Sat, 10am-4pm Sun).

ℹ Information

Tourist Office (☑ 01584-875053; www.ludlow. org.uk; Castle Sq; ⊗ 10am-5pm daily Apr-Sep, to 4pm Mon-Sat Oct-Mar) Contains a small local-history museum (adult/child £1/free).

ℹ Getting There & Around

Bus 435 runs to Shrewsbury (£4.50, 1½ hours, hourly Monday to Saturday) via Church Stretton (£2.70, 40 minutes). From mid-April to September, the Castle Connect Shuttle links Ludlow with Bishop's Castle (Day Rover ticket/single £7/1.30, 1¼, three daily).

Trains run frequently from the station on the north edge of town to Hereford (£9.50, 25 minutes, half-hourly) and Shrewsbury (£14.20, 30 minutes, half-hourly) via Church Stretton (£6.80, 20 minutes).

Hire bikes from **Wheely Wonderful** (☑ 01568-770755; www.wheelywonderfulcycling.co.uk; Petchfield Farm; adult/child bikes per day from £20/10; ☺ 9am-5pm Mon-Sat, by reservation Sun Apr-Oct), 5 miles west of Ludlow.

NOTTINGHAMSHIRE

Say Nottinghamshire and people think of one thing – Robin Hood. Whether the hero woodsman existed is debated, but the county plays up its connections to the outlaw. Storytelling seems to be in Nottinghamshire's blood – local wordsmiths include provocative writer DH Lawrence, of *Lady Chatterley's Lover* fame, and hedonist poet Lord Byron. The city of Nottingham is the bustling hub, but venture into the surrounding countryside and you'll discover historic towns and stately homes surrounding the Sherwood Forest.

ℹ Information

Experience Nottinghamshire (www.experience nottinghamshire.com)

ℹ Getting There & Around

National Express and **Trent Barton** (☑ 01773-712265; www.trentbarton.co.uk) buses provide the majority of bus services. See **Traveline** (☑ 0871 200 2233; www.travelineeastmidlands.co.uk) for timetables. Trains run frequently to most large towns, and many smaller villages in the Peak District.

Nottingham

POP 289,300

Forever associated with men in tights and a sheriff with anger-management issues – aka the Robin Hood legend – Nottingham is a dynamic county capital with big-city aspirations, atmospheric historical sights, and a buzzing music and club scene thanks to its spirited student population.

◉ Sights & Activities

★ Nottingham Castle & Art Gallery
CASTLE, GALLERY

(☑ 0115-876 1400; www.nottinghamcity.gov.uk/ nottinghamcastle; adult/child £5.50/4, Mortimer's Hole tours £3/free; ☺ 10am-5pm daily mid-Feb–Oct, to 4pm Wed-Sun Nov–mid-Feb, Mortimer's Hole tours 11am, 1pm, 2pm & 3pm) Nottingham's namesake castle crowns a sandstone outcrop worm-holed with caves and tunnels. The original castle was founded by William the Conqueror and held by a succession of English kings before falling in the English Civil War. Its 17th-century manor-house-like replacement contains a local-history museum and an art gallery.

Burrowing through the bedrock, the underground passageway **Mortimer's Hole** emerges at Brewhouse Yard, where you can visit five atmospheric 17th-century cottages housing the **Museum of Nottingham Life at Brewhouse Yard** (☑ 0115-876 1400; www. nottinghamcity.gov.uk; Castle Blvd; adult/child £2.50/free; ☺ noon-4pm Sat & Sun year-round).

In 1330 supporters of Edward III used Mortimer's Hole to breach the castle security and capture Roger Mortimer, the machiavellian earl of March, who briefly appointed himself ruler of England after deposing Edward II.

City of Caves
CAVE

(☑ 0115-988 1955; www.cityofcaves.com; adult/ child £7.50/5.50, incl Galleries of Justice £12.75/9.75; ☺ 10.30am-5pm) Over the centuries, the sandstone underneath Nottingham has been carved into a honeycomb of caverns and passageways. Audio tours (Monday to Friday) and performance tours (weekends and school holidays) lead you from the top level of the Broadmarsh shopping centre through a WWII air-raid shelter, a medieval underground tannery, several pub cellars and a mock-up of a Victorian slum dwelling. Book ahead.

Galleries of Justice
MUSEUM

(☑ 0115-952 0555; www.galleriesofjustice.org.uk; High Pavement; adult/child £9.50/7.50, incl City of Caves £12.75/9.75; ☺ 9am-5.30pm Mon-Fri, 10am-5pm Sat & Sun, tours 10am-4pm Mon-Fri, 10.30am-4.30pm Sat & Sun) In the grand Georgian Shire Hall, the Galleries of Justice offers a ghoulish stroll through centuries of British justice, including medieval trials by fire and water. Audio tours run on Mondays and Tuesdays; live-action tours with 'gaolers' run from Wednesday to Sunday (daily during school holidays).

Nottingham

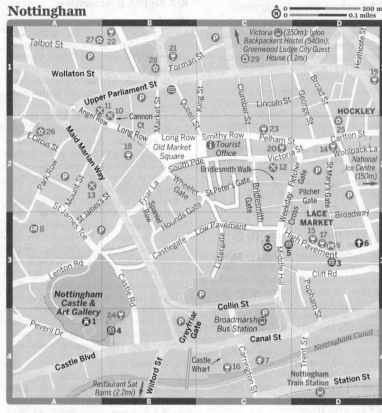

Nottingham Contemporary   GALLERY
(☑ 0115-948 9755; www.nottinghamcontemporary.
org; Weekday Cross; ☺ 10am-7pm Tue-Fri, to 6pm Sat,
11am-5pm Sun) **FREE** Behind its lace-patterned
concrete facade, Nottingham Contemporary
holds edgy, design-driven exhibitions of paintings, prints, photography and sculpture.

St Mary's Church   CHURCH
(www.nottinghamchurches.org; High Pavement;
☺ 10am-3pm Mon-Sat) The most atmospheric
time to visit this historic church dating from
Saxon times is during evensong at 6.15pm.

National Ice Centre   SKATING
(☑ 0843 373 3000; www.national-ice-centre.com;
Bolero Sq; skating £6, skate hire £2) On Bolero
Sq (named for Nottingham skaters Jayne
Torvill and Christopher Dean's iconic 1984
gold-medal-winning routine) lies the UK's
first ice centre with twin Olympic-sized (60m
x 30m) rinks. The complex incorporates the
East Midland's premier entertainment venue,

the **Capital FM Arena**, which hosts sporting
fixtures, competitions and performances.
Daily skating session times are posted online.

☞ Tours

★ **Ezekial Bone Tours**   WALKING TOUR
(☑ 07941 210986; www.bonecorporation.co.uk; Robin Hood Town Tours adult/child £12/7, Guts & Gore
tours £7; ☺ Sat May-Sep) Entertaining history
tours are led by Nottingham's 'modern day
Robin Hood' Ezekial Bone, aka Ade Andrews.
In addition to the 2½-hour Robin Hood town
tours, Bone/Andrews runs regular 80-minute
Guts & Gore ghost tours, plus Robin Hood
Sherwood Forest tours and various other
walks year-round by request. Over 10s only.

Nottingham Princess   CRUISE
(☑ 0115-910 0400; www.princessrivercruises.co.uk;
2/3hr cruises from £14.85/16.35) Lunch, afternoon tea and dinner (and dance) cruises
along the River Trent.

Nottingham

✹ Festivals & Events

Nottingham hosts an intriguing selection of festivals – search events online at www.experiencenottinghamshire.com.

Splendour   MUSIC
(www.splendourfestival.com; ⊙ mid-Jul) The city's biggest live-music festival.

Goose Fair   CULTURAL
(www.nottinghamcity.gov.uk; ⊙ Oct) Early October's medieval Goose Fair has evolved from a travelling market to a modern funfair.

Robin Hood Beer &
Cider Festival   FOOD & DRINK
(www.beerfestival.nottinghamcamra.org; ⊙ Oct) In the castle grounds, this tasting festival in early October features more than 1000 beers and 200 ciders.

Robin Hood Pageant   CULTURAL
(www.experiencenottinghamshire.com; ⊙ Oct) A family-friendly pageant in late October.

⊨ Sleeping

Igloo Backpackers Hostel   HOSTEL £
(☑ 0115-947 5250; www.igloohostel.co.uk; 110 Mansfield Rd; dm/d from £16/44; 🛜) A favourite with international backpackers, this independent hostel is opposite the Golden Fleece pub and a 24-hour supermarket (handy for the self-

catering kitchen). As well as its private-room Annexe, a spiffing new Pods building has private rooms with retro-vintage furniture, grafitti murals, memory foam mattresses and flatscreen TVs.

★**Lace Market Hotel**   BOUTIQUE HOTEL ££
(☑ 0115-852 3232; www.lacemarkethotel.co.uk; 29-31 High Pavement; s/d incl breakfast from £65/85; P🅿🛜) Within an elegant Georgian town house in the heart of the trendy Lace Market, sleek rooms have state-of-the-art furnishings and amenities; some have air-conditioning. Its fine-dining restaurant, Merchants (p450), and adjoining genteel pub, the Cock & Hoop (☑ 0115-852 3231; 25 High Pavement; ⊙ noon-11pm Mon-Thu, to midnight Fri, to 1am Sat, to 10.30pm Sun), are both superb.

Greenwood Lodge
City Guest House   B&B ££
(☑ 0115-962 1206; www.greenwoodlodgecityguesthouse.co.uk; Third Ave, Sherwood Rise; s/d from £51.50/86.50; P🛜) A B&B set in a large Victorian house north of the centre. The location is quiet; the house and frilly rooms are full of period character; and there's a pretty courtyard garden. Children under 10 aren't permitted.

Hart's   BOUTIQUE HOTEL £££
(☑ 0115-988 1900; www.hartsnottingham.co.uk; Standard Hill, Park Row; d from £125; P@🛜)

DON'T MISS

WOLLATON HALL

Built in 1588 for land owner and coal mogul Sir Francis Willoughby by avant-garde architect Robert Smythson, fabulous Wollaton Hall (www.nottinghamcity.gov.uk; Wollaton Park, Derby Rd; parking per 3hr/day £2/4, tours adult/child £5/3; ⊙10am-5pm daily mid-Feb–Oct, 11am-4pm Thu-Mon Nov–mid-Feb, tours 11am, 2pm & 3pm) sits within 200 hectares of grounds roamed by fallow and red deer. Along with extravagant rooms from the Tudor, Regency and Victorian periods, there's a natural history museum and industrial museum.

Wollaton Hall is 2.5 miles west of Nottingham city centre; take bus 30 or 2 from Victoria bus station (£2, 15 minutes, every 15 minutes Monday to Saturday, half-hourly Sunday).

The hall starred as Wayne Manor in 2012's Batman film *The Dark Knight Rises*.

Within the former Nottingham General Hospital compound, the city's swishest hotel has ultracontemporary rooms in a striking modernist building, and its renowned restaurant (☑0115-988 1900; www.hartsnottingham.co.uk; Standard Hill, Park Row; mains £15-29.50; ⊙noon-2.30pm & 6-10pm; ☑) is housed in a historic red-brick wing. Work out in the small gym or unwind in the private garden.

✗ Eating

Nottingham reputedly has more restaurants, pubs and bars per square mile than anywhere else in Europe.

★ Delilah Fine Foods   DELI, CAFE £

(www.delilahfinefoods.co.uk; 12 Victoria St; dishes £6-11; ⊙8am-7pm Mon-Fri, 9am-7pm Sat, 11am-5pm Sun) ✔ Impeccably selected cheeses (more than 150 varieties), pâtés, meats and more from artisan producers are available to take away or eat on-site at this gourmand's dream, housed in a grand former bank with mezzanine seating.

Aubrey's Traditional Crêperie   CREPERIE £

(www.aubreystraditionalcreperie.com; 14-16 West End Arcade; dishes £2.75-7.50; ⊙10am-6pm Mon-Sat) Traditional down to its savoury galettes made with buckwheat flour, its sweet crêpes including salted caramel and its Breton ciders, this little hole-in-the-wall is a charming spot for an inexpensive lunch. Alongside the classics, there are galettes you'll never see in Brittany, such as smoked tofu (with balsamic and plum chutney, beetroot, walnuts, baby spinach and orange zest) too.

Alley Cafe Bar   VEGETARIAN £

(☑0115-955 1013; www.alleycafe.co.uk; 1a Cannon Ct; mains £5.50-8; ⊙11am-9pm Mon & Tue, to 1am Wed-Sat, noon-5pm Sun; ☑) ✔ Down a narrow alleyway, this beat-spinning hippie haven serves dishes such as tofu, tempeh and hemp-seed burgers alongside organic beers,

wines and ciders. It hosts events such as open-mic nights and exhibits local art.

Memsaab   INDIAN ££

(☑0115-957 0009; www.mem-saab.co.uk; 12-14 Maid Marian Way; mains £8.50-19; ⊙5.30-10.30pm Mon-Thu, to 11pm Fri & Sat, 5-10pm Sun) The best of the glamorous modern Indian eateries on Maid Marian Way, Memsaab serves fabulous regional specialities in dinner-date friendly surroundings.

Merchants   GASTRONOMIC £££

(☑0115-852 3232; www.thefinessecollection.com; 29-31 High Pavement; mains £19-30; ⊙noon-2pm & 7-9.30pm Tue-Thu, noon-2pm & 6-10pm Fri, noon-4pm & 6-10pm Sat) A stunning, coffered-ceilinged dining room sets the stage for some of Nottingham's finest dining. Knock-out combinations include smoked eels and pork-belly risotto with lime gel, crackling lollypop, wasabi caviar, and flower and citrus salad. Follow up with desserts such as butternut-squash bavarois with candied purée, basil ice cream and a black-pepper cookie.

Restaurant Sat Bains   GASTRONOMIC £££

(☑0115-986 6566; www.restaurantsatbains.com; Lenton Lane; tasting menu £75-99; ⊙noon-2pm & 7-9pm Tue-Thu, noon-2pm & 6.30-9.30pm Fri, noon-2pm & 6-10pm Sat; ☑) Two miles southwest of the centre off the A52, chef Sat Bains has been awarded two Michelin stars for his wildly inventive Modern European cooking. Book well in advance and beware of hefty cancellation charges. It also has eight chic guest rooms (double from £129).

▼ Drinking & Nightlife

Weekends in Nottingham are boisterous affairs, when the streets throng with lads on stag nights, girls on hens' parties, student revellers and intoxicated grown-ups who really should know better, but there are plenty of low-key alternatives.

★ **Ye Olde Trip to Jerusalem** PUB
(☎0115-947 3171; www.triptojerusalem.com; Brew house Yard, Castle Rd; ⊙11am-11pm Sun-Thu, to midnight Fri & Sat) Carved into the cliff below the castle, this atmospheric alehouse claims to be England's oldest pub. Founded in 1189, it supposedly slaked the thirst of departing crusaders, and its rooms and cobbled court-yards are still the most ambient place in Nottingham for a pint. Book informal tours (£2.50) of its cellars and caves at least two weeks ahead.

Boilermaker COCKTAIL BAR
(http://boilermakerbar.co.uk; 36b Carlton St, Hock-ley; ⊙5pm-1am Mon-Sat, 7pm-1am Sun) Entering what appears to be an industrial boilermak-er's shop and navigating your way through two secret doors brings you into this cav-ernous speakeasy spinning chilled lounge music. The obligatory table service can be slow, and the lighting's so low it's hard to read the inventive cocktails listed (eg Cereal Killer, with rum-soaked cornflakes), but it's a unique-and-then-some experience.

Dragon PUB
(www.the-dragon.co.uk; 67 Long Row; ⊙noon-11pm Mon-Thu, to 1am Fri & Sat, 11am-10pm Sun) The Dragon has a fabulous atmosphere at any time, thanks to homemade food, a good beer garden and funky music on weekends. But it peaks from 8pm on Tuesdays when it hosts the Racing Room (race entry £5) – an awe-some Scalextric slot-car race around a scale model of Nottingham along 180 feet of track.

Tilt COCKTAIL BAR
(www.tiltbar.co.uk; 9 Pelham St; ⊙5pm-midnight Tue-Thu, to 1.30am Fri & Sat) This tiny 1st-floor cocktail bar serves up a brilliant array of live blues offerings as well as cocktails that are giving their competition (in Nottingham, that's a lot of bars) a run for their money. House specialities include a Blues Blazer (cognac and Drambuie flamed with vanilla sugar and orange peel).

Pit & Pendulum PUB
(www.eerie-pubs.co.uk/pit-pendulum; 17 Victoria St; ⊙noon-11pm Sun & Mon, to midnight Tue-Thu, to 1am Fri & Sat; ☎) Local goths flock to this dimly lit pub for the vampire vibe and the-atrical decor (push the floor-to-ceiling base-ment 'bookcase' to reach the toilets), as well as 'seven deadly sins' cocktails and occasion-al live music.

Brass Monkey BAR
(www.brassmonkeybar.co.uk; High Pavement; ⊙5pm-3am Mon-Sat, 8pm-3am Sun) Notting-ham's original cocktail bar rocks the Lace Market with DJ sets and quirky takes on favourites such as elderflower mojitos. The roof terrace gets packed on summer evenings.

Rocket@Saltwater BAR
(☎0115-924 2664; www.rocketrestaurants.co.uk; The Cornerhouse, Forman St; ⊙noon-midnight Mon-Thu, to 2am Fri & Sat, to 11pm Sun) Slick hip-ster rooftop bar and restaurant with a great open-air terrace.

BIRMINGHAM, THE MIDLANDS & THE MARCHES NOTTINGHAM

LOCAL KNOWLEDGE

EZEKIAL BONE AKA ADE ANDREWS

Ade Andrews is a writer, actor, producer and tour guide.

Your background? I did a history degree and worked as a Heritage Ranger at Sherwood Forest, then set up Ezekial Bone Tours to deconstruct the Robin Hood myths and focus on the historic building blocks.

Did Robin Hood actually exist? He's a composite hero: many real outlaws in the me-dieval period were woven together over time by minstrels and storytellers. St Mary's Church (p448) is mentioned in the 1450 *Ballad of Robin Hood and the Monk*, and Old Market Sq in *Robin Hood and the Potter* circa 1500. It was only at the end of the 16th century that playwright Antony Munday elevated Robin Hood from a yeoman to a dis-placed Saxon earl as a symbol of the gentry's dissatisfaction with the Crown.

Robin Hood's relevance in the 21st century? Robin Hood was an original ecowarrior in harmony with the land. I want to put him on the pedestal he deserves – as a figurehead of culture and the environment.

Best places to experience Nottingham's history? The Lace Market area, the City of Caves (p447), Nottingham Castle (p447) and Ye Olde Trip to Jerusalem.

Canal House
PUB

(☑ 0115-955 5060; http://thecanalhouse.co.uk; 48-52 Canal St; ☺ 11am-11pm Mon-Wed, to midnight Thu, to 1am Fri & Sat, to 10.30pm Sun) The best of the canal-front pubs, run by the independent Castle Rock Brewery, and split in two by a watery inlet.

Malt Cross
PUB

(www.maltcross.com; 16 St James's St; ☺ 11am-11pm Mon-Thu, to 1am Fri & Sat, noon-6pm Sun) A fine place for a pint in a stately old Victorian music hall, where past performers included Charlie Chaplin. It's now a community space run by the Christian Charity Trust hosting art exhibitions and live music.

NG1
GAY, CLUB

(☑ 0115-958 8440; www.ng1club.co.uk; 76-80 Lower Parliament St; ☺ 11pm-4am Wed, to 6am Fri, to 6.30am Sat, to 4am Sun) Gay-friendly mixed club NG1 is unpretentious, hedonistic fun, with two dance floors belting out house, electro, pop and more.

Stealth
CLUB

(☑ 0845 413 4444; www.stealthattack.co.uk; Masonic Pl, Goldsmith St; ☺ 10pm-5am Fri & Sat) An underground club for those who like their bass heavy and their beats supercharged. The attached Rescue Rooms has a varied line-up of live bands and DJs.

☆ Entertainment

Theatre Royal & Royal Concert Hall
THEATRE, LIVE MUSIC

(☑ 0115-989 5555; www.trch.co.uk; Theatre Sq; ☺ booking office 9.30am-8.30pm Mon-Sat, 1hr before performance Sun) Sharing the same building and booking office, the Theatre Royal and Royal Concert Hall host musicals, touring theatre shows and veteran music acts. Backstage tours can be arranged (£6, 90 minutes).

Rock City
LIVE MUSIC

(☑ 0845 413 4444; www.rock-city.co.uk; 8 Talbot St) This monster venue hosts everything from Goth rock and Midlands metal to Northern Soul.

Rescue Rooms
LIVE MUSIC

(☑ 0115-828 3173; www.rescuerooms.com; ☺ 4pm-3am) Attached to Stealth nightclub; has a varied line-up of live bands and DJs.

Nottingham Playhouse
THEATRE

(☑ 0115-941 9419; www.nottinghamplayhouse.co.uk; Wellington Circus) Beside Anish Kapoor's enormous *Sky Mirror* dish, the Playhouse puts on serious theatre, from stage classics to the avant-garde. Nottingham's artistic community congregates at its attached restaurant and bar.

Broadway Cinema
CINEMA, GALLERY

(www.broadway.org.uk; 14-18 Broad St) Artistic hub with an independent cinema, media arts gallery and a cafe-bar where you can actually hear yourself talk.

ℹ Information

Tourist Office (☑ 0844 477 5678; www.experiencenottinghamshire.com; The Exchange, 1-4 Smithy Row; ☺ 9.30am-5.30pm Mon-Sat year-round, 11am-5pm Sun late Jul-Aug & mid-late Dec) Friendly office with racks of info and Robin Hood merchandise.

ℹ Getting There & Away

AIR

East Midlands Airport (p400) is about 18 miles south of Nottingham; Skylink buses pass the airport (one-way/return £5/8, one hour, at least hourly, 24 hours).

BUS

Local services run from the Victoria bus station, behind the **Victoria Shopping Centre** (Lower Parliament St) on Milton St. Bus 100 runs to Southwell (£4.15, 50 minutes, every 20 minutes Monday to Saturday, hourly Sunday) and bus 90 to Newark (£4.90, 55 minutes, hourly, every two hours Sunday).

Long-distance buses operate from the dingy **Broadmarsh bus station** (Collin St).

National Express services include the following:
Birmingham £10.60, 2¼ hours, five daily
Derby £6.80, 40 minutes, seven daily
Leicester £4.80, 45 minutes, every 20 minutes
London Victoria £13, 3½ hours, 11 daily

TRAIN

The train station is just south of the town centre. Useful services include the following:
Derby £6.60, 25 minutes, four hourly
Lincoln £10.60, one hour, hourly
London King's Cross/St Pancras £23.50, two hours, half-hourly
Manchester £21.50, two hours, two per hour

ℹ Getting Around

For information on buses within Nottingham, call **Nottingham City Transport** (☑ 0115-950 6070; www.nctx.co.uk). A Kangaroo ticket gives you unlimited travel on buses and trams within the city for £4.20.

The single tram line operated by **Nottingham Express Transit** (www.thetram.net; single/day from £2/3.50) runs from Nottingham train station to Hucknall, passing near Broadmarsh bus station, the tourist office and Theatre Royal.

Bunneys Bikes (☑ 0115-947 2713; www.bunneysbikes.com; 97 Carrington St; per day £12.99; ☺ 9am-5.30pm Mon, Thu & Fri, 8am-5.30pm Tue, 9am-7pm Wed, 10am-5pm Sat) is near the train station. Hire bicycles are also available from Nottingham's tourist office and Broadmarsh bus station for £4 per day through a Nottingham City Council bike-share scheme. Bonus: hire includes unlimited use of Nottingham city buses, trams and trains.

Around Nottingham

Newstead Abbey

The evocative lakeside ruins of Newstead Abbey (☑ 01623-455900; www.newsteadabbey.org.uk; adult/child £5/1, garden only £1; ☺ house noon-4pm Sat & Sun, garden 9am-dusk) are inextricably associated with the original tortured romantic, Lord Byron (1788–1824), who owned the house until 1817. Founded as an Augustinian priory in around 1170, it was converted into a residence in 1539.

Newstead Abbey is 12 miles north of Nottingham, off the A60. Pronto buses from Victoria bus station stop at Newstead Abbey gates (£3.10, 25 minutes, every 10 minutes Monday to Saturday, half-hourly Sunday), a mile from the house and gardens.

Byron's old living quarters are full of suitably eccentric memorabilia, and the landscaped grounds include a monument to his yappy dog, Boatswain.

Sherwood Forest National Nature Reserve

If Robin Hood wanted to hide out in Sherwood Forest today, he'd have to disguise himself and the Merry Men as day-trippers on mountain bikes. Now covering just 182 hectares of old-growth forest, it's a major destination for Nottingham city dwellers.

Until a proposed new visitor centre opens, the Sherwood Forest visitor centre (www.nottinghamshire.gov.uk; Swinecote Rd, Edwinstowe; parking £3; ☺ 10am-5pm Easter-Oct, to 4.30pm Nov-Mar), on the B6034, is an uninspiring collection of faded late 20th-century buildings housing cafes, gift shops et al. It's the departure point for walking trails passing Sherwood Forest landmarks such as the Major Oak (1 mile return), a broad-boughed

oak tree (propped up by supporting rods) alleged to have sheltered Robin of Locksley.

🏃 Activities

For informative guided walks try Ezekial Bone Tours (p448).

Sherwood Pines Cycles   CYCLING
(☑ 01623-822855; www.sherwoodpinescycles.co.uk; Sherwood Pines Forest Park, Clipstone; bike hire adult/child per hr £8/7, per day £24/18; ☺ 9am-5pm Thu-Tue, to 7pm Wed) In the Sherwood Pines Forest Park woodlands area, 2 miles south of Sherwood Forest on the B6030, Sherwood Pines Cycles rents mountain bikes for exploring the area's trails.

🎉 Festivals & Events

Robin Hood Festival   CULTURAL
(www.nottinghamshire.gov.uk; ☺ Aug) The week-long Robin Hood Festival is a massive medieval re-enactment that takes place every August.

🛏 Sleeping

Sherwood Forest YHA   HOSTEL £
(☑ 0845 371 9139; www.yha.org.uk; Forest Corner; dm/d £13/39; P) An arrow's flight from the visitor centre, Sherwood Forest YHA is a modern hostel with comfortable dorms, a bar, a self-catering kitchen and meals.

❶ Getting There & Away

From Nottingham, take the Sherwood Arrow bus (£3.50, 50 minutes, hourly Monday to Saturday, five on Sunday).

Southwell

POP 6760

A graceful scattering of grand, wisteria-draped country houses, Southwell is straight out of the pages of a novel from the English Romantic period.

◉ Sights

Southwell Minster   CHURCH
(www.southwellminster.org; suggested donation £5; ☺ 8am-7pm) Rising from the village centre, the awe-inspiring Southwell Minster, built over Saxon and Roman foundations, blends 12th- and 13th-century features including zigzag doorframes and curved arches. Its chapterhouse features some unusual stained glass and detailed carvings of faces, animals and leaves of forest trees.

Southwell Workhouse   MUSEUM

(NT; www.nationaltrust.org.uk; Upton Rd; adult/
child £7.70/3.85; ⊙noon-4pm Wed-Sun Mar-Oct)
On the road to Newark, Southwell Workhouse is a sobering reminder of the tough
life faced by paupers in the 19th century. You
can explore the factory floors and workers'
chambers accompanied by an audioguide
narrated by 'inmates' and 'officials'.

🛏 Sleeping & Eating

Enticing gourmet delis and tearooms line
the village streets.

Saracen's Head Hotel   HISTORIC HOTEL ££

(☑01636-812701; www.saracensheadhotel.com;
Market Pl; s/d incl breakfast from £75/95,
2-/3-course menus £15.95/19.95; 🅿🛜) This
rambling, timbered coaching inn has 27
beautifully refurbished rooms and an
oak-panelled restaurant.

Mosedales Bakery   BAKERY £

(7 King St; dishes £3-6.50; ⊙9am-4pm Mon-Fri,
8.30am-4pm Sat, 9.30am-3pm Sun) Queues at
this superb bakery regularly extend out the
door.

❶ Getting There & Away

Bus 100 runs from Nottingham (£4.15, 50 minutes, every 20 minutes, hourly on Sunday). For
Newark-on-Trent, take bus 28 or 29 (£2.50, 20
minutes, half-hourly).

Newark-on-Trent

POP 37,080

Newark-on-Trent paid the price for back-
ing the wrong side in the English Civil
War. After surviving four sieges by Oliver
Cromwell's men, the town was ransacked by
Roundheads when Charles I surrendered in
1646. Today, the riverside town is a peaceful
place worth a stop to wander its castle ruins.

◎ Sights

Newark Castle   CASTLE

(www.newark-sherwooddc.gov.uk/newarkcastle;
Castlegate; grounds admission free, tours adult/
child £3/1.50; ⊙9am-6pm, tours 11am, 1pm &
3pm Wed & Fri-Sun) Set in a pretty park overlooking the River Trent, the ruins include
an impressive Norman gate and a series of
underground passages and chambers. The
real King John, portrayed as a villain in the
Robin Hood legend, died here in 1216. Contact the tourist office about tours.

Newark Air Museum   MUSEUM

(☑01636-707170; www.newarkairmuseum.org;
adult/child £7.50/4; ⊙10am-5pm Mar-Oct, to 4pm
Nov-Feb) About 2 miles east of Newark by the
Winthorpe Showground, this air museum
has an impressive collection of aircraft, including a fearsome Vulcan bomber.

🍴 Eating & Drinking

Old Bakery Tea Rooms   TEAROOM £

(☑01636-611501; www.oldbakerytearooms.co.uk;
4 Queens Head Ct; mains £6-12; ⊙9.30am-5pm
Mon-Sat; 🍴) Everything, including to-die-
for scones, is baked fresh on the premises at the Old Bakery Tea Rooms, housed
in an enchanting *Hansel and Gretel*-like
15th-century Tudor building. Lunch specials include soups, frittata, bruschetta and
smoked-salmon brioche.

Castle Barge   BAR

(www.castlebarge.co.uk; The Wharf; ⊙11am-11pm)
Moored on the River Trent overlooking
Newark Castle, this barge is an idyllic spot
for a local ale. It serves decent food, and
there's picnic seating on the riverbanks.

❶ Information

Tourist Office (☑01636-655765; www.new-
ark-sherwooddc.gov.uk/newarkcastle; Gilstrap
Centre, Castlegate; ⊙10am-4pm) In the castle
grounds; can help find accommodation.

❶ Getting There & Away

Newark has two train stations. Trains on the
East Coast Main Line between London King's
Cross (£25, two hours, one to two hourly) and
the north stop at Newark North Gate, while East
Midlands trains between Leicester (£12.40, two
hours, hourly), Nottingham (£6.10, one hour,
hourly) and Lincoln (£4.90, 50 minutes, hourly)
stop at Newark Castle station.

Bus 90 runs hourly to Nottingham (£4.90, 55
minutes, every two hours Sunday).

LINCOLNSHIRE

One of the most sparsely populated corners
of England, Lincolnshire's farmland unfolds
over low hills and the pancake-flat Fens. It
is dotted with windmills and, more recently,
wind turbines. Surrounding the charming
county town of Lincoln you'll find seaside
resorts, scenic waterways, serene nature reserves and stone-built towns tailor-made for
English period dramas.

🏃 Activities

The 140-mile Viking Way walking trail snakes across the gentle hills of the Lincolnshire Wolds from the banks of the River Humber to Oakham in Leicestershire.

Cyclists can find information on routes across the county in any of the local tourist offices; the Water Rail Way is a flat, sculpture-lined on-road cycling route that follows the River Witham through classic Fens countryside between Lincoln and Boston.

ℹ Information

Visit Lincolnshire (www.visitlincolnshire.com)

ℹ Getting There & Around

East Midlands trains connect Lincoln, Newark Castle and Nottingham. Newark North Gate and Grantham lie on the East Coast Main Line between London King's Cross and Edinburgh.

Local buses link Lincolnshire's towns but services are slow and infrequent. Check the transport pages at www.lincolnshire.gov.uk, which also has cycling route info.

Lincoln

POP 100,160

Ringed by historic city gates – including the Newport Arch on Bailgate, a relic from the original Roman settlement – this beautiful city is a tangle of cobbled medieval streets surrounding its colossal 12th-century cathedral. The lanes that topple over the edge of Lincoln Cliff are lined with Tudor town houses, ancient pubs and quirky independent stores.

Flanking the River Witham at the base of the hill, the new town is less absorbing, but the revitalised Brayford Waterfront development by the university is an idyllic spot to watch the boats go by.

◉ Sights

The tourist office sells the three-day Visit Lincoln Pass (adult/family £12/35), giving access to several heritage sites including the castle, cathedral and Bishops' Palace.

★ Lincoln Cathedral   CATHEDRAL
(☏ 01522-561600;   http://lincolncathedral.com; Minster Yard; adult/child £8/1 Mon-Sat, by donation Sun; ⊙ 7.15am-8pm Mon-Fri, to 6pm Sat & Sun, evensong 5.30pm Mon-Sat, 3.45pm Sun) Towering over Lincoln like a medieval skyscraper, Lincoln's magnificent cathedral is a breathtaking representation of divine power on earth. The great tower rising above the crossing is the third-highest in England at 83m, but in medieval times, a lead-encased wooden spire added a further 79m, topping even the great pyramids of Giza.

One-hour guided tours take place at least twice daily; there are less-frequent tours of the roof and the tower. All are included in admission; booking is essential.

The vast interior of the church is too large for modern congregations – services take place instead in St Hugh's Choir, a church within a church running east from the crossing. The choir stalls are accessed through a

---

LINCOLNSHIRE: BOMBER COUNTY

Following WWI the Royal Air Force (RAF) was formed in 1918 and two years later its college was established in Lincolnshire. During WWII, England's 'Bomber County' was home to numerous squadrons and by 1945 had more airfields (49) than any other in the country. US Navy flying boats flew antisubmarine patrols and B-29 bombers were based here. Lincoln's tourist office has details of the county's aviation legacy.

Battle of Britain Memorial Flight Visitor Centre (☏ 01522-552222; www.lincolnshire. gov.uk/bbmf; Dogdyke Rd, Coningsby; hangar tours adult/child £6.50/4.50; ⊙ 10am-5pm Mon-Fri) See Spitfires and the four-engined Lancaster City of Lincoln at the Battle of Britain Memorial Flight Visitor Centre on 90-minute hangar tours. Interconnect bus 5 (£3.95, 50 minutes, hourly Monday to Saturday) runs here from Lincoln.

Lincolnshire Aviation Heritage Centre (☏ 01790-763207; www.lincsaviation.co.uk; East Kirkby, near Spilsby; adult/child £7/3; ⊙ 9.30am-5pm Mon-Sat Easter-Oct, 10am-4pm Mon-Sat Nov-Easter) Sited on an original WWII Bomber Command airfield complete with its original wartime control tower. It's 30 miles southeast of Lincoln via the A153; there's no public transport.

Waddington Air Show (www.waddingtonairshow.co.uk; ⊙ Jul) The RAF's Waddington Air Show takes place 3 miles south of Lincoln on the first weekend in July. Book well ahead.

Lincoln

magnificent carved stone screen; look north to see the stunning rose window known as the Dean's Eye (c 1192), mirrored to the south by the floral flourishes of the Bishop's Eye (1330). There's more stained glass in the three Services Chapels in the North Transept.

Beyond St Hugh's Choir, the Angel Choir is supported by 28 columns topped by carvings of angels and foliate scrollwork. Other interesting details include the 10-sided chapterhouse – where Edward I held his parliament and where the climax of the *Da Vinci Code* was filmed in 2005.

The best time to hear the organ resounding through the cathedral is during evensong.

★ Lincoln Castle
CASTLE

(www.lincolnshire.gov.uk/lincolncastle; adult/child £2/1.20; ⊙10am-6pm May-Aug, to 5pm Apr & Sep, to 4pm Oct-Mar) One of the first castles erected by the victorious William the Conqueror to keep his new kingdom in line, Lincoln Castle offers awesome views over the city and miles of surrounding countryside. Highlights include the chance to view one of the four surviving copies of the Magna Carta (dated 1215) and the grim Victorian prison chapel, from when this was the county jailhouse and execution ground.

Free 75-minute guided tours run once or twice daily (on weekends only in December and January).

Bishops' Palace
HISTORIC SITE

(EH; ☎01522-527468; www.english-heritage.org.uk; adult/child £4.70/2.80; ⊙10am-6pm Wed-Sun Apr-Sep, to 5pm Wed-Sun Oct, to 4pm Sat & Sun Nov-Mar) Beside Lincoln Cathedral lie the time-ravaged but still imposing ruins of the 12th-century Bishops' Palace, gutted by parliamentary forces during the Civil War. From here, the local bishops once controlled a diocese stretching from the Humber to the Thames. Entertaining audioguides are included in admission.

Lincoln

Collection MUSEUM
(www.thecollectionmuseum.com; Danes Tce; ⊙10am-4pm, from 10.45am 1st Mon of month) FREE Archaeology bursts into life with loads of hands-on displays. Kids can handle artefacts and dress up in period costume. Check out the crushed skull of a 4000-year-old 'yellowbelly' (the local term for the locals), pulled from a Neolithic burial site near Sleaford.

Usher Gallery GALLERY
(www.thecollectionmuseum.com; Danes Tce; ⊙10am-4pm, from 10.45am 1st Mon of month) FREE A handsome Edwardian building decorated with carvings of cow skulls houses an impressive collection of works by greats such as Turner, Lowry and English watercolourist Peter de Wint (1784–1849).

Museum of Lincolnshire Life MUSEUM
(Old Barracks, Burton Rd; ⊙10am-4pm daily Apr-Sep, closed Sun Oct-Mar) FREE Displays at this charming community museum housed in an old Victorian barracks span everything from Victorian farm implements to the tin-can tank built in Lincoln for WWI. Around the corner from the museum is the cute little **Ellis Mill** (www.lincolnshire.gov.uk; Mill Rd; ⊙2-5pm Sat & Sun Apr-Sep, 2pm-dusk Sun Oct-Mar) FREE, which ground the town's flour in the 18th century and is still in use today.

☞ Tours

Walking Tours WALKING TOUR
(☎01522-521256; www.lincolnguidedtours.co.uk; adult/child £4/free; ⊙tours 11am daily Jul & Aug,

Sat & Sun Jun, Sep & Oct) History-focused 90-minute guided walking tours run from outside the tourist office.

Ghost Walks WALKING TOUR
(☎01522-874056; adult/child £4/2; ⊙7pm Wed-Sat year-round) Genuinely spooky 75-minute ghost walks depart adjacent to the tourist office in Castle Sq.

Brayford Belle BOAT TOUR
(☎01522-881200; www.lincolnboattrips.co.uk; adult/child £6.50/4) Boat trips along the River Witham and Fossdyke Navigation, a canal system dating back to Roman times, start from Brayford Waterfront. The *Brayford Belle* runs five times daily from Easter to September, and weekends only in October. No credit cards.

⌂ Sleeping

★**Castle Hotel** BOUTIQUE HOTEL ££
(☎01522-538801; www.castlehotel.net; Westgate; s £90, d £110-140, incl breakfast; P🅿🛜) Each of the 18 rooms at this boutique hotel have been exquisitely refurbished in olive, truffle and oyster tones. Built on the site of Lincoln's Roman forum in 1852, the red-brick building's incarnations variously include a school and WWII lookout station. Take advantage of the great-value dinner, bed and breakfast deals linked to its award-winning restaurant Reform (p458).

Bail House B&B ££
(☎01522-541000; http://bailhouse.jpchotelsandleisure.co.uk; 34 Bailgate; d from £79; P@🍴🛏)

ℹ️ MINIMISING LINCOLN'S HILLS

Walking between Lincoln's old and new towns can feel like an Everest expedition, but fortunately there are alternatives.

Walk & Ride (single ticket adult/child £1.50/70p, all-day pass £3/1.60; ⏱9.10am-5.22pm Mon-Sat) Lincoln's 'Little Green Bus' runs every 20 minutes from the Stonebow at the corner of High St and Saltergate to the cathedral and Newport Arch, then back via Brayford Waterfront and the train station.

Tour Lincoln (adult/child £10/4; ⏱10am-3pm Jul & Aug, to 3pm Sat & Sun Mar-May & Jun-Oct) To tour the city in comfort, hop aboard the open-topped Tour Lincoln bus. Tickets are sold at the tourist office and on board. Tours last one hour; tickets are valid all day.

Stone walls, worn flagstones, secluded gardens and one room with an extraordinary timber-vaulted ceiling are just some of the charms of this lovingly restored Georgian town house in central Lincoln. There's limited on-site parking, a garden and children's playground, and even a seasonal heated outdoor swimming pool.

White Hart Hotel HOTEL ££
(☏01522-526222; www.whitehart-lincoln.co.uk; Bailgate; s/d from £70/90; P@🖲) You can't get more venerable than this grand dame of Lincoln hotels, sandwiched between castle and cathedral, with a history dating back 600 years through flowing countrified rooms.

✗ Eating

Tearooms are dotted along Steep Hill. Restaurant reservations are generally recommended in the evenings.

La Bottega Delitalia CAFE, DELI £
(9 West Pde; dishes £2.15-7.45; ⏱9am-4pm Mon-Wed, to 9pm Thu & Fri, 8.30am-3pm Sat) Authentic Italian fare such as lobster ravioli in creamy tomato and basil sauce is made from scratch at this inexpensive cafe-deli. Cash only.

Reform MODERN BRITISH ££
(☏01522-538801; www.castlehotel.net; The Castle Hotel, Westgate; mains £13.50-23.95; ⏱noon-2.30pm & 7-9pm Mon-Sat, noon-3pm & 7-9pm Sun) Inspired by local, seasonal produce, the Castle Hotel's sophisticated restaurant serves starters such as feta beignets with pomegranate and mint-and-coriander Israeli cous-cous, followed by mains such as pork confit with artichoke risotto and sage onion rings. The real showstoppers, however, are desserts such as warm plum-and-raspberry crumble tart with white-chocolate ice cream and quince purée.

Bronze Pig MODERN BRITISH ££
(☏01522-524817; http://thebronzepig.co.uk; 6 West Pde; mains £15-24; ⏱dinner by reservation Wed-Sat) BBC Masterchef 2012 finalist, Irishman Eamonn Hunt, and Sicilian chef Pompeo Siracusa have taken Lincoln's dining scene by storm since opening the Bronze Pig. Their exceptional Modern British cooking has an Italian accent and food is locally sourced. Reserve well ahead and prepare to be wowed.

Brown's Pie Shop BRITISH ££
(☏01522-527330; www.brownspieshop.co.uk; 33 Steep Hill; takeaway pies £1.50-3.50, lunch mains £9-12, dinner mains £10-25; ⏱noon-2.30pm & 5-11pm Mon-Sat, noon-8pm Sun) One of Lincoln's top tables, this long-established pie shop encompasses a smart upstairs dining room and cosy brick-lined basement. Hearty pies are stuffed with locally sourced beef, rabbit and game.

Jew's House MODERN EUROPEAN ££
(☏01522-524851; www.jewshouserestaurant.co.uk; 15 The Strait (Steep Hill); 2-/3-course lunch menu £16.50/19.95, mains £15.50-21.50; ⏱7-9.30pm Tue, noon-2pm & 7-9.30pm Wed-Sat) This local favourite serves up gourmet fare in atmospheric surrounds in one of England's oldest houses; the Romanesque Jew's House was constructed around 1160. For the ultimate indulgence, go for the six-course tasting menu (by reservation, £59.50).

Wig & Mitre PUB ££
(www.wigandmitre.com; 30 Steep Hill; mains £10.50-14.50; ⏱8.30am-10.30pm Mon-Sat, to 10pm Sun; 🖲) Civilised pub-restaurant the Wig & Mitre has an excellent menu yet retains the ambience of a friendly local. Food is served throughout the day, from morning fry-ups to lunchtime sandwiches and filling evening roasts. Bookings not necessary.

Drinking & Nightlife

Strugglers Inn   PUB
(83 Westgate; ⊙noon-midnight Tue & Wed, to
1am Thu-Sat, to 11pm Sun & Mon) A sunny
walled-courtyard beer garden out back, a
cosy interior and a superb selection of real
ales on tap make this the pick of Lincoln's
independent pubs.

Cloud Bar   BAR
(1 St Pauls Lane; ⊙10.30am-11pm Sun-Thu, to 1am
Fri & Sat; ⊙) The roof terrace at this new bar
near Lincoln Cathedral is a winner on sunny
days. Good tapas menu, too.

Electric Bar & Restaurant   BAR
(⊙01522-565182; www.electricbarandrestaurant.
co.uk; 5th fl, DoubleTree by Hilton Lincoln, Brayford
Wharf North; ⊙11am-11pm Sun-Thu, to midnight Fri
& Sat; ⊙) On the top floor of Lincoln's snazzy four-star DoubleTree Hilton Hotel, this
swish spot with glittering river views has a
great cocktail list, regular live jazz and a restaurant serving sophisticated British dishes
with a retro twist (such as ham-hock terrine
and coconut-ice parfait).

☆ Entertainment

Check www.lovelincoln.co.uk or www.visit
lincolnshire.com for events listings.

Lincoln Drill Hall   ARTS CENTRE
(www.lincolndrillhall.com; Freeschool Lane) Downhill from the station, this stern-looking
building hosts bands, orchestras, stage
shows, comedy and daytime festivals.

Home Nightclub   LIVE MUSIC
(http://homelincoln.co.uk; Park St; ⊙11.30am-11pm
Mon & Wed, to 3am Tue & Thu-Sat, noon-3am Sun)
Spread over six rooms with live music, dance
tunes and a total of eight bars, this cavernous
venue is home to Lincoln's students.

ℹ Information

Tourist Office (⊙01522-545458; www.
visitlincoln.com; 9 Castle Hill; ⊙10am-5pm
Mon-Sat, 10.30am-4pm Sun) Friendly office in
a handsome 16th-century building.

ℹ Getting There & Away

BUS
National Express runs direct bus services from
Lincoln to London Victoria (£19.60, 5¼ hours,
two daily) and Birmingham (£16.80, three hours,
daily).

Local Stagecoach buses include bus 1 to
Grantham (£4.40, 1¼ hours, hourly Monday to
Saturday, five on Sunday).

TRAIN
Boston £15.10, two hours, hourly, change at
Sleaford
Newark-on-Trent (Newark Castle) £4.90, 25
minutes, every 15 minutes Monday to Saturday,
10 on Sunday
Nottingham £10.60, one hour, hourly
Sheffield £14.10, 80 minutes, hourly
York £36.30, two hours, two per hour

Stamford

POP 19,700
One of England's prettiest towns, Stamford
seems frozen in time, with elegant streets
lined with honey-coloured limestone buildings and hidden alleyways dotted with
alehouses, interesting eateries and small
independent boutiques. A forest of historic
church spires rises overhead and the gently
gurgling River Welland meanders through
the town centre. It's a favourite with film-
makers seeking the postcard vision of England, and appears in everything from *Pride
and Prejudice* to the *Da Vinci Code*.

◉ Sights

Simply strolling Stamford's streets is a delight.

★ Burghley House   HISTORIC BUILDING
(www.burghley.co.uk; adult/child incl sculpture
garden £13/6.50, garden only £7.50/6.50; ⊙11am-
5pm Sat-Thu mid-Mar–late Oct) Lying just a mile
south of Stamford, opulent Burghley House
('bur-lee') was built by Queen Elizabeth's
chief adviser William Cecil, whose descendants still live here.

Set in more than 810 hectares of grounds,
landscaped by the famous Lancelot 'Capability' Brown, the house bristles with cupolas,
pavilions, belvederes and chimneys. A particular highlight is the lavish staterooms.

The renowned Burghley Horse Trials take
place here in early September.

Follow the marked path for 15 minutes
through the park by Stamford train station.

St Mary's Church   CHURCH
(http://stamfordstmary.weebly.com; St Mary's St;
⊙hours vary) A charmingly wonky broach
spire tops St Mary's Church.

WORTH A TRIP

GRANTHAM & AROUND

Grantham would be just another country town were it not for two famous 'yellowbellies' (as Lincolnshire locals call themselves) – Sir Isaac Newton and the late former prime minister Margaret Thatcher, the daughter of a humble Grantham greengrocer, who plied his trade at 2 North Pde. The town itself has just a few sights, but there are some fascinating properties in the surrounding countryside.

Woolsthorpe Manor (NT; www.nationaltrust.org.uk; Water Lane; adult/child £6.65/3.35; ⊙ 11am-5pm Wed-Mon Mar-Oct, 11am-5pm Fri-Sun Nov-Feb) Newton fans may feel the gravitational pull of the great man's birthplace, about 8 miles south of Grantham. The 17th-century house contains reconstructions of Newton's rooms; the apple that inspired the theory of gravity allegedly fell from the tree in the garden. There's a nifty kids' science room and a cafe. Take Centrebus 28 from Grantham (£2.50, 25 minutes, four per day Monday to Saturday).

Belvoir Castle (☑ 01476-871001; www.belvoircastle.com; adult/child £15/8, gardens only £8/5; ⊙ castle tours 11.15am, 1.15pm & 3.15pm Sun & Mon May-Aug, gardens 11am-5pm Sun & Mon May-Aug) The Duke and Duchess of Rutland's ancestral home, Belvoir (pronounced 'beaver') is a 19th-century baroque and Gothic fantasy built over the ruins of three previous castles. Still inhabited by the Manners family, it overflows with tapestries, priceless furniture and ancient oil paintings. Belvoir Castle is technically in Leicestershire, but Grantham, 6 miles east, is the nearest town. Bus 9 (£1.60, 20 minutes, four per day Monday to Friday) stops at the Chequers Inn, from where it's a 20-minute walk.

Chequers Inn (☑ 01476-870701; www.chequersinn.net; Main St, Woolsthorpe by Belvoir; mains £11-20; ⊙ kitchen noon-2.30pm & 6-9.30pm Mon-Sat, noon-4pm & 6-8.30pm Sun) Dine on some of the finest food in the Midlands in the rambling garden bordering a sheep-filled paddock or inside by the open fire of this charming inn, about 7 miles southwest of Grantham. There's a fabulous range of ciders and real ales on tap and, across the lane, the former stables house four simple but stylish guest rooms (single/double £50/70). The inn's sunny front patio overlooks Belvoir Castle.

William Browne Hospital　　　MUSEUM
(Broad St; adult/child £2.50/1; ⊙ 11am-4pm Sat, 2-4.30pm Sun May-Sep) Explore the 15th-century chapel and chambers of the medieval almshouse, William Browne Hospital.

🛏 Sleeping

Stamford Lodge　　　B&B ££
(☑ 01780-482932; www.stamfordlodge.co.uk; 66 Scotgate; s/d £65/85; 🐾) Centrally situated, this 18th-century former bakehouse has five fresh, modern rooms and excellent breakfasts.

★ George Hotel　　　HISTORIC HOTEL £££
(☑ 01780-750750; www.georgehotelofstamford.com; 71 St Martin's; s/d from £95/165, 4-poster d £250; P @ 🐾) Stamford's luxurious landmark inn opened its doors in 1597. Today its 47 rooms impeccably blend period charm and modern elegance, while its restaurant serves superior Modern British cuisine.

William Cecil at Stamford　HISTORIC HOTEL £££
(☑ 01780-750070; www.thewilliamcecil.co.uk; High St, St Martins; s/d midweek £101/111, weekends £120/130; P 🐾) Within the Burghley Estate, rooms at this stunningly renovated hotel are inspired by Burghley House, with period furnishings and luxuries such as claw-foot baths. The smart restaurant opens to a wicker-chair-furnished patio.

🍴 Eating

The finest dining in town is at the George and William Cecil hotels.

Tobie Norris　　　PUB ££
(www.tobienorris.com; 12 St Pauls St; mains £8-20; ⊙ kitchen noon-2.30pm & 6-9.30pm Mon-Sat, to 4pm & 6-8.30pm Sun) A wonderful stone-walled, flagstone-floored pub with a warren of rooms and a sunny courtyard. It serves international dishes such as wasabi chicken with crushed plum-chutney potatoes and wholesome local ales.

Jim's Yard　　　MODERN BRITISH ££
(☑ 01780-756080; www.jimsyard.biz; 3 Ironmonger St; mains £12.50-21; ⊙ noon-2.30pm & 6-9.30pm Tue-Sat) Tucked away in a courtyard off a narrow laneway, Jim's Yard serves upmarket fare sourced from local producers.

ℹ️ Information

Tourist Office (📞 01780-755611; www.stamford artscentre.com; 27 St Mary's St; ⏰ 9.30am-5pm Mon-Sat; 📶) In the Stamford Arts Centre.

ℹ️ Getting There & Away

Centrebus 4 runs to Grantham (£4, one hour, three per day Monday to Friday, two Saturday) and National Express to London Victoria (£13.50, four hours, one daily).

Trains run to Birmingham (£21.90, 1½ hours, hourly), Leicester (£12.90, 40 minutes, hourly) and Stansted Airport (£31.40, 1¾ hours, hourly) via Cambridge (£24, 1¼ hours) and Peterborough (£7.70, 15 minutes).

Boston
POP 41,340

It's hard to believe that sleepy Boston was the inspiration for its larger and more famous American cousin. Although no Boston citizens sailed on the *Mayflower,* the town became a conduit for persecuted Puritans fleeing Nottinghamshire for religious freedom in the Netherlands and America. In the 1630s, the fiery sermons of Boston vicar John Cotton inspired many locals to follow their lead, among them the ancestors of John Quincy-Adams, the sixth American president. These pioneers founded a namesake town in the new colony of Massachusetts and the rest, as they say, is history.

👁️ Sights

St Botolph's Church   CHURCH
(www.parish-of-boston.org.uk; tower adult/child £3/1; ⏰ church 8.30am-4.30pm daily, tower 10am-3.30pm Mon-Sat, last climb 3pm) Built in the early 14th century, St Botolph's Church (the name Boston is a corruption of 'St Botolph's Stone') is known locally as the Stump, in reference to the truncated appearance of its 88m-high tower. Walk up the 365 steps on a clear day and you'll see out to Lincoln, 32 miles away.

Guildhall   MUSEUM
(📞 01205-365954; www.bostonguildhall.co.uk; South St; ⏰ 10.30am-3.30pm Wed-Sat) Before escaping to the New World, the Pilgrim Fathers were briefly imprisoned in the 14th-century Guildhall. It's one of Lincolnshire's oldest brick buildings, dating from the 1390s and situated close to the River Witham. Inside are fun, interactive exhibits, as well as a restored 16th-century courtroom and a re-created Georgian kitchen.

Maud Foster Windmill   MILL
(📞 01205-352188; www.maudfoster.co.uk; adult/child £4/2; ⏰ 10am-5pm Wed & Sat) About 800m northeast of Market Pl, England's tallest working windmill has seven floors that creak and tremble with every turn of the sails; it sells bags of flour milled on-site. Self-caterers can stay in the granary next door (double from £195 for two nights including a windmill tour; children not permitted).

🛏️ Sleeping & Eating

White Hart   PUB ££
(📞 01205-311900; www.whitehartboston.com; 1-5 High St; s/d £49.50/67.50; 🅿️ @) Right in the middle of town, this handsome pub-hotel is part of the Best Western chain. Rooms are tastefully modernised and there's a decent Modern British menu (mains £9 to £18).

ℹ️ Information

Tourist Office (📞 01205-365954; www. bostonguildhall.co.uk; South St; ⏰ 10.30am-3.30pm Wed-Sat) Inside the Guildhall.

ℹ️ Getting There & Away

Trains connect Boston with Leicester (£22.10, 2½ hours, hourly) and Lincoln (£15.10, two hours, hourly) via a change at Sleaford.

NORTHAMPTONSHIRE

Dotted with villages full of pincushion cottages with thatched rooves and Tudor timbers, Northamptonshire also has a string of stately manors, including the ancestral homes of George Washington and Diana, Princess of Wales.

Motoring fans won't want to miss the Formula One British Grand Prix (www.silverstone.co.uk), which roars around Silverstone Circuit, near Towcester, for three days in early July.

ℹ️ Information

Visit Northamptonshire (www.visitnorth amptonshire.co.uk; 📶)

ℹ️ Getting Around

Northampton is the county's hub for bus services; see the 'Transport & Streets' pages at www.northamptonshire.gov.uk for routes and timetables. Trains run by London Midland are useful for getting to/from Northampton.

Northampton

POP 215,170

Rebuilt after a devastating fire in 1675, Northamptonshire's county town was one of the prettiest in the Midlands before WWII bombers and postwar town planners wreaked havoc. Still, the city's heart retains some grand architecture. Northampton played a significant role in the Wars of the Roses and the English Civil War, before shifting its attention to manufacturing shoes.

◎ Sights

All Saints' Church CHURCH
(www.allsaintsnorthampton.com; George Row; ⊙9am-6pm) Constructed after the 1675 fire, All Saints' Church owes an obvious debt to the churches built by Sir Christopher Wren after the Great Fire of London, with an ornate barrel-vaulted ceiling and dark-wood organ and reredos.

Guildhall HISTORIC BUILDING
(St Giles St) Built between 1861 and 1864, Northampton's landmark Guildhall is adorned with carvings and 14 statues of monarchs, local luminaries and patron saints, including St Michael, patron saint of corporations. Now housing the council offices, it's closed to the public except during heritage events.

Northampton Museum & Art Gallery MUSEUM, GALLERY
(www.northampton.gov.uk/museums; Guildhall Rd; ⊙10am-5pm Tue-Sat, 2-5pm Sun) FREE Even those without a shoe fetish will get a kick out of the impressive displays, where you can learn about the history of shoemaking and footwear fashions.

St Peter's Church CHURCH
(⊙10am-4pm Wed-Sat Mar-Oct, 11am-3pm Wed-Sat Nov-Feb) West of the central Market Sq, St Peter's Church is a marvellous Norman edifice built in 1150 and adorned with ancient carvings. The sign on the door tells you where you can collect the key to peek inside.

Church of the Holy Sepulchre CHURCH
(www.stseps.org; ⊙2-4pm Wed, 11am-3pm Sat May-Sep) North of the centre, beyond the eyesore bus station, Church of the Holy Sepulchre is one of the few surviving round churches in the country. It was founded when the first earl of Northampton returned from the Crusades in 1100.

🛏 Sleeping & Eating

The tourist office can advise on B&Bs in the area.

Church Bar & Restaurant MODERN EUROPEAN ££
(☑01604-603800; www.thechurchrestaurant.com; 67-83 Bridge St; mains £15; ⊙noon-2.30pm & 6-9.30pm Mon-Sat) At this superbly converted old church, you can feast on modern European cooking (bookings recommended), or sip a cocktail under the stained-glass windows in the bar.

❶ Information

Tourist Office (☑01604-838800; www.visitnorthampton.co.uk; George Row; ⊙8am-5.30pm Mon-Fri year-round, 10am-2pm Sat Apr-Sep) Housed in the historic Sessions House, built in 1675.

❶ Getting There & Away

Greyfriars bus station is on Lady's Lane, just north of the Grosvenor shopping centre. National Express coach services include the following:
Birmingham £7.40, 2¾ hours, eight daily
London Victoria £13, 2¼ hours, 12 daily
Nottingham £13.20, 2½ hours, two daily

Northampton has good rail links with Birmingham (£14, one hour, every 20 minutes) and London Euston (£26.20, one hour, three hourly). The train station is about half a mile west of town along Gold St.

Around Northampton

Northamptonshire has a cache of ancient churches, some dating back to Saxon times. Many open only from May to September; Northampton's tourist office has information including bus schedules.

Althorp

The ancestral home of the Spencer family, **Althorp House** (☑01604-770107; www.spencerofalthorp.com; adult/child £18.50/11; ⊙1-5pm Sun May–mid-Jul & Sep, 1-5pm daily mid-Jul–Aug) – pronounced 'altrup' – is the final resting place of Diana, Princess of Wales, commemorated by a memorial. The outstanding art collection features works by Rubens, Gainsborough and Van Dyck. Tickets are limited and must be booked by phone or online.

Althorp is off the A428, 5.5 miles northwest of Northampton. Stagecoach bus 96

(Northampton–Rugby, £4.60, hourly, Monday to Saturday) passes the estate gates, from where it's a 20-minute walk.

Profits go to charities supported by the Princess Diana Memorial Fund.

Stoke Bruerne

POP 375

About 8 miles south of Northampton, brightly painted barges frequent this charming little village nestled against the Grand Union Canal, the main drag of England's canal network. From here, you can follow the waterways all the way to Leicester, Birmingham or London.

○ Sights & Activities

Several boat owners offer summertime cruises.

Canal Museum   MUSEUM

(http://canalrivertrust.org.uk/the-canal-museum/stoke-bruerne; adult/child £4.75/2.75; ⊙10am-5pm Apr-Oct, 11am-3pm Wed-Fri, to 4pm Sat & Sun Nov-Mar) Set in a converted corn mill, the entertaining Canal Museum charts the history of the canal network and its bargemen, lock keepers and pit workers. Scale models abound; outside you can see the historic narrowboat *Sculptor*, listed on the National Historic Boat Register.

Indian Chief   CRUISE

(☑ 01604-862428; www.boatinn.co.uk; adult/child from £3/2.50; ⊙11.30am-3pm Sun & bank holiday weekends) Year-round you can take trips lasting 25 minutes aboard the Boat Inn's narrowboat, the *Indian Chief*.

⌂ Sleeping & Eating

Waterways Cottage   B&B ££

(☑ 01604-863865; www.waterwayscottage.co.uk; Bridge Rd; d £75) For overnight stays, try Waterways Cottage, an adorable thatched cottage right off the front of a biscuit box.

Boat Inn   PUB ££

(☑ 01604-862428; www.boatinn.co.uk; mains £7.75-24; ⊙9.30am-3pm & 6-9pm Mon-Fri, to 9pm Sat, to 8.30pm Sun) Meals and brews are served up at the canalside Boat Inn.

❶ Getting There & Away

Buses 86 and 87 run between Stoke Bruerne and Northampton (£4.40, 30 minutes, four per day Monday to Saturday, four Sunday).

Sulgrave Manor

This impressively preserved Tudor mansion (www.sulgravemanor.org.uk; adult/child £7.90/3.60, garden only £3.60/free; ⊙11am-4pm Sat & Sun Apr-Jul, Sep & Oct, to 4pm Tue-Sun Aug) was built by Lawrence Washington in 1539. The Washington family lived here for almost 120 years before Colonel John Washington, the great-grandfather of America's first president George Washington, sailed to Virginia in 1656.

Sulgrave Manor is about 20 miles southwest of Northampton, just off the B4525 near Banbury; you'll need your own wheels to get here.

LEICESTERSHIRE

Leicestershire was a vital creative hub during the Industrial Revolution, but its factories were a major target for German air-raids in WWII and most towns in the county still bear the scars of war-time bombing. Nevertheless, there are some impressive remains, from Elizabethan castles to Roman ruins. The busy, multicultural capital Leicester is enjoying new-found fame due to the recent discovery of King Richard III's remains.

❶ Information

Leicestershire Tourism (www.goleicestershire.com)

❶ Getting There & Around

Leicester is well served by buses and trains. For bus routes and timetables, visit the 'Roads & Transport' pages at www.leics.gov.uk. Regular buses connect Rutland to Leicester, Stamford and other surrounding towns.

Leicester

POP 329,840

Built over the buried ruins of two millennia of history, Leicester (*les*-ter) suffered at the hands of the Luftwaffe and postwar planners. A massive influx of textile workers from India and Pakistan since the 1960s, however, has transformed the city into a bustling global melting pot, with dozens of mosques and temples in and around the centre.

Leicester

Historical treasures include one of England's finest medieval guildhalls. The 2012 discovery and 2013 identification of the remains of King Richard III in a Leicester car park has sparked a flurry of developments, including a spiffing new visitor centre on the site.

◉ Sights

★ King Richard III: Dynasty, Death & Discovery
HERITAGE CENTRE

(http://kriii.com; St Martin's Pl; adult/child £7.95/4.75; ⊙10am-4pm Mon-Fri, to 5pm Sat & Sun) Leicester's brand-new, high-tech King Richard III visitor centre is split into three sections. Dynasty explores his rise to become the final Plantagenet king. Death delves into the Battle of Bosworth, when Richard became the last English king to be killed in battle. Discovery details the University of Leicester's archaeological dig and identification, allowing you to visit the site of the grave in which he was found.

Guildhall
HISTORIC BUILDING

(www.leicester.gov.uk/museums; Guildhall Lane; ⊙11am-4.30pm Mon-Wed & Sat, 1-4.30pm Sun Feb-Nov) FREE Leicester's perfectly preserved 14th-century guildhall is reputed to be the most haunted building in Leicester. You can search for spooks in the magnificent Great Hall, the wood-panelled 'Mayor's Parlour' and the old police cells, which contain a reconstruction of a 19th-century gibbet.

New Walk Museum & Art Gallery
MUSEUM, GALLERY

(www.leicester.gov.uk/museums; New Walk; ⊙10am-5pm Mon-Sat, from 11am Sun) FREE Highlights of this grand Victorian museum include the dinosaur galleries, the painting collection (with works by Turner and Degas) and the Egyptian gallery, where real mummies rub shoulders with displays about Boris Karloff's *The Mummy* film. Littlies under five can let loose in the interactive Den.

National Space Centre
MUSEUM

(www.spacecentre.co.uk; adult/child £13/11; ⊙10am-4pm Tue-Fri, to 5pm Sat & Sun) Leicester's space museum is a fascinating introduction to the mysteries of the spheres. Although British space missions usually launch from French Guiana or Kazakhstan, the ill-fated *Beagle 2* mission to Mars was controlled from here. Fun, kid-friendly displays cover everything from astronomy to the status of current space missions. The centre is off the A6 about 1.5 miles north of the city centre. Take bus 54 (£1.80, 15 minutes, every 20 minutes) from Charles St.

Newarke Houses Museum
MUSEUM

(www.leicester.gov.uk/museums; The Newarke; ⊙10am-5pm Mon-Sat, from 11am Sun) Sprawling over two 16th-century mansions, exhibits at this entertaining museum detail the lifestyle of locals through the centuries. Don't miss the walk-through re-creation of a WWI trench, and the trophies of the Royal Leicestershire Regiment, including an outrageous snuff box made from a tiger's head.

Leicester Castle
CASTLE

Scattered around the Newarke Houses Museum are the ruins of Leicester's medieval castle, where Richard III spent his final

BIRMINGHAM, THE MIDLANDS & THE MARCHES LEICESTER

KING RICHARD III

It's an amazing story. Philippa Langley, a member of the Richard III Society, spent four-and-a-half years researching the whereabouts of King Richard's remains after his demise at Bosworth (p468). The society, founded in 1924, aims to research the king's life and to achieve a more balanced characterisation of him than that of a cruel and calculating figure, as portrayed by Shakespeare and various authors and historians. Langley narrowed it down to a Leicester car park, built over the site of the long-since-demolished Greyfriars church. But it took her another three years to persuade the city council to excavate.

Archaeologists from the University of Leicester carried out the dig in August 2012, unearthing a skeleton just three weeks later. In February 2013, the bones were confirmed by DNA analysis as those of the late king.

The university was also able to undertake a facial reconstruction using the king's skull, giving the modern world its first true image of Richard III. The reconstruction is on permanent display at Leicester's new King Richard III: Dynasty, Death & Discovery (p465) visitor centre.

A free Richard III Audio Tour app covers key Richard sites in the city and county.

Leicester Cathedral's arrangements to bury the king were derailed by the Plantagenet Alliance, a group of distant relatives, some of whom wanted Richard to be buried in York, while others sought a public consultation. A High Court ruling in 2014 ordered that the Leicester Cathedral burial go ahead – it's slated for spring 2015, preceded by a procession from Bosworth.

days before the Battle of Bosworth. The most impressive chunk of masonry is the monumental gateway known as the Magazine (Newarke St), once a storehouse for cannonballs and gunpowder. Clad in Georgian brickwork, the 12th-century Great Hall (Castle Yard) stands behind a 15th-century gate near the church of St Mary de Castro (Castle St), where Geoffrey Chaucer was married in 1336.

Jewry Wall Museum
MUSEUM

(www.leicester.gov.uk/museums; St Nicholas Circle; ☉11am-4.30pm Feb-Oct) FREE You can see fine Roman mosaics and frescos in this museum exploring the history of Leicester from Roman times to the modern day. In front of the museum is the Jewry Wall, part of Leicester's Roman baths. Tiles and masonry from the baths were incorporated in the walls of neighbouring St Nicholas Church.

★ Leicester Cathedral
CATHEDRAL

(http://leicestercathedral.org; ☉8am-6pm Mon-Sat, 7am-4.30pm Sun) FREE Look for the striking carvings on the roof supports of this substantial medieval cathedral. Free hour-long tours take place at 2pm from Monday to Saturday.

✳ Festivals & Events

Leicester Comedy Festival
COMEDY

(☏0116-242 3595; www.comedy-festival.co.uk; ☉Feb) England's longest-running comedy festival draws big names as well as fresh talent.

Leicester Caribbean Carnival
CULTURAL

(http://leicestercarnival.com; ☉Aug) The biggest Caribbean celebration in the country (after London's Notting Hill Carnival), with colourful costumes galore on the first Saturday in August.

🛏 Sleeping

★ Hotel Maiyango
HOTEL ££

(☏0116-251 8898; www.maiyango.com; 13-21 St Nicholas Pl; d from £89; ✲@☎) At the end of the pedestrian High St, this sophisticated pad has spacious rooms, decorated with handmade Asian furniture, contemporary art and massive plasma TVs. In addition to its candlelit Maiyango Restaurant & Bar, it also has a fabulous Kitchen Deli gourmet cafe and store.

Belmont Hotel
HOTEL ££

(☏0116-254 4773; www.belmonthotel.co.uk; De Montfort St; s/d from £59/79; P✲@☎) Owned and run by the same family for four generations, the 19th-century Belmont has stylish contemporary, individually designed rooms and a fantastic location overlooking leafy New Walk. Its restaurant is highly regarded; the two bars, Jamie's and Will's, open to a terrace and a conservatory respectively.

🍴 Eating

A visit to Leicester isn't complete without singeing your tastebuds on a curry along the Golden Mile. Self-caterers should head to the Leicester Market (p467). The glitzy Highcross Leicester (www.highcrossleicester. com; Shires Lane; ☉9.30am-8pm Mon-Fri, 9am-7pm Sat, 11am-5pm Sun; ☎) shopping mall has upmarket chain restaurants.

Good Earth
VEGETARIAN £

(☏0116-262 6260; 19 Free Lane; mains £3.50-6.50; ☉10am-3pm Mon-Fri, to 4pm Sat; ☑) ✦ Justifiably popular for its daily changing wholesome veggie bakes; huge, fresh salads; and homemade cakes.

Boot Room
BISTRO ££

(☏0116-262 2555; www.thebootroomeaterie.co. uk; 29 Millstone Lane; mains £13-19.50; ☉noon-2.30pm & 5.30-9.30pm Tue-Fri, noon-10pm Sat) A

DON'T MISS

THE GOLDEN MILE

Lined with sari stores, jewellery emporiums and curry houses, Belgrave Rd – aka the Golden Mile – is an essential stop for authentic Indian vegetarian food.

There are more top-notch eateries than you can shake a chapatti at. Top pick is Bobby's (☏0116-266 0106; www.eatatbobbys.com; 154-156 Belgrave Rd; dishes £3.75-6; ☉11am-9pm Mon, to 10pm Wed-Fri, 10am-10pm Sat & Sun; ☑), famed for its *namkeen* – lentil-flour snacks that come in myriad shapes and sizes. Shops along the strip sell *mithai* (Indian sweets), which involve sugary combinations of nuts, fruit and milk curds.

Belgrave Rd is about 1 mile northeast of the centre – follow Belgrave Gate and cross Burleys Flyover, or take bus 5A, 25, 54, or 126 (£1.80, seven minutes, every five minutes) from St Margaret's bus station.

former shoe factory now houses this contemporary independent bistro. Premium ingredients are used in dishes from roast Cornish cod with smoked tomato risotto to duck leg with Clonakilty black pudding. Save room for the soufflé of the day for dessert.

White Peacock MODERN BRITISH £££
(☑ 0116-254 7663; www.the-white-peacock.co.uk; 14-16 King St; lunch 2-/3-course menu £16/19, dinner 2-/3-course menu £26.50/28.50; ⊙noon-3pm & 6-9.30pm Tue-Sat, to 3pm Sun) Leicester lacked an independent fine-dining restaurant until it arrived in this beautiful Grade II–listed building overlooking the New Walk pedestrian path. Chef Phillip Sharpe's ambitious dishes span starters such as goats cheese mousse with fig, beetroot and walnut to mains such as chicken with crayfish, mango and tamarind jus, and sublime desserts.

Drinking & Nightlife

The Moroccan-style bar of the Hotel Maiyango mixes Leicester's best cocktails.

Globe PUB
(www.everards.co.uk; 43 Silver St; ⊙11am-11pm Sun-Thu, to 1am Fri & Sat) In the atmospheric Lanes – a tangle of alleys south of the High St – this old-fashioned pub has fine draught ales and a crowd that rates its drinks by quality rather than quantity.

XY Club CLUB
(www.superfly-city.com; 2 King St; ⊙10pm-3am Wed & Thu, to 6am Fri & Sat) Behind a towering mock-Tudor facade, XY serves up diverse beats, with resident and visiting DJs.

Entertainment

Curve Theatre THEATRE
(☑ 0116-242 3595; www.curveonline.co.uk; Rutland St; backstage tours adult/child £3/2) A sleek artistic space with big-name shows and some innovative modern theatre. Call the ticket office to book backstage tours. The bar is a sophisticated place for a sundowner.

Phoenix Square CINEMA
(☑ 0116-242 2800; http://phoenix.org.uk; 4 Midland St) Leicester's premier venue for arthouse films and digital media.

De Montfort Hall LIVE MUSIC
(☑ 0116-233 3111; www.demontforthall.co.uk; Granville Rd) Big orchestras, ballets, musicals and other big song-and-dance performances are on the bill at this huge venue.

Shopping

Leicester Market MARKET
(www.leicestermarket.co.uk; Market Pl; ⊙outdoor market 7am-6pm Mon-Sat, indoor market 8am-5pm Tue-Sat) More than 300 stalls at Leicester's indoor and outdoor markets sell everything from organic vegetables to aromatic spices, fish and shellfish, new and secondhand clothes, and homewares, electronic goods, cosmetics, jewellery, flowers and fabrics.

Information

Tourist Office (☑ 0116-299 4444; www.goleicestershire.com; 51 Gallowtree Gate; ⊙9.30am-5.30pm Mon-Sat, 11am-5pm Sun) Helpful office with reams of city and county info. Sells the *Richard III Walking Trail* map (50p), which is also downloadable. Ask about guided walking tours (£5).

Getting There & Away

BUS
Inter-city buses operate from **St Margaret's bus station** (Gravel St), located north of the centre. The useful Skylink bus runs to East Midlands airport (£7, 50 minutes, at least hourly, 24 hours). Bus 440 runs to Derby (£7.70, one hour, at least hourly).

National Express services include the following:
Coventry £6.60, 45 minutes, four daily
London Victoria £10, 2¾ hours, hourly
Nottingham £4.60, 45 minutes, one to two hourly
Rugby £3.60, one hour, hourly

WORTH A TRIP

WYMESWOLD

The cute village of Wymeswold, 16 miles north of Leicester via the A46, warrants a visit for a mind-blowing meal. Set in bucolic gardens at the edge of the village, everything is at this idyllic **Hammer & Pincers** (☑ 01509-880735; www.hammerandpincers.co.uk; 5 East Rd; mains £15-24, 8-course menu £45, with wine £65; ⊙noon-2pm & 6-9.30pm Tue-Sat, to 4pm Sun; ☑) gastropub is homemade, down to the breads and condiments. Steaks are a speciality; value for money is exceptional. Best reached by car; buses from Leicester require changing at Loughborough or Ashfordby.

TRAIN

East Midlands services include the following:

Birmingham £12.90, 50 minutes, hourly

London St Pancras £57, 1¼ hours, two to four hourly

ℹ Getting Around

The centre is cut off from the suburbs by a tangle of underpasses and flyovers, but downtown Leicester is easy to get around on foot. For unlimited transport on local buses, buy a Flexi Day Ticket (£5).

Around Leicester

Bosworth Battlefield

Given a few hundred years, every battlefield ends up simply a field, but the site of the Battle of Bosworth – where Richard III met his maker in 1485 – is enlivened by an entertaining heritage centre (☑ 01455-290429; www.bosworthbattlefield.com; adult/child £7.95/4.75; ☺ 10am-5pm Apr-Oct, to 4pm Nov-Mar)

SPLASHING ABOUT ON RUTLAND WATER

Tiny Rutland was merged with Leicestershire in 1974, but in 1997 regained its 'independence' as England's smallest county.

Rutland centres on Rutland Water, a vast artificial reservoir created by the damming of the Gwash Valley in 1976. Covering 1255 hectares, the reservoir attracts some 20,000 birds, including ospreys.

Oakham, the main hub, is 20 miles east of Leicester, linked by train (£11.80, 30 minutes, hourly or better). The hail-and-ride Rutland Shore Link bus service (single/day ticket £2.50/4, round trip 1½ hours) runs from Oakham around the lake.

Rutland Water Visitor Centre (☑ 01780-686800; www.anglianwater.co.uk; ☺ 10am-4pm Mar-Oct, hours vary Nov-Feb) At Skyes Lane near Empingham, the Rutland Water Visitor Centre has a snack kiosk, walking and cycling trails, and information on the area.

Rutland Water Nature Reserve (www.rutlandwater.org.uk; adult/child incl parking £5.65/3.30; ☺ 9am-5pm Mar-Oct, to 4pm Nov-Feb) Near Oakham, Rutland Water Nature Reserve has hides where you can view the abundant bird life.

Normanton Church (☑ 01780-686800; www.anglianwater.co.uk; adult/child £3/2; ☺ 12.30-3pm Sun-Wed Apr-Aug) This quaint church is saved from inundation by a limestone barrier wall. Inside are displays on the history of the Rutland reservoir.

Rockblok (☑ 01780-460060; www.rockblok.com; Whitwell Leisure Park, Bull Brigg Lane, Whitwell; climbing/high ropes £4/10, bike hire adult/child £17/10; ☺ 10am-4.30pm) Tackle a vertigo-inducing high-ropes course, an outdoor climbing wall or rent bikes for a gentle pedal around the Rutland lakeshore. See also www.rutlandcycling.com.

Rutland Watersports (☑ 01780-460154; www.anglianwater.co.uk/leisure; Whitwell Leisure Park, Bull Brigg Lane, Whitwell; sailboat/windsurf/kayak rental per hr from £17.50/20/7; ☺ 9am-7pm Fri-Tue, to 8pm Wed & Thu Apr-Oct, reduced hours Nov-Mar) Aquatic activities at Rutland include sailing and windsurfing. You can rent gear, take lessons or do certified courses.

Rutland Belle (☑ 01572-787630; www.rutlandwatercruises.com; adult/child £8.50/5.50; ☺ hourly 1-3pm Mon-Sat, 11am-3pm Sun May-Sep, hourly 1-3pm Sat, noon-3pm Sun Apr & Oct) Cruise from Whitwell to Normanton on the southern shore of the Rutland reservoir, where a stone causeway leads out across the water to Normanton Church.

Giant-Bike (☑ 01780-720888; www.giant-rutland.co.uk; adult/child per day £17/10; ☺ 9am-5.30pm) Close to the Normanton boat jetty, Giant-Bike rents bicycles.

Rutland Sailing School (☑ 01780-721999; www.rutlandsc.co.uk; Gibbet Lane, Edith Weston; sail boat hire per hr from £20, half-day sailing courses from £125; ☺ 7.30am-dusk) Rents boats and runs sailing courses.

Hambleton Hall (☑ 01572-756991; www.hambletonhall.com; s/d incl breakfast from £220/285, 2-/3-course lunch menu £25.50/31.50, 3-course dinner menu £65; 🅿 📶) One of England's finest country hotels, Hambleton Hall sits on a peninsula jutting out into Rutland Water, 3 miles east of Oakham. Its luxuriant floral rooms and Michelin-starred restaurant are surrounded by gorgeous gardens.

full of skeletons and musket balls. Enthusiasts in period costume re-enact the battle each August.

The battlefield is 16 miles southwest of Leicester at Sutton Cheny, off the A447. A taxi from Leicester costs around £25.

Although it lasted just a few hours, the Battle of Bosworth marked the end of the Plantagenet dynasty and the start of the Tudor era. This was where the mortally wounded Richard III famously proclaimed: 'A horse, a horse, my kingdom for a horse'. Well, actually, he didn't: the quote was invented by that great Tudor propagandist William Shakespeare.

Conkers & the National Forest

The National Forest (www.forestry.gov.uk/nationalforest) is an ambitious project to generate new areas of sustainable woodland by planting 30 million trees in Leicestershire, Derbyshire and Staffordshire. More than eight million saplings have already taken root, and all sorts of visitor attractions are springing up in the forest.

◉ Sights & Activities

Conkers NATURE CENTRE
(☑ 01283-216633; www.visitconkers.com; Rawdon Rd; adult/child £8.95/7.25; ⊙ 10am-6pm Easter–mid-Oct, to 5pm mid-Oct–Easter) A family-oriented nature centre, it has interactive displays, indoor and outdoor playgrounds, and lots of hands-on activities. It's 20 miles northwest of Leicester off the A444; take bus 29 (£3.30, 35 minutes, half-hourly).

Hicks Lodge CYCLING
(☑ 01751-460011; www.purplemountain.co.uk; Willesley Wood Side; bike rental per day adult/child £30/15; ⊙ trails 8am-dusk, bike hire 10am-4pm Mon-Fri, 9am-5pm Sat & Sun) Bike trails run through the National Forest, including a flat 2km path around the lake, from this cycle centre. Hicks Lodge rents wheels; has a cafe; and also organises guided tours and night rides.

🛏 Sleeping

National Forest YHA HOSTEL £
(☑ 0845 371 9672; www.yha.org.uk; dm/d from £13/52; P @ 🖰) 🚲 Situated 300m west of Conkers visitor centre along Bath Lane, this hostel has impressive ecofriendly features (such as greywater and solar biomass boiler usage), en suite rooms, and a restaurant serving local produce and organic wines.

> ### STEAMING AROUND LEICESTER
>
> Steam locomotives chug from Leicester North station on Redhill Circle to Loughborough Central, following the 8-mile route of the Great Central Railway (☑ 01509-632323; www.gcrailway.co.uk; return adult/child £15/9) along which Thomas Cook ran the original package tour in 1841. The locos operate several days a week from June to August, and at weekends for the rest of the year – check timetables online.
>
> To reach Leicester North station, take bus 125 (£2.30, 20 minutes, every five minutes) from Leicester's Haymarket bus station on Charles St (take bus 126 to return).

DERBYSHIRE

The Derbyshire countryside is painted in two distinct tones – the lush green of rolling valleys, criss-crossed by dry stone walls, and the barren mottled brown hilltops of the high moorlands. The biggest draw here is the Peak District National Park, which preserves some of England's most evocative scenery, attracting legions of hikers, climbers, cyclists and cave enthusiasts.

ℹ Getting There & Around

East Midlands Airport (p400) is the nearest air hub, and Derby is well served by trains, but connecting services to smaller towns are few. In the Peak District, the Derwent Valley Line runs from Derby to Matlock. Edale and Hope lie on the Hope Valley Line from Sheffield to Manchester. For a comprehensive list of Derbyshire bus routes, visit the 'Transport' pages at www.derbyshire.gov.uk.

Derby

POP 255,390

Derby was one of the crucibles of the Industrial Revolution. Almost overnight, a sleepy market town was transformed into a major manufacturing centre, producing everything from silk to bone china, and later locomotives and Rolls-Royce aircraft engines. The city suffered the ravages of industrial decline in the 1980s, but has bounced back with impressive cultural developments and a rejuvenated riverfront.

◎ Sights

Derby Cathedral
CATHEDRAL

(www.derbycathedral.org; 18 Irongate; ⊙ 9.30am-4.30pm Mon-Sat & services Sun) Founded in AD 943 and reconstructed in the 18th century, Derby Cathedral's vaulted ceiling towers above a fine collection of medieval tombs, including the opulent grave of the oft-married Bess of Hardwick, who at various times held court at Hardwick Hall, Chatsworth House and Bolsover Castle. Peregrine falcons nest in the tower – follow their progress at www.derbyperegrines.blogspot.com.

Derby Museum & Art Gallery
MUSEUM

(www.derbymuseums.org; The Strand; ⊙ 10am-5pm Tue-Sun) FREE Local history and industry displays include fine ceramics produced by Royal Crown Derby and an archaeology gallery.

Quad
GALLERY, CINEMA

(✆ 01332-290606; www.derbyquad.co.uk; Market Pl; gallery & mediatheque free, cinema £7-15; ⊙ gallery 11am-6pm, from noon Sun, BFI Mediatheque 11am-8pm, from noon Sun) A striking modernist cube on Market Pl, Quad contains a cinema, futuristic art gallery and mediatheque – an archive of films and TV covering decades of broadcasting, run by the British Film Institute (BFI).

Royal Crown Derby Factory
CERAMICS

(✆ 01332-712800; www.royalcrownderby.co.uk; Osmaston Rd; tour & museum adult/child £5/2.50; ⊙ 10am-5pm Mon-Sat, tours 11am & 1.30pm Tue-Thu, 11am Fri by reservation) Derby's historic potteries still turn out some of the finest bone china in England, from edgy Asian-inspired designs to the kind of stuff your grandma collects.

⌂ Sleeping

Cathedral Quarter Hotel
HOTEL ££

(✆ 01332-546080; www.cathedralquarterhotel.com; 16 St Mary's Gate; s/d incl breakfast from £59/69; @☎) A bell's peal from the cathedral, this grand Georgian edifice houses Derby's finest digs. The service is as polished as the grand marble staircase and there's an on-site spa and fine-dining restaurant.

Chuckles
B&B ££

(✆ 01332-367193; www.chucklesguesthouse.co.uk; 48 Crompton St; s/d £38/64; ☎) A friendly and cosy B&B just south of the centre, Chuckles is run by an arty couple and is renowned for its bountiful breakfasts. Take Green Lanes and turn onto Crompton St by the church.

✕ Eating

★ Jack Rabbits
CAFE, DELI £

(✆ 01332-349966; www.jackrabbitskitchen.co.uk; 50-55 Queen St; mains £6-11; ⊙ 8.30am-6pm Mon-Sat, 10am-2pm Sun; ✐) Jack Rabbits serves gourmet sandwiches, quiches, deli goods (including homemade jams and chutneys) and ready-to-eat meals that are perfect for a riverside picnic. It's proved so popular that it opened an adjoining sunlit cafe for lazy grazing on platters, cheese-boards and scrumptious cakes and slices.

Wonky Table
BISTRO ££

(✆ 01332-295000; www.wonkytable.co.uk; 32 Sadler Gate; lunch mains £5.50-7.25, lunch 2-course menu £11, dinner 2-/3-course menu £15/19; ⊙ 5pm-midnight Mon, 11.30am-3pm & 5pm-midnight Tue-Sat) Inside a retro-vintage dining room with exposed brick walls, Wonky Table features a slimmed-down daytime menu plus sandwiches such as warm goats cheese with caramelised onion and walnuts. But it comes into its own at dinner with dishes including honey and balsamic goose breast, rosemary-crusted lamb rump, and beetroot and goats-cheese risotto balls with watercress cream.

Darleys
MODERN BRITISH £££

(✆ 01332-364987; www.darleys.com; Waterfront, Darley Abbey; mains £19.75-22.50; ⊙ noon-2pm & 7-9.30pm Mon-Sat, to 2.30pm Sun) Two miles north of the centre, this upmarket restaurant has a gorgeous setting in a bright, converted mill overlooking the river. Classy fare includes warm fig tart, goats-cheese mousse and toasted hazelnuts.

╤ Drinking & Entertainment

Derby has a wonderful selection of historic real-ale pubs, many of which have live music.

Catch art-house films at Quad, or check what's showing at the two theatre spaces run by Derby Live (✆ 01332-255800; www.derbylive.co.uk; Market Pl).

★ Old Bell Hotel
PUB, TEAROOM

(51 Sadler Gate; ⊙ 8.30am-5pm Mon, to 11pm Tue-Thu, to 12.30am Fri & Sat, 10am-10pm Sun) Dating from 1680 and hosting Bonnie Prince Charlie's soldiers in 1745, this history-steeped black-and-white inn languished from late last century until its recent restoration by valiant local entrepreneur Paul Hurst. There's a crackling open fire and a central courtyard (and, allegedly, more than a few ghosts); boutique accommodation and a microbrewery are planned.

Ye Olde Dolphin PUB
(☎01332-267711; www.yeoldedolphin.co.uk; 5a Queen St; ◷10.30am-11pm Mon-Wed, to midnight Thu-Sat, noon-11pm Sun) Dating from 1530, Derby's oldest pub has a hearty menu, live music in the beer garden on weekends, and it also organises ghost tours.

Brewery Tap PUB
(www.brewerytap-dbc.co.uk; 1 Derwent St; ◷noon-11pm Mon-Wed, to midnight Thu, to 1am Fri, 11am-1am Sat, 1-11pm Sun) This pub serves its own brews and guest ales in elegant Victorian surrounds.

Silk Mill PUB
(www.silkmillderby.co.uk; 19 Full St; ◷noon-11pm Mon-Thu, 11am-midnight Fri & Sat, noon-10.30pm Sun; 🔊) Live music several times a week including Sunday afternoon jazz.

🔒 Shopping

Bennetts DEPARTMENT STORE
(www.bennettsirongate.co.uk; 8 Irongate; ◷9am-5pm Mon-Sat) Founded as an ironmongers in 1734 and still retaining an ironmongery, Derby's historic department store has evolved over the centuries to sell beautiful clothes, homewares, gifts and more. There's a tearoom and cafe, and, on the 1st-floor interior balcony, the excellent Michael Frith at Bennetts Brasserie (☎01332-344621; www.michaelfrithcuisine.co.uk; 8 Irongate; mains £8.50-11.50, 3-course champagne breakfast £23; ◷9am-3pm Mon-Sat), specialising in three-course champagne breakfasts (served until 2pm).

❶ Information

Tourist Office (☎01332-643411; www.visitderby.co.uk; Market Pl; ◷9.30am-4.30pm Mon-Sat) Under the Assembly Rooms in the main square.

❶ Getting There & Away

AIR
East Midlands Airport, 8 miles northwest of Derby, is served by regular Skylink buses (£4.20, 30 minutes, at least hourly, 24 hours).

BUS
Local and long-distance buses run from Derby's bus station, immediately east of the Westfield shopping mall. From Monday to Saturday, Transpeak has hourly buses between Derby and Buxton (£5.70, 1¾ hours), via Matlock (£4.20, 35 minutes) and Bakewell (£4.70, 1¼ hours). Five buses continue to Manchester (£7.70, 2¼ hours).

Other services include the following:
Leicester National Express; £7.70, one to two per hour
Nottingham Red Arrow; £7.20, 30 minutes, nine daily

TRAIN
The train station is about half a mile southeast of the centre on Railway Tce. Services include the following:
Birmingham £15.90, 45 minutes, four hourly
Leeds £37.30, 1½ hours, every 30 minutes
London St Pancras £65, 1¾ hours, half-hourly

Around Derby

Ashbourne
POP 8375
Perched at the southern edge of the Peak District National Park, Ashbourne is a pretty spread of steeply slanting stone streets, lined with cafes, pubs and antique shops.

The main attraction, however, is the chance to walk or cycle along the Tissington Trail, part of NCN Route 68, which runs north for 13 miles to Parsley Hay, connecting with the Pennine Cycleway (NCN Route 68) and the High Peak Trail towards Buxton or Matlock. The track climbs gently along the tunnels, viaducts and cuttings of the disused railway line that once transported local milk to London.

🛏 Sleeping & Eating

Compton House B&B ££
(☎01335-343100; www.comptonhouse.co.uk; 27-31 Compton St; s/d/f from £45/65/85; 🅿🔊) Fresh, clean, frilly rooms, a warm welcome and a central location make this the pick of Ashbourne's B&Bs.

Bramhalls DELI, CAFE £
(☎01335-342631; www.bramhallsdeli.co.uk; 22 Market Pl; dishes £3.25-8; ◷8am-5pm Mon-Sat, 9am-5pm Sun) A great little deli and cafe with posh light meals and sandwiches, and excellent homemade pastries, breads, cold meats and 60 varieties of cheese.

Flower Cafe CAFE £
(www.theflowercafe.co.uk; 5 Market Pl; mains £6-7; ◷8.30am-5pm Sun-Fri, to 8pm Sat) Soups such as parsnip, chorizo and chestnut, broccoli and stilton, and spicy bean and lentil are a speciality at this cute-as-a-button cafe where everything is homemade.

ROYAL SHROVETIDE FOOTBALL

Some people celebrate Mardi Gras aka Shrove Tuesday (the last day before Lent) by eating pancakes or dressing up in carnival finery. But Ashbourne marks the occasion with a riotous game of football, where the ball is wrestled as much as kicked from one end of town to the other by crowds of revellers.

Following 12th-century rules, villagers are split into two teams – those from north of the river and those from south – and the 'goals' are two millstones, set 3 miles apart. Participants are free to kick, carry or throw the ball, though it's usually squeezed through the crowds like a rugby scrum. Sooner or later, players and the ball end up in the river. Local shops board up their windows and the whole town comes out to watch or play.

Fearless visitors are welcome to participate in the melee but, under a quirk of the rules, only locals are allowed to score goals.

Drinking & Nightlife

Smith's Tavern   PUB
(36 St John's St; ⊙noon-11pm Mon-Thu & Sun, to midnight Fri & Sat) A tiny pub on the main shopping street, with a big selection of real ales and an old piano at the back.

Getting There & Away

Bus services include the following:

Buxton Highpeak 441 and 442; £4.20, 80 minutes, every two hours Monday to Saturday, four Sunday

Derby Trent Barton Swift; £4, 30 minutes, hourly Monday to Saturday, five Sunday

Getting Around

Cycle Hire Centre (☑ 01335-343156; www.peakdistrict.gov.uk/visiting/cycle; Mapleton Lane; half-day/day from £13/16; ⊙9.30am-5.30pm Mar-Oct, reduced hours Nov-Feb) About a mile above town, the Cycle Hire Centre is right on the Tissington Trail, at the end of a huge and atmospheric old railway tunnel leading under Ashbourne. You can also rent children's bikes, bikes with baby seats, trailers for buggies and tandems.

Matlock Bath

POP 640

Unashamedly tacky, Matlock Bath (not to be confused with the larger, work-a-day town of Matlock 2 miles north) looks like a seaside resort that somehow lost its way and ended up at the foot of the Peak District National Park. Following the River Derwent through a sheer-walled gorge, the main promenade is lined with amusement arcades, tearooms, fish-and-chip shops, pubs and shops catering to the bikers who congregate here on summer weekends. Outside summer, the town is considerably quieter and many lodgings and eateries shut.

Sights & Activities

Steep paths climb the eastern side of the gorge, reached by pedestrian bridges from the A6. The tourist office has details of longer, more challenging walks in the hills.

Beware: many of the lanes up the side of the valley are too narrow for cars, with no space for turning.

Peak District Mining Museum & Temple Mine   MUSEUM
(www.peakmines.co.uk; The Grand Pavilion, South Pde; museum adult/child £3.50/2.50, mine £3.50/2.50, combined ticket £6/4; ⊙10am-5pm Apr-Oct, 11am-3pm Wed-Fri, to 4pm Sat & Sun Nov-Mar) An educational introduction to the mining history of Matlock is provided by this enthusiast-run museum. Set in an old Victorian dancehall, the museum has a maze of tunnels and shafts that kids can wriggle through while adults browse historical displays. At noon and 2pm daily (at weekends only from November to March) you can go into the workings of the Temple Mine and pan for 'gold' (well, shiny minerals).

Gulliver's Kingdom   AMUSEMENT PARK
(☑ 01925-444888; www.gulliversfun.co.uk; admission £16; ⊙hours vary) This old-fashioned amusement park offers plenty of splashing, churning, looping attractions for anyone as tall as the signs at the start of the rides. Call for opening days and times or check seasonal schedules online.

Heights of Abraham   AMUSEMENT PARK
(☑ 01629-582365; www.heightsofabraham.com; adult/child £14/9.50; ⊙10am-4.30pm daily early Feb–mid-Feb & mid-Mar–Nov, 10am-4.30pm Sat & Sun mid-Feb–mid-Mar) A spectacular cable-car

ride (via admission ticket only) from the base of the gorge brings you to this hilltop leisure park, whose cave and mine tours and fossil exhibitions are a winner with kids.

Peak Rail HISTORIC RAILWAY
(☑ 01629-580381; www.peakrail.co.uk; adult/child £8/4.30) From a tiny platform by Sainsbury's supermarket on the outskirts of Matlock (not Matlock Bath), nostalgic steam trains trundle along a 4-mile length of track to the nearby village of Rowsley, home to Caudwell's Mill, which includes a craft centre. Tickets include unlimited travel on the day of purchase. Services run five times a day Saturday and Sunday (and some weekdays) from May to October, and some weekends at other times of the year – check timetables online.

Would-be engineers can also do a one-hour train-driving course (9.45am March to November, 9.15am January and February; £115); you must be aged between 18 and 70. From March to November, there are also two-hour courses (8.45am; £200)

🛏 Sleeping & Eating

Despite its inland location, Matlock Bath's signature dish is fish and chips, which is served at cafes, tearooms and pubs along the strip.

Hodgkinson's Hotel & Restaurant HOTEL ££
(☑ 01629-582170; www.hodgkinsons-hotel.co.uk; 150 South Pde; s/d incl breakfast from £77/95,

2-/3-course meal £29.50/34; ☺ restaurant noon-2.30pm & 6.30-10.30pm; 🅿 🛜) Rooms at this central Grade II–listed Victorian beauty conjure up Matlock's golden age with antique furnishings, flowery wallpaper and cast-iron fireplaces. The restaurant has just 16 seats so bookings are advised. Service is superb.

Ashdale Guest House B&B ££
(☑ 01629-57826; www.ashdaleguesthouse.co.uk; 92 North Pde; s/d from £45/65; 🅿) 🍃 A tall stone house just beyond the bling of the amusement-arcade-lined main promenade, with tasteful rooms and organic breakfasts.

🛍 Shopping

For arts, crafts and discounted clothing brands, check out the Derwent Valley mills.

Scarthin Books BOOKS
(www.scarthinbooks.com; The Promenade, Cromford; ☺ 9am-6pm Mon-Sat, noon-6pm Sun) More than 100,000 new and secondhand books cram 12 rooms in this biblioparadise, which hosts regular literary events and has a vegetarian cafe serving organic pizza, wraps, pies and burritos.

ℹ Information

Tourist Office (☑ 01335-343666; www.visit-peakdistrict.com; The Grand Pavilion, South Pde; ☺ 10am-5pm daily Apr-Oct, 11am-3pm Wed-Fri, to 4pm Sat & Sun Nov-Mar) Visitor information point at the Peak District Mining Museum.

DERWENT VALLEY MILLS

Unlikely as it may sound, the industrial mills that line the Derwent Valley are ranked up there with the Taj Mahal on the Unesco World Heritage list.

Cromford Mill (☑ 01629-823256; www.cromfordmills.org.uk; Mill Lane, Cromford; tour adult/child £3.50/2.50; ☺ 9am-5pm, tours 11am, 1pm & 2.30pm Sat-Thu, 11am Fri by reservation) Three miles south of Matlock Bath, the Cromford Mill was founded in the 1770s by Richard Arkwright. It was the first modern factory, producing cotton on automated machines, powered by a series of waterwheels along the River Derwent. This prototype inspired a succession of mills, ushering in the industrial age. The Arkwright Society runs atmospheric tours. It's one train stop from Matlock Bath (60p, three minutes, hourly).

Masson Mills (☑ 01629-581001; www.massonmills.co.uk; Derby Rd; adult/child £3/2; ☺ 10am-4pm Mon-Sat, 11am-4pm Sun, closed Dec) A museum tells the story of the valley's textile mills at this large complex 1 mile south of Matlock Bath. The attached shopping village is full of outlet stores for big clothing brands.

Caudwell's Mill (☑ 01629-734374; www.caudwellsmillcraftcentre.co.uk; Rowsley; mill tours adult/child £4.50/2; ☺ 9.30am-4.30pm) A chugging, grinding, water-powered mill that still produces flour the old-fashioned way, and has various craft workshops and a tearoom. You can get to Rowsley direct from Matlock Bath by Highpeak bus (£2.70, 15 minutes, hourly Monday to Saturday, two services Sunday) on the route to Bakewell, or take the Peak Rail steam train and follow the riverside path from the station.

❶ Getting There & Away

Matlock is a hub for buses around the Peak District.

Bakewell Highpeak; £3.20, 30 minutes, hourly Monday to Saturday

Derby Transpeak; £4.20, 45 minutes, hourly Monday to Saturday, two services Sunday

Trains run hourly between Matlock Bath and Derby (£5, 70 minutes, hourly).

Chesterfield

POP 88,480

The eastern gateway to the Peaks, Chesterfield is worth a stop to see the astonishing crooked spire rising atop St Mary & All Saints Church (☑ 01246-206506; www.chesterfieldparishchurch.org.uk; spire tours adult/child £3.50/1.50; ☺ spire tours 11.30am & 2pm Tue & Thu, 11.30am & 2.30pm Mon, Wed, Fri & Sat). Dating from 1360, the 68m-high spire is twisted in a right-handed corkscrew and leans several metres southwest. It's the result of the lead casing on the south-facing side having buckled in the sun. Learn more at the engaging Chesterfield Museum & Art Gallery (☑ 01246-345727; www.chesterfieldmuseum.co.uk; St Mary's Gate; ☺ 10am-4pm Mon & Thu-Sat) FREE.

The tourist office (☑ 012246-345777; www.visitchesterfield.info; Rykneld Sq; ☺ 9am-5.30pm Mon-Sat Easter-early Nov, to 5pm Mon-Sat early Nov-Easter) is directly opposite the crooked spire.

Chesterfield lies on the main rail line between Nottingham/Derby (£8, 30 minutes, up to two per hour) and Sheffield (£4.90, 15 minutes, up to two per hour). The station is just east of the centre. From Chesterfield coach station on Beetwell St, bus 170 serves Bakewell (£3.10, 45 minutes, hourly).

Hardwick Hall

One of the most complete Elizabethan mansions in the country, Hardwick Hall (NT; www.nationaltrust.org.uk; house & garden adult/child £12/6, garden only £6/3; ☺ house noon-4.30pm Wed-Sun, garden 9am-6pm daily) was designed by eminent architect Robert Smythson. The hall featured all the latest mod-cons of the time, including fully glazed windows. The atmospheric interiors are decked out with magnificent tapestries and oil paintings of forgotten dignitaries.

Hardwick Hall is 10 miles southeast of Chesterfield, just off the M1; it's best reached by your own wheels.

The hall was home to the 16th-century's second-most powerful woman, Elizabeth, Countess of Shrewsbury – known to all as Bess of Hardwick – who amassed a staggering fortune by marrying wealthy noblemen with one foot in the grave. Hardwick Hall was constructed using her inheritance from hubby number four, who shuffled off this mortal coil in 1590.

Set aside time to explore the formal gardens or the longer walking trails of Hardwick Park.

Next door to the manor is Bess' first house, Hardwick Old Hall (EH; www.english-heritage.org.uk; adult/child £5/3, incl Hardwick Hall £14/7; ☺ 10am-5pm Wed-Sun Apr-early Nov, to 5pm Sat & Sun early Nov-Mar), now a romantic ruin administered by English Heritage.

PEAK DISTRICT

Rolling across the southernmost hills of the Pennines is the glorious Peak District. Ancient stone villages are folded into creases in the landscape, and the hillsides are littered with stately homes and rocky outcrops that attract hordes of walkers, climbers and cavers. No one knows how the Peak District got its name – certainly not from the landscape, which has hills and valleys, gorges and lakes, wild moorland and gritstone escarpments, but no peaks. The most popular theory is that the region was named for the Pecsaetan, the Anglo-Saxon tribe who once populated this part of England.

Founded in 1951, the Peak District National Park was England's first national park and is Europe's busiest. But escaping the crowds is easy if you avoid summer weekends. Even at peak times, there are 555 sq miles of open English countryside in which to soak up the scenery.

Locals divide the Peak District into the Dark Peak – dominated by exposed moorland and gritstone 'edges' – and the White Peak, made up of the limestone dales to the south.

Although there are several YHA hostels (www.yha.org.uk) in the Peak District, they're often booked out in advance by groups, so contact them before turning up.

🏃 Activities

Caving & Climbing

The limestone sections of the Peak District are riddled with caves and caverns, includ-

Peak District National Park

ing a series of 'showcaves' in Castleton, Buxton and Matlock Bath. For serious caving (or potholing) trips, the first port of call should be the website www.peakdistrictcaving.info, run by the caving store **Hitch n Hike** (www.hitchnhike.co.uk; Mytham Bridge, Bamford), near Castleton, which has gear and advice for climbing.

England's top mountaineers train in this area, which offers rigorous technical climbing on a series of limestone gorges, exposed tors (crags) and gritstone 'edges' that extend

Driving Tour
Peak District

START BAKEWELL
END BUXTON
LENGTH 52 MILES; ONE TO TWO DAYS

Although you can drive this route in just a few hours, there's a lot to see and even more to do, so pack your hiking boots and consider breaking your journey overnight.

Fuel your car and yourself at ❶ **Bakewell** (p484), famed for its distinctive Bakewell Pudding. Head south on the A6 for 3.5 miles to Rowsley and turn left on winding Church Lane for 2 miles to visit the atmospheric medieval manor ❷ **Haddon Hall** (p484).

Return to Rowsley, turn left on the A6 and left on the B6012 – follow it for 2.9 miles before turning right to reach the 'Palace of the Peak', ❸ **Chatsworth House** (p485).

Back on the B6012, turn right to join the A619. At Baslow, home to the country hotel and Michelin-starred restaurant Fischer's Baslow Hall, turn left at the roundabout and travel along the A623 for 3.4 miles to the turn-off for ❹ **Eyam** (p483). Drive up the hill to reach its quaint museum, where you can

learn about the town's poignant plague history. There's fantastic walking here.

Continue up the hill and turn right on Edge Rd, then right on Sir William Hill Rd and left on the B601 at Grindleford. Continue to Hathersage and turn left on the A6187 to Hope Valley. From here, turn right on the A6013, passing Ladybower Reservoir, to reach the ❺ **Derwent Dam Museum** (p482). Pop in to learn about the Dambusters squadron's 'bouncing bombs' tests here during WWII.

It's 5.8 miles back to the Hope Valley turn-off. Then turn right onto Hathersage Rd, right again on Edale Rd and follow the valley to stretch your legs at another prime walking destination, ❻ **Edale** (p482).

Scenery peaks when you travel southwest towards Castleton, climbing the steep hill near 517m-high Mam Tor, to Winnats Rd, then following the former coral reef canyon Winnats Pass to explore ❼ **Speedwell Cavern** (p481), half-a-mile west of charming Castleton.

From Speedwell Cavern, head west along Arthurs Way on to Winnats Rd. Turning right on the A623 brings you to the riot of Victoriana in the former spa town of ❽ **Buxton** (p478).

south into the Staffordshire Moorlands. Gritstone climbing in the Peak District is predominantly on old-school trad routes, requiring a decent rack of friends, nuts and hexes. Bolted sport routes are found on several limestone crags in the Peak District, but many use ancient pieces of gear and most require additional protection. The crags are best reached with your own transport; check seasonal bus services with tourist offices in Trent Barton or Buxton.

Cycling

Plunging dales and soaring scarps provide a perfect testing ground for cyclists, and local tourist offices are piled high with cycling maps and pamphlets. For easy traffic-free riding, head for the 17.5-mile High Peak Trail, which follows the old railway line from Cromford, near Matlock Bath, to Dowlow near Buxton. The trail winds through beautiful hills and farmland to Parsley Hay, where the Tissington Trail, part of NCN Route 68, heads south for 13 miles to Ashbourne. Trails are off-road on dedicated cycle paths, suitable for road bikes.

Mirroring the Pennine Way, the Pennine Bridleway is another top spot to put your calves through their paces. Around 120 miles of trails have been created between Middleton Top and the South Pennines, and the route is suitable for horse riders, cyclists and walkers. You could also follow the Pennine Cycleway (NCN Route 68) from Derby to Buxton and beyond. Other popular routes include the Limestone Way, running south from Castleton to Staffordshire, and the Monsal Trail & Tunnels between Bakewell and Wyedale, near Buxton.

Peak Tours (www.peak-tours.com; mountain bike per day £20) delivers rental bikes anywhere in the Peak District, and offers guided cycling tours. From March to October, the Peak District National Park Authority (☑ 01629-816200; www.peakdistrict.gov.uk; bicycle hire per half-day/day adult £13/16, child £9/11) operates several cycle-hire centres.

Walking

The Peak District is one of England's most popular walking areas, with awe-inspiring vistas of hills, dales and sky that attract legions of hikers in summer. The White Peak is perfect for leisurely strolls, which can start from pretty much anywhere. Be sure to close gates behind you as you go. When exploring the rugged territory of the Dark Peak, make sure your boots are waterproof and beware of slipping into rivulets and marshes.

The Peak's most famous walking trail is the Pennine Way, which runs north from Edale for more than 250 miles, finishing in the Scottish Borders. If you don't have three weeks to spare, you can reach the pretty town of Hebden Bridge in Yorkshire comfortably in three days.

The 46-mile Limestone Way winds through the Derbyshire countryside from Castleton to Rocester in Staffordshire, following footpaths, tracks and quiet lanes. Many people walk the 26-mile section between Castleton and Matlock in one long, tiring day, but two days is better. Tourist offices have a detailed leaflet.

Other popular routes include the High Peak Trail, Tissington Trail, and Monsal Trail & Tunnels. Numerous short walks are available.

ℹ Information

Tourist offices or national park visitor centres include Buxton, Bakewell, Castleton and Edale, The Peak District National Park Authority website (www.peakdistrict.gov.uk) has reams of information on transport, activities and local events.

ℹ Getting There & Away

Buses run from regional centres such as Sheffield and Derby to destinations across the Peak District. Be aware that buses are much more frequent at weekends, and many services close down completely in winter. Bakewell and Matlock (not Matlock Bath) are the two main hubs – from here you can get anywhere in the Peak District. Timetables are available from all the tourist offices, or online at www.derbyshire.gov.uk/transport. Trains run to Matlock Bath, Buxton, Edale and several other towns and villages.

ℹ PEAK DISTRICT TRANSPORT PASSES

Handy bus passes covering travel in the Peak District include the Peaks Plus (adult/child £6/4), offering all-day travel on Trent Barton buses and the Transpeak between Derby and Buxton. The Derbyshire Wayfarer (adult/child £11.60/5.80) covers buses and trains throughout the county and as far afield as Manchester and Sheffield.

Buxton

POP 22,110

The 'capital' of the Peak District National Park, albeit just outside the park boundary, Buxton is a confection of Georgian terraces, Victorian amusements and parks in the rolling hills of the Derbyshire dales. The town built its fortunes on its natural warm-water springs, which attracted health tourists in Buxton's turn-of-the-century heyday.

Today, visitors are drawn here by the flamboyant Regency architecture and the natural wonders of the surrounding countryside. Tuesdays and Saturdays are market days, bringing colour to the grey limestone market place.

◎ Sights

Buxton's historic centre overflows with Victorian pavilions, concert halls and glasshouse domes. Its most famous building is the turreted Opera House (p480).

★ **Pavilion Gardens**   GARDENS
(www.paviliongardens.co.uk;   ⊙9.30am-5pm)
FREE Adjoining Buxton's opulent Opera House is the equally flamboyant Pavilion Gardens, dotted with domed pavilions. The main building contains a tropical greenhouse, a nostalgic cafe and the tourist office.

Devonshire Dome   HISTORIC BUILDING
A glorious piece of Victoriana, the Devonshire Dome forms part of the campus of the University of Derby. It is also home to **Devonshire Spa** (☑01298-338408; www.devonshiredome.co.uk; 1 Devonshire Rd; 2hr body spa £20, ocean or frangipani wrap £50, day package from £95), which offers a full range of pampering treatments.

Buxton Baths   HISTORIC BUILDING
In Victorian times, spa activities centred on the extravagant Buxton Baths complex, built in grand Regency style in 1854. The various bath buildings are fronted by a grand, curving facade, known as the **Crescent**, inspired by the Royal Crescent in Bath. It's expected to re-open in 2016 as a five-star hotel and spa.

Slopes   PARK
Opposite the Crescent, a small park called the Slopes rises steeply in a series of grassy terraces. Climbing them provides the definitive view over Buxton's Victorian rooftops.

Pump Room   HISTORIC BUILDING
At the base of the Slopes is the Pump Room, which dispensed Buxton's spring water for nearly a century. Modern-day health-tourists queue up to fill plastic bottles from a small spout known as **St Ann's Well**.

**Buxton Museum
& Art Gallery**   MUSEUM, GALLERY
(www.derbyshire.gov.uk/buxtonmuseum; Terrace Rd; ⊙9.30am-5.30pm Tue-Fri, to 5pm Sat year-round, 10.30am-5pm Sun Easter-Sep) **FREE** In a handsome Victorian building, the town museum displays local historical bric-a-brac and curiosities from Castleton's Victorian-era 'House of Wonders', including Harry Houdini's handcuffs.

🏃 Activities

★ **Buxton Tram**   BUS TOUR
(☑01298-79648;   http://discoverbuxton.co.uk; adult/child £6/4; ⊙hourly 10am-4pm) From the Pavilion Gardens, this vintage milk float takes you on a 12mph, hour-or-so circuit of the centre on its entertaining Wonder of the Peak tour. There are only eight seats, so booking ahead is recommended.

Poole's Cavern   CAVE
(☑01298-26978; www.poolescavern.co.uk; adult/child £9/5; ⊙9.30am-5pm Mar-Oct, 10am-4pm Sat & Sun Nov-Feb) A pleasant mile stroll southwest from the centre brings you to Poole's Cavern. This magnificent natural limestone cavern is reached by descending 28 steps; the temperature is a cool 7°C. Tours lasting 50 minutes run every 20 minutes from March to October and at 10.30am, 12.30pm and 2.30pm from November to February.

From the cavern's car park, a 20-minute walk leads up through Grin Low Wood to **Solomon's Temple**, a ruined tower with fine views over the town.

Parsley Hay Cycle Hire   CYCLING
(☑01298-84493; www.peakdistrict.gov.uk; bike hire per half-/full day adult £13/16, child £9/11; ⊙9.30am-5pm Mar-Oct) Rent bikes from the Peak District National Park Authority's Parsley Hay Cycle Hire, about 8 miles south of Buxton at the junction of the High Peak and Tissington Trails.

🛏 Sleeping

Buckingham Hotel   HOTEL **£**
(☑01298-70481; www.buckinghamhotel.co.uk; 1 Burlington Rd; d £55-65, f £67.50-80; **P** 🛜) The eccentric decor isn't for everyone – framed

Buxton

BIRMINGHAM, THE MIDLANDS & THE MARCHES BUXTON

Buxton

photos of Hollywood stars such as Pierce Brosnan or Bruce Willis adorn each of the 57 old-fashioned rooms, and there are more lining the hallways – but there's still a lot to recommend this oddball town-centre hotel. Rooms are clean and spacious, parking's free, and there's a lively downstairs bar and restaurant.

Old Hall Hotel
HISTORIC HOTEL ££

(☎ 01298-22841; www.oldhallhotelbuxton.co.uk; The Square; s/d incl breakfast from £69/79; @ ☎) There's a tale to go with every creak of the floorboards at this history-soaked establishment, supposedly the oldest hotel in England. Among other esteemed residents, Mary, Queen of Scots, stayed here from 1576 to 1578, albeit against her will. The rooms are still the grandest in town, and there are several bars, lounges and dining options.

Roseleigh Hotel
B&B ££

(☎ 01298-24904; www.roseleighhotel.co.uk; 19 Broad Walk; s/d from £41/80; P @ ☎) This gorgeous family-run B&B in a roomy old Victorian house has lovingly decorated rooms, many with fine views out over the Pavilion Gardens. The owners are a welcoming couple, both seasoned travellers, with plenty of interesting stories.

Victorian Guest House
B&B ££

(☎ 01298-78759; www.buxtonvictorian.co.uk; 3a Broad Walk; d from £95; P ☎) Overlooking the Pavilion Gardens, this elegant house has eight individually decorated bedrooms furnished with Victorian and Edwardian antiques. The home-cooked breakfasts are renowned.

✕ Eating

Number 13
MODERN BRITISH ££

(☎ 01298-25397; www.number13.co.uk; cnr Market St & South Ave; mains £11-16; ☺ noon-10.30pm Mon-Thu, to midnight Fri & Sat, to 7pm Sun) 🍴 Don't be fooled by the low prices – this is serious cooking that just happens to be affordable too. Dishes such as coq au vin in garlic and red wine or sausage and root mash with smoked onion marmalade are expertly prepared and exquisitely presented. Live jazz swings in the bar on Sunday afternoons.

Columbine Restaurant
MODERN BRITISH ££

(☎ 01298-78752; www.columbinerestaurant.co.uk; 7 Hall Bank; mains £13.50-17.50; ☺ 7-10pm Mon-Sat May-Oct & Dec, 7-10pm Wed-Sat Jan-Apr & Nov) 🍴 On the lane leading down beside the Town Hall, this understated restaurant is the top choice among in-the-know Buxtonites. The chef conjures up imaginative dishes primarily made from local produce. Bookings recommended.

🍷 Drinking & Entertainment

Barbarella's
WINE BAR

(www.barbarellaswinebar.co.uk; 7 The Quadrant; ☺ noon-11pm Sun-Thu, to midnight Fri & Sat; ☎) Black-and-white paisley wallpaper, chandeliers and glossy timber tables make this sleek retro wine bar the hottest drinking den in Buxton. Stellar food too.

Old Sun Inn
PUB

(www.theoldsuninnbuxton.com; 33 High St; ☺ noon-11pm Mon & Wed, to 11.30pm Tue, Thu & Sun, to midnight Fri & Sat) The cosiest of Buxton's pubs, with a warren of rooms full of original features, a dozen ales on tap, and a lively crowd that spans the generations.

Opera House
OPERA

(☎ 0845 127 2190; www.buxtonoperahouse.org.uk; Water St; tours £2.50; ☺ tours 11am Sat) Buxton's gorgeously restored Opera House hosts a full program of drama, dance, concerts and comedy. It's the focal point for festivities including the Buxton Festival (www.buxtonfestival.co.uk; ☺ Jul).

🛍 Shopping

Scrivener's Books & Bookbinding
BOOKS

(☎ 01298-73100; www.scrivenersbooks.co.uk; 42 High St; ☺ 9am-5pm Mon-Sat, noon-4pm Sun) A delightfully chaotic bookshop, sprawling over five floors, where books are filed in piles and the Dewey system has yet to be discovered.

ℹ Information

Tourist Office (☎ 01298-25106; www.visitpeakdistrict.com; Pavilion Gardens; ☺ 9.30am-5pm; ☎) Helpful, well-organised office with useful leaflets on walks in the area. Hour-long Roman Buxton town walks, by donation, depart at 11am and 2pm Saturdays.

ℹ Getting There & Away

Buses stop on both sides of the road at Market Pl. The hourly Highpeak runs to Derby (£5.70, 1½ hours), via Bakewell (£3.70, 30 minutes) and Matlock Bath (£3.20, one hour). Five Highpeak services run to Manchester (£5.20, 1¼ hours).

To reach Sheffield take bus 65 (£5.70, 1¼ hours, every two hours Monday to Saturday, three services Sunday).

Northern Rail has trains to/from Manchester (£9.80, one hour, hourly).

Castleton & Around
POP 735

Guarding the entrance to the forbidding Winnats Pass gorge, charming Castleton is a magnet on summer weekends for Midlands visitors – come mid-week if you want to enjoy the sights in relative peace and quiet. The village's streets are lined with leaning stone houses, and walking trails criss-crossing the surrounding hills. An atmospheric castle crowns the ridge above, and the bedrock below is riddled with fascinating caves.

◎ Sights

Peveril Castle   CASTLE
(EH;   www.english-heritage.org.uk;   adult/child £4.70/2.80; ⊙10am-6pm Apr-Sep, to 5pm Oct, to 4pm Sat & Sun Nov-Mar) Topping the ridge to the south of Castleton, this evocative castle has been so ravaged by the centuries that it almost looks like a crag itself. Constructed by William Peveril, son of William the Conqueror, the castle was used as a hunting lodge by Henry II, King John and Henry III, and the crumbling ruins offer swooping views over the Hope Valley.

Castleton Museum   MUSEUM
(☑01629-816572;   Buxton Rd;   ⊙10am-5.30pm Apr–mid-Sep, to 5pm mid-Sep–Oct, reduced hours Nov-Mar) FREE Attached to the tourist office, the cute town museum has displays on everything from mining and geology to rock climbing, hang-gliding and the curious Garland Festival.

Peak Cavern   CAVE
(☑01433-620285;   http://devilsarse.com;   adult/child £9.25/7.25, incl Speedwell Cavern £15.50/11.75;   ⊙10am-5pm Apr-Oct, to 5pm Sat & Sun Nov-Mar) Castleton's most convenient cave is easily reached by a pretty streamside walk from the village centre. It has the largest natural cave entrance in England, known (not so prettily) as the Devil's Arse. Dramatic limestone formations are lit with fibre-optic cables.

Speedwell Cavern   CAVE
(☑01433-620512;   www.speedwellcavern.co.uk; adult/child £10/8, incl Peak Cavern £15.50/11.75; ⊙9.30am-4pm) About half a mile west of Castleton at the mouth of Winnats Pass, this claustrophobe's nightmare is reached via an eerie boat ride through flooded tunnels, emerging by a huge subterranean lake called the Bottomless Pit. New chambers are discovered here all the time by potholing expeditions.

Treak Cliff Cavern   CAVE
(☑01433-620571;   www.bluejohnstone.com;   adult/child £8.95/9.95;   ⊙10am-5pm Mar-Oct, to 4pm Nov-Feb) Captivating Treak Cliff has a forest of stalactites and exposed seams of colour-

ful Blue John Stone, which is still mined to supply the jewellery trade. Tours focus on the history of mining; kids can polish their own Blue John Stone during school holidays.

Blue John Cavern   CAVE
(☑01433-620638;   www.bluejohn-cavern.co.uk; adult/child £10/5;   ⊙9.30am-5.30pm Apr-Oct, 9.30am-dusk Nov-Mar) Up the side of Mam Tor, Blue John is a maze of natural caverns with rich seams of Blue John Stone that are still mined every winter. You can get here on foot up the closed section of the Mam Tor road.

🏃 Activities

At the base of 517m-high Mam Tor, Castleton is the northern terminus of the Limestone Way, which follows narrow, rocky Cave Dale, far below the east wall of the castle. The tourist office has maps and leaflets, including details of numerous easier walks.

🎉 Festivals & Events

Garland Festival   CULTURAL
(www.visitpeakdistrict.co.uk;   ⊙May) Castleton celebrates Oak Apple Day on 29 May (28 May if the 29th is a Sunday) as it has for centuries, with the Garland King (buried under an enormous floral headdress) and Queen parading through the village on horseback.

🛏 Sleeping

Prices are often higher at weekends, when booking ahead is advised.

Ye Olde Nag's Head Hotel   PUB £
(☑01433-620248;   www.yeoldenagshead.co.uk; Cross St; d from £50; 🛜) The cosiest of the 'residential' pubs along the main road, offering 10 comfortable, well-appointed rooms (some with four-poster beds and spas), ale-tasting trays and a popular restaurant, plus regular live music.

Rowter Farm   CAMPSITE £
(☑01433-620271;   2-person sites £10;   ⊙Easter-Oct; 🅿) A simple campsite about 1 mile west of Castleton in a stunning location up in the hills. Drivers should approach via Winnats Pass; on foot, follow the Cave Dale path.

Causeway House   B&B ££
(☑01433-623921;   www.causewayhouse.co.uk; Back St; s/d from £35/70) The floors within this ancient character-soaked stone cottage are worn and warped with age, but the quaint bedrooms are bright and welcoming.

Doubles have en suites but the two single rooms (one of which can be used as a twin) share a bathroom.

Eating & Drinking

Tearooms abound in Castleton. The village shop has limited stocks of provisions for walkers and is open seven days.

Three Roofs Cafe CAFE £
(www.threeroofscafe.co.uk; The Island; dishes £6-9.50; ⊙ 9.30am-5pm Mon-Fri, to 5.30pm Sat & Sun; ⊛⬛) The most popular purveyor of cream teas, opposite the turn-off to the tourist office.

1530 ITALIAN ££
(⎙ 01433-621870; www.1530therestaurant. co.uk; Cross St; mains £9.50-17; ⊙ noon-2pm & 6-8.30pm Wed & Thu, to 2pm & 6-9.30pm Fri & Sat, to 2pm & 6-8pm Sun & Mon; ⬛) Crispy thin-crust pizzas and fresh pastas such as king prawn, crab, crayfish and calamari linguine are the speciality of Castleton's swish Italian flag-bearer.

★ Samuel Fox MODERN BRITISH £££
(⎙ 01433-621562; www.samuelfox.co.uk; Stretfield Rd, Bradwell; lunch mains £6-18.50, dinner mains £13.50-22.50; ⊙ kitchen 6-9pm Tue, noon-2pm & 6-9pm Tue-Sat, to 3.30pm Sun) In the Hope Valley village of Bradwell, 2.5 miles southeast of Castleton, this enchanting inn owned by pedigreed chef James Duckett serves exceptional food such as rare roasted venison with pickled red cabbage, and roast pheasant with braised sprouts, bacon and parsnips. Rates for the gorgeous pastel-shaded guestrooms upstairs (single/double £95/130) include a sumptuous breakfast as well as sherry, grapes and chocolates.

Look out for dinner, bed and breakfast deals.

ⓘ Information

Tourist Office (⎙ 01433-620679; www.peak-district.gov.uk; Buxton Rd; ⊙10am-5.30pm Apr–mid-Sep, to 5pm mid-Sep–Oct, reduced hours Nov-Mar) In the Castleton Museum.

ⓘ Getting There & Away

Bus services include the following:

Bakewell Bus 173; £3, 50 minutes, four daily via Hope (10 minutes) and Tideswell (25 minutes)

Buxton Buses 68 and 173; £3.80, one hour (departs Castleton in the morning and returns in the afternoon from Monday to Saturday)

The nearest train station is at Hope, about 2 miles east of Castleton on the line between Sheffield (£6.60, 30 minutes, half-hourly) and Manchester (£10.80, 50 minutes, half-hourly). On summer Saturdays, a bus runs between Hope station and Castleton to meet the trains, but otherwise it's an easy walk.

Derwent Reservoirs

North of the Hope Valley, the upper reaches of the Derwent Valley were flooded between 1916 and 1935 to create three huge reservoirs to supply Sheffield, Leicester, Nottingham and Derby with water. These constructed lakes soon proved their worth – the Dambusters squadron carried out practice runs over Derwent Reservoir before unleashing their 'bouncing bombs' on the Ruhr Valley in Germany in WWII. Their exploits are detailed in the Derwent Dam Museum (www.peakdistrict.gov.uk; Fairholmes; ⊙10am-4pm Sun) FREE in a tower atop the dam.

These days, the Ladybower, Derwent and Howden Reservoirs are popular destinations for walkers, cyclists and mountain bikers – and lots of ducks, so drive slowly! Fairholmes has a tourist office (⎙ 01433-650953; www.peakdistrict.gov.uk; Fairholmes; ⊙10am-5pm Apr-Oct, to 3.30pm Nov-Mar), which dispenses walking and cycling advice, a car park, a snack bar and a good cycle hire centre (⎙ 01433-651261; per half-/full day adult £13/16, child £9/11; ⊙9.30am-5.30pm).

Fairholmes is 2 miles north of the A57, the main road between Sheffield and Manchester. Buses are limited at best, so you really need your own wheels.

Edale

POP 290

Surrounded by majestic Peak District countryside, this cluster of stone houses set around a pretty parish church is an enchanting place to pass the time. Edale lies between the White and Dark Peak areas, and is the southern terminus of the Pennine Way. Despite the remote location, the Manchester–Sheffield line passes through the village, bringing throngs of weekend visitors.

🏃 Activities

Walking is the number one drawcard, with plenty of diverting strolls for less committed hill walkers.

As well as trips to Hollins Cross and Mam Tor, on the ridge dividing Edale from Castleton, you can walk north onto the **Kinder Plateau**, dark and brooding in the mist, gloriously high and open when the sun's out. This was the setting for a famous act of civil disobedience by ramblers in 1932 that paved the way for the legal 'right to roam' and the creation of England's national parks.

Weather permitting, a fine circular walk starts by following the **Pennine Way** through fields to **Upper Booth**, then up a path called Jacobs Ladder and along the southern edge of Kinder, before dropping down to Edale via the steep rocky valley of Grindsbrook Clough, or the ridge of Ringing Roger.

About 1.5 miles east of Edale, **Ladybooth Equestrian Centre** (☑ 01433-670205; www.ladybooth.co.uk; Nether Booth; horse riding per hour/day from £25/100) offers horseback trips around the Peak District, lasting anything from one hour to a full day, plus pony farm rides for kids.

Sleeping

Fieldhead Campsite CAMPSITE £
(☑ 01433-670386; www.fieldhead-campsite.co.uk; sites per person/car from £5/2.50; P) Right next to the Moorland Tourist Office, this pretty and well-equipped campsite spreads over six fields, with some pitches right by the river.

Edale YHA HOSTEL £
(☑ 0845 371 9514; www.yha.org.uk; dm/d from £5/58; P @ ☎) Spectacular views across to Back Tor unfold from this country-house hostel 1.5 miles east of Edale. The attached **activity centre** is very popular with student groups. It's signposted from the Hope road.

Stonecroft B&B ££
(☑ 01433-670262; www.stonecroftguesthouse.co. uk; Grindsbrook; d from £80; P ☎) ✹ This handsomely fitted-out stone house, built in the 1900s, has two comfortable bedrooms. Vegetarians and vegans are well catered for – host Julia is an award-winning chef and the organic breakfast is excellent. Picnic baskets (£12) are availble by request when booking.

Eating

Cooper's Cafe CAFE £
(☑ 01433-670401; Cooper's Camp; dishes £2.20-4.80; ☺8am-4pm daily Apr-Sep, 9.30am-3pm Thu-Sun Nov-Mar; ☎) Load up on carbs at this cheerful cafe close to the village school.

Rambler Inn PUB ££
(☑ 01433-670268; www.theramblerinn.com; Grindsbrook; mains £9.25-12; ☎ ⊞) Cosy stone pub with real ales, hearty steaks, pies and casseroles; also B&B rooms and occasional live music.

ℹ️ Information

Moorland Tourist Office (☑ 01433-670207; www.edale-valley.co.uk; Grindsbrook; ☺9.30am-5pm Mon-Fri, to 5.30pm Sat & Sun Apr-Sep, 10.30am-3.30pm Sat & Sun Oct-Mar) Visitor centre with maps, displays on the moors, a kiosk and a campsite.

ℹ️ Getting There & Away

Trains run from Edale to Manchester (£10.80, every hour, 45 minutes) and Sheffield (£6.90, every two hours, 40 minutes) via Hope.

Eyam
POP 970

Quaint little Eyam (ee-em), a former lead-mining village, has a poignant history. In 1665, the town was infected by the dreaded Black Death plague, carried here by fleas on a consignment of cloth from London, and the village rector, William Mompesson, convinced villagers to quarantine themselves. Some 270 of the village's 800 inhabitants succumbed, while surrounding villages remained relatively unscathed. Today, Eyam's sloping streets of old cottages backed by rows of green hills are delightful to wander.

◉ Sights

Eyam Parish Church CHURCH
(www.eyam-church.org; ☺9am-6pm) Many victims of the village's 1665 Black Death plague outbreak were buried at Eyam's church. You can view stained-glass panels and moving displays telling the story of the outbreak. The churchyard contains a Celtic cross carved in the 8th century.

Eyam Hall HISTORIC BUILDING
(NT; www.nationaltrust.org.uk; craft centre admission free, house & garden adult/child £7.15/3.70; ☺ craft centre 10am-4.30pm daily year-round, house & garden noon-4pm Wed, Thu & Sun Easter-early May & late Jul-Aug) This solid-looking 17th-century manor house with stone windows and doorframes, home to a craft centre and several eateries, is surrounded by a traditional English walled garden.

Eyam Museum
MUSEUM

(www.eyammuseum.demon.co.uk; Hawkhill Rd; adult/child £2.50/2; ⊙10am-4.30pm Tue-Sun late Mar-early Nov) Vivid displays on the Eyam plague are the centrepiece of the engaging town museum, alongside exhibits on the village's history of lead-mining and silk-weaving.

🏃 Activities

Eyam makes a great base for walking and cycling in the White Peak area. For an interesting short walk, follow Water Lane out of the village from the main square, then turn right and climb the hill to reach Mompesson's Well, where supplies were left during the Black Death plague time for Eyam folk by friends from other villages. The goods were paid for using coins sterilised in vinegar. To return to Eyam, retrace your steps down the lane, then take a path that leads directly to the church. This 2-mile circuit takes about 1½ hours.

🛏 Sleeping & Eating

Miner's Arms
PUB ££

(☎01433-630853; Water Lane; s/d £45/70; 🛜) Although its age isn't immediately obvious, this traditional village inn was built shortly before the Black Death hit Eyam in 1665. Inside you'll find beamed ceilings, affable staff, a cosy stone fireplace, comfy en suite rooms and good-value pub food.

Crown Cottage
B&B ££

(☎01433-630858; www.crown-cottage.co.uk; Main Rd; s/d from £50/70; 🅿) Opposite the post office, this walker- and cyclist-friendly stone house full of pottery ornaments is crammed to the rafters most weekends, when there's a minimum two-night stay.

Village Green
CAFE £

(http://cafevillagegreen.com; The Square; dishes £2-6; ⊙10am-4pm; 🛜) On the village square, with tables on the cobblestones outside, this sweet cafe has a mouth-watering array of slices and decent coffee.

ℹ Getting There & Away

Services include the following:

Bakewell Buses 275 and 350; £3.50, 20 minutes, four per day Monday to Saturday

Buxton Buses 65 and 66; £3.50, 40 minutes, five per day Monday to Saturday, three Sunday

Sheffield Bus 65; £5.60, 40 minutes, five per day Monday to Saturday, three Sunday

Bakewell & Around

POP 3950

The second-largest town in the Peak District, pretty Bakewell is a great base for exploring the White Peak. The town is ringed by famous walking trails and stately homes, but it's probably best known for its famous pudding, a pastry shell filled with jam and frangipane invented in 1820. Like other Peak towns, Bakewell is mobbed during the summer months – expect traffic jams and cut-throat competition for accommodation at weekends. The centre of town is Rutland Sq, the meeting point of the roads from Matlock, Buxton and Chesterfield.

◎ Sights

All Saints Church
CHURCH

(www.bakewellchurch.co.uk; ⊙9am-4pm Mon-Sat, to 6pm Sun Apr-Oct, 10am-3.45pm daily Nov-Mar) Up on the hill above Rutland Sq, All Saints Church is packed with ancient features, including a 14th-century font, a pair of Norman arches, some fine heraldic tombs, and a collection of crude stone gravestones and crosses dating from the 12th century.

Old House Museum
MUSEUM

(www.oldhousemuseum.org.uk; Cunningham Pl; adult/child £3.50/2, incl Spirit of the 1940s £5/2; ⊙11am-4pm Apr-early Nov) Set in a time-worn stone house near All Saints Church, the Old House Museum explores local history. Check out the Tudor loo and the displays on wattle and daub, a traditional technique for building walls using woven twigs and cow dung.

Spirit of the 1940s
MUSEUM

(www.oldhousemuseum.org.uk; Tanners Yard; adult/child £2/50p, incl Old House Museum £5/2; ⊙10.30am-4pm Fri-Mon Apr-early Nov) The Spirit of the 1940s museum incorporates an evocative 1940s street scene, letters and photographs, and wartime memorabilia.

Haddon Hall
HISTORIC SITE

(www.haddonhall.co.uk; adult/child £10/5.50; ⊙noon-5pm daily May-Sep, noon-5pm Sat-Mon Mar-Apr & Oct) With stone turrets, time-worn timbers and walled gardens, Haddon Hall, 2 miles south of Bakewell on the A6, looks exactly like a medieval manor house should. Founded in the 12th century, it was expanded and remodelled throughout medieval times. The 'modernisation' stopped when the house was abandoned in the 18th century. Take the Highpeak bus from Bakewell

(£2.10, 10 minutes, hourly) or walk along the footpath through the fields, mostly on the east side of the river.

Spared from the more florid excesses of the Victorian period, Haddon Hall has been used as the location for numerous period blockbusters (such as *Elizabeth*).

Chatsworth House   HISTORIC BUILDING

(☑ 01246-565300; www.chatsworth.org; house & gardens adult/child £18/10, gardens only £12/7, playground £6, park admission free; ⊙ 11am-4.30pm mid-Mar–late Dec, garden 11am-6pm mid-Mar–late Dec) Known as the 'Palace of the Peak', this vast edifice 3 miles northeast of Bakewell has been occupied by the earls and dukes of Devonshire for centuries. Inside, the lavish apartments and mural-painted staterooms are packed with priceless paintings and period furniture. The house sits in 25 sq miles of grounds and ornamental gardens, some landscaped by Lancelot 'Capability' Brown. Kids will love the farmyard adventure playground.

From Bakewell, take bus 215 (£2.10, 20 minutes, hourly).

The manor was founded in 1552 by the formidable Bess of Hardwick and her second husband, William Cavendish, who earned grace and favour by helping Henry VIII dissolve the English monasteries. Mary, Queen of Scots was imprisoned at Chatsworth on the orders of Elizabeth I in 1569.

Look out for the portraits of the current generation of Devonshires by Lucian Freud.

Walkers can take the footpaths through Chatsworth park via the mock-Venetian village of Edensor (en-sor), while cyclists can pedal via Pilsley.

🏃 Activities

Walking and cycling are, of course, the main activities in the area. The scenic Monsal Trail follows the path of a disused railway line from Combs Viaduct on the outskirts of Bakewell to Topley Pike in Wye Dale, about 3 miles east of Buxton, including a number of reopened old railway tunnels, covering 8½ miles in all.

For a rewarding shorter walk, follow the Monsal Trail for 3 miles to the dramatic viewpoint at Monsal Head, where you can pause for refreshment at the Monsal Head Hotel (☑ 01629-640250; www.monsalhead.com; s/d incl breakfast from £85/100, mains £11.50-16; ⊙ kitchen 8am-10am & noon-9.30pm; ℗), which serves real ales and excellent Modern British cuisine. With more time to kill, continue to Miller's Dale, where viaducts give a spectacular vista across the steep-sided valley. The tourist offices at Bakewell and Buxton have full details.

Other walking routes go to the stately homes Haddon Hall and Chatsworth House.

🛏️ Sleeping

Melbourne House & Easthorpe   B&B ££

(☑ 01629-815357; www.bakewell-accommodation. co.uk; Buxton Rd; d from £70; ℗) In a picturesque, creeper-covered building dating back more than three centuries and a new annexe, this inviting B&B is handily situated on the main road leading to Buxton.

Rutland Arms Hotel   HOTEL £££

(☑ 01629-812812; www.rutlandarmsbakewell.co.uk; The Square; s £82-95, d £139-195; ℗ 🛜) Jane Austen is said to have stayed in room 2 of this aristocratic, recently refurbished stone coaching inn while working on *Pride and Prejudice*. The more expensive of its 33 rooms have lots of Victorian flourishes.

🍴 Eating & Drinking

Bakewell's streets are lined with sweet tearooms and bakeries selling the famous Bakewell Pudding.

Old Original Bakewell
Pudding Shop   BAKERY, TEAROOM £

(www.bakewellpuddingshop.co.uk; The Square; dishes £6.50-17; ⊙ 8.30am-6pm) One of the claimants of the Bakewell Pudding, this place has a lovely 1st-floor tearoom with exposed beams that serves light meals and afternoon teas on tiered trays.

Bloomers Original
Bakewell Puddings   BAKERY £

(☑ 01629-814844; Water St; dishes 80p-£4.50; ⊙ 9am-5pm Mon-Sat, 10.30am-5pm Sun) Claims to be the progenitor of the famous Bakewell Pudding. No sit-down dining; head to the pretty riverbanks.

Piedaniel's   FRENCH ££

(☑ 01629-812687; www.piedaniels-restaurant.com; Bath St; mains £17, 2-/3-course lunch £16/18 Tue-Fri; ⊙ noon-2pm & 7-9pm Tue-Sat) Chefs Eric and Christiana Piedaniel's Modern French cuisine is the toast of in-town restaurants. A whitewashed dining room is the exquisite setting for the likes of lobster bisque with *quenelles* (feather-light flour, egg and cream dumplings) followed by monkfish in salmon mousse. Weekday lunch menus are exceptional value.

Fischer's Baslow Hall   GASTRONOMIC £££

(☎ 01246-583259; www.fischers-baslowhall.co.uk; 259 Calver Rd, Baslow; lunch 2-/3-course menu from £20/27, dinner 1-/2-/3-course menu from £34/55/72; ⏰ kitchen noon-1.30pm & from 7pm daily by reservation) Just over 4 miles northeast of Bakewell, this stately 1907-built stone manor house has a magnificent Michelin-starred dining room showcasing a roll-call of British produce (Derbyshire lamb, Yorkshire game, Cornish crab...) along with vegetables from its kitchen garden.

Six sumptuous floral bedrooms are in the main house, with another five larger but less atmospheric rooms in the adjacent garden house (doubles from £155 to £250).

Castle Inn   PUB

(☎ 01629-812103; www.oldenglishinns.co.uk; Bridge St; 🛜🅿️) The ivy-draped Castle Inn is one of the better pubs in Bakewell, with four centuries of practice in rejuvenating ham-strung hikers. Gourmet burgers are a menu highlight (mains from £8 to £17).

ℹ️ Information

Tourist Office (☎ 01629-813227; www.visit-peakdistrict.com; Bridge St; ⏰ 9.30am-5pm Apr-Oct, 10.30am-4.30pm Nov-Mar) In the old Market Hall; the helpful staff can book accommodation.

ℹ️ Getting There & Away

Bakewell lies on the Highpeak bus route. Buses run hourly to Derby (£4.70, 1¼ hours), Matlock Bath (£3.20, 30 minutes) and Buxton (£3.20, 30 minutes). Five services a day continue to Manchester (£5.90, 1¾ hours).

Other services include the following:

Castleton Bus 173; £3, 25 minutes, three per day

Chesterfield Bus 170; £3.10, 45 minutes, hourly

Yorkshire

Best Places to Eat

➡ Pipe and Glass Inn (p541)

➡ Van Zeller (p506)

➡ Star Inn (p513)

➡ Crafthouse (p530)

➡ Mannion's (p500)

Best Places to Stay

➡ Millgate House (p526)

➡ Devonshire Fell (p522)

➡ Helaina (p509)

➡ Quebecs (p530)

Why Go?

With a population as big as Scotland's and an area half the size of Belgium, Yorkshire is almost a country in itself. It has its own flag, its own dialect and its own celebration, Yorkshire Day (1 August). While local folk are proud to be English, they're even prouder to be natives of 'God's Own County'.

What makes Yorkshire so special? First, there's the landscape – with its brooding moors and green dales rolling down to a dramatic coastline, Yorkshire has some of Britain's finest scenery. Second, there's the sheer breadth of history – every facet of the British experience is represented here, from Roman times to the 20th century.

But Yorkshire's greatest appeal lies in its people. Industrious and opinionated, they have a wry wit and shrewd friendliness. Stay here for a while and you'll come away believing, like the locals, that God is indeed a Yorkshirewoman.

When to Go

➡ The week-long Jorvik Festival in February sees York taken over by a Viking invasion.

➡ Spring brings drifts of yellow daffodils to brighten the roadsides in the Dales and North York Moors; the Three Peaks Race takes place in Horton-in-Ribblesdale.

➡ Agriculture is celebrated at the Great Yorkshire Show in Harrogate in July. At the same time of year Yorkshire's coastal sea cliffs become a frenzy of nesting seabirds.

➡ September is the ideal time for hiking in the Yorkshire Dales; the Walking Festival in Richmond also takes place in this month. York goes all gourmet with its annual 10-day food festival, while Harrogate gets green-fingered during its Autumn Flower Show.

Yorkshire Highlights

1 Exploring the medieval streets of **York** (p492) and its awe-inspiring cathedral

2 Getting off the beaten track and exploring the lesser-known corners of the **Yorkshire Dales** (p520)

3 Wandering among the atmospheric medieval ruins of **Fountains Abbey** (p510)

4 Being beside the seaside at **Scarborough** (p506) with its traditional bucket-and-spade atmosphere

5 Riding on the **North Yorkshire Moors Railway** (p514), one of England's most scenic train lines

6 Sitting on the pier at **Whitby** (p515) and tucking into the world's best fish and chips

7 Reliving the story of *Brideshead Revisited* amid the aristocratic splendour of **Castle Howard** (p503)

8 Pulling on your hiking boots and tackling the steep paths around scenic **Malham Cove** (p522)

9 Discovering mining's dark side at the **National Coal Mining Museum for England** (p533)

10 Enjoying the high-tech, hands-on exhibits at Bradford's **National Media Museum** (p533)

N 0 —————————— 20 km
0 —————————— 10 miles

Billingham

Middlesbrough

A174

Stokesley

A171

Danby

6 Whitby

Hawsker

Grosmont

Robin Hood's Bay

A171

North York Moors National Park

5 North Yorkshire Moors Railway

NORTH SEA

The Hambleton Hills

Hutton-le-Hole

Lastingham

Helmsley

Pickering

Derwent

Hertford

Filey

Bempton Cliffs Nature Reserve

Thirsk

Cleveland Hills

Malton

7

Castle Howard

Kirkham Priory

Flamborough Head

Bridlington

oughbridge

B1363

A64

A166

A59

Great Driffield

York

A1079

EAST RIDING OF YORKSHIRE

South Dalton

Hull

Hornsea

etherby

A19

Beverley

Selby

Barlby

A164

Hull

Hull Ferry Terminal

Monk Fryston

Howden

Ouse

Patrington

To Rotterdam & Zeebrugge

Easington

Kilnsea

Humber

NORTH LINCOLNSHIRE

Thorne

Scunthorpe

A15

Grimsby

Cleethorpes

Spurn Head

Doncaster

NORTHEAST LINCOLNSHIRE

therham

A15

Gainsborough

Market Rasen

LINCOLNSHIRE

Worksop

NOTTINGHAMSHIRE

A57

Lincoln

A158

terfield

RBYSHIRE

History

As you drive through Yorkshire on the main A1 road, you're following in the footsteps of the Roman legions who conquered northern Britain in the 1st century AD. In fact, many Yorkshire towns – including York, Catterick and Malton – were founded by the Romans, and many modern roads (including the A1, A59, A166 and A1079) follow the alignment of Roman roads.

When the Romans departed in the 5th century, native Britons battled for supremacy with invading Teutonic tribe the Angles and, for a while, Yorkshire was part of the Kingdom of Northumbria. In the 9th century the Vikings arrived and conquered most of northern Britain, an area that became known as the Danelaw. They divided the territory that is now Yorkshire into *thridings* (thirds), which met at Jorvik (York), their thriving commercial capital.

In 1066 Yorkshire was the scene of a pivotal showdown in the struggle for the English crown, when the Anglo-Saxon king, Harold II, rode north to defeat the forces of the Norwegian king, Harold Hardrada, in the Battle of Stamford Bridge, before returning south for his appointment with William the Conqueror – and a fatal arrow – in the Battle of Hastings.

The inhabitants of northern England did not take the subsequent Norman invasion lying down. In order to subdue them, the Norman nobles built a chain of formidable castles throughout Yorkshire, including those at York, Richmond, Scarborough, Pickering and Helmsley. The Norman land grab formed the basis of the great estates that supported England's medieval aristocrats.

By the 15th century, the duchies of York and Lancaster had become so wealthy and powerful that they ended up battling for the English throne in the Wars of the Roses (1455–87). The dissolution of the monasteries by Henry VIII from 1536 to 1540 saw the wealth of the great abbeys of Rievaulx, Fountains and Whitby fall into the hands of noble families, and Yorkshire quietly prospered for 200 years, with fertile farms in the north and the Sheffield cutlery business in the south, until the big bang of the Industrial Revolution transformed the landscape.

South Yorkshire became a centre of coal mining and steel-making while west Yorkshire nurtured a massive textile industry, and the cities of Leeds, Bradford, Sheffield and Rotherham flourished. By the late 20th century another revolution was taking place. The heavy industries had died out, and the cities of Yorkshire were reinventing themselves as shiny, high-tech centres of finance, higher education and tourism.

🏃 Activities

Yorkshire's varied landscape of wild hills, tranquil valleys, high moors and spectacular coastline offers plenty of opportunities for outdoor activities. See www.outdooryorkshire.com for more details.

Cycling

Yorkshire's hosting of the start of the 2014 Tour de France saw a huge upsurge in interest in cycling. The county has a vast network of country lanes that are perfect for road cyclists, although the national parks also attract lots of motorists so even minor roads can be busy at weekends.

North York Moors   MOUNTAIN BIKING
(www.mtb-routes.co.uk/northyorkmoors) Off-road bikers can avail themselves of the network of bridleways, former railways and disused mining tracks now converted for two-wheel use. Dalby Forest (www.forestry.gov.uk/dalbyforest), near Pickering, sports purpose-built mountain-biking trails of all grades from green to black, and there are newly waymarked trails at the Sutton Bank visitor centre.

Moor to Sea Cycle Route   CYCLING
(www.moortoseacycle.net) A network of routes between Pickering, Danby and the coast includes a 20-mile traffic-free route that follows a disused railway line between Whitby and Scarborough.

White Rose Cycle Route   CYCLING
(www.sustrans.org.uk; NCN Route 65) A 131-mile road cruise from Middlesbrough to York and on to Hull and Hornsea, via the dramatic western scarp of the North York Moors and the rolling Yorkshire Wolds. There is a traffic-free section on the old railway between Selby and York.

Yorkshire Dales Cycleway   CYCLING, MOUNTAIN BIKING
(www.cyclethedales.org.uk) An exhilarating 130-mile loop, taking in the best of the national park; the website also details the route followed by Stage 1 of the 2014 Tour de France. There's scope for off-road riding, with about 500 miles of bridleways and trails – for inspiration, check out www.mtbthedales.org.uk.

Walking

For shorter walks and rambles, the best area is the Yorkshire Dales, with a great selection of walks through scenic valleys or over wild hilltops, with a few higher summits thrown in for good measure. The East Riding's Yorkshire Wolds hold hidden delights, while the quiet valleys and dramatic coast of the North York Moors also offer many opportunities.

Cleveland Way   WALKING
(www.nationaltrail.co.uk/clevelandway) A venerable moor-and-coast classic that circles the North York Moors National Park on its 109-mile, nine-day route from Helmsley to Filey.

Coast to Coast Walk   WALKING
(www.wainwright.org.uk/coasttocoast.html) One of England's most popular walks: 190 miles across northern England from the Lake District through the Yorkshire Dales and North York Moors National Parks. The Yorkshire section takes a week to 10 days and offers some of the finest walking of its kind in England.

Dales Way   WALKING
(www.dalesway.org.uk) A charming and not-too-strenuous amble from the Yorkshire Dales to the Lake District, following the River Wharfe through the heart of the Dales and finishing at Bowness-on-Windermere.

Pennine Way   WALKING
(www.nationaltrail.co.uk/pennineway) The Yorkshire section of England's most famous walk runs for more than 100 miles via Hebden Bridge, Malham, Horton-in-Ribblesdale and Hawes, passing near Haworth and Skipton.

White Rose Way   WALKING
(www.whiteroseway.co.uk) A long-distance trail covering the 104 miles from Leeds city centre to Scarborough, taking in remote and picturesque Yorkshire villages along the way.

Wolds Way   WALKING
(www.nationaltrail.co.uk/yorkshirewoldsway) This beautiful but oft-overlooked walk winds through the most scenic part of Yorkshire's East Riding district.

ⓘ Information

Yorkshire Tourist Board (www.yorkshire.com) Plenty of general leaflets and brochures are available, for postal and email enquiries only. For more detailed information, contact local tourist offices.

ⓘ Getting There & Around

The major north–south road transport routes – the M1 and A1 motorways – run through the middle of Yorkshire, serving the key cities of Sheffield, Leeds and York. If you're arriving by sea from northern Europe, Hull in the East Riding district is the region's main port.

Traveline Yorkshire (☑ 0871 200 22 33; www.yorkshiretravel.net) provides public transport information for all of Yorkshire.

BUS

Long-distance coaches operated by **National Express** (☑ 08717 81 81 81; www.nationalexpress.com) serve most cities and large towns in Yorkshire from London, the south of England, the Midlands and Scotland.

Bus transport around Yorkshire is frequent and efficient, especially between major towns. Services are more sporadic in the national parks, but are still adequate for reaching most places, particularly in summer months (June to September).

TRAIN

The main rail line between London and Edinburgh runs through Yorkshire, with at least 10 trains calling each day at York and Doncaster, where you can change trains for other Yorkshire destinations. There are also direct services between the major towns and cities of Yorkshire and other northern cities such as Manchester and Newcastle. For timetables, contact **National Rail Enquiries** (☑ 08457 48 49 50; www.nationalrail.co.uk).

NORTH YORKSHIRE

This, the largest of Yorkshire's four counties – and the largest county in England – is also the most beautiful. Unlike the rest of northern England, it survived almost unscathed by the Industrial Revolution. Since the Middle Ages, North Yorkshire has been almost exclusively about sheep and the woolly wealth they produce.

Rather than closed-down factories, mills and mines, the artificial monuments dotting the landscape in these parts are of the stately variety – the great houses and wealthy abbeys that sit, ruined or restored, as a reminder that there was plenty of money to be made off the sheep's back.

All the same, North Yorkshire's biggest attraction is an urban one. While the genteel spa town of Harrogate and the bright and breezy seaside resorts of Scarborough and Whitby have many fans, nothing compares to the unparalleled splendour of York, England's most-visited city outside London.

York

POP 198,000

Nowhere in northern England says 'medieval' quite like York, a city of extraordinary cultural and historical wealth that has lost little of its pre-industrial lustre. A magnificent circuit of 13th-century walls encloses a medieval spider's web of narrow streets. At its heart lies the immense, awe-inspiring York Minster, one of the most beautiful Gothic cathedrals in the world. York's long history and rich heritage are woven into virtually every brick and beam, and the modern, tourist-oriented city – with its myriad museums, restaurants, cafes and traditional pubs – is a carefully maintained heir to that heritage.

Try to avoid the inevitable confusion by remembering that around these parts, *gate* means street and *bar* means gate.

History

In AD 71 the Romans built a garrison called Eboracum, which in time became a large fort with a civilian settlement around it. Hadrian used it as the base for his northern campaign, while Constantine the Great was proclaimed emperor here in AD 306. When the Roman Empire collapsed, the town was taken by the Anglo-Saxons, who renamed it Eoforwic and made it the capital of the independent kingdom of Northumbria.

In 625 a Roman priest, Paulinus, arrived and converted King Edwin and his nobles to Christianity; two years later they built the first wooden church here. For most of the next century, the city was a major centre of learning, attracting students from all over Europe. In 866 the next wave of invaders arrived, this time the Vikings, who gave the town a more tongue-friendly name, Jorvik. It was their capital for the next 100 years, and during that time they turned the city into an important trading port.

King Eadred of Wessex drove out the last Viking ruler in 954 and reunited Danelaw with the south, but trouble quickly followed. In 1066 King Harold II fended off a Norwegian invasion at Stamford Bridge, east of York, but was defeated by William the Conqueror a few months later in the Battle of Hastings.

After William's two wooden castles were captured by an Anglo-Scandinavian army, he torched the entire city (and Durham) and the surrounding countryside. The Normans then set about rebuilding it, adding a grand new minster. Over the next 300 years York (a contraction of the Viking name Jorvik) prospered through royal patronage, textiles, trade and the Church.

Throughout the 18th century the city was a fashionable social centre dominated by the aristocracy, who were drawn by its culture and new racecourse. When the railway arrived in 1839, thousands of people were employed in new industries that sprang up around it, such as confectionery (the Terry's and Rowntree's brands were founded here). These industries went into decline in the latter half of the 20th century, but by then a new invader was asking for directions at the city gates, armed only with a guidebook.

◉ Sights

★ **York Minster** CATHEDRAL
(www.yorkminster.org; Deangate; adult/child £10/free, combined ticket incl tower £15/5; ⊙9am-5.30pm Mon-Sat, 12.45-5.30pm Sun, last admission 5pm) The remarkable York Minster is the largest medieval cathedral in all of Northern Europe, and one of the world's most beautiful Gothic buildings. Seat of the archbishop of York, primate of England, it is second in importance only to Canterbury, seat of the primate of *all* England – the separate titles were created to settle a debate over the true centre of the English church. If this is the only cathedral you visit in England, you'll still walk away satisfied.

The first church on this site was a wooden chapel built for the baptism of King Edwin of Northumbria on Easter Day 627, whose location is marked in the crypt. It was replaced with a stone church built on the site of a Roman basilica, parts of which can be seen in the foundations. The first Norman minster was built in the 11th century and, again, you can see surviving fragments in the foundations and crypt.

The present minster, built mainly between 1220 and 1480, manages to encompass all the major stages of Gothic architectural development. The transepts (1220–55) were built in Early English style; the octagonal chapter house (1260–90) and nave (1291–1340) in the Decorated style; and the west towers, west front and central (or lantern) tower (1470–72) in Perpendicular style.

➜ Choir, Chapter House & Nave
Entrance to the minster is via the south transept, which was badly damaged by fire in 1984, but has now been fully restored. The stained-glass windows, choir screen and

chapter house within are superb examples of English Gothic architecture.

As you enter the transept, facing you is the magnificent Five Sisters Window, with five lancets over 15m high. This is the minster's oldest complete window; most of its tangle of coloured glass dates from around 1250. Just beyond it to the right is the 13th-century chapter house, a fine example of the Decorated style. Sinuous and intricately carved stonework – there are more than 200 expressive carved heads and figures – surrounds an airy, uninterrupted space.

Back in the main church, take note of the unusually tall and wide nave, the aisles of which (to the sides) are roofed in stone in contrast to the central roof, which is wood painted to look like stone. On both sides of the nave are painted stone shields of the nobles who met with Edward II at a parliament in York. Also note the dragon's head projecting from the gallery – it's a crane believed to have been used to lift a font cover. There are several fine windows dating from the early 14th century, but the most impressive is the Great West Window (1338), with its beautiful heart-shaped stone tracery.

Beyond the screen and the choir is the lady chapel and, behind it, the huge Great East Window (1405). At 23.7m by 9.4m – roughly the size of a tennis court – it is the world's largest medieval stained-glass window and the cathedral's single most important treasure. Needless to say, its epic size matches the epic theme depicted within: the beginning and end of the world as described in Genesis and the Book of Revelations.

➧ Undercroft, Treasury & Crypt

A set of stairs in the south transept of York Minster leads down to the architecturally outstanding undercroft, treasury and crypt. The treasury houses 11th-century artefacts including relics from the graves of medieval archbishops. The crypt contains fragments from the Norman cathedral, including the font showing King Edwin's baptism, which also marks the site of the original wooden chapel. Look out for the Doomstone, a 12th-century carving showing a scene from the Last Judgment with demons casting doomed souls into Hell.

In 1967 the minster foundations were shored up when the central tower threatened to collapse; while engineers worked frantically to save the building, archaeologists uncovered Roman and Norman remains that attest to the site's ancient history – one of the most extraordinary finds is a Roman culvert, still carrying water to the Ouse.

A new interactive exhibit in the Undercroft, Revealing York Minster, leads visitors through 2000 years of history on the site of the cathedral.

➧ Tower

At the heart of York's cathedral is the massive tower, which is well worth climbing for the unparalleled views of York. You'll have to tackle a fairly claustrophobic climb of 275 steps and, most probably, a queue of people with cameras in hand.

Access to the tower is near the entrance in the south transept, dominated by the exquisite Rose Window, commemorating the union of the royal houses of Lancaster and York through the marriage of Henry VII and Elizabeth of York, which ended the Wars of the Roses and began the Tudor dynasty.

★ National Railway Museum   MUSEUM
(www.nrm.org.uk; Leeman Rd; ☉10am-6pm; P ♿)
FREE While many railway museums are the sole preserve of lone men in anoraks comparing dog-eared notebooks and getting high on the smell of machine oil, coal smoke and nostalgia, this place is different. York's National Railway Museum – the biggest in the world, with more than 100 locomotives – is so well presented and crammed with fascinating stuff that it's interesting even to folk whose eyes don't mist over at the thought of a 4-6-2 A1 Pacific class thundering into a tunnel.

Highlights for the trainspotters among us include a replica of George Stephenson's Rocket (1829), the world's first 'modern' steam locomotive; the sleek and streamlined Mallard, which set the world speed record for a steam locomotive in 1938 (126mph); a 1960s Japanese Shinkansen bullet train; and the world-famous Flying Scotsman, the first steam engine to break the 100mph barrier (scheduled to return to the tracks in

---

ⓘ **THE YORK PASS**

If you plan on visiting a number of sights, you can save yourself some money by using a York Pass (www.yorkpass.com; 1/2/3 days adult £36/48/58, child £20/24/28). It gives you free access to more than 30 pay-to-visit sights in and around York, including York Minster, Jorvik and Castle Howard. You can buy it at York Tourist Office or online.

YORKSHIRE YORK

summer 2015, but still undergoing restoration at the time of writing). There's also a massive 4-6-2 loco from 1949 that's been cut in half so you can see how it works.

Even if you're not a rail nerd, you'll enjoy looking through the gleaming, silk-lined carriages of the royal trains used by Queen Victoria and Edward VII, or having a *Brief Encounter* moment over tea and scones at the museum's station platform cafe called, erm, Brief Encounter. Allow at least two hours to do the museum justice.

The museum is about 400m west of the train station and if you don't fancy walking you can ride the road train (adult/child £2/1, April to October) that runs between the minster and museum every 30 minutes from 11am to 4pm.

★ **Jorvik Viking Centre**   MUSEUM
(www.jorvik-viking-centre.co.uk; Coppergate; adult/child £9.95/6.95; ☺10am-5pm Apr-Oct, to 4pm Nov-Mar) Interactive multimedia exhibits aimed at bringing history to life often achieve exactly the opposite, but the much-hyped Jorvik manages to pull it off with aplomb. It's a smells-and-all reconstruction of the Viking settlement unearthed here during excavations in the late 1970s, brought to you courtesy of a 'time-car' monorail that transports you through 9th-century Jorvik. You can reduce time waiting in the queue by booking your tickets online and choosing the time you want to visit (£1 extra).

While some of the 'you will now travel back in time' malarkey is a bit naff, it's all done with a sense of humour tied to historical authenticity that will give you a pretty good idea of what life must have been like in Viking-era York. In the exhibition at the end of the monorail, look out for the Lloyds Bank coprolite, a fossilised human stool that measures an eye-watering nine inches long and half a pound in weight, and must be the only turd in the world to have its own Wikipedia entry.

★ **City Walls**   ARCHAEOLOGICAL SITE
(☺8am-dusk) **FREE** If the weather's good, don't miss the chance to walk the City Walls, which follow the line of the original Roman walls and give a whole new perspective on the city. Allow 1½ to two hours for the full circuit of 4.5 miles or, if you're pushed for time, the short stretch from Bootham Bar to Monk Bar is worth doing for the views of the minster.

Start and finish in the Museum Gardens or at Bootham Bar (on the site of a Roman gate), where a multimedia exhibit provides

York

some historical context, and travel clockwise. Highlights include Monk Bar, which is the best-preserved medieval gate and still has a working portcullis, and **Walmgate Bar**, England's only city gate with an intact barbican.

At Monk Bar you'll find the **Richard III Museum** (www.richardiiimuseum.co.uk; adult/child £2.50/free; ⊙9am-5pm Mar-Oct, 9.30am-4pm Nov-Feb), which sets out the case of the murdered 'Princes in the Tower' and invites visitors to judge whether their uncle, Richard III, killed them. **Micklegate Bar Museum** (www.micklegatebar.com; Micklegate; adult/child £3.50/free; ⊙10am-4.30pm May-Sep, 11am-3.30pm Feb-Apr, Oct & Nov) charts the history of

the city walls and the Battle of Towton, chief conflict in the Wars of the Roses.

Yorkshire Museum   MUSEUM
(www.yorkshiremuseum.org.uk; Museum St; adult/child £7.50/free; ⊙10am-5pm) Most of York's Roman archaeology is hidden beneath the medieval city, so the recently revamped displays in the Yorkshire Museum are invaluable if you want to get an idea of what Eboracum was like. There are maps and models of Roman York, funerary monuments, mosaic floors and wall paintings, and a 4th-century bust of Emperor Constantine.

There are excellent exhibits on Viking and medieval York as well, including priceless artefacts such as the beautifully decorated 9th-century York helmet and the exquisite 15th-century Middleham Jewel, an engraved gold pendant adorned with a giant sapphire. Kids will enjoy the dinosaur exhibit, centred around giant ichthyosaur fossils from Yorkshire's Jurassic Coast.

Museum Gardens   GARDENS

(entrances on Museum St & Marygate; ⊘dawn-dusk) In the grounds of the peaceful Museum Gardens, you can see the Multangular Tower, a part of the City Walls that was once the western tower of the Roman garrison's defensive ramparts. The Roman stonework at the base has been built over with 13th-century additions. On the other side of the gardens are the ruins of St Mary's Abbey dating from 1270 to 1294. The ruined Gatehall was its main entrance, providing access from the abbey to the river.

The adjacent Hospitium dates from the 14th century, although the timber-framed upper storey is a much-restored survivor from the 15th century, used as the abbey guesthouse. St Mary's Lodge was built in about 1470 to provide VIP accommodation.

Shambles   STREET

The Shambles takes its name from the Saxon word *shamel*, meaning 'slaughterhouse' – in 1862 there were 26 butcher shops on this street. Today the butchers are long gone, but this narrow cobbled lane, lined with 15th-century Tudor buildings that overhang so much they seem to meet above your head, is the most picturesque in Britain, and one of the most visited in Europe, often crammed with visitors intent on buying a tacky souvenir before rushing back to the tour bus.

York Castle Museum   MUSEUM

(www.yorkcastlemuseum.org.uk; Tower St; adult/child £8.50/free; ⊘9.30am-5pm) This excellent museum has displays of everyday life through the centuries, with reconstructed domestic interiors, a Victorian street and a prison cell where you can try out a condemned man's bed – in this case, that of highwayman Dick Turpin (imprisoned here before being hanged in 1739). There's a bewildering array of evocative objects from the past 400 years, gathered together by a certain Dr Kirk from the 1920s onwards for fear the items would become obsolete and disappear completely.

Treasurer's House   HISTORIC BUILDING

(NT; www.nationaltrust.org.uk; Chapter House St; adult/child £7/3.50; ⊘11am-4.30pm Sat-Thu Apr-Oct, to 3pm Nov) Once home to York Minster's medieval treasurers, this historic house – substantially rebuilt in the 17th and 18th centuries – contains a fine collection of furniture and offers a fascinating insight into 18th-century life. It is also the setting for one of York's most enduring ghost stories: during the 1950s a plumber working in the basement swore he saw a band of Roman soldiers marching *through* the walls.

Dig   MUSEUM

(www.digyork.com; St Saviour's Church, St Saviourgate; adult/child £6/5.50, Dig & Jorvik combined £14.45/11; ⊘10am-5pm, last admission 4pm; ⓘ) Under the same management as Jorvik, Dig cashes in on the popularity of archaeology programs on TV by giving you the chance to be an 'archaeological detective', unearthing the secrets of York's distant past as well as learning something of the archaeologist's world – what they do, how they do it, and so on. Aimed mainly at kids, it's much more hands-on than Jorvik and a lot of its merit depends on how good – and entertaining – your guide is.

Clifford's Tower   CASTLE

(EH; www.english-heritage.org.uk; Tower St; adult/child £4.30/2.60; ⊘10am-6pm Apr-Sep, to 5pm Oct, to 4pm Nov-Mar) There's precious little left of York Castle except for this evocative stone tower, a highly unusual figure-of-eight design built into the castle's keep after the original one was destroyed in 1190 during anti-Jewish riots. An angry mob forced 150 Jews to be locked inside the tower and the hapless victims took their own lives rather than be killed. There's not much to see inside, but the views over the city are excellent.

Church of the Holy Trinity   CHURCH

(Goodramgate; ⊘10am-5pm Tue-Sat May-Sep, to 4pm Oct-Apr) FREE Tucked away behind an inconspicuous gate and seemingly cut off from the rest of the town, the Church of the Holy Trinity is a fantastically atmospheric old building, having survived almost unchanged for the past 200 years (it has no electricity or running water). Inside are rare 17th- to 18th-century box pews, 15th-century stained glass and wonky walls that seem to have been built without plumb line or spirit level.

York City Art Gallery
GALLERY

(www.yorkartgallery.org.uk; Exhibition Sq; ⊙10am-5pm) FREE Artists represented here include Joshua Reynolds, Paul Nash, Eugène Boudin, LS Lowry and the controversial York artist William Etty, who, back in the 1820s, was the first major British artist to specialise in painting nudes. Closed for redevelopment at the time of writing, the gallery is due to reopen sometime in 2015.

☞ Tours

There's a bewildering range of tours in York, from historic walking tours to ever more competitive night-time ghost tours (York is considered England's most haunted city).

Ghost Hunt of York
WALKING TOUR

(www.ghosthunt.co.uk; adult/child £5/3; ⊙tours 7.30pm) The kids will just love this award-winning and highly entertaining 75-minute tour laced with authentic ghost stories. It begins at the Shambles, whatever the weather (it's never cancelled) and there's no need to book, just turn up and wait till you hear the handbell ringing...

Yorkwalk
WALKING TOUR

(www.yorkwalk.co.uk; adult/child £6/5; ⊙tours 10.30am & 2.15pm Feb-Nov) Offers a series of two-hour walks on a range of themes, from the classics – Roman York, the snickelways (narrow alleys) and City Walls – to walks focused on chocolates and sweets, women in York, and the inevitable graveyard, coffin and plague tour. Walks depart from Museum Gardens Gate on Museum St; there's no need to book.

YorkBoat
BOAT TOUR

(www.yorkboat.co.uk; King's Staith; adult/child from £7.50/3.50; ⊙tours 10.30am, noon, 1.30pm & 3pm Feb-Nov) Hour-long cruises on the River Ouse, departing from King's Staith and, 10 minutes later, Lendal Bridge. Special lunch, dinner and evening cruises are also offered.

Original Ghost Walk of York
WALKING TOUR

(www.theoriginalghostwalkofyork.co.uk; adult/child £5/3; ⊙tours 8pm) An evening of ghouls, ghosts, mystery and history, courtesy of a well-established group departing from the King's Arms pub by Ouse Bridge.

York Citysightseeing
BUS TOUR

(www.city-sightseeing.com; day ticket adult/child £12/5; ⊙9am-5pm mid-Feb–Nov) Hop-on/hop-off route with 16 stops, calling at all the main sights. Buses leave every 20 to 30 minutes from Exhibition Sq near York Minster.

Association of Voluntary Guides
WALKING TOUR

(www.avgyork.co.uk; ⊙tours 10.15am & 2.15pm Apr-Oct, also 6.45pm Jun-Aug, 10.15am Nov-Mar) FREE Two-hour walking tours of the city, setting out from Exhibition Sq in front of York City Art Gallery.

✯ Festivals & Events

Check out the city's full calendar of events at www.yorkfestivals.com.

Jorvik Viking Festival
HISTORY

(www.jorvik-viking-centre.co.uk/festivals) For a week in mid-February, York is invaded by Vikings once again as part of this festival, which

---

LOCAL KNOWLEDGE

ANDY DEXTROUS: GHOST TOUR GUIDE

I love York's outstanding architecture, the maze of 'snickleways' (narrow alleys), the array of small independent shops, the street entertainment and festivals, and the central, green spaces like Museum Gardens. All year round, the streets are full of appreciative visitors from all over the world enjoying the city, relaxing and adding to the atmosphere.

York's Spookiest Spots Haunted pubs like the Old White Swan (p502), plus the Antiques Centre (p502) on Stonegate, which is also haunted. In the streets around the Minster you're always within a breath of a ghost tale.

Best of York For beer and atmosphere, the Blue Bell (p501). For veggie and vegan food and a place that welcomes children, El Piano (p500). And for sheer ambience, Grays Court (p501).

Best of Yorkshire Take the North Yorkshire Moors Railway to Goathland, then walk to Mallyan Spout waterfall. Include a drink at the Birch Hall Inn (p519) at Beck Hole. For a special meal, there's the Star Inn (p513) at Harome or the Stone Trough Inn (p503) at Kirkham; stroll down to the abbey ruins before or after your meal.

features battle re-enactments, themed walks, markets and other bits of Viking-related fun.

York Food Festival FOOD & DRINK

(www.yorkfoodfestival.com) For 10 days in September, discover all that's good to eat and drink in Yorkshire, with food stalls, tastings, a beer tent, cookery demonstrations and more.

York Christmas CHRISTMAS

(www.visityork.org/christmas) Kicking off with St Nicholas Fayre market in late November, the run-up to Christmas is an extravaganza of street decorations, market stalls, carol singers and mulled wine.

🛏 Sleeping

Beds are hard to find in midsummer, even with inflated high season rates. The tourist office's accommodation booking service charges £4, which might be the best four quid you spend if you arrive without a reservation.

Needless to say, prices get higher the closer you are to the city centre. However, there are plenty of decent B&Bs on the streets north and south of Bootham. Southwest of the town centre, B&Bs are clustered around Scarcroft Rd, Southlands Rd and Bishopthorpe Rd.

It's also worth looking at serviced apartments if you're planning to stay two or three nights. **In York Holidays** (☑01904-632660; www.inyorkholidays.co.uk) offers a good selection of places from about £110 a night for a two-person apartment.

★ Fort HOSTEL £

(☑01904-620222; www.thefortyork.co.uk; 1 Little Stonegate; dm from £22, d from £68; ☎) This new boutique hostel showcases the work of young British designers, combining affordable accommodation with a dash of character and flair. There are six- and eight-bed dorms, along with half a dozen doubles, but don't expect a peaceful retreat – the central location is in the middle of York's nightlife, and there's a lively club downstairs (earplugs are provided!).

York YHA HOSTEL £

(☑0845 371 9051; www.yha.org.uk; 42 Water End, Clifton; dm/q from £21/99; ☻@☎) Originally the Rowntree (Quaker confectioners) mansion, this handsome Victorian house makes a spacious and child-friendly youth hostel, with most of its rooms four-bed dorms. Often busy, so book early. It's about a mile northwest of the city centre; there's a riverside footpath from Lendal Bridge (poorly lit, so avoid after dark). Alternatively, take bus 2 from the train station or Museum St.

Safestay York HOSTEL £

(☑01904-627720; www.safestayyork.co.uk; 88-90 Micklegate; dm £16-34, tw £60-72; @☎) Housed in a Grade I Georgian building that was once home to the High Sheriff of Yorkshire, and recently taken over by London hostel group Safestay, this is a large and well-equipped boutique hostel popular with school groups and stag and hen parties – don't come here looking for peace and quiet!

Abbeyfields B&B ££

(☑01904-636471; www.abbeyfields.co.uk; 19 Bootham Tce; s/d from £55/84; ☎) ✦ Expect a warm welcome and thoughtfully arranged bedrooms here, with chairs and bedside lamps for comfortable reading. Breakfasts are among the best in town, with sausage and bacon from the local butcher, freshly laid eggs from a nearby farm and the aroma of newly baked bread.

Elliotts B&B B&B ££

(☑01904-623333; www.elliottshotel.co.uk; 2 Sycamore Pl; s/d from £55/75; ☐@☎) A beautifully converted 'gentleman's residence', Elliotts leans towards the boutique end of the guesthouse market, with stylish and elegant rooms and some designer touches such as contemporary art and colourful textiles. An excellent location, both quiet and central.

Hedley House Hotel HOTEL ££

(☑01904-637404; www.hedleyhouse.com; 3 Bootham Tce; r from £113; ☐☎) ✦ This red-brick terrace-house hotel sports a variety of smart, family-friendly accommodation, including rooms that sleep up to five, and some self-catering apartments – plus it has a spa bath on the outdoor terrace at the back, and is barely five minutes' walk from the city centre through the Museum Gardens.

Dairy Guesthouse B&B ££

(☑01904-639367; www.dairyguesthouse.co.uk; 3 Scarcroft Rd; d/f from £80/110; ☎) A lovely Victorian home that has retained many of its original features, including pine doors, stained glass and cast-iron fireplaces. But the real treat here is the flower- and plant-filled courtyard leading to the cottage-style rooms. Minimum two-night stay at weekends.

Arnot House B&B ££

(☑01904-641966; www.arnothouseyork.co.uk; 17 Grosvenor Tce; r £80-88; ☎) ✦ With three beautifully decorated rooms (provided you're a fan of Victorian frills and floral patterns), including two with impressive four-poster beds, Arnot House has an authentically old-fashioned atmosphere that appeals to a more mature clientele. No children allowed.

Brontë House
B&B ££

(☑ 01904-621066; www.bronte-guesthouse.com; 22 Grosvenor Tce; s/d/f from £45/80/100; 📶) The Brontë has five homely en suite rooms, each individually decorated. Our favourite is the double with a carved 19th-century canopied bed, William Morris wallpaper and assorted bits and pieces from another era.

23 St Mary's
B&B ££

(☑ 01904-622738; www.23stmarys.co.uk; 23 St Mary's; s/d from £52/85; 📶) A smart and stately town house with nine chintzy, country-house-style rooms. Some have hand-painted furniture for that rustic look, others are decorated with antiques, lace and polished mahogany.

Briar Lea Guest House
B&B ££

(☑ 01904-635061; www.briarlea.co.uk; 8 Longfield Tce; s/d from £40/66; 📶) Clean, basic rooms and a friendly welcome in a central location.

St Raphael
B&B ££

(☑ 01904-645028; www.straphaelguesthouse.co. uk; 44 Queen Anne's Rd; s/d from £75/82; 📶) Historic house with that distinctive half-timbered look, a great central location and home-baked bread for breakfast.

Monkgate Guesthouse
B&B ££

(☑ 01904-655947; www.monkgateguesthouse.com; 65 Monkgate; s/d/f from £45/78/117; 🅿📶) Attractive guesthouse with a special family suite that has a separate bedroom for two children.

★ Middlethorpe Hall
HOTEL £££

(☑ 01904-641241; www.middlethorpe.com; Bishopthorpe Rd; s/d from £139/199; 🅿📶) This breathtaking 17th-century country house is set in 8 hectares of parkland, once the home of diarist Lady Mary Wortley Montagu. The rooms are divided between the main house, restored courtyard buildings and three cottage suites. All the rooms are beautifully decorated with original antiques and oil paintings that have been carefully selected to reflect the period.

Mount Royale
HOTEL £££

(☑ 01904-628856; www.mountroyale.co.uk; The Mount; s/d/ste from £95/125/225; 🅿📶🏊) A grand, early-19th-century heritage-listed building converted into a superb luxury hotel, complete with a solarium, beauty spa

and outdoor heated tub and swimming pool. The rooms in the main house are gorgeous, but best of all are the open-plan garden suites, reached via an arcade of tropical fruit trees and bougainvillea.

🍴 Eating

★ Mannion's
CAFE, BISTRO £

(☑ 01904-631030; www.mannionandco.co.uk; 1 Blake St; mains £5-9; ☉ 9am-5.30pm Mon-Sat, 10am-5pm Sun) Expect to queue for a table at this busy bistro (no reservations), with its maze of cosy, wood-panelled rooms and selection of daily specials. Regulars on the menu include eggs Benedict for breakfast, a chunky Yorkshire rarebit made with home-baked bread, and lunch platters of cheese and charcuterie from the attached deli. Oh, and pavlova for pudding.

Your Bike Shed
CAFE £

(☑ 01904-633777; www.yourbikeshed.co.uk; 148-150 Micklegate; mains £3-7; ☉ 9am-5pm Mon-Sat, 10am-5pm Sun; 📶🅿🚲) 🚲 Reinvigorated by the 2014 Tour de France, York's cycling scene has latched onto this cool new cafe and bike workshop. Fitted out with recycled furniture and colourful artwork, it serves reviving portions of halloumi burger, pie and peas or carrot cake to hungry cyclists, washed down with excellent coffee.

Cafe No 8
CAFE, BISTRO ££

(☑ 01904-653074; www.cafeno8.co.uk; 8 Gillygate; 2-/3-course meal £18/22, Fri & Sat £22/27; ☉ 10am-10pm; 📶🚲) 🚲 A cool little place with modern artwork mimicking the Edwardian stained glass at the front, No 8 offers a day-long menu of classic bistro dishes using fresh local produce, including duck breast with blood orange and juniper, and Yorkshire pork belly with star anise, fennel and garlic. It also does breakfast daily (mains £5) and Sunday lunch (three courses £25). Booking recommended.

El Piano
VEGAN ££

(☑ 01904-610676; www.el-piano.com; 15 Grape Lane; mains £10; ☉ 11am-11pm Mon-Sat, noon-9pm Sun; 📶🅿🚲) 🚲 With a menu that's 100% vegan, nut-free and gluten-free, this colourful, Hispanic-style spot is a vegetarian haven. Downstairs there's a lovely cafe and upstairs, three themed rooms. The menu offers dishes such as falafel, onion bhaji, corn fritters and mushroom-and-basil salad, either in tapas-size portions or as mixed platters. There's also a takeaway counter.

Parlour at Grays Court
CAFE ££

(www.grayscourtyork.com; Chapter House St; mains £8-14; ⊙10am-5pm; 🐾) An unexpected find in the heart of York, this 16th-century house (now a hotel) has more of a country atmosphere. Enjoy gourmet coffee and cake in the sunny garden, or indulge in a light lunch in the historic setting of the oak-panelled Jacobean gallery. The menu runs from Yorkshire rarebit to confit duck, and includes traditional afternoon tea (£18.50).

Ate O'Clock
BISTRO ££

(☑01904-644080; www.ateoclock.co.uk; 13a High Ousegate; mains £9-20; ⊙5.30-9pm Mon, noon-2pm & 6-9.30pm Tue-Sat; 🐾) 🍴 A tempting menu of classic bistro dishes (sirloin steak, slow-roasted pork belly, pan-fried duck breast) made with fresh Yorkshire produce has made this place hugely popular with locals – best to book a table to avoid disappointment. A three-course dinner costs £19 from 6pm to 7.55pm, Tuesday to Thursday.

Bettys
TEAHOUSE ££

(www.bettys.co.uk; St Helen's Sq; mains £6-14, afternoon tea £18.50; ⊙9am-9pm; 🐾) Old-school afternoon tea, with white-aproned waiters, linen tablecloths and a teapot collection ranged along the walls. The house speciality is the Yorkshire Fat Rascal, a huge fruit scone smothered in melted butter, but the smoked haddock with poached egg and hollandaise sauce (seasonal) is our favourite lunch dish. No bookings – queue for a table at busy times.

Olive Tree
MEDITERRANEAN ££

(☑01904-624433; www.theolivetreeyork.co.uk; 10 Tower St; mains £10-21; ⊙noon-2pm & 5.30-10pm) Local produce gets a Mediterranean makeover at this bright and breezy bistro. Classic pizza and pasta dishes are complemented by more ambitious recipes such as crayfish and chorizo risotto, and Moroccan lamb stew. The set menu (lunch and dinner, pre-6.30pm Friday and Saturday) offers two courses for £15.

1331
STEAK ££

(☑01904-661130; www.1331-york.co.uk; 13 Grape Lane; mains £9-17; ⊙6-10pm Mon-Thu, 11am-1am Fri & Sat, 11am-10pm Sun; 🐾🌿🐾) This courtyard complex houses a bar, cocktail lounge and even a private cinema, along with this appealing 1st-floor restaurant serving a menu of crowd-pleasing classics ranging from sausage and mash with onion gravy or slow-braised lamb shank, to good old steak and chips. Vegetarians are catered for,

too, with a good selection of dishes such as chickpea and coriander burgers.

Café Concerto
CAFE, MEDITERRANEAN ££

(☑01904-610478; www.cafeconcerto.biz; 21 High Petergate; mains lunch £5-9, dinner £13-18; ⊙8.30am-10pm) Walls papered with sheet music, chilled jazz on the stereo, and battered, mismatched tables and chairs set the bohemian tone in this comforting coffee shop–cum-bistro. Expect breakfasts, bagels and cappuccinos big enough to float a boat in during the daytime, and a sophisticated Mediterranean-style menu in the evening.

Melton's Too
CAFE, BISTRO ££

(www.meltonstoo.co.uk; 25 Walmgate; tapas £3-6, mains £11-18; ⊙10.30am-midnight Mon-Sat, to 11pm Sun; 🐾) A comfortable, chilled-out cafe, bar and bistro, Melton's Too serves everything from cake and cappuccino to tapas-style snacks and three-course dinners (an early-bird special, served before 7pm, offers three courses for £14).

🍷 Drinking & Nightlife

With only a couple of exceptions, the best drinking holes in town are the older, traditional pubs. There are some nice cocktail bars with outdoor seating on Swinegate Court (off Grape Lane), but the area around Ousegate and Micklegate can get a bit rowdy, especially at weekends.

★ Blue Bell
PUB

(53 Fossgate; ⊙11am-11pm Mon-Sat, noon-10.30pm Sun) This is what a real English pub looks like: a tiny, 200-year-old wood-panelled room with a smouldering fireplace, decor untouched since 1903, a pile of ancient board games in the corner, friendly and efficient bar staff, and Timothy Taylor and Black Sheep ales on tap. Bliss, with froth on top – if you can get in (it's often full).

Ye Olde Starre
PUB

(www.taylor-walker.co.uk; 40 Stonegate; ⊙11am-11pm Sun-Wed, to midnight Thu-Sat) Licensed since 1644, this is York's oldest pub – a warren of small rooms and a small beer garden, with a half-dozen real ales on tap. It was used as a morgue by the Roundheads (supporters of parliament) during the Civil War, but the atmosphere has improved a lot since then.

Pivní
PUB

(pivni.co.uk; 6 Patrick Pool; ⊙noon-11.30pm Sun-Thu, 11am-11.30pm Fri & Sat; 🐾) A slick, modern pub set in an ancient half-timbered house, Pivní provides an atmospheric setting for sampling its range of more than 80 draught and bottled craft beers from all over the world.

Old White Swan
PUB

(www.nicholsonspubs.co.uk; 80 Goodramgate; ⏱10am-midnight Sun-Thu, to 1am Fri & Sat) Popular and atmospheric old pub with a small beer garden and a good range of guest real ales.

King's Arms
PUB

(King's Staith; ⏱11am-11pm Sun-Thu, to 1am Fri & Sat) York's best-known pub enjoys a fabulous riverside location, with tables spilling out onto the quayside. It's the perfect spot on a summer evening, but be prepared to share it with a few hundred other people.

☆ Entertainment

There are a couple of good theatres in York and an interesting art-house cinema.

York Theatre Royal
THEATRE

(☎01904-623568; www.yorktheatreroyal.co.uk; St Leonard's Pl) Well-regarded productions of theatre, opera and dance are staged here.

Grand Opera House
LIVE MUSIC, COMEDY

(☎0844 871 3024; www.grandoperahouseyork. org.uk; Clifford St) Despite the name, there's no opera here; instead, there's a wide range of entertainment from live bands and popular musicals to stand-up comics and pantomime.

City Screen Picturehouse
CINEMA

(☎0871 902 5726; www.picturehouses.co.uk; 13-17 Coney St) An appealing modern building in a converted printing works, screening both mainstream and art-house films. There's also a nice cafe-bar on the terrace overlooking the river.

🛍 Shopping

Coney St, Davygate and the adjoining streets are the hub of York's central-city shopping scene, but the real treat are the antique, bric-a-brac and secondhand bookshops, concentrated in Colliergate, Fossgate and Micklegate.

Ken Spelman Booksellers
BOOKS

(www.kenspelman.com; 70 Micklegate; ⏱9am-5.30pm Mon-Sat) This fascinating shop has been selling rare, antiquarian and secondhand books since 1910. With an open fire crackling in the grate in winter, it's a browser's paradise.

Antiques Centre
ANTIQUES

(www.theantiquescentreyork.co.uk; 41 Stonegate; ⏱9am-5.30pm Mon-Sat, to 4pm Sun) A Georgian town house with a veritable maze of rooms and corridors, showcasing the wares of about 120 dealers selling everything from lapel pins and snuff boxes to oil paintings and longcase clocks. And the house is haunted as well…

Red House
ANTIQUES

(www.redhouseyork.co.uk; Duncombe Pl; ⏱9.30am-5.30pm Mon-Sat, 10.30am-5pm Sun) The goods of about 60 antiques dealers are displayed in 10 showrooms spread over two floors, with items ranging from jewellery and porcelain to clocks and furniture.

ℹ Information

Post Office (22 Lendal; ⏱8.30am-5.30pm Mon-Sat)

York Hospital (☎01904-631313; www.york-hospitals.nhs.uk; Wigginton Rd) Located a mile north of the centre.

York Tourist Office (☎01904-550099; www.visityork.org; 1 Museum St; ⏱9am-6pm Mon-Sat, 10am-5pm Sun Apr-Sep, shorter hours Oct-Mar) Visitor and transport info for all of Yorkshire, plus accommodation bookings, ticket sales and internet access.

ℹ Getting There & Away

BUS

For timetable information, call **Traveline Yorkshire** (☎0871 200 2233; www.yorkshiretravel. net) or check the computerised 24-hour information points at the train station and Rougier St. All local and regional buses stop on Rougier St, about 200m northeast of the train station.

York connections:

Birmingham £29, 3½ hours, one daily

London £31, 5½ hours, three daily

Newcastle £15.20, 2¾ hours, two daily

CAR

A car is more hindrance than help in the city centre, so use one of the Park & Ride car parks at the edge of the city. If you want to explore the surrounding area, rental options include **Europcar** (☎0844 846 4003; www.europcar. co.uk; Train Station, Station Rd; ⏱8am-8.30pm Mon-Sat, 9am-8.30pm Sun), located in the long-stay car park at the train station; Europcar also stores luggage for £4 per bag.

TRAIN

York is a major railway hub, with frequent direct services to British cities. York connections:

Birmingham £45, 2¼ hours, every 30 minutes

Cambridge (change at Peterborough) £65, three hours, hourly

Edinburgh £80, 2½ hours, every 30 minutes

Leeds £13.50, 25 minutes, every 15 minutes

London Kings Cross £80, two hours, every 30 minutes

Manchester £17, 1½ hours, every 15 minutes

Newcastle £16, one hour, every 30 minutes

Scarborough £8, 50 minutes, hourly

❶ Getting Around

Central York is easy to get around on foot – you're never more than 20 minutes' walk from any of the major sights.

BICYCLE

The tourist office has a useful free map showing York's cycle routes, or visit **iTravel-York** (www.itravelyork.info/cycling). Castle Howard (15 miles northeast of York via Haxby and Strensall) is an interesting destination, and there's also a section of the **Trans-Pennine Trail cycle path** (www.transpenninetrail.org.uk) from Bishopthorpe in York to Selby (15 miles) along the old railway line.

You can rent bikes from **Cycle Heaven** (☑ 01904-622701; www.cycle-heaven.co.uk; York Railway Station, Station Rd; ☺ 8.30am-5.30pm Mon-Fri, 9am-6pm Sat & Sun, closed Sun Sep-Apr) at the train station for £20 per day.

BUS

Local bus services are operated by **First York** (www.firstgroup.com/ukbus/york). Single fares range from £1 to £3, and a day pass valid for all local buses is £3.70 (available at Park & Ride car parks).

TAXI

Station Taxis (☑ 01904-623332; www.yorkstationtaxis.co.uk; Train Station, Station Rd) has a kiosk outside the train station.

Castle Howard

Stately homes may be two-a-penny in England, but you'll have to try pretty damn hard to find one as breathtakingly stately as **Castle Howard** (www.castlehoward.co.uk; adult/child house & grounds £14/7.50, grounds only £9.50/6; ☺ house 11am-4.30pm Apr-Oct, grounds 10am-5pm Mar-Oct & Dec, to 4pm Nov, Jan & Feb; ℗), a work of theatrical grandeur and audacity set in the rolling Howardian Hills. This is one of the world's most beautiful buildings, instantly recognisable from its starring role in the 1980s TV series *Brideshead Revisited* and in the 2008 film of the same name (both based on Evelyn Waugh's 1945 novel of nostalgia for the English aristocracy).

When the Earl of Carlisle hired his pal Sir John Vanbrugh to design his new home in 1699, he was hiring a bloke who had no formal training and was best known as a playwright. Luckily, Vanbrugh hired Nicholas Hawksmoor who had worked as Christopher Wren's clerk of works – not only would Hawksmoor have a big part to play in the house's design, but he and Vanbrugh would later work wonders with Blenheim Palace. Today the house is still home to the Hon Simon Howard and his family and he can often be seen around the place.

If you can, try to visit on a weekday when it's easier to find the space to appreciate this hedonistic marriage of art, architecture, landscaping and natural beauty. As you wander about the peacock-haunted grounds, views open up over the hills, Vanbrugh's playful Temple of the Four Winds and Hawksmoor's stately mausoleum, but the great baroque house with its magnificent central cupola is an irresistible visual magnet. Inside, the house is full of treasures – the breathtaking Great Hall with its soaring Corinthian pilasters, Pre-Raphaelite stained glass in the chapel, and corridors lined with classical antiquities.

WORTH A TRIP

KIRKHAM PRIORY & STONE TROUGH INN

While crowds queue up to get into Castle Howard, you could turn off on the other side of the A64 along the minor road to the hamlet of Kirkham. Here, the picturesque ruins of Kirkham Priory (EH; www.english-heritage.org.uk; adult/child £3.60/2.20; ☺ 10am-6pm Wed-Sun Apr-Sep, daily Aug; ℗) rise gracefully above the banks of the River Derwent, sporting an impressive 13th-century gatehouse encrusted with heraldic symbols.

After a stroll by the river, head up the hill on the far side to the Stone Trough Inn (☑ 01653-618713; www.stonetrough-inn.co.uk; Kirkham; mains £12-18; ☺ noon-2.30pm & 5.30-9pm Mon-Fri, noon-9pm Sat, to 8pm Sun; ℗ 🌐 📶 🐾) for a spot of lunch. This traditional country inn serves gourmet-style pub grub (try the roast belly pork with black pudding and tarragon cream sauce) and its outdoor terrace has a great view over the valley.

The entrance courtyard has a good cafe, a gift shop and a farm shop filled with foodie delights from local producers.

Castle Howard is 15 miles northeast of York, off the A64. There are several organised tours from York – check with the tourist office for up-to-date schedules. Stephenson's of Easingwold (www.stephensonsofeasingwold.co.uk) operates a bus service (£7.50 return, 40 minutes, three times daily Monday to Saturday) linking York with Castle Howard.

Harrogate

POP 73,580

The quintessential Victorian spa town, prim and pretty Harrogate has long been associated with a certain kind of old-fashioned Englishness – the kind that seems the preserve of retired army majors and formidable dowagers who take the *Daily Telegraph* and vote Tory. They come to Harrogate to enjoy the flower shows and gardens that fill the town with magnificent displays of colour, especially in spring and autumn. It is fitting that the town's most famous visitor was Agatha Christie, who fled here incognito in 1926 to escape her broken marriage.

And yet, this picture of Victoriana redux is not quite complete. While it's undoubtedly true that Harrogate remains a firm favourite of visitors in their golden years, the town has plenty of smart hotels and trendy eateries catering to the boom in Harrogate's newest trade – conferences. All those dynamic young sales-and-marketing guns have to eat and sleep somewhere.

◎ Sights & Activities

Royal Pump Room Museum   MUSEUM
(www.harrogate.gov.uk; Crown Pl; adult/child £3.95/2.30; ⊙10.30am-5pm Mon-Sat, 2-5pm Apr-Oct, to 4pm Jan-Mar) You can learn all about Harrogate's history as a spa town in the ornate Royal Pump Room, built in 1842 over the most famous of the town's sulphurous springs. It gives an insight into how the phenomenon of visiting spas to 'take the waters' shaped the town and records the illustrious visitors it attracted. At the end, you get the chance to sample the spa water, if you dare.

The ritual of visiting spa towns as a health cure became fashionable in the 19th century and peaked during the Edwardian era in the years before WWI. Charles Dickens visited Harrogate in 1858 and described it as 'the queerest place, with the strangest people in it, leading the oddest lives of dancing, newspaper-reading and dining' – sounds quite pleasant, really.

Montpellier Quarter   NEIGHBOURHOOD
(www.montpellierharrogate.com) The most attractive part of town is the Montpellier Quarter, overlooking Prospect Gardens between Crescent Rd and Montpellier Hill. It's an area of pedestrianised streets lined

---

EAT & DRINK LIKE A LOCAL

Yorkshire pudding *The* classic local dish, these puffy batter puddings are traditionally served with roast beef, but Yorkshire tearooms often serve them as a dish in themselves, with gravy. Try them at Ye Olde Naked Man (p523) in Settle.

Theakston's ale Theakston's was turning out best bitter long before the term 'craft beer' had ever been thought of. Try it at pubs all over Britain, or at Theakston's Brewery (p509) in Masham.

Wensleydale cheese Famous as the favourite snack of animated characters Wallace and Gromit, this crumbly white cheese is made in the heart of the Yorkshire Dales. Try it at the source, at Wensleydale Creamery (p524) in Hawes.

Yorkshire rhubarb Traditionally grown in the 'rhubarb triangle' near Wakefield, Yorkshire forced rhubarb (early season rhubarb grown in darkness) has achieved Protected Designation of Origin status. Try the Michelin-starred rhubarb trifle at the Pipe and Glass (p541) near Beverley.

Curd tart A very old Yorkshire dish, a bit like cheesecake, traditionally baked for the Whitsun holiday. Try it at Bettys (p506) in Harrogate.

Parkin A rich and sticky cake made with oatmeal and flavoured with ginger and treacle. Try it at Thomas of Helmsley (p513).

with restored 19th-century buildings that are now home to art galleries, antique shops, fashion boutiques, cafes and restaurants – an upmarket annexe to the main shopping area around Oxford and Cambridge Sts.

Turkish Baths SPA
(☎ 01423-556746; www.turkishbathsharrogate.co.uk; Parliament St; admission £17-29.50, guided tours per person £3.75; ⊙ check website, guided tours 9-10am Wed) Plunge into Harrogate's past at the town's fabulously tiled Turkish Baths. This mock-Moorish facility is gloriously Victorian and offers a range of watery delights – hot rooms, steam rooms, plunge pools and so on. A visit is likely to last about 1½ hours. There's a complicated schedule of opening hours that are by turns ladies-only and mixed, so call or check online for details. If you prefer to stay dry, there are also guided tours of the building.

🎉 Festivals & Events

All three of Harrogate's major events are held at the Great Yorkshire Showground, just off the A661 on the southeastern edge of town.

Spring Flower Show HORTICULTURE
(www.flowershow.org.uk; admission £14.50-16) The year's main event, held in late April. A colourful three-day extravaganza of blooms and blossoms, flower competitions, gardening demonstrations, market stalls, crafts and gardening shops.

Great Yorkshire Show AGRICULTURE
(www.greatyorkshireshow.co.uk; adult/child £25/11) Staged over three days in mid-July. The Yorkshire Agricultural Society. Expect all manner of primped and prettified farm animals competing for prizes, and entertainment ranging from show jumping and falconry to cookery demonstrations and hot-air-balloon rides.

Autumn Flower Show HORTICULTURE
(www.flowershow.org.uk; admission £14.50-16) Held in late September, this show has vegetable-and fruit-growing championships, cookery demonstrations, a heaviest-onion competition and children's events.

🛏 Sleeping

There are lots of excellent B&Bs and guesthouses just north of Harrogate town centre, in and around Franklin and Ripon Rds.

Bijou B&B ££
(☎ 01423-567974; www.thebijou.co.uk; 17 Ripon Rd; s/d from £74/104; P@ 🖙) Bijou by name and bijou by nature, this Victorian villa sits firmly at the boutique end of the B&B spectrum – you can tell that a lot of thought and care has gone into its design. The husband-and-wife team who own the place make fantastic hosts, warm and helpful but unobtrusive.

Acorn Lodge B&B ££
(☎ 01423-525630; www.acornlodgeharrogate.co.uk; 1 Studley Rd; s/d from £49/89; P 🖙) Attention to detail makes the difference between an average and an excellent B&B, and the details at Acorn Lodge are spot on – stylish decor, crisp cotton sheets, powerful showers and perfect poached eggs for breakfast. The location is good too, just 10 minutes' walk from the town centre.

Harrogate Brasserie Hotel BOUTIQUE HOTEL ££
(☎ 01423-505041; www.harrogatebrasserie.co.uk; 26-30 Cheltenham Pde; s/d/f from £85/110/120; P🖙) Stripped pine, leather armchairs and subtle colour combinations make this one of Harrogate's most appealing places to stay. The cheerful and cosy accommodation is complemented by an excellent restaurant and bar, with live jazz every evening except Saturday.

Arden House Hotel B&B ££
(☎ 01423-509224; www.ardenhousehotel.co.uk; 69-71 Franklin Rd; s/d from £50/80; P 🖙) This grand old Edwardian house has been given a modern makeover with stylish contemporary furniture, Egyptian-cotton bed linen and posh toiletries, but still retains some lovely period details, including tiled cast-iron fireplaces. Attentive service, good breakfasts and a central location are the icing on the cake.

Hotel du Vin BOUTIQUE HOTEL £££
(☎ 01423-856800; www.hotelduvin.com; Prospect Pl; r/ste from £155/315; P@🖙) An extremely stylish boutique hotel that has made the other lodgings in town sit up and take notice. The loft suites with exposed oak beams, hardwood floors and designer bathrooms are among the nicest rooms in town, but even the standard bedrooms are spacious and very comfortable (though they can be noisy), each with a huge bed draped in soft Egyptian cotton.

🍴 Eating

Le Jardin BISTRO £
(☎ 01423-507323; www.lejardin-harrogate.com; 7 Montpellier Pde; lunch mains £5-9, 2-/3-course dinner £10/13; ⊙ 11.30am-2.30pm Tue-Fri, 6-8.30pm

Tue-Sat, noon-3pm Sun;) This cool little bistro has a snug atmosphere, especially in the evening when candlelight adds a romantic glow. During the day, locals throng to the tables to enjoy great salads, sandwiches and homemade ice cream.

Bettys TEAROOM ££
(www.bettys.co.uk; 1 Parliament St; afternoon tea £18.50; 9am-9pm) A classic tearoom in a classic location with views across the park, Betty's is a local institution. It was established in 1919 by a Swiss immigrant confectioner who took the wrong train, ended up in Yorkshire and decided to stay. There are exquisite home-baked breads, scones and cakes, quality tea and coffee, and a gallery hung with art-nouveau marquetry.

Le D2 BISTRO, FRENCH ££
(www.led2.co.uk; 7 Bower Rd; 2-/3-course dinner £21/25; noon-2pm & 6-11.30pm Tue-Sat) This bright and airy bistro is always busy, with diners drawn back again and again by its relaxed atmosphere, warm and friendly service, and hearty menu that takes fresh local produce and adds a twist of French sophistication. A one-course lunch costs £8.95 including a drink.

Tannin Level MODERN BRITISH ££
(01423-560595; www.tanninlevel.co.uk; 5 Raglan St; mains £15-25; noon-9pm Mon-Thu, to 9.30pm Fri & Sat, to 8pm Sun) Old terracotta floor tiles, polished mahogany tables and gilt-framed mirrors and paintings create a relaxed yet elegant atmosphere at this popular neighbourhood bistro. A competitively priced menu based on seasonal British produce – think beef braised in Yorkshire ale, or hazelnut-crusted sea bream – means you'd best book a table or face being turned away.

Sasso ITALIAN ££
(01423-508838; www.sassorestaurant.co.uk; 8-10 Princes Sq; mains £10-22; noon-3pm & 6pm-midnight Mon-Sat) A top-class basement trattoria where homemade pasta is served in a variety of traditional and authentic ways, along with a host of other Italian specialities.

★ **Van Zeller** MODERN BRITISH £££
(01423-508762; www.vanzellerrestaurants.co.uk; 8 Montpellier St; 3-course lunch/dinner £35/50; noon-2pm & 6-10pm Tue-Sat) Michelin-trained Yorkshire chef Tom van Zeller (who began his career in Bettys) offers exquisite and unusual interpretations of classic British dishes in a refreshingly relaxed atmosphere – 'fine food without the fuss' is his motto. Imaginative starters include smoked hen's egg with morels and a wild garlic and pine nut pesto. The 10-course chef's tasting menu is £85.

☆ Entertainment

Harrogate Theatre THEATRE
(01423-502116; www.harrogatetheatre.co.uk; Oxford St) A historic Victorian building that dates from 1900, staging variety, comedy, musicals and dancing.

Royal Hall MUSIC
(01423-500500; www.royalhall.co.uk; Ripon Rd) A gorgeous Edwardian theatre that is now part of the conference and events venue Harrogate International Centre. The musical program covers orchestral and choral performances, piano recitals, jazz and more.

ⓘ Information

Harrogate Tourist Office (01423-537300; www.visitharrogate.co.uk; Crescent Rd; 9am-5.30pm Mon-Sat, 10am-1pm Sun Apr-Oct, 9.30am-5pm Mon-Sat Nov-Mar)
Post Office (11 Cambridge Rd; 9.30am-5.30pm Mon-Sat)

ⓘ Getting There & Away

Bus National Express coaches run from Leeds (£3.90, 40 minutes, four daily). Bus 36 comes from Ripon (£6, 30 minutes, every 15 minutes) and continues to Leeds.

Train Trains run to Harrogate from Leeds (£7.90, 40 minutes, every 30 minutes) and York (£8.10, 45 minutes, hourly).

Scarborough

POP 61,750

Scarborough is where the tradition of English seaside holidays began – and it began earlier than you might think. It was in the 1660s that a book promoting the medicinal properties of a local spring (now the site of Scarborough Spa) pulled in the first flood of visitors. A belief in the health-giving effects of sea bathing saw wheeled bathing carriages appear on the beach in the 1730s and with the arrival of the railway in 1845 Scarborough's fate was sealed. By the time the 20th century rolled in, it was all donkey rides, fish and chips, and boat trips round the bay, with saucy postcards, beauty contests and slot-machine arcades only a decade or two away.

Scarborough

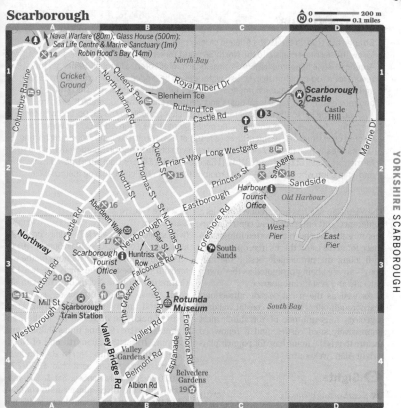

N ▲ | 0 ———————— 200 m
0 ———————— 0.1 miles

Naval Warfare (80m); Glass House (500m);
Sea Life Centre & Marine Sanctuary (1mi)
Robin Hood's Bay (14mi)

North Bay

Cricket Ground

Royal Albert Dr

Columbus Ravine

Queen's Pde

North Marine Rd

Blenheim Tce

Rutland Tce

Castle Rd

Scarborough Castle

Castle Hill

Marine Dr

Friars Way

Long Westgate

Sandgate

Sandside

St Thomas St

Queen St

North St

Princess St

Harbour Tourist Office

Old Harbour

Aberdeen Walk

Eastborough

Newborough

St Nicholas St

Foreshore Rd

West Pier

East Pier

Northway

Castle Rd

Huntriss Row

Bar St

Falconers Rd

South Sands

Scarborough Tourist Office

Vernon Rd

The Crescent

Valley Rd

Rotunda Museum

South Bay

Victoria Rd

Mill St

Westborough

Scarborough Train Station

Valley Bridge Rd

Valley Gardens

Belmont Rd

Esplanade

Foreshore Rd

Albion Rd

Belvedere Gardens

YORKSHIRE SCARBOROUGH

Scarborough

◎ Top Sights
1 Rotunda Museum	B3
2 Scarborough Castle	D1

◎ Sights
3 Grave of Anne Brontë	C1
4 Peasholm Park	A1
5 St Mary's Church	C1

✪ Activities, Courses & Tours
6 Secretspot Surf Shop	B3

🛏 Sleeping
7 Helaina	B1
8 Interludes	C2
9 North Bay Guest House	A1
10 Regency Central Hotel	B3
11 Windmill	A3

✕ Eating
12 Bonnet's	B3
13 Golden Grid	C2
14 Jeremy's	A1
15 Lanterna	B2
16 Naylor's	B2
17 Roasters	B3
18 Tunny Club	C2

✿ Entertainment
19 Scarborough Spa	B4
20 Stephen Joseph Theatre	A3

Like all British seaside towns, Scarborough suffered a downturn in recent decades as people jetted off to the Costa Blanca on newly affordable foreign holidays, but things are looking up again. The town retains all the trappings of the classic seaside resort, but is in the process of reinventing itself as a centre for the creative arts and digital industries.

THE TUNNY CLUB

Strange but true: in the 1930s Atlantic bluefin tuna (also known as tunny) started to follow the herring shoals into the North Sea, and Yorkshire became the hub of an American-style big-game fishery. Professional hunter Lorenzo Mitchell-Henry set the record for a rod-caught fish in British waters when he landed a 386kg monster in 1933, and Scarborough was soon home to the Tunny Club of Great Britain. Visiting millionaires and movie stars chartered local boats and vied with each other to smash the record.

Overfishing led to the disappearance of the herring shoals in the 1950s, and with them the tunny. However, in recent years the ocean giants have returned to British waters, attracted by warmer sea temperatures (a result of climate change) and recovering herring stocks. Meanwhile, the only evidence that remains of the fishery in Scarborough is the former premises of the Tunny Club (1 Sandgate; mains £4-7; ⊙11am-11pm), now a fish-and-chip shop whose upstairs dining room is filled with big-game fishing memorabilia.

The Victorian spa has been redeveloped as a conference and entertainment centre, a former museum has been converted into studio space for artists, and there's free, open-access wi-fi along the promenade beside the harbour – an area being promoted as the town's bar, cafe and restaurant quarter.

As well as the usual seaside attractions, Scarborough offers excellent coastal walking, a geology museum, one of Yorkshire's most impressively sited castles, and a renowned theatre that is the home base for popular playwright Alan Ayckbourn.

⊙ Sights

★ Scarborough Castle   CASTLE

(EH; www.english-heritage.org.uk; adult/child £5/3; ⊙10am-6pm Apr-Sep, to 5pm Oct, to 4pm Sat & Sun only Nov-Mar) The massive medieval keep of Scarborough Castle occupies a commanding position atop its headland. Legend has it that Richard I loved the views from here so much that his ghost just keeps coming back. Take a walk out to the edge of the cliffs, where you can see the 2000-year-old remains of a Roman signal station; clearly the Romans appreciated this viewpoint, too.

★ Rotunda Museum   MUSEUM

(www.rotundamuseum.co.uk; Vernon Rd; adult/child £3/free; ⊙10am-5pm Tue-Sun; ⊞) The Rotunda Museum is dedicated to the coastal geology of northeast Yorkshire, which has yielded many of Britain's most important dinosaur fossils. The strata in the local cliffs were also important in deciphering England's geological history. Founded by William Smith, 'the father of English geology', who lived in Scarborough in the 1820s, the museum has original Victorian exhibits as well as a hands-on gallery for kids.

Sea Life Centre & Marine Sanctuary   AQUARIUM

(www.sealife.co.uk; Scalby Mills; admission £16.20, family per person £13.20; ⊙10am-5pm; ⓟⓕ) Of all the family-oriented attractions on the waterfront, the best of the lot is the Sea Life Centre overlooking North Bay. You can see coral reefs, turtles, octopuses, seahorses, otters and many other fascinating creatures, though the biggest draw is the Seal Rescue Centre (feeding times 11.30am and 2.30pm). It's at the far north end of North Beach – the miniature North Bay Railway (www.nbr.org.uk; return adult/child £3.30/2.70; ⊙10.30am-3pm daily Apr-Sep, Sat & Sun year-round) runs the three-quarter-mile route. A lot of the attractions are outdoors, so it's not an ideal rainy-day refuge.

Peasholm Park   PARK

(www.peasholmpark.com; Columbus Ravine; ⊙24hr) Set back from North Bay, Scarborough's beautiful Edwardian pleasure gardens are famous for their summer sessions of Naval Warfare (adult/child £3.90/2.10; ⊙3pm selected dates Jun-Aug), when large model ships re-enact famous naval battles on the boating lake (check the website for dates).

St Mary's Church   CHURCH

(Castle Rd; ⊙10am-4pm Mon-Fri, 1-4pm Sun May-Sep) This church dates from the 12th to the 15th centuries (boards inside explain its history), but it is most notable for the little cemetery across the lane that contains the grave of Anne Brontë.

🏃 Activities

There are some decent waves on England's northeast coast, supporting a growing surf scene. A top spot is Cayton Bay, 4 miles south of town, where you'll find **Scarborough Surf School** (☑ 01723-585585; www.scarboroughsurfschool.co.uk; Cayton Bay; parking £2) offering full-day lessons for £45 per person and surfboard hire for £18 per day.

Back in town, you can get information and advice from the **Secretspot Surf Shop** (www.secretspot.co.uk; 4 Pavilion Tce) near the train station.

🛏 Sleeping

In Scarborough, if a house has four walls and a roof it will offer B&B. Competition is intense, and in such a tough market multi-night-stay special offers are a dime a dozen, which means single-night rates are the highest of all.

Scarborough YHA   HOSTEL £
(☑ 01723-361176; www.yha.org.uk; Burniston Rd; dm/q from £18/60; ℗) An idyllic hostel set in a converted 17th-century water mill, 2 miles north of town along the A166 to Whitby. Take bus 3 or 3A from York Pl.

★ Helaina   B&B ££
(☑ 01723-375191; www.hotelhelaina.co.uk; 14 Blenheim Tce; s/d from £79/89; ⊙ daily Apr-Nov, Fri & Sat only Feb & Mar; 🕾) Location, location, location – you'd be hard pushed to find a place with a better sea view than this elegant guesthouse perched on the clifftop overlooking North Beach. And the view inside is pretty good, too, with sharply styled contemporary furniture and cool colours. It's well worth paying extra for the deluxe sea-view room with bay window (£119).

Waves   B&B ££
(☑ 01723-373658; www.scarboroughwaves.co.uk; 39 Esplanade Rd, South Cliff; s/d from £39/68; ℗🕾) 🍃 Crisp cotton sheets and powerful showers make for comfortable accommodation at this B&B, but it's the second B that's the real star – the breakfasts range from vegan-friendly fruit salads and smoothies to fry-ups, kippers and kedgeree. A unique selling point is the jukebox in the lounge, loaded with 1960s and '70s hits.

The property is 0.75 miles south of the centre, off the A165 (Ramshill Rd).

North Bay Guest House   B&B ££
(☑ 01723-374406; www.northbay-scarborough.co.uk; 137 Columbus Ravine; s/d from £28/60; 🕾🖵) Cosy and colourful bedrooms, big breakfasts and wonderfully welcoming owners come together to create exceptional value at this excellent B&B, within easy walking distance of Peasholm Park, North Bay Railway and the beach at North Bay.

Windmill   B&B ££
(☑ 01723-372735; www.windmill-hotel.co.uk; Mill St; d from £85; ℗🕾) Quirky doesn't begin to

---

WORTH A TRIP

BLACK SHEEP OF THE BREWING FAMILY

The village of Masham (pronounced 'Massam') is a place of pilgrimage for connoisseurs of real ale – it's the frothing fountainhead of Theakston's beers, brewed here since 1827. The company's most famous brew, Old Peculier, takes its name from the Peculier of Masham, a parish court established in medieval times to deal with religious offences, including drunkenness, brawling and 'taking a skull from the churchyard and placing it under a person's head to charm them to sleep'. The court seal is used as the emblem for Theakston Ales.

To the horror of real-ale fans, and after much falling-out among Theakston family members, the Theakston Brewery was taken over by megabrewer Scottish & Newcastle in 1987. Five years later, Paul Theakston, who refused to work for S&N and was determined to keep small-scale artisan brewing alive, bought an old maltings building in Masham and set up his own brewery, which he named Black Sheep. He managed to salvage all kinds of traditional brewing equipment, including six Yorkshire 'stone square' brewing vessels, and was soon running a successful enterprise.

History came full circle in 2004 when Paul's four brothers took the Theakston brewery back into family ownership. Both **Black Sheep Brewery** (☑ 01765-680101; www.black-sheepbrewery.com; tours £6.95; ⊙ 10am-5pm Sun-Wed, to 11pm Thu-Sat) and **Theakston's Brewery** (☑ 01765-680000; www.theakstons.co.uk; tours £6.95; ⊙ 10.30am-5.30pm Jul & Aug, to 4.30pm Sep-Jun) have visitor centres and offer guided tours (best booked in advance).

Masham is 9 miles northwest of Ripon on the A6108 to Leyburn. Bus 159 from Richmond to Ripon stops at Masham (£4, 30 minutes, two or three daily).

describe this place, a beautifully converted 18th-century windmill in the middle of town. There are two self-catering cottages and three four-poster doubles around a cobbled courtyard, but try to secure the balcony suite (from £110 a night) in the upper floors of the windmill itself, with great views from the wraparound balcony.

Interludes B&B ££
(☎01723-360513; www.interludeshotel.co.uk; 32 Princess St; s/d £45/70; ☎) Owners Ian and Bob have a flair for the theatrical and have enacted it with visible success on this lovely, gay-friendly Georgian home plastered with old theatre posters, prints and other thespian mementos. The individually decorated rooms are guaranteed to put a smile on your face. No children.

Regency Central Hotel HOTEL £££
(☎01723-365766; www.regencycentralhotel.com; 1-3 The Crescent; s/d from £100/149; P☎) Set in an elegant Georgian terrace in the middle of town, on a quiet street overlooking gardens, this recently refurbished hotel combines old-fashioned style – think swagged drapes and sink-up-to-your-waist sofas – and spacious rooms with attentive but friendly and informal service.

✕ Eating

Glass House CAFE £
(☎01723-368791; www.glasshousebistro.co.uk; Burniston Rd; mains £4-8; ⊙10am-4.30pm; ☎) Homemade lasagne, steak-and-ale pie and filled baked potatoes pull in the lunchtime crowds at this appealing (and always busy) cafe beside the start of the North Bay Rail-

---

FOUNTAINS ABBEY & STUDLEY ROYAL

Nestled in the secluded valley of the River Skell are two of Yorkshire's most beautiful attractions, an absolute must on any northern itinerary.

The alluring and strangely obsessive water gardens of the Studley Royal estate were built in the 18th century to enhance the picturesque ruins of 12th-century Fountains Abbey (NT; www.fountainsabbey.org.uk; adult/child £10.50/5.25; ⊙10am-6pm Apr-Sep, to 5pm Sat-Thu Oct-Mar). Together, they present a breathtaking picture of pastoral elegance and tranquillity that have made them a Unesco World Heritage Site and the most visited of all the National Trust's pay-to-enter properties.

After falling out with the Benedictines of York in 1132, a band of rebel monks came here to establish their own monastery. Struggling to make it alone, they were formally adopted by the Cistercians in 1135. By the middle of the 13th century, the new abbey had become the most successful Cistercian venture in the country. After the Dissolution, when Henry VIII confiscated church property, the abbey's estate was sold into private hands, and between 1598 and 1611 Fountains Hall was built using stone from the abbey ruins. The hall and ruins were united with the Studley Royal estate in 1768.

Studley Royal was owned by John Aislabie, once Chancellor of the Exchequer, who dedicated his life to creating the park after a financial scandal saw him expelled from parliament. The main house of Studley Royal burnt down in 1946, but the superb landscaping, with its serene artificial lakes, survives almost unchanged from the 18th century.

A choice of scenic walking trails leads for a mile to the famous water gardens, designed to enhance the romantic views of the ruined abbey. Don't miss St Mary's Church (Studley Royal; ⊙noon-4pm Apr-Sep) FREE above the gardens, a neo-Gothic jewel designed by William Burgess, and ask the attendant to point out the trademark mouse carved into the stone of the mausoleum.

The remains of the abbey are impressively grandiose, gathered around the sunny Romanesque cloister, with a huge vaulted cellarium leading off the west end of the church. Here, the abbey's 200 lay brothers lived, and food and wool from the abbey's farms were stored. At the east end is the soaring Chapel of Nine Altars and on the outside of its northeast window is a Green Man carving (a pre-Christian fertility symbol).

Fountains Abbey is 4 miles west of Ripon off the B6265. Bus 139 travels from Ripon to Fountains Abbey visitor centre year-round (£2.60 return, 15 minutes, four times daily Monday to Saturday, seven on Sundays in summer).

way. Fried breakfasts, sandwiches, cakes and scones fill the menu for the rest of the day.

Roasters CAFE £

(www.roasterscoffee.co.uk; 8 Aberdeen Walk; mains £4-6; ⊘9am-5pm) A funky coffee shop with chunky pine tables, bentwood chairs and an excellent range of freshly ground coffees. There's a juice and smoothie bar, too, and the lunch menu includes ciabatta sandwiches, salads and jacket potatoes.

Bonnet's TEAROOM £

(38-40 Huntriss Row; mains £5-9; ⊘9am-5pm Mon-Sat, 11am-4pm Sun) One of the oldest cafes in town (established in 1880), Bonnet's serves delicious cakes and light meals in a quiet courtyard.

Naylor's FISH & CHIPS £

(45 Aberdeen Walk; mains £4-5; ⊘11.30am-6pm Mon-Thu, to 7pm Fri & Sat) Currently riding high in the local charts for best fish and chips in Scarborough.

★ **Jeremy's** BRITISH, FRENCH ££

(🖉01723-363871; www.jeremys.co; 33 Victoria Park Ave; mains £16-24, 3-course Sun lunch £25; ⊘6-9.30pm Wed-Sat, noon-3pm Sun; 🖼) 🖋 A fantastic neighbourhood bistro run by a chef who won his Michelin credential with Marco Pierre White, this off-the-beaten-track gem sports an art-deco ambience and a menu that blends the best of Yorkshire and British produce with French inventiveness and flair. Best to book at weekends.

Golden Grid FISH & CHIPS ££

(www.goldengrid.co.uk; 4 Sandside; mains £8-18; ⊘11.30am-11pm; 🖼) Whoever said fish and chips can't be eaten with dignity hasn't tried the Golden Grid, a sit-down fish restaurant that has been serving the best cod in Scarborough since 1883. Its starched white tablecloths and starched white aprons are staunchly traditional, as is the menu – as well as seafood there's sausage and mash, liver and bacon, and steak and chips.

★ **Lanterna** ITALIAN £££

(🖉01723-363616; www.lanterna-ristorante.co.uk; 33 Queen St; mains £15-24; ⊘7-10pm Mon-Sat) 🖋 A snug, old-fashioned Italian trattoria that specialises in fresh local seafood (including lobster from £32) and classic dishes from the old country such as *stufato de ceci* (chickpea stew with oxtail) and white-truffle dishes in season (October to December; £30 to £45). As well as sourcing Yorkshire produce, the chef imports delicacies direct from Italy.

☆ **Entertainment**

Stephen Joseph Theatre THEATRE

(🖉01723-370541; www.sjt.uk.com; Westborough) A good range of drama is staged here, including the premieres of plays by the renowned chronicler of middle-class mores, Alan Ayckbourn.

Scarborough Spa VARIETY

(🖉01723-821888; www.scarboroughspa.co.uk; Foreshore Rd) The revitalised spa complex stages a varied program of entertainment, especially in the summer months – orchestral performances, variety shows, popular musicals and old-fashioned afternoon-tea dances.

ℹ️ **Information**

FreeBay Wifi (🛜) Free wi-fi internet access along the harbourfront from West Pier to East Pier.

Harbour Tourist Office (Sandside; ⊘10am-5.30pm Easter-Oct, to 9pm Jul & Aug)

Post Office (11-15 Aberdeen Walk; ⊘9am-5.30pm Mon-Fri, to 12.30pm Sat)

Scarborough Tourist Office (🖉01723-383637; www.discoveryorkshirecoast.com; Brunswick Shopping Centre, Westborough; ⊘9.30am-5.30pm Apr-Oct, 10am-4.30pm Mon-Sat Nov-Mar; 🛜)

ℹ️ **Getting There & Away**

Bus Bus 128 travels along the A170 from Helmsley to Scarborough (£7.60, 1½ hours, hourly Monday to Saturday, six on Sunday) via Pickering, while buses 93 and X93 come from Whitby (£5.60, one hour, every 30 minutes) via Robin Hood's Bay (hourly). Bus 843 goes to Scarborough from Leeds (£12, 2¾ hours, hourly) via York (£11, 1¾ hours, hourly).

Train There are regular trains from Hull (£15.10, 1½ hours, hourly), Leeds (£18, 1¼ hours, hourly) and York (£15, 50 minutes, hourly).

ℹ️ **Getting Around**

Tiny Victorian-era **funicular railways** (per person 80p; ⊘9.30am-5.30pm Feb-Oct) rattle up and down Scarborough's steep cliffs between town and beach. Local buses leave from the western end of Westborough and outside the train station.

For a taxi, call **Station Taxis** (🖉01723-366366; www.taxisinscarborough.co.uk); £5 should get you to most places in town.

NORTH YORK MOORS NATIONAL PARK

Inland from the north Yorkshire coast, the wild and windswept North York Moors rise in desolate splendour. Three-quarters of all the world's heather moorland is to be found in Britain, and this is the largest expanse in England. Ridge-top roads climb up from lush green valleys to the bleak open moors, where weather-beaten stone crosses mark the lines of ancient roadways. In summer, heather blooms in billowing drifts of purple haze.

This is classic walking country. The moors are criss-crossed with footpaths old and new, and dotted with pretty, flower-bedecked villages. The national park is also home to one of England's most picturesque steam railways.

The park produces the useful *Out & About* visitor guide, available from tourist offices and hotels, with information on things to see and do. See also www.northyorkmoors.org.uk.

ⓘ Information

There are two national park visitor centres, providing information on walking, cycling, wildlife and public transport:

Moors National Park Centre (☑ 01439-772737; www.northyorkmoors.org.uk; Lodge Lane, Danby; ⏰ 10am-5pm Apr-Oct, 10.30am-4pm Nov-Mar, Sat & Sun only Jan-Feb)

Sutton Bank National Park Centre (☑ 01845-597426; www.northyorkmoors.org.uk; Sutton Bank, by Thirsk; ⏰ 10am-5pm Apr-Oct, 10.30am-4pm Nov-Mar, Sat & Sun only Jan-Feb; 🛜)

ⓘ Getting Around

On Sundays and bank holiday Mondays from late May to September, the **Moors Explorer** (☑ 01482-592929; www.eyms.co.uk) bus service runs from Hull to the Moors National Park Centre in Danby, via Beverley, Pickering, Hutton-le-Hole and the Lion Inn at Blakey, with a shuttle between Danby and Pickering. An all-day hop-on/hop-off ticket costs £12.50.

If you're planning to drive on the minor roads over the moors, beware of wandering sheep and lambs – hundreds are killed by careless drivers every year.

Helmsley

POP 1515

Helmsley is a classic North Yorkshire market town, a handsome huddle of old stone houses, historic coaching inns and – inevitably – a cobbled market square (market day is Friday), all basking under the watchful gaze of a sturdy Norman castle. Nearby are the romantic ruins of Rievaulx Abbey and a fistful of country walks.

North York Moors National Park

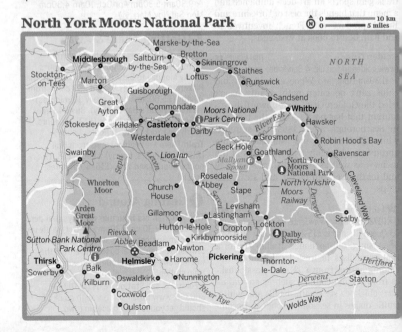

⊙ Sights & Activities

Helmsley Castle
CASTLE

(EH; www.english-heritage.org.uk; adult/child £5.20/3.10; ⊙ 10am-6pm Apr-Sep, to 5pm Oct, to 4pm Sat & Sun Nov-Mar) The impressive ruins of 12th-century Helmsley Castle are defended by a striking series of deep ditches and banks, to which later rulers added the thick stone walls and defensive towers. Only one tooth-shaped tower survives today, following the dismantling of the fortress by Sir Thomas Fairfax after the Civil War. The castle's tumultuous history is well explained in the visitor centre.

Helmsley Walled Garden
GARDENS

(www.helmsleywalledgarden.org.uk; adult/child £6/free; ⊙ 10am-5pm Apr-Oct) Helmsley Walled Garden would be just another plant and produce centre were it not for its dramatic position next to Helmsley Castle and fabulous selection of flowers, fruits and vegetables (some of them rare), not to mention the herbs, which include 40 varieties of mint. If you're into horticulture with a historical twist, this is Eden.

Duncombe Park Gardens
GARDENS

(www.duncombepark.com; adult/child £5/3; ⊙ 10.30am-5pm Sun-Fri May-Aug) South of Helmsley lies the superb landscape of Duncombe Park estate, with the stately home of Duncombe Park House at its heart. From the house (not open to the public) and formal gardens, grassy walkways and terraces lead through woodland to mock-classical temples, while longer walking trails are set out in the landscaped parkland, now protected as a nature reserve. You could easily spend a day here, especially if you take in one of the many walks. Cream of the crop is the 3.5-mile route to Rievaulx Abbey, and the tourist office can provide route leaflets and advise on buses if you don't want to walk both ways. This route is also the opening section of the Cleveland Way.

🛏 Sleeping

Helmsley YHA
HOSTEL £

(☏ 0845 371 9638; www.yha.org.uk; Carlton Lane; dm/q £21/91; ℗) This hostel's location, just 400m east of the market square at the start of the Cleveland Way, means it's often busy, so book in advance.

Wrens of Ryedale
CAMPSITE £

(☏ 01439-771260; www.wrensofryedale.co.uk; Gale Lane; site & 1 person £12, with car & 2 people £20; ⊙ Apr-Oct; 🐕) A sheltered campsite with more than a hectare of pristine parkland 3 miles east of Helmsley, just south of Beadlam.

Feathers Hotel
INN ££

(☏ 01439-770275; www.feathershotelhelmsley.co.uk; Market Pl; s/d from £70/80) One of a number of old coaching inns on the market square that offer B&B, decent grub and a pint of hand-pumped real ale. There are four-poster beds in some rooms and historical trimmings throughout.

Feversham Arms
HOTEL £££

(☏ 01439-770766; www.fevershamarms.com; High St; r from £130; ℗ 🐕 🛜 🏊) A rustic hotel given a designer makeover, the Feversham Arms has a snug and sophisticated atmosphere where country charm meets boutique chic. Individually decorated bedrooms are complemented by an excellent restaurant, spa treatments and a heated outdoor pool in the central courtyard.

🍴 Eating

Helmsley is a bit of a foodie town, sporting a couple of quality delicatessens on the main square. There's Thomas of Helmsley (18 Market Pl; ⊙ 7.30am-5.30pm Mon-Sat, 10am-4pm Sun), a butcher and deli specialising in local produce, and Hunters of Helmsley (www.huntersofhelmsley.com; 13 Market Pl; ⊙ 8am-5.30pm), offering a cornucopia of locally made chutneys, jams, beers, cheeses, bacon, humbug sweets and ice cream – a great place to stock up for a gourmet picnic.

★ Star Inn
GASTROPUB £££

(☏ 01439-770397; www.thestaratharome.co.uk; Harome; mains £19-29; ⊙ 11.30am-2pm Tue-Sat, 6.15-9.30pm Mon-Sat, noon-6pm Sun; ℗ 🐕) 🍴 This thatch-roofed country pub is home to one of Yorkshire's best restaurants, with a menu specialising in top-quality produce from the surrounding countryside: Whitby turbot with smoked eel and beetroot or roast English quail with wild mushrooms and truffle. There's also a set three-course menu for £25 (Monday to Saturday). Harome is about 2 miles southeast of Helmsley off the A170.

The Star is the sort of place you won't want to leave, and the good news is you don't have to – the adjacent lodge has eight magnificent bedrooms (£170 to £260), each decorated in classic but luxurious country style.

ⓘ Information

The tourist office (☏ 01439-770173; Castlegate; ⊙ 9.30am-5.30pm Mar-Oct, 10am-4pm Fri-Sun Nov-Feb) at the castle entrance sells maps and books, and can help with accommodation.

ⓘ Getting There & Away

All buses stop in the main square. Bus 31X runs from York to Helmsley (£7.60, 1¼ hours, four daily Monday to Saturday). From Scarborough, take bus 128 (£7.60, 1½ hours, hourly Monday to Saturday, four times on Sunday) via Pickering.

Rievaulx

In the secluded valley of the River Rye, amid fields and woods loud with birdsong, stand the magnificent ruins of Rievaulx Abbey (www.english-heritage.org.uk; adult/child £6.20/3.70; ⊙10am-6pm Apr-Sep, to 5pm Oct, to 4pm Sat & Sun only Nov-Mar; P), pronounced 'ree-voh'. The extensive remains give a wonderful sense of the size and complexity of the community that once lived here, and their story is fleshed out in a series of fascinating exhibits in the neighbouring visitor centre.

This idyllic spot was chosen by Cistercian monks in 1132 as a base for their missionary activity in northern Britain. St Aelred, the third abbot, famously described the abbey's setting as 'everywhere peace, everywhere serenity, and a marvellous freedom from the tumult of the world'. But the monks of Rievaulx were far from unworldly and soon created a network of commercial interests ranging from sheep farms to lead mines.

In the 1750s, landscape-gardening fashion favoured a Gothic look and many aristocrats had mock ruins built in their parks. The Duncombe family were able to go one better, as their lands contained a real medieval ruin, Rievaulx Abbey. They built Rievaulx Terrace and Temples (www.nationaltrust.org.uk; adult/child £5.95/3; ⊙11am-5pm Mar-Oct; P) so that lords and ladies could stroll effortlessly in 'the wilderness' and admire the abbey in the valley below. Visitors today can do the same, with views over Ryedale and the Hambleton Hills forming a perfect backdrop.

Rievaulx is located about 3 miles west of Helmsley. Note that there's no direct access between the abbey and the terrace. Their entrance gates are about a mile apart, though easily reached along a lane (steeply uphill if you're heading from the abbey to the terrace).

Pickering

POP 6590

Pickering is a lively market town with an imposing Norman castle that advertises itself as the 'gateway to the North York Moors'. That gateway is the terminus of the wonderful North Yorkshire Moors Railway, a picturesque survivor from the great days of steam. The tourist office (☏01751-473791; The Ropery; ⊙9.30am-5.30pm Mon-Sat, to 4pm Sun Mar-Oct, 10am-4pm Mon-Sat Nov-Feb) has the usual details, as well as plenty of railway-related info.

◉ Sights

North Yorkshire Moors Railway HERITAGE RAILWAY
(NYMR; www.nymr.co.uk; Pickering-Whitby Day Rover ticket adult/child £25/12.50; ⊙May-Oct) The privately owned North Yorkshire Moors Railway runs for 18 miles through beautiful countryside from Pickering to Grosmont. Lovingly restored steam locos pull period carriages resplendent with polished brass and bright paintwork, and the railway appeals to train buffs and day trippers alike. For visitors without wheels, it's excellent for reaching out-of-the-way spots. Grosmont is on the main railway line between Middlesbrough and Whitby, which opens up yet more possibilities for walking or sightseeing day trips.

Pickering Castle CASTLE
(EH; www.english-heritage.org.uk; adult/child £4.20/2.50; ⊙10am-6pm Apr-Sep, to 5pm Oct) Pickering Castle is a lot like the castles we drew as kids: thick stone outer walls circle the keep, and the whole lot is perched atop a high motte (mound) with great views of the surrounding countryside. Founded by William the Conqueror, it was added to and altered by later kings.

⌕ Sleeping & Eating

There's a strip of B&Bs on tree-lined Eastgate (on the A170 to Scarborough) and a few more on Westgate (heading towards Helmsley). Decent options include Eleven Westgate (☏01751-475111; www.elevenwestgate.co.uk; 11 Westgate; s/d from £49/75; 🕸), a pretty house with patio and garden, and the elegant Georgian town house at 17 Burgate (☏01751-473463; www.17burgate.co.uk; 17 Burgate; s/d from £85/99; @🕸).

There are several cafes and teashops on Market Pl, but don't overlook the tearoom (mains £4-6; ⊙8.30am-4pm) at Pickering station, which serves excellent home-baked goodies and tasty lunch specials such as Yorkshire pudding with roast beef and gravy.

★ **White Swan Hotel** HOTEL £££
(☏01751-472288; www.white-swan.co.uk; Market Pl; r from £149; P🕸) ✿ The top spot in town

successfully combines a smart pub, a superb restaurant serving local produce cooked with a continental twist (mains £14 to £25), and a luxurious boutique hotel. Nine modern rooms in the converted coach house up the ante, with flatscreen TVs and other stylish paraphernalia adding to the luxury found throughout the hotel.

❶ Getting There & Away

In addition to the NYMR trains, bus 128 between Helmsley (£4.50, 40 minutes) and Scarborough (£5.50, 50 minutes) runs hourly via Pickering. Bus 840 between Leeds and Whitby links Pickering with York (£8.80, 70 minutes, hourly).

Whitby

POP 13,215

Whitby is a town of two halves, split down the middle by the mouth of the River Esk. It's also a town with two personalities – on the one hand, a busy commercial and fishing port with a bustling quayside fish market; on the other, a traditional seaside resort, complete with sandy beach, amusement arcades and promenading holidaymakers slurping ice-cream cones in the sun.

It's the combination of these two facets that makes Whitby more interesting than your average resort. The town has managed to retain much of its 18th-century character, recalling the time when James Cook – Whitby's most famous adopted son – was making his first forays out to sea on his way to becoming one of the best-known explorers in history. The narrow streets and alleys of the old town hug the riverside, now lined with restaurants, pubs and cute little shops, all with views across the handsome harbour where colourful fishing boats land their catch. Keeping a watchful eye over the whole scene is the atmospheric ruined abbey atop the East Cliff.

But Whitby also has a darker side. Most famously, it was the inspiration and setting for part of Bram Stoker's Gothic horror story *Dracula*. Less well known is the fact that Whitby is famous for the jet (fossilised wood) that has been mined from its sea cliffs for centuries. This smooth black substance was popularised in the 19th century when Queen Victoria took to wearing mourning jewellery made from Whitby jet. In recent years these morbid associations have seen the rise of a series of hugely popular goth festivals.

◉ Sights

★ Whitby Abbey RUIN

(EH; www.english-heritage.org.uk; adult/child £6.60/4; ☺10am-6pm Apr-Sep, to 5pm Oct, to 4pm Sat & Sun only Nov-Mar; ⓟ) There are ruined abbeys; and there are picturesque ruined abbeys; and then there's Whitby Abbey, dominating the skyline above the East Cliff like a great Gothic tombstone silhouetted against the sky. Looking as though it was built as an atmospheric film set rather than a monastic establishment, it is hardly surprising that this medieval hulk inspired the Victorian novelist Bram Stoker (who holidayed in Whitby) to make it the setting for Count Dracula's dramatic landfall.

From the end of Church St, which has many shops selling jet jewellery, the 199 steps of Church Stairs will lead you steeply up to Whitby Abbey, passing the equally atmospheric St Mary's Church (☺10am-5pm Apr-Oct, to 4pm Nov-Mar) and its spooky graveyard, a favourite haunt of courting goth couples.

★ Captain Cook
Memorial Museum MUSEUM

(www.cookmuseumwhitby.co.uk; Grape Lane; adult/child £4.80/3.30; ☺9.45am-5pm Apr-Oct, 11am-3pm Mar) This fascinating museum occupies the house of the ship owner with whom Cook began his seafaring career. Highlights include the attic where Cook lodged as a young apprentice, Cook's own maps and letters,

---

CAPTAIN COOK – WHITBY'S ADOPTED SON

Although he was born in Marton (now a suburb of Middlesbrough), the renowned explorer Captain James Cook has been adopted by Whitby. Ever since the first tourists got off the train in Victorian times, local entrepreneurs have mercilessly cashed in on Cook's memory, as endless Endeavour Cafes and Captain Cook Chip Shops testify.

Still, Whitby played a key role in Cook's eventual success as a world-famous explorer. It was here that he first went to sea, serving his apprenticeship with local ship owners, and the designs of the ships used for his voyages of discovery – including the *Endeavour* – were based on the design of Whitby 'cats', flat-bottomed ships that carried coal from Newcastle to London.

Whitby

Whitby

etchings from the South Seas, and a wonderful model of the *Endeavour,* with the crew and stores all laid out for inspection.

Whitby Sands   BEACH

Whitby Sands, stretching west from the harbour mouth, offers donkey rides, ice-cream vendors and bucket-and-spade escapades. The beach can be reached from West Cliff via the **cliff lift** (per person 60p; ⊙10am-5.30pm May-Sep), an elevator that has been in service

since 1931. Atop the cliff at the beach's east end, the **Captain Cook Monument** shows the great man looking out to sea, often with a seagull perched on his head. Nearby is the **Whalebone Arch**, which recalls Whitby's days as a whaling port.

Whitby Museum   MUSEUM

(www.whitbymuseum.org.uk; Pannett Park; adult/child £5/free; ⊙9.30am-4.30pm Tue-Sun) Set in a park to the west of the town centre is the wonderfully eclectic Whitby Museum, with displays of fossil plesiosaurs and dinosaur footprints, Captain Cook memorabilia, ships in bottles, jet jewellery and even the 'Hand of Glory', a preserved human hand reputedly cut from the corpse of an executed criminal.

🏃 Activities

For a cracking day out, take a bus to Robin Hood's Bay, explore the village, have lunch, and then hike the 6-mile clifftop footpath back to Whitby (allow three hours).

First choice for a bike ride is the excellent 20-mile Whitby to Scarborough Coastal Cycle Trail, which starts a mile south of the town centre and follows the route of an old railway line via Robin Hood's Bay. Bikes can be hired for £15 to £25 a day from Dr Crank's Bike Shack (☑01947-606661; 20 Skinner St; ⊙10am-4.30pm Mon, Tue & Thu-Sat) in Whitby, or Trailways (☑01947-820207; www.trailways.info; Old Railway Station, Hawsker; ⊙9.30am-6pm) at Hawsker.

🎉 Festivals & Events

Whitby Goth Weekends   COUNTER CULTURE
(www.whitbygothweekend.co.uk; tickets £55) Goth heaven, with gigs, events and the Bizarre Bazaar – dozens of traders selling goth gear, jewellery, art and music. Held twice yearly on the last weekends of April and October.

Whitby Spring Session   MUSIC, ART
(www.moorandcoast.co.uk; tickets from £40) Beards, sandals and real ale abound at this traditional festival of folk music, dance and dubious Celtic art on the May Bank Holiday weekend.

🛏 Sleeping

B&Bs are concentrated in West Cliff in the streets to the south and east of Royal Cres. If a house here ain't offering B&B, the chances are it's derelict. Accommodation can be hard to find at festival times when it's wise to book ahead.

Whitby YHA   HOSTEL £
(☑0845 371 9049; www.yha.org.uk; Church Lane; dm/q £25/109; ⓟ@🛜) With an unbeatable position next to the abbey, this hostel is incredibly popular – you'll have to book well in advance to get your body into one of the bunks here. Hike up the 199 steps from the town, or take bus 97 from the train station to Whitby Abbey (twice hourly Monday to Saturday).

Harbour Grange   HOSTEL £
(☑01947-600817; www.whitbybackpackers.co.uk; Spital Bridge; dm from £18) Overlooking the harbour and less than 10 minutes' walk from the train station, this clean and basic hostel is conveniently located and has great views, but has an 11.30pm curfew – just the ticket for a night when you don't want to paint the town red.

★La Rosa Hotel   HOTEL ££
(☑01947-606981; www.larosa.co.uk/hotel; 5 East Tce; d £86-135; 🛜) 🗡 Weird, but wonderful. Lewis Carroll, author of *Alice in Wonderland*, once stayed in this house while holidaying in Whitby. And entering today is like stepping through the looking-glass into an antique world of love-it-or-hate-it Victorian bric-a-brac and kitsch. Eight quirky and atmospheric bedrooms (one with a wooden bath!), great sea views, no TVs, and breakfast served in a basket in your room.

Langley Hotel   B&B ££
(☑01947-604250; www.langleyhotel.com; 16 Royal Cres; s/d from £70/105; 🛜) With its cream-and-crimson colour scheme, and a gilt four-poster bed in one room, this grand old guesthouse exudes a whiff of Victorian splendour. Go for room 1 or 2, if possible, to make the most of the panoramic views – the same as those enjoyed in 1897 by Bram Stoker, who holidayed a few doors along at No 6.

Shepherd's Purse   GUESTHOUSE ££
(☑01947-820228; www.theshepherdspurse.com; 95 Church St; r £60-75) This place combines

---

DRACULA IN WHITBY

The famous story of *Dracula*, inspiration for a thousand lurid horror movies, was written by Bram Stoker while holidaying in Whitby in 1897 (a blue plaque at 6 Royal Cres marks the house where he stayed). Although most Hollywood versions of the tale concentrate on deepest, darkest Transylvania, a large part of the original book was set in Whitby, and many of the sites can still be seen today.

The tourist office sells a *Dracula Trail* leaflet (£1), which will direct you to the Bram Stoker memorial seat on Khyber Pass. From here, you can see all the Whitby-based settings used in the novel.

a beads-and-baubles boutique and wholefood shop with guest accommodation in the courtyard at the back. The cheaper rooms share a bathroom and are perfectly adequate, but we recommend the rustic en suite bedrooms; while the four-poster beds feel a bit as though they've been shoehorned in, the atmosphere is cute rather than cramped. Breakfast is not provided.

Trailways SELF-CATERING **££**
(☑ 01947-820207; www.trailways.info; Hawsker; per week high season £699; ℗) If travelling on the North Yorkshire Moors Railway has given you a taste for trains, how about sleeping in one? Trailways has a beautifully converted InterCity 125 coach parked at the old Hawsker train station on the Whitby–Scarborough cycle route, offering luxurious self-catering accommodation with all mod cons for two to six people.

Rosslyn House B&B **££**
(☑ 01947-604086; www.rosslynhousewhitby.co.uk; 11 Abbey Tce; s/d from £65/75; ☎) Bright and cheerful with a friendly welcome.

Bramblewick B&B **££**
(☑ 01947-604504; www.bramblewickwhitby.com; 3 Havelock Pl; s/d £35/78; ℗ ☎) Friendly owners, hearty breakfasts and abbey views from the top-floor room.

Argyle House B&B **££**
(☑ 01947-602733; www.argyle-house.co.uk; 18 Hudson St; per person £37-43; ☎) ✐ It's as comfortable as old slippers, and serves kippers for breakfast.

★ **Marine Hotel** INN **£££**
(☑ 01947-605022; www.the-marine-hotel.co.uk; 13 Marine Pde; r £135-150; ☎) Feeling more like mini-suites than ordinary hotel accommodation, the four bedrooms at the Marine are quirky, stylish and comfortable; it's the sort of place that makes you want to stay in rather than go out. Ask for one of the two rooms with a balcony – they have great views across the harbour.

✖ Eating & Drinking

Humble Pie 'n' Mash BRITISH **£**
(www.humblepienmash.com; 163 Church St; mains £6; ☺ noon-8pm Mon-Sat, to 4pm Sun) Superb homemade pies with fillings ranging from lamb, leek and rosemary to roast veg and goats cheese, served in a cosy timber-framed cottage.

Java Cafe-Bar CAFE **£**
(2 Flowergate; mains £5-8; ☺ 8am-6pm; ☎) A cool little diner with stainless-steel counters and retro decor, music videos on the flatscreen and a menu of healthy salads, sandwiches and wraps washed down with excellent coffee.

★ **Green's** SEAFOOD **££**
(☑ 01947-600284; www.greensofwhitby.com; 13 Bridge St; mains £10-20; ☺ noon-2pm & 6-9pm Mon-Fri, noon-10pm Sat & Sun) ✐ The classiest eatery in town is ideally situated to take its pick of the fish and shellfish freshly landed at the harbour. Grab a hearty lunch in the ground-floor bistro (mussels and chips, sausage and mash, fish and chips), or head to the upstairs restaurant for a sophisticated dinner date. Two-course lunch for £10 Monday to Friday.

Moon & Sixpence BRASSERIE **££**
(☑ 01947-604416; www.moon-and-sixpence.co.uk; 5 Marine Pde; mains £10-20; ☺ 9am-midnight; ☎) ✐ This brasserie and cocktail bar has a prime position, with views across the harbour to the abbey ruins. The seafood-dominated menu concentrates on hearty, straightforward dishes such as chunky vegetable soup, seafood chowder, fish pie, homemade burgers, and mussels and chips. Good breakfasts, too, including local kippers with brown bread and butter.

Magpie Cafe SEAFOOD **££**
(www.magpiecafe.co.uk; 14 Pier Rd; mains £7-23; ☺ 11.30am-9pm; ⏶) ✐ The Magpie flaunts its reputation for serving the 'World's Best Fish and Chips'. Damn fine they are, too, but the world and his dog knows about it and summertime queues can stretch along the street. Takeaway fish and chips cost £4.95; the sit-down restaurant is more expensive, but offers a wide range of seafood dishes, from grilled sea bass to paella.

Quayside FISH & CHIPS **££**
(www.quaysidewhitby.co.uk; 7 Pier Rd; mains £10-14; ☺ 11am-7pm Sun-Thu, to 8pm Fri & Sat; ⏶) Top-notch fish and chips minus the 'world's best' tag line – this place is your best bet if you want to avoid queues. Takeaway fish and chips are £4.40.

Station Inn PUB
(www.stationinnwhitby.co.uk; New Quay Rd; ☺ 10am-midnight Mon-Sat, to 11.30pm Sun; ☎) The best place in town for atmosphere

and real ale, with its impressive range of cask-conditioned beers including Timothy Taylor's Golden Best and Ossett Silver King. Live music Wednesday, Friday, Saturday and Sunday.

Duke of York PUB
(www.dukeofyork.co.uk; Church St; ⊘11am-11pm Sun-Thu, to midnight Fri, to 1am Sat; 🛜) A popular watering hole at the bottom of the Church Stairs, serving Timothy Taylor ales and great views over the harbour.

ⓘ Information

Post Office (Langbourne Rd; ⊘8.30am-5.30pm Mon-Sat) Located inside the Co-op supermarket.

Whitby Tourist Office (📞 01947-602674; www.visitwhitby.com; Langbourne Rd; ⊘9.30am-6pm Apr-Oct, to 4.30pm Nov-Mar)

ⓘ Getting There & Away

Bus Buses 93 and X93 run south to Scarborough (£5.60, one hour, every 30 minutes), with every second bus going via Robin Hood's Bay (£3.90, 15 minutes, hourly); and north to Middlesbrough (£5.60, one hour, hourly), with fewer services on Sunday. The Coastliner service 840 runs from Leeds to Whitby (£13, 3¼ hours, six times daily Monday to Saturday) via York and Pickering.

Train Coming from the north, you can get to Whitby by train along the Esk Valley Railway from Middlesbrough (£6, 1½ hours, four per day), with connections from Durham and Newcastle. From the south, it's easier to get a train from York to Scarborough, and then a bus from Scarborough to Whitby.

Robin Hood's Bay

Picturesque **Robin Hood's Bay** (www.robin-hoods-bay.co.uk) is the end point of the Coast to Coast Walk (p491). It has nothing to do with the hero of Sherwood Forest – the origin of its name is a mystery, and the locals call it Bay Town or just Bay. But there's no denying that this fishing village is one of the prettiest spots on the Yorkshire coast.

Leave your car at the parking area in the upper village (£3.50 for four hours), where 19th-century ships' captains built comfortable Victorian villas, and walk downhill to Old Bay, the oldest part of the village (don't even think about driving down). This maze of narrow lanes and passages is dotted with

WORTH A TRIP

GOATHLAND

This picture-postcard halt on the North Yorkshire Moors Railway (p514) stars as Hogsmeade train station in the Harry Potter films, and the village appears as Aidensfield in the British TV series *Heartbeat*. It's also the starting point for lots of easy and enjoyable walks, often with the chuff-chuff-chuff of passing steam engines in the background.

One of the most popular hikes is to head northwest from the station (via a gate on the platform on the far side from the village) to the hamlet of Beck Hole, where you can stop for a pork pie and a pint of Black Sheep at the wonderfully atmospheric **Birch Hall Inn** (www.beckhole.info; ⊘11am-11pm mid-Apr–mid Sep, shorter hours & closed Tue mid-Sep–mid-Apr), where it's like stepping into the past. Return to Goathland via the waterfall at **Mallyan Spout** (total 4 miles).

An alternative to the hike is to walk or cycle from Goathland along Beck Hole Rd (just over 1 mile); it's best not to drive, as the road is narrow and twisty and there's nowhere to park.

tearooms, pubs, craft shops and artists' studios (there's even a tiny cinema) and at low tide you can go down onto the beach and fossick around in the rock pools. The NT-listed **Old Coastguard Station** (www.nationaltrust.org.uk; The Dock; ⊘10am-5pm Apr-Oct, to 4pm Sat & Sun Nov-Mar) FREE houses an exhibition about local geology and natural history.

There are several pubs and cafes. The best pub for ambience and real ale is **Ye Dolphin** (King St; ⊘11.30am-11pm), while the **Swell Cafe** (www.swell.org.uk; Chapel St; mains £3-8; ⊘10am-4pm Mon-Fri, to 4.30pm Sat & Sun; 🛜♿) does great coffee and has a terrace with a view over the beach.

Robin Hood's Bay is 6 miles southeast of Whitby. You can walk here along the coastal path in two or three hours, or bike to it along the cycle trail in 40 minutes. Bus 93 runs hourly between Whitby and Scarborough via Robin Hood's Bay – the bus stop is at the top of the hill, in the new part of town.

YORKSHIRE DALES NATIONAL PARK

The Yorkshire Dales – named from the old Norse word *dalr,* meaning 'valleys' – is the central jewel in the necklace of three national parks strung across the neck of northern England, with the dramatic fells of the Lake District to the west and the brooding heaths of the North York Moors to the east.

From well-known names such as Wensleydale and Ribblesdale to the obscure and evocative Langstrothdale and Arkengarthdale, the park's glacial valleys are characterised by a distinctive landscape of high heather moorland, stepped skylines and flat-topped hills. Down in the green valleys, patchworked with drystone dykes and little barns, are picture-postcard villages where sheep and cattle still graze on village greens. And in the limestone country of the southern Dales you'll find England's best examples of karst scenery (a landscape created by rainwater dissolving the underlying limestone bedrock).

The Dales have been protected as a national park since the 1950s, assuring their status as a walker's and cyclist's paradise. But there's plenty for nonwalkers as well, from exploring the legacy of literary vet James Herriot of *All Creatures Great and Small* fame to sampling the favourite teatime snack of the British TV characters Wallace and Gromit at the Wensleydale Creamery.

The *Visitor* newspaper, available from tourist offices, lists local events and walks guided by park rangers, as well as many places to stay and eat. The official park website (www.yorkshiredales.org.uk) is also useful.

ℹ Getting There & Around

About 90% of visitors to the park arrive by car, and the narrow roads can become extremely crowded in summer. Parking can also be a serious problem. If you can, try to use public transport as much as possible.

Yorkshire Dales National Park

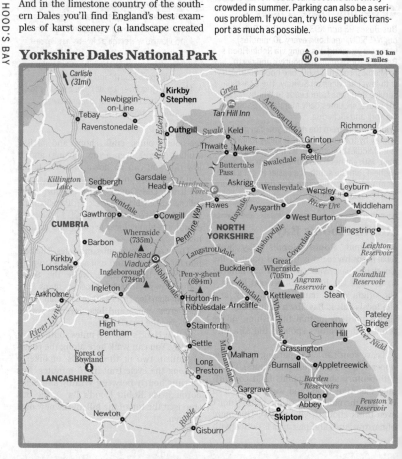

Pick up a DalesBus Timetable from tourist offices, or consult the **DalesBus** (www.dalesbus.org) website.

By train, the best and most interesting access to the Dales is via the famous Settle–Carlisle Line (p525). Trains run between Leeds and Carlisle, stopping at Skipton, Settle and numerous small villages, offering unrivalled access to the hills straight from the station platform.

Skipton

POP 14,625

This busy market town on the southern edge of the Dales takes its name from the Anglo-Saxon *sceape ton* (sheep town). There are no prizes for guessing how it made its money. Monday, Wednesday, Friday and Saturday are market days, bringing crowds from all over and giving the town something of a festive atmosphere. The tourist office (01756-792809; www.welcometoskipton.com; Town Hall, High St; 9.30am-4pm Mon-Sat, 10am-4pm 1st Sun of month) is in the town hall.

Sights & Activities

High Street STREET

Skipton's pride and joy is the broad and bustling High St, one of the most attractive shopping streets in Yorkshire. There's a general market on High St four days a week, and on the first Sunday of the month the nearby canal basin hosts the Northern Dales Farmers Market (www.northerndalesfarmersmarkets.com; 8.30am-2.30pm 1st Sun of month).

Skipton Castle CASTLE

(www.skiptoncastle.co.uk; High St; adult/child £7.30/4.50; 10am-6pm Mon-Sat, noon-6pm Sun Mar-Sep, to 4pm Oct-Feb) A gate to the side of the church at the north end of High St leads to Skipton Castle, one of the best-preserved medieval castles in England and a fascinating contrast to the ruins you'll see elsewhere.

Pennine Cruisers BOAT CRUISE

(www.penninecruisers.com; The Wharf, Coach St; per person £4; 10.30am-dusk Mar-Oct) No trip to Skipton is complete without a cruise along the Leeds–Liverpool Canal, which runs through the middle of town. Pennine Cruisers runs half-hour trips to Skipton Castle and back.

Sleeping

There's a strip of B&Bs just outside the centre on Keighley Rd.

OFF THE BEATEN TRACK

DELVE INTO THE DALES

Whether on two wheels or four, one of the joys of the Yorkshire Dales is exploring the hidden corners of the lesser known valleys. From Swaledale, climb up to the moors above Arkengarthdale in search of the Tan Hill Inn (01833-628246; www.tanhillinn.com; Tan Hill; 8am-11.30pm Jul & Aug, noon-9.30pm Sep-Jun;), Britain's highest pub, or seek out the picture-postcard village green at West Burton, at the entrance to Bishopdale. From Grassington, make your way north along lovely Littondale and stop for a pint at the Falcon Inn (www.thefalconinn.com; Arncliffe), where beer is still served from a jug on the counter.

Park Hill B&B ££

(01756-792772; www.parkhillskipton.co.uk; 17 Grassington Rd; d £80;) From the complimentary glass of sherry on arrival to the hearty breakfasts based on local produce, farm-fresh eggs and homegrown tomatoes, this B&B provides a real Yorkshire welcome. It enjoys an attractive rural location half a mile north of the town centre, on the B6265 road towards Grassington.

Carlton House B&B ££

(01756-700921; www.carltonhouseskipton.co.uk; 46 Keighley Rd; s/d from £30/60) A handsome house with five pretty and comfortable rooms – there are no frills, but lots of floral prints. This B&B is deservedly popular on account of its friendly welcome.

Eating & Drinking

Cafe 76 BRITISH £

(01756-795460; www.cafe76.co.uk; 76 High St; mains £4-8; 8.15am-4.30pm Mon, Wed, Fri & Sat, 9am-4.30pm Thu & Sun;) Squeezed into a tall and narrow building (best seats are upstairs), this popular local lunch spot serves hearty homemade food including roast chicken, cheese burgers, roast beef sandwiches, and daily specials such as minted lamb and vegetable pasty with onion gravy. Full English breakfast served all day.

Bizzie Lizzies FISH & CHIPS £

(www.bizzielizzies.co.uk; 36 Swadford St; mains £4-8; 11am-9pm;) An award-winning sit-down fish-and-chip restaurant overlooking the canal. There's also a takeaway counter offering fish and chips for £5; it's open until 11.30pm.

Bean Loved
CAFE £

(www.beanloved.co.uk; 17 Otley St; mains £5-9; ⏱7.30am-5pm Mon-Sat, 9am-5pm Sun; 🛜) This place just off High St serves the best coffee in town, along with good cakes and freshly prepared sandwiches.

Le Caveau
FRENCH ££

(☎01756-794274; www.lecaveau.co.uk; 86 High St; mains £13-20; ⏱noon-2pm & 7-9.30pm Tue-Fri, 5-10pm Sat) 🍴 Set in a stylishly decorated 16th-century cellar with barrel-vaulted ceilings, this friendly bistro offers a seasonal menu built lovingly around fresh local produce. Daily specials include dishes such as a light and flavourful quiche made with black pudding, bacon and mushrooms, and a succulent smoked haddock and leek pie. On weekdays you can get a two-course lunch for £11.

Narrow Boat
PUB

(www.markettowntaverns.co.uk; 38 Victoria St; ⏱noon-11pm) A traditionally styled pub with a great selection of local ales and foreign beers, friendly service and bar meals.

ⓘ Getting There & Away

Skipton is the last stop on the Metro rail network from Leeds and Bradford (£9.10, 45 minutes, half-hourly, hourly on Sunday). Three buses a day (weekdays only) link Skipton with Settle (£6, 40 minutes).

Grassington

The perfect base for jaunts around the south Dales, Grassington's handsome Georgian centre teems with walkers and visitors throughout the summer months, soaking up an atmosphere that – despite the odd touch of faux rusticity – is as attractive and traditional as you'll find in these parts.

Highlight of the year is the **Grassington Festival** (www.grassington-festival.org.uk), a two-week arts extravaganza held in June that attracts many big names in music, theatre and comedy, and also includes offbeat events like drystone-walling workshops.

The **tourist office** (☎01756-751690; Hebden Rd; ⏱10am-5pm Apr-Oct, Fri-Sun only Nov-Mar) is beside the big car park on the edge of town.

🍽 Sleeping & Eating

Ashfield House
B&B ££

(☎01756-752584; www.ashfieldhouse.co.uk; Summers Fold; r from £100; 🅿@🛜) A secluded 17th-century country house behind a walled garden, with exposed stone walls, open fireplaces and an all-round cosy feel. It's just off the main square.

★ Devonshire Fell
HOTEL £££

(☎01756-718111; www.devonshirefell.co.uk; Burnsall; r from £140; 🅿@🛜) A sister property to Bolton Abbey's Devonshire Arms Country House Hotel, this former gentleman's club for mill owners has a much more contemporary feel, with beautiful modern furnishings crafted by local experts. The conservatory (used as a lounge and breakfast room) has a stunning view over the valley. It's 3 miles southeast of Grassington on the B6160.

Whimsical Cottage
CAFE £

(☎01756-752414; 1 Garr's Lane; mains £4-9; ⏱10am-4pm; 🌱) This cute little white cottage, just uphill from the village square, serves good coffee and unusual homemade cakes (parsnip and apple sponge is unexpectedly delicious), as well as hot pies for lunch – chicken, ham and leek, or steak and Guinness. Breakfast served till 11.30am.

Malham
POP 120

Stretching west from Grassington to Ingleton is the largest area of limestone country in England, a distinctive landscape pockmarked with potholes, dry valleys, limestone pavements and gorges. Two of the most spectacular features – Malham Cove and Gordale Scar – lie near the pretty village of Malham.

The **national park centre** (☎01969-652380; www.yorkshiredales.org.uk; ⏱10am-5pm Apr-Oct, to 4pm Sat & Sun only Nov-Mar) at the southern edge of the village has the usual wealth of information. See also www.malhamdale.com.

⊙ Sights & Activities

A 0.75-mile walk north from Malham village leads to **Malham Cove**, a huge rock amphitheatre lined with 80m-high vertical cliffs. Peregrine falcons nest here in spring, when the Royal Society for the Protection of Birds (RSPB) sets up a birdwatching lookout. You can hike up the steep steps on the left-hand side of the cove (on the Pennine

Way footpath) to see the extensive limestone pavement above the cliffs. Another 1.5 miles further north is **Malham Tarn**, a glacial lake and nature reserve.

A mile east of Malham along a narrow road (with very limited parking) is spectacular **Gordale Scar**, a deep limestone canyon with scenic cascades and the remains of an Iron Age settlement. The national park centre has a leaflet describing the **Malham Landscape Trail**, a 5-mile circular walk that takes in Malham Cove, Gordale Scar and the Janet's Foss waterfall.

The Pennine Way (p491) passes through Malham, with Horton-in-Ribblesdale a day's hike away to the northwest.

🛏 Sleeping

Malham YHA HOSTEL £
(📞 0845 371 9529; www.yha.org.uk; dm/tw £22/49; 🅿) You will find this recently refurbished, purpose-built hostel in the village centre. The facilities are top-notch, including a restaurant, and young children are well catered for.

Beck Hall HOTEL ££
(📞 01729-830332; www.beckhallmalham.com; s/d from £45/65; 🅿 🛜) This rambling 17th-century country house on the edge of the village, a gurgling stream flowing through the garden, has 18 individually decorated rooms; we recommend the Green Room, with its old-style furnishings and antique four-poster bed.

ℹ Getting There & Away

There are between two and five buses a day (except Tuesday and Thursday) from Skipton to Malham (45 minutes), and the Malham Tarn Shuttle bus links Settle and Malham (25 minutes) four times daily on Sundays only, Easter to October. Check the DalesBus website or ask at Skipton tourist office for details.

Note that Malham is reached via narrow roads that can get very congested in summer, so leave your car at the national park centre and walk into the village.

Ribblesdale & the Three Peaks

Scenic Ribblesdale cuts through the southwestern corner of the Yorkshire Dales National Park, where the skyline is dominated by a trio of distinctive hills known as the **Three Peaks** – Whernside (735m), Ingleborough (724m) and Pen-y-ghent (694m).

Easily accessible via the Settle–Carlisle railway line, this is one of England's most popular areas for outdoor activities, attracting thousands of hikers, cyclists and cavers each weekend.

Settle

POP 3660

The busy market town of Settle, dominated by its grand neo-Gothic town hall, is the gateway to Ribblesdale and marks the beginning of the scenic part of the famous Settle–Carlisle railway line. Narrow cobbled streets lined with shops and pubs lead out from the central market square (Tuesday is market day), and the town offers plenty of accommodation options.

The **tourist office** (📞 01729-825192; Town Hall, Cheapside; ⊙ 9.30am-4pm Mon, Tue & Thu-Sat, to 1pm Wed) has maps and guidebooks.

Around the main square are several good cafes, including **Ye Olde Naked Man** (Market Pl; mains £4-8; ⊙ 9am-5pm Thu-Tue, to 4pm Wed; 🚼), formerly an undertaker's (look for the 'naked man' on the outside wall, dated 1663), which serves superb Yorkshire pudding with a choice of fillings.

Trains from Leeds heading to Carlisle stop at Settle station near the town centre (£12, one hour, eight daily). Those heading for Morecambe (on the west coast) stop at Giggleswick, about 1.5 miles outside town.

Horton-in-Ribblesdale

POP 560

A favourite with outdoor enthusiasts, the little village of Horton and its railway station is 5 miles north of Settle. Everything centres on the Pen-y-Ghent Cafe, which acts as the village tourist office, wet-weather retreat and hikers' information centre.

Horton is the starting point for climbing Pen-y-ghent and doing the **Three Peaks Walk**; it's also a stop on the Pennine Way. At the head of the valley, 5 miles north of Horton, is the spectacular 30m-high **Ribblehead Viaduct**, built in 1874 and, at 400m, the longest on the Settle–Carlisle Line (p525). You can hike there along the Pennine Way and travel back by train from Ribblehead station.

🛏 Sleeping & Eating

Horton is popular, so it's advisable to book accommodation in advance.

Golden Lion INN £

(☑ 01729-860206; www.goldenlionhotel.co.uk; s/d from £45/70, bunkhouse per person £12) The Golden Lion is a lively pub that offers comfortable B&B rooms, a 15-bed bunkhouse, and three public bars where you can tuck into a bit of grub washed down with a pint of hand-pulled ale.

Holme Farm Campsite CAMPSITE £

(☑ 01729-860281; Horton-in-Ribblesdale; tent sites per person £5, shower £1) A basic, no-frills campsite next door to the Golden Lion pub, much used by Pennine Way hikers.

Pen-y-Ghent Cafe CAFE £

(mains £3-6; ☺ 9am-5.30pm Mon & Wed-Fri, 8.30am-5pm Sat & Sun; ☑ ♠) A traditional cafe run by the same family since 1965, the Pen-y-Ghent fills walkers' fuel tanks with fried eggs and chips, homemade scones and pint-sized mugs of tea. It also sells maps, guidebooks and walking gear.

Hawes

POP 885

Hawes is the beating heart of Wensleydale, a thriving and picturesque market town (market day is Tuesday) that has the added attraction of its own waterfall in the village centre. On busy summer weekends, however, Hawes' narrow arteries can get seriously clogged with traffic. Leave the car in the parking area beside the national park centre (☑ 01969-666210; Station Yard; ☺ 10am-5pm Apr-Oct, limited hours Nov-Mar, closed Jan) at the eastern entrance to the village.

◉ Sights

Dales Countryside Museum MUSEUM

(☑ 01969-666210; Station Yard; adult/child £4, free; ☺ 10am-5pm, closed Jan; ℗) Sharing a building with the national park centre is the Dales Countryside Museum, a beautifully presented social history of the area that explains the forces shaping the landscape, from geology to lead mining to land enclosure.

Wensleydale Creamery MUSEUM

(www.wensleydale.co.uk; adult/child £2.50/1.50; ☺ 10am-4pm; ♠) This museum is devoted to the production of the animated TV characters Wallace and Gromit's favourite crumbly white cheese. You can visit the cheese museum, see cheesemakers in action in the viewing gallery, and then try-before-you-buy in the shop, which is free to enter.

Hardraw Force WATERFALL

About 1.5 miles north of Hawes is 30m-high Hardraw Force. It's the highest unbroken waterfall in England, but by international standards not really all that impressive (except after heavy rain). Access is through the Green Dragon Inn, which levies a £2 admission fee.

Sheepdog Demonstrations FARM

(www.sheepdogdemo.co.uk; adult/child £4/1; ☺ 6.30pm Thu May-Aug, 2.30pm Thu Sep; ℗) On Thursdays from May to September a local farmer gives demonstrations of working sheepdogs, held in a field 800m north of Hawes on the minor road towards Hardraw.

🛏 Sleeping & Eating

Bainbridge Ings
Caravan & Camp Site CAMPSITE £

(☑ 01969-667354; www.bainbridge-ings.co.uk; hikers & cyclists per person £6, site, car & 2 adults £15; 🚉🐾) An attractive site set around a spacious farmhouse in stone-walled fields about half a mile east of Hawes. Fresh-laid eggs are sold on-site.

Hawes YHA HOSTEL £

(☑ 0845 371 9120; www.yha.org.uk; Lancaster Tce; dm/tw £19.50/47) A modern place on the western edge of town, at the junction of the main A684 (Aysgarth Rd) and B6255, this is a family-friendly hostel with great views of Wensleydale.

Herriot's Guest House B&B ££

(☑ 01969-667536; www.herriotsinhawes.co.uk; Main St; d from £75; 🐾) A delightful guesthouse set in an old stone building close to the bridge by the waterfall, Herriot's has seven comfy en suite bedrooms set above an art gallery and coffee shop.

Green Dragon Inn INN ££

(☑ 01969-667392; www.greendragonhardraw.co.uk; Hardraw; B&B per person £35-50; 🐾) A fine old pub with flagstone floors, low timber beams, ancient oak furniture and Theak-ston's on draught. The Dragon serves up a tasty steak-and-ale pie and offers bunkhouse accommodation (per person £15), camping (per person £8) or B&B in plain but adequate rooms, as well as a pair of larger, more comfortable suites. One mile northwest of Hawes.

Cart House TEAROOM £

(☑ 01969-667691; Hardraw; mains £4-7; ⏱ 10am-5pm mid-Mar–Oct) This craft shop and tearoom offers a healthier diet of homemade soup, organic bread and a 'Fellman's Lunch' of Wensleydale cheese, pickle and salad. There's a basic campsite at the back (per person £7, including tent and car). One mile northwest of Hawes.

ℹ Getting There & Away

Buses 156 and 157 run from Hawes to Leyburn (50 minutes, four daily Monday to Saturday), where you can connect with buses to or from Richmond.

From Garsdale station on the Settle–Carlisle Line, bus 113 runs to Hawes (20 minutes, three daily Monday to Friday). On Sundays and bank holidays from April to October, bus 831 goes to Hawes from Ribblehead station (25 minutes, one daily). Check bus times with Traveline Yorkshire or a tourist office before using these routes.

THE SETTLE–CARLISLE LINE

The 72-mile Settle–Carlisle Line (SCL; www.settle-carlisle.co.uk), built between 1869 and 1875, offers one of England's most scenic railway journeys. The line's construction was one of the great engineering achievements of the Victorian era: 5000 labourers armed with picks and shovels built 325 bridges and 21 viaducts and blasted 14 tunnels in horrific conditions – nearly 200 of them died in the process. Trains run between Leeds and Carlisle via Settle about eight times per day.

The first section of the journey from Leeds is along the Aire Valley, stopping at Keighley, where the Keighley & Worth Valley Railway (p537) branches off to Haworth, Skipton (gateway to the southern Dales) and Settle. The train then labours up the valley beside the River Ribble, through Horton-in-Ribblesdale, across the spectacular Ribblehead Viaduct and then through Blea Moor Tunnel to reach remote Dent station, at 350m the highest main-line station in the country.

The line reaches its highest point (356m) at Ais Gill, where it leaves the Dales behind before easing down to Kirkby Stephen. The last halts are Appleby and Langwathby, just northeast of Penrith (a jumping-off point for the Lake District), before the train finally pulls into Carlisle.

The entire journey from Leeds to Carlisle takes two hours and 40 minutes and costs £28/34 for a single/day return. Various hop-on/hop-off passes are also available for one or three days. You can pick up a free SCL timetable – which includes a colour map of the line and brief details about places of interest – from most Yorkshire stations. For more information, contact National Rail Enquiries (www.nationalrail.co.uk) or see www.settle-carlisle.co.uk.

Richmond

POP 8415

The handsome market town of Richmond is one of England's best-kept secrets, perched on a rocky outcrop overlooking the River Swale and guarded by the ruins of a massive castle. A maze of cobbled streets radiates from the broad, sloping market square (market day is Saturday), lined with elegant Georgian buildings and photogenic stone cottages, with glimpses of the surrounding hills and dales peeking through the gaps.

In September/October the town hosts the **Richmond Walking & Book Festival** (www.booksandboots.org), 10 days of guided walks, talks, films and other events.

◉ Sights

Richmond Castle　　　　　CASTLE
(www.english-heritage.org.uk; Market Pl; adult/child £4.90/2.90; ⊙10am-6pm Apr-Sep, to 5pm Oct, to 4pm Sat & Sun only Nov-Mar) The impressive heap that is Richmond Castle, founded in 1070, was one of the first castles in England since Roman times to be built of stone. It's had many uses through the years, including a stint as a prison for conscientious objectors during WWI (there's a small and sobering exhibition about their part in the castle's history). The best part of a visit is the view from the top of the remarkably well-preserved 30m-high keep, which towers over the town.

Green Howards Museum　　　　MUSEUM
(www.greenhowards.org.uk; Trinity Church Sq; adult/child £4/2; ⊙10am-4.30pm Mon-Sat Feb-Dec, also 12.30-4.30pm Sun Apr-Oct) Military buffs will enjoy the three floors of this museum (recently reopened after a major revamp), which pays tribute to the famous Yorkshire regiment.

Richmondshire Museum　　　　MUSEUM
(www.richmondshiremuseum.org.uk; Ryder's Wynd; adult/child £3/free; ⊙10.30am-4pm Apr-Oct) The Richmondshire Museum is a delight, with local history exhibits including an early Yorkshire cave-dweller and displays about lead mining, which forever altered the Swaledale landscape a century ago. You can also see the original set that served as James Herriot's surgery in the TV series *All Creatures Great and Small*.

Georgian Theatre Royal　　HISTORIC BUILDING
(www.georgiantheatreroyal.co.uk; Victoria Rd; tour per person £3.50; ⊙tours hourly 10am-4pm Mon-Sat mid-Feb–mid-Nov) The Georgian Theatre

Royal, built in 1788, is the most complete Georgian playhouse in Britain. Tours include a look at the country's oldest surviving stage scenery, painted between 1818 and 1836.

🏃 Activities

Walkers can follow paths along the River Swale both upstream and downstream from the town. A longer option is to follow part of the famous long-distance Coast to Coast Walk (p491) all the way to Reeth (11 miles) and take the bus back (see www.dalesbus.info/richmond).

Cyclists can also follow Swaledale – as far as Reeth may be enough, while a trip along Arkengarthdale and then over the high wild moors to Kirkby Stephen via the Tan Hill Inn is a more serious (but very rewarding) 40-mile undertaking.

🛏 Sleeping

There's a batch of pleasant places to stay along Frenchgate, and a couple more on Pottergate (the road into town from the east).

Frenchgate Hotel　　　　HOTEL ££
(☎01748-822087; www.thefrenchgate.co.uk; 59-61 Frenchgate; s/d from £88/118; P) Nine elegant bedrooms occupy the upper floors of this converted Georgian town house, now a boutique hotel decorated with local art. The rooms have cool designer fittings that set off a period fireplace here, a Victorian roll-top bath there. Downstairs there's an excellent restaurant (three-course dinner £39) and a hospitable lounge with oak beams and an open fire.

Willance House　　　　B&B ££
(☎01748-824467; www.willancehouse.com; 24 Frenchgate; s/d £55/75; 🐾) This oak-beamed house, built in 1600, has three immaculate rooms (one with a four-poster bed) that combine old-fashioned charm and all mod cons.

66 Frenchgate　　　　B&B ££
(☎01748-823421; www.66frenchgate.co.uk; 66 Frenchgate; s/d/f £70/84/120; 🐾) Three of the six stylish bedrooms have superb river views.

★ Millgate House　　　　B&B £££
(☎01748-823571; www.millgatehouse.com; Market Pl; r £110-145; P @ 🐾) 🐾 Behind an unassuming grey door lies the unexpected pleasure of one of the most attractive guesthouses in England. While the house itself is a Georgian gem crammed with period details, it is overshadowed by the multi-award-winning garden at the back, which offers superb views

over the River Swale and the Cleveland Hills. If possible, book the Garden Suite.

✖ Eating & Drinking

Cross View Tearooms　　　　TEAROOM **£**
(www.crossviewtearooms.co.uk; 38 Market Pl; mains £5-8; ⊙9am-5.30pm; �ⓦ) ✎ So popular with locals that you might have to queue for a table at lunchtime, the Cross View is the place to go for a hearty breakfast, homemade cakes, a hot lunch, or just a nice cup of tea.

Barkers　　　　FISH & CHIPS **£**
(Trinity Church Sq; mains £6-10; ⊙11am-9.30pm) The best fish and chips in town, sit-down or takeaway.

Rustique　　　　FRENCH **££**
(☑01748-821565; www.rustiqueyork.co.uk; Chantry Wynd, Finkle St; mains £10-21; ⊙noon-9pm) Tucked away in an arcade, this cosy bistro has consistently impressed with its mastery of French country cooking, from *confit de canard* (duck slow roasted in its own fat) to *paupiette de poulet* (chicken breast stuffed with brie and sun-dried tomatoes). Booking is recommended.

Black Lion Hotel　　　　PUB
(www.blacklionhotelrichmond.co.uk; Finkle St; ⊙11am-11pm) Cosy bars, low beams and good beer and food.

Unicorn Inn　　　　PUB
(2 Newbiggin; ⊙10.30am-11pm Mon-Thu, to midnight Fri & Sat, to 10.30pm Sun) A determinedly old-fashioned free house, serving Theakston's and Old Speckled Hen.

❶ Information

The **tourist office** (☑01748-850549; www.richmond.org; 2 Queens Rd; ⊙10am-4pm Mon-Sat), in Calverts shop on the central traffic roundabout, has the usual maps and guides, plus several leaflets showing walks in town and the surrounding countryside.

❶ Getting There & Away

From Darlington (on the railway between London and Edinburgh), it's easy to reach Richmond on bus X26 or X27 (£4.50, 30 minutes, every half hour, hourly on Sunday). All buses stop in Market Pl.

On Sundays and bank holiday Mondays only, from May to October, the Northern Dalesman bus 830 runs from Richmond to Hawes (£6.25, 1½ hours, one daily) via Reeth, and continues on to Ribblehead and Ingleton (£8.90, two hours, one daily).

WEST YORKSHIRE

It was the tough and unforgiving textile industry that drove West Yorkshire's economy from the 18th century onward. The woollen mills, factories and canals built to transport raw materials and finished products defined much of the county's landscape. But that's all in the past, and recent years have seen the transformation of this once hard-bitten area into quite the picture postcard.

Leeds and Bradford, two adjoining cities so big they've virtually become one, are the perfect case in point. Though both were founded amid the dark satanic mills of the Industrial Revolution, both are undergoing radical redevelopment and reinvention, prettifying their town centres and trying to tempt the more adventurous tourist with a host of new museums, galleries, restaurants and bars.

Beyond the cities, West Yorkshire is a landscape of bleak moorland dissected by deep valleys dotted with old mill towns and villages. The relics of the wool and cloth industries are still visible in the rows of weavers' cottages and workers' houses built along ridges overlooking the towering chimneys of the mills in the valleys – landscapes that were so vividly described by the Brontë sisters, West Yorkshire's most renowned literary export and biggest tourist draw.

❶ Getting Around

The Metro is West Yorkshire's highly efficient train and bus network, centred on Leeds and Bradford – which are also the main gateways to the county. For transport information, contact **West Yorkshire Metro** (☑0113-245 7676; www.wymetro.com).

Day Rover tickets (£7.70) are good for one day's unlimited travel on Metro buses and trains after 9.30am on weekdays and all day at weekends. A range of additional Rover tickets covering buses and/or trains, plus heaps of useful Metro maps and timetables, are available from bus and train stations and most tourist offices in West Yorkshire.

Leeds

POP 751,500

One of the fastest-growing cities in the UK, Leeds is the glitzy embodiment of rediscovered northern self-confidence. More than a decade of redevelopment has seen the city centre transform from near-derelict mill town into a vision of 21st-century urban chic, with towering office blocks, glass-and-steel

Leeds

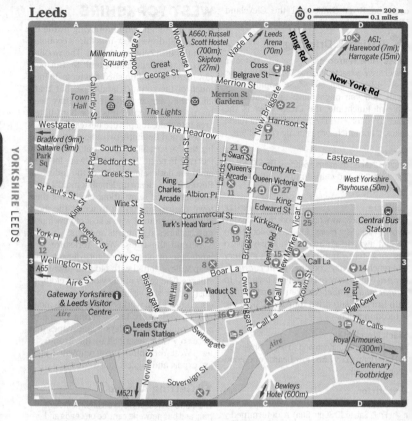

waterfront apartment complexes and renovated Victorian shopping arcades. The financial crisis of 2008–10 saw many flagship development projects grind to a halt, but tower cranes are beginning to sprout on the skyline again and a massive new entertainment venue, the Leeds Arena (www.firstdirectarena.com; Clay Pit Lane), opened in 2013.

Known as the 'Knightsbridge of the North', Leeds has made itself a shopping mecca, its streets lined with bustling malls sporting the top names in fashion. And when you've shopped till you've dropped, there's a plethora of pubs, clubs and excellent restaurants to relax in. From cutting-edge couture to contemporary cuisine, Leeds will serve it to you on a plate (or more likely in a stylishly designed bag). Amid all this fashion-conscious finery, it seems fitting that the network of city bus routes includes peach, mauve and magenta lines as well as the more humdrum red, orange and blue.

◉ Sights

Royal Armouries   MUSEUM

(www.royalarmouries.org; Armouries Dr; ◷10am–5pm; **P**▮) **FREE** Leeds' most interesting museum was originally built in 1996 to house armour and weapons from the Tower of London, but subsequently expanded to cover 3000 years' worth of combat and self-defence. It all sounds a bit macho, but the exhibits are as varied as they are fascinating, covering subjects as diverse as jousting and Indian elephant armour. To get here, walk east along the river from Centenary Footbridge (10 minutes), or take bus 28 from Albion St.

Leeds Industrial Museum   MUSEUM

(www.leeds.gov.uk/armleymills; Canal Rd; adult/child £3.60/1.80; ◷10am–5pm Tue–Sat, 1–5pm Sun; **P**▮) One of the world's largest textile mills has been transformed into a museum telling the story of Leeds' industrial past, both glorious and ignominious. The city grew rich

Leeds

from the textile industry, but at some cost in human terms – working conditions were Dickensian. As well as a selection of mill machinery, there's a particularly informative display about how cloth is made. The museum is 2 miles west of the city centre; take bus 5 from the train station.

Leeds Art Gallery GALLERY
(www.leeds.gov.uk/artgallery; The Headrow; ◷10am-5pm Mon, Tue & Thu-Sat, noon-5pm Wed, 1-5pm Sun) FREE The municipal gallery is packed with 19th- and 20th-century British heavyweights – Turner, Constable, Stanley Spencer, Wyndham Lewis et al – along with contemporary pieces by more recent arrivals such as Antony Gormley, sculptor of the *Angel of the North*.

Henry Moore Institute GALLERY
(www.henry-moore.org; The Headrow; ◷11am-5.30pm Tue & Thu-Sun, to 8pm Wed) FREE Housed in a converted Victorian warehouse in the city centre, this gallery showcases the work of 20th-century sculptors, but not, despite the name, anything by Henry Moore (1898–1986), who graduated from the Leeds School of Art. To see works by Moore, head to the Yorkshire Sculpture Park (p534).

🎪 Festivals & Events

Leeds Festival MUSIC
(www.leedsfestival.com) The August Bank Holiday (the weekend preceding the last Monday in August) sees 50,000-plus music fans converge on Bramham Park, 10 miles outside the city centre, for the Leeds Festival. Spread across four stages, it's one of Englands's biggest rock-music extravaganzas.

🛏 Sleeping

There are no budget options in the city centre, and the midrange choices here are either chain hotels or places we wouldn't recommend. If you want somewhere cheapish you'll be forced to head for the suburbs, where there are plenty of decent B&Bs and smallish hotels.

Russell Scott Hostel HOSTEL £
(✆0113-245 9046; www.rshostels.co.uk; 47a Well Close Rise, Woodhouse; dm £15; ☏) There's a reason there are no photos of this new hostel on its website – it's just an anonymous red-brick suburban semi on a council estate. But it's the only hostel in Leeds, and if you can find it, the facilities are fine and the location is quiet. It's 1.5 miles (a half-hour walk) north of the train station.

Roomzzz Leeds City APARTMENT ££
(✆0844 499 4888; www.roomzzz.co.uk; 10 Swinegate; 2-person apt from £82; @☏) This outfit offers bright and modern luxury apartments complete with fitted kitchen, with the added advantage of 24-hour hotel reception, and a great city centre location; a second branch, Roomzzz Leeds City West, is half a mile west on Burley Rd.

Headingley Lodge HOTEL ££
(✆0844 858 2858; www.headingleylodge.co.uk; Headingley Stadium, St Michael's Lane; d/f from £60/75; 𝗣☏) Smart, comfortable rooms

with views of Headingley cricket ground; part of the stadium complex.

Bewleys Hotel
HOTEL **££**

(☎ 0113-234 2340; www.bewleyshotels.com/leeds; City Walk, Sweet St; r from £68; P@🐾) Bewleys is super-convenient for motorists, just off Junction 3 on the M621, but also just 10 minutes' walk from the city centre and with secure basement parking. Rooms are stylish and well appointed, with soundproofed walls and windows. The flat rate accommodates up to two adults plus two children under 12.

★ Quebecs
BOUTIQUE HOTEL **£££**

(☎ 0113-244 8989; www.quebecshotel.co.uk; 9 Quebec St; d/ste from £110/300; @🐾) Victorian grace at its opulent best is the theme of our favourite hotel in town, a conversion of the former Leeds & County Liberal Club. The elaborate wood panelling and heraldic stained-glass windows in the public areas are matched by the contemporary design of the bedrooms. Booking online can get you a suite for as little as half the rack rate.

42 The Calls
BOUTIQUE HOTEL **£££**

(☎ 0113-244 0099; www.42thecalls.co.uk; 42 The Calls; r/ste from £150/280; @🐾) A snazzy boutique hotel in what was once a 19th-century grain mill overlooking the river, this place is a big hit with the trendy business crowd, who love its sharp, polished lines and designer aesthetic. The smaller 'study' rooms are pretty compact and breakfast is not included – it'll cost you an extra £15 for the full English.

✗ Eating

The Leeds restaurant scene is constantly evolving, with new places springing up in the wake of new shopping and residential developments.

Pickles & Potter
DELI, CAFE **£**

(www.picklesandpotter.co.uk; 18-20 Queens Arcade; mains £4-7; ⊙9am-5pm Mon-Fri, to 6pm Sat, 10.30am-5pm Sun; 🖉) 🐾 This rustic cafe is famous for its superb sandwiches, especially the sumptuous roast-beef version complete with mustard, onion marmalade and fresh salad. There's also homemade soup, delicious cakes and a meat or vegetarian main course of the day.

Hansa's Gujarati
INDIAN, VEGETARIAN **£**

(www.hansasrestaurant.com; 72-74 North St; mains £6-8; ⊙5-10pm Mon-Fri, 6-11pm Sat, noon-2pm Sun; 🖉🐾) A Leeds institution, Hansa's has been dishing up wholesome Gujarati vegetarian cuisine for almost 20 years. The restaurant is plain and unassuming (save for a Hindu shrine), but the food is exquisite – specialities of the house include *samosa chaat,* a mix of spiced potato and chickpea samosas with a yoghurt and tamarind sauce.

Dish
MODERN BRITISH **££**

(☎ 0113-318 2274; www.dishdining.co.uk; 19 Boar Lane; mains £11-22; ⊙5-10pm Tue-Sat, noon-2.30pm Fri & Sat; 🖉) 🐾 One of Yorkshire's best up-and-coming restaurants, Dish offers fine dining in an informal setting, while the menu takes an imaginative approach to the best of British and especially Yorkshire produce – the Yorkshire beef Wellington (£55 for two) is not to be missed. Unusually, vegetarians are not forgotten, with several gourmet options to choose from. Two-/three-course set menu £16.50/19.50.

Brasserie Blanc
FRENCH **££**

(☎ 0113-220 6060; www.brasserieblanc.com; Victoria Mill, Sovereign St; mains £10-20; ⊙noon-2.45pm & 5.30-10pm Mon-Fri, noon-10.30pm Sat, to 9pm Sun; 🖬) Raymond Blanc manages to create a surprisingly intimate and romantic space amid the cast-iron pillars and red brick of an old Victorian warehouse, with a scattering of outdoor tables for sunny lunchtimes beside the river. The menu is unerringly French, from *escargots* (edible snails) to Toulouse sausage. The lunch and pre-7pm menu (except Sunday) offers three courses for £14.

Art's Cafe Bar & Restaurant
INTERNATIONAL **££**

(www.artscafebar.co.uk; 42 Call Lane; mains £11-17; ⊙noon-11pm; 🐾) Local art on the walls and a bohemian vibe throughout make this a popular place for quiet reflection, a chat and a really good cup of coffee. The dinner menu offers a half-dozen classic dishes, while the early bird menu (pre-7pm, except Saturday) offers three courses for £15.

★ Crafthouse
MODERN BRITISH **£££**

(☎ 0113-897 0444; www.crafthouse-restaurant.com; Level 5, Trinity Leeds, 70 Boar Lane; mains £14-21; ⊙noon-3pm & 5-11pm Mon-Sat, noon-10pm Sun; 🐾) 🐾 This new rooftop restaurant makes a big impression, with cool grey and black decor and huge picture windows overlooking the neighbouring church tower. The food is similarly striking, with bold flavour combinations such as ham hock and dandelion salad or sea bream with fennel salad and sautéed beetroot. The three-course set menu (£22.50) is available lunchtimes and from 5pm to 6.30pm.

🍷 Drinking & Nightlife

Leeds is renowned for its selection of pubs and bars. Glammed-up hordes of party animals crawl the cluster of venues around Boar and Call Lanes, where bars are opening (and closing) all the time. Most bars open till 2am and many turn into clubs after 11pm or midnight.

The tremendous club scene attracts people from miles around. In true northern tradition, people brave the cold wearing next to nothing, even in winter, which is a spectacle in itself. Clubs charge a variety of admission prices, ranging from as little as £1 on a slow weeknight to £10 or more on Saturday. In order to make sense of the ever-evolving scene, check out **Leeds Guide** (www.leedsguide.co.uk). The tourist office provides a free *Gay Leeds* map and guide.

North Bar   BAR
(www.northbar.com; 24 New Briggate; ⊙ 11am-1am Mon & Tue, to 2am Wed-Sat, noon-midnight Sun; ⊚) There's a Continental feel to this long and narrow, minimalist bar, enhanced by the unfamiliar beer labels, from Dortmunder and Duvel to Schneider and Snake Dog. In fact, North is dedicated to the best of world beers, with more than a dozen ales on tap and scores more in bottles. Good selection of malt whisky, too.

Duck & Drake   PUB
(www.duckndrake.co.uk; 43 Kirkgate; ⊙ 10am-midnight Mon-Thu, to 1am Fri & Sat, 11am-midnight Sun; ⊚) A down-to-earth, traditional boozer with a well-worn atmosphere, a cast of regular characters, a pub piano, pork pie and mushy peas on the menu, and no fewer than 15 hand-pulled real ales to choose from. It also provides a stage for local rock and blues bands from Wednesday to Sunday nights.

Whitelocks   PUB
(www.whitelocksleeds.com; 6-8 Turk's Head Yard; ⊙ 11am-midnight Mon-Thu, to 1am Fri & Sat, to 11.30pm Sun; ⊚🍴🍽) There's lots of polished wood, gleaming brass and colourful stained glass in this popular traditional pub, which dates from 1715. Theakston's, Deuchars IPA and several other real ales are on tap, there's a log fire in winter, and in summer the crowds spill out into the courtyard.

Baby Jupiter   BAR
(www.babyjupiter.co.uk; 11 York Pl; ⊙ noon-midnight Mon-Wed, to 2am Thu & Fri, 5pm-2am Sat) A retro gem with lots of purple velvet, hanging fishbowls and images from old sci-fi films, this basement bar sports a cool soundtrack that ranges from indie, funk and soul to punk, new wave and electro.

Sandinista   COCKTAIL BAR
(www.sandinistaleeds.co.uk; 5/5a Cross Belgrave St; ⊙ 11am-3am Sun-Fri, 10am-4am Sat; ⊚) This laid-back bar has a Latin look, but a unifying theme, attracting an eclectic clientele with its mixed bag of music and unpretentious atmosphere. If you enjoy a well-mixed cocktail, but aren't too fussed about looking glam, this is the spot for you.

Bar Fibre   GAY
(www.barfibre.com; 168 Lower Briggate; ⊙ noon-1am Sun-Wed, to 3am Thu & Fri, to 4am Sat) Leeds' most popular gay bar, which spills out onto the cheekily named Queen's Court, is where the beautiful people congregate. There's another cluster of gay bars downhill at the junction of Lower Briggate and The Calls.

HiFi Club   CLUB
(www.thehificlub.co.uk; 2 Central Rd; ⊙ 11pm-3am Wed & Fri-Sun) This intimate club is a good break from the hardcore sound of electronic dance: if it's Tamla Motown or the percussive beats of dance-floor jazz that shake your booty, this is the spot for you.

Mission   CLUB
(www.clubmission.com; Viaduct St; ⊙ 11pm-4am Mon & Fri, to 6am Sat, 10pm-3.30am Thu) Fresh from a huge refit, this massive club redefines the term 'up for it'. Thursday sees the Full Moon Thai Beach Party student night, while Saturdays offer a range of house, dance and classic-anthem club nights, plus the Queer-Do gay club (11pm to 6am).

Wire   CLUB
(www.wireclub.co.uk; 2-8 Call Lane; ⊙ 10pm-3am) This small, atmospheric basement club, set in a forest of Victorian cast-iron pillars, throbs to a different beat every night, from rock and roll to drum and bass. Popular with local students.

☆ Entertainment

City Varieties   VARIETY
(www.cityvarieties.co.uk; Swan St) Founded in 1865, City Varieties is the world's longest running music hall, where the likes of Harry Houdini, Charlie Chaplin and Lily Langtry once trod the boards. Reopened after a major revamp, the program now features stand-up comedy, live music, pantomime and old-fashioned variety shows.

Grand Theatre & Opera House THEATRE, OPERA (www.leedsgrandtheatre.com; 46 New Briggate) Hosts musicals, plays and opera, including performances by the acclaimed Opera North (www.operanorth.co.uk).

West Yorkshire Playhouse THEATRE (www.wyp.org.uk; Quarry Hill Mount) The Playhouse has a reputation for excellent live drama, from the classics to cutting-edge new writing. It's on the eastern edge of the city centre.

🛍 Shopping

Leeds' city centre has so many shopping arcades they all seem to blend into one giant mall. The latest development, Trinity Leeds (www.trinityleeds.com; ⊙9am-8pm Mon-Sat, 11am-5pm Sun), opened in 2013, is the city's biggest, while the historic Corn Exchange (www.leedscornexchange.co.uk; ⊙10am-6pm Mon-Sat, 10.30am-4.30pm Sun; 🐾), with its dramatic wrought-iron dome, is reinventing itself as a home for designer boutiques and fashion markets.

Victoria Quarter MALL (www.v-q.co.uk) The mosaic-paved, stained-glass-roofed Victorian arcades of Victoria Quarter, between Briggate and Vicar Lane, are well worth visiting for aesthetic reasons alone. Dedicated shoppers can join the footballers' wives browsing boutiques by Louis Vuitton, Vivienne Westwood and Swarovski. The flagship store here, of course, is Harvey Nichols (www.harveynichols.com; 107-111 Briggate; ⊙10am-6pm Mon-Wed, to 8pm Thu, to 7pm Fri, 9am-7pm Sat, 10.30am-5pm Sun).

Leeds City Market MARKET (www.leedsmarket.com; Kirkgate; ⊙9am-5pm Mon, Tue & Thu-Sat, to 1pm Wed, open-air market Thu-Tue) Sitting at the opposite end of the retail spectrum to its flashy Victoria Quarter neighbour, this is Britain's largest covered market, selling fresh meat, fish and fruit and vegetables, as well as household goods. It was once the home of Michael Marks, who later joined forces with Spencer to become the retailing giant.

ℹ Information

Gateway Yorkshire & Leeds Visitor Centre (☎0113-242 5242; www.visitleeds.co.uk; The Arcade, Leeds City Train Station; ⊙10am-5.30pm Mon, 9am-5.30pm Tue-Sat, 10am-4pm Sun)

Post Office (St John's Centre, 116 Albion St; ⊙9am-5.30pm Mon-Sat)

ℹ Getting There & Away

Air Eleven miles northwest of the city via the A65, Leeds Bradford International Airport (www.leedsbradfordairport.co.uk) has flights to a range of domestic and international destinations. The Metroconnect 757 bus (£3.50, 40 minutes, every 30 minutes, hourly on Sunday) runs between Leeds bus station and the airport. A taxi costs about £20.

Bus National Express (www.nationalexpress.com) serves most major cities, including services from London (from £12, 4½ hours, hourly) and Manchester (from £5, 1¼ hours, every 30 minutes). Yorkshire Coastliner (www.coastliner.co.uk) buses run from Leeds to York (£6.20, 1¼ hours), Whitby (£13, 3¾ hours) and Scarborough (£12, three hours). A Freedom Ticket (£15) gives unlimited bus travel on all of these services for a day.

Train Leeds City Train Station has hourly services from London King's Cross (£90, 2½ hours), Sheffield (£14, one hour), Manchester (£16, one hour) and York (£13.50, 25 minutes, every 15 minutes). Leeds is also the starting point for trains on the famous Settle–Carlisle railway line (p525).

ℹ Getting Around

Leeds City Bus (www.wymetro.com; flat fare 50p) runs every few minutes from 6.30am to 7.30pm Monday to Saturday, linking the bus and train stations with all the main shopping areas in the city centre.

The various WY Metro DayRover passes covering trains and/or buses are good for reaching Bradford, Haworth and Hebden Bridge.

Bradford

Their suburbs may have merged into one sprawling urban conurbation, but Bradford remains far removed from its much more glamorous neighbour, Leeds. Thanks to its role as a major player in the wool trade, Bradford attracted large numbers of immigrants from Bangladesh and Pakistan during the 20th century. Despite occasional racial tensions, these new arrivals have helped reinvigorate the city and give it new energy (plus a reputation for superb curry restaurants). A high point of the year is the colourful Bradford Mela, now incorporated into the mid-June Bradford Festival (www.bradfordfestival.org.uk), a celebration of Asian music, dance, arts, crafts and food.

Bradford is on the Metro train line from Leeds (£3.60, 20 minutes, three or four per hour).

⊙ Sights

★ National Media Museum   MUSEUM
(www.nationalmediamuseum.org.uk; off Little Horton Lane; ⊙10am-6pm) FREE Bradford's top attraction is the National Media Museum, an impressive glass-fronted building that chronicles the story of photography, film, TV, radio and the web from 19th-century cameras and early animation to digital technology and the psychology of advertising. There's lots of hands-on stuff, too. You can film yourself in a bedroom scene, pretend to be a TV newsreader, or play 1970s and '80s video games. The IMAX cinema (adult/child £11.50/9) here shows the usual combination of in-your-face nature films, space documentaries and 3D animations.

The museum looks out over City Park, Bradford's new central square, which is home to the Mirror Pool, the country's largest urban water feature.

✗ Eating

Bradford is famous for its curries – it was voted the UK's Curry Capital for three years running from 2011 to 2013 – so don't miss out on trying one of the city's hundred or so restaurants. A great help is the Bradford Curry Guide (www.visitbradford.com/explore/Bradford_Curry_Guide.aspx).

Kashmir   INDIAN £
(27 Morley St; mains £4-6; ⊙11am-3am; ✐) Bradford's oldest curry house has top tucker, served with no frills and no booze (although it is BYO). Whatever you do, go for a table upstairs, as the soul-destroying, windowless basement has all the character of a 1950s factory canteen. It's just around the corner from the National Media Museum.

Zouk Tea Bar   INDIAN ££
(www.zoukteabar.co.uk; 1312 Leeds Rd; mains £7-13; ⊙11am-midnight; 🛜✐💺) This modern and stylish cafe-restaurant staffed by chefs from Lahore serves everything from *chana puri* (curried chickpeas) for breakfast to legendary lamb Nihari (slow-cooked lamb with a thick and spicy sauce) for dinner.

Saltaire

A Victorian-era landmark, Saltaire was a model industrial village built in 1851 by philanthropic wool baron and teetotaller Titus Salt. The rows of neat, honey-coloured cottages – now a Unesco World Heritage Site –

overlook what was once the largest factory in the world.

The factory is now Salts Mill (www.saltsmill.org.uk; ⊙10am-5.30pm Mon-Fri, to 6pm Sat & Sun; P) FREE, a splendidly bright and airy building where the main attraction is a permanent exhibition of 1970s and '80s artworks by local boy David Hockney (1937–). In a fitting metaphor for the shift in the British economy from making things to selling them, this former engine of industry is now a shrine to retail therapy, with shops selling books, crafts and outdoor equipment, and a cafe and restaurant.

Saltaire's tourist office (📞01274-437942; www.saltairevillage.info; Salts Mill, Victoria Rd; ⊙10am-5pm Apr-Sep, to 4pm Oct-Mar) has maps of the village and provides information on local walks.

Saltaire is 9 miles west of Leeds city centre and 3 miles north of Bradford centre, and is easily reached by Metro rail from either.

National Coal Mining Museum for England

For close to three centuries, West and South Yorkshire were synonymous with coal production. The collieries shaped and scarred the landscape and entire villages grew up around the pits. The industry came to a shuddering halt in the 1980s, but the imprint of coal is still very much in evidence, even if there's only a handful of collieries left. One of these, the former Caphouse Colliery, is now this fascinating museum (www.ncm.org.uk; Overton, near Wakefield; ⊙10am-5pm, last tour 3.15pm; P💺) FREE, a superb testament to the inner workings of a coal mine.

The highlight of a visit is the underground tour (departing every 10 minutes): equipped with helmet and head-torch, you descend almost 140m in the 'cage', then follow subterranean passages to the coal seam where massive drilling machines now stand idle. Former miners work as guides and explain the detail – sometimes with a suitably authentic and almost impenetrable mix of local dialect (known in Yorkshire as 'Tyke') and technical terminology.

At ground level there are audiovisual displays, some fascinating memorabilia (including sketches by Henry Moore), and exhibits about trade unions, strikes and the wider mining communities – only a bit over-romanticised in parts. You can also stroll round the pit-pony stables (their equine inhabitants also now retired) or the slightly eerie bathhouse, unchanged since the miners scrubbed off the coal dust for the last time and emptied their lockers.

The museum is 10 miles south of Leeds on the A642 between Wakefield and Huddersfield, reached via Junction 40 on the M1. By public transport, take a train from Leeds to Wakefield (£3.30, 15 minutes, at least hourly), and then bus 232 towards Huddersfield (£3, 25 minutes, hourly).

Yorkshire Sculpture Park

One of England's most impressive collections (www.ysp.co.uk; Bretton Park, near Wakefield; admission free, 4hr parking £4; ☺ 10am-6pm Apr-Oct, to 5pm Nov-Mar; Ⓟ) of sculpture is scattered across the formidable 18th-century estate of Bretton Park, 200-odd hectares of lawns, fields and trees. A bit like the art world's equivalent of a safari park, the Yorkshire Sculpture Park showcases the work of dozens of sculptors both national and international. But the main focus of this outdoor gallery is the work of local kids Barbara Hepworth (1903–75), who was born in nearby Wakefield, and Henry Moore (1898–1986).

The rural setting is especially fitting for Moore's work, as the artist was hugely influenced by the outdoors and preferred his art to be sited in the landscape rather than indoors. Other highlights include pieces by Andy Goldsworthy and Eduardo Paolozzi, and Richard Hiorns' famous work *Seizure 2008/2013*, an apartment coated in blue copper sulphate crystals (open weekends only). There's also a program of temporary exhibitions and installations by visiting artists, plus a bookshop and cafe.

The park is 12 miles south of Leeds and 18 miles north of Sheffield, just off Junction 38 on the M1 motorway. If you're on public transport, take a train from Leeds to Wakefield (£3.30, 15 minutes, at least hourly), or from Sheffield to Barnsley (£3.80, 20 minutes, at least hourly), and then take bus 9, which runs between Wakefield and Barnsley via Bretton Park (£3, 30 minutes, hourly Monday to Saturday).

Hepworth Wakefield

West Yorkshire's standing in the international arts scene got a boost in 2011 when the Yorkshire Sculpture Park was joined by this award-winning gallery (☑ 01924-247360; www.hepworthwakefield.org; Gallery Walk, Wakefield; admission free, parking £4.50; ☺ 10am-5pm Tue-Sun; Ⓟ) of modern art, housed in a stunningly angular building on the banks of the River Calder. The gallery has been built around the works of Wakefield-born sculptor Barbara Hepworth, perhaps best known for her work *Single Form*, which graces the United Nations Headquarters in New York.

The gallery showcases more than a dozen Hepworth originals, as well as works by other 20th-century British artists including Ivon Hitchens, Paul Nash, Victor Pasmore, John Piper and Henry Moore. The Gott Collection of 19th-century art includes a 1793 painting of Wakefield Bridge and Chantry Chapel, which you can compare with the real thing by looking out the neighbouring window.

The gallery is near the centre of Wakefield, a 10-minute walk south of Wakefield Kirkgate train station, easily reached from Leeds (£3.30, minutes, at least hourly).

Hebden Bridge

POP 4235

Tucked tightly into a fold of a steep-sided valley, Yorkshire's funkiest little village is a former mill town that refused to go gently with the dying of industry's light. Instead, it raged a bit and then morphed into an attractive little tourist trap with a distinctly bohemian atmosphere. The town is home to university academics, artists, die-hard hippies and a substantial gay community. All of this explains the abundance of craft shops, organic cafes and secondhand bookstores.

◉ Sights

Alternative Technology Centre INTERPRETATION CENTRE

(www.alternativetechnology.org.uk; Hebble End Mill; ☺ 10am-5pm Mon-Fri, noon-5pm Sat, noon-4pm Sun) FREE From the town centre, a short stroll along the attractive waterfront of the Rochdale Canal leads to the Alternative Technology Centre, which promotes renewable energy, recycling and sustainable lifestyles through a series of intriguing exhibits and workshops.

Heptonstall VILLAGE

Above Hebden Bridge is the much older village of Heptonstall, its narrow cobbled street lined with 500-year-old cottages and the ruins of a beautiful 13th-century church. But it's the churchyard of the newer **St Thomas' Church** that draws literary pilgrims, for here is buried the poet Sylvia Plath (1932–63), wife of another famous poet, Ted Hughes (1930–98), who was born in nearby Mytholmroyd.

Gibson Mill   HISTORIC BUILDING
(www.nationaltrust.org.uk; adult/child £3.60/1.80; ⊙11am-4pm Tue-Thu, Sat & Sun Mar-Oct, to 3pm Sat & Sun Nov-Feb; P) ✎ This renovated 19th-century cotton mill houses a visitor centre with exhibitions covering the industrial and social history of the mill and its former workers.

🛏 Sleeping & Eating

Hebden Bridge Hostel   HOSTEL £
(☎01422-843183; www.hebdenbridgehostel.co.uk; Birchcliffe Centre, Birchcliffe Rd; dm/tw £20/55; ⊙Easter-early Nov; P 🐾) ✎ Just 10 minutes' walk uphill from the town centre, this hostel is set in a peaceful stone building, complete with sunny patio, tucked behind a former Baptist chapel (look for the green hostel signs). There's a cosy library, comfy and clean en suite rooms, and a vegetarian-food-only kitchen. The hostel is closed from 10.30am to 5pm daily.

Thorncliffe B&B   B&B ££
(☎01422-842163; Alexandra Rd; s/d £50/70; 🐾) This delightful Victorian house is perched on the hill above town, and the guest accommodation is perched at the top of the house – a spacious attic double with en suite and lovely views across the valley (there's a second double room, but without views and en suite). A continental, vegetarian breakfast is served in your room.

Mooch   CAFE £
(www.moochcafebar.co.uk; 24 Market St; mains £4-9; ⊙9am-8pm Mon-Thu, to 11pm Fri, 10am-11pm Sat, to 8pm Sun; 🐾✎) This chilled-out little cafe-bar exemplifies Hebden's alternative atmosphere, with a menu that includes a full-vegan breakfast, brie-and-grape ciabatta, and Mediterranean lunch platters of olives, hummus, stuffed vine leaves, tabouli and more. There's also Krombacher beer on draught, and excellent espresso.

Organic House   CAFE £
(www.organic-house.co.uk; 2 Market St; mains £6-13; ⊙9am-5pm Mon-Sat, 10am-5pm Sun; 🐾✎🍴) ✎ Practically everything on the menu at this busy local cafe is organic, locally produced or fair-trade, from the veggie breakfast to the *pâté du jour* (served with toast

and chutney). There are outdoor tables in the garden, and a shiatsu and reflexology studio upstairs.

★**Green's Vegetarian Café**   VEGETARIAN ££
(☎01422-843587; www.greensvegetariancafe.co.uk; Old Oxford House, Albert St; mains £11; ⊙11am-3pm Wed-Sun, 6.30-9pm Fri & Sat; ✎) ✎ One of Yorkshire's best vegetarian restaurants, Green's adopts a gourmet attitude towards veggie and vegan cuisine, serving dishes such as Sicilian *caponata* (aubergines, red pepper, celery, olives and capers) with spaghetti, and Thai green curry with chickpeas, squash and tofu. Best book a table to avoid disappointment, especially for dinner.

ℹ Information

Hebden Bridge Visitor & Canal Centre
(☎01422-843831; www.hebdenbridge.co.uk; Butlers Wharf, New Rd; ⊙10am-5pm mid-Mar–mid-Oct, shorter hours rest of year) Has a good stock of maps and leaflets on local walks, including a saunter to Hardcastle Crags, the local beauty spot, and the nearby NT-listed Gibson Mill.

ℹ Getting There & Away

Hebden Bridge is on the train line from Leeds (£5.30, 50 minutes, every 20 minutes Monday to Saturday, hourly on Sunday) to Manchester.

Haworth

POP 6380

It seems that only Shakespeare himself is held in higher esteem than the beloved Brontë sisters – Emily, Anne and Charlotte – judging by the 8 million visitors a year who trudge up the hill from the train station to pay their respects at the handsome parsonage where the literary classics *Jane Eyre* and *Wuthering Heights* were penned.

Not surprisingly, the whole village is given over to Brontë-linked tourism, but even without the literary associations Haworth is still worth a visit, though you'll be hard pushed not to be overwhelmed by the cottage industry that has grown up around the Brontës and their wonderful creations.

◉ Sights

Haworth Parish Church   CHURCH
(Church St; ⊙9am-5.30pm) Your first stop in Haworth should be the parish church, a lovely old place of worship built in the late 19th century on the site of the older

church that the Brontë sisters knew, which was demolished in 1879. In the surrounding churchyard, gravestones are covered in moss or pushed to one side by gnarled tree roots, giving the place a tremendous feeling of age.

Brontë Parsonage Museum MUSEUM
(www.bronte.info; Church St; adult/child £7.50/3.75; ⏱10am-5.30pm) Set in a pretty garden overlooking the church and graveyard, the house where the Brontë family lived from 1820 to 1861 is now a museum. The rooms are meticulously furnished and decorated exactly as they were in the Brontë era, including Charlotte's bedroom, her clothes and her writing paraphernalia. There's also an informative exhibition, which includes the fascinating miniature books the Brontës wrote as children.

🏃 Activities

Above Haworth stretch the bleak moors of the South Pennines – immediately familiar to Brontë fans – and the tourist office has leaflets on local walks to endless Brontë-related places. A 6.5-mile favourite leads to Top Withins, a ruined farm thought to have inspired *Wuthering Heights*, even though a plaque clearly states that the farmhouse bore no resemblance to the one Emily wrote about.

Other walks can be taken around the Brontë Way, a longer route linking Bradford and Colne via Haworth. Alternatively, you can walk or cycle the 8 miles south to Hebden Bridge via the scenic valley of Hardcastle Crags.

🛏 Sleeping & Eating

Virtually every second house on Main St offers B&B; they're mostly indistinguishable from each other, but some are just that little bit cuter. There are a couple of good restaurants in town, and many of the B&Bs have small cafes that are good for a spot of lunch.

Apothecary Guest House B&B £
(☎ 01535-643642; www.theapothecaryguesthouse.co.uk; 86 Main St; s/d £35/55; 🛜) Oak beams and narrow, slanted passageways lead to smallish rooms with cheerful decor.

Haworth YHA HOSTEL £
(☎ 0845 371 9520; www.yha.org.uk; Longlands Dr; dm/tw £18.50/47; 🅿 @) A big old house with a games room, lounge, cycle store and laundry. It's on the northeastern edge of town, off Lees Lane.

BAD-LUCK BRONTËS

The Reverend Patrick Brontë, his wife Maria and six children moved to Haworth Parsonage in 1820. Within four years Maria and the two eldest daughters had died from cancer and tuberculosis. This triple tragedy led the good reverend to keep his remaining family close to him, and for the next few years the children were home-schooled in a highly creative environment.

The children conjured up mythical heroes and fantasy lands, and produced miniature homemade books. It was an auspicious start, at least for the three girls, Charlotte, Emily and Anne. The lone boy, Branwell, was more of a painter, but lacked his sisters' drive and discipline. After a short stint as a professional artist, he ended up spending most of his days in the Black Bull pub, drunk and stoned on laudanum obtained across the street at Rose & Co Apothecary.

While the three sisters were setting the London literary world alight with the publication of three superb novels – *Jane Eyre, Wuthering Heights* and *Agnes Grey* – in one extraordinary year (1847), Branwell was fading quickly and died of tuberculosis in September 1848. The family was devastated, but things quickly got worse. Emily fell ill with tuberculosis soon after her brother's funeral; she never left the house again, and died on 19 December. Anne, who had also been sick, was next; Charlotte took her to Scarborough to seek a sea cure, but she died on 28 May 1849.

The remaining family never recovered. Despite her growing fame, Charlotte struggled with depression and never quite adapted to her high position in literary society. Despite her misgivings, she eventually married, but died in the early stages of pregnancy on 31 March 1855. All things considered, it's hardly surprising that poor old Patrick Brontë spent the remainder of his life going steadily insane.

Old Registry
B&B ££

(☎01535-646503; www.theoldregistryhaworth.co.uk; 2-4 Main St; r £75-120; 🛜) This place is a bit special. It's an elegantly rustic guesthouse where each of the carefully themed rooms has a four-poster bed, whirlpool bath or valley view. The Blue Heaven room is just that – at least for fans of Laura Ashley's delphinium blue.

Ye Sleeping House
B&B ££

(☎01535-546992; www.yesleepinghouse.co.uk; 8 Main St; s/d from £29/58; 🅿🛜) This welcoming B&B has a cosy, country-cottage atmosphere, with just three small rooms and two friendly resident cats.

Try to get the one en suite room, which can sleep a family of four and has great views over the valley.

Old White Lion Hotel
INN ££

(☎01535-642313; www.oldwhitelionhotel.com; West Lane; s/d from £70/98; 🅿🛜) Pub-style accommodation, comfortable if not spectacular – though some rooms have good views – above an oak-panelled pub and highly rated restaurant.

Cookhouse
CAFE, BISTRO £

(☎01535-958904; www.thecookhousehaworth.co.uk; Main St; mains £4-9; ⊙10am-5.30pm; 🛜🌐) A bright and breezy cafe that serves a bracing breakfast menu (till 11.45am) that includes eggs Benedict and bacon, cheese and onion hash, and mouth-watering lunch dishes such as bangers and mash with onion gravy, pulled pork sandwiches with barbecue sauce or toasted crumpets with Wensleydale cheese and chutney.

Cobbles & Clay
CAFE £

(www.cobblesandclay.co.uk; 60 Main St; mains £5-8; ⊙9am-5pm; 🌐🌐) This attractive, child-friendly cafe not only offers fair-trade coffee and healthy salads and snacks – Tuscan bean stew, or hummus with pita bread and raw veggie sticks – but also provides the opportunity to indulge in a bit of pottery painting.

Haworth Old Hall
PUB ££

(☎01535-642709; www.hawortholdhall.co.uk; Sun St; mains £10-15) A 16th-century pub serving real ale and decent food, with a glorious beer garden for alfresco drinking and dining. If you want to linger longer, two comfortable doubles cost from £60 each.

STEAM ENGINES & RAILWAY CHILDREN

The **Keighley & Worth Valley Railway** (www.kwvr.co.uk; adult/child return £11/5.50, Day Rover £15/7.50) runs steam and classic diesel engines between Keighley and Oxenhope via Haworth, of Brontë fame. It was here, in 1969, that the classic 1970 movie *The Railway Children* was shot: Mr Perks was station master at Oakworth, where the Edwardian look has been meticulously maintained. Trains operate about hourly at weekends all year, and in holiday periods they run hourly every day.

ℹ Information

Haworth Tourist Office (☎01535-642329; www.haworth-village.org.uk; 2-4 West Lane; ⊙9am-5.30pm) The tourist office has an excellent supply of information on the village, the surrounding area and, of course, the Brontës.

ℹ Getting There & Away

From Leeds, the easiest approach is via Keighley, which is on the Metro rail network. Bus 500 runs from Keighley bus station to Haworth (£2.10, 15 minutes, hourly) and continues to Todmorden and Hebden Bridge. However, the most interesting way to get from Keighley to Haworth is via the Keighley & Worth Valley Railway (see above).

SOUTH YORKSHIRE

What wool was to West Yorkshire, so steel was to South Yorkshire. A confluence of natural resources – coal, iron ore and ample water – made the region a crucible of the British iron and steel industries. From the 18th to the 20th centuries, the region was the industrial powerhouse of northern England.

Sheffield's and Rotherham's blast furnaces and the coal pits of Barnsley and Doncaster may have closed long ago, but the hulking reminders of that irrepressible Victorian dynamism remain, not only in the old steelworks and pit heads (some of which have been converted into museums and exhibition spaces), but also in the grand civic buildings that grace Sheffield's city centre, fitting testaments to the untrammelled ambitions of their 19th-century patrons.

Sheffield

POP 551,800

Steel is everywhere in Sheffield. Today, however, it's not the steel of the foundries, mills and forges that made the city's fortune, nor the canteens of cutlery that made 'Sheffield Steel' a household name, but the steel of scaffolding and cranes, of modern sculptures and supertrams, and of new steel-framed buildings rising against the skyline.

The steel industry that made the city famous is long since gone, but after many years of decline Sheffield is on the up again – like many of northern England's cities, it has grabbed the opportunities presented by urban renewal with both hands and is working hard to reinvent itself. The new economy is based on services, shopping and the 'knowledge industry' that flows from the city's universities.

◉ Sights

Since 2000 the city centre has been in the throes of a massive redevelopment that will continue into 2020 and beyond, so expect building sites and roadworks for several years to come.

Winter Gardens   GARDENS

(Surrey St; ⊙8am-6pm) Pride of place in Sheffield's city centre goes to this wonderfully ambitious public space with a soaring glass roof supported by graceful arches of laminated timber. The 21st-century architecture contrasts sharply with the Victorian town hall nearby, and is further enhanced by the Peace Gardens – complete with fountains, sculptures, and lawns full of lunching office workers whenever there's a bit of sun.

Millennium Gallery   GALLERY, MUSEUM

(www.museums-sheffield.org.uk; Arundel Gate; ⊙10am-5pm Mon-Sat, 11am-4pm Sun) FREE Sheffield's cultural revival is spearheaded by the Millennium Gallery, a collection of four galleries under one roof. Inside, the Ruskin Gallery houses an eclectic collection of paintings, drawings and manuscripts established and inspired by Victorian artist, writer, critic and philosopher John Ruskin, while the Metalwork Gallery charts the transformation of Sheffield's steel industry into craft and design – the 'Sheffield steel' stamp on locally made cutlery and tableware now has the cachet of designer chic.

Graves Gallery   GALLERY

(www.museums-sheffield.org.uk; Surrey St; ⊙10am-5pm Mon-Sat) This gallery has a neat and accessible display of British and European modern art. The big names represented include Cézanne, Gaugin, Miró, Klee and Picasso.

Abbeydale Industrial Hamlet   MUSEUM

(www.simt.co.uk; Abbeydale Rd S; adult/child £4/free; ⊙10am-4pm Mon-Thu, 11am-4.45pm Sun; 🅿🖼) In the days before steel mills, metalworking was a cottage industry (just like wool and cotton). For a glimpse of that earlier, more innocent era, explore the restored 18th-century forges, workshops and machines at the Abbeydale Industrial Hamlet, 4 miles southwest of the centre on the A621 (towards the Peak District).

🛌 Sleeping & Eating

Tourism has not quite taken off in Sheffield, and most of the city-centre hotels cater primarily to business travellers. New restaurants are springing up, but the main restaurant areas are outside the centre.

There's a mile-long strip of bars, restaurants, cafes and takeaways on Ecclesall Rd, a mile to the southwest of the city centre, while London Rd, a mile south of the central city, has a concentration of good-value ethnic restaurants ranging from Turkish to Thai. To find student bars and eateries, head along Division St and Devonshire St just west of the city centre.

Leopold Hotel   BOUTIQUE HOTEL ££

(📋0845 078 0067; www.leopoldhotel.co.uk; 2 Leopold St; r from £65; 🕾) Housed in a former grammar school building, Sheffield's first boutique hotel brings some much-needed style and sophistication to the city's accommodation scene (but without a London-sized price tag). Rooms can suffer late-night noise from the bars on Leopold Sq – ask for a quiet room at the back.

Houseboat Hotels   HOUSEBOAT ££

(📋01909-569393; www.houseboathotels.com; Victoria Quays, Wharfe St; s/d/q from £79/99/159; 🅿) Here's something a bit different: kick off your shoes and relax on board your very own permanently moored houseboat, complete with self-catering kitchen and patio area. Guests are entitled to use the gym and pool facilities at the Hilton across the road.

Marmaduke's CAFE £

(www.marmadukescafedeli.co.uk; 22a Norfolk Row; mains £6-9; ⊙ 9am-5pm Mon-Sat, 10am-4pm Sun; 🖥️🞄) 🍴 This appealingly cramped and chaotic cafe, crammed with recycled furniture and run by a young and enthusiastic crew, serves an imaginative breakfast menu (until 11.30am) that includes corn fritters with avocado salsa, and lunch dishes that range from deli sandwiches and quiche to vegetarian specials. Cash only.

Blue Moon Cafe VEGETARIAN £

(2 St James St; mains £6-7; ⊙ 8am-8pm Mon-Sat; 🞄) A Sheffield institution offering tasty veggie and vegan creations, soups and other healthy dishes, all served with the ubiquitous salad, in a very pleasant atmosphere – perfect for a spot of Saturday afternoon lounging.

★ **Vero Gusto** ITALIAN ££

(🞄 0114-276 0004; www.gustosheffield.com; 12 Norfolk Row; mains £9-25; ⊙ 4-10pm Tue-Sat; 🖥️) Gusto is a *real* Italian restaurant, from the Italian owners serving homemade Italian food to the genuine Italian coffee enjoyed by Italian customers reading Italian newspapers...you get the idea. Coffee and home-baked Italian cakes and pastries are served in the late afternoon, plus a dinner menu of exquisite Italian cuisine. It's best to book for dinner.

🛈 Information

Post Office (Norfolk St; ⊙ 8.30am-5.30pm Mon-Fri, to 3pm Sat)

Sheffield Tourist Office (🞄 0114-221 1900; www.welcometosheffield.co.uk; Winter Gardens, Surrey St; ⊙ 9.30am-5pm Mon-Fri, to 4pm Sat, closed 1-1.30pm)

🛈 Getting There & Away

For all travel-related info for Sheffield and South Yorkshire, contact **Travel South Yorkshire** (🞄 01709-515151; www.travelsouthyorkshire.com).

Bus The bus station, called the Interchange, is just east of the centre, about 250m north of the train station. National Express services link Sheffield with most major centres in the north. There are frequent buses to Leeds (£4.50, one hour, hourly), Manchester (£8.60, 1½ hours, four daily) and London (£14, four hours, four daily).

Train Sheffield is served by trains from all directions: Leeds (£12, one hour, twice hourly); London St Pancras (£65, 2½ hours, hourly) via Derby or Nottingham; Manchester (£14, one hour, twice hourly); and York (£15, 1¼ hours, twice hourly).

EAST RIDING OF YORKSHIRE

The rolling farmland of the East Riding of Yorkshire meets the sea at Hull itself, a no-nonsense port that looks to the North Sea and the broad horizons of the Humber estuary for its livelihood. Just to its north, and in complete contrast to Hull's salt and grit, is Beverley, the East Riding's most attractive town, with lots of Georgian character and one of England's finest churches.

Hull

POP 284,320

Properly known as Kingston-upon-Hull – the ancient harbour on the River Hull was granted a royal charter in 1299 and became King's Town – Hull has long been the principal port of England's east coast, with an economy that grew up around carrying wool out and bringing wine in. It was also a major whaling and fishing port until the trawling industry died out.

Though it's not going to win any prizes for prettiness, the city has a gritty appeal for those who appreciate Britain's industrial past and enjoy getting away from the beaten tourist path. Famous as the home of poet Philip Larkin, Hull harbours a clutch of fascinating museums and one of Britain's best aquariums. Named as UK City of Culture 2017, the town has set about the regeneration of its waterfront.

A minor cultural renaissance has taken place in the Fruitmarket district around Humber St, where derelict buildings have been reclaimed as artists' studios and performance spaces, but progress is slow.

👁 Sights & Activities

Deep AQUARIUM

(www.thedeep.co.uk; Tower St; adult/child £11.50/9.50; ⊙ 10am-6pm, last entry 5pm; 🅿️♿) Hull's biggest tourist attraction is the Deep, a vast aquarium housed in a colossal angular building that appears to lunge above the muddy waters of the Humber like a giant shark's head. Inside, it's just as dramatic, with echoing commentaries and computer-generated interactive displays that guide you through the formation of the oceans and the evolution of sea life.

The largest aquarium is 10m deep, filled with sharks, stingrays and colourful coral fishes, with moray eels draped over rocks like scarves of iridescent slime. A glass elevator plies up and down inside the tank, though you'll get a better view by taking the stairs. Don't miss the cafe on the top floor, which has a great view of the Humber estuary.

Streetlife Museum   MUSEUM
(www.hullcc.gov.uk/museums; ⊙10am-5pm Mon-Sat, 1.30-4.30pm Sun) **FREE** This fascinating museum contains re-created street scenes from Georgian and Victorian times and from the 1930s, with all sorts of historic vehicles to explore, from stagecoaches to bicycles, buses and trams.

Hull & East Riding Museum   MUSEUM
(www.hullcc.gov.uk/museums; ⊙10am-5pm Mon-Sat, 1.30-4.30pm Sun) **FREE** This museum traces local history and archaeology from Roman times to the present, with new Anglo-Saxon, medieval and geology galleries.

Arctic Corsair   HISTORIC SHIP
(www.hullcc.gov.uk/museums; ⊙10am-4.30pm Wed & Sat, 1.30-4.30pm Sun Apr-Oct) **FREE** Behind the Streetlife Museum, marooned in the mud of the River Hull, is the Arctic Corsair. Tours of this Atlantic trawler, a veteran of the 1970s so-called 'Cod Wars', when the UK and Iceland clashed over fishing rights, demonstrate the hardships of fishing north of the Arctic Circle.

Spurn Lightship   MUSEUM
(Castle St; ⊙1.30-4pm Sun late Jun-mid Sep) **FREE** Built in 1927, Hull's lighthouse-ship once served as a navigation mark for ships entering the notorious Humber estuary. Now safely retired in the marina, it houses an engaging exhibition about its own history, and offers an interesting contrast between the former living quarters of captain and crew.

Old Town   NEIGHBOURHOOD
Hull's Old Town, whose grand public buildings retain a sense of the prosperity the town once knew, occupies the thumb of land between the River Hull to the east and Princes Quay to the west. The most impressive legacy is the Guildhall (Low Gate; ⊙8.30am-4.30pm Mon-Thu, to 3.30pm Fri) **FREE**, a huge neoclassical building that dates from 1916 and houses vast areas of polished marble, and oak and walnut panelling, plus the Hull Tapestry, which records the city's history (on view near reception).

Wilberforce House   MUSEUM
(www.hullcc.gov.uk/museums; High St; ⊙10am-5pm Mon-Sat, 1.30-4.30pm Sun) **FREE** Wilberforce House (1639) was the birthplace in 1759 of politician and antislavery crusader William Wilberforce. It is now a museum chronicling the slave trade and its abolition.

Larkin Trail   WALKING TOUR
(www.thelarkintrail.co.uk) Hull's most famous son, the poet Philip Larkin, is commemorated in this self-guided walking tour, which begins beside a bronze statue of the man himself in the railway station. It leads past places mentioned in his poetry, and on to some of his favourite pubs. Pick up a free leaflet at the tourist office.

🛏 Sleeping & Eating

Good accommodation in the city centre is pretty thin on the ground and is mostly business-oriented chain hotels and a few mediocre guesthouses. The tourist office will help book accommodation for free.

The best concentration of eating places is found around Dock St in the city centre, and along Princes Ave, from Welbeck St to Blenheim St, a mile northwest of the centre.

Kingston Theatre Hotel   HOTEL ££
(☏01482-225828; www.kingstontheatrehotel.com; 1-2 Kingston Sq; s/d/ste from £60/80/110; ☏) Overlooking leafy Kingston Sq, close to the New Theatre, this hotel is one of the best options in the city centre, with elegant bedrooms, friendly service and an excellent breakfast.

Fudge   CAFE, BRASSERIE ££
(☏01482-441019; www.fudgefood.com; 93 Princes Ave; mains £7-21; ⊙10.30am-2.30pm Tue-Thu & Sun, 9am-3pm Fri & Sat, 6-9pm Tue-Sun) This funky cafe decked out in pink and peppermint colours serves hearty breakfasts, cakes and coffee all day, but also offers a tempting brasserie menu at lunch and dinner, with dishes that include juicy burgers (beef or veggie), herby crab cakes and Portuguese fish stew.

Hitchcock's
Vegetarian Restaurant   VEGETARIAN ££
(☏01482-320233; www.hitchcocksrestaurant.co.uk; 1 Bishop Lane, High St; buffet £18; ⊙8-10.30pm Tue-Sat; 🗷) The word 'quirky' could have been invented to describe this place. It's an atmospheric maze of small rooms, with an all-you-can-eat vegetarian buffet whose theme – Thai, Indian, Spanish, whatever – is chosen by the first person to book that evening. But, hey, the food is excellent and the welcome is warm. Bookings required.

1884 Dock
Street Kitchen
MODERN BRITISH £££

(☎01482-222260; www.1884dockstreetkitchen.co.
uk; Humber Dock St; mains £17-32; ⊙noon-2pm
& 6-9.30pm Tue-Sat, noon-3pm Sun; 🛜) 🍴
Poster boy for the city's redeveloping waterfront, this big and bold enterprise tries
to blend British cuisine with a sepia-tinted,
late-19th-century New York steakhouse look,
and just about pulls it off. As well as the
steaks, the menu is strong on Scottish seafood, Yorkshire pork and Lancashire lamb,
and dishes dotted with wild garlic and duck
egg. Three-course set menu £22.

🍷 Drinking & Entertainment

Come nightfall – especially at weekends –
Hull can be raucous and often rowdy, especially in the streets around Trinity Sq
in the Old Town and on the strip of pubs
along Beverley Rd to the north of the city
centre.

Minerva
PUB

(Nelson St; ⊙11am-11pm Mon-Sat, noon-10.30pm
Sun) If you're more into pubbing than clubbing, try a pint of Black Sheep at this lovely
200-year-old pub down by the waterfront.
On a sunny day you can sit outdoors and
watch the ships go by.

Fruitspace
LIVE MUSIC, COMEDY

(☎01482-221113; www.fruitspace.co.uk; 62-63
Humber St) A focus for the cultural revival of
Hull's Fruitmarket district, this former industrial space is now a multipurpose venue
incorporating a bar, cinema and stage. There
are regular live gigs by local bands (and occasional big names), a monthly comedy club
and, on the third Sunday of the month, the
Humber Street Market.

Hull Truck Theatre
THEATRE, JAZZ

(www.hulltruck.co.uk; Spring St) Home to acclaimed playwright John Godber, who made
his name with the gritty comedies *Bounc-
ers* and *Up 'n' Under* (Godber is one of the
most-performed playwrights in the English-
speaking world), Hull Truck presents a lively
program of drama, comedy and Sunday jazz.
It's just northwest of the Old Town.

ℹ️ Information

Hull Tourist Office (☎0844-811 2070; www.
visithullandeastyorkshire.com; 1 Paragon St;
⊙10am-5pm Mon-Sat, 11am-3pm Sun)
Post Office (63 Market Pl; ⊙9am-5.30pm
Mon-Sat)

ℹ️ Getting There & Away

Boat The ferry port is 3 miles east of the centre
at King George Dock. A bus connects the train
station with the ferries. There are ferry services
to Zeebrugge and Rotterdam.

Bus There are buses direct from London (£26,
6½ hours, one daily), Leeds (£9, 1¾ hours,
hourly) and York (£6.90, 1¾ hours, six daily).

Train Hull has rail links north and south to
Newcastle (£40, 2½ hours, hourly, change at
York or Doncaster) and London Kings Cross
(£75, 2¾ hours, every two hours), and west to
York (£25, 1¼ hours, hourly) and Leeds (£15,
one hour, hourly).

Beverley

POP 30,590

Handsome, unspoilt Beverley is one of the
most attractive towns in Yorkshire, largely on
account of its magnificent minster – a rival to
any cathedral in England – and the tangle of
streets that lie beneath it, each brimming with
exquisite Georgian and Victorian buildings.

All the sights are a short walk from either
train or bus station. There's a large market
in the main square on Saturday, and a smaller one on Wednesday on the square called...
Wednesday Market.

◎ Sights

★ **Beverley Minster**
CHURCH

(www.beverleyminster.org; ⊙9am-4.45pm Mon-
Sat, noon-5.30pm Sun) One of the great glories
of English religious architecture, Beverley
Minster is the most impressive church in
the country that is not a cathedral. The soaring lines of the exterior are imposing, but it
is inside that the charm and beauty lie. The

YORKSHIRE BEVERLEY

WORTH A TRIP

PIPE & GLASS INN

Set in a picturesque hamlet 4 miles
northwest of Beverley, this charming
country pub (☎01430-810246; www.
pipeandglass.co.uk; West End, South Dalton;
mains £11-27; ⊙noon-2pm & 6.30-9.30pm
Tue-Fri, noon-11pm Sat, noon-4pm Sun;
🅿️🛜🍴♿) has held a Michelin star since
2010. The setting may be delightfully
informal, with weathered timber tables,
stone hearths and leather sofas, but a
great deal of care is lavished on the
food – even seemingly simple dishes
such as fish pie are unforgettable.

14th-century north aisle is lined with original stone carvings, mostly of musicians. Much of our knowledge of early musical instruments comes from these images. You'll also see goblins, devils and grotesque figures. Look out for the bagpipe player.

Construction began in 1220 – the third church to be built on this site, with the first dating from the 7th century – and continued for two centuries, spanning the Early English, Decorated and Perpendicular periods of the Gothic style.

Close to the altar, the elaborate and intricate Percy Canopy (1340), a decorative frill above the tomb of local aristocrat Lady Eleanor Percy, is a testament to the skill of the sculptor and the finest example of Gothic stone carving in England. In complete contrast, in the nearby chancel is the 10th-century Saxon frith stool, a plain and polished stone chair that once gave sanctuary to anyone escaping the law.

In the roof of the tower is a restored treadwheel crane, where workers ground around like hapless hamsters to lift the huge loads necessary to build a medieval church. Access to the roof is by guided tour only (per person £5).

St Mary's Church CHURCH
(⊘ 9.30am-4.30pm Mon-Fri, 10am-4pm Sat, 2-4pm Sun Apr-Sep, shorter hours Oct-Mar) Doomed to play second fiddle to Beverley Minster, St Mary's Church at the other end of town was built between 1120 and 1530. The west front (early 15th century) is considered one of the finest of any parish church in England. In the north choir aisle there is a carving (c 1330) of a rabbit dressed as a pilgrim, said to have inspired Lewis Carroll's White Rabbit.

🛏 Sleeping & Eating

Friary YHA HOSTEL £
(⊘ 0845 371 9004; www.yha.org.uk; Friar's Lane; dm/d £18.50/69; ℗) In Beverley, the cheapest accommodation also has the best setting and location. This hostel is housed in a beautifully restored 14th-century Dominican friary mentioned in Chaucer's *The Canterbury Tales*, and is only 100m from the minster and a short walk from the train station.

Kings Head INN ££
(⊘ 01482-868103; www.kingsheadpubbeverley.co.uk; 38 Saturday Market; s/d £70/80; @ 🤶) A Georgian coaching inn given a modern makeover, the Kings Head is a lively pub with 12 bright and cheerful rooms above the bar. The pub opens late on weekend nights, but earplugs are supplied for those who don't want to join the revelry!

Vanessa Delicafe CAFE ££
(⊘ 01482-868190; www.vanessadelicafe.co.uk; 21-22 Saturday Market; mains £7-15; ⊘ 9am-4.30pm Mon, Tue, Fri & Sat, to 9pm Wed & Thu, 10am-3.30pm Sun; 🤶 🖐) This popular cafe sits above a delicatessen, with sofas and bookshelves scattered among the tables, and window seats overlooking the market square. Settle down for cappuccino and cake with the Sunday papers, or tuck into hearty lunch and dinner specials such as homemade lasagne or venison burger.

Grant's Bistro 22 MODERN BRITISH £££
(⊘ 01482-887624; 22 North Bar Within; mains £16-25; ⊘ noon-2pm Fri & Sat, 6-9.30pm Mon-Sat) ✐ A great place for a romantic dinner *à deux*, with dark-wood tables, fresh flowers and candlelight. The menu makes the most of fresh local beef, game and especially seafood, with dishes such as pan-fried scallops with black pudding. A two-/three-course lunch is £15/20.

🛈 Information

Beverley Tourist Office (⊘ 01482-391672; www.beverley.gov.uk; 34 Butcher Row; ⊘ 9.30am-5.30pm Mon-Fri, to 4.30pm Sat year-round, also 10am-3.30pm Sun Apr-Sep)
Post Office (Register Sq; ⊘ 9am-5.30pm Mon-Fri, to 12.30pm Sat)

🛈 Getting There & Away

Bus There are frequent bus services from Hull, including numbers 121, 122, 246 and X46/X47 (£4.05, 30 minutes, every 20 minutes). Bus X46/X47 links Beverley with York (£6.45, 1¼ hours, hourly).
Train Trains run regularly to Scarborough (£13.70, 1¼ hours, every two hours) and Hull (£6.60, 15 minutes, twice hourly).

Manchester, Liverpool & Northwest England

Best Places to Eat

→ Australasia (p553)
→ Monro (p569)
→ Lime Tree (p553)
→ Upstairs at the Grill (p561)
→ Tanroagan (p576)

Best Places to Stay

→ Stone Villa (p560)
→ Great John Street Hotel (p553)
→ Hope Street Hotel (p568)
→ Malmaison (p553)
→ Richmond Hotel (p568)

Why Go?

If you're looking for clues as to what once made Britain great, you'll find plenty of them in the Northwest. Dominating the region is Manchester, a paradigm of reinvention that has transformed itself from 20th-century industrial hulk into a modern city with accompanying distractions – from football to fine food. Nearby Liverpool has plenty of its own diversions including a fine collection of galleries and museums, terrific shopping and a sporting pedigree every bit as impressive as that of its neighbour across the Pennines. Within easy reach of both is Chester, a historic postcard to its Tudor past and beyond, to when it was the Roman Castra Devana. And, for a bit of respite from humankind's concrete pawprint, some of Britain's most beautiful – and walkable – countryside can be found in northern Lancashire and on the Isle of Man.

When to Go

→ The world's most famous steeplechase – the Aintree Grand National – is run just outside Liverpool over the first weekend in April.

→ May and June are Tourist Trophy (TT) Festival season on the Isle of Man – beloved of motor enthusiasts the world over.

→ In the arts, the highlight is the Manchester International Festival, a biennial showstopper held in July.

→ Music buffs should visit Liverpool in the last week of August for madness at Creamfields dance-fest and for the Mathew St Festival, an ode to all things Beatles.

→ The football (soccer) season runs from late August until May.

Manchester, Liverpool & Northwest England Highlights

1 Learning a valuable history lesson at Liverpool's **International Slavery Museum** (p566)

2 Having your insides churned at Blackpool's **Pleasure Beach** (p571)

3 Learning exactly what kind of hell war is in the **Imperial War Museum North** (p551) in Manchester

4 Tramping Chester's **City Walls** (p559) like the Romans did 2000 years ago

5 Sampling Manchester's culinary delights at one (or more!) of its superb **restaurants** (p553)

6 Getting to grips

with wild, exciting **Isle of Man** (p575)

7 Going for a rural constitutional in the **Ribble Valley** (p573)

🏃 Activities

Walking & Cycling

In between the urban bits, the northwest is surprisingly good for walking and cycling options, notably in northern Lancashire's Ribble Valley, home to plenty of good walks including the 70-mile Ribble Way. The historic village of Whalley, in the heart of the Ribble Valley, is the meeting point of the two circular routes that make up the 260-mile Lancashire Cycle Way.

The Isle of Man has top-notch walking and cycling opportunities. Regional tourism websites contain walking and cycling information, and tourist offices stock free leaflets as well as maps and guides (usually £1 to £5) that cover walking, cycling and other activities.

Boating

Explore the historic Peak Forest Canal between Manchester and the Peak District on the Wandering Duck (www.wanderingduck. co.uk; 2-night trip per person incl meals from £145), a combined budget hostel and boat tour.

ℹ️ Information

Visit England's Northwest (www.visitnorthwest.com) is the centralised tourist authority; for the Isle of Man, check out the main **Isle of Man Public Services** (www.gov.im) site.

ℹ️ Getting Around

The towns and cities covered are all within easy reach of each other, and are well linked by public transport. The two main cities, Manchester and Liverpool, are only 34 miles apart and are linked by hourly bus and train services. Chester is 18 miles south of Liverpool, but is also easily accessible from Manchester by train or via the M56. Blackpool is 50 miles to the north of Manchester and Liverpool, and is also well connected.

Transport for Greater Manchester (www. tfgm.com) Extensive info on Manchester and its environs.

Merseytravel (www.merseytravel.gov.uk) Taking care of all travel in the county of Merseyside, including Liverpool.

National Express (www.nationalexpress.com) Extensive coach services in the northwest; Manchester and Liverpool are major hubs.

MANCHESTER

POP 503,100

Raised on lofty ambition and not afraid to declare its considerable bona fides, Manchester is – by dint of geography and history – England's second city (apologies to Birmingham), although if you were to ask a Mancunian what it's like to be second they might reply, 'Don't know, ask a Londoner'.

Even accounting for northern bluster, the uncrowned capital of the north is well deserving of the title. It has a rich history and culture, easily explored in its myriad museums and galleries. And while history and heritage make the city interesting, its dis-

MANCHESTER IN...

Two Days

Explore the **Museum of Science & Industry** (p547) and visit the **People's History Museum** (p547) to get a sense of Manchester's huge historical influence. For food, try **Oast House** (p554) or go for afternoon tea in the **Rosylee Tearooms** (p553) before stopping by one of the bars in the Northern Quarter.

On day two, take the Metrolink to Salford and explore the **Imperial War Museum North** (p551), the **Lowry** (p551) and the **Manchester United Museum at Old Trafford** (p551). Take a tour of the BBC spread at **MediaCityUK** (p552). Back in the city, indulge some retail *chi* at the high-end shops of **Spinningfields** (p557) or the offbeat boutiques of the **Northern Quarter** (p554). Treat yourself with dinner at **Australasia** (p553).

Four Days

Follow the two-day itinerary and tackle some of the city's lesser-known museums like the **John Rylands Library** (p550) and examine the riches of the **Manchester Art Gallery** (p550). End the day with a gig at one of the city's excellent **live music venues** (p556). The next day, take a walking tour – the tourist office has details of a whole host of themed ones – and if you're serious about clubbing, make the pilgrimage to Ancoats for the absolutely fabulous **Sankey's** (p555).

tractions of pure pleasure make Manchester fun: you can dine, drink and dance yourself into happy oblivion in the swirl of hedonism that is one of Manchester's most cherished characteristics.

History

Canals and steam-powered cotton mills were what transformed Manchester from a small disease-infested provincial town into a big disease-infested industrial city. It all happened in the 1760s, with the opening of the Bridgewater Canal between Manchester and the coal mines at Worsley in 1763, and with Richard Arkwright patenting his super cotton mill in 1769. Thereafter Manchester and the world would never be the same again. When the canal was extended to Liverpool and the open sea in 1776, Manchester – dubbed 'Cottonopolis' – kicked into high gear and took off on the coal-fuelled, steam-powered gravy train.

There was plenty of gravy to go around, but the good burghers of 19th-century Manchester made sure that the vast majority of the city's swollen citizenry (with a population of 90,000 in 1801, and two million 100 years later) who produced most of it never got their hands on any of it. Their reward was life in a new kind of urban settlement: the industrial slum. Working conditions were dire, with impossibly long hours, child labour, work-related accidents and fatalities commonplace. Mark Twain commented that he would like to live here because the 'transition between Manchester and Death would be unnoticeable'. So much for Victorian values.

The wheels started to come off towards the end of the 19th century. The USA had begun to flex its own industrial muscles and was taking over a sizeable chunk of the textile trade; production in Manchester's mills began to slow, and then it stopped altogether. By WWII there was hardly enough cotton produced in the city to make a tablecloth. The postwar years weren't much better: 150,000 manufacturing jobs were lost between 1961 and 1983, and the port – still the UK's third largest in 1963 – finally closed in 1982 due to declining traffic. The nadir came on 15 June 1996, when an IRA bomb wrecked a chunk of the city centre, but the subsequent reconstruction proved to be the beginning of the glass-and-chrome revolution so much in evidence today.

◉ Sights & Activities

◉ City Centre

⭐**Museum of Science & Industry**   MUSEUM
(MOSI; ☑0161-832 2244; www.msim.org.uk; Liverpool Rd; charges vary for special exhibitions; ⊙10am-5pm) **FREE** If there's anything you want to know about the Industrial (and post-Industrial) Revolution and Manchester's key role in it, you'll find the answers here among this collection of steam engines and locomotives, factory machinery from the mills, and the excellent exhibition telling the story of Manchester from the sewers up.

It's an all-ages kind of museum, but the emphasis is on making sure the young 'uns don't get bored – they could easily spend a whole day poking about this 'urban heritage park', testing an early electric-shock machine here and trying out a printing press there. A unifying theme is that Manchester and Mancunians had a key role to play: this is the place to discover that Manchester was home to the world's first stored-program computer (a giant contraption nicknamed 'baby') in 1948 and that the world's first submarine was built to the designs of local curate Reverend George Garrett in 1880.

⭐**People's History Museum**   MUSEUM
(☑0161-838 9190; www.phm.org.uk; Left Bank, Bridge St; ⊙10am-5pm) **FREE** The story of Britain's 200-year march to democracy is told in all its pain and pathos at this superb museum, housed in a refurbished Edwardian pumping station. You clock in on the 1st floor (literally: punch your card in an old mill clock, which managers would infamously fiddle with so as to make employees work longer) and plunge into the heart of Britain's struggle for basic democratic rights, labour reform and fair pay.

Amid displays like the (tiny) desk at which Thomas Paine (1737–1809) wrote *Rights of Man* (1791), and an array of beautifully made and colourful union banners, are compelling interactive displays, including a screen where you can trace the effects of all the events covered in the museum on five generations of the same family. The 2nd floor takes up the struggle for equal rights from WWII to the current day, touching on gay rights, antiracism initiatives and the defining British sociopolitical landmarks of the last 50 years, including the founding of the National Health Service (NHS), the Miners' Strike and the widespread protests against the Poll Tax.

Manchester

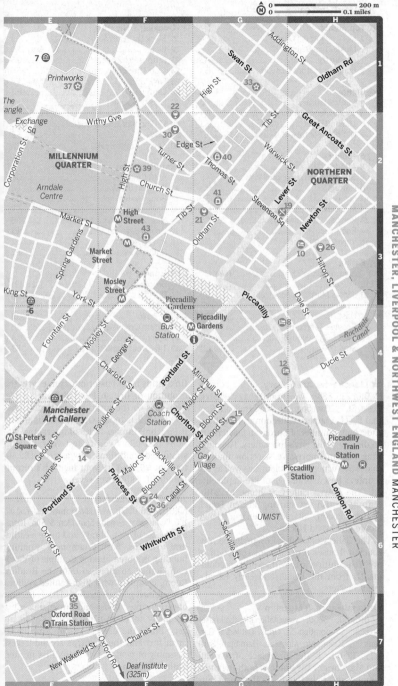

MANCHESTER, LIVERPOOL & NORTHWEST ENGLAND MANCHESTER

0 200 m
0 0.1 miles

Addington St
Swan St
33
Oldham Rd
Great Ancoats St
High St
Printworks
37
The angle
Exchange Sq
Corporation St
Withy Gve
MILLENNIUM QUARTER
Arndale Centre
22
30
Edge St
40
Thomas St
Turner St
Church St
High St
39
Tib St
Warwick St
NORTHERN QUARTER
Lever St
Stevenson Sq
19
41
Newton St
Market St
Spring Gardens
High Street
43
Tib St
21
Oldham St
10
26
Hilton St
Market Street
York St
Mosley Street
Piccadilly Gardens
Piccadilly
Dale St
8
Rochdale Canal
King St
6
Fountain St
Mosley St
Piccadilly Gardens
Bus Station
Ducie St
12
Portland St
Minshull St
Major St
Piccadilly Train Station
George St
Charlotte St
Coach Station
Chorlton St
Bloom St
15
Piccadilly Station
Manchester Art Gallery
1
Faulkner St
CHINATOWN
Richmond St
Gay Village
St Peter's Square
George St
14
Major St
Sackville St
Bloom St
Canal St
London Rd
St James St
Princess St
24
36
UMIST
Portland St
Oxford St
Whitworth St
Sackville St
35
Oxford Road Train Station
27
25
New Wakefield St
Oxford Rd
Charles St
Deaf Institute (325m)

Manchester

★ **Manchester Art Gallery**   GALLERY
(☎0161-235 8888; www.manchestergalleries.org;
Mosley St; ⊙10am-5pm Mon-Wed & Fri-Sun, to 9pm
Thu) **FREE** A superb collection of British art
and a hefty number of European masters are
on display at the city's top gallery. The older
wing has an impressive selection that includes 37 Turner watercolours, as well as the
country's best assemblage of Pre-Raphaelite
art. The newer gallery is home to 20th-
century British art starring Lucien Freud,
Francis Bacon, Stanley Spencer, Henry
Moore and David Hockney.

The Gallery of Craft & Design, in the Ath-
enaeum, houses a permanent collection of
pre-17th-century art, with works predominantly from the Dutch and early Renaissance masters.

National Football Museum   MUSEUM
(☎0161-605 8200; www.nationalfootballmuse-
um.com; Corporation St, Urbis, Cathedral Gardens; ⊙10am-5pm Mon-Sat, 11am-5pm Sun)
FREE Britain is the birthplace of football
and Manchester the home of both the most
popular and richest clubs in the world. Fittingly, this blockbuster museum charts the
evolution of British football from its earliest days to the multi-billion pound phenomenon it is today. One of the highlights
is Football Plus, a series of interactive stations that allow you to test your skills in
simulated conditions; buy a credit (£2.50,
four for £9) and try your luck – it's recommended for kids over seven.

John Rylands Library   LIBRARY
(☎0161-306 0555; www.library.manchester.ac.uk;
150 Deansgate; ⊙noon-5pm Mon & Sun, 10am-
5pm Tue-Sat) Less a library and more a cathedral to books, Basil Champneys' stunning
building is a breathtaking example of Victorian Gothic, no more so than the Reading
Room, complete with high-vaulted ceilings
and stained-glass windows. The collection
of early printed books and rare manuscripts
is equally impressive, and includes a Gutenberg Bible, the earliest extant New Testament text and the country's second-largest
assembly of works by Britain's first printer,
William Caxton.

◉ Salford Quays

Just west of the city centre lies Salford Quays, home to some of Manchester's big-ticket attractions and the new hub of the BBC's northern HQ. It is easily reached via Metrolink (£2). Check out www.thequays.co.uk for more info.

Imperial War Museum North   MUSEUM
(☏ 0161-836 4000; www.iwm.org.uk/north; Trafford Wharf Rd; ◷10am-5pm; 🚇Harbour City, MediaCityUK) **FREE** War museums generally appeal to those with a fascination for military hardware and battle strategy (toy soldiers optional), but Daniel Libeskind's visually stunning Imperial War Museum North takes a radically different approach. War is hell, it tells us, but it's a hell we revisit with tragic regularity.

The exhibits cover the main conflicts of the 20th century through a broad selection of displays, including regular screenings of the Big Picture Show, which include three permanent 15-minute films (*Children and War, The War at Home* or *Weapons of War*) and other topical ones, including (in 2014) *Al-Mutanabbi Street: A Reaction*, about a 2007 street bombing in Baghdad.

Although the audiovisuals and displays are quite compelling, the extraordinary aluminium-clad building itself is a huge part of the attraction, and the exhibition spaces are genuinely breathtaking.

Old Trafford (Manchester United Museum & Tour)   STADIUM
(☏ 0161-868 8000; www.manutd.com; Sir Matt Busby Way; tours adult/child £18/12; ◷museum 9.30am-5pm, tours every 10min except match days 9.40am-4.30pm; 🚇Old Trafford) You don't have to be a fan of the world's most famous football club to enjoy a visit to their impressive 75,000-plus capacity stadium, but it helps. The museum tour includes a walk down the tunnel onto the edge of the playing surface of the 'Theatre of Dreams', where Manchester United's superstar footballers exercised their Premier League supremacy for 20 years, guided by the peerless Sir Alex Ferguson.

Fergie retired in 2013 and the team's fortunes dipped accordingly; the success of their cross-town rivals Manchester City (league winners in 2012 and 2014) puts added pressure on United to reclaim the top spot, and the appointment of Dutchman Louis Van Gaal as manager in 2014 (replacing the hapless David Moyes, Fergie's successor) is a measure of their intent.

Other highlights of the excellent tour include a seat in the stands, a stop in the changing rooms and a peek at the players' lounge (from which the manager is banned unless invited by the players) – all ecstatic experiences for a Man United devotee. The museum has a comprehensive history of the club and a state-of-the-art call-up system that means you can view your favourite goals.

Lowry   ARTS CENTRE
(☏ 0161-876 2020; www.thelowry.com; Pier 8, Salford Quays; ◷11am-6pm Sun-Fri, 10am-8pm Sat; 🚇Harbour City, MediaCity UK) Looking more like a shiny steel ship than an arts centre, the Lowry is the quays' most notable success. With multiple performance spaces, bars, restaurants and shops, it attracts more than a million visitors a year to its myriad functions, which include everthing from big-name theatrical productions to comedy, kids' theatre and even weddings. The centre is also home to 300 beautifully humanistic

---

MORE NOTABLE BUILDINGS

Demonstrating a vibrant medley of architectural styles, Manchester has no shortage of eye-catching buildings dating from the 19th century (when the city was flush with industrial wealth). Keep an eye out for these showstoppers on your travels.

Town Hall (☏ 0161-234 5000; www.manchester.gov.uk; Albert Sq) The Victorian town hall is Manchester's most impressive building. It is crowned by an 85m-high tower and features an especially ornate interior.

Central Library (☏ 0161-234 1900; www.manchester.gov.uk; St Peter's Sq) Built in 1934 to resemble the Roman Pantheon, this is Britain's largest municipal library. It reopened in late 2014 after a two-year restoration.

Midland Bank (100 King St) The year 1935 saw the opening of Edwin Lutyens' stunning art-deco Midland Bank, now home to a branch of Jamie's Italian (p554) – even if you don't eat there it's well worth having a look inside; be sure to go downstairs and peek in at the deposit vaults.

depictions of urban landscapes by LS Lowry (1887–1976), who was born in nearby Stretford, and after whom the complex is named.

MediaCityUK
MEDIA CENTRE

(☑ 0161-886 5300; www.mediacityuk.co.uk; Salford Quays; adult/child £10/6.50; ☺ tours 10.30am, 12.30pm & 3pm Mon-Wed, Sat & Sun; ⌕ MediaCity UK) The BBC's northern home is but one significant element of this vast, 81-hectare site. Besides hosting six departments of the national broadcaster (BBC Breakfast, Children's, Sport, Radio 5 Live, Learning, and Future Media & Technology), it is also home to the set of the world's longest-running soap opera, the perennially popular *Coronation Street* (which broadcasts on ITV).

There are no plans as yet to offer tours of the Corrie set, but you can visit the BBC's impressive set-up and see the sets of some of TV's most iconic programs on a guided 90-minute tour that also includes a chance for kids to 'make' a program in an interactive studio; see www.bbc.co.uk/shows andtours. For refuelling, there are plenty of cafes and restaurants in the area.

☞ Tours

The tourist office (p557) sells tickets for guided walks on all aspects of the city, from architecture to radical history, which operate almost daily year-round and cost £7/6 per adult/child.

✺ Festivals & Events

Screenfields
FILM

(www.spinningfieldsonline.com; Spinningfields; admission £3; ☺ 8pm Thu May-Jul) Summer season of outdoor films, complete with deckchairs and picnics beginning in May.

Manchester Day
ARTS, PARADE

(www.themanchesterdayparade.co.uk) A day to celebrate all things Manchester: art, music and performances, including a parade through the city centre.

Manchester International Festival
ARTS

(☑ 0161-238 7300; www.mif.co.uk) A three-week-long biennial arts festival of new work across visual arts, performance and popular culture. The next festival is scheduled for July 2015.

Manchester Pride
GAY & LESBIAN

(☑ 0161-831 7700; www.manchesterpride.com) One of England's biggest celebrations of gay, lesbian, bisexual and transgender life, held over 10 days in late August.

Manchester Food & Drink Festival
FOOD

(www.foodanddrinkfestival.com) Manchester's superb foodie scene shows off its wares over 10 days in mid-October. Farmers markets, pop-up restaurants and gourmet events are just part of the UK's biggest urban food fest.

🛏 Sleeping

Manchester's hotels cater primarily for business travellers and sports fans but, keeping up the capital-of-chic reputation, there are a handful of designer digs and cool hotels around town. Beds can be tough to get during home matches during the football season (August to May). The tourist office has a free accommodation service.

Manchester YHA
HOSTEL £

(☑ 0845 371 9647; www.yha.org.uk; Potato Wharf; dm/d from £11/58; ⓟ@⌖) This canalside hostel in the Castlefield area is one of the best in the country. It's a top-class option with four- and six-bed dorms, all with bathroom, as well as three doubles and a host of good facilities. Potato Wharf is just left off Liverpool Rd.

Hatters
HOSTEL £

(☑ 0161-236 9500; www.hattersgroup.com; 50 Newton St; dm/s/d/tr from £16/30/55/70; ⓟ@⌖) The old-style lift and porcelain sinks are the only leftovers of this former milliner's factory, now one of the best hostels in town, with location to boot – smack in the heart of the Northern Quarter, you won't have to go far to get the best of alternative Manchester.

ABode
HOTEL ££

(☑ 0161-247 7744; www.abodehotels.co.uk; 107 Piccadilly St; r from £100; @⌖) The original fittings at this converted textile factory have been combined successfully with 61 bedrooms divided into four categories of ever-increasing luxury: Comfortable, Desirable, Enviable and Fabulous, the latter being five seriously swanky top-floor suites. Vispring beds, monsoon showers, LCD-screen TVs and stacks of Aquae Sulis toiletries are standard. In the basement, star chef Michael Caines has a champagne-and-cocktail bar adjacent to his very own restaurant.

Roomzzz
APARTMENT ££

(☑ 0161-236 2121; www.roomzzz.co.uk; 36 Princess St; r £65-180; @⌖) The inelegant name belies the designer digs inside this beautifully restored Grade II building, which features serviced apartments equipped with a kitchen and the latest connectivity gadgetry including sleek iMac computers and free wi-fi throughout. There's a small pantry with food for sale downstairs. Highly recommended if you're planning a longer stay.

Radisson Blu Edwardian HOTEL ££

(☑ 0161-835 9929; www.radissonblu-edwardian.com/manchester; Peter St; r from £100; ⚹@⚹) Gladstone, Dickens and Fitzgerald...just some of the names associated with the historic Free Trade Hall, now a business hotel with high-end decor. It has done its best to preserve the memories of the building's most famous visitors: suites are named after Bob Dylan and Shirley Bassey, while meeting rooms carry the names of Disraeli, Thackeray and Pankhurst.

★ Great John Street Hotel HOTEL £££

(☑ 0161-831 3211; www.greatjohnstreet.co.uk; Great John St; r £160-320; @⚹) Elegant designer luxury? Present. Fabulous rooms with all the usual delights (Egyptian cotton sheets, fabulous toiletries, free-standing baths and lots of high-tech electronics)? Present. This former schoolhouse (ah, now you get it) is small but sumptuous – beyond the art-deco lobby are the fabulous bedrooms, each an example of style and luxury. If only school left such comfortable memories.

Malmaison HOTEL £££

(☑ 0161-278 1000; www.malmaison.com; Piccadilly St; r from £119; ⚹Piccadilly) Drop-dead trendy and full of crushed-red velvet, deep purples, art-deco ironwork and signature black-and-white tiles, Malmaison Manchester follows the chain's quirky design style and passion for cool, although rarely at the expense of comfort: the rooms are terrific. The **Smoak Grill** (☑ 0161-278 1000; www.smoak-grill.com; mains £13-25) downstairs is hugely popular.

Velvet Hotel BOUTIQUE HOTEL £££

(☑ 0161-236 9003; www.velvetmanchester.com; 2 Canal St; r from £119; ⚹) Nineteen beautiful bespoke rooms each oozing style: there's the sleigh bed in room 24, the double bath of room 34, the saucy framed photographs of a stripped-down David Beckham (this is Gay Village, after all!). Despite the tantalising decor and location, this is not an exclusive hotel and is as popular with straight visitors as it is with the same-sex crowd.

Lowry HOTEL £££

(☑ 0161-827 4000; www.roccofortecollection.com; 50 Dearman's Pl; r £120-950; ⚹@⚹) Visiting rock stars and luxury hunters tend to favour this modern, five-star hotel (not to be confused with the arts centre in Salford

Quays), where the fabulous bedrooms have enormous beds and ergonomically designed furniture...for maximum comfort, of course. There's an excellent restaurant on the premises, and a health spa where you can soothe yourself with a skin-brightening treatment or an aromatherapy head-massage.

🍴 Eating

With a choice of restaurants unrivalled outside of London, there's something for every palate and budget. You can eat well throughout the city. Spinningfields, just off Deansgate, has a handful of trendy contemporary restaurants; the Northern Quarter is the spot to go for organic eats; while the outlying suburb of Didsbury (5 miles south of the city centre, and easily reached by Metrolink) is where in-the-know Mancunians like to dine.

Rosylee Tearooms CAFE £

(www.rosyleetearooms.com; 11 Stevenson Sq; lunch £6.95, 2-/3-course menu £15.95/17.95; ⊙noon-10pm Tue-Thu, 10am-10pm Fri-Sun) One of the nicest of the Northern Quarter's cafes opened in 2014, combining Edwardian and Georgian decor with a touch of Parisian bistro. The room is bright, the cakes are fabulous and the afternoon tea (£18.95), with its selection of freshly made sandwiches, is one of the nicer experiences to be had in Manchester.

★ Australasia MODERN AUSTRALIAN ££

(☑ 0161-831 0288; www.australasia.uk.com; 1 The Avenue, Spinningfields; mains £13-26; ⊙noon-midnight; ⚹) One of Manchester's most successful building conversions has been that of the basement archive of the *Manchester Evening News* into this suprisingly bright and beautiful restaurant, which serves contemporary Australian cuisine with flavours of Southeast Asia – the lunchtime selection of fresh sushi

> **WORTH A TRIP**
>
> ### FINE DINING IN DIDSBURY
>
> The ambience at **Lime Tree** (☑ 0161-445 1217; www.thelimetreerestaurant.co.uk; 8 Lapwing Lane; mains £16-26; ⊙noon-2.30pm Tue-Fri, 5.30-10pm Mon-Sat, noon-8pm Sun; ⚹ West Didsbury) is refined without being stuffy, the service is relaxed but spot on, and the food is divine – Mancunians book in advance and travel from far afield just to enjoy the superb menu. The 21-day dry-aged fillet steak in peppercorn sauce (£21) is to die for.

is particularly good, as are the specials. A late licence sees it turn into a very cool bar.

Sam's Chop House · BRITISH ££

(☎0161-834 3210; www.samschophouse.co.uk; Back Pool Fold, Chapel Walks, off Cross St; mains £12.50-20; ☉noon-3pm & 5-9.30pm Mon-Fri, 12.30-10pm Sat, noon-8pm Sun) Arguably the city's top gastropub, Sam's is a Victorian classic that serves dishes straight out of a Dickens novel. The highlight is the crispy corned beef hash cake starter, which is salt-cured for 10 days on the premises. The gravy-loving Mrs Todgers from *Martin Chuzzlewit* would certainly approve.

James Martin Manchester · MODERN BRITISH ££

(☎0161-828 0345; www.jamesmartinmanchester.co.uk; Manchester235, Great Northern, Watson St; mains £16-18; ☉5-11pm) Inside the opulent Manchester235 casino, itself a converted linen warehouse, this elegant restaurant is all wooden floors, exposed brick walls and wonderfully comfortable seating. The perfect ambience to enjoy celebrity chef James Martin's terrific menu, a tasty exploration of modern British dishes like slow roast belly of Redhill pork or West Coast plaice, served with herb dumplings.

Oast House · INTERNATIONAL ££

(☎0161-829 3830; www.theoasthouse.uk.com; Crown Sq, Spinningfields; mains £9-15; ☉noon-midnight) An oast house is a 16th-century kiln used to dry out hops as part of the beer-making process. In Manchester, the Oast House is Tim Bacon's exciting BBQ restaurant, a slice of medieval charm in the heart of (slightly) po-faced Spinningfields' contemporary designer chic.

The kitchen is an outdoor covered grill, so staff have to shuttle the barbecued delights (nothing fancy: burgers, kebabs, steaks and rotisserie chickens) to diners inside, but it works brilliantly. The deli boards (lots of cheeses and cured meats) are equally delicious.

Jamie's Italian · ITALIAN ££

(☎0161-241 3901; www.jamieoliver.com; 100 King St; mains £11-18; ☉noon-11.30pm) The magnificent banking hall of Edwin Lutyens' castle-like art-deco Midland Bank (1935) is now home to a branch of Jamie Oliver's fast-expanding gourmet empire. And while the food is perfectly adequate – it's an appealing blend of British staples given the Italian treatment – the real treat is the building itself. In the basement, the old deposit vaults have been converted into private dining rooms.

French · MODERN BRITISH £££

(☎0161-236 3333; www.the-french.co.uk; Midland Hotel, Peter St; 6-/10-course menu £59/84; ☉noon-1.30pm Wed-Sat, 6.30-9.30pm Tue-Sat) 🍴 The revamped restaurant of the Midland Hotel (where Rolls met Royce to make motoring history) is now home to Simon Rogan's exquisite Modern British cuisine, which uses exclusively local produce grown on his farm in Cartmel, Cumbria, home to his Michelin-starred L'Enclume restaurant. The 10-course tasting menu is a feast you won't soon forget.

🍷 Drinking & Nightlife

There are all kinds of bars in town – from old-fashioned watering holes where nostalgia is on tap to trendy cocktail lounges where the beautiful people take selfies and update their social media profiles. Like most other British cities, club nights generally take place in bars with late licences and dance floors. Check the *Manchester Evening News* for details of what's on.

Bluu · BAR

(☎0161-839 7740; www.bluu.co.uk; Smithfield Market Bldgs, Thomas St; ☉10am-midnight; 🛜) Our favourite of the Northern Quarter's collection of great bars. Bluu is cool, comfortable and comes with a great terrace on which to enjoy a pint and listen to music selected by folks with really good taste.

Black Dog Ballroom · BAR

(www.blackdogballroom.co.uk; 52 Church St; ☉10am-midnight; 🛜) A basement bar with a speakeasy vibe, but there's nothing illicit about drinking here: the cocktails are terrific, the atmosphere is always buzzing and the music always good and loud.

Britons Protection · PUB

(☎0161-236 5895; www.britons-protection.com; 50 Great Bridgewater St; ☉noon-11pm) Whisky (over 300 different kinds) is the beverage of choice at this liver-threatening, proper English pub that also does home-style meals. An old-fashioned boozer with open fires in the back rooms and a cosy atmosphere...perfect on a cold evening.

Lass O'Gowrie · PUB

(☎0161-273 6932; 36 Charles St; ☉noon-11pm) A Victorian classic off Princess St that brews its own beer in the basement. It's a favourite with students, old-timers and anyone looking for an authentic pub experience. It also does good-value bar meals.

Liar's Club
BAR

(www.theliarsclub.co.uk; 19a Back Bridge St; ⏥5pm-4am; 🛜) A basement bar designed in the style of a speakeasy/tiki lounge, the Liar's Club serves strong cocktails to an assorted clientele of revellers, students and off-duty barstaff. A great atmosphere any night of the week.

Odd
BAR

(📞0161-833 0070; www.oddbar.co.uk; 30-32 Thomas St; ⏥11am-midnight Sun-Wed, to 1am Thu, to 2am Fri & Sat) This eclectic little bar – with its oddball furnishings, wacky tunes and anti-establishment crew of customers – is the perfect antidote to the increasingly similar look of so many modern bars. A slice of Mancuniana to be treasured.

Mr Thomas' Chop House
PUB

(www.tomschophouse.com; 52 Cross St; ⏥11am-11pm Mon-Thu, to midnight Fri & Sat, noon-10.30pm Sun) An old-style boozer that is very popular for a pint as well as a meal (mains £13).

Peveril of the Peak
PUB

(📞0161-236 6364; 127 Great Bridgewater St; ⏥11am-11pm) An unpretentious pub with wonderful Victorian glazed tilework outside.

Sankey's
CLUB

(📞0161-950 4201; www.sankeys.info; Radium St, Ancoats; admission free-£12; ⏥10pm-3am Thu & Fri, to 4am Sat) If you're a fan of techno, electro or any kind of nonmainstream house music, then a pilgrimage to Manchester's best nightclub should on no account be missed. Its commitment to top-class music is unwavering, with world-renowned DJs mixing it up with residents.

Sankey's has earned itself legendary status for being at the vanguard of dance music (The Chemical Brothers, Daft Punk and others got their start here); these days, you'll hear the likes of Timo Maas, Séb Léger and Thomas Schumacher mix it up to an ever-adoring crowd. Choon! The best way to get here is to board the free Disco Bus that picks up at locations throughout the city from Thursday to Saturday night; see the website for details.

Fac251
CLUB

(📞0161-272 7251; www.factorymanchester.com; 112-118 Princess St; admission £1-6; ⏥11pm-3am Mon-Sat) Located in Tony Wilson's former Factory Records HQ, Fac251 is one of the most popular venues in town. There are three rooms, all with a broad musical appeal, from drum and bass to Motown and indie rock. Something for everybody.

☆ Entertainment

Cinemas

Cornerhouse
CINEMA

(www.cornerhouse.org; 70 Oxford St; ⏥11am-8.30pm Mon-Thu, to 11pm Fri-Sun) Your only destination for good art-house releases; also has a gallery, bookshop and cafe.

Odeon Cinema
CINEMA

(www.odeon.co.uk; The Printworks, Exchange Sq; ⏥noon-11pm) A 20-screen complex in the middle of the Printworks centre.

GAY & LESBIAN MANCHESTER

The city's gay scene is unrivalled outside London and caters to every taste. Its healthy heart beats loudest in the Gay Village, centred on handsome Canal St. Here you'll find bars, clubs, restaurants and – crucially – karaoke joints that cater almost exclusively to the pink pound.

Manchester Pride (p552) is a 10-day festival that runs from the middle of August each year and attracts more than 500,000 people.

There are bars to suit every taste, but you won't go far wrong in Lammar's (www.lammarsbar.com; 57 Hilton St; ⏥noon-late Wed-Sat, to 6pm Sun), which was voted best bar in the city two years running in the Pride of Manchester awards.

For your clubbing needs, look no further than Club Alter Ego (105-107 Princess St; ⏥11pm-5am Thu-Sat).

And then there's karaoke, the ultimate choice for midweek fun. The best of the lot is at the New Union Hotel & Showbar (📞0161-228 1492; 111 Princess St; r from £40; ⏥noon-10pm Mon, to 2am Tue-Thu & Sun, to 3.30am Fri, to 4am Sat), where you can find your inner Madonna and Cyndi Lauper every Tuesday and Thursday – for a top prize of £50.

For more information, check with the Lesbian & Gay Foundation (📞0161-235 8035; www.lgf.org.uk; 105-107 Princess St; ⏥4-10pm). Up-to-date information is also available at www.visitmanchester.com under LGBT.

AMC Cinemas
CINEMA

(www.amccinemas.co.uk; The Great Northern, 235 Deansgate; ☉noon-11pm) A 16-screen multiplex in a retail centre that was formerly a goods warehouse for the Northern Railway Company.

Theatre

Royal Exchange
THEATRE

(☎0161-833 9833; www.royalexchange.co.uk; St Anne's Sq) Interesting contemporary plays are standard at this magnificent, modern theatre-in-the-round.

Live Music

Band on the Wall
LIVE MUSIC

(☎0161-834 1786; www.bandonthewall.org; 25 Swan St) A top-notch venue that hosts everything from rock to world music, with splashes of jazz, blues and folk thrown in.

Deaf Institute
LIVE MUSIC

(www.thedeafinstitute.co.uk; 135 Grosvenor St; ☉10am-midnight) Excellent midsized venue in a former institute for the deaf; also includes a smaller venue in the basement and a cafe on the ground floor.

MEN Arena
CONCERT VENUE

(www.men-arena.com; Great Ducie St) A giant arena north of the centre that hosts rock concerts (as well as being the home of the city's ice-hockey and basketball teams). It's about 300m north of Victoria Station.

Ruby Lounge
LIVE MUSIC

(☎0161-834 1392; www.therubylounge.com; 28-34 High St; ☉noon-midnight) Terrific live-music venue in the Northern Quarter that features mostly rock bands. It gets very loud.

Classical Music

Bridgewater Hall
CONCERT VENUE

(☎0161-907 9000; www.bridgewater-hall.co.uk; Lower Mosley St) The world-renowned Hallé Orchestra has its home at this enormous and impressive concert hall, which hosts up to 250 concerts and events a year. It has a widespread program that includes opera, folk music, children's shows, comedy and contemporary music.

THE MADCHESTER SOUND

It's often claimed that Manchester was the engine room of British pop and that its chief engineer was TV presenter and music impresario Tony Wilson (1950–2007), founder of Factory Records, owner of the Hacienda and the man responsible for Joy Division and New Order. In 1983, Wilson released New Order's ground-breaking 'Blue Monday', whose successful fusion of punk and a pulsating dance beat laid the foundations for the trippy, soul-infused dance music that became known as the Manchester Sound.

The Hacienda was open from 1982 to 1997, and even though it struggled financially for much of its existence (the club was supported by New Order's record sales) it was the HQ of acid house and then rave, as the club embraced the house music coming out of Chicago and Detroit. By the late 1980s, ecstasy hit the scene and it seemed every kid in town was 'mad for it'.

Meanwhile, the city's homegrown guitar bands took notice and began shaping their sound to suit the clubbers' needs. Happy Mondays and the Stone Roses were particularly good at it, as were the Charlatans and other local producers like A Guy Called Gerald ('Voodoo Ray') and 808 State ('Pacific'). Taking no part in the revolution, but admired by everybody in it, were The Smiths, who brought a sardonic and literate tone to the grey-grim state of play that was 1980s Britain before disappearing just as the party known as Madchester was taking off.

Overdanced and overdrugged, the city awoke with a terrible hangover in 1992. Within a year or so the party was over and the fertile crossover scene, which had seen clubbers go mad at rock gigs, and rock bands play the kind of dance sounds that kept the floor thumping until the early hours, virtually disappeared and the two genres withdrew into a more familiar isolation. Taking its place was a new generation of bands, led by Oasis, the self-styled biggest band in the world, and then followed on by a host of other names like The Verve, The Chemical Brothers, Badly Drawn Boy and Elbow.

If you missed the party, you can get a terrific sense of what it was like by watching Michael Winterbottom's *24-Hour Party People* (2002), which captures the hedonism, extravagance and genius of Madchester's cast of characters, and the superb *Control* (2007) by Anton Corbijn, which tells the story of Ian Curtis, Joy Division's tragic lead singer.

Lowry CONCERT VENUE

(☎ 0161-876 2020; www.thelowry.com; Pier 8, Salford Quays) Two separate venues in one: the Lyric Theatre, with the country's largest stage outside the West End, hosts all kinds of performances including Opera North. The smaller Quays hosts more intimate gigs.

Sport

For most people, Manchester plus sport equals football, and football means Manchester United (p551). But the last few years has seen the arrival on the main stage of their cross-town rivals Manchester City, whose ambition is to match United's global footprint.

Manchester City FOOTBALL

Perennial underdogs turned 2014 league champions, Manchester City is now one the world's wealthiest clubs, and fans from all over the world come for the **Etihad Stadium Tour** (☎ 0161-444 1894; www.mcfc.co.uk; tours adult/child £14/10; ⊙ tours 11am, 1.30pm & 3.30pm Mon-Sat, 11.45am, 1.45pm & 3.30pm Sun except match days), a circuit of the ground, dressing rooms and museum before the inevitable steer into the kit shop. Tours must be booked in advance.

The club owes its new-found success to Sheikh Mansour of Abu Dhabi, who bought the club in 2008 and transformed them into big-time contenders. A lineup of mediocre talent was replaced at great expense with some of the brightest stars of the game, and success followed soon after: two league championships and an FA Cup win in three years.

Take bus 53, 54, 185, 186, 216, 217, 230–37, X36 or X37 from Piccadilly Gardens.

Lancashire County Cricket Club CRICKET

(☎ 0161-282 4000; www.lccc.co.uk; Warwick Rd; matches £11-17; 🚇 Old Trafford) The genteel game of cricket is a big deal here and the biggest game of Lancashire's season is the Roses match against Yorkshire. They play their matches at Old Trafford (same name, different but adjacent ground to the football stadium) where international test matches are also played occasionally.

Lancashire – founded in 1816 as the Aurora before changing their name in 1864 – are one of the most beloved of England's county teams, despite the fact that they haven't won the county championship since 1934. Still, a match at the ground remains a great day out.

🛍 Shopping

From the boho indie boutiques of the Northern Quarter to the swanky stores of **Spinningfields** (www.spinningfieldsonline.com), including **Emporio Armani** (☎ 0161-220 2980; Unit G1 & 2, The Avenue; ⊙ 10am-6pm Mon-Sat, 11am-6pm Sun), **Brooks Brothers** (☎ 0161-834 6649; Unit G19, The Avenue; ⊙ 10am-6pm Mon-Sat, 11am-6pm Sun) and **DKNY** (☎ 0161-833 3277; Unit G18, The Avenue; ⊙ 10am-6pm Mon-Sat, 11am-6pm Sun), Manchester's retail credentials are assured. New Cathedral St, part of the Millennium Quarter, and King St also have fancy shops, while the Arndale Centre is the city's equivalent of the English high street.

Oi Polloi CLOTHING

(www.oipolloi.com; 63 Thomas St) Besides the impressive range of casual footwear, this hip boutique also stocks a range of designers including APC, Lyle & Scott, Nudie Jeans and Fjällräven.

Tib Street Market MARKET

(☎ 0161-234 7357; Tib St; ⊙ 10am-5pm Sat) Up-and-coming local designers get a chance to display their wares at this weekly market where you can pick up everything from purses to lingerie and hats to jewellery.

Oxfam Originals VINTAGE

(Unit 8, Smithfield Bldg, Oldham St; ⊙ 10am-6pm Mon-Sat, 11am-6pm Sun) If you're into retro, this terrific store has high-quality gear from the 1960s and '70s. Shop in the knowledge that it's for a good cause.

ℹ Information

EMERGENCY

Ambulance (☎ 0161-436 3999)
Police Station (☎ 0161-872 5050; Bootle St)

MEDICAL SERVICES

Cameolord Chemist (St Peter's Sq; ⊙ 10am-10pm) A pharmacy conveniently located in the city centre.

Manchester Royal Infirmary (Oxford Rd; ⊙ 24hr) The most centrally located of the city's hospitals.

POST

Post Office (Brazennose St; ⊙ 9am-5.30pm Mon-Fri)

TOURIST INFORMATION

Tourist Office (www.visitmanchester.com; Piccadilly Plaza, Portland St; guided tours daily £7/6 per adult/child; ⊙ 10am-5.15pm Mon-Sat, to 4.30pm Sun) This is mostly a self-service tourist office, with brochures and interactive maps to help guide visitors.

WEBSITES

Manchester City Council (www.manchester.gov.uk) The council's official website, which includes a visitors section.

Manchester Evening News (www.menmedia.co.uk) The city's evening paper in electronic form.

Real Manchester (www.realmanchester.com) Online guide to nightlife.

Restaurants of Manchester (www.restaurantsofmanchester.com) Thorough, reliable and up-to-date reviews of restaurants in the city and suburbs.

Visit Manchester (www.visitmanchester.com) The official website for Greater Manchester.

ⓘ Getting There & Away

AIR

Manchester Airport (☎ 0161-489 3000; www.manchesterairport.co.uk) is the largest airport outside London and is served by 13 locations throughout Britain as well as more than 50 international destinations.

BUS

National Express (☎ 08717 81 81 81; www.nationalexpress.com) serves most major cities almost hourly between the coach station (Chorlton St) in the city centre. Destinations include Leeds (£9.70, one hour, hourly), Liverpool (£7.10, 1¼ hours, hourly) and London (£26.20, 3¾ hours, hourly).

TRAIN

Manchester Piccadilly (east of the Gay Village) is the main station for trains to and from the rest of the country, although Victoria station (north of the National Football Museum) serves Halifax and Bradford. The two stations are linked by Metrolink. Off-peak fares are considerably cheaper. Destinations include Blackpool (£16.30, 1¼ hours, half-hourly), Liverpool Lime St (£11.90, 45 minutes, half-hourly), London Euston (£78.70, three hours, seven daily) and Newcastle (£62.70, three hours, six daily).

ⓘ Getting Around

TO/FROM THE AIRPORT

The airport is 12 miles south of the city. A train to or from Victoria station costs peak/off-peak £4.10/3.50, and a coach is £3.50. A taxi is nearly four times as much in light traffic.

PUBLIC TRANSPORT

The excellent public transport system can be used with a variety of Day Saver tickets. For enquiries about local transport, including night buses, contact **Travelshop** (☎ 0161-228 7811; www.tfgm.com; 9 Portland St, Piccadilly Gardens; ⊙ 8am-8pm).

Bus

Centreline bus 4 provides a free service around the heart of Manchester every 10 minutes. Pick up a route map from the tourist office. Most local buses start from Piccadilly Gardens.

Metrolink

The **Metrolink** (www.metrolink.co.uk) is the best way to get between Victoria and Piccadilly train stations (and the G-Mex for Castlefield), as well as further afield to Salford Quays and other suburbs. Buy your tickets from the platform machine.

Train

Castlefield is served by Deansgate station with rail links to Piccadilly, Oxford Rd and Salford stations.

CHESHIRE

Cheshire is genteel, southern hinterland to both Liverpool and Manchester, the postal code of choice for many of its better-off citizens (including the cities' football millionaires) who opt for the amenity-laden bucolic charm of the county's contemporary version of ye olde Englande – complete with fields of Friesian cows, half-timbered Tudor houses and high-speed internet and transport links. For everybody else, Cheshire is really about Chester.

Chester

POP 90,525

Chester is one of English history's greatest gifts to the contemporary visitor. Its red-sandstone wall, which today gift-wraps a tidy collection of Tudor and Victorian buildings, was built during Roman times. The town was then called Castra Devana, and was the largest Roman fortress in Britain.

Beyond the cruciform-shaped historic centre, Chester is an ordinary, residential town; it's hard to believe today, but throughout the Middle Ages Chester made its money as the most important port in the northwest. However, the River Dee silted up over time and Chester fell behind Liverpool in importance.

◉ Sights & Activities

★ City Walls
LANDMARK

A good way to get a sense of Chester's unique character is to walk the 2-mile circuit along the walls that surround the historic centre. Originally built by the Romans around AD 70, the walls were altered substantially over the following centuries but have retained their current position since around 1200. The tourist office's *Walk Around Chester Walls* leaflet is an excellent guide.

Of the many features along the walls, the most eye-catching is the prominent **Eastgate**, where you can see the most famous clock in England after London's Big Ben, built for Queen Victoria's Diamond Jubilee in 1897.

At the southeastern corner of the walls are the **wishing steps**, added in 1785. Local legend claims that if you can run up and down these uneven steps while holding your breath your wish will come true.

Just inside Southgate, known here as **Bridgegate** (as it's located at the northern end of the Old Dee Bridge), is the **Bear & Billet** (www.bearandbillet.com; Southgate; ☺noon-11pm) pub, Chester's oldest timber-framed building, built in 1664, and once a toll gate into the city.

★ Rows
ARCHITECTURE

Besides the city walls, Chester's other great draw is the Rows, a series of two-level galleried arcades along the four streets that fan out in each direction from the **Central Cross**. The architecture is a handsome mix of Victorian and Tudor (original and mock) buildings that house a fantastic collection of individually owned shops.

The origin of the Rows is a little unclear, but it is believed that as the Roman walls slowly crumbled, medieval traders built their shops against the resulting rubble banks, while later arrivals built theirs on top.

Chester Cathedral
CATHEDRAL

(☑01244-324756; www.chestercathedral.com; 12 Abbey Sq; admission £3; ☺9am-5pm Mon-Sat, 1-4pm Sun) Originally a Benedictine abbey built on the remains of an earlier Saxon church dedicated to St Werburgh (the city's patron saint), it was shut down in 1540 as part of Henry VIII's dissolution frenzy, but reconsecrated as a cathedral the following year. Although the cathedral itself was given a substantial Victorian facelift, the 12th-century cloister and its surrounding buildings are essentially unaltered and retain much of the structure from the early monastic years.

Grosvenor Museum
MUSEUM

(☑01244-972197; www.grosvenormuseum.co.uk; 27 Grosvenor St; ☺10.30am-5pm Mon-Sat, 2-5pm Sun) **FREE** Excellent museum with the country's most comprehensive collection of Roman tombstones. At the back of the museum is a preserved Georgian house, complete with kitchen, drawing room, bedroom and bathroom.

Dewa Roman Experience
MUSEUM

(☑01244-343407; www.dewaromanexperience.co.uk; Pierpoint Lane; adult/child £5.50/3.75; ☺9am-5pm Mon-Sat, 10am-5pm Sun) Walk through a reconstructed Roman street to reveal what Roman life was like.

Roman Amphitheatre
ARCHAEOLOGICAL SITE

(Little St John St) **FREE** Just outside the city walls is what was once an arena that seated 7000 spectators (making it the country's largest); some historians have suggested that it may have also been the site of King Arthur's Camelot and that his knights' 'round table' was really just this circular construction. Excavations continue; during summer months there are occasional shows held here.

St John the Baptist Church
CHURCH

(Vicar's Lane; ☺9.15am-6pm) Built on the site of an older Saxon church in 1075, it's been a peaceful ruin since 1581. It includes the remains of a Norman choir and medieval chapels.

Boat Hire
BOATING

(The Groves; per hr £6-8; ☺9am-6pm Apr-Sep) Steps at the back of St John the Baptist Church (Vicar's Lane) lead down to the riverside promenade known as the Groves. Here you can hire different kinds of boats with pedals, oars or small engines.

☞ Tours

Chester Visitor Information Centre offers a broad range of walking tours departing from the town hall, including food, historical and ghost tours. Each lasts between 1½ and two hours. Recommended are the cruises up and down the Dee run by **Chester Boat** (☑01244-325394; www.chesterboat.co.uk; Boating Station, Souters Lane, The Groves; tours £6.50-15), which include a foray into the gorgeous Eaton Estate, home of the duke and duchess of Westminster.

MANCHESTER, LIVERPOOL & NORTHWEST ENGLAND CHESTER

Chester

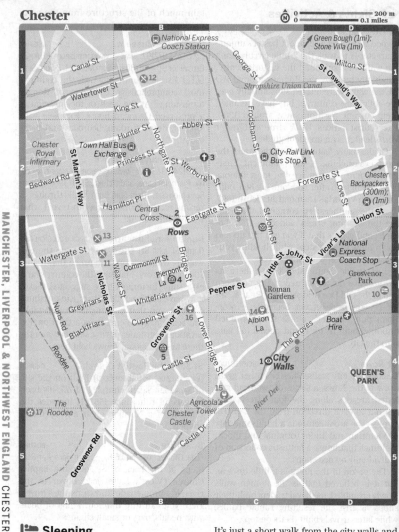

🛏 Sleeping

If you're visiting between Easter and September, you'd better book early if you want to avoid going over budget or settling for far less than you hoped for. Except for a handful of options, most of the accommodation is outside the city walls, but within easy walking distance of the centre.

Chester Backpackers HOSTEL **£**
(☎01244-400185; www.chesterbackpackers.co.uk; 67 Boughton; dm/s/d from £16/22/34; ☎) Comfortable dorm rooms with nice pine beds in a typically Tudor white-and-black building.

It's just a short walk from the city walls and there's also a pleasant garden.

★Stone Villa B&B **££**
(☎01244-345014; www.stonevillachester.co.uk; 3 Stone Pl, Hoole Rd; s/d from £45/75; 🅿🛜; 🚍9) Twice winner of Chester's B&B of the Year in the last 10 years, this beautiful villa has everything you need for a memorable stay. Elegant bedrooms, a fabulous breakfast and welcoming, friendly owners all add up to one of the best lodgings in town. The property is about a mile from the city centre.

Chester

Grove Villa B&B **££**

(☎01244-349713; www.grovevillachester.com; 18 The Groves; r from £75; P) A wonderfully positioned Victorian home overlooking the Dee. The rooms have antique beds and great river views.

Chester Grosvenor Hotel & Spa HOTEL **£££**

(☎01244-324024; www.chestergrosvenor.com; 58 Eastgate St; r from £175; P@☎) Perfectly located, the Chester Grosvenor has huge rooms with exquisite period furnishings and all mod cons. The spa, which is also open to nonguests, offers a range of body treatments, including reiki, LaStone therapy, Indian head massage and four-handed massage. There's also a Michelin-starred restaurant downstairs.

✕ Eating

Chester has great food – it's just not in any of the tourist-oriented restaurants that line the Rows. Besides the better restaurants, you'll find the best grub in some of the pubs.

Joseph Benjamin MODERN BRITISH **££**

(☎01244-344295; www.josephbenjamin.co.uk; 134-140 Northgate St; mains £13-17; ⊗9am-5pm Tue & Wed, 9am-midnight Thu-Sat, 10am-5pm Sun) A bright star in Chester's culinary firmament is this combo restaurant, bar and deli that delivers carefully prepared local produce to take out or eat in. Excellent sandwiches and gorgeous salads are the mainstay of the takeout menu, while the more formal dinner menu features fine examples of modern British cuisine.

Bar Lounge MODERN BRITISH **££**

(www.barlounge.co.uk; 75 Watergate St; mains £11-18) One of the most popular spots in town is this bistro-style bar that serves up good burgers, pies and a particularly tasty beer-battered haddock and chips. There's a heated outdoor terrace for alfresco drinks.

Upstairs at the Grill STEAKHOUSE **£££**

(☎01244-344883; www.upstairsatthegrill.co.uk; 70 Watergate St; mains £17-29; ⊗5-11pm Mon-Thu, noon-11pm Fri-Sun) This two-storey Manhattan-style steakhouse is the place to devour every cut of meat from American-style porterhouse to a sauce-sodden chateaubriand. All of the cuts are locally sourced and dry aged for five weeks to guarantee succulence; most cuts are available in 225g or 340g except for the bone-in rib eye, which comes in a daunting racket-sized 680g hunk of meat.

🍷 Drinking & Nightlife

Albion PUB

(4 Albion St; ⊗noon-11pm) No children, no music and no machines or big screens (but plenty of Union Jacks). This 'family hostile' Edwardian classic pub is a throwback to a time when ale-drinking still had its own rituals. Still, this is one of the finest pubs in northwest England precisely because it doggedly refuses to modernise.

Falcon PUB

(Lower Bridge St; ⊗noon-11pm) An old-fashioned boozer with a lovely atmosphere, the Falcon is great for a pint, especially the selection of Samuel Smyth ales, wheat beers and ciders – they also serve organic fruit beers.

☆ Entertainment

Roodee HORSE RACING

(www.chester-races.co.uk; The Racecourse; ⊗May-Sep) Chester's ancient and very beautiful racetrack, on the western side of the walls, has been hosting races since the 16th century. Highlights of the summer flat season include the two-day July Festival and the August equivalent.

ℹ Information

Cheshire Constabulary (☎ 01244-350000; Town Hall, Northgate St)

Countess of Chester Hospital (☎ 01244-365000; Health Park, Liverpool Rd)

Post Office (2 St John St; ⊙ 9am-5.30pm Mon-Sat)

Tourist Office (☎ 01244-402111; www.visitchester.com; Town Hall, Northgate St; ⊙ 9am-5.30pm Mon-Sat, 10am-4pm Sun May-Oct, 10am-5pm Mon-Sat Nov-Apr)

ℹ Getting There & Away

BUS

National Express (☎ 08717 81 81 81; www.nationalexpress.com) coaches stop on Vicar's Lane, just opposite the tourist office by the Roman amphitheatre. Destinations include Birmingham (£14.30, two hours, four daily), Liverpool (£8.20, one hour, four daily), London (£23, 5½ hours, three daily) and Manchester (£7.70, 1¼ hours, three daily).

For information on local bus services, ring the **Cheshire Bus Line** (☎ 01244-602666). Local buses leave from the **Town Hall Bus Exchange** (Princess St).

TRAIN

The train station is about a mile from the city centre via Foregate St and City Rd, or Brook St. City-Rail Link buses are free for people with rail tickets, and operate between the station and **Bus Stop A** (Frodsham St). Destinations include Liverpool (£6.65, 45 minutes, hourly), London Euston (£78.70, 2½ hours, hourly) and Manchester (£16.10, one hour, hourly).

ℹ Getting Around

Much of the city centre is closed to traffic from 10.30am to 4.30pm, so a car is likely to be a hindrance. The city is easy to walk around anyway, and most places of interest are close to all.

Around Chester

The largest of its kind in the country, **Chester Zoo** (www.chesterzoo.org; Upton-by-Chester; adult/child £20/16, monorail £2/1.50, waterbus £2/1.50; ⊙ 10am-dusk, last admission 4pm Mon-Fri, to 5pm Sat & Sun) is about as pleasant a place as caged animals in artificial renditions of their natural habitats could ever expect to live. It's so big that there's even a **monorail** and a **waterbus** for getting around. The zoo is on the A41, 3 miles north of Chester's city centre. Bus 1 (return £8, 15 minutes, every 15 minutes Monday to Saturday, every 30 minutes Sunday) runs between Chester's Town Hall Bus Exchange and the zoo.

LIVERPOOL

POP 466,400

Few English cities are as shackled by reputation as Liverpool, and none has worked so hard to outgrow the clichés that for so long have been used to define it.

A hardscrabble town with a reputation for wit and an obsessive love of football, Liverpool also has an impressive cultural heritage: it has more listed museums than any other city outside London, its galleries are among the best in the country, and it has recently undergone an impressive program of urban regeneration. And then there's the Beatles. Liverpool cherishes them not because it's stuck in the past and hasn't gotten over the fact that they're long gone – it's because their worldwide popularity would make it crazy *not* to do so.

The main attractions are Albert Dock (west of the city centre), and the trendy Ropewalks area (south of Hanover St and west of the two cathedrals). Lime St station, the bus station and the Cavern Quarter – a mecca for Beatles fans – lie just to the north.

History

Liverpool grew wealthy on the back of the triangular trading of slaves, raw materials and finished goods. From 1700 ships carried cotton goods and hardware from Liverpool to West Africa, where they were exchanged for slaves, who in turn were carried to the West Indies and Virginia, where they were exchanged for sugar, rum, tobacco and raw cotton.

As a great port, the city drew thousands of Irish and Scottish immigrants, and its Celtic influences are still apparent. Between 1830 and 1930, however, nine million emigrants – mainly English, Scots and Irish, but also Swedes, Norwegians and Russian Jews – sailed from here to the New World.

The start of WWII led to a resurgence of Liverpool's importance. More than one million American GIs disembarked here before D-Day and the port was, once again, hugely important as the western gateway for transatlantic supplies. The GIs brought with them the latest American records, and Liverpool was thus the first European port of call for the new rhythm and blues that would eventually become rock and roll. Within 20 years, the Mersey Beat was *the* sound of British pop, and four mop-topped Scousers had formed a skiffle band...

⦿ Sights

The wonderful Albert Dock is the city's biggest tourist attraction and the key to understanding the city's history, but the city centre is where you'll find most of Liverpool's real day-to-day life.

⦿ City Centre

★ World Museum   MUSEUM
(☏0151-478 4399; www.liverpoolmuseums.org.uk/wml; William Brown St; ☺10am-5pm) FREE Natural history, science and technology are the themes of the oldest museum in town, which opened in 1853 and whose exhibits range from live bugs to human anthropology. This vastly entertaining and educational museum is spread across five themed floors, from the live fish aquarium on the 1st floor to the planetarium on the 5th, where you'll also find exhibits dedicated to space (moon rocks, telescopes etc) and time (clocks and timepieces from the 1500s to 1960). Highly recommended.

★ Liverpool Cathedral   CATHEDRAL
(☏0151-709 6271; www.liverpoolcathedral.org.uk; Upper Duke St; visitor centre & tower admission £5; ☺8am-6pm) Liverpool's Anglican cathedral is a building of superlatives. Not only is it Britain's largest church, it's also the world's largest Anglican cathedral. It is the work of Sir Gilbert Scott, who also gave us the red telephone box and the Southwark Power Station in London, now the Tate Modern. The central bell is the world's third largest (with the world's highest and heaviest peal), while the organ, with its 9765 pipes, is likely the world's largest operational model.

The visitor centre features *Great Space*; this 10-minute, panoramic high-definition movie about the history of the cathedral is followed by your own audiovisual tour, courtesy of a headset. Your ticket also gives you access to the cathedral's 101m tower, from which there are terrific views of the city and beyond – on a clear day you can see Blackpool Tower.

★ Walker Art Gallery   GALLERY
(☏0151-478 4199; www.liverpoolmuseums.org.uk/walker; William Brown St; ☺10am-5pm) FREE The city's foremost art gallery is the national gallery for northern England, housing an outstanding collection of art from the 14th to the 21st centuries. Its strong suits are pre-Raphaelite art, modern British art and sculpture – not to mention the rotating exhibits of contemporary expression. It's a family-friendly place, too: the ground-floor Big Art for Little People gallery is designed for under-eights and features interactive exhibits and games that will (hopefully) result in a lifelong love affair with art.

St George's Hall   CULTURAL CENTRE
(☏0151-707 2391; www.stgeorgesliverpool.co.uk; William Brown St; ☺10am-5pm Tue-Sat, 1-5pm Sun) FREE Arguably Liverpool's most impressive building is the Grade I–listed St George's Hall, a magnificent example of neoclassical architecture that is as imposing today as it was when it was completed in 1854.

LIVERPOOL IN...

Two Days

Start at the waterfront's collection of superb museums. Visit the **Museum of Liverpool** (p567) and, just south, the **International Slavery Museum** (p566) in Albert Dock.

Pay the Fab Four their due at the **Beatles Story** (p566) before heading into town to the Cavern Quarter around Mathew St. The **Monro** (p569) is worth a visit for lunch and the **London Carriage Works** (p569) for dinner. Round off the day with a pint at the marvellous **Philharmonic** (p569), and wrap yourself in the crisp sheets of the **Malmaison** (p569). Night hawks can tear it up in the bars and clubs of the hip **Ropewalks** area. The next day, explore the city's two **cathedrals** and check out the twin delights of the **World Museum** (p563) and the **Walker Art Gallery** (p563).

Four Days

Follow the two-day itinerary and make a pilgrimage to **Mendips** and **20 Forthlin Road** (p567), the childhood homes of John Lennon and Paul McCartney respectively. For dinner, try **HoSt** (p569). The next day, walk on holy ground at Anfield, home of **Liverpool Football Club** (p570). Race junkies can head to the visitor centre at Aintree racecourse, which hosts England's beloved race, the **Grand National** (p568).

Liverpool

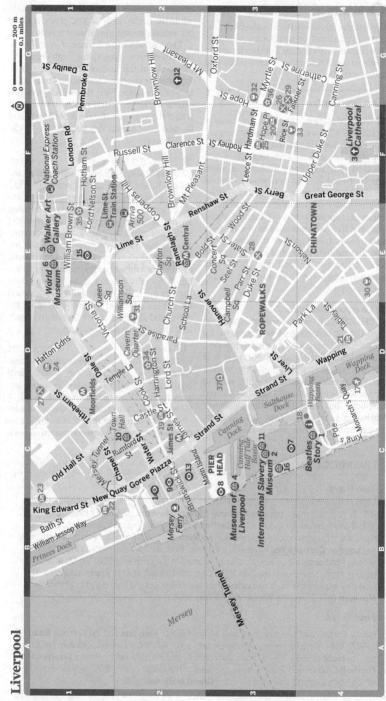

0 200 m
0 0.1 miles

Liverpool

Curiously, it was built as law courts and a concert hall – presumably a judge could pass sentence and then relax to a string quartet.

Inside, you can visit the recently refurbished courtroom and robing room, stop by the cells below, and get a nice vantage point on the Great Hall, home to Britain's second-largest organ (its 7000 pipes are pipped by the organ in London's Albert Hall). The building also hosts concerts, corporate gigs and a host of other civic get-togethers; it is also the focal point of any city-wide celebration.

**Metropolitan Cathedral
of Christ the King** CATHEDRAL
(☑ 0151-709 9222; www.liverpoolmetrocathedral.org.uk; Brownlow Hill; ☺ 7.30am-6pm) Known colloquially as Paddy's Wigwam, Liverpool's Catholic cathedral is a mightily impressive modern building that looks like a soaring concrete tepee, hence its nickname. It was completed in 1967 according to the design of Sir Frederick Gibberd after the original plans by Sir Edwin Lutyens, whose crypt is inside. The central tower frames the world's largest stained-glass window, created by John Piper and Patrick Reyntiens.

Liverpool War Museum MUSEUM
(www.liverpoolwarmuseum.co.uk; 1 Rumford St; adult/child £6/4; ☺ 10.30am-4.30pm Mon-Thu & Sat Mar-Oct) The secret command centre for the Battle of the Atlantic, the Western Approaches, was abandoned at the end of the war with virtually everything left intact. You can get a good glimpse of the labyrinthine nerve centre of Allied operations, including the all-important map room, where you can imagine playing a real-life, full-scale version of Risk.

◉ Albert Dock

Liverpool's biggest tourist attraction is Albert Dock (☑ 0151-708 8854; www.albertdock.com) FREE, 2.75 hectares of water ringed by enormous cast-iron columns and impressive five-storey warehouses that make up the country's largest collection of protected buildings and are a World Heritage Site. A fabulous development program has really brought the dock to life – here you'll find several outstanding museums and an extension of London's Tate Gallery, as well as a couple of top-class restaurants and bars.

MANCHESTER, LIVERPOOL & NORTHWEST ENGLAND LIVERPOOL

LIVERPOOL FOR CHILDREN

The waterfront museums are extremely popular with kids, especially the Museum of Liverpool (p567) and the Merseyside Maritime Museum (p566), which has a couple of boats for kids to mess about on. A visit to Anfield Rd (p570) is a must if your kids have any kind of interest in football. The Big Art for Little People gallery at the Walker Art Gallery (p563) is perfect for kids who want to find out that art is more than just something that adults stare at.

MANCHESTER, LIVERPOOL & NORTHWEST ENGLAND LIVERPOOL

★ **International Slavery Museum** MUSEUM
(☎0151-478 4499; www.liverpoolmuseums.org. uk/ism; Albert Dock; ☺10am-5pm) **FREE** Museums are, by their very nature, like a still of the past, but the extraordinary International Slavery Museum resonates very much in the present. It reveals slavery's unimaginable horrors – including Liverpool's own role in the triangular slave trade – in a clear and uncompromising manner. It does this through a remarkable series of multi-media and other displays, and it doesn't baulk at confronting racism, slavery's shadowy ideological justification for this inhumane practice.

The history of slavery is made real through a series of personal experiences, including a carefully kept ship's log and captain's diary. These tell the story of one slaver's experience on a typical trip, departing Liverpool for West Africa. The ship then purchased or captured as many slaves as it could carry before embarking on the gruesome 'middle passage' across the Atlantic to the West Indies. The slaves that survived the torturous journey were sold for sugar, rum, tobacco and raw cotton, which were then brought back to England for profit. Exhibits include original shackles, chains and instruments used to punish rebellious slaves – each piece of metal is more horrendous than the next.

It's heady, disturbing stuff, but as well as providing an insightful history lesson, we are reminded of our own obligations to humanity and justice throughout the museum, not least in the Legacies of Slavery exhibit, which explores the continuing fight for freedom and equality.

★ **Beatles Story** MUSEUM
(☎0151-709 1963; www.beatlesstory.com; Albert Dock; adult/child £12.95/7, incl Elvis & Us £15.95/7; ☺9am-7pm, last admission 5pm) Liverpool's most popular museum won't illuminate any dark corners in the turbulent history of the world's most famous foursome – there's ne'er a mention of internal discord, drugs or Yoko Ono – but there's plenty of genuine memorabilia to keep a Beatles fan happy. You can also get a combo ticket for the Elvis & Us (p567) exhibit at the Beatles Story extension on Pier Head.

Particularly impressive is the full-size replica Cavern Club (which was actually tiny) and the Abbey Rd studio where the lads recorded their first singles, while George Harrison's crappy first guitar (now worth half a million quid) should inspire budding, penniless musicians to keep the faith.

Merseyside Maritime Museum MUSEUM
(☎0151-478 4499; www.liverpoolmuseums.org.uk/ maritime; Albert Dock; ☺10am-5pm) **FREE** The story of one of the world's great ports is the theme of this excellent museum and, believe us, it's a graphic and compelling page-turner. One of the many great exhibits is Emigration to a New World, which tells the story of nine million emigrants and their efforts to get to North America and Australia; the walkthrough model of a typical ship shows just how tough conditions on board really were.

Tate Liverpool GALLERY
(☎0151-702 7400; www.tate.org.uk/liverpool; Albert Dock; special exhibitions adult/child from £5/4; ☺10am-5.50pm Jun-Aug, closed Mon Sep-May) **FREE** Touted as the home of modern art in the north, this gallery features a substantial checklist of 20th-century artists across its four floors, as well as touring exhibitions from the mother ship on London's Bankside. But it's all a little sparse, with none of the energy we'd expect from the world-famous Tate.

⊙ North of Albert Dock

The area to the north of Albert Dock is known as Pier Head, after a stone pier built in the 1760s. This is still the departure point for ferries across the River Mersey, and was for millions of migrants their final contact with European soil.

The Museum of Liverpool is an impressive architectural interloper, but pride of place in this part of the dock still goes to the trio of Edwardian buildings known as the 'Three Graces', dating from the days when Liverpool's star was still ascending. The southernmost, with the dome mimicking St Paul's Cathedral, is the Port of Liverpool

Building, completed in 1907. Next to it is the Cunard Building, in the style of an Italian palazzo, once HQ to the Cunard Steamship Line. Finally, the Royal Liver Building (pronounced *lie*-ver) was opened in 1911 as the head office of the Royal Liver Friendly Society. It's crowned by Liverpool's symbol, the famous 5.5m copper Liver Bird.

★ **Museum of Liverpool**   MUSEUM
(☎ 0151-478 4545; www.liverpoolmuseums.org.uk/mol; Pier Head; ⊙ 10am-5pm) FREE Liverpool's storied past is explored through an interactive exploration of the city's cultural and historical milestones – the railroad, poverty, wealth, *Brookside* (a popular '80s TV soap opera set in the city), the Beatles and football (the film on the meaning of the game to the city is worth the 15 minutes). The desire to tell all of the city's rich story means there isn't a huge amount of depth, but the kids will love it.

Beatles Story: Elvis & Us   EXHIBITION
(☎ 0151-709 1963; www.elvisandus.com; Mersey Ferries Terminal, Pier Head; admission £6; ⊙ 9am-7pm Apr-Sep, 10am-6pm Oct-Mar) The meeting of pop music's most iconic figures on 27 August 1965 forms the basis of this exhibit atop the Pier Head ferry terminal. Want to gawk at the white Fender bass Paul played at the meeting? Stare lovingly at the shirt Elvis wore in *Jailhouse Rock*? Look at rare footage and examine a ticket to the '68 comeback special? Then this is the place to do it.

☞ Tours

Beatles Fab Four Taxi Tour   TAXI TOUR
(☎ 0151-601 2111; www.thebeatlesfabfourtaxitour.co.uk; 2/3hr tour £45/55) Themed tours of the city's mop-top landmarks – there's the three-hour original Lennon tour or the two-hour Epstein express tour. Pick-ups arranged when booking. Up to five people per tour.

Liverpool Beatles Tour   GUIDED TOUR
(☎ 0151-281 7738; www.beatlestours.co.uk; tours from £65) Your own personalised tour of every bit of Beatles minutiae, from cradle to grave. Tours range from the three-hour Helter Skelter excursion to the Fantastic All-Day Tour, by the end of which, presumably, you'll be convinced you were actually in the band. Pick-ups are arranged upon booking.

Magical Mystery Tour   GUIDED TOUR
(☎ 0151-709 3285; www.cavernclub.org; per person £16.95; ⊙ tours 10.30am, 11.30am, 1pm & 2pm) This two-hour tour takes in all Beatles-related landmarks – their birthplaces, childhood homes, schools and places such as Penny Lane and Strawberry Field – before finishing up in the Cavern Club (which isn't the original). Departs from opposite the tourist office on Albert Dock.

MANCHESTER, LIVERPOOL & NORTHWEST ENGLAND LIVERPOOL

(NEVER) LET IT BE

They broke up more than 40 years ago and two of their members are dead, but the Beatles are bigger business than ever in Liverpool.

Most of it centres around tiny Mathew St, site of the original Cavern Club, which is now the main thoroughfare of the 'Cavern Quarter'. Here you can shuck oysters in the Rubber Soul Oyster Bar, buy a George pillowcase in the From Me to You shop and put it on the pillows of the Hard Day's Night Hotel. Ringo may have disparaged the city in 2008 by declaring that he missed nothing about it, but the city's tourist authorities continue to exploit Liverpool's ties to the world's most famous group and have done so with enormous success – the original, Beatles-oriented Mathew St Festival was enormously popular, attracting over 350,000 fans (it's now the Liverpool International Music Festival (p568) and explores music beyond the Fab Four).

Wandering around Mathew St is plenty of fun – and the Beatles Shop is best for memorabilia – but if you really want a bit of Beatles lore, you'll have to visit the National Trust–owned Mendips, the home where John lived with his Aunt Mimi from 1945 to 1963 (which is also the time period covered by Sam Taylor-Wood's superb 2009 biopic of the young Lennon, *Nowhere Boy*) and 20 Forthlin Road, the plain terraced home where Paul grew up; you can only do so by prebooked tour (☎ 0151-427 7231; www.nationaltrust.org.uk; Jury's Inn, 31 Keel Wharf, Wapping Dock; adult/child £22/7; ⊙ 10am, 11am & 2.15pm Wed-Sun Mar-Nov). Tours also leave from Speke Hall (☎ 0151-427 7231; www.nationaltrust.org.uk; The Walk, Speke; ⊙ 3.15pm Wed-Sun Mar-Oct).

If you'd rather do it yourself, the tourist offices stock the *Discover Lennon's Liverpool* guide and map, and Ron Jones' *The Beatles' Liverpool*.

✦ Festivals & Events

Creamfields MUSIC, DANCE
(www.cream.co.uk) An alfresco dance-fest that brings together some of the world's best DJs and dance acts during the last weekend in August. It takes place at the Daresbury Estate near Halton, Cheshire.

International Beatleweek MUSIC
(www.cavernclub.org) Tribute bands keep the crowds entertained across a week in late August of Beatles-inspired music and talks organised by the Cavern Club.

**Liverpool International
Music Festival** MUSIC
(☑0151-239 9091; www.limfestival.org) A festival showcasing local bands and international acts across five different venues spread throughout the city during the last two weeks of August.

⊨ Sleeping

Liverpool's choice of accommodation ranges from sexy boutique to strictly functional. Rooms are at a premium when Liverpool FC are playing at home and during the mobbed-out music festivals of late August. If you fancy self-catering options, the tourist office has all the information you need.

⊨ City Centre

★**Richmond Hotel** HOTEL **££**
(www.richmondliverpool.com; 24 Hatton Garden; d from £80, 2-bedroom apt from £199) Centrally located and fully renovated, the Richmond offers a convenient choice of accommodation, from classic doubles and suites to fully equipped, self-catering one-, two- and three-bedroom apartments. All of the rooms have high-spec decor, including 50in

---

THE GRAND NATIONAL

The world's most famous **steeple-chase** (☑0151-522 2929; www.aintree.co.uk) – and one of England's most cherished events – takes place on the first Saturday in April across 4.5 miles and over the most difficult fences in world racing. Its protagonists are 40-odd veteran stalwarts of the jumps, ageing bruisers full of the oh-so-English qualities of grit and derring-do. If you want to attend the race, you'd better book tickets far in advance.

---

flatscreen TVs and fancy toiletries. Guests also have access to the hotel spa.

Radisson Blu HOTEL **££**
(☑0151-966 1500; www.radissonblu.co.uk; 107 Old Hall St; r from £95; @ ☎) The rooms at this funky Scandinavian design hotel are divided into 'Ocean', with regal blues and views of the docks and the Mersey, and 'Urban', with luscious reds and purples and city views. Each comes with all the designer gadgetry you'd expect: flatscreen TVs, free highspeed wi-fi and super-hip bathrooms. They're not especially huge, but they're very cool, baby.

62 Castle St BOUTIQUE HOTEL **££**
(☑0151-702 7898; www.62castlest.com; 62 Castle St; r from £80; P @ ☎) This elegant property successfully blends the traditional Victorian features of the neoclassical building with a sleek, contemporary style. The 20 fabulously different suites come with high-definition plasma-screen TVs, drench showers and luxe toiletries as standard.

Roscoe House BOUTIQUE HOTEL **££**
(☑0151-709 0286; www.roscoehouse.com; 27 Rodney St; r from £70; ☎) A handsome Georgian home once owned by Liverpool-born writer and historian William Roscoe (1753–1831) has been given the once-over and is now a chic boutique hotel. The elegant rooms combine period touches (original coving, fireplaces and furnishings) with contemporary comforts such as flatscreen TVs and fancy Egyptian cotton sheets.

★**Hope Street Hotel** BOUTIQUE HOTEL **£££**
(☑0151-709 3000; www.hopestreethotel.co.uk; 40 Hope St; r/ste from £130/190; @ ☎) Luxurious Liverpool's pre-eminent flag-waver is this stunning boutique hotel on the city's most elegant street. King-sized beds draped in Egyptian cotton, oak floors with underfloor heating, LCD TVs and sleek modern bathrooms (with REN bath and beauty products) are but the most obvious touches of class at this supremely cool address. Breakfast, taken in the marvellous London Carriage Works, is not included.

⊨ Around Albert Dock

Liverpool YHA HOSTEL **£**
(☑0845 371 9527; www.yha.org.uk; 25 Tabley St; dm from £18; P ☎) It may have the look of an Eastern European apartment complex, but this award-winning hostel, adorned with plenty of Beatles memorabilia, is one of the

most comfortable you'll find anywhere in the country. The dorms with en suite bathrooms even have heated towel rails.

⭐ **Malmaison** — HOTEL ££

(📞0151-229 5000; www.malmaison.com; 7 William Jessop Way, Princes Dock; r from £89; 🅿@🛜) Malmaison's preferred colour scheme of plum and black is everywhere in this purpose-built hotel, which gives it an air of contemporary sophistication. Everything about the Liverpool Mal is plush, from the huge beds and the deep baths to the heavy velvet curtains and the excellent buffet breakfast.

✖ Eating

Top-grade international cuisine, the best of British and the greasy spoon...you'll find plenty of choices to satisfy every taste. Best spots include Ropewalks, along Hardman St and Hope St.

Monro — GASTROPUB ££

(📞0151-707 9933; www.themonro.com; 92 Duke St; 2-course lunch £11.95, dinner mains £14-20; ⏰11am-11pm) 🌿 The Monro has fast become one of the city's favourite spots for lunch, dinner and, especially, weekend brunch. The constantly changing menu of classic British dishes made with ingredients sourced as locally as possible has transformed this handsome old pub into a superb dining experience. It's tough to find pub grub this good elsewhere, unless you go to its sister pub, the James Monro (📞0151-236 9700; www.thejamesmonro. com; 69 Tithebarn St; ⏰11am-11pm).

HoSt — ASIAN, FUSION ££

(www.ho-st.co.uk; 31 Hope St; mains £9.50-13; ⏰11am-11pm; 🚼🌿) A bright, airy room with the look of a chic, contemporary New York brasserie serves up excellent pan-Asian dishes like Indonesian braised lamb with fried rice and red duck coconut curry with lychees. The starter nibbles are pretty delicious, too.

Quarter — BISTRO ££

(📞0151-707 1965; www.thequarteruk.com; 7-11 Falkner St; mains £9-15; ⏰8am-11pm Mon-Fri, 9am-11pm Sat & Sun) A gorgeous little wine bar and bistro with outdoor seating for that elusive summer's day.

London Carriage Works — MODERN BRITISH £££

(📞0151-705 2222; www.thelondoncarriageworks. co.uk; 40 Hope St; 2-/3-course meal £17.50/22.50, mains £16-30; ⏰7-10am & noon-10pm Mon-Fri, 8-11am & noon-10pm Sat, to 9pm Sun) Liverpool's dining revolution is being led by Paul Askew's award-winning restaurant, which successfully blends ethnic influences from around the globe with staunch British favourites and serves up the result in a beautiful dining room – actually more of a bright glass box divided only by a series of sculpted glass shards. Reservations are recommended.

🍷 Drinking & Nightlife

Unless specified, all the bars included here open from 11am until 2am Monday to Saturday, and most have a nominal entry charge after 11pm. Most of the city's clubs are concentrated in Ropewalks, where they compete for customers with a tonne of late-night bars; considering the number of punters in the area on a Friday or Saturday night, we're guessing there's plenty of business for everyone.

Everyman Bistro — BAR

(www.everymanplayhouse.com; Williamson Sq; ⏰10am-10pm) This Liverpool institution reopened in 2014 in a new location and is better than ever. The downstairs bar and bistro are packed most evenings, making this one of the best places in town for a drink and a bite. The wi-fi is stronger than in most other bars.

Philharmonic — PUB

(36 Hope St; ⏰10am-11.30pm) This extraordinary bar, designed by the shipwrights who built the *Lusitania,* is one of the most beautiful bars in all of England. The interior is resplendent with etched and stained glass, wrought iron, mosaics and ceramic tiling – and if you think that's good, just wait until you see inside the marble men's toilets, the only heritage-listed lav in the country.

Ye Cracke — PUB

(13 Rice St; ⏰11am-11pm) A traditional pub with a beer garden; the fact that John and Cynthia Lennon liked coming here when they were students is completely incidental to its charms.

DON'T MISS

BEST PUBS FOR A PINT IN THE NORTHWEST

➡ Philharmonic (p569), Liverpool

➡ Britons Protection (p554), Manchester

➡ Albion (p561), Chester

➡ Peveril of the Peak (p555), Manchester

24 Kitchen Street CLUB
(www.facebook.com/24kitchenstreet; 24 Kitchen St; tickets £8-12; ⊘9pm-4am Fri & Sat) A multipurpose venue that splits its focus between the arts and electronic music. The converted Victorian building is one of the best places in town to dance in.

☆ Entertainment

Philharmonic Hall CLASSICAL MUSIC
(☑0151-709 3789; www.liverpoolphil.com; Hope St) One of Liverpool's most beautiful buildings, the art-deco Phil is home to the city's main classical orchestra, but it also stages the work of avant-garde musicians such as John Cage and Nick Cave.

O2 Academy LIVE MUSIC
(☑0151-794 6868; www.o2academyliverpool.co.uk; Liverpool University, 11-13 Hotham St) Good spot to see midsize bands on tour.

Cavern Club LIVE MUSIC
(☑0151-236 1965; www.cavernclub.org; 8-10 Mathew St; admission before/after 2pm free/£4; ⊘10am-midnight Mon-Wed & Sun, to 1.30am Thu, to 2am Fri & Sat) It's a reconstruction, and not even on the same spot, but the 'world's most famous club' is still a great spot to see local bands.

Liverpool FC FOOTBALL
(☑0151-263 9199, ticket office 0151-220 2345; www.liverpoolfc.com; Anfield Rd) Doff o' the cap to Evertonians and Beatle-maniacs, but no single institution represents the Mersey spirit and strong sense of identity more powerfully than Liverpool FC, who dominated British football in the '70s and '80s, but have had to watch as their bitter rivals Manchester United did the same in the decades since.

New manager Brendan Rodgers was appointed in 2012 and has re-established the club as viable contenders for the league title: in 2014 they were pipped to the prize by Manchester City, but the club's millions of fans worldwide have a renewed sense of hope for the future.

After years of discussion, plans to enlarge the utterly marvellous Anfield Road were approved in 2014 and the 60,000-capacity ground should be ready by 2017. In the meantime, the experience of a live match remains a sporting highlight of a visit to England, especially the sound of 40,000 fans singing the club's anthem, 'You'll Never Walk Alone'. The **Anfield Stadium Tour** (www.liverpoolfc.com; Anfield Stadium; stadium tour adult/child £16.50/10) brings fans to the home dressing room and down the tunnel past the famous 'This is Anfield' sign into the pitchside dugout. Take bus 26 or 27 from Paradise St Interchange or bus 17 or 217 from the Queen St Bus Station.

Everton Football Club FOOTBALL
(☑0151-330 2400, ticket office 0151-330 2300; www.evertonfc.com; Goodison Park) Founded in 1878, Liverpool's blue half, Everton FC, consoles itself for existing in the shadow of its more successful neighbour with the historical truth of 'we were there first'. **Goodison Park Tours** (☑0151-530 5212; www.evertonfc.com; adult/child £10/5; ⊘11am & 1pm Mon, Wed, Fri & Sun) run throughout the year, except on the Friday before home matches. Take bus 19, 20 or 21 from Paradise St Interchange or Queen St Bus Station.

🔒 Shopping

Sandwiched between Albert Dock, the Cavern Quarter and Ropewalks, the simply enormous **Liverpool ONE** (www.liverpool-one.com; ⊘9.30am-8pm Mon-Fri, 9am-7pm Sat, 11am-5pm Sun) shopping district ('centre' just feels too small) – 17 hectares of retail and restaurant pleasure.

ℹ Information

There is a small **tourist office** (☑0151-707 0729; www.visitliverpool.com; Anchor Courtyard; ⊘10am-6pm) in Albert Dock, and a separate **accommodation hotline** (☑0845 601 1125; ⊘9am-5.30pm Mon-Fri, 10am-4pm Sat).

Liverpool Magazine (www.liverpool.com) Insiders' guide to the city run by the *Liverpool Echo*, including lots of great recommendations for food and nights out.

Mars Pharmacy (68 London Rd) Open until 10pm every night.

Mersey Guide (www.merseyguide.co.uk) Guide to the Greater Mersey area.

Merseyside Police Headquarters (☑0151-709 6010; Canning Pl) Opposite Albert Dock.

Post Office (Ranelagh St; ⊘9am-5.30pm Mon-Sat)

Royal Liverpool University Hospital (☑0151-706 2000; Prescot St)

ℹ Getting There & Away

AIR

Liverpool John Lennon Airport (☑0870 750 8484; www.liverpoolairport.com; Speke Hall Ave) serves a variety of international destinations as well as destinations in the UK (Belfast, London and the Isle of Man).

BUS

The **National Express Coach Station** (www.nationalexpress.com; Norton St) is 300m north of Lime St station. There are services to/from most major towns including Birmingham (£13.80, 2¾ hours, five daily), London (£28, five to six hours, six daily), Manchester (£7.10, 1¼ hours, hourly) and Newcastle (£25.70, 6½ hours, three daily).

TRAIN

Liverpool's main station is Lime St. It has hourly services to almost everywhere, including Chester (£6.65, 45 minutes), London Euston (£78.70, 3¼ hours) and Manchester (£11.90, 45 minutes).

ⓘ Getting Around

TO/FROM THE AIRPORT

The airport is 8 miles south of the centre. **Arriva Airlink** (www.arriva.co.uk; adult £2; ⊗ 6am-11pm) buses 80A and 180 depart from Paradise St Interchange, and **Arriva 500** (www.arriva.co.uk; £2.50; ⊗ 5.15am-12.15am) buses leave from outside Lime St station. Buses from both stations take half an hour and run every 20 minutes. A taxi to the city centre should cost no more than £18.

BOAT

The famous **Mersey ferry** (www.merseyferries.co.uk; one way/return £2.30/2.80) crossing for Woodside and Seacombe departs from Pier Head Ferry Terminal, next to the Royal Liver Building (to the north of Albert Dock).

CAR & MOTORCYCLE

You won't have much use for a car in Liverpool, and it'll no doubt end up costing you in parking fees. If you have to drive, there are parking meters around the city and a number of open and sheltered car parks. Car break-ins are a significant problem, so leave nothing of value in the car.

PUBLIC TRANSPORT

Local public transport is coordinated by **Merseytravel** (www.merseytravel.gov.uk). Highly recommended is the Saveaway ticket (adult/child £5/2.50), which allows for one day's off-peak (after 9.30am) travel on all bus, train and ferry services throughout Merseyside. Tickets are available at shops and post offices throughout the city. Paradise St Interchange is in the city centre.

Merseyrail (www.merseyrail.org) is an extensive suburban rail service linking Liverpool with the Greater Merseyside area. There are four stops in the city centre: Lime St, Central (handy for Ropewalks), James St (close to Albert Dock) and Moorfields (for the Liverpool War Museum).

TAXI

Mersey Cabs (☑ 0151-298 2222) operates tourist taxi services and also has some wheelchair-accessible cabs.

LANCASHIRE

As you travel north, past the concrete blanket that covers much of the southern half of the county, Lancashire's undulating landscape begins to reveal itself in all its bucolic glory. Beyond Blackpool – the faded queen of beachside holidays – the Ribble Valley is a gentle and beautiful warm-up for the Lake District that lies beyond the county's northern border. North of the Ribble Valley is the county's handsome Georgian capital, Lancaster.

Blackpool

POP 148,185

Blackpool is the queen of England's faded fun-by-the-seaside resorts, a defiant tribute to a traditional past before the advent of low-cost airlines and sun holidays in Spain. It's tacky, trashy and a little tawdry, but Blackpool doesn't care because 15 million-plus annual visitors don't either.

The town is famous for its tower, its three piers, its Pleasure Beach and its Illuminations, the latter being a successful ploy to extend the brief summer holiday season. From early September to early November, 5 miles of the Promenade are illuminated with thousands of electric and neon lights.

⊙ Sights

Blackpool Pleasure Beach AMUSEMENT PARK (www.blackpoolpleasurebeach.com; Central Promenade; Pleasure Beach Pass £6, Unlimited Ride wristband 1-day adult/child £30/27, Speedy Pass/VIP Speedy Pass per person £12/42; ⊗ hours vary) The main reason for Blackpool's immense popularity is the Blackpool Pleasure Beach, a 16-hectare collection of more than 145 rides that attracts some seven million visitors annually. As amusement parks go, it's easily the best in Britain.

Rides are divided into categories, and once you've gained entry to the park with your Freedom Ticket you can buy tickets for individual categories or for a mixture of them all. Alternatively, an Unlimited Ride wristband includes the £5 entrance fee; there are great discounts if you book your tickets online in advance. The Speedy Pass saves you the hassle of queuing for rides by allocating you a specific ride time; rent it and add as many people to it as you want; they've just added a VIP Speedy Pass that allows you get in ahead of regular Speedy Pass users.

There are no set times for closing; it depends how busy it is.

Blackpool Tower
ENTERTAINMENT COMPLEX

(☑ 0844 856 1000; www.theblackpooltower.com; Tower Ticket adult/child £52/40; ⊙ hours vary) Built in 1894, this 154m-high tower is Blackpool's most recognisable landmark. Watch a 4D film on the town's history in the **Blackpool Tower Eye** (a 2011 addition), before taking the elevator 154m up to the observation deck, which has splendid views and only a (thick) glass floor between you and the ant-sized people below.

Back at ground level, the **dungeon** exhibit sits alongside the old Moorish circus and the magnificent rococo ballroom, with its extraordinary sculptured and gilded plasterwork, murals, chandeliers and couples gliding across the beautifully polished wooden floor to the melodramatic tones of a huge Wurlitzer organ. There's also **Jungle Jim's** adventure playground for kids.

Visitors are strongly urged to buy their tickets online as buying them at the door can be up to 50% more expensive.

Sandcastle Waterpark
AMUSEMENT PARK

(www.sandcastle-waterpark.co.uk; adult/child £14.50/11.50, Hyperzone £5/2.50; ⊙ hours vary) Across from Pleasure Beach is this indoor water complex with 15 different slides and rides, including the Hyperzone, which has the complex's most popular slides: Aztec Falls, Montezooma, the Sidewinder and Master Blaster, the world's largest indoor water slide.

North Pier
LANDMARK

(Promenade) **FREE** Built in 1862 and opening a year later, the most famous of the three Victorian piers once charged a penny for admission; its plethora of unexciting rides are now free.

🛏 Sleeping

If you want to stay close to the waterfront, prepare for a noisy, boisterous night; accommodation along Albert and Hornby Rds, 300m back from the sea, is that little bit quieter. The tourist office will assist you in finding a bed.

Number One
BOUTIQUE HOTEL **££**

(☑ 01253-343901; www.numberoneblackpool.com; 1 St Lukes Rd; s/d from £70/100; P ☏) Far fancier than anything else around, this stunning boutique guesthouse is all luxury and contemporary style. Everything exudes a kind of discreet elegance, from the dark-wood furniture and high-end mod cons to the top-notch breakfast. It's on a quiet road just set back from the South Promenade near the Pleasure Beach amusement park.

Big Blue Hotel
HOTEL **££**

(☑ 01253-400045; www.bigbluehotel.com; Blackpool Pleasure Beach; r from £80; P @ ☏) A handsome family hotel with smartly kitted-out rooms. Kids are looked after with DVD players and computer games, while its location at the southern entrance to Blackpool Pleasure Beach should ensure that everyone has something to do.

🍴 Eating

Forget gourmet meals – the Blackpool experience is all about stuffing your face with burgers, doughnuts, and fish and chips. Most people eat at their hotels, where roast and three vegetables often costs just £5 per head.

There are a few restaurants around Talbot Sq (near the tourist office) on Queen St, Talbot Rd and Clifton St.

ℹ Information

Tourist Office (☑ 01253-478222; www.visitblackpool.com; 1 Clifton St; ⊙ 9am-5pm Mon-Sat)

ℹ Getting There & Away

BUS

The central coach station is on Talbot Rd, near the town centre. Services include London (£34.20, seven hours, four daily) and Manchester (£8.90, 1¾ hours, four daily).

TRAIN

The main train station is Blackpool North, about five blocks east of the North Pier on Talbot Rd. There is a direct service from Manchester (£16.30, 1¼ hours, half-hourly) and Liverpool (£17.60, 1½ hours, seven daily), but most other arrivals change in Preston (£7.60, 30 minutes, half-hourly).

ℹ Getting Around

A host of travel-card options for trams and buses ranging from one day to a week are available at the tourist office and most newsagents. With more than 14,000 car-parking spaces in Blackpool, you'll have no problem parking. The (recently upgraded) **tramway** (one stop £1, up to 16 stops £2; ⊙ from 10.30am Apr-Oct) shuttles funsters for 11 miles, including along the pier as far as the Fylde Coast (also serving the central corridor car parks), every eight minutes or so throughout the day. Otherwise, the town's **bike hire scheme** (www.hourbike.com; per hr £1) has bikes available for hire from stations along the Promenade and in Stanley Park.

Lancaster

POP 44,500

Lancashire's county seat is genteel, austere and much, much quieter than it was in its 18th-century heyday, when it served as an important trading port for all manner of goods, including people. The city's handsome Georgian architecture was one of the slave trade's ancillary benefits.

◉ Sights

Lancaster Castle & Priory　　CASTLE
(☑01524-64998; www.lancastercastle.com; Castle Park; adult/child £8/6.50; ◉10am-5pm, guided tours every 30min 10am-4pm) Lancaster's imposing castle was originally built in 1150. Later additions include the Well Tower, more commonly known as the Witches' Tower because it was used to incarcerate the accused of the famous Pendle Witches Trial of 1612, and the impressive twin-towered gatehouse, both from the 14th century. Visits are by guided tour only as the castle is used as a Crown Court.

The castle was heavily restored in the 18th and 19th centuries to suit a new function as a prison, and it continued to house Category C prisoners until 2011.

Immediately next to the castle is the equally fine priory church (Priory Cl; ◉9.30am-5pm), founded in 1094 but extensively remodelled in the Middle Ages.

Judges' Lodgings　　MUSEUM
(Church St; adult/child £3/2; ◉10am-4pm Jun & Jul, 1-4pm Easter-May & Aug-Oct) Once the home of witch-hunter Thomas Covell (who 'caught' the poor Pendle women), Lancaster's oldest town house, a Grade I–listed Georgian building, is now home to a Museum of Furnishings by master builders Gillows of Lancaster, whose work graces the Houses of Parliament. It also houses a Museum of Childhood with memorabilia from the turn of the 20th century.

**Williamson Park &
Tropical Butterfly House**　　GARDENS
(Tropical Butterfly House adult/child £3.70/2.70; ◉10am-5pm Apr-Sep, to 4pm Oct-Mar) Lancaster's highest point is the 22-hectare spread of this elegant park, whose highlights are (besides the views) the Tropical Butterfly House, full of exotic and stunning species, and the Ashton Memorial, a 67m-high baroque folly built by Lord Ashton (the son of the park's founder, James Williamson) for his wife. Take bus 25 or 25A from the station, or else it's a steep, short walk up Moor Lane.

🛏 Sleeping & Eating

Sun Hotel & Bar　　HOTEL ££
(☑01524-66006; www.thesunhotelandbar.co.uk; 63 Church St; r from £90; ᴾ🖥) An excellent hotel in a 300-year-old building with a rustic, old-world look that stops at the bedroom doors – beyond them are 16 stylish and contemporary rooms. The pub downstairs is one of the best in town and a top spot for a bit of grub; the two-course roast of the day (£8) is excellent.

Whale Tail Cafe　　VEGETARIAN £
(www.whaletailcafe.co.uk; 78a Penny St; mains £8-11; ◉10am-4pm Mon-Fri, to 5pm Sat, to 3pm Sun; 🍴) This gorgeous 1st-floor veggie restaurant has an elegant dining room and a more informal plant-filled courtyard for lunch on a sunny day. The spicy bean burger is particularly good. Food here is locally produced and, where possible, organic.

❶ Information

Tourist Office (☑01524-582394; www.citycoastcountryside.co.uk; Storey Creative Industries Centre, Meeting House Lane; ◉9am-5pm Mon-Sat)

❶ Getting There & Away

Lancaster is on the main west coast railway line and on the Cumbrian coast line. Destinations include Carlisle (£19.50, one hour, hourly), Manchester (£8.60, one hour, hourly) and Morecambe (£2.30, 15 minutes, half-hourly).

Ribble Valley

Known locally as 'Little Switzerland', Lancashire's most attractive landscapes lie east of the brash tackiness of Blackpool and north of the sprawling urban areas of Preston and Blackburn.

The northern half of the valley is dominated by the sparsely populated moorland of the Forest of Bowland, which is a fantastic place for walks, while the southern half features rolling hills, attractive market towns and ruins, with the River Ribble flowing between them.

🏃 Activities

Ribble Way　　WALKING
(www.visitlancashire.com) The Ribble Way, a 70-mile footpath that follows the River Ribble from its source at Ribblehead (in the Yorkshire Dales) to the estuary at Preston, is one of the more popular walks in the area and passes through Clitheroe.

THE PENDLE WITCHES

A lovely walk brings you to the top of Pendle Hill (558m) from which there are marvellous views of the surrounding countryside.

In 1612, however, the surrounding villages in the shadow of Pendle Hill were the scene of dramatic witch trials. Ten people, two of them older women who were known locally as 'healers', were accused of practising witchcraft, including murder, and were convicted to hang based on the sole testimony of a nine-year-old child (a legal reference point that would later influence the Salem Witch Trials of the New World). Every Halloween a pseudomystical ceremony is performed here to commemorate their 'activities'. If that's not enough, in 1652 George Fox, the founder of the Quakers, felt compelled to climb Pendle Hill and experienced visions there – an event that was to add momentum to the growth of the Quaker religion.

Lancashire Cycle Way   CYCLING

The Ribble Valley is well covered by the northern loop of the Lancashire Cycle Way; for more information about routes, safety and so on, contact Blazing Saddles (01442-844435; www.blazingsaddles.co.uk; 35 West End, Hebden Bridge, West Yorkshire), a Yorkshire-based bike shop.

Clitheroe

POP 14,700

Located northeast of Preston, the Ribble Valley's largest market town is best known for its impressive Norman keep (dawn-dusk) FREE, built in the 12th century and now, sadly, standing empty; from it there are great views of the river valley below. The extensive grounds are home to the newly refurbished Castle Museum (Castle Hill; adult/child £4/3; 11am-4pm Mar-Oct, noon-4pm Mon, Tue & Fri-Sun Nov-Feb), which explores 350 million years of local history.

Sleeping & Eating

Old Post House Hotel   HOTEL ££

(01200-422025; www.posthousehotel.co.uk; 44-48 King St; s/d from £50/70; P) A former post office is now Clitheroe's most handsome hotel, with 11 superbly decorated rooms.

Halpenny's of Clitheroe   TEAROOM £

(Old Toll House, 1-5 Parson Lane; mains £7-9) A traditional teashop that serves sandwiches, and dishes such as Lancashire hotpot.

Information

Tourist Office (01200-425566; www.visitribblevalley.co.uk; Church Walk; 9am-5pm Mon-Sat) Info on the town and surrounding area.

Forest of Bowland

This vast grouse-ridden moorland is somewhat of a misnomer. The use of 'forest' is a throwback to an earlier definition, when it served as a royal hunting ground. Today it is an Area of Outstanding Natural Beauty (AONB), which makes for good walking and cycling. The Pendle Witch Way, a 45-mile walk from Pendle Hill to northeast of Lancaster, cuts right through the area, and the Lancashire Cycle Way runs along the eastern border. The forest's main town is Slaidburn, about 9 miles north of Clitheroe on the B6478.

Other villages worth exploring are Newton, Whitewell and Dunsop Bridge.

Sleeping & Eating

Slaidburn YHA   HOSTEL £

(0845 371 9343; www.yha.org.uk; King's House; dm £18; Apr-Oct) A converted 17th-century village inn that is especially popular with walkers and cyclists.

Inn at Whitewell   INN ££

(01200-448222; www.innatwhitewell.com; s/d from £90/119) Once the home of Bowland's forest keeper, this is now a superb guesthouse with antique furniture, peat fires and Victorian claw-foot baths. The restaurant specialises in traditional English game dishes (mains £11 to £19).

Hark to Bounty Inn   INN ££

(01200-446246; www.harktobounty.co.uk; Slaidburn; s/d from £45/90) This marvellous 13th-century inn has atmospheric rooms with exposed oak beams. An excellent restaurant downstairs specialises in homemade herb breads (mains £9 to £17).

Getting There & Away

Clitheroe is served by regular buses from Preston and Blackburn and hourly trains from Manchester (£9.30, 75 minutes) and Preston (£6.70, 50 minutes). Once here, you're better off having your own transport: there is only a Sunday bus service between Clitheroe and the rest of the valley villages.

ISLE OF MAN

Deliberately different and not-so-ferociously independent, the Isle of Man (Ellan Vannin in Manx, the local lingo) has doggedly held onto its semi-autonomous status (it is home to the world's oldest continuous parliament, the Tynwald) so as to continue doing its own thing, which really means operating as a popular tax haven.

The islanders' rejection of England's warm embrace has led to an oft-quoted prejudice that there's something odd about them, but the only thing that's odd here is the local tailless cat.

Crass commercialism and mass tourism have no place here, except of course for the world-famous summer season of Tourist Trophy (TT) motorbike racing, which attracts around 50,000 punters and bike freaks every May and June, bringing noise and mayhem to the otherwise lush valleys, barren hills and rugged coastlines of this beautiful island. Needless to say, if you want a slice of silence, be sure to avoid the high-rev bike fest.

🏃 Activities

With plenty of great marked trails, the Isle of Man is a firm favourite with walkers and is regularly voted one of the best walking destinations in Britain. Ordnance Survey (OS) Landranger Map 95 (£6.99) covers the whole island, while the free *Walks on the Isle of Man* is available from the tourist office in Douglas. The Millennium Way is a walking path that runs the length of the island amid some spectacular scenery. The most demanding of all the island's walks is the 95-mile Raad ny Foillan (Road of the Gull), a well-marked path that makes a complete circuit of the island and normally takes about five days to complete. The Isle of Man Walking Festival (www.iomevents.com; ⊙ mid-May) takes place over five days in May.

The island has six designated off-road mountain-biking trails, each with varying ranges of difficulty. See www.visitisleofman.com for details.

ℹ Information

Most of the island's historic sites are operated by Manx Heritage, which offers free admission for National Trust or English Heritage members. Unless otherwise indicated, **Manx Heritage** (www.manxnational.im) sites are open 10am to 5pm daily, from Easter to October. The Manx Heritage **Holiday Pass** (www.manxheritageshop.com; adult/child £20/10) grants you entry to all nine of the island's heritage attractions; pick it up at any of the tourist offices or online.

You can also check out www.iomevents.com for listings of what's on in the Isle of Man, along with accommodation and other tourist information.

ℹ Getting There & Away

AIR

Ronaldsway Airport (www.iom-airport.com) is 10 miles south of Douglas near Castletown. Airlines that service the region:

Aer Lingus Regional (www.aerlingus.com; from £75) From Dublin.

Citywing (www.citywing.com; from £50) From Belfast, Blackpool, Leeds-Bradford, Gloucester M5, Newcastle and East Midlands.

EasyJet (www.easyjet.com; from £59) From Liverpool and London Gatwick.

Flybe (www.flybe.com; from £21) From Birmingham, Bristol, Jersey, London Gatwick, Luton, Liverpool, Manchester, Glasgow and Edinburgh.

BOAT

Isle of Man Steam Packet (www.steampacket.com; foot passenger single/return £22/40, car & 2 passengers return from £115) Isle of Man Steam Packet is a car ferry and high-speed catamaran service from Liverpool and Heysham to Douglas. There is also a summer service (mid-April to mid-September) to Dublin (three hours) and Belfast (three hours). It's usually cheaper to buy a return ticket than to pay the single fare.

ℹ Getting Around

Buses link the airport with Douglas every 30 minutes between 7am and 11pm; a taxi should cost you no more than £18.

The island has a comprehensive **bus service** (www.gov.im); the tourist office in Douglas has timetables and sells tickets. It also sells the **Island Explorer** (1-day adult/child £16/8, 3-day £32/16), which gives you unlimited public transport use, including the tram to Snaefell and Douglas' horse-trams.

Bikes can be hired from **Eurocycles** (www.eurocycles.co.im; 8 Victoria Rd; per day £14-20; ⊙9am-5.30pm Mon-Sat).

Petrolheads will love the scenic, sweeping bends that make for some exciting driving – and the fact that outside of Douglas town there's no speed limit. Naturally, the most popular drive is along the TT route. Car-hire operators have desks at the airport, and charge from around £38 per day.

The 19th-century electric and steam **rail services** (☏ 01624-663366; www.iombusandrail.info; ⊙ Mar-Oct) are a thoroughly satisfying way of getting from A to B:

Douglas–Castletown–Port Erin Steam Train
(return £10.80)
Douglas–Laxey–Ramsey Electric Tramway
(return £10.80)
Laxey–Summit Snaefell Mountain Railway
(return £10.80)

Douglas

POP 28,940

Much like Blackpool across the water, Douglas' heyday was in the middle of the 19th century, when it was a favourite destination for Victorian mass tourism. It's not nearly as popular – or as pretty – today, but it still has the best of the island's hotels and restaurants – as well as the bulk of the finance houses that are frequented so regularly by tax-allergic Brits.

The Manx Museum (www.gov.im/mnh; Kingswood Grove; ⊙10am-5pm Mon-Sat) FREE gives an introduction to everything from the island's prehistoric past to the latest TT race winners.

🛏 Sleeping

The seafront promenade is crammed with B&Bs. Unless you booked back at the beginning of the millennium, however, there's little chance of finding accommodation during TT week and the weeks either side of it. The tourist office's camping information sheet lists sites all around the island.

Sefton Hotel　　　　　　　　HOTEL ££
(☑01624-645500; www.seftonhotel.co.im; Harris Promenade; r from £70; P🗢) Douglas' best hotel is an upmarket oasis with its own indoor water garden and rooms that range from plain and comfy to elegant and very luxurious. The rooms overlooking the water garden are superb, even better than the ones with sea views. Save up to 10% by booking online.

Admiral House　　　　　　　　　B&B ££
(☑01624-629551; www.admiralhouse.com; Loch Promenade; s/d from £60/75; P🗢) This elegant guesthouse overlooks the harbour near the ferry port. The 23 spotless and modern rooms are a cheerful alternative to the worn look of a lot of other seafront B&Bs.

Palace Hotel　　　　　　　　　HOTEL ££
(☑01624-662662; www.palacehotel.co.im; Central Promenade; r from £75; P@🗷) Tidy, modern rooms, a small gym and a casino – a Best Western hotel that takes care of your every need.

🍴 Eating & Drinking

There are a few good drinking spots around, including Bar George (www.bargeorge.im; St George's Chambers, 3 Hill St), an elegant option for a glass of wine, and Rover's Return (11 Church St), which specialises in the local brew, Bushy Ales.

14North　　　　　　　　MEDITERRANEAN ££
(☑01624-664414; www.14north.im; mains £14-21; ⊙noon-2.30pm & 6-9.30pm Mon-Sat) An old timber merchant's house is now home to this smart eatery serving North African–style flatbreads (basically gourmet pizzas with a variety of toppings) and a selection of fish and meat dishes.

Tanroagan　　　　　　　　　SEAFOOD £££
(☑01624-472411; www.tanroagan.co.uk; 9 Ridgeway St; mains £19-31; ⊙noon-2pm & 6.30-9.30pm Mon-Sat) The place for all things from the sea, this elegant eatery is Douglas' smartest. It serves fresh fish straight off the boats, giving them the merest of Continental twists or just a spell on the hot grill. Reservations are recommended.

ℹ Information

Tourist Office (☑01624-686766; www.visit isleofman.com; Sea Terminal Bldg; ⊙9.15am-7pm May-Sep, closed Sun Oct-Apr) Makes free accommodation bookings.

Around Douglas

You can follow the TT circuit up and over the mountain or wind around the coast. The mountain route goes close to the summit of Snaefell (621m), the island's highest point. It's an easy walk up to the summit, or take the electric tram from Laxey, near the coast.

On the edge of Ramsey, on the north of the island, is the Grove Museum of Victorian Life (MH; Andreas Rd; admission £5; ⊙10am-5pm Apr-Oct), where you can see the summer home of a well-to-do family preserved in aspic – and learn what it was like to be a scullery maid! The church in the small village of Maughold is on the site of an ancient monastery; a small shelter houses quite a good selection of stone crosses and ancient inscriptions.

It's no exaggeration to describe the Lady Isabella Laxey Wheel (MH; Mines Rd, Laxey; admission £5; ⊙10am-5pm Apr-Oct), built in 1854 to pump water from a mine, as a 'great' wheel: it measures 22m across and can draw 1140L of water per minute from a depth of 550m. The largest wheel of its kind in the world, it's named after the wife of the then lieutenant-governor.

The wheel-headed cross at Lonan Old Church, just north of Douglas, is the island's most impressive early Christian cross.

Castletown & Around

At the southern end of the island is Castletown, a quiet harbour town that was originally the capital of the Isle of Man. The town is dominated by the impressive 13th-century Castle Rushen (MH; Castletown Sq; admission £6; ☉ 10am-5pm Apr-Oct). The flag tower affords fine views of the town and coast. There's also a small Nautical Museum (MH; Bridge St; admission £5; ☉ 10am-5pm Easter-Oct) displaying, among other things, its pride and joy, *Peggy*, a boat built in 1791 and still housed in its original boathouse. There is a school dating back to 1570 in St Mary's Church (MH; ☉ 10am-5pm Mar-Nov) FREE, behind the castle.

The Garrison Tapas Bar (www.thegarrison. co.im; 5 Castle St; tapas £7-8; ☉ 10am-4pm Mon, to 9pm Tue-Sat) brings Iberian flavour to a handsome 17th-century building in the town centre. The paella is fantastic and huge, so is best shared.

Between Castletown and Cregneash, the Iron Age hill fort at Chapel Hill encloses a Viking ship burial site.

On the southern tip of the island, the Cregneash Village Folk Museum (MH; admission £5; ☉ 10am-5pm Apr-Oct) recalls traditional Manx rural life. The Calf of Man, the small island just off Cregneash, is a bird sanctuary. Calf Island Cruises (☎01624-832339; adult/child £14/7; ☉ 10.15am, 11.30am & 1.30pm Apr-Oct, weather permitting) run between Port Erin and the island.

Port Erin & Port St Mary

Port Erin, another Victorian seaside resort, plays host to the small Railway Museum (Station Rd; adult/child £2/1; ☉ 10am-5pm Apr-Oct), which reveals the history of steam railway on the island.

Port Erin has a good range of accommodation, as does Port St Mary, across the headland and linked by steam train. The Victorian Falcon's Nest Hotel (☎01624-834077; www.falconsnesthotel.co.uk; Station Rd, Port Erin; d from £80; ☎), once supremely elegant, is now just handsome in a nostalgic sort of way. The rooms aren't noteworthy, but the views over the water are superb. The slightly more splendid Victorian-style Aaron House (☎01624-835702; www.aaronhouse.co.uk; The Promenade, Port St Mary; s/d from £38/70) is a B&B that has fussed over every detail, from the gorgeous brass beds and claw-foot baths to the old-fashioned photographs on the walls. The sea views are also sensational.

Peel & Around

The west coast's most appealing town has a fine sandy beach, but its real attraction is the 11th-century Peel Castle (MH; admission £5; ☉ 10am-5pm Apr-Oct), stunningly positioned atop St Patrick's Island and joined to Peel by a causeway.

The House of Manannan (MH; admission £6; ☉ 10am-5pm Apr-Oct) museum uses interactive displays to explain Manx history and its seafaring traditions.

Three miles east of Peel is Tynwald Hill at St John's, where the annual parliamentary ceremony takes place on 5 July.

Peel has several B&Bs, including the Fernleigh Hotel (☎01624-842435; www.isleofman-bedandbreakfast.com; Marine Pde; d from £72; ☉ Feb-Nov), which has 12 decent bedrooms. For a better-than-average bite, head for the Creek Inn (☎01624-842216; www.thecreekinn. co.uk; East Quay; mains around £8, r from £35; ☉ 10am-11pm), opposite the House of Manannan, which serves Manx queenies (scallops served with white cheese sauce).

The Lake District & Cumbria

Best Traditional Inns

➡ Drunken Duck (p597)

➡ Wasdale Head Inn (p601)

➡ Pheasant Inn (p604)

➡ Mortal Man (p590)

➡ Kirkstile Inn (p607)

Best Beauty Spots

➡ Wasdale (p600)

➡ Tarn Hows (p596)

➡ Great Langdale (p599)

➡ Buttermere (p607)

➡ Derwentwater (p603)

Why Go?

'No part of the country is more distinguished by its sub-limity', mused the grand old bard of the lakes, William Wordsworth, and a couple of centuries on his words still ring true. In terms of natural splendour, nowhere in England can compare to the Lake District. For centuries, poets, painters and perambulators alike have been flocking here in search of inspiration and escape, and it's still the nation's favourite place to revel in the majesty of the English landscape.

The main draw here is undoubtedly the Lake District National Park – England's largest, at 885 sq miles. Every bend in the road reveals more eye-popping views: deep valleys, plunging passes, glittering lakes, whitewashed inns, barren hills. But it's worth exploring beyond the national park's boundaries too: the old towns of Carlisle, Kendal and Penrith are full of historical interest, and Cumbria's coast has a windswept charm all of its own.

When to Go

➡ The Lake District is the UK's most popular national park; visit in early spring and late autumn for the fewest crowds. Its weather is also notoriously fickle – showers can strike at any time of year, so bring wet-weather gear just in case.

➡ Cumbria's largest mountain festival is held in Keswick in mid-May, while the Beer Festival in June welcomes ale aficionados from across the globe.

➡ Ambleside's traditional sports day on the last Saturday in July features events such as hound trailing and Cumbrian wrestling; Grasmere's annual sports day takes place on the August Bank Holiday.

➡ In November, the world's greatest liars congregate on Santon Bridge for their annual fibbing contest.

History

Neolithic settlers arrived in the Lake District around 5000 BC. The region was subsequently occupied by Celts, Angles, Vikings and Romans, and during the Dark Ages marked the centre of the ancient kingdom of Rheged.

During the Middle Ages, Cumbria marked the start of the 'Debatable Lands', the wild frontier between England and Scotland. Bands of raiders known as Border Reivers regularly plundered the area, prompting the construction of defensive *pele* towers and castles at Carlisle, Penrith and Kendal.

The area became a centre for the Romantic movement during the 19th century, largely thanks to the Cumbrian-born poet William Wordsworth, who also championed the need to protect the Lake District's landscape from overdevelopment – a dream that was achieved in 1951, when the Lake District National Park was formed.

The present-day county of Cumbria was formed from the neighbouring districts of Cumberland and Westmorland in 1974.

⚘ Activities

Cycling

Cycling is a great way to explore the Lake District and Cumbria, as long as you don't mind the hills. For short mountain-bike rides, the trails of Grizedale Forest (p596) and Whinlatter Forest Park (p602) are very popular.

Long-distance touring routes include the 70-mile Cumbria Way between Ulverston, Keswick and Carlisle; the 140-mile Sea To Sea Cycle Route (C2C; NCN 7; www.c2c-guide.co.uk), which begins in Whitehaven and cuts east across the northern Pennines to Newcastle; and the 173-mile Reivers Route (NCN 10; www.reivers-route.co.uk) from the River Tyne to Whitehaven.

Several local buses (including bus 599 from Bowness to Grasmere, bus X33 from Ambleside to Ravenglass and the Cross Lakes Experience) have space for bikes. There's also the new summer-only bus 800 along Windermere's eastern shore, which can carry 12 bikes. It runs several times a day in July and August, plus on weekends in May and June. You pay the standard bus fare plus £1.50 for each bike. For more information see www.golakes.co.uk/travel/New-Bike-Bus.aspx.

Walking

For many people, hiking is the main reason for a visit to the Lake District. All tourist offices and bookshops sell maps and guidebooks, such as Collins' *Lakeland Fellranger* and Ordnance Survey's *Pathfinder Guides*. Purists prefer Alfred Wainwright's seven-volume *Pictorial Guides to the Lakeland Fells* (1955–66) – part walking guides, part illustrated artworks, part philosophical memoirs, with painstakingly hand-penned maps and text.

Maps are essential: the Ordnance Survey's 1:25,000 *Landranger* maps are used by most official bodies, while some hikers prefer the Harvey *Superwalker* 1:25,000 maps.

Long-distance trails which pass through Cumbria include the 54-mile Allerdale Ramble from Seathwaite to the Solway Firth, the 70-mile Cumbria Way from Ulverston to Carlisle and the 191-mile Coast to Coast from St Bees to Robin Hood's Bay in Yorkshire. Door-to-door baggage services such as Coast to Coast Packhorse (☑ 017683-71777; www.c2cpackhorse.co.uk) or Sherpa Van (☑ 0871 520-0124; www.sherpavan.com) transport luggage from one destination to the next.

Other Activities

Cumbria is a haven for outdoor activities, including rock climbing, orienteering, horse riding, archery, fell (mountain) running and *ghyll* (waterfall) scrambling. Contact the Holmescales Activity Centre (☑ 01539-722147; www.holmescales.com; Old Hutton, Kendal), Rookin House (☑ 017684-83561; www.rookinhouse.co.uk; Troutbeck) or Keswick Adventure Centre (☑ 017687-75687; www.keswickadventurecentre.co.uk; Newlands).

❶ Getting There & Away

Carlisle is on the main West Coast train line from London Euston to Manchester and Glasgow. To get to the Lake District, you need to change at Oxenholme for Kendal and Windermere. The lines around the Cumbrian coast and between Settle and Carlisle are particularly scenic.

National Express coaches run direct from London Victoria and Glasgow to Windermere, Carlisle and Kendal.

❶ Getting Around

Traveline (☑ 0871 200 22 33; www.travelinenortheast.info) provides comprehensive travel information. Bus timetables are available from tourist offices.

There are round-the-lake ferry services on Windermere, Coniston Water, Ullswater and Derwentwater. Windermere also has a ferry service (p589).

Traffic can be heavy during peak season and holiday weekends. Many Cumbrian towns use

THE LAKE DISTRICT & CUMBRIA

The Lake District & Cumbria Highlights

1 Conquering England's highest mountain, **Scafell Pike** (p600)

2 Spotting the inspirations for Beatrix Potter's tales at **Hill Top** (p596)

3 Cruising Coniston Water aboard the **Steam Yacht Gondola** (p598)

4 Cycling the trails of **Grizedale Forest** (p596)

5 Delving into the slate mines of **Honister Pass** (p607)

6 Catching the miniature steam trains of **La'al Ratty** (p612) into Eskdale

7 Visiting Wordsworth's houses, **Dove Cottage** (p594) and **Rydal Mount** (p591)

8 Patrolling the battlements of **Carlisle Castle** (p612)

9 Sampling world-famous gingerbread at **Sarah Nelson's shop** (p595) in Grasmere

timed parking permits for on-street parking, which you can pick up free from local shops and tourist offices.

The main bus operator is **Stagecoach** (www. stagecoachbus.com). Services on most routes are reduced in winter. You can download timetables from the Stagecoach website or the Cumbria County Council website.

Bus 505 (Coniston Rambler) Kendal, Windermere, Ambleside and Coniston.

Bus 555 (Lakeslink) Lancaster to Keswick, stopping at all the main towns including Windermere and Ambleside.

Bus X4/X5 Penrith to Workington via Troutbeck, Keswick and Cockermouth.

TRAVEL PASSES

Several travel passes are available in Cumbria.

Central Lakes Dayrider (adult/child/family £8/6/20) This pass covers buses around Bowness, Ambleside, Grasmere, Langdale and Coniston; it includes buses 599, 505 and 516.

Cumbria Day Ranger (adult/child £40.50/20.25) This provides one day's train travel in Cumbria and parts of Lancashire, North Yorkshire, Northumberland and Dumfries and Galloway.

Keswick & Honister Dayrider (adult/child/family £8/6/20) Buses from Keswick through Borrowdale, Buttermere, Lorton and the Whinlatter Forest Park.

Lakes Day Ranger (adult/child/family £21.50/11.75/42) The best-value ticket, allowing one day's unlimited travel on trains and buses. It also includes a boat cruise on Windermere, 10% discount on the steam railways and 20% discount on the Coniston Launch, Keswick Launch and Ullswater Steamers.

North West Explorer (adult/child/family £10.50/7.50/25) Includes one day's travel in Cumbria and Lancashire, and cross-border services to/from Dumfries. The £30 Group ticket can be used by five adults.

THE LAKE DISTRICT

The Lake District (or Lakeland, as it's often known round these parts) is by far and away the UK's most popular national park. Every year, some 15 million people pitch up to explore the region's fells and countryside, and it's not hard to see why. Ever since the Romantic poets arrived in the 19th century, its postcard panorama of craggy hilltops, mountain tarns and glittering lakes has been stirring the imaginations of visitors.

It's awash with outdoor opportunities, from lake cruises to mountain walks, but many people visit for the region's literary connections; William Wordsworth, Beatrix Potter, Arthur Ransome and John Ruskin all found inspiration here.

ℹ Information

The national park's main visitor centre is at Brockhole (p589), just outside Windermere, and there are tourist offices in Windermere, Bowness, Ambleside (p593), Keswick (p605), Coniston (p599) and Carlisle (p614). All have information on local sights, activities, accommodation and public transport, and can help with accommodation bookings.

Windermere & Around

POP 5423

Stretching for 10.5 miles between Ambleside and Newby Bridge, Windermere isn't just the queen of Lake District lakes – it's also the largest body of water anywhere in England, closer in stature to a Scottish loch. It's been a centre for tourism since the first trains chugged into town in 1847, and it's still one of the national park's busiest spots.

Confusingly, the town of Windermere is split in two: Bowness-on-Windermere (usually shortened to Bowness) sits on the lake's eastern shore, while Windermere Town is actually 1.5 miles inland, at the top of a steep hill called Lake Road. Bowness is a bustling tourist town, with a gaggle of teashops, ice-cream stalls, restaurants and souvenir shops that make it feel more like an old-fashioned British seaside resort. Windermere Town is home to a busy high street and orderly ranks of Victorian- and Edwardian-era villas, as well as the town's bus and train stations.

Accommodation (and parking) can be hard to come by during holidays and busy periods, so plan accordingly.

◉ Sights

Windermere's four main attractions – the Lakeland Motor Museum, Lakeside Haverthwaite Railway, Lakes Aquarium and Windermere Lake Cruises – offer combination tickets. Savings depend on which attractions you want to combine: as an example, a ticket including a cruise from Bowness, a return trip on the railway, admission to the Lakeland Motor Museum and a bus back to Bowness costs adult/child/family £21/12.65/58.35.

Tickets can be bought at any of the four sights.

World of Beatrix Potter

MUSEUM

(www.hop-skip-jump.com; Crag Brow, Bowness-on-Windermere; adult/child £6.95/3.65; ⊘ 10am-5.30pm Apr-Sep, to 4.30pm Oct-Mar) This themed attraction brings to life various scenes from Beatrix Potter's books, including Peter Rabbit's garden, Mr McGregor's greenhouse, Mrs Tiggywinkle's kitchen, Jemima Puddle-Duck's glade (there's even a themed tearoom). It's squarely aimed at kids, but adult Potter fans might enjoy indulging their inner child. Be prepared for queues (and lots of Japanese tourists) during holiday times.

Blackwell House

HISTORIC BUILDING

(www.blackwell.org.uk; adult/child under 16yr £7.25/free; ⊘ 10.30am-5pm Apr-Oct, to 4pm Feb-Mar, Nov & Dec) Two miles south of Bowness on the B5360, Blackwell House is a glorious example of the 19th-century Arts and Crafts Movement, which championed the importance of handmade goods and craftsmanship over the mass-produced mentality of the Industrial Revolution.

Designed by Mackay Hugh Baillie Scott for a wealthy brewer, the house has many hallmarks of Arts and Crafts design: light, airy rooms, detailed decor and bespoke craftwork (including wood panelling, stained glass and Delft tiles).

Of note are the huge wood-panelled Great Hall and the serene White Drawing Room. The cafe has brilliant views over Windermere.

Fell Foot Park

GARDENS

(NT; www.nationaltrust.org.uk/fell-foot-park; ⊘ 8am-8pm Apr-Sep, 9am-5pm Oct-Mar) **FREE** Located at the southern end of Windermere, 7 miles south of Bowness, this 7-hectare lakeside estate originally belonged to a manor house. It's now owned by the National Trust, and its shoreline paths and grassy lawns are ideal for a sunny-day picnic. The small cafe is open 10am to 5pm, and rowing boats are available for hire.

1. Mountain biking in Peak District National Park (p477) **2.** Walking in Yorkshire Dales National Park (p520) **3.** Surfing in Newquay (p334) 4. Horse riding in Northumberland National Park (p639)

England's Great Outdoors

The English love the great outdoors, and every weekend sees a mass exodus from the towns and cities to the hills, moors and coastline. Hiking and biking are the most popular pursuits but there's a huge range of activities available – and getting wet and muddy can actually be a highlight of your trip!

Walking

England can seem crowded, but away from the cities there are many beautiful areas, perfect for walking. You can go for a short riverside stroll or a major hike over mountain ranges – or anything in between. The best places include the Cotswolds, Lake District and Yorkshire Dales.

Cycling

A bike is ideal for getting to know England's countryside. Areas such as Suffolk, Yorkshire and Wiltshire offer a vast network of quiet country roads ideal for cycle touring. For off-road fun, mountain bikers can go further into the wilds in places such as the Peak District, the North Yorkshire Moors and the South Downs.

Horse Riding

If you want to explore the hills and moors at a more leisurely place, seeing the wilder parts of England from horseback is the way to go. In rural areas and national parks such as Dartmoor and Northumberland, there are riding centres catering to all levels of proficiency.

Surfing

England may not be an obvious destination for surfers, but conditions can be surprisingly good at key locations. Top of the list are the west-facing coasts of Cornwall and Devon, while there are smaller scenes on the east coast, notably in Norfolk and Yorkshire.

Windermere Town

Windermere Town

Sleeping
1 1 Park Road...C3
2 Archway...B1
3 Lake District Backpackers
　Lodge...B1
4 Rum Doodle...B4
5 The Boundary..B4
6 Wheatlands Lodge.................................B2

Eating
7 Hooked..B2
8 Lazy Daisy's Lakeland Kitchen............C2
9 Lighthouse..C1
10 Mojo's Bistro.......................................C1

Lakes Aquarium　　　　　　　　　AQUARIUM
(☎015395-30153; www.lakesaquarium.co.uk; Lakeside; adult/child £6.95/4.95; ☉9am-6pm Apr-Oct)
At the southern end of the lake near Newby Bridge, this aquarium explores a range of underwater habitats from tropical Africa

through to Morecambe Bay. Windermere Lake Cruises and the Lakeside & Haverthwaite Railway stop right beside the aquarium, or you could catch bus 618 from Bowness. Discounts for tickets purchased online.

Lakeland Motor Museum　　　　MUSEUM
(www.lakelandmotormuseum.co.uk; Backbarrow; adult/child £8/5; ☉9.30am-5.30pm Apr-Sep, to 4.30pm Oct-Mar) In a purpose-built new home 2 miles south of Newby Bridge, this car museum houses a wonderful collection of antique cars: classic (Minis, Austin Healeys, MGs), sporty (DeLoreans, Audi Quattros, Aston Martins) and plain odd (Scootacars, Amphicars).

The museum is on the A590 from Newby Bridge towards Kendal. Bus X35 (hourly Monday to Saturday, three on Sunday) from Newby Bridge to Ulverston and Kendal stops nearby.

A separate building explores Donald and Malcolm Campbell's record attempts on

Coniston Water, with replicas of the 1935 Bluebird car and 1967 boat, *Bluebird K7.*

Lakeside & Haverthwaite Railway   HERITAGE RAILWAY

(☑ 015395-31594; www.lakesiderailway.co.uk; adult/child/family return £6.50/3.25/18; ☺ mid-Mar–Oct) Originally built to carry ore and timber to the ports at Ulverston and Barrow, these vintage steam trains puff their way between Haverthwaite, near Ulverston, to Newby Bridge and Lakeside. There are five to seven trains a day, timed to correspond with the Windermere cruise boats.

🏃 Activities

Windermere Lake Cruises   BOATING

(☑ 015395-31188; www.windermere-lakecruises.co.uk; tickets from £2.70) Since the launch of the first passenger ferry in 1845, cruising has been an essential part of every Windermere itinerary. Some of the vessels are modern, but there are a couple of period beauties dating back to the 1930s. All cruises allow you to disembark as you please and catch a later ferry back.

There are various colour-coded cruise options available. The **Freedom of the Lake** ticket (adult/child/family £18.50/9.25/50) remains valid all day, and allows unlimited travel on all routes.

The **Blue Cruise** (adult/child/family £7.50/3.80/20) is a 45-minute circular cruise around Windermere's shoreline and islands. The north-lake **Red Cruise** (adult/child/family £10/6/29) goes from Bowness to Ambleside, while the south-lake **Yellow Cruise** (adult/child/family £10.50/6.30/30) heads down to Lakeside and the Lakes Aquarium.

Running in summer only, the **Green Cruise** (adult/child/family £7.50/3.80/20) takes in Waterhead/Ambleside via Wray Castle and Brockhole Visitor Centre. For a cross-lake dash, the **Bowness to Ferry House** (adult/child/family £2.70/1.60/7.60) service links up with buses to Hill Top and Hawkshead. Seasonal twilight cruises are also available.

If you're visiting other attractions such as the Lakeland Motor Museum and the Lakes Aquarium, look out for combination tickets; see p589.

🛌 Sleeping

Windermere's popularity means accommodation is pricier than elsewhere.

Archway   B&B £

(☑ 015394-45613; www.the-archway.com; 13 College Rd, Windermere Town; d £50-86) Value is the name of the game here: this place is a no-nonsense, old-fashioned, home-away-from-home. Some of the rooms have fell views, and the breakfast is enormous, but there's no parking.

Lake District Backpackers Lodge   HOSTEL £

(☑ 015394-46374; www.lakedistrictbackpackers.co.uk; High St, Windermere Town; dm £16, r £36; @) Not the fanciest hostel in the Lake District, but these Windermere digs are about the only option in town for backpackers. There are two small four-bed dorms, plus two private rooms with a double bed and a single bed above.

Boundary   B&B ££

(☑ 015394-48978; www.theboundaryonline.co.uk; Lake Rd, Windermere Town; d £100-191; P ☎) Not the cheapest sleep in Windermere, but definitely one of the swishest. Owners Steve and Helen have given this Victorian house a sleek, boutique makeover: chic decor, monochrome colours, retro furniture and all. Steve's a cricket obsessive, so all the rooms are named after famous batsmen.

Rum Doodle   B&B ££

(☑ 015394-45967; www.rumdoodlewindermere.com; Sunny Bank Rd, Windermere Town; d £85-119; P ☎) Forget boutique B&B: this little place is all about quirky English style. Each of the nine rooms is named after an explorer with corresponding decorative twist: Jungle has old suitcases and giant map, Wish has a four-poster and faux-bookcase wallpaper, while Summit and Burley hunker under attic eaves. There's a two-night minimum in summer.

Wheatlands Lodge   B&B ££

(☑ 015394-43789; www.wheatlandslodge-windermere.co.uk; Old College Lane; d £80-170; P ☎)

> **WORTH A TRIP**
>
> ### WRAY CASTLE & CLAIFE HEIGHTS
>
> Windermere's quieter west side is a good place to escape the crowds. North of the ferry landings at Ferry House, a network of woodland paths winds across **Claife Heights**, while the nearby National Trust–owned estate of **Wray Castle** (NT; www.nationaltrust.org.uk/wray-castle; adult/child £7.20/3.60; ☺ 10am-5pm) encompasses 25 hectares of lakeside grounds and a turreted 19th-century mansion, once used as a holiday home by Beatrix Potter's family.

WINDERMERE & THE ISLANDS

Like many places in Cumbria, Windermere gets its name from the old Norse, Vinandr mere, or Vinandr's lake (so Lake Windermere is actually a tautology). Encompassing 5.7 sq miles between Ambleside and Newby Bridge, the lake is a mile wide at its broadest point, with a maximum depth of about 220m.

The lake's shoreline is owned by a combination of private landholders, the National Park Authority and the National Trust, but the lake bed itself (and thus the lake itself) officially belongs to the people of Windermere (local philanthropist Henry Leigh Groves purchased it on their behalf in 1938).

There are 18 islands on Windermere: the largest is **Belle Isle**, encompassing 16 hectares and an 18th-century Italianate mansion, while the smallest is **Maiden Holme**, little more than a patch of soil and a solitary tree.

From April to October, rowing boats can be hired for £12. Motorboats cost from £18 to £22 for two adults per hour; children under 16 go free. There's a 10mph speed limit.

Between Bowness and Windermere, this detached house looks Victorian, but the eight rooms are nice and modern. They're split into three categories (Comfortable, Deluxe and Master); extra money buys more space and luxury spa baths. Breakfast is a high point, with homemade muesli, local bacon and sausages, plus smoked salmon from Loch Ewe.

1 Park Road　　B&B ££
(www.1parkroad.com; 1 Park Rd, Windermere Town; d £76-104; P ⊚) It's the little treats that keep this cosy guesthouse a cut above: bath goodies from Pure Lakes and The White Company, iPod docks in every room, and home-made baked beans and marmalade for breakfast. Rooms are comfortable, and the rates stay reasonable year-round – a rarity in Windermere.

Cranleigh　　HOTEL ££
(☑ 015394-43293; www.thecranleigh.com; Kendal Rd, Bowness-on-Windermere; d £109-189, ste £220-425; P ⊚) This guesthouse has gone all-out on the decor, but strip away the snazziness and it's still just a B&B. It's worth bumping up to the Superior for the spacious bathrooms, or maybe blowing the budget on one of the two over-the-top suites (check out the Sanctuary, complete with Bose stereo, glass bath and picture-fireplace).

Samling　　HOTEL £££
(☑ 015394-31922; www.thesamlinghotel.co.uk; Ambleside Rd; r £220-670) If money's no object, this deluxe country house is the choice. The chic rooms and cottages are classically styled, and feature luxury touches such as split-level mezzanines, rain showers and private lounges. Its restaurant has recently scooped a Michelin star, too. Early bookings score a substantial

discount. The hotel is 3 miles northwest of Windermere Town, off the A591.

✕ Eating

Lazy Daisy's Lakeland Kitchen　　CAFE £
(☑ 015394-43877; 31-33 Crescent Rd, Windermere Town; lunch £4-10, dinner £10-16; ⊙ 10am-9pm Mon-Sat) Filling comfort food is the order of the day at this trad cafe: the cakes and giant Yorkshire puddings are a highlight.

Lighthouse　　CAFE £
(Main Rd, Windermere Town; mains £8-15; ⊙ 8.30am-5.30pm) This three-storey cafe downhill from the train station offers a continental-style menu, quality coffee and freshly baked pastries.

Hooked　　SEAFOOD ££
(☑ 015394-48443; www.hookedwindermere.co.uk; Ellerthwaite Sq, Windermere Town; mains £16.95-19.95; ⊙ 5.30-10.30pm Tue-Sun) This seafood restaurant in Windermere Town has a loyal following. Fish arrives daily from the Fleetwood docks, and chef Paul White dabbles in everything from fish classics to fusion concoctions: *moules marinières* (mussels in white wine) to start, perhaps, then a whole Thai-spiced sea bass or king scallops with pea purée and black pudding. The only drawback is the limited space: bookings essential.

Brown Horse Inn　　PUB ££
(☑ 015394-43443; www.thebrownhorseinn.co.uk; Winster; mains £11.95-17.95; ⊙ lunch noon-2pm, dinner 6-9pm) Three miles from Windermere in Winster, the Brown Horse is one of Windermere's top dining pubs. Produce is sourced from the Brown Horse Estate, furnishing the chefs with meat and game such as venison, spring lamb and roast pigeon. Beams and

fireplaces conjure rustic atmosphere, and there are two home-brewed ales on tap (Old School and Best Bitter). Worth the drive.

Watermill   PUB **££**
(☑ 01539-821309; www.watermillinn.co.uk; Ings; mains £12-20; ☺ 11am-11pm Mon-Sat, to 10.30pm Sun) Two miles from Windermere in Ings, this resolutely traditional inn is exactly what you'd expect from a Cumbrian pub – beamed ceilings, whitewashed walls, log fires, hand-pumps and all. Throw in good food and a choice of 16 ales – including home-brewed Collie Wobbles – and it's no wonder it's scooped lots of local awards.

Mason's Arms   PUB **££**
(☑ 015395-68486; www.masonsarmsstrawberry bank.co.uk; Winster; mains £13-20) Three miles east of the lake near Bowlands Bridge, the marvellous Mason's Arms is a local secret. The rafters, flagstones and cast-iron range haven't changed in centuries, and the patio has to-die-for views across fields and fells. In short, a cracker.

Mojo's Bistro   BRITISH **££**
(☑ 015394-449540; www.mojosbistro.co.uk; 4 High St, Windermere Town; 2-/3-course menu £13.95/ 17.95; ☺ 6-9pm Mon-Sat) Quality bistro-style food and a handy High St location make Mojo's a winner. The menu is largely old British classics: bangers-and-mash, beef-and-ale cobbler, chargrilled chicken with mushroom sauce.

Angel Inn   GASTROPUB **££**
(☑ 015394-44080; www.the-angelinn.com; Helm Rd, Bowness-on-Windermere; mains £10.95-16.50; ☺ 11.30am-4pm & 5-9pm) Bowness' gastropub is on a hummock behind the shoreline. Settle into a sofa and order a sharing platter, or go upmarket with a paupiette of plaice. The front lawn is the spot when the sun shines.

Postillion   BISTRO **££**
(☑ 015394-45852; www.postillionrestaurant.co.uk; Ash St, Bowness-on-Windermere; mains £12-16, set menu £18.95; ☺ 6-10pm) Reliable bistro tucked away off Ash St with a French-Mediterranean menu.

🍷 Drinking & Nightlife

Hole in T' Wall   PUB
(Falbarrow Rd, Bowness-on-Windermere; ☺ 11am-11pm) Bowness' best-loved boozer is also the town's oldest, dating back to 1612, and offering lashings of rough-beamed, low-ceilinged atmosphere.

Hawkshead Brewery   BREWERY
(☑ 01539-822644; www.hawksheadbrewery.co.uk; Mill Yard, Staveley) This craft brewery has its own brewhall in Staveley, 3 miles east of Windermere. Core beers include Hawkshead Bitter, dark Brodie's Prime and fruity Red. Guided tours can be arranged in advance.

ℹ Information

Bowness Tourist Office (☑ 015394-42895; bownesstic@lake-district.gov.uk; Glebe Rd, Bowness-on-Windermere; ☺ 9.30am-5.30pm Easter-Oct, 10am-4pm Fri-Sun Nov-Easter) Beside the lake jetties.

Brockhole National Park Visitor Centre (☑ 015394-46601; www.lake-district.gov.uk; ☺ 10am-5pm Easter-Oct, to 4pm Nov-Easter) In a 19th-century mansion 3 miles north of Windermere on the A591, this is the Lake District's flagship visitor centre, and also has a teashop, an adventure playground and gardens.

Windermere Tourist Office (☑ 015394-46499; windermeretic@southlakeland.gov.uk; Victoria St, Windermere Town; ☺ 9am-5.30pm Mon-Sat, 9.30am-5.30pm Sun Apr-Oct, shorter hours winter) Opposite Natwest bank.

ℹ Getting There & Away

BOAT
The **Windermere Ferry** (car/bike/pedestrian £4.30/1/50p; ☺ 6.50am-9.50pm Mon-Fri, 9.10am-9.50pm Sat & Sun Mar-Oct, to 8.50pm

winter) carries vehicles and pedestrians from Ferry Nab, just south of Bowness, across to Ferry House on the lake's west side. There's a ferry roughly every 20 minutes, although queues can be horrendous in summer. You can also take lake cruises (p587).

BUS

There's one daily National Express coach from London (£31.50, eight hours) via Lancaster and Kendal.

Combo tickets include a day's bus travel and one boat journey: the Central Lakes version costs adult/child/family £12/8/32, or there's an Explorer version for £15/11/36.

Bus 505 Coniston Rambler (hourly including Sundays) Travels from Windermere to Coniston (£4, 50 minutes) via Troutbeck, Brockhole, Ambleside, Skelwith Fold, Hawkshead and Hawkshead Hill. Two buses a day serve Kendal.

Bus 555/556 Lakeslink (at least hourly including Sundays) Starts at the train station, stopping at Troutbeck Bridge (five minutes), Brockhole Visitor Centre (seven minutes), Ambleside (£6.30, 15 minutes), Grasmere (£6.80, 30 minutes) and Keswick (£8.55, one hour). In the opposite direction it continues to Kendal (£9.30, 25 minutes) and Lancaster (one hour 40 minutes).

Bus 599 Lakes Rider (£4 to £6, three times hourly including weekends) Open-top bus between Bowness, Troutbeck, Brockhole, Rydal Church (for Rydal Mount), Dove Cottage and Grasmere. Some buses stop at Windermere train station.

TRAIN

Windermere is the only town inside the national park accessible by train. It's on the branch line to Kendal and Oxenholme.

Edinburgh (£59.10, 2½ hours)
Glasgow (£51.50, 2¼ to 2¾ hours)
Kendal (£4.50, 15 minutes)
Lancaster (£13.50, 45 minutes)
London Euston (£99, 3½ hours)
Manchester Piccadilly (£22.70, 1½ hours)

Troutbeck

Nestled among the fells to the north of Windermere, on the road towards Kirkstone Pass, this rural hamlet feels a world away from the Bowness bustle, with wonderful views over Windermere.

◉ Sights

Townend HISTORIC BUILDING
(NT; ☎ 01539-432628; www.nationaltrust.org.uk/townend; adult/child £5.25/2.60; ◷ 1-5pm Wed-Sun Mar-Oct, daily school holidays) The historic farmhouse at Townend contains a collection of vintage farming tools and furniture that belonged to the Browne family, who owned the house until 1943. Public visiting hours are from 1pm to 5pm, but you can join hourly guided tours from 11am to 1pm.

🛏 Sleeping & Eating

Windermere YHA HOSTEL £
(☎ 0845 371 9352; www.yha.org.uk/hostel/windermere; Bridge Lane; dm £15, r £29; ◷ reception 7.30-11.30am & 1-11pm; P @) Downhill from Troutbeck village is the Windermere YHA, the closest YHA to Windermere. The rooms are modern, and facilities include a well-stocked shop, canteen and gear-drying room. Buses stop about a mile downhill from the village, at the river crossing of Troutbeck Bridge.

★ Mortal Man PUB ££
(☎ 015394-33193; www.themortalmaninn.co.uk; mains £8.95-14.95, r £85-130; P 🐾) Troutbeck has a couple of excellent pubs; top of the heap is the 17th-century Mortal Man, which has a lovely beer garden offering panoramic fell and lake views.

ℹ Getting There & Away

Bus 508 from Windermere costs £3.20.

Ambleside & Around

POP 2529

Once a busy mill and textile centre at Windermere's northern tip, Ambleside is an attractive little town, built from the same slate and stern grey stone that's so characteristic of the rest of Lakeland. Ringed by fells, it's a favourite base for hikers, with a cluster of outdoors shops and plenty of cosy pubs and cafes providing fuel for their adventures.

◉ Sights & Activities

Bridge House HISTORIC BUILDING
The town's best-known landmark is Bridge House, a tiny cottage that spans the clattering brook of Stock Ghyll; now occupied by a National Trust shop, it's thought to have originally been built as an apple store.

Armitt Museum MUSEUM
(www.armitt.com; Rydal Rd; adult £2.50; ◷ 10am-5pm) Ambleside's excellent little museum hosts some intriguing seasonal exhibitions alongside its core collection, populated with artefacts relating to important Lakeland

FIVE CLASSIC LAKELAND HIKES

The Lake District's most famous fell-walker, the accountant-turned-author Alfred Wainwright, recorded 214 official fells in his seven-volume *Pictorial Guides* (as if that weren't enough, he usually outlined at least two possible routes to the top, or in the case of Scafell Pike, five). If you only have limited time, here are five hikes which offer a flavour of what makes fell-walking in the Lake District so special.

Scafell Pike (978m) The daddy of Lakeland hikes, a six- to seven-hour slog to the top of England's highest peak. The classic route is from Wasdale Head.

Helvellyn (950m) Not for the faint-hearted; a vertiginous scramble along the knife-edge ridge of Striding Edge. It takes at least six hours starting from Glenridding or Patterdale.

Blencathra (868m) A mountain on its own, Blencathra offers a panoramic outlook on Keswick and the northern fells. Count on four hours from Threlkeld.

Haystacks (597m) Wainwright's favourite mountain, and the place where his ashes were scattered. It's a steep three-hour return hike from Buttermere village.

Catbells (451m) The fell for everyone, accessible to six-year-olds and septuagenarians. It's on the west side of Derwentwater, and takes a couple of hours to climb.

characters such as Beatrix Potter, National Trust founder Canon Hardwicke Rawnsley and pioneering photographers Herbert Bell and the Abraham Brothers. There are also original canvases by the modernist artist Kurt Schwitters, a German refugee who settled in Ambleside after WWII.

★ **Rydal Mount** HISTORIC BUILDING
(www.rydalmount.co.uk; adult/child £7/3; ◉9.30am-5pm Mar-Oct, 11am-4pm Wed-Mon Nov, Dec & Feb) The poet William Wordsworth's most famous residence in the Lake District is Dove Cottage, but he actually spent a great deal more time at Rydal Mount, a much grander house halfway between Ambleside and Grasmere. This was the Wordsworth family's home from 1813 until the poet's death in 1850, and the house contains a treasure trove of Wordsworth memorabilia. The house is 1.5 miles northwest of Ambleside, off the A591. Bus 555 (and bus 599 from April to October) stops at the end of the drive.

Downstairs you can wander around the library, dining room and drawing room (look out in the cabinets for William's pen, inkstand and picnic box, and a famous portrait of the poet by the American painter Henry Inman hanging above the fireplace). Upstairs are the family bedrooms and Wordsworth's attic study, containing his encyclopedia and a sword belonging to his brother John, who was lost in a shipwreck in 1805. Below the house is Dora's Field, which Wordsworth planted with daffodils in memory of his eldest daughter, who died from tuberculosis in 1847.

Stock Ghyll Force WALKING
Ambleside's most popular walk is the half-hour stroll up to the 18m waterfall of Stock Ghyll Force; the trail is signposted behind the old Market Hall at the bottom of Stock Ghyll Lane. If you feel energetic, you can follow the trail beyond the falls up **Wansfell Pike** (482m), a reasonably steep walk of about two hours.

Low Wood Watersports BOATING
(☑015394-39441; www.englishlakes.co.uk/watersports; Low Bay Marina) This water-sports centre offers water-skiing, sailing and kayaking, and also has rowboats and motorboats for hire.

🛏 Sleeping

Ambleside YHA HOSTEL £
(☑0845 371 9620; ambleside@yha.org.uk; Windermere Rd; dm £20-23; ℗ 🛜) One of the YHA's flagship Lake District hostels, this huge lakeside house is a fave for activity holidays (everything from kayaking to *ghyll* scrambling). Great facilities (kitchen, bike rental, boat jetty and bar) mean it's heavily subscribed, so book well ahead. Families can book out dorms as private rooms. The hostel is halfway between Ambleside and Windermere on Lake Rd (the A591).

Ambleside Backpackers HOSTEL £
(☑015394-32340; www.amblesidehostel.co.uk; Old Lake Rd; dm £21-25; ℗ @) Independent cottage hostel a short walk south from Ambleside's centre.

ℹ NATIONAL TRUST CAMPSITE BOOKINGS

The National Trust has four fantastic campsites in the Lake District at **Low Wray** near Ambleside, **Hoathwaite** near Coniston, **Wasdale** and **Great Langdale**.

The centralised **National Trust Lake District Campsite Bookings** (☑ 01539-432733; www.nationaltrust.org.uk/holidays/camping/camping-in-the-lake-district; ☉ 10am-3pm Mon-Fri) service handles reservations for all NT campsites in the Lake District. Bookings can be made up to 24 hours before arrival. There's a fee of £5 for booking online, or £7.50 by telephone and email, and stays must be for a minimum of two nights.

Low Wray   CAMPSITE £

(NT; ☑ bookings 015394-63862; www.ntlakescampsites.org.uk; 2 adults & tent £14.50-19, eco-pods £35-55; ☉ campsite arrivals 3-7pm Sat-Thu, to 9pm Fri Mar-Oct) Lakeside camping courtesy of the National Trust. It's 3 miles from town along the B5286, near the Wray Castle estate; bus 505 stops nearby. Yurts and tepees also available.

Regent Hotel   HOTEL ££

(☑ 015394-32254; www.regentlakes.co.uk; Waterhead Bay; d £89-159; ☑ 🐕) This attractive hotel has a near-the-lake location, but for once doesn't charge sky-high prices. The rooms offer different settings: some have balconies overlooking the garden, others have bunks for the kids or walk-in wet rooms, and a few sneak in views over Windermere. The top-floor Sail Loft has its own private deck terrace.

Lakes Lodge   B&B ££

(☑ 015394-33240; www.lakeslodge.co.uk; Lake Rd; r £99-129; ☑ 🐕) This modish mini-hotel offers a touch more luxury than Ambleside's other guesthouses. The 16 rooms are all about clean lines, stark walls and zero clutter, and most have a full-size wall mural featuring a local beauty spot. Some are in the main building, while others are in an attached annexe.

Gables   B&B ££

(☑ 015394-33272; www.thegables-ambleside.co.uk; Church Walk; s £45-50, d £90-120; ☑ 🐕) One of the best value of Ambleside's B&Bs, in a quiet spot overlooking the recreation ground. Spotty cushions and colourful prints keep things cheery, but room sizes are variable (in this instance, bigger is definitely better).

Guests receive discounts at the owner's restaurant, Sheila's Cottage.

Compston House Hotel   B&B ££

(☑ 015394-32305; www.compstonhouse.co.uk; Compston Rd; s from £45, d from £65; 🐕) Americans will feel at home here: the owners are expat New Yorkers, and each room is themed after a different state: sunny Hawaii, bright Florida, maritime Maine. Breakfast includes blueberry muffins and maple pancakes. There's a three-night minimum in season.

Waterhead Hotel   HOTEL £££

(☑ 0845 850 4503; www.englishlakes.co.uk; r £135-215; ☑ 🐕) Ambleside's main hotel has a super position beside the lakeshore. The exterior is classic Lakeland, all solid stone and bay windows, but inside it's very much a modern hotel, with spacious rooms stocked with heritage furniture and designer fabrics, and a sophisticated restaurant, the Mountain View.

Cote How   B&B £££

(☑ 015394-32765; www.bedbreakfastlakedistrict.com; Rydal; d £150-180; ☑ 🐕) 🌿 In Rydal, 1.5 miles from Ambleside, this detached house is all about the good life. Food is 100% local and organic, power's sourced from an eco-supplier, and there's a discount for non-drivers. The three rooms are olde Edwardian, with cast-iron beds, roll-top baths and fireplaces (ex-president Woodrow Wilson once visited the Rydal Suite). Two-night minimum at weekends.

🍴 Eating

Zeffirelli's   ITALIAN £

(☑ 015394-33845; www.zeffirellis.com; Compston Rd; pizzas & mains £8-12; ☉ 11am-10pm) A beloved local landmark, Zeff's is often packed out for its quality pizza and pasta. The £19.75 Double Feature deal includes two courses and a ticket to the cinema next door.

Lucy 4   TAPAS £

(2 St Mary's Lane; tapas £4-10; ☉ 5-10.30pm Mon-Fri, noon-10.30pm Sat & Sun) A cosy wine-bar that also does good tapas.

Apple Pie   CAFE £

(Rydal Rd; lunches £4-10; ☉ 9am-5.30pm) Sunny cafe popular for its sandwiches, buns and hearty pies.

Atelier   BISTRO ££

(☑ 015394-31156; www.atelier-ambleside.co.uk; Kelsick Rd; mains £11.95-20.95; ☉ 6.30-10pm Thu-Sat) Sometimes, simplicity is strength. This small street-corner bistro specialises in fresh, zesty Mediterranean flavours, served in an intimate modern dining room, characterised by framed prints and Arne Jacobsen–style chairs. Dishes are classic but accomplished: eg Barbary duck with sautéed potatoes, or balsamic-marinated Lakeland lamb.

Fellini's   VEGETARIAN ££

(☑ 015394-32487; www.fellinisambleside.com; Church St; mains £11.95; ☺ 5.30-10pm; ✍) Fear not, veggies: even in the land of the Cumberland sausage and the tattie hotpot, you won't go hungry thanks to Fellini's sophisticated 'vegeterranean' food. It's run by Zeffirelli's owners; a small upstairs cinema shows art-house and opera performances.

Glass House   MEDITERRANEAN ££

(☑ 015394-32137; www.theglasshouserestaurant. co.uk; Rydal Rd; mains £10.25-14.75; ☺ noon-2pm & 6.30-10pm) Classy dining in a converted fulling mill (with original mill wheels and machinery still in place). It's known for its accomplished French-inspired food, so expect plenty of rich flavours underpinned by Lakeland ingredients.

🍸 Drinking & Entertainment

Ambleside has plenty of pubs: locals favour the Golden Rule (Smithy Brow) for its ale selection, while the Royal Oak (Market Pl) packs in the post-hike punters.

Zeffirelli's Cinema   CINEMA

(☑ 015394-33100; Compston Rd) Ambleside's two-screen Zeffirelli's Cinema is next to Zeffirelli's, with extra screens in a converted church down the road.

🛍 Shopping

Gaynor Sports   OUTDOOR EQUIPMENT

(☑ 01524-734938; www.gaynors.co.uk; Market Cross) Compston Rd has enough equipment shops to launch an assault on Everest. The largest is Gaynor Sports, with three floors of outdoor gear.

ⓘ Information

Hub (☑ 015394-32582; tic@thehubofambleside.com; Central Bldgs, Market Cross; ☺ 9am-5pm) The tourist office and the post office are both here.

ⓘ Getting There & Around

BICYCLE

Bikes and gear can be hired from **Biketreks** (☑ 015394-31505; www.biketreks.net; Rydal Rd; per day £20) and **Ghyllside Cycles** (☑ 015394-33592; www.ghyllside.co.uk; The Slack; per day £18).

BUS

Bus 505 to Hawkshead and Coniston (£4, hourly including Sundays).

THE LAKE DISTRICT & CUMBRIA AMBLESIDE & AROUND

LOCAL KNOWLEDGE

TOP LAKE DISTRICT CAMPSITES

In addition to the four excellent campsites run by the National Trust (near Ambleside, Great Langdale, Wasdale and Coniston), there are more great places to sleep under the stars. Here's our top five:

The Quiet Site (☑ 07768 727016; www.thequietsite.co.uk; sites £18-30, pods £50; ☺ year-round; 📶) Eco-camping on the fells above Ullswater, with pre-erected tents and eco-pods available.

Syke Farm (☑ 01768-770222; adult/child £7/3.50; ☺ Easter-Oct) Back-to-basics camping beside the river in Buttermere. Fresh milk and homemade ice cream are sold at the farm shop.

Bowkerstead Farm (☑ 01229-860208; www.grizedale-camping.co.uk; Satterthwaite; adult/child £7/3, camping pods £30; ☺ Apr-Sep) Pitch beside the trees of Grizedale Forest, either in your own tent, a luxury yurt or a timber eco-pod.

Seatoller Farm (☑ 01768-777232; www.seatollerfarm.co.uk; adult/child £6/3; ☺ Easter-Oct) A tucked-away site on a 500-year-old farm near Seatoller in Borrowdale, with a choice of riverside or woodland pitches.

Fisherground Farm (☑ 019467-23349; www.fishergroundcampsite.co.uk; adult/child £6.50/3.50, car £2.50; ☺ Mar-Oct) Family-friendly camping in idyllic Eskdale, handy for the Ravenglass & Eskdale Railway (see p612).

Bus 516 to Elterwater and Langdale (£3.60, seven daily).

Bus 555 to Grasmere and Windermere (£6.30, at least hourly including Sundays).

Grasmere

POP 1458

Even without its connections to the Romantic poets, gorgeous Grasmere would still be one of the Lakes' biggest draws. It's one of the prettiest of the Lakeland hamlets, huddled at the edge of an island-studded lake surrounded by woods, pastures and slate-coloured hills, but most of the thousands of trippers come in search of its famous former resident, the poet William Wordsworth, who set up home at nearby Dove Cottage in 1799. With such a rich literary heritage, Grasmere unsurprisingly gets busy.

⊙ Sights

★ **Dove Cottage**   HISTORIC BUILDING
(☎ 015394-35544; www.wordsworth.org.uk; adult/child £7.50/4.50; ⊙ 9.30am-5.30pm) On the edge of Grasmere, this tiny, creeper-clad cottage (formerly a pub called the Dove & Olive Bough) was famously inhabited by William Wordsworth between 1799 and 1808. The cottage's cramped rooms are full of artefacts: try to spot the poet's passport, a pair of his spectacles and a portrait of his favourite dog Pepper, given to him by Sir Walter Scott. Entry is by timed ticket to avoid overcrowding, and includes an informative guided tour.

Wordsworth lived here happily with his sister Dorothy, wife Mary and three children John, Dora and Thomas until 1808, when the family moved to another nearby house at Allen Bank, and the cottage was rented by Thomas de Quincey (author of *Confessions of an English Opium Eater*).

Tickets also include admission to the **Wordsworth Museum & Art Gallery** next door, which houses one of the nation's main collections relating to the Romantic movement – including many original manuscripts and some creepy death masks of some famous Romantic figures.

St Oswald's Church   CHURCH
(Church Stile) In the churchyard of this tiny chapel in the centre of Grasmere are the Wordsworths' family graves: look out for tombstones belonging to William, Mary, Dorothy and all three children. Samuel Taylor Coleridge's son Hartley is also buried here.

Grasmere Lake & Rydal Water   LAKE
Quiet paths lead along the shorelines of Grasmere's twin-set lakes. Rowing boats can be hired at the northern end of Grasmere Lake from the **Faeryland Tea Garden** (⊙ 10.30am-4pm), a five-minute walk from the village centre.

🏃 Activities

Popular hikes starting from Grasmere include **Helm Crag** (405m), often known as the 'Lion and the Lamb', thanks to its distinctive shape, Silver Howe (394m), **Loughrigg Fell** (335m) and the multipeak circuit known as the **Easedale Round** (five to six hours, 8.5 to 9 miles).

A less taxing option is to follow the **Old Coffin Trail** between Grasmere and Rydal Mount, which was once used by pallbearers carrying coffins to St Oswald's Church. The trail begins near Dove Cottage.

🛏 Sleeping

Butharlyp How YHA   HOSTEL £
(☎ 0845 371 9319; www.yha.org.uk; Easedale Rd; dm £18-21; ⊙ reception 7am-10pm daily Feb-Nov, Sat & Sun Dec & Jan; [P] [@]) Grasmere's YHA is in a large Victorian house set among grassy grounds. There's a good range of different-sized dorms and a cafe-bar.

Grasmere Hostel   HOSTEL £
(☎ 015394-35055; www.grasmerehostel.co.uk; Broadrayne Farm; dm £20-22; [P] [@]) This independent hostel is in a converted farmhouse on the A591, near the Traveller's Rest pub. There are two kitchens, and each dorm has its own en suite bathroom. There's even a Nordic sauna.

Thorney How   HOSTEL £
(☎ 015394-35597; www.thorneyhow.co.uk; Easedale Rd; dm £21-5) Now independent, this former YHA is in a Grade II–listed farmhouse off Easedale Rd, 15 minutes' walk from Grasmere. Accommodation is in six- to 10-bed dorms, and it all feels pretty cramped – although there are a few double rooms available. Facilities include a kitchen, cafe and bike shelter.

How Foot Lodge   B&B ££
(☎ 015394-35366; www.howfoot.co.uk; Town End; d £75-80; [P]) Just a stroll from Dove Cottage, this stone house has six rooms finished in fawns and beiges; the nicest are the Deluxe Doubles, one with sun terrace and the other with private sitting room. Rates are an absolute bargain considering the location.

Raise View House
B&B ££

(☑ 015394-35215; www.raiseviewhouse.co.uk; White Bridge; s £53-58, d £106-116; 🅿 🛜) Fell views unfurl from nearly every room here: Helm Crag, Easedale and Stone Arthur are particularly impressive. On the edge of Grasmere, the house is smartly appointed: Farrow & Ball paints, Gilchrist & Soames bathstuffs and Wedgwood china on the breakfast table.

Heidi's Grasmere Lodge
B&B ££

(☑ 015394-35248; www.heidisgrasmerelodge. co.uk; Red Lion Sq; d £79-110; 🛜) This plush B&B plonked above Heidi's cafe offers six super-feminine rooms full of frilly cushions and Cath Kidston–style patterns. They're quite small but very comfy: room 6 has its own sun patio, reached via a spiral staircase.

★ Moss Grove Organic
HOTEL £££

(☑ 015394-35251; www.mossgrove.com; r Sun-Thu £114-209, Fri & Sat £129-259; 🅿 🛜) 🍴 This eco-chic hotel champions its green credentials: sheep-wool insulation, organic paints, reclaimed timber beds, but for once, eco also equals elegance. Rooms are enormous, and bathrooms sparkle with sexy showers and underfloor heating. Breakfast is served buffet-style in the kitchen-diner downstairs.

✕ Eating

Heidi's of Grasmere
CAFE £

(Red Lion Sq; mains £4-8; ⏱ 9am-5.30pm) This cute pine-clad cafe makes a welcome refuge if the weather turns. Thick-cut sandwiches and hot soups are its mainstay, but the house special, 'cheese smokeys', is the choice if you're hungry.

Baldry's Tea Room
CAFE £

(Red Lion Sq; lunch £3-8; ⏱ 10am-5pm) This lacy cafe is the spot for a classic cream tea, served in a bone-china pot and accompanied by buttery scones or Victoria sponges.

★ Jumble Room
MODERN BRITISH ££

(☑ 015394-35188; www.thejumbleroom.co.uk; Langdale Rd; dinner mains £14.50-21; ⏱ 5.30-10pm Wed-Mon) Husband-and-wife team Andy and Crissy Hill have turned this village bistro into a dining landmark. It's a really fun and friendly place to dine. Spotty crockery, cow murals and primary colours set the boho tone, matched by a magpie menu taking in everything from Dithose chicken to a 9oz 'flatiron' steak.

Sara's Bistro
BISTRO ££

(Broadgate; mains £10-16; ⏱ 6-9pm Tue-Sun) Hearty homespun cooking is Sara's raison d'être – big portions of roast chicken, honey-roasted duck and thyme-infused belly pork. There's nothing fancy about the food or the decor, but warm welcomes are guaranteed.

Miller Howe Cafe
CAFE ££

(Red Lion Sq; mains £5-14; ⏱ 8.30am-5.30pm) A smart cafe on the main square, serving up-market lunch fare: smoked-salmon muffins, club toasties and excellent Farrers coffee.

🔒 Shopping

★ Sarah Nelson's Gingerbread Shop
FOOD

(www.grasmeregingerbread.co.uk; Church Cottage; ⏱ 9.15am-5.30pm Mon-Sat, 12.30-5pm Sun) In business since 1854, this famous sweetshop next to the village church makes Grasmere's essential souvenir: traditional gingerbread with a half-biscuit, half-cakey texture, cooked according to the same top-secret recipe (12 pieces for £4.95). Friendly service by ladies dressed in frilly pinafores and starched bonnets is an added bonus.

ℹ Getting There & Away

The regular 555 bus runs from Windermere to Grasmere (15 minutes), via Ambleside, Rydal Church and Dove Cottage.

The open-top 599 (two or three per hour in summer) runs from Grasmere via Ambleside, Troutbeck Bridge, Windermere and Bowness.

Both buses charge the same fares: Grasmere to Ambleside is £6.30, to Windermere it's £6.80.

Hawkshead & Around

POP 1640

Lakeland villages don't come much more perfect than Hawkshead, a jumble of whitewashed cottages, cobbled lanes and old pubs lost among bottle-green countryside between Ambleside and Coniston. The village has literary cachet too – Wordsworth went to school here, and Beatrix Potter's husband, William Heelis, worked here as a solicitor for many years (his old office is now an art gallery).

Cars are banned in the village centre.

⦿ Sights

Hawkshead Grammar School
HISTORIC BUILDING

(www.hawksheadgrammar.org.uk; admission £2; ⏱ 10am-1pm & 2-5pm Mon-Sat, 1-5pm Sun Apr-Sep) In centuries past, promising young gentleman were sent to Hawkshead's village school for their educational foundation.

DON'T MISS

GRIZEDALE FOREST

Sprawling across the hills between Coniston Water and Esthwaite Water, Grizedale Forest (from the Old Norse for 'wild boar') is one of the Lake District's most beautiful woodlands – not to mention its largest outdoor art project. More than 90 large-scale artworks and sculptures are sprinkled throughout the forest, from an enormous xylophone to a Tolkienesque 'man of the forest'.

Bus X30, the Grizedale Wanderer (four daily March to November), runs from Haverthwaite to Grizedale via Hawkshead and Moor Top.

Grizedale Visitors Centre (☏ 01229-860010; www.forestry.gov.uk/grizedaleforestpark; ⊙ 10am-5pm, 11am-4pm winter) The main information point has lots of leaflets and maps covering activities in the forest.

Grizedale Mountain Bikes (☏ 01229-860369; www.grizedalemountainbikes.co.uk; adult/child per day from £25/18; ⊙ 9am-5pm) Rents out mountain bikes and supplies trail maps. Last hire at 3pm.

Go Ape (www.goape.co.uk; adult/child £30/24; ⊙ 9-5pm daily Mar-Oct, Sat & Sun Nov-Feb) Children (big and little) will love this treetop assault course.

Among the former pupils was a certain William Wordsworth, who attended the school from 1779 to 1787.

The curriculum was punishing: 10 hours' study a day, covering weighty subjects such as Latin, Greek, geometry, science and rhetoric. Hardly surprising young William felt the urge to carve his name into a desk.

Upstairs is a small exhibition exploring the history of the school.

Beatrix Potter Gallery　　　　GALLERY
(NT; www.nationaltrust.org.uk/beatrix-potter-gallery; Red Lion Sq; adult/child £5/2.50; ⊙ 10.30am-5pm Sat-Thu mid-Mar–Oct) As well as being a children's author, Beatrix Potter was also a talented botanical painter and amateur naturalist. This small gallery (housed in the offices of Potter's husband, solicitor William Heelis) contains a collection of her watercolours depicting local flora and fauna. She was particularly fascinated by mushrooms.

There's discounted admission if you show your ticket from Hill Top.

★ **Tarn Hows**　　　　　　　LAKE
(NT; www.nationaltrust.org.uk/coniston-and-tarn-hows) FREE Two miles off the B5285 from Hawkshead, a winding country lane wends its way to this famously photogenic artificial lake, now owned by the National Trust. Trails wind their way around the lakeshore and surrounding woodland – keep your eyes peeled for red squirrels in the treetops.

There's a small National Trust car park, but it fills quickly. Several buses, including the 505 and X30, stop nearby.

Hill Top　　　　　HISTORIC BUILDING
(NT; ☏ 015394-36269; www.nationaltrust.org.uk/hill-top; adult/child £9/4.50; ⊙ 10.30am-4.30pm Sat-Thu mid-Feb–Oct, longer hours Jul & Aug) In the tiny village of Near Sawrey, 2 miles south of Hawkshead, this idyllic farmhouse is a must for Beatrix Potter buffs: it was the first house she lived in after moving to the Lake District, and also where she wrote and illustrated many of her famous tales. Purchased in 1905 (largely on the proceeds of her first bestseller, *The Tale of Peter Rabbit*), Hill Top is crammed with decorative details fans will recognise from the author's illustrations. Entry is by timed ticket; try visiting later in the day to avoid the worst crowds.

The house features directly in *Samuel Whiskers, Tom Kitten* and *Jemima Puddle-Duck*, and you might recognise the cast-iron kitchen range from many of Potter's underground burrows.

Thanks to its fame (helped by the 2006 biopic *Miss Potter*), Hill Top is one of the Lakes' most popular spots, so queues are inevitable in season.

🛏 Sleeping & Eating

Hawkshead YHA　　　　HOSTEL £
(☏ 0845 371 9321; hawkshead@yha.org.uk; dm £15-21; P @) This large hostel occupies a Regency house a mile along the Newby Bridge road. The dorms and kitchen are spacious, there's on-site bike rental and buses stop outside the door.

Yewfield B&B ££

(☑015394-36765; www.yewfield.co.uk; Hawkshead Hill; s £49-65, d £98-130; 🅿🛜) 🡒 This detached house occupies a hilltop spot near Tarn Hows, halfway between Coniston and Hawkshead. It's run by the owners of Zeffirelli's, and though the building itself is Victorian, it's run along eco lines: breakfast is veggie and organic, power comes from a wood-mass boiler, and produce comes from the kitchen garden.

Randy Pike B&B £££

(☑015394-36088; www.randypike.co.uk; r Mon-Fri £200, Sat & Sun £225) Managed by the owners of Grasmere's Jumble Room restaurant, Andy and Chrissy Hill, this former hunting lodge feels more like a stay in the country with friends than a night in a B&B. The three rooms ooze bohemian style: distressed wood floors, quirky furniture and mix-and-match fabrics, plus iPods loaded up with music. There's even a Tardis in the garden.

Love Shack COTTAGE £££

(☑015394-41242; www.lakedistrictloveshack.com; Cunsey; 🕒r Sat & Sun £350-650, per week £600-850) 🡒 A cooler cottage you simply will not find. Built on the site of a 1960s love shack (hence the name), this eco-friendly cabin is the brainchild of artists Karen Guthrie and Adam Sutherland. It's a mix of modern and retro – reclaimed timber, organic paints and oak floors meet funky furnishings and shagadelic love seats, all in a secluded woodland location not far from Near Sawrey.

Hawkshead Relish Company DELI £

(☑015394-36614; www.hawksheadrelish.com; The Square; 🕒9.30am-5pm winter, 9am-5.30pm summer) This village chutney company sells an enormous choice of relishes and jams.

Queen's Head PUB ££

(☑015394-36271; www.queensheadhawkshead.co.uk; Main St; mains £14-22, s £70, d £100-130; 🕒noon-3pm & 6-10pm) Hawkshead has several decent pubs, but the old Queen's Head beats them all in age and atmosphere. Head-knockingly low ceilings and the oak-panelled walls give it period character, and the food is packed with local flavour (roast Herdwick lamb, shepherd's pie, sticky toffee pudding). Rooms in the main inn are small and prim, decked out in elegant gingham checks and neutral tones.

⭐**Drunken Duck** PUB £££

(☑015394-36347; www.drunkenduckinn.co.uk; Barngates; mains £13-25; 🕒noon-2pm & 6-10pm; 🅿🛜) For top-class dining in the Lakes, nowhere beats the Drunken Duck. It's become one of the region's premier foodie destinations, closer to a fine-dining restaurant than a country pub. The food is full of flair, and ales come from the pub's own Barngates Brewery out back. You'll need to book weeks in advance for dinner, although lunch is first-come, first-served.

If you fancy staying, you'll find the rooms (£95 to £275) are just as fancy as the food. The pub's tricky to find: drive along the B5286 from Hawkshead towards Ambleside, and look out for the brown signs.

🛈 Getting There & Away

Hawkshead is linked with Windermere (£6.50), Ambleside (£4) and Coniston (£4) by bus 505 (hourly including Sundays).

Coniston

POP 641

Hunkered beneath the pockmarked peak known as the **Old Man of Coniston** (803m), this lakeside village was originally established to support the local mining industry, and the surrounding hilltops are littered with the remains of old copper workings. These days most people visit with two things in mind: to cruise on the lovely old Coniston Launch, or to tramp to the top of the Old Man, a steep but rewarding return hike of around 7 miles.

Coniston's other claim to fame is as the location for a string of world-record speed attempts made here by Sir Malcolm Campbell and his son, Donald, between the 1930s and 1960s. Tragically, after beating the record several times, Donald was killed during an attempt in 1967, when his futuristic jet-boat *Bluebird* flipped at around 320mph. The boat and its pilot were recovered in 2001, and Campbell was buried in the cemetery of St Andrew's church.

◉ Sights

Brantwood HISTORIC BUILDING

(☑015394-41396; www.brantwood.org.uk; adult/child £7.20/free, gardens only £4.95/free; 🕒10.30am-5pm mid-Mar–mid-Nov, to 4pm Wed-Sun mid-Nov–mid-Mar) John Ruskin (1819–1900), who lived at Brantwood for 28 years, was one of the great thinkers of 19th-century society. A polymath, philosopher, painter and critic, as well as an inveterate shell collector, he expounded views on everything from Venetian architecture to the finer points of lace-making.

In 1871 Ruskin purchased this lakeside house and spent the next 20 years expanding and modifying it, championing his passion for traditional 'Arts and Crafts' over factory-made materials. He even dreamt up the wallpaper designs.

Of particular note are Ruskin's enormous shell collection in the downstairs study, and several works by JMW Turner (Ruskin's favourite artist) in an upstairs bedroom. The formal gardens are also delightful to wander, with unsurprisingly majestic views.

The best way to arrive is by boat from Coniston (you also get a 50p discount on admission). While you wait, you can have lunch at the Jumping Jenny (lunches £4-8) in the house's former stables. If you'd prefer to drive, take the B5285 towards Coniston from Hawkshead and follow the signs.

Ruskin Museum   MUSEUM

(www.ruskinmuseum.com; adult/child £5.25/2.50; ⊙10am-5.30pm Easter–mid-Nov, 10.30am-3.30pm Wed-Sun mid-Nov–Easter) Coniston's little museum explores the village's history, touching on copper mining, Arthur Ransome and the Campbell story. There's also a section on John Ruskin, with displays of his writings, watercolours and sketchbooks.

The new Bluebird Wing currently houses the recovered engine from Donald Campbell's *Bluebird* boat, but it's hoped that the whole boat will be displayed here when (and if) it's finally restored.

🏃 Activities

Lake Coniston famously inspired Arthur Ransome's classic children's tale *Swallows and Amazons*. Peel Island, towards the southern end of Coniston Water, doubles in the book as Wild Cat Island, while the *Gondola* steam yacht allegedly gave Ransome the idea for Captain Flint's houseboat.

Steam Yacht Gondola   BOATING

(NT; ☑ 015394-63850; www.nationaltrust.org.uk/gondola; Coniston Jetty; half-lake return adult/child £11/5.50) 🕑 Built in 1859 and restored in the 1980s by the National Trust, this wonderful steam yacht looks like a cross between a Venetian *vaporetto* and an English houseboat, complete with cushioned saloons and polished wood seats. It's a stately way of seeing the lake, especially if you're visiting Brantwood, and it's even ecofriendly: since 2008 it's been powered by waste-wood.

There are several 'Half Lake' trips a day from mid-March to October. Longer 'Full

Lake' cruises run a few times a week, and cover the history of Ransome, the Campbells and Ruskin. Special picnic and Sunday afternoon tea cruises also run in summer. There's a 10% discount for online bookings.

Coniston Launch   BOATING

(☑ 015394-36216;   www.conistonlaunch.co.uk; Coniston Jetty; northern service adult/child return £10.50/5.25, southern £15.50/7.75) 🕑 Coniston's two launches have been solar-powered since 2005. The regular 45-minute northern service calls at the Waterhead Hotel, Torver and Brantwood, while the 105-minute southern service sails from Monday to Thursday with a different theme depending on the day; it's Swallows and Amazons on Monday and Wednesday, and the Campbells on Coniston on Tuesday and Thursday.

Coniston Boating Centre   BOATING

(☑ 015394-41366;   www.conistonboatingcentre. co.uk; Coniston Jetty) Hires out rowing boats, Canadian canoes and motorboats.

🛌 Sleeping

Coniston Holly How YHA   HOSTEL £

(☑ 0845 371 9511; conistonhh@yha.org.uk; Far End; dm £15-21.50; ⊙reception 7.30-10am & 5-10pm) A fine period house offering the usual YHA standards: decent dorms, well-equipped kitchens, organised walks and an in-house cafe.

Coppermines YHA   HOSTEL £

(☑ 0845 371 9630; coppermines@yha.org.uk; dm from £16; ⊙reception 7-11am & 5-10pm Easter-Oct) Up a steep rock road 1.5km from the village, this rustic hostel once provided accommodation for local copper miners. It's now a walkers' favourite; dorms are small but there's a kitchen, showers and even a licensed bar.

Hoathwaite Campsite   CAMPSITE £

(NT; ☑ bookings 015394-63862; www.ntlakescamp sites.org.uk; adult, tent & car from £6; ⊙Easter-Nov) This 'back-to-basics' National Trust–owned campsite is on the A5394 between Coniston and Torver. There's a toilet block, water taps and not much else – but the views over Coniston Water are super.

Bank Ground Farm   B&B ££

(☑ 015394-41264; www.bankground.com; East of the Lake; d from £90, 2-night minimum; ℗) This lakeside farmhouse has literary cachet: Arthur Ransome used it as the model for Holly Howe Farm in *Swallows and Amazons*. Parts of the house date back to the 15th century, so the rooms are snug. Some have sleigh beds, others exposed beams. The tearoom is a beauty, too, and there are cottages for longer stays. Two-night minimum.

Lakeland House   B&B ££
(☎ 015394-41303; www.lakelandhouse.co.uk; Tilberthwaite Ave; s £30-55, d £60-95) Perched above the village's internet cafe is this no-fuss B&B. Budget doubles border on the utilitarian, so it's worth stretching to Superior for space and comfort. The Lookout Suite has its own sitting room.

✖ Eating & Drinking

Bluebird Cafe   CAFE £
(Lake Rd; mains £4-8; ⊙ 9.30am-5.30pm) This lakeside cafe does a brisk trade from people waiting for the Coniston launches. The usual salads and sandwiches are on offer, and there are lots of outside tables.

Sun Hotel   PUB ££
(www.thesunconiston.com; mains £12-20; ⊙ 10am-11pm) A Coniston landmark, this 400-year-old gabled inn was famously used as an HQ by Donald Campbell during his final fateful campaign. There's lots of Campbell memorabilia to spot inside, dotted around the inn's beamed interior, and a pleasant garden overlooking the lake. The food is solid (beer-battered fish, oak-smoked roast chicken), washed down with guest ales from local breweries.

Black Bull   PUB
(www.conistonbrewery.com/black-bull-coniston.htm; Yewdale Rd; mains £8-16; ⊙ 10am-11pm) Coniston's main meeting spot, the old Black Bull offers a warren of rooms and a popular outside terrace. The pub grub's good, but it's mainly known for its home-brewed ales: Bluebird Bitter and Old Man Ale are always on tap, and there are seasonal ones too.

❶ Information

Coniston Tourist Office (☎ 015394-41533; www.conistontic.org; Ruskin Ave; ⊙ 9.30am-5.30pm Easter-Oct, to 4pm Nov-Easter) Sells the Coniston Loyalty Card offering local discounts.

❶ Getting There & Away

Bus 505 runs to Windermere (£4, hourly including Sundays), via Ambleside (£4), with a couple of daily connections to Kendal (£9.30, 1¼ hours).

The Coniston Bus-and-Boat ticket (adult/child £17.90/7.50) includes return bus travel on the 505, plus a trip on the launch and entry to Brantwood.

Elterwater & Great Langdale

Travelling north from Coniston, the road passes into the wild, empty landscape of Great Langdale, one of Lakeland's iconic hiking valleys. As you pass the pretty village of Elterwater, imposing fells stack up like dominoes along the horizon, looming over a pastoral patchwork of tumbledown barns and lime-green fields.

Langdale's best-known hike is the multipeak route up and over the Langdale Pikes: Pike O' Stickle (709m), Loft Crag (682m), Harrison Stickle (736m) and Pavey Ark (700m). Across the valley are the rippled summits of Bowfell (902m) and the Crinkle Crags, which represent a serious challenge even for experienced walkers.

🛏 Sleeping

Great Langdale Campsite   CAMPSITE £
(NT; ☎ 015394-63862; www.ntlakescampsites.org.uk; tent sites £10.50-13, extra adult £6, pods £35-50; ⊙ arrivals 3-7pm Sat-Thu, 3-9pm Fri; P) Quite possibly the most spectacularly positioned campsite in the Lake District, spread out over grassy meadows overlooked by Langdale's fells. It gets crowded in season, but around three-quarters of the sites can be booked in advance; the remainder are available on a first-come, first-served basis. Camping pods and yurts are also available.

Langdale YHA   HOSTEL £
(☎ 0845 371 9748; langdale@yha.org.uk; High Close, Loughrigg; dm £15-21; ⊙ reception 7-10am & 5-10.15pm Mar-Oct; P @) Hostel in a grand Victorian house on the road towards Grasmere. It's a rambling old affair, with big rooms, high ceilings and a huge communal lounge.

Elterwater YHA   HOSTEL £
(☎ 0845 371 9017; elterwater@yha.org.uk; dm £15-21; ⊙ reception 7.30-10am & 5-10.30pm Easter-Oct; @) A pleasant hostel in a former farmhouse, a stone's throw from Elterwater's village green.

★ Old Dungeon Ghyll   HOTEL ££
(☎ 015394-37272; www.odg.co.uk; d from £106, half-board £156; P 🛜 🐾) Affectionately known as the ODG, this historic inn is awash with Lakeland heritage: many famous walkers have stayed here, including Prince Charles and mountaineer Chris Bonington. It's endearingly olde-worlde (well-worn furniture, four-poster beds), and even if you're not staying here, the Hiker's Bar is a must for a

THE STEEPEST ROAD IN ENGLAND?

Zigzagging over fells between the valleys of **Little Langdale** and **Eskdale** is one of the Lake District's most infamous mountain roads. Used since ancient times and later substantially improved by the Romans, this old packhorse route provided a vital trading link between the central valleys of Lakeland and the ports dotted along the Cumbrian coast. En route, it traverses both of England's highest road passes, **Wrynose** and **Hardknott**, and in places the road reaches forbidding gradients of 1 in 3. At the top of Hardknott Pass, there's a ruined Roman fort, where you can still see the remains of the walls, parade ground and commandant's house. The views from here to the coast are stunning.

It's perfectly driveable if you take things slow and steady, but probably best avoided if you're a hesitant reverser or don't like driving next to steep drops (caravans and buses should definitely steer clear). Things to note: it's single-carriage most of the way, and passing places few and far between, so be prepared for vehicles going the opposite way. Also, make sure your brakes are in good order, and top up the water in your radiator – you'll do most of it in first or second gear.

To get to the passes from Ambleside, follow road signs on the A593 to Skelwith Bridge, then turn off to Little Langdale. When you reach the Three Shires Inn, the road becomes really steep. Alternatively, you can approach from the west; drive along the A595 coast road and turn off towards Eskdale, and follow the road past Boot to the passes.

post-hike pint – it's been the hub of Langdale's social life for decades.

★ **Eltermere Inn**   HOTEL **£££**
(☑ 015394-37207; www.eltermere.co.uk; r £125-225) Lovingly refurbished by hoteliers Mark and Ruth Jones, this Elterwater inn is one of Lakeland's loveliest backwater bolt-holes. Rooms are simple and classic, tastefully decorated in fawns and taupes, with quirky features such as window seats and free-standing tubs. The food's excellent, too, served in the inn's snug bar, and afternoon tea is served on the lawn on sunny days.

Brimstone Hotel   HOTEL **£££**
(☑ 015394-38062; www.brimstonehotel.co.uk; Langdale Estate; r £200-300) This lavish cottage complex on the Langdale Estate takes luxury to another level. The huge suites are more London-chic than Lakeland-cosy; mezzanine floors, sleek tiles, private patios and futuristic log-burners are standard, and then of course there's a reading room, spa, restaurant and private woodland.

✗ Eating

Stickle Barn   PUB **£**
(☑ 015394-37356; mains £6-12) A walkers' fave, this lively pub near the ODG serves filling food such as curries, chillies and hotpots.

Chesters by the River   CAFE **££**
(☑ 015394-32553; www.chestersbytheriver.co.uk; lunch mains £8-14; ☺10am-5pm) A fine riverside cafe handily placed between Amble-

side and Elterwater, serving gastro-gourmet grub and superb cakes. There's a gift shop, too, and you can pick up slate souvenirs from the workshop around the corner.

ⓘ Getting There & Away

Bus 516 (seven daily) is the only bus, with stops at Ambleside, Skelwith Bridge, Elterwater, and the Old Dungeon Ghyll Hotel in Great Langdale. Fares from Ambleside are £3.60 to all destinations.

Wasdale

Carving its way for 5 miles from the Cumbrian coast, the craggy, wind-lashed valley of Wasdale is where the Lake District scenery takes a turn for the wild. Ground out by a long-extinct glacier, the valley is home to the Lake District's highest and wildest peaks, as well as the steely grey expanse of Wastwater, England's deepest and coldest lake.

Wasdale's fells are an irresistible draw for hikers, especially those looking to conquer England's tallest mountain, **Scafell Pike** (978m). The classic route starts from Wasdale Head and is well within the reach of most walkers, although it's long, steep and hard to navigate in bad weather. You're looking at around six to seven hours out on the mountain, so you'll need proper supplies.

The valley is also home to one of England's tiniest chapels, 16th-century **St Olaf's Church**. Legend claims the roof beams were salvaged from a Viking longboat.

The Barn Door Shop (☎019467-26384; www.wasdaleweb.com), next door to the Wasdale Head Inn, sells camping and walking supplies.

🛏 Sleeping

Wasdale Head Campsite
CAMPSITE £

(NT; ☎ bookings 015394-63862; www.ntlakescampsites.org.uk; sites £10.50-13, extra adult £6, pods £35-50; ☺reception 8-10.30am Mon-Fri, 8-10.30am & 5-6.30pm Sat & Sun) This campsite is in a fantastically wild spot, nestled beneath the Scafell range. Facilities are basic (laundry room, showers), but the views are out of this world.

Wastwater YHA
HOSTEL £

(☎0845 371 9350; wasdale@yha.org.uk; Wasdale Hall, Nether Wasdale; dm £18-23; ☺reception 8-10am & 5-10.30pm; ℗) This lakeside hostel on the shores of Wastwater has the kind of location you'd normally pay through the nose for. It's in a 19th-century mansion that still boasts most of its period architecture, including original roof trusses and latticed windows. It has the usual self-catering facilities plus a decent restaurant.

★Wasdale Head Inn
B&B ££

(☎019467-26229; www.wasdale.com; s £59, d £118-130, tr £177; ℗) Hunkering beneath the brooding bulk of Scafell Pike is this 19th-century hostelry full of hill-walking heritage. It's wonderfully old-fashioned, covered in vintage photos and climbing memorabilia. The rooms are cosy, with roomier suites in a converted stable. The wood-panelled dining room serves fine food, with humbler grub and ales from the Great Gable Brewing Co available in Ritson's Bar.

❶ Getting There & Away

There are no longer any scheduled bus services to Wasdale Head, but you could order a taxi from Gosforth Taxis (☎01946-734800).

Cockermouth

POP 9146

Set along the River Cocker, the Georgian town of Cockermouth is best known as the birthplace of William Wordsworth and the home base of the renowned Jenning's Brewery, but hit the headlines in 2009 when the town suffered serious flooding. Since then, Cockermouth's elegant streets have been restored, and the town makes an interesting detour from the better-known and busier Lakeland towns.

◉ Sights

★Wordsworth House
HISTORIC BUILDING

(NT; ☎01900-824805; Main St; adult/child £6.70/3.35; ☺11am-5pm Sat-Thu Mar-Oct) William Wordsworth was born on 7 April 1770 at this handsome Georgian house at the end of Main St. Built around 1745, the house has been restored based on accounts from the Wordsworth archive. Costumed guides help bring the house to life.

The kitchen garden (mentioned in Wordsworth's autobiographical poem *The Prelude*) was badly damaged during the floods, but has since been carefully replanted.

Jenning's Brewery
BREWERY

(☎01900-821011; www.jenningsbrewery.co.uk; adult/child £8/4.50; ☺guided tours noon & 2pm Mon-Sat Apr-Oct, fewer in winter) Real ale aficionados will be well familiar with the name of Jenning's, a renowned brewery that's been in business since 1874. It's possible to take a guided tour to see the brewing process, followed by a tasting session in the Old Cooperage Bar. Take your pick from golden Cocker Hoop, classic Bitter and the superbly named Sneck Lifter. Children must be over 12.

OFF THE BEATEN TRACK

ENNERDALE

If you really want to leave the outside world behind, the remote valley of Ennerdale is definitely the place. Just to the north of Wasdale, this valley and its namesake lake was once home to slate mines and large timber plantations, but these are slowly being removed and the valley is being returned to nature as part of the Wild Ennerdale project (www.wildennerdale.co.uk).

Needless to say, the valley is paradise if you prefer your trails quiet. Several popular routes head over the fells to Wasdale, while walking towards Buttermere takes you past the Black Sail YHA (☎0845 371 9680; www.yha.org.uk/hostel/black-sail; dm £20.50-22.50), a marvellously remote hostel inside a shepherd's bothy. Much-loved by mountaineers and hikers, it's become a YHA landmark. and has recently been kitted out with solar panels, LED lighting and double glazing at a cost of around £260,000. Space is very limited, so make sure you book ahead.

🛏 Sleeping

Six Castlegate B&B ££
(☑ 01900-826749; www.sixcastlegate.co.uk; 6 Castlegate; s £45-50, d £70-80; 🛜) A Grade II–listed town house combining Georgian heritage with a modern twist, and feathery pillows, lofty ceilings and shiny showers in all six rooms.

Croft House B&B ££
(☑ 01900-827533; www.croft-guesthouse.com; 6/8 Challoner St; s £50, d £70-80; 🛜) This swish lemon-yellow B&B offers rooms in a Georgian house, all with exposed stone and reclaimed maple-wood floors.

🍴 Eating & Drinking

Merienda CAFE £
(7a Station St; mains £4-8; ⏰ 9am-5pm Mon-Sat) The town's best bet for lunch, this bright cafe serves fresh soups and open-face sandwiches.

Quince & Medlar VEGETARIAN ££
(www.quinceandmedlar.co.uk; 13 Castlegate; mains £13.95; ⏰ 7-10pm Tue-Sat; 🖉) 🌿 Imaginative veggie food served in the refined surrounds of one of Castlegate's Georgian houses, complete with panelled walls and flickering candles. Even committed carnivores will be tempted by the creative creations. Butternut squash layered with spiced ginger and cumin quinoa, anyone?

Honest Lawyer BISTRO ££
(☑ 01900-824888; 2 Main St; 2-course meal £18.95; ⏰ 5.30-9.30pm) Tucked away by the river, this attractive bistro specialises in French-Italian fusion: grilled sea bass with scallops with sauce vierge, perhaps, or supreme of duck with pommes Anna. There's a range of veggie options too. They can usually squeeze you in even at the busiest of times.

Bitter End PUB
(☑ 01900-828993; www.bitterend.co.uk; 15 Kirkgate; mains £10-15; ⏰ noon-2.30pm & 6-10pm) This well-regarded brewpub produces its own award-winning beers such as Cockermouth Pride, Lakeland Honey Beer and Cuddy Lugs. You can watch the vats at work through a glass partition in the bar.

ℹ Information

Tourist Office (☑ 01900-822634; cockermouthtic@co-net.com; ⏰ 10am-4pm Mon-Fri, to 2pm Sat) Inside the town hall.

ℹ Getting There & Away

Bus X4/X5 (half-hourly Monday to Saturday, hourly Sunday) travels from Penrith to Keswick and Cockermouth (£6.40), and Workington (£7.60, 1¼ hours).

Keswick

POP 4821

The most northerly of the Lake District's major towns, Keswick has perhaps the most beautiful location of all: encircled by cloud-capped fells and nestled alongside the idyllic, island-studded lake of Derwentwater, a silvery curve criss-crossed by puttering cruise boats. It's also brilliantly positioned for further adventures into the nearby valleys of Borrowdale and Buttermere.

◉ Sights

The heart of Keswick is the old Market Place, in the shadow of the town's former prison and meeting rooms at the **Moot Hall** (now occupied by the tourist office). Keswick's oddball museum is still closed for refurbishment; ask at the tourist office for the latest news.

Castlerigg Stone Circle MONUMENT
FREE Set on a hilltop a mile east of town, this jaw-dropping stone circle consists of 48 stones that are between 3000 and 4000 years old, surrounded by a dramatic ring of mountain peaks.

Pencil Museum MUSEUM
(www.pencilmuseum.co.uk; Southy Works; adult/child £4.25/3.25; ⏰ 9.30am-5pm) Vying for top spot in Cumbria's weirdest museum chart, this pencil-themed museum's exhibits include the world's longest pencil (8m from end to end) and a replica of a Borrowdale slate mine. There is method in the madness, though – when graphite was discovered in the Borrowdale fells during the 17th century, Keswick became one of the world's main pencil producers. You can buy luxury Derwent colouring pencils in the shop.

Whinlatter Forest Park FOREST
(www.forestry.gov.uk/whinlatter) **FREE** Encompassing 1200 hectares of pine, larch and spruce, Whinlatter is England's only true mountain forest, rising sharply to 790m about 5 miles from Keswick. The forest is a designated red squirrel reserve; you can check out live video feeds from squirrel cams at the **visitor centre** (☑ 017687-78469; ⏰ 10am-4pm).

It's also home to two exciting mountain-bike trails and the Go Ape (www.goape.co.uk/days-out/whinlatter; adult/child £30/25; ☺9am-5pm mid-Mar–Oct) tree-top assault course. You can hire bikes from Cyclewise (☑017687-78711; www.cyclewise.co.uk; ☺10am-5pm), next to the visitor centre.

Entry to the forest is free, but you have to pay for parking. Bus 77 (four daily) runs from Keswick. If you're driving, head west on the A66 and look for the brown signs near Braithwaite.

🏃 Activities

Keswick has a wealth of fantastic walks on its doorstep. The most popular is the family-friendly fell of Catbells (451m), on the lake's west side; the trailhead starts next to the jetty at Hawse End, served by the Keswick Launch. There's also an easy trail along the old railway path to Threlkeld.

Hardcore hikers will prefer the more challenging slog up Skiddaw (931m), the huge mountain that looms on Keswick's northern skyline. Alternatively, near Threlkeld is the lonely fell of Blencathra (868m), which was recently put up for sale by the Earl of Lonsdale with a price tag of £1.75 million.

Keswick Launch BOATING
(☑017687-72263; www.keswick-launch.co.uk; round-the-lake adult/child £9.25/4.50) Said to have been Beatrix Potter's favourite lake (she's supposed to have got the idea for Squirrel Nutkin while watching red squirrels on the shoreline), Derwentwater is certainly a real beauty. As always, the best way to appreciate its charms is by getting out on the water. There are six daily boats from March to November, with a couple of extra afternoon sailings and a twilight cruise in summer, dropping to just a couple of sailings a day in winter.

Apart from the main jetties in Keswick, the lake's other landing stages are at Ashness Gate, Lodore Falls, High Brandlehow, Low Brandlehow, Hawse End and Nichol End. Departures run clockwise and anticlockwise. Rowboats and motorboats can be hired next to the launch jetties.

🎆 Festivals & Events

Keswick Mountain Festival OUTDOORS
(www.keswickmountainfestival.co.uk) This May festival celebrates all things mountainous.

Keswick Beer Festival BEER
(www.keswickbeerfestival.co.uk) Lots of beer is drunk during Keswick's real ale fest in June.

THE BASSENTHWAITE OSPREYS

In 2001 the first wild ospreys to breed in England for 150 years set up home at Bassenthwaite Lake, near Keswick. Over the last few years, the birds have usually arrived at Bassenthwaite in April, spending the summer at the lake before heading for Africa in late August or early September.

There are two official viewpoints, both in Dodd Wood, about 3 miles north of Keswick on the A591 (follow signs for Dodd Wood and Cattle Inn). The lower hide (open 10am to 5pm) is about 15 minutes' walk from the car park at Mirehouse, and the new upper hide (open 10.30am to 4.30pm) is half an hour further. Find out more at www.ospreywatch.co.uk.

🛏 Sleeping

Keswick is simply crammed with good-value B&Bs, especially around Stanger and Helvellyn Sts.

Keswick YHA HOSTEL £
(☑0845 371 9746; keswick@yha.org.uk; Station Rd; dm £13-21; @) Keswick's YHA is a beauty, lodged inside a converted woollen mill by the clattering River Rothay, and renovated thanks to the benevolence of a generous doctor. Dorms are cosy, there's an excellent cafe, and some rooms even have balconies over Fitz Park.

★ **Howe Keld** B&B ££
(☑017687-72417; www.howekeld.co.uk; 5-7 The Heads; s £58, d £110-130; ℙ☎) This B&B pulls out all the stops: goose-down duvets, slate-floored bathrooms, chic colours and locally made furniture. The best rooms have views across Crow Park and the golf course, and the breakfast is a pick-and-mix delight. Free parking is available on the Heads if there's space.

Linnett Hill B&B ££
(☑017687-44518; www.linnetthillkeswick.co.uk; 4 Penrith Rd; s/d £45/80; ☎) Much recommended by travellers, this lovingly run B&B has lots going for it: crisp white rooms, a great location near Fitz Park and keen prices that stay the same year-round. Breakfast is good too: there's a blackboard of specials to choose from, and the dining room has

gingham-check tablecloths and a crackling woodburner.

Oakthwaite House
B&B ££

(☑ 017687-72398; www.oakthwaite-keswick.com; 35 Helvellyn St; d £76-90; 🛜) One of the top choices in the B&B-heavy neighbourhood around Helvellyn St. There are just four rooms (so it's not too crowded), all with power showers, white linen and soothingly neutral tones. Rooms 4 and 5 are up in the eaves, while Room 2 is the most spacious, with views of Walla Crag.

★ Cottage in the Wood
HOTEL £££

(☑ 017687-78409; www.thecottageinthewood. co.uk; Braithwaite; d £110-190; ⊘ restaurant 6.30-9pm Tue-Sat) For a secluded spoil, this out-of-the-way hotel is a real find. It's on the way to Whinlatter Forest, in a 17th-century coaching inn that's been thoroughly modernised. Elegant rooms survey woods and countryside: the Mountain View rooms overlook the Skiddaw Range, but we liked the super-private Attic Suite and Garden Room, with its wood floors and wet-room. The restaurant's fantastic, too.

🍴 Eating & Drinking

Abraham's Tea Rooms
CAFE £

(2 Borrowdale Rd; mains £6-10; ⊘ 10am-5pm Mon-Sat, 10.30am-4.30pm Sun) On the top floor of George Fishers, in the former photography studio of the Abraham brothers, this cosy cafe is great for a country lunch: hot rarebit (toasted-cheese-on-toast), mackerel paté or a classic baked spud.

Lakeland Pedlar Wholefood Cafe
CAFE £

(www.lakelandpedlar.co.uk; Hendersons Yard; mains £4-10; ⊘ 9am-5pm) 🌿 Down a narrow side alley off the high street, this veggie-organic wholefood emporium is a hallowed destination for hikers and bikers, renowned for its chunky sandwiches, homemade soups and enormous cakes. There's a bike shop upstairs.

Bryson's
CAFE £

(42 Main St; cakes £2-5; ⊘ 8.30am-5.30pm) An old-fashioned bakery known for its fruitcakes, Battenbergs and Florentines.

Pumpkin Cafe
CAFE £

(19 Lake Rd; lunches £3-6; ⊘ 8.30am-5pm Mon-Sat) Metropolitan cafe culture comes to Keswick: order a make-your-own salad or a deli sandwich, followed by a fresh-baked croissant and a flat white. There's seating upstairs, or you can order to go.

★ Pheasant Inn
PUB ££

(☑ 017687-72219; www.the-pheasant.co.uk; Bassenthwaite; mains £14-18; ⊘ restaurant 7-9pm Tue-Sat, noon-2pm Sun, bistro noon-4.30pm & 6-9pm) A short drive along Bassenthwaite Lake is this fine dining pub. Hunting prints and pewter tankards cover the old bar, stocked with vintage whiskies and Lakeland ales, and the brace of restaurants (informal bistro and smart restaurant) both serve superior country food. The afternoon tea's done in the proper English fashion, too, complete with cucumber sandwiches.

★ Chalet
BISTRO ££

(☑ 017687-72757; www.thechaletportinscale.co.uk; lunch £5-8.50, dinner £12.95-17.95; ⊘ 9am-5pm Tue & Wed, 9am-5pm & 6.30-11pm Thu-Mon) This cafe-bistro opened in 2013 in Portinscale and has fast become one of Keswick's gastronomic hot spots. The architecture blends old (wood-burners, log piles) and new (plate glass, Scandinavian minimalism), and the food's a similar blend of styles; comforting crumpets and sharing platters for lunch, sophisticated plates of confit duck and dry-aged steak for supper, all accompanied by a suggested wine. Classy.

Morrel's
BRITISH ££

(☑ 017687-72666; www.morrels.co.uk; Lake Rd; 3-course menu £21.95, mains £12.50-16.50; ⊘ 5.30-9pm Tue-Sun) A reliable bistro that serves Mediterranean-tinged food. The stripped-back interior and spotlights make it feel formal, but it's actually a very relaxed affair.

Cafe-Bar 26
CAFE, BAR

(26 Lake Rd; tapas £4-10; ⊘ 9am-11pm Mon-Sat, 10am-10pm Sun) An attractive corner wine-bar that also serves good tapas.

Dog & Gun
PUB

(2 Lake Rd; ⊘ 11am-11pm) Benches, beams, hearths, rugs: the old Dog is the picture of a Lakeland pub. Look out for Thirst Rescue ale, which donates part of its proceeds to the Keswick Mountain rescue team.

🛍 Shopping

George Fisher
OUTDOOR EQUIPMENT

(2 Borrowdale Rd; ⊘ 9am-5.30pm Mon-Sat, 10am-4pm Sun) Keswick has plenty of outdoor shops, but the traditionalists' choice is George Fisher, one of the Lake District's oldest outdoors suppliers. There are three floors of boots, tents and gear, and the boot-fitting service is superb.

ℹ Information

Tourist Office (☑ 017687-72645; keswicktic@
lake-district.gov.uk; Moot Hall, Market Pl;
⊙ 9.30am-5.30pm Apr-Oct, to 4.30pm Nov-Mar)
Sells discounted tickets for the Keswick Launch.

ℹ Getting There & Away

The Keswick & Honister Dayrider (adult/child/
family £8/6/22) buys unlimited travel on buses
in the Keswick area.

Useful buses from Keswick:

555/556 Lakeslink Hourly to Ambleside
(£7.95, 40 minutes), Windermere (£8.55, 50
minutes) and Kendal (£9.30, 1½ hours).

77/77A Honister Rambler Circular route (Keswick & Honister Dayrider adult/child £8/6, four
daily) from Keswick via Portinscale, Catbells,
Grange, Seatoller, Honister Pass, Buttermere,
Lorton and Whinlatter.

78 Borrowdale Rambler (Keswick & Honister
Dayrider adult/child £8/6, at least hourly Mon-
day to Friday, half-hourly weekends) The main
Borrowdale bus, with stops at Lodore, Grange,
Rosthwaite and Seatoller.

X4/X5 Penrith to Workington via Keswick
(£6.40, hourly Monday to Friday, six on Sunday).

ℹ Getting Around

Keswick Mountain Bikes (☑ 017687-75202;
www.keswickmountainbikes.co.uk; 133 Main St;
adult bikes per day £15-40; ⊙ 9.30am-5.30pm)
Mountain bikes can be hired from Keswick
Mountain Bikes. The road-specific shop is
above the Lakeland Pedlar Wholefood Cafe.

Borrowdale

With their patchwork of craggy hills, broad
fields, tinkling streams and drystone walls,
the side-by-side valleys of Borrowdale and
Buttermere are many people's idea of the
quintessential Lakeland landscape. Once
a centre for mineral mining (especially for
slate, coal and graphite), this is walkers'
country these days, and apart from the odd
rickety barn or puttering tractor, there's precious little to spoil the view.

South of Keswick, the B5289 tracks Derwentwater into the heart of Borrowdale,
winding past the small farming villages
of Grange-in-Borrowdale, Rosthwaite and
Stonethwaite.

◉ Sights & Activities

Lodore Falls   WATERFALL
At the southern end of Derwentwater, this
famous waterfall featured in a poem by Rob-

ert Southey, but it's only worth visiting after a
spell of rain. It's in the grounds of the Lodore
Hotel; there's an honesty box for donations.

Bowder Stone   OUTDOORS
A mile south from Grange, a turn-off leads
up to the geological curiosity known as the
Bowder Stone, a 1696-tonne lump of rock
left behind by a retreating glacier. A small
stepladder leads up to the top of the rock.

Watendlath Tarn   LAKE
This National Trust–owned tarn is reached
via a turn-off on the B5285 south of Keswick.
On the way, the road passes over one of the
Lake District's most photographed packhorse crossings at **Ashness Bridge**. Parking
at the tarn is free for NT members, but the
road is narrow and has few passing places,
so it's more pleasant to walk up in summer.

Platty+   BOATING
(☑ 017687-76572; www.plattyplus.co.uk; kayaks &
canoes per hr £8-15) Based at the Lodore Boat
Landings, this company hires out kayaks, canoes and sailing dinghies, and runs instruction courses.

🛏 Sleeping

Derwentwater Independent Hostel HOSTEL **£**
(☑ 017687-77246; www.derwentwater.org; Barrow
House; dm £19-21, r from £66; 🅿 @) Built as a
19th-century mansion for the local notable
George Pocklington, this grand hostel was
previously YHA-owned, but it's now inde-
pendently run and offers clean, basic dorms
(most have four to eight beds, but one has 22
beds) plus self-catering facilities. The house
still has many of its original architectural
features, and sits in 7-hectare grounds complete with waterfall.

Borrowdale YHA   HOSTEL **£**
(☑ 0845 371 9624; borrowdale@yha.org.uk; Long-
thwaite; dm £19-23; ⊙ Feb-Dec) Purpose-built
chalet hostel, specialising in walking and
activity trips.

Langstrath Inn   B&B **££**
(☑ 017687-77239; www.thelangstrath.com; Stonethwaite; d £100-128, mains from £11.30; ⊙ restaurant
noon-10.30pm Tue-Sun; 🅿 🛜) Borrowdale's
country hotels are expensive, so you'll be better off basing yourself at this out-of-the-way
inn in Stonethwaite. The eight rooms feature
white walls, crimson throws and pleasant en
suites, and the countryside views are to die
for. Hearty food and beers from Hawkshead
Brewery are served in the restaurant.

🏃 Driving Tour
Borrowdale & Buttermere

START KESWICK
END KESWICK
LENGTH 28 MILES, THREE TO FOUR HOURS

This is one of the Lakes' most beautiful road trips, taking in the unspoilt scenery of the Borrowdale, Buttermere and Lorton Valleys. Begin with breakfast in **❶ Keswick**, then head along the B5289 into Borrowdale. First stop is **❷ Lodore Falls** (p605), a pretty cascade at the southern end of Derwentwater. Next, detour to the little hamlet of **❸ Grange-in-Borrowdale**, where a trail leads up the slate-strewn sides of Castle Crag, a small fell with great views over Borrowdale.

From Grange, carry on to the huge boulder known as the **❹ Bowder Stone** (p605), shifted into position by the glacier which carved out the Borrowdale Valley. Pootle on to **❺ Rosthwaite** for tea and cake at the Flock-In tearoom, or continue to **❻ Seatoller** for lunch.

In the afternoon, tackle the steep crawl up to **❼ Honister Pass** (p607), where you can pick up some slate souvenirs or take a mine tour. From here, the road drops down into the beautiful valley of **❽ Buttermere**. Spot the zigzag peaks of High Stile, Haystacks and Red Pike looming on your left-hand side over the lake, stop off for a drink at the Fish Inn, and remember to pay your respects to Alfred Wainwright inside St James' Church.

Continue along the shore of Crummock Water past **❾ Loweswater**, where you could make an optional but very worthwhile detour via the excellent Kirkstile Inn. When you reach **❿ Low Lorton**, a right-hand turn carries you over Whinlatter Pass to **⓫ Whinlatter Forest Park** (p602). The forest park makes a good spot for a late-afternoon stop; there's a pleasant cafe at the visitor centre, as well as displays on the local wildlife.

There are a couple of great options for dinner on your way back to Keswick such as the **⓬ Cottage in the Wood** (p604) just before Braithwaite.

Seatoller House
B&B ££

(☑ 017687-77218; www.seatollerhouse.co.uk; s £55, d £90-100; ℗) A tiny hideaway in Seatoller that feels like a Beatrix Potter burrow. It's tucked beneath Honister Pass and all the rooms are named after animals: attic Osprey has skylight views, Rabbit is pine-filled and Badger looks over the garden. Rooms including a four-course dinner for two cost £139.

Yew Tree Farm
B&B ££

(☑ 017687-77675; www.borrowdaleherdwick.co.uk; Rosthwaite; d £80; ℗) There are floral patterns galore at this sturdy Cumbrian farmhouse in rural Rosthwaite, with three rooms snuggled among cob walls and tiny windows (no wi-fi or TVs!). It's run by working sheep farmers, and you'll be able to spot Herdwicks in the nearby fields. Breakfast is huge, and the Flock-In tearoom over the road serves delicious cakes and puddings.

⊙ Getting There & Away

Buses 77/77A and 78 connect Borrowdale and Buttermere with Keswick. Get the Keswick & Honister Dayrider pass (adult/child £8/6).

Honister Pass

From Borrowdale, a narrow, perilously steep road snakes up the fellside to Honister Pass and Buttermere Valley beyond.

Overlooking the top of the pass is the Honister Slate Mine (☑ 017687-77230; www.honister-slate-mine.co.uk; mine tour adult/child £12.50/7.50, all-day pass £34/25; ⊙ tours 10.30am, 12.30pm & 3.30pm Mar-Oct), where underground tours venture deep into the bowels of the old 'Edge' and 'Kimberley' mines (a tour into the 'Cathedral' mine runs on Friday by request, but you'll need eight people and it costs £19.75).

Honister is also home to the UK's first Via Ferrata (Classic route adult/child £35/25, Xtreme £39.50/29.50), a vertiginous system of clifftop ropes and ladders once used by slate miners. It's exhilarating and great fun, but unsurprisingly you'll need a head for heights. Combination tickets are available for both activities.

A brand-new attraction opened in April 2014 combines the mining-and-climbing experience: a subterranean 'Burma Bridge', which involves clambering along underground passages on fixed ropes. It costs adult/child £19.95/14.95, and you need to be 10 or older.

Buttermere

From the high point of Honister, the road drops sharply into the deep bowl of Buttermere, skirting the lakeshore to Buttermere village, 4 miles from Honister and 9 miles from Keswick. From here, the B5289 cuts past Crummock Water before exiting the valley's northern edge.

Buttermere marks the start of Alfred Wainwright's all-time favourite circuit: up Red Pike (755m), and along High Stile (807m), High Crag and Haystacks (597m). In fact, the great man liked it so much, he stayed here for good: after his death in 1991, his ashes were scattered across the top of Haystacks as requested in his will. A small plaque in Buttermere's little chapel, St James' Church, commemorares the great man.

🛏 Sleeping & Eating

Buttermere YHA
HOSTEL £

(☑ 0845 371 9508; buttermere@yha.org.uk; dm £17-22; ⊙ reception 8.30-10am & 5-10.30pm) A fine YHA, with a lake-view location halfway between Honister and Buttermere village.

★ Kirkstile Inn
PUB ££

(☑ 01900-85219; www.kirkstile.com; mains £12-16, s £63.50-90, d £99-109) A finer country pub you could not hope to find. Hidden away near the little lake of Loweswater, a mile or so north of Buttermere, the Kirkstile is a joy: crackling fires, oak beams, worn carpets, wooden bar and all. It's particularly known for its award-winning ales (try the Loweswater Gold). Rooms are quaint; some have views across Lorton Vale.

Fish Inn
PUB ££

(☑ 017687-70253; www.fishinnbuttermere.co.uk; mains £8-14, d £90-110; ℗) This inn once employed the 18th-century beauty known as the 'Maid of Buttermere', but these days it's just a welcoming local's pub, serving staples such as lasagne and battered haddock, washed down with ales from several local breweries.

⊙ Getting There & Away

Bus 77/77A serves Buttermere and Honister Pass from Keswick. Use the Keswick & Honister Dayrider (adult/child £8/6).

Ullswater & Around

After Windermere, the second-largest lake in the Lake District is Ullswater, stretching for 7.5 miles between Pooley Bridge, and Glenridding and Patterdale in the south. Carved out by a long-extinct glacier, the deep valley in which the lake sits is flanked by an impressive string of fells, most notably the razor ridge of Helvellyn, Cumbria's third-highest mountain at 950m.

It's also famous as the place where William Wordsworth was inspired to write his best-known poem, 'Daffodils'.

Sights & Activities

Gowbarrow Park & Aira Force
PARK, WATERFALL

FREE This rolling park stretches out across the lakeshore between Pooley Bridge and Glenridding. Well-marked paths lead up to the impressive 20m waterfall of Aira Force. Another waterfall, High Force, is further up the hillside.

South of Gowbarrow Park is Glencoyne Bay, where the springtime daffodils inspired Wordsworth to pen the immortal lines: 'I wandered lonely as a cloud/That floats on high over hills and dales/When all at once I saw a crowd/A host, of golden daffodils...'

February and March are the best months if you want to see the flowers for yourself.

Ullswater 'Steamers'
BOATING

(☑ 017684-82229; www.ullswater-steamers.co.uk; round-the-lake adult/child £13.20/6.60) Ullswater's historic steamer service has been running since 1855. There are now four boats, all dressed in the company's distinctive livery; the stately *Lady of the Lake* was launched in 1888, making it the oldest passenger boat still working in the world.

The boats run east–west from Pooley Bridge, stopping at the village of Howtown on the southern shore en route to Glenridding. There are up to 11 sailings a day in summer, dropping to four in winter.

Sleeping

Helvellyn YHA
HOSTEL £

(☑ 0845 371 9742; helvellyn@yha.org.uk; Greenside; dm £13-18; ⊙ Easter-Oct) A high-level hostel, in an old miners' cottage 275m above the valley at the end of a rough track. It's a favourite with hikers looking to get a headstart on Helvellyn; dorms are small and facilities are basic, but meals are provided by hostel staff.

Patterdale YHA
HOSTEL £

(☑ 0845 371 9337; patterdale@yha.org.uk; Patterdale; dm £17-22.50; ⊙ reception 7.30-10am &

5-10.30pm Easter-Oct) This 1970s hostel lacks the heritage of some of the Lakeland YHAs, but it has a great location by the lake and all the usual YHA trappings (kitchen, cafe, TV lounge) – as long as you don't mind the institutional architecture.

Lowthwaite Farm
B&B ££

(☑ 017684-82343; www.lowthwaiteullswater.com; Matterdale; d £86-90; ℗) This lovely farmhouse in Matterdale is all about the good life. The owners have filled the place with souvenirs collected on their travels, such as chunky wooden beds made in Tanzania that match the house's hefty wooden beams. It's a couple of miles from the lake, off the A5091 to Dockray; ring ahead for directions, as it's tricky to find. Two-night minimum on weekends.

Old Water View
B&B ££

(☑ 017684-82175; www.oldwaterview.co.uk; Patterdale; d £72-86) Patterdale has several B&Bs, but this one's the pick. It's a simple place focusing on the essentials: friendly service, comfy rooms and good value. The split-level Bothy room is ideal for families, with attic beds for the kids, while Little Gem overlooks a stream and Place Fell is said to have been a favourite of Alfred Wainwright.

Eating

Traveller's Rest
PUB ££

(Glenridding; mains £5.50-15; ⊙ 10am-11pm) Down a pint with a view of the fells at Traveller's Rest, a Glenridding stalwart. The food might be plain (steaks, pies, prawn cocktails) but the portions are huge.

Fellbites
CAFE ££

(Glenridding; mains £5-15; ⊙ 11am-8.30pm, to 5.30pm Wed) Popular Glenridding cafe that serves a good selection of spuds, sarnies and all-day breakfasts, plus a daily roast and chunky steaks.

Information

Ullswater Information Centre (☑ 017684-82414; ullswatertic@lake-district.gov.uk; Glenridding; ⊙ 9am-5.30pm Apr-Oct)

Getting There & Away

The Ullswater Bus-and-Boat Combo ticket (adult/child/family £15.50/8.50/33) includes a day's travel on bus 108 with a return trip on an Ullswater Steamer; buy the ticket on the bus.

108 Travels from Penrith to Patterdale via Pooley Bridge and Glenridding (£5.50 to £6.50, five daily Monday to Friday, four on weekends).

Kendal

POP 28,586

Technically Kendal isn't in the Lake District, but it's a major gateway town. Often known as the 'Auld Grey Town' thanks to the sombre grey stone used for many of its buildings, Kendal is a bustling shopping centre with some good restaurants, a funky arts centre and intriguing museums. But it'll forever be synonymous in many people's minds with its famous mint cake, a staple item in the nation's hiking packs ever since Edmund Hillary and Tenzing Norgay munched it during their ascent of Everest in 1953.

◉ Sights

Kendal Museum MUSEUM

(www.kendalmuseum.org.uk; Station Rd; ⊙10.30am-5pm Tue-Sat) FREE Founded in 1796 by the inveterate Victorian collector William Todhunter, this mixed-bag museum features everything from stuffed beasts and transfixed butterflies to medieval coin hoards. There's also a reconstruction of the office of Alfred Wainwright, who served as honorary curator at the museum from 1945 to 1974: look out for his pipe and knapsack.

Abbot Hall Art Gallery GALLERY

(www.abbothall.org.uk; adult/child £5/free; ⊙10.30am-5pm Mon-Sat Apr-Oct, to 4pm Nov-Mar) Kendal's fine art gallery houses one of the northwest's best collections of 18th- and 19th-century art. It's especially strong on portraiture and Lakeland landscapes: look out for works by Constable, John Ruskin and local boy George Romney, a key figure in the Kendal School.

Museum of Lakeland Life & Industry MUSEUM

(www.lakelandmuseum.org.uk; adult/child £5/free; ⊙10.30am-5pm Mon-Sat Mar-Oct, to 4pm Nov-Feb) Directly opposite Abbot Hall, this museum recreates various scenes from Lakeland life during the 18th and 19th centuries, including a farmhouse parlour, a Lakeland kitchen, an apothecary and the study of Arthur Ransome, author of *Swallows and Amazons*.

★☆ Festivals & Events

Kendal Mountain Festival OUTDOORS

(www.mountainfest.co.uk) An annual mountain-themed celebration that encompasses films, books and talks in November.

🛏 Sleeping

Crosthwaite House B&B ££

(☎015395-68264; www.crosthwaitehouse.co.uk; d £80; 🅿🛜) Zingy and zesty, this bright number has lots of imagination: the six rooms are colourfully decorated with swirly wallpapers, funky fabrics and retro furniture, and all named after a type of damson fruit. Tasty breakfast options include blueberry pancakes and huevos rancheros. It's in Crosthwaite, about 6 miles west of Kendal.

Beech House B&B ££

(☎01539-720385; www.beechhouse-kendal.co.uk; 40 Greenside; d £75-100; 🅿🛜) Top Kendal honours go to this extremely elegant B&B at the top of the steep hill of Beast Banks. Rooms are a prim-and-proper treat: some feature sleigh beds and fluffy cushions, others free-standing baths and comfy sofas.

✕ Eating

Baba Ganoush DELI £

(☎01539-738210; Finkle St; mains £5-8; ⊙9.30am-4pm Tue-Sat) Down a side alley, this super cafe-deli serves delicious Mediterranean-tinged food such as falafels, lamb stews, veggie mezze and Moroccan tagines.

Waterside Wholefoods CAFE £

(Kent View; light meals £4-10; ⊙8.30am-4.30pm Mon-Sat) 🌱 Kendal's veggies make a beeline for this riverside cafe, a long-standing staple for sandwiches, pancakes and naughty-but-nice cakes.

1657 Chocolate House CAFE £

(54 Branthwaite Brow; lunches £3-8) A chocoholics' delight: handmade chocolates and Kendal mint cake in the basement, plus umpteen varieties of hot chocolate in the upstairs cafe.

New Moon BISTRO ££

(☎01539-729254; www.newmoonrestaurant.co.uk; 129 Highgate; mains £11.95-16.95; ⊙11.30am-2.15pm & 5.30-9pm Tue-Sat) A good bet for a pre-theatre supper, the New Moon is one of Kendal's longest-standing bistros, strong on filling dishes spiced with Asian and African flavours. The two-course pre-7pm menu is great value at £13.50.

Grain Store BISTRO ££

(Highgate; pizzas £6.50-10, mains £10-16.50; ⊙10am-11pm Mon-Sat) The Brewery Arts Centre's restaurant does a decent line in pub grub and stone-baked pizzas.

★ **Punch Bowl Inn** PUB £££

(☑ 015395-68237; www.the-punchbowl.co.uk; Crosthwaite; mains £14.50-19.95; ☺ noon-4pm & 5.30-8.30pm; ℗) This country inn in Crosthwaite, halfway between Kendal and Bowness, is one of the Lake District's epicurian pubs par excellence. Chef Scott Fairweather favours classic flavours, but his menu is sprinkled with cheffy ingredients such as salsify, pickled carrot, pak choi and cep purées. The elegant rooms are lovely too (£105 to £305), with reclaimed beams and Roberts Revival radios.

☆ Entertainment

Brewery Arts Centre THEATRE, CINEMA

(☑ 01539-725133; www.breweryarts.co.uk; Highgate) One of the best arts centres in the northwest, it has a gallery, cafe, theatre and two cinemas, with regular live events to boot.

❶ Getting There & Around

The train line from Windermere runs to Kendal (£4.50, 15 minutes, hourly) en route to Oxenholme.

Bus 106 To Penrith (£4.50, 80 minutes, six to eight daily Monday to Saturday).

Bus 505 To Windermere, Ambleside, Hawkshead and Coniston (£9.30, hourly including Sundays).

Buses 555/556 Regular bus (£8 to £9.30, half-hourly Monday to Saturday, hourly at weekends) to Windermere (30 minutes), Ambleside (40 minutes) and Grasmere (1¼ hours).

Around Kendal

The countryside around Kendal feels gentler than the dramatic fells and valleys of the rest of the Lakes. It's mainly worth visiting for its stately homes and one of the county's top farm shops.

◉ Sights

Sizergh Castle CASTLE

(NT; ☑ 015395-60070; www.nationaltrust.org.uk/sizergh-castle; adult/child £9.45/4.73, gardens only £5.85/2.93; ☺ house 1-5pm Sun-Thu, gardens 11am-5pm daily) Three-and-a-half miles south of Kendal along the A591, this castle is the feudal seat of the Strickland family. Set around a *pele* tower, its finest asset is the lavish wood panelling on display in the Great Hall. There are private house tours between noon and 1pm.

Levens Hall HISTORIC BUILDING

(☑ 015395-60321; www.levenshall.co.uk; adult/child £12.50/free, garden only £8.50/free; ☺ house noon-4.30pm, gardens 10am-5pm Sun-Thu Mar-Oct) This Elizabethan manor is built around a mid-13th-century *pele* tower, and fine Jacobean furniture litters the house, although the real draw is the 17th-century topiary garden: a surreal riot of pyramids, swirls, curls, pom-poms and peacocks straight out of *Alice in Wonderland*. It's 2 miles south from Sizergh Castle along the A6. The 555/556 bus runs past the castle gates.

ⓐ Shopping

Low Sizergh Barn FOOD

(☑ 015395-60426; www.lowsizerghbarn.co.uk; ☺ 9am-5.30pm) A prodigious selection of Lakeland goodies are available at this beamed farm shop, one of the Lake District's very best. Breads from Grange Bakery, meats from Mansergh Hall, cheeses from Thornby Moor Dairy and beers from the Coniston Brewery Co are just some of the gourmet treats in store. There's also a farm trail and woodland walk to follow if the weather's nice. Look out for the signs just outside Kendal on the A590.

CUMBRIAN COAST

While the central lakes and fells pull in a never-ending stream of visitors, surprisingly few ever make the trek west to explore Cumbria's coastline. And that's a shame: while it might not compare to the wild grandeur of Northumberland or the rugged splendour of Scotland's shores, Cumbria's coast is well worth exploring. Less attractive is the nuclear plant of Sellafield, still stirring up controversy some 50 years after its construction.

◉ Sights

Holker Hall HISTORIC BUILDING

(☑ 015395-58328; www.holker.co.uk; adult/child £12/free; ☺ house 11am-4pm Sun-Fri, grounds 10.30am-4.30pm Mar-Oct, longer hours Jul & Aug) Holker Hall has been the family seat of the Cavendish family for nigh on 400 years. Though parts of the house date from the 16th century, the house was almost entirely rebuilt following a devastating fire in 1871. It's a typically ostentatious Victorian affair, covered with mullioned windows, gables and copper-topped turrets outside, and filled inside with a warren of lavishly over-the-top rooms. The estate is about 3 miles east of Cartmel on the B5278.

Of particular note are the library and lavish Long Gallery (renowned for its elaborate plasterwork) and the amazing Wedgwood Dressing Rooms, covered in blue-and-white Wedgwood Jasperware. Also look out for various pieces of priceless Chippendale furniture, especially in the Drawing Room.

Outside, Holker's grounds sprawl for more than 10 hectares, encompassing a rose garden, a woodland, ornamental fountains and a 22m-high lime tree. There's also a food hall stocking produce from the estate, including venison and saltmarsh lamb.

Muncaster Castle CASTLE
(www.muncaster.co.uk; adult/child £13/7.50; ⊙gardens & owl centre 10.30am-5pm, castle noon-4.30pm Sun-Fri) Like many Cumbrian castles, Muncaster was originally built around a 14th-century *pele* tower, constructed to resist Reiver raids. Home to the Pennington family for seven centuries, the castle's architectural highlights are its great hall and octagonal library, and outside you'll find an ornamental maze and owl centre.

The castle is also known for its numerous ghosts: keep your eyes peeled for the Muncaster Boggle and a malevolent jester known as Tom Fool (hence 'tomfoolery'). The castle is about 1.5 miles east of Ravenglass.

Laurel & Hardy Museum MUSEUM
(☎01229-582292; www.laurel-and-hardy.co.uk; Brogden St, Ulverston; adult/child £4.50/2.50; ⊙10am-5pm Tue & Thu-Sun) Founded by avid Laurel and Hardy collector Bill Cubin back in 1983, this madcap museum in Ulverston (the birthplace of Stan Laurel) has new premises inside the town's old Roxy cinema. It's crammed floor-to-ceiling with cinematic memorabilia, from original posters to film props, and there's a shoebox-sized cinema showing back-to-back Laurel and Hardy classics.

Furness Abbey ABBEY
(EH; adult/child £4.20/2.50; ⊙10am-6pm) Eight-and-a-half miles southwest of Ulverston, the rosy ruins of Furness Abbey are all that remains of one of northern England's largest and most powerful monasteries. Founded

CARTMEL

Tiny Cartmel is known for three things: its 12th-century **priory** (⊙9am-5.30pm May-Oct, to 3.30pm Nov-Apr) FREE, its **miniature racecourse** and its world-famous sticky toffee pudding, sold at the **Cartmel Village Shop** (☎015395-36280; www.stickytoffeepudding.co.uk; ⊙9am-5pm Mon-Sat, 10am-4.30pm Sun).

More recently it's become known as the home of chef Simon Rogan (dubbed Cumbria's answer to Heston Blumenthal). His flagship restaurant, **L'Enclume** (☎015395-36362; www.lenclume.co.uk; Cavendish St; set lunch £45, dinner menu £120; ⊙noon-1pm Wed-Sun & 6.30-9pm daily), showcases his boundary-pushing cuisine and madcap presentation, as well as his passion for foraged ingredients.

He also runs a less formal bistro, **Rogan & Company** (☎015395-35917; www.roganandcompany.co.uk; The Square; 3-course menu £40; ⊙noon-2pm Tue-Sat, 6.30-9pm Mon-Sat), across the village. Bookings for both are essential.

in the 12th century, it met an ignominious end in 1537 during the Dissolution. You can make out its footprint; arches, windows and some transept walls are still standing, along with the shell of the bell tower.

A recently unearthed gold crozier and gemstone ring are displayed in the abbey museum with other archaeological finds. Several buses, including bus X35, stop nearby.

St Bees Head WILDLIFE RESERVE
(RSPB; stbees.head@rspb.org.uk) Five-and-a-half miles south of Whitehaven and 1.5 miles north of the tiny town of St Bees, this wind-battered headland is one of Cumbria's most important reserves for nesting seabirds. Depending on the season, species nesting here include fulmars, kittiwakes and razorbills, as well as Britain's only population of resident black guillemots. There are over 2 miles of cliff paths to explore.

ℹ **Getting Around**

The Furness and Cumbrian Coast railway lines loop 120 miles from Lancaster to Carlisle,

---

DON'T MISS

LA'AL RATTY

Officially known as the Ravenglass & Eskdale Railway (☑ 01229-717171; www. ravenglass-railway.co.uk; adult/child/family return £13/16.50/33), but universally known hereabouts as La'al Ratty, this pocket-sized railway was originally built to ferry iron ore from the Eskdale mines out to the coast. These days it's one of Cumbria's most beloved family attractions, with miniature steam trains that chug for 7 miles down the Eskdale valley between the coastal town of Ravenglass and the village of Dalegarth.

Even if you're not a train nerd, it's a fabulously odd way to see the Lake District countryside. There are between seven and 14 trains a day depending on the season, and the trains stop at various stations en route.

---

stopping at the coastal resorts of Grange, Ulverston, Ravenglass, Whitehaven and Workington. The Cumbrian Coast Day Ranger (adult/child £19/9.50) covers a day's unlimited travel on the line, and works out cheaper than a return journey from Carlisle or Lancaster.

NORTHERN & EASTERN CUMBRIA

Many visitors speed through the northern and eastern reaches of Cumbria in a headlong dash for the Lake District, but it's worth taking the time to venture inland from the national park. It might not have the big-name fells and chocolate-box villages, but it's full of interest: traditional towns, crumbling castles, abandoned abbeys and sweeping moors, all set alongside the magnificent Roman engineering project of Hadrian's Wall.

Carlisle

POP 75,306

Carlisle isn't Britain's prettiest city, but it has history and heritage aplenty. Precariously perched on the frontier between England and Scotland, in the area once ominously dubbed the 'Debatable Lands', Cumbria's capital is a city with a notoriously stormy past: sacked by the Vikings, pillaged by the Scots, and plundered by the Border Reivers,

the city has been on the frontline of England's defences for more than 1000 years.

Reminders of the past are evident in its great crimson castle and cathedral, built from the same rosy-red sandstone as most of the city's houses. On English St, you can also see two massive circular towers which once flanked the city's gateway.

The nearest section of Hadrian's Wall begins at nearby Brampton; see p637 for details.

◉ Sights

★ Carlisle Castle   CASTLE
(EH; www.english-heritage.org.uk/daysout/proper ties/carlisle-castle; Castle Way; adult/child £5.90/ 3.50; ⊙ 9.30am-5pm Apr-Sep, 10am-4pm Oct-Mar) Carlisle's brooding, rust-red castle lurks on the north side of the city. Founded around a Celtic and Roman stronghold, the Norman keep was added in 1092 by William Rufus, and later refortified by Henry II, Edward I and Henry VIII (who added the supposedly cannon-proof towers). From the battlements, the stirring views stretch as far as the Scottish borders.

The castle has witnessed some dramatic events over the centuries: Mary, Queen of Scots was imprisoned here in 1568, and the castle was the site of a notorious eight-month siege during the English Civil War, when the Royalist garrison survived by eating rats, mice and the castle dogs before finally surrendering in 1645. Look out for some medieval graffiti and the 'licking stones' in the dungeon, which Jacobite prisoners supposedly lapped for moisture.

Admission includes entry to the Kings Own Royal Border Regiment Museum, which details the history of Cumbria's Infantry Regiment. There are guided tours from April to September.

Carlisle Cathedral   CATHEDRAL
(www.carlislecathedral.org.uk; 7 The Abbey; suggested donation £5, photography £1; ⊙ 7.30am-6.15pm Mon-Sat, to 5pm Sun) Built from the same red sandstone as the castle, Carlisle's cathedral began life as a priory church in 1122, and became a cathedral when its first abbot, Athelwold, became the first Bishop of Carlisle. Among its notable features are the 15th-century choir stalls, the barrel-vaulted roof and the 14th-century East Window, one of the largest Gothic windows in England. Surrounding the cathedral are other priory relics, including the 16th-century Fratry and the Prior's Tower.

Tullie House Museum MUSEUM

(www.tulliehouse.co.uk; Castle St; adult/child £7/ free; ⊙10am-5pm Mon-Sat, 11am-4pm Sun) Carlisle's main museum covers the city's past, from Roman foundations to the present day. There's an awesome view of the castle from the rooftop Lookout.

The highlight is the Roman Frontier Gallery, which uses a mix of archaeological exhibits and interactive displays to tell the story of the Roman occupation of Carlisle. Upstairs, the Border Galleries cover the rest of the city's history, from the Bronze Age through to the Border Reivers, the Jacobite Rebellion and the Industrial Revolution. The Carlisle Life Gallery details the city's social history through photos, films and archive recordings, and Old Tullie House has a collection of art, sculpture and porcelain.

🛏 Sleeping

Carlisle's accommodation leaves a lot to be desired. The B&Bs in the centre are pretty uninspiring, so you're better off heading further out.

Warwick Lodge B&B £

(☑01228-523796; www.warwicklodgecarlisle.co. uk; 112 Warwick Rd; s/d £40/75) Decent budget B&B, with clean rooms, flouncy furnishings and a generous breakfast.

Willowbeck Lodge B&B ££

(☑01228-513607; www.willowbeck-lodge.com; Lambley Bank, Scotby; d £100-130; P🅿🛜) Escape the city hustle at this modern house, 3 miles from the centre. Six deluxe rooms are closer to hotel standard than B&B, offering tasteful shades of beige and taupe, luxurious bathrooms and a gabled lounge overlooking a private pond.

Premier Inn Carlisle Central HOTEL ££

(☑0871 527 8210; www.premierinn.com; Warwick Rd; d from £60; P🛜) A Premier Inn it may be, but this is actually one of Carlisle's best-value and best-located options. It's about a mile from the centre along Warwick Rd, and offers the usual bog-standard facilities: decent-sized rooms, generic decor, wi-fi and plenty of parking. It's about a mile east of the centre on Warwick Rd.

Warwick Hall B&B £££

(☑01228-561546; www.warwickhall.org; Warwick-on-Eden; s £95, d £126-180) This fine country house 2 miles from the centre along Warwick Rd is a real country retreat. With its huge rooms, high ceilings and antique decor, it feels a bit like staying on an aristocratic friend's estate. There are hectares of grounds and it even has its own stretch of river for fishing.

🍴 Eating

Shabby Scholar CAFE £

(☑01228-402813; 11-13 Carlyle Ct; mains £7-10; ⊙9.30am-9pm Tue-Sat) As its name suggests, this popular place is stylishly shabby, with scruffy furniture, a bar made out of old crates and a determinedly chilled vibe. It's great for tapas and light bites such as pulled-pork rolls, mackerel salad and 'carnivore' nachos, but it does not take bookings.

Prior's Kitchen Restaurant CAFE £

(Carlisle Cathedral; lunches £4-6; ⊙9.45am-4pm Mon-Sat) Carlisle's best place for traditional afternoon tea is in the cathedral's fratry, once used as a monk's mess hall.

Foxes Cafe Lounge CAFE £

(www.foxescafelounge.co.uk; 18 Abbey St; mains £4-10; ⊙10am-7pm Tue-Thu, to 11pm Fri, to 4.30pm Sat) This cool cafe-gallery provides a venue for all kinds of creative happenings, from open-mic nights and live gigs to photo exhibitions. Count on Continental cafe food and excellent coffee.

David's BRITISH ££

(☑01228-523578; www.davidsrestaurant.co.uk; 62 Warwick Rd; 2-course lunch £13.95, 2-course dinner £18.95; ⊙noon-3.30pm & 6.30-11pm Tue-Sat) For sit-down dining in Carlisle, David's townhouse restaurant is definitely the place. Gourmet gastronomy is the order of the day here – herb-crusted lamb, saffron-infused cod or roast Goosnargh duck – with a formal setting to match (think chandeliers, fireplaces, cornicing).

Holme Bistro BRITISH ££

(☑01228-534343; www.holmebistro.co.uk; 56-58 Denton St; mains £10.95-15.95; ⊙12.30-2pm & 6-9pm Tue-Sat) This slick bistro is run by brother-and-sister team Rob Don and Kirsty Robson, and has earned a loyal clientele for its unpretentious cuisine.

🍸 Drinking & Entertainment

Botchergate's the centre of Carlisle's nightlife, but it gets rowdy at closing time.

Fats PUB

(☑01228-511774; 48 Abbey St; ⊙11am-11pm) A less hectic alternative to Botchergate's pubs. DJs and comedy nights are held regularly.

Hell Below & Co
BAR

(✆ 01228-548481; 14 Devonshire St; ⊘ noon-1am)
Bare brick and wood floors give this lively
bar a hint of hipsterdom; the house special-
ties are mojitos and craft beer, ideally served
with a wood-fired pizza.

Brickyard
CONCERT VENUE

(www.thebrickyardonline.com; 14 Fisher St) Carlisle's grungy gig venue, housed in the former
Memorial Hall.

ℹ Information

Tourist Office (✆ 01228-625600; www.histor-
ic-carlisle.org.uk; Greenmarket; ⊘ 9.30am-5pm
Mon-Sat, 10.30am-4pm Sun)

ℹ Getting There & Away

BUS

National Express coaches depart from the bus
station on Lonsdale St for destinations including
London (£22 to £34.80, 7½ hours, two direct
daily), Manchester (£22.90 to £27.40, three to
3½ hours, four daily) and Glasgow (£16.40 to
£19.50, two hours, four to six daily).

104 To Penrith (£5.40, 40 minutes, half-hourly
Monday to Saturday, nine on Sunday).

554 To Keswick (£7.75, 70 minutes, four daily
Monday to Saturday, three on Sunday).

TRAIN

Carlisle is on the west coast line from London
to Glasgow. It's also the terminus for the scenic
Cumbrian Coast and Tyne Valley Lines, as well
as the historic **Settle to Carlisle Railway** (www.
settle-carlisle.co.uk; anytime single to Settle
£20.30, anytime return £26.20) across the
Yorkshire Dales. Main destinations:

Glasgow £27, 1¼ hours

Lancaster £29.70, 45 minutes

London Euston £109.70, 3½ hours

Manchester £53, two hours

Newcastle-upon-Tyne £15.50, 1½ hours

ℹ Getting Around

To book a taxi, call **Radio Taxis** (✆ 01228-
527575) or **Cumbria Cabs** (✆ 01228-899599).

Alston

POP 1105

Surrounded by the bleak hilltops of the Pennines, isolated Alston's main claim to fame
is its elevation: at 305m above sea level, it's
thought to be the highest market town in
England (despite no longer having a market). It's also famous among steam enthusi-

asts thanks to the **South Tynedale Railway**
(✆ 01434-381696, timetable 01434-382828; www.
south-tynedale-railway.org.uk; adult/child return
to Lintley £10/4; ⊘ Apr-Oct), which puffs and
clatters through the hilly country between
Alston and Lintley, along a route that originally operated from 1852 to 1976.

The line was partly reopened by enthusiasts in 1983. It's now run as a registered charity, and a recent £4.2 million lottery grant will
fund the long-awaited extension of the line all
the way to Slaggyford over the next few years.

The return trip takes about an hour; there
are up to five daily trains in midsummer.

Penrith

POP 15,181

Just outside the borders of the national
park, red-brick Penrith perhaps has more
in common with the stout market towns of
the Yorkshire Dales. It's a solid, traditional
place, with plenty of cosy pubs and quaint
teashops, and a lively market on Tuesdays.
It's also the main gateway for exploring the
picturesque Eden Valley.

Two miles west of Penrith, the **Rheged
visitor centre** (www.rheged.com; ⊘ 10am-6pm)
houses a large-screen Imax cinema and retail hall. The name commemorates the Celtic kingdom of Rheged, of which the Eden
Valley was once the centre.

◉ Sights

Penrith Castle
RUIN

(⊘ 7.30am-9pm Easter-Oct, to 4.30pm Nov-Easter)
The ruins of Penrith Castle loom on the edge
of town, opposite the train station. Built
in the 14th century, by William Strickland
(later Bishop of Carlisle and Archbishop of
Canterbury), it was later expanded by Richard III to resist Scottish raids, one of which
razed the town in 1345.

⌷ Sleeping

Brooklands
B&B ££

(✆ 01768-863395; www.brooklandsguesthouse.com;
2 Portland Pl; s £40, d £80-90; ☎) The town's
most elegant B&B is this Victorian red-brick
on Portland Pl. Rich furnishings and posh
extras (such as White Company toiletries,
fridges and chocolates on the tea tray) keep
it a cut above the competition.

★ Augill Castle
HOTEL £££

(✆ 01768-341967; www.stayinacastle.com; Kirkby
Stephen; r £170-240; P ☎) If you've always

HAWESWATER & LOWTHER

The most easterly of the Lake District's waters, Haweswater is also one of its most remote; it can only be reached via a narrow, winding road. In fact, it's not actually a lake but an artificial reservoir, created in 1935; sometimes during exceptionally dry spells, the remains of the drowned village of Mardale appear above the water-line. It's a great area to escape the hiking crowds, and is popular with wildlife-spotters too; sometimes golden eagles can be seen soaring over the fells.

Nearby is the sprawling estate of Lowther (☏01931-712192; www.lowthercastle.org; admission £8; ☉10am-5pm), which belonged to one of the Lake District's most venerable families and is currently undergoing a huge, multimillion-pound restoration project. The 400-year-old crenellated castle and the estate's grounds are now open to the public for the first time in many years; though the castle itself is to remain a ruin, restoration work is slowly breathing life back into the gardens, which have been largely forgotten since the estate fell into disrepair following WWII. The estate has a new cafe and shop, but the nearby George & Dragon (☏01768-865381; www.georgeanddragonclifton.co.uk; mains £12.95-21.95; ☉noon-2.30pm & 6-9pm) in Clifton is the best bet for lunch.

dreamt of staying in a bona-fide British castle, then this stately pile in Kirkby Stephen is definitely the place. All the trappings are here – crenellated turrets, stained-glass windows, cavernous rooms – and inside the design vibe is rather groovy, with a mix of antique furniture and contemporary furnishings. There's even a mini-cinema. It's 25 miles southeast of Penrith.

George Hotel HOTEL £££
(☏01768-862696; www.lakedistricthotels.net/georgehotel; Devonshire St; d £134-204; P☎) Penrith's venerable red-brick coaching inn offers classically decorated rooms in prim stripes and country patterns, plus a quaint bar and restaurant.

✖ Eating

No 15 CAFE £
(15 Victoria Rd; lunches £6-10; ☉9am-5pm Mon-Sat) Lively cafe-cum-art emporium specialising in gourmet lunch fare such as ciabattas, burgers, salads and veggie quiches. After lunch, browse the latest exhibition in the attached gallery.

★ Four & Twenty BISTRO ££
(☏01768-210231; www.fourandtwentypenrith.co.uk; 14 King St; mains £13-16; ☉noon-2.30pm

&6.30-9.30pm) Proper fine dining with a reasonable price tag is the modus operandi at this much-admired new bistro, which blends sleek decor with rustic wood, banquette seats and mix-and-match furniture. Expect sophisticated dishes such as twice-baked Stilton soufflé and braised blade of beef with caramelised onion rosti. If you're going to eat out in Penrith, this is the place to do it.

❶ Information

Tourist Office (☏01768-867466; pen.tic@eden.gov.uk; Middlegate; ☉9.30am-5pm Mon-Sat, 1-4.45pm Sun) Also houses Penrith's tiny museum.

❶ Getting There & Away

There are frequent train connections to Carlisle (£7.30, 15 minutes) and Lancaster (£16.80, one hour).

The bus station is northeast of the centre, off Sandgate.

104 To Carlisle (£5.40, 40 minutes, half-hourly Monday to Saturday, nine on Sunday).

X4/X5 Via Rheged, Keswick and Cockermouth to the Cumbrian coast (£6.40 to £7.60, half-hourly Monday to Saturday, hourly Sunday).

Newcastle & Northeast England

Best Places to Eat

➤ Jolly Fisherman (p642)

➤ Mizen Head (p644)

➤ Bouchon Bistrot (p637)

➤ Blackfriars (p624)

➤ Broad Chare (p624)

Best Places to Stay

➤ Otterburn Castle (p640)

➤ Jesmond Dene House (p623)

➤ Ashcroft (p638)

➤ 2 The Crofts (p636)

Why Go?

The irrepressible city of Newcastle-upon-Tyne anchors England's northeast. Set on the mighty River Tyne, this former industrial powerhouse's steep hills are lined with handsome Victorian buildings, and many of its one-time factories and warehouses have been transformed into galleries, museums, bars and entertainment venues. Newcastle's nightlife is legendary and revelling in an evening on the tiles here is a quintessential experience.

Newcastle is also an ideal gateway for escaping into the northeast's utterly wild, starkly beautiful countryside – from the rounded Cheviot Hills to brooding Northumberland National Park and the remote North Pennines. Spectacular Hadrian's Wall cuts a lonely path through the landscape, dotted with dramatic fortress ruins that are haunting reminders of the bloody struggle with the Scots to the north, while the region's unspoilt coastline takes in long, desolate beaches, wind-worn castles and tiny, magical islands offshore.

When to Go

➤ May in the northeast brings the chance to celebrate all things Roman at the week-long Hadrian's Wall Festival.

➤ The best time to discover the region's miles of wide sandy beaches is during the summer season (June to August), although for surfers, Tynemouth's world-class waves are best (if chilliest) in winter and spring.

➤ September through October is great for losing yourself in the autumnal landscapes of the North Pennines.

➤ September is also the month to grab a Newkie Brown ale, or your running shoes, and join the party along the route of Tyneside's Great North Run, one of the world's biggest half marathons.

History

Violent history has shaped this region more than any other in England, primarily because of its frontier position. Although Hadrian's Wall didn't serve as a defensive barrier, it marked the northern limit of Roman Britain and was the empire's most heavily fortified line. Following the Romans' departure, the region became part of the Anglian kingdom of Bernicia, which united with the kingdom of Deira (encompassing much of modern-day Yorkshire) to form Northumbria in 604.

The kingdom changed hands and borders shifted several times over the next 500 years as Anglo-Saxons and Danes struggled to seize it. The land north of the River Tweed was finally ceded to Scotland in 1018, while the nascent kingdom of England kept everything below it.

The arrival of the Normans in 1066 saw William I eager to secure his borders against the Scots. He commissioned most of the castles you see along the coast, and cut deals with the prince bishops of Durham to ensure their loyalty. The new lords of Northumberland became very powerful because, as Marcher Lords (from the use of 'march' as a synonym of 'border'), they kept the Scots at bay.

Northumberland's reputation as a hotbed of rebellion intensified during the Tudor years, when the largely Catholic north, led by the seventh duke of Northumberland, Thomas Percy, rose up against Elizabeth I in the defeated Rising of the North in 1569. The Border Reivers, raiders from both sides of the border in the 16th century, kept the region in a perpetual state of lawlessness that only subsided after the Act of Union between England and Scotland in 1707.

Coal mines were the key to the 19th-century industrialisation of the northeast, powering steelworks, shipyards and armament works that grew up along the Tyne and Tees. In 1825 the mines also spawned the world's first steam railway, the Stockton & Darlington, built by local engineer George Stephenson. Social strife emerged in the 20th century, however, with mines, shipbuilding, steel production and the railway industry all winding down during the Great Depression and postwar years. Reinventing the northeast has been a mammoth task but regeneration continues apace.

🏃 Activities

Walking and cycling opportunities abound in this region, but be prepared for wind and rain at any time of year and for very harsh conditions in winter. Regional tourism websites all contain walking and cycling information, and tourist offices stock free leaflets, plus maps and guides covering walking, cycling and other activities.

Cycling

The northeast has some of England's most inspiring cycle routes. Part of the National Cycle Network (NCN), a longtime favourite is the Coast & Castles Cycle Route (www.coast-and-castles.co.uk; NCN Route 1), which runs south–north along the glorious Northumberland coast between Newcastle-upon-Tyne and Berwick-upon-Tweed and Edinburgh, Scotland.

The 140-mile Sea to Sea Cycle Route (C2C; www.c2c-guide.co.uk) runs across northern England between the Cumbrian coast (Whitehaven or Workington) and Tynemouth or Sunderland via the northern Lake District and wild North Pennines' hills.

The other coast-to-coast option is the Hadrian's Cycleway (www.cycle-routes.org), a 175-mile route between South Shields or Tynemouth and Ravenglass in Cumbria along Hadrian's Wall.

Walking

The North Pennines – along with the Cheviots further north – are considered 'England's last wilderness'. Long routes through the hills include the famous Pennine Way National Trail, which keeps mainly to the high ground between the Yorkshire Dales and the Scottish border, but also crosses sections of river valley and some tedious patches of plantation. The whole route is around 270 miles, but the 70-mile section between Bowes and Hadrian's Wall is a fine four-day taster.

Hadrian's Wall has a huge range of easy loop walks taking in forts and other historical highlights.

One of the finest walks along the windswept Northumberland coast, between the villages of Craster and Bamburgh via Dunstanburgh, includes two of the region's most spectacular castles.

ℹ️ Getting There & Around

BUS

Bus transport around the region can be difficult, particularly around the more remote reaches of western Northumberland. Contact **Traveline** (☑ 0871 200 2233; www.travelinenortheast. info) for information on connections, timetables and prices.

Newcastle & Northeast England Highlights

❶ Exploring a coal wagon tunnel and WWII air-raid shelter beneath Newcastle's streets on a **Victoria Tunnel Tour** (p622)

❷ Stargazing from **Kielder Observatory** (p639) in the newly minted Northumberland International Dark Sky Park

❸ Negotiating the tidal causeway to reach otherworldly **Holy Island (Lindisfarne)** (p644)

❹ Viewing extraordinary objets d'art in the chateau-housed **Bowes Museum** (p631) at Barnard Castle

❺ Circumnavigating the Elizabethan **walls** (p645) of England's

---

SCOTLAND

EAST LOTHIAN

Cockburnspath • Grantshouse •
• Coldingham
• St Abbs
• Eyemouth

Duns •

Chirnside

BERWICKSHIRE

❺ Berwick-upon-Tweed

❸ Holy Island (Lindisfarne)

FARNE ISLANDS

Earlston •
St Boswell's •
Melrose •

Kelso •

Coldstream

Etal •
Ford •

Crookham •

Wooler •

Bamburgh •

Seahouses •

Belford •

NORTH SEA

Jedburgh •

Town
Yetholm

Kirk Yetholm •

ROXBURGHSHIRE

Bonchester
Bridge •

❹ Kielder Observatory

Kielder
Forest
Park

▲ Cheviot (815m)

Northumberland
National Park

High Newton-
by-the-Sea
Low Newton-
by-the-Sea
Embleton

Embleton Bay

❼ Dunstanburgh Castle
Craster

Otterburn •

Danger Area
(MOD Live
Firing Range)

Rothbury •

NORTHUMBERLAND

❿ Alnwick

Alnmouth •

Warkworth •
Amble •

Newbiggin-
by-the-Sea

Ashington •

0   20 km
0   10 miles

northernmost city,
Berwick-upon-Tweed

6 Cruising on
the tranquil **River
Wear** (p629), taking
in Durham's city,
castle and wondrous
cathedral

7 Hiking along
the Roman remains
of **Hadrian's Wall**
(p632)

8 Learning about
the fascinating
maritime and wartime
history of **Hartlepool**
(p628)

9 Reliving the
northeast's Industrial
Age at **Beamish
Open-Air Museum**
(p629)

10 Wandering
the halls of Harry
Potter's Hogwarts,
aka **Alnwick Castle**
(p640)

Several one-day Explorer tickets are available; always ask if one might be appropriate. The Explorer North East (adult/child £9/8), available on buses, covers Berwick-upon-Tweed south to Scarborough, and allows unlimited travel for one day, as well as numerous admission discounts.

TRAIN

The East Coast Main Line runs north from London King's Cross to Edinburgh via Durham, Newcastle and Berwick; Northern Rail operates local and inter-urban services in the north, including west to Carlisle.

There are numerous Rover tickets for single-day travel and longer periods; check www.railrover.org.

NEWCASTLE-UPON-TYNE

POP 279,100

Against its dramatic backdrop of Victorian elegance and industrial grit, this fiercely independent city harbours a spirited mix of heritage and urban sophistication, with excellent new art galleries and a magnificent concert hall, along with boutique hotels, some exceptional restaurants and, of course, interesting bars; Newcastle is renowned throughout Britain for its thumping nightlife, bolstered by an energetic student population.

The city retains deep-rooted traditions, embodied by the no-nonsense, likeable locals. Raised and subsequently abandoned by coal and steel, Geordies (as locals are dubbed, possibly due to support for George II during the 1745 Jacobite Rebellion or to miners' use of safety lamps designed by George Stephenson – no one knows for sure) are united through history, adversity and that impenetrable dialect – the closest language to 1500-year-old Anglo-Saxon left in England.

Allow at least a few days to explore the Victorian city centre and quayside areas along the Tyne and across the river in Gateshead, as well as the rejuvenated Ouseburn Valley to the east, shabby-chic Jesmond to the north, and, on the coast, the surf beaches of Tynemouth.

◎ Sights

◎ City Centre

Newcastle's grand Victorian centre, a compact area bordered roughly by Grainger St to the west and Pilgrim St to the east, is one of the most compelling examples of urban rejuvenation in England. Down by the quays

are the city's most recognisable attractions the iconic bridges that span the Tyne an the striking buildings that flank it.

Castle Garth Keep   CASTL

(www.castlekeep-newcastle.org.uk; Castle Garth adult/child £4/free; ⊙10am-5pm Mon-Sat, noon 5pm Sun) The stronghold that put both th 'new' and 'castle' into Newcastle has bee largely swallowed up by the train station leaving only the square Norman keep a one of the few remaining fragments. Insid you'll discover a fine chevron-covered chap el and an exhibition of architectural model ranging from Hadrian's Wall to 20th-centur eyesores. The 360-degree city views from th rooftop are the best in town.

★ Discovery Museum   MUSEUM

(www.discoverymuseum.org.uk; Blandford Sq ⊙10am-4pm Mon-Fri, 11am-4pm Sat & Sun) FREE Tyneside's rich history is explored at thi unmissable museum. Exhibitions are sprea across three floors of the former Co-operativ Wholesale Society building around th mightily impressive 30m-long *Turbinia* the fastest ship in the world in 1897 and th first to be powered by steam turbine. Othe highlights are a section on shipbuilding or the Tyne, with a scale model of the river in 1929, and the 'Story of Newcastle' spanning the city's history from Pons Aelius (Roman Newcastle) to Cheryl Cole.

★ Great North Museum   MUSEUM

(✆0191-208 6765; www.greatnorthmuseum.org uk; Barras Bridge; general admission free, planetarium adult/child £3/2; ⊙10am-5pm Mon-Fri, to 4pm Sat, 11am-4pm Sun) The contents of Newcastle University's museums and the prestigious Hancock Museum's natural history exhibits come together in the latter's neoclassical building. The result is a fascinating jumble of dinosaurs, Roman altar stones, Egyptian mummies, Samurai warriors and impressive taxidermy. Standout exhibits include a life-size Tyrannosaurus rex recreation and an interactive model of Hadrian's Wall showing every milecastle and fortress. There's also lots of hands-on stuff for kids and a planetarium with screenings throughout the day.

Laing Art Gallery   GALLERY

(www.laingartgallery.org.uk; New Bridge St; ⊙10am-5pm Tue-Sat, 2-5pm Sun) FREE The exceptional collection at the Laing includes works by Gainsborough, Gauguin and Henry Moore, and an important collection of paintings by Northumberland-born artist

Newcastle-upon-Tyne

Newcastle-upon-Tyne

John Martin (1789–1854). Check the 'What's On' section of the website for free events including talks and tours.

★ **Life Science Centre**　SCIENCE CENTRE
(☎0191-243 8210; www.life.org.uk; Times Sq; family/adult/concession £29.50/12.00/£9.50, child 2-17yr £7.50, child under 2yr free; ☺10am-6pm Mon-Sat, 10am-8pm Thu, 11am-6pm Sun) Part of a sober-minded institute devoted to the study of genetic science, this centre lets you discover the secrets of life through a fascinating series of hands-on exhibits. The highlight is the Motion Ride, a simulator that lets you 'experience' bungee jumping and the like (the 3D film changes every year). There are lots of thought-provoking arcade-style games, and if the information sometimes gets lost on the way, never mind, kids will love it. Book ahead at busy times.

Bessie Surtees House　HISTORIC BUILDING
(EH; www.english-heritage.org.uk; 41-44 Sandhill; ☺10am-4pm Mon-Fri) FREE The Tyne's northern bank was the hub of commercial Newcastle in the 16th century and on Sandhill a row of leaning merchant houses has survived from that era. One of them is Bessie Surtees House, where three rooms are open to the public. The daughter of a wealthy banker, feisty Bessie annoyed Daddy by falling in love with pauper John Scott (1751–1838). It all ended in smiles as John went on to become Lord Chancellor.

◉ **Ouseburn Valley**

Around a mile east of the city centre, Newcastle's 19th-century industrial heartland, Ouseburn Valley, is now an up-and-coming, semi-regenerated district, with potteries, glass-blowing studios and other creative workspaces, along with pubs, bars and entertainment venues.

★ **Victoria Tunnel**　HISTORIC SITE
(☎0191-261 6596; www.ouseburntrust.org.uk; adult/child £6/3; ☺by reservation) Walking Newcastle's streets, you'd never know this extraordinary tunnel runs for 4km beneath your feet. Built between 1839 and 1842 as a thoroughfare for coal wagons, it was used as an air-raid shelter during WWII. Volunteer-led, two-hour tours take you through an atmospheric 700m-long level section of the tunnel. Book ahead as numbers are limited to 12 participants, and wear good shoes and a washable jacket for the limewashed walls. Tours usually depart from Ouseburn Farm.

Ouseburn Farm　FARM
(☎0191-232 3698; www.bykerbridge.org.uk/farm; Ouseburn Rd, adjacent Lime St; admission by donation; ☺9.30am-4.30pm) Shetland ponies, pigs, sheep, goats, chickens and agricultural crops are the last thing you'd expect to find in Newcastle, but you can see them all at this community farm.

Biscuit Factory　GALLERY
(www.thebiscuitfactory.com; 16 Stoddart St; ☺10am-5pm Mon-Fri, to 6pm Sat, 11am-5pm Sun) No prizes for guessing what this commercial art gallery used to be. These days, it's the UK's biggest contemporary art shop, where you can peruse and/or buy works by artists from near and far in a variety of mediums, including painting, sculpture, glassware and furniture, many with a northeast theme.

Seven Stories – The Centre for Children's Books　MUSEUM
(www.sevenstories.org.uk; 30 Lime St; adult/child £7/6; ☺10am-5pm Mon-Sat, to 4pm Sun) A marvellous conversion of a handsome Victorian mill has resulted in Seven Stories, a very hands-on museum dedicated to the

BRIDGING THE TYNE

The most famous view in Newcastle is the cluster of Tyne bridges, the most famous of these being the **Tyne Bridge** (1925–28). Its resemblance to Australia's Sydney Harbour Bridge (1923–32) is no coincidence, as both were built by the same company, Dorman Long of Middlesbrough. The quaint little **Swing Bridge** (1876) pivots in the middle to let ships through. Nearby, the **High Level Bridge** (1849) designed by Robert Stephenson, was the world's first combined road and railway bridge. The most recent addition is the multiple-award-winning **Millennium Bridge** (aka Blinking Bridge; 2002), which opens like an eyelid to let ships pass.

Beneath the Tyne between Howdon in North Tyneside and Jarrow in South Tyneside, east of the centre, are the Grade II–listed, 1951-built **Tyne Pedestrian and Cyclist Tunnels** (www.tynepedestrianandcyclisttunnels.co.uk) as well as two tollway **vehicle tunnels** (TT2; www.tt2.co.uk; one-way £1.60, notes & copper coins not accepted).

wondrous world of children's literature. Across the seven floors you'll find original manuscripts and artwork from the 1930s onwards, and a constantly changing program of kid-oriented exhibitions, activities and events designed to encourage the AA Milnes of the new millennium.

⊙ Gateshead

The area of Newcastle south of the Tyne is the 'town' of Gateshead. Local authorities are now promoting the whole kit-and-caboodle-on-Tyne as 'NewcastleGateshead'.

★ BALTIC – Centre for Contemporary Art   GALLERY

(www.balticmill.com; Gateshead Quays; ⊙10am-6pm) **FREE** Once a huge mustard-coloured grain store, the BALTIC is now a huge mustard-coloured art gallery rivalling London's Tate Modern. There are no permanent exhibitions; instead, rotating shows feature the work and installations of some of contemporary art's biggest show-stoppers. The complex has artists in residence, a performance space, a cinema, a bar, a spectacular rooftop restaurant (bookings essential) and a ground-floor restaurant with riverside tables. A 4th-floor outdoor platform and 5th-floor viewing box offer fabulous panoramas of the Tyne.

🛏 Sleeping

Although the number of city-centre accommodation options is increasing, they are still generally restricted to the chain variety – either budget or business – catering to party people and execs. Most of the other properties are in the handsome northern suburb of Jesmond, where the forces of gentrification and student power fight it out for territory.

🛏 City Centre

Backpackers Newcastle   HOSTEL **£**
(☑0191-340 7334; www.backpackersnewcastle.com; 262 Westgate Rd; dm from £18; 🖱) This clean, well-run budget hostel has just 26 beds, lending it a bit more of a backpacker vibe than its competitors in the city. Great facilities include bike storage, a kitchen, a big games room with an X-box, and power-showers.

Grey Street Hotel   BOUTIQUE HOTEL **££**
(☑0191-230 6777; www.greystreethotel.com; 2-12 Grey St; d from £80; ❄🖱) On the classiest

street in the city centre, this beautiful Grade II–listed building has been adapted for contemporary needs, including triple-glazing on the sash windows. Gorgeous, individually designed rooms boast flatscreen TVs, big beds and handsome modern furnishings.

Royal Station Hotel   HOTEL **££**
(☑0191-232 0781; www.royalstationhotel.com; Neville St; s £53-93, d £80-150, f £90-120; P🖱⛱) Newcastle's hotels don't come better located than this Grade I– and II–listed Victorian beauty attached to Central Station. Above the chandeliered lobby, the 144 streamlined, unfussy rooms include cheaper 'small doubles' (from £55). Staff couldn't be friendlier or more helpful. Arrive early – the 20 free on-street car spaces are first-come, first-served.

Malmaison   BOUTIQUE HOTEL **£££**
(☑0191-245 5000; www.malmaison.com; Quayside; d/ste from £99/174; P@🖱) The affectedly stylish Malmaison touch has been applied to this former warehouse with considerable success, even down to the French-speaking lifts. Big beds, sleek lighting and designer furniture embellish the bouncy boudoirs and slick chambers.

🛏 Jesmond

About a mile-and-a-half north of the centre, Jesmond has a host of budget and midrange accommodation. Catch the Metro to Jesmond or West Jesmond.

Newcastle Jesmond Hotel   HOTEL **££**
(☑0191-239 9943; www.newcastlejesmondhotel.co.uk; 105 Osborne Rd; s/d from £55/65; P🖱) Rooms aren't huge at this freshly refurbished red-brick property footsteps from the bars and restaurants of Osborne Rd, but they're cosy, comfy and come with the bonus of free parking (though spaces are limited, so get in quick). Wi-fi can be patchy.

★ Jesmond Dene House   HOTEL **£££**
(☑0191-212 3000; www.jesmonddenehouse.co.uk; Jesmond Dene Rd; s/d/ste from £115/130/180; P@🖱) Large, gorgeous bedrooms at this exquisite property are furnished in a modern interpretation of the Arts and Crafts style and are bedecked with all manner of technological goodies (flatscreen digital TVs, digital radios). Wonderful bathrooms come complete with underfloor heating. The fine-dining restaurant (p624) is sublime.

✗ Eating

The Geordie palate is pretty refined and there are a host of dining options in all price ranges.

✗ City Centre

Quay Ingredient
CAFE £

(✆ 0191-447 2327; www.quayingredient.co.uk; 4 Queen St; dishes £2-7; ⏱ 8am-5pm Tue-Sun; 🕏) Beneath the Tyne Bridge's soaring steel girders, this chic little hole-in-the-wall has a devoted following for its eggs Benedict (and Florentine, and Montreal), but don't discount the rest of the menu – Craster kippers with pickled beetroot, scampi with homemade tartar sauce, pulled beef with bourbon...

★ Broad Chare
GASTROPUB ££

(✆ 0191-211 2144; www.thebroadchare.co.uk; 25 Broad Chare; mains £11.50-18.50; ⏱ kitchen noon-2.30pm & 5.30-10pm Mon-Sat, noon-5pm Sun) Spiffing English classics – the grilled pork chop with black pudding and cider sauce is divine – and splendid cask ales are served in the dark-wood bar and mezzanine of this perfect gastropub.

Oak Newcastle
INTERNATIONAL ££

(✆ 0191-232 3200; www.oaknewcastle.co.uk; Milburn House, Dean St; mains £8-20; ⏱ restaurant 7.30am-11pm Mon-Fri, 10am-11pm Sat & Sun, bar noon-2am daily) This hybrid restaurant/deli/bar is an equally good spot to pick up takeaways like pies, dine on dishes spanning black truffle risotto to Moroccan lamb burgers, or sip a cocktail while listening to DJs or live music. Energetic staff ensure it all comes together.

Silk Room
INTERNATIONAL ££

(✆ 0191-260 3506; www.silkroom.co.uk; Pandon Bankside, Trinity Gardens; mains £13-28; ⏱ 11am-2pm & 5pm-midnight Mon-Fri, 5pm-midnight Sat & Sun) Glamorous fare like Kobe wagyu burgers and kangaroo with port and caramelised pears is complemented with over 25 brands of bubbly and 16 champagne cocktails at this glitzy Quayside establishment.

★ Blackfriars
BRITISH £££

(✆ 0191-261 5945; www.blackfriarsrestaurant.co.uk; Friars St; mains £12-25; ⏱ noon-2.30pm & 5.30-11pm Mon-Sat, noon-4pm Sun) 🖉 A 12th-century friary is the atmospheric setting for 'modern medieval' cuisine. Check the tablemat map for the provenance of your cod, woodpigeon or rare-breed pork. Everything else is made from scratch on-site, including breads, pastries, ice creams and sausages. Bookings recommended.

✗ Jesmond

Fat Hippo
BURGERS ££

(✆ 0191-340 8949; www.fat-hippo.co.uk; 35a St Georges Tce, West Jesmond; burgers £7.50-14.50; ⏱ 11.30am-9.30pm Tue-Fri, 9am-9.30pm Sat, 9am-3.30pm Sun) Humongous burgers arrive on wooden planks with stainless-steel buckets of triple-fried, hand-cut chips at this local success story. The Shenton's three beef patties weigh in at one-and-a-half pounds; veggie options include My Big Fat Bean Burger with halloumi and garlic mayo. Sides (if you can squeeze them in) span deep-fried gherkins to breaded jalapeno poppers with sour cream.

Around the corner, the Little Hippo (✆ 0191-447 2114; www.fat-hippo.co.uk; 7 Acorn Rd, West Jesmond; dishes £4-5.50; ⏱ 11am-8.30pm) has smaller burgers, street food and specials like pulled pork and mac 'n' cheese.

Pizzeria Francesca
PIZZERIA ££

(134 Manor House Rd; pizza & pasta £5-7, other mains £9-17; ⏱ noon-2.30pm & 5-9.30pm Mon-Sat) This chaotic, cheerful place is how all Italian restaurants should be. Excitable waiters and huge portions of pizza and pasta keep locals queuing at the door – get in line and wait because you can't book in advance.

Jesmond Dene House
MODERN BRITISH £££

(✆ 0191-212 5555; www.jesmonddenehouse.co.uk; Jesmond Dene Rd; mains £20-35; ⏱ 7am-9.30pm) 🖉 Head chef Michael Penaluna is the architect of an exquisite regional menu – venison from County Durham, oysters from Lindisfarne and herbs plucked straight from the garden. The result is a gourmet extravaganza.

🍷 Drinking & Nightlife

Are you up for it? You'd better be, because Newcastle's nightlife doesn't mess about. While it's no secret that Geordies love a night on the razzle, the nightlife beyond the coloured cocktails of the boisterous Bigg Market (just south of Newgate St) is infinitely less raucous. Jesmond has loads of bars, while Ouseburn Valley attracts a mellower crowd.

🍷 City Centre

QB Tea House
TEAHOUSE

(✆ 0191-261 4861; www.quilliambrothers.com; Claremont Bldgs, 1 Eldon Pl; ⏱ 10am-midnight Mon-Fri, 9am-midnight Sat) Set up by a trio of brothers as 'an alternative to Newcastle's boozy scene', this hip Hungarian-style teahouse with post-industrial decor has over 100 types of tea as well as a tiny cinema screening cult films (dates vary), plus various gigs and art events.

Centurion Bar
BAR

(www.centurion-newcastle.com; Central Station; ⊘noon-11pm Mon-Thu, 11am-midnight Fri, noon-midnight Sat, to 10.30pm Sun) Dating from 1893, with floor-to-ceiling ornate Victorian tiling, Central Station's former first-class waiting room is ideal for a pre-club drink in style.

World Headquarters
CLUB

(www.welovewhq.com; Curtis Mayfield House, Carliol Sq; ⊘from 11pm, days vary) Dedicated to the genius of black music – funk, rare groove, dance-floor jazz, northern soul, genuine R&B, lush disco, proper house, reggae and more – this brilliant club is a world away from commercial blandness.

Trent House
PUB

(1-2 Leazes Lane; ⊘noon-11pm) Old-school boozer Trent House out-cools every other bar because it isn't trying. There's a free jukebox and fabulous atmosphere.

Digital
CLUB

(www.yourfutureisdigital.com; Times Sq; ⊘11pm-3am Mon & Wed-Sat) A two-floored cathedral to dance music, this megaclub was voted one of the top 20 clubs in the world by *DJ Magazine* thanks to one of the best sound systems you're ever likely to hear. Live acts rock the house, too.

Ouseburn Valley

★ Tyne Bar
PUB

(☑0191-265 2550; www.thetyne.com; 1 Maling St; ⊘11am-1pm Sun-Thu, to midnight Fri & Sat; ☎) An outdoor stage hosting free gigs, a disco ball spinning beneath the Glasshouse Bridge and a sprawling expanse of grass with knock-out river views make this tucked-away waterfront pub a magnet for in-the-know locals.

Ship Inn
PUB

(☑0191-222 1322; www.ship-inn.co.uk; Stepney Bank; ⊘3-11.30pm Mon-Wed, noon-11.30pm Thu, to 12.30am Fri & Sat, to 11pm Sun) Maritime memorabilia and historic photos of the Ouseburn Valley fill this red-brick charmer, which has been pouring pints since the early 1800s. On busy days the elbow-bending spills out onto the small green in front.

Cumberland Arms
PUB

(www.thecumberlandarms.co.uk; off Byker Bank, Ouseburn Valley; ⊘11am-1am Mon-Sat, noon-12.30am Sun; ☎) Sitting on a hill at the top of the Ouseburn, this 19th-century bar has a sensational selection of ales and ciders as well as a range of Northumberland meads. There's a terrace, regular live music and if you can't bear to leave, four comfy B&B rooms upstairs (double £80).

☆ Entertainment

Free monthly magazine *The Crack* (www. thecrackmagazine.com), available from clubs, tourist offices and some hotels, contains comprehensive theatre, music, cinema and club listings for the entire northeast.

Sage Gateshead
LIVE MUSIC

(☑0191-443 4666; www.sagegateshead.com; Gateshead Quays) Norman Foster's magnificent chrome-and-glass horizontal bottle is a stunner in itself but as the home of the Northern Sinfonia and Folkworks also presents outstanding live music.

Tyneside Cinema
CINEMA

(www.tynesidecinema.co.uk; Pilgrim St) Opened in 1937 as Newcastle's first newsreel cinema, this art-deco picture house with plush red-velvet seats still screens newsreels (11.15am daily) as well as mainstream and offbeat movies, and archive British Pathé films. Free one-hour guided tours of the building run at 11am on Monday, Tuesday, Friday and Saturday.

GAY & LESBIAN NEWCASTLE

Newcastle's dynamic gay scene centres on the 'Pink Triangle', formed by Waterloo, Neville and Collingwood Sts, though venues stretch south to Scotswood Rd. Check www.negayscene.co.uk for venues, parties and events.

Eazy Street (www.eazy-street.co.uk; 8-10 Westmorland Rd; ⊘noon-3am) Called Camp David in a previous life, this gay and all-welcoming bar draws a crowd for its nightly feast of DJs and cabaret drag shows.

Loft (10a Scotswood Rd; ⊘11pm-3am Sun-Thu, to 4am Fri & Sat) Small but supremely popular late-night bar.

Powerhouse (www.clubph.co.uk; 9-19 Westmorland Rd; ⊘11pm-4am Thu-Mon) Mixed but mainly gay, this massive four-floor club has flashing lights, a pumping sound system and suggestive posing.

Theatre Royal
THEATRE

(☑08448 11 21 21; www.theatreroyal.co.uk; 100 Grey St) The winter home of the Royal Shakespeare Company is full of Victorian splendour and has an excellent program of drama, along with major musicals, pantomimes, opera, ballet, comedy and contemporary dance.

Head of Steam @ The Cluny
LIVE MUSIC

(☑0191-230 4474; www.headofsteam.co.uk; 36 Lime St; ☺noon-11pm Mon-Thu, to midnight Fri & Sat, to 10.30pm Sun) Based at the artist cooperative 36 Lime St, touring acts and local talent – from experimental prog-rock heads to up-and-coming pop goddesses – fill the bill every night of the week.

Newcastle United Football Club
FOOTBALL

(NUFC; www.nufc.co.uk) NUFC is more than just a football team – it's the collective expression of Geordie hope and pride. The club's hallowed ground, St James Park (Strawberry Pl), is always packed, but you can get a stadium tour (☑0844 372 1892; adult/child £15/8; ☺11.30am, 12.30pm & 2.30pm daily, 10.30am match days) that includes the dugout and changing rooms. Match tickets go on public sale about two weeks before a game.

🛍 Shopping

Newcastle Quayside Market
MARKET

(☑0191-211 5533; under the Tyne Bridge; ☺9am-4pm Sun) Stalls displaying jewellery, photographic prints, art, clothing, homewares and more set up along the quays around the Tyne Bridge every Sunday. Buskers and food stalls add to the street-party atmosphere.

Grainger Market
MARKET

(www.graingermarket.org.uk; btwn Grainger & Clayton Sts; ☺9am-5pm Mon-Sat) Trading since 1835, Newcastle's gorgeous, heritage-listed covered market has over 100 stalls selling everything from fish, farm produce, meat and vegetables to clothes, accessories and homewares. Between alleys 1 and 2, look out for the historic Weigh House, where goods were once weighed.

ℹ Information

Newcastle City Centre Police Station (☑emergency 999, nonemergency 101; www.northumbria.police.uk; Forth Banks; ☺24hr)

Tourist Office Main Branch (☑0191-277 8000; www.visitnewcastlegateshead.com; Central Arcade, Market St; ☺9.30am-5pm Mon-Sat, 2-5pm Sun Jul & Aug, 10am-5pm Mon-Sat Sep-Jun)

ℹ Getting There & Away

AIR

Newcastle International Airport (☑0871 882 1121; www.newcastleairport.com) Seven miles north of the city off the A696, the airport has direct services to many UK and European cities as well as long-haul flights to Dubai. Tour operators fly charters to the USA, Middle East and Africa.

BUS

Local and regional buses leave from Haymarket or Eldon Sq bus stations. National Express buses arrive and depart from the coach station (St James Blvd). For local buses around the northeast, the excellent-value Explorer North East ticket (£9.30) is valid on most services.

Buses X15 and X18 run north to Berwick-upon-Tweed (£6.50, two hours, nine daily). National Express offers services to Edinburgh (£14.90, three hours, two daily), London (£16, seven hours, nine daily) and Manchester (£12.50, 4½ hours, four daily).

TRAIN

Newcastle is on the main rail line between London and Edinburgh and is the starting point of the scenic Tyne Valley Line west to Carlisle.

Alnmouth (for bus connections to Alnwick) £9.70, 25 minutes, hourly

Berwick-upon-Tweed £23.60, 45 minutes, hourly

Carlisle £15.50, 1½ hours, hourly

Edinburgh £48, 1½ hours, every 30 minutes

Hartlepool £8.90, 45 minutes, hourly

London King's Cross £121, three hours, every 30 minutes

York £32, one hour, every 20 minutes

ℹ Getting Around

TO/FROM THE AIRPORT

The airport is linked to town by the Metro (£3.30, 20 minutes, every 12 minutes).

PUBLIC TRANSPORT

There's a large bus network, but the best means of getting around is the excellent Metro, with fares from £1.80. Several saver passes are also available. The tourist office can supply you with route plans for the bus and Metro networks.

The DaySaver (£2.60 to £4.50) gives unlimited Metro travel for one day for travel after 9am, and the DayRover (adult/child £6.80/3.70) gives unlimited travel on all modes of transport in Tyne and Wear for one day for travel any time.

TAXI

On weekend nights taxis can be rare; try **Noda Taxis** (☑0191-222 1888; www.noda-taxis.co.uk), which has a kiosk outside Central Station.

AROUND NEWCASTLE

Angel of the North

Nicknamed the Gateshead Flasher, this extraordinary 200-tonne, rust-coloured, winged human frame has loomed over the A1 (M) some 6 miles south of Newcastle since 1998. At 20m high and with a wingspan wider than a Boeing 767, Sir Antony Gormley's iconic work (which saw him knighted in 2014) is the UK's largest sculpture and most viewed public artwork. Buses 21 and 22 from Newcastle's Eldon Sq (£2, 20 minutes) stop here. There's a free car park by the base.

Tynemouth

POP 67,520

One of the most popular Geordie days out is to this handsome seaside resort some 9 miles east of Newcastle. The mouth of the Tyne is one of the best surf spots in England, with great all-year breaks off the immense, crescent-shaped Blue Flag beach, which occasionally hosts the National Surfing Championships.

◉ Sights & Activities

Tynemouth Priory RUIN

(EH; www.english-heritage.org.uk; adult/child £4.80/2.90; ☺10am-6pm Apr-Sep, to 4pm Oct, 10am-4pm Sat & Sun Nov-Mar) Built by Benedictine monks on a strategic bluff above the mouth of the Tyne in the 11th-century ruins, Tynemouth Priory was ransacked during the Dissolution in 1539. The military took over for four centuries, only leaving in 1960, and today the skeletal remains of the priory church sit alongside old military installations, their guns aimed out to sea at an enemy that never came.

Tynemouth Surf Company SURFING

(☎0191-258 2496; www.tynemouthsurf.co.uk; Grand Pde; ☺10am-5.30pm) For all your surfing needs, call into this friendly surf company, which also provides two-hour group lessons for £25 per person.

✖ Eating & Drinking

Opposite the priory, village-like Front St runs inland from the ocean and is lined with bars, restaurants, cafes and arty shops.

Barca Art Cafe CAFE ££

(☎0191-257 7959; www.barcaart.co.uk; 68 Front St; mains £10.50-19; ☺kitchen 5-10pm Mon-Sat, noon-4pm Sun, bar noon-1am) This funky hybrid restaurant, bar and art gallery (the works by local artists are all for sale) has an ambitious, contemporary menu, though vegetarian options, aside from starters like mezze boards to share, are few. DJs spin on Saturday nights from 10pm.

Turks Head PUB

(☎0191-257 6547; www.johnbarras.com; 41 Front St; ☺11am-11pm Mon-Wed, to 11.30pm Thu-Sat, noon-11.30pm Sun; ☜) Encased in ivory-coloured tiles, this salt-of-the-earth 1850-built traditional pub is great for a pint of real ale while watching a Newcastle United match.

❶ Getting There & Away

From Newcastle, the easiest way to reach Tynemouth is by Metro (£3.20, 25 minutes).

Segedunum

The last strong post of Hadrian's Wall was the fort of **Segedunum** (☎0191-236 9347; www.twmuseums.org.uk; Buddle St, Wallsend; adult/child £5.50/free; ☺10am-5pm Apr-Aug, to 4pm Sep & Oct, 10am-2.30pm Mon-Fri Nov-Mar), 5 miles east of Newcastle at the 'wall's end', now the Newcastle suburb of Wallsend. Beneath the 35m-high tower, which you can climb for terrific views, is an absorbing site that includes a reconstructed Roman bathhouse (with steaming pools and frescoes) and a museum offering a fascinating insight into life during Roman times.

Segedunum is a three-minute walk from the Wallsend Metro station (from Newcastle £3.95, 20 minutes).

HARTLEPOOL

POP 88,895

Steelworks and shipyards made this North Sea coastal town's fortunes in the 19th century, but also made it a WWI target. On 16 December 1914, it was hit by 1150 shells, killing 117 people including 29-year-old Durham Light Infantry Private Theophilus Jones, the war's first soldier killed on British soil. Hartlepool's defence batteries returned fire, damaging three enemy ships and becoming England's only coastal battery to fire its guns in the conflict.

After WWII, the collapse of both the steel and ship-building industries saw Hartlepool languish until the revitalisation of its marina around the turn of the millennium, and it makes a fascinating stop to explore its wartime and maritime heritage.

Sights

Hartlepool's Maritime Experience INTERPRETATION CENTRE
(☎01429-860077; www.hartlepoolsmaritimeexperience.com; Jackson Dock, Maritime Ave; adult/child £8.95/6.85, museum free; ⊙10am-5pm Apr-Oct, 11am-4pm Nov-Mar) This superb family attraction incorporates both the Museum of Hartlepool, with exhibits from the Bronze Age to today, and the 1817-built HMS *Trincomalee*, the oldest British warship still afloat, as well as recreated businesses – gunsmith, swordsmith and so on – along its historic quayside. Costumed staff and audioguides do a great job of bringing it to life.

Heugh Gun Battery Museum MUSEUM
(☎01429-270746; www.heughbattery.com; Moor Tce; adult/child £5/3; ⊙10am-4pm Thu-Sun) Atop the windswept Hartlepool Headland, about 2 miles west of the centre, you can visit the underground magazines, parade ground, museum and panoramic observation tower at the 19th-century Heugh (pronounced 'yuff') Gun Battery – one of Hartlepool's two defence batteries to return WWI fire.

Sleeping

Hillcarter Hotel HOTEL ££
(☎01429-855800; www.hillcarterhotel.com; 31-32 Church St, enter via Whitby St; s £65, d £75-85, f £95; P🖨) This central Hartlepool landmark was built in 1887 as the Hill and Carter department store and converted to a hotel a century later. Rooms are spacious and comfortable, service is top notch and there's an enclosed rooftop restaurant, a bar serving meals, and two nightclubs, plus nearby late bars, so beware noisy Friday and Saturday nights (other nights are quiet).

Eating & Drinking

By far the best place to eat and/or drink is Navigation Point, where a slew of bars, cafes and restaurants serving a wide range of cuisines – traditional and contemporary British, Chinese, Indian, Italian – overlook the boats moored at Hartlepool Marina.

Cinnamons BANGLADESHI £
(☎01429-269666; 29 Navigation Point, Hartlepool Marina; mains £6-11; ⊙noon-2pm & 5.30-11.30pm Mon-Sat, 5.30-11.30pm Sun) Fresh, fiery Bangladeshi cuisine at this elegant restaurant spans clay oven tikka and tandoori favourites, Bengal curries, baltis and countless *chingri* (prawn) dishes.

Information

Tourist Office
(☎01429-869706; www.destinationhartlepool.com; Church Sq; ⊙10am-5.30pm Tue-Sat, 2-5pm Sun) At the Hartlepool Art Gallery.

Getting There & Away

Trains link Hartlepool with Newcastle (£8.90, 45 minutes, hourly). Bus 22 to/from Durham (£5.70, 1¼ hours, hourly) stops at the train station.

COUNTY DURHAM

Spread across the lonely, rabbit-inhabited North Pennines and Teesdale's ochre hills, County Durham's star attraction is its county town. Its cathedral and adjoining castle were the seat of the once powerful prince bishops, rulers since 1081 of the Palatinate of Durham, a political entity created by William the Conqueror as a bulwark against Saxons and Scots.

The county was at the heart of the region's coal-mining industry, a brutal business that saw the last pit close in 1984 and left the landscape with some fast-dissolving yet evocative scarring.

Durham

POP 47,785

England's most beautiful Romanesque cathedral, a huge castle, and, surrounding them both, a cobweb of hilly, cobbled streets usually full of upper-crust students attending England's third university of choice (after Oxford and Cambridge) make Durham an ideal day trip from Newcastle or overnight stop.

Sights

★ Durham Cathedral CATHEDRAL
(www.durhamcathedral.co.uk; by donation, tower £5, guided tours adult/child £5/free; ⊙7.30am-6pm Mon-Sat, to 5.30pm Sun) This monumental cathedral is the definitive structure of the Anglo-Norman Romanesque style, a resplendent monument to the country's ecclesiastical history and, since 1986, a Unesco World Heritage Site. Beyond the main door and the famous Sanctuary Knocker, which medieval felons would strike to gain 37 days

asylum within the cathedral before standing trial or leaving the country – the interior is spectacular. Climbing the tower's 325 steps rewards you with show-stopping vistas.

Durham was the first European cathedral to be roofed with stone-ribbed vaulting, which upheld the heavy stone roof and made it possible to build pointed transverse arches – the first in England, and a great architectural achievement. The central tower dates from 1262, but was damaged in a fire caused by lightning in 1429 and unsatisfactorily patched up until it was entirely rebuilt in 1470. The western towers were added in 1217–26.

The northern side of the beautiful, 1175-built Galilee Chapel features rare surviving examples of 12th-century wall painting (thought to feature portraits of Sts Cuthbert and Oswald). Galilee Chapel also contains the tomb of the Venerable Bede, the 8th-century Northumbrian monk turned historian: his *Ecclesiastical History of the English People* is still the prime source of information on the development of early Christian Britain. Among other things, Bede introduced the numbering of years from the birth of Jesus. He was first buried at Jarrow, but in 1022 a miscreant monk stole his remains and brought them here.

Other highlights include the 14th-century Bishop's Throne; the beautiful stone Neville Screen (1372–80), which separates the high altar from St Cuthbert's tomb; and the mostly 19th-century Cloisters where you'll find the Monk's Dormitory, now a library of 30,000 books, with Anglo-Saxon carved stones. There are audiovisual displays on the building of the cathedral and the life of St Cuthbert.

★ **Durham Castle** CASTLE
(☑ 0191-334 2932; www.dur.ac.uk/durham.castle; admission by guided tour only, adult/child £5/3.50; ⊗ by reservation) Built as a standard motte-and-bailey fort in 1072, Durham Castle was the prince bishops' home until 1837, when it became the University of Durham's first college. It remains a university hall, and it's possible to stay here (contact the castle for information and availability). Highlights of the 45-minute tour include the groaning 17th-century Black Staircase and the beautifully preserved Norman chapel (1080).

Each successive prince bishop sought to put his particular imprint on the place, but heavy restoration and reconstruction were necessary in any case as the castle is built of soft stone on soft ground.

BEAMISH OPEN-AIR MUSEUM

County Durham's living, breathing, working museum (☑ 0191-370 4000; www.beamish.org.uk; adult/child £17.50/10; ⊗ 10am-5pm Apr-Oct, 10am-4pm Tue-Thu, Sat & Sun Nov-Mar) offers an unflinching glimpse into industrial life in the northeast during the 19th and 20th centuries. Spread over 121 hectares, it is instructive and fun for all ages. Allow at least three hours here, but check ahead in the winter months as some sections close.

Beamish is about 8 miles northwest of Durham. Take buses 28 and 28A from Newcastle (£4.70, one hour, every 30 minutes) or 128 from Durham (£3.20, 30 minutes, hourly).

Highlights include going underground, exploring mine heads, visiting a working farm, school, dentist and pub, and marvelling at how every cramped pit cottage seemed to find room for a piano. Don't miss a ride behind an 1815 Steam Elephant locomotive or a replica of Stephenson's *Locomotion No 1*.

🏃 Activities

Prince Bishop River Cruiser BOAT CRUISE
(☑ 0191-386 9525; www.princebishoprc.co.uk; Browns Boathouse, Elvet Bridge; adult/child £7/4; ⊗ cruises 12.30pm, 2pm & 3pm Jun-Sep, call for times Oct-May) Wonderfully scenic one-hour cruises on the Wear.

Browns Boathouse BOATING
(☑ 0191-386 3779; Elvet Bridge; per hr adult/child £5/4; ⊗ dawn-dusk Apr-Oct) Rent a row boat for a romantic river excursion.

🛏 Sleeping

Honest Lawyer INN ££
(☑ 0191-378 3780; www.honestlawyerhotel.com; Croxdale; d £68-88; P 🛜) An easy 3-mile drive south of Durham on the A167, this handy spot has mostly motel-style rooms with countrified chequered fabrics and parking outside the door. The main building has a timber bar and restaurant serving good pub grub in generous portions.

Cathedral View B&B ££
(☑ 0191-386 9566; www.cathedralview.com; 212 Gilesgate; s/d from £75/90; P 🛜) This discreet Georgian house has no sign, but inside, two of its six large rooms decorated with lots of

Durham

cushions and coordinated bed linen and window dressings indeed have sensational cathedral views. Breakfast, including home-baked bread, is cooked to order and served on the terrace or in the art-lined dining room.

Gadds Townhouse BOUTIQUE HOTEL **£££**
(☑ 0191-384 1037; www.gaddstownhouse.com; 34 Old Elvet; d £110-250; ☎) Each of Gadds' 11 opulent rooms has a theme, with Le Jardin featuring a shed and garden furniture, a huge projection screen and popcorn machine in Premiere, and the Edwardian Express recreating a night in a yesteryear sleeper compartment. The most 'normal' room is the Garden Lodge, with outdoor tub and underfloor heating. The restaurant is superb.

✖ Eating

Tealicious CAFE **£**
(☑ 0191-340 1393; www.tealicioustearoom.co.uk; Elvet Bridge; dishes £2-5.25; ⏱ 10am-4pm Tue-Sat)

A gingerbread-house replica of this quaint pastel-blue and white building sits in the window, while inside, amid vintage decor, treats include homemade cakes (such as white chocolate cheesecake or ginger and lime), soups, and over a dozen blends of tea served from individual pots on fine bone china. It's tiny so book ahead.

Cellar Door Durham MODERN BRITISH **££**
(☑ 0191-383 1856; www.thecellardoordurham.co.uk; 41 Saddler St; mains £14-17.50; ⏱ 11.30am-10.30pm) Accessed from an inconspicuous door on Saddler St, this 12th-century building boasts glorious river views, including from the outdoor terrace. The Mediterranean-meets-Britain menu features starters such as twice-baked goats cheese soufflé, mains such as seared venison with chestnut dressing, and desserts including brioche bread-and-butter pudding. Service is spot on.

Durham

Oldfields   BRITISH ££
(☑ 0191-370 9696; www.oldfieldsrealfood.co.uk; 18 Claypath; 2-/3-course lunch £10/13, dinner mains £12-17.50; ⊘ noon-10pm; ☎) ✍ Serving strictly seasonal menus that use only local or organic ingredients sourced within a 60-mile radius of Durham – such as North Sea fish casserole, pan haggerty and wild boar pie – this award-winning restaurant, in the 1881 boardroom of the former HQ of the Durham Gas Company, is passionate about great British food.

Drinking & Nightlife

Shakespeare Tavern   PUB
(www.shakespearedurham.com; 63 Saddler St; ⊘ 11am-11.30pm) Built in 1190, this authentic-as-it-gets locals' boozer is complete with dartboard, cosy snugs, a terrific selection of beers and spirits and wise-cracking characters propping up the bar – as well as, allegedly, a resident ghost. Folk music jam sessions take place on Wednesday evenings.

Information

Tourist Office (World Heritage Site Visitor Centre; ☑ 0191-334 3805; www.thisisdurham.com; 7 Owengate; ⊘ 9.30am-6pm Jul & Aug, to 5pm late Mar-Jun & Sep, to 4.30pm Oct-late Mar) Small but helpful, with all the usual tourist information.

Getting There & Away

BUS

Destinations include Hartlepool (bus 22; £5.70, 1¼ hours, hourly), London (National Express; £32, 6½ hours, four daily) and Newcastle (bus 21, 43, 44, X2, X21, X41; £3.60, one hour to 1¾ hours, several hourly).

TRAIN

The East Coast Main Line provides speedy connections to many destinations including Edinburgh (£56.20, two hours, hourly), London King's Cross (£121, three hours, hourly), Newcastle (£5.10, 15 minutes, four hourly) and York (£30.50, 50 minutes, four hourly).

Getting Around

Pratt's (☑ 0191-386 0700; www.prattstaxis.co.uk) Reliable taxi company.

Barnard Castle

POP 7040

The charming market town of Barnard Castle, better known as 'Barney', is a traditionalist's dream, full of antiquarian shops and atmospheric old pubs that serve as a wonderful setting for its twin draws: a daunting ruined castle at its edge and an extraordinary French chateau. If you can drag yourself away, it's also a terrific base for exploring Teesdale and the North Pennines.

Sights

Barnard Castle   CASTLE
(EH; www.english-heritage.org.uk; adult/child £4.60/2.80; ⊘ 10am-6pm Apr-Sep, to 5pm Oct, 10am-4pm Sat & Sun Nov-Mar) Built on a cliff above the River Tees by Guy de Bailleul and rebuilt around 1150, Barnard Castle was partly dismantled some four centuries later, but still manages to cover more than two very impressive hectares with wonderful river views.

★ **Bowes Museum**   MUSEUM
(www.thebowesmuseum.org.uk; adult/child £9/free; ⊘ 10am-5pm) About half a mile east of town a monumental chateau contains the lavishly furnished Bowes Museum. Funded by 19th-century industrialist John Bowes, and opened in 1892, this brainchild of his Parisian actress wife, Josephine, was built by French architect Jules Pellechet to display a collection the Bowes had travelled the world to assemble. The star attraction is the marvellous 18th-century mechanical swan, which performs every day at 2pm. If you miss it, a film shows it in action.

Look for works by Canaletto, El Greco and Goya as well as 55 paintings by Josephine herself. Among the 15,000 other objets d'art are incredible dresses from the 17th century through to the 1970s as part of an exhibit on

RABY CASTLE

About 7 miles northeast of Barnard Castle, sprawling Raby Castle (www.rabycastle.com; adult/child £10/4.50; ⊙ 1-4.30pm Sun-Fri Jul & Aug, Sun-Wed May, Jun & Sep) was a stronghold of the Catholic Neville family until it engaged in some ill-judged plotting (the 'Rising of the North') against the oh-so Protestant Queen Elizabeth in 1569. Most of the interior dates from the 18th and 19th centuries, but the exterior remains true to the original design, built around a courtyard and surrounded by a moat. Bus 8 zips between Barnard Castle and Raby (£3, 15 minutes, eight daily).

There are beautiful formal gardens and a deer park.

textiles through the ages, and clocks, watches and tableware in gold and silver in the precious-metals section.

🛏 Sleeping & Eating

Old Well Inn INN ££
(☑ 01833-690130; www.theoldwellinn.co.uk; 21 The Bank; s/d/f from £50/70/96; ☎) Built over a huge well (not visible), this old coaching inn has 10 enormous rooms. No 9 is the most impressive with its own private entrance, flagstone floors and a bath. The pub has a reputation for excellent grub like rabbit and black pudding casserole (mains £7.50 to £9) as well as regional real ales that you can sip in the leafy beer garden in fine weather.

Jersey Farm Country Hotel HOTEL ££
(☑ 01833-638223; www.jerseyfarmhotel.co.uk; Darlington Rd; s/d from £72/99; ☺ kitchen noon-2pm & 6-9pm; P ☎) Another genteel farmhouse conversion, right? Wrong. Rooms here sport cool retro colour schemes and gadgets galore. The restaurant is a clean-cut affair (mains £10 to £19). It's a mile east of town just off the A67.

❶ Information

Tourist Office (☑ 01833-631107; www.thewitham.org.uk; 3 Horsemarket; ⊙ 10am-4pm Mon & Wed-Sat) In the Witham building's new arts and community centre.

❶ Getting There & Away

From Durham, take bus 75 via Darlington (£3.80, 1½ hours, twice hourly).

North Pennines

The North Pennines stretch from western Durham to just short of Hadrian's Wall in the north. In the south is Teesdale, the gently undulating valley of the River Tees; to the north is the much wilder Weardale, carved by the River Wear. Both dales are marked by ancient quarries and mines – industries that date back to Roman times. The wilds of the North Pennines are also home to the picturesque Derwent and Allen Valleys, north of Weardale.

For information on the area check out www.northpennines.org.uk and www.exploreteesdale.co.uk.

HADRIAN'S WALL

What exactly have the Romans ever done for us? The aqueducts. Law and order. And this enormous wall, built between AD 122 and 128 to separate Romans and Scottish Picts. Named in honour of the emperor who ordered it built, Hadrian's Wall was one of Rome's greatest engineering projects, a spectacular 73-mile testament to ambition and the practical Roman mind. Even today, almost 2000 years after the first stone was laid, the awe-inspiring sections that remain are proof that when the Romans wanted something done, they just knuckled down and did it.

It wasn't easy. When completed, the mammoth structure ran across the narrow neck of the island, from the Solway Firth in the west almost to the mouth of the Tyne in the east. Every Roman mile (0.95 miles) there was a gateway guarded by a small fort (milecastle) and between each milecastle were two observation turrets. Milecastles are numbered right across the country, starting with Milecastle 0 at Wallsend (where you can visit the wall's last stronghold, Segedunum (p627)) and ending with Milecastle 80 at Bowness-on-Solway.

A series of forts were developed as bases some distance south (and may predate the wall), and 16 lie astride it.

Carlisle, in Cumbria, and Newcastle are logical start/end points; Haltwhistle, Hexham and Corbridge make good bases. The B6318 follows the course of the wall from the outskirts of Newcastle to Birdoswald. The main A69 road and the railway line follow 3 or 4 miles to the south.

Every May the Hadrian's Wall Festival features lots of recreations of Roman life along the wall – contact tourist offices for details.

🏃 Activities

Hadrian's Wall Path   WALKING
(www.nationaltrail.co.uk/hadrianswall) This 84-mile National Trail runs the length of the wall from Wallsend in the east to Bowness-on-Solway in the west. The entire route should take about seven days on foot, giving plenty of time to explore the rich archaeological heritage along the way. Local bookshops and tourist offices sell detailed guides.

ℹ️ Information

Hadrian's Wall Country (www.visithadrianswall.co.uk) The official portal for the whole of Hadrian's Wall Country.

Northumberland National Park Visitor Centre (📞 01434-344396; www.northumberlandnationalpark.org.uk; Bardon Mill, Once Brewed; ⏰ 9.30am-5.30pm Apr-Oct, 10am-3pm Sat & Sun Nov-Mar) On Military Rd (B6318).

ℹ️ Getting There & Around

BUS

The AD122 Hadrian's Wall bus (one-day adult/child £12/6, five daily, April to October) is a hail-and-ride service that runs between Hexham and Carlisle, with one bus a day starting and ending at Newcastle's Central Station and not all services covering the entire route. Bikes can be taken aboard AD122 buses, but space is limited. Bus 185 zips from Haltwhistle to Carlisle the rest of the year (Monday to Saturday only).

West of Hexham the wall runs parallel to the A69, which connects Carlisle and Newcastle. Bus 685 runs along the A69 hourly, passing 2 miles to 3 miles south of the main sites throughout the year.

All these services can be used with the **Hadrian's Wall Rover Ticket** (adult/child one-day £9/4.50, three-day £18/9, seven-day £36/18), available from bus drivers and tourist offices, where you can also get timetables.

Hadrian's Wall & Northumberland National Park

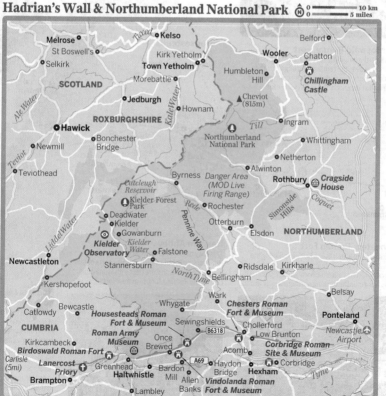

Hadrian's Wall

ROME'S FINAL FRONTIER

Of all Britain's Roman ruins, Emperor Hadrian's 2nd-century wall, cutting across northern England from the Irish Sea to the North Sea, is by far the most spectacular; Unesco awarded it world cultural heritage status in 1987.

We've picked out the highlights, one of which is the prime remaining Roman fort on the wall, Housesteads, which we've reconstructed here.

Housesteads' granaries
Nothing like the clever underground ventilation system, which kept vital supplies of grain dry in Northumberland's damp and drizzly climate, would be seen again in these parts for 1500 year

Milecastle

North Gate

Interval Tower

Birdoswald Roman Fort
Explore the longest intact stretch of the wall, scramble over the remains of a large fort then head indoors to wonder at a full-scale model of the wall at its zenith. Great fun for the kids.

Housesteads Roman Fort
See Illustration Right

Chesters Roman Fort
Built to keep watch over a bridge spanning the River North Tyne, Britain's best-preserved Roman cavalry fort has a terrific bathhouse, essential if you have months of nippy northern winter ahead.

Hexham Abbey
This may be the finest non-Roman sight near Hadrian's Wall, but the 7th-century parts of this magnificent church were built with stone quarried by the Romans for use in their forts.

Housesteads' hospital
Operations perform at the hospital would have been surprisingly effecti even without anaes thetics; religious rituals and prayers to Aesculapius, the Roman god of heal were possibly less helpful for a hernia appendicitis.

Map labels:
10 km / 5 miles
N
Birdoswald Roman Fort
Irthing
Roman Army Museum
Housesteads Roman Fort & Museum
Hadrian's Wall
Sewingshields
B6318
Chesters Roman Fort & Museum
Chollerford
Low Brunton
Harrow Scar Milecastle
Vindolanda Roman Fort & Museum
Acomb
Greenhead
Once Brewed
A69
Haltwhistle
South Tyne
Bardon Mill
Haydon Bridge
Hexham
Brampton

Housesteads' latrines

Communal toilets were the norm in Roman times and Housesteads' are remarkably well preserved – fortunately no traces remain of the vinegar-soaked sponges that were used instead of toilet paper.

QUICK WALL FACTS & FIGURES

» **Latin name** Vallum Aelium

» **Length** 73.5 miles (80 Roman miles)

» **Construction date** AD 122–128

» **Manpower for construction**
Three legions (around 16,000 men)

» **Features** At least 16 forts, 80 milecastles, 160 turrets

» **Did you know** Hadrian's wasn't the only wall in Britain – the Antonine Wall was built across what is now central Scotland in the AD 140s, but it was abandoned soon after

Commanding
Officer's House

Farms

FREE GUIDES

At some sites knowledgeable volunteer heritage guides are on hand to answer questions and put meat on the wall's stony bones.

Workshop

Headquarters

Barracks

West Gate

Angle
Tower

SCALING THE WALL

The main concentration of sights is in the central, wildest part of the wall, roughly between Corbridge in the east and Brampton in the west. All our suggested stops are within this area and follow an east–west route. The easiest way to travel is by car, scooting along the B6318, but special bus AD122 will also get you there. Hiking along the designated Hadrian's Wall Path (84 miles) allows you to appreciate the achievement up close.

Housesteads' gatehouses
Unusually at Housesteads neither of the gates faces the enemy, as was the norm at a Roman fort – builders aligned them east-west. Ruts worn by cart wheels are still visible in the stone.

CAR & MOTORCYCLE

Your own wheels are the easiest way to get around, with one fort or garrison usually just a short hop from the next. Parking costs £4/15 per day/week; tickets are valid at all sites along the wall.

TRAIN

The railway line between Newcastle and Carlisle (Tyne Valley Line; £12.20, one hour, hourly) has stations at Corbridge, Hexham, Haydon Bridge, Bardon Mill, Haltwhistle and Brampton. Not all services stop at all stations.

Corbridge

POP 2950

Above a green-banked curve in the Tyne, Corbridge's shady, cobbled streets are lined with old-fashioned shops and pubs. Inhabited since Saxon times when there was a substantial monastery, many of its charming buildings feature stones nicked from nearby Corstopitum.

◉ Sights

Corbridge Roman
Site & Museum   HISTORIC SITE

(EH; www.english-heritage.org.uk; adult/child £5.60/3.40; ◷10am-6pm Apr-Sep, to 5pm Oct, 10am-4pm Sat & Sun Nov-Mar) What's left of the Roman garrison town of Corstopitum lies about half a mile west of Market Pl on Dere St, once the main road from York to Scotland. It's the oldest fortified site in the area, predating the wall itself by some 40 years. Most of what you see here though dates from around AD 200, when the fort had developed into a civilian settlement and was the main base along the wall.

You get a sense of the domestic heart of the town from the visible remains. The Corbridge Museum displays Roman sculpture and carvings, including the amazing 3rd-century Corbridge Lion.

⌂ Sleeping & Eating

★ 2 The Crofts   B&B ££

(☑01434-633046; www.2thecrofts.co.uk; B6530; d from £80; P ☎) By far the best place in town to drop your pack, this secluded B&B occupies a beautiful period home around half a mile's walk east of the town centre on Newcastle Rd. The three high-ceilinged, spacious rooms are all en suite and the energetic owners cook a mean breakfast.

Corbridge Larder   DELI, CAFE £

(☑01434-632948; www.corbridgelarder.co.uk; 18 Hill St; dishes £4-7; ◷9.30am-5pm Mon-Fri, 9am-5.30pm Sat) Gourmet picnic fare at this fabulous deli includes bread, over 100 varieties of cheese, chutneys, cakes, chocolates and wine (you can get hampers made up) as well as made-to-order sandwiches, pies, quiches, tarts, and antipasti and mezze delicacies. Upstairs from the wonderland of provisions there's a small sit-down cafe.

Black Bull   BRITISH ££

(Middle St; mains £8-17; ◷kitchen noon-9pm; ☎ 🐾) A menu of British comfort food, such as beef burgers, fish in beer batter and slow-cooked lamb, and a series of low-ceilinged, atmospheric dining rooms, make this tavern a cosy spot to hole up. Sundays offer a choice of five different roasts.

ⓘ Information

Tourist Office (☑01434-632815; www.thisiscorbridge.co.uk; Hill St; ◷10am-4.30pm Mon-Sat Easter-Oct, 11am-4pm Wed, Fri & Sat Nov-Mar) Occupies a corner of the library.

ⓘ Getting There & Away

Buses 85, 685 and X85 between Newcastle and Carlisle come through Corbridge (£4.70 to either, up to one hour, every 30 minutes), as does the half-hourly bus 10 from Newcastle (£5, one hour) to Hexham (£2.90, 20 minutes), where you can connect with the Hadrian's Wall bus AD122.

Corbridge is also on the Newcastle–Carlisle railway line.

Hexham

POP 11,390

Bustling Hexham is a handsome if somewhat scuffed market town centred on its grand Augustinian abbey. Its cobbled alleyways have more shops and amenities than any other wall town between Carlisle and Newcastle, making it a good place to pick up supplies if you're heading out into the windswept wilds beyond.

◉ Sights

Hexham Abbey   MONASTERY

(www.hexhamabbey.org.uk; ◷9.30am-5pm, Saxon crypt 11am & 3.30pm) Dominating tiny Market Pl, Hexham's stately abbey is a marvellous example of Early English architecture. It cleverly escaped the Dissolution of 1537 by rebranding as Hexham's parish church, a role it still has today. The highlight is the 7th-century Saxon crypt, the only surviving element of St Wilifrid's Church, built with inscribed stones from Corstopitum in 674.

Old Gaol HISTORIC BUILDING
(adult/child £4/2; ⊙11am-4.30pm Tue-Sat Apr-Sep, Tue & Sat only Oct-Nov & Feb-Mar) Completed in 1333 as England's first purpose-built prison, today this strapping stone structure's four floors tell the history of the jail in all its gruesome glory. The history of the Border Reivers – a group of clans who fought, kidnapped, blackmailed and killed each other in an effort to exercise control over a lawless tract of land along the Anglo-Scottish border throughout the 16th century – is also retold, along with tales of the punishments handed out in the prison.

🛏 Sleeping & Eating

Hallbank Guest House B&B ££
(☑01434-605567; www.hallbankguesthouse.com; Hallgate; s/d from £70/90; [P]🛜) Behind the Old Gaol, this fine Edwardian house combines period elegance with stylishly furnished rooms equipped with flatscreen TVs and huge beds. It's very popular so book ahead.

Deli at Number 4 DELI, CAFE £
(☑01434-608091; www.deliatnumber4.co.uk; 4 Beaumont St; dishes £2-5; ⊙9am-5pm Mon-Sat, 11am-4pm Sun) Opposite Hexham's abbey, colourful window displays of breads, cheeses, olives, jams, homemade cakes and more entice you in, and the aromas from the kitchen tempt you upstairs to dine on soups, sandwiches and various specials.

★ Bouchon Bistrot FRENCH ££
(www.bouchonbistrot.co.uk; 4-6 Gilesgate; mains £12-20; ⊙noon-2pm & 6-9.30pm Mon-Sat) Hexham may be an unlikely setting for some true fine dining, but this Gallic affair has an enviable reputation. Classically inspired dishes range from proper French onion soup with gruyère or garlic snails to pan-fried Coley fillet with watercress velouté. Ingredients are as fresh as nature can provide and the wine list is an elite selection of champagnes, reds and whites.

ℹ Information

Tourist Office (☑01434-652220; www.visitnorthumberland.com/hexham; Wentworth Car Park; ⊙9.30am-5pm Mon-Sat, 11am-4pm Sun Apr-Oct, 10am-4.30pm Mon-Sat Nov-Mar) Northeast of the town centre.

ℹ Getting There & Away

Buses 85, 685 and X85 between Newcastle and Carlisle come through Hexham (£4.70, 1¼ hours, every 30 minutes); the AD122 Hadrian's Wall bus connects with other towns along the wall. Bus 10 (£5.40, 1¼ hours, every 30 minutes) links Hexham with Newcastle.

Hexham is on the scenic railway line between Newcastle (£6.60, 30 minutes, hourly) and Carlisle (£5, one hour, hourly).

Chesters Roman Fort & Museum

This Roman cavalry fort's (EH; ☑01434-681379; www.english-heritage.org.uk; adult/child £5.60/3.40; ⊙10am-6pm Apr-Sep, to 5pm Oct, 10am-4pm Sat & Sun Nov-Mar) superbly preserved remains are set among green woods and meadows near the village of Chollerford. Originally constructed to house a unit of troops from Asturias in northern Spain, they include part of a bridge (best appreciated from the eastern bank), four gatehouses, a bathhouse and an underfloor heating system. The museum has a large Roman sculpture collection. It's served by Hadrian's Wall bus AD122.

Haltwhistle & Around
POP 3790

It's one of the more intriguing debates in Britain: where exactly is the centre of the mainland? The residents of Haltwhistle, basically one long street just north of the A69, claim it's here. But then so do the folks in Dunsop Bridge, 71 miles to the south.... No matter, Haltwhistle is a handy spot to get some cash and load up on gear and groceries. Thursday is market day.

◉ Sights

Vindolanda Roman Fort & Museum HISTORIC SITE
(www.vindolanda.com; adult/child £6.50/4, with Roman Army Museum £10/5.50; ⊙10am-6pm Apr-Sep, to 5pm Oct, to 4pm Nov & Dec) The extensive site of Vindolanda offers a fascinating glimpse into the daily life of a Roman garrison town. The time-capsule museum is just one part of this large, extensively excavated site, which includes impressive parts of the fort and town (excavations continue) and reconstructed turrets and temple.

It's 1.5 miles north of Bardon Mill between the A69 and B6318 and a mile from Once Brewed.

Highlights of the Vindolanda museum displays include leather sandals, signature Roman toothbrush-flourish helmet decorations, and numerous writing tablets recently returned from the British Library. These include a student's marked work ('sloppy'), and a parent's note with a present of socks and underpants (things haven't changed – in this climate you can never have too many).

Roman Army Museum
MUSEUM

(www.vindolanda.com; adult/child £5.25/3, with Vindolanda £10/5.50; ⏰10am-6pm Apr-Sep, to 5pm Oct, 10am-4pm Sat & Sun Nov & Dec) A mile northeast of Greenhead, near Walltown Crags, this kid-pleasing museum provides lots of colourful background detail to Hadrian's Wall life, such as how the soldiers spent their R&R time in this lonely outpost of the empire.

Housesteads Roman
Fort & Museum
HISTORIC SITE

(EH; www.english-heritage.org.uk; adult/child £6.40/3.80; ⏰10am-6pm Apr-Sep, to 5pm Oct, to 4pm Nov-Mar) The most dramatic site of Hadrian's Wall – and the best-preserved Roman fort in the whole country – is at Housesteads, 2.5 miles north of Bardon Mill on the B6318, and about 6 miles from Haltwhistle. From here, high on a ridge and covering 2 hectares, you can survey the moors of Northumberland National Park, and the snaking wall, with a sense of awe at the landscape and the aura of the Roman lookouts.

Housesteads' remains include an impressive hospital, granaries with a carefully worked out ventilation system and barrack blocks. Most memorable are the spectacularly situated communal flushable latrines. Information boards show what the individual buildings would have looked like in their heyday. There's a scale model of the entire fort in the small museum at the ticket office.

Birdoswald Roman Fort
HISTORIC SITE

(EH; ☎01697-747602; www.english-heritage.org.uk; adult/child £5.60/3.40; ⏰10am-6pm Apr-Sep, to 5pm Oct, 10am-4pm Sat & Sun Nov-Mar) Technically in Cumbria, the remains of this once-formidable fort on an escarpment overlooking the beautiful Irthing Gorge are on a minor road off the B6318, about 3 miles west of Greenhead; a fine stretch of wall extends from here to Harrow's Scar Milecastle.

Lanercost Priory
RUIN

(EH; www.english-heritage.org.uk; adult/child £3.60/2.20; ⏰10am-6pm Apr-Sep, to 5pm Oct, 10am-4pm Sat & Sun Nov-Mar) Situated 2.6 miles northeast of Brampton, these peaceful ruins are all that remain of a priory founded in 1166 by Augustinian canons. Post-dissolution it became a private house and a priory church was created from the Early English nave.

🛏 Sleeping

Once Brewed YHA
HOSTEL £

(☎0845 371 9753; www.yha.org.uk; Military Rd, Bardon Mill; dm/d from £19.50/37.50; ⏰Mar-Nov; 🅿) This modern, well-equipped hostel, with a kitchen, laundry and meals available, is central for visiting the Roman forts of Vindolanda, 1 mile away, and Housesteads, 3 miles away. The Hadrian's Wall bus AD122 drops you at the door.

Greenhead
HOSTEL £

(☎01697-747411; www.greenheadhotelandhostel.co.uk; Greenhead; dm from £15) A converted Methodist chapel by a stream and a pleasant garden houses this independent hostel 3 miles west of Haltwhistle near the Roman Army Museum. There's a laundry and kitchen, but if you don't feel like cooking, Greenhead's hotel across the road has a restaurant and bar. It's served by the Hadrian's Wall bus AD122.

★ Ashcroft
B&B ££

(☎01434-320213; www.ashcroftguesthouse.co.uk; Lanty's Lonnen, Haltwhistle; s/d from £65/89; 🅿🐾) British B&Bs don't get better than this elegant Edwardian vicarage surrounded by nearly a hectare of beautifully manicured, terraced lawns and gardens. Inside, the nine rooms – some with private balconies and terraces – have soaring ceilings and come with every gadget 21st-century beings need. The dining room is grander than some snooty hotels and the welcome certainly more genuine.

Holmhead Guest House
B&B ££

(☎01697-747402; www.bandbhadrianswall.com; Greenhead Brampton; dm/s/d from £12.50/56/72, camping per person £7; 🅿🐾) Built using recycled bits of the wall on whose foundations it stands, this superb farmhouse half a mile north of Greenhead offers comfy rooms, a basic bunk barn and unpowered campsites. The Pennine Way and the Hadrian's Wall Path pass through the grounds and Thirlwall Castle's jagged ruins loom above. Ask to see the 3rd-century Roman graffiti.

ℹ Information

Tourist Office (☎01434-322002; www.northumberland.gov.uk; Mechanics Institute, Westgate; ⏰10am-4.30pm Mon-Sat Apr-Oct)

NORTHUMBERLAND NATIONAL PARK

England's last great wilderness is the 405 sq miles of natural wonderland that make up the country's least populated national park. The finest sections of Hadrian's Wall run along its southern edge and the landscape is dotted with prehistoric remains and fortified houses – the thick-walled *peles* were the only solid buildings built here until the mid-18th century.

Adjacent to the national park itself, the Kielder Water & Forest Park is home to Kielder Water, Europe's largest artificial lake, holding 200,000 million litres. Surrounding its 27-mile-long shoreline is England's largest forest, with 150 million spruce and pine trees.

The lack of population here helped see the area awarded dark-sky status by the International Dark Skies Association in late 2013 (the largest such designation in Europe), with controls to prevent light pollution.

The towns of Wooler (population 1990) and Rothbury (population 2330) make handy bases for exploring the area.

◎ Sights

★ Kielder Observatory
OBSERVATORY
(☑ 07805-638469; www.kielderobservatory.org; off Shilling Pot; public observing session adult/child £15/10; ⊙ by reservation) For the best views of the Northumberland International Dark Sky Park, attend a stargazing session at this state-of-the-art, 2008-built observatory. In addition to public observing there are a host of events including family astronomy, astrophotography and star camps. Book well ahead for all events, which sell out quickly, and dress as you would for the ski slopes (it's seriously chilly here at night). At the signs towards Kielder Observatory and Skyspace, turn left; it's a 2-mile drive up the track.

Cragside House, Garden & Estate
HISTORIC BUILDING, GARDENS
(NT; ☑ 01669-620333; www.nationaltrust.org.uk; adult/child £15.85/7.90, gardens & estate only £10.20/5.20; ⊙ house 1-5pm or 11am-5pm Tue-Sun depending on the month, gardens 10.30am-5pm Tue-Sun mid-Mar–Oct) Situated 1 mile northeast of Rothbury is the astonishing country retreat of the first Lord Armstrong. In the 1880s the house had hot and cold running water, a telephone and alarm system, and was the first in the world to be lit by electricity, generated through hydropower. The sprawling Victorian gardens feature lakes, moors and one of Europe's largest rock gardens. Visit late May to mid-June to see Cragside's famous rhododendrons in bloom. It's just off the B6341.

Chillingham Castle
CASTLE
(☑ 01668-215359; www.chillingham-castle.com; adult/child £9/5; ⊙ noon-5pm Sun-Fri Apr-Oct) Steeped in history, warfare, torture and ghosts, Chillingham is said to be one of the country's most haunted places, with spectres from a phantom funeral to Lady Mary Berkeley seeking her errant husband. Owner Sir Humphrey Wakefield has passionately restored the castle's extravagant medieval staterooms, stone-flagged banquet halls and grisly torture chambers. Chillingham is 6 miles southeast of Wooler. Bus 470 (three daily Monday to Saturday) between Alnwick (£3.70, 25 minutes) and Wooler (£3.10, 20 minutes) stops at Chillingham.

It's possible to stay at the medieval fortress in one of eight self-catering apartments where the likes of Henry III and Edward I once snoozed. Doubles start from £100.

🏃 Activities

The most stretch of the Hadrian's Wall Path is between Sewingshields and Greenhead in the south of the park.

There are many fine walks through the Cheviots (including a clamber to the top of the 815m-high Cheviot, the highest peak in the range), frequently passing by prehistoric remnants; local tourist offices can provide maps, guides and route information.

Though at times strenuous, cycling is a pleasure here; roads are good and traffic is light.

Kielder Water is a water-sports playground (and midge magnet; bring insect repellent). There are also walking and cycling trails here as well as great birdwatching. Visit www.visitkielder.com for more information.

🛏 Sleeping & Eating

Wooler YHA
HOSTEL £
(☑ 01668-281365; www.yha.org.uk; 30 Cheviot St; dm/d from £15.50/32; ⊙ Mar-Nov; P 🛜) In a low, red-brick building above Wooler, this handy hostel contains 57 beds in a variety of rooms including four handcrafted 'shepherds' huts', a modern lounge and a small restaurant.

★ **Otterburn Castle**
Country House Hotel   HISTORIC HOTEL **££**
(☑ 01830-520620; www.otterburncastle.com; Main St, Otterburn; s £59-69, d £99-119, f £129; P 🛜) Founded by William the Conqueror's cousin Robert Umfraville in 1086 and set in 13 hectares of grounds, this storybook castle's 18 rooms (some with four-poster beds) are recently refurbished and astonishing value. Rates include breakfast, served in the wood-panelled Oak Room restaurant. Cheaper meals are available in the Stable Bar & Bistro.

Katerina's Guest House   B&B **££**
(☑ 01669-620691; www.katerinasguesthouse.co.uk; High St, Rothbury; d £78; 🛜) Beamed ceilings, stone fireplaces and en suite rooms with fridges and canopied four-poster beds make Katerina's one of Rothbury's best choices. Bakeries, cafes and pubs abound along the street.

ℹ Information

For information, contact the **National Park** (☑ 01434-605555; www.northumberlandnationalpark.org.uk). As well as tourist offices in towns including **Wooler** (☑ 01668-282123; www.wooler.org.uk; Cheviot Centre, 12 Padgepool Pl; ⊙10am-4.30pm Apr-Oct, 10am-4.30pm Mon-Sat Nov-Mar) and **Rothbury** (☑ 01669-620887; www.theheartofnorthumberland.co.uk; Church St; ⊙10am-4.30pm), there's a national park office in **Once Brewed** (☑ 01434-344396; Military Rd; ⊙9.30am-5pm Apr-Oct, 10am-3pm Sat & Sun Nov-Mar). All offices can help find accommodation.

ℹ Getting There & Around

Public transport options are limited – to explore properly you really need your own wheels.
Kielder Bus 880 (£3.50, 50 minutes, two daily, Tuesday, Friday and Saturday) runs between Hexham and Kielder.
Otterburn Bus 808 (£3.50, 55 minutes, three daily, Monday to Saturday) runs between Otterburn and Newcastle. A National Express service calls at Otterburn (£5.80, 50 minutes, daily) between Newcastle and Edinburgh.
Rothbury Bus 14 runs hourly between Morpeth and Rothbury (£5, 1¼ hours, hourly, Monday to Saturday).
Wooler Buses 470 and 473 link Wooler and Alnwick (£3.70, 50 minutes, nine daily). Buses 267 and 464 run between Wooler and Berwick-upon-Tweed (£3.70, 50 minutes, nine daily).

NORTHUMBERLAND COAST

Like Northumberland's wild and remote interior, its coast is also sparsely populated. You won't find any hurdy-gurdy seaside resorts, but instead charming, castle-crowned villages strung along miles of wide, sandy beaches that you might just have to yourself.

Alnwick

POP 8120
Northumberland's historic ducal town, Alnwick (pronounced 'annick') is an elegant maze of narrow cobbled streets beneath the watchful gaze of a colossal medieval castle. Alnwick is also home to an enchanting bookshop and spectacular Alnwick Garden.

◉ Sights

★ **Alnwick Castle**   CASTLE
(www.alnwickcastle.com; adult/child £14.50/7.50, with Alnwick Garden £26.25/10.40; ⊙10am-5.30pm Apr-Oct) The outwardly imposing ancestral home of the Duke of Northumberland, and a favourite set for film-makers (it was Hogwarts for the first couple of Harry Potter films), has changed little since the 14th century. The interior is sumptuous and extravagant; the six rooms open to the public – staterooms, dining room, guard chamber and library – have an incredible display of Italian paintings, including Titian's *Ecce Homo* and many Canalettos.

Various free tours include several focusing on Harry Potter and other productions that have used the castle as a backdrop, including British comedy series *Blackadder*.

The castle is set in parklands designed by Lancelot 'Capability' Brown. The woodland walk offers some great aspects of the castle, or for a view looking up the River Aln, take the B1340 towards the coast.

Alnwick Garden   GARDENS
(www.alnwickgarden.com; adult/child £13.75/4.40; ⊙10am-7pm Jan-Oct, noon-6pm Nov & Dec) This 4.8-hectare walled garden has been transformed from a derelict site into a series of magnificent green spaces surrounding the breathtaking Grand Cascade – 120 separate jets spurting more than 30,000L of water down 21 weirs for everyone to marvel at and kids to splash around in.

There are six other gardens, including the Franco-Italian-influenced Ornamental

🏃 Driving Tour
Northumberland Coast

START NEWBIGGIN-BY-THE-SEA
END BERWICK-UPON-TWEED
LENGTH 78 MILES; ONE DAY

It's possible to shadow the coast to the Scottish border from Tynemouth, but the scenery really picks up at ① **Newbiggin-by-the-Sea**. Newbiggin's beach was recently restored, when over 500,000 tonnes of Skegness' sand was relocated here to counteract erosion, and Sean Henry's gigantic bronze sculpture *The Couple* was installed offshore.

Continuing north along the A1068 coast road for 13 miles brings you to the fishing port of ② **Amble**, with a boardwalk along the seafront and puffin cruises. Less than 2 miles north, biscuit-coloured ③ **Warkworth** is a cluster of houses around a loop in the River Coquet, dominated by the craggy ruin of 14th-century Warkworth Castle. The castle features in Shakespeare's *Henry IV Parts I and II*, and the 1998 film *Elizabeth* was shot here. A few hundred yards upriver, the tiny 14th-century Warkworth Hermitage is carved into the rock.

Some 5 miles north of Warkworth is ④ **Alnmouth**, with brightly painted houses and pretty beaches. It's another 5 miles inland to the bustling town of ⑤ **Alnwick** to see its imposing castle – which starred as Harry Potter's Hogwarts – and glorious Alnwick Garden. Turn back towards the coast and follow the B1339 for 4.7 miles before turning east on Windside Hill to ⑥ **Craster**, famed for its smoked kippers, which you can buy direct from the smokery. Don't miss a meal at the Jolly Fisherman, which has spectacular views of brooding Dunstanburgh Castle. Around 5 miles north at ⑦ **Low Newton-by-the-Sea**, in Embleton Bay, pause for a pint brewed at the Ship Inn.

Past the village of Seahouses (jumping-off point for the Farne Islands), quaint ⑧ **Bamburgh** is home to the most dramatic castle yet. Another 17 miles on, via a tidal causeway (check tide times!), the sacred priory ruins of isolated, other-worldly ⑨ **Holy Island (Lindisfarne)** still attract spiritual pilgrims. Return to the mainland where, 14 miles north, you can walk almost the entire length of the Elizabethan walls encircling England's northernmost city, beautiful ⑩ **Berwick-upon-Tweed**.

Garden (with more than 15,000 plants), the Rose Garden and the fascinating Poison Garden, home to some of the deadliest – and most illegal – plants in the world, including cannabis, magic mushrooms, belladonna and tobacco.

Sleeping & Eating

Alnwick fills up at weekends from Easter onwards so book ahead. B&Bs cluster near the castle.

★ Alnwick Lodge
B&B ££

(01665-604363; www.alnwicklodge.com; West Cawledge Park, A1; sites from £12, s/d/f £55/72/100; P🐾) Situated 2 miles south off the A1, this gorgeous Victorian farmstead has 15 antique-filled rooms with quirky touches like free-standing, lidded baths. Cooked breakfasts are served around a huge circular banqueting table. You can also go 'glamping' in restored gypsy caravans, wagons and shepherds' huts (from £45, linen per bed £15; shared bathrooms), or pitch up on the sheltered meadow.

White Swan Hotel
HOTEL ££

(01665-602109; www.classiclodges.co.uk; Bondgate Within; d/f from £105/115; P🐾) Alnwick's top address is this 300-year-old coaching inn in the heart of town. Its rooms are all superbly appointed (LCD TVs, DVD players and free wi-fi), but its showpiece is the fine-dining restaurant (mains £11 to £19), fitted with the original dining room decor from the *Olympic,* sister ship to the *Titanic* – elaborate panelling, ceiling and stained-glass windows included.

Art House
INTERNATIONAL ££

(www.arthouserestaurant.com; 14 Bondgate Within; mains £10-16; ⏰11am-11pm Thu-Mon) Located partially within the 15th-century Hotspur Tower (aka Bondgate Tower), this hip restaurant/art gallery serves upmarket comfort food like sausages with wholegrain mustard mash, pulled pork burgers and steaks with Alnwick rum sauce.

Shopping

★ Barter Books
BOOKS

(01665-604888; www.barterbooks.co.uk; Alnwick Station; ⏰9am-7pm Mon-Sat Apr-Sep, 9am-5pm Mon-Fri, to 7pm Sat Oct-Mar) If you're familiar with the renaissance of the WWII 'Keep Calm and Carry On' slogan, it's thanks to this wonderfully atmospheric secondhand bookshop in Alnwick's Victorian former railway station. While converting the station, the owner came across a set of posters – the framed original is above the till – and turned it into a successful industry.

Coal fires, velvet ottomans, reading rooms and a cafe make this a place you could spend days in, the silence interrupted only by the tiny rumble of the toy train that runs along the track above your head.

❶ Information

Tourist Office (01670-622152; www.visitalnwick.org.uk; 2 The Shambles; ⏰9am-5pm Mon-Sat, 10am-4pm Sun Easter-Oct, 9.30am-4.30pm Mon-Fri, 10am-4pm Sat Nov-Easter) By the marketplace.

❶ Getting There & Away

Alnwick's nearest train station is at Alnmouth, connected to Alnwick by bus X18 (£2.65, 10 minutes, hourly). Buses X15 and X18 run to Berwick-upon-Tweed (£5.90, 50 minutes, 10 daily) and Newcastle (£5.90, one hour, 10 daily).

Craster
POP 435

Sandy, salty Craster is a small, sheltered fishing village about 6 miles northeast of Alnwick, and is famous for its kippers. In the early 20th century, 2500 herring were smoked here daily. The kippers they still produce today often grace the Queen's breakfast table, no less.

◉ Sights

Dunstanburgh Castle
CASTLE

(EH & NT; www.english-heritage.org.uk; adult/child £4.30/2.60; ⏰10am-6pm Apr-Sep, to 4pm Oct, 10am-4pm Sat & Sun Nov-Mar) The dramatic 1.5-mile walk along the coast from Craster (not accessible by car) is the most scenic path to this moody, weather-beaten castle. Its construction began in 1314, it was strengthened during the Wars of the Roses, but left to crumble, becoming ruined by 1550. Parts of the original wall and gatehouse keep are still standing and it's a tribute to its builders that so much remains.

You can also reach the castle on foot from Embleton (1.5 miles).

✖ Eating

★ Jolly Fisherman
PUB ££

(01665-0576461; www.thejollyfishermancraster. co.uk; Haven Hill, Craster; lunch mains £7-10, dinner mains £12-20; ⏰kitchen 11am-3pm & 5-8.30pm

Mon-Sat, noon-7pm Sun; 🅿) Crab (in sensational soup, sandwiches, fish platters and more) is the speciality of this superb gastropub, but Paul Bocuse–trained chef John Blackmore's other amazing creations include apricot-stuffed pheasant leg and Northumbrian venison with juniper berry jus. Great wine list, wonderful real ales, a roaring fire in the bar and a stunning beer garden overlooking Dunstanburgh Castle, too.

🛍 Shopping

Robson & Sons   FOOD
(☑ 01665-576223; www.kipper.co.uk; Haven Hill, Craster; kippers per kilo £6) Four generations have operated this traditional fish smokers. It's best known for its kippers, but also smokes salmon and other fish.

ℹ Information

Tourist Office (☑ 01665-576007; Quarry Car Park; ⊙10am-5pm Easter-Oct)

ℹ Getting There & Away

Bus X18 runs to Berwick-upon-Tweed (£5.90, 1½ hours, nine daily) and Newcastle (£5.40, 1½ hours, nine daily). Bus 418 links Craster to Alnwick (£4.90, 30 minutes, hourly).

Embleton Bay

Beautiful Embleton Bay, a pale wide arc of sand, stretches from Dunstanburgh past the endearing, sloping village of Embleton and curves in a broad vanilla-coloured strand around to end at Low Newton-by-the-Sea, a tiny whitewashed, National Trust–preserved village.

⊙ Sights & Activities

Behind the bay is a path leading to the Newton Pool Nature Reserve, an important spot for breeding and migrating birds such as black-headed gulls and grasshopper warblers. There are a couple of hides where you can peer out at them. You can continue walking along the headland beyond Low Newton, where you'll find Football Hole, a delightful hidden beach between headlands.

Dunstanburgh Castle Golf Club   GOLF
(☑ 01665-576562; www.dunstanburgh.com; green fee per round weekday/weekend £26/30; ⊙ by reservation) First laid out in 1900, this stunning course was improved upon by golf legend and 'inventor' of the dogleg, James Braid (1870–1950) in 1922.

🛏 Sleeping & Eating

Joiners Arms   PUB £££
(☑ 01665-576112; www.joiners-arms.com; High Newton-by-the-Sea; d £140-155; 🅿🖲) Locals love this gastropub and for good reason: ingredients are sourced nearby, the seafood and steaks are excellent (mains £8 to £21) and families are warmly welcomed. But for visitors, it's also a fantastic place to stay – five contemporary guest rooms are individually and exquisitely decorated with details like exposed brick, free-standing baths and four-poster beds.

Ship Inn   PUB ££
(☑ 01665-576262; www.shipinnnewton.co.uk; Low Newton-by-the-Sea; mains £8.50-18; ⊙ bar 11am-11pm Mon-Sat, noon-11pm Sun, kitchen noon-2.30pm daily & 7-8pm Wed-Sat) ✎ Set around a village green, this wonderful pub brews 20 different beers – blond, wheat, rye, bitter, stout and seasonal – using local Coquet river water. Food is first-rate, too, from local crab to slow-cooked Peelham Farm lamb shanks with lemon and parsley couscous. No credit cards.

ℹ Getting There & Away

Bus X18 to Newcastle (£5.40, 1¾ hours, nine daily) and Berwick-upon-Tweed (£5.40, 1¼ hours, nine daily) stops outside the Joiners Arms. Bus 418 (£4.90, 40 minutes, hourly) links the village of Embleton with Alnwick.

Farne Islands

During breeding season (roughly May to July), you can see feeding chicks of 20 species of seabird, including puffin, kittiwake, Arctic tern, eider duck, cormorant and gull, as well as some 6000 grey seals on this rocky archipelago (NT; ☑ 07901-922143; www.nationaltrust.org.uk; adult/child excl boat transport £6.80/3.50; ⊙ by reservation, season and conditions permitting) about 3 miles offshore from the fishing village of Seahouses, reached from its dock with operators including Billy Shiel (☑ 01665-720308; www.farne-islands.com; 2½hr tour adult/child £13/9, 6hr tour £30/18).

Crossings can be rough (impossible in bad weather); wear warm, waterproof clothing and an old hat to guard against the birds!

Inner Farne is the more interesting of the two islands accessible to the public (along with Staple Island); its tiny chapel (1370; restored 1848) commemorates St Cuthbert, who lived here for a spell and died here in 687.

ℹ️ Information

Tourist Office (☑ 01670-625593; www.
seahouses.org; Seafield car park; ⊙10am-5pm
Apr-Oct, 11am-3pm Sat & Sun Nov-Mar)

ℹ️ Getting There & Away

Seahouses bus connections include bus X18
to Berwick-upon-Tweed (£5.70, nine daily, 45
minutes) and Newcastle (£6.20, nine daily, two
hours). Bus 418 runs to Alnwick (£5.10, 55 minutes, hourly).

Bamburgh

POP 280

Roosting high up on a basalt crag, Bamburgh's mighty castle looms over the
quaint village – a clutch of houses around
a pleasant green – which continues to commemorate the valiant achievements of local heroine, Grace Darling.

⊙ Sights

Bamburgh Castle   CASTLE
(www.bamburghcastle.com; adult/child £9.95/4.50;
⊙10am-5pm mid-Feb–Oct, 11am-4.30pm Nov-
mid-Feb) Northumberland's most dramatic
castle was built around a powerful 11th-
century Norman keep by Henry II. The castle played a key role in the border wars of the
13th and 14th centuries, and in 1464 was the
first English castle to fall during the Wars of
the Roses. It was restored in the 19th century by the great industrialist Lord Armstrong,
and is still home to the Armstrong family.

Its name is a derivative of Bebbanburgh,
after the wife of Anglo-Saxon ruler Aedel-
frip, whose fortified home occupied this
basalt outcrop 500 years earlier. Antique
furniture, suits of armour, priceless ceramics and artworks cram the castle's rooms
and chambers, but top billing goes to the
neo-Gothic King's Hall with wood panelling, leaded windows and hefty beams supporting the roof.

RNLI Grace Darling Museum   MUSEUM
(www.rnli.org; 1 Radcliffe Rd; ⊙10am-5pm Easter-
Sep, 10am-4pm Tue-Sun Oct-Easter) FREE Born
in Bamburgh, Grace Darling was the lighthouse keeper's daughter on Outer Farne
who rowed out to the grounded, flailing SS
Forfarshire in 1838 and saved its crew in the
middle of a dreadful storm. This recently refurbished museum even has her actual coble
(row boat) as well as a film on the events of

that stormy night. Grace was born just three
houses down from the museum and is buried in the churchyard opposite.

Her ornate wrought-iron and sandstone
tomb was built tall so as to be visible to
passing ships.

🍴 Eating

★**Mizen Head**   MODERN BRITISH £££
(☑01668-214254; www.mizenheadhotel.co.uk; Luc-
ker Rd; mains £10-29; ⊙noon-2pm & 6-9pm; P🐕）
Since it opened in 2011, Bamburgh's best
place to eat and/or stay is this stunning restaurant with rooms. Local seafood (lobster
thermidor, and roast turbot with asparagus,
tarragon and lemon butter) is the kitchen's
speciality, along with chargrilled steaks. Its
six rooms with chequered fabrics and black-
and-white coastal prints are light, bright
and spacious (doubles from £100 to £140).
Switched-on staff know their stuff.

There's wi-fi in public areas only.

ℹ️ Getting There & Away

Take bus X18 north to Berwick-upon-Tweed
(£5.90, 35 minutes, nine daily) or south to Newcastle (£5.90, two hours, nine daily).

Holy Island (Lindisfarne)

POP 160

There's something almost other-worldly
about this tiny, 2-sq-mile island. Connected
to the mainland by a narrow causeway that
only appears at low tide, it's fiercely desolate
and isolated, scarcely different from when St
Aidan arrived to found a monastery in 635.

As you cross the empty flats, it's easy to
imagine the marauding Vikings who repeatedly sacked the settlement between 793 and
875, when the monks finally took the hint
and left. They carried with them the illuminated *Lindisfarne Gospels* (now in the British Library in London) and the miraculously
preserved body of St Cuthbert, who lived
here for a couple of years but preferred the
hermit's life on Inner Farne. A priory was
re-established in the 11th century, but didn't
survive the Dissolution in 1537.

Pay close attention to the crossing-time
information, posted at tourist offices and
on notice boards throughout the area, and
at www.holy-island.info. Every year drivers
are caught midway by the incoming tide and
have to abandon their cars.

Sights

Lindisfarne Priory
RUIN

(EH; www.english-heritage.org.uk; adult/child £5.40/ 3.20; ⊙ 10am-6pm Apr-Sep, to 5pm Oct, 10am-4pm Sat & Sun Nov-Mar) The skeletal, red and grey ruins of the priory are an eerie sight and give a glimpse into the isolated life led by the Lindisfarne monks. The later 13th-century St Mary the Virgin Church is built on the site of the first church between the Tees and the Firth of Forth, and the adjacent museum displays the remains of the first monastery and tells the story of the monastic community before and after the Dissolution.

Lindisfarne Heritage Centre
MUSEUM

(www.lindisfarne-centre.com; Marygate; adult/child £4/2; ⊙ 10am-5pm Apr-Oct, reduced hours Nov-Mar) Twenty pages of the luminescent *Lindisfarne Gospels* can be flicked through on touch-screens here, though there's normally a queue. While you wait your turn there are fascinating exhibitions on the Vikings and the sacking of Lindisfarne in 793.

Lindisfarne Castle
CASTLE

(NT; www.nationaltrust.org.uk; adult/child £7.40/ 3.70; ⊙ 10am-3pm Tue-Sun Mar-Oct) Half a mile from the village stands this tiny, storybook castle, moulded onto a hunk of rock in 1550, and extended and converted by Sir Edwin Lutyens from 1902 to 1910 for Mr Hudson, the owner of *Country Life* magazine – you can imagine some of the decadent Gatsby-style parties to have graced its alluring rooms. Opening times can vary due to tide times.

Sleeping & Eating

It's possible to stay on the island, but you'll need to book well in advance.

Crown & Anchor
INN ££

(☑ 01289-389215; www.holyislandcrown.co.uk; Market Pl; d £75-100) The only locally run inn on the island is a relaxed, down-to-earth spot with brightly coloured guest rooms and solid pub grub (steak-and-ale pie, rib-eye steak with onion rings; mains £8 to £18), but the biggest winner is the beer garden with a postcard panorama of the castle, priory and harbour.

Lindisfarne Inn
INN ££

(☑ 01289-381223; www.lindisfarneinn.co.uk; Beal; s/d from £60/85; 🛜) Although on the mainland (on the A1 next to the turn-off to the causeway), this is a handy alternative to staying and/or dining on the island if you're cutting it fine with crossing times. Its 21 spotless, modern rooms are set far back enough that road noise isn't a problem. The well-above-average bar food includes a catch-of-the-day fisherman's pie (mains £9 to £15).

There's wi-fi in the bar only.

Open Gate
GUESTHOUSE ££

(☑ 01289-389222; www.aidanandhilda.org; Marygate; s £48-58, d £78-85) An Elizabethan farmhouse is the setting for this Christian retreat. In addition to four en suite rooms, the top floor has some cheaper single rooms that share bathrooms (£38).

🛈 Getting There & Around

The sea covers the causeway and cuts the island off from the mainland for about five hours each day.

Holy Island can sometimes be reached by bus 477 from Berwick-upon-Tweed (£4.50, 40 minutes, depends on tides); check with Berwick's tourist offices for updated information.

Drivers need to park in one of the signposted car parks (£4.60 per day). A shuttle bus (£2 return) runs from the car park to the castle every 20 minutes.

Berwick-upon-Tweed

POP 13,265

England's northernmost city is a picturesque fortress town, cleaved by the River Tweed, which is spanned by the Grade I–listed Berwick Bridge (aka Old Bridge), built from sandstone between 1611 and 1624, and the Royal Tweed (1925–28).

Berwick is the stubborn holder of two unique honours: it is the most fought-over settlement in European history (between 1174 and 1482 it changed hands 14 times between the Scots and the English); and its football team, Berwick Rangers, are the only English team to play in the Scottish League (albeit in lowly Scottish League Two). Although firmly English since the 15th century, Berwick retains its own identity, with locals south of the border speaking with a noticeable Scottish whirr.

Sights & Activities

Berwick Walls
WALLS

(EH; ⊙ daylight hours) FREE You can walk almost the entire length of Berwick's hefty Elizabethan walls, begun in 1558 to reinforce an earlier set built during the reign of Edward II. The mile-long walk is a must, with wonderful, wide-open views. Only a small fragment remains of the once-mighty border castle, most of the building having been replaced by the train station.

Berwick Barracks
MUSEUM, GALLERY

(EH; www.english-heritage.org.uk; The Parade; adult/child £4.20/2.50; ⊙10am-6pm Mon-Fri Apr-Sep, to 4pm Oct) Designed by Nicholas Hawksmoor, Britain's oldest purpose-built barracks (1717) now house an assortment of museums and art galleries, covering a history of the town and British soldiery since the 17th century. The Gymnasium Gallery hosts big-name contemporary art exhibitions.

Cell Block Museum
MUSEUM

(Marygate; adult/child £2/50p; ⊙tours 10.30am & 2pm Mon-Fri Easter-Sep) The original jail cells in the upper floor of the town hall (1750–61) have been preserved as a chilling museum devoted to crime and punishment. Tours take in the public rooms, museum, jail and belfry.

☞ Tours

Time to Explore Guided Tours
WALKING TOUR

(☑01289-330218; www.visitberwick.com; 106 Marygate; Town & Walls adult/child £5/free, Hidden Berwick adult/child £6/free; ⊙by reservation Easter-Oct) Passionate local Derek Sharman leads 1¼-hour Town & Walls tours taking in the town's highlights, and 1¾-hour Hidden Berwick tours including entry to an Elizabethan bastion and the 18th-century gunpowder magazine, which aren't normally open to the public. Tours depart from the tourist office.

🛏 Sleeping

Accommodation in Berwick is limited – the tourist office can help find places to stay.

Berwick YHA
HOSTEL £

(☑01629-592700; www.yha.org.uk; Dewars Lane; dm/d from £18/59; @ 🛜) A 240-year-old granary has been converted into a state-of-the-art hostel with contemporary facilities: comfortable dorms, a handful of en suite doubles, a TV room, a laundry and wi-fi in common areas. Staff are terrifically friendly and helpful.

Granary Guesthouse
BOUTIQUE B&B ££

(☑01289-304403;www.granaryguesthouse.co.uk; 11 Bridge St; s/d from £80/96; 🅿🛜) ✐ In a charming town-centre location, Berwick's most romantic B&B has three fresh, elegant and contemporary guest rooms, locally sourced and/or organic breakfasts and an on-site beauty treatment room offering massages.

✗ Eating & Drinking

Audela
MODERN BRITISH ££

(☑01289-308827; www.audela.co.uk; 41-47 Bridge St; breakfast dishes £3-8, lunch mains £5-9.50, dinner mains £8-19; ⊙9am-9pm; 🖫) ✐ Named for the last vessel to be built at Berwick Shipyard (in 1979), this brand-new addition to Berwick's dining scene has become the town's top table. Local suppliers provide the ingredients for dishes like twice-baked blue cheese soufflé, halibut with lemon butter sauce and herb-crusted rack of lamb, served in a striking sage-green dining room.

Barrels Alehouse
PUB

(59-61 Bridge St; ⊙noon-midnight; 🛜) Berwick's best watering hole attracts a mixed, laid-back crowd who can be found sipping real ales and micro-distilled gins and whiskies at all hours. There's regular live music in the atmospherically dingy basement bar.

ⓘ Information

Tourist Office (☑01670-622155; www.visitberwick.com; 106 Marygate; ⊙10am-5pm Apr-Oct, 10am-4pm Mon-Sat Nov-Mar)

ⓘ Getting There & Away

BUS

Buses stop on Golden Sq (where Marygate becomes Castlegate). National Express coaches between Edinburgh (£11.60, 1¼ hours, twice daily) and London (£36.50, eight hours, twice daily) stop here. Other options include buses X15 (via Alnwick) and X18 to Newcastle (£6.50, 2½ hours, nine daily) and bus 477 to Holy Island (£4.50, 35 minutes, depends on tides; check with Berwick's tourist offices for updated information).

TRAIN

Berwick is almost exactly halfway between Edinburgh (£19.90, 40 minutes, every 30 minutes) and Newcastle (£23.60, 45 minutes, every 30 minutes) on the East Coast Main Line linking London and Edinburgh.

Understand England

England Today

For England and the English, the first 15 years of the 21st century have been a time of change, conflict, controversy and national soul-searching. Despite a boost to the national mood from the successful London Olympics in 2012 and signs of the economy emerging from recession, there is a nagging uncertainty about the future.

Best in Print

Notes from a Small Island (Bill Bryson) It's dated, but this American's fond take on British behaviour is a classic, and still spot on today.

Icons of England (Bill Bryson) It's that man again, still in love with his adopted home.

Watching the English (Kate Fox) A fascinating field guide to the nation's peculiar habits.

I Never Knew That About England (Christopher Winn) A treasure trove of bizarre facts.

The English (Jeremy Paxman) A perceptive take on the national character.

Best on Film

Brief Encounter (1945) Classic tale of buttoned-up English love affair.

This Sporting Life (1961) Gritty exploration of the realities of postwar life in northern England.

My Beautiful Laundrette (1985) Touching and comic study of racism and homophobia in Thatcher-era London.

The Full Monty (1997) Unemployed steel workers become male strippers.

War Horse (2011) Rite-of-passage story of a young man surviving WWI.

British or English?

Where once the United Kingdom of Great Britain and Northern Ireland was a single political entity, it's now anything but united. From 1999 onwards, the process of devolution has seen the nations of Scotland, Wales and Northern Ireland get their own ruling bodies with power over domestic affairs such as health and education.

Although England has been part of the UK for more than 300 years, its status as the biggest member state by far – with 84% of the UK population – means that until recently, there was no clamour for English devolution. A referendum in 2004 overwhelmingly rejected the creation of regional assemblies in northern England by 78% to 22%. For many English people, the difference between being British and being English remained pretty hazy. As far as they were concerned, England and the UK were effectively the same thing – an attitude widely resented by the Scots, Welsh and Northern Irish.

However, in the wake of the Scottish independence referendum of 2014 (when Scotland voted by 55% to 45% to remain in the UK), the very identity of England has become the subject of fierce debate. The independence campaign stirred up all kinds of questions about the values, beliefs and institutions that bind the UK together. Would an independent Scotland be able to continue using the pound sterling (issued by the Bank of England)? Would there be border controls between Scotland and England? Would the Queen still be head of state?

As part of the Westminster government's campaign for a 'No' vote in the independence referendum, it promised greater powers for the Scottish parliament if the Scots voted to stay in the UK. But after the referendum, this promise soon stirred up an indignant response from English MPs – why should Scottish MPs be able to vote at Westminster on matters affecting only England, while English MPs have no say on matters decided in Edinburgh and affecting only Scotland? 'English votes for English laws' became the rallying cry for a surge of English national feeling.

A Crumbling Coalition

A key milestone in England's recent history was the general election of 2010, when the Labour government was ousted after 13 years in power, but no party won an overall majority. An agreement between the Conservative and Liberal Democrat parties created the first coalition government in Westminster since WWII.

But the relationship between the coalition parties has been turbulent, battered by disagreements over how to tackle the country's problems. Conservative 'rebels' blocked Lib Dem moves to reform the House of Lords, and the Lib Dems vetoed Tory plans to cut taxes on the rich, ditch the Human Rights Act and reduce the number of MPs at Westminster.

The constraints of coalition have also forced the Lib Dems to abandon some of their 2010 election pledges, notably a promise not to raise tuition fees for university students in England and Wales. As a result, their support plummeted. Nonetheless, opinion polls suggest that, once again, no party will win an overall majority in the 2015 UK general election, raising the prospect of minority government, or yet another uneasy coalition.

The Rise of UKIP

Although British politics since 2010 has been dominated by austerity measures supposed to combat the impact of the global financial crisis, by the start of 2014 the economy had been joined by immigration as the issue of most concern. The same year saw the rise to prominence of the United Kingdom Independence Party (UKIP), a right-wing, libertarian party whose flagship policies include cutting back on immigration and taking Britain out of the EU.

UKIP is particularly popular in England, being favoured by around 30% of the electorate (compared to 20% in Wales and 10% in Scotland). The party took first place in the European elections of May 2014 with 27.5% of the vote (on a turnout of 34%) – the first time any party other than Labour or Conservative had come first in a UK-wide election since 1906 – and went on to gain its first two elected Members of Parliament in a by-election later that year. The result threw Britain into a spin. Did this herald a fundamental change in the direction of British politics? Or was it a protest vote from an electorate fed up with Westminster politicians?

Opinion polls suggesting that UKIP might win more Westminster seats in the 2015 election saw both Labour and the Conservatives harden their positions on immigration, while the Tory leader David Cameron pledged that he would offer the country a referendum on whether to stay in the EU if he remained as prime minister after 2015.

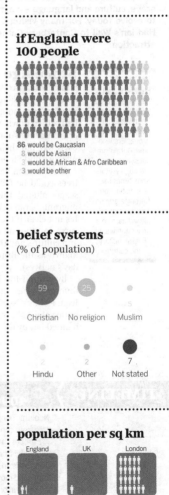

POPULATION: **53 MILLION**

AREA: **50,000 SQ MILES (130,000 SQ KM)**

GDP PER CAPITA (UK): **£21,800**

GDP GROWTH (UK): **1.8%**

INFLATION (UK): **2%**

UNEMPLOYMENT (UK): **7.2%**

if England were 100 people

86 would be Caucasian
8 would be Asian
3 would be African & Afro Caribbean
3 would be other

belief systems
(% of population)

59 Christian
25 No religion
5 Muslim
2 Hindu
2 Other
7 Not stated

population per sq km

England | UK | London

♟ ≈ 250 people

History

England may be a small country on the edge of Europe, but its multifaceted history is not short on drama and intrigue. For thousands of years, invaders and incomers have arrived, settled and made their mark. The result is England's fascinating mix of landscape, culture and language – a dynamic pattern that shaped the nation and continues to evolve today. For many visitors, this rich historical legacy – from Stonehenge and Hadrian's Wall to Canterbury Cathedral and the Tower of London – is England's main attraction.

The country of England is part of the island of Great Britain (along with Wales and Scotland). The words 'England' and 'Britain' are not synonymous, although visitors sometimes miss the distinction. Getting a grip on this basic principle will ease your understanding of English history and culture.

Stone Age & Iron Age

Stone tools discovered near Lowestoft in Suffolk show that human habitation in England stretches back at least 700,000 years. These early peoples were nomadic hunter-gatherers, but by around 4000 BC, most had settled down, notably in open areas such as Salisbury Plain in southern England. Alongside fields they built burial mounds (today called barrows), but their most enduring legacies are the great stone circles of Avebury and Stonehenge, still clearly visible today.

Move on a millennium or two and it's the Iron Age. Better tools meant trees could be felled and more land turned over to farming. As landscapes altered, this was also a time of cultural change: a new wave of migrants – the Celts – arrived in Britain from the European mainland. It's not clear if the new arrivals absorbed the indigenous people, or vice versa, but the end result was the widespread adoption of Celtic language and culture, and the creation of a Celtic-British population – today often known as the Britons (or Ancient Britons to distinguish them from today's natives).

By around 100 BC, the Ancient Britons had separated into about 20 different tribes, including the Cantiaci (in today's county of Kent), the Iceni (today's Norfolk) and the Brigantes (northwest England). Did you notice the Latin-sounding names? That's because the tribal tags were handed out by the next arrivals on England's shores...

TIMELINE	4000 BC	c 55 BC	AD 43
	Neolithic peoples migrate from continental Europe. They differ significantly from previous arrivals: instead of hunting and moving on, they settle in one place and start farming.	Relatively small groups of Roman invaders under the command of Emperor Julius Caesar make forays into southern England from the northern coast of Gaul (today's France).	Emperor Claudius leads the first proper Roman invasion of Britain. His army wages a ruthless campaign, and the Romans control most of southern England by AD 50.

The Romans

Although there had been some earlier expeditionary campaigns, the main Roman invasion of what is now England began in AD 43. They called their newly won province Britannia, and within a decade most of southern England was under Roman control. It wasn't a walkover though: some locals fought back, most famously the warrior-queen Boudica, who led a rebel army against Londinium, the Roman port on the present site of London.

Opposition was mostly sporadic, however, and no real threat to Roman military might. By around AD 80 Britannia comprised much of today's England and Wales. Though it's tempting to imagine noble natives battling courageously against occupying forces, Roman control and stability was probably welcomed by the general population, tired of feuding chiefs and insecure tribal territories.

Roman settlement in Britain continued for almost four centuries, and intermarriage was common between locals and incomers (many from other parts of the empire – including modern-day Belgium, Spain and Syria – rather than Rome itself). A Romano-British population thus evolved, particularly in the towns, while indigenous Celtic-British culture remained in rural areas.

Along with stability and wealth, the Romans introduced another cultural facet: a new religion called Christianity, after it was recognised by Emperor Constantine in the 4th century. (Recent research, however, indicates that Celtic Christians may have brought the religion to Britain even earlier.) But by this time, although Romano-British culture was thriving in Britannia, back in its Mediterranean heartland the Empire was already in decline.

> Probably built around 3000 BC, Stonehenge has stood on Salisbury Plain for more than 5000 years, making it older than the Great Pyramids of Egypt.

HISTORY THE ROMANS

LEGACY OF THE LEGIONS

To control their new territory, the Romans built garrisons across England. Many developed into towns, which can be recognised by names ending in 'chester' or 'caster' (from the Latin castrum, meaning military camp) – Lancaster, Winchester, Manchester and, of course, Chester, to name but a few. The Romans also built roads, initially so soldiers could march quickly from place to place, and later so that trade could develop. Wherever possible the roads were straight lines (because it was efficient, not – as the old joke goes – to stop Ancient Britons hiding round corners) and included Ermine St between London and York, Watling St between Kent and Wales, and the Fosse Way between Exeter and Lincoln. As you travel around England, you'll notice many modern highways still follow Roman roads. In a country better known for old lanes and turnpike routes winding through the landscape, these ruler-straight highways stand out on the map.

60	200	c 410	5th century
The Iceni warrior queen Boudica (also known as Boadicea) leads a rebel army against the Romans, destroys the Roman town of Colchester and gets as far as their port at Londinium (now London).	The Romans build a defensive wall around the city of London with four main entrance gates, still remembered today by the districts of Aldgate, Ludgate, Newgate and Bishopsgate.	As the classical world's greatest empire declines after more than three centuries of relative peace and prosperity, Roman rule ends in Britain with more of a whimper than a bang.	Teutonic tribes – known today as the Anglo-Saxons – from the area now called Germany migrate to England, and quickly spread across much of the country.

It was an untidy finale. The Romans were not driven out by the Ancient Britons (after more than 300 years, Romano-British culture was so established there was nowhere for many to go 'home' to). In reality, Britannia was simply dumped by the rulers in Rome, and the colony slowly fizzled out. But historians are tidy folk, and the end of Roman power in England is generally dated at AD 410.

Fledgling England

When Roman power faded, the province of Britannia went downhill. Romano-British towns were abandoned and rural areas became no-go zones as local warlords fought over fiefdoms. The vacuum didn't go unnoticed, and once again invaders crossed from the European mainland – this time Germanic tribes called Angles and Saxons.

Historians disagree on what happened next; either the Anglo-Saxons largely overcame or absorbed the Romano-British and Celts, or the indigenous tribes simply adopted Anglo-Saxon language and culture. Either way, by the late 6th century much of England was predominantly Anglo-Saxon, divided into separate kingdoms dominated by Wessex (in southern England), Mercia (today's Midlands) and Northumbria (northern England).

A History of England in 100 Places by John Julius Norwich is a fascinating handbook mixing history with geography, covering a range of locations 'from Stonehenge to the Gherkin'.

Some areas remained unaffected by the incomers, but the overall impact was immense – the name England means 'land of the Angles', and today the core of the English language is Anglo-Saxon, many place names have Anglo-Saxon roots, and the very term 'Anglo-Saxon' has become a (much abused and factually incorrect) byword for 'pure English'.

The Vikings & Alfred the Great

In the 9th century England was yet again invaded by a bunch of pesky Continentals. This time it was the Vikings from today's Scandinavia. They quickly conquered the eastern and northeastern areas of England, then started to expand into central England. Blocking their route were the Anglo-Saxon armies heading north, led by Alfred the Great, the king of Wessex and one of English history's best-known characters.

Thus England was divided in two: north and east was the Viking land, known as 'Danelaw', while south and west was Anglo-Saxon territory. Alfred was hailed as king of the English – the first time the Anglo-Saxons regarded themselves as a truly united people. His capital was Winchester; if you come to visit the famous cathedral, look out for the nearby statue of Alfred in the city centre.

Alfred's son and successor was Edward, known as Edward the Elder. After more battles, he gained control of Danelaw, and thus became the first king to rule the whole country – a major milestone in English history.

8th century	850	927	1066
King Offa of Mercia orders the construction of a clear border between his kingdom and Wales – a defensive ditch called Offa's Dyke that is still visible today.	Vikings come from what is today Denmark and conquer east and northeast England. They establish their capital at Yorvik, today's city of York.	Athelstan, grandson of Alfred the Great, son of Edward the Elder, is the first monarch to be crowned king of England, building on his ancestors' success in regaining Viking territory.	Incumbent King Harold is defeated by an invading Norman army at the Battle of Hastings, and England finds itself with a new monarch: William the Conqueror.

But it was hardly cause for celebration. Later in the 10th century, more raids from Scandinavia threatened the fledgling English unity, and as England came to the end of the 1st millennium AD, the future was anything but certain.

1066 & All That

When King Edward the Confessor died, the crown passed to Harold, his brother-in-law. That should've settled things, but Edward had a cousin in Normandy (in northern France) called William, who thought *he* should have succeeded to the throne of England.

The end result was the Battle of Hastings in 1066, the most memorable of dates for anyone who has studied English history. William sailed from Normandy with an army, the Saxons were defeated, and King Harold was killed – by an arrow in the eye, according to legend. William became king of England, earning himself the prestigious epithet Conqueror.

In the years after the invasion, the French-speaking Normans and the English-speaking Anglo-Saxons kept pretty much to themselves. At the top of the feudal system came the monarch, and below that came the landowning nobles: barons and baronesses, dukes and duchesses, plus the bishops. Then came earls, knights and lords – and their ladies. At the bottom were landless peasants or 'serfs', and this strict hierarchy became the basis of a class system that to a certain extent still exists in England today.

Royal & Holy Squabbling

William's successor, William II, was assassinated during a hunting trip and succeeded by Henry I, Stephen of Blois then Henry II, establishing the House of Plantagenet. This period also established the long-standing English tradition of competition for the throne, and introduced an equally enduring tendency of bickering between royalty and the Church. Things came to a head in 1170 when Henry II had the 'turbulent priest' Thomas Becket murdered in Canterbury Cathedral.

Perhaps the next king, Richard I, wanted to make amends for his forebears' unholy sentiments by fighting against Muslim 'infidels' in the Holy Land (today's Israel and the Palestinian territories, plus parts of Syria, Jordan and Lebanon). Unfortunately, he was too busy crusading to bother about governing England – although his bravery earned Richard the sobriquet Lionheart – and in his absence the country fell into disarray.

Richard was succeeded by his brother John. According to legend, it was during this time that a noble named Robert of Loxley, better known as Robin Hood, hid in Sherwood Forest and engaged in a spot of wealth redistribution.

Despite Anglo-Saxon dominance from around AD 500, the Celtic language was still being spoken in parts of southern England when the Normans invaded in the 11th century.

Medieval Women by Henrietta Leyser looks through a female lens at the period of English history from AD 500 to 1500; a life of work, marriage, sex and children – not necessarily in that order.

1085–86	1095	12th century	1215
The Norman invaders compile the Domesday Book – a thorough census of England's stock and future potential; it's still a vital historical document today.	The start of the First Crusade – a campaign of Christian European armies against the Muslim occupation of Jerusalem and the 'Holy Land'. A series of crusades continues until 1272.	Oxford University founded. There's evidence of teaching in the area since 1096, but King Henry II's 1167 ban on students attending the University of Paris solidifies Oxford's importance.	King John signs the Magna Carta, limiting the monarch's power for the first time in English history: an early step on the path towards constitutional rule.

Plantagenet Progress

By the early 13th century King John's erratic rule was too much for the powerful barons, and they forced him to sign a document called the Magna Carta (Great Charter), which set limits on the power of the monarch. It was signed at Runnymede, near Windsor; you can still visit the site today.

The next king was Henry III, followed in 1272 by Edward I – a skilled ruler and ambitious general. During a busy 35-year reign, he was unashamedly expansionist, leading campaigns into Wales and Scotland, where his ruthless activities earned him the title 'Hammer of the Scots'.

Edward I was succeeded by Edward II, who lacked his forebear's military success. He failed in the marriage department too, and came to a grisly end when his wife, Isabella, and her lover, Roger Mortimer, had him murdered in Berkeley Castle. Today, fans of ghoulish ends can visit the very spot where it happened.

Today, more than 500 years after the Wars of the Roses, Yorkshire's symbol is still a white rose, while Lancashire's is still a red rose, and rivalry between these two counties is still very strong – especially when it comes to cricket and football.

Houses of Lancaster & York

In 1399, Richard II was ousted by a powerful baron called Henry Bolingbroke, who became Henry IV – the first monarch of the House of Lancaster. He was followed, neatly, by Henry V, who decided it was time to end the Hundred Years' War, a long-standing conflict between England and France. Henry's victory at the Battle of Agincourt and the patriotic speech he was given by Shakespeare in his namesake play ('cry God for Harry, England and St George!') ensured his position among the most famous of English monarchs.

Still keeping things neat, Henry V was followed by Henry VI. His main claims to fame were overseeing the building of great places of worship –

RULING THE ROOST

The gallop through the story of England's ruling dynasties clearly shows that life is never dull for the person at the top. Despite immense power and privilege, the position of monarch (or, perhaps worse, *potential* monarch) probably ranks as one of history's least safe occupations. English kings to meet an untimely end include Harold (killed in battle), William II (assassinated), Charles I (beheaded by Republicans), Edward V (allegedly murdered by an uncle), Richard II (probably starved to death), John (too much eating and drinking), James II (deposed), Edward II (dispatched by his queen and her lover) and William III (died after his horse tripped over a molehill). As you visit the castles and battlefields of England, you may feel a touch of sympathy – but only a touch – for those all-powerful figures continually looking over their shoulders.

1337–1453	1348	1415	1459–71
England battles France in a long conflict known as the Hundred Years' War. It was actually a series of small conflicts. And it lasted for more than a century too...	The arrival of the Black Death. Commonly attributed to bubonic plague, the pandemic killed more than 1.5 million people, over a third of the country's population.	The invading English army under Henry V defeats the French army at the Battle of Agincourt – a crucial battle in the Hundred Years' War. (The war itself continues for almost another 40 years.)	The Wars of the Roses: a conflict between two competing dynasties – the Houses of Lancaster and York. The Yorkists are successful, and King Edward IV gains the throne.

King's College Chapel, in Cambridge, Eton Chapel, near Windsor – and suffering from great bouts of insanity.

The Hundred Years' War finally ground to a halt in 1453, but just a few years later, England was plunged into a civil conflict dubbed the Wars of the Roses. Briefly it went like this: Henry VI of the House of Lancaster (emblem: a red rose) was challenged by Richard, duke of York (emblem: a white rose). Henry was weak and it was almost a walkover for Richard, but Henry's wife, Margaret of Anjou, was made of sterner stuff and her forces defeated the challenger. Then Richard's son Edward entered with an army, turned the tables, drove out Henry, and became King Edward IV – the first monarch of the House of York.

Dark Deeds in the Tower

Edward IV hardly had time to catch his breath before facing a challenge from the earl of Warwick, who teamed up with the energetic Margaret of Anjou to shuttle Edward into exile and bring Henry VI to the throne. A year later Edward IV came bouncing back, killed Warwick, captured Margaret and had Henry executed in the Tower of London.

Edward IV was succeeded by his 12-year-old son, Edward V. But in 1483 the boy-king was mysteriously murdered, along with his brother, and once again the Tower of London was the scene of the crime.

With the 'little princes' dispatched, the throne was open for their old Uncle Richard. Whether he was the princes' killer remains the subject of debate, but his rule as Richard III was short-lived: in 1485 he was tumbled from the top job (thus concluding the House of Plantagenet) by a Welsh nobleman named Henry Tudor, who became King Henry VII.

Peace & Dissolution

With the Wars of the Roses only recently ended, Henry VII's Tudor neutrality was important. He also mended fences with his northern neighbours by marrying off his daughter to James IV of Scotland, thus linking the Tudor and Stuart lines. The result was a much-welcomed period of peace for England.

The next king, Henry VIII, is one of England's best-known monarchs, mainly thanks to his six wives – the result of a desperate quest for a male heir. He also had a profound impact on England's religious history: his excommunication from the Roman Catholic Church led to the separation of the Church of England from papal rule, and to the 'Dissolution' – the infamous closure of many monasteries, the ruins of which can still be seen today at places such as Fountains Abbey and Rievaulx Abbey in Yorkshire.

The 1955 film version of Shakespeare's *Richard III*, starring Laurence Olivier and John Gielgud, was the award-winning drama of its time, and is well worth watching for a view on this turbulent period in English history.

Shakespeare's *Henry V* was filmed in 1989 as a superb epic, starring Kenneth Branagh as the eponymous king. Also worth catching is the earlier movie of the same name starring Laurence Olivier, made in 1944 as a patriotic rallying cry.

1485	1509–47	1558–1603	1605
Henry Tudor defeats Richard III at the Battle of Bosworth to become King Henry VII, establishing the Tudor dynasty and ending York-Lancaster rivalry for the throne.	Reign of King Henry VIII. The Pope's disapproval of Henry's serial marriage and divorce results in the English Reformation – the founding of the Church of England.	Reign of Queen Elizabeth I, a period of boundless English optimism. Enter stage right playwright William Shakespeare. Exit due west navigators Walter Raleigh and Francis Drake.	King James' attempts to smooth religious relations are set back by an anti-Catholic outcry following the infamous Gunpowder Plot, a terrorist attempt to blow up Parliament led by Guy Fawkes.

The Elizabethan Age

Henry VIII was succeeded by his son Edward VI, then his daughter Mary I, but their reigns were short. And so Elizabeth, third in line, unexpectedly came to the throne.

As Elizabeth I, she inherited a nasty mess of religious strife and divided loyalties, but after an uncertain start she gained confidence and turned the country around. Refusing marriage, she borrowed biblical motifs and became known as the Virgin Queen – perhaps the first English monarch to create a cult image.

Highlights of her 45-year reign included the naval defeat of the Spanish Armada, the far-flung explorations of English seafarers Walter Raleigh and Francis Drake and the expansion of England's trading network, including newly established colonies on the east coast of America – not to mention a cultural flourishing, thanks to writers such as William Shakespeare and Christopher Marlowe.

Meanwhile, Elizabeth's cousin Mary Stuart (daughter of Scottish King James V, and a Catholic) had become Queen of Scotland. She'd spent her childhood in France and had married the French dauphin (crown prince), thereby becoming queen of France as well. Why stop at two? After her husband's death (so no longer France's queen), Mary returned to Scotland, and from there ambitiously claimed the English throne as well – on the grounds that Elizabeth was illegitimate.

Mary's plans failed; she was imprisoned and forced to abdicate, but escaped to England and appealed to Elizabeth for help. This could have been a rookie error, or she might have been advised by courtiers with their own agenda. Either way, it was a bad move. Mary was, not surprisingly, seen as a security risk and imprisoned once again. In an uncharacteristic display of indecision, before finally ordering her execution Elizabeth held Mary under arrest for nearly 19 years, moving her frequently from house to house. As you travel around England today, you can visit many stately homes (and even a few pubs) that proudly claim, 'Mary Queen of Scots slept here'.

The movie *Elizabeth*, directed by Shekhar Kapur (1998) and starring Cate Blanchett, covers the early years of the Virgin Queen's rule, as she graduates from princess to commanding monarch – a time of forbidden love, unwanted suitors, intrigue and death.

United & Disunited Britain

Elizabeth died in 1603, but despite a bountiful reign, the Virgin Queen had failed to provide an heir. She was succeeded by her closest relative, the Scottish King James, the safely Protestant son of the murdered Mary. Thus, he became James I of England and VI of Scotland, the first English monarch of the House of Stuart. James did his best to soothe Catholic-Protestant tensions and united England, Wales and Scotland into one kingdom for the first time – another step towards British unity, at least on paper.

1644–49	1749	1776–83	1799–1815
English Civil War. Royalist forces supporting the king are pitted against Oliver Cromwell's army of 'parliamentarians'. Cromwell is victorious, and England becomes a republic.	Author and magistrate Henry Fielding founds the Bow Street Runners, London's first professional police force. A 1792 Act of Parliament allowed the Bow Street model to spread across England.	The American War of Independence is the British Empire's first major reversal. William Pitt the Younger becomes the country's youngest-ever prime minister at the age of 24.	The Napoleonic Wars see a weakened Britain threatened with invasion by Napoleon, whose ambitions are curtailed at the famous battles of Trafalgar (1805) and Waterloo (1815).

But the divide between king and Parliament continued to smoulder, and the power struggle worsened during the reign of Charles I, eventually degenerating into the English Civil War. The antiroyalist (or 'parliamentarian') forces were led by Oliver Cromwell, a Puritan who preached against the excesses of the monarchy and established Church. His army (known as the Roundheads) was pitched against the king's forces (the Cavaliers) in a conflict that tore England apart, although it was the final civil war in English history. It ended with victory for the Roundheads – the king was executed and England declared a republic, with Cromwell hailed as 'Protector'.

The Return of the King

By 1653 Cromwell was finding Parliament too restricting and assumed dictatorial powers, much to his supporters' dismay. On his death in 1658, he was followed half-heartedly by his son, but in 1660 Parliament decided to reestablish the monarchy, as republican alternatives were proving far worse.

Charles II (the exiled son of Charles I) came to the throne, and his rule – known as 'the Restoration' – saw scientific and cultural activity bursting forth after the strait-laced ethics of Cromwell's time. Exploration and expansion were also on the agenda. Backed by the army and navy (which had been modernised by Cromwell), colonies stretched down the American coast, while the East India Company set up headquarters in Bombay, laying foundations for what was to become the British Empire.

The next king, James II, had a harder time. Attempts to ease restrictive laws on Catholics ended with his defeat at the Battle of the Boyne by William III, the Protestant king of Holland, aka William of Orange. William was married to James' daughter Mary. William and Mary had equal rights to the throne, and their joint accession in 1688 was known as the Glorious Revolution.

Empire Building

In 1694 Mary died, leaving William as monarch. He died a few years later and was succeeded by his sister-in-law, Anne. During her reign, in 1707, the Act of Union was passed, uniting England, Wales and Scotland under one Parliament – based in London – for the first time.

Queen Anne died without an heir in 1714, marking the end of the Stuart line. The throne passed to distant (but still safely Protestant) German relatives – the House of Hanover.

Meanwhile, the British Empire – which, despite its title, was predominantly an English entity – continued to grow in the Americas as well as in Asia, while claims were made to Australia after James Cook's epic voyage in 1768.

A History of England in a Nutshell by John Mathew provides exactly what it says on the cover: a quick overview of the nation's key events in less than 200 pages.

The Isles: A History by Norman Davies provides much-acclaimed and highly readable coverage of the past 10,000 years in England, within the broader history of the British Isles.

HISTORY THE RETURN OF THE KING

1837–1901	1914	1926	1939–45
Reign of Queen Victoria. The British Empire – 'the Empire where the sun never sets' – expands from Canada through Africa and India to Australia and New Zealand.	Archduke Franz Ferdinand of Austria is assassinated in the Balkan city of Sarajevo – the final spark in a decade-long crisis that starts the Great War, now called WWI.	Increasing mistrust of the government, fuelled by soaring unemployment, leads to the General Strike. Millions of workers – train drivers, miners, shipbuilders – down tools and bring the country to a halt.	WWII rages across Europe, and much of Africa and Asia. Britain and Allies, including America, Russia, Australia, India and New Zealand, eventually defeat the armies of Germany, Japan and Italy.

The Industrial Era

While the Empire expanded abroad, at home Britain had become the crucible of the Industrial Revolution. Steam power (pioneered by James Watt in 1781) and steam trains (launched by George Stephenson in 1830) transformed methods of production and transport, and the towns of the English Midlands became the first industrial cities.

Industrial growth led to Britain's first major period of internal migration, as vast numbers of people from the countryside came to the cities in search of work. At the same time, medical advances improved life expectancy, creating a sharp population increase. For many ordinary people the effects of Britain's economic blossoming were dislocation and poverty.

But despite the social turmoil of the early 19th century, by the time Queen Victoria took the throne in 1837 Britain's factories and fleets dominated world trade. The rest of the 19th century was seen as Britain's Golden Age – a period of patriotic confidence not seen since the days of the last great queen, Elizabeth I.

The times were optimistic, but it wasn't all tub-thumping jingoism. Prime Minister Disraeli and his successor, William Gladstone, also introduced social reforms to address the exploitative excesses of the Industrial Revolution. Education became universal, trade unions were legalised and the right to vote was extended in a series of reform acts, finally being granted to all men over the age of 21 in 1918, and to all women in 1928.

London is an epic novel by Edward Rutherfurd – or rather around 50 separate mini-novels – each set in a key historical era, from the Roman invasion to the Blitz of WWII. Exhaustive and exhausting, but great for a sense of each period.

World War I

When Queen Victoria died in 1901, it seemed that all of Britain's energy fizzled out too, and the country entered a period of decline. Meanwhile, in continental Europe, the military powers of Russia, Austro-Hungary, Turkey and Germany were sabre-rattling in the Balkan states, a dispute that eventually started the 'Great War' (now known as WWI). By the war's weary end in 1918, millions had died, with hardly a street or village untouched, as the sobering lists of names on war memorials all over England still show.

For the soldiers that did return from WWI, disillusion with the old social order helped make the Labour Party – which represented the working class – a political force, upsetting the balance long enjoyed by the Liberal and Conservative parties.

The Labour Party came to power for the first time, in coalition with the Liberals, in the 1923 election, but by the mid-1920s the Conservatives were back. The world economy was now in decline and industrial unrest had become widespread.

The situation worsened in the 1930s as the Great Depression meant another decade of misery and political upheaval, and even the royal fam-

One of the finest novels about WWI is *Birdsong* by Sebastian Faulks. Understated, perfectly paced and intensely moving, it tells of passion, fear, waste, incompetent generals and the poor bloody infantry.

1945	1946–48	1948	1952
WWII ends, and in the immediate postwar election the Labour Party under Clement Attlee defeats the Conservatives under Winston Churchill, despite the latter's pivotal rule in Britain's WWII victory.	The Labour Party nationalises key industries such as shipyards, coalmines and steel foundries. Britain's 'big four' train companies are combined into British Railways.	Aneurin Bevan, the Health Minister in the Labour government, launches the National Health Service: free medical care for all – the core of Britain as a 'welfare state'.	Princess Elizabeth becomes Queen Elizabeth II when her father, George VI, dies. Her coronation takes place in Westminster Abbey in June 1953.

ily took a knock when Edward VIII abdicated in 1936 so he could marry Wallis Simpson, a woman who was twice divorced and – horror of horrors – American.

World War II

The next monarch was Edward's less-than-charismatic brother, George VI, and Britain dithered through the rest of the decade, with mediocre government failing to confront the country's deep-set problems.

Meanwhile, Adolf Hitler came to power in Germany and in 1939 invaded Poland. Two days later Britain was once again at war. The German army swept through Europe and pushed back British forces to the beaches of Dunkirk, in northern France. In June 1940 an extraordinary flotilla

WINSTON CHURCHILL

More than a century after he became part of the British government, Winston Churchill is still one of the country's best-known political figures. He was born in 1874 and, although from an aristocratic family, his early years were not auspicious; he was famously a 'dunce' at school, an image he actively cultivated in later life.

As a young man Churchill joined the British Army and also acted as a war correspondent for various newspapers, and wrote several books about his exploits. In 1901 he was elected to Parliament as a Conservative MP. In 1904 he defected to the Liberals, the main opposition party at the time. A year later, after a Liberal election victory, he became a government minister. Churchill rejoined the Conservatives in 1922, and held various ministerial positions through the rest of the 1920s. Notable statements during this period included calling Mussolini a 'genius' and Gandhi 'a half-naked fakir'.

Churchill criticised Prime Minister Neville Chamberlain's 1938 'appeasement' of Hitler and called for British rearmament to face a growing German threat, but his political life was generally quiet – so he concentrated on writing. His multivolume *A History of the English-Speaking Peoples* was drafted during this period; although biased and flawed, it remains his best-known work.

In 1939 Britain entered WWII, and by 1940 Churchill was prime minister, taking additional responsibility as Minister of Defence. Hitler had expected an easy victory in the war, but Churchill's extraordinary dedication (not to mention his radio speeches – most famously offering 'nothing but blood, toil, tears and sweat' and promising to 'fight on the beaches...') inspired the British people to resist.

Between July and October 1940 the Royal Air Force withstood Germany's aerial raids to win what became known as the Battle of Britain – a major turning point in the war, and a chance for land forces to rebuild their strength. Britain's refusal to negotiate terms with Germany and the decision to stand alone against Hitler's forces was an audacious strategy, but it paid off and Churchill was lauded as a national hero – praise that continued beyond his death in 1965 and which continues today.

1960–66	1971	1970s	1979
The era of African and Caribbean independence brings the freedom of Nigeria, Tanzania, Jamaica, Trinidad & Tobago, Kenya, Malawi, Gambia and Barbados.	Britain adopts the 'decimal' currency (one pound equals 100 pence) and drops the ancient system of 20 shillings or 240 pennies per pound, the centuries-old bane of school maths lessons.	Much of the decade is characterised by inflation, inept governments (on the left and right), trade-union disputes, strikes, shortages and blackouts, culminating in the 1978–9 'Winter of Discontent'.	A Conservative government led by Margaret Thatcher wins the general election, a major milestone in Britain's 20th-century history, ushering in a decade of dramatic political and social change.

of rescue vessels turned total disaster into a brave defeat – and Dunkirk Day is still remembered with pride and sadness in Britain every year.

By mid-1940, most of Europe was controlled by Germany. Russia had negotiated a peace agreement and the USA was neutral, leaving Britain virtually isolated. Into this arena came a new prime minister called Winston Churchill.

Between September 1940 and May 1941, the German air force launched 'The Blitz', a series of (mainly night-time) bombing raids on London and other cities. But morale in Britain remained strong, thanks partly to Churchill's regular radio broadcasts. The USA entered the war after the Japanese bombing of Pearl Harbor, and in late 1941 the tide began to turn.

By 1944 Germany was in retreat. Russia pushed back from the east, and Britain, the USA and other Allies were again on the beaches of France. The Normandy landings (D-Day, as it's remembered) marked the start of the liberation of Europe's western side. By 1945 Hitler was dead and the war was over.

Swinging & Sliding

The aftermath of WWII saw an unexpected swing on the political front. An electorate tired of war tumbled Churchill's Conservatives from power in favour of the Labour Party. There was change abroad too, as parts of the British Empire became independent, including India and Pakistan in 1947 and Malaya in 1957, followed by much of Africa and the Caribbean.

But while the Empire's sun may have been setting, Britain's royal family was still going strong. In 1952 George VI was succeeded by his daughter, Elizabeth II.

By the late 1950s, postwar recovery was strong enough for Prime Minister Harold Macmillan to famously remind the British people they had 'never had it so good'. Some saw this as a boast for a confident future, others as a warning about difficult times ahead. But many people didn't care either way, as the 1960s had arrived and grey old England was suddenly more fun and lively than it had been for generations.

The '60s may have been swinging, but by the 1970s decline had set in, thanks to a combination of inflation, an oil crisis and international competition revealing the weaknesses of Britain's economy.

The rest of the decade was marked by strikes, disputes and general all-round gloom, but neither the Conservatives (also known as the Tories) under Prime Minister Edward Heath, nor Labour, under Prime Ministers Harold Wilson and Jim Callaghan, proved capable of controlling the strife. The British public had had enough, and the elections of May 1979 saw the arrival of a new prime minister: a previously little-known Conservative politician named Margaret Thatcher.

Handy History Websites

www.royal.gov.uk

www.bbc.co.uk/history

www.victorianweb.org

1990	1992	1997	2003
Thatcher ousted as leader, and the Conservative party enters a period of decline, but remains in power largely due to inept Labour opposition.	Labour remains divided between 'traditionalists' and 'modernists'. The Conservatives, under new leader John Major, confound the pundits and unexpectedly win the general election.	The general election sees Tony Blair lead 'New' Labour to victory in the polls, with a record-breaking parliamentary majority, ending 18 years of Conservative rule.	Britain joins the USA in the invasion of Iraq, initially with some support from Parliament and the public – despite large antiwar demonstrations held in London and other cities.

The Thatcher Years

Soon everyone had heard of Margaret Thatcher. Love her or hate her, no one could argue that her methods weren't dramatic, and many policies had a lasting impact, one of the most prominent being the privatisation of state-run industries that had been nationalised in the late 1940s.

Looking back from a 21st-century vantage point, most commentators agree that by economic measures the Thatcher government's policies were largely successful, but by social measures they were a failure and created a polarised Britain: on one side were the people who gained from the prosperous wave of opportunities in the 'new' industries, while on the other side were those who had become unemployed and dispossessed as the 'old' industries such as coal mining and steel production became an increasingly small part of the country's economic picture.

Despite policies that were frequently described as uncompromising, by 1988 Margaret Thatcher was the longest-serving British prime minister of the 20th century, although her repeated electoral victories were helped considerably by the Labour Party's ineffective campaigns and destructive internal struggles.

New Labour, New Millennium, New Government

The pendulum started to swing again in the early 1990s. Margaret Thatcher was replaced as leader by John Major, but the voters still regarded Labour with suspicion, allowing the Conservatives to unexpectedly win the 1992 election. It all came to a head in the 1997 election, when 'New' Labour swept to power under a new fresh-faced leader called Tony Blair.

Blair and the Labour party enjoyed an extended honeymoon period, and the next election (in 2001) was another walkover. The Conservative party continued to struggle, allowing Labour to win a historic third term in 2005, and a year later Blair became the longest-serving Labour prime minister in British history.

In May 2010 a record 14 years of Labour rule came to an end, and a new coalition between the Conservative and Liberal Democrat parties formed the new government.

2005	2007	2010	2014
The Labour government faces several internal crises but, thanks largely to inept Conservative opposition, still wins the general election for a historic third term.	Tony Blair, Britain's longest-serving Labour prime minister, resigns and Gordon Brown, Chancellor of the Exchequer, takes over as Labour leader and prime minister.	Labour is narrowly defeated in the general election as the minority Liberal Democrats align with the Conservatives to form the first coalition government in Britain's postwar history.	An independence referendum in neighbouring Scotland sparks a debate on the possibility of a separate English parliament within the UK.

Food & Drink

Wherever you travel in England, for every greasy spoon or fast-food joint, there's a local pub or speciality restaurant serving up enticing homemade meals. For decades most towns have boasted Italian, Chinese and Indian restaurants, so spaghetti carbonara, chow mein or vindaloo are no longer considered exotic. London is now regarded as a global gastronomic capital, and it's increasingly easy to find decent food options in other cities, towns and villages across the country.

Rick Stein is a TV chef, energetic restaurateur and good-food evangelist. His books *Food Heroes* and *Food Heroes – Another Helping* extol small-scale producers and top-notch local food, from organic veg to wild-boar sausages.

The Full English

For the locals, the English culinary day is punctuated by the three traditional main meals of breakfast, lunch and dinner. And just to keep you on your toes, the last two meals are also called dinner and tea, or lunch and supper – depending on social class and location.

Breakfast

Many people in England make do with toast or a bowl of cereal before dashing to work, but visitors staying in hotels and B&Bs will undoubtedly encounter a phenomenon called the 'Full English Breakfast'. This usually consists of bacon, sausages, eggs, tomatoes, mushrooms, baked beans and fried bread. If you don't feel like eating half a farmyard first thing in the morning it's OK to ask for just the eggs and tomatoes, for example. Some B&Bs offer other alternatives such as kippers (smoked fish) or a 'continental breakfast' – which completely omits the cooked stuff and may even add something exotic such as croissants.

Lunch

One of the many great inventions that England gave the world is the sandwich, often eaten as a midday meal. Slapping a slice of cheese or ham between two bits of bread may seem a simple concept, but no one apparently thought of it until the 18th century: the Earl of Sandwich (his title comes from a town in southeast England that originally got its name from the Viking word for 'sandy beach') ordered his servants to bring cold meat between bread so he could keep working at his desk or, as some historians claim, keep playing cards late at night.

In Yorkshire, the eponymous pudding is traditionally a *starter*, a reminder of days when food was scarce and the pudding was a premeal stomach-filler.

Another English classic – served especially in pubs – is the ploughman's lunch. Basically it's bread and cheese, and although hearty yokels probably did carry such food to the fields in the days of yore, the meal was actually invented in the 1960s by the national cheesemakers' organisation to boost consumption, neatly cashing in on public nostalgia and fondness for tradition.

You can still find a basic ploughman's lunch offered in some pubs – and it undeniably goes well with a pint or two of local ale at lunchtime – but these days the meal has usually been smartened up to include butter, salad, pickle, pickled onion and dressings. At some pubs you get a selection of cheeses. You'll also find other variations, such as a farmer's lunch (bread and chicken), stockman's lunch (bread and ham), Frenchman's lunch (brie and baguette) and fisherman's lunch (you guessed it, with fish).

Dinner

For generations, a typical English dinner has been 'meat and two veg'. Dressed up as 'evening meal' or dressed down as 'cooked tea', there was little variation: the meat would be pork, beef or lamb, one of the vegetables would be potatoes and the other would inevitably be carrots, cabbage or cauliflower – just as inevitably cooked long and hard. Although tastes and diets are changing, this classic combination still graces the tables of many English families several times a week.

Traditionally, the beef is roast beef (always roast, never 'roasted') and with the beef – especially at Sunday lunches – comes Yorkshire pudding. It's simply roast batter, but very tasty when properly cooked. Another classic English dish brings Yorkshire pudding and sausages together, with the delightful name of 'toad-in-the-hole'.

Yorkshire pudding also turns up in another guise, especially in pubs and cafes in northern England, where a big bowl-shaped pudding is filled with stew, gravy or vegetables. You can even find multicultural crossover Yorkshire puddings filled with curry.

Perhaps the best-known classic English meal is fish and chips, often bought from the 'chippie' as a takeaway wrapped in paper to eat on the spot or enjoy at home. For visitors, English fish and chips can be an acquired taste. Sometimes the chips can be limp and the fish tasteless, especially once you get away from the sea, but in towns with salt in the air this classic deep-fried delight is always worth trying.

In the 16th century, Queen Elizabeth I decreed that mutton could only be served with bitter herbs – intended to stop people eating sheep in order to help the wool trade – but her subjects discovered mint sauce, and it's been a favourite condiment ever since.

Dessert

After the main course – usually at an evening meal, or if you're enjoying a hearty lunch – comes dessert or 'pudding'. A classic English pudding is rhubarb crumble, the juicy stem of a large-leafed garden plant, stewed and sweetened, then topped with a crunchy mix of flour, butter and more sugar – and served with custard or ice cream. Other favourites include treacle sponge, bread-and-butter pudding and plum pudding, a dome-shaped cake with fruit, nuts and brandy or rum, traditionally eaten at Christmas.

Regional Specialities

With the country's large coastline, it's no surprise that seafood is a speciality in many English regions. Yorkshire's seaside resorts are particularly famous for huge servings of cod – despite it becoming an endangered species thanks to overfishing – while restaurants in Devon and Cornwall regularly conjure up prawns, oysters, mussels and scallops. Other local seafood you may encounter elsewhere on your travels includes Norfolk crab and Northumberland kippers.

In northern and central England you'll find Cumberland sausage – a tasty mix of minced pork and herbs, so large it has to be spiralled to fit on your plate. Look out too for Melton Mowbray pork pies – cooked ham in a casing of pastry, eaten cold. A legal victory in 2005 ensured that only

NAME THAT PASTY

A favourite speciality in southwest England is the Cornish pasty. Originally a mix of cooked vegetables wrapped in pastry, it's often available in meat varieties (much to the scorn of the Cornish people) and now sold everywhere in England. Invented long before Tupperware, the pasty was an all-in-one-lunch pack that tin miners carried underground and left on a ledge ready for mealtime. So pasties weren't mixed up, they were marked with their owners' initials – always at one end, so the miner could eat half and safely leave the rest to snack on later without it mistakenly disappearing into the mouth of a workmate. Before going back to the surface, the miners traditionally left the last few crumbs of the pasty as a gift for the spirits of the mine, known as 'knockers', to ensure a safe shift the next day.

NOSE-TO-TAIL CUISINE

One of the many trends enjoyed by modern British cuisine is the revival of nose-to-tail cooking – that is, using the whole animal, not just the more obvious cuts such as chops and fillet steaks. This does not mean boiling or grilling a pig or sheep all in one go – although spit-roasts are popular. It means utilising the parts that may at first seem unappetising or, frankly, inedible. So as well as dishes involving liver, heart, chitterlings (intestines) and other offal, traditional delights such as bone marrow on toast, or tripe (stomach) and onions once again grace the menus of fashionable restaurants. The movement is particularly spearheaded by chef Fergus Henderson at his St John restaurant in London and via his influential recipe books *Nose to Tail Eating: A Kind of British Cooking* and *Beyond Nose To Tail*.

---

pies from the eponymous Midlands town could carry the Melton Mowbray moniker, in the same way that only fizzy wine from the Champagne region of France can carry that name. Another English speciality that enjoys the same protection is Stilton – a strong white cheese, either plain or in a blue-vein variety. Only five dairies in all of England are allowed to produce cheese with this name.

Perhaps less appealing is black pudding, a large sausage made with pig's blood and oatmeal, and traditionally served for breakfast in northern England.

For more on regional specialities, see the Eat & Drink Like A Local boxed text on p400 and p504.

Eating Out

In England, 'eating out' means simply going to a restaurant or cafe – anywhere away from home. There's a huge choice across the country.

Picnics & Self-Catering

When shopping for food, as well as the more obvious chain stores and corner shops, markets can be a great place for bargains – everything from dented tins of tomatoes to home-baked cakes and organic goat's cheese. Farmers markets are always worth a visit; they're a great way for producers to sell good food direct to consumers, with both sides avoiding the grip of the supermarkets.

Cafes & Teashops

The traditional English cafe is nothing like its continental European namesake. For a start, asking for a brandy with your coffee may cause confusion, as cafes in England rarely serve alcohol. Most are simple places serving simple meals such as meat pie, beans on toast, baked potato or omelette with chips (costing around £3 to £4) and stuff like sandwiches, cakes and other snacks (£1 to £2). Quality varies enormously: some cafes definitely earn their 'greasy spoon' handle, while others are neat and clean.

In London and some other cities, a rearguard of classic cafes – with formica tables, seats in booths and decor unchanged from their 1950s glory days – stand against the onslaught of the international chains. In rural areas, many market towns and villages have cafes catering for tourists, walkers, cyclists and other outdoor types, and in summer they're open every day. Whether you're in town or country, good English cafes are a wonderful institution and always worth a stop during your travels.

Smarter cafes are called teashops – also more often found in country areas – where you might pay a bit more for extras such as neat decor and table service.

Like meat, but not battery pens? Go to the Freedom Food website of the Royal Society for the Prevention of Cruelty to Animals (www.freedomfood.co.uk).

As well as the traditional establishments, in most cities and towns you'll also find coffee shops – independents and international chains – and a growing number of Euro-style cafe-bars, serving decent lattes and espressos and offering bagels or ciabattas rather than beans on toast (you'll probably be able to get that brandy too). Some of these modern places even have outdoor chairs and tables – rather brave considering the narrow pavements and inclement weather much of England enjoys.

Restaurants

London has scores of excellent restaurants that could hold their own in major cities worldwide, while places in Bath, Leeds and Manchester can give the capital a fair run for its money (actually, often for rather less money). We've taken great pleasure in seeking out some of the best and best-value restaurants in England.

Prices vary considerably across the country, with a main course in a straightforward restaurant costing around £9 or less, and anywhere between £9 and £18 at midrange places. Excellent food, service and surroundings can be enjoyed for £20 to £50 – although in London you can, if you want, pay double this.

For vegetarians, England is not too bad. Many restaurants and pubs have at least one token vegetarian dish, while better places offer much more imaginative choices. Vegans will find the going trickier, except of course at dedicated veggie/vegan restaurants.

Pubs & Gastropubs

Not so many years ago, a pub was the place to go for a drink. And that was it. If you felt peckish, your choice might be a ham or cheese sandwich, with pickled onions if you were lucky. Today many pubs serve a wide range of food, and it's usually a good-value option, whether you want a toasted sandwich between museum visits in London, or a three-course meal in the evening after touring castles and stately homes in Yorkshire.

While the food in many pubs is good quality and good value, some places raised the bar to such a degree that a whole new genre of eatery – the gastropub – was born. The finest gastropubs are effectively restaurants (with smart decor, neat menus and uniformed table service; a few have won Michelin stars; while others have gone for a more relaxed atmosphere, with mismatched cutlery, waiters in T-shirts and the day's choices chalked up on a blackboard. The key for all, though, is top-notch no-frills food and drink. For visitors relaxing after a hard day's sightseeing, nothing beats the luxury of a wholesome shepherd's pie washed down with a decent ale without the worry of guessing which fork to use.

Drinking in England

The two beverages most associated with England are probably tea and beer. Both are unlike drinks of the same name found elsewhere in the world, and well worth trying on your travels around the country.

Many towns and cities in England hold regular farmers markets – a good chance for food producers large and small to sell direct to the public. For more info and a searchable database, see www.localfoods. org.uk.

WHERE THERE'S SMOKE

All restaurants and cafes in England are nonsmoking throughout. Pubs have the same rule, which is why there's often a small crowd of smokers standing on the pavement outside. Some pubs provide specific outdoor smoking areas, ranging from a simple yard to elaborate gazebos with canvas walls and the full complement of lighting, heating, piped music and TV screens – you'd never need to know you were 'outside' at all, apart from the pungent clouds of burning tobacco.

THE OLDEST PUB IN ENGLAND?

Many drinkers are often surprised to learn that the word 'pub' (short for 'public house'), although apparently steeped in history, dates only from the 19th century. But places selling beer have been around for much longer, and 'the oldest pub in England' is a hotly contested title.

One of the country's oldest pubs, with the paperwork to prove it, is Ye Olde Trip to Jerusalem in Nottingham, which was serving ale to departing crusaders in the 12th century.

Other contenders dismiss Ye Olde Trip as a mere newcomer. A fine old inn called the Royalist Hotel in Stow-on-the-Wold, Gloucestershire claims to have been selling beer since AD 947, while another pub called Ye Olde Fighting Cocks in St Albans (Hertfordshire) apparently dates back to the 8th century – although the 13th is more likely.

But then back comes Ye Olde Trip with a counterclaim: one of its bars is a cave hollowed out of living rock, and that's more than a million years old.

Tea & Coffee

In England, if a local asks 'Would you like a drink?' don't automatically expect a gin and tonic. They may well mean a 'cuppa' (cup of tea), England's best-known beverage. It's usually made with dark tea leaves to produce a strong brown drink, more bitter in taste than tea served in some other Western countries, which is partly why it's usually served with a dash of milk.

The Campaign for Real Ale promotes the understanding of traditional British beer. Look for endorsement stickers on pub windows, and for more info see www.camra.org.uk.

Although tea is often billed as the national drink – in 2008 Brits consumed 165 million cups a day – coffee is becoming ever more popular (around 90 million cups a day). The British coffee market is worth almost £1 billion a year, but with the prices some coffee shops charge, maybe that's not surprising. A final word of warning: when you're ordering a coffee and the server says 'white or black', don't panic. It simply means 'do you want milk in it?'.

Beer & Wine

Among alcoholic drinks, England is probably best known for its beer. As you travel around the country you should definitely try some local brews. English beer typically ranges from dark brown to bright amber in colour, and is often served at room temperature. Technically it's ale but it's often called 'bitter'. This is to distinguish it from lager – the drink that most of the rest of the word calls 'beer' – which is generally yellow and served cold.

Beer that's brewed and served traditionally is called 'real ale' to distinguish it from mass-produced brands, and there are many regional varieties. But be ready! If you're used to the 'amber nectar' or 'king of beers', a traditional British brew may come as a shock – a warm, flat and expensive shock. This is partly to do with Britain's climate, and partly to do with the beer being served by hand pump rather than gas pressure. Most important, though, is the integral flavour: traditional British beer doesn't need to be chilled or fizzed to make it palatable.

On hot summer days, you could go for shandy – beer and lemonade mixed in equal quantities. You'll usually need to specify 'lager shandy' or 'bitter shandy'. It may seem an astonishing combination for outsiders, but it's very refreshing and of course not very strong.

Another option is cider – available in sweet and dry varieties. In western and southwestern counties, you could try 'scrumpy', a very strong dry cider traditionally made from local apples.

Many visitors are surprised to learn that wine is produced in England, and has been since the time of the Romans. Today, more than 400 vineyards and wineries produce around two million bottles a year, many winning major awards. English white sparkling wines have been a particular success story, especially those produced in the southeast, where the growing conditions are similar to those of the Champagne region in France.

Bars & Pubs

In England, the difference between a bar and a pub is sometimes vague, but generally bars are smarter and louder than pubs, possibly with a younger crowd. Drinks are more expensive too, unless there's a gallon-of-vodka-and-Red-Bull-for-a-fiver promotion – which there often is.

As well as beer and wine, pubs and bars offer the usual choice of spirits, often served with a 'mixer', producing English favourites such as gin and tonic, rum and coke or vodka and lime. These drinks are served in measures called 'singles' and 'doubles'. A single is usually 35ml – just over one US fluid ounce. Only more upmarket city bars have a large array of cocktail options.

And finally, two tips: First, if you see a pub called a 'free house', it means it doesn't belong to a brewery or pub company, and thus is 'free' to sell any brand of beer. It doesn't mean the booze is free of charge. Second, remember that drinks in English pubs are ordered and paid for at the bar. You can always spot the freshly arrived tourists – they're the ones sitting forlornly at an empty table hoping to spot a server.

When it comes to gratuities, it's not usual to tip pub and bar staff. However, if you're ordering a large round, or the service has been good all evening, you can say to the person behind the bar '…and one for yourself'. They may not have a drink, but they'll add the monetary equivalent to the total you pay and keep it as a tip.

Food & Drink Glossary

aubergine	large purple-skinned vegetable; 'eggplant' in the USA and Australia
bangers	sausages (colloquial)
bap	a large, wide, flat, soft bread roll
bevvy	drink (slang; originally from northern England); abbreviation of 'beverage'
bill	the total you need to pay after eating in a restaurant ('check' to Americans)
bitter	ale; a type of beer
black pudding	type of sausage made from dried blood and other ingredients
bun	bread roll, usually sweet, eg currant bun, cream bun
BYO	bring your own (usually in the context of bringing your own drink to a restaurant)
caff	abbreviated form of cafe
candy floss	light sugar-based confectionery; called 'cotton candy' in the USA, 'fairy floss' in Australia
chips	sliced, deep-fried potatoes, eaten hot (what Americans call 'fries')
cider	alcoholic drink made from fermented apple juice
clotted cream	cream so heavy or rich that it's become almost solid (but not sour)
corkage	a small charge levied by the restaurant when you BYO
courgette	green vegetable ('zucchini' to Americans)
cream cracker	white unsalted savoury biscuit
cream tea	cup of tea and a scone loaded with jam and cream
crisps	thin slices of fried potato bought in a packet, eaten cold; called 'chips' or 'potato chips' in the USA and Australia
crumpet	circular piece of doughy bread, toasted before eating, usually covered with butter
double cream	heavy or thick cream

dram	whisky measure
fish fingers	strips of fish pieces covered in breadcrumbs, usually bought frozen and cooked by frying or grilling
greasy spoon	cheap cafe (colloquial)
ice lolly	flavoured ice on a stick; called 'popsicle' in the USA, 'icy pole' in Australia
icing	thick, sweet and solid covering on a cake
jam	fruit conserve often spread on bread
jelly	sweet dessert of flavoured gelatine; called 'jello' in the US
joint	cut of meat used for roasting
kippers	salted and smoked fish, traditionally herring
pickle	food, usually vegetables (eg onions or beetroot), preserved in vinegar
Pimm's	popular English spirit mixed with lemonade, mint and fresh fruit
pint	beer (as in 'let me buy you a pint')
pop	fizzy drink
salad cream	creamy vinegary salad dressing, much sharper than mayonnaise
scrumpy	a type of strong dry cider
shandy	beer and lemonade mixed together in equal quantities
shepherd's pie	two-layered dish with a minced (ground) beef and onion mixture on the bottom and mashed potato on the top, cooked in an oven
shout	to buy a group of people drinks, usually reciprocated (colloquial)
single cream	light cream (to distinguish from double cream and clotted cream)
snug	a small room in a pub, usually just inside the door
squash	fruit-drink concentrate mixed with water
stout	dark, full-bodied beer made from malt; Guinness is the most famous variety
swede	large root vegetable; sometimes called 'yellow turnip' or 'rutabaga' in the USA
sweets	what Americans call 'candy' and Australians call 'lollies' or 'cakes'
treacle	dark treacle is molasses, but in England treacle often means golden syrup

Architecture in England

The history of English architecture spans more than three millenniums, from the mysterious stone circles of Stonehenge and Avebury to the glittering skyscrapers of modern London. The country's built heritage includes Roman baths and parish churches, mighty castles and magnificent cathedrals, humble cottages and grand stately homes, and exploring it all is one of the great joys of a visit to England.

Early Foundations

The oldest surviving structures in England are the grass-covered mounds of earth, called 'tumuli' or 'barrows', used as burial sites by England's prehistoric residents. These mounds – measuring anything from a rough semisphere just 2m high to much larger, elongated semiovoids 5m high and 10m long – are dotted across the countryside from Cornwall to Cumbria, and are especially common in chalk areas such as Salisbury Plain and the Wiltshire Downs in southern England.

Perhaps the most famous barrow – and certainly the largest and most mysterious – is Silbury Hill (p267), near Marlborough. Historians are not sure exactly why this huge conical mound was built – there's no evidence of it actually being used for burial. Theories suggest it was used at cultural ceremonies or as part of the worship of deities in the style of South American pyramids, but whatever its original purpose, it's still very impressive today, many centuries after it was built.

Even more impressive than giant tumuli are another legacy of the Neolithic era: menhirs (standing stones), especially well known when they're set out in rings. These include the iconic stone circle of Stonehenge (p261) and the even larger Avebury Stone Circle (p265), both in Wiltshire. Again, their original purpose is a mystery, providing fertile ground for hypothesis and speculation. The most recent theories suggest that Stonehenge may have been a place of pilgrimage for the sick, like modern-day Lourdes, though it was also used as a burial ground and a place of ancestor worship.

Bronze Age & Iron Age

Compared with the large stone circles of the Neolithic era, the architecture of the Bronze Age that we can see today is on a more domestic scale. Hut circles from this period can still be seen in several parts of England, most notably on Dartmoor.

By the time we reach the Iron Age, the early peoples of England were organising themselves into clans or tribes. Their legacy includes the forts they built to defend territory and protect themselves from rival tribes or other invaders. Most forts consisted of a large circular or oval ditch, with a steep mound of earth behind. A famous example is Maiden Castle (p247) in Dorset.

The construction of Stonehenge pushed the limits of technology in the Neolithic era. Some giant menhirs were brought from a great distance, and many were shaped slightly wider at the top to take account of perspective – a trick used by the Greeks many centuries later.

There are more than a thousand Iron Age hill forts in England. Impressive examples include: Danebury Ring, Hampshire; Barbury Castle, Wiltshire; Uffington Castle, Oxfordshire; Carl Wark, Derbyshire; and Cadbury Castle, Somerset.

Roman Baths (p311), Bath

The Roman Era

Roman remains are found in many English towns and cities, including Chester, Exeter and St Albans – as well as the lavish Roman spa and bathing complex in Bath. But England's largest and most impressive Roman relic is the 73-mile sweep of Hadrian's Wall (p632), built in the 2nd century AD as a defensive line stretching coast to coast across the country. Originally built to separate marauding Pictish warriors to the north of the wall (in modern Scotland) from the Empire's territories to the south, it later became as much a symbol of Roman power as a necessary defence mechanism.

Medieval Masterpieces

In the centuries following the Norman Conquest of 1066, the perfection of the mason's art saw an explosion of architecture in stone, inspired by the two most pressing concerns of the day: religion and defence. Early structures of timber and rubble were replaced with churches, abbeys and monasteries built in dressed stone. The round arches, squat towers and chevron decoration of the Norman or Romanesque style (11th to 12th centuries) slowly evolved into the tall pointed arches, ribbed vaults and soaring spires of the Gothic (13th to 16th centuries), a history that can often be seen all in the one church – construction often took a couple of hundred years to complete. Many cathedrals remain modern landmarks, such as Salisbury, Winchester, Canterbury and York.

Stone was also put to good use in the building of elaborate defensive structures. Castles range from the atmospheric ruins of Tintagel and Dunstanburgh, and the feudal keeps of Lancaster and Bamburgh, to the sturdy fortresses of Warwick and Windsor. And then there's the most impressive of them all: the Tower of London (p70), guarding the capital for more than 900 years.

England's Top Castles

Alnwick Castle

Bamburgh Castle

Berkeley Castle

Carlisle Castle

Corfe Castle

Ludlow Castle

Richmond Castle

Skipton Castle

Tintagel Castle

Tower of London

Warwick Castle

Windsor Castle

Stately Homes of England

The medieval period was tumultuous, but by around 1600 life became more settled, and the nobility started to have less need for their castles. While they were excellent for keeping out rivals or the common riff-raff, they were often too dark, cold and draughty to be comfortable. So many castles saw the home improvements of the day – the installation of larger windows, wider staircases and better drainage. Others were simply abandoned for a brand-new dwelling next door; an example of this is Hardwick Hall (p474) in Derbyshire.

Following the Civil War, the trend away from castles gathered pace, as through the 17th century the landed gentry developed a taste for fine 'country houses' designed by the most famous architects of the day. Many became the 'stately homes' that are a major feature of the English landscape, celebrated by Noël Coward's famous song, and a major attraction for visitors. Among the most extravagant are Holkham Hall (p394) in Norfolk, Chatsworth House (p485) in Derbyshire, and Blenheim Palace (p189) in Oxfordshire.

The great stately homes all display the proportion, symmetry and architectural harmony so in vogue during the 17th and 18th centuries, styles later reflected in the fashionable town houses of the Georgian era – most notably in the city of Bath, where the stunning Royal Crescent (p313) is the epitome of the genre.

England's Finest Stately Homes

Audley End House

Blickling Hall

Burghley House

Blenheim Palace

Castle Howard

Chastleton House

Chatsworth House

Leeds Castle

Snowshill Manor

Waddesdon Manor

ARCHITECTURE IN ENGLAND STATELY HOMES OF ENGLAND

Victoriana

The Victorian era was a time of great building. A style called Victorian-Gothic developed, echoing the towers and spires that were such a feature of the original Gothic cathedrals. The most famous example of this style is the Palace of Westminster (better known as the Houses of Parliament; p57) and Elizabeth Tower (home to Big Ben), in London. Other highlights include London's Natural History Museum and St Pancras train station.

Through the early 20th century, as England's cities grew in size and stature, the newly moneyed middle classes built streets and squares of smart town houses. Meanwhile, in other suburbs the first town planners oversaw the construction of endless terraces of red-brick two-up-two-down houses to accommodate the massive influx of workers required to fuel the country's factories – not especially scenic but perhaps the most enduring mark of all on the English architectural landscape today.

Postwar Pains & Pride

During WWII many of England's cities were damaged by bombing, and the rebuilding that followed showed scant regard for the overall aesthetic of the cities, or for the lives of the people who lived in them. The rows of terraces were swept away in favour of high-rise tower blocks, while the 'brutalist' architects of the 1950s and '60s employed the modern and efficient materials of steel and concrete, leaving legacies such as London's South Bank Centre.

HOUSE & HOME

It's not all about big houses. Alongside the stately homes, ordinary domestic architecture from the 16th century onwards can also still be seen in rural areas: black-and-white 'half-timbered' houses still characterise counties such as Worcestershire, while brick-and-flint cottages pepper Suffolk and Sussex, and hardy centuries-old farms built with slate or local gritstone are a feature of areas such as Derbyshire and the Lake District.

THE STIRLING PRIZE FOR ARCHITECTURE

The highlight of the year for aficionados of modern architecture is the announcement of the shortlist for the Stirling Prize, an annual award for excellence in architecture organised by the Royal Institute of British Architects (RIBA). Established in 1996, this prestigious award is for 'the building that has made the greatest contribution to the evolution of architecture in the past year'. Famous winners include the Millennium Bridge in Gateshead (2002), 30 St Mary Axe (better known as the Gherkin) in London (2004), the Scottish Parliament Building in Edinburgh (2005) and the Everyman Theatre in Liverpool (2014).

Perhaps this is why, on the whole, the English are conservative in their architectural tastes, and often resent ambitious or experimental designs, especially when they're applied to public buildings, or when form appears more important than function. But a familiar pattern often unfolds: after a few years of resentment, first comes a nickname, then grudging acceptance, and finally – once the locals have got used to it – comes pride and affection for the new building. The English just don't like to be rushed, that's all.

With this attitude in mind, over the last few decades, English architecture has started to redeem itself, and many big cities now have contemporary buildings their residents can be proud of and enjoy. Highlights in London's financial district include the bulging cone with the official address of 30 St Mary Axe (but widely known by its nickname, the Gherkin), and the former Millennium Dome (now rebranded as simply the O2), which has been transformed from a source of national embarrassment into one of the capital's leading live-music venues.

Twenty-First Century

Through the first decade of the 21st century, many areas of England placed a new importance on progressive, popular architecture as a part of wider regeneration. Top examples include Manchester's Imperial War Museum North (p551), The Deep (p539) aquarium in Hull, Cornwall's futuristic Eden Project (p349) and the Sage (p625) concert hall in Gateshead, near Newcastle.

From around 2010, development slowed and some plans were shelved, thanks to the global slowdown, but several significant projects continued, including the Turner Contemporary Gallery (p148) in Margate (opened 2011) and the futuristic Library of Birmingham (p401; 2013).

But England's largest and most high-profile architectural project of recent times was of course the Olympic Park (p99), the centrepiece of the 2012 Games, in the London suburb of Stratford. As well as the main Olympic Stadium, other arenas include the Velodrome and Aquatics Centre – all dramatic structures in their own right, using cutting-edge construction techniques. The Velodrome also won the construction industry's 2011 Better Public Buildings Award.

Meanwhile, in the centre of the capital, the London Bridge Tower – its tall and jagged shape means it was quickly nicknamed the Shard (p83) – was officially opened in July 2012; at 306m, it's one of Europe's tallest buildings. On the other side of the River Thames, two more giant skyscrapers were completed in 2014: 20 Fenchurch St (nickname: the Walkie-Talkie) and the Leadenhall Building (the Cheese-grater).

So London continues to grow upwards, and English architecture continues to push new boundaries of style and technology. The buildings may look a little different, but it's great to see the spirit of Stonehenge alive and well after all these years.

Glossary of English Architecture

bailey	outermost wall of a castle
bar	fortified gate (York, and some other northern cities)
barrel vault	semicircular arched roof
brass	memorial consisting of a brass plate set into the side or lid of a tomb, or into the floor of a church to indicate a burial place below
buttress	vertical support for a wall; see also flying buttress
campanile	free-standing belfry or bell tower
chancel	eastern end of the church, usually reserved for choir and clergy
choir	area in the church where the choir is seated
cloister	covered walkway linking the church with adjacent monastic buildings
close	buildings grouped around a cathedral
cob	mixture of mud and straw for building
corbel	stone or wooden projection from a wall supporting a beam or arch
flying buttress	supporting buttress in the form of one side of an open arch
lancet	pointed window in Early English style
lierne vault	vault containing many tertiary ribs
Martello tower	small, circular tower used for coastal defence
minster	church connected to a monastery
nave	main body of the church at the western end, where the congregation gather
oast house	building containing a kiln for drying hops
pargeting	decorative stucco plasterwork
pele	fortified house
precincts	see close
priory	religious house governed by a prior
quire	medieval term for choir
rood	archaic word for cross (in churches)
transepts	north–south projections from a church's nave, giving church a cruciform (cross-shaped plan)
undercroft	vaulted underground room or cellar
vault	roof with arched ribs, usually in a decorative pattern

The English Landscape

When it comes to landscapes, England is not a place of extremes; there are no Alps or Himalayas here, no Amazon or Sahara. But there's plenty to keep you enthralled. The country may be small, but even a relatively short journey takes you through a surprising mix of scenery. Seeing the change – subtle in some areas, dramatic in others – as you travel is one of this country's great attractions.

Landscape Online

www.wildaboutbrit-ain.co.uk

www.environment-agency.gov.uk

www.nationalparks.gov.uk

www.landscapes-forlife.org.uk

Beaches

England has a great many beaches – from tiny hidden coves in Cornwall to vast neon-lined strands such as Brighton or Blackpool. Other great beaches can be found in Devon, Somerset and along the south coast, in Suffolk, Norfolk, Lancashire, Yorkshire and Northumberland – each with their own distinct character. The best resort beaches earn the coveted international **Blue Flag** (www.blueflag.org) award, meaning sand and water are clean and unpolluted. Other parameters include the presence of life-guards, litter bins and recycling facilities – meaning some wild beaches may not earn the award, but are stunning nonetheless.

National Parks

In 1810, English poet William Wordsworth suggested that the wild land-scape of the Lake District in Cumbria should be 'a sort of national property, in which every man has a right'. More than a century later, the Lake District did indeed become a national park, along with Dartmoor, Exmoor, the New Forest, Norfolk and Suffolk Broads, Northumberland, the North York Moors, the Peak District, the South Downs and the Yorkshire Dales.

But the term 'national park' can cause confusion. First, in England the parks are not state owned: nearly all land is private, belonging to farm-ers, private estates and conservation organisations. Second, they are *not* areas of wilderness as in many other countries.

In England's national parks you'll see crop fields in lower areas and grazing sheep on the uplands, as well as roads, railways and villages, and even towns, quarries and factories in some parks. It's a reminder of the balance that is struck in this crowded country between protecting the natural environment and catering for the people who live in it.

Despite these apparent anomalies, England's national parks still con-tain mountains, hills, downs, moors, lakes, woods, river valleys and other areas of quiet countryside, all ideal for enjoying nature however you like to experience it.

Protected Areas

As well as national parks, other parts of the English countryside are des-ignated as Areas of Outstanding Natural Beauty (AONBs), the second tier of protected landscape after national parks. Some of the finest AONBs in England include the Chilterns, Cornwall, the Cotswolds, the Isles of Scilly, the North Pennines, the Northumberland Coast, the Suffolk Coast and the Wye Valley.

There are also Conservation Areas, Sites of Special Scientific Interest (SSSIs) and many other types of protected landscape that you can enjoy as you travel around.

Wildlife

For a small country, England has a diverse range of plants and animals. Many native species are hidden away, but there are some undoubted gems – from lowland woods carpeted in shimmering bluebells to stately herds of deer on the high moors. Having a closer look will enhance your trip enormously, especially if you have the time and inclination to enjoy some walking through the English landscape.

Animals

Farmland

In rural areas, rabbits are everywhere, but if you're hiking through the countryside be on the lookout for the much larger brown hares, an increasingly rare species. Males who battle for territory by boxing on their hind legs in early spring are, of course, as 'mad as a March hare'.

Common birds of farmland areas (and urban gardens) include the robin, with its instantly recognisable red breast and cheerful whistle; the

ENGLAND'S NATIONAL PARKS

NATIONAL PARK	FEATURES	ACTIVITIES	BEST TIME TO VISIT
Dartmoor	rolling hills, rocky outcrops, serene valleys; Iron Age relics; wild ponies, deer, peregrine falcons	walking, mountain biking, horse riding	May-Jun (wildflowers bloom)
Exmoor	sweeping moors, craggy sea cliffs; red deer, wild ponies, horned sheep	horse riding, walking	Sep (heather flowering)
Lake District	majestic fells, rugged mountains, shimmering lakes; literary heritage; ospreys, red squirrels, golden eagles	water sports, walking, mountaineering, rock climbing	Sep-Oct (summer crowds departed, autumn colours abound)
New Forest	woodlands, heath; wild ponies, otters, Dartford warbler, southern damselfly	walking, cycling, horse riding	Apr-Sep (lush vegetation)
Norfolk & Suffolk Broads	expansive shallow lakes, rivers, marshlands, water lilies; windmills; wildfowl, otters	walking, cycling, boating	Apr-May (birds most active)
North York Moors	heather-clad hills, deep-green valleys, isolated villages; merlins, curlews, golden plovers	walking, mountain biking	Aug-Sep (heather flowering)
Northumberland	wild rolling moors, heather, gorse; Hadrian's Wall; black grouse, red squirrels	walking, cycling, mountain biking, climbing	Apr-May (lambs) & Sep (heather flowering)
Peak District	high moors, tranquil dales, limestone caves; kestrels, badgers, grouse	walking, cycling, mountain biking, hang-gliding, climbing	Apr-May (even more lambs)
South Downs	rolling grassy chalky hills, chalky sea-cliffs, gorse, heather; Adonis blue butterfly	walking, mountain biking	Aug (heather flowering)
Yorkshire Dales	rugged hills, lush valleys, limestone pavements; red squirrels, hares, curlews, lapwings, buzzards	walking, cycling, mountain biking, climbing	Apr-May (visitors outnumbered by, you guessed it, lambs)

wren, whose loud trilling song belies its tiny size; and the yellowhammer, with a song that sounds like (if you use your imagination) 'a-little-bit-of-bread-and-no-cheese'. In open fields, the warbling cry of a skylark is another classic, but now threatened, sound of the English outdoors. You're more likely to see a pheasant, a large bird originally introduced from Russia to the nobility's shooting estates, but now considered naturalised.

Alongside rivers the once-rare otter is making a comeback. Elsewhere, the black-and-white striped badger is under threat from farmers who believe they transmit bovine tuberculosis to cattle, although conservationists say the case is far from proven. Also at the centre of controversy is the fox; this animal is widespread in the countryside and well adapted to a scavenging life in rural towns, and even city suburbs.

Woodland

In woodland areas, mammals include the small white-spotted fallow deer and the even smaller roe deer. Woodland is full of birds too, but you'll hear them more than see them. Listen out for willow warblers (which have a warbling song with a descending cadence), chiffchaffs (which make a repetitive 'chiff chaff' noise), and the rat-a-tat-tat of woodpeckers.

If you hear rustling among the fallen leaves it might be a hedgehog – a spiny-backed insect eater – but it's an increasingly rare sound these days; conservationists say they'll be extinct in Britain by 2025, thanks to farming insecticides, decreased habitat and their inability to safely cross roads.

Grey squirrels (introduced from North America) have proved very adaptable, to the extent that England's native red squirrels are severely endangered because the greys eat all the food.

Perhaps unexpectedly, England is home to herds of 'wild' ponies, notably in the New Forest, Exmoor and Dartmoor, but although these animals roam free they are privately owned and regularly managed. There's even a pocket of wild goats near Lynmouth in Devon, where they've apparently gambolled merrily for almost 1000 years.

Mountains & High Moors

On mountains and high moors the most visible mammal is the red deer. Males of the species grow their famous large antlers between April and July, and shed them again in February. Also on the high ground, well-known and easily recognised birds include the red grouse, which often hides in the heather until almost stepped on then flies away with a loud warning call, and the curlew, with its stately long legs and elegant curved bill. Look hard, and you may see beautifully camouflaged golden plovers, while the spectacular aerial displays of lapwings are impossible to miss.

Wildlife of Britain by George McGavin et al is subtitled 'the definitive visual guide'. Although too heavy to carry around during your travels, this beautiful photographic book is great for pretrip inspiration or posttrip memories.

WILDLIFE IN YOUR POCKET

Is it a rabbit or a hare? A gull or a tern? Buttercup or cowslip? If you need to know a bit more about England's plant and animal kingdoms the following field guides are ideal for entry-level naturalists:

➡ *Complete Guide to British Wildlife* by Paul Sterry is portable and highly recommended, covering mammals, birds, fish, plants, snakes, insects and even fungi, with brief descriptions and excellent photos.

➡ If feathered friends are enough, the *Complete Guide to British Birds* by Paul Sterry has clear photos and descriptions, plus when and where each species may be seen.

➡ *Wildlife of the North Atlantic* by world-famous film-maker Tony Soper beautifully covers the animals seen from beach, boat and clifftop in the British Isles and beyond.

➡ The Collins GEM series includes handy little books on wildlife topics such as *Birds, Trees, Fish* and *Wild Flowers*.

BLACKCATPHOTOS / LONELY PLANET IMAGES ©

Grey seals

Coastal Areas

By the sea, two seal species frequent English coasts: the larger grey seal, which is more often seen, and the misnamed common seal. In areas such as Norfolk and Northumberland, boat trips to see seal colonies are a popular attraction. Dolphins, porpoises, minke whales and basking sharks can also be seen off the western coasts, especially from about May to September when viewing conditions are better – although you may need to go with someone who knows where to look. Boat trips are available from many coastal holiday resorts.

England's estuaries and mudflats are feeding grounds for numerous migrant wading birds; easily spotted are black-and-white oystercatchers with their long red bills, while flocks of ringed plovers skitter along the sand. On the coastal cliffs in early summer, particularly in Cornwall and Yorkshire, countless thousands of guillemots, razorbills, kittiwakes and other breeding seabirds fight for space on crowded rock ledges, and the air is thick with their sound. Even if you're not into birdwatching, this is one of England's finest wildlife spectacles.

Plants

In the rolling hills of southern England and the limestone areas further north (such as the Peak District and Yorkshire Dales), the best places to see wildflowers are the fields that evade large-scale farming – many erupt with great profusions of cowslips and primroses in April and May.

For woodland flowers, the best time is also April and May, before the leaf canopy is fully developed so sunlight can reach plants such as bluebells – a beautiful and rare species. Another classic English plant is gorse: you can't miss this spiky bush in heath areas like the New Forest. Its vivid yellow flowers show year-round and have a distinctive, coconut-like scent.

In contrast, the blooming season for heather is quite short, but no less dramatic; through August and September areas such as the North York Moors and Dartmoor are covered in a riot of purple.

Perhaps surprisingly, England's most wooded county is Surrey, despite its proximity to London. The soil is too poor for agriculture, so while woodland areas elsewhere in England were cleared, Surrey's trees got a stay of execution.

'THE UNSPEAKABLE IN PURSUIT OF THE INEDIBLE'

The red fox, a doglike animal with a characteristic bushy tail and an anthropomorphic reputation for cunning, is a controversial creature in England. The controversy focuses on hunting, and specifically fox hunting with hounds. Supporters say it's been a traditional English rural activity for centuries, and helps control the fox population; opponents say it's a savage blood sport that has virtually no impact on overall numbers. Distaste for this type of hunting is not a new phenomenon; the activity was famously described as 'the unspeakable in pursuit of the inedible' by Oscar Wilde more than a century ago. Today, observers say the hunting debate has come to represent much bigger issues: town versus country, or the relative limits of privilege, state control and individual freedom. Either way, fox hunting with dogs was banned in 2005 by law. And opinion is still very strongly divided.

Environmental Issues

With England's long history of human occupation, it's not surprising that the country's appearance is almost totally the result of human interaction with the environment. Since the earliest times, trees have been chopped down and fields created for crops or animals, but the biggest changes to rural areas came after WWII in the late 1940s, continuing into the '50s and '60s, when a drive to be self-reliant in food meant new – intensive and large-scale – farming methods. The result was dramatic: an ancient patchwork of small meadows became a landscape of vast prairie-like fields, as walls were demolished, woodlands felled, ponds filled, wetlands drained and, most notably, hedgerows ripped out.

In most cases the hedgerows were lines of dense bushes, shrubs and trees forming a network that stretched across the countryside, protecting fields from erosion, supporting a varied range of flowers, and providing shelter for numerous insects, birds and small mammals. But in the rush to improve farm yields, thousands of miles of hedgerows were destroyed in the postwar decades, and between the mid-1980s and the early 2000s another 25% disappeared.

Hedgerows have come to symbolise many other environmental issues in rural areas, and in recent years the destruction has abated, partly because farmers recognise their anti-erosion qualities, and partly because they're encouraged – with financial incentives from UK or European agencies – to 'set aside' such areas as wildlife havens.

In addition to hedgerow clearance, other farming techniques remain hot environmental issues. Studies have shown that the use of pesticides and intensive irrigation results in rivers being poisoned or simply running dry. Meanwhile, monocropping means the fields have one type of grass and not another plant to be seen. These 'green deserts' support no insects, so in turn wild-bird populations have plummeted. This picture is not a case of wizened old peasants recalling the idyllic days of their forbears; you only have to be aged about 40 in England to remember a countryside where birds such as skylarks or lapwings were visibly much more numerous.

But all is not lost. In the face of apparently overwhelming odds, England still boasts great biodiversity, and some of the best wildlife habitats are protected (to a greater or lesser extent) by the creation of national parks and similar areas, or private reserves owned by conservation campaign groups such as the **Wildlife Trusts** (www.wildlifetrusts.org), **National Trust** (www.nationaltrust.org.uk), **Woodland Trust** (www.woodlandtrust.org.uk) and the **Royal Society for the Protection of Birds** (www.rspb.org.uk). Many of these areas are open to the public – ideal spots for walking, birdwatching or simply enjoying the peace and beauty of the countryside – and well worth a visit as you travel around.

Although the hedgerows around fields have been reduced, new 'hedgerows' have appeared in the landscape: the long strips of grass and bushes alongside motorways and major roads. These areas support thousands of insect species plus mice, shrews and other small mammals, so kestrels are often seen hovering nearby, unconcerned by traffic.

The Arts

England's contributions to the worlds of literature, drama, cinema and pop are celebrated around the world, thanks in no small part to the global dominance of the English language. As you travel around England today you'll see landscapes made famous as movie sets and literary locations, or mentioned in songs, so here we've picked some major milestones and focused on works with a connection to real places where you can experience something of your favourite artist.

English Literature

The roots of England's poetic and storytelling heritage stretch back to Nordic sagas and early English epics such as *Beowulf*, but modern English literature starts around 1387 (yes, that is 'modern' in history-soaked England) when Geoffrey Chaucer produced *The Canterbury Tales*. This mammoth poem is a collection of fables, stories and morality tales using travelling pilgrims – the Knight, the Wife of Bath and so on – as a narrative hook.

For extra insight, the *Oxford Guide to Literary Britain and Ireland*, edited by Daniel Hahn and Nicholas Robins, gives details of towns, villages and countryside immortalised by writers, from Geoffrey Chaucer's Canterbury to Jane Austen's Bath.

William Shakespeare

The next big name in English literature came in the 16th century, when William Shakespeare entered the scene. Best known for his plays, he was also a remarkably prolific and influential poet. 'Shall I compare thee to a summer's day?' is just one of his famous lines still widely quoted today.

The Romantic Era

During the late 18th and early 19th centuries, a new generation of writers drew inspiration from human imagination and the natural world. Leading lights of the movement were William Blake, John Keats, Percy Bysshe Shelley, Lord Byron and Samuel Taylor Coleridge, and perhaps the best-known English poet of all, William Wordsworth. His famous line from 'Daffodils' – 'I wandered lonely as a cloud' – was inspired by a waterside walk in the Lake District in northern England.

JANE AUSTEN & THE BRONTËS

The beginning of the 19th century saw the emergence of some of English literature's best-known and beloved writers: Jane Austen and the Brontë sisters.

Austen's fame stems from her exquisite observations of love, friendship, intrigues and passions boiling beneath the strait-laced surface of middle-class social convention, and from the endless stream of movies and TV costume dramas based on her works, such as *Pride and Prejudice* and *Sense and Sensibility*. For visitors today, the location most associated with Jane Austen is the city of Bath – a beautiful place even without the literary link. As one of her heroines said, 'who can ever be tired of Bath?'.

Of the Brontë sisters' prodigious output, Emily Brontë's *Wuthering Heights* is the best known – an epic tale of obsession and revenge, where the dark and moody landscape plays a role as great as any human character. Charlotte Brontë's *Jane Eyre* and Anne Brontë's *The Tenant of Wildfell Hall* are classics of passion and mystery. Fans still flock to their former home in the Yorkshire town of Haworth, perched on the edge of the wild Pennine moors that inspired so many of their books.

Victoriana

As industrialisation expanded during the reign of Queen Victoria, so key novels of the time explored social themes. Charles Dickens tackled many prevailing issues of his day: in *Oliver Twist*, he captures the lives of young pickpockets in the London slums; *Bleak House* is a critique of the English legal system; and *Hard Times* criticises the excesses of capitalism. At around the same time, but choosing a rural setting, George Eliot (the pen name of Mary Ann Evans) wrote *The Mill on the Floss* – where the central character struggles against society's expectations.

Thomas Hardy's classic *Tess of the D'Urbervilles* deals with the peasantry's decline, and *The Trumpet Major* paints a picture of idyllic English country life interrupted by war and encroaching modernity. Many of Hardy's works are based in the fictionalised county of Wessex, largely based on today's Dorset and surrounding counties, where towns such as Dorchester are popular stops on tourist itineraries.

The 20th Century

The end of WWI and the ensuing social disruption fed into the modernist movement, with DH Lawrence perhaps its finest exponent; *Sons and Lovers* follows the lives and loves of generations in the English Midlands as the country changes from rural idyll to an increasingly industrial landscape, while his controversial exploration of sexuality in *Lady Chatterley's Lover* was originally banned as 'obscene'. Other highlights of this period included Daphne du Maurier's romantic suspense novel *Rebecca*, set on the Cornish coast, and Evelyn Waugh's *Brideshead Revisited*, an exploration of moral and social disintegration among the English aristocracy.

The 1970s saw the arrival of two novelists who became prolific for the remainder of the century and beyond. Martin Amis published *The Rachel Papers* then went on to produce a string of novels where common themes included the absurdity and unappealing nature of modern life, such as *London Fields* (1989) and *Lionel Asbo: State of England* (2012). Meanwhile, Ian McEwan debuted with *The Cement Garden,* and earned critical acclaim for finely observed studies of the English character such as *The Child in Time* (1987), *Atonement* (2001) and *On Chesil Beach* (2007).

Helen Fielding's book Bridget Jones's Diary, originally a series of newspaper articles, is a fond look at the heartache of a modern single woman's blundering search for love, and the epitome of the late-1990s 'chick-lit' genre. It's also (very loosely) based on Pride and Prejudice by Jane Austen.

New Millennium

As the 20th century came to a close, the nation's multicultural landscape proved a rich inspiration for contemporary novelists: Hanif Kureishi sowed the seeds with his groundbreaking *The Buddha of Suburbia*, about a group of Anglo-Asians in suburban London; Zadie Smith published her acclaimed debut *White Teeth* in 2000, followed by a string of bestsellers including *The Autograph Man* and 2012's *NW;* Andrea Levy published *Small Island*, about a Jamaican couple settled in postwar London; and Monica Ali's *Brick Lane* was shortlisted for the high-profile Man Booker Prize in 2003.

Other contemporary writers include Will Self, known for his surreal, satirical novels including *The Book of Dave;* and Nick Hornby, best known for novels like *Fever Pitch,* a study of the insecurities of English blokishness. Others are Julian Barnes, whose books include *England, England,* a darkly ironic study of nationalism and tourism among other themes, and *The Sense of An Ending,* winner of the 2011 Man Booker Prize; and Hilary Mantel, author of many novels on an astoundingly wide range of subjects, and winner of the Man Booker Prize twice, first in 2009 for historical blockbuster *Wolf Hall* (about Henry VIII and his ruthless advisor Thomas Cromwell), and then in 2012 for its sequel *Bring Up the Bodies* (at the time of research, Mantel was writing the third and final instalment, *The Mirror and the Light*).

For other worlds and other-worldly humour, try two of England's funniest – and most successful – writers: Douglas Adams (The Hitchhiker's Guide to the Galaxy and several sequels) and Terry Pratchett (the Discworld series).

England's greatest literary phenomenon of the 21st century is JK Rowling's *Harry Potter* books, a series of other-worldly adventures that have entertained millions of children (and many grown-ups too) since the first book was published in 1996. The magical tales are the latest in a long line of British children's classics enjoyed by adults, stretching back to the works of Lewis Carroll *(Alice's Adventures in Wonderland),* E Nesbit *(The Railway Children),* AA Milne *(Winnie-the-Pooh)* and CS Lewis *(The Chronicles of Narnia).*

Cinema

English cinema has a long history, with many early directors cutting their teeth in the silent-film industry. Perhaps the best known of these was Alfred Hitchcock, who directed *Blackmail,* one of the first English 'talkies' in 1929, and who went on to direct a string of films during the 1930s before emigrating to Hollywood in the early 1940s.

War & Postwar

During WWII, films such as *In Which We Serve* (1942) and *We Dive at Dawn* (1943) were designed to raise public morale, while a young director called David Lean produced *Brief Encounter* (1945), the classic tale of buttoned-up English passion, before graduating to Hollywood epics including *Lawrence of Arabia* and *Doctor Zhivago.*

Following the hardships of war, British audiences were in the mood for escape and entertainment. During the late 1940s and early '50s, the domestic film industry specialised in eccentric British comedies epitomised by the output of Ealing Studios: notable titles include *Passport to Pimlico* (1949), *Kind Hearts and Coronets* (1949) and *The Titfield Thunderbolt* (1953).

Swinging Sixties

In the late 1950s 'British New Wave' and 'Free Cinema' explored the gritty realities of British life in semidocumentary style, with directors Lindsay Anderson and Tony Richardson crystallising the movement in films such as *This Sporting Life* (1961) and *A Taste of Honey* (1961). At the other end of the spectrum were the *Carry On* films, the cinematic equivalent of the smutty seaside postcard, packed with bawdy gags and double entendres. The 1960s also saw the birth of another classic English genre: the James Bond films, starring Sean Connery (who is actually Scottish).

Brit Flicks

The 1970s was a tough decade for the British film industry, but the 1980s saw a recovery, thanks partly to David Puttnam's Oscar success with *Chariots of Fire* (1981), and the newly established Channel Four investing in edgy films such as *My Beautiful Laundrette* (1985).

> *The Ladykillers* (1955) is a classic Ealing comedy about a band of hapless bank robbers holed up in a London guesthouse, and features Alec Guinness sporting the most outrageous set of false teeth ever committed to celluloid.

> The British Film Institute (BFI; www.bfi.org.uk) is dedicated to promoting film and cinema in Britain, and publishes the monthly academic journal *Sight & Sound.*

A GRAND SUCCESS

One of the great success stories of English TV and cinema has been Bristol-based animator Nick Park and the production company Aardman Animations, best known for the award-winning man-and-dog duo Wallace and Gromit. This lovable pair first appeared in Park's graduation film, *A Grand Day Out* (1989), and went on to star in *The Wrong Trousers* (1993), *A Close Shave* (1995) and their full-length feature debut, *The Curse of the Were-Rabbit* (2005). Known for their intricate plots, film homages and amazingly realistic animation, the Wallace and Gromit films scooped Nick Park four Oscars. Other Aardman features include *Chicken Run* (2000), *Flushed Away* (2006) and *The Pirates! – In an Adventure with Scientists* (2012).

Another minor renaissance occurred in the 1990s, ushered in by the massively successful *Four Weddings and a Funeral* (1994), introducing Hugh Grant in his trademark role as a floppy-haired, self-deprecating Englishman, a character type he reprised in subsequent hits, including *Notting Hill*, *About a Boy* and *Love Actually*.

The 'Brit Flick' genre – characterised by themes such as irony, social realism and humour in the face of adversity – went on to include: *Brassed Off* (1996), about a struggling colliery band; *The Full Monty* (1997), following a troupe of laid-off steel workers turned male strippers; and *Billy Elliot* (2000), the story of an aspiring young ballet dancer striving to escape the slag heaps and boarded-up factories of the industrial north.

Meanwhile, films such as *East Is East* (1999) and *Bend it Like Beckham* (2002) explored the tensions of modern multicultural Britain, while veteran director Mike Leigh, known for his heavily improvised style, found success with *Life Is Sweet* (1991), *Naked* (1993) and the Palme d'Or–winning *Secrets and Lies* (1996).

The UK's biggest film magazine is *Empire* (www.empireonline.com). For less mainstream opinion check out *Little White Lies* (www.littlewhitelies.co.uk).

Twenty-First-Century Box

In the early part of the 21st century, literary adaptations have continued to provide the richest seam of success in the English film industry, including 2012's *Anna Karenina*, directed by Joe Wright and staring Keira Knightley, and of course the blockbuster *Harry Potter* franchise. Biopics are also a perennial favourite: recent big-screen subjects include Elizabeth I (*Elizabeth: The Golden Age,* 2007), Margaret Thatcher (*The Iron Lady,* 2011) and the 19th-century artist JMW Turner (*Mr Turner,* 2014).

Meanwhile the oldest of English film franchises trundles on: a tough, toned 21st-century James Bond appeared in 2006 courtesy of Daniel Craig and the blockbuster *Casino Royale* (2006), followed by *Quantum of Solace* (2008), *Skyfall* (2012) and *Spectre* (2015).

Pop & Rock Music

England has been putting the world through its musical paces ever since some mop-haired lads from Liverpool created The Beatles. And while Elvis may have invented rock 'n' roll, it was the Fab Four that transformed it into a global phenomenon, backed by the other bands of the 1960s 'British Invasion' – The Rolling Stones, The Who, Cream and The Kinks.

ROCK 'N' ROLL LOCATIONS...

Fans buy the single, then the T-shirt. But true fans visit the location featured on the album cover. Here are a few favourites:

➡ Abbey Rd, St John's Wood, London – *Abbey Road,* The Beatles

➡ Battersea Power Station, London – *Animals,* Pink Floyd (the inflatable pig has gone)

➡ Berwick St, Soho, London – *(What's the Story) Morning Glory,* Oasis

➡ Big Ben plus a corner of plinth under Boudica's statue, London – *My Generation* (US version), The Who

➡ Durdle Door, Dorset – *North Atlantic Drift,* Ocean Colour Scene

➡ Salford Boys Club, Manchester – *The Queen is Dead,* The Smiths

➡ Thor's Cave, Manifold Valley, near Ashbourne, Peak District National Park – *A Storm in Heaven,* The Verve

➡ Yes Tor, Dartmoor, Devon – *Tomato,* Yes

Glam to Punk

Glam rock arrived in the 1970s, fronted by artists such as chameleon-like David Bowie and the anthemic Queen, while Led Zeppelin laid down the blueprint for heavy metal, and the psychedelia of the previous decade morphed into the prog rock of Pink Floyd and Yes.

At the end of the decade, it was all swept aside as punk exploded onto the scene, most famously with the Sex Pistols, ably assisted by The Clash, The Damned, the Buzzcocks and The Stranglers. Then punk begat New Wave, with acts including The Jam and Elvis Costello blending spiky tunes and sharp lyrics into a more radio-friendly sound.

The '80s

The conspicuous consumption of the early 1980s influenced the era's pop scene. Big hair and shoulder pads became the uniform of the day, with big names including Wham! (a boyish duo headed by an up-and-coming popster called George Michael) and New Romantic bands such as Spandau Ballet and Duran Duran. Away from the glitz, fans enjoyed the doom-laden lyrics of The Cure, the heavy metal of Iron Maiden and Black Sabbath, and the 'miserabilism' of The Smiths.

Indie & Britpop

The 1990s saw the rise of ecstasy-fuelled rave culture, centred on famous clubs like Manchester's Haçienda and London's Ministry of Sound. Manchester was also a focus for the burgeoning British 'indie' scene, driven by guitar-based bands such The Stone Roses, James, Happy Mondays and Oasis. Then indie morphed into Britpop, with Oasis, Pulp, Supergrass and Blur, whose distinctively British music chimed with the country's reborn sense of optimism after the landslide election of New Labour in 1997.

New Millennium Sounds

The first decade of the new millennium saw no let-up in the music scene's continual shifting and reinventing. Jazz, soul, R&B and hip hop fused into a new 'urban' sound epitomised by artists like Dizzee Rascal, Tinie Tempah and Plan B. Dance acts like Calvin Harris and Disclosure enjoyed major international success. Meanwhile, singer-songwriters – such as Katie Melua, Ed Sheeran and the all-conquering Adele - have made a comeback, and the spirit of British punk and indie stays alive thanks to the likes of Arctic Monkeys, Florence & the Machine, Snow Patrol, Coldplay, Muse, Kasabian, Radiohead and The Horrors.

But the biggest commercial success of all were boy-band One Direction: their first three albums debuted at number one on the US charts, and in 2013 they released the year's biggest-selling British album and were named the top global act.

Movies on the English music scene include: *Backbeat* (1994), about The Beatles' early days; *Sid & Nancy* (1986), Sex Pistols' bassist and girlfriend; *Quadrophenia* (1979), mods and rockers; *Velvet Goldmine* (1998), glam rock; *24 Hour Party People* (2002), Manchester scene; and *Nowhere Boy* (2009), John Lennon pre-Beatles.

Painting & Sculpture

For many centuries, continental Europe – especially the Netherlands, Spain, France and Italy – set the artistic agenda. The first artist with a truly British style and sensibility was arguably William Hogarth, whose riotous canvases exposed the vice and corruption of 18th-century London. His most celebrated work is *A Rake's Progress,* which kick-started a long tradition of British caricatures that can be traced right through to the work of modern-day cartoonists such as Gerald Scarfe and Steve Bell. You can see it at Sir John Soane's Museum in London.

Portraits

While Hogarth was busy satirising society, other artists were hard at work showing it in its best light. The leading figures of 18th-century English portraiture were Sir Joshua Reynolds, Thomas Gainsborough

ANISH KAPOOR

The sculptor Anish Kapoor has been working in London since the 1970s. He is best known for his large outdoor installations, which often feature curved shapes and reflective materials, such as highly polished steel. His recent works include a major new installation in London, called *ArcelorMittal Orbit,* to celebrate the 2012 Olympic Games. At over 110m high, this is the largest piece of public art in Britain.

and George Romney, while George Stubbs is best known for his intricate studies of animals (particularly horses). Most of these artists are represented at Tate Britain or the National Gallery in London.

Landscape & Fables

In the 19th century leading painters favoured the English landscape. John Constable's best-known works include *Salisbury Cathedral* and *The Hay Wain,* depicting a mill in Suffolk (National Gallery), while JMW Turner was fascinated by the effects of light and colour on English scenes, with his works becoming almost entirely abstract by the 1840s.

In contrast, the Pre-Raphaelite painters of the late 19th century preferred a figurative style reflecting the Victorian taste for English fables and fairy tales. Key members of the movement included Dante Gabriel Rossetti, John Everett Millais and William Holman Hunt, all represented at London's Tate Britain or Victoria & Albert Museum.

Stones & Sticks

Some of Henry Moore's work can be seen at the Yorkshire Sculpture Park. Barbara Hepworth is celebrated at the eponymous gallery in Wakefield, and is also associated with St Ives, Cornwall.

In the tumultuous 20th century, English art became increasingly experimental. Francis Bacon placed Freudian psychoanalysis on the canvas in his portraits, while pioneering sculptors such as Henry Moore and Barbara Hepworth experimented with natural forms in stone and new materials. At about the same time, the painter LS Lowry was setting his 'matchstick men' among the smokestacks of northern England, and is today remembered by the major art centre that bears his name in Manchester.

Pop Art

The mid-1950s and early '60s saw an explosion of English 'pop art', as artists plundered popular culture for inspiration. Leaders of this new movement included David Hockney. His bold colours and simple lines were ground-breaking at the time, and are still used to great effect half a century later. A contemporary, Peter Blake, designed the cut-up collage cover for The Beatles' landmark album *Sgt Pepper's Lonely Hearts Club Band.* The '60s also saw the rise of sculptor Anthony Caro; creating large abstract works in steel and bronze, he was one of England's most influential sculptors.

Britart & Beyond

Thanks partly to the support (and money) of advertising tycoon Charles Saatchi, a new wave of British artists came to the fore in the 1990s. The movement was dubbed, inevitably, 'Britart'; its leading members included Damien Hirst, famous (or infamous) initially for works involving pickled sharks, semidissected human figures and more recently for a diamond-encrusted skull entitled *For the Love of God.*

A contemporary is Tracey Emin. Once considered an *enfant terrible*, she incurred the wrath of the tabloids for works such as *My Bed* (a messed-up bedroom scene which sold for £2.2 million in 2014), but is now a respected figure and patron of the new Turner Gallery in Margate, named for the famous English artist JMW Turner.

JMW Turner also gives his name to the Turner Prize, a high-profile and frequently controversial annual award for British visual artists. As well as Hirst, other winners have included Martin Creed (his work was a room with lights going on and off), Mark Wallinger (a collection of anti-war objects), Simon Starling (a shed converted to a boat and back again), Rachel Whiteread (a plaster cast of a house) and Antony Gormley (best known in England for his gigantic *Angel of the North*).

Theatre

English theatre can trace its roots back to medieval morality plays, court jesters and travelling storytellers, and possibly even to dramas during Roman times in amphitheatres – a few of which still remain, such as at Chester and Cirencester. But most scholars agree that the key milestone in the story is the opening of England's first theatre – called simply The Theatre – in London in 1576. A few years later, the Rose and the Globe Theatres appeared, and the stage was set for the entrance of England's best-known playwright.

William Shakespeare

For most visitors to England (and for most locals) English drama means just one name: William Shakespeare. Born in 1564, in the Midlands town of Stratford-upon-Avon, Shakespeare made his mark in London between around 1590 and 1610, where most of his plays were performed at the Globe Theatre. His brilliant plots and spectacular use of language, plus the sheer size of his canon of work (including classics such as *Hamlet, Romeo and Juliet, Henry V* and *A Midsummer Night's Dream*), have turned him into a national – and international – icon, so that today, almost 400 years after shuffling off his mortal coil, The Bard's plays still pull in big crowds.

You can enjoy Shakespeare plays at the rebuilt Globe Theatre in London or at the Royal Shakespeare Company's own theatre in Stratford-upon-Avon.

English Theatre Today

However you budget your time and money during your visit to England, make sure that you see some English theatre as part of your travels. It easily lives up to its reputation as the finest in the world, especially in London, while other big cities around the country boast their own top-class venues, such as the Birmingham Repertory Theatre, the Bristol Old Vic, Chichester Festival Theatre and the Nottingham Playhouse.

Many accomplished British actors, including Judi Dench, Ralph Fiennes, Brenda Blethyn, Toby Stephens and Simon Callow juggle high-paying Hollywood roles with appearances on the British stage, while over the last decade or so several American stars have taken hefty pay cuts to tread the London boards, including Glenn Close, Kevin Spacey, Gwyneth Paltrow, Gillian Anderson, Christian Slater and Danny DeVito.

Other options in London include the Donmar Warehouse and Royal Court Theatre, best known for new and experimental works. For big names, most people head for the West End, where famous spots include the Shaftesbury, Adelphi and Theatre Royal at Drury Lane. These venues are mostly the preserve of classic plays, including *The Mousetrap,* the legendary whodunit and world's longest-running play, showing continuously since 1952.

West End Musicals

As well as drama, London's West End means big musicals, with a long history of crowd-pullers such as *Cats, The Wizard of Oz, Les Misérables, Sweeney Todd, The Phantom of the Opera* and *The Lion King,* with many of today's shows raiding the pop world for material, such as *We Will Rock You,* inspired by the music of Queen, and Abba-based *Mamma Mia!*

Sporting England

If you want a short cut into the heart of British culture, then watch the British at play. They're passionate about their sport – as participants or spectators. Every weekend thousands of people turn out to cheer their favourite team, and sporting highlights such as Wimbledon keep the entire nation enthralled.

Football (Soccer)

For the dates and details of major football and cricket matches, horse racing and other sporting fixtures across the country, a great place to start is the sports pages of www.britevents.com.

The English Premier League (www.premierleague.com) has some of the finest teams in the world, dominated in recent years by four top teams – Arsenal, Liverpool, Chelsea and Manchester United – joined in 2012 by a fifth big player in the shape of Manchester City. Down in quality from the Premiership, 72 other teams play in the English divisions called the Championship, League One and League Two.

The football season is the same for all divisions (August to May), so seeing a match can easily be tied into most visitors' itineraries, but tickets for the biggest games are like gold dust – your chances of bagging one are low unless you're a club member, or know someone who is. You're better off buying a ticket to see the less fashionable teams – they're cheaper and more easily available. You can often buy tickets on the spot, or at online agencies like www.ticketmaster.co.uk and www.myticketmarket.com.

Cricket

Along with Big Ben, The Beatles and a nice cup of tea, cricket is quintessentially English. Dating from the 18th century (although its roots are much older) the sport spread throughout the Commonwealth during Britain's colonial era. Australia, the Caribbean and the Indian subcontinent took to the game with gusto, and today the former colonies delight in giving the old country a good spanking on the cricket pitch.

While many English people follow cricket like a religion, to the uninitiated it can be an impenetrable enigma. Spread over one-day games or five-day 'test matches', progress seems so *slow,* and dominated by arcane terminology like 'innings', 'cover drives', 'googlies', 'outswingers', 'leg-byes'

THE SWEET FA CUP

The Football Association held its first interclub knockout tournament in 1871: 15 clubs took part, playing for a nice piece of silverware called the FA Cup – then worth about £20.

Nowadays, around 600 clubs compete for this legendary and priceless trophy. It differs from many other competitions in that every team – from the lowest-ranking part-timers to the stars of the Premier League – is in with a chance. The preliminary rounds begin in August, and the Cup Final is held in May at the iconic Wembley Stadium in London.

Manchester United and Arsenal have the most FA Cups, but public attention – and affection – is invariably focused on the 'giant-killers': minor clubs that claw their way up through the rounds, unexpectedly beating higher-ranking competitors. One of the best-known giant-killing events occurred in 1992, when Wrexham, then ranked 24th in Division 3, famously beat league champions Arsenal in the third round.

THE ASHES

The historic test-cricket series between England and Australia known as the Ashes has been played every other year since 1882 (bar a few interruptions during the World Wars). It is played alternately in England and Australia with each of the five matches in the series held at a different cricket ground, always in the summer in the host location.

The contest's name dates back to the landmark test match of 1882, won (for the very first time) by the Australians. Defeat of the mother country by the colonial upstarts was a source of profound national shock: a mock obituary in the *Sporting Times* lamented the death of English cricket and referred to the sport's ashes being taken to Australia.

Later the name was given to a terracotta urn presented the following year to the English captain Ivo Bligh (later Lord Darnley), purportedly containing the cremated ashes of a stump or bail used in this landmark match. Since 1953 this hallowed relic has resided at the Marylebone Cricket Club (MCC) Museum at Lord's. Despite the vast importance given to winning the series, the urn itself is a diminutive 6in high (150mm).

The recent history of the Ashes is not without drama. In the 2010–11 series England thrashed Australia, winning on Australian turf for the first time since the 1986–87 series. Then in 2013 Australia thrashed England 5-0, repeating the humiliating clean sweep they had inflicted in 2006–07.

and 'silly-mid-off'. Nonetheless, at least one cricket match should be a feature of your travels around England. If you're patient and learn the intricacies, you could find cricket as absorbing as it is for all the Brits who remain glued to their radio or computer all summer long, 'just to see how England's getting on'.

Causing ructions is Twenty20 cricket, a new format which limits the time each team has to play, putting the emphasis on fast, big-batting scores. Traditionalists see it changing the character of the game, though there's no doubting its popularity – most Twenty20 matches sell out.

One-day games and international tests are played at grounds including Lord's in London, Edgbaston in Birmingham and Headingley in Leeds. Tickets cost from £30 to well over £200. The County Championship pits the best teams from around the country against each other; tickets cost £5 to £25, and only the most crucial games tend to sell out. Details are on the website of the English Cricket Board (www.ecb.co.uk).

The easiest way to watch cricket – and often the most enjoyable – is by stumbling across a local game on a village green as you travel around the country. There's no charge for spectators, and no one will mind if you nip into the pub during a quiet period.

Horse Racing

The tradition of horse racing in Britain stretches back centuries, and there's a 'meeting' somewhere pretty much every day. For all but the major events you should be able to get a ticket on the day, or buy in advance from the British Horse Racing Authority's website (www.lovetheraces.com), which also has lots of information about social events such as music festivals that coincide with the races.

The top event in the calendar is Royal Ascot (www.ascot.co.uk) at Ascot Racecourse in mid-June, where the rich and famous come to see and be seen, and the fashion is almost as important as the nags. Even the queen turns up to put a fiver each way on Lucky Boy in the 3.15.

Other highlights include the Grand National steeplechase at Aintree (www.aintree.co.uk) in early April; and the Derby at Epsom (www.epsomdowns.co.uk) on the first Saturday in June. The latter is especially popular with the masses so, unlike at Ascot, you won't see many morning suits or outrageous hats.

Queen Elizabeth II is a great horse-racing fan, and the royal stables have produced many winners. The 2005 Grand National famously clashed with the marriage of Prince Charles; rumours abound that the start was delayed so the Queen could attend the nuptials *and* see the race.

England's enthralling sports have equally fascinating histories. No one can say when football was invented, but the word 'soccer' (the favoured term in countries where 'football' means another game) is reputedly derived from 'sock'. In medieval times this was a tough leather foot-cover worn by peasants – ideal for kicking around a pig's bladder in the park on a Saturday afternoon.

In contrast, rugby can trace its roots to a football match in 1823 at Rugby School, in Warwickshire. A player called William Webb Ellis, frustrated at the limitations of mere kicking, reputedly picked up the ball and ran with it towards the goal. True to the sense of English fair play, rather than Ellis being dismissed from the game, a whole new sport was developed around his tactic, and the Rugby Football Union was formally inaugurated in 1871. The Rugby World Cup is named the Webb Ellis Trophy after this enterprising young tearaway.

Rugby

A wit once said that football was a gentlemen's game played by hooligans, while rugby was a hooligans' game played by gentlemen. That may be true, but rugby is very popular, especially since England became world champions in 2003 (and nearly did it again in 2007). It's worth catching a game for the display of skill (OK, and brawn), and the fun atmosphere in the grounds. Tickets for games cost around £15 to £50 depending on the club's status and fortunes.

A highlight of the international rugby calendar is the annual Six Nations Championship (www.rbs6nations.com), in which England battles against teams from Wales, Scotland, Ireland, France and Italy.

There are two versions of the game: Rugby Union (www.rfu.com) is played more in southern England, Wales and Scotland, and is traditionally thought of as the game of the middle and upper classes. Rugby League (www.therfl.co.uk) is played predominantly in northern England, traditionally by the working classes. Today, leading rugby-union clubs include Leicester, Bath and Gloucester, while London has a host of good-quality teams (including Wasps and Saracens). In rugby league, teams to watch include the Wigan Warriors, Bradford Bulls and Leeds Rhinos.

The Rugby League World Cup is dominated by Australia and New Zealand (the 2017 tournament will be held in Australia and New Zealand), but the 2015 Rugby Union World Cup will be hosted by England, with the final played at Twickenham. For details see www.rugbyworldcup.com.

Tennis

Tennis is widely played at club and regional level, but the best-known tournament is the All England Championships – known to all as Wimbledon (www.wimbledon.com) – when tennis fever sweeps through the country in the last week of June and first week of July. There's something quintessentially English about the combination of grass courts, polite applause and umpires in straw hats, with strawberries and cream devoured by the truckload.

Over 27 tonnes of strawberries and 7000L of cream are consumed every year during the two weeks of the Wimbledon Tennis Championships.

Demand for seats at Wimbledon always outstrips supply, but to give everyone an equal chance tickets are sold through a public ballot. You can also take your chance on the spot; about 6000 tickets are sold each day (excluding the final four days), but you'll need to be an early riser: dedicated fans start queuing before dawn. See the website for more information.

Survival Guide

Directory A–Z

Accommodation

B&Bs & Guesthouses

The B&B (bed and breakfast) is a great English institution. At smaller places it's pretty much a room in somebody's house; larger places may be called a 'guesthouse' (half-way between a B&B and a full hotel). Prices start from around £25 per person for a simple bedroom and shared bathroom; for around £30 to £35 per person you get a private bathroom – either down the hall or en suite.

In cities, some B&Bs are for long-term residents or people on welfare; they don't take passing tourists. In country areas, most B&Bs cater for walkers and cyclists, but some don't, so let them know if you'll be turning up with dirty boots or wheels.

When booking, check where your B&B actually is. In country areas, postal addresses include the nearest town, which may be 20 miles away – important if you're walking! Some B&B owners will pick you up by car for a small charge.

Prices Usually quoted per person, based on two people sharing a room. Single rooms for solo travellers are harder to find, and attract a 20% to 50% premium. Some B&Bs simply won't take single people (unless you pay the full double-room price), especially in summer.

Booking Advance reservations are preferred at B&Bs and are essential during popular periods. You can book many B&Bs via online agencies but rates may be cheaper if you book directly. If you haven't booked in advance, most towns have a main drag of B&Bs; those with spare rooms hang up a 'Vacancies' sign. Many B&Bs require a minimum two-night stay on weekends. Some places reduce rates for longer stays (two or three nights) midweek. If a B&B is full, owners may recommend another place nearby (possibly a private house taking occasional guests, not in tourist listings).

Food Most B&Bs serve enormous breakfasts; some offer packed lunches (around £6) and evening meals (around £15 to £20).

Bunkhouses & Camping Barns

A bunkhouse in England is a simple place, usually in country areas, with a communal sleeping area and bathroom, plus stoves for self-catering. You provide sleeping bag and possibly cooking gear. Most charge around £12 per person per night.

Camping barns are even more basic: usually converted farm buildings. Take everything you'd need to camp except the tent. Charges are from around £6 per person.

Camping

Campsites range from farmers' fields with a tap and basic toilet, costing from £3 per person per night, to smarter affairs with hot showers and many other facilities, charging up to £13. You usually need all your own kit.

A few campsites also offer self-catering accommodation in chalets, caravans, tepees, yurts and stylish wooden camping 'pods', often dubbed 'glamping'.

If you're touring Britain with a tent or campervan (motorhome), consider joining the **Camping & Caravanning Club** (www.campingandcaravanningclub.co.uk), which provides a 30% discount on its sites for an annual membership fee of £37. The club owns almost 100 campsites and lists thousands more in the invaluable Big Sites Book (free to members).

Hostels

There are two types of hostel in England: those run by the **Youth Hostel Association** (YHA; www.yha.org.uk) and independent hostels – most listed in the **Independent Hostels** (www.independenthostelguide.co.uk).

Hostels can be found in rural areas, towns and cities, and are aimed at all types of traveller, young and old. Some hostels are converted cottages, country houses and even castles – often in wonderful locations. Sleeping is usually in dormitories; some hostels also have twin or four-bed rooms.

YHA HOSTELS

The simplest YHA hostels cost around £15 per person per night. Larger hostels with more facilities are £18 to £25. London's YHA hostels cost from £30. Advance bookings and payments with credit card are usually possible.

You don't have to be a member of the YHA (or another Hostelling International organisation) to stay, but most hostels charge extra if you're not a member (£3 at YHA hostels), so it's usually worth joining. Annual YHA membership costs £20; younger people and families get discounts.

Most hostel prices vary according to demand and season. Book early for a Tuesday night in May and you'll get the best rate. Book late for a weekend in August and you'll pay top price – if there's space at all. We have generally quoted the cheaper rates (in line with those listed on the YHA's website); you may find yourself paying more.

YHA hostels tend to have complicated opening times and days, especially in remote locations or out of tourist season, so check before turning up.

INDEPENDENT HOSTELS

In rural areas some independent hostels are little more than simple bunkhouses (charging around £12), or almost up to B&B standard (£20 or more). In cities, independent backpacker hostels are usually aimed at young budget travellers. Most are open 24 hours, with a lively atmosphere, a range of rooms (doubles or dorms), bar, cafe, wi-fi and laundry. Prices go from around £20 for a dorm bed to £40 for a bed in a private room.

Hotels

There's a massive choice of hotels in England, from small town houses to grand country mansions, from no-frills locations to boutique hideaways. At the bargain end, single/double rooms cost from £40/50. Move up the scale and you'll pay £100/150 or beyond.

If all you want is a place to put your head down, budget chain hotels can be a good option. Most are lacking in ambience, but who cares? You'll only be there for 12 hours, and eight of them you'll be asleep. Prices vary on demand: at quiet times twin-bed rooms start from £30; at the height of the

---

tourist season you'll pay £60 or more. Options include the following:

Ibis Hotels (www.ibis.com)

Premier Inn (www.premierinn.com)

Travelodge (www.travelodge.co.uk)

Houseboats

A popular English holiday option is renting a houseboat on one of England's picturesque waterways, combining accommodation and transport for a few days or a week.

UK Boat Hire (www.ukboathire.com)

Hoseasons (www.hoseasons.co.uk)

Wandering Duck 'Floating hostels' for budget travellers.

Pubs & Inns

As well as selling drinks, many pubs and inns offer lodging, particularly in country areas. For bed and breakfast, you'll pay around £25 per person for a basic room, around £40 for something better. An advantage for solo tourists: pubs often have single rooms.

Rental Accommodation

If you want to stay in one place, renting for a week

NO 'STANDARD' HOTEL RATES

There's no such thing as a 'standard' hotel rate in England. Many hotels, especially larger places or chains, vary prices according to demand – or have different rates for online, phone or walk-in bookings – just like airlines and train operators. So if you book early for a night when the hotel is likely to be quiet, rates are cheap. If you book late, or aim for a public-holiday weekend, you'll pay a lot. But wait until the very last minute, and you can sometimes get a bargain as rates drop again. The end result: you can pay anything from £25 to £200 for the very same hotel room. With that in mind, the hotel rates we quote are often guide prices only. (In contrast, B&B prices tend to be much more consistent.)

can be ideal. Choose from neat apartments in cities or quaint old houses (always called 'cottages', whatever the size) in country areas. Cottages for four people cost between £250 and £650 in high season. Rates fall at quieter times and you may be able to rent for a long weekend. Handy websites include the following:

Bed & Breakfast Nationwide (www.bedandbreakfastnationwide.com)

Cottages & Castles (www.cottages-and-castles.co.uk)

Cottages4U (www.cottages4you.co.uk)

Hoseasons (www.hoseasons.co.uk)

National Trust (www.nationaltrust.org.uk/holidays)

Stilwell's (www.stilwell.co.uk)

University Accommodation

During vacations, many universities offer accommodation to visitors. You usually get a functional single bedroom, and self-catering flats are also available. Prices range from £25 to £60 per person. A handy portal is www.universityrooms.co.uk.

Climate

London

Bath

York

Customs Regulations

Britain has a two-tier customs system: one for goods bought duty-free outside the EU; the other for goods bought in another EU country where tax and duty is paid. Below is a summary of the rules; for more details go to www.hmrc.gov.uk and search for 'Customs Allowances'.

Duty Free

The duty-free limit for goods from *outside* the EU includes 200 cigarettes or equivalent in cigars, 4L of wine, 1L of spirits, 60cc of perfume and other goods worth up to £390.

Tax & Duty Paid

There is no limit on goods from within the EU (if taxes have been paid), but customs officials use the following guidelines to distinguish personal use from commercial imports: 800 cigarettes, 200 cigars, 10L of spirits, 90L of wine and 110L of beer. Still enough to have one hell of a party.

Electricity

230V/50Hz

Embassies & Consulates

This is a selection of embassies, consulates and high commissions in London. For a complete list, go to www.fco.gov.uk and search for 'foreign embassies'.

Australia (☑020-7379 4334; www.uk.embassy.gov.au; The Strand, WC2B 4LA)

Canada (☑020-7258 6600; www.canadainternational.gc.ca; 1 Grosvenor Sq, W1X 0AB)

China (☑020-7299 4049; www.chinese-embassy.org.uk; 49-51 Portland Pl, W1B 4JL)

France (☑020-7073 1000; www.ambafrance-uk.org; 58 Knightsbridge, SW1 7JT)

Germany (☑020-7824 1300; www.london.diplo.de; 23 Belgrave Sq, SW1X 8PX)

Ireland (☑020-7235 2171; www.embassyofireland.co.uk; 17 Grosvenor Pl, SW1X 7HR)

Japan (☑020-7465 6500; www.uk.emb-japan.go.jp; 101 Piccadilly, W1J 7JT)

Netherlands (☑020-7590 3200; www.dutchembassyuk.org; 38 Hyde Park Gate, SW7 5DP)

New Zealand (☑020-7930 8422; www.nzembassy.com/uk; 80 Haymarket, SW1Y 4TQ)

Poland (☑020-7291 3520; www.london.mfa.gov.pl; 47 Portland Pl, W1B 1HQ)

USA (☑020-7499 9000; www.usembassy.org.uk; 24 Grosvenor Sq, W1A 1AE)

Food

To whet your appetite for English cuisine, see the Food & Drink chapter on p662.

Gay & Lesbian Travellers

England is generally a tolerant place for gays and lesbians. London, Manchester and Brighton have flourishing gay scenes, and in other sizeable cities you'll find communities not entirely in the closet. That said, you'll still find pockets of homophobic hostility in some areas. Resources include the following:

Diva (www.divamag.co.uk)

Gay Times (www.gaytimes.co.uk)

London Lesbian & Gay Switchboard (☑0300 330 0630; www.llgs.org.uk; ⊙10am-11pm)

Health

➡ If you're an EU citizen, a European Health Insurance Card (EHIC) – available from health centres or, in the UK, post offices – covers you for most medical care. An EHIC will not cover you for non-urgent cases, or emergency repatriation.

➡ Citizens from non-EU countries should find out if there is a reciprocal arrangement for free medical care between their country and the UK.

➡ If you do need health insurance, make sure you get a policy that covers you for the worst possible scenarios, including emergency flights home.

➡ No jabs (vaccinations) are required to travel to Britain. For more information, check with your medical provider in your own country before you travel.

➡ Chemists (pharmacies) can advise on minor ailments such as sore throats and earaches. In large cities, there's always at least one 24-hour chemist.

Insurance

Although everyone in England receives free emergency treatment, regardless of nationality, travel insurance is still highly recommended. It will usually cover medical and dental consultation and treatment at private clinics – which can be quicker than National Health Service (NHS) places – as well as the cost of any emergency flights, plus all the usual stuff like loss of baggage.

Worldwide travel insurance is available at www.lonelyplanet.com/travel-insurance. You can buy, extend and claim online anytime – even if you're already on the road.

Internet Access

➡ 3G and 4G mobile broadband coverage is good in large population centres, but limited or nonexistent in rural areas. However, beware high charges for data roaming – check with your mobile-/cell-phone provider before travelling.

PRACTICALITIES

→ **Newspapers** Tabloids include the *Sun*, *Daily Mail* and *Mirror;* quality 'broadsheets' include (from right to left, politically) the *Telegraph*, *Times*, *Independent* and *Guardian*.

→ **TV** All TV in England is digital. Leading broadcasters include BBC, ITV and Channel 4. Satellite and cable-TV providers include Sky and Virgin Media.

→ **Radio** Main BBC stations and wavelengths are Radio 1 (98–99.6MHz FM), Radio 2 (88–92MHz FM), Radio 3 (90–92.2 MHz FM), Radio 4 (92–94.4MHz FM) and Radio 5 Live (909AM or 693AM). National commercial stations include Virgin Radio (1215Hz MW) and non-highbrow classical specialist Classic FM (100–102MHz FM). All are available on digital.

→ **DVD** PAL format (incompatible with NTSC and Secam).

→ **Weights & Measures** England uses a mix of metric and imperial measures (eg petrol is sold by the litre but beer by the pint; mountain heights are in metres but road distances in miles).

→ Most hotels, B&Bs, hostels, stations and coffee shops (even some trains and buses) have wi-fi access, charging anything from nothing to £6 per hour.

→ Internet cafes are surprisingly rare in England, especially away from big cities and tourist spots. Most charge from £1 per hour, but out in the sticks you can pay £5 per hour.

→ Public libraries often have computers with free internet access, but only for 30-minute slots, and demand is high. All the usual warnings apply about keystroke-capturing software and other security risks.

→ We've indicated accommodation and eating and drinking options that have wi-fi with the 🛜 symbol in the text. Wi-fi is often free, but some places (usually upmarket hotels) charge.

→ If you see the @ symbol, then the place has an internet terminal.

Legal Matters

→ Police have the power to detain, for up to six hours, anyone suspected of having committed an offence punishable by imprisonment (including drugs offences). Police have the right to search anyone they suspect of possessing drugs.

→ You must be over 18 to buy alcohol and cigarettes. You usually have to be 18 to enter a pub or bar, although rules are different for under-18s if eating. Some bars and clubs are over-21 only.

→ Illegal drugs are widely available, especially in clubs. Cannabis possession is a criminal offence; punishment for carrying a small amount may be a warning, a fine or imprisonment. Dealers face stiffer penalties, as do people caught with other drugs.

→ On buses and trains (including the London Underground), people without a valid ticket are fined on the spot – usually around £20.

Money

The currency of Britain is the pound sterling (£). Paper money ('notes') comes in £5, £10, £20 and £50 denominations. Some shops don't accept £50 notes because fakes circulate.

Other currencies are very rarely accepted, except at some gift shops in London, which may take euros, US dollars, yen and other major currencies.

See the Need to Know chapter, p20, for exchange rates.

ATMs

ATMs (usually called 'cash machines' in England) are common in cities and even small towns. Cash withdrawals from some ATMs may be subject to a small charge, but most are free. If you're not from the UK, your home bank will likely charge you for withdrawing money overseas. Watch out for ATMS that have been tampered with; one ruse by scammers is to attach a card-reader or minicamera.

Credit & Debit Cards

Visa and MasterCard credit and debit cards are widely accepted in England. Most businesses will assume your card is 'Chip and PIN' enabled (using a PIN instead of signing). If it isn't, you should be able to sign instead, but some places may not accept your card. Some smaller country B&Bs don't take cards, so you'll need to pay with cash.

Money Changers

Cities and larger towns have banks and exchange bureaux for changing your money into pounds. Check rates first; some bureaux offer poor rates or levy outrageous commissions. You can also change money at some post offices – very handy in country areas, and exchange rates are fair.

Tipping

In England you're not obliged to tip if the service or food was unsatisfactory (even if it's been automatically added to your bill as a 'service charge').

Restaurants Around 10%. Also at teashops and smarter cafes with full table service. At smarter restaurants waiters expect tips nearer 12% or 15%.

Taxis Around 10%, or rounded up to the nearest pound, especially in London. It's less usual to tip minicab drivers.

Pubs Around 10% if you order food at the table and your meal is brought to you. If you order and pay at the bar (food or drinks), tips are not expected.

Opening Hours

Banks

➡ 9.30am to 4pm or 5pm Monday to Friday.

➡ Main branches 9.30am to 1pm Saturday.

Bars, Pubs & Clubs

➡ Standard hours for pubs and bars: 11am to 11pm Monday to Thursday, 11am to 1am Friday and Saturday, 12.30pm to 11pm Sunday.

➡ Clubs open any time from 8pm to 11pm, until 2am or beyond.

Cafes & Restaurants

Most restaurants and cafes are open for lunch or dinner or both.

➡ Standard hours for cafes: 9am to 5pm. Most cafes open daily.

➡ In cities, some cafes open at 7am for breakfast, then shut at 6pm or later.

➡ In country areas, some cafes open until 7pm or later in the summer. In winter months hours are reduced; some cafes close completely from October to Easter.

➡ Standard hours for restaurants: lunch is noon to 3pm, dinner 6pm to 9pm or 10pm (to midnight or later in cities). Most restaurants open daily; some close Sunday evening or all day Monday.

➡ A few restaurants open for breakfast (usually 9am), but mainly cafes do this.

Museums & Sights

➡ Large museums and sights usually open daily.

➡ Some smaller places open Saturday and Sunday but close Monday and/or Tuesday.

➡ Smaller places open daily in high season but operate weekends only or completely close in low season.

Post Offices

➡ 9am to 5pm (5.30pm or 6pm in cities) Monday to Friday.

➡ 9am to 12.30pm Saturday; main branches to 5pm.

Shops

➡ 9am to 5.30pm (or 6pm in cities) Monday to Saturday, and often 11am to 5pm Sunday. London and other cities have convenience stores open 24/7.

➡ In smaller towns and country areas shops often shut for lunch (normally 1pm to 2pm) and on Wednesday or Thursday afternoon.

Public Holidays

Holidays for the whole of Britain:

New Year's Day 1 January

Easter March/April (Good Friday to Easter Monday inclusive)

May Day First Monday in May

Spring Bank Holiday Last Monday in May

Summer Bank Holiday Last Monday in August

Christmas Day 25 December

Boxing Day 26 December

If a public holiday falls on a weekend, the nearest Monday is usually taken instead. Most businesses and banks close on official public holidays (hence the quaint term 'bank holiday').

On public holidays, some small museums and places of interest close, but larger attractions have their busiest times. If a place closes on Sunday, it'll probably be shut on bank holidays as well.

Virtually everything – attractions, shops, banks, offices – closes on Christmas Day, although pubs are open at lunchtime. There's usually no public transport on Christmas Day, and a very minimal service on Boxing Day.

SCHOOL HOLIDAYS

Roads get busy and hotel prices go up during school holidays. Exact dates vary from year to year and region to region, but are roughly as follows:

Easter Holiday Week before and week after Easter.

Summer Holiday Third week of July to first week of September.

Christmas Holiday Mid-December to first week of January.

There are also three week-long 'half-term' school holidays – usually late February (or early March), late May and late October. These are staggered, so the whole country is not on holiday during the same week.

Safe Travel

England is a remarkably safe country, but crime is not unknown in London and other cities.

➡ Watch out for pickpockets and hustlers in crowded areas popular with tourists, such as around Westminster Bridge in London.

➡ When travelling by tube, tram or urban train services at night, choose a carriage containing other people.

➡ Many town centres can be rowdy on Friday and Saturday nights when the pubs and clubs are emptying.

➡ Unlicensed minicabs – a bloke with a car earning money on the side – operate in large cities, and are worth avoiding unless you know what you're doing.

Telephone
Mobile Phones

The UK uses the GSM 900/1800 network, which covers the rest of Europe, Australia and New Zealand, but isn't compatible with the North American GSM 1900.

Most modern mobiles can function on both networks, but check before you leave home just in case.

Though roaming charges within the EU are due to be entirely eliminated in December 2015, other international roaming charges can be prohibitively high, and you'll probably find it cheaper to get a UK number. This is easily done by buying a SIM card (around £10 including calling credit) and sticking it in your phone. Your phone may be locked to your home network, however, so you'll have to either get it unlocked, or buy a pay-as-you-go phone along with your SIM card (around £50).

Pay-as-you-go phones can be recharged by buying vouchers from shops.

Phone Codes

Dialling to the UK Dial your country's international access code then ☎44 (the UK country code), then the area code (dropping the first ☎0) followed by the telephone number.

Dialling from the UK The international access code is ☎00; dial this, then add the code of the country you wish to dial.

Reverse-charge (collect) international call Dial ☎155 for the operator. It's an expensive option, but not for the caller.

Area codes in the UK No standard format or length, eg Edinburgh ☎0131, London ☎020, Ambleside ☎015394.

Directory assistance A host of agencies compete for your business and charge from 10p to 40p; numbers include ☎118 192, ☎118 118, ☎118 500 and ☎118 811.

Mobile phones Codes usually begin with ☎07.

Free calls Numbers starting with ☎0800 are free; calls to ☎0845 numbers are charged at local rates.

National operator ☎100

International operator ☎155

Time

Britain is on GMT. The clocks go forward for 'summer time' one hour at the end of March, and go back at the end of October. The 24-hour clock is used for transport timetables.

Time Differences

Paris, Berlin, Rome One hour ahead of Britain.

New York Five hours behind.

Sydney Nine hours ahead between April and September, 10 hours October, 11 hours between November and March.

Los Angeles Eight hours behind.

Mumbai 5½ hours ahead, 4½ hours bewteen March and October.

Tokyo Nine hours ahead, eight hours between March and October.

Tourist Information

Most English cities and towns, and some villages, have a tourist-information centre or visitor-information centre – for ease we've called all these places 'tourist offices'. Such places

---

HERITAGE ORGANISATIONS

A highlight of a journey through England is visiting the numerous castles and historic sites that pepper the country. Membership of a heritage organisation gets you free admission (usually a good saving) as well as information handbooks and so on.

National Trust (NT; www.nationaltrust.org.uk) A charity protecting historic buildings and land with scenic importance across England and Wales. Annual membership is £58 (discounts for under-26s and families). A Touring Pass allows free entry to NT properties for one/two weeks (£25/30 per person); families and couples get cheaper rates.

English Heritage (EH; www.english-heritage.org.uk) State-funded organisation responsible for numerous historic sites. Annual membership is £49 (couples and seniors get discounts). An Overseas Visitors Pass allows free entry to most sites for nine/16 days for £25/30 (cheaper rates for couples and families).

have helpful staff, books and maps for sale, leaflets to give away and advice on things to see or do. Some can also assist with booking accommodation. Some are run by national parks and often have small exhibits about the area.

Most tourist offices keep regular business hours; in quiet areas they close from October to March, while in popular areas they open daily year-round. In recent years, cost-cutting has seen many smaller tourist offices close down.

Before leaving home, check the comprehensive website of England's official tourist board, **Visit England** (www.visitengland.com), which covers all the angles of national tourism, with links to numerous other sites.

Travellers with Disabilities

All new buildings have wheelchair access, and even hotels in grand old country houses often have lifts, ramps and other facilities. Hotels and B&Bs in historic buildings are often harder to adapt, so you'll have less choice here.

Modern city buses and trams have low floors for easy access, but few have conductors who can lend a hand when you're getting on or off. Many taxis take wheelchairs, or just have more room in the back.

For long-distance travel, coaches may present problems if you can't walk, but the main operator, **National Express** (www.nationalexpress.com), has wheelchair-friendly coaches on many routes. For details, ring its dedicated **Disabled Passenger Travel Helpline** (☎08717 81 81 79).

On intercity trains there's more room and better facilities, and usually station staff around; just have a word and they'll be happy to help out. A **Disabled Person's Railcard** (www.disabledpersons-railcard.co.uk) costs £20 and gets you 33% off most train fares.

Useful organisations:

Disability Rights UK (www.disabilityrightsuk.org) Published titles include a *Holiday Guide*. Other services include a key for 7000 public disabled toilets across the UK.

Good Access Guide (www.goodaccessguide.co.uk)

Tourism For All (www.tourismforall.org.uk)

Visas

➡ If you're a citizen of the European Economic Area (EEA) nations or Switzerland, you don't need a visa to enter or work in the UK – you can enter using your national identity card.

➡ Visa regulations are always subject to change, and immigration restriction is currently big news in the UK, so it's essential to check with your local British embassy, high commission or consulate before leaving home.

➡ Currently, if you're a citizen of Australia, Canada, New Zealand, Japan, Israel, the USA and several other countries, you can stay for up to six months (no visa required), but are not allowed to work.

➡ Nationals of many countries, including South Africa, will need to obtain a visa; for more info, see www.ukvisas.gov.uk.

➡ The Youth Mobility Scheme, for Australian, Canadian, Japanese, Hong Kong, Monégasque, New Zealand, South Korean and Taiwanese citizens aged 18 to 31, allows working visits of up to two years, but must be applied for in advance.

➡ Commonwealth citizens with a UK-born parent may be eligible for a Certificate of Entitlement to the Right of Abode, which entitles them to live and work in the UK.

➡ Commonwealth citizens with a UK-born grandparent could qualify for a UK Ancestry Employment Certificate, allowing them to work full time for up to five years in the UK.

➡ British immigration authorities have always been tough; dress neatly and carry proof that you have sufficient funds with which to support yourself. A credit card and/or an onward ticket will help.

Transport

GETTING THERE & AWAY

Most overseas visitors reach England by air. As London is a global transport hub, it's easy to fly to England from just about anywhere. In recent years the massive growth of budget ('no-frills') airlines has increased the number of routes – and reduced the fares – between England and other countries in Europe.

The other main option for travel between England and mainland Europe is ferry, either port-to-port or combined with a long-distance bus trip, although journeys can be long and financial savings not huge compared with budget airfares.

International trains are much more comfortable and a 'green' option; the Channel Tunnel allows direct rail services between England, France and Belgium, with onward connections to many other European destinations.

Flights, cars and rail tickets can be booked online at lonelyplanet.com/bookings.

Air

London Airports

Heathrow (LHR; www.heathrowairport.com) The UK's main airport for international flights; often chaotic and crowded. About 15 miles west of central London.

Gatwick (LGW; www.gatwickairport.com) Britain's number-two airport, mainly for international flights; 30 miles south of central London.

Stansted (STN; www.stanstedairport.com) About 35 miles northeast of central London, mainly handling charter and budget European flights.

Luton (LTN; www.londonluton.co.uk) Some 35 miles north of central London, well known as a holiday-flight airport.

London City (LCY; www.londoncityairport.com) A few miles east of central London, specialising in flights to/from European and other UK airports.

Regional Airports

Some planes on European and long-haul routes avoid London and use major regional airports including Manchester and Newcastle. Smaller regional airports such as Southampton and Birmingham are served by flights to and from continental Europe and Ireland.

Land

Bus & Coach

You can easily get between England and other European countries via long-distance bus (called coach in England). The international network **Eurolines** (www.eurolines.com) connects a huge number of destinations; you can buy tickets online via one of the national operators.

Services to/from England are operated by **National Express** (www.nationalexpress.com). Sample journey times to/from London include Amsterdam 12 hours; Barcelona 24 hours; Dublin 12 hours; and Paris eight hours.

If you book early, and can be flexible with timings (ie travel when few other people want to), you can get some very good deals. For example, between London and Paris or Amsterdam from about £20 one way (although paying £30 to £40 is more usual).

Train

CHANNEL TUNNEL PASSENGER SERVICE

High-speed **Eurostar** (☎08705 186 186; www.eurostar.com) passenger services shuttle at least 10 times daily between London and Paris (2½ hours) or Brussels (two hours). Buy tickets from travel agencies, major train stations or the Eurostar website.

The normal one-way fare between London and Paris/Brussels costs £140 to £180; advance booking and off-peak travel gets cheaper fares as low as £39 one way.

CHANNEL TUNNEL CAR SERVICE

Drivers use **Eurotunnel** (www.eurotunnel.com). At Folkestone in England or Calais in France, you drive onto a train, get carried through the tunnel and drive off at the other end.

Trains run about four times an hour from 6am to 10pm, then hourly through the night. Loading and unloading takes an hour; the journey lasts 35 minutes.

Book in advance online or pay on the spot. The one-way cost for a car and passengers is between £75 and £165 depending on time of day; promotional fares often bring it down to £55.

TRAIN & FERRY CONNECTIONS

As well as Eurostar, many 'normal' trains run between England and mainland Europe. You buy one ticket, but get off the train at the port, walk onto a ferry, then get another train on the other side. Routes include Amsterdam–London (via Hook of Holland and Harwich). Travelling between Ireland and England, the main train-ferry-train route is Dublin to London, via Dun Laoghaire and Holyhead (Wales). Ferries also run between Rosslare and Fishguard or Pembroke (Wales), with train connections on either side.

Sea

Ferry Routes

The main ferry routes between England and other European countries include the following:

➡ Dover to Calais (France)

➡ Dover to Boulogne (France)

➡ Newhaven to Dieppe (France)

➡ Harwich to Hook of Holland (Netherlands)

➡ Hull to Zeebrugge (Belgium)

➡ Hull to Rotterdam (Netherlands)

➡ Portsmouth to Santander (Spain)

➡ Portsmouth to Bilbao (Spain)

Ferry Fares

Most ferry operators offer flexible fares, meaning great bargains at quiet times of day or year. For example, short cross-channel routes such as Dover to Calais or Boulogne can be as low as £20 for a car plus up to five passengers, although around £50 to £90 is more likely. If you're a foot passenger, or cycling, there's less need to book ahead; fares on short crossings cost about £10 to £30 each way.

Ferry Booking

You can book directly with one of the ferry operators listed below, or use the very handy www.ferrybooker.com, a single site covering all sea-ferry routes, plus Eurotunnel.

Brittany Ferries (www.brittany-ferries.com)

DFDS Seaways (www.dfdsseaways.co.uk)

Irish Ferries (www.irishferries.com)

P&O Ferries (www.poferries.com)

Stena Line (www.stenaline.com)

GETTING AROUND

For getting around England your first big decision is to travel by car or public transport.

Having your own car makes the best use of time, and helps reach remote places, but rental and fuel costs can be expensive for budget travellers (while traffic jams in major cities hit everyone) – public transport is often the better choice. As long as you have time, using a mix of train, bus, taxi, walking and occasionally hiring a bike, you can get almost anywhere in England without having to drive.

The main public-transport options are train and long-distance bus (coach). Services between major towns and cities are generally good, although at peak times you must book in advance to be sure of getting a ticket. If you book ahead early or travel at off-peak periods – ideally both – train and coach tickets can be very cheap.

Air

England's domestic airline companies include British Airways, FlyBe/Loganair, easyJet and Ryanair. If you're really pushed for time, flights on longer routes across England (eg Exeter or Southampton to Newcastle) are handy, although you miss the glorious scenery in between. On some shorter routes (eg London to Newcastle or Manchester to Newquay) trains compare favourably with planes on time, once airport downtime is factored in. On costs, you might get a bargain airfare, but trains can be cheaper if you buy tickets in advance.

Bicycle

England is a compact country, and hiring a bike – for an hour or two, or a week or longer – is a great way to really see the country if you've got time to spare.

London

London is famous for its Barclays Cycle Hire Scheme, known as 'Boris bikes' after the mayor that introduced them to the city. Bikes can be hired on the spot from automatic docking stations. For more information visit the Transport for London website (www.tfl.gov.uk). Other rental options in the capital are listed at www.lcc.org.uk (under Advice/Bike Shops).

Around the Country

The **nextbike** (www.nextbike.co.uk) bike-sharing scheme has stations in Bath, while towns such as Oxford and Cambridge have plenty of bike-rental options. Bikes can also be hired in national parks or forestry sites now primarily used for leisure activities, such as Kielder Water in Northumberland and Grizedale Forest in the Lake District. In some areas, disused railway lines are now bike routes, notably the Peak District in Derbyshire. Rental rates start at about £10 per day, or £20 for something half decent.

Bikes on Trains

Bicycles can be taken free of charge on most local urban trains (although they may not be allowed at peak times when the trains are crowded with commuters). Also on shorter trips in rural areas, on a first-come, first-served basis – though there may be space limits.

Bikes can be carried on long-distance train journeys free of charge, but advance booking is required for most conventional bikes. (Folding bikes can be carried on pretty much any train at any time.) In theory, this shouldn't be too much trouble as most long-distance rail trips are best bought in advance anyway, but you have to go a long way down the path of booking your seat before you start booking your bike – only to find space isn't available. A better course of action is to buy in advance at a major rail station, where the booking clerk can help you through the options.

A final warning: when railways are repaired, cancelled trains are replaced by buses – and they won't take bikes.

A very useful leaflet called *National Rail Cycling by Train* is available at major stations or downloadable from www.nationalrail.co.uk (from the homepage follow links to 'Stations & on train' then 'Cyclists').

Bus & Coach

If you're on a tight budget, long-distance buses (coaches) are nearly always the cheapest way to get around, although they're also the slowest – sometimes by a considerable margin. Many towns have separate stations for local buses and long-distance coaches; make sure you go to the right one!

National Express (www.nationalexpress.com) The main coach operator, with a wide network and frequent services between main centres. Fares vary: they're cheaper if you book in advance and travel at quieter times, and more expensive if you buy your ticket on the spot and it's Friday afternoon. As a guide, a 200-mile trip (eg London to York) will cost £15 to £30 if you book a few days in advance.

Megabus (www.megabus.com) Operates a budget coach service serving more than 100 destinations around the country. Go at a quiet time, book early and your ticket will be very cheap. Book later, for a busy time and... You get the picture.

Passes & Discounts

National Express offers discount passes to full-time students and under-26s, called Young Persons Coachcards. They cost £10 and give you 30% off standard adult fares. Also available are coachcards for people over 60, families and disabled travellers.

For touring the country, National Express offers Brit Xplorer passes, allowing unlimited travel for seven/14/28 days (£79/139/219). You don't need to book journeys in advance: if the coach has a spare seat, you can take it.

Car & Motorcycle

Travelling by car or motorbike around England means you can be independent and flexible, and reach remote places. Downsides for drivers include traffic jams, the high price of fuel and high parking costs in cities.

Car Rental

Compared with many countries (especially the USA), hire rates are expensive in Britain; the smallest cars start from about £120 per week, and it's around £250 per week for a medium car. All rates include insurance and unlimited mileage, and can rise at busy times (or drop at quiet times).

Some main players:

Avis (www.avis.co.uk)

Budget (www.budget.co.uk)

Europcar (www.europcar.co.uk)

Sixt (www.sixt.co.uk)

Thrifty (www.thrifty.co.uk)

Another option is to look online for small, local car-hire companies in Britain that can undercut the international franchises. Generally those in cities are cheaper than in rural areas. Using a rental-broker or comparison site such as **UK Car Hire** (www.ukcarhire.net) or **Kayak** (www.kayak.com) can also help find bargains.

Motorhome Rental

Hiring a motorhome or campervan (£500 to £900 a week) is more expensive than hiring a car, but saves on accommodation costs and gives almost unlimited freedom. Sites to check include the following:

Just Go (www.justgo.uk.com)

Wild Horizon (www.wildhorizon.co.uk)

Motoring Organisations

Motoring organisations in Britain include the **Automobile Association** (www.theaa.com) and the **Royal Automobile Club** (www.rac.co.uk). For both, annual membership starts at around £50, including 24-hour roadside breakdown assistance. A greener alternative is the

Environmental Transport Association (www.eta.co.uk); it provides breakdown assistance but doesn't campaign for more roads.

Insurance

It's illegal to drive a car or ride a motorbike in England without (at least) third-party insurance. This will be included with all rental cars. If you're bringing your own car, you will need to arrange this.

Parking

Many cities have short-stay and long-stay car parks; the latter are cheaper though may be less convenient. 'Park & Ride' systems allow you to park on the edge of the city then ride to the centre on frequent nonstop buses for an all-in-one price.

Yellow lines (single or double) along the edge of the road indicate restrictions. Nearby signs spell out when you can and can't park. In London and other big cities, traffic wardens operate with efficiency; if you park on the yellow lines at the wrong time, your car will be clamped or towed away, and it'll cost you £100 or more to get driving again. In some cities there are also red lines, which mean no stopping at all. Ever.

Roads

Motorways and main A-roads deliver you quickly from one end of the country to another. Lesser A-roads, B-roads and minor roads are much more scenic – ideal for car or motorcycle touring. You can't travel fast, but you won't care.

Speed limits are usually 30mph (48km/h) in built-up areas, 60mph (96km/h) on main roads and 70mph (112km/h) on motorways and most (but not all) dual carriageways.

Road Rules

A foreign driving licence is valid in Britain for up to 12 months.

Drink driving is taken very seriously; you're allowed a maximum blood-alcohol level of 80mg/100mL (0.08%) – campaigners want it reduced to 50mg/100mL (0.05%), in line with most European countries.

Some other important rules:

➡ Drive on the left (!).

➡ Wear fitted seatbelts in cars.

➡ Wear helmets on motorcycles.

➡ Give way to your right at junctions and roundabouts.

➡ Always use the left lane on motorways and dual carriageways unless overtaking (although so many people ignore this rule, you'd think it didn't exist).

➡ Don't use a mobile phone while driving unless it's fully hands free (another rule frequently flouted).

Local Transport

English cities usually have good public-transport systems (a combination of bus, train and tram), often run by a confusing number of separate companies. Tourist offices can provide maps and information.

Local Bus

There are good local bus networks year-round in cities and towns. Buses also run in some rural areas year-round, although timetables are designed to serve schools and businesses, so there aren't many noon and weekend services (and they may stop running during school holidays), or buses may link local villages to a market town on only one day each week.

In tourist areas (especially national parks), there are frequent services from Easter to September. However, it's always worth double-checking at a tourist office before planning your day's

activities around a bus that may not actually be running.

In this book, along with the local bus-route number, frequency and duration, we have provided indicative fares.

LOCAL BUS PASSES

If you're taking a few local bus rides in one area, day passes (with names like Day Rover, Wayfarer or Explorer) are cheaper than buying several single tickets. Often they can be bought on your first bus, and may include local rail services. It's always worth asking ticket clerks or bus drivers about your options.

Taxi

There are two sorts of taxi in England: those with meters that can be hailed in the street; and minicabs, which are cheaper but can only be called by phone. Unlicensed minicabs operate in some cities.

In London, most taxis are the famous 'black cabs' (some with advertising livery in other colours), which charge by distance and time. Depending on the time of day, a 1-mile journey takes five to 10 minutes and costs £6 to £9. Longer journeys are proportionally cheaper.

In rural areas, taxis need to be called by phone; the best place to find the local taxi's phone number is the local pub. Fares are £2 to £4 per mile.

Traintaxi (www.traintaxi. co.uk) is a portal site that helps 'bridge the final gap' between the train station and your hotel or other final destination.

Train

For long-distance travel around England, trains are generally faster and more comfortable than coaches but can be more expensive, although with discount tickets they're competitive – and often take you through beautiful countryside. The English like to moan about their trains, but around 85% run on time. The other 15% that get delayed or cancelled mostly impact commuter services rather than long-distance journeys.

Train Operators

About 20 different companies operate train services in England, while Network Rail operates tracks and stations. For some passengers this system can be confusing at first, but information and ticket-buying services are mostly centralised. If you have to change trains, or use two or more train operators, you still buy one ticket – valid for the whole journey. The main railcards and passes are also accepted by all train operators.

Where more than one train operator services the same route, eg York to Newcastle, a ticket purchased from one company may not be valid on trains run by another. So if you miss the train you originally booked, it's worth checking which later services your ticket will be valid for.

Information

Your first stop should be **National Rail Enquiries** (☎08457 48 49 50; www.nationalrail.co.uk), the nationwide timetable and fare information service. Its website advertises special offers and has real-time links to station departure boards and downloadable maps of the rail network.

Tickets & Reservations

BUYING TICKETS

Once you've found the journey you need on the National Rail Enquiries website, links take you to the relevant train operator to buy the ticket. This can be mailed to you (UK addresses only) or collected at the station on the day of travel from automatic machines. There's usually no booking fee on top of the ticket price.

You can also use a centralised ticketing service to buy your train ticket. These cover all train services in a single site, and make a small booking fee on top of every ticket price. The main players include the following:

QJump (www.qjump.co.uk)

Rail Easy (www.raileasy.co.uk)

Train Line (www.thetrainline.com)

To use operator or centralised ticketing websites, you always have to state a preferred time and day of travel, even if you don't mind when you go, but you can change it as you go through the process, and with a little delving around you can find some real bargains.

You can also buy train tickets on the spot at stations, which is fine for short journeys (under about 50 miles), but discount tickets for longer trips are usually not available and these must be bought in advance by phone or online.

COSTS

For longer journeys, on-the-spot fares are always available, but tickets are much cheaper if bought in advance. The earlier you book, the cheaper it gets. You can also save if you travel off-peak. Advance purchase usually gets a reserved seat too.

Whichever operator you travel with and wherever you buy tickets, these are the three main fare types:

Anytime Buy any time, travel any time – usually the most expensive option.

Off-peak Buy ticket any time, travel off-peak (what is off-peak depends on the journey).

Advance Buy ticket in advance, travel only on specific trains – usually the cheapest option.

For an idea of the price difference, an Anytime single ticket from London to York will cost £125 or more, an Off-peak around £95, with an Advance around £30 to £40, and possibly less if you book early enough or don't mind arriving at midnight.

The cheapest fares are nonrefundable, so if you miss your train you'll have to buy a new ticket.

ONWARD TRAVEL

If the train doesn't get you all the way to your destination, you can add a **PlusBus** (www.plusbus.info) supplement when making your reservation to validate your train ticket for onward travel by bus. This is more convenient, and usually cheaper, than buying a separate bus ticket.

Classes

There are two classes of rail travel: first and standard. First class costs around 50% more than standard fare (up to double at busy periods) and gets you bigger seats, more leg-room, and usually a more peaceful business-like atmosphere, plus extras such as complimentary drinks and newspapers. At weekends some train operators offer 'upgrades' to 1st class for an extra £5 to £25 on top of your standard-class fare, payable on the spot.

Train Passes

DISCOUNT PASSES

If you're staying in England for a while, passes known as **Railcards** (www.railcard.co.uk) are available:

16-25 Railcard For those aged 16 to 25, or a full-time UK student.

Senior Railcard For anyone over 60.

Family & Friends Railcard Covers up to four adults and four children travelling together.

Railcards cost £30 (valid for one year, available from major stations or online) and get a 33% discount on most train fares, except those already heavily discounted.

With the Family card, adults get 33% and children get 60% discounts, so the fee is easily repaid in a couple of journeys.

LOCAL & REGIONAL PASSES

Local train passes usually cover rail networks around a city (many include bus travel too). These are detailed in the relevant sections throughout this guide.

If you're concentrating your travels on southeast England (eg London to Dover, Weymouth, Cambridge or Oxford), a **Network Railcard** (www.railcard.co.uk/network; per year £30) covers up to four adults and up to four children travelling together outside peak times.

NATIONAL PASSES

For countr-wide travel, **Brit-Rail** (www.britrail.net) passes are available for visitors from overseas. They must be bought in your country of origin (not in England) from a specialist travel agency. Available in different versions (eg England only; all Britain; UK and Ireland) for periods from four to 30 days.

Behind the Scenes

SEND US YOUR FEEDBACK

We love to hear from travellers – your comments keep us on our toes and help make our books better. Our well-travelled team reads every word on what you loved or loathed about this book. Although we cannot reply individually to your submissions, we always guarantee that your feedback goes straight to the appropriate authors, in time for the next edition. Each person who sends us information is thanked in the next edition – the most useful submissions are rewarded with a selection of digital PDF chapters.

Visit **lonelyplanet.com/contact** to submit your updates and suggestions or to ask for help. Our award-winning website also features inspirational travel stories, news and discussions.

Note: We may edit, reproduce and incorporate your comments in Lonely Planet products such as guidebooks, websites and digital products, so let us know if you don't want your comments reproduced or your name acknowledged. For a copy of our privacy policy visit lonelyplanet.com/privacy.

OUR READERS

Many thanks to the travellers who used the last edition and wrote to us with helpful hints, useful advice and interesting anecdotes:

Gayle Galletta, Hannah Layford, Heather Monell, Katharina Asghari, Margaret Nash, Nick Adams, Paul Hegenbarth, Safia Weeks, Sain Alizada, Sandra Meinert, Walter Rask

AUTHOR THANKS

Neil Wilson

Many thanks to all the helpful and enthusiastic staff at tourist information centres throughout the country, and to the many travellers I met on the road who chipped in with advice and recommendations. Thanks also to Carol Downie, and to Steven Fallon and Keith Jeffrey, Steve Hall, Russell Leaper, Brendan Bolland, Jenny Neil, and Tom and Christine Duffin. Finally, many thanks to all my co-authors and to the ever-helpful and patient editors and cartographers at Lonely Planet.

Oliver Berry

Thanks for help and assistance on this book go to Alice Sommerlad, Thom Hunt, Rupert Ellis, Dave Grimstead, Jim Burns, Lucy Granger, Simon Timms and Hetty at Koru Kayaking. Special thanks to Susie & Gracie Berry, to Belinda Dixon for co-authoring skills, to Neil Wilson for steering

the ship, and James Smart and all the folks at Lonely Planet for guidance and sage advice.

Fionn Davenport

Thanks to Andy Parkinson at Visit Manchester and Joe Keggin at Marketing Liverpool for their help; big thanks to Saralinda Turner at Lonely Planet for her patience and perseverance, and also to Neil for being the good steward and James for, well, everything else.

Marc Di Duca

A huge 'ta' goes to all the staff at tourist offices across the Southeast (those that haven't been axed that is) but especially to the helpful guys in Hastings, Canterbury and Rye. Also thanks to Therese at Canterbury Cathedral and my Kyiv parents-in-law Mykola and Vira for looking after sons Taras and Kirill while I was on the road. And last, but certainly not least, heartfelt gratitude must go to my wife Tanya, for all those long days we spend apart.

Belinda Dixon

Huge thanks go to: James Smart for having faith (and the gig!), Lonely Planet's behind the scenes teams, and fellow authors for humour, wisdom and travellers' tales. Everyone encountered on southwest-wide travels for tips, facts and countless kindnesses. And JL for sharing the road trips (especially kayaking, fossil-hunting and afternoon tea drinking) and still making me smile.

Peter Dragicevich

Many thanks to the friends on the road who made this such an enjoyable assignment, especially Kerri Tyler, Tim Benzie, Paul Joseph and Kurt Crommelin. Extra special thanks to Matt, Clare, Charlie and Artie Swaine for the Bristol bonhomie. Much love to Phillippa Steel – an absolute inspiration and a true friend.

Damian Harper

Many thanks to a long list of helpful individuals: John Patrick Egan, Fiona Jenkins, Stephanie Francis, Daisy Harper, Amy Williams, Arlene Fraser, Matthew Scudamore, Daniel Hands and last but certainly not least, Timothy Benjamin and Emma Rosalind. A tip of the hat also to the people of London who make this city such an exciting and fascinating place to call home.

Catherine Le Nevez

Cheers first and foremost to Julian, and to all of the locals, tourism professionals and fellow travellers who provided insights, inspiration and good times. Thanks especially to Ade Andrews for the interview, and to Steven, Jeremy, Jayni and Alan in Birmingham, Nadia in Nottingham, and Raisa and Jonny in Newcastle. Thanks too to Neil Wilson, James Smart, Cliff Wilkinson, Joe Revill and everyone at Lonely Planet. As ever, merci encore to my parents, brother, *belle-sœur* and *neveu*.

ACKNOWLEDGEMENTS

Climate map data adapted from Peel MC, Finlayson BL & McMahon TA (2007) 'Updated World Map of the Köppen-Geiger Climate Classification', Hydrology and Earth System Sciences, 11, 1633–44.

Cover photograph: Wensleydale, Yorkshire Dales National Park, Paul Harris/AWL.

Illustrations: pp74-5 and pp634-5 by Javier Zarracina; pp80-1 by Javier Zarracina and Michael Weldon.

BEHIND THE SCENES

THIS BOOK

This 8th edition of Lonely Planet's *England* guidebook was researched and written by Neil Wilson, Oliver Berry, Fionn Davenport, Marc Di Duca, Belinda Dixon, Peter Dragicevich, Damian Harper and Catherine Le Nevez. This guidebook was produced by the following:

Destination Editors James Smart, Clifton Wilkinson

Product Editor Elin Berglund

Senior Cartographer Mark Griffiths

Book Designer Cam Ashley

Assisting Editors Nigel Chin, Charlotte Orr

Cover Researcher Naomi Parker

Thanks to Penny Cordner, Ryan Evans, Anna Harris, Jouve India, Andi Jones, Elizabeth Jones, Claire Naylor, Karyn Noble, Katie O'Connell, Ellie Simpson, Lauren Wellicome

Index

Map Pages **000**
Photo Pages **000**

Map Legend

Sights
- Beach
- Bird Sanctuary
- Buddhist
- Castle/Palace
- Christian
- Confucian
- Hindu
- Islamic
- Jain
- Jewish
- Monument
- Museum/Gallery/Historic Building
- Ruin
- Shinto
- Sikh
- Taoist
- Winery/Vineyard
- Zoo/Wildlife Sanctuary
- Other Sight

Activities, Courses & Tours
- Bodysurfing
- Diving
- Canoeing/Kayaking
- Course/Tour
- Sento Hot Baths/Onsen
- Skiing
- Snorkelling
- Surfing
- Swimming/Pool
- Walking
- Windsurfing
- Other Activity

Sleeping
- Sleeping
- Camping

Eating
- Eating

Drinking & Nightlife
- Drinking & Nightlife
- Cafe

Entertainment
- Entertainment

Shopping
- Shopping

Information
- Bank
- Embassy/Consulate
- Hospital/Medical
- Internet
- Police
- Post Office
- Telephone
- Toilet
- Tourist Information
- Other Information

Geographic
- Beach
- Hut/Shelter
- Lighthouse
- Lookout
- Mountain/Volcano
- Oasis
- Park
- Pass
- Picnic Area
- Waterfall

Population
- Capital (National)
- Capital (State/Province)
- City/Large Town
- Town/Village

Transport
- Airport
- Border crossing
- Bus
- Cable car/Funicular
- Cycling
- Ferry
- Metro station
- Monorail
- Parking
- Petrol station
- S-Bahn/Subway station
- Taxi
- T-bane/Tunnelbana station
- Train station/Railway
- Tram
- Tube station
- U-Bahn/Underground station
- Other Transport

Note: Not all symbols displayed above appear on the maps in this book

Routes
- Tollway
- Freeway
- Primary
- Secondary
- Tertiary
- Lane
- Unsealed road
- Road under construction
- Plaza/Mall
- Steps
- Tunnel
- Pedestrian overpass
- Walking Tour
- Walking Tour detour
- Path/Walking Trail

Boundaries
- International
- State/Province
- Disputed
- Regional/Suburb
- Marine Park
- Cliff
- Wall

Hydrography
- River, Creek
- Intermittent River
- Canal
- Water
- Dry/Salt/Intermittent Lake
- Reef

Areas
- Airport/Runway
- Beach/Desert
- Cemetery (Christian)
- Cemetery (Other)
- Glacier
- Mudflat
- Park/Forest
- Sight (Building)
- Sportsground
- Swamp/Mangrove

Belinda Dixon

Bath & Southwest England; Cambridge & East Anglia Belinda made a gleeful bolt for the sunny southwest for her post-grad, having been drawn there by the palm trees on campus. Like the best Westcountry limpets, she's proved hard to shift since and now writes and broadcasts in the region. Research highlights for this latest adventure included fossil hunting on the Jurassic Coast, white-water kayaking on Dartmoor, pony spotting on Exmoor, 'researching' cider in Dorset and sampling afternoon tea in Lyme.

Peter Dragicevich

Oxford, Cotswolds & Around Wales has held a fascination for Peter ever since he was sent to write about Welsh castles for one of his first ever newspaper travel features. Since then he's co-authored dozens of Lonely Planet titles, including the Wales guidebook. And while his name may not be very Welsh, it does at least have over half a dragon in it.

Damian Harper

London Born off the Strand within earshot of Bow Bells (favourable wind permitting), Damian grew up in Notting Hill way before it was discovered by Hollywood. A onetime Shakespeare and Company bookseller and radio presenter, Damian has been authoring guidebooks for Lonely Planet since the late 1990s. He lives in South London with his wife and two kids, frequently returning to China (his second home).

Catherine Le Nevez

Birmingham, the Midlands & the Marches; Newcastle & Northeast England Catherine first roadtripped around Great Britain aged four and she's been roadtripping here at every opportunity since, completing her Doctorate of Creative Arts in Writing, Masters in Professional Writing, and post-grad qualifications in editing and publishing along the way. She's also written dozens of Lonely Planet guidebooks and newspaper, magazine and online articles covering the UK, Europe and beyond. Roaming castle ruins and corridors of stately homes were highlights of researching this book, as was discovering idyllic countryside pubs.

OUR STORY

A beat-up old car, a few dollars in the pocket and a sense of adventure. In 1972 that's all Tony and Maureen Wheeler needed for the trip of a lifetime – across Europe and Asia overland to Australia. It took several months, and at the end – broke but inspired – they sat at their kitchen table writing and stapling together their first travel guide, *Across Asia on the Cheap*. Within a week they'd sold 1500 copies. Lonely Planet was born.

Today, Lonely Planet has offices in Franklin, London, Melbourne, Oakland, Beijing and Delhi, with more than 600 staff and writers. We share Tony's belief that 'a great guidebook should do three things: inform, educate and amuse'.

OUR WRITERS

Neil Wilson

Coordinating Author; Yorkshire Neil was born in Scotland and, save for a few years spent abroad, has lived there most of his life. A lifelong enthusiasm for the great outdoors has inspired hiking, biking and sailing expeditions to every corner of Britain. Researching this edition took him from the country's most westerly point at Ardnamurchan Lighthouse to its most easterly at Fraserburgh, and to every corner of Yorkshire. Neil has been a full-time author since 1988 and has written around 65 guidebooks for various publishers, including Lonely Planet's *Scotland* and *Scotland's Highlands & Islands*.

Oliver Berry

Bath & Southwest England; The Lake District & Cumbria A professional writer and photographer based in Cornwall and Bristol, Oliver likes nothing better than exploring his local beaches and clifftops in the name of research. For this book he covered his home county, and also ventured across the Tamar to write the sections on Somerset, Bristol, Bath and Cumbria. Research highlights included kayaking down the Helford River and watching the sunset from the top of Scafell Pike. You can see his latest work at www.oliverberry.com.

Fionn Davenport

Manchester, Liverpool & Northwest England As a Dubliner, Fionn feels an affinity with the Northwest. Maybe it's his lifelong support of Liverpool Football Club, or his longtime love of The Smiths, but a visit to Liverpool or Manchester is always that little bit special. Over the years and various editions of this guide he's had plenty of occasion to visit and get to know the region better, exploring Chester and the Wirral, and tramping through Lancaster and into the north Lancashire hills.

Marc Di Duca

Canterbury & Southeast England Originally from Darlington, County Durham, Marc has been a northerner-gone-south since 2000 and has covered his adopted corner of weald and down for the past three editions of Lonely Planet's *England* and *Great Britain*. A full-time travel author for a decade, Marc has updated and written Lonely Planet guides to Ukraine, Russia, the Trans-Siberian Railway, Poland, Austria and Germany, though he can usually be found in Sandwich, K where he lives with wife Tanya and their two sons.

Read more about Mar
lonelyplanet.com/members/ma

OVER MORE
PAGE WRITERS

Published by Lonely Planet Publications Pty Ltd
ABN 36 005 607 983
8th edition – April 2015
ISBN 978 1 74321 467 1
© Lonely Planet 2015   Photographs © as indicated 2015
10 9 8 7 6 5 4 3 2 1
Printed in China

Although the authors and Lonely Planet have taken all reasona ble care in preparing this book, we make no warranty about th accuracy or completeness of its content and, to the maximum extent permitted, disclaim all liability arising from its use.

All rights reserved. No part of this publication may be copied, stored in a retrieval system, or transmitted in any form by any means, electronic, mechanical, recording or otherwise, except brief extracts for the purpose of review, and no part of this publication may be sold or hired, without written permission of the publisher. Lonely Planet and the Lonely Planet logo are trademarks of Lonely Planet and are registered in the US Patent Trademark Office and in other countries. Lonely Planet does not allow its name or logo to be appropriated by commercial establishments, such retailers, restaurants or hotels. Please let us know of any misuses: lonelyplanet.com/ip.

OKANAGAN REGIONAL LIBRARY
3 3132 03741 3269